Standard Normal Distribution Table

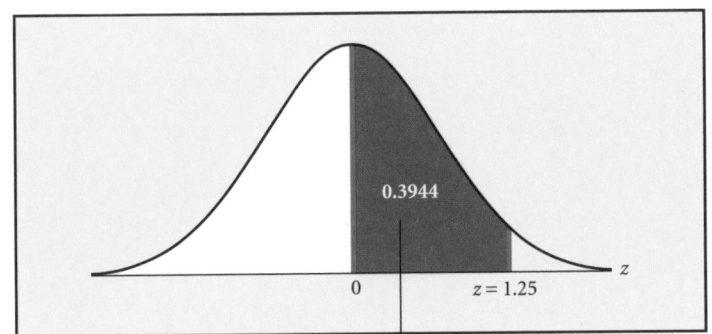

z	0	0.01	0.02	0.03	0.04	0.05	0.06	0.07	0.08	0.09
0.0	0.0000	0.0040	0.0080	0.0120	0.0160	0.0199	0.0239	0.0279	0.0319	0.0359
0.1	0.0398	0.0438	0.0478	0.0517	0.0557	0.0596	0.0636	0.0675	0.0714	0.0753
0.2	0.0793	0.0832	0.0871	0.0910	0.0948	0.0987	0.1026	0.1064	0.1103	0.1141
0.3	0.1179	0.1217	0.1255	0.1293	0.1331	0.1368	0.1406	0.1443	0.1480	0.1517
0.4	0.1554	0.1591	0.1628	0.1664	0.1700	0.1736	0.1772	0.1808	0.1844	0.1879
0.5	0.1915	0.1950	0.1985	0.2019	0.2054	0.2088	0.2123	0.2157	0.2190	0.2224
0.6	0.2257	0.2291	0.2324	0.2357	0.2389	0.2422	0.2454	0.2486	0.2517	0.2549
0.7	0.2580	0.2611	0.2642	0.2673	0.2704	0.2734	0.2764	0.2794	0.2823	0.2852
0.8	0.2881	0.2910	0.2939	0.2967	0.2995	0.3023	0.3051	0.3078	0.3106	0.3133
0.9	0.3159	0.3186	0.3212	0.3238	0.3264	0.3289	0.3315	0.3340	0.3365	0.3389
1.0	0.3413	0.3438	0.3461	0.3485	0.3508	0.3531	0.3554	0.3577	0.3599	0.3621
1.1	0.3643	0.3665	0.3686	0.3708	0.3729	0.3749	0.3770	0.3790	0.3810	0.3830
1.2	0.3849	0.3869	0.3888	0.3907	0.3925	0.3944	0.3962	0.3980	0.3997	0.4015
1.3	0.4032	0.4049	0.4066	0.4082	0.4099	0.4115	0.4131	0.4147	0.4162	0.4177
1.4	0.4192	0.4207	0.4222	0.4236	0.4251	0.4265	0.4279	0.4292	0.4306	0.4319
1.5	0.4332	0.4345	0.4357	0.4370	0.4382	0.4394	0.4406	0.4418	0.4429	0.4441
1.6	0.4452	0.4463	0.4474	0.4484	0.4495	0.4505	0.4515	0.4525	0.4535	0.4545
1.7	0.4554	0.4564	0.4573	0.4582	0.4591	0.4599	0.4608	0.4616	0.4625	0.4633
1.8	0.4641	0.4649	0.4656	0.4664	0.4671	0.4678	0.4686	0.4693	0.4699	0.4706
1.9	0.4713	0.4719	0.4726	0.4732	0.4738	0.4744	0.4750	0.4756	0.4761	0.4767
2.0	0.4772	0.4778	0.4783	0.4788	0.4793	0.4798	0.4803	0.4808	0.4812	0.4817
2.1	0.4821	0.4826	0.4830	0.4834	0.4838	0.4842	0.4846	0.4850	0.4854	0.4857
2.2	0.4861	0.4864	0.4868	0.4871	0.4875	0.4878	0.4881	0.4884	0.4887	0.4890
2.3	0.4893	0.4896	0.4898	0.4901	0.4904	0.4906	0.4909	0.4911	0.4913	0.4916
2.4	0.4918	0.4920	0.4922	0.4925	0.4927	0.4929	0.4931	0.4932	0.4934	0.4936
2.5	0.4938	0.4940	0.4941	0.4943	0.4945	0.4946	0.4948	0.4949	0.4951	0.4952
2.6	0.4953	0.4955	0.4956	0.4957	0.4959	0.4960	0.4961	0.4962	0.4963	0.4964
2.7	0.4965	0.4966	0.4967	0.4968	0.4969	0.4970	0.4971	0.4972	0.4973	0.4974
2.8	0.4974	0.4975	0.4976	0.4977	0.4977	0.4978	0.4979	0.4979	0.4980	0.4981
2.9	0.4981	0.4982	0.4982	0.4983	0.4984	0.4984	0.4985	0.4985	0.4986	0.4986
3.0	0.4987	0.4987	0.4987	0.4988	0.4988	0.4989	0.4989	0.4989	0.4990	0.4990

HAVE YOU THOUGHT ABOUT
Customizing THIS BOOK?

THE PRENTICE HALL JUST-IN-TIME PROGRAM IN DECISION SCIENCE

You can combine chapters from this book with chapters from any of the Prentice Hall titles listed on the following page to create a text tailored to your specific course needs. You can add your own material or cases from our extensive case collection. By taking a few minutes to look at what is sitting on your bookshelf and the content available on our Web site, you can create your ideal textbook.

The Just-In-Time program offers:

➡ **Quality of Material to Choose From**—In addition to the books listed, you also have the option to include any of the cases from Prentice Hall Custom Business Resources, which gives you access to cases (and teaching notes where available) from Darden, Harvard, Ivey, NACRA, and Thunderbird. Most cases can be viewed online at our Web site.

➡ **Flexibility**—Choose only that material you want, either from one title or several titles (plus cases) and sequence it in whatever way you wish.

➡ **Instructional Support**—You have access to the text-specific CD-ROM that accompanies the traditional textbook and desk copies of your JIT book.

➡ **Outside Materials**—There is also the option to include up to 20% of the text from materials outside of Prentice Hall Custom Business Resources.

➡ **Cost Savings**—Students pay only for material you choose. The base price is $6.00, plus $2.00 for case material, plus $.09 per page. The text can be shrink-wrapped with other Pearson textbooks for a 10% discount. Outside material is priced at $.10 per page plus permission fees.

➡ **Quality of Finished Product**—Custom cover and title page—including your name, school, department, course title, and section number. Paperback, perfect bound, black-and-white printed text. Customized table of contents. Sequential pagination throughout the text.

Visit our Web site at www.prenhall.com/custombusiness and create your

custom text on our bookbuildsite or download order forms online.

THE PRENTICE HALL

 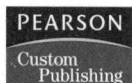 Just-In-Time program

You can customize your textbook with chapters from any of the following Prentice Hall titles: *

BUSINESS STATISTICS

- Berenson/Levine/Krehbiel, BASIC BUSINESS STATISTICS, 10/e
- Groebner/Shannon/Fry/Smith, BUSINESS STATISTICS: A DECISION-MAKING APPROACH, 7/e
- Levine/Stephan/Krehbiel/Berenson, STATISTICS FOR MANAGERS USING MICROSOFT EXCEL, 4/e
- Levine/Krehbiel/Berenson, BUSINESS STATISTICS: A FIRST COURSE, 4/e
- Newbold/Carlson/Thorne, STATISTICS FOR BUSINESS AND ECONOMICS, 5/e
- Groebner/Shannon/Fry/Smith, A COURSE IN BUSINESS STATISTICS, 4/e

OPERATIONS MANAGEMENT

- Anupindi/Chopra/Deshmukh/Van Mieghem/Zemel, MANAGING BUSINESS PROCESS FLOWS, 2/e
- Bozarth/Handfield, INTRODUCTION TO OPERATIONS AND SUPPLY CHAIN MANAGEMENT
- Chopra/Meindl, SUPPLY CHAIN MANAGEMENT, 3e
- Foster, MANAGING QUALITY, 3/e
- Handfield/Nichols, Jr., SUPPLY CHAIN MANAGEMENT
- Heineke/Meile, GAMES AND EXERCISES FOR OPERATIONS MANAGEMENT
- Heizer/Render, OPERATIONS MANAGEMENT, 8/e
- Krajewski/Ritzman/Malhotra, OPERATIONS MANAGEMENT, 8/e
- Latona/Nathan, CASES AND READINGS IN PRODUCTION AND OPERATIONS MANAGEMENT
- Ritzman/Krajewski, FOUNDATIONS OF OPERATIONS MANAGEMENT
- Schmenner, PLANT AND SERVICE TOURS IN OPERATIONS MANAGEMENT, 5/e

MANAGEMENT SCIENCE/SPREADSHEET MODELING

- Render/Stair/Hanna, QUANTITATIVE ANALYSIS FOR MANAGEMENT, 9/e
- Balakrishnan/Render/Stair, MANAGERIAL DECISION MODELING WITH SPREADSHEETS, 2/e
- Render/Greenberg/Stair, CASES AND READINGS IN MANAGEMENT SCIENCE, 2e
- Taylor, INTRODUCTION TO MANAGEMENT SCIENCE, 9/e

For more information, or to speak to a customer service representative, contact us at 1-800-777-6872.

www.prenhall.com/custombusiness

* Selection of titles on the JIT program is subject to change.

Business Statistics
A DECISION-MAKING APPROACH

Seventh **EDITION**

Business Statistics
A DECISION-MAKING APPROACH

DAVID F. GROEBNER
Boise State University, Emeritus

PATRICK W. SHANNON
Boise State University

PHILLIP C. FRY
Boise State University

KENT D. SMITH
California Polytechnic University at San Luis Obispo

PEARSON

Prentice
Hall

Prentice Hall, Upper Saddle River, New Jersey 07458

Library of Congress Cataloging-in-Publication Data

Business statistics: a decision-making approach / David F. Groebner . . . [et al.].—7th ed.
    p. cm.
    Includes bibliographical references and index.
    ISBN 978-0-13-224001-7
    1. Commercial statistics. 2. Statistical decision. I. Groebner, David F.
HF1017.G73 2008
519.5—dc22

2006100022

AVP/Executive Editor: Mark Pfaltzgraff
VP/Editorial Director: Jeff Shelstad
Manager, Product Development: Pamela Hersperger
Assistant Editor: Barbara Witmer
Editorial Assistant: Kelly Loftus
Product Development Manager, Media: Nancy Welcher
Marketing Assistant: Laura Cirigliano
Associate Director, Production Editorial: Judy Leale
Senior Managing Editor: Cynthia Zonneveld
Senior Production Editor: Carol Samet
Permissions Coordinator: Charles Morris
Associate Director, Manufacturing: Vinnie Scelta
Manufacturing Buyer: Michelle Klein
Design/Composition Manager: Christy Mahon
Composition Liaison: Suzanne Duda
Art Director: Steve Frim
Interior Design: Kim Buckley
Cover Design: Steve Frim
Cover Illustration/Photo: McDonald's Corporation
Composition: GGS Book Services
Full-Service Project Management: GGS Book Services
Printer/Binder: Quebecor
Typeface: 10/12 Times

Microsoft® and Windows® are registered trademarks of the Microsoft Corporation in the U.S.A. and other countries. Screen shots and icons reprinted with permission from the Microsoft Corporation. This book is not sponsored or endorsed by or affiliated with the Microsoft Corporation.

Portions of the input and output contained in this publication/book are printed with permission of Minitab Inc. All materials remain the exclusive property and copyright of Minitab Inc. All rights reserved.

Pearson Education LTD.
Pearson Education Singapore, Pte. Ltd
Pearson Education, Canada, Ltd
Pearson Education—Japan

Pearson Education Australia PTY, Limited
Pearson Education North Asia Ltd
Pearson Educación de Mexico, S.A. de C.V.
Pearson Education Malaysia, Pte. Ltd.

10 9 8 7 6 5 4 3 2 1
ISBN-13: 978-0-13-224001-7
ISBN-10: 0-13-224001-7

To Jane and my family, who survived the process one more time.

David F. Groebner

To Kathy, my wife and best friend; to our children, Jackie and Jason; and to my parents, John and Ruth Shannon.

Patrick W. Shannon

To my wonderful family: Susan, Alex, Allie, Candace, and Courtney.

Phillip C. Fry

To Dottie, my loving wife, who dances much better than I write.

Kent D. Smith

About the Authors

David F. Groebner is a Professor Emeritus of Production Management in the College of Business and Economics at Boise State University. He has bachelor's and master's degrees in Engineering and a Ph.D. in Business Administration. After working as an engineer, he has taught statistics and related subjects for 27 years. In addition to writing textbooks and academic papers, he has worked extensively with both small and large organizations, including Hewlett-Packard, Boise Cascade, Albertson's, and Ore-Ida. He has worked with numerous government agencies, including Boise City and the U.S. Air Force.

Patrick W. Shannon, Ph.D. is Professor of Production and Operations Management in the College of Business and Economics at Boise State University. He teaches graduate and undergraduate courses in business statistics, quality management, and production and operations management. In addition, Dr. Shannon has lectured and consulted in the statistical analysis and quality management areas for over 20 years. Listed among his consulting clients are Boise Cascade Corporation, Hewlett-Packard; PowerBar, Inc.; Potlatch Corporation; Woodgrain Millwork, Inc.; J.R. Simplot Company; Zilog Corporation; and numerous other public- and private-sector organizations. Professor Shannon has co-authored several university-level textbooks and has published numerous articles in such journals as *Business Horizons, Interfaces, Journal of Simulation, Journal of Production and Inventory Control, Quality Progress,* and *Journal of Marketing Research.* He obtained B.S. and M.S. degrees from the University of Montana and a Ph.D. in Statistics and Quantitative Methods from the University of Oregon.

Phillip C. Fry is a Professor in the College of Business and Economics at Boise State University, where he has taught since 1988. Phil received his B.A. and M.B.A degrees from the University of Arkansas, and his M.S. and Ph.D. degrees from Louisiana State University.His teaching and research interests are in the areas of business statistics, production management, and quantitative business modeling. In addition to his academic responsibilities, Phil has consulted with and provided training to small and large organizations, including Boise Cascade Corporation; Hewlett-Packard Corporation; The J.R. Simplot Company; United Water of Idaho; Woodgrain Millwork, Inc.; Boise City; and Micron Electronics.

Phil spends most of his free time with his wife Susan and his four children, Phillip Alexander, Alejandra Johanna, and twins, Courtney Rene and Candace Marie.

Kent D. Smith received a Ph.D. in Applied Statistics from the University of California, Riverside in 1981. He holds a Master of Science degree in Statistics from the University of California, Riverside and a Master of Science degree in Systems Analysis from the Air Force Institute of Technology. His Bachelor of Arts degree in Mathematics was obtained from the University of Utah. Dr. Smith has served as a University Statistical Consultant at the University of California, Riverside and at California Polytechnic State University, San Luis Obispo. While at the University of California, he served as a consultant for the Biometrical Services Unit of the Biometrical Project at the University of California, Riverside. His private consulting has ranged from serving as an expert witness in legal cases, survey sampling for corporations and private researchers, medical and orthodontic research, and assisting graduate students with analysis required for master and doctoral degrees in various disciplines.

Dr. Smith began teaching as a part-time lecturer at the California State University, San Bernardino. While completing his doctoral dissertation, he served as a lecturer at the University of California, Riverside. Currently, he is a Professor of Statistics at the California Polytechnic State University, San Luis Obispo, one of the minority of universities that offer an undergraduate degree in statistics. The subjects he teaches include upper-division courses in regression, analysis of variance, nonparametrics, linear models, and probability and mathematical statistics, as well as a full array of service courses.

Brief Contents

Contents

Preface

In today's workplace, students can have an immediate competitive edge over both new graduates and experienced employees if they know how to apply statistical analysis skills to real-world decision-making problems.

Our intent in writing ***Business Statistics: A Decision-Making Approach,*** **Seventh Edition** is to provide an introductory business statistics text for students who do not necessarily have an extensive mathematics background but who need to understand how statistical tools and techniques are applied in business decision making.

This text differs from its competitors in three key ways. First, it uses a direct approach and consistently presents concepts and techniques in a systematic and ordered way. Second, it presents the content at a level that makes it accessible to students of all levels of mathematical maturity. The text features clear, step-by-step explanations that make learning business statistics straightforward. Third, the text integrates engaging examples, drawn from our years of experience as authors, educators, and consultants, to show the relevance of the statistical techniques in realistic business decision situations.

Regardless of how accessible or engaging a textbook is, we recognize that many students do not read the chapters from front to back. Instead, they use the text "backwards." That is, they go to the assigned exercises, try them, and if they get stuck they turn to the text to look for examples to help them. Thus, this text features clearly marked, step-by-step examples that students can follow. Each detailed example is linked to a section exercise, which may be used by students to build specific skills needed to work exercises in the section.

Each chapter begins with a clear set of specific chapter outcomes and objectives. The examples and practice exercises are designed to reinforce these objectives and lead the students toward the desired outcomes. The exercises are ordered from easy to more difficult and are divided into categories: Conceptual, Skill Development, Business Applications, and Database Exercises.

Another difference is the importance this text places on data and how data are obtained. Many business statistics texts assume that data have already been collected. We have decided to underscore a more modern theme: Data are the starting point. We believe that effective decision making relies on a good understanding of the different types of data and the different data collection options that exist. To highlight our theme, we begin a discussion of data and collecting data in Chapter 1 before any discussion of data analysis is presented. In Chapters 2 and 3, where the important descriptive statistical techniques are introduced, we tie these statistical techniques to the type and level of data for which they are best suited.

Although we know that the role of the computer is important in applying business statistics, it can be overdone at the beginning level to the point where instructors are required to spend too much time teaching the software and too little time teaching statistical concepts. This text features Excel and Minitab but limits the inclusion of software output to those areas where it is of particular advantage to beginning students.

Key Features of the Seventh Edition

■ *Step-by-Step Approach*
  Continued and improved emphasis on providing concise, step-by-step details to reinforce chapter material.
  • **NEW! Text design** allows for a clearer visual relationship between the content Summary Boxes and Textual Examples.

- **Summary Boxes** are provided throughout each chapter to summarize major techniques and reinforce fundamental concepts.
- **Textual Examples** throughout the text provide step-by-step details enabling students to follow solution techniques easily. Students can then apply the methodology to solve other problems. These examples are provided in addition to the vast array of business applications to give students a real-world, competitive edge.

■ *Real-World Application*

- **NEW! McDonald's Corporation Video Cases**—The authors have established a relationship with McDonald's to provide students with real-world statistical data and a brand new, integrated video case series.
- **Chapter Cases**—These are provided in nearly every chapter and are designed to give students the opportunity to apply statistical tools. The cases challenge students to define the problem, determine the appropriate tool to use, apply it, and then write a summary report.
- Not only do the chapters and cases feature real companies, actual applications, and rich data sets, but the authors have concentrated their efforts on addressing how students apply this statistical knowledge to the decision-making process.
- **NEW! Virtual Office Hours**—The seventh edition includes a new and unique feature in which the authors appear in 3 to 5 minute video clips in which they work examples taken directly from the book. In addition to reading a step-by-step example in the text, now students can watch and listen to the instructor walk through the example and obtain even greater clarity with respect to how the example is worked and how the results are interpreted.

■ *Computer Integration*

The text seamlessly integrates computer applications with textual examples and figures, always focusing on interpreting the output. The goal is for students to be able to know which tools to use, how to apply them, and how to analyze their results for making decisions.

- **NEW! Microsoft Excel 2007** integration instructs students in how to use the new Excel user interface for statistical applications.
- **New PHStat2** release is featured in the text for compatibility with the new Microsoft Excel 2007.
- **Minitab 14** is also featured with associated instructions.

■ *Pedagogical Tools*

- **Chapter Outcomes**—Each chapter begins with a bullet point list of key outcomes and objectives to be gained from completing the chapter. Then, throughout each chapter, specially marked icons are used to tie the material to specific outcomes
- **Business Applications**—One of the strengths of the previous editions of the Groebner, Shannon, Fry, and Smith text has been the emphasis on business applications and decision making. This feature is expanded even more in the seventh edition. Many new applications are included, and all applications are highlighted in the text with specially marked icons making them easier for students to locate as they use the text.
- **Special Review Sections**—For Chapters 1 to 3 and Chapters 8 to 12, these provide a summary and review of the key issues and statistical techniques. Highly effective flow diagrams help the student sort out which statistical technique is appropriate to use in a given problem or exercise. These flow diagrams serve as a mini-decision support system that takes the emphasis off memorization and encourages the students to seek a higher level of understanding and learning. Integrative questions and exercises are included that ask students to demonstrate their comprehension of the topics covered in these sections.

■ *Problems and Exercises*
- This edition includes an extensive revision of exercise sections, featuring over 600 new problems.
- The exercise sets are broken down into three categories for ease of use and assignment purposes:
  1. **Skill Development**—These problems help students build and expand upon statistical methods learned in the chapter.
  2. **Business Applications**—These problems involve realistic situations in which students apply decision-making techniques.
  3. **NEW! Computer Applications**—In addition to the problems that may be worked out manually, many problems have associated data files and can be solved using Excel, Minitab, or other statistical software.

■ *Specific Chapter Changes*
- **Chapters 5 and 6**—The sixth edition's Chapter 5 is separated into two distinct chapters: "Introduction to Discrete Probability Distributions" (Chapter 5) and "Introduction to Continuous Probability Distributions" (Chapter 6).
- **Chapters 8 to 11**—The use of the t or standard normal distribution in estimation and hypothesis testing is now based exclusively on whether the population standard deviation is known.
- **Chapter 9**—A new discussion has been included that clarifies how the null and alternative hypotheses should be formulated in a hypothesis testing application.
- **Chapter 15**—An expanded section on stepwise regression analysis has been added.
- **Chapter 16**—The time-series and forecasting chapter has been expanded to include a section on using dummy variables to represent seasonality in a regression-based forecasting model.
- **Chapter 19**—The "Introduction to Decision Analysis" chapter, formerly available only on the Student CD-ROM, has been placed back into the text as Chapter 19.

■ *PH Grade Assist* allows students to go online and work on a virtually unlimited number of practice problems associated with the text. Problems are algorithmically generated so that no student receives exactly the same question. Answers can be submitted online for instant feedback or they can be printed and turned in to instructors.

This homework system allows instructors to create, assign, and grade assignments quickly and easily. Problems can be selected from the text, created by hand, or both. By registering and using the site, instructors can post assignments, receive grades, and build detailed information on class performance. Contact your local Prentice Hall sales representative for more details.

Student Resources

Student CD-ROM

The CD-ROM for this edition contains all the resources and tools your students need to succeed:

■ **Excel and Minitab Tutorials** These customized PowerPoint tutorials for both Minitab and Excel use data sets from text examples. Separate tutorials for Excel 2003 and Excel 2007 are provided. Students who need additional instruction in Excel or Minitab can access the menu-driven tutorial, which will show the exact steps needed to replicate all computer examples in the text.
■ **Data Files** An extensive number of data files for examples, cases, and exercises in the text are included on the CD-ROM in Excel and Minitab.
■ **Excel Simulations** Several interactive simulations illustrate key statistical topics and allow students to do "what-if" scenarios.
■ **PHStat2**
- This specially developed Excel add-in package is compatible with the new Excel 2007 release. It performs a number of statistical features not included with Excel.

The added functions and procedures are useful in the study and application of business statistics. When installed, PHStat2 attaches itself to the Excel menu bar, providing users with a pull-down menu of topics that supplement the Data Analysis add-in tools in Microsoft Excel.

- PHStat2 uses a set of simple and consistent dialog boxes that allow students to specify values and options for almost 50 tools included in the software. PHStat2 produces Excel worksheets organized into areas for the input data, intermediate calculations, and the results of analysis. Unlike some competitors' add-ins, most of these worksheets contain live formulas that allow students to engage immediately in further "what-if" explorations of the data. (Where applicable, these worksheets contain special cell tints that distinguish the cells that contain user-modifiable input values from the cells containing the results, making "what-if" analysis even easier.) Completing the package is an excellent online help system.

Student Solutions Manual

The Student Solutions Manual contains worked-out solutions to odd-numbered problems in the text. It displays the detailed process that students should use to work through the problems. The manual also provides interpretation of the answers and serves as a valuable learning tool for the student.

Student Companion Web Site

- **Online Study Guide** contains practice or homework quizzes consisting of multiple-choice, true/false, and essay questions that effectively review textual material.
- **PowerPoint slides** are available for each chapter.

Student DVD

This DVD features McDonald's video cases and the new Virtual Office Hour videos.

Instructor Resources

Instructor Resource Center

The Instructor's Resource Center is available online at www.prenhall.com/groebner. It contains electronic versions of the Instructor's Solutions Manual and Test Item File as well as Lecture PowerPoint Presentations and TestGen conversion files and data files.

Instructor's Solutions Manual

The Instructor's Solutions Manual contains worked-out solutions to all problems and cases in the text.

Test Item File

This Testbank, by Donna Retzlaff-Roberts of University of South Alabama, contains a variety of true/false, multiple-choice, and short-answer questions for each chapter.

Lecture PowerPoint Presentations

A PowerPoint presentation created by Dirk Yandell, University of San Diego, is available for each chapter.

Instructor's Resource CD-ROM

This Instructor's Resource CD-ROM contains all the resources included on the Student CD-ROM as well as all the instructor ancillaries in electronic format.

DVD—Video Cases

Contains the McDonald's-based video case series.

Acknowledgments

Publishing this seventh edition of *Business Statistics: A Decision-Making Approach* has been a team effort involving the contribution of many people. At the risk of overlooking someone, we express our sincere appreciation to the many key contributors. Throughout the two years we have worked on this revision, many of our colleagues from colleges and universities around the country have taken time from their busy schedules to provide valuable input and suggestions for improvement. We would like to thank the following people:

Donald I. Bosshardt, *Canisius College*

Sara T. DeLoughy, *Western Connecticut State University*

Nicholas R. Farnum, *California State University—Fullerton*

Kent E. Foster, *Winthrop University*

John Gum, *University of South Florida—St. Petersburg*

Jeffery Guyse, *California State Polytechnic University, Pomona*

Chaiho Kim, *Santa Clara University*

David Knopp, *Chattanooga State Technical Community College*

Linda Leighton, *Fordham University*

Sally A. Lesik, *Central Connecticut State University*

Merrill W. Liechty, *Drexel University*

Robert M. Lynch, *University of Northern Colorado—Monfort College of Business*

Jennifer Martin, *York College of Pennsylvania*

Constance McLaren, *Indiana State University*

Carl E. Miller, *Northern Kentucky University*

Tariq Mughal, *David Eccles, School of Business, University of Utah*

Kenneth Paetsch, *Cleveland State University*

Ed Pappanastos, *Troy University*

Michael D. Polomsky, *Cleveland State University*

Peter Royce, *University of New Hampshire*

Rose Sebastianelli, *University of Scranton*

Bulent Uyar, *University of Northern Iowa*

Tom Wheeler, *Georgia Southwestern State University*

We also wish to thank Professor Dirk Yandell who designed and developed the PowerPoint slides that accompany this text. Thanks also to David Stephen for his expert work in developing the PHStat add-ins for Excel that accompany the text.

Thanks too to Annie Puciloski who checked the solutions to every exercise. This is a very time-consuming but extremely important role, and we greatly appreciate her efforts. In addition, we wish to thank Donna Retzlaff-Roberts of the University of South Alabama for developing the test manual. This too requires a huge commitment of time and effort, and we appreciate her contributions to the package of materials that accompany the text. Howard Flomberg at the Metropolitan State College of Denver contributed his skills and creative abilities to develop the Excel and Minitab tutorials that are so useful to students, and we thank him for all his contributions. Thanks too to Bob Donnelly of Goldey Beacom College for his development of the Online Study Guide.

Finally, we wish to give our utmost thanks and appreciation to the Prentice Hall publishing team that have assisted us in every way possible to make this seventh edition a reality. Steve Frim was responsible for the text design. Nancy Welcher oversaw all the media products that accompany this text. Carol Samet, in her role as senior production editor, guided the development of the book from its initial design all the way through to final printing. Barbara Witmer, assistant editor, served as our day-to-day contact and expertly facilitated the project in every way imaginable. And finally, we wish to give the highest thanks possible to Mark Pfaltzgraff, the executive editor for decision sciences, who has provided valuable guidance, motivation, and leadership from beginning to end on this project. It has been a great pleasure to work with Mark and his team at Prentice Hall.

—David F. Groebner

—Patrick W. Shannon

—Phillip C. Fry

—Kent D. Smith

The Where, Why, and How of Data Collection

CHAPTER OUTCOMES

After studying the material in Chapter 1, you should:

1. Know the key data collection methods.
2. Know the difference between a population and a sample.
3. Understand the similarities and differences between different sampling methods.
4. Understand how to categorize data by type and level of measurement.

PREPARING FOR CHAPTER ONE

- Locate a recent copy of a business periodical, such as *Fortune* or *Business Week*, and take note of the graphs, charts, and tables that are used in the articles and advertisements.

- Recall any recent experiences you have had in which you were asked to complete a written survey or respond to a telephone survey.

- Make sure that you have access to Excel or Minitab software. Open either Excel or Minitab and familiarize yourself with the software.

WHY YOU NEED TO KNOW

Although you may not realize it yet, by taking this business statistics course, you will be learning about some of the most useful business tools available for decision makers. In today's workplace, you can have an immediate competitive edge over other new employees, and even those with more experience, by applying statistical analysis skills to real-world decision-making problems. The purpose of this text is to assist in your learning process and to complement your instructor's efforts in conveying how to apply a variety of important statistical tools. Each chapter introduces one or more statistical tools and techniques that regardless of your major will be useful in your career.

Wal-Mart, the world's largest retail chain, collects and manages massive amounts of data related to the operation of its stores throughout the world. Its highly sophisticated database systems contain sales data, detailed customer data, employee satisfaction data, and much more. General Motors maintains databases with information on production, quality, customer satisfaction, safety records, and much more. Governmental agencies amass extensive data on such things as unemployment, interest rates, incomes, and education. However, access to data is not limited to large companies. The relatively low cost of computer hard drives with 100 gigabyte or larger capacities makes it possible for small firms, and even individuals, to store vast amounts of data on desktop computers. But without some way to transform the data into useful information, the data any of these companies has gathered are of little value.

Transforming data into information is where business statistics comes in—the statistical tools introduced in this text are those that are used to help transform data into information. This text focuses on the practical application of statistics; we do not develop the theory you would find in a mathematical statistics course. Will you need to use math in this course? The answer is yes, but mainly the concepts covered in your college algebra course.

Statistics does have its own terminology. You will need to learn various terms that have special statistical meaning. You will also learn certain do's and don'ts related to statistics. But most importantly you will learn specific methods to effectively convert data into information. Don't try to memorize the concepts; rather, go to the next level of learning called *understanding*. Once you understand the underlying concepts, you will be able to *think statistically*.

Because data are the starting point for any statistical analysis, Chapter 1 is devoted to discussing various aspects of data, from how to collect data to the different types of data that you will be analyzing. You need to gain an understanding of the where, why, and how of data and data collection because the remaining chapters deal with the techniques for transforming data into useful information.

1.1 What is Business Statistics?

Every day, your local newspaper contains stories that report descriptors such as stock prices, crime rates, and government agency budgets. Such descriptors can be found in many places. However, they are just a small part of the discipline called **business statistics** which provides a wide variety of methods to assist in data analysis and decision making. Business is one important area of application for these methods.

Business Statistics
A collection of tools and techniques that are used to convert data into meaningful information in a business environment.

Descriptive Statistics

The tools and techniques that comprise business statistics include those specially designed to *describe data*, such as charts, graphs, and numerical measures. Also included are inferential tools that help decision makers *draw inferences* from a set of data. Inferential tools include estimation and hypothesis testing. A brief discussion of these tools and techniques follows. The examples illustrate data that have been entered into the Microsoft Excel and Minitab software packages.

BAKER CITY HOSPITAL Because health care companies in the United States are facing increased competition, hospital administrators must become more efficient in managing operations. This demand means they must better understand their customers.

The financial vice president for Baker City Hospital recently collected data for 138 patients. The VP has entered these data into an Excel spreadsheet called **Baker**, as illustrated in Figure 1.1. Each column in the figure corresponds to a different factor for which data were collected. Each row corresponds to a different patient. Many statistical tools might help the VP describe these patients' data, including *charts*, *graphs*, and *numerical measures*.

FIGURE 1.1

Excel 2007 Spreadsheet of Baker City Hospital Patient Data

Excel 2007 Instructions:
1. Open file: Baker.xls.

Charts and Graphs Although we develop an extensive variety of methods to describe data using graphs and charts in Chapter 2, a few examples are offered here to give you an idea of what is possible. Figure 1.2 shows a graph called a *histogram*. This graph gives us some insight into how long patients stay at the Baker City Hospital by visually showing how many patients appear in each length-of-stay category. It displays the shape and spread of the patient length-of-stay distribution. The *bar chart* shown in Figure 1.3 breaks down the patient data, showing the percentage of male and female patients. We can tell, looking at this chart, that the mix of patients has a higher percentage of females.

Chapter 2 will discuss in detail the conditions under which either a histogram or a bar chart should be used, but we can point out now two basic differences between these two important graphical tools. First, a bar chart is used to display data that have been categorized (for example, males and females in Figure 1.3.) A histogram is used to display data over a range of values for the factor being considered (for example, days in the hospital between 0 and 18 in Figure 1.2). A second difference is that a histogram should have no gaps between the bars, but we typically do insert gaps between the bars on a bar chart. These differences will be emphasized again in Chapter 2. Bar charts and histograms are only two of the graphical techniques that the Baker City Hospital VP might use to help describe her patient population. In Chapter 2 you will learn more about these and other techniques.

FIGURE 1.2

Histogram

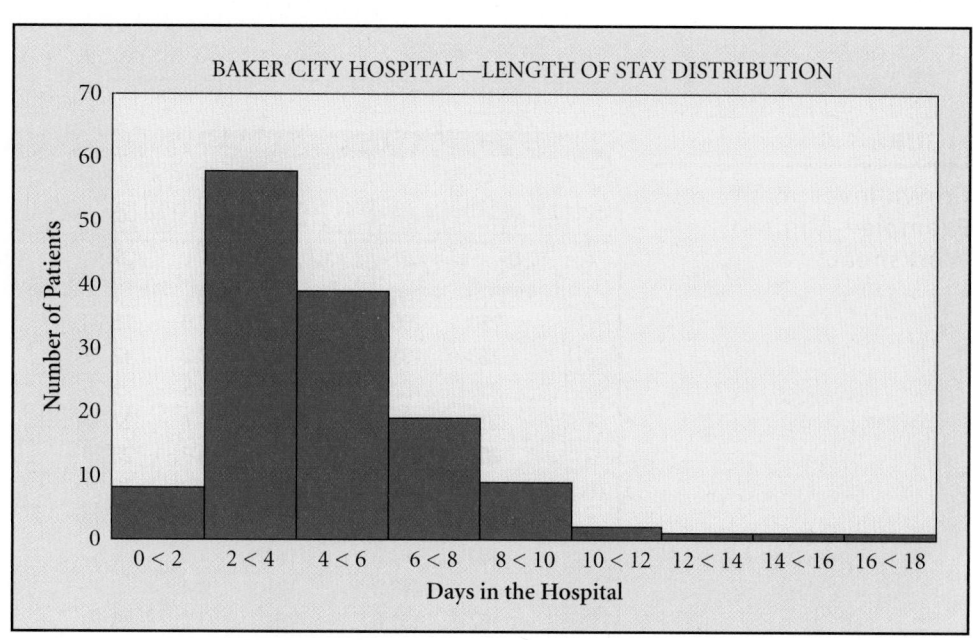

FIGURE 1.3

Bar Chart of Baker City Hospital

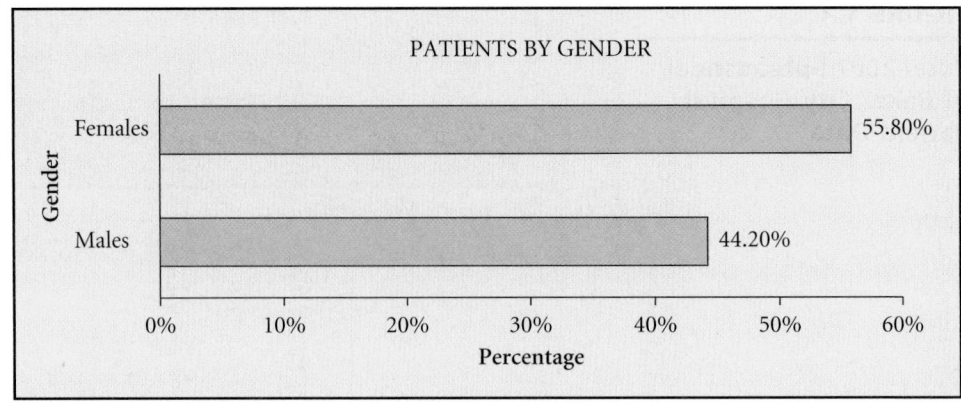

CROWN INVESTMENTS During the 1990s and early 2000s, many major changes occurred in the financial services industry. Numerous banks merged. Money flowed into the stock market at rates far surpassing anything the U.S. economy had previously witnessed. The international financial world fluctuated greatly. All these developments have spurred the need for more financial analysts who can critically evaluate financial data and explain them to customers.

At Crown Investments, a senior analyst is preparing to present data to upper management on the 100 fastest-growing companies on the Hong Kong Stock Exchange. Figure 1.4 shows a Minitab worksheet containing a subset of the data. The columns correspond to the different items of interest (growth percentage, sales, and so on). The data for each company are in a single row. The data file is called **Fast100**.

In addition to preparing appropriate graphs, the analyst will compute important numerical measures. One of the most basic and most useful measures in business statistics is one with which you are already familiar: the **arithmetic mean** or **average**.

Average

The sum of all the values divided by the number of values. In equation form:

$$\text{Average} = \frac{\sum_{i=1}^{N} x_i}{N} = \frac{\text{Sum of All Data Values}}{\text{Number of Data Values}} \tag{1.1}$$

where:

N = Number of data values
x_i = ith data value

FIGURE 1.4

Crown Investment Example—Minitab Worksheet

MINITAB - Fast100.MPJ - [Fast100.MTW ***]

File Edit Manip Calc Stat Graph Editor Window Help

	C5	C6	C7	C8	C9	C10	C11	C12
	Growth %	Sales	EPS	Profits	Stk-Price	Last Yr Price	P/E ratio	Stk Market
1	256	185.3	-99	6.8	18.00	8.50	17	1
2	228	183.2	243	43.2	42.25	12.50	31	1
3	215	187.5	-99	26.5	21.25	11.13	17	1
4	209	229.8	129	35.4	27.38	26.25	16	1
5	209	249.9	97	8.9	23.38	15.00	53	2
6	203	399.7	18	4.2	2.31	1.13	17	1
7	200	731.4	95	77.7	11.63	10.00	24	2
8	180	93.0	116	8.6	6.63	-99.00	21	2
9	179	440.9	72	8.4	8.25	-99.00	9	1
10	167	131.8	-99	3.7	16.50	-99.00	66	1

FIGURE 1.5

The Role of Business Statistics

The analyst may be interested in the average profit (that is, the average of the column labeled "Profits") for the 100 companies. The total profit for the 100 companies is $3,193.60, but profits are given in millions of dollars, so the total profit amount is actually $3,193,600,000. The average is found by dividing this total by the number of companies:

$$\text{Average} = \frac{\$3,193,600,000}{100} = \$31,936,000, \text{ or } \$31.936 \text{ million dollars}$$

As we will discuss in greater depth in Chapter 3, the average or mean is a measure of the center of the data. In this case, the analyst may use the average profit as an indicator—firms with above-average profits are rated higher than firms with below-average profits.

The graphical and numerical measures illustrated here are only some of the many descriptive tools that will be introduced in Chapters 2 and 3. The key to remember is that the purpose of the descriptive tools is to describe data. Your task will be to select the tool or tools that best accomplish this. As Figure 1.5 reminds you, the role of statistics is to convert data into meaningful information.

Inferential Tools

How do television networks determine which programs people prefer to watch? How does the network that carries the Super Bowl know how many people were watching the game? Advertisers pay for TV ads based on the audience level, so these numbers are important; millions of dollars are at stake. Clearly, the networks don't check with everyone in the country. Instead, they use **statistical inference tools** to come up with the information.

Statistical Inference Tools
Tools that allow a decision maker to reach a conclusion about a set of data based on a subset of that data.

There are two primary categories of statistical inference tools: *estimation* and *hypothesis testing*. These tools are closely related but serve very different purposes.

Estimation In situations in which we would like to know about all the data in a large data set but it is impractical to work with all the data, decision makers can use techniques to estimate what the larger data set looks like. The estimates are formed by looking closely at a subset of the larger data set.

TV RATINGS The television networks cannot know for sure how many people watched last year's Super Bowl. They cannot possibly ask everyone what he or she saw that day on television. Instead, the networks rely on organizations that conduct surveys to supply program ratings. For example, the Nielsen Company asks people from only a small number of homes across the country what shows they watched, and then it uses the data from the survey to estimate the number of viewers per show for the entire population.

Advertisers and television networks enter into contracts in which price per ad is based on a certain minimum viewership. If the Nielsen ratings estimate an audience smaller than this minimum, then a network must refund some money to its advertisers. You can go to the Web site www.nielsenmedia.com/whatratingsmean to learn more about TV ratings.

In Chapter 8 we will discuss the estimating techniques that companies such as Nielsen use.

Hypothesis Testing Television advertising is full of product claims. For example, we might hear that "Goodyear tires will last at least 60,000 miles" or that "More doctors recommend Bayer Aspirin than any other brand." Other claims might include statements like "General Electric lightbulbs last longer than any other brand" or "Customers prefer McDonald's over Burger King." Are these just idle boasts, or are they based on actual data? Probably some of both! However, consumer research organizations such as *Consumer Reports* regularly test these types of claims. For example, in the hamburger case, *Consumer Reports* might select a sample of customers who would be asked to blind taste test Burger King's and McDonald's hamburgers, under the hypothesis that there is no difference in customer preferences between the two restaurants. If the sample data show a substantial difference in preferences, then the hypothesis of no difference would be rejected. If only a slight difference in preferences were detected, then *Consumer Reports* writers could not reject the hypothesis. Chapters 9 and 10 introduce basic hypothesis-testing techniques that are used to test claims about products and services using information taken from samples.

1-1: Exercises

Skill Development

1-1. Consider the following situation and determine whether the statistical application is primarily descriptive or inferential.

"The owner of the Holden Pet Store has collected data for 10 years on the number of each type of pet that have been sold at his establishment. He is interested in making a presentation that will illustrate these data effectively."

1-2. The following graph appeared in a company annual report. Indicate whether this graph is a bar chart or a histogram and explain your reasoning.

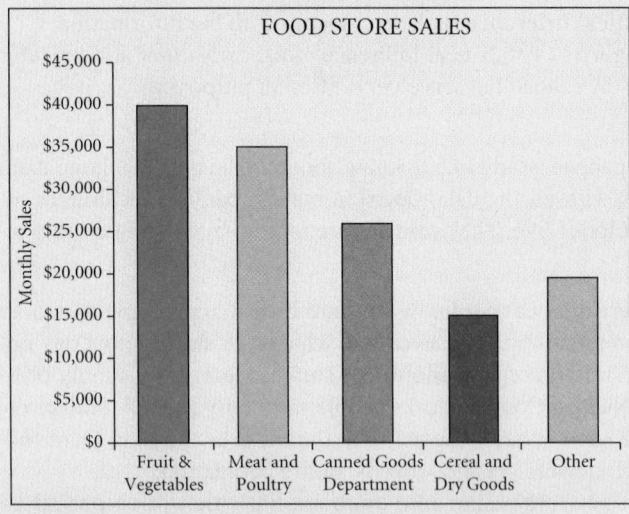

FOOD STORE SALES

1-3. What are the important differences between a bar chart and a histogram?

1-4. Provide an example of how hypothesis testing can be used to evaluate a product claim.

1-5. In what situations might a decision maker need to use statistical inference tools?

1-6. Define what is meant by hypothesis testing. Provide an example in which you personally have tested a hypothesis (even if you didn't use formal statistical techniques to do so.)

1-7. It is important to know when to employ estimation and when to employ hypothesis testing. Explain under what circumstances you would use hypothesis testing as opposed to an estimation procedure.

1-8. Discuss any advantages a single measure, such as an average, has over a table showing a whole set of data.

1-9. Discuss any advantages a graph showing a whole set of data has over a single measure, such as an average.

Business Applications

1-10. The manager of human resources for the eastern region for the office-supply company Staples has collected the following data showing how many employees there were in each of five categories for the number of days missed due to illness or injury during the past year.

Missed Days	0–2 days	3–5 days	6–8 days	8–10 days
Employees	159	67	32	10

Construct the appropriate chart for these data. Be sure to use labels and add a title to your chart.

1-11. Describe how statistics it could be used by a business to determine if the light bulbs it produces last longer than the competitor's brand.

1-12. Suppose *The New York Times* would like to determine the average age and income of its subscribers. How could statistics be of use in determining these values?

1-13. Locate a business periodical such as *Fortune* or *Forbes* or a business newspaper such as *The Wall Street Journal*. Find three examples of the use of a graph to display data. For each graph.
  a. Give the name, date, and page number of the periodical in which the graph appeared.
  b. Describe the main point made by the graph.
  c. Analyze the effectiveness of the graphs.

1-14. Considering the types of jobs you might have after graduating in your own major, discuss one or more situations where statistical analyses would be used. Base your answer on research (Internet, business periodicals, personal interviews, etc.). Indicate whether the situations you are describing involve descriptive statistics or inferential statistics or a combination of both.

1-15. A group of executives at a local company is considering introducing a new product into a market area. It is important to know the age characteristics of the people in the market area.
  a. If the executives wish to calculate a number that would characterize the "center" of the age data, what statistical technique would you suggest? Explain your answer.
  b. The executives need to know the percentage of people in the market area that are senior citizens. Name the basic category of statistical tools they would use to determine this information.
  c. Describe a hypothesis which the executives might wish to test concerning the percentage of senior citizens in the market area.

1-16. Locate an example from a business periodical or newspaper in which estimation has been used.
  a. What specifically was estimated?
  b. What conclusion was reached using the estimation?
  c. Describe how the data were extracted and how they were used to produce the estimation.
  d. Keeping in mind the goal of the estimation, discuss whether you believe that the estimation was successful and why.
  e. Describe what inferences were drawn as a result of the estimation.

CHAPTER OUTCOME #1

1.2 Tools for Collecting Data

We have defined business statistics as a set of tools that are used to transform data into information. Before you learn how to use statistical tools, it is important that you become familiar with different types of data collection methods.

Data Collection Methods

There are many methods and tools available for collecting data. The following are considered some of the most useful and frequently used data collection methods:

- experiments
- telephone surveys
- written questionnaires and surveys
- direct observation and personal interviews

Experiments

FOOD PROCESSING A company often must conduct a specific experiment or set of experiments to get the data managers need to make informed decisions. For example, the J. R. Simplot Company in Idaho is a primary supplier of french fries to companies such as McDonald's. At its Caldwell factory, Simplot has a tech center that, among other things, houses a mini–french fry plant used to conduct experiments on its potato manufacturing process. McDonald's has strict standards on the quality of the french fries it buys. One important attribute is the color of the fries after cooking. They should be uniformly "golden brown"—not too light or too dark.

French fries are made from potatoes that are peeled, sliced into strips, blanched, partially cooked, and then freeze-dried—not a simple process. Because potatoes differ in many ways (such as sugar content and moisture), blanching time, cooking temperature, and other factors vary from batch to batch.

FIGURE 1.6

Data Layout for the French Fry Experiment

Blanch Time	Blanch Temperature	Potato Category			
		1	2	3	4
10 minutes	100 110 120				
15 minutes	100 110 120				
20 minutes	100 110 120				
25 minutes	100 110 120				

Experiment
Any process that generates data as its outcome.

Experimental Design
A plan for performing an experiment in which the variable of interest is defined. One or more factors are identified to be manipulated, changed, or observed so that the impact (or influence) on the variable of interest can be measured or observed.

Simplot tech-center employees start their **experiments** by grouping the raw potatoes into batches with similar characteristics. They run some of the potatoes through the line with blanch time and temperature settings set at specific levels defined by an **experimental design**. After measuring one or more output variables for that run, they change the settings and run another batch, again measuring the output variables.

Figure 1.6 shows a typical data collection form. The output variable (for example, percentage of fries without dark spots) for each combination of potato category, blanch time, and temperature is recorded in the appropriate cell in the table. Chapter 12 introduces the fundamental concepts related to experimental design and analysis.

Telephone Surveys

PUBLIC ISSUES One common method of obtaining data about people and their opinions is the telephone survey. Chances are that you have been on the receiving end of one. "Hello. My name is Mary Jane and I represent the XYZ organization. I am conducting a survey on. . . ." Political groups use telephone surveys to poll people about candidates and issues.

Telephone surveys are a relatively inexpensive and efficient data collection tool. Of course, some people will refuse to respond to a survey, others are not home when the calls come, and some people do not have phones, only have a cell phone, or cannot be reached by phone for one reason or another.

Figure 1.7 shows the major steps in conducting a telephone survey. This example survey was run by a Seattle television station to determine public support for using tax dollars to build a new football stadium for the NFL Seattle Seahawks. The survey was aimed at property-tax payers only.

Closed-End Questions
Questions that require the respondent to select from a short list of defined choices.

Because most people will not stay on the line very long, the phone survey must be short—usually 1 to 3 minutes. The questions are generally what are called **closed-end questions**. For example, a closed-end question might be, "To which political party do you belong? Republican? Democrat? Or other?"

The survey instrument should have a short statement at the beginning explaining the purpose of the survey and reassuring the respondent that his or her responses will remain confidential. The initial section of the survey should contain questions relating to the central issue of the survey. The last part of the survey should contain **demographic questions** (such as gender, income level, and education level) that will allow you to break down the responses and look deeper into the survey results.

Demographic Questions
Questions relating to the respondents' characteristics, backgrounds, and attributes.

A survey budget must be considered. For example, if you have $3,000 to spend on calls and each call costs $10 to make, you obviously are limited to making 300 calls. However, keep in mind that 300 calls may not result in 300 usable responses.

FIGURE 1.7

**Major Steps for a
Telephone Survey**

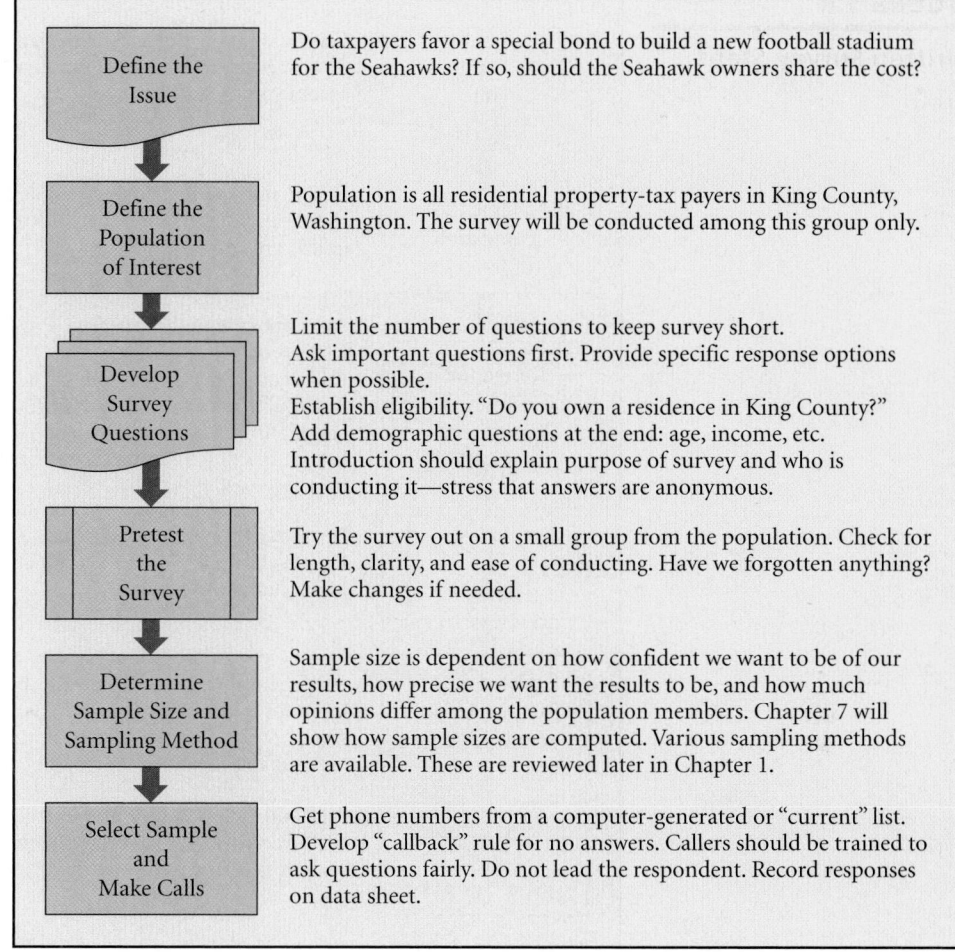

Define the Issue	Do taxpayers favor a special bond to build a new football stadium for the Seahawks? If so, should the Seahawk owners share the cost?
Define the Population of Interest	Population is all residential property-tax payers in King County, Washington. The survey will be conducted among this group only.
Develop Survey Questions	Limit the number of questions to keep survey short. Ask important questions first. Provide specific response options when possible. Establish eligibility. "Do you own a residence in King County?" Add demographic questions at the end: age, income, etc. Introduction should explain purpose of survey and who is conducting it—stress that answers are anonymous.
Pretest the Survey	Try the survey out on a small group from the population. Check for length, clarity, and ease of conducting. Have we forgotten anything? Make changes if needed.
Determine Sample Size and Sampling Method	Sample size is dependent on how confident we want to be of our results, how precise we want the results to be, and how much opinions differ among the population members. Chapter 7 will show how sample sizes are computed. Various sampling methods are available. These are reviewed later in Chapter 1.
Select Sample and Make Calls	Get phone numbers from a computer-generated or "current" list. Develop "callback" rule for no answers. Callers should be trained to ask questions fairly. Do not lead the respondent. Record responses on data sheet.

The phone survey should be conducted in a short time period. Typically, the prime calling time for a voter survey is between 7:00 P.M. and 9:00 P.M. However, some people are not home in the evening and will be excluded from the survey unless there is a plan for conducting callbacks.

Written Questionnaires and Surveys The most frequently used method to collect opinions and factual data from people is a written questionnaire. In some instances, the questionnaires are mailed to the respondent. In others, they are administered directly to the potential respondents. Written questionnaires are generally the least expensive means of collecting survey data. If they are mailed, the major costs include postage to and from the respondents, questionnaire development and printing costs, and data analysis.

Figure 1.8 shows the major steps in conducting a written survey. Note how written surveys are similar to telephone surveys; however, written surveys can be slightly more involved and, therefore, take more time to complete than those used for a telephone survey. However, you must be careful to construct a questionnaire that can be easily completed without requiring too much time.

A written survey can contain both closed-end and **open-end questions**.

Open-end questions provide the respondent with greater flexibility in answering a question; however, the responses can be difficult to analyze. Note that telephone surveys can use open-end questions, too. However, the caller may have to transcribe a potentially long response and may misinterpret what is being said.

Written surveys also should be formatted to make it easy for the respondent to provide accurate and reliable data. This means that proper space must be provided for the responses and the directions must be clear about how the survey is to be completed.

Open-End Questions
Questions that allow respondents the freedom to respond with any value, words, or statements of their own choosing.

FIGURE 1.8

Written Survey Steps

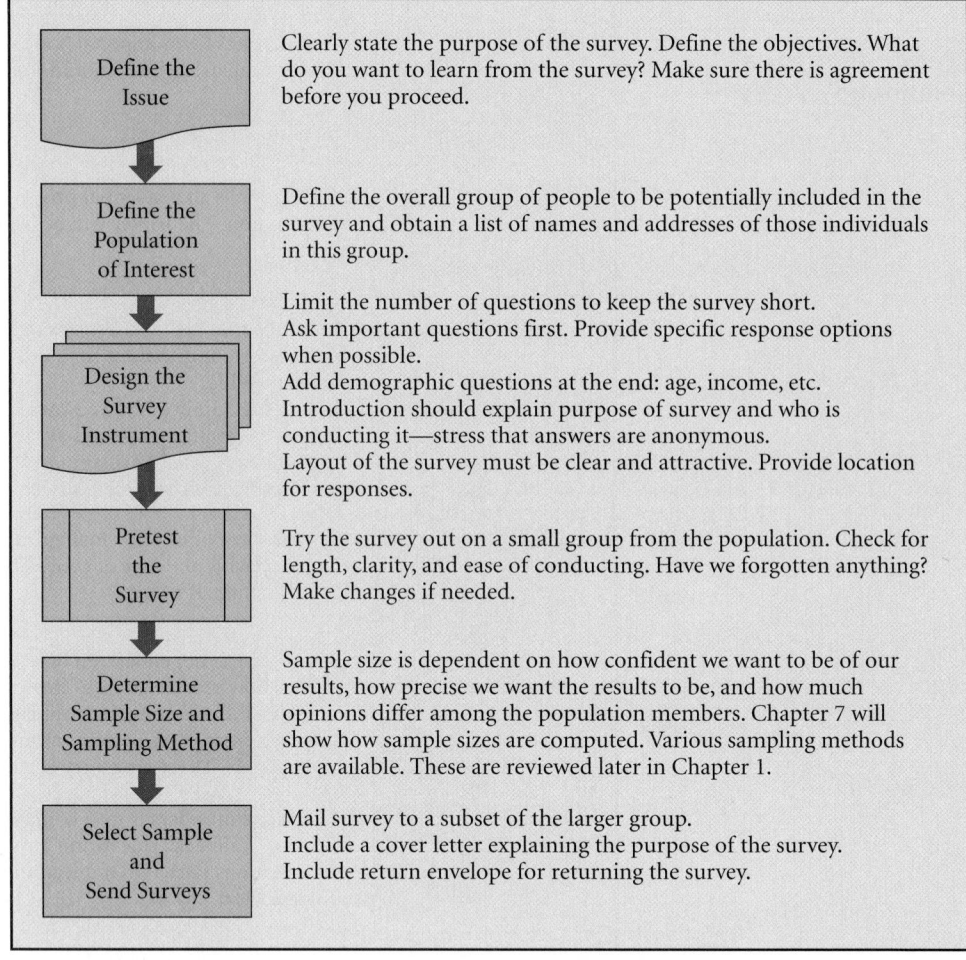

A written survey needs to be pleasing to the eye. How it looks will affect the response rate, so it must look professional.

You also must decide whether to manually enter or scan the data gathered from your written survey. The survey design will be affected by the approach you take. If you are administering a large number of surveys, scanning is preferred. It cuts down on data entry errors and speeds up the data gathering process. However, you may be limited in the form of responses that are possible if you use scanning.

If the survey is administered directly to the desired respondents, you can expect a high response rate. For example, you probably have been on the receiving end of a written survey many times in your college career, when you were asked to fill out a course evaluation form at the end of the term. Most students will complete the form. On the other hand, if a survey is administered through the mail, you can expect a low response rate—typically 5% to 20%. Therefore, if you want 200 responses, you should mail out 1,000 to 4,000 questionnaires.

Overall, written surveys can be a low-cost, effective means of collecting data if you can overcome the problems of low response. Be careful to pretest the survey and spend extra time on the format and look of the survey instrument.

Developing a good written questionnaire or telephone survey instrument is a major challenge. Among the potential problems are the following:

■ Leading Questions
  Example: "Do you agree with most other reasonably minded people that the city should spend more money on neighborhood parks?"
  Issue: In this case, the phrase "Do you agree" may suggest that you should agree. Also, by suggesting that "most reasonably minded people" already

agree, the respondent might be compelled to agree so that he or she can also be considered "reasonably minded."

    Improvement: "In your opinion, should the city increase spending on neighborhood parks?"

Example: "To what extent would you support paying a small increase in your property taxes if it would allow poor and disadvantaged children to have food and shelter?"

    Issue: The question is ripe with emotional feeling and may imply that if you don't support additional taxes, you don't care about poor children.

    Improvement: "Should property taxes be increased to provide additional funding for social services?"

■ Poorly Worded Questions

Example: "How much money do you make at your current job?"

    Issue: The responses are likely to be inconsistent. When answering, does the respondent state the answer as an hourly figure or as a weekly or monthly total? Also, many people refuse to answer question regarding their income.

    Improvement: "Which of the following categories best reflects your monthly income from your current job?

       _____ Under $500   _____ $500–$1,000

       _____ Over $1,000"

Example: "After trying the new product, please provide a rating from 1 to 10 to indicate how you like its taste and freshness."

    Issue: First, is a low number or a high number on the rating scale considered a positive response? Second, the respondent is being asked to rate two factors, taste and freshness, in a single rating. What if the product is fresh but does not taste good?

    Improvement: "After trying the new product, please rate its taste on a 1 to 10 scale with 1 being best. Also rate the product's freshness using the same 1 to 10 scale.

       _____ Taste   _____ Freshness"

Another problem is inappropriate choice of vocabulary. If you don't match the terms used to the reading and knowledge level of the respondents, they will struggle to complete the survey and may simply leave questions blank. The best advice is to use simple vocabulary and very direct questions.

Example: "Please provide your response to each of the following statements using the Likert scale provided:"

	Strongly Agree	Agree	Neutral	Disagree	Strongly Disagree
The cuisine was above reproach.	1	2	3	4	5
The ambiance was divine.	1	2	3	4	5
The service was impeccable.	1	2	3	4	5

    Issue: First, how many respondents will be confused by the term *Likert scale*? There is no need to name the scale being used. Second, terms like *cuisine*, *ambiance*, *divine*, and *impeccable* might be unfamiliar to some respondents.

    Improvement: Please indicate your degree of agreement or disagreement with each of the following by circling the appropriate number:

	Strongly Agree	Agree	Neutral	Disagree	Strongly Disagree
The food was excellent.	1	2	3	4	5
The atmosphere was pleasant.	1	2	3	4	5
The service was great.	1	2	3	4	5

Direct Observation and Personal Interviews *Direct observation* is another tool that is often used to collect data. As implied by the name, this technique requires that the process from which the data are being collected is physically observed and the data recorded based on what takes place in the process.

Possibly the most basic way to gather data on human behavior is to watch people. If you are trying to decide whether a new method of displaying your product at the supermarket will be more pleasing to customers, change a few displays and watch customers' reactions. If, as a member of a state's transportation department, you want to determine how well motorists are complying with the state's seat belt laws, place observers at key spots throughout the state to monitor people's seat belt habits. If, as a movie producer, you want information on whether your new movie will be a success, hold a preview showing and observe the reactions and comments of the movie patrons as they exit the screening. The major constraints when collecting observations are the time and money it takes to carry out the observations. For observations to be effective, trained observers must be used, which increases the cost. Personal observation is also time-consuming. Finally, personal perception is subjective. There is no guarantee that different observers will see a situation in the same way, much less report it the same way.

Personal interviews are often used to gather data from people. Interviews can be either **structured** or **unstructured**, depending on the objectives, and they can utilize either open-end or closed-end questions.

Regardless of the tool used for data collection, care must be taken that the data collected are accurate and reliable and that they are the right data for the purpose at hand.

Structured Interview

Interviews in which the questions are scripted.

Unstructured Interview

Interviews that begin with one or more broadly stated questions, with further questions being based on the responses.

Other Data Collection Methods

Data collection methods that take advantage of new technologies are becoming more prevalent all the time. For example, many people believe that Wal-Mart is the best company in the world at collecting and using data about the buying habits of its customers. Most of the data are collected automatically as checkout clerks scan the UPC bar codes on the products customers purchase. Not only are Wal-Mart's inventory records automatically updated, but information about the buying habits of customers is recorded. The data help managers organize their stores to increase sales. For instance, Wal-Mart apparently decided to locate beer and disposable diapers close together when it discovered that many male customers also purchase beer when they are sent to the store for diapers.

Bar code scanning is used in many different data collection applications. In a DRAM wafer fabrication plant, batches of silicon wafers have bar codes. As the batches travel through the plant's workstations, their progress and quality are tracked through the data that are automatically obtained by scanning.

Every time you use your credit card, data are automatically collected by the retailer and the bank. Computer information systems are developed to store the data and to provide decision makers with tools to access the data.

In many instances your data collection method will require you to use *physical measurement*. For example, the Anderson Window Company has quality analysts physically measure the width and height of its windows to assure that they meet customer specifications, and a state Department of Weights and Measures will physically test meat and produce scales to determine that customers are being properly charged for their purchases.

Data Collection Issues

There are several data collection issues of which you need to be aware. When you need data to make a decision, we suggest that you first see if appropriate data have already been collected, because it is usually faster and less expensive to use existing data than to collect data yourself. However, before you rely on data that were collected by someone else for another purpose, you need to check out the source to make sure that the data were collected and recorded properly.

Such organizations as *Value Line* and *Fortune* have built their reputations on providing quality data. Although data errors are occasionally encountered, they are few and far between. You really need to be concerned with data that come from sources with which you are not familiar. This is an issue for many sources on the World Wide Web. Any organization, or any individual, can post data to the Web. Just because the data are there doesn't mean they are accurate. Be careful.

Interviewer Bias There are other general issues associated with data collection. One of these is the potential for *bias* in the data collection. There are many types of bias. For example, in a personal interview, the interviewer can interject bias (either accidentally or on purpose) by the way she asks the questions, by the tone of her voice, or by the way she looks at the subject being interviewed. We recently allowed ourselves to be interviewed at a trade show. The interviewer began by telling us that he would only get credit for the interview if we answered all of the questions. Next, he asked us to indicate our satisfaction with a particular display. He wasn't satisfied with our less-than-enthusiastic rating and kept asking us if we really meant what we said. He even asked us if we would consider upgrading our rating! How reliable do you think these data will be?

Nonresponse Bias Another source of bias that can be interjected into a survey data collection process is called *nonresponse bias*. We stated earlier that mail surveys suffer from a high percentage of unreturned surveys. Phone calls don't always get through, or people refuse to answer. Subjects of personal interviews may refuse to be interviewed. There is a problem with nonresponse. Those who respond may provide data that are quite different from the data that would be supplied by those who choose not to respond. If you aren't careful, the responses may be heavily weighted by people who feel strongly one way or another on an issue.

Selection Bias Bias can be interjected through the way subjects are selected for data collection. This is referred to as *selection bias*. A study on the virtues of increasing the student athletic fee at your university might not be best served by collecting data from students attending a football game. Sometimes, the problem is more subtle. If we do a telephone survey during the evening hours, we will miss all of the people who work nights. Do they share the same views, income, education levels, and so on as people who work days? If not, the data are biased.

   Written and phone surveys and personal interviews can also yield flawed data if the interviewees *lie* in response to questions. For example, people commonly give inaccurate data about such sensitive matters as income. Sometimes, the data errors are not due to lies. The respondents may not know or have accurate information to provide the correct answer.

Observer Bias Data collection through personal observation is also subject to problems. People tend to view the same event or item differently. This is referred to as *observer bias*. One area in which this can easily occur is in safety check programs in companies. An important part of behavioral-based safety programs is the safety observation. Trained data collectors periodically conduct a safety observation on a worker to determine what, if any, unsafe acts might be taking place. We have seen situations in which two observers will conduct an observation on the same worker at the same time, yet record different safety data. This is especially true in areas in which judgment is required on the part of the observer, such as the distance a worker is from an exposed gear mechanism. People judge distance differently.

Measurement Error A few years ago we were working with a window manufacturer. The company was having a quality problem with one of its saws. A study was developed to measure the width of boards that had been cut by the saw. Two people were trained to use digital calipers and record the data. This caliper is a U-shaped tool that measures distance (in inches) to three decimal places. The caliper was placed around the board and squeezed tightly against the sides. The width was indicated on the display. Each person measured 500 boards during an 8-hour day. When the data were analyzed, it looked like the widths were coming from two different saws; one set showed considerably wider widths than the other.

Upon investigation, we learned that the person with the narrower width measurements was pressing down on the calipers much more firmly. The soft wood reacted to the pressure and gave narrower readings. Fortunately, we had separated the data from the two data collectors. Had they been merged, the measurement error might have gone undetected.

Internal Validity When data are collected through experimentation, you need to make sure that proper controls have been put in place. For instance, suppose a drug company such as Pfizer is conducting tests on a drug that it hopes will reduce cholesterol. One group of test participants is given the new drug while a second group (a control group) is given a placebo. Suppose that after several months, the group using the drug did see significant cholesterol reduction. For the results to have **internal validity**, the drug company would have had to make sure the two groups did not have statistically different values for the many other factors that might affect cholesterol, such as smoking, diet, weight, gender, race, and exercise habits. Issues of internal validity are generally addressed by randomly assigning subjects to the test and control groups. However, if the extraneous factors are not controlled, there could be no assurance that the drug was the factor influencing reduced cholesterol. For data to have internal validity, the extraneous factors must be controlled.

Internal Validity
A characteristic of an experiment in which data are collected in such a way as to eliminate the effects of variables within the experimental environment that are not of interest to the researcher.

External Validity Even if experiments are internally valid, you will always need to be concerned that the results can be generalized beyond the test environment. For example, if the cholesterol drug test had been performed in Europe, would the same basic results occur for people in North America, South America, or elsewhere? For that matter, the drug company would also be interested in knowing whether the results could be replicated if other subjects are used in a similar experiment. If the results of an experiment can be replicated for groups different than the original population, then there is evidence the results of the experiment have **external validity**.

External Validity
A characteristic of an experiment whose results can be generalized beyond the test environment so that the outcomes can be replicated when the experiment is repeated.

An extensive discussion of how to measure the magnitude of bias and how to reduce bias and other data collection problems is beyond the scope of this text. However, you should be aware that data may be biased or otherwise flawed. Always pose questions about the potential for bias and determine what steps have been taken to reduce its affect.

1-2: Exercises

Skill Development

1-17. What is a leading question? Provide an example.

1-18. Briefly explain what is meant by an experiment and an experimental design.

1-19. If a bank wishes to determine the level of customer satisfaction with its services, would it be appropriate to conduct an experiment? Explain.

1-20. What type of bias is most likely to occur when a personal interview is conducted? Explain.

1-21. For each of the following situations, indicate what type of data collection method you would recommend and discuss why you have made that recommendation:
   a. collecting data on the percentage of bike riders who wear helmets.
   b. collecting data on the price of regular unleaded gasoline at gas stations in your state.
   c. collecting data on customer satisfaction with the service provided by a major U.S. airline.

1-22. Suppose a survey is conducted using a telephone survey method. The survey is conducted from 9 A.M. to 11 A.M. on Tuesday. Indicate what potential problems the data collectors might encounter.

1-23. Assume you have received a class assignment to determine the attitude of students in your school toward the school's registration process. What are the validity issues you should be concerned with?

Business Applications

1-24. Briefly describe how new technologies can assist businesses in their data collection efforts.

1-25. The U.S. Department of Agriculture (USDA) estimates that the Southern fire ants spread at a rate of 4 to 5 miles a year. What data collection method do you think was used to collect this data? Explain your answer.

1-26. Assume you have made an airline reservation using an online service (like Orbitz or Travelocity). The following day you receive an e-mail containing a questionnaire asking you to rate the quality of the experience. Discuss both the advantages and disadvantages of using this form of questionnaire delivery.

1-27. Suppose you are asked to survey students at your university to determine if they are satisfied with the food service choices on campus. What types of biases must you guard against in collecting your data?

1-28. An end-of-aisle display is a common method retail stores use to promote new products. A regional manager of a national chain is experimenting with two new displays of the same product. You have been hired to determine which is more effective. Two measures you have decided to take are which display causes the highest percentage of people to stop, and for those who stop, which causes people to view the display the longest. Discuss how you would gather such data.

1-29. Assume that you work for Gold's Gym, a large fitness chain. You have been asked to survey the customers of your location to determine whether they want to convert the racquetball courts to aerobics

exercise space. The plan calls for a written survey to be handed out to customers when they arrive at the fitness center. Your task is to develop a short questionnaire with at least three "issue" questions and at least three "demographic" questions. You also need to provide the finished layout design for the questionnaire.

1-30. In your capacity as assistant sales manager for a large office products retailer, you have been assigned the task of interviewing purchasing managers for medium and large companies in the San Francisco Bay area. The objective of the interview is to determine the office products buying plans of the company in the future year. Develop a personal interview form that asks both issue-related questions as well as demographic questions.

1-31. According to a national CNN/USA/Gallup survey of 1,007 adults, conducted August 28–30, 2005, 69% of Americans say they have experienced a hardship because of rising gasoline prices. How do you believe the survey was conducted and what types of bias could occur in the data collection process?

Population
The set of all objects or individuals of interest or the measurements obtained from all objects or individuals of interest.

Sample
A subset of the population.

Business Application

Census
An enumeration of the entire set of measurements taken from the whole population.

1.3 Populations, Samples, and Sampling Techniques

Populations and Samples

Two of the most important terms in statistics are **population** and **sample**.

The list of all objects or individuals in the population is referred to as the *frame*. The choice of the frame depends on what objects or individuals you wish to study and on the availability of the list of these objects or individuals. Once the frame is defined, it forms the list of sampling units. The next example illustrates what we mean.

CPA FIRM We can use a certified public accounting (CPA) firm to illustrate the difference between a population and a sample. When preparing to audit the financial records of a business, a CPA firm must determine the number of accounts to examine. Until recently, good accounting practice dictated that the auditors verify the balance of every account and each financial transaction. Though this is still done in some audits, the size and complexity of most businesses have forced accountants to select only some accounts and some transactions to audit.

Suppose one part of the financial audit is to verify the accounts receivable balances. A population includes measurements made on all the items of interest to the data gatherer. In our example, the accountant would define the population as *all accounts receivable balances* on record. The list of these accounts, possibly by account number, forms the frame. If she examines the entire population, she is taking a **census**. But suppose there are too many accounts receivable balances to work through. The CPA would then select a subset of the accounts, called a *sample*. The accountant uses the sample results to make inferences about the population. If the sample balances look good, she might conclude that the population balances also are acceptable. How inferences are drawn will be discussed at greater length in later chapters.

There are trade-offs between taking a census and taking a sample. Usually the main trade-off is whether the information gathered in a census is worth the extra cost.

In organizations in which data are stored on computer files, the additional time and effort of taking a census may not be substantial. However, if there are many accounts that must be manually checked, a census may be impractical.

Another consideration is that the measurement error in census data may be greater than in sample data. A person obtaining data from fewer sources tends to be more complete and thorough in both gathering and tabulating the data. As a result, with a sample there are likely to be fewer human errors.

Parameters and Statistics Descriptive numerical measures, such as an average or a proportion, that are computed from an entire population are called *parameters*. Corresponding measures for a sample are called *statistics*. In the previous example, if the CPA examined every accounts receivable balance, the proportion of correct balances would be a parameter, because it reflects the value for the population. However, if she selected a sample of balances from the population, the proportion of accurate balances in this sample is a statistic. These concepts are more fully discussed in Chapters 3 and 7.

Sampling Techniques

> **Statistical Sampling Techniques**
> Those sampling methods that use selection techniques based on chance selection.

> **Nonstatistical Sampling Techniques**
> Those methods of selecting samples using convenience, judgment, or other nonchance processes.

Once a manager decides to gather information by sampling, he can use a sampling technique that falls into one of two categories: **statistical** or **nonstatistical**.

Both nonstatistical and statistical sampling techniques are commonly used by decision makers. Regardless of which technique is used, the decision maker has the same objective—to obtain a sample that is a close representative of the population. There are some advantages to using a statistical sampling technique, as we will discuss at many places throughout this text. However, in many cases, nonstatistical sampling represents the only feasible way to sample, as illustrated in the following example.

Nonstatistical Sampling

> **Business Application**

> **Convenience Sampling**
> A sampling technique that selects the items from the population based on accessibility and ease of selection.

FORD MOTOR COMPANY In 2002, Ford opened an assembly plant in Bahia, Brazil. Parts arrive at the plant in large quantities from a variety of suppliers at various locations around the world. As parts are unloaded, quality analysts select a small sample of parts from the top of each container in the shipment to verify that the parts meet Ford's specifications. One or two parts are selected from each container, and based on the findings in the sample, a decision is made whether to accept the entire shipment. Because of the volume of parts, the assembly plant uses a nonstatistical sampling method called **convenience sampling**. In doing so, the quality analysts are willing to assume that the defective parts are evenly spread throughout the container. That is, the parts near the top of each container are no more likely or less likely to meet specifications than parts located anywhere else in the container.

There are other nonstatistical sampling methods, such as *judgment sampling* and *ratio sampling*, which we will not discuss here. Instead, we now turn your attention to the most frequently used statistical sampling techniques.

Statistical Sampling

Statistical sampling methods (also called *probability sampling*) allow every item in the population to have a known or calculable chance of being included in the sample. The fundamental statistical sample is called a *simple random sample*. Other types of statistical sampling discussed in this text include *stratified random sampling, systematic sampling*, and *cluster sampling*.

Simple Random Sampling

> **Business Application**

BAIRD LIFE AND CASUALTY A salesperson at Baird Life and Casualty in Charleston, West Virginia, wishes to estimate the percentage of people in a local subdivision who already have life insurance policies. The result would indicate the potential market. The population of interest consists of all families living in the subdivision.

For this example, we simplify the situation by saying that there are only five families in the subdivision: James, Sanchez, Lui, White, and Fitzpatrick. We will let N be the population size and n be the sample size. From the five families ($N = 5$), we select three ($n = 3$) for the sample. There are 10 possible samples of size 3 that could be selected.

{James, Sanchez, Lui}   {James, Sanchez, White}   {James, Sanchez, Fitzpatrick}
{James, Lui, White}   {James, Lui, Fitzpatrick}   {James, White, Fitzpatrick}
{Sanchez, Lui, White}   {Sanchez, Lui, Fitzpatrick}   {Sanchez, White, Fitzpatrick}
{Lui, White, Fitzpatrick}

Note that no family is selected more than once in a given sample. This method is called *sampling without replacement* and is the most commonly used method. If the families could be selected more than once, the method would be called *sampling with replacement*.

Simple Random Sampling
A method of selecting items from a population such that *every possible sample of a specified size has an equal chance of being selected.*

Simple random sampling is the method most people think of when they think of random sampling.

In a correctly performed simple random sample, each of these samples would have an equal chance of being selected. A simplified way of doing this would be to put each sample of three names on a piece of paper in a bowl and then blindly reach in and select one piece of paper. This method would be difficult to do if the number of possible samples were large. For example, if $N = 50$ and a sample of size $n = 10$ is to be selected, there are more than 10 billion possible samples. Try finding a bowl big enough to hold those!

Simple random samples can be obtained in a variety of ways. We will present several examples to illustrate how simple random samples are selected in practice.

Business Application

Excel and Minitab Tutorial

NORDSTROM'S PAYROLL Suppose the personnel manager at Nordstrom's Department Store in Seattle is considering changing the payday from once a month to once every two weeks. Before making any decisions, he wants to survey a sample of 10 employees from the store's 300 employees. He first assigns employees a number (001 to 300). He can then use the random number function in either Excel or Minitab to determine which employees to include in the sample. Figure 1.9, shows the results when Excel chooses 10 random numbers. The first employee sampled is number 115, followed by 31, and so forth. The important thing to remember is that assigning each employee a number and then randomly selecting a sample from those numbers gives each possible sample an equal chance of being selected.

Random Number Table If you don't have access to computer software such as Excel or Minitab, the items in the population to be sampled can be determined by using the *random numbers table* in Appendix A. Begin by selecting a starting point in the random numbers table (row and digit). Suppose we use row 5, digit 8 as the starting point. Go down 5 rows and over 8 digits. Verify that the digit in this location is 1. Ignoring the blanks between

FIGURE 1.9

Excel 2007 Output of Random Numbers for Nordstrom's Example

Excel 2007 Instructions:
1. On the **Data** tab, click **Data Analysis**.
2. Select **Random Number Generation** option.
3. Select **Uniform** as the distribution.
4. Define range as between 1 and 300.
5. Indicate where the results are to go.
6. Click **OK**.

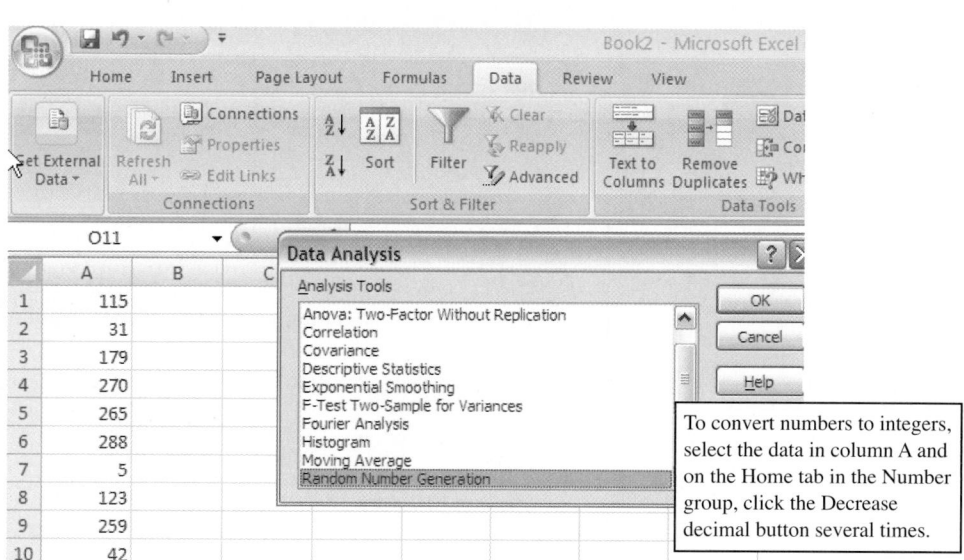

columns that are there only to make the table more readable, the first three-digit number is 149. Employee number 149 is the first one selected in the sample. Each subsequent random number is obtained from the random numbers in the next row down. For instance, the second number is 127. The procedure continues selecting numbers from top to bottom in each subsequent column. Numbers exceeding 300 and duplicate numbers are skipped. When enough numbers are found for the desired sample size, the process is completed. Employees whose numbers are chosen are then surveyed.

Stratified Random Sampling

Business Application

Stratified Random Sampling
A statistical sampling method in which the population is divided into subgroups called *strata* so that each population item belongs to only one stratum. The objective is to form strata such that the population values of interest within each stratum are as much alike as possible. Sample items are selected from each stratum using the simple random sampling method.

FEDERAL RESERVE BANK Sometimes, the sample size required to obtain a needed level of information from a simple random sampling may be greater than our budget permits. At other times, it may take more time to collect than is available. **Stratified random sampling** is an alternative method that has the potential to provide the desired information with a smaller sample size. The following example illustrates how stratified sampling is performed.

Each year, the Federal Reserve Board asks its staff to estimate the total cash holdings of U.S. financial institutions as of July 1. The staff must base its estimate on a sample. Note that not all financial institutions (banks, credit unions, and the like) are the same size. A majority are small, some are medium-sized, and only a few are large. However, the few large institutions have a substantial percentage of the total cash on hand. To make sure that a simple random sample includes an appropriate number of small, medium, and large institutions, the sample size might have to be quite large.

As an alternative to the simple random sample, the Federal Reserve staff could divide the institutions into three groups called *strata*: small, medium, and large. Staff members could then select a simple random sample of institutions from each stratum and estimate the total cash on hand for all institutions from this combined sample. Figure 1.10 shows the stratified random sampling concept. Note that the combined sample size $(n_1 + n_2 + n_3)$ is the sum of the simple random samples taken from each stratum.

The key behind stratified sampling is to develop strata for the characteristic of interest (such as cash on hand), that have items that are quite *homogeneous*. In this example, the size of the financial institution may be a good factor to use in stratifying. Here the combined sample size $(n_1 + n_2 + n_3)$ will be less than the sample size that would have been required if no stratification had occurred. Because sample size is directly related to cost (in both time and money), a stratified sample can be more cost-effective than a simple random sample.

FIGURE 1.10

Stratified Sampling Example

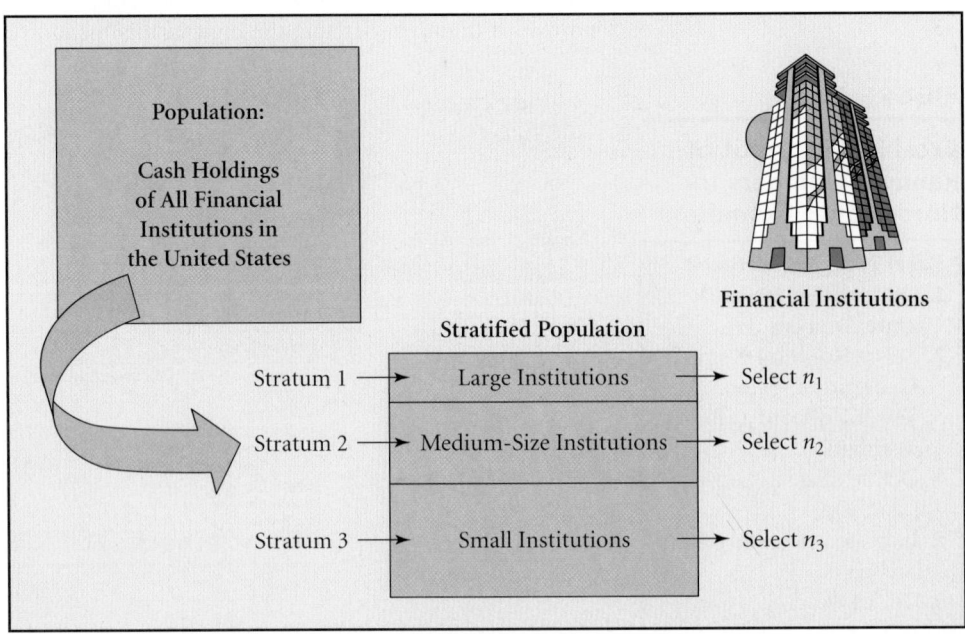

Multiple layers of stratification can further reduce the overall sample size. For example, the Federal Reserve might break the three strata in Figure 1.10 into *substrata* based on type of institution: state bank, interstate bank, credit union, and so on.

Most large-scale market research studies use stratified random sampling. The well-known political polls, such as the Gallup and Harris polls, use this technique also. For instance, the Gallup poll typically samples between 1,800 and 2,500 people nationwide to estimate how more than 60 million people will vote in a presidential election. We encourage you to go to the Web site www.gallup.com/help/FAQs/poll1.asp to read a very good discussion about how the Gallup polls are conducted. It talks about how samples are selected and many other interesting issues associated with polling.

Systematic Random Sampling

Business Application

Systematic Random Sampling
A statistical sampling technique that involves selecting every kth item in the population after a randomly selected starting point between 1 and k. The value of k is determined as the ratio of the population size over the desired sample size.

NATIONAL ASSOCIATION OF ACCOUNTANTS A few years ago, the National Association of Accountants (NAA) considered establishing a code of ethics. To determine the opinion of its 20,000 members, a questionnaire was sent to a sample of 500 members. Although simple random sampling could have been used, an alternative method called **systematic random sampling** was chosen.

The NAA's systematic random sampling plan called for it to send the questionnaire to every 40th member (20,000/500 = 40) from the list of members. The list was in alphabetical order. It could have begun by using Excel or Minitab to generate a single random number in the range 1 to 40. Suppose this value was 25. The 25th person in the alphabetic list would be selected. After that, every 40th member would be selected (25, 65, 105, 145, . . .) until there were 500 NAA members.

Systematic sampling is frequently used in business applications. Use it as an alternative to simple random sampling only when you can assume the population is randomly ordered with respect to the measurement being addressed in the survey. In this case, peoples' views on ethics are likely unrelated to the spelling of their last name.

Cluster Sampling

Business Application

WASHINGTON GROUP INTERNATIONAL When using a telephone survey or a mail questionnaire, the geographical location of the respondents is not a significant data collection issue. However, in some instances when physical measurement or observation is required to collect the data, location can be an important issue.

Suppose Washington Group International, a large worldwide construction company, wants to develop a new corporate bidding strategy. Upper management wants input on possible new strategies from its middle-level managers. Assume that Figure 1.11 illustrates the current distribution of middle-level managers throughout the world. For example, there are 25 middle-level managers in Algeria, 47 in Illinois, and so forth. Upper management decides to hold face-to-face personal interviews with a sample of these mid-level managers.

One sampling technique is to select a simple random sample of size n from the population of middle managers. Unfortunately, this technique would likely require that interviewer(s) go to each state or country in which Washington Group International has middle-level managers. This would prove to be an expensive and time-consuming process. A systematic or stratified sampling procedure also would probably require visiting each location. The geographical spread in this case causes problems.

FIGURE 1.11

Mid-Level Managers by Location for Washington Group International

Algeria	Illinois	Scotland	California	Alaska	New York	Florida	Idaho	Mexico	Australia
25	47	22	105	20	36	52	152	76	37

Cluster Sampling
A method by which the population is divided into groups, or clusters, that are each intended to be mini-populations. A simple random sample of m clusters is selected. The items chosen from a cluster can be selected using any probability sampling technique.

A sampling technique that overcomes the traveling (time and money) problem is **cluster sampling**. Ideally, the clusters would each have the same characteristics as the population as a whole. In the Washington Group International example, the states or countries where the company has managers would be the clusters.

After the clusters have been defined, a sample of m clusters is selected at random from the list of possible clusters. The number of clusters to select depends on various factors, including our survey budget. Suppose WGI selects $m = 3$ clusters randomly as follows:

Scotland   Florida   Illinois

These are the *primary clusters*. Next, the company can either survey all the managers in each cluster or select a simple random sample of managers from each cluster, depending on time and budget considerations.

1-3: Exercises

Skill Development

1-32. A parts file has 18,000 different part items. The file is ordered by part number from 1 to 18,000. If a sample of 100 parts is to be selected from the 18,000 parts using systematic random sampling, within what range of part numbers will the first part selected come from?

1-33. Indicate which sampling method would most likely be used in each of the following situations:
  a. an interview conducted with mayors of a sample of cities in Florida
  b. a poll of voters regarding a referendum calling for a national value-added tax
  c. a survey of customers entering a shopping mall in Minneapolis

1-34. Briefly describe the difference between a parameter and a statistic.

1-35. Describe how systematic random sampling could be used to select a random sample of 1,000 customers who have a certificate of deposit at a commercial bank. Assume that the bank has 25,000 customers who own a certificate of deposit.

1-36. If a manager surveys a sample of 100 customers to determine how many miles they live from the store, is the mean travel distance for this sample considered a parameter or a statistic? Explain.

1-37. Why is convenience sampling considered to be a nonstatistical sampling method?

1-38. Explain the difference between stratified random sampling and cluster sampling.

1-39. Explain why a census does not necessarily have to involve a population of people. Use an example to illustrate.

1-40. Use Excel or Minitab to generate five random numbers between 1 and 900.

Business Applications

1-41. Give the name of the kind of sampling that was most likely used in each of the following cases:
  a. a *Washington Post*/ABC News poll of 2,000 people to determine the president's approval rating
  b. a poll taken of each of the General Motor dealerships in Ohio in December 2006 to determine an estimate of the average number of 2006 model Chevrolets not yet sold by GM dealerships in the United States
  c. a quality assurance procedure within a BF Goodrich manufacturing plant that tests every 1,000th tire produced for cord strength of the tire
  d. a sampling technique in which a random sample from each of the tax brackets is obtained by the Internal Revenue Service to audit tax returns

1-42. Your manager has given you an Excel file that contains the names of the company's 500 employees and has asked you to sample 50 employees from the list. You decide to take your sample as follows. First, you assign a random number to each employee using Excel's random number function Rand(). Because the random number is volatile (it recalculates itself whenever you modify the file), you freeze the random numbers using the Copy—Paste Special—Values feature. You then sort by the random numbers in ascending order. Finally, you take the first 50 sorted employees as your sample. Does this approach constitute a statistical or a nonstatistical sample?

1-43. According to the U.S. Bureau of Labor Statistics, the annual percentage increase in U.S. college tuition and fees in 1995 was 6.0%; in 1999 it was

4.0%; and in 2004 it was 9.5%. Are these percentages statistics or parameters? Explain.

1-44. According to an article in the *Idaho Statesman*, a poll taken the day before elections in Germany showed Chancellor Gerhard Schroeder behind his challenger by 6 to 8 percentage points. Is this a statistic or a parameter? Explain.

Computer Applications

1-45. The Craigthorp Company is a statewide food distributor to restaurants, universities, and other establishments that prepare and sell food. The company has a very large warehouse where the food is stored until it is pulled from the shelves to be delivered to the customers. The warehouse has 64 storage racks numbered 1–64. Each rack is three shelves high, labeled A, B, and C, and each shelf is divided into 80 sections, numbered 1–80. Products are located by rack number, shelf letter, and section number. For example, breakfast cereal is located at 43-A-52 (rack 43, shelf A, section 52).

Each week, employees perform an inventory for a sample of products. Certain products are selected and counted. The *actual count* is compared to the *book count* (the quantity in the records that should be in stock). To simplify things, assume that the company has selected breakfast cereals to inventory. Also for simplicity sake, suppose the cereals occupy racks 1 through 5.

a. Assume that you plan to use simple random sampling to select the sample. Use Excel or Minitab to determine the sections on each of the five racks to be sampled.

b. Assume that you wish to use cluster random sampling to select the sample. Discuss the steps you would take to carry out the sampling.

c. In this case, why might cluster sampling be preferred over simple random sampling? Discuss.

1-46. United Airlines established a discount airline named Ted. The managers were interested in determining how flyers using Ted rate the airline service. They plan to question a random sample of flyers from the November 12 flights between Denver and Fort Lauderdale. A total of 578 people were on the flights that day. United has a list of the travelers together with their mailing addresses. Each traveler is given an identification number (here, from 001 to 578). Use Excel or Minitab to generate a list of 40 flyer identification numbers so that those identified can be surveyed.

1-47. The U.S. Forest Service has started charging a user fee to park at selected trailheads and cross-country ski lots. Some users object to this fee, claiming they already pay taxes for these areas. The agency has decided to randomly question selected users at fee areas in Colorado.

a. Define the population of interest.

b. Assume a sample of 250 is required. Describe the technique you would use to select a sample from the population. Which sampling technique did you suggest?

c. Assume the population of users is 4,000. Use either Minitab or Excel to generate a list of users to be selected for the sample.

1-48. The Fairview Title Company has over 4,000 customer files listed alphabetically in its computer system. The office manager wants to survey a statistical sample of these customers to determine how satisfied they were with service provided by the title company. She plans to use a telephone survey of 100 customers.

a. Describe how you would attach identification numbers to the customer files; for example, how many digits (and which digits) would you use to indicate the first customer file?

b. Describe how the first random number would be obtained to begin a simple random sample method.

c. How many random digits would you need for each random number you selected?

d. Use Excel or Minitab to generate the list of customers to be surveyed.

CHAPTER OUTCOME #4

1.4 Data Types and Data Measurement Levels

Chapters 2 and 3 will introduce a variety of techniques for describing data and transforming the data into information. As you will see in those chapters, the statistical techniques deal with different types of data. The level of measurement may vary greatly from application to application. In general, there are four types of data: *quantitative, qualitative, time-series,* and *cross-sectional*. A discussion of each follows.

Quantitative and Qualitative Data

Quantitative Data
Measurements whose values are inherently numerical.

In some cases, data values are best expressed in purely numerical, or **quantitative** terms, such as in dollars, pounds, inches, or percentages. As an example, a study of college students at your campus might obtain data on the number of hours each week that students work at a paying job and the income level of the students' parents.

In other cases, the observation may signify only the category to which an item belongs. Categorical data are referred to as **qualitative** data.

Qualitative Data

Data whose measurement scale is inherently categorical.

For example, a study might be interested in the class standings—*freshman, sophomore, junior, senior*, or *graduate*—of college students. The same study also might ask the students to judge the quality of their education as *very good, good, fair, poor*, or *very poor*. Note, even if the students are asked to record a number (1 to 5) to indicate the quality level at which the numbers correspond to a category, the data would still be considered qualitative because the numbers are just codes for the categories.

Time-Series Data and Cross-Sectional Data Data may also be classified as being either **time-series** or **cross-sectional**.

Time-Series Data

A set of consecutive data values observed at successive points in time.

Cross-Sectional Data

A set of data values observed at a fixed point in time.

The data collected from the study of college students about their quality ratings would be cross-sectional because the data from each student relates to a fixed point in time. In another case, if we sampled 100 stocks from the stock market and determined the closing stock price on March 15, the data would be considered cross-sectional because all measurements corresponded to one point in time.

On the other hand, Ford Motor Company tracks the sales of its Explorer SUVs on a monthly basis. Data values observed at intervals over time are referred to as time-series data. If we determined the closing stock price for a particular stock on a daily basis for a year, the stock prices would be time-series data.

Data Measurement Levels

Data can also be identified by their *level of measurement*. This is important because the higher the data level, the more sophisticated the analysis that can be performed. This will be clear when you study the material in the remaining chapters of this text.

We shall discuss and give examples of four levels of data measurements: *nominal, ordinal, interval*, and *ratio*. Figure 1.12 illustrates the hierarchy among these data levels, with nominal data being the lowest level.

Nominal Data *Nominal data* are the lowest form of data, yet you will encounter this type of data many times. Assigning codes to categories generates nominal data. For example, a survey question that asks for marital status provides the following responses:

1. Married   2. Single   3. Divorced   4. Other

FIGURE 1.12

Data Level Hierarchy

For each person, a code of 1, 2, 3, or 4 would be recorded. These codes are nominal data. Note that the values of the code numbers have no specific meaning, because the order of the categories is arbitrary. We might have shown it this way:

    1. Single   2. Divorced   3. Married   4. Other

With nominal data we also have complete control over what codes are used. For example, we could have used

    88. Single   11. Divorced   33. Married   55. Other

All that matters is that you know which code stands for which category. Recognize also that the codes need not be numeric. We might use

    S = Single   D = Divorced   M = Married   O = Other

Ordinal Data *Ordinal*, or *rank data* are one notch above nominal data on the measurement hierarchy. At this level, the data elements can be rank-ordered on the basis of some relationship among them, with the assigned values indicating this order. For example, a typical market research technique is to offer potential customers the chance to use two unidentified brands of a product. The customers are then asked to indicate which brand they prefer. The brand eventually offered to the general public depends on how often it was the preferred test brand. The fact that an ordering of items took place makes this an ordinal measure.

    Bank loan applicants are asked to indicate the category corresponding to their household incomes:

_____ Under $20,000	_____ $20,000 to $40,000	_____ over $40,000
(1)	(2)	(3)

The codes 1, 2, and 3 refer to the particular income categories, with higher codes assigned to higher incomes.

    Ordinal measurement allows decision makers to equate two or more observations or to rank-order the observations. In contrast, nominal data can be compared only for equality. You cannot order nominal measurements. Thus, a primary difference between ordinal and nominal data is that ordinal data contain both an equality (=) and a greater than (>) relationship, whereas nominal data contain only an equality (=) relationship.

Interval Data If the distance between two data items can be measured on some scale and the data have ordinal properties (>, <, or =), the data are said to be *interval data*. The best example of interval data is the temperature scale. Both the Fahrenheit and Celsius temperature scales have ordinal properties of ">" and "=." In addition, the distances between equally spaced points are preserved. For example, 32°F > 30°F, and 80°C > 78°C. The difference between 32°F and 30°F is the same as the difference between 80°F and 78°F, two degrees in each case. Thus, interval data allow us to precisely measure the difference between any two values. With ordinal data this is not possible, because all we can say is that one value is larger than another.

Ratio Data Data that have all the characteristics of interval data but also have a true zero point (at which zero means "none") are called *ratio data*. Ratio measurement is the highest level of measurement.

    Packagers of frozen foods encounter ratio measures when they pack their products by weight. Weight, whether measured in pounds or grams, is a ratio measurement because it has a unique zero point—zero meaning no weight. Many other types of data encountered in business environments involve ratio measurements, for example, distance, money, and time.

    The difference between interval and ratio measurements can be confusing because it involves the definition of a true zero. If you have $5 and your brother has $10, he has twice as much money as you. If you convert the dollars to pounds, lire, yen, or marks, your brother will still have twice as much. If your money is lost or stolen, you have no dollars. Money has a true zero. Likewise, if you travel 100 miles today and 200 miles tomorrow, the ratio of distance traveled will be 2/1, even if you convert the distance to kilometers. If on the third day you rest, you have traveled no miles. Distance has a true zero. Conversely, if today's temperature is 35°F (1.67°C) and tomorrow's is 70°F (21.11°C), is tomorrow twice as warm as today? The answer is no. One way to see this is to convert the Fahrenheit temperature to Celsius: The ratio will no longer be 2/1 (12.64/1). Likewise, if the temperature reads 0°F (−17.59°C), this does not imply that there is no temperature. It's simply colder than 10°F (−12.22°C). Also, 0°C (32°F) is not the same temperature as 0°F. Thus, temperature, measured with either the Fahrenheit or Celsius scale (an interval-level variable), does not have a true zero.

As was mentioned earlier, a major reason for categorizing data by level and type is that the methods you can use to analyze the data are partially dependent on the level and type of data you have available.

EXAMPLE 1-1   Categorizing Data

For many years *U.S. News and World Report* has published annual rankings based on various data collected from more than 1,300 U.S. colleges and universities. Figure 1.13 shows a portion of the data in the file named **Colleges**. Each column corresponds to a different factor for which data were collected. Before doing any statistical analyses with these data, *U.S. News and World Report* employees need to determine the type and level for each of the factors. Limiting the effort to only those factors that are shown in Figure 1.13, this is done using the following steps:

Step 1 Identify each factor in the data set.
The factors (later to be called variables) in the data set shown in Figure 1.13 are

College Name	State	Public (1) Private (2)	Math SAT	Verbal SAT	ACT	# appli. rec'd.	# appli. accepted.	# new stud. enrolled	% new stud. from top 10%	% new stud. from top 25%	# FT under-grad	# PT under-grad	in-state tuition

Each of the 14 columns represents a different factor. As shown in Figure 1.13, data are missing for some colleges and universities.

Step 2 Determine whether the data are time-series or cross-sectional.
Because each row represents a different college or university and the data are for the same year, the data are cross-sectional. Time-series data are measured over time—say, over a period of years.

Step 3 Determine which factors are quantitative data and which are qualitative data.
Qualitative data are codes or numerical values that represent categories. Quantitative data are those that are purely numerical. In this case, the data for the following factors are qualitative:

College Name
State
Code for Public or Private College or University

FIGURE 1.13

Data for U.S. Colleges and Universities

Data for the following factors are considered quantitative:

Math SAT	Verbal SAT	ACT
# appl. rec'd.	# appl. accepted	# new stud. enrolled
% new stud. from top 10%	% new stud. from top 25%	# FT undergrad
# PT. undergrad	in-state tuition	

Step 4   Determine the level of data measurement for each factor.

The four levels of data are nominal, ordinal, interval, and ratio. This data set has only nominal-and ratio-level data. The three nominal level factors are

College Name
State
Code for Public or Private College or University

The others are all ratio-level data.

1-4: Exercises

Skill Development

1-49. What is the difference between qualitative and quantitative data?

1-50. For each of the following variables, indicate the level of data measurement:
   a. marital status {single, married, divorced, other}
   b. home ownership {own, rent, other}
   c. college grade point average
   d. product rating {1 = excellent, 2 = good, 3 = fair, 4 = poor, 5 = very poor}

1-51. For each of the following, indicate whether the data are cross-sectional or time-series:
   a. monthly sales
   b. unemployment rates by state
   c. quarterly unemployment rates
   d. employment satisfaction data for a company

1-52. What is the difference between ordinal and nominal data?

1-53. *Consumer Reports*, in its rating of cars, indicates repair history with circles. The circles are either white, black, or half-and-half. To which level of data does this correspond? Discuss.

Business Applications

1-54. The manufacturer of a top-selling brand of laser printers has a support center where customers can call to get questions answered about their printer. The manager in charge of the support center has recently conducted a study in which she surveyed 2,300 customers. The customers who called the support center were transferred to a third party who asked the customer a series of questions.

   a. Indicate whether the data generated from this study will be considered cross-sectional or time-series. Explain why.

   b. One of the questions asked customers was approximately how many minutes they had been on hold waiting to get through to a support person. What level of data measurement is obtained from this question? Explain.

   c. Another question asked the customer to rate the service on a scale of 1–7, with 1 being the worst possible service and 7 being the best possible service. What level of data measurement is achieved from this question? Will the data be quantitative or qualitative? Explain.

1-55. The following information can be found in the Murphy Oil Corporation 2004 Annual Report to Shareholders. For each variable, indicate the level of data measurement.

   a. List of Principal Offices (e.g., El Dorado, New Orleans, Houston, and so on)

   b. Income (in millions of dollars) from Continuing Operations

   c. List of Principal Subsidiaries (for example, Murphy Oil USA, Inc., Murphy Exploration & Production Company-International, and so on)

   d. Number of New Stations Added in 2004

   e. Barrels of Gasoline Sold Per Day in North America

   f. Major Exploration and Production Areas (for example, Malaysia, Congo, Ecuador, and so on)

   g. Capital Expenditures (in millions of dollars) for example by Function

1-56. You have collected the following information on 15 different real estate investment trusts (REITs). Identify whether the data are cross-sectional or time-series.

   a. Income distribution by region in 2006

   b. Per share (diluted) funds from operations (FFO) for the years 2000 to 2006

   c. Income distribution by region in 2006

   d. Number of properties owned as of December 31, 2006

   e. The overall percentage of leased space for the 119 properties in service as of December 31, 2006

   f. Dividends per share for the years 2000–2006

1-57. A loan manager for Farmers and Merchants Bank has the responsibility for approving automobile loans. In 2004, to assist her in this matter, she has compiled data on 428 cars and trucks. These data are in the file called **2004-Automobiles**. The variables for which she has collected data are

Columns Variables

Vehicle Name
Sports Car? (1=yes, 0=no)
Sport Utility Vehicle? (1=yes, 0=no)
Wagon? (1=yes, 0=no)
Minivan? (1=yes, 0=no)
Pickup? (1=yes, 0=no)
All-Wheel Drive? (1=yes, 0=no)
Rear-Wheel Drive? (1=yes, 0=no)
Suggested Retail Price, what the manufacturer
   thinks the vehicle is worth, including adequate
   profit for the automaker and the dealer (U.S.
   Dollars)
Dealer Cost (or "invoice price"), what the dealer-
   ship pays the manufacturer (U.S. Dollars)
Engine Size (liters)
Number of Cylinders ($=-1$ if rotary engine)
Horsepower
City Miles Per Gallon
Highway Miles Per Gallon
Weight (Pounds)
Wheel Base (inches)
Length (inches)
Width (inches)

Indicate the level of data measurement for each of the variables in this data file.

1-58. Recently the manager of the call center for a large Internet bank asked his staff to collect data on a random sample of the bank's customers. Data on the following variables were collected and placed in a file called **Bank Call Center**:

Column A	Column B	Column C	Column D	Column E	Column F
Account Number	**Caller Sex**	**Account Holder Sex**	**Past Due Amount**	**Current Amount Due**	**Was this a Billing Question?**
Unique tracking #	1 = Male	1 = Male	Numerical Value	Numerical Value	3 = Yes
	2 = Female	2 = Female			4 = No

A small portion of the data is as follows:

Account Number	Caller Gender	Account Holder Sex	Past Due Amount	Current Amount Due	Was this a Billing Question?
4348291	2	2	40.35	82.85	3
6008516	1	1	0	−129.67	4
17476479	1	2	0	76.38	4
13846306	2	2	0	99.24	4
21393711	1	1	0	37.98	3

a. Would you classify these data as time-series or cross-sectional? Explain.

b. Which of the variables are quantitative and which are qualitative?

c. For each of the six variables, indicate the level of data measurement.

Summary and Conclusions

Business statistics is about converting data into useful information. There are three main components in this process: *descriptive statistics, probability*, and *inferential statistics*. The tools for descriptive statistics include graphs, charts, tables, and various numerical measures. Chapters 2 and 3 will introduce the important descriptive tools.

Probability is the way decision makers express their uncertainty about whether some event will take place. We use probability distributions as a means of defining the chances of any outcome occurring based on a set of business conditions. Chapters 4 and 5 introduce the key rules and concepts you will need to work effectively with probability.

Drawing inferences about a population based on sample data takes up a good portion of the remainder of the text. We will introduce you to a variety of inferential tools to help you learn to think statistically. Figure 1.14 summarizes the differences between populations and samples and the different types of sampling techniques you may have reason to use.

Businesses have access to more data than ever. Much of this data they generate internally through normal operations. In other cases, the data they need is found outside the organization. We have discussed the fact that there are numerous ways to gather data. *Surveys* (phone or written) are effective when gathering data from people. *Observation* and *direct measurement* are appropriate when collecting data from a process. Figure 1.15 summarizes the most frequently used data collection techniques and the advantages and disadvantages of each.

The type of data that is collected varies, too. The data may be *quantitative* or *qualitative*, it may be *time-series* or

FIGURE 1.14

Sampling Techniques

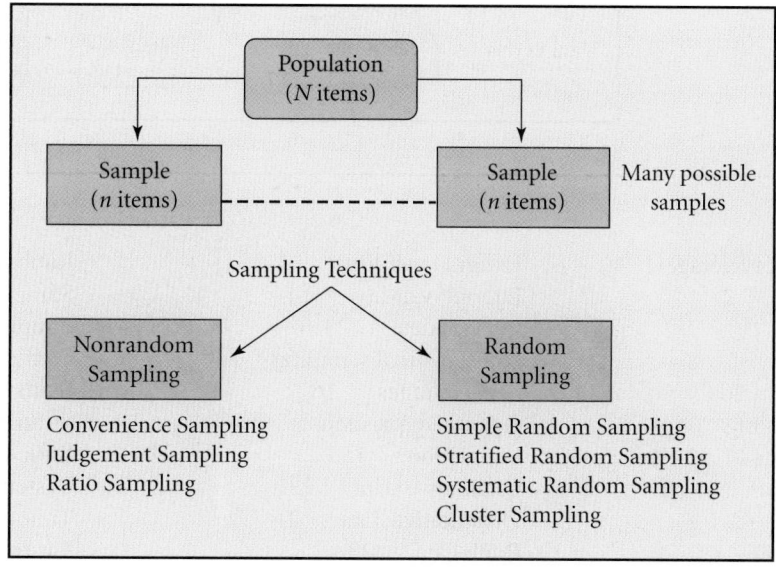

FIGURE 1.15

Data Collection Techniques

Data Collection Method	Advantages	Disadvantages
Experiments	Provide controls Preplanned objectives	Costly Time-consuming Requires planning
Telephone Surveys	Timely Relatively inexpensive	Poor reputation Limited scope and length
Mail Questionnaires Written Surveys	Inexpensive Can expand length Can use open-ended questions	Low response rate Requires exceptional clarity
Direct Observation Personal Interview	Expands analysis opportunities No respondent bias	Potential observer bias Costly

cross-sectional, and it may be *nominal, ordinal, interval*, or *ratio* level. The type and level of data that we have is important in determining the type of analysis we can perform. Please refer to Figure 1.16 for a quick summary of the ways in which we classify data.

Many of the things you will be doing in this course can be better done using computer software. The software selected for this text is Microsoft Excel and Minitab. Although not a special-purpose statistics software package, Excel contains a great many tools and techniques for performing descriptive and inferential statistical analysis. Minitab is a fully functional statistics package with a spreadsheet look and feel. You will find that whichever software package is used during this course, it will be a valuable tool that will free you from tedious computations, allowing you more time to analyze and interpret the output to make better business decisions.

FIGURE 1.16

Data Classification

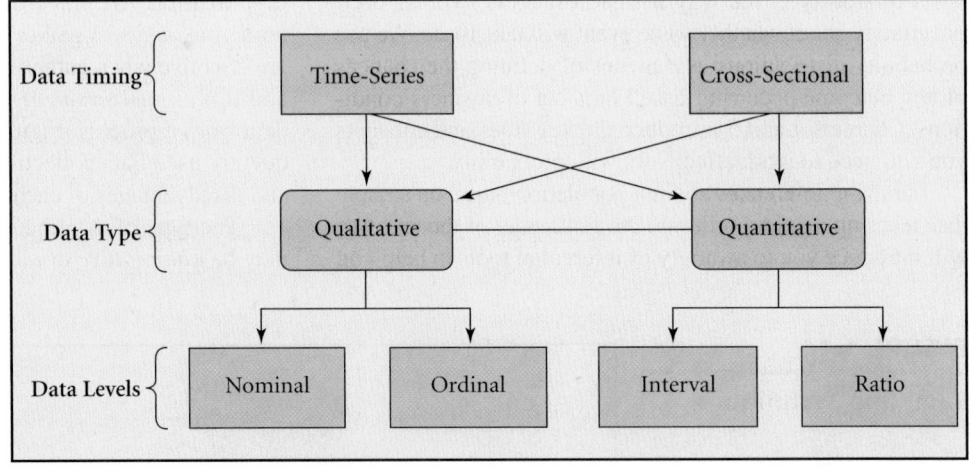

Key Terms

Chapter Exercises

Conceptual Questions

1-59. What level of data is a bar chart most appropriately used with?

1-60. What level of data is a histogram most appropriately used with?

1-61. Two people see the same movie; one says it was average and the other says it was exceptional. What level of data are they using in these ratings? Discuss how the same movie could receive different reviews.

1-62. Several organizations publish the results of presidential approval polls. Movements in these polls are seen as an indication of how the general public views presidential performance. Comment on these polls within the context of what was covered in this chapter.

1-63. The University of Michigan publishes a monthly measure of consumer confidence. This is taken as a possible indicator of future economic performance. Comment on this process within the context of what was covered in this chapter.

Business Applications

1-64. In a business publication such as *The Wall Street Journal* or *Business Week*, find a graph or chart representing time-series data. Discuss how the data were gathered and the purpose of the graph or chart.

1-65. In a business publication such as *The Wall Street Journal* or *Business Week*, find a graph or chart representing cross-sectional data. Discuss how the data were gathered and the purpose of the graph or chart.

1-66. A local television station has asked its viewers to call in and respond to the question "Do you believe police officers are using too much force in routine traffic stops?"

    a. Would the results of this phone-in survey be considered a random sample?

    b. What type of bias might be associated with a data collection system such as this? Discuss what options might be used to reduce this bias potential.

1-67. The maker of Creamy Good Ice Cream is concerned about the quality of ice cream being produced by its Illinois plant. The particular trait of the ice cream of concern is the texture of the ice cream in each carton.

    a. Discuss a plan by which the Creamy Good managers might determine the percentage of cartons of ice cream believed to have an unacceptable texture by potential purchasers of a particular flavor of their ice cream. (1) Define the sampling procedure to be used, (2) the randomization method to be used to select the sample, and (3) the measurement to be obtained.

    b. Explain why it would or wouldn't be feasible (or, perhaps, possible) to take a census to address this issue.

1-68. A beer manufacturer is considering abandoning can containers and going exclusively to bottles because the sales manager believes beer drinkers prefer drinking beer from bottles. However, the vice president in charge of marketing is not convinced the sales manager is correct.

    a. Indicate the data collection method you would use.

    b. Indicate what procedures you would follow to apply this technique in this setting.

    c. State which level of data measurement applies to the data you would collect. Justify your answer.

    d. Is the data qualitative or quantitative? Explain.

VIDEO CASE #1

Statistical Data Collection @ McDonald's

Think of any well-known, successful business in your community. What do you think has been their secret? Competitive products or services? Talented managers with vision? Dedicated employees with great skills? There's no question these all play an important part in their success. But there's more, lots more. It's "data." That's right, data.

The data collected by a business in the course of running its daily operations form the foundation of every decision made. Those data are analyzed using a variety of statistical techniques to provide decision makers with a succinct and clear picture of the company's activities. The resulting statistical information then plays a key role in decision making, whether those decisions are made by an accountant, marketing manager, or operations specialist. To better understand just what types of business statistics organizations employ, let's take a look at one of the world's most well-respected companies: McDonald's.

McDonald's operates more than 30,000 restaurants in over 118 countries around the world. Total annual revenues recently surpassed the $20 billion mark. Wade Thoma, vice president of US Menu Management for McDonalds, helps drive those sales but couldn't do it without statistics.

"When you're as large as we are, we can't run the business on simple gut instinct. We rely heavily on all kinds of statistical data to help us determine whether our products are meeting customer expectations, when products need to be updated, and much more," says Wade. "The cost of making an educated guess is simply too great a risk."

McDonald's Restaurant owner/operators and managers also know the competitiveness of their individual restaurants depends on the data they collect, and the statistical techniques used to analyze the data into meaningful information. Each restaurant has a sophisticated cash register system that collects data such as individual customer orders, service times and methods of payment, to name a few. Periodically, each US-based restaurant undergoes a restaurant operations improvement process, or ROIP, study. A special team of reviewers monitors restaurant activity over a period of several days, collecting data about everything from front-counter service and kitchen efficiency, to drive-thru service times. The data are analyzed by McDonald's US Consumer and Business Insights group at McDonald's headquarters near Chicago to help the restaurant owner/operator and managers better understand what they're doing well, and where they have opportunities to grow.

Steve Levigne, VP of Consumer and Business Insights manages the team that supports the company's decision making efforts. Both qualitative and quantitative data are collected and analyzed all the way down to the individual store level. "Depending on the audience, the results may be rolled up to an aggregate picture of operations," says Steve. Software packages such as Microsoft Excel, SAS, and SPSS do most of the number crunching and are useful for preparing the graphical representations of the information so decision makers can quickly see the results.

Not all companies have an entire department staffed with specialists in statistical analysis, however. That's where you come in. The more you know about the tools for collecting and analyzing data, and how to use them, the better decision maker you'll be, regardless of your career aspirations. So it would seem there's a strong relationship here – knowledge of statistics and your success.

Discussion Questions:

1. You will recall that McDonald's vice president of US Menu Management, Wade Thoma, indicated that McDonald's relied heavily on statistical data to determine, in part, if their products were meeting customer expectations. The narrative indicated that two important sources of data were the sophisticated register system and the restaurant operations improvement process, ROIP. Describe the types of data that could be generated by these two methods and discuss how these data could be used to determine if their products were meeting customer expectations.

2. One of McDonald's uses of statistical data is to determine when products need to be updated. Discuss the kinds of data McDonald's would require to make this determination. Also provide how these types of data would be used to determine when a product needed to be updated.

3. This video case presents the types of data collected and used by McDonald's in the course of running its daily operations. For a moment, imagine that McDonald's did not collect this data. Attempt to describe how they might make a decision concerning, for instance, how much their annual advertising budget would be.

4. Visit a McDonald's in your area. While there take note of the different types of data that could be collected using observation only. For each variable you identify, determine the level of data measurement. Select three different variables from your list and outline the specific steps you would use to collect the data. Discuss how each of the variables could be used to help McDonald's manage the restaurant.

References

Berenson, Mark L., and David M. Levine, *Basic Business Statistics: Concepts and Applications*, 10th ed. (Upper Saddle River, NJ: Prentice Hall, 2006).

Cryer, Jonathan D., and Robert B. Miller, *Statitics for Business: Data Analysis and Modeling*, 2nd ed. (Belmont, CA: Duxbury Press, 1994).

Fowler, Floyd J., *Survey Research Methods*, 3rd ed. (Thousand Oaks, CA: Sage Publications, 2001).

Hildebrand, David, and R. Lyman Ott, *Statistical Thinking for Managers*, 4th ed. (Belmont, CA: Duxbury Press, 1998).

John, J. A., D. Whitiker, and D. G. Johnson, *Statistical Thinking for Managers*. (Boca Raton, FL: CRC Press, 2001).

Microsoft Excel 2007 (Redmond, WA: Microsoft Corp., 2007).

Minitab for Windows Version 15 (State College, PA: Minitab, 2007).

Pelosi, Marilyn K., and Theresa M. Sandifer, *Doing Statistics for Business with Excel*, 2nd ed. (New York: John Wiley & Sons, 2001).

Scheaffer, Richard L., William Mendenhall, and Lyman Ott, *Elementary Survey Sampling*, 6th ed. (Brooks/Cole, 2005).

Siegel, Andrew F., *Practical Business Statistics*, 5th ed. (Burr Ridge, IL: Irwin, 2003).

Graphs, Charts, and Tables— Describing Your Data

CHAPTER OUTCOMES

After studying the material in Chapter 2, you should:

1. Be able to construct frequency distributions both manually and with your computer.
2. Be able to construct and interpret a frequency histogram.
3. Be able to develop and interpret joint frequency distributions.
4. Know how to construct and interpret various types of bar charts.
5. Be able to build a stem and leaf diagram.
6. Be able to create a line chart and interpret the trend in the data.
7. Be able to construct a scatter plot and interpret it.

PREPARING FOR CHAPTER TWO

- Review the definitions for nominal, ordinal, interval, and ratio data in Section 1-4.

- Examine the statistical software, such as Excel or Minitab, which you will be using during this course to make sure you are aware of the tools for constructing graphs and tables. For instance, in Excel, look at the Charts group on Insert tab and also the *Pivot Table* feature on the Insert tab. In Minitab, acquaint yourself with the *Graph* menu and the *Tables* command within the *Stat* menu.

- Look at issues of popular newspapers such as *USA Today* and such business periodicals as *Fortune*, *Business Week*, or *The Wall Street Journal* for instances where charts, graphs, or tables are used to convey information.

We live in an age where we are constantly bombarded with visual images and stimuli. Much of our time is spent watching television, playing video games, or working at a computer monitor. These technologies are advancing rapidly, making the images sharper and more attractive to our eyes. Flat-panel screens, high-resolution monitors, and high-definition televisions represent significant improvements over the original technologies that they replaced. However, this phenomenon is not limited to video technology, but has also become an important part of the way businesses communicate with customers, employees, suppliers, and other constituents.

Presentations and reports are expected to include high-quality graphs and charts that effectively transform data into information. While the written word is still vital, words become even more powerful when coupled with an effective visual illustration of data. The adage that "a picture is worth a thousand words" is particularly relevant in business decision making.

As a business major, upon graduation you will find yourself on both ends of the data analysis business. On the one hand, regardless of what you end up doing for a career, you will almost certainly be involved in preparing reports and making presentations requiring the use of the visual descriptive statistical tools presented in this chapter. You will be on the "do it" end of the data analysis process. Thus, you need to know *how to* use these statistical tools.

On the other hand, you will also find yourself reading reports or listening to presentations that others have made. In many instances, you will be required to make important decisions, or reach conclusions, based on the information in those reports or presentations. Thus, you will be on the "use it" end of the data analysis process. You need to be knowledgeable about these tools in order to effectively screen and critique the work that others do for you.

Charts and graphs are not just tools used internally by businesses. Business periodicals such as *Fortune* and *Business Week* use graphs and charts extensively in articles to help readers better understand key concepts. Many advertisements will even use graphs and charts effectively to convey their message. Virtually every issue of *The Wall Street Journal* contains different graphs, charts, or tables that display data in an informative way.

Thus, you will find yourself as both a producer and a consumer of the descriptive statistical techniques known as graphs, charts, and tables. You will create a competitive advantage for yourself throughout your career if you obtain a solid understanding of the techniques introduced in Chapter 2.

This chapter introduces some of the most frequently used tools and techniques for describing data with graphs, charts, and tables. Although this analysis can be done manually, we will provide output from Excel and Minitab showing that these software packages can be used as tools for doing the analysis easily, quickly, and with a finished quality that once required a graphic artist.

CHAPTER OUTCOME #1

2.1 Frequency Distributions and Histograms

As we discussed in Chapter 1, in today's business climate, companies collect massive amounts of data they hope will be useful for making decisions. Every time a customer makes a purchase at a store like Wal-Mart or Sears, data from that transaction is updated to the store's database. For example, one item of data that is captured is the number of different product categories included in each "market basket" of items purchased. Table 2.1 shows these data for all customer transactions for a single day at one store in Atlanta. A total of 450 customers made purchases on the day in question. The first value, 4, in Table 2.1 indicates that the customer's purchase included four different product categories (for example food, sporting goods, photography supplies, and dry goods).

While the data in Table 2.1 are easy to capture with the technology of today's cash registers, in this form the data provide little or no information that managers could use to determine the buying habits of their customers. However, these data can be converted into useful information through descriptive statistical analysis.

Frequency Distribution

One of the first steps would be to construct a **frequency distribution**.

The product data in Table 2.1 take on only a few possible values (1, 2, 3, . . . , 11). The minimum number of product categories is 1 and the maximum number of categories in these data is 11. These data are called **discrete data**.

Frequency Distribution
A summary of a set of data that displays the number of observations in each of the distribution's distinct categories or classes.

Discrete Data
Data that can take on a countable number of possible values.

TABLE 2.1 Product Categories Per Customer at the Atlanta Retail Store

4	2	5	8	8	10	1	4	8	3	4	1	1	3	4
1	4	4	5	4	4	4	9	5	4	4	10	7	11	4
10	2	6	7	10	5	4	6	4	6	2	3	2	4	5
5	4	11	1	4	1	9	2	4	6	6	7	6	2	3
6	5	3	4	5	6	5	3	10	6	5	7	7	4	3
8	2	2	6	5	11	9	9	5	5	6	5	3	1	7
6	6	5	3	8	4	3	3	4	4	4	7	6	4	9
1	6	5	5	4	4	7	5	6	6	9	5	6	10	4
7	5	8	4	4	7	4	6	6	4	4	2	10	4	5
4	11	8	7	9	5	6	4	2	8	4	2	6	6	6
6	4	6	5	7	1	6	9	1	5	9	10	5	5	10
5	4	7	5	7	6	9	5	3	2	1	5	5	5	5
5	9	5	3	2	5	7	2	4	6	4	4	4	4	4
6	5	8	5	5	5	5	5	2	5	5	6	4	6	5
5	7	10	2	2	6	8	3	1	3	5	6	3	3	6
5	4	5	3	3	7	9	4	4	5	10	6	10	5	9
4	3	8	7	1	8	4	3	1	3	6	7	5	5	5
4	7	4	11	6	6	3	7	9	4	4	2	9	7	5
1	6	6	8	3	8	4	4	1	9	3	9	3	4	2
9	5	5	7	10	5	3	4	7	7	6	2	2	4	4
4	7	3	5	4	9	2	3	4	3	2	1	6	4	6
1	8	1	4	3	5	5	10	4	4	4	6	9	2	7
9	4	5	3	6	5	5	3	4	6	5	7	3	6	8
3	6	1	5	7	7	5	4	6	6	6	3	6	9	5
4	5	10	1	5	5	7	8	9	1	6	5	6	6	4
10	6	5	5	5	1	6	5	6	4	7	9	10	2	6
4	4	6	11	9	5	4	4	3	5	4	6	2	6	7
3	5	6	7	4	5	4	6	9	4	3	3	6	9	4
3	7	5	6	11	4	4	8	4	2	8	2	4	2	3
6	5	1	10	5	9	5	4	5	1	4	9	5	4	4

When you encounter discrete data, where the variable of interest can take on only a reasonably small number of possible values, a frequency distribution is constructed by counting the number of times each possible value occurs in the data set. We organize these counts into a *frequency distribution table* as shown in Table 2.2. Now, from this frequency distribution we are able to see how the data values are spread over the different number of possible product categories. For instance, you can see that the most frequently occurring number of product categories in a customer's "market basket" is 4, which occurred 92 times. You can also see that the three most common number of product categories are 4, 5, and 6. Only a very few times do customers purchase 10 or 11 product categories in their shopping trip to the store.

Consider another example in which a consulting firm surveyed random samples of residents in two cities, Dallas, Texas, and Knoxville, Tennessee. The firm is investigating the labor markets in these two communities for a client that is thinking of relocating its corporate offices to one of the two locations. Education level of the workforce in the two cities is a key factor in making the relocation decision. The consulting firm surveyed 160 randomly selected adults in Dallas and 330 adults in Knoxville and recorded the number

TABLE 2.2 Atlanta Store Product Categories Frequency Distribution

Number of Product Catagories	Frequency
1	25
2	29
3	42
4	92
5	83
6	71
7	35
8	19
9	29
10	18
11	7
	Total = 450

TABLE 2.3 Frequency Distributions of Years of College Education

Dallas		Knoxville	
Years of College	Frequency	Years of College	Frequency
0	35	0	187
1	21	1	62
2	24	2	34
3	22	3	19
4	31	4	14
5	13	5	7
6	6	6	3
7	5	7	4
8	3	8	0
	Total = 160		Total = 330

Relative Frequency
The proportion of total observations that are in a given category. Relative frequency is computed by dividing the frequency in a category by the total number of observations. The relative frequencies can be converted to percentages by multiplying by 100.

of years of college attended. The responses ranged from zero to eight years. Table 2.3 shows the frequency distributions for each city.

Suppose now we wished to compare the college years distribution for Dallas with that for Knoxville. How do the two cities' distributions compare? Do you see any difficulties in making this comparison? Because the surveys contained different numbers of people, it is difficult to compare the frequency distributions directly. When the number of total observations differs, comparisons are aided if **relative frequencies** are computed. Equation 2-1 is used to compute the relative frequencies.

Relative Frequency

$$\text{Relative frequency} = \frac{f_i}{n} \qquad\qquad (2.1)$$

where:

f_i = Frequency of the ith value of the discreate variable

$$n = \sum_{i=1}^{k} f_i$$

k = The number of different values for the discrete variable

Table 2.4 shows the relative frequencies for each city's distribution. This makes a comparison of the two much easier. We see that Knoxville has relatively more people without any college (56.7%) or one year of college (18.8%) than Dallas (21.9% and 13.1%). At all other levels of education, Dallas has relatively more people than Knoxville.

The frequency distributions shown in Table 2.2 and Table 2.3 were developed from *quantitative data*. That is, the variable of interest was numerical (number of product categories or number of years of college). However, a frequency distribution can also be developed when the data are *qualitative data* or nonnumerical data. For instance, if a survey asked individuals for their marital status, the following possible responses could be listed:

Single

Married

Divorced

Other

Table 2.5 shows the frequency distribution from a survey of 200 people.

TABLE 2.4 Relative Frequency Distributions of Years of College

Years of College	Dallas		Knoxville	
	Frequency	Relative Frequency	Frequency	Relative Frequency
0	35	35/160 = 0.219	187	187/330 = 0.567
1	21	21/160 = 0.131	62	62/330 = 0.188
2	24	24/160 = 0.150	34	34/330 = 0.103
3	22	22/160 = 0.138	19	19/330 = 0.058
4	31	31/160 = 0.194	14	14/330 = 0.042
5	13	13/160 = 0.081	7	7/330 = 0.021
6	6	6/160 = 0.038	3	3/330 = 0.009
7	5	5/160 = 0.031	4	4/330 = 0.012
8	3	3/160 = 0.019	0	0/330 = 0.000
Total	160		330	

TABLE 2.5 Marital Status Frequency Distribution

Marital Status	Frequency
Single	80
Married	90
Divorced	20
Other	10
	Total = 200

SUMMARY Developing Frequency and Relative Frequency Distributions for Discrete Data

To develop a discrete data frequency distribution, perform the following steps:

1. List all possible values of the variable. If the variable is ordinal level or higher, order the possible values from low to high.
2. Count the number of occurrences at each value of the variable and place this value in a column labeled "frequency."

To develop a relative frequency distribution, do the following:

3. Use Equation 2.1 and divide each frequency count by the total number of data values and place in a column headed "relative frequency."

TRY PROBLEM 2.3

EXAMPLE 2-1 Frequency and Relative Frequency Distributions

International Airline Travel Following the tragic events of September 11, 2001, there was a sharp reduction in international travel by U.S. citizens. A travel magazine recently surveyed 16 business executives to determine how many international trips they made in 2006. The following data were observed:

3	0	0	1
1	2	2	0
0	2	1	0
2	1	4	2

The editors wish to construct a frequency distribution and a relative frequency distribution for the number of international trips taken by these executives.

Step 1 **List the possible values.**
The possible values listed in order for the discrete variable are 0, 1, 2, 3, 4.

Step 2 **Count the number of occurrences at each value.**
The frequency distribution follows:

International Trips	Frequency	Relative Frequency
0	5	5/16 = .3125
1	4	4/16 = .2500
2	5	5/16 = .3125
3	1	1/16 = .0625
4	1	1/16 = .0625
	Total = 16	1.0000

Step 3 **Determine the relative frequencies.**
The relative frequencies are determined by dividing each frequency by 16, as shown. Thus, just over 31% of those responding took no trips during 2006.

EXAMPLE 2-2 Frequency Distribution for Qualitative Data

Lawn Care Companies A subdivision in northern California has 20 homes. Recently a survey was conducted to determine which lawn service the homeowners used last summer. Fifteen homeowners responded to the survey with the following results:

Emerald	Green Thumb	Green Thumb	Self	Self
Master Care	Emerald	Self	Master Care	Green Thumb
Emerald	Self	Master Care	Emerald	Self

The frequency distribution for this qualitative variable is found as follows:

Step 1 List the possible values.
The possible values for the variable are Emerald, Green Thumb, Master Care, and Self.

Step 2 Count the number of occurrences at each value.
The frequency distribution is

Lawn Company	Frequency
Emerald	4
Green Thumb	3
Master Care	3
Self	5
	Total = 15

Business Application

Excel and Minitab Tutorial

ATHLETIC SHOE SURVEY In recent years, a status symbol for many students has been the brand and style of athletic shoes they wear. Companies such as Nike and Adidas compete for the top position in the sport shoe market. A survey was recently conducted in which 100 college students at a southern state school were asked a number of questions, including how many pairs of Nike shoes they currently own. The data are in a file called **SportsShoes** on the CD-ROM that comes with this text.

The variable *Number of Nike* is a discrete quantitative variable. Figures 2.1 and 2.2 show frequency distributions (Excel and Minitab versions) for the number of Nike shoes owned by those surveyed. These frequency distributions show that, although a few people own more than six pairs of Nike shoes, the bulk of those surveyed own two or fewer pairs.

CHAPTER OUTCOME #1

Continuous Data
Data whose possible values are uncountable and which may assume any value in an interval.

Grouped Data Frequency Distributions

In the previous examples, the variable of interest was a discrete variable and the number of possible values for the variable was limited to only a few. However, there are many instances in which the variable of interest will be either **continuous** (weight, time, length) or discrete and have many possible outcomes (age, income, stock prices), yet we want to describe the variable using a frequency distribution.

BLOCKBUSTER INC. Blockbuster is one of the largest video rental and sales companies in the United States. Its stores rent and sell both VHS tapes and DVD products. Recently, a district manager for Blockbuster in Arkansas conducted a survey of customers in her district. Among the questions asked on the written survey was, "How many DVD movies do

FIGURE 2.1

Excel 2007 Output— Nike Shoes Frequency Distribution

Excel 2007 Instructions:
1. Open File: SportsShoes.xls.
2. Enter the Possible Values for the Variable; i.e., 0, 1, 2, 3, 4, etc.
3. Select the cells to contain the Frequency values.
4. Select the **formulas** tab.
5. Click on the f_x button.
6. Select the **Statistics— FREQUENCY** function.
7. Enter the range of data and the bin range (the cells containing the possible number of shoes).
8. Press **ctrl-shift-enter** to determine the frequency values.

	A	B	C	D	E	F	G	H	I	J	K	L	M
1		Annual	Pairs per	Pairs at	Number of	Number	Brand					Level of	
2	Age	Income	Year	This Time	Nike	Adidas	Preference	Comfort	Advertising	Appearance	Price	Activity	Gender
91	65	27,500	1	2	1	0	1	1	2	1	1	1	2
92	29	21,000	5	1	0	1	2	1	2	2	2	2	2
93	56	63,000	2	7	4	2	1	1	1	1	1	1	1
94	24	13,000	2	3	2	1	2	2	2	1	1	2	1
95	72	80,000	2	5	1	4	2	2	2	1	1	1	2
96	25	23,000	1	6	6	0	1	1	2	2	1	3	2
97	21	32,000	3	2	1	0	1	1	2	1	2	1	1
98	56	51,000	2	3	0	1	2	1	1	1	1	1	2
99	27	26,500	6	3	2	0	1	1	2	2	1	3	2
100	19	11,000	1	2	1	1	2	1	2	1	2	1	1
101	26	32,000	1	2	1	0	1	1	2	1	2	2	2
102	51	90,000	2	5	4	1	1	1	2	1	1	2	1
103													
104													
105					Number of Nikes								
106					0	27							
107					1	27							
108					2	20							
109					3	9							
110					4	6							
111					5	4							
112					6	4							
113					7	1							
114					8	2							

you own?" A total of 230 people completed the survey; Table 2.6 shows the responses to the DVD ownership question. These data are discrete, quantitative data. The values range from 0 to 30.

The manager is interested in transforming these data into useful information by constructing a frequency distribution. Table 2.7 shows one approach where the possible values for the number of DVD movies owned is listed from 0 to 30. While this frequency distribution is a step forward in transforming the data into information, because of the large number of possible values for DVD movies owned, the 230 observations are spread over a large range, making analysis difficult. In this case, the manager might consider forming a *grouped data frequency distribution* by organizing the possible number of DVD movies owned into discrete categories or *classes*.

The first step in constructing a grouped frequency distribution is to sort the quantitative data from low to high. The sorted data is called a *data array*. Next, define the classes

FIGURE 2.2

Minitab Output—Nike Shoes Frequency Distribution

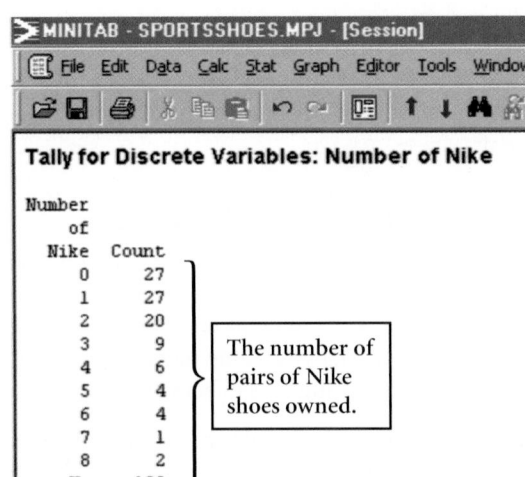

Minitab Instructions:
1. Open file: SportsShoes.MTW.
2. Choose **Stat > Tables > Tally Individual Variables**.
3. In **Variables**, enter data column.
4. Under **Display**, check **Counts**.
5. Click **OK**.

TABLE 2.6 DVD Movies Owned: Blockbuster Survey

9	4	13	10	5	10	13	14	10	19
0	10	16	9	11	14	8	15	7	15
10	11	9	7	6	12	12	14	15	16
15	14	10	13	9	12	12	10	10	11
15	14	9	19	3	9	16	19	15	9
4	2	4	5	6	2	3	4	7	5
6	2	2	0	0	8	3	4	3	2
2	5	2	5	2	2	6	2	5	6
5	2	7	3	5	1	6	4	3	6
3	7	7	1	6	2	7	1	3	2
4	0	2	2	4	6	2	5	3	7
4	16	9	10	11	7	10	9	10	11
11	12	9	8	9	7	9	17	8	13
14	13	10	6	12	5	14	7	13	12
9	6	10	15	7	7	9	9	13	10
9	3	17	5	11	9	6	9	15	8
11	13	4	16	13	9	11	5	12	13
0	3	3	3	2	1	4	0	2	0
3	7	1	5	2	2	3	2	1	3
2	3	3	3	0	3	3	3	1	1
13	24	24	17	17	15	25	20	15	20
21	23	25	17	13	22	18	17	30	21
18	21	17	16	25	14	15	24	21	15

for the variable of interest. Care needs to be taken when constructing these classes to ensure each data point is put into one, and only one, possible class. Therefore, the classes should meet four criteria.

First, they must be **mutually exclusive**.

Second, they must be **all-inclusive**.

Third, if at all possible, they should be of **equal width**.

Equal-width classes make analyzing and interpreting the frequency distribution easier. However, there are some instances in which the presence of extreme high or low values makes it necessary to have an open-ended class. For example, annual family incomes in the United States are mostly between $15,000 and $200,000. However, there are some families with much higher family incomes. In order to best accommodate these high incomes, you might consider having the highest income class be "over $200,000" or "$200,000 and over" as a catchall for the high-income families.

Fourth, avoid **empty classes** if possible.

Empty classes are those for which there are no data values. If this occurs, it may be because you have set up classes that are too narrow.

Steps for Grouping Data into Classes There are four steps for grouping data, such as that found in Table 2.6, into classes.

Step 1 **Determine the number of groups or classes to use.** Although there is no absolute right or wrong number of classes, the rule of thumb is to have *between 5 and 20 classes*. Another guideline for helping you determine how many classes to use is the $2^k \geq n$ rule, where $k =$ the number of classes and $n =$ the number of data values. For example, for $n = 230$, the $2^k \geq n$ rule would suggest $k = 8$ classes ($2^8 = 256 \geq 230$).

Mutually Exclusive Classes
Classes that do not overlap so that a data value can be placed in only one class.

All-Inclusive Classes
A set of classes that contains all the possible data values.

Equal-Width Classes
The distance between the lowest possible value and the highest possible value in each class is equal for all classes.

TABLE 2.7 Frequency Distribution of DVD Movies Owned

DVD Movies Owned	Frequency
0	8
1	8
2	22
3	22
4	11
5	13
6	12
7	14
8	5
9	19
10	14
11	9
12	8
13	12
14	8
15	12
16	6
17	7
18	2
19	3
20	2
21	4
22	1
23	1
24	3
25	3
26	0
27	0
28	0
29	0
30	1
	Total = 230

Remember, these are only guidelines for the number of classes. There is no specific right or wrong number. In general, use fewer classes for smaller data sets; more classes for larger data sets. However, using too few classes tends to condense data too much, and information is lost. Using too many classes spreads out the data so much that little advantage is gained over the original raw data.

Step 2 Establish the class width.
The minimum **class width** is determined by Equation 2.2

Class Width

The distance between the lowest possible value and the highest possible value for a frequency class.

Class Width

$$W = \frac{\text{Largest Value} - \text{Smallest Value}}{\text{Number of Classes}} \qquad (2.2)$$

For the Blockbuster data using eight classes, we get:

$$W = \frac{\text{Largest} - \text{Smallest}}{\text{Classes}} = \frac{30 - 0}{8} = 3.75$$

This means we could construct eight classes that are each 3.75 units wide to provide mutually exclusive and all-inclusive classes. However, because our purpose is to make the data more understandable, we suggest that you *round up to a more convenient class width*, such as 4.0.

Class Boundaries
The upper and lower values of each class.

Step 3 Determine the class boundaries for each class.
The **class boundaries** determine the lowest possible value and the highest possible value for each class. In the Blockbuster example, if we start the first class at 0, we get the class boundaries shown in the first column of the table below. Notice the classes have been formed to be *mutually exclusive* and *all-inclusive*.

DVD Movies Owned (Classes)	Frequency
0–3.99	60
4–7.99	50
8–11.99	47
12–15.99	40
16–19.99	18
20–23.99	8
24–27.99	6
28–31.99	1
	Total = 230

Cumulative Frequency Distribution
A summary of a set of data that displays the number of observations with values less than or equal to the upper limit of each of its classes.

Cumulative Relative Frequency Distribution
A summary of a set of data that displays the proportion of observations with values less than or equal to the upper limit of each of its classes.

Another step we can take to help analyze the Blockbuster data is to construct a **cumulative frequency distribution** and a **cumulative relative frequency distribution**.

DVD Movies	Frequency	Relative Frequency	Cumulative Frequency	Cumulative Relative Frequency
0–3.99	60	0.261	60	0.261
4–7.99	50	0.217	110	0.478
8–11.99	47	0.204	157	0.683
12–15.99	40	0.174	197	0.857
16–19.99	18	0.078	215	0.935
20–23.99	8	0.035	223	0.970
24–27.99	6	0.026	229	0.996
28–31.99	1	0.004	230	1.000
Total = 230				

The cumulative frequency distribution is shown in the Cumulative Frequency column. We can then form the cumulative relative frequency distribution as shown in the Cumulative Relative Frequency column. The cumulative relative frequency distribution indicates, as an example, that 85.7% of the sample own fewer than 16 DVD movies.

SUMMARY Developing Frequency Distributions for Continuous Variables

To develop a continuous data frequency distribution, perform the following steps:

1. Determine the desired number of classes or groups. The rule of thumb is to use 5 to 20 classes. The $2^k \geq n$ rule can be used.

2. Determine the minimum class width using:

$$W = \frac{\text{Largest Value} - \text{Smallest Value}}{\text{Number of Classes}}$$

Round the class width up to a more convenient value.

3. Define the class boundaries, making sure that the classes that are formed are *mutually exclusive* and *all-inclusive*. Ideally, the classes should have equal widths and should all contain at least one observation.

4. Count the number of values in each class.

EXAMPLE 2-3 Frequency Distribution for Continuous Variables

TRY PROBLEM 2.9

Airport Security Screening Example 2-1 referred to the international travel difficulties after the September 11, 2001, attack on the World Trade Center in New York City and the Pentagon in Washington D.C. As a result, airports throughout the world have stepped up their security, and passengers have had to spend more time waiting to pass through security screening. At the Miami, Florida, airport, officials each week select a random sample of passengers. For each person selected, the time spent in the security screening line is recorded. The waiting times (already sorted from high to low), in seconds, for one such sample of 72 passengers are as follows:

35	339	650	864	1,025	1,261
38	340	655	883	1,028	1,280
48	395	669	883	1,036	1,290
53	457	703	890	1,044	1,312
70	478	730	934	1,087	1,341
99	501	763	951	1,091	1,355
138	521	788	969	1,126	1,357
164	556	789	985	1,176	1,360
220	583	789	993	1,199	1,414
265	595	802	997	1,199	1,436
272	596	822	999	1,237	1,479
312	604	851	1,018	1,242	1,492

The airport security manger wishes to construct a frequency distribution for the time passengers wait for security screening. The frequency distribution is determined as follows:

Step 1 Group the data into classes.
The number of classes is arbitrary but typically will be between 5 and 20, depending on the volume of data. In this example, we have $n = 72$ data items. Using the $2^k \geq n$ guideline we get $k = 7$ classes ($2^7 = 128 \geq 72$).

Step 2 Determine the class width.

$$W = \frac{\text{Largest Value} - \text{Smallest Value}}{\text{Number of Classes}} = \frac{1,492 - 35}{7} = 208.1429 \Rightarrow 225$$

Note, we have rounded the class width up from the minimum required value of 208.1429 to the more convenient value of 225.

Step 3 Define the class boundaries.

0	and under	225
225	and under	450
450	and under	675
675	and under	900
900	and under	1,125
1,125	and under	1,350
1,350	and under	1,575

These classes are mutually exclusive, all-inclusive, and have equal widths.

Step 4 Count the number of values in each class.

Waiting Time	Frequency
0 and under 225	9
225 and under 450	6
450 and under 675	12
675 and under 900	13
900 and under 1,125	14
1,125 and under 1,350	11
1,350 and under 1,575	7

This frequency distribution shows that for this sample of passengers, most people wait between 450 and 1,350 seconds.

Histograms

Although frequency distributions are useful for analyzing large sets of data, they are presented in table format and may not be as visually informative as a graph. If a frequency distribution has been developed from a quantitative variable, a **frequency histogram** can be constructed directly from the frequency distribution. In many cases, the histogram offers a superior format for transforming the data into useful information. (Note, histograms cannot be constructed from a frequency distribution where the variable of interest is qualitative. However, a similar graph, called a *bar chart*, is used when qualitative data are involved.)

A histogram shows three general types of information:

1. It provides a visual indication of where the approximate center of the data is. Look for the center point along the horizontal axes in the histograms in Figure 2.3. Even though the shapes of the histograms are the same, there is a clear difference in where the data are centered.
2. We can gain an understanding of the degree of spread (or variation) in the data. The more the data cluster around the center, the smaller the variation in the data. If the data are spread out from the center, the data exhibit greater variation. The examples in Figure 2.4 all have the same center but are different in terms of spread.
3. We can observe the shape of the distribution. Is it reasonably flat, is it weighted to one side or the other, is it balanced around the center, or is it bell-shaped?

CAPITAL CREDIT UNION Even for applications with small amounts of data, such as the Blockbuster example, constructing grouped data frequency distributions and histograms is a time-consuming process. Decision makers may hesitate to try different numbers of classes and different class limits because of the effort involved and the "best" presentation of the data may be missed.

Frequency Histogram
A graph of a frequency distribution with the horizontal axis showing the classes, the vertical axis showing the frequency count, and (for equal class widths) the rectangles having a height equal to the frequency in each class.

CHAPTER OUTCOME #2

Business Application

Excel and Minitab Tutorial

FIGURE 2.3

Histograms Showing Different Centers

We showed earlier that Excel and Minitab both provide the capability of constructing frequency distributions. Both software packages are also quite capable of generating grouped data frequency distributions and histograms.

Consider Capital Credit Union (CCU) in Mobile, Alabama, which recently began issuing a new credit card. Managers at CCU have been wondering how customers have been using the card, so a sample of 300 customers was selected. Data on the current credit card balance (rounded to the nearest dollar) and the genders of the cardholders appear in the file **Capital**, which is stored on your CD-ROM.

As with the manual process, the first step in Excel or Minitab is to determine the number of classes. Recall that the rule of thumb is to use between 5 and 20 classes, depending on the amount of data. Suppose we decide to use 10 classes.

FIGURE 2.4

Histograms—Same Center, Different Spread

Next, we determine the class width using Equation 2.2. The highest account balance in the sample is $1,493.00. The minimum is $99.00. Thus, the class width is

$$W = \frac{1,493.00 - 99.00}{10} = 139.40$$

which we round up to $150.00.

Our classes will be

$90–239.99

$240–389.99

$390–539.99

etc.

The resulting histogram in Figure 2.5 shows that the data are centered between $690 and $840. The customers vary considerably in their credit card balances, but the distribution is quite symmetrical and somewhat bell-shaped. Capital Credit Union managers must decide whether the usage rate for the credit card is sufficient to warrant the cost of maintaining the credit card accounts.

FIGURE 2.5

Excel 2007 Output of Credit Card Balance Histogram

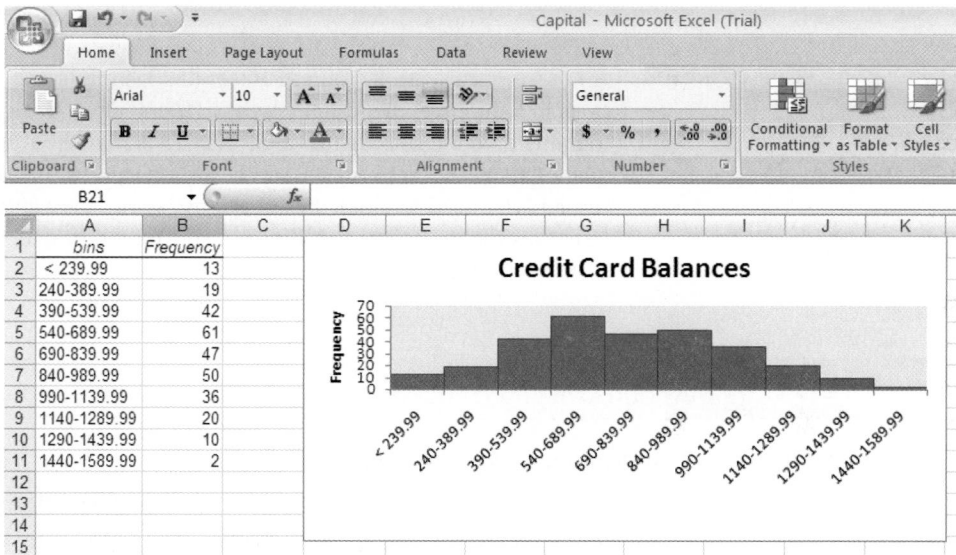

Excel 2007 Instructions:
1. Open file: Capital.xls
2. Set up an area on the worksheet for the bins defined as 239.99, 389.99, etc. up to 1589.99 Be sure to include a label such as "Bins."
3. On the **Data** tab, click **Data Analysis**.
4. Select **Histogram**.
5. Input Range specifies the actual data values as the **Credit Card Account Balance** column and the bin range as the area defined in Step 2.
6. Put on a new worksheet and include the Chart Output.
7. Right-mouse-click on the bars and use the **Format Data Series Options** to set gap width to zero and add lines to the bars.
8. Convert the bins to actual class labels by typing labels in Column A. Note, the bin 239.99 is labeled 0-239.99.

FIGURE 2.6

Minitab Output of Credit Card Balance Histogram

Minitab Instructions:
1. Open file: Capital.MTW.
2. Choose **Graph >
   Histogram**.
3. Click **Simple**.
4. Click **OK**.
5. In **Graph variables**,
   enter data column.
6. Click **OK**.

Issues with Excel If you use Excel to construct a histogram as indicated in the instructions in Figure 2.5, the initial graph will come up with gaps between the bars. Because histograms illustrate the distribution of data across the range of all possible values for the quantitative variable, *histograms do not have gaps*. Therefore, to get the proper histogram format, you need to close these gaps by setting the gap width to zero, as indicated in the Excel instructions shown in Figure 2.5. Minitab provides no gaps with its default output, as shown in Figure 2.6.

SUMMARY Constructing Frequency Histograms

To construct a frequency histogram, perform the following steps:

1. Follow the steps for constructing a frequency distribution (see Examples 2-1 or 2-3).
2. Use the horizontal axis to represent the variable of interest. Use the vertical axis to represent the frequency in each class.

3. Draw vertical bars for each class or data value so that the heights of the bars correspond to the frequencies. Make sure there are no gaps between the bars. (Note, if the classes do not have equal widths, the bar height should be adjusted to make the area of the bar proportional to the frequency.)
4. Label the histogram appropriately.

TRY PROBLEM   2.10

EXAMPLE 2-4 Frequency Histograms

Emergency Response Times The director of emergency responses in Montreal, Canada, is interested in analyzing the time needed for response teams to reach their destinations in emergency situations after leaving their stations. She has acquired the response times for 1,220 calls last month. To develop the frequency histogram, perform the following steps:

Step 1 Construct a frequency distribution.

Because response time is a continuous variable measured in seconds, the data should be broken down into classes and the steps given in Example 2-3 should be used. The following frequency distribution with 10 classes was developed:

Response Time	Frequency	Response Time	Frequency
0 and under 30	36	180 and under 210	145
30 and under 60	68	210 and under 240	80
60 and under 90	195	240 and under 270	43
90 and under 120	180	270 and under 300	31
120 and under 150	260		Total = 1,220
150 and under 180	182		

Step 2 Construct the axes for the histogram.

The horizontal axis will be response time and the vertical axis will be frequency.

Step 3 Construct bars with heights corresponding to the frequency of each class and label appropriately.

This is shown as follows:

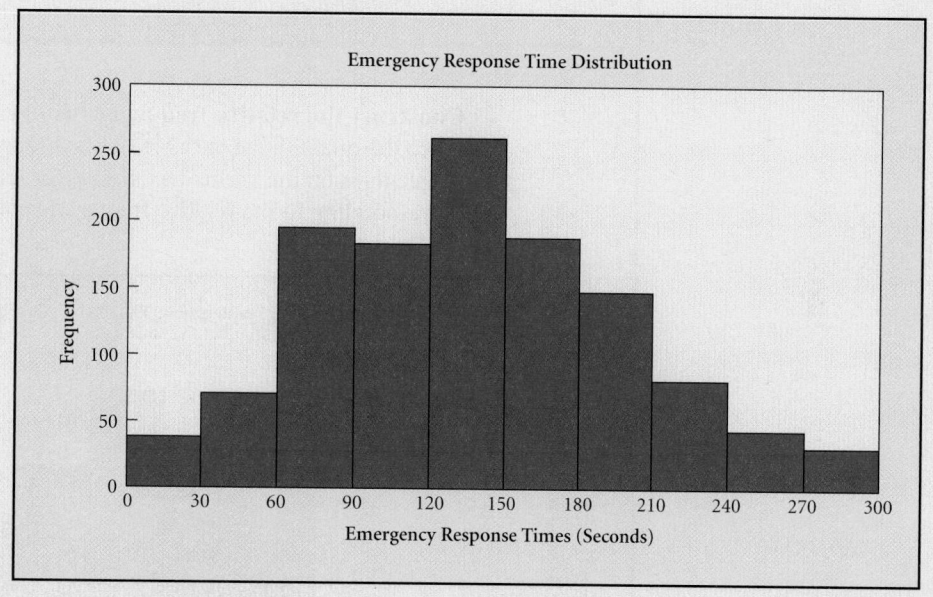

This histogram indicates that the response times vary considerably. The center is somewhere in the range of 120 to 180 seconds.

Relative Frequency Histograms and Ogives

Histograms can also be used to display relative frequency distributions and cumulative relative frequency distributions. A relative frequency histogram is formed in the same manner as a frequency histogram, but relative frequencies are used rather than frequencies. The cumulative relative frequency is presented using a graph called an **ogive**. Example 2-5 illustrates each of these graphical tools.

EXAMPLE 2-5 Relative Frequency Histograms and Ogives

TRY PROBLEM 2.16

Emergency Response Times (continued) Example 2-4 introduced the situation facing the emergency response manager in Montreal. In that example, she formed a frequency distribution for a sample of 1,220 response times. She is now interested in graphing the relative frequencies and the cumulative relative frequencies. To do so, use the following steps:

Step 1 Convert the frequency distribution into relative frequencies and cumulative relative frequencies.

Response Time	Frequency	Relative Frequency	Cumulative Relative Frequency
0 and under 30	36	36/1220 = 0.0295	0.0295
30 and under 60	68	68/1220 = 0.0557	0.0852
60 and under 90	195	195/1220 = 0.1598	0.2451
90 and under 120	180	180/1220 = 0.1475	0.3926
120 and under 150	260	260/1220 = 0.2131	0.6057
150 and under 180	182	182/1220 = 0.1492	0.7549
180 and under 210	145	145/1220 = 0.1189	0.8738
210 and under 240	80	80/1220 = 0.0656	0.9393
240 and under 270	43	43/1220 = 0.0352	0.9746
270 and under 300	31	31/1220 = 0.0254	1.0000
	1,220	1.0000	

Step 2 Construct the relative frequency histogram.
Place the quantitative variable on the horizontal axis and the relative frequencies on the vertical axis. The vertical bars are drawn to heights corresponding to the relative frequencies of the classes.

Note the relative frequency histogram has exactly the same shape as the frequency histogram. However, the vertical axis has a different scale.

Step 3 Construct the ogive.
Draw a line connecting the points plotted above the *upper limit* of each class at a height corresponding to the cumulative relative frequency.

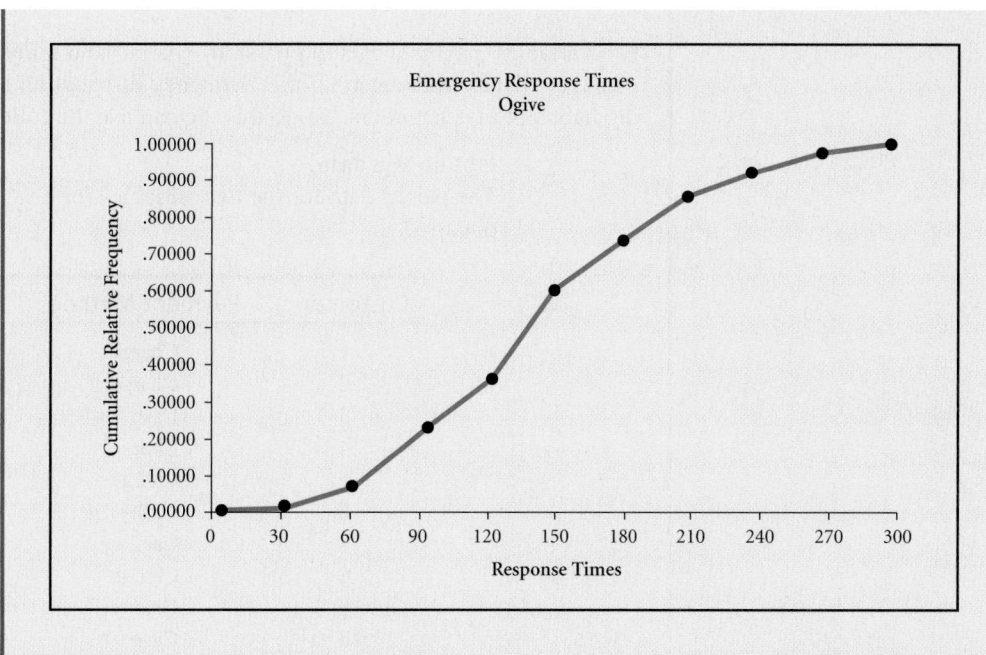

Joint Frequency Distributions

CHAPTER OUTCOME #3

Frequency distributions are effective tools for describing data. Thus far we have discussed how to develop grouped and ungrouped frequency distributions for one variable at a time. For instance, in the Capital Credit Union example, we were interested in customer credit card balances for all customers. We constructed a frequency distribution and histogram for that variable. However, often we need to examine the data more closely. This may involve constructing a *joint frequency distribution* for two variables. Joint frequency distributions can be constructed for qualitative or quantitative variables.

SUMMARY   Constructing Joint Frequency Distributions

A joint frequency distribution is constructed using the following steps:

1. Obtain a set of data consisting of paired responses for two variables. The responses can be qualitative or quantitative. If the responses are quantitative, they can be discrete or continuous.

2. Construct a table with *r* rows and *c* columns, in which the number of rows represents the number of categories (or numeric classes) of one variable and the number of columns corresponds to the number of categories (or numeric classes) of the second variable.

3. Count the number of joint occurrences at each row level and each column level for all combinations of row and column values and place these frequencies in the appropriate cells.

4. Compute the row and column totals, which are called the *marginal frequencies*.

5. If a joint relative frequency distribution is desired, divide each cell frequency by the total number of paired observations.

EXAMPLE 2-6   Joint Frequency Distribution

Pizza Hut   Pizza Hut is a national pizza chain that has franchises in every major city in the United States and many foreign countries. Recently, the manager at a Minnesota store collected data dealing with customer purchases. Among the data collected were two variables: payment method (cash or charge) and number of pizzas purchased. The manager wishes to develop a joint frequency distribution to better understand the buying habits of his customers. To do this, he can use the following steps:

TRY PROBLEM 2.12

Step 1 Obtain the data.

The paired data for the two variables for a sample of 12 customers are obtained.

Customer	Payment Method	Pizzas Purchased
1	Charge	2
2	Charge	1
3	Cash	2
4	Charge	2
5	Charge	1
6	Cash	1
7	Cash	3
8	Charge	1
9	Charge	3
10	Cash	2
11	Cash	1
12	Charge	1

Step 2 Construct the rows and columns of the joint frequency table.

The row variable will be the payment method, and two rows will be used, corresponding to the two payment methods. The column variable is pizzas purchased, and it will have three levels, because the data for this variable contain only the values 1, 2, and 3. (Note, if a variable is continuous, classes should be formed using the methods discussed in Example 2-3.)

		Pizzas Purchased		
		1	2	3
Payment	Charge			
	Cash			

Step 3 Count the number of joint occurrences at each row level and each column level for all combinations of row and column values and place these frequencies in the appropriate cells.

		Pizzas Purchased			
		1	2	3	Total
Payment	Charge	4	2	1	7
	Cash	2	2	1	5
	Total	6	4	2	12

Step 4 Calculate the row and column totals (see Step 3).

The manager can now see that for this sample, most people charged their purchase (seven people) and most people purchased only one pizza (six people). Likewise, four people both purchased one pizza and charged their purchase.

**Business
Application**

Excel and Minitab Tutorial

CAPITAL CREDIT UNION (*CONTINUED*) Recall that the Capital Credit Union discussed earlier was interested in evaluating the success of its new credit card. Figures 2.5 and 2.6 showed the frequency distribution and histogram for a sample of customer credit card balances. Although this information is useful, the managers would like to know more. Specifically, what does the credit card balance distribution look like for male versus female cardholders?

One way to approach this is to sort the data by the gender variable and develop frequency distributions and histograms for males and females separately. You could then make a visual comparison of the two to determine what, if any, difference exists between males and females. However, an alternative approach is to jointly analyze the two variables: gender and credit card balance.

Although the process is different for Excel and Minitab, both software packages provide methods for analyzing two variables jointly. In Figure 2.5, we constructed the frequency distribution for the 300 credit card balances using 10 classes. The class width was set at $150. Figure 2.7 shows a table that is called a *joint frequency distribution*. This type of table is also called a *cross-tabulation* table.[1]

The Capital Credit Union managers can use a joint frequency table to analyze the credit card balances for males versus females. For instance, for the 61 customers with balances of $540 to $689, Figure 2.7 shows that 45 were males and 16 were females. Previously, we discussed the concept of relative frequency (proportions, which Excel converts to percentages) as a useful tool for making comparisons between two data sets. In this example, comparisons between males and females would be easier if the frequencies were converted to proportions (or percentages). The result is the *joint relative frequency table* shown in Figure 2.8. Notice that the percentages in each cell are percentages of the

FIGURE 2.7

Excel 2007 Output of the Capital Credit Union Joint Frequency Distribution

Excel 2007 Instructions.
1. Open file: Captital.xls.
2. Place cursor anywhere in the data.
3. On the **Insert** tab, click on **PivotTable** and click **OK**.
4. Drag **Credit Card Account Balance** to "*Drop Row Field Here*" area. (Note, you may need to use Pivot Table **Options** under **Display** and make sure **Classical Pivot Table Layout** is checked.)
5. Right-click in **Credit Card Account Balance** numbers and click **Group**.
6. Change **Start at** to 90. Change **End** to 1589. Change **By** to 150.
7. Drag **Gender** to "*Drop Column Fields Here*" area.
8. Drag **Credit Card Account Balance** to "*Drop Data Items Here*" area.
9. Place cursor in the *Data Item* area, right click, and select **Summarize Data By** and select **Count**.

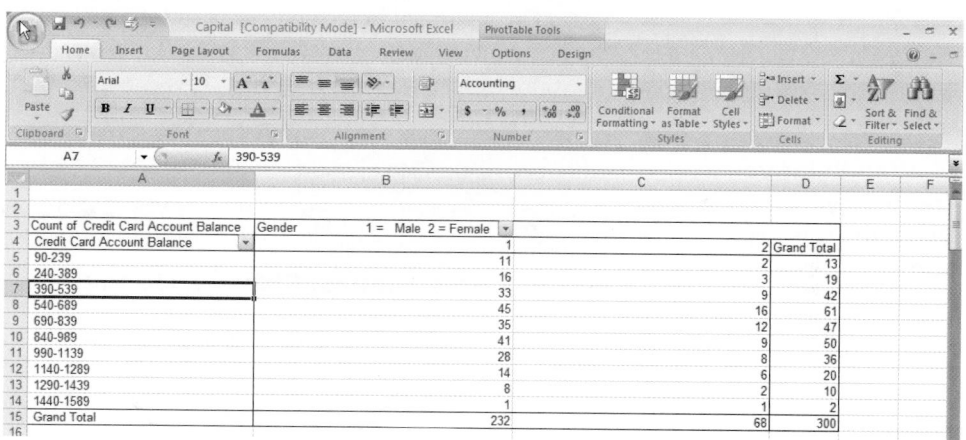

Minitab Instructions (for similar results):
1. Open file: Capital.MTW.
2. Click on **Data > Code > Numeric to Text**.
3. Under **Code data from columns**, select data column.
4. Under **Into columns**, specify destination column: Classes.
5. In **Original values**, define each data class range.
6. In **New**, specify code for each class.
7. Click **OK**.
8. Click on **Stat > Tables > Cross Tabulation and Chi-Square**.
9. Under **Categorical Variables For rows** enter Classes column and **For columns** enter *Gender* column.
10. Under **Display** check **Counts**.
11. Click **OK**.

---

[1] In Excel, the joint frequency distribution is developed using a tool called Pivot tables. In Minitab, the joint frequency distributions are constructed using the Cross Tabulation option.

FIGURE 2.8

Excel 2007 Output of the Joint Relative Frequencies

Excel 2007 Instructions:
1. Place cursor in the **Gender** numbers of the PivotTable.
2. Right-click and select **Value Field Settings**.
3. On the **Show values as** tab, click on the down arrow and select % **of total**.
4. Click **OK**.

In Figure 2.8 we have used the **Data Field Settings** of the Excel PivotTable to represent the data as percentages.

total 300 people in the survey. For example, the \$540-to-\$689 class had 20.33% (61) of the 300 customers. The male customers with balances in the \$540-to-\$689 range constituted 15% (45) of the 300 customers, whereas females with that balance level made up 5.33% (16) of all 300 customers. On the surface, this result seems to indicate a big difference between males and females at this credit balance level.

Suppose we really wanted to focus on the male-versus-female issue and control for the fact that there are far more male customers than female. We could compute the percentages differently. Rather than using a base of 300 (the entire sample size), we might instead be interested in the percentages of the males who have balances at each level, and the same measure for females.[2] Figure 2.9 shows the relative frequencies converted to

FIGURE 2.9

Minitab Relative Frequency Distribution—Males and Females

Tabulated statistics: Classes, Gender

Rows: Classes   Columns: Gender

	1	2	All
90-239	4.74	2.94	4.33
240-389	6.90	4.41	6.33
390-539	14.22	13.24	14.00
540-689	19.40	23.53	20.33
690-839	15.09	17.65	15.67
840-989	17.67	13.24	16.67
990-1139	12.07	11.76	12.00
1140-1289	6.03	8.82	6.67
1290-1439	3.45	2.94	3.33
1440-1589	0.43	1.47	0.67
All	100.00	100.00	100.00

Cell Contents: % of Column

Minitab Instructions:
1. Open file: Capital.MTW.
2. Steps 2–7 as in Figure 2.7.
8. Click on **Stat > Tables > Cross Tabulation and Chi-square**.
9. Under **Categorical variables For rows** enter *Classes* column and **For columns** enter *Gender* column.
10. Under **Display**, check **Total Percents**.
11. Click **OK**.

---
[2] Such distributions are known as *marginal distributions*.

percentages of the column total. In general, there seems to be little difference in the male and female distributions with respect to credit card balances.

There are many options for transferring data into useful information. Thus far, we have introduced frequency distributions, joint frequency tables, and histograms. In the next section, we discuss one of the most useful graphical tools: the bar chart.

2-1: Exercises

Skill Development

2-1. Assuming you have data for a variable with 2,000 values, using the $2^k \geq n$ guideline, what is the least number of groups that should be used in developing a grouped data frequency distribution?

2-2. A study is being conducted in which a variable of interest has 1,000 observations. The minimum value in the data set is 300 points and the maximum is 2,900 points.

   a. Use the $2^k \geq n$ guideline to determine the minimum number of classes to use in developing a grouped data frequency distribution.

   b. Based on the answer to part a, determine the class width that should be used. (Round up to the nearest 100 points.)

2-3. Given the following data, develop a frequency distribution:

5	3	2	6	6
7	3	3	6	7
7	9	7	5	3
12	6	10	7	2
6	8	0	7	4

2-4. You have the following data:

8	6	11	14	10
11	9	7	2	8
9	5	5	5	12
7	8	4	17	8
12	7	8	8	7
10	8	6	9	9
11	16	2	7	4
8	4	4	5	5
9	9	6	6	7
7	9	5	4	5
14	2	9	0	6
1	1	12	11	4

   a. Construct a frequency distribution for these data. Use the $2^k \geq n$ guideline to determine the number of classes to use.

   b. Develop a relative frequency distribution using the classes you constructed in part a.

   c. Develop a cumulative frequency distribution and a cumulative relative frequency distribution using the classes you constructed in part a.

   d. Develop a histogram based on the frequency distribution you constructed in part a.

2-5. Fill in the missing components of the following frequency distribution constructed for a sample size of 50:

Class	Frequency	Relative Frequency	Cumulative Relative Frequency
7.85 – < ____	____	____	0.12
____ – < 8.05	____	____	0.48
8.05 – < ____	____	.24	____
____ – < 8.25	____	.10	____
8.25 – < ____	____	____	____

2-6. Produce the relative frequency distribution from a sample of size 50 that gave rise to the following ogive:

2-7. The following cumulative relative frequency distribution summarizes data obtained in a study of the ending overages (in dollars) for the cash register balance at a business:

Class	Frequency	Relative Frequency	Cumulative Relative Frequency
−60.00 – < −40.00	2	0.04	0.04
−40.00 – < −20.00	2	0.04	0.08
−20.00 – < 00.00	8	0.16	0.24
00.00 – < 20.00	16	0.32	0.56
20.00 – < 40.00	20	0.40	0.96
40.00 – < 60.00	2	0.04	1.00

a. Determine the proportion of the days in which there were no shortages
b. Determine the proportion of the days the cash register was less than $20 off.
c. Determine the proportion of the days in which the cash register was less than $40 over or at most $20 short.

2-8. You are given the following data:

6	10	6	4	9	5
5	5	5	7	6	2
5	5	5	4	5	7
6	7	8	6	8	4
7	5	5	5	5	7
8	7	6	7	5	4
6	4	4	7	4	6
6	7	8	6	7	6
7	8	5	6	5	7
3	6	4	7	4	4

a. Construct a frequency distribution for these data.
b. Based on the frequency distribution, develop a histogram.
c. Construct a relative frequency distribution.
d. Develop a relative frequency histogram.
e. Compare the two histograms. Why do they look alike?

2-9. Using the data from Problem 2-8,
a. Construct a grouped data relative frequency distribution of the data. Use the $2^k \geq n$ guideline to determine the number of classes.
b. Construct a cumulative frequency distribution of the data.
c. Construct a relative frequency histogram.
d. Construct an ogive.

Business Applications

2-10. Wendy's is one of the largest fast-food chains in the world. Recently, the district manager for Wendy's in Las Vegas conducted a study in which she selected a random sample of sales receipts. She was interested in the number of line items on the receipts. For instance, if a customer ordered two $1/4$-pound hamburgers, one side of fries, and two soft drinks, the number of line items would be five. The following data were observed:

7	5	7	6	5	5	4	8	6	5
8	7	6	5	6	2	9	4	4	5
8	4	9	6	6	5	8	9	9	1
6	5	10	6	7	6	5	5	5	6
8	7	6	8	6	6	9	6	12	7
5	6	7	11	4	4	3	4	1	4
11	2	5	5	8	2	3	4	9	6
6	5	8	6	3	6	4	5	8	10

a. Develop a frequency distribution for these data. Discuss briefly what the frequency distribution tells you about these sample data.
b. Based on the results in part a, construct a frequency histogram for these sample data.

2-11. In a survey conducted by NFO Interactive, investors were asked to rate how knowledgeable they felt they were as investors. Both online and traditional investors were included in the survey. The survey resulted in the following data:
   Of the online investors, 8%, 55%, and 37% responded they were "savvy," "experienced," and "novice," respectively.
   Of the traditional investors, the percentages were 4, 29, and 67, respectively.
Six hundred investors were surveyed, of which 200 were traditional investors.
a. Use the information to construct a joint frequency distribution.
b. Use the information to construct a joint relative frequency distribution.
c. Determine the proportion of investors who were both online investors and rated themselves experienced.
d. Calculate the proportion of investors who were online investors.

2-12. KXGH Television, Channel 7, is the NBC affiliate in a mid-size southeastern city. Recently, the station's sales manager surveyed 20 advertisers and asked each one to rate the service of the station on the following scale:

VERY GOOD	GOOD	FAIR	POOR	VERY POOR
1	2	3	4	5

He also tracked the general time slot when the advertiser's commercials were shown on the station. The following codes were used:

1 = morning   2 = afternoon
3 = evening   4 = various times

The following sample data were observed:

Rating	Time Slot	Rating	Time Slot
2	1	4	3
1	1	2	2
3	3	3	3
2	1	3	3
1	1	2	1
4	4	1	1
2	2	1	1
1	1	5	3
2	1	2	4
2	2	3	4

a. Construct separate relative frequency distributions for each of the two variables.
b. Construct a joint frequency distribution for these two variables.
c. Construct a joint relative frequency distribution for these two variables. Write a short paragraph describing what the data imply.

2-13. In a study to evaluate the time required to turn around its airplanes, an airline company has randomly sampled 49 airplane records. The turnaround times, measured in minutes, for the sampled planes are as follows:

89	83	97	101	86	89	86
91	84	89	87	93	86	90
86	92	92	88	88	92	86
93	80	93	77	98	94	95
94	88	95	87	99	98	90
91	87	89	89	96	88	94
95	79	94	86	92	94	85

a. Create a data array of the turnaround times.
b. Develop a frequency distribution using five classes having equal widths.
c. Develop a histogram from the frequency distribution you created in part b.
d. Develop a relative frequency and a cumulative relative frequency distribution for the turnaround times using the same five classes created in part b. What percent of the sampled planes have turnaround times greater than 96 minutes?

2-14. Hurricane Katrina in 2005 caused massive damage to the states of Louisiana, Mississippi, and Alabama. In addition to the loss of life, a large amount of property was damaged by the wind and floods that resulted from the storm. Many of the properties were covered by insurance. One of the country's largest insurance companies recently released data on a sample of 100 residential properties showing the dollars in claims paid on each property. The sample data are as follows:

$172,229	$211,021	$159,205	$247,697	$247,469
$176,736	$240,815	$195,056	$315,097	$257,150
$129,779	$207,451	$165,225	$178,970	$319,101
$87,429	$219,808	$242,761	$277,389	$213,803
$153,468	$205,696	$210,447	$179,029	$241,331
$117,808	$188,909	$376,644	$185,523	$168,145
$158,094	$135,461	$131,457	$263,232	$256,262
$240,034	$289,973	$302,341	$178,684	$226,998
$176,440	$268,106	$181,507	$118,752	$251,009
$196,457	$195,249	$195,986	$201,680	$233,182
$271,552	$123,262	$212,411	$246,462	$177,673
$103,699	$252,375	$192,335	$265,992	$232,247
$320,004	$213,020	$192,546	$295,660	$211,876
$265,787	$207,443	$203,043	$133,014	$289,645
$251,560	$302,054	$185,381	$284,345	$184,869
$237,485	$282,506	$278,783	$335,920	$199,630
$248,272	$232,234	$188,833	$168,905	$357,612
$241,894	$186,956	$114,601	$301,728	$251,865
$207,040	$221,614	$318,154	$156,611	$219,730
$201,473	$174,840	$196,622	$263,686	$159,029

a. Using the $2^k \geq n$ guideline, what is the minimum number of classes that should be used to display these data in a grouped data frequency distribution?
b. Referring to part a, what should the class width be, assuming you round the width up to nearest $1,000?
c. Referring to parts a and b, develop a grouped data frequency distribution for these insurance data.
d. Based on your answer to part c, construct and interpret a frequency histogram for the insurance data.

2-15. Wageweb exhibits salary data obtained from surveys. It provides compensation information on over 170 benchmark positions, including finance positions. It reported that salaries of Chief Finance Officers (CFOs) ranged from $127,735 to $209,981 (Wageweb.com, April 12, 2004) for data as of October 1, 2003. Suppose the following data represent a sample of the annual salaries for

25 CFOs. Assume that data are in thousands of dollars.

173.1	171.2	141.9	112.6	211.1	156.5	145.4	134.0
192.0	185.8	168.3	131.0	214.4	155.2	164.9	123.9
161.9	162.7	178.8	161.3	182.0	165.8	213.1	177.4
159.3							

a. Using 11 classes, construct a cumulative frequency distribution.

b. Determine the proportion of CFO salaries that are larger than $175,000.

c. Determine the proportion of CFO salaries that are at most $205,000 and at least $135,000.

2-16. The *San Diego Union Tribune* reported ("Mortgage Interest Rates Rise," September 16, 2005) that the 30-year fixed-rate mortgage rates had risen to an average of 5.74% in September 2005. A sample of mortgage rates in the San Diego area produced the following interest rates:

5.84	5.73	5.58	5.69	5.84	5.68	5.73
5.79	5.77	5.67	5.76	5.70	5.70	5.66
5.71	5.80	5.81	5.75	5.81	5.78	5.79
5.77	5.73	5.67	5.74	5.76	5.76	5.74
5.73	5.71	5.71	5.72	5.80	5.69	5.88
5.70	5.75	5.75	5.68	5.72	5.70	5.67
5.83	5.76	5.80				

a. Construct a histogram with eight classes beginning at 5.58.

b. Determine the proportion of mortgage rates that are at least 5.74%.

c. Generate an ogive for this data.

Computer Database Exercises

2-17. The Franklin Tire Company is interested in demonstrating the durability of its steel-belted radial tires. To do this, the managers have decided to put four tires on 100 different sport utility vehicles and drive them throughout Alaska. The data collected indicate the number of miles (rounded to the nearest 1,000 miles) that each of the SUVs traveled before one of the tires on the vehicle did not meet minimum federal standards for tread thickness. The data file is called **Franklin**.

a. Construct a frequency distribution and histogram using 8 classes. Use 51 as the lower limit of the first class.

b. The marketing department wishes to know the tread life of at least 50% of the tires, the 10% that had the longest tread life, and the longest tread life of these tires. Provide this information to the marketing department. Also provide any other significant items that point out the desirability of this line of steel-belted tires.

c. Construct a frequency distribution and histogram using 12 classes, using 51 as the lower limit of the first class. Compare your results with those in parts a and b. Which distribution gives the best information about the desirability of this line of steel-belted tires? Discuss.

2-18. The United States Golf Association recently conducted a survey of its members. Among other questions, the members were asked to indicate the number of 18-hole rounds that they played last year. Data for a sample of 294 members is provided in the data file called **golf survey**.

a. Using the $2^k \geq n$ guideline, what is the minimum number of classes that should be used to display these data in a grouped data frequency distribution?

b. Referring to part a, what should the class width be, assuming you round the width up to nearest integer?

c. Referring to parts a and b, develop a grouped data frequency distribution for these golf data.

d. Based on your answer to part c, construct and interpret a frequency histogram for the data.

2-19. J.D. Power and Associates' annual customer-satisfaction survey, the Automotive Performance, Execution and Layout (APEAL) Study[SM], in its 10th year, was released on September 21, 2005. The study measures owners' satisfaction with the design, content, layout, and performance of their new vehicles. A file entitled **APEAL** contains the satisfaction ratings for 2005 for each make of car.

a. Construct a histogram for the APEAL ratings that starts at 825 and has class widths of 10.

b. The past industry average APEAL rating was 855. What does the 2005 data suggest in terms of the relative satisfaction with the 2005 models?

c. Determine if any class is vacant and indicate what that would signify with respect to these data.

2-20. *Ars Technia, LLD* published a news release (Eric Bangeman, "Dell still king of market share," January 18, 2005) that presented the results of a study concerning the world market share for the major manufacturers of personal computers. It indicated that Dell held 17.9% of this market. The file entitled **PCMarket** contains a sample of the market shares alluded to in the article.

a. Construct a histogram from this set of data and identify the market shares for each of the listed manufacturers.

b. Excluding the data referred to as "other," determine the total market share of the manufacturers that have headquarters in the United States.

2-21. Orlando, Florida, is a vacation destination for travelers from across the United States and around the world. As a result, the Orlando International Airport is very busy throughout the year. The Greater Orlando Airport Authority (GOAA) maintains a variety of data pertaining to airport operations. For example, the GOAA tracks the number of people who get on and off airplanes by airline. For the year 2004, these data are in a file called **Orlando Airport 2004**. These data can also be located on the airport's Web site at sun6.dms.state.fl.us/goaa. Suppose the airport manager is interested in analyzing the passenger data. In particular, she wishes you to help her with the following. (*Hint*: Use the variable called Total.)

a. Using the $2^k \geq n$ guideline, what is the minimum number of classes that should be used to display these data in a grouped data frequency distribution?

b. Referring to part a, what should the class width be, assuming you round the width up to nearest 1,000 passengers?

c. Referring to parts a and b, develop a grouped data frequency distribution for these airport data.

d. Based on your answer to part c, construct and interpret a frequency histogram for the data.

2-22. The manager of AJ's Fitness center, a full-service heath and exercise club, recently conducted a survey of 1,214 members. The objective of the survey was to determine the satisfaction level of his club's customers. In addition, the survey asked for several demographic factors such as age and gender. The data from the survey are in a file called **AJFitness**.

a. One of the key variables is "Overall Customer Satisfaction." This variable is measured on an ordinal scale as follows:

5 = very satisfied   4 = satisfied   3 = neutral
2 = dissatisfied   1 = very dissatisfied

Develop a frequency distribution for this variable and discuss the results.

b. Develop a joint relative frequency distribution for the variables "Overall Customer Satisfaction" and "Typical of Visits Per Week." Discuss the results.

2-23. The file **German Coffee** contains data on individual coffee consumption (in kg) for 144 randomly selected German coffee drinkers.

a. Construct a data array of the coffee consumption data.

b. Construct a frequency distribution of the coffee consumption data. Within what class do more of the observations fall?

c. Construct a histogram of the coffee consumption data. Briefly comment on what the histogram reveals concerning the data.

d. Develop a relative frequency distribution and a cumulative relative frequency distribution of the coffee data. What percentage of the coffee drinkers sampled consumes 8.3 kg or more annually?

Bar Chart

A graphical representation of a categorical data set in which a rectangle or bar is drawn over each category or class. The length or height of each bar represents the frequency or percentage of observations or some other measure associated with the category. The bars may be vertical or horizontal. The bars may all be the same color or they may be different colors depicting different categories. Additionally, multiple variables can be graphed on the same bar chart.

Business Application

2.2 Bar Charts, Pie Charts, and Stem and Leaf Diagrams

Bar Charts

Section 2-1 introduced some of the basic tools for describing numerical variables, both discrete and continuous, when the data are in their raw form. However, in many instances, you will be working with categorical data or data that have already been summarized to some extent. In these cases, an effective presentation tool is often a **bar chart**.

NEW CAR SALES The automobile industry is a significant part of the U.S., Japanese, and German economies. When car sales are up, the economies of these countries are up, and vice-versa. Table 2.8 displays data showing the total number of cars sold in March 2005,

TABLE 2.8 March 2005 New Car Sales for the Top Six Automobile Companies (United States)

Car Company	March 2005 Sales
General Motors	426,114
Ford	305,173
DaimlerChrysler	243,165
Toyota	203,443
Honda	128,548
Nissan	106,042

Source: www.theautochannel.com/news/2005/04/22/046636.html

CHAPTER OUTCOME #4

by the six largest automobile companies in the world. Although the table format is informative, a graphical presentation is often desirable. Because the car sales data are summarized by car company, a bar chart would work well in this instance. The bars on a bar chart can be vertical (called a *column bar chart*) or horizontal (called a *horizontal bar chart*.) Figure 2.10 illustrates an example of a column bar chart. The height of the bars corresponds to the number of cars sold by each company. This gives you an idea of the sales advantage held by General Motors in March 2005.

One strength of the bar chart is its capability of displaying multiple variables on the same chart. For instance, a bar chart can conveniently compare new car sales data for March 2005 and sales for the same month the previous year. Figure 2.11 is a horizontal bar chart that does just that. Notice that both GM and Ford had a decline in car sales in March between 2004 and 2005.

People sometimes confuse histograms and bar charts. Although there are some similarities, they are two very different graphical tools. Histograms are used to represent a frequency distribution associated with a quantitative (ratio or interval-level) variable. Refer to the histogram illustrations in Section 2-1. In every case, the variable on the horizontal axis was numerical, with values moving from low to high. There are no gaps between the histogram bars. On the other hand, bar charts are used when the variable of interest is categorical, as in this case in which the category is car company.

FIGURE 2.10

Bar Chart Showing March 2005 New Car Sales

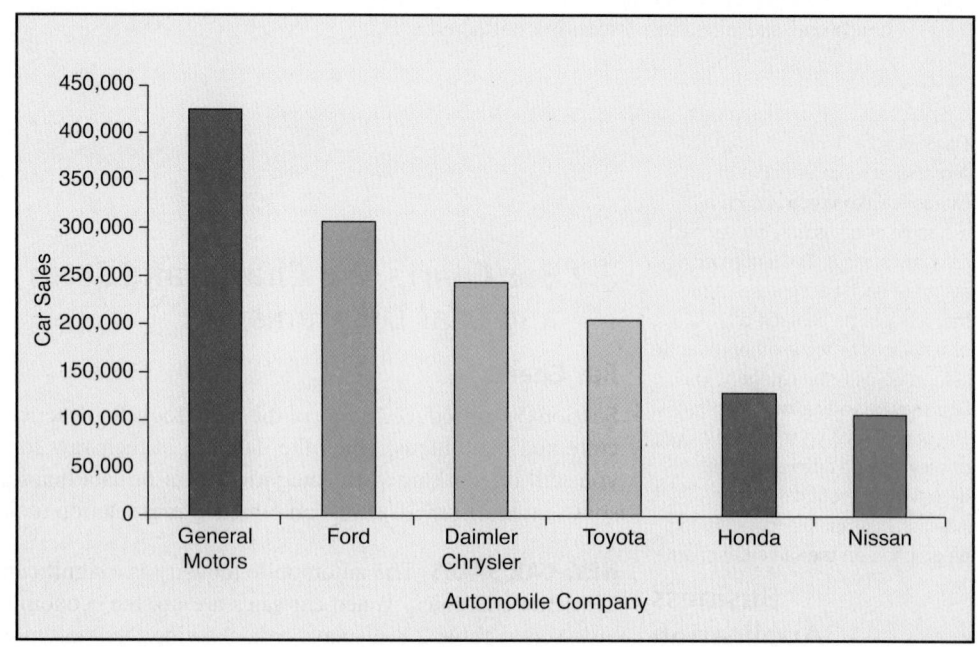

FIGURE 2.11

Bar Chart Comparing March 2004 and March 2005 Car Sales

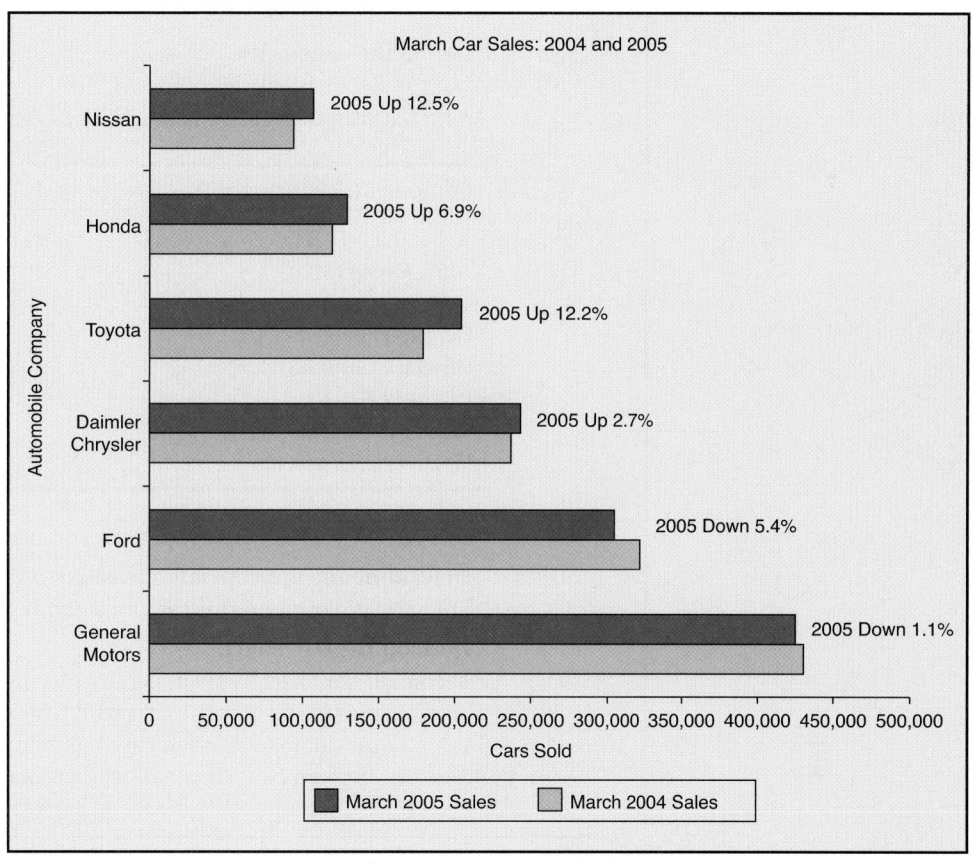

TRY PROBLEM   2.27

SUMMARY Constructing Bar Charts

A bar chart is constructed using the following steps:

1. Define the categories for the variable of interest.
2. For each category, determine the appropriate measure or value.
3. For a column bar chart, locate the categories on the horizontal axis. The vertical axis is set to a scale

corresponding to the values in the categories. For a horizontal bar chart, place the categories on the vertical axis and set the scale of the horizontal axis in accordance with the values in the categories. Then construct bars, either vertical or horizontal, for each category such that the length or height corresponds to the value for the category.

EXAMPLE 2-7 Bar Charts

Investment Recommendations   In the July 11, 2005 issue of *Fortune*, David Stires authored "The Best Stocks to Buy Now." The article identified 40 companies as good investment opportunities. These companies were divided into five categories: Growth and Income, Bargain Growth, Deep Value, Small Wonders, and Foreign Value. For each company, data for several key variables were reported, including the price/earnings ratio based on the previous 12-months' reported earnings. We are interested in constructing a bar chart of the PE ratios for the eight companies classified as Growth and Income.

Step 1 **Define the categories.**

Data are available for the June 24, 2005 stock price and price/earnings ratio for each of eight companies. These data are shown as follows:

Company (ticker symbol)	PE Ratio	Stock Price
Abbott Labs (ABT)	21	$49
Altria Group (MO)	14	$65
Coca-Cola (KO)	21	$42
Colgate-Palmolive (CL)	20	$51
General Mills (GIS)	17	$51
Pfizer (PFE)	13	$29
Proctor & Gamble (PG)	21	$53
Wyeth (WYE)	15	$43

The category to be displayed is the company.

Step 2 **Determine the appropriate measure to be displayed.**

The measure of interest is the price/earnings ratio.

Step 3 **Develop the bar chart.**

A column bar chart is developed by placing the eight companies on the horizontal axis and constructing bars whose heights correspond to the value of the company's price/earnings ratio. Each company is assigned a different-colored bar. The resulting bar chart is

Step 4 **Interpret the results.**

The bar chart shows three companies with especially low PE ratios. These are Altria Group, Pfizer, and Wyeth. Thus, of the eight recommended companies in the Growth and Income group, these three have the lowest PE ratios.

You might be interested in seeing how these eight companies have done since this article was published in July 2005. Go to one of the online services (for example, Yahoo Finance) to get the current stock prices and PE ratios and compare those with the values listed above.

TABLE 2.9 Salary Data for Bach, Lombard, & Wilson

Year	Males: Average Starting Salaries	Females: Average Starting Salaries
2000	$44,456	$41,789
2001	$47,286	$46,478
2002	$56,234	$53,854
2003	$57,890	$58,600
2004	$63,467	$59,070
2005	$61,090	$55,321
2006	$67,543	$64,506

Business Application

Excel and Minitab Tutorial

BACH, LOMBARD, & WILSON One of the most useful features of bar charts is that they can display multiple issues. Consider Bach, Lombard, & Wilson, the New England law firm. Recently, the firm handled a case in which a woman was suing her employer, a major electronics firm, claiming the company gave higher starting salaries to men than to women. Consequently, she stated, even though the company tended to give equal percentage raises to women and men, the gap between the two groups widened.

Attorneys at Bach, Lombard, & Wilson had their staff assemble massive amounts of data. Table 2.9 provides an example of the type of data they collected. A bar chart is a more effective way to convey this information, as Figure 2.12 shows. From this graph we can quickly see that in all years except 2003 the starting salaries for males did exceed that of females. The bar chart also illustrates that the general trend in starting salaries for both groups has been increasing, though with a slight downturn in 2005. Do you think the information in Figure 2.12 alone is sufficient to rule in favor of the claimant in this lawsuit?

FIGURE 2.12

Bar Chart of Starting Salaries

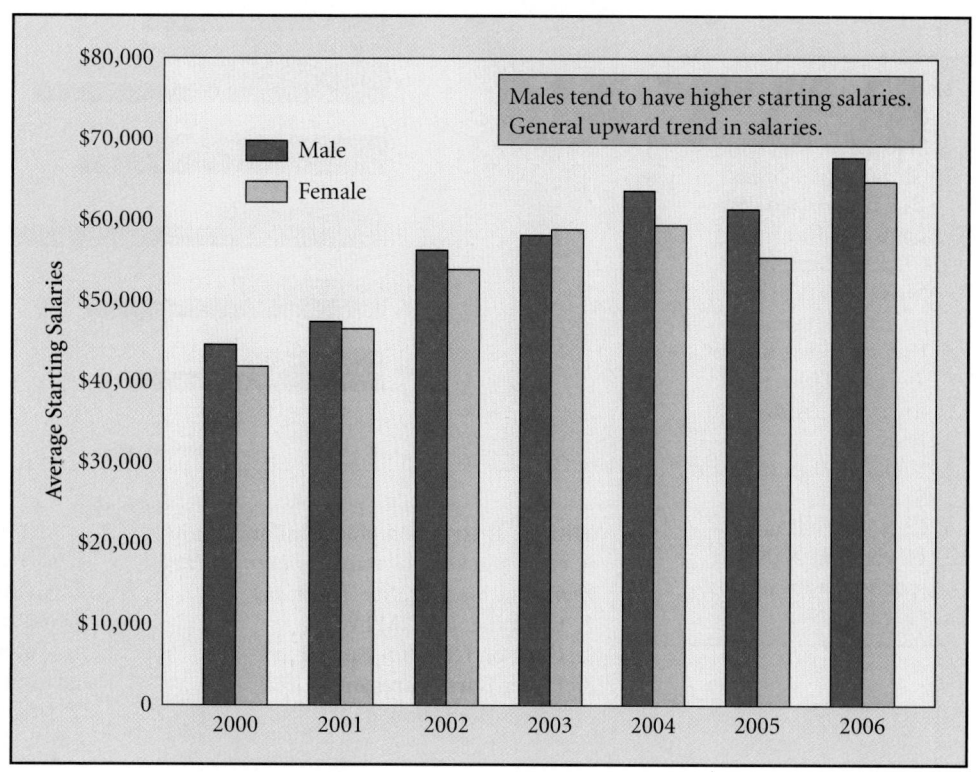

TABLE 2.10 Salary Data for the Bach, Lombard, & Wilson Example

Year	Males: Average Starting Salaries	Males: Percentage with MBA	Females: Average Starting Salaries	Females: Percentage with MBA
2000	$44,456	35	$41,789	18
2001	$47,286	39	$46,478	20
2002	$56,234	49	$53,854	22
2003	$57,890	40	$58,600	30
2004	$63,467	46	$59,070	25
2005	$61,090	32	$55,321	24
2006	$67,543	48	$64,506	26

Bar charts like the one in Figure 2.12 that display two or more variables are referred to as *cluster bar charts*.

Suppose other data are available showing the percentage of new hires having MBA degrees by gender, as illustrated in Table 2.10. The cluster bar chart in Figure 2.13 presents

FIGURE 2.13

Excel 2007 Output—Bar Chart of MBA Hire Data

Excel 2007 Instructions:
1. Open file: Bach.xls.
2. Select data for chart.
3. On **Insert** tab, click **Bar Chart**, and then click **2-D Bar** option.
4. Click on **Design** and **Move Chart** to put chart on a separate page.
5. Use the **Layout** tab of the **Axis Titles** to add titles and remove grid lines.
6. Under **Design**, click on **Select Data**.
7. Click on **Edit** under **Horizontal Axis** and specify the location of year variable.

Minitab Instructions for Similar Results:
(**Create stacked columns** for *Percent Hired*, *Years*, and *Gender*, *See Tutorial*.)
1. Open file: Bach.MTW.
2. Click on **Graph > Bar Chart**.
3. Under **Bars represent**, select *Values from a table*.
4. Under **One column of values**, select *Cluster*, click **OK**.
5. In **Graph variables**, enter *Percent Hired* column.
6. In **Categorical variables for grouping (1-4 outer-most first)**, enter *Year* and *Gender columns*.
7. Click **OK**.

FIGURE 2.14

Excel 2007 Output—Bar Chart of Average Starting Salaries by Degree Type

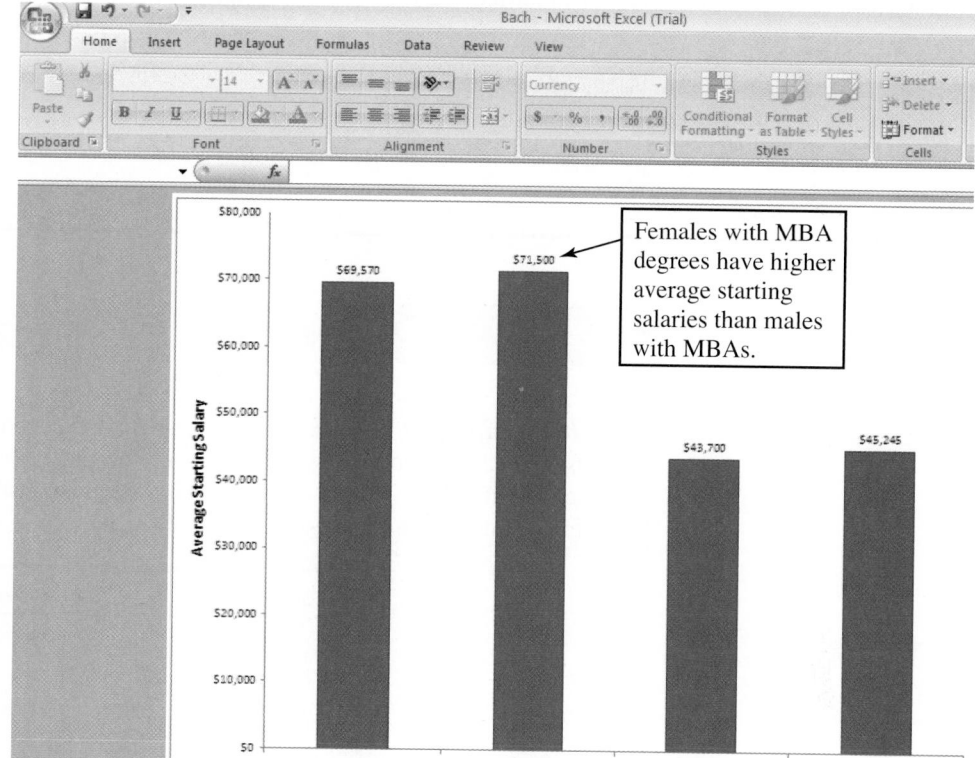

Excel 2007 Instructions:
1. Open file: Bach.xls.
2. Select data for chart.
3. On **Insert** tab, click **Bar Chart**, and then click **2-D Bar** option.
4. Click on **Design** and **Move Chart** to put chart on a separate page.
5. Use the **Layout** tab of the **Axis Titles** to add titles and remove grid lines.
6. Under **Design**, click on **Select Data**.
7. Click on **Edit** under **Horizontal Axis** and specify the location x-axis labels.

these data clearly. The chart shows that every year the percentage of new hires with MBA degrees was substantially higher for male hires than for female hires. What might this imply about the reason for the difference in starting salaries?

After viewing the bar chart in Figure 2.13, the lead attorney had her staff look at the average starting salary for MBA and non-MBA graduates for the combined seven-year period, broken down by male and female employees. Figure 2.14 shows the bar chart for those data.

Figure 2.14 shows an interesting result. Over the seven-year period, females actually had higher starting salaries than males for those with and without MBA degrees. Then how can Figure 2.12 be correct, when it shows that in almost every year the male average starting salary exceeded the female average starting salary? The answer lies in Figure 2.13, which shows that far more of the newly hired males had MBAs. Because MBAs tend to get substantially higher starting salaries, the overall male average salary was higher. In this case, the initial data looked like the electronics firm had been discriminating against females by paying lower starting salaries. After digging deeper, we see that females actually get the higher starting average salaries with and without MBA degrees. However, does this prove that the company is not discriminating in its hiring practices? Perhaps it purposefully hires fewer female MBAs or fewer females in general. More research is needed.

Pie Chart

A graph in the shape of a circle. The circle is divided into "slices" corresponding to the categories or classes to be displayed. The size of each slice is proportional to the magnitude of the displayed variable associated with each category or class.

Pie Charts

Another graphical tool that can be used to transform data into information is the **pie chart**.

A pie chart is constructed using the following steps:

1. Define the categories for the variable of interest.
2. For each category, determine the appropriate measure or value. The value assigned to each category is the proportion the category is to the total for all categories.

3. Construct the pie chart by displaying one slice for each category that is proportional in size to the proportion the category value is to the total of all categories.

EXAMPLE 2-8 Pie Charts

TRY PROBLEM 2.28

Gold Equipment A survey was recently conducted of 300 golfers that asked questions about the impact of new technology on the game. One question asked the golfers to indicate which area of golf equipment is most responsible for improving an amateur golfer's game. The following data were obtained:

Equipment	Frequency
Golf Ball	81
Club Head Material	66
Shaft Material	63
Club Head Size	63
Shaft Length	3
Don't Know	24

To display these data in pie chart form, use the following steps:

Step 1 Define the categories.
The categories are the six equipment-response categories.

Step 2 Determine the appropriate measure.
The appropriate measure is the proportion of the golfers surveyed. The proportion for each category is determined by dividing the number of

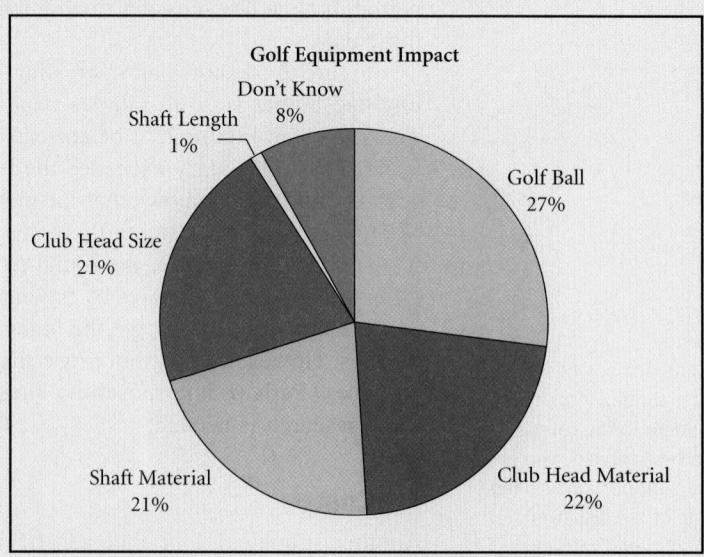

golfers in a category by the total sample size. For example, for the category golf ball, the percentage is $81/300 = 0.27 = 27\%$.

Step 3 **Construct the pie chart.**

The pie chart is constructed by dividing a circle into six slices (one for each category) such that each slice is proportional to the percentage of golfers in the category.

Pie charts are sometimes mistakenly used when a bar chart would be more appropriate. For example, a few years ago the student leaders at Boise State University wanted to draw attention to the funding inequities among the four public universities in Idaho. To do so, they rented a large billboard adjacent to a major thoroughfare through downtown Boise. The billboard contained a large pie chart like the one shown in Figure 2.15, where each slice indicated the funding per student at a given university. However, for a pie chart to be appropriate, the slices of the pie should represent parts of a total. But in the case of the billboard, that was not the case. The amounts merely represented the dollars of state money spent per student at each university. The sum of the four dollar amounts on the pie chart was a meaningless number. In this case, a bar chart like that shown in Figure 2.16 would have been more appropriate.

Stem and Leaf Diagrams

CHAPTER OUTCOME #5

Another graphical technique that is useful for doing a preliminary analysis of quantitative data is called the *stem and leaf diagram*. The stem and leaf diagram is similar to the histogram introduced in Section 2-1 in that it displays the distribution for the quantitative variable. However, unlike the histogram, in which the individual values of the data are lost if the variable of interest is broken into classes, the stem and leaf diagram shows the individual data values.

Minitab has a procedure for constructing stem and leaf diagrams. Although Excel does not have a stem and leaf procedure, the PHStat add-ins to Excel that are included on the CD-ROM do have a stem and leaf procedure.

FIGURE 2.15

Pie Chart: Per Student Funding for Universities

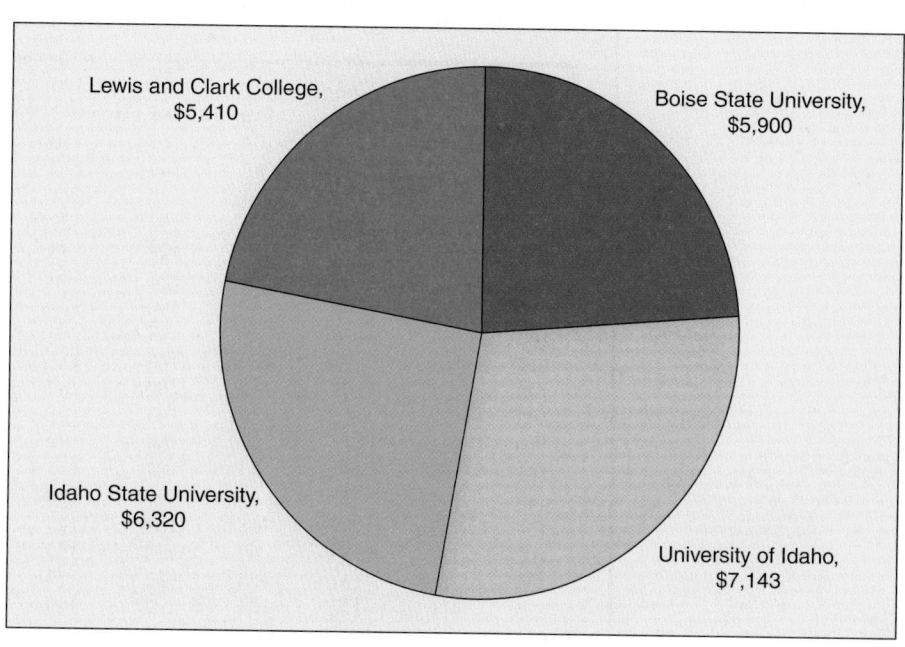

FIGURE 2.16

Bar Chart: Per Student Funding for Universities

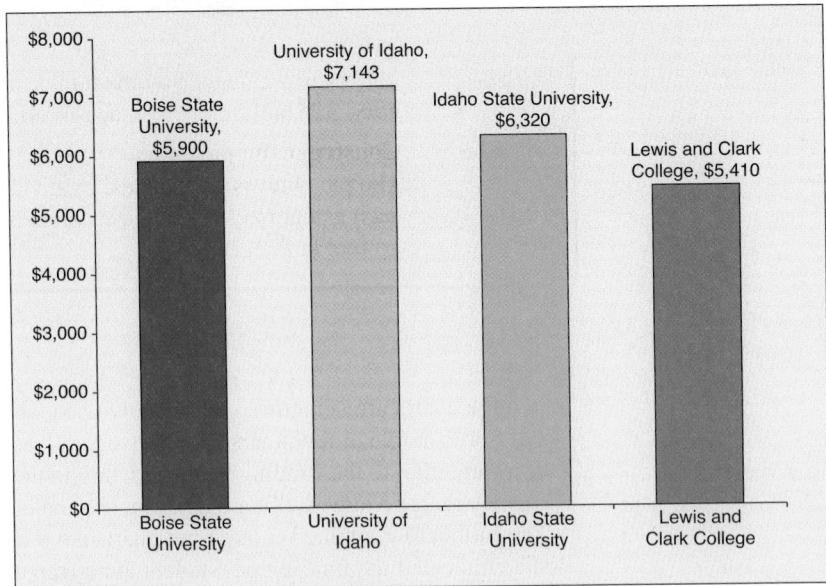

SUMMARY — Constructing Stem and Leaf Diagrams

To construct the stem and leaf diagram for a quantitative variable, use the following steps:

1. Sort the data from low to high.
2. Analyze the data for the variable of interest to determine how you wish to split the values into a stem and a leaf.
3. List all possible stems in a single column between the lowest and highest values in the data.
4. For each stem, list all leaves associated with the stem.

TRY PROBLEM 2.24

EXAMPLE 2-9 — Stem and Leaf Diagrams

Regis Auto Rental   The operations manager for Regis Auto Rental is interested in performing an analysis of the miles driven for the cars the company rents on weekends. One method for analyzing the data for a sample of 200 rentals is the stem and leaf diagram. The following data represent the miles driven in the cars:

113	112	63	127	110	129	142	115	192	94
165	121	105	140	85	93	105	140	93	126
183	118	67	104	162	110	76	109	91	132
88	96	132	80	144	112	57	139	123	124
172	149	198	114	88	111	133	117	138	134
53	147	108	109	153	89	159	99	130	93
161	118	115	117	128	98	125	184	134	132
117	127	166	72	122	109	124	92	82	69
110	128	151	67	142	177	135	121	143	89
160	115	138	79	104	76	89	110	44	140
117	103	59	109	145	117	162	108	141	139
148	175	107	117	87	87	150	152	80	168
88	127	131	85	143	101	137	111	128	147
110	81	111	149	154	90	150	117	101	116
153	176	112	147	87	177	190	66	62	154
143	122	176	153	97	106	86	62	146	98
134	135	127	118	109	143	146	152	140	95
102	137	158	69	122	135	136	129	91	136
135	86	131	154	132	59	136	85	142	137
155	190	120	154	102	109	97	157	144	149

The stem and leaf diagram is constructed using the following steps:

Step 1 Sort the data from low to high.

The lowest value is 44 miles and the highest value is 198 miles.

Step 2 Split the values into a stem and leaf.

Stem = tens place   leaf = units place

For example, for the value 113, the stem is 11 and the leaf is 3. We are keeping one digit for the leaf.

Step 3 List all possible stems from lowest to highest.

Step 4 Itemize the leaves from lowest to highest and place next to the appropriate stems.

4	4
5	3 7 9 9
6	2 2 3 6 7 7 9 9
7	2 6 6 9
8	0 0 1 2 5 5 5 6 7 7 7 8 8 8 9 9 9
9	0 1 1 2 3 3 3 4 5 6 7 7 8 8 9
10	1 1 2 2 3 4 4 5 5 6 7 8 8 9 9 9 9 9 9
11	0 0 0 0 1 1 1 2 2 2 3 4 5 5 5 6 7 7 7 7 7 7 7 8 8 8
12	0 1 1 2 2 2 3 4 4 5 6 7 7 7 7 8 8 8 9 9
13	0 1 1 2 2 2 2 3 4 4 4 5 5 5 5 6 6 6 7 7 7 8 8 9 9
14	0 0 0 0 1 2 2 2 3 3 3 3 4 4 5 6 6 7 7 7 8 9 9 9
15	0 0 1 2 2 3 3 3 4 4 4 4 5 7 8 9
16	0 1 2 2 5 6 8
17	2 5 6 6 7 7
18	3 4
19	0 0 2 8

The stem and leaf diagram shows that most people drive the rental car between 80 and 160 miles, with the most frequent value in the 110- to 120-mile range.

2-2: Exercises

Skill Development

2-24. Given the following data, construct a stem and leaf diagram:

0.7	1.7	2.8	3.8
0.8	1.8	3.3	4.3
1.0	2.0	4.4	5.4
1.1	2.1	5.3	6.3
1.4	2.4	5.4	6.4
2.0	3.0		

2-25. A university has the following number of students at each grade level.

Freshman	3,450
Sophomore	3,190
Junior	2,780
Senior	1,980
Graduate	750

a. Construct a bar chart that effectively displays these data.

b. Construct a pie chart to display these data.

c. Referring to the graphs constructed in parts a and b, indicate which you would favor as the most effective way of presenting these data. Discuss.

2-26. The following data reflect the percentages of employees with different levels of education:

Education Level	Percentage
Less than HS Graduate	18
HS Graduate	34
Some College	14
College Graduate	30
Graduate Degree	4
	Total = 100

a. Develop a pie chart to illustrate these data.

b. Develop a horizontal bar chart to illustrate these data.

2-27. Given the following sales data for product category and sales region, construct at least two different bar charts that display the data effectively:

		Region			
		East	West	North	South
	XJ-6 Model	200	300	50	170
Product	X-15-Y Model	100	200	20	100
Type	Craftsman	80	400	60	200
	Generic	100	150	40	50

2-28. The 2004 Annual Report to shareholders of Murphy Oil Corporation contains the following information concerning the number of barrels of product sold per day by product category for North America and the United Kingdom.

Product Sold—Barrels Per Day (Murphy Oil Corporation 2004 Annual Report To Shareholders)	
North America 2004	
Gasoline	207,786
Kerosene	4,811
Diesel & Home Heating Oils	66,648
Residuals	13,699
Asphalt, LPG, and Other	8,857
United Kingdom 2004	
Gasoline	11,435
Kerosene	2,756
Diesel & Home Heating Oils	14,649
Residuals	4,062
Asphalt, LPG, and Other	4,205

a. Construct a pie chart that displays North American sales.

b. Construct a pie chart that displays United Kingdom sales.

c. Develop a bar chart that effectively compares the daily product sales for North America and the United Kingdom.

2-29. Boston Properties is a real estate investment trust (REIT) that owns first-class office properties in selected markets. According to its 2004 annual report, its income distribution by region (in percent) was as follows:

Region	2004 Income Distribution (in %)
Boston	24
San Francisco	14
Washington, D.C.	21
Princeton	5
New York City	36

a. Construct a pie chart to display the income distribution by region for 2004.

b. Construct a bar chart to display the income distribution by region for 2004.

c. Which chart do you think more effectively displays the information?

2-30. A large technology corporation recently released the following data concerning its operating profits (in $billions) for the last five years:

Year	2001	2002	2003	2004	2005
Profit	0.5	0.1	0.7	0.5	0.2

a. Construct a bar chart to graphically display these data.

b. Construct a pie chart to graphically display these data.

c. Select the display that most effectively displays the data and provide reasons for your choice.

2-31. As reported in *Business Week* ("Dark Days for Daimler," August 15, 2005), DaimlerChrysler stated its first-half revenues (in $billions) for 2005 as follows:

Division	Mercedes	Chrysler	Commercial Vehicles	Financial Services	Total
Revenues	27.7	30.5	23.2	8.9	90.3

a. Produce a bar chart for these data

b. Determine the proportion of first-half revenues accounted for by its vehicle divisions.

Business Applications

2-32. In September 2005, an Associated Press article by David Caruso, titled "Million-Dollar Homes Are

Now A Dime A Dozen," discussed the rapid growth of residential real estate prices in the United States. In the article he reports the U.S. Census data indicate that ". . . for first time, there are more than one million owner-occupied homes in the United States worth $1 million or more." The following data reflect the number of $1 million homes in the United States in the five years prior to 2005:

Year	Number of $1 Million Homes
2000	394,878
2001	495,600
2002	595,441
2003	714,467
2004	1,034,386

Develop a horizontal bar chart to represent these data in graphical form.

2-33. At the March meeting of the board of directors for the Graystone Services Company, one of the regional managers put the following data on the overhead projector to illustrate the ratio of the number of units manufactured divided by the number of employees at each of Graystone's five manufacturing plants:

Plant Location	Units Manufactured/Employees
Bismarck ND	14.5
Boulder CO	9.8
Omaha NE	13.0
Harrisburg PA	17.6
Portland ME	5.9

a. Discuss whether a pie chart or a bar chart would be most appropriate to present these data graphically.

b. Based on your analysis in part a, construct the chart you have recommended.

2-34. The pharmaceutical industry is a very fast-growing segment of the U.S. and international economies. Recently, there has been controversy over how studies are done to show that drugs are both safe and effective. One drug product, Cymbalta, which is an antidepressant, was purported in a published abstract of an article in a medical journal to be superior to other competing products. Yet, the article itself stated that no studies had actually been done to show such comparisons between Cymbalta and other competing products. In an August 2005 report in *The Wall Street Journal*, an article titled "Reading Fine Print, Insurers Question Drug Studies," the following data were presented showing the U.S. sales of antidepressant drugs by major brand. The sales data for the first half of 2005 are

Antidepressant Drug	Sales (First Half 2005 in billions)
Effexor XR	$1.29
Lexapro	$1.03
Zoloft	$1.55
Cymbalta	$0.27
Other	$0.97

Construct an appropriate graph to display these data.

2-35. The number of branded retail outlets for Murphy Oil Corporation as of December 31 of each year from 2001 to 2004 is shown here (2004 Annual Report to Shareholders Murphy Oil Corporation).

Branded Retail Outlets	2001	2002	2003	2004
North America	387	506	623	752
Other	428	408	371	375

Develop a chart that effectively compares the number of branded retail outlets over time between North America and Other.

2-36. The 2005 Annual Report to Shareholders of the Procter & Gamble Company reports its geographic sales split, based on fiscal year 2005 net sales, as follows:

Geographic Region	Sales Split
North America	48%
Western Europe	24%
Northeast Asia	5%
Developing Geographies	23%

a. Construct a bar chart that displays this information.

b. Construct a pie chart that displays this information.

2-37. A fast-food restaurant monitors its drive-thru service times electronically to ensure that its speed of service is meeting the company's goals. A sample of 28 drive-thru times was recently taken and is shown here.

Speed of Service (time in seconds)			
83	138	145	147
130	79	156	156
90	85	68	93
178	76	73	119
92	146	88	103
116	134	162	71
181	110	105	74

a. Construct a stem and leaf diagram of the speed of service times.

b. What range of time might the restaurant say is the most frequent speed of service?

2-38. A random sample of 30 customer records for a physician's office showed the following time (in days) to collect insurance payments:

Number of Days to Collect Payment				
34	55	36	39	36
32	35	30	47	31
60	66	48	43	33
24	37	38	65	35
22	45	33	29	41
38	35	28	56	56

a. Construct a stem and leaf diagram of these data.

b. Within what range of days are most payments collected?

2-39. *USA Today* presented data (Marilyn Adams and Dan Reed, "Difficult times battered airlines," September 16, 2005) to show that major airlines accounting for more than half of capacity were expected to be in bankruptcy court. The total seat capacity of major airlines was 858 billion at the time. For airlines expected to be in bankruptcy court, the following data were presented:

2004 airline seat capacity (in billions)				
Airline	United	Delta	Northwest	U.S. Airways	ATA
Capacity	145	130	92	54	21

a. Construct a bar graph representing the contribution to the total seat capacity of the major airlines for the five airlines indicated.

b. Produce a pie chart exhibiting the percentage of the total seat capacity for the five major airlines expected to be in bankruptcy court and the combined capacity of all others.

c. Calculate the percent of the capacity of the airlines expected to be in bankruptcy court. Was *USA Today* correct in the percentage stated?

2-40. The NPD Group provides global sales and marketing information that helps clients make more informed, fact-based decisions in order to optimize their businesses. Many of the world's most successful companies rely on them for insight on what is selling, where, and why so that they can understand and leverage the latest trends. They recently (July 2005) released the following results of a survey intended to determine the market share distribution for the major corporations that make digital music devices:

Corporation	Apple	SanDisk	Creative Technology	iRiver	Samsung
Market Share	74%	6.4%	3.9%	3.6%	2.6%

a. Generate a bar chart to display these data.

b. Generate a pie chart to display these data.

c. Which of the two displays most effectively presents the data? Explain your answer.

Computer Database Exercises

2-41. The manager for Capital Educators Federal Credit Union has selected a random sample of 300 of the credit union's credit card customers. The data are in a file called **Capital**. The manager is interested in graphically displaying the percentage of card holders of each gender.

a. Determine the appropriate type of graph to use in this application.

b. Construct the graph and interpret it.

2-42. Amazon.com celebrated its 10th anniversary in July 2005. Its growth can seen by examining its increasing sales volume (in $billions) and the net income/loss during Amazon's 10 years of existence as reported in *USA Today* ("Amazon CEO takes long view," September 6, 2005). A file entitled **Amazon** contains these data.

a. Construct one bar graph illustrating the relationship between sales and income for each separate year of Amazon's existence.

b. Describe the type of relationship that exists between the years in business and Amazon's sales volume.

c. Amazon's sales rose sharply. However, its net income yielded losses, which increased during the first few years. In which year did this situation reverse itself and show improvement in the net income balance sheet?

2-43. The Honda Ridgeline was the highest-ranked compact pickup in J.D. Power and Associates annual customer-satisfaction survey released on

September 21, 2005. The study also found that models with high ratings have a tendency to stay on dealers' lots a shorter period of time. As an example, the Honda Ridgeline had stayed on dealers' lots an average of 24 days. The file entitled **Honda** contains 50 lengths of stay on dealers' lots for Ridgeline trucks.

a. Construct a stem and leaf display for these data.

b. Determine the average length of stay on dealers' lots by the Honda Ridgeline. Does this agree with the average obtained by J.D. Power and Associates? Explain the difference.

2-44. In your capacity as assistant to the administrator at Freedom Hospital, you have been asked to develop a graphical presentation that focuses on the insurance carried by the geriatric patients at the hospital. The data file **Patients** contains data for a sample of geriatric patients. In developing your presentation, please do the following:

a. Construct a pie chart that shows the percentage of patients with each health insurance payer.

b. Develop a bar chart that shows total charges for patients by insurance payer.

c. Develop a stem and leaf diagram for the length-of-stay variable.

d. Develop a bar chart that shows the number of males and females by insurance carrier.

2-45. Recently, a study was conducted in which a random sample of hospitals was selected from each of four categories of hospitals: university related, religious related, community owned, and privately owned. At issue is the hospital charges associated with outpatient gall bladder surgery. The following data are in the file called **Hospitals**:

University Related	Religious Affiliated	Municipally Owned	Privately Held
$6,120	$4,010	$4,320	$5,100
$5,960	$3,770	$4,650	$4,920
$6,300	$3,960	$4,575	$5,200
$6,500	$3,620	$4,440	$5,345
$6,250	$3,280	$4,900	$4,875
$6,695	$3,680	$4,560	$5,330
$6,475	$3,350	$4,610	$5,415
$6,250	$3,250	$4,850	$5,150
$6,880	$3,400		$5,380
$6,550			

a. Compute the average charge for each hospital category.

b. Construct a bar chart showing the averages by hospital category.

c. Discuss why a pie chart would not in this case be an appropriate graphical tool.

CHAPTER OUTCOME #6

Line Chart
A two-dimensional chart showing time on the horizontal axis and the variable of interest on the vertical axis.

Business Application

Excel and Minitab Tutorial

2.3 Line Charts and Scatter Diagrams

Line Charts

Most of the examples that have been presented thus far have involved *cross-sectional data*, or data gathered from many observations, all taken at the same time. However, if you have *time-series* data that are measured over time (e.g., monthly, quarterly, or annually), an effective tool for presenting such data is a **line chart**.

MCGREGOR VINEYARDS McGregor Vineyards owns and operates a winery in the Sonoma Valley in northern California. At a recent company meeting, the financial manager expressed concern about the company's profit trend over the past 20 weeks. He presented weekly profit and sales data to McGregor management personnel. The data are on the CD-ROM that accompanies this text in the file **McGregor**.

Initially, the financial manager developed two separate line charts for this data: one for sales, the other for profits. These are displayed in Figures 2.17a and 2.17b. These line charts provide an indication that, although sales have been increasing, the profit trend is downward. But to fit both Excel graphs on one page, he had to compress the size of the graphs. This "flattened" the lines somewhat, masking the magnitude of the problem.

What the financial manager needed is one graph with both profits and sales. Figure 2.18 shows his first attempt. This is better, but there still is a problem: The sales and profit variables are of different magnitudes. This results in the profit line being flattened out to almost a straight line. The profit trend is hidden.

To overcome this problem, the financial manager needed to construct his graph using two scales, one for each variable. Figure 2.19 shows the improved graph. We can now clearly see that although sales are moving steadily higher, profits are headed downhill. For some reason, costs are rising faster than revenues, and this graph should motivate McGregor Vineyards to look into the problem.

FIGURE 2.17A

Excel 2007 Output Showing McGregor Line Charts

Excel 2007 Instructions:
1. Open file: McGregor.xls.
2. Select the **Sales (dollars)** data to be graphed.
3. On the **Insert** tab, click the **Line** chart.
4. Click the **Line with Markers** option.
5. Use the **Layout** tab in the **Chart Tools** to remove the Legend, change the Chart Title, add the Axis Titles, and remove the grid lines.
6. Repeat Steps 2–5 for the **Profit** data.

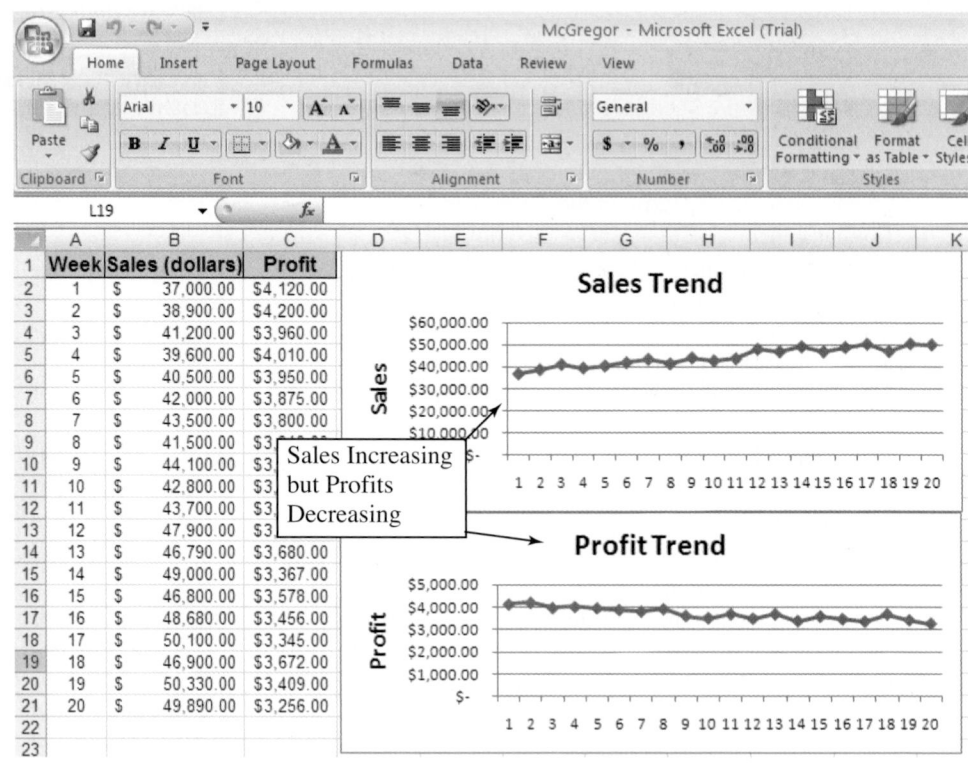

FIGURE 2.17B

Minitab Output Showing McGregor Line Charts

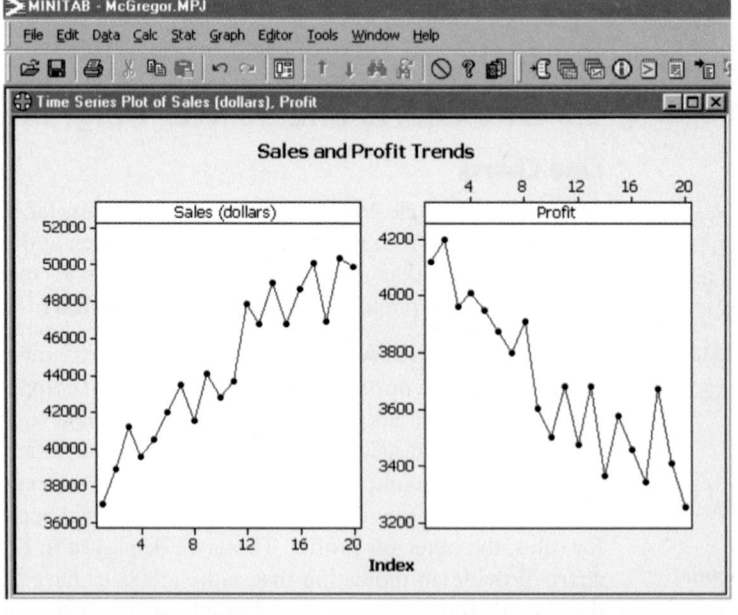

Minitab Instructions:
1. Open file: McGregor.MTW.
2. Choose **Graph > Times Series Plot.**
3. Select **Simple.**
4. Click **OK.**
5. In Series enter *Sales* and *Profit* columns.
6. Select **Multiple Graphs.**
7. Under **Show Graph Variables**, select **In separate panels of the same graph.**
8. Click **OK. OK.**

FIGURE 2.18

Excel 2007 Line Charts
of McGregor Profit and
Sales Using Same Value
Axis

Excel 2007 Instructions:
1. Open file: McGregor.xls.
2. Select the two variables,
   Sales (dollars) and
   Profit, to be graphed.
3. On the **Insert** tab, click
   the **Line** chart.
4. Click the **Line with
   Markers** option.
5. Use the **Layout** tab in
   the **Chart Tools** to
   change the Chart Title,
   add the Axis Titles,
   remove the border, and
   remove the grid lines.

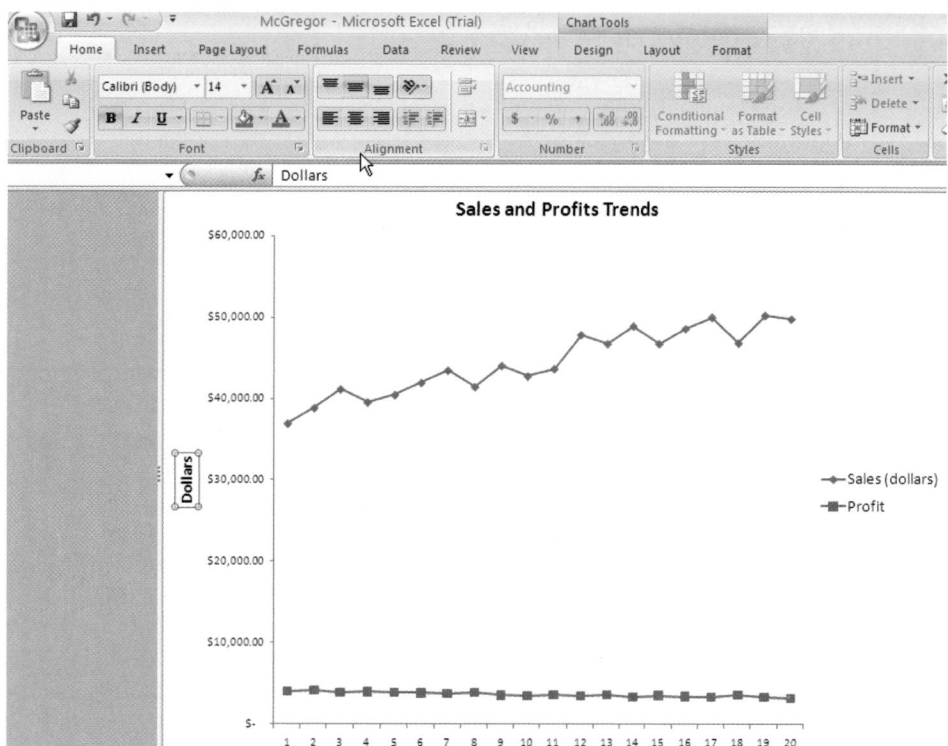

Minitab Instructions (for similar results):

1. Open File: McGregor.MTW.
2. Choose **Graph > Times Series Plot**.
3. Select **Multiple**.
4. Click **OK**.
5. In **Series** enter *Sales and Profit* columns.
6. Select **Multiple Graphs**.
7. Under **Show Graph Variables**, select
   Overlaid on the same graph.
8. Click **OK. OK**.

FIGURE 2.19

Excel 2007 Sales and
Profits Line Chart Using
Different Value Axes

Excel 2007 Instructions:
1. Open file: McGregor.xls.
2. Select data from the profit
   and sales columns.
3. Click on **Insert**.
4. Click on **Line Chart**.
5. Move graph to separate
   page.
6. Select Profit line on graph
   and right click.
7. Click on **Format Data
   Series**.
8. Click on **Secondary Axis**.
9. Click on **Layout** and add
   titles as desired.

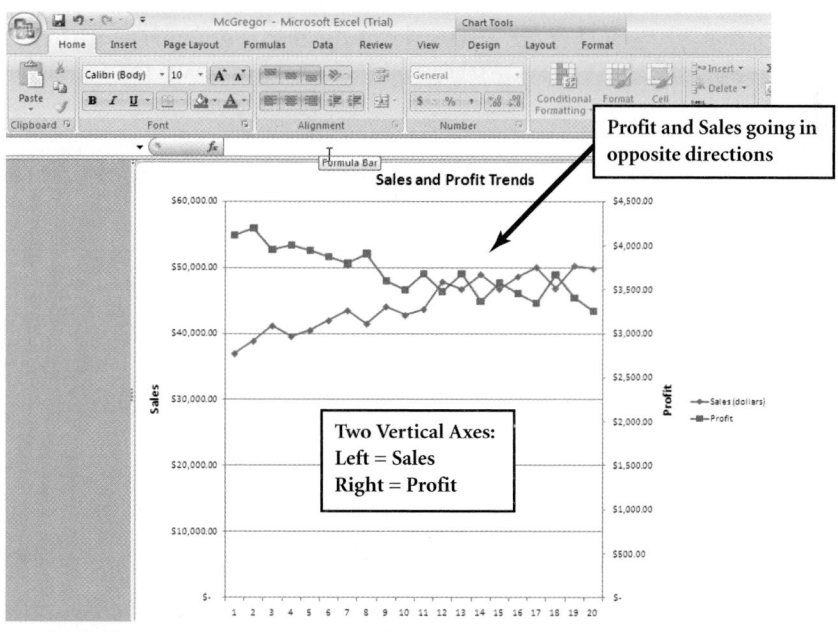

Minitab Instructions (for similar results):

1. Open File: McGregor.MTW.
2. Choose **Graph > Times Series Plot**.
3. Select **Multiple**.
4. Click **OK**.
5. In **Series**, enter *Sales* and *Profit* columns.
6. Select **Multiple Graphs**.
7. Click **OK**.

SUMMARY   Constructing Line Charts

A line chart, also commonly called a *trend chart*, is developed using the following steps:

1. Identify the time-series variable of interest and determine the maximum value and the range of time periods covered in the data.
2. Construct the horizontal axis for the time periods using equal spacing between each time period. Construct the vertical axis with a scale appropriate for the range of values of the time-series variable.
3. Plot the points on the graph and connect the points with straight lines.

EXAMPLE 2-10   Line Charts

TRY PROBLEM 2.46

Grogan Builders   Grogan Builders produces mobile homes in Alberta, Canada. The owners are planning to expand the manufacturing facilities. To do so requires additional financing. In preparation for the meeting with the bankers, the owners have assembled data on total annual sales for the past 10 years. These data are shown as follows:

1997	1998	1999	2000	2001	2002	2003	2004	2005	2006
1,426	1,678	2,591	2,105	2,744	3,068	2,755	3,689	4,003	3,997

The owners wish to present these data in a line chart to effectively show the company's sales growth over the 10-year period. To construct the line chart, the following steps are used:

Step 1 **Identify the time-series variable.**
The time-series variable is units sold measured over 10 years, with a maximum value of 4,003.

Step 2 **Construct the horizontal and vertical axes.**
The horizontal axis will have the 10 time periods equally spaced. The vertical axis will start at zero and go to a value exceeding 4,003. We will use 4,500. The vertical axis will also be divided into 500-unit increments.

Step 3 **Plot the data values on the graph and connect the points with straight lines.**

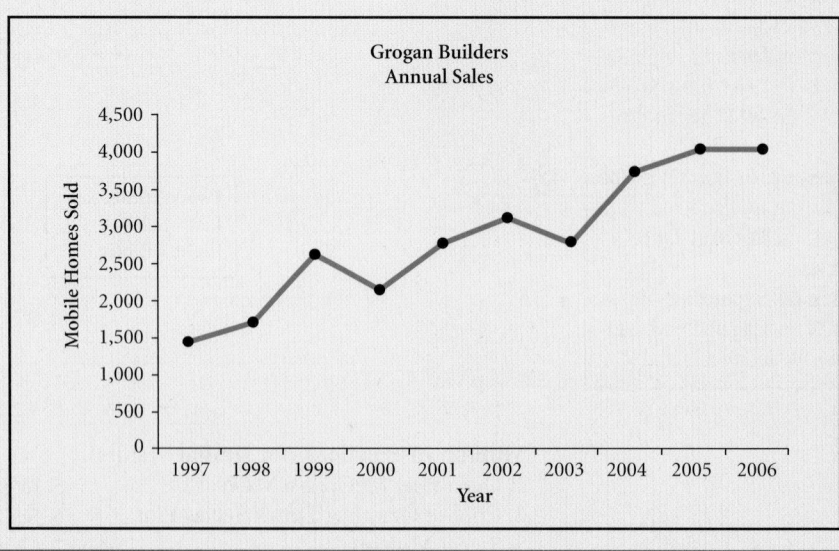

CHAPTER OUTCOME #7

Scatter Diagrams

In Section 2.1 we introduced a set of statistical tools known as joint frequency distributions that allow the decision maker to examine two variables at the same time. Another tool used to study two quantitative variables simultaneously is the **scatter diagram**, or the **scatter plot**.

There are many situations in which we are interested in understanding the *bivariate* relationship between two *quantitative* variables. For example, a company would like to know the relationship between sales and advertising. A bank might be interested in the relationship between savings account balances and credit card balances for its customers. A real estate agent might wish to know the relationship between the selling price of houses and the number of days that the houses have been on the market. The list of possibilities is almost limitless.

Regardless of the variables involved, there are several key relationships we are looking for when we develop a scatter diagram. Figure 2.20 shows scatter diagrams representing some key bivariate relationships that might exist between two quantitative variables.

Chapters 14 and 15 make extensive use of scatter diagrams. They introduce a statistical tool called *regression analysis* that focuses on the relationship between two variables. These variables are known as **dependent** and **independent variables**.

PERSONAL COMPUTERS Can you think of any product that has increased in quality and capability as rapidly as personal computers? Not that long ago an 8-MB RAM system with a 486 processor and a 640-K hard drive sold in the mid-$2500 range. Now the same money would buy a 3.0 GHz or faster machine with a 100+ GB hard drive and 512-MB RAM or more!

In September 2005 we examined various Internet Web sites looking for the best prices on personal computers. The data file called **Personal Computers** contains data on several characteristics, including processor speed, hard drive capacity, RAM, whether a monitor is included, and the price for 13 personal computers. Of particular interest is the relationship between the computer price and processing speed. Our objective is to develop a scatter diagram to graphically depict what, if any, relationship exists between these two variables. The dependent variable is price and the independent variable is processor speed. Figure 2.21 shows the Excel scatter diagram output. The relationship between processor speed and price is somewhat curvilinear and positive.

Scatter Diagram
A two-dimensional graph of plotted points in which the vertical axis represents values of one quantitative variable and the horizontal axis represents values of the other quantitative variable. Each plotted point has coordinates whose values are obtained from the respective variables.

Dependent Variable
A variable whose values are thought to be a function of, or dependent on, the values of another variable called the *independent variable*. On a scatter plot, the dependent variable is placed on the *y* axis and is often called the response variable.

Independent Variable
A variable whose values are thought to impact the values of the *dependent variable*. The independent variable, or explanatory variable, is often within the direct control of the decision maker. On a scatter plot, the independent variable, or explanatory variable, is graphed on the *x* axis.

FIGURE 2.20

Scatter Diagrams Showing Relationships Between x and y

Excel and Minitab Tutorial

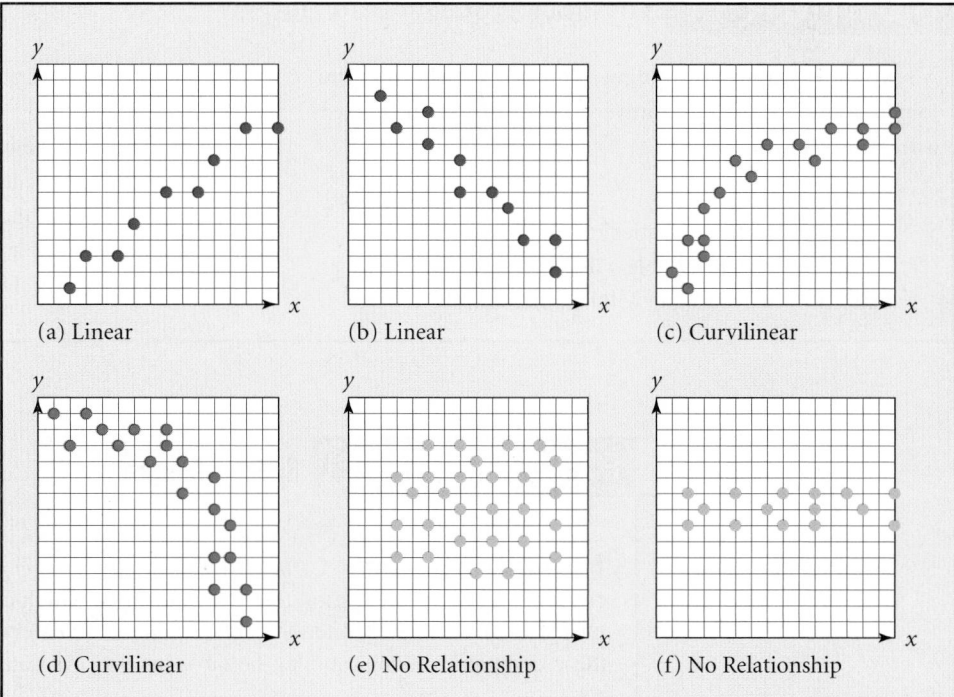

FIGURE 2.21

Excel 2007 Output of Scatter Diagrams for Computers Data

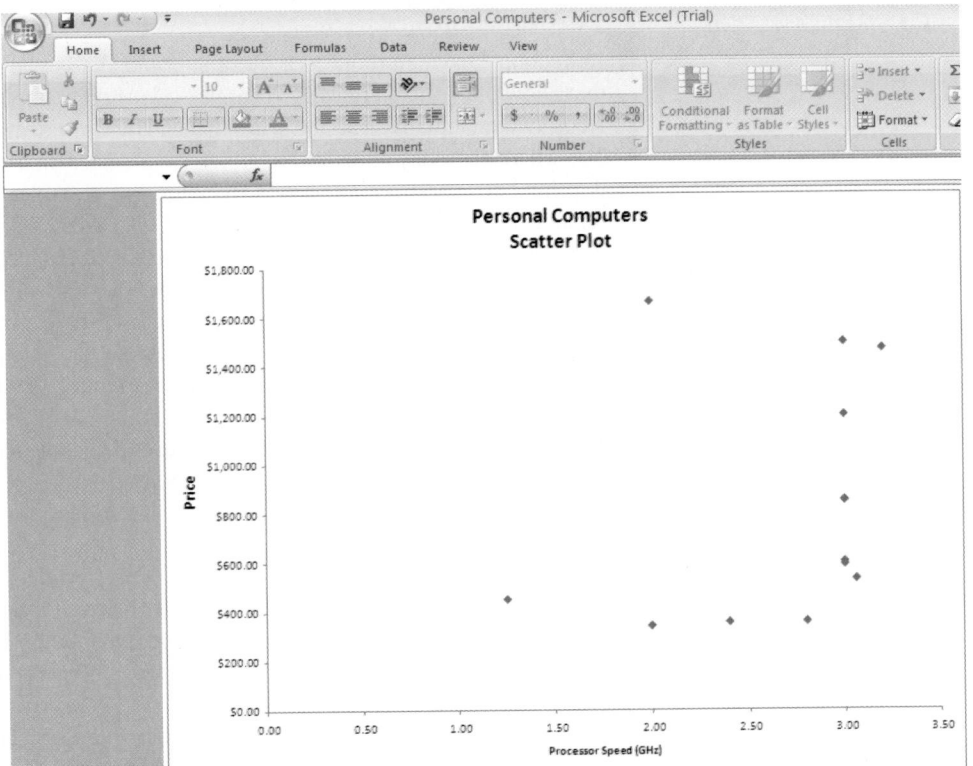

Excel 2007 Instructions:
1. Open file: Personal Computer.xls.
2. Select data for chart (Processor GHz and Price). (Hint, use Ctrl key to select just the two desired columns.)
3. On **Insert** tab, click **XY (Scatter)**, and then click **Scatter with only Markers** option.
4. Move the chart to a separate page.
5. Use the **Layout** tab of the **Chart Tools** to add titles and remove grid lines.

Minitab Instructions (for similar result):
1. Open file: Personal Computers.MTW.
2. Choose **Graph > Scatterplot**.
3. Select **Simple**.
4. Click **OK**.
5. In **Y**, enter *Price* column. In **X**, enter *Processor Speed* column.
6. Click **OK**.

SUMMARY Constructing Scatter Diagrams

A scatter diagram is a two-dimensional graph showing the joint values for two quantitative variables. It is constructed using the following steps:

1. Identify the two quantitative variables and collect paired responses for the two variables.
2. Determine which variable will be placed on the vertical axis and which variable will be placed on the horizon-tal axis. Often the vertical axis can be considered the dependent variable (y) and the horizontal axis can be considered the independent variable (x).
3. Define the range of values for each variable and define the appropriate scale for the x and y axes.
4. Plot the joint values for the two variables by placing a point in the x,y space. Do not connect the points.

TRY PROBLEM 2.47

EXAMPLE 2-11 Scatter Diagrams

Fortune's Best Eight Companies Each year, *Fortune* magazine surveys employees regarding job satisfaction to try to determine which companies are the "best" companies to work for in the United States. *Fortune* also collects a variety of data associated with these companies. For example, the table here shows data for the top eight companies on three variables: number of U.S. employees; number of training hours per year per employee; and total revenue in millions of dollars.

Company	U.S. Employees	Training Hr/Yr	Revenues
Southwest Airlines	24,757	15	$3,400
Kingston Technology	552	100	$1,300
SAS Institute	3,154	32	$653
Fel-Pro	2,577	60	$450
TD Industries	976	40	$127
MBNA	18,050	48	$3,300
W.L. Gore	4,118	27	$1,200
Microsoft	14,936	8	$8,700

To better understand these companies, we might be interested in the relationship between number of U.S. employees and revenue and between training hours and U.S. employees. To construct these scatter diagrams, we can use the following steps:

Step 1 **Identify the two variables of interest.**

In the first case, one variable is U.S. employees and the second is revenue. In the second case, one variable is training hours and the other is U.S. employees.

Step 2 **Identify the dependent and independent variables.**

In each case, think of U.S. employees as the independent (x) variable. Thus,

Case 1: y = revenue (vertical axis) x = U.S. employees
                                                              (horizontal axis)

Case 2: y = training hours x = U.S. employees
              (vertical axis)   (horizontal axis)

Step 3 **Establish the scales for the vertical and horizontal axes.**

The maximum value for each variable is

revenue = $8,700   U.S. employees = 24,757   training hours = 100

Step 4 **Plot the joint values for the two variables by placing a point in the x, y space.**

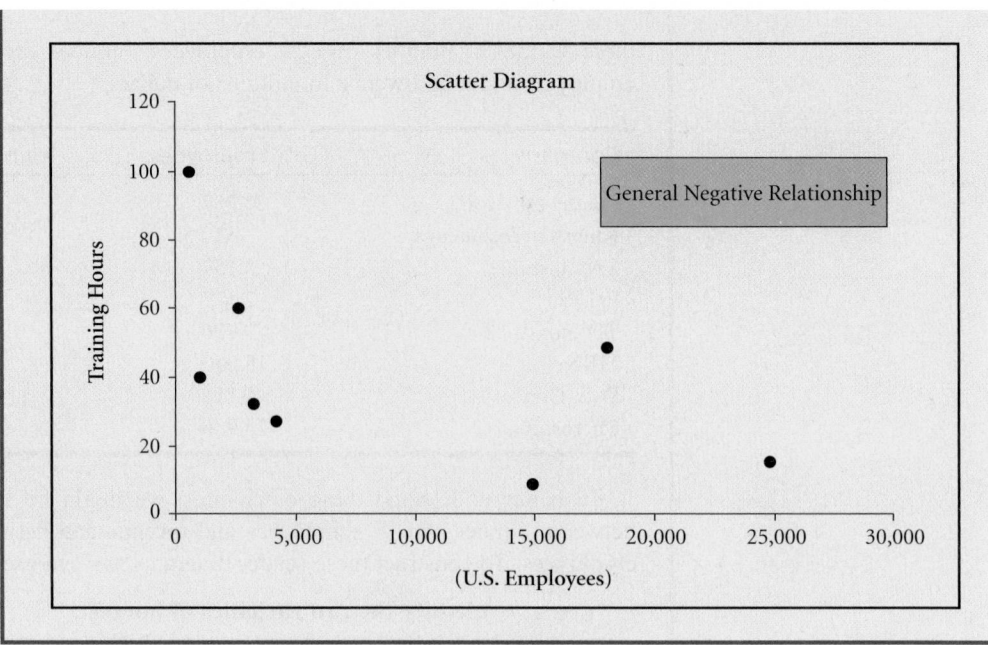

2-3: Exercises

Skill Development

2-46. You have the following sales data for the past 12 months. Develop a line graph for these data.

Month	Jan	Feb	Mar	Apr	May	Jun
Sales	200	230	210	300	320	290

Month	Jul	Aug	Sep	Oct	Nov	Dec
Sales	300	360	400	410	390	450

2-47. The following data have been selected on two variables, y and x. Construct a scatter plot for these two variables and indicate what type, if any, relationship appears to be present.

y	x
100	23.5
250	17.8
70	28.6
130	19.3
190	15.9
250	19.1
40	35.3

2-48. The following information shows the year-end dollar value (in millions) of deposits for Bank of the Ozarks, Inc. for the years 1997–2004. (*Source: Bank of the Ozarks, Inc., 2004 Annual Report.*)

Year	Deposits (in $millions)
1997	296
1998	529
1999	596
2000	678
2001	678
2002	790
2003	1062
2004	1380

Prepare a line chart of the data and briefly describe what the chart shows.

2-49. The following data represent 11 observations of two quantitative variables:

x = contact hours with client,

y = profit generated from client.

x	y	x	y	x	y	x	y
45	2,345	54	3,811	34	−700	24	1,975
56	4,200	24	2,406	45	3,457	32	206
26	278	23	3,250	47	2,478		

a. Construct a scatter plot of the data. Indicate whether the plot suggests a linear or nonlinear relationship between the dependent and independent variables.

b. Determine how much influence one data point will have upon your perception of the relationship between the independent and dependent variables by deleting the data point with the smallest *x*-value. What appears to be the relationship between the dependent and independent variables?

2-50. The district manager for a corporation has collected the following data on annual sales and the years of experience of members of his sales staff:

Sales $K:	200	191	135	236	305	183	50	192	184	73
Years:	10	4	5	9	12	6	2	7	6	2

a. Construct a scatter plot representing these data.
b. Determine the kind of relationship that exists (if any) between years of experience and sales.
c. Approximate the increase in sales that accrues with each additional year of experience for a member of the salesforce.

Business Applications

2-51. In July 2005, Greg Sandoval of the Associated Press authored a study of the video game industry that focused on the efforts of the industry to interest women in the games. In that study, he cited another report by the Entertainments Software Association that indicated the percentage of women who play video games in 2004 was 43% while only 12.5% of the software developers were female. Sandoval also presented the following data showing the U.S. computer/video game sales:

Year	Sales (Billions)
1996	$3.80
1997	$4.30
1998	$5.70
1999	$6.10
2000	$6.00
2001	$6.30
2002	$6.95
2003	$7.00
2004	$7.30

Construct a line chart showing these computer/video game sales data. Write a short statement describing the graph.

2-52. Recent changes in the U.S. federal tax code have increased the popularity of dividend-paying stocks for some investors. Shown here are the diluted net earnings per common share and the dividends per common share for the Procter & Gamble Company for the years 1996–2005. (*Source:* 2005 P&G Annual Report.)

Year	Diluted Net Earnings per Common Share	Dividends per Common Share
1996	$1.00	$0.40
1997	$1.14	$0.45
1998	$1.28	$0.51
1999	$1.29	$0.57
2000	$1.23	$0.64
2001	$1.03	$0.70
2002	$1.54	$0.76
2003	$1.85	$0.82
2004	$2.32	$0.93
2005	$2.66	$1.03

a. Construct a line chart of diluted net earnings per common share for the years 1996–2005.
b. Construct a line chart of dividends per common share for the years 1996–2005.
c. Construct a chart that can be used to determine whether there is a relationship between the two variables for the years 1996–2005. What relationship, if any, appears to exist between the two variables?

2-53. Amazon.com celebrated its 10th anniversary in July 2005. Its growth can be seen by examining its increasing sales volume (in $billions) as reported by Hoovers Inc.

Sales	0.0005	0.0157	0.1477	0.6098	1.6398
Year	1995	1996	1997	1998	1999
Sales	2.7619	3.1229	3.9329	5.2637	6.9211
Year	2000	2001	2002	2003	2004

a. Construct a line plot for Amazon's sales.
b. Describe the type of relationship that exists between the years in business and Amazon's sales volume.
c. In which year does it appear that Amazon had the sharpest increase in sales?

2-54. *Business Week* (Reed, Stanley, et al., "Open Season on Big Oil," September 26, 2005) reported on data provided by A. G. Edwards & Sons concerning the profits ($billions) for 10 of the largest integrated oil and gas companies over the period from 1999 to 2005.

Year	1999	2000	2001	2002	2003	2004	2005
Profit	33.3	62.5	58.3	41.7	66.7	91.7	118.0

a. Produce a line plot of the profit versus the year.

b. Describe the types of relationship that exist between years and profits during the specified time period.

c. Which of the relationships would you use to project the companies' profits in the year 2006? Explain your answer.

Computer Database Exercises

2-55. Major League Baseball is played in 30 North American cities, including Toronto, Canada. Having a team in a city is generally considered to provide an economic boost to the community. Although winning is the stated goal for all teams, the business side of baseball has to do with attendance. The data file **MLB Attendance-2005** contains data for both home and road game attendance for all 30 MLB teams for 2005. Of interest is the relationship between average home attendance and average road attendance. Using the 2005 attendance data, construct the appropriate graph to help determine the relationship between these two variables and discuss the implications of the graph.

2-56. In the October 17, 2005 issue of *Fortune*, a special advertising section focused on private jets. Included in the section was an article about "fractional" jet ownership, where wealthy individuals and also companies

share ownership in private jets. The idea is that the expensive airplanes can be better utilized if more than one individual or company has an ownership stake. AvData, Inc. provided data showing the number of fractional ownerships since 1986. These data are in the file called **JetOwnership**. Using these data, develop a line chart that displays the trend in fractional ownership between 1986 and 2004. Discuss.

2-57. In 2005, a chain of events, including the war in Iraq and hurricane Katrina, lead to a sharp increase in fuel costs. As a result, the U.S. airline industry has been hit hard financially. Some airlines are substituting smaller planes on certain routes in an attempt to reduce fuel costs. As an analyst for one of the major airlines, you have been asked to analyze the relationship between passenger capacity and fuel consumption per hour. Data for 19 commonly flown planes is presented in the file called **Airplanes**. Develop the appropriate graph to illustrate the relationship between fuel consumption per hour and passenger capacity. Discuss.

2-58. Japolli Bakery tracks sales of its different bread products on a daily basis. The following data show sales for 22 consecutive days at one of its retail outlets in Nashville. Develop a line chart that displays these data. The data are also located in a data file called **Japolli Bakery**. Discuss what, if any, conclusions you might be able to reach from the line chart.

Japolli Bakery

Day of Week	White	Wheat	Multigrain	Black	Cinnamon Raisin	Sourdough French	Light Oat
Friday	436	456	417	311	95	96	224
Saturday	653	571	557	416	129	140	224
Sunday	496	490	403	351	114	108	228
Monday	786	611	570	473	165	148	304
Tuesday	547	474	424	365	144	104	256
Wednesday	513	443	380	317	100	92	180
Thursday	817	669	622	518	181	152	308
Friday	375	390	299	256	124	88	172
Saturday	700	678	564	463	173	136	248
Sunday	597	502	457	383	140	144	312
Monday	536	530	428	360	135	112	356
Tuesday	875	703	605	549	201	188	356
Wednesday	421	433	336	312	100	104	224
Thursday	667	576	541	438	152	144	304
Friday	506	461	406	342	135	116	264
Saturday	470	352	377	266	84	92	172
Sunday	748	643	599	425	153	148	316
Monday	376	367	310	279	128	104	208
Tuesday	704	646	586	426	174	160	264
Wednesday	591	504	408	349	140	120	276
Thursday	564	497	415	348	107	120	212
Friday	817	673	644	492	200	180	348

2-59. Federal flood insurance underwritten by the federal government was initiated in 1968. This federal flood insurance coverage has, according to *USA Today* ("How you pay for people to build in flood zones," September 21, 2005), more than tripled in the past 15 years. A file entitled **Flood** contains the amount of federal flood insurance coverage for each of the years from 1990 to 2004.
   a. Produce a line plot for these data.
   b. Describe the type of relationship between the year and the amount of federal flood insurance.
   c. Determine the average increase per year in federal flood insurance.

2-60. The Office of Management and Budget keeps data on many facets of corporations. One item that has become a matter of concern in the number of applications for patents submitted compared to the backlog of applications that have not been processed by the end of the year. A file entitled **Patent** provides data extracted from a *USA Today* article (Kevin Maney, "Patent applications so abundant that examiners can't catch up," September 21, 2005) that addresses the problem.
   a. Construct the two line plots on the same axes.
   b. Determine the types of relationship that exist between the years and the two patent-related variables.
   c. During which year(s) did the backlog of applications at the end of year equal approximately the same number of patent applications?

2-61. Energy prices have been a major source of economic and political debate in the United States and around the world. Consumers have seen gasoline prices at the pump rise and the impact of fuel prices has been blamed for economic problems in the United States at different points in time. The following data (also found in the file called **Gasoline Prices**) reflect the average price of regular unleaded gasoline in the state of California for the years between 1970 and 2005. The first price column is the actual average price of gasoline during each of those years. The second column is the average price adjusted for inflation, with 2005 being the base year. (Note, for each year prior to 2005, the average gasoline price is adjusted downward to reflect the inflation adjustment compared to the base year of 2005.)
   a. Construct an appropriate chart showing the actual average price of gasoline in California over the years between 1970 and 2005.
   b. Add to the graph developed in part a the data for the adjusted gasoline prices.

c. Based on this graph from part b, what conclusions might be reached about the price of gasoline over the years between 1970 and 2005?

Year	Actual Average Price	Inflation Adjusted Price (Base Year = 2005)
1970	$0.34	$1.36
1971	$0.36	$1.36
1972	$0.35	$1.27
1973	$0.39	$1.38
1974	$0.53	$1.67
1975	$0.59	$1.69
1976	$0.61	$1.67
1977	$0.65	$1.66
1978	$0.65	$1.57
1979	$0.90	$1.98
1980	$1.23	$2.49
1981	$1.35	$2.50
1982	$1.25	$2.18
1983	$1.12	$1.88
1984	$1.13	$1.83
1985	$1.11	$1.75
1986	$0.87	$1.35
1987	$0.89	$1.33
1988	$0.90	$1.31
1989	$0.97	$1.36
1990	$1.09	$1.47
1991	$1.15	$1.50
1992	$1.10	$1.40
1993	$1.22	$1.52
1994	$1.21	$1.47
1995	$1.23	$1.47
1996	$1.32	$1.54
1997	$1.33	$1.53
1998	$1.16	$1.32
1999	$1.36	$1.53
2000	$1.66	$1.82
2001	$1.64	$1.75
2002	$1.51	$1.60
2003	$1.83	$1.90
2004	$2.12	$2.15
2005	$2.39	$2.39

Source: The California Energy Commission, September 2005

2-62. Existing-home sales rose in August of 2005 to the second-highest pace on record, with strong price gains in a market of tight supply, according to the National Association of Realtors® (Walter Molony and Lucien Salvant, "Existing Home Sales Second Highest on Record," September 26, 2005). A file entitled **EHSales** contains the number of existing homes sold (millions) from August of 2004 to August 2005.

a. Construct a line plot for these data.
b. The data file also contains data concerning the median selling price ($thousands). Construct a graph containing the line plot for both the number of sales (*tens* of thousands) and the median

($thousands) price of these sales for the indicated time period.
c. Describe the relationship between the two line plots constructed in part b.

Summary and Conclusions

This chapter has introduced some of the most commonly used statistical techniques for organizing data and presenting them in a meaningful way to aid in the decision-making process. Organizing raw data into a frequency distribution is a major step in transforming data into information. We have outlined the steps for developing frequency distributions and for producing histograms.

The chapter also has introduced other graphical techniques for displaying data to make them more usable to a decision maker. The choices for effective graphical data displays are

numerous. Histograms, bar charts, pie charts, stem and leaf diagrams, scatter diagrams, and line graphs are among the more commonly used techniques. Figure 2.22 summarizes the conditions under which each descriptive technique is appropriate.

Software packages, such as Excel and Minitab, have made graphical representation of data much easier. You are now able to analyze large volumes of data quickly and easily. The output from these packages can be pasted directly into word-processing documents to create professional-looking business reports.

Equations

Relative Frequency

$$\text{Relative Frequency} = \frac{f_i}{n} \quad \text{(2.1)}$$

Class Width

$$W = \frac{\text{Largest Value} - \text{Smallest Value}}{\text{Number of Classes}} \quad \text{(2.2)}$$

FIGURE 2.22

Summary: Descriptive Statistical Techniques

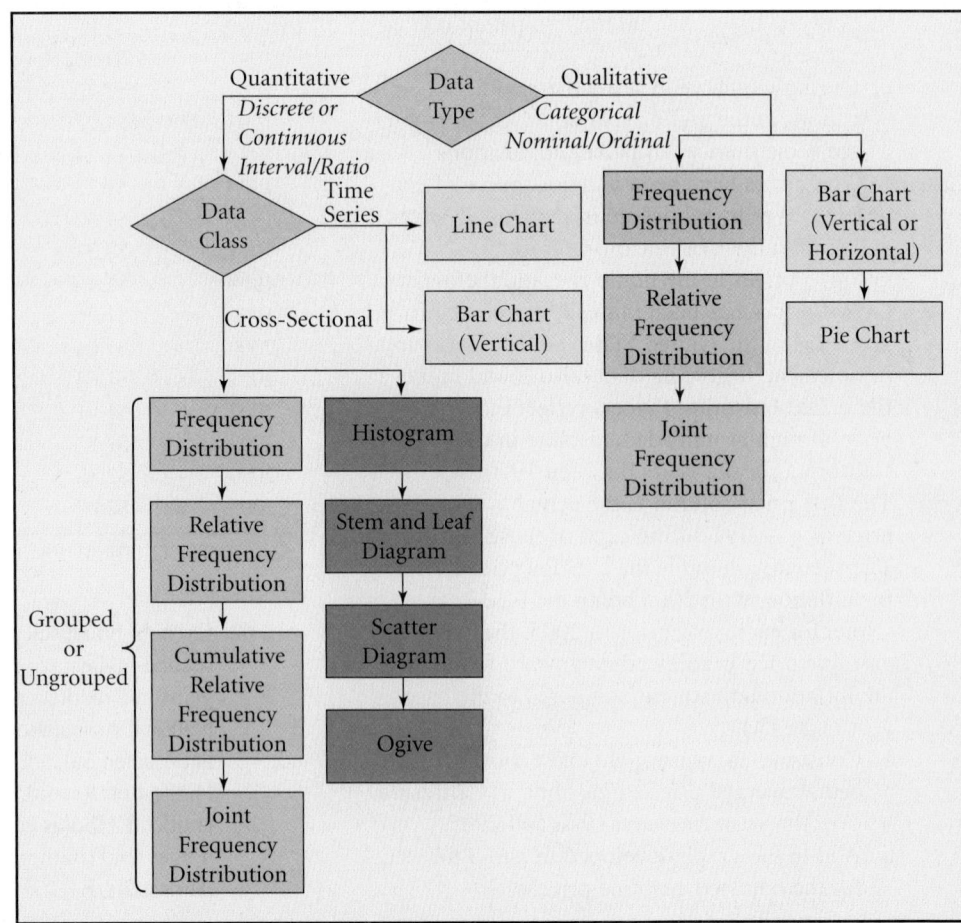

Key Terms

All-inclusive classes   39
Bar chart   57
Class boundaries   41
Class width   40
Continuous data   37
Cumulative frequency
    distribution   41

Cumulative relative frequency
    distribution   41
Dependent variable   75
Discrete data   32
Equal-width classes   39
Frequency distribution   32
Frequency histogram   43

Independent variable   75
Line chart   71
Mutually exclusive classes   39
Pie chart   63
Relative frequency   34
Scatter diagram   75
Stem and Leaf Plot   66

Chapter Exercises

Conceptual Questions

2-63. Discuss the advantages of constructing a relative frequency distribution as opposed to a frequency distribution.

2-64. What are the characteristics of a data set that would lead you to construct a bar chart?

2-65. What are the characteristics of a data set that would lead you to construct a pie chart?

2-66. Discuss the differences in data that would lead you to construct a line chart as opposed to a scatter plot.

Business Applications

2-67. In a *USA Today* article (Adrienne Lewis, "Tuition outstrips inflation," January 5, 2004), it was disclosed that college tuition had risen at a faster pace than inflation for more than two decades. The article presented the average college tuition and fees for four-year institutions from 1984 to 2004. Those data for the selected years are

Year	1984	1989	1994	1999	2004
Private College Tuition	$9,202	$12,146	$13,844	$16,454	$19,710
Public College Tuition	$2,074	$2,395	$3,188	$3,632	$4,694

a. Construct one bar graph illustrating the relationship between private and public university tuition for the displayed years.

b. Describe the tuition trend for both private and public college tuition.

2-68. *USA Today* ("Big (lack of) men on campus," September 23, 2005) used the following data to illustrate the decline in the percentage of men who receive college and advanced degrees:

	Bachelor			Doctorate		
	1989	2003	2014*	1989	2003	2014*
Men	47	43	40	64	57	49
Women	53	57	60	36	43	51

*Education Department projection

a. Use one graph that contains two bar charts, each of which represents the kind of degree received, to display the relationship between the percentages of men and women receiving each type of degree.

b. Describe any trends that might be evident.

2-69. *USA Today* reported (Anthony Breznican and Gary Strauss, "Where have all the moviegoers gone?" June 23, 2005) that in the summer of 2005 ticket sales to movie theaters had fallen 17 straight weeks, the industry's longest losing streak since 1985. To determine the long-term trends in ticket sales, the following data representing the number of admissions (billions) were obtained from the National Association of Theatre Owners:

Year	1987	1988	1989	1990	1991	1992	1993	1994	1995
Admissions	1.09	1.08	1.26	1.19	1.14	1.17	1.24	1.28	1.26

Year	1996	1997	1998	1999	2000	2001	2002	2003	2004
Admissions	1.34	1.39	1.48	1.47	1.42	1.49	1.63	1.57	1.53

a. Produce a line plot of the data.

b. Describe any trends that you detect.

2-70. The Minnesota State Fishing Bureau has contracted with a university biologist to study the length of walleyes (fish) caught in Minnesota lakes. The biologist has collected data on a sample of 1,000 fish caught and developed the following relative frequency distribution:

Class Length (inches)	Relative Frequency f_i
8 to less than 10	.22
10 to less than 12	.15
12 to less than 14	.25
14 to less than 16	.24
16 to less than 18	.06
18 to less than 20	.05
20 to less than 22	.03

a. Construct a frequency distribution from this relative frequency distribution and then produce a histogram based on the frequency distribution.

b. Construct a pie chart from the relative frequency distribution. Discuss which of the two graphs, the pie chart or the histogram, you think is more effective in presenting the fish length data.

2-71. The following data represent the commuting distances for employees of the Pay-and-Carry Department store.

a. The personnel manager for Pay-and-Carry would like you to develop a frequency distribution and histogram for these data.

b. Develop a stem and leaf diagram for these data.

c. Break the data into three groups (under 3 miles, 3 and under 6 miles, and 6 and over). Construct a pie chart to illustrate the proportion of employees in each category.

Commuting Distance (miles)							
3.5	2.0	4.0	2.5	0.3	1.0	12.0	17.5
3.0	3.5	6.5	9.0	3.0	4.0	9.0	16.0
3.5	0.5	2.5	1.0	0.7	1.5	1.4	12.0
9.2	8.3	1.0	3.0	7.5	3.2	2.0	1.0
3.5	3.6	1.9	2.0	3.0	1.5	0.4	6.4
11.0	2.5	2.4	2.7	4.0	2.0	2.0	3.0

d. Referring to part c, construct a bar chart to depict the proportion of employees in each category.

2-72. A computer software company has been looking at the amount of time customers spend on hold after their call is answered by the central switchboard. The company would like to have at most 2% of the callers wait two minutes or more. The company's calling service has provided the following data showing how long each of last month's callers spent on hold:

Class	Number
Less than 15 seconds	456
15 to less than 30 seconds	718
30 to less than 45 seconds	891
45 to less than 60 seconds	823
60 to less than 75 seconds	610
75 to less than 90 seconds	449
90 to less than 105 seconds	385
105 to less than 120 seconds	221
120 to less than 150 seconds	158
150 to less than 180 seconds	124
180 to less than 240 seconds	87
More than 240 seconds	153

a. Develop a relative frequency distribution and ogive for these data.

b. The company estimates it loses an average of $30 in business from callers who must wait two minutes or more before receiving assistance. The company thinks that last month's distribution of waiting times is typical. Estimate how much money the company is losing in business per month because people have to wait too long before receiving assistance.

2-73. The regional sales manager for American Toys, Inc. recently collected data on weekly sales (in dollars) for the 15 stores in his region. He also collected data on the number of salesclerk work hours during the week for each of the stores. The data are as follows:

Store	Sales	Hours	Store	Sales	Hours
1	23,300	120	9	27,886	140
2	25,600	135	10	54,156	300
3	19,200	96	11	34,080	254
4	10,211	102	12	25,900	180
5	19,330	240	13	36,400	270
6	35,789	190	14	25,760	175
7	12,540	108	15	31,500	256
8	43,150	234			

a. Develop a scatter plot of these data. Determine which variable should be the dependent variable and which should be the independent variable.

b. Based on the scatter plot, what, if any, conclusions might the sales manager reach with respect to the relationship between sales and number of clerk hours worked? Do any stores stand out as being different? Discuss.

Computer Database Exercises

2-74. *USA Today* reported (Jefferson Graham, "Looks like the new iPod's a hit," September 19, 2005) that Apple had 74% of the digital music device market, according to researcher The NPD Group. The NPD Group provides global sales and marketing information that helps clients make more informed, fact-based decisions in order to optimize their businesses. The data in the file entitled **Digital** provide the brand of digital devices owned by a sample of consumers that would produce the market shares alluded to in the article. Produce a pie chart that represents the market shares obtained from the referenced sample. Indicate the market shares and the identity of those manufacturers in the pie chart.

2-75. The file **Home-Prices** contains information about single-family housing prices in 100 metropolitan areas in the United States.

a. Construct a frequency distribution and histogram of 1997 median single-family home prices. Use the $2^k \geq n$ guideline to determine the appropriate number of classes.

b. Construct a cumulative relative frequency distribution and ogive for 1997 median single-family home prices.

c. Repeat parts a and b but this time use half again as many class intervals as recommended by the $2^k \geq n$ guideline. What was the impact of using more class intervals?

2-76. Elliel's Department Store tracks its inventory on a monthly basis. Monthly data for the years 1996–2000 are in the file called **Elliels**.

a. Construct a line chart showing the monthly inventory over the five years. Discuss what this graph implies about inventory.

b. Sum the monthly inventory figures for each year. Then present the sums in bar chart form. Discuss whether you think this is an appropriate graph to describe the inventory situation at Elliels.

2-77. The Energy Information Administration (EIA) surveys the price of diesel fuel. The EIA-888 is a survey of diesel fuel outlet prices from truck stops and service stations across the country. It produces estimates of national and regional prices. The diesel fuel prices that are released are used by the trucking industry to make rate adjustments in hauling contracts. The file entitled **Diesel$** contains the average on-highway diesel prices for each of 53 weeks from September 27, 2004 to September 26, 2005.

a. Construct a histogram with 11 classes beginning at $1.85.

b. Are there any data points that are unusually larger than the rest of the data? In which classes do these points occur? What is the interpretation of this phenomenon?

2-78. The Energy Information Administration published a press release on September 26, 2005 (Paula Weir and Pedro Saavedra, "Two Multi-Phase Surverys That Combine Overlapping Sample Cycles at Phase I"). The file entitled **Diesel$** contains the average on-highway diesel prices for each of 53 weeks from September 27, 2004 to September 26, 2005. It also contains equivalent information for the state of California, recognized as having the highest national prices.

a. Construct a chart containing line plots for both the national average and California's diesel prices. Describe the relationship between the diesel prices in California versus the national average.

b. In what week did the California average diesel price surpass $3.00 a gallon?

c. Determine the smallest and largest price paid in California for a gallon of diesel. At what weeks did these occur? Use this information to project when California gas prices might exceed $4.00, assuming a linear trend between California diesel prices and the week in which they occurred.

VIDEO CASE 3

Drive-Thru Service Times @ McDonald's

When you're on the go and looking for a quick meal, where do you go? If you're like millions of people every day, you make a stop at McDonald's. Known as "quick service restaurants" in the industry (not "fast food"), companies such as McDonald's invest heavily to determine the most efficient and effective ways to provide fast, high quality service in all phases of their business.

Drive-thru operations play a vital role. It's not surprising that attention is focused on the drive-thru process. After all, over 60% of individual restaurant revenues in the United States come from the drive-thru experience. Yet understanding the process is more complex than just counting cars. Marla King, professor at the company's international training center, Hamburger University, got her start 25 years ago working at a McDonald's drive-thru. She now coaches new restaurant owners and managers. "Our stated drive-thru service time is 90 seconds or less. We train every manager and team member to understand that a quality customer experience at the drive-thru depends on them," says Marla. Some of the factors that affect customers' ability to complete their purchases within 90 seconds include restaurant staffing, equipment layout in the restaurant, training, and efficiency of the grill team, and frequency of customer arrivals to name a few. Also, customer order patterns also play a role. Some customers will just order drinks, while others seem to need enough food to feed an entire soccer team. And then there are the special orders. Obviously, there is plenty of room for variability here.

Yet that doesn't stop the company from using statistical techniques to better understand the drive-thru action. In particular, McDonald's utilizes graphical techniques to display data and to help transform the data into useful information. In order for restaurant managers to achieve the goal in their own restaurants, they need training in proper restaurant and drive-thru operations. Hamburger University, McDonald's training center located near Chicago, Illinois, satisfies that need. In the mock-up restaurant service lab, managers go through a "before and after" training scenario. In the "before scenario," they run the restaurant for thirty minutes as if they were back in their home restaurants. Managers in the training class are assigned to be crew, customers, drive-thru cars, special needs guests (such as hearing impaired, indecisive, or clumsy), or observers. Statistical data about the operations, revenues, and service times are collected and analyzed. Without the right training, the restaurant's operations usually start breaking down after 10–15 minutes. After debriefing and analyzing the data collected, the managers make suggestions for adjustments and head back to the service lab to try again. This time, the results usually come in well within standards. "When presented with the quantitative results, managers are pretty quick to make the connections between better operations, higher revenues, and happier customers," Marla states.

When managers return to their respective restaurants, the training results and techniques are shared with staff who are charged with implementing the ideas locally. The results of the training eventually are measured when McDonald's conducts a restaurant operations improvement process study, or ROIP. The goal is simple: improved operations. When the ROIP review is completed, statistical analyses are performed and managers are given their results. Depending on the results, decisions might be made that require additional financial resources, building construction, staff training, or reconfiguring layouts. Yet one thing is clear: statistics drive the decisions behind McDonald's drive-thru service operations.

Discussion Questions:

1. After returning from the training session at Hamburger University, a McDonald's store owner selected a random sample of 362 drive-thru customers and carefully measured the time it took from when a customer entered the McDonald's property until the customer had received the order at the drive-thru window. These data are in the file called **McDonald's Drive-Thru Waiting Times**. Note, the owner selected some customers during the breakfast period, others during lunch and others during dinner. Construct any appropriate graphs and charts that will effectively display these drive-thru data. Prepare a short discussion indicating the conclusions that this store owner might reach after reviewing the graphs and charts you have prepared.

2. Referring to question 1, suppose the manager comes away with the conclusion that his store is not meeting the 90 second customer service goal. As a result he plans to dig deeper into the problem by collecting more data from the drive-thru process. Discuss what other measures you would suggest the manager collect. Discuss how these data could be of potential value in helping the store owner understand his problem.

3. Visit a local McDonald's that has a drive-thru facility. Randomly sample 20 drive-thru customers and collect the following data:
   a. the total time from arrival on the property to departure from the drive-thru window.
   b. the time from when customers place the order until they receive their order and exit the drive-thru process
   c. the number of cars in the line when the sampled vehicle enters the drive-thru process.

Using the data that you have collected, construct appropriate graphs and charts to describe these data. Write a short report discussing the data.

CASE 2.1

Server Downtime

After getting outstanding grades in high school and scoring very high on his ACT and SAT tests, Clayton Haney had his choice of colleges but wanted to follow his parents legacy and enrolled at Northwestern University. Clayton soon learned that there is a big difference between getting high grades in high school and being a good student. While he was recognized as being quite bright and very quick to pick up on things, he had never learned how to study. As a result, after slightly more than two years at Northwestern, Clayton was asked to try his luck at another university. To the chagrin of his parents, Clayton decided that college was not for him.

After short stints working for a computer manufacturer and as a manager for a Blockbuster video store, Clayton landed a job working for the EDS company. EDS contracts to support information technology implementation and application for companies in the United States and throughout the world. Clayton had to train himself in virtually all aspects of personal computers and local area networks and was assigned to work for a client in the Chicago area.

Clayton's first assignment was to research the downtime on one of the client's primary network servers. He was asked to study the downtime data for the month of April and to make a short presentation to the company's management. The downtime data are in a file called **Server Downtime**. These data are also shown in Table C-2.1-A. Although Clayton is very good at solving computer problems, he has had no training or experience in analyzing data, so he is going to need some help.

Required Tasks:

a. Construct a frequency distribution showing the number of times during the month that the server was down for each downtime cause category.
b. Develop a bar chart that displays the data from the frequency distribution in part a.
c. Develop a histogram that displays the downtime data.
d. Develop a pie chart that breaks down the percentage of total downtime that is attributed to each downtime cause during the month.
e. Prepare a short written report that discusses the downtime data. Make sure you merge the graphs and charts into the report.

TABLE C-2.1-A

Date	Problem Experienced	Downtime Minutes
04/01/06	Lockups	25
04/02/06	Lockups	35
04/05/06	Memory Errors	10
04/07/06	Lockups	40
04/09/06	Weekly Virus Scan	60
04/09/06	Lockups	30
04/09/06	Memory Errors	35
04/09/06	Memory Errors	20
04/12/06	Slow Startup	45
04/12/06	Weekly Virus Scan	60
04/13/06	Memory Errors	30
04/14/06	Memory Errors	10
04/19/06	Manual Re-start	20
04/20/06	Memory Errors	35
04/20/06	Weekly Virus Scan	60
04/20/06	Lockups	25
04/21/06	Memory Errors	35
04/22/06	Memory Errors	20
04/27/06	Memory Errors	40
04/28/06	Weekly Virus Scan	60
04/28/06	Memory Errors	15
04/28/06	Lockups	25

CASE 2.2

Yakima Apples, Inc.

As a rule, Julie Fredrick preferred to work in the field rather than do "office" work in her capacity as a midlevel manager with Yakima Apples, Inc., a large grower and processor of apples in the state of Washington. However, after just leaving a staff meeting where she was asked to prepare a report of apple consumption in the United States, Julie was actually looking forward to spending some time at her computer "crunching some numbers." Arden Golchein, senior marketing manager, indicated that he would e-mail her a data file that contained apple consumption data from 1970 through 2002 and told her that he wanted a very nice report using graphs, charts, and tables to describe apple consumption.

When she got to her desk, the e-mail was waiting and she saved the file under the name **Yakima Apples**. These data are also shown in Table C-2.2-A. Julie had done quite a bit of descriptive analysis in her previous job with the

Washington State Department of Agriculture, so she had several ideas for types of graphs and tables that she might construct. She began by creating a list of the tasks that she thought would be needed.

Required Tasks:

a. Construct a line chart showing the total annual consumption of apples.
b. Construct one line chart that shows two things: the annual consumption of fresh apples and the annual consumption of processed apples.
c. Construct a line chart that shows the annual consumption for each type of processed apples.
d. Construct a histogram for the total annual consumption of apples.
e. Write a short report that discusses the historical pattern of apple consumption. The report will include all pertinent charts and graphs.

TABLES C-2.2-A Apples: Per Capita Consumption in Pounds (fresh weight equivalent)

| Year | Total | Fresh | Processed | | | | | |
			Total	Canned	Juice	Frozen	Dried	Other
1970	31.4	17.0	14.4	5.6	6.4	0.8	0.9	0.7
1971	30.7	16.4	14.3	5.3	7.0	0.9	0.5	0.6
1972	28.0	15.5	12.5	4.7	5.4	1.1	0.6	0.6
1973	29.5	16.1	13.3	6.0	4.6	1.0	1.1	0.6
1974	30.5	16.4	14.1	5.8	5.9	0.6	0.9	0.9
1975	33.3	19.5	13.8	4.8	6.9	0.8	1.0	0.4
1976	29.7	17.1	12.6	4.3	6.3	0.6	1.1	0.3
1977	31.5	16.5	15.0	4.9	7.9	0.7	1.0	0.5
1978	35.5	17.9	17.5	5.5	9.6	0.6	1.0	0.8
1979	35.9	17.1	18.8	5.9	10.6	0.6	1.1	0.6
1980	39.6	19.2	20.4	5.3	13.0	0.6	0.8	0.7
1981	34.5	16.8	17.7	4.4	11.5	0.6	0.8	0.4
1982	39.5	17.5	22.0	5.4	14.6	0.7	0.9	0.5
1983	41.4	18.3	23.1	5.1	15.8	0.5	1.2	0.4
1984	44.1	18.4	25.7	5.0	18.4	0.6	1.3	0.4
1985	43.0	17.3	25.7	5.3	18.4	0.6	1.2	0.3
1986	42.8	17.8	25.0	4.9	18.2	0.7	0.8	0.4
1987	48.0	20.8	27.2	5.4	19.4	0.9	1.2	0.3
1988	47.0	19.8	27.2	5.7	19.1	0.8	1.2	0.3
1989	46.1	21.2	24.8	5.3	17.4	0.8	1.1	0.2
1990	47.4	19.6	27.9	5.5	20.7	0.7	0.8	0.3
1991	43.3	18.1	25.2	5.1	18.1	0.8	0.8	0.4
1992	46.3	19.1	27.1	5.8	18.7	0.8	1.2	0.6
1993	47.8	19.0	28.8	5.1	21.3	0.6	1.4	0.3
1994	48.5	19.3	29.1	5.3	21.3	0.5	1.5	0.5
1995	44.7	18.7	26.0	4.9	18.9	0.8	1.2	0.3
1996	46.1	18.7	27.4	4.9	20.3	0.8	1.2	0.2
1997	44.5	18.1	26.5	5.6	18.5	0.8	0.9	0.7
1998	47.1	19.0	28.1	4.4	21.5	0.7	1.2	0.4
1999	46.8	18.5	28.3	4.8	21.4	0.6	1.0	0.5
2000	45.3	17.5	27.9	4.4	21.4	0.9	0.8	0.5
2001	43.7	15.6	28.0	4.6	21.3	0.9	0.8	0.5
2002	43.4	16.0	27.5	4.0	21.4	0.7	0.8	0.5

Source: USDA/Economic Research Service

CASE 2.3

Welco Lumber Company— Part A

Gene Denning wears several hats at the Welco Lumber Company, including process improvement team leader, shipping manager, and assistant human resources manager. Welco Lumber makes cedar fencing materials at its Naples, Idaho, facility employing about 160 people.

Over 75% of the cost of the finished cedar fence boards is in the cedar logs that the company buys on the open market. Therefore, it is very important that the company get as much finished product as possible from each log. One of the most

FIGURE C-2.3-A

Log Breakdown at the Head Rig

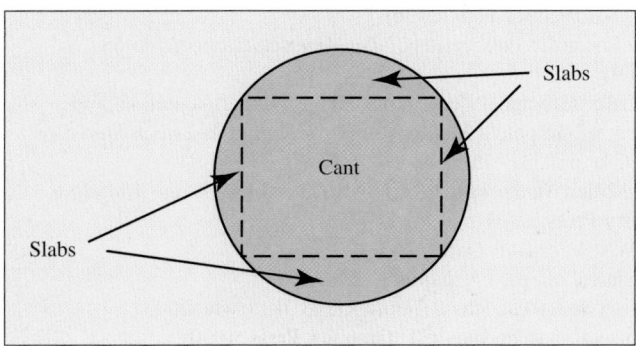

important steps in the manufacturing process is referred to as the head rig. The Head Rig is a large saw that breaks down the logs into slabs and cants. Figure C-2.3-A shows the concept. From small logs with diameters of 12 inches or less, one cant and four or fewer usable slabs are obtained. From larger logs, multiple cants as well as four slabs are obtained. Finished fence boards can be produced from both the slabs and the cants.

At some companies, the head rig cutting operation is automated and the cuts are made based on a scanner system and computer algorithms. However, at Welco Lumber, the head rig is operated manually by operators who must look at a log as it arrives and determine how best to break the log down to get the most finished product. In addition, the operators are responsible for making sure that the cants are "centered" so that maximum product can be gained from them.

Recently, Gene Denning headed up a study in which he videotaped 365 logs being broken down by the head rig. All three operators, April, Sid and Jim, were involved. Each log was marked as to its true diameter. Then Gene observed the way the log was broken down and the degree to which the cants were properly centered. He then determined the projected value of the finished product from each log given the way it was actually cut. In addition, he also determined what the value would have been had the log been cut in the optimal way. Data for this study is in a file called **Welco Lumber**. A portion of the data is shown in Table C-2.3-A.

You have been asked to assist Gene by analyzing these data using graphs, charts, and tables as appropriate. He wishes to focus on the lost profit to the company and whether there are differences among the operators. Also, do the operators tend to do a better job on small logs than on large logs? In general, he is hoping to learn as much as possible from this study and needs your help with the analysis.

TABLE C-2.3-A Head Rig Data—Welco Lumber Company

5-Nov-06	Thru		21-Nov-06						
			Head Rig Log Study			Baseline			
Log #	Operator	Log Size	Large/Small Log	Correct Cut (Yes or No)	Error Category		Actual Value	Potential Value	Potential Gain
1	Sid	15	Large	No	Excessive Log Breakdown		$59.00	$65.97	$6.97
2	Sid	17	Large	No	Excessive Log Breakdown		$79.27	$85.33	$6.06
3	Sid	11	Small	Yes	No Error		$35.40	$35.40	$0.00
4	Sid	11	Small	No	Off Center Cant		$31.61	$35.40	$3.79
5	Sid	14	Large	No	Reduced Value Cut		$47.67	$58.86	$11.19
6	Sid	17	Large	Yes	No Error		$85.33	$85.33	$0.00
7	Sid	8	Small	Yes	No Error		$16.22	$16.22	$0.00
8	Sid	11	Small	Yes	No Error		$35.40	$35.40	$0.00
9	Sid	9	Small	Yes	No Error		$21.54	$21.54	$0.00
10	Sid	9	Small	No	Off Center Cant		$18.92	$21.54	$2.62
11	Sid	10	Small	Yes	No Error		$21.54	$21.54	$0.00
12	Sid	8	Small	Yes	No Error		$16.22	$16.22	$0.00
13	Sid	10	Small	No	Off Center Cant		$25.71	$28.97	$3.26
14	Sid	12	Small	Yes	No Error		$41.79	$41.79	$0.00
15	Sid	11	Small	Yes	No Error		$35.40	$35.40	$0.00

References

Berenson, Mark L., and David M. Levine, *Basic Business Statistics: Concepts and Applications*, 10th ed. (Upper Saddle River, NJ: Prentice Hall, 2006).

Cleveland, William, S., "Graphs in Scientific Publications," *The American Statistician* 38 (November 1984), pp. 261–269.

Cleveland, William S., and R. McGill, "Graphical Perception: Theory, Experimentation, and Application to the Development of Graphical Methods," *Journal of the American Statistical Association* 79 (September 1984), pp. 531–554.

Cryer, Jonathan D., and Robert B. Miller, *Statistics for Business: Data Analysis and Modeling*, 2nd ed. (Belmont, CA: Duxbury Press, 1994).

Microsoft Excel 2007 (Redmond, WA: Microsoft Corp., 2007).

Minitab for Windows Version 15 (State College, PA: Minitab, 2007).

Siegel, Andrew F., *Practical Business Statistics*, 5th ed. (Burr Ridge, IL: Irwin, 2003).

Tufte, Edward R., *Envisioning Information* (Cheshire, CT: Graphics Press, 1990).

Tufte, Edward R., *The Visual Display of Quantitative Information*, 2nd ed. (Cheshire, CT: Graphics Press, 2001).

Tukey, John W., *Exploratory Data Analysis* (Reading, MA: Addison-Wesley, 1977).

Describing Data Using Numerical Measures

CHAPTER OUTCOMES

After studying the material in Chapter 3, you should be able to:

1. Compute the mean, median, mode, and weighted average for a set of data and understand what these values represent.
2. Know how to construct a box and whisker graph and be able to interpret it.
3. Compute the range, variance, and standard deviation and know what these values mean.
4. Compute the coefficient of variation and z-scores and understand how they are applied in decision-making situations.

PREPARING FOR CHAPTER THREE

- Review the definitions for nominal, ordinal, interval, and ratio data in Section 1.4.

- Examine the statistical software, such as Excel or Minitab, used during this course to identify the tools for computing descriptive measures. For instance, in Excel, look at the function wizard and the descriptive statistics tools on the Data tab under Data Analysis. In Minitab acquaint yourself with the *Basic Statistics* menu within the *Stat* menu.

- Review the material on frequency histograms in Section 2.1 with special attention on how histograms help determine where the data is centered and how the data are spread around the center.

◆WHY YOU NEED TO KNOW

Graphs and charts provide effective tools for transforming data into information; however, they are only a starting point. Graphs and charts do not reveal all the information contained in a set of data. To make your descriptive toolkit complete, you need to become familiar with the key descriptive measures that quantify the center of the data and its spread.

Suppose you are an advertising manager for a major tire company and you want to develop an ad campaign touting how much longer your company's tires last than the competition's. You must be careful that your claims are valid. First, the Federal Trade Commission (FTC) is charged with regulating advertising and requires that advertising be truthful. Second, customers who could show that they were misled by an incorrect claim about your tires could sue you and your company. You have no choice. You must use statistical procedures to determine the validity of any claim you might want to make about your tires.

You might start by sampling tires from your company and from the competition. You could measure the number of miles each tire lasts before a specified portion of the tread is depleted. You might graph the data for each company as a histogram, but a clear comparison with this graph might be difficult. Instead, you could compute the mileage numbers for the various tires and show these values side-by-side, perhaps in a bar chart. Thus, to effectively describe data, you will need to combine the graphical tools discussed in Chapter 2 with the numerical measures introduced in this chapter.

3.1 Measures of Center and Location

You learned in Chapter 2 that frequency histograms are an effective way of converting quantitative data into useful information. The histogram provides a visual indication of where data are centered and how much spread there is in the data around the center. However, to fully describe a quantitative variable, we also need to compute measures of its center and spread. These measures can then be coupled with the histogram to give a clear picture of the variable's distribution. This section focuses on measures of the center of data. Section 3-2 introduces measures of the spread of data.

Parameters and Statistics

Depending on whether we are working with a population or a sample, a numerical measure is known as either a **parameter** or a **statistic**.

Parameter
A measure computed from the entire population. As long as the population does not change, the value of the parameter will not change.

Statistic
A measure computed from a sample that has been selected from a population. The value of the statistic will depend on which sample is selected.

Mean
A numerical measure of the center of a set of quantitative measures computed by dividing the sum of the values by the number of values in the data.

Population Mean

There are three important measures of the center of a set of data. The first of these is the **mean**, or average of the data. To find the mean, we sum the values and divide the sum by the number of data values, as shown in Equation 3.1.

Population Mean

$$\mu = \frac{\sum_{i=1}^{N} x_i}{N} \tag{3.1}$$

where:

μ = Population mean (mu)
N = Population size
x_i = ith individual value of variable x

The **population mean** is represented by the Greek symbol μ, pronounced "mu." The formal notation in the numerator for the sum of the x values reads

$$\sum_{i=1}^{N} x_i \rightarrow \text{sum all } x_i \text{ value where } i \text{ goes from 1 to } N$$

In other words, we are summing all N values in the population.

Because you almost always sum all the data values, to simplify notation in this text, we generally will drop the subscripts after the first time we introduce a formula. Thus the formula for the population mean will be written as

$$\mu = \frac{\sum x}{N}$$

Business Application

CHAPTER OUTCOME #1

FOSTER CITY HOTEL The manager of a small hotel in Foster City, California, was asked by the corporate vice president to analyze the Sunday night registration information for the past eight weeks. Data on three variables were collected:

x_1 = Total number of rooms rented

x_2 = Total dollar revenue from the room rentals

x_3 = Number of customer complaints that came from guests each Sunday

These data are shown in Table 3.1. They are a population because they include all data that interest the vice president.

Figure 3.1 shows the frequency histogram for the number of rooms rented. If the manager wants to describe the data further, she can locate the center of the data by finding the balance point for the histogram. Think of the horizontal axis as a plank and the histogram bars as weights proportional to their area. The center of the data would be the point at which the plank would balance. As shown in Figure 3.1, the balance point seems to be about 15 rooms.

Eyeing the histogram might yield a reasonable approximation of the center. However, computing a numerical measure of the center directly from the data is preferable. The most frequently used measure of the center is the mean. The population mean for number of rooms rented is computed using Equation 3.1 as follows:

$$\mu = \frac{\sum x}{N} = \frac{22 + 13 + 10 + 16 + 23 + 13 + 11 + 13}{8}$$

$$= \frac{121}{8}$$

$$\mu = 15.125$$

TABLE 3.1 Foster City Hotel Data

Week	Rooms Rented	Revenue	Complaints
1	22	$1,870	0
2	13	$1,590	2
3	10	$1,760	1
4	16	$2,345	0
5	23	$4,563	2
6	13	$1,630	1
7	11	$2,156	0
8	13	$1,756	0

FIGURE 3.1

Balance Point, Rooms Rented at Foster City Hotel

Thus, the average number of rooms rented each Sunday for the past eight weeks is 15.125. This is the true balance point for the data. Turn to Table 3.2, where we calculate what is called a *deviation* $(x - \mu)$ by subtracting the mean from each value.

Note that the sum of the deviations of the data from the mean is zero. This is not a coincidence. *For any set of data, the sum of the deviations around the mean will be zero.*

SUMMARY Computing the Population Mean

When the available data constitute the population of interest, the population mean is computed using the following steps:

1. Collect the data for the variable of interest for all items in the population. The data must be quantitative.

2. Sum all values in the population (Σx).

3. Divide the sum (Σx) by the number of values (N) in the population to get the population mean. The formula for the population mean is

$$\mu = \frac{\Sigma x}{N}$$

EXAMPLE 3-1 Computing the Population Mean

United Airlines   In order to stay competitive, United Airlines, headquartered in Chicago, must update its airplane fleet. Suppose United selects its planes from a list of 17 possible planes, including such models as the Boeing 747-100, Air Bus 300-B4, and the DC 9-10. At a recent meeting, the chief operating officer asked a member of his staff to determine the mean fuel consumption rate per hour of operation for the population of 17 planes.

Step 1   Collect data for the quantitative variable of interest.
The manufacturers for each of the 17 planes were asked to provide the hourly fuel consumption in gallons for a flight between Chicago and New York City. These data are recorded as follows:

Airplane	Fuel Consumption (gal/hr)
B747-100	3,529
L-1011-100/200	2,215
DC-10-10	2,174
A300-B4	1,482
A310-300	1,574
B767-300	1,503
B767-200	1,377
B757-200	985
B727-200	1,249
MD-80	882
B737-300	732
DC-9-50	848
B727-100	806
B737-100/200	1,104
F-100	631
DC-9-30-11	804
DC-9-10	764

Step 2 Add the data values.

$$\Sigma x = 3,529 + 2,215 + 2,174 + \cdots + 764 = 22,659$$

Step 3 Divide the sum by the number of values in the population using Equation 3.1.

$$\mu = \frac{\Sigma x}{N} = \frac{22,659}{17} = 1,332.9$$

The mean number of gallons of fuel consumed per hour on a flight between New York and Chicago is 1,332.9.

TABLE 3.2 Centering Concept of the Mean Using Hotel Data

x	$(x - \mu)$ = Deviation
22	$22 - 15.125 = 6.875$
13	$13 - 15.125 = -2.125$
10	$10 - 15.125 = -5.125$
16	$16 - 15.125 = 0.875$
23	$23 - 15.125 = 7.875$
13	$13 - 15.125 = -2.125$
11	$11 - 15.125 = -4.125$
13	$13 - 15.125 = -2.125$
	$\Sigma (x - \mu) = \overline{0.000}$ ← Sum of deviations equals zero.

FIGURE 3.2A

Excel 2007 Output Showing Mean Revenue for the Foster City Hotel

Excel 2007 Instructions:
1. Open File: Foster.xls.
2. On the **Data** tab, click on **Data Analysis**.
3. Click on **Descriptive Statistics**.
4. Define data range for the variables.
5. Check **Summary Statistics**.
6. Name output sheet.
7. On the **Home** tab, adjust decimal point.

	A	B	C	D	E	F
1	Rooms Rented		Revenue		Complaints	
2						
3	Mean	15.13	Mean	2208.75	Mean	0.75
4	Standard Error	1.73	Standard Error	348.54	Standard Error	0.31
5	Median	13	Median	1875	Median	0.5
6	Mode	13	Mode	#N/A	Mode	0
7	Standard Deviation	4.88	Standard Deviation	985.81	Standard Deviation	0.89
8	Sample Variance	23.84	Sample Variance	971821.93	Sample Variance	0.79
9	Kurtosis	-0.60	Kurtosis	6.38	Kurtosis	-1.48
10	Skewness	0.95	Skewness	2.46	Skewness	0.62
11	Range	13	Range	2973	Range	2
12	Minimum	10	Minimum	1590	Minimum	0
13	Maximum	23	Maximum	4563	Maximum	2
14	Sum	121	Sum	17670	Sum	6
15	Count	8	Count			8

Mean Rooms Rented = 15.13
Mean Revenue   = $2,208.75
Mean Complaints = 0.75

Business Application

Excel and Minitab Tutorial

FOSTER CITY HOTEL (*CONTINUED*) In addition to collecting data on the number of rooms rented on Sunday nights, the Foster City Hotel manager also collected data on the room-rental revenue generated, and the number of complaints, on Sunday nights. Both Excel and Minitab have procedures for computing numerical measures such as the mean. Because these data are the population of all nights of interest to the hotel manager, she can compute the population mean, μ, revenue per night. The population mean is μ = $2,208.75 (rounded to $2,209 in Minitab), as shown in the Excel and Minitab outputs in Figure 3.2A and 3.2B. Likewise, the mean number of complaints is μ = 0.75 per night. (Note, there are other measures shown in the figures. We will discuss several of these later in the chapter.)

Now, for these eight Sunday nights, the manager can report to the corporate vice president that the mean number of rooms rented is 15.125 ≈ 15.13. This level of business generated an average nightly revenue of $2,208.75. The number of complaints averaged 0.75 (less than 1) per night. These values are the true means for the population and are, therefore, called parameters.

Sample Mean

CHAPTER OUTCOME #1

The data for the Foster City Hotel constituted the population of interest. Thus, μ = 15.13 nights is the parameter measure. However, if we have a sample rather than a population, the mean for the sample is computed using Equation 3.2.

Sample Mean

$$\bar{x} = \frac{\sum_{i=1}^{n} x_i}{n} \qquad (3.2)$$

where:

$\bar{x}$ = Sample mean (pronounced "*x*-bar")

n = Sample size

FIGURE 3.2B

Minitab Output Showing Mean Revenue for the Foster City Hotel

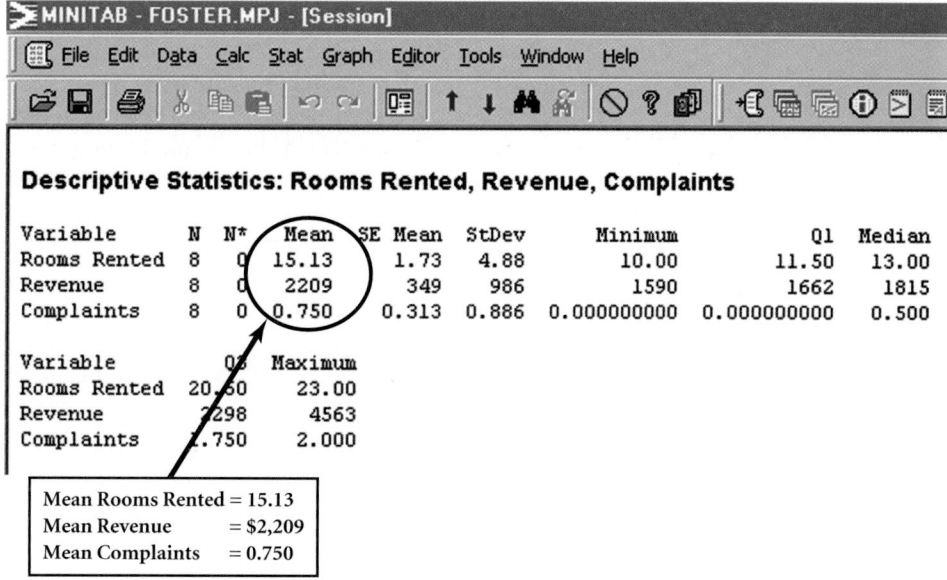

Minitab Instructions:
1. Open file: Foster.MTW.
2. Choose **Stat > Basic Statistics > Display Descriptive Statistics**.
3. In **Variables**, enter columns *Rooms Rented*, *Revenue*, and *Complaints*.
4. Click **Statistics**.
5. Check required statistics.
6. Click **OK**.

Notice, Equation 3.2 is the same as Equation 3.1 *except* that we sum the sample values, not the population values, and divide by the sample size, not the population size.

The notation for the sample mean is $\bar{x}$. Sample descriptors (statistics) are usually assigned a Roman character. (Recall that population values usually are assigned a Greek character.)

TRY PROBLEM 3.3

EXAMPLE 3-2 Computing a Sample Mean

Housing Prices   Consider a sample of seven house prices in Modesto, California. The real estate agency is interested in computing the mean price for this sample of homes. The following steps can be used:

Step 1 Collect the sample data.

$$\{x_i\} = \{\text{house prices}\} = \{\$144{,}000; \$98{,}000; \$204{,}000; \\ \$177{,}000; \$155{,}000; \$316{,}000; \$100{,}000\}$$

Step 2 Add the values in the sample.

$$\sum x = \$144{,}000 + 98{,}000 + 204{,}000 + 177{,}000 + 155{,}000 + 316{,}000 + 100{,}000$$

$$= \$1{,}194{,}000$$

Step 3 Divide the sum by the sample size (Equation 3.2).

$$\bar{x} = \frac{\sum x}{n} = \frac{\$1{,}194{,}000}{7} = \$170{,}571.43$$

Therefore, the mean price for the sample of seven houses in Modesto is $170,571.43.

The Impact of Extreme Values on the Mean

The mean (population or sample) is the balance point for data, so using the mean as a measure of the center generally makes sense. However, the mean does have one potential disadvantage: *The mean can be affected by extreme values*. There are many instances in business when this may occur. For example, in a population or sample of income data, there likely will be extremes on the high end that will pull the mean upward from the center. Example 3-3 illustrates how an extreme value can affect the mean. In these situations, a second measure called the *median* may be more appropriate.

TRY PROBLEM 3.15

EXAMPLE 3-3 | Impact of Extreme Values

Housing Prices Suppose the sample of house prices in Modesto (see Example 3-2) had been slightly different. If the house recorded as $316,000 had actually been $1,000,000, how would the mean be affected? We can see the impact as follows:

Step 1 Collect the sample data.

$$\{x_i\} = \{\text{house prices}\} = \{\$144{,}000; \$98{,}000; \$204{,}000;$$
$$\$177{,}000; \$155{,}000; \$1{,}000{,}000; \$100{,}000\}$$

extreme value

Step 2 Add the values.

$$\Sigma x = \$144{,}000 + 98{,}000 + 204{,}000 + 177{,}000 + 155{,}000 + 1{,}000{,}000 + 100{,}000$$
$$= \$1{,}878{,}000$$

Step 3 Divide the sum by the number of values in the sample.

$$\bar{x} = \frac{\Sigma x}{n} = \frac{\$1{,}878{,}000}{7} = \$268{,}285.71$$

Recall, in Example 3-2, the sample mean was $170,571.43.

With only one value in the sample changed, the mean is now substantially higher than before. Because the mean is affected by extreme values, it may be a misleading measure of the data's center. In this case, the mean is larger than all but one of the seven house prices.

Median

CHAPTER OUTCOME #1

Another measure of the center is called the **median**.

The median is found by first arranging data in numerical order from smallest to largest. Data that are sorted in order are referred to as a **data array**.

Equation 3.3 is used to find the index point corresponding to the median value for a set of data placed in numerical order from low to high.

Median
The median is a center value that divides a data array into two halves. We use $\tilde{\mu}$ to denote the population median and M_d to denote the sample median.

Data Array
Data that have been arranged in numerical order.

Median Index Point
$$i = \frac{1}{2}n \qquad \qquad (3.3)$$

where:

i = the index point in the data set corresponding to the median value
n = sample size

> If i is not an integer, round up to the next highest integer. The next integer greater than i corresponds to the position of the median in the data set.
>
> If i is an integer, the median is the average of the values in position i and position $i + 1$.

For instance, suppose a personnel manager has hired 10 new employees. The ages of each of these employees sorted from low to high is listed as follows:

23   25   25   34   35   45   46   47   52   54

Using Equation 3.3 to find the median index, we get

$$i = \frac{1}{2}n = \frac{1}{2}(10) = 5$$

Since the index is an integer, the median value will be the average of the 5th and 6th values in the data set. Thus, the median is

$$M_d = \frac{35 + 45}{2} = 40$$

Consider another case in which customers at a restaurant are asked to rate the service they received on a scale of 1 to 100. A total of 15 customers were asked to provide the ratings. The data, sorted from low to high, are presented as follows:

60   68   75   77   80   80   80   85   88   90   95   95   95   95   99

Using Equation 3.3, we get the median index

$$i = \frac{1}{2}n = \frac{1}{2}(15) = 7.5$$

Since the index is not an integer. We round 7.5 up to 8. Thus, the median is the 8th data value from either end. In this case,

$$M_d = 85$$

EXAMPLE 3-4 Computing the Median

TRY PROBLEM 3.3

Housing Prices   Consider again the original Modesto, California, house-price data shown in Example 3-2. The median for these data is computed using the following steps:

Step 1 Collect the sample data.

$\{x_i\}$ = {house prices} = {$144,000; $98,000; $204,000; $177,000; $155,000; $316,000; $100,000}

Step 2 Sort the data from smallest to largest, forming a data array.

$\{x_i\}$ = {$98,000; $100,000; $144,000; $155,000; $177,000; $204,000; $316,000}

Step 3 Locate the middle value in the data.

Using Equation 3.3, we get: $i = \frac{1}{2}(7) = 3.5$. Rounding up, the median is the fourth value from either end of the data array.

$\{x_i\}$ = {$98,000; $100,000; $144,000; $155,000; $177,000; $204,000; $316,000}

fourth value = M_d

The median-price house is $155,000. The notation for the sample median is M_d.

Note, if the number of data values in a sample or population is an even number, the median is the average of the two middle values.

FIGURE 3.3

Skewed and Symmetric Distributions

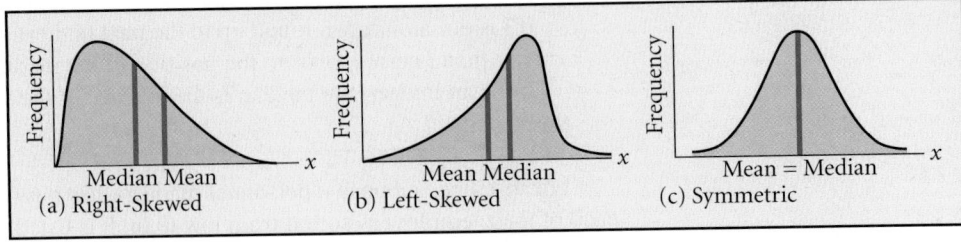

(a) Right-Skewed   (b) Left-Skewed   (c) Symmetric

Skewed and Symmetric Distributions

Symmetric Data
Data sets whose values are evenly spread around the center. For symmetric data, the mean and median are equal.

Skewed Data
Data sets that are not symmetric. For skewed data, the mean will be larger or smaller than the median.

Right-Skewed Data
A data distribution is right skewed if the mean for the data is larger than the median.

Left-Skewed Data
A data distribution is left skewed if the mean for the data is smaller than the median.

Data in a population or sample can be either **symmetric** or **skewed**, depending on how the data are distributed around the center.

In the original Modesto house-price example (Example 3-2), the mean for the sample of seven homes was $170,571.43. In Example 3-4, the median home price was $155,000. Thus, for these data the mean and the median are not equal. This sample data set is **right skewed**, because $\bar{x} = \$170.571.43 > M_d = \$155,000$.

Figure 3.3 illustrates examples of right-skewed, left-skewed, and symmetric distributions. The greater the difference between the mean and the median, the more skewed the distribution. *Example 3-5 shows that an advantage of the median over the mean is that the median is not affected by extreme values.* Thus, the median is particularly useful as a measure of the center when the data are highly skewed.[1]

EXAMPLE 3-5   Impact of Extreme Values on the Median

Housing Prices (Continued)   In Example 3-3, when we substituted a $1,000,000 price for the house priced at $316,000, the sample mean increased from $170,571.43 to $268,285.71. What will happen to the median? The median is determined using the following steps:

Step 1   **Collect the sample data.** The sample house-price data (including the extremely high-priced house) are

$$\{x_i\} = \{\text{house prices}\} = \{\$144,000; \$98,000; \$204,000; \$177,000;$$
$$\$155,000; \$1,000,000; \$100,000\}$$

Step 2   **Sort the data from smallest to largest, forming a data array.**

$$\{x_i\} = \{\$98,000; \$100,000; \$144,000; \$155,000; \$177,000; \$204,000; \$1,000,000\}$$

Step 3   **Locate the middle value in the data.**

Using Equation 3.3, we get $i = \frac{1}{2}(7) = 3.5$. Rounding up, the median is the fourth value from either end of the data array.

$$\{x_i\} = \{\$98,000; \$100,000; \$144,000; \$155,000; \$177,000; \$204,000; \$1,000,000\}$$

fourth value $= M_d$

The median-price house is $155,000, the same value as in Example 3-4, when the high house price was not included in the data. Thus, the median is not affected by the extreme values in the data.

---

[1] Both Minitab and Excel will provide a skewness statistic. The sign on the skewness statistic implies the direction of skewness. The higher the absolute value, the more the data are skewed.

CHAPTER OUTCOME #1

Mode
The mode is the value in a data set that occurs most frequently.

Mode

The mean is the most commonly used measure of central location, followed closely by the median. However, the **mode** is another measure that is occasionally used as a measure of central location.

A data set may have more than one mode if two or more values tie for the most frequently occurring value. Example 3-6 illustrates this concept and shows how the mode is determined.

TRY PROBLEM 3.3

EXAMPLE 3-6 | Determining the Mode

Smoky Mountain Pizza   The owners of Smoky Mountain Pizza are planning to expand their restaurant to include an open-air patio. Before finalizing the design, the managers want to know what the most frequently occurring group size is so that they can organize the seating arrangements to best meet demand. They wish to know the mode, which can be calculated using the following steps:

Step 1 Collect the sample data.
A sample of 20 groups was selected at random. These data are
$\{x_i\} = \{\text{people}\} = \{2, 4, 1, 2, 3, 2, 4, 2, 3, 6, 8, 4, 2, 1, 7, 4, 2, 4, 4, 3\}$

Step 2 Organize the data into a frequency distribution.

x_i	Frequency
1	2
2	6
3	3
4	6
5	0
6	1
7	1
8	1
	Total = 20

Step 3 Determine the value that occurs most frequently.
In this case, there are two modes, because the values 2 and 4 each occurred six times. Thus the modes are 2 and 4.

A common mistake is to state the mode as being the frequency of the most frequently occurring value. In Example 3-6, you might be tempted to say that the mode = 6 because that was the highest frequency. Instead, there were two modes, 2 and 4, each of which occurred six times.

If no value occurs more frequently than any other, the data set is said to not have a mode. The mode might be particularly useful in describing the central location value for clothes sizes. For example, shoes come in full and half sizes. Consider the following sample data that have been sorted from low to high:

$$\{x\} = \{7.5, 8.0, 8.5, 9.0, 9.0, 10.0, 10.0, 10.0, 10.5, 10.5, 11.0, 11.5\}$$

The mean for these sample data is

$$\bar{x} = \frac{\sum x}{n} = \frac{7.5 + 8.0 + \cdots + 11.5}{12} = \frac{115.50}{12} = 9.63$$

Although 9.63 is the numerical average, the mode is 10, because more people wore that size shoe than any other. In making purchasing decisions, a shoe store manager would order more shoes at the modal size than at any other size. The mean isn't of any particular value in her purchasing decision.

Business Application

Excel and Minitab Tutorial

Applying the Measures of Central Tendency

There are two fundamental categories used to classify a company: public or private. A public company's stock is available for purchase by the public. The shares of stock in publicly traded companies are typically listed on a stock exchange such as the New York Stock Exchange. These public companies are required to report financial information to the Securities Exchange Commission (SEC). The data file **US Companies 2005** contains data on 6,992 public companies and stock funds. Suppose a financial analyst is interested in the 2005 closing stock prices for these companies and funds and wishes to conduct a descriptive analysis of this quantitative variable.

Figure 3.4 shows a frequency histogram generated using Excel. This histogram is a good place to begin the descriptive analysis since it allows the analyst to get a good indication of the center value, the spread around the center, and the general shape of the

FIGURE 3.4

An Excel 2007 Frequency Histogram of Stock Prices

Minitab Instructions (for similar results):
1. Open file: US Companies 2005.MTW.
2. Choose **Graph > Histogram**.
3. Click **Simple**.
4. Click **OK**.
5. In **Graph variables**, enter data column *stock price*.
6. Click **OK**.

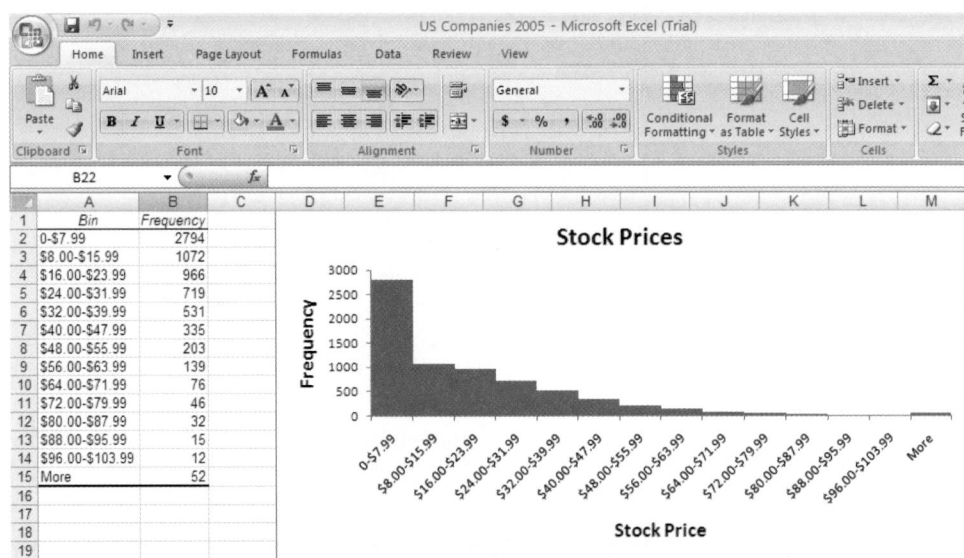

Excel 2007 Instructions:
1. Open file: US Companies 2005.xls.
2. Set up an area on the worksheet for the bins defined as 7.99,15.99, etc, up to 103.99. Be sure to include a label such as "Bins."
3. On the **Data** tab, click **Data Analysis**.
4. Select **Histogram**.
5. Input Range specifies the actual data values as the **Stock Price** column and the bin range as the area defined in Step 2.
6. Put on a new worksheet and include the **Chart Output**.
7. Right-mouse-click on the bars and use the **Format Data Series Options** to set gap width to zero and add lines to the bars.
8. Convert the bins to actual class labels by typing labels in column A. Note, the bin 7.99 is labeled $0–$7.99.
9. Click on **Layout** and set titles as desired.

FIGURE 3.5

Excel 2007 Descriptive Statistics Output

Excel 2007 Instructions:
1. Open File: US Companies 2005.xls.
2. On the **Data** tab, click on **Data Analysis**.
3. Click on **Descriptive Statistics**.
4. Define data range for the variable.
5. Check **Summary Statistics**.
6. Name output sheet.
7. On the **Home** tab, adjust decimals.

	A	B
1	*Stock Price*	
2		
3	Mean	34.9867
4	Standard Error	12.6375
5	Median	13.05
6	Mode	0.08
7	Standard Deviation	1056.7225
8	Sample Variance	1116662.3912
9	Kurtosis	6748.6620
10	Skewness	81.5668
11	Range	87599.9895
12	Minimum	0.0105
13	Maximum	87600
14	Sum	244627.0035
15	Count	6992

Mean, median, and mode for each variable

Note: The Skewness statistic is positive, implying a right skew in the data. The higher the absolute value of this measure, the greater the skewness.

Minitab Instructions (for similar results):
1. Open file: U.S. Companies 2005. MTW.
2. Choose **Stat > Basic Statistics > Display Descriptive Statistics**.
3. In **Variables**, enter columns *Stock Price*.
4. Click **Statistics**.
5. Check required statistics.
6. Click **OK. OK**.

distribution of share prices for these companies. Using the $2^k \geq n$ rule introduced in Chapter 2, the analyst will use $k = 13$ classes. Note, there are 52 companies and funds with stock prices of $104 or more per share. These include First National Bank Alaska at $2,400, the Dow-Jones Industrial Average at $10,773.77, and Warren Buffet's company, Berkshire Hathaway, at $87,600. These 52 companies are in the "More" category in Figure 3.4. Based on this histogram what would you conclude about the distribution of stock prices? Is it skewed right or left?

The analysis can be extended by computing appropriate descriptive measures for the distribution of stock prices. Specifically, we want to look at measures of central location. Figure 3.5 shows the Excel output with descriptive measures for stock price. First focus on the primary measures of central location, mean and median. These are

$$\text{Mean} = \$34.99 \qquad \text{Median} = \$13.05$$

These statistics provide measures of the center of the stock price variable. The mean closing price in 2005 was $34.99 while the median closing price was $13.05. Because the mean exceeds the median, we conclude that the data are right skewed—the same conclusion you should have reached by looking at the histogram in Figure 3.4.

Issues with Excel In many instances, data files will have "missing values." That is, the values for one or more variables may not be available for some of the observations. The data may have been lost, or they were not measured when the data were collected. Many times when you receive data like this, the missing values will be coded in a special way. For example, the code "N/A" might be used or a "−99" might be entered to signify that the data for that observation is missing.

Statistical software packages typically have flexible procedures for dealing with missing data. Minitab provides you with missing data options and properly adjusts the results to account for the missing data. *However, Excel does not contain a missing-value option.* If you attempt to use certain data analysis options in Excel, such as Descriptive Statistics, in the presence of nonnumeric ("N/A") data, you will get an error message. When that happens you must clear the missing values, generally by deleting all rows with missing values. In some instances, you can save the good data in the row by using **Edit-Clear-All** for the cell in question. However, a bigger problem exists when the missing value has been coded as an arbitrary numeric value (−99). In this case, unless you go into the data and clear these values, Excel will use the −99 values in the computations as if they are real values. The result will be incorrect calculations.

Also, if a data set contains more than one mode, Excel will only show the first mode in the list of modes and will not warn you that multiple modes exist. For instance, if you look at Figure 3.5, Excel has computed a mode = $0.08. If you examine these data, you will see that a stock price of $0.08 occurred 26 times. This is the most frequently occurring value. However, had other, higher prices occurred 26 times too, Excel would not have so indicated. (Minitab does not have a mode output option in its Descriptive Statistics tool.)

Other Measures of Location

CHAPTER OUTCOME #1

Weighted Mean The arithmetic mean is the most frequently used measure of central location. Equations 3.1 and 3.2 are used when you have either a population or a sample. For instance, the sample mean is computed using

$$\bar{x} = \frac{\sum x}{n} = \frac{x_1 + x_2 + x_3 + \cdots + x_n}{n}$$

In this case, each x-value is given an equal weight in the computation of the mean. However, in some applications there is reason to weight the data values differently. In those cases, we need to compute a **weighted mean**.

Equations 3.4 and 3.5 are used to find the weighted mean (or weighted average) for a population and for a sample, respectively.

Weighted Mean
The mean value of data values that have been weighted according to their relative importance.

Weighted Mean for a Population

$$\mu_W = \frac{\sum w_i x_i}{\sum w_i} \qquad (3.4)$$

Weighted Mean for a Sample

$$\bar{x}_w = \frac{\sum w_i x_i}{\sum w_i} \qquad (3.5)$$

where:

w_i = The weight of the ith data value
x_i = The ith data value

TRY PROBLEM 3.8

EXAMPLE 3-7 Calculating a Weighted Population Mean

Myers & Associates   Recently, the law firm of Myers & Associates was involved in litigating a discrimination suit concerning ski instructors at a ski resort in Colorado. One ski instructor from Germany had sued the operator of the ski resort, claiming that he had not received equitable pay compared with the other ski instructors from Norway and the United States. In preparing a defense, the Myers attorneys planned to compute the mean annual income for all seven Norwegian ski instructors at the resort. However, because these instructors worked different numbers of days during the ski season, a weighted mean needed to be computed. This was done using the following steps:

Step 1 Collect the desired data and determine the weight to be assigned to each data value.

In this case, the variable of interest was the income of the ski instructors. The population consisted of seven Norwegian instructors. The weights were the number of days that the instructors worked. The following data and weights were determined:

x_i = Income:	$7,600	$3,900	$5,300	$4,000	$7,200	$2,300	$5,100
w_i = Days:	50	30	40	25	60	15	50

Step 2 Multiply each weight by the data value and sum these.

$$\sum w_i x_i = (50)(\$7,600) + (30)(\$3,900) + \cdots + (50)(\$5,100) = \$1,530,500$$

Step 3 Sum the weights for all values (the weights are the days).

$$\sum w_i = 50 + 30 + 40 + 25 + 60 + 15 + 50 = 270$$

Step 4 Compute the weighted mean.

Divide the weighted sum by the sum of the weights. Because we are working with the population, the result will be the population weighted mean.

$$\mu_W = \frac{\sum w_i x_i}{\sum w_i} = \frac{\$1,530,500}{270} = \$5,668.52$$

Thus, taking into account the number of days worked, the Norwegian ski instructors had a mean income of $5,668.52.

One weighted-mean example that you are probably very familiar with is your college grade point average (GPA). At most schools, A = 4 points, B = 3 points, and so forth. Each course has a certain number of credits (usually 1 to 5). The credits are the weights. Your GPA is computed by summing the product of points earned in a course times the credits for the course, and then dividing this sum by the total number of credits earned.

Percentiles In some applications, we might wish to describe the location of the data in terms other than the center of the data. For example, prior to enrolling at your university you took the SAT or ACT test and received a **percentile** score in math and verbal skills.

If you received word that your standardized exam score was at the 90th percentile, it means that you scored as high or higher than 90% of the other students who took the exam. The score at the 50th percentile would indicate that you were at the median, where at least 50% scored at or below and at least 50% scored at or above your score.[2]

Percentiles

The *p*th percentile in a data array is a value that divides the data set into two parts. The lower segment contains at least *p*%, and the upper segment contains at least (100 − *p*)%, of the data. The 50th percentile is the median.

---

[2] More rigorously, the percentile is that value (or set of values) such that at least *p*% of the data is as small or smaller than that value and at least (100 − *p*)% of the data is at least as large as that value. For introductory courses, a convention has been adopted to average the largest and smallest values that qualify as a certain percentile. This is why the median was defined as it was earlier for data sets with an even number of data values.

To illustrate how to manually approximate a percentile value, consider a situation in which you have 309 customers enter a bank during the course of a day. The time (rounded to the nearest minute) that each customer spends in the bank is recorded. If we wish to approximate the 10th percentile, we would begin by first sorting the data in order from low to high, then assign each data value a location indicator from 1 to 309, and next determine the location indicator that corresponds to the 10th percentile using Equation 3.6.

Percentile Location Value

$$i = \frac{p}{100}(n) \qquad\qquad (3.6)$$

where:

p = Desired percent
n = Number of values in the data set

If i is not an integer, round up to the next highest integer. The next integer greater than i corresponds to the position of the pth percentile in the data set.

If i is an integer, the pth percentile is the average of the values in position i and position $i + 1$.

Thus, the index value associated with the 10th percentile is

$$i = \frac{p}{100}(n) = \frac{10}{100}(309) = 30.90$$

Because $i = 30.90$ is not an integer, we round to the next highest integer, which is 31. Thus, the 10th percentile corresponds to the value in the 31st position from the low end of the sorted data.

SUMMARY Calculating Percentiles

To calculate a specific percentile for a set of quantitative data, you can use the following steps:

1. Sort the data in order from the lowest to highest value.
2. Determine the percentile location value, i, using Equation 3.6.

$$i = \frac{p}{100}(n)$$

where

p = Desired percent
n = Number of values in the data set

3. If i is not an integer, then round to next highest integer. The pth percentile is located in the rounded position.
   If i is an integer, the pth percentile is the average of the values in position i and $i + 1$.

EXAMPLE 3-8 Calculating Percentiles

TRY PROBLEM 3.7

Henson Trucking The Henson Trucking Company is a small company that is in the business of moving people from one home to another within the Dallas, Texas, area. Historically, the owners have charged the customers on an hourly basis, regardless of the distance of the move within the Dallas city limits. However, they are now considering adding a surcharge for moves over a certain distance. They have decided to base this charge on the 80th percentile. They have a sample of travel-distance data for 30 moves. These data are as follows:

13.5	8.6	16.2	21.4	21.0	23.7	4.1	13.8	20.5	9.6
11.5	6.5	5.8	10.1	11.1	4.4	12.2	13.0	15.7	13.2
13.4	13.1	21.7	14.6	14.1	12.4	24.9	19.3	26.9	11.7

The 80th percentile can be computed using these steps.

Step 1 **Sort the data from lowest to highest.**

4.1	4.4	5.8	6.5	8.6	9.6	10.1	11.1	11.5	11.7
12.2	12.4	13.0	13.1	13.2	13.4	13.5	13.8	14.1	14.6
15.7	16.2	19.3	20.5	21.0	21.4	21.7	23.7	24.9	26.9

Step 2 **Determine percentile location value, *i*, using Equation 3.6.**
The 80th percentile location value is

$$i = \frac{p}{100}(n) = \frac{80}{100}(30) = 24$$

Step 3 **Locate the appropriate percentile.**
Because $i = 24$ is an integer value, the 80th percentile is found by averaging the values in the 24th and 25th positions. These are 20.5 and 21.0. Thus, the 80th percentile is (20.5 + 21.0)/2 = 20.75 therefore, any distance exceeding 20.75 miles will be subject to a surcharge.

Quartiles

Quartiles in a data array are those values that divide the data set into four equal-sized groups. The median corresponds to the second quartile.

Quartiles Another location measure that can be used to describe data is **Quartiles**.

The first quartile corresponds to the 25th percentile. That is, it is the value at or below which there is at least 25% (one quarter) of the data and at or above which there is at least 75% of the data. The third quartile is also the 75th percentile. It is the value at or below which there is at least 75% of the data and at or above which there is at least 25% of the data. The second quartile is the 50th percentile and is also the median.

A quartile value can be approximated manually using the same method as for percentiles using Equation 3.6. For the 309 bank customer-service times mentioned earlier, the location of the first-quartile (25th percentile) value is found, after sorting the data, as

$$i = \frac{p}{100}(n) = \frac{25}{100}(309) = 77.25$$

Because 77.25 is not an integer value, we round up to 78. The first quartile is the 78th value from the low end of the sorted data.

CHAPTER OUTCOME #2

Box and Whisker Plot
A graph that is composed of two parts: a box and the whiskers. The box has a width that ranges from the first quartile (Q_1) to the third quartile (Q_3). A vertical line through the box is placed at the median. Limits are located at a value that is 1.5 times the difference between Q_1 and Q_3 below Q_1 and above Q_3. The whiskers extend to the left to the lowest value within the limits and to the right to the highest value within the limits.

Issues with Excel The procedure that Excel uses to compute quartiles *is not standard*. Therefore, the quartile and percentile values from Excel will be slightly different from those we found using Equation 3.6 and from what other statistical software packages, including Minitab, will provide. For example, referring to Example 3-8, when Excel is used to compute the 80th percentile for the moving distances, the value returned is 20.58 miles. This is slightly different from the 20.75 we found in Example 3-8. Equation 3.6, the method used by Minitab, is generally accepted by statisticians to be correct. Therefore, if you need precise values for quartiles, use software such as Minitab. However, Excel will give reasonably close percentile and quartile values.

Box and Whisker Plots

A descriptive tool that many decision makers like to use is called a **box and whisker plot** (or a box plot). The box and whisker plot incorporates the median and the quartiles to graphically display quantitative data. It is also used to identify *outliers* that are unusually small or large data values that lie mostly by themselves.

SUMMARY   Constructing a Box and Whisker Plot

A box and whisker plot is a graphical summary of a quantitative variable. It is constructed using the following steps:

1. Sort the data values from low to high.
2. Use Equation 3.6 to find the 25th percentile (Q_1 = first quartile), the 50th percentile (Q_2 = median), and the 75th percentile (Q_3 = third quartile).
3. Draw a box so that the ends of the box are at Q_1 and Q_3. This box will contain the middle 50% of the data values in the population or sample.
4. Draw a vertical line through the box at the median. Half the data values in the box will be on either side of the median.

5. Calculate the *interquartile range* ($IQR = Q_3 - Q_1$). (The interquartile range will be discussed more fully in Section 3-2.) Compute the lower limit for the box and whisker plot as $Q_1 - 1.5(Q_3 - Q_1)$. The upper limit is $Q_3 + 1.5(Q_3 - Q_1)$. Any data values outside these limits are referred to as outliers.
6. Extend dashed lines (called the whiskers) from each end of the box to the lowest and highest value within the limits.
7. Any value outside the limits (outlier) found in step 5 is marked with an asterisk (*).

EXAMPLE 3-9   Constructing a Box and Whisker Plot

TRY PROBLEM 3.5

Rolling Hills Golf Course   Rolling Hills is a semiprivate golf club in rural North Carolina. Like most golf courses, Rolling Hills constantly battles the slow-play issue. Recently, the course manager collected a random sample of times for 18-hole rounds at the course. He plans to make a presentation to the board of directors and wishes to construct a box and whisker plot as part of the presentation. The sorted sample data (time measured in minutes) for 45 rounds are as follows:

231	236	241	242	242	243	243	243	248
248	249	250	251	251	252	252	254	255
255	256	256	257	259	260	260	260	260
262	262	264	265	265	265	266	268	268
270	276	277	277	280	286	300	324	345

The box and whisker plot is computed using the following steps:

Step 1   Sort the data from low to high.

Step 2   Calculate the 25th percentile (Q_1), the 50th percentile (median), and the 75th percentile (Q_3).
The location for Q_1 is

$$i = \frac{p}{100}(n) = \frac{25}{100}(45) = 11.25$$

Thus, Q_1 will be the 12th value, which is 250.
    The median location is

$$i = \frac{p}{100}(n) = \frac{50}{100}(45) = 22.5$$

In the sorted data, the median is the 23rd value, which has a value of 259 minutes. The third-quartile location is

$$i = \frac{p}{100}(n) = \frac{75}{100}(45) = 33.75$$

Thus, Q_3 is the 34th data value. This is 266.

Step 3 **Draw the box so the ends correspond to Q_1 and Q_3.**

Step 4 **Draw a vertical line through the box at the median.**

Step 5 **Compute the upper and lower limits.**

The lower limit is computed as $Q_1 - 1.5(Q_3 - Q_1)$. This is

Lower Limit $= 250 - 1.5(266 - 250) = 226$

The upper limit is $Q_3 + 1.5(Q_3 - Q_1)$. This is

Upper Limit $= 266 + 1.5(266 - 250) = 290$

Any value outside these limits is identified as an outlier.

Step 6 **Draw the whiskers.**

The whiskers are drawn to the smallest and largest values within the limits.

Step 7 **Plot the outliers.**

The outliers are plotted as values outside the limits.

Data-Level Issues

You need to be very aware of the level of data you are working with before computing the numerical measures introduced in this chapter. A common mistake is to compute means on nominal-level data. For example, a major electronics manufacturer recently surveyed a sample of customers to determine whether they preferred black, white, or colored stereo cases. The data were coded as follows:

$$1 = \text{black}$$
$$2 = \text{white}$$
$$3 = \text{colored}$$

A few of the responses are

$$\text{Color code} = \{1, 1, 3, 2, 1, 2, 2, 2, 3, 1, 1, 1, 3, 2, 2, 1, 2\}$$

Using these codes, the sample mean is

$$\bar{x} = \frac{\sum x}{n}$$

$$= \frac{30}{17} = 1.765$$

As you can see, reporting that customers prefer a color somewhere between black and white but closer to white would be meaningless. The mean should not be used with nominal data. This type of mistake tends to happen when people use computer software to perform their calculations. It is easy to ask Excel, Minitab, or other statistical software to compute the mean, median, and so on for all the variables in the data set. Then a table is created and, before long, the meaningless measures creep into your report.

There is also some disagreement about whether means should be computed on ordinal data. For example, in market research a 5- or 7-point scale is often used to measure customers' attitudes about products or TV commercials. For example, we might set up the following scale:

$$1 = \text{Strongly Agree}$$
$$2 = \text{Agree}$$
$$3 = \text{Neutral}$$
$$4 = \text{Disagree}$$
$$5 = \text{Strongly Disagree}$$

Customer responses to a particular questions are obtained on this scale from 1 to 5. For a sample of $n = 10$ people, we might get the following responses to a question.

$$\text{Response} = \{2, 2, 1, 3, 3, 1, 5, 2, 1, 3\}$$

The mean rating is 2.3. We could then compute the mean for a second issue and compare the means. However, what exactly do we have? First, when we compute a mean for a scaled variable, we are making two basic assumptions:

1. We are assuming the distance between a rating of 1 and 2 is the same as the distance between 2 and 3. We are also saying these distances are exactly the same for the second issue's variable to which you wish to compare it. Although from a numerical standpoint this is true, in terms of what the scale is measuring, is the difference between strongly agree and agree the same as the difference between agree and neutral? If not, is the mean really a meaningful measure?

2. We are also assuming people who respond to the survey have the same definition of what "strongly agree" means or what "disagree" means. When you mark a 4 (disagree) on your survey, are you applying the same criteria as someone else who also marks a 4 on the same issue? If not, then the mean might be misleading.

FIGURE 3.6

Descriptive Measures of the Center

Descriptive Measure	Computation Method	Data Level	Advantages/ Disadvantages
Mean	Sum of values divided by the number of values	Ratio Interval	• Numerical center of the data • Sum of deviations from the mean is zero • Sensitive to extreme values
Median	Middle value for data that have been sorted	Ratio Interval Ordinal	• Not sensitive to extreme values • Computed only from the center values • Does not use information from all the data
Mode	Value(s) that occur most frequently in the data	Ratio Interval Ordinal Nominal	• May not reflect the center • May not exist • Might have multiple modes

Although these difficulties exist with ordinal data, we see many examples in which means are computed and used for decision purposes. In fact, we once had a dean who focused on one particular question on the course evaluation survey that was administered in every class each semester. This question was "Considering all factors of importance to you, how would you rate this instructor?"

1 = Excellent   2 = Good   3 = Average   4 = Poor   5 = Very Poor

The dean then had his staff compute means for each class and for each professor. He then listed classes and faculty in order based on the mean values, and he based a major part of the performance evaluation on where a faculty member stood with respect to mean score on this one question. By the way, he carried the calculations for the mean out to three decimal places!

In general, the median is the preferred measure of central location for ordinal data instead of the mean.

Figure 3.6 summarizes the three measures of the center that have been discussed in this section.

3-1: Exercises

Skill Development

3-1. The following data reflect the number of vacation days that all employees at a small company in Indiana have left to take before the end of the year.

3	0	2	0	1	3	5	2
5	1	3	0	0	1	3	3
4	3	1	8	4	2	4	0

a. Compute the mean number of vacation days for this population of employees.

b. Compute the median number of vacation days for this population of employees.

c. Determine if there is a mode number of vacation days and, if so, indicate the mode value.

3-2. A national fast-food chain recently sampled 20 of its large size french fry packages to determine the weights of the fries in each package. These sample data, measured in ounces, are as follows:

14.7	16.3	14.3	14.2	18.7	13.2	13.1	14.4	16.2	12.8
13.6	17.1	14.4	11.5	15.5	15.9	13.8	14.2	15.1	13.5

Calculate the first and third quartiles for these sample data.

3-3. A random sample of 15 term papers in a senior-level economics course revealed the following word counts per paper:

5176	6005	5052	5310	4188
4132	5736	5381	4983	4423
5002	4573	4209	5611	4568

Compute the mean, median, first quartile, and third quartile for these sample data.

3-4. The time (in seconds) required to process an ATM banking transaction for 16 randomly selected customers at a bank is

106	153	169	116
135	78	51	129
100	141	72	101
130	125	128	139

Compute the mean, median, first quartile, and third quartile range for the sample data.

3-5. A random sample of 20 pledges to a public radio fund-raiser revealed the following dollar pledges:

90	85	100	150
125	75	50	100
75	60	35	90
100	125	75	85
50	100	50	80

Develop a box and whisker plot for the sample data.

3-6. Examine the following data:

23	65	45	19	35	28	39	100	50	26	25	27
24	17	12	106	23	19	39	70	20	18	44	31

a. Compute the quartiles.
b. Calculate the 90th percentile.
c. Develop a box and whisker plot.
d. Calculate the 20th and the 30th percentiles.

3-7. Consider the following data:

3.1	4.7	8.4	11.6	12.1	13.0	13.4	16.1	17.3	20.8
22.8	24.3	26.2	26.6	26.7	31.2	32.2	35.8	35.8	39.8

a. Determine the 80th percentile.
b. Determine numbers that are the 25th and 75th percentiles.
c. Determine a number that qualifies as a median for these data.

3-8. A professor wishes to develop a numerical method for giving grades. He intends to base the grade on homework, two midterms, a project, and a final examination. He wishes the final exam to have the largest influence on the grade. He wants the project to have 10%, each midterm to have 20%, and the homework to have 10% of the influence of the semester grade.

a. Determine the weights the professor should use to produce a weighted average for grading purposes.

b. For a student with the following grades during the quarter, calculate a weighted average for the course:

Instrument	Final	Project	Midterm 1	Midterm 2	Homework
Percentage	64	98	67	63	89

c. Calculate an (unweighted) average of these five scores and discuss why the weighted average would be preferable here.

Business Applications

3-9. The Soccer Shoppe was recently opened in Sonoma, California, to provide soccer equipment and supplies to players and teams in the area. During the first month that it was open, the managers kept track of the number of customers who entered the store each day. The following data were collected:

21	19	21	19	19	20	18	12	20	19	17	14
21	22	25	21	22	23	10	19	25	14	17	18

a. Compute the mean, median, and mode for these data.
b. Indicate whether the data are skewed or symmetrical.
c. Construct a box and whisker plot for these data. Referring to your answer in part a, does the box plot support your conclusion about skewness? Discuss.

3-10. The Ollander Corporation operates five food-processing plants in western Europe. Recently, the company was considering modifying its financial reward system for the plant managers. In doing the analysis, the director of human resources collected information on the profits (in thousands of U.S. dollars) generated from each plant last year. She also collected data on number of employees at the plants. These data are as follows:

Profits	$7,400	$14,400	$12,300	$6,200	$3,100
Employees	123	402	256	109	67

a. Compute the weighted mean profit for these five plants using number of employees as the weights.
b. Explain why the human resource director would desire that a weighted average be computed in this situation rather than a simple numeric average.

3-11. The Paradise Pool and Spa Company maintains swimming pools and spas for customers throughout the San Diego area. Recently, the operations manager for the company tracked the time his field employees spent at a sample of customer locations. He was hoping to use these data to help him with his scheduling and to establish billing rates. The following sample data, in minutes, were recorded:

31	27	29	22	24	30	28	21	29	26
22	17	17	20	38	10	38	25	27	23
23	13	17	34	25	29	22	22	14	11
29	26	29	29	37	32	27	26	18	22

Describe the central tendency of these data by computing the mean, median, and mode. Based on these measures, can you conclude that the distribution of time spent at customer locations is skewed or symmetric?

3-12. During the past few years, there has been a lot of discussion about the price of university textbooks. The complaints have come from many places, including students, faculty, parents, and even government officials. The publishing companies have been called on to explain why textbooks cost so much. Recently, one of the major publishing companies was asked to testify before a congressional panel in Washington DC. As part of the presentation, the president of the company organized his talk around four main areas: production costs, author royalties, marketing costs, and bookstore markup. He used one of his company's business statistics texts as an example when he pointed out the production costs— including editing, proofing, printing, binding, inventory holding, and distribution—come to about $32 per book sold. Authors receive $12 per copy for the hundreds of hours of creative work in writing the book and supplementary materials. Marketing costs are pegged at about $5 per copy sold and go to pay for the book salesforce and examination copies sent to professors. The book is then sold to bookstores for $70 per copy, a markup on costs of about 40% to cover overhead and the publishing costs associated with many upper-division, low-market texts that lose money for the company. Once university bookstores purchase the book, they mark it up, place it on the shelf, and sell it to the student. If books go unsold, they are returned to the publisher for a full refund. The following data reflect the dollar markup on the business statistics text for a sample of 20 college bookstores:

$33	$32	$42	$31	$31
$37	$37	$34	$47	$31
$42	$29	$36	$32	$25
$29	$47	$26	$32	$40

a. Compute the mean markup on the business statistics text by university bookstores in the sample.

b. Compute the median markup.
c. Determine the mode markup.
d. Write a short paragraph discussing the statistics computed in parts a–c.

3-13. A fast-food restaurant monitors its drive-thru service times electronically to ensure that its speed of service is meeting the company's goals. A sample of 28 drive-thru times was recently taken and is shown here.

Speed of Service (time in seconds)			
83	138	145	147
130	79	156	156
90	85	68	93
178	76	73	119
92	146	88	103
116	134	162	71
181	110	105	74

a. Compute the mean, median, and mode for these sample data.
b. Indicate whether the data are symmetrical or skewed.
c. Construct a box and whisker plot for the sample data. Does the box and whisker plot support your conclusions in part b concerning the symmetry or skewness of these data?

3-14. The Natchez Trace Company, a real estate investment trust, owns six office buildings in Mississippi that it leases to businesses. The lease price per square foot differs by building due to location and building amenities. Currently, all six buildings are fully leased at the prices shown here.

	Price Per Square Foot	Number of Square Feet
Building 1	$75	125,000
Building 2	$85	37,500
Building 3	$90	77,500
Building 4	$45	35,000
Building 5	$55	60,000
Building 6	$110	130,000

a. Compute the weighted average (mean) price per square foot for these buildings.
b. Why is the weighted average price per square foot preferred to a simple average price per square foot in this case?

3-15. *Business Week* reported ("War of the Screens," August 12, 2005) that L. G. Philips LCD Co. would soon complete the construction of a new factory in Paju, South Korea, at a cost of $5 billion. It will be the world's largest maker of liquid-crystal display panels. The arrival of the plant means that flat-panel LCD TVs could soon become affordable. The average retail cost of a 20″ LCD TV in 2000 was $5,139. To obtain what the average retail cost was in 2005, a survey yielded the following data:

606.70	558.12	625.82	533.70	464.37
511.15	400.56	538.20	531.64	632.14
474.86	567.46	588.39	528.78	610.32
564.71	912.68	475.87	545.25	589.15

a. Calculate the mean cost for these data.
b. Examine the data presented. Choose an appropriate measure of the center of the data, justify the choice, and calculate the measure.
c. The influence an observation has on a statistic may be calculated by deleting the observation and calculating the difference between the original statistic and the statistic with the data point removed. The larger the difference, the more influential is the data point. Identify the data points that have the most and the least influence in the calculation of the sample mean.

3-16. *Wageweb.com* exhibits salary data obtained from surveys. It provides compensation information on over 170 benchmark positions, including finance positions. It reported that salaries of chief finance officers (CFOs) ranged from $127,735 to $209,981 (*Wageweb.com*, April 12, 2004) as of October 1, 2003. Suppose that a sample is taken of the annual salaries for 25 CFOs. Assume the data are in thousands of dollars.

173.1	171.2	141.9	112.6	211.1	156.5	145.4	134.0	192.0
185.8	168.3	131.0	214.4	155.2	164.9	123.9	161.9	162.7
178.8	161.3	182.0	165.8	213.1	177.4	159.3		

a. Calculate the mean salary of the CFOs.
b. Based upon measures of the center of the data, determine if the CFO salary data are skewed.
c. Construct a box and whisker plot and summarize the characteristics of the CFO salaries that it reveals.

3-17. The Federal Deposit Insurance Corporation (FDIC) insures deposits in banks and thrift institutions for up to $100,000. As of October 6, 2005, there were 8,885 FDIC-insured institutions, with deposits of $6,826,804,000,000. Bank of America had deposits of $681,570,000,000 in nearly 6,000 banking centers during 2004.
a. Calculate the average deposits per bank for both FDIC-insured institutions and Bank of America.
b. Describe the relationship between the two averages calculated in part a. Provide a reason for the disparity.

c. Would the two averages be considered to be parameters or statistics? Explain.

Computer Database Exercises

3-18. DRAM memory chips are made from silicon wafers in manufacturing facilities through a very complex process called wafer fabs. The wafers are routed through the fab machines in an order that is referred to as a recipe. The wafers may go through the same machine several times as the chip is created. The data file **DRAM Chips** contains a sample of processing times, measured in fractions of hours, at a particular machine center for one chip recipe.
a. Compute the mean processing time.
b. Compute the median processing time.
c. Determine what the mode processing time is.
d. Calculate the 80th percentile for processing time.

3-19. Japolli Bakery tracks sales of its different bread products on a daily basis. The data for 22 consecutive days at one of its retail outlets in Nashville are in a file called **Japolli Bakery**. Calculate the mean, mode, and median sales for each of the bread categories and write a short report that describes these data. Use any charts or graphs that may be helpful in more fully describing the data.

3-20. Each year, *Business Week* publishes information and rankings of MBA programs. The data file **MBA Analysis** contains data on several variables for eight reputable MBA programs as presented in the October 2, 2000 issue of *Business Week*. The variables include pre- and post-MBA salary, percentage salary increase, undergraduate GPA, average GMAT score, annual tuition, and expected annual student cost. Compute the mean and median for each of the variables in the database and write a short report that summarizes the data. Include any appropriate charts or graphs to assist in your report.

3-21. Homeowners and businesses pay taxes on the assessed value of their property. As a result, property taxes can be a problem for elderly homeowners who are on a fixed retirement income. While these retirement incomes remain basically constant, because of rising real estate prices, the property taxes in many areas of the country have risen dramatically. In some cases, homeowners are required to sell their homes because they can't afford the taxes. In Phoenix, Arizona, government officials are considering giving certain elderly homeowners a property tax reduction based on income. One proposal calls for all homeowners over the age of 65 with incomes at or below the 20th percentile to get a reduction in property taxes. A random sample of 50 people over the age of 65 was selected and the household income (as reported on the most current federal tax return) was recorded. These data are also in the file called **Property Tax Incomes.** Use these data to establish the income cutoff point to qualify for the property tax cut.

$35,303	$56,855	$ 7,928	$26,006	$28,278
$54,215	$38,850	$15,733	$29,786	$65,878
$46,658	$62,874	$49,427	$19,017	$46,007
$32,367	$31,904	$35,534	$66,668	$37,986
$10,669	$54,337	$ 8,858	$45,263	$37,746
$14,550	$ 8,748	$58,075	$23,381	$11,725
$45,044	$55,807	$54,211	$42,961	$62,682
$32,939	$38,698	$11,632	$66,714	$31,869
$57,530	$59,233	$14,136	$ 8,824	$42,183
$58,443	$34,553	$26,805	$16,133	$61,785

3-22. Suppose a random sample of 137 households in Detroit was taken as part of a study on annual household spending for food at home. The sample data are contained in the file **Detroit Eats**.
  a. For the sample data, compute the mean and the median and construct a box and whisker plot.
  b. Are the data skewed or symmetric?
  c. Approximately what percent of the data values are between $2,900 and $3,250?

3-23. The National Association of Realtors® reported ("NAR Launches New Leading Indicator for Housing Market," March 7, 2005) the development of the Pending Home Sales Index (PHSI), a new leading indicator for the housing market. An index of 100 is equal to the average level of contract activity during 2001, the first year to be analyzed. The index is based on a large national sample, representing about 20% of home sales The file entitled **Pending** contains the PHSI from January 2004 to August 2005.
  a. Determine the mean and median for the PHSI between January 2004 and August 2005. Specify the shape of the PHSI's distribution.
  b. The PHSI was at 111.0 in January 2004 and it was at 129.5 in August of 2005. Determine the average monthly increase in the PHSI for this period.
  c. Using your answer to part b, suggest a weighting scheme to calculate the weighted mean for the months between January 2005 and August 2005. Use the scheme to produce the weighted average of the PHSI in this time period.
  d. Does the weighted average seem more appropriate here? Explain.

3-24. *USA Today* reported (Jon Swartz, "Survey: ID theft takes time to wipe clean," September 29, 2005) a study made by Nationwide Mutual Insurance. The survey indicated that the average amount of time spent to resolve identity crises was 81 hours. The file entitled **Theft** contains data that would produce this statistic.
  a. Construct a stem and leaf display. Indicate the shape of data displayed by the stem and leaf display.
  b. Use measures that indicate the shape of the distribution. Do these measures give results that agree with the shape shown in part a?
  c. Considering your answers to part a and b, indicate which measure you would recommend using to indicate the center of the data.

3.2 Measures of Variation

Business Application

BRYCE LUMBER COMPANY Consider the situation involving two manufacturing facilities for the Bryce Lumber Company. The division vice president asked the two plant managers to record their production output for five days. The resulting sample data are shown in Table 3.3.

Instead of reporting these raw data, the managers reported only the mean and median for their data. The following are the computed statistics for the two plants:

TABLE 3.3
Manufacturing Output for Bryce Lumber

Plant A	Plant B
15 units	23 units
25 units	26 units
35 units	25 units
20 units	24 units
30 units	27 units

Plant A	Plant B
$\bar{x} = 25$ units	$\bar{x} = 25$ units
$M_d = 25$ units	$M_d = 25$ units

The division vice president looked at these statistics and concluded:

  1. Average production is the same at both plants.
  2. At both plants, the output is at or more than 25 units half the time and at or fewer than 25 units half the time.
  3. Because the mean and median are equal, the distribution of production output at the two plants is symmetrical.

4. Based on these statistics, there is no reason to believe that the two plants are different in terms of their production output.

However, if he had taken a closer look at the raw data, he would have seen there is a very big difference between the two plants. The difference is the production **variation** from day to day. Plant B is very stable, producing almost the same amount every day. Plant A varies considerably, with some high-output days and some low-output days. Thus, looking at only measures of the data's central location can be misleading. To fully describe a set of data, we need a measure of variation or spread.

There is variation in everything that is made by humans or that occurs in nature. The variation may be small, but it is there. Given a fine enough measuring instrument, we can detect the variation. Variation is either a natural part of a process (or inherent to a product) or can be attributed to a special cause that is not considered random.

There are several different measures of variation that are used in business decision making. In this section, we introduce four of these measures: range, interquartile range, variance, and standard deviation.

Variation
A set of data exhibits variation if all the data are not the same value.

CHAPTER OUTCOME #3

Range
The range is a measure of variation that is computed by finding the difference between the maximum and minimum values in a data set.

Range

The simplest measure of variation is the **range**. It is both easy to compute and easy to understand.

The range is computed using Equation 3.7.

Range

$$R = \text{Maximum Value} - \text{Minimum Value} \qquad \textbf{(3.7)}$$

BRYCE LUMBER (*CONTINUED*) Table 3.3 showed the production-volume data for the two Bryce Lumber Company plants. The range for each plant is determined using Equation 3.7 as follows:

Plant A	Plant B
$R = \text{Maximum} - \text{Minimum}$	$R = \text{Maximum} - \text{Minimum}$
$R = 35 - 15$	$R = 27 - 23$
$R = 20$	$R = 4$

We see Plant A has a range that is five times as great as Plant B.

Although the range is quick and easy to compute, it does have some limitations. First, because we use only the high and low values to compute the range, it is very sensitive to extreme values in the data. Second, regardless of how many values are in the sample or population, the range is computed from only two of these values. For these reasons, it is considered a weak measure of variation.

CHAPTER OUTCOME #3

Interquartile Range
The interquartile range is a measure of variation that is determined by computing the difference between the third and first quartiles.

Interquartile Range

A measure of variation that tends to overcome the range's susceptibility to extreme values is called the **interquartile range**.

Equation 3.8 is used to compute the interquartile range.

Interquartile Range

$$\text{Interquartile Range} = \text{Third Quartile} - \text{First Quartile} \qquad \textbf{(3.8)}$$

EXAMPLE 3-10 Computing the Interquartile Range

TRY PROBLEM 3.29

D.C. Hilton Investment Company The D.C. Hilton Investment Company, head-quartered in New Orleans, has a number of individual clients who have recently opened a Roth IRA. Each client must decide on how much to contribute on a monthly basis. The manager in charge of Roth investments at D.C. Hilton has collected a random sample of 100 clients who make monthly contributions to a Roth IRA. He has recorded the net dollars, after brokerage fees, that each client deposits into his or her account. He wishes to analyze the variation in these data by computing the range and the interquartile range. He could use the following steps to do so:

Step 1 **Sort the data into a data array from lowest to highest.**
The 100 sorted deposit values, in dollars, are as follows:

$33	$164	$173	$184	$190	$197	$207	$216	$224	$237
53	164	175	186	191	197	207	217	225	240
150	164	175	186	191	198	208	217	225	240
152	166	175	186	192	200	208	217	229	240
157	166	178	187	193	200	208	219	231	250
160	168	178	188	193	201	210	222	231	251
161	169	179	188	194	202	211	223	234	259
162	171	180	188	194	204	212	223	234	270
162	171	182	190	196	205	213	223	235	379
163	172	183	190	196	205	216	224	236	479

Step 2 **Compute the range using Equation 3.7.**

$$R = \text{Maximum Value} - \text{Minimum Value}$$
$$R = \$479 - \$33 = \$446$$

Note, the range is sensitive to extreme values. The small value of $33 and the high value of $479 cause the range value to be very large.

Step 3 **Compute the first and third quartiles.**
Equation 3.6 can be used to find the location of the third quartile (75th percentile) and the first quartile (25th percentile).

For Q_3, the location $i = \dfrac{75}{100}(100) = 75$. Thus, Q_3 is halfway between the 75th and 76th data values, which is found as follows:

$$Q_3 = (219 + 222)/2 = 220.5$$

For Q_1, the location is $i = \dfrac{25}{100}(100) = 25$. Then Q_1 is halfway between the 25th and 26th data values.

$$Q_1 = (178 + 178)/2 = 178$$

Step 4 **Compute the interquartile range.**
The interquartile range overcomes the range's sensitivity to extreme values problem. It is computed using Equation 3.8:

$$\text{Interquartile Range} = Q_3 - Q_1$$
$$= 220.50 - 178 = 42.50$$

Note, the interquartile range would be unchanged even if the values on the high or low end of the distribution were even more extreme than those shown in these sample data.

CHAPTER OUTCOME #3

Variance
The population variance is the average of the squared distances of the data values from the mean.

Standard Deviation
The standard deviation is the positive square root of the variance.

Business Application

Population Variance and Standard Deviation

Although the range is easy to compute and understand and the interquartile range is designed to overcome the range's sensitivity to extreme values, neither measure uses all the available data in its computation. Thus, both measures ignore potentially valuable information in data.

Two measures of variation that incorporate all the values in a data set are the **variance** and the **standard deviation**.

These two measures are closely related. The standard deviation is the square root of the variance. The standard deviation is in the original units (dollars, pounds, etc.), whereas the units of measure in the variance are squared. Because dealing with original units is easier than dealing with the square of the units, we usually use the standard deviation to measure variation in a population or sample.

BRYCE LUMBER (*CONTINUED*) Recall the Bryce Lumber application, in which we compared the production output for two of the company's plants. Table 3.3 showed the data, which are considered a population for our purposes here.

Previously we examined the variability in the output from these two plants by computing the ranges. Although those results gave us some sense of how much more variable Plant A is than Plant B, we also pointed out some of the deficiencies of the range. The variance and standard deviation offer alternatives to the range for measuring variation in data.

Equation 3.9 is the formula for the population variance. Like the population mean, the population variance and standard deviation are assigned a Greek symbol.

Population Variance

$$\sigma^2 = \frac{\sum_{i=1}^{N}(x_i - \mu)^2}{N}$$

(3.9)

where:

μ = Population mean
N = Population size
σ^2 = Population variance (sigma squared)

We begin by computing the variance for the output data from Plant A. The first step in manually calculating the variance is to find the mean using Equation 3.1.

$$\mu = \frac{\sum x}{N} = \frac{15 + 25 + 35 + 20 + 30}{5} = \frac{125}{5} = 25$$

Next, subtract the mean from each value, as shown in Table 3.4. Notice the sum of the deviations from the mean is 0. Recall from Section 3.1 that this will be true for any set of

TABLE 3.4 Computing the Population Variance: Squaring the Deviations

x	$(x - \mu)$	$(x - \mu)^2$
15	$15 - 25 = -10$	100
25	$25 - 25 = 0$	0
35	$35 - 25 = 10$	100
20	$20 - 25 = -5$	25
30	$30 - 25 = 5$	25
	$\Sigma = 0$	$\Sigma = 250$

data. The positive differences are cancelled out by the negative differences. To overcome this fact when computing the variance, we square each of the differences and then sum the squared differences. These calculations are also shown in Table 3.4.

The final step in computing the population variance is to divide the sum of the squared differences by the population size, $N = 5$.

$$\sigma^2 = \frac{\Sigma(x-\mu)^2}{N} = \frac{250}{5} = 50$$

The population variance is 50 *products squared.*

Manual calculations for the population variance may be easier if you use an alternative formula for σ^2 that is the algebraic equivalent. This is shown as Equation 3.10.

Population Variance Shortcut

$$\sigma^2 = \frac{\Sigma(x-\mu)^2}{N} = \frac{\Sigma x^2 - \frac{(\Sigma x)^2}{N}}{N} \qquad (3.10)$$

Example 3-11 will illustrate using Equation 3.10 to find a population variance.

Because we squared the deviations to keep the plus values and minus values from canceling, the units of measure were also squared, but the term *products squared* doesn't have a meaning. To get back to the original units of measure, take the square root of the variance. The result is the standard deviation. Equation 3.11 shows the formula for the population standard deviation.

Population Standard Deviation

$$\sigma = \sqrt{\sigma^2} = \sqrt{\frac{\sum_{i=1}^{N}(x_i - \mu)^2}{N}} \qquad (3.11)$$

Therefore, the population standard deviation of Plant A's production output is

$$\sigma = \sqrt{50}$$
$$\sigma = 7.07 \, \text{products}$$

The population standard deviation is a parameter and will not change unless the population values change.

We could repeat this process using the data for Plant B, which also had a mean output of 25 products. You should verify that the population variance is

$$\sigma^2 = \frac{\Sigma(x-\mu)^2}{N} = \frac{10}{5} = 2 \, \text{products squared}$$

The standard deviation is found by taking the square root of the variance.

$$\sigma = \sqrt{2}$$
$$\sigma = 1.414 \, \text{products}$$

Thus, Plant A has an output standard deviation that is five times larger than Plant B's. The fact that Plant A's range was also five times larger than the range for Plant B is merely a coincidence.

SUMMARY — Computing the Population Variance and Standard Deviation

The population variance and standard deviation are computed using the following steps:

1. Collect quantitative data for the variable of interest for the entire population.
2. Use either Equation 3.9 or Equation 3.10 to compute the variance.
3. If Equation 3.10 is used, find the sum of the x-values (Σx) and then square this sum ($\Sigma x)^2$.
4. Square each x-value and sum these squared values (Σx^2).

5. Compute the variance using

$$\sigma^2 = \frac{\Sigma x^2 - \frac{(\Sigma x)^2}{N}}{N}$$

6. Compute the standard deviation by taking the square root of the variance:

$$\sigma = \sqrt{\sigma^2}$$

EXAMPLE 3-11 — Computing a Population Variance and a Standard Deviation

TRY PROBLEM 3.27

Boydson Shipping Company Boydson Shipping Company owns and operates a fleet of tanker ships that carry commodities between the countries of the world. In the past six months, the company has had seven contracts that called for shipments between Vancouver, Canada, and London, England. For many reasons, the travel time varies between these two locations. The scheduling manager is interested in knowing the variance and standard deviation in shipping times for these seven shipments. To find these values, he can follow these steps:

Step 1 Collect the data for the population.
These shipping times are shown as follows:

$$x = \text{shipping weeks}$$
$$= \{5, 7, 5, 9, 7, 4, 6\}$$

Step 2 Select Equation 3.10 to find the population variance.

$$\sigma^2 = \frac{\Sigma x^2 - \frac{(\Sigma x)^2}{N}}{N}$$

Step 3 Add the x-values and square the sum.

$$\Sigma x = 5 + 7 + 5 + 9 + 7 + 4 + 6 = 43$$
$$(\Sigma x)^2 = (43)^2 = 1{,}849$$

Step 4 Square each of the x-values and sum these squares.

$$\Sigma x^2 = 5^2 + 7^2 + 5^2 + 9^2 + 7^2 + 4^2 + 6^2 = 281$$

Step 5 Compute the population variance.

$$\sigma^2 = \frac{\Sigma x^2 - \frac{(\Sigma x)^2}{N}}{N} = \frac{281 - \frac{1{,}849}{7}}{7} = 2.4082$$

The variance is in units squared, so in this example the population variance is 2.4082 weeks squared.

> **Step 6** **Calculate the standard deviation as the square root of the variance.**
>
> $$\sigma = \sqrt{\sigma^2} = \sqrt{2.4082} = 1.5518 \text{ weeks}$$
>
> Thus, the standard deviation for the number of shipping weeks between Vancouver and London for the seven shipments is 1.5518 weeks.

Sample Variance and Standard Deviation

Equations 3.9, 3.10, and 3.11 are the equations for the population variance and standard deviation. Any time you are working with a population, these are the equations that are used. However, in most instances, you will be describing sample data that have been selected from the population. In addition to using different notation for the sample variance and standard deviation, the equations are also slightly different. Equations 3.12 and 3.13 can be used to find the sample variance. Note that Equation 3.13 is considered the shortcut formula for manual computations.

Sample Variance

$$s^2 = \frac{\displaystyle\sum_{i=1}^{n}(x_i - \bar{x})^2}{n-1} \tag{3.12}$$

Sample Variance Shortcut

$$s^2 = \frac{\sum x^2 - \dfrac{(\sum x)^2}{n}}{n-1} \tag{3.13}$$

where:

$$n = \text{Sample size}$$
$$\bar{x} = \text{Sample mean}$$
$$s^2 = \text{Sample variance}$$

The sample standard deviation is found by taking the square root of the sample variance, as shown in Equation 3.14.

Sample Standard Deviation

$$s = \sqrt{s^2} = \sqrt{\frac{\displaystyle\sum_{i=1}^{n}(x_i - \bar{x})^2}{n-1}} \tag{3.14}$$

Take note in Equations 3.12, 3.13, and 3.14 that the denominator is $n-1$ (sample size minus 1). This may seem strange, given that the denominator for the population variance and the standard deviation is simply N, the population size. The mathematical justification for the $n-1$ divisor is outside the scope of this text. However, the general reason for this is that we want the average sample variance to equal the population variance. If we were to select all possible samples of size n from a given population and for each sample we computed the sample variance using Equation 3.12 or Equation 3.13, the average of all the sample variances would equal σ^2 (the population variance), provided we used $n-1$ as the divisor. Using n instead of $n-1$ in the denominator would produce an average sample variance that would be smaller than σ^2, the population variance. Because we do not want an estimator on average to underestimate the population variance, we use $n-1$ in the denominator of s^2.

EXAMPLE 3-12	Computing a Sample Variance and Standard Deviation

TRY PROBLEM 3.25

Red Line Taxi The managers at Red Line Taxi selected a random sample of 10 taxi-cabs and recorded the number of round-trips made to the local international airport on November 15. The manager can find the sample variance and the sample standard deviation using the following steps:

Step 1 **Select the sample and record the data for the variable of interest.**

Cab	Round-trips = x
1	4
2	7
3	1
4	0
5	5
6	0
7	3
8	2
9	6
10	2

Step 2 **Select either Equation 3.12 or Equation 3.13 to compute the sample variance.**
If we use Equation 3.12,

$$s^2 = \frac{\Sigma(x - \bar{x})^2}{n-1}$$

Step 3 **Compute $\bar{x}$.**
The sample mean number of trips is

$$\bar{x} = \frac{\Sigma x}{n} = \frac{30}{10} = 3.0$$

Step 4 **Determine the sum of the squared deviations of each x-value from $\bar{x}$.**

Cab	Round-trips = x	$(x - \bar{x})$	$(x - \bar{x})^2$
1	4	1	1
2	7	4	16
3	1	−2	4
4	0	−3	9
5	5	2	4
6	0	−3	9
7	3	0	0
8	2	−1	1
9	6	3	9
10	2	−1	1
	$\Sigma = 30$	$\Sigma = 0$	$\Sigma = 54$

Step 5 Compute the sample variance using Equation 3.12.

$$s^2 = \frac{\sum(x-\bar{x})^2}{n-1} = \frac{54}{9} = 6$$

The sample variance is measured in squared units. Thus, the variance in this example is 6 trips squared.

Step 6 Compute the sample standard deviation by taking the square root of the variance (see Equation 3.14).

$$s = \sqrt{\frac{\sum(x-\bar{x})^2}{n-1}} = \sqrt{\frac{54}{9}} = \sqrt{6}$$
$$s = 2.4495 \text{ trips}$$

This sample standard deviation measures the variation in the sample data for daily round-trips to the airport for Red Line Taxi.

Business Application

Excel and Minitab Tutorial

US COMPANIES 2005 (*CONTINUED*) In the previous section we considered the financial analyst who was interested in describing the closing stock prices for 6,992 publicly traded companies. The data for these companies is in the file **US Companies 2005**. Previously we determined the following descriptive measures of the center:

Mean = $34.99

Median = $13.05

Mode = $0.08

The large difference between the mean and median is due to the extreme high stock prices for some companies.

Next, the analyst will turn her attention to measures of variability. The range (maximum − minimum) is one measure of variability. Both Excel and Minitab can compute the range. Both software packages can also be used to compute the standard deviation in stock prices, which is a more powerful measure of variation than the range. Figure 3.7 shows the Excel descriptive statistics results. We find the following measures of variation:

Range = $87,599.99

Standard Deviation = $1,056.72

Both of these values are inflated due to the one extremely high stock price (Berkshire Hathaway, at $87,600). Figure 3.8 shows the descriptive statistics with this company removed from the calculations. We see big differences in the mean, range, and standard deviation, all of which are affected by extremes. These differences are summarized as follows:

	With High Stock Price Included	With High Stock Price Excluded
Mean	$34.99	$22.46
Median	$13.05	$13.05
Mode	$0.08	$0.08
Range	$87,599.99	$10,773.76
Standard Deviation	$1,056.72	$140.44

FIGURE 3.7

Excel 2007 Descriptive Statistics Output—U.S. Company Stock Prices

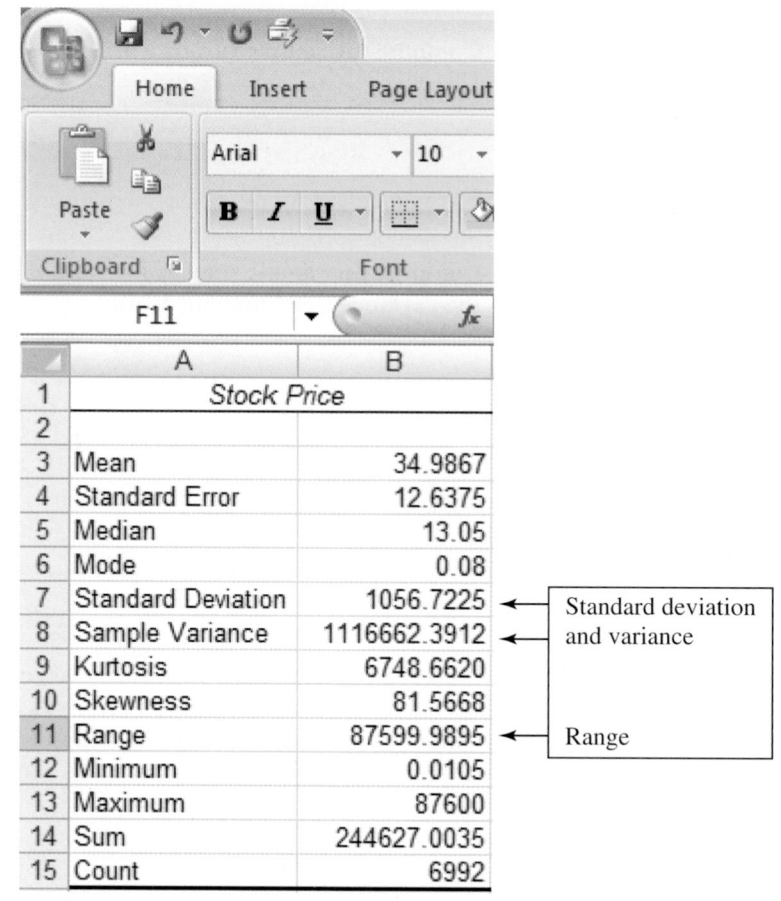

Excel 2007 Instructions:
1. Open File: US Companies 2005.xls.
2. On the **Data** tab, click on **Data Analysis**.
3. Click on **Descriptive Statistics**.
4. Define data range for the variable.
5. Check **Summary Statistics**.
6. Name output sheet.
7. On the **Home** tab, adjust decimals.

Minitab Instructions (for similar results):
1. Open file: U.S. Companies 2005.MTW.
2. Choose **Stat > Basic Statistics > Display Descriptive Statistics**.
3. In **Variables**, enter columns *Stock Price*.
4. Click **Statistics**.
5. Check required statistics.
6. Click **OK. OK**.

Consider how the analyst's report would differ depending on whether or not she included the company with the high stock price.

This brings up an important issue—what do you do with an *outlier*? An outlier can be a data value that has been incorrectly recorded in the data set or one that does not belong with the other data because it is part of a different population. These data values should be removed from the data set. An outlier can also be a very unusual data value that is simply much higher or lower than the other data values. In this case, you should be very careful before removing the data value and make sure that you can justify doing so, or your analysis may be subject to criticism.

One guideline for identifying outliers is the ±3 standard deviation rule. That is, if a value falls outside ±3 standard deviations from the mean, it is considered an outlier. In the case of the U.S. companies data, when the high stock price is included, data within the range:

$$\$34.99 \pm 3(\$1,056.72) \quad \text{or} \quad 0 - \$3,205.15$$

would be considered normal. A close look at the data in the **US Companies 2005** data file shows only Berkshire Hathaway and the index for the Dow-Jones Industrial Average, at $87,600 and $10,773.77, being outside the ±3 standard deviation range. Although these prices are correctly recorded and they do come from the population of U.S. publicly traded equity investments, they are so different from the rest that a good argument could be made for eliminating them from the analysis as outliers. Figure 3.8 shows the descriptive statistics with Berkshire Hathaway removed.

FIGURE 3.8

Excel 2007 Descriptive Statistics—Berkshire Hathaway Stock Removed

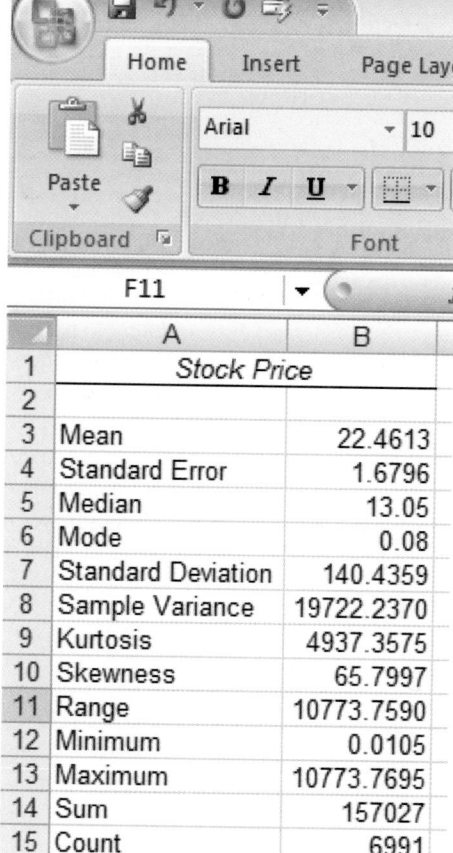

	A	B
1	Stock Price	
2		
3	Mean	22.4613
4	Standard Error	1.6796
5	Median	13.05
6	Mode	0.08
7	Standard Deviation	140.4359
8	Sample Variance	19722.2370
9	Kurtosis	4937.3575
10	Skewness	65.7997
11	Range	10773.7590
12	Minimum	0.0105
13	Maximum	10773.7695
14	Sum	157027
15	Count	6991

Excel 2007 Instructions:
1. Open File: US Companies 2005.xls.
2. On the **Data** tab, click on **Data Analysis**.
3. Click on **Descriptive Statistics**.
4. Define data range for the variable.
5. Check **Summary Statistics**.
6. Name output sheet.
7. On the **Home** tab, adjust decimals.

3-2: Exercises

Skill Development

3-25. The following data reflect the number of vacation days that a sample of employees at Hewlett-Packard have left to take before the end of the year:

3	0	2	0	1	3	5	2
5	1	3	0	0	1	3	3
4	3	1	8	4	2	4	0

a. Compute the range for these sample data.
b. Compute the variance for these sample data.
c. Compute the standard deviation for these sample data.

3-26. You are given the following data for the number of times a population of six families dined out during the previous month:

4	6	9	4	5	7

a. Compute the range for these data.
b. Compute the variance and standard deviation.
c. Assuming that these data represent a sample rather than a population, compute the variance and standard deviation. Discuss the difference between the values computed here and in part b.

3-27. The following data constitute the population of interest:

16	15	17	15	15	15
14	9	16	15	13	10
8	18	20	17	17	17
18	23	7	15	20	10
14	14	12	12	24	21

a. Compute the population variance.
b. Compute the population standard deviation.

3-28. A random sample of 15 term papers in a senior-level economics course revealed the following word counts per paper:

5176	6005	5052	5310	4188
4132	5736	5381	4983	4423
5002	4573	4209	5611	4568

Determine the range, variance, and standard deviation for the sample data.

3-29. The folllowing data show the number of hours spent watching television for 12 randomly selected freshmen attending a liberal arts college in the Midwest:

Hours of Television Viewed Weekly			
7.5	11.5	14.4	7.8
13	10.3	5.4	12
12.2	8.9	8.5	6.6

Calculate the range, variance, standard deviation, and interquartile range for the sample data.

3-30. Consider the two following samples:

27 27 25 12 15 10 20 37 31 35

and

1 3 2 16 18 16 16 4 16 118

a. Calculate the range, variance, standard deviation, and the interquartile range for each data set.
b. Which data set is most spread out based on these statistics?
c. Now remove the largest number from each data set and repeat the calculations called for in part a.
d. Compare the results of parts a and c. Which stastistic seems to be most affected by outliers?

3-31. Consider the following set of data:

24	16	23	26	30	21	15	9
18	27	14	6	14	10	12	

a. Assume the data set is a sample. Calculate the range, variance, standard deviation, and interquartile range for the data set.
b. Assume the data set is a population. Calculate the range, variance, standard deviation, and interquartile range for the data set.
c. Indicate the relationship between the statistics and the respective parameters calculated in parts a and b.

Business Applications

3-32. Computer labs at most universities are busy places. Lab managers monitor the use to make sure that the capacity of the lab is sufficient to meet the needs of the students. Recently, one lab manager collected data on a sample of students. He tracked the time the students arrived at the lab and the time they left. The elapsed times, in minutes, are shown as follows:

40	42	18	32	43	35	11	39	36	37
8	34	34	50	20	39	31	75	33	17

Compute appropriate measures of the center and variation to describe the time students spend in the computer lab.

3-33. A random sample of 20 pledges to a public radio fund-raiser revealed the following dollar pledges:

90	85	100	150
125	75	50	100
75	60	35	90
100	125	75	85
50	100	50	80

a. Compute the range, variance, standard deviation, and interquartile range for these sample data.
b. Briefly explain the difference between the range and the interquartile range as a measure of dispersion.

3-34. The Stop N Go convenience chain recently selected a random sample of 10 customers. The store monitored the number of times each customer made a purchase at the store over a two-month period. The following data were collected:

10 19 17 19 12 20 20 15 16 13

Store executives are considering a promotion in which they reward frequent purchasers with a small gift. They have decided that they will only give gifts to those shoppers whose number of visits in the past two-month period is above the mean plus 1 standard deviation. Find the minimum number of visits required to receive a gift.

3-35. The marketing director for South East Insurance has been worried about the increasing age of the company's policyholder base. She wants to determine whether a new advertising campaign has had the desired effect of attracting younger customers. She has taken a sample of 10 new policies and has found the following ages:

32 22 24 27 27 33 28 23 24 21

a. Compute the range, interquartile range, and the standard deviation for these data.
b. Before the new advertising campaign, the average age of the customers was 37.8. Based on your calculations in part a, has the advertising campaign been effective in reducing the average age of the customers?

3-36. The branch manager for Farmers and Merchants Bank has been asked to prepare a presentation for next week's board meeting. At the presentation, she will discuss the status of her branch's automobile loans. In particular, she will analyze the loan balances for a sample of 10 automobile loans. The following data were collected:

$11,509	$8,088	$13,415	$17,028	$16,754
$18,626	$4,917	$11,740	$16,393	$8,757

a. Compute the mean loan balance.
b. Compute the loan balance standard deviation.
c. Write a one-paragraph statement that uses the statistics computed in parts a and b to describe the automobile loan data at the branch.

3-37. A fast-food restaurant monitors its drive-thru service times electronically to ensure that its speed of service is meeting the company's goals. A sample of 28 drive-thru times was recently taken and is shown here.

Speed of Service (time in seconds)			
83	138	145	147
130	79	156	156
90	85	68	93
178	76	73	119
92	146	88	103
116	134	162	71
181	110	105	74

a. Calculate the range, interquartile range, variance, and standard deviation for these sample data.
b. If the minimum time and the maximum time in the sample data are both increased by 10 seconds, would this affect the value for the interquartile range that you calculated in part a? Why or why not?
c. Suppose the clock that electronically recorded the times was not working properly when the sample was taken and each of the sampled times needs to be increased by 10 seconds. How would adding 10 seconds to each of the sampled speed of service times change the sample variance of the data?

3-38. Nielsen Monitor-Plus, a service of Nielsen Media Research, is one of the leaders in advertising information services in the United States, providing advertising activity for 16 media, including television tracking, in all 210 Designated Market Areas (DMAs). One of the issues it has researched is the increasing amount of "clutter"—nonprogram minutes in an hour of prime time—including network and local commercials and advertisements for other shows. In 2004, the average nonprogramming minutes in an hour of prime-time broadcasting for network TV was 15:48 minutes. For cable TV, the average was 14:55 minutes.
a. Calculate the difference in the average "clutter" between network and cable TV.
b. Suppose the standard deviation in the amount of "clutter" for both the network and cable TV was either 5 minutes or 15 seconds. Which standard deviation would lead you to conclude that there was a major difference in the two "clutter" averages? Comment.

3-39. The Bureau of Labor Statistics in its *Monthly Labor Review* published the "over-the-month" percent change in the price index for imports from April 2004 to April 2005. This data is reproduced next.

Month	Apr	May	Jun	Jul	Aug	Sep	Oct
ΔIndex	0.2	1.5	−0.2	0.4	1.5	0.5	1.6
Month	Nov	Dec	Jan	Feb	Mar	Apr	
ΔIndex	−0.3	−1.4	0.6	.9	2.0	0.8	

a. Calculate the mean, standard deviation, and the interquartile range for the 9 months of 2004 and the 4 months of 2005.
b. Compare the two averages that were calculated in part a. What do these two measurements indicate about the price index in each time period?
c. Compare the two standard deviations that were calculated in part a. What do these two measurements indicate about the price index in each time period?

3-40. The U.S. Government Accountability Office indicated in July 29, 2005 that the price of college textbooks had been rising an average of 6% annually since the academic year 1987–88. The report estimated that the average cost of books and supplies for first-time, full-time students at four-year public universities for the academic year 2003–2004 had reached $898. A data set ($) that would produce this average follows:

537.51	1032.52	1119.17	877.27	856.87	739.91	963.79
847.92	1393.81	524.68	1012.91	1176.46	944.60	708.26
1074.35	778.87	967.91	562.55	789.50	1051.65	

a. Calculate the mean and standard deviation.
b. Determine the number of standard deviations the most extreme cost is away from the mean. If you were to advise a prospective student concerning the money the student should save to afford the cost of books and supplies for at least 90% of the colleges, determine the amount you would suggest. (*Hint*: Don't forget the yearly inflation of the cost of books and supplies.)

Computer Database Exercises

3-41. Each year, *Business Week* publishes information and rankings of MBA programs. The data file **MBA Analysis** contains data on several variables for eight reputable MBA programs as presented in the October 2, 2000 issue of *Business Week*. The variables include pre- and post-MBA salary, percentage salary increase, undergraduate GPA, average GMAT score, annual tuition, and expected annual student cost. Compute the mean, median, range, variance, and the standard deviation for each of the variables in the database and write a short report that summarizes the data using these measures. Include any appropriate charts or graphs to assist in your report.

3-42. The First City Real Estate Company lists and sells residential real estate property in and around Yuma, Arizona. At a recent company meeting, the managing partner asked the office administrator to provide a descriptive analysis of the asking prices of the homes the company currently has listed. Currently, this list includes 319 homes; the price data, along with other home characteristics, are included in the data file called **First City Real Estate**. These data constitute a population.

a. Compute the mean listing price.

b. Compute the median listing price.

c. Compute the range in listing prices.

d. Compute the standard deviation in listing prices.

e. Write a short report using the statistics computed in parts a–d to describe the prices of the homes currently listed by First City Real Estate.

3-43. The manager of a phone kiosk in the Valley Mall recently collected data on a sample of 50 customers who purchased a cell phone and a monthly call plan. The data she recorded are in the data file called **Phone Survey**.

a. The manager is interested in describing the difference between male and female customers with respect to the price of the phone purchased. She wants to compute mean and standard deviation of phone purchase price for each group of customers.

b. The manager is also interested in an analysis of the phone purchase price based on whether the use will be for home or business. Again, she wants to compute mean and standard deviation of phone purchase price for each group of customers.

3-44. Suppose an investigation to determine whether the increased availability of generic drugs, Internet drug purchases, and cost controls has reduced

out-of-pocket drug expenses. As a part of the investigation, a random sample of 196 privately insured adults with incomes above 200% of the poverty level was taken, and their 2005 out-of-pocket medical expenses for prescription drugs were collected. The data are in the file **Drug Expenses**.

a. Calculate the mean and median for the sample data.

b. Calculate the range, variance, standard deviation, and interquartile range for the sample data.

c. Construct a box and whisker plot for the sample data.

d. Write a short report that describes out-of-pocket drug expenses for privately insured adults whose incomes are greater than 200% of the poverty level.

3-45. In an article entitled "The Best Executive MBAs" (Louis Lavelle, October 24, 2005), *Business Week* provided data concerning the top 25 Executive MBA programs. The tuition for each of the schools selected was given. A file entitled **EMBA** contains this data.

a. Calculate the 20th, 40th, 60th, and 80th percentile among the ranks.

b. Calculate the mean and standard deviation of the tuition for the five subgroups defined by the rank percentiles in part a. (*Hint*: For this purpose, are the data subgroups, samples, or populations?)

c. Do the various subgroups' descriptive statistics echo their standing among the listed programs? Comment.

3-46. PricewaterhouseCoopers Saratoga released its 2005/2006 Human Capital Index Report. It indicated that the average hiring cost for an American company to fill a job vacancy in 2004 was $3,270. Sample data for recent job hires is in a file entitled **Hired**.

a. Calculate the variance and standard deviation for the sample data.

b. Construct a box and whisker plot. Does this plot indicate that extreme values (outliers) may be inflating the measures of spread calculated in part a?

c. Suggest and calculated a measure of spread that is not affected by outliers.

3.3 Using the Mean and the Standard Deviation Together

In the previous sections, we introduced several important descriptive measures that are useful for transforming data into meaningful information. Two of the most important of these measures are the mean and the standard deviation. In this section, we discuss several statistical tools that combine these two.

CHAPTER OUTCOME #4

Coefficient of Variation

The standard deviation measures the variation in a set of data. For decision makers, the standard deviation indicates how spread out a distribution is. For distributions having the same mean, the distribution with the largest standard deviation has the greatest relative spread. When two or more distributions have different means, the relative spread cannot be determined by merely comparing standard deviations.

Coefficient of Variation
The ratio of the standard deviation to the mean expressed as a percentage. The coefficient of variation is used to measure variation relative to the mean.

The **coefficient of variation**, (*CV*), is used to measure the relative variation for distributions with different means.

The coefficient of variation for a population is computed using Equation 3.15, whereas Equation 3.16 is used for sample data.

Population Coefficient of Variation

$$CV = \frac{\sigma}{\mu}(100)$$

(3.15)

Sample Coefficient of Variation

$$CV = \frac{s}{\bar{x}}(100)$$

(3.16)

When the coefficients of variation for two or more distributions are compared, the distribution with the largest *CV* is said to have the greatest relative spread.

In finance, the *CV* measures the relative risk of a stock portfolio. Assume portfolio A has a collection of stocks that average a 12% return with a standard deviation of 3% and portfolio B has an average return of 6% with a standard deviation of 2%. We can compute the *CV* values for each as follows:

$$CV(A) = \frac{3}{12}(100) = 25\%$$

and

$$CV(B) = \frac{2}{6}(100) = 33\%$$

Even though portfolio B has a lower standard deviation, it would be considered more risky than portfolio A because B's *CV* is 33% and A's *CV* is 25%.

EXAMPLE 3-13 Computing the Coefficient of Variation

TRY PROBLEM 3.47

Agra-Tech Industries   Agra-Tech Industries has recently introduced feed supplements for both cattle and hogs that will increase the rate at which the animals gain weight. Three years of feedlot tests indicate that steers fed the supplement will weigh an average of 125 pounds more than those not fed the supplement. However, not every steer on the supplement has the same weight gain; results vary. The standard deviation in weight-gain advantage for the steers in the three-year study has been 10 pounds.

Similar tests with hogs indicate those fed the supplement average 40 additional pounds compared with hogs not given the supplement. The standard deviation for the hogs was also 10 pounds. Even though the standard deviation is the same for both cattle and hogs, the mean weight gain differs. Therefore, the coefficient of variation is needed to compare relative variability. The coefficient of variation for each is computed using the following steps:

Step 1 **Collect the sample (or population) of data for the variable of interest.**
In this case, we have two samples: weight gain for cattle and weight gain for hogs.

Step 2 **Compute the mean and the standard deviation.**
For the two samples in this example, we get

$$\text{Cattle: } \bar{x} = 125 \text{ lb and } s = 10 \text{ lb}$$
$$\text{Hogs: } \bar{x} = 40 \text{ lb and } s = 10 \text{ lb}$$

Step 3 **Compute the coefficient of variation using Equation 3.15 (for populations) or Equation 3.16 (for samples).**
Because the data in this example are from samples, the *CV* is computed using

$$CV = \frac{s}{\bar{x}}(100)$$

For each data set, we get

$$CV(\text{cattle}) = \frac{10}{125}(100) = 8\%$$

$$CV(\text{hogs}) = \frac{10}{40}(100) = 25\%$$

These results indicate that hogs exhibit much greater relative variability in weight gain compared with cattle.

CHAPTER OUTCOME #4

Empirical Rule
If the data distribution is bell-shaped, then the interval

$\mu \pm 1\sigma$ contains approximately 68% of the values

$\mu \pm 2\sigma$ contains approximately 95% of the values

$\mu \pm 3\sigma$ contains virtually all of the data values

Business Application

Excel and Minitab Tutorial

The Empirical Rule

A tool that is helpful in describing data in certain circumstances is called the **Empirical Rule**. In order for the Empirical Rule to be used, the frequency distribution must be bell-shaped, such as the one shown in Figure 3.9.

BURGER N' BREW The standard deviation can be thought of as a measure of distance from the mean. Consider the Phoenix Burger n' Brew restaurant chain, which records the number of each hamburger option it sells each day at each location. The number of chili burgers sold each day for the past 365 days are in the file called **Burger N' Brew**. Figure 3.10 shows the frequency histogram for those data. The distribution is nearly *symmetrical* and approximately *bell-shaped*. The mean number of chili burgers sold was 15.1, with a standard deviation of 3.1.

The Empirical Rule is a very useful statistical concept for helping us understand the data in a bell-shaped distribution. In the Burger n' Brew example, with $\bar{x} = 15.1$ and $s = 3.1$, if we move 1 standard deviation in each direction from the mean, *approximately* 68% of the data should lie within the range:

$$15.1 \pm 1(3.1)$$

$$12.0 - - - - - - - - - - - - - - 18.2$$

The actual number of days Burger n' Brew sold between 12 and 18 chili burgers is 262. Thus, out of 365 days, 72% of the days Burger n' Brew sold between 12 and 18 chili burgers. (The reason that we didn't get exactly 68% is that the distribution in Figure 3.10 is not perfectly bell-shaped.)

FIGURE 3.9

Illustrating the Empirical Rule for the Bell-Shaped Distribution

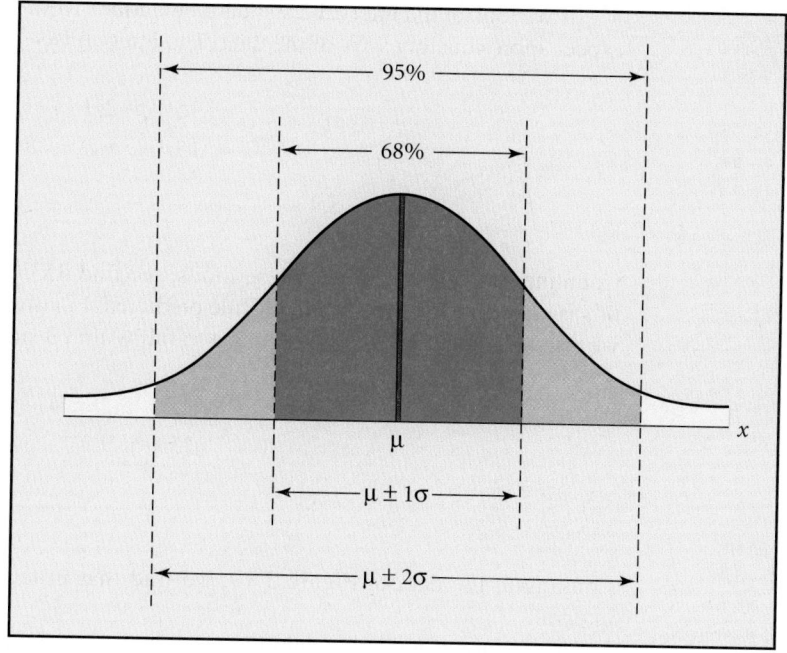

FIGURE 3.10

Excel 2007 Histogram for Burger n' Brew Data

Minitab Instructions (for similar results):

1. Open file: BurgerNBrew. MTW.
2. Choose **Graph > Histogram**.
3. Click **Simple**.
4. Click **OK**.
5. In **Graph variables**, enter data column *Chili-Burgers Sold.*
6. Click **OK**.

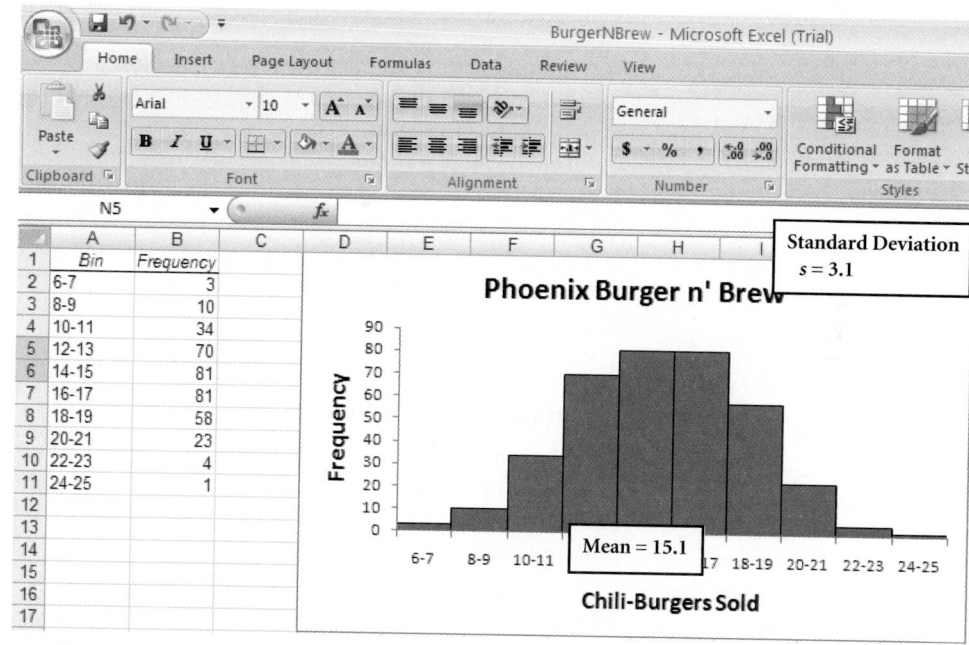

Excel 2007 Instructions:

1. Open file: BurgerNBrew.xls.
2. Set up Bins (upper limit of each class).
3. On the **Data** tab, click on **Data Analysis—Histogram**.
4. Supply data range and bin range.
5. Put on a new worksheet ply and include the **Chart Output**.

6. Right-mouse-click on the bars and use the **Formal Data Series Options** to set gap width to zero and add lines to the bars.
7. Convert the bins to actual class labels by typing labels in column A. Note, bin 7 is labeled 6-7.

If we look at the interval 2 standard deviations from either side of the mean, we would expect approximately 95% of the data. The interval is

$$15.1 \pm 2(3.1)$$
$$15.1 \pm 6.2$$

$$8.9 - - - - - - - - - - - - - 21.30$$

Counting the values between these limits, we find 353 of the 365 values, or 97%. Again this is close to what the Empirical Rule predicted. Finally, according to the Empirical Rule, we would expect almost all of the data to fall within 3 standard deviations. The interval is

$$15.1 \pm 3(3.1)$$
$$15.1 \pm 9.3$$

$$5.80 - - - - - - - - - - - - - - 24.40$$

Looking at the data in Figure 3.10, we find that in fact all the data do fall within this interval.

Therefore, if we know only the mean and the standard deviation for a set of data, the Empirical Rule gives us a tool for describing how the data are distributed, if the distribution is bell-shaped.

Tchebysheff's Theorem

Tchebysheff's Theorem
Regardless of how data are distributed, *at least* $(1 - 1/k^2)$ of the values will fall within k standard deviations of the mean. For example:

At least $\left(1 - \dfrac{1}{1^2}\right) = 0 = 0\%$ of the values will fall within $k = 1$ standard deviation of the mean.

At least $\left(1 - \dfrac{1}{2^2}\right) = \dfrac{3}{4} = 75\%$ of the values will lie within $k = 2$ standard deviation of the mean.

At least $\left(1 - \dfrac{1}{3^2}\right) = \dfrac{8}{9} = 89\%$ of the values will lie within $k = 3$ standard deviation of the mean.

The Empirical Rule applies when a distribution is bell-shaped. But what about the many situations when a distribution is skewed and not bell-shaped? In these cases, we can use **Tchebysheff's theorem**.

Tchebysheff's theorem is conservative. It tells us nothing about the data within 1 standard deviation of the mean. Tchebysheff indicates that *at least* 75% of the data will fall within 2 standard deviations—it could be more. If we applied Tchebysheff's theorem to bell-shaped distributions, the percentage estimates are very low. The thing to remember is that Tchebysheff's theorem applies to *any distribution*. This gives it great flexibility.

Standardized Data Values

CHAPTER OUTCOME #4

Standardized Data Values
The number of standard deviations a value is from the mean. Standardized data values are sometimes referred to as *z*-scores.

When you are dealing with quantitative data, you will sometimes want to convert the measures to a form called **standardized data values**. This is especially useful when we wish to compare data from two or more distributions when the data scales for the two distributions are substantially different.

Business Application

HUMAN RESOURCES Consider a company that uses placement exams as part of its hiring process. The company currently will accept scores from either of two tests: AIMS Hiring and BHS-Screen. The problem is that the AIMS Hiring test has an average score of 2,000 and a standard deviation of 200, whereas the BHS-Screen test has an average score of 80 with a standard deviation of 12. (These means and standard deviations were developed from a large number of people who have taken the two tests.) How can the company compare applicants when the average scores and measures of spread are so different for the two tests? One approach is to *standardize* the test scores.

Suppose the company is considering two applicants, John and Mary. John took the AIMS Hiring test and scored 2,344, whereas Mary took the BHS-Screen and scored 95. Their scores can be standardized using Equation 3.17.

Standardized Population Data

$$z = \frac{x - \mu}{\sigma} \tag{3.17}$$

where:

x = Original data value
μ = Population mean
σ = Population standard deviation
z = Standard score (number of standard deviations x is from μ)

If you are working with sample data rather than a population, Equation 3.18 can be used to standardize the values.

Standardized Sample Data

$$z = \frac{x - \bar{x}}{s} \tag{3.18}$$

where:

x = Original data value
$\bar{x}$ = Sample mean
s = Sample standard deviation
z = The standard score

We can standardize the test scores for John and Mary using

$$z = \frac{x - \mu}{\sigma}$$

For the AIMS Hiring test, the mean, μ, is 2,000, and the standard deviation, σ, equals 200. John's score of 2,344 converts to

$$z = \frac{2,344 - 2,000}{200}$$
$$z = 1.72$$

The BHS Screen has $\mu = 80$ and $\sigma = 12$. Mary's score of 95 converts to

$$z = \frac{95 - 80}{12}$$
$$z = 1.25$$

Compared to the average score on the AIMS Hiring test, John's score is 1.72 standard deviations higher. Mary's score is only 1.25 standard deviations higher than the average score on the BHS-Screen test. Therefore, even though the two tests used different scales, standardizing the data allows us to conclude John scored relatively better on his test than Mary did on her test.

SUMMARY   Converting Data to Standardized Values

For a set of quantitative data, each data value can be converted to a corresponding standardized value by determining how many standard deviations the value is from the mean. Here are the steps to do this.

1. Collect the population or sample values for the quantitative variable of interest.
2. Compute the population mean and standard deviation or the sample mean and standard deviation.

3. Convert the values to standardized z-values using Equation 3.17 or Equation 3.18. For populations,

$$z = \frac{x - \mu}{\sigma}$$

For samples,

$$z = \frac{x - \bar{x}}{s}$$

EXAMPLE 3-14   Converting Data to Standardized Values

TRY PROBLEM 3.51

SAT and ACT Exams   Many colleges and universities require students to submit either SAT or ACT scores or both. One eastern university requires both exam scores. However, in assessing whether to admit a student, the university uses whichever exam score favors the student among all the applicants. Suppose the school receives 4,000 applications for admission. To determine which exam will be used for each student, the school will standardize the exam scores from both tests. To do this, it can use the following steps:

Step 1   Collect data.
The university will collect the data for the 4,000 SAT scores and the 4,000 ACT scores for those students who applied for admission.

Step 2   Compute the mean and standard deviation.
Assuming that these data reflect the population of interest for the university, the population mean is computed using

$$\text{SAT:} \quad \mu = \frac{\sum x}{N} = 1,255 \qquad \text{ACT:} \quad \mu = \frac{\sum x}{N} = 28.3$$

The standard deviation is computed using

$$\text{SAT:} \quad \sigma = \sqrt{\frac{\sum (x - \mu)^2}{N}} = 72 \qquad \text{ACT:} \quad \sigma = \sqrt{\frac{\sum (x - \mu)^2}{N}} = 2.4$$

Step 3   Standardize the data.
Convert the x-values to z-values using

$$z = \frac{x - \mu}{\sigma}$$

Suppose a particular applicant has an SAT score of 1,228 and an ACT score of 27. These test scores can be converted to standardized scores.

$$\text{SAT:} \quad z = \frac{x - \mu}{\sigma} = \frac{1,228 - 1,255}{72} = -0.375$$

$$\text{ACT:} \quad z = \frac{x - \mu}{\sigma} = \frac{27 - 28.3}{2.4} = -0.542$$

The negative z-values indicate that this student is below the mean on both the SAT and ACT exams. Because the university wishes to use the score that most favors the student, it will use the SAT score. The student is only 0.375 standard deviations below the SAT mean, compared with 0.542 standard deviations below the ACT mean.

3-3: Exercises

Skill Development

3-47. You are given the following parameters for two populations:

Population 1	Population 2
$\mu = 700$	$\mu = 29,000$
$\sigma = 50$	$\sigma = 5,000$

a. Compute the coefficient of variation for each population.
b. Based upon the answers to part a, which population has data values that are more variable relative to the size of the population mean?

3-48. Two distributions of data are being analyzed. Distribution A has a mean = 500 and a standard deviation equal to 100. Distribution B has a mean = 10 and a standard deviation equal to 4.0. Based on this information, use the coefficient of variation to determine which distribution has greater relative variation.

3-49. Given two distributions with the following characteristics:

Distribution A	Distribution B
$\mu = 45,600$	$\mu = 33.40$
$\sigma = 6,333$	$\sigma = 4.05$

If a value from distribution A is 50,000 and a value from distribution B is 40.0, convert each value to a standardized z-value and indicate which one is relatively closer to its respective mean.

3-50. A population of unknown shape has a mean of 3,000 and a standard deviation of 200.
a. Find the minimum proportion of observations in the population that are in the range 2,600 to 3,400.
b. Determine the maximum proportion of the observations that are above 3,600.
c. What statement could you make concerning the proportion of observations that are smaller than 2,400?

3-51. The mean time that a certain model of light bulb will last is 400 hours with a standard deviation equal to 50 hours.

a. Calculate the standardized value for a light bulb that lasts 500 hours.
b. Assuming that the distribution hours that light bulbs last is bell-shaped, what percentage of bulbs could be expected to last longer than 500 hours?

3-52. Consider the following set of sample data:

78	121	143	88	110	107	62	122	130	95	78	139	89	125

a. Compute the mean and standard deviation for these sample data.
b. Calculate the coefficient of variation for these sample data and interpret its meaning.
c. Using Tchebysheff's Theorem, determine the range of values that should include at least 89% of the data. Count the number of data values that fall into this range and comment on whether your interval range was conservative or not.

3-53. If a sample mean is 1,000 and the sample standard deviation is 250, then determine the standardized value for
a. $x = 800$
b. $x = 1,200$
c. $x = 1,000$

3-54. The following data represent random samples taken from two different populations, A and B:

A	31	10	69	25	62	61	46	74	57
B	1030	1111	1155	978	943	983	932	1067	1013

a. Compute the mean and standard deviation for the sample data randomly selected from population A.
b. Compute the mean and standard deviation for the sample data randomly selected from population B.
c. Which population has the greater spread when measured by the standard deviation?
d. Compute the coefficient of variation for the sample data selected from population A and from population B. Which sample exhibits the greater relative variation?

3-55. Consider the following sample:

22	46	25	37	35	84	33	54	80	37
76	34	48	86	41	13	49	45	62	47
72	70	91	51	91	43	56	25	12	65

a. Calculate the mean and standard deviation for this data.

b. Determine the percentage of data values that fall in each of the following intervals: $\bar{x} \pm s, \bar{x} \pm 2s, \bar{x} \pm 3s$.

c. Compare these with the percentages that should be expected from a bell-shaped distribution. Does it seem plausible that this data came from a bell-shaped population? Explain.

3-56. Consider the following population:

71	89	65	97	46	52	99	41	62	88
73	50	91	71	52	86	92	60	70	91
73	98	56	80	70	63	55	61	40	95

a. Determine the mean and variance.

b. Determine the percentage of data values that fall in each of the following intervals: $\bar{x} \pm 2s, \bar{x} \pm 3s, \bar{x} \pm 4s$.

c. Compare these with the percentages specified by Tchebysheff's Theorem.

Business Applications

3-57. A company's call center has both Spanish-speaking and English-speaking service representatives. A random sample of 11 calls to English-speaking service representatives and a random sample of 14 calls to Spanish-speaking service representatives was taken and the time to complete the call was measured. The results (in seconds) are as follows:

Time to Complete the Call (in seconds)
English-Speaking 131 80 140 118 79 94 103 145 113 100 122
Spanish-Speaking 170 177 150 208 151 127 147 140 109 184 119 149 129 152

a. Compute the mean and standard deviation for the time to complete calls to English-speaking service representatives.

b. Compute the mean and standard deviation for the time to complete calls to Spanish-speaking service representatives.

c. Compute the coefficient of variation for the time to complete calls to English-speaking and Spanish-speaking service representatives. Which group has the greater relative variability in the time to complete calls?

d. Construct box and whisker plots for the time required to complete the two types of calls and briefly discuss.

3-58. A pharmaceutical company is developing a new pain medication. Two drugs are currently under development. One consideration in the evaluation of the medication is how long the pain-killing effects of the drug last. A random sample of 12 tests for each drug revealed the following times (in minutes) until the effects of the drug were neutralized. The random samples are as follows:

Drug A	Drug B
258	219
214	283
243	291
227	277
235	258
222	273
240	289
245	260
245	286
234	265
243	284
211	266

a. Calculate the mean and standard deviation for each of the two drugs.

b. Based on the sample means calculated in part a, which drug appears to be effective longer?

c. Based on the sample standard deviations calculated in part a, which drug appears to have the greater variability in effect time?

d. Calculate the sample coefficient of variation for the two drugs. Based on the coefficient of variation, which drug has the greater variability in its time until the effect is neutralized?

3-59. The Cirus Group is a parts supplier for the aerospace industry. Recently, the company was considering switching to a new supplier for one of the component parts it needs for an assembly that Cirus sells to Boeing. At issue is the variability of the components supplied by the new supplier compared to that of the existing supplier. The existing supplier makes the desired part with a mean diameter of 3.75 inches and a standard deviation of 0.078 inches. Unfortunately, Cirus does not have any of the exact same parts from the new supplier. Instead, the new supplier has sent a sample of 20 parts of a different size that it claims are representative of the type of work it can do. These sample data are shown here and in the data file called **Cirus**.

Diameters (in inches)									
18.018	17.856	18.095	17.992	18.086	17.812	17.988	17.996	18.129	18.003
17.983	18.153	17.996	17.908	18.214	18.313	17.948	18.219	18.079	17.799

Prepare a short letter to The Cirus Group indicating which supplier you would recommend based on relative variability.

3-60. Robinson & Associates performs employment screening for large companies in southern California. It usually follows a two-step process. First, potential applicants are given a test that covers basic knowledge and intelligence. If applicants score between a certain range, they are called in for an interview. If they score below a certain point, they are sent a rejection letter. If applicants score above a certain point, they are sent directly to the client's human resources office without the interview. Recently, Robinson & Associates began working with a new client and formulated a new test just for this company. Thirty people were given the test, which is supposed to produce scores that are distributed according to a bell-shaped distribution. The following data reflect the scores of those 30 people. The data are also in a file called **Robinson & Associates**.

76	75	74	56	61	76
62	96	68	62	78	76
84	67	60	96	77	59
67	81	66	71	69	65
58	77	82	75	76	67

Robinson & Associates has in the past issued a rejection letter with no interview to the lower 16% taking the test. They also send the upper 2.5% directly to the company without an interview. Everyone else is interviewed. Based on the data and the assumption of a bell-shaped distribution, what score should be used for the two cutoffs?

3-61. The College Board's Annual Survey of Colleges provides up-to-date information on tuition and other expenses associated with attending public and private nonprofit institutions of postsecondary education in the United States. Each fall, the College Board releases the survey results on how much colleges and universities are charging undergraduate students in the new academic year. The survey indicated that the average published tuition and fees for 2005–2006 were $5,491 at public four-year colleges and universities and $21,235 at private, nonprofit four-year colleges and universities. The standard deviation was approximately $3,000 at public four-year colleges and universities and approximately $10,000 for private colleges and universities.

a. Do the private, nonprofit four-year colleges and universities have the largest relative variability? Provide statistical evidence to support your answer.

b. If the data on published tuition and fees were bell-shaped, determine the largest and smallest amount paid at the four-year private, nonprofit colleges and universities.

c. Based upon your answer to part b, do you believe that the data are bell-shaped? Support your answer using statistical reasoning.

3-62. Robert J. Samuelson of *The Washington Post Weekly Edition* ("Homes as Hummers," July 18–24, 2005) indicated that "In 2005, about 80% of the estimated $200 billion of federal housing subsidies consists of tax breaks (mainly deductions for mortgage interest payments and preferential treatment for profits on home sales). . . . Federal housing benefits average $8,268 for those with incomes between $50,000 and $200,000 and $365 for those with income of $40,000 to $50,000." Suppose the standard deviations of the housing benefits in these two categories were equal to $2,750 and $120, respectively.

a. Examine the two standard deviations. What do these indicate about the range of benefits enjoyed by the two groups?

b. Repeat part a using the coefficient of variation as the measure of relative variation.

Computer Database Exercises

3-63. Nike ONE Black is one of the golf balls Nike, Inc. produces. It must meet the specifications of the United States Golf Association (USGA). The USGA mandates that the diameter of the ball shall not be less than 1.682 inches (42.67 mm). In order to verify that this specification is met, sample golf balls are taken from the production line and measured. This data are found in the file entitled **Diameter**.

a. Calculate the mean and standard deviation of this sample.

b. Examine the specification for the diameter of the golf ball again. Does it seem that the data could possibly be bell-shaped? Explain.

c. Determine the proportion of diameters in the following intervals: $\bar{x} \pm 2s, \bar{x} \pm 3s, \bar{x} \pm 4s$. Compare these with the percentages specified by Tchebysheff's Theorem.

3-64. The Centers for Disease Control and Prevention (CDC) started the Vessel Sanitation Program (VSP) in the early 1970s because of several disease outbreaks on cruise ships. VSP was established to protect the health of passengers and crew by minimizing the risk of gastrointestinal illness on cruise ships. Inspections are scored on a point system of maximum 100, and cruise ships earn a score based on the criteria. Ships that score an 86 or higher have a satisfactory sanitation level. Data from the most recent inspection date (up to October 8, 2005) are contained in a file entitled **Cruiscore**.

a. Calculate the mean, standard deviation, the median, and the interquartile range. Which of these measures would seem most appropriate to characterize this data set?

b. Produce a box and whisker plot of the data. Would the Empirical Rule or Tchebysheff's Theorem be appropriate for describing this data set? Explain.

c. If you wished to travel only on those ships that are at the 90th percentile or above in terms of sanitation, what would be the lowest sanitation score you would find acceptable?

3-65. Airfare prices were collected on October 23, 2005 for a round-trip from Los Angeles (LAX) to San Francisco (SFO). Airfare prices were also collected for a round-trip from Los Angeles (LAX) to Barcelona, Spain (BCN). Airfares were obtained for the designated and nearby airports. The passenger was to fly coach class round-trip, staying seven days. The data are contained in a file entitled **Airfare**.

a. Calculate the mean and standard deviation for each of the flights.

b. Calculate an appropriate measure of the relative variability of these two flights.

c. A British friend of yours is currently in Barcelona and wishes to fly to Los Angeles. If the flight fares are the same but priced in English pounds, determine his mean, standard deviation, and measure of relative dispersion for that data. (*Note*: $1 = 0.566 GBP.)

3-66. April 15th every year is a day that most adults in the United States can relate to—the day that federal and state income taxes are due. Although there have been several attempts by Congress and the Internal Revenue Service over the past few years to simplify the income tax process, many people still have a difficult time completing their tax return properly. To draw attention to this problem, a West Coast newspaper has asked 50 CPA firms to complete the same tax return for a hypothetical head of household. The CPA firms have their tax experts complete the return with the objective of determining the total federal income tax liability. The data in the file called **Taxes** shows the taxes owed as figured by each of the 50 CPA firms. Theoretically, they should all come up with the same taxes owed.

Based on these data, write a short article for the paper that describes the results of this experiment. Include in your article such descriptive statistics as the mean, median, and standard deviation. You might consider using percentiles, the coefficient of variation, and Tchebysheff's Theorem to help describe the data.

3-67. Doing business internationally is no longer something reserved for the largest companies. In fact, medium-size and, in some cases, even small companies are finding themselves with the opportunity to do business internationally. One factor that will be important for world trade is the growth rate of the population of the world's countries. The data file called **Countries** contains data on the 2000 population and the growth rate between 1990 and 2000 for 74 countries throughout the world. Based on these data, which countries had growth rates that exceeded 2 standard deviations higher than the mean growth rate? Which countries had growth rates more than 2 standard deviations below the mean growth rate?

Summary and Conclusions

Transforming data into useful information is an important activity for business decision makers. Chapter 3 has introduced a variety of numerical measures that can be used either by themselves or in conjunction with the graphical techniques introduced in Chapter 2. These measures can be computed for the population as a whole or from a sample taken from the population.

Two main categories of measures were introduced. These were measures of the center and measures of spread or variation. The two most frequently used measures of central location are the mean and the median. Generally, the mean is preferred. However, when the data are highly skewed or when the data level is ordinal, the median is preferred. Other measures of location, including the mode, percentiles, and quartiles, were introduced.

The most frequently used measure of variation is the standard deviation. This measure uses all the data and measures the spread of the individual observations around the mean. Other measures include the range and the interquartile range. Figure 3.11 summarizes the measures of location and spread that were discussed in this chapter.

When the numerical measures introduced in this chapter are effectively combined with the graphical techniques from Chapter 2, you will have the capability of transforming data into information. These concepts and skills will be utilized throughout the remainder of this text and will be highly valuable to you in other courses and in your careers after graduation.

FIGURE 3.11

Summary of Numerical Statistical Measures

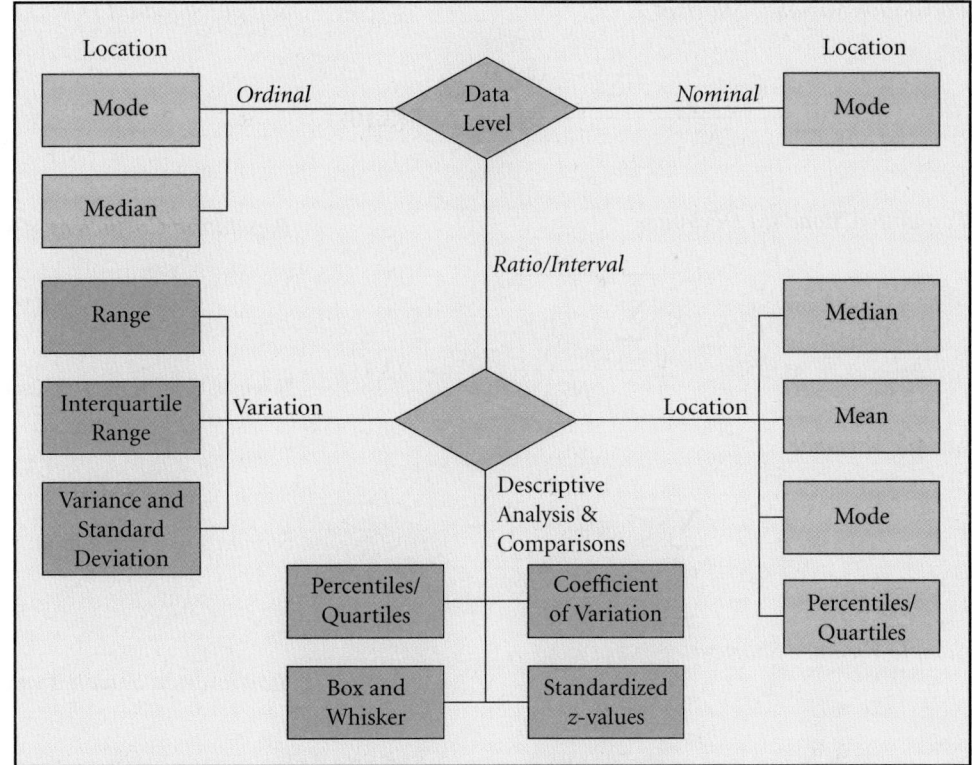

Equations

Population Mean

$$\mu = \frac{\sum_{i=1}^{N} x_i}{N} \qquad \textbf{(3.1)}$$

Sample Mean

$$\bar{x} = \frac{\sum_{i=1}^{n} x_i}{n} \qquad \textbf{(3.2)}$$

Median Index Point

$$i = \frac{1}{2}(n) \qquad \textbf{(3.3)}$$

Weighted Mean for a Population

$$\mu_w = \frac{\sum w_i x_i}{\sum w_i} \qquad \textbf{(3.4)}$$

Weighted Mean for a Sample

$$\bar{x}_w = \frac{\sum w_i x_i}{\sum w_i} \qquad \textbf{(3.5)}$$

Percentile Location Value

$$i = \frac{p}{100}(n) \qquad \textbf{(3.6)}$$

Range

$$R = \text{Maximum Value} - \text{Minimum Value} \qquad \textbf{(3.7)}$$

Interquartile Range

$$\text{Interquartile Range} = \text{Third Quartile} - \text{First Quartile} \qquad \textbf{(3.8)}$$

Population Variance

$$\sigma^2 = \frac{\sum_{i=1}^{N} (x_i - \mu)^2}{N} \qquad \textbf{(3.9)}$$

Population Variance Shortcut

$$\sigma^2 = \frac{\Sigma(x-\mu)^2}{N} = \frac{\Sigma x^2 - \frac{(\Sigma x)^2}{N}}{N} \qquad \textbf{(3.10)}$$

Population Standard Deviation

$$\sigma = \sqrt{\sigma^2} = \sqrt{\frac{\sum_{i=1}^{N}(x_i-\mu)^2}{N}} \qquad \textbf{(3.11)}$$

Sample Variance

$$s^2 = \frac{\sum_{i=1}^{n}(x_i-\bar{x})^2}{n-1} \qquad \textbf{(3.12)}$$

Sample Variance Shortcut

$$s^2 = \frac{\Sigma x^2 - \frac{(\Sigma x)^2}{n}}{n-1} \qquad \textbf{(3.13)}$$

Sample Standard Deviation

$$s = \sqrt{s^2} = \sqrt{\frac{\sum_{i=1}^{n}(x_i-\bar{x})^2}{n-1}} \qquad \textbf{(3.14)}$$

Population Coefficient of Variation

$$CV = \frac{\sigma}{\mu}(100) \qquad \textbf{(3.15)}$$

Sample Coefficient of Variation

$$CV = \frac{s}{\bar{x}}(100) \qquad \textbf{(3.16)}$$

Standardized Population Data

$$z = \frac{x-\mu}{\sigma} \qquad \textbf{(3.17)}$$

Standardized Sample Data

$$z = \frac{x-\bar{x}}{s} \qquad \textbf{(3.18)}$$

Key Terms

Box and whisker plots 107	Parameter 92	Standardized data
Coefficient of variation 129	Percentiles 105	values 132
Data array 98	Population mean 92	Statistic 92
Empirical Rule 130	Quartiles 107	Symmetric data, 100
Interquartile range 116	Range 116	Tchebysheff's
Left-skewed data 100	Right-skewed data 100	Theorem 132
Mean 92	Sample mean 96	Variance 118
Median 98	Skewed data 100	Variation 116
Mode 101	Standard deviation 118	Weighted mean 104

Chapter Exercises

Conceptual Questions

3-68. Consider the following questions concerning the sample variance:

a. Is it possible for a variance to be negative? Explain.

b. What is the smallest value a variance can be? Under what conditions does the variance equal this smallest value?

c. Under what conditions is the sample variance smaller than the corresponding sample standard deviation?

3-69. For a continuous variable that has a bell-shaped distribution, determine the percentiles associated with the endpoints of the intervals specified in the Empirical Rule.

3-70. Consider that the Empirical Rule stipulates that virtually all of the data values are within the interval $\mu \pm 3\sigma$. Use this stipulation to determine an approximation for the standard deviation involving the range.

3-71. At almost every university in the United States, the university computes student grade point averages. The following scale is typically used by universities:

A = 4 points   B = 3 points   C = 2 points
D = 1 point   F = 0 points

Discuss what, if any, problems might exist when GPAs for two students are compared? What about comparing GPAs for students from two different universities?

3-72. Since the standard deviation of a set of data requires more effort to compute than does the range, what advantages does the standard deviation have when discussing the spread in a set of data?

3-73. The mode seems like a very simple measure of the location of a distribution. When would the mode be preferred over the median or the mean?

Business Applications

3-74. The *Detroit News* reported (February 15, 2004) that over 221 million computer and video games were sold in 2002—nearly two games for every U.S. household. Sixty percent of Americans age 6 or older—about 145 million people—play computer and video games. Gamers spend an average of 3 to 4 hours playing games online every day. The average age of players is 28. Video games and gamers have even created a new form of marketing—called "advergaming." "Advergaming is taking games—something that people do for recreation—and inserting a message," said Julie Roehm, director of marketing communications for DaimlerChrysler AG's Chrysler Group, which sells Chrysler, Jeep, and Dodge brand vehicles. "It's important we go to all the places our consumers are." Suppose it is possible to assume the standard deviation of the ages of video game users is 9 years and that the distribution is bell-shaped. To assist the marketing department in obtaining demographics to increase sales, determine the proportion of players who are
a. between 19 and 28.
b. between 28 and 37.
c. older than 37.

3-75. Travelers are facing increased costs for both driving and flying to chosen destinations. With rising costs for both modes of transportation, what really weighs on the decision to drive or to fly? To gain a better understanding of the "fly or drive" decision, Runzheimer International reviewed ("The 'Fly or Drive' Decision: Runzheimer International Analyzes Costs," October 21, 2005) costs for trips between Los Angeles to San Francisco, 425 miles one way. Los Angeles to San Francisco round-trip costs $617.90 by car and $407.00 by plane. Cost flexibility is greater with the flying trips because of greater airfare choices. The driving trip costs, except for the on-road lunches, are pretty much set in place. Assume the standard deviation for the cost of flying trips is approximately $100.
a. If a flight to San Francisco from Los Angeles was chosen at random, determine the proportion

of the time that the cost would be smaller than $507. Assume the flight costs are bell-shaped.
b. Determine a flight cost that would qualify as the 25th percentile.
c. If nothing can be assumed about the distribution of the flight costs, determine the largest percentile that could be attributed to an airfare of $250.

3-76. Grover's Pay n' Pak sells hardware supplies to "do-it-yourselfers." One of the things the company prides itself on is fast service. It uses a number system and takes customers in the order that they arrive at the store. Recently, the assistant manager tracked the time customers spent in the store from the time they took a number until they left. A sample of 16 customers was selected and the following data (measured in minutes) were recorded:

15	14	16	14	14	14	13	8
12	9	7	17	10	15	16	16

a. Compute the mean, median, mode, range, interquartile range, and standard deviation.
b. Develop a box and whisker plot for these data.

3-77. The division manager for Northern Pipe and Steel Company has decided to implement a new incentive system for the managers of the three plants. The plan calls for a bonus to be paid next month to the manager whose plant has the greatest relative improvement over the average monthly production volume. The following data reflect the historical production volumes at the three plants:

Plant 1	Plant 2	Plant 3
$\mu = 700$	$\mu = 2300$	$\mu = 1200$
$\sigma = 200$	$\sigma = 350$	$\sigma = 30$

At the close of next month, the monthly output for the three plants was

Plant 1 = 810   Plant 2 = 2,600   Plant 3 = 1,320

Suppose the division manager has awarded the bonus to the manager of Plant 2 since her plant increased its production by 300 units over the mean. This was more than that for any of the other managers. Do you agree with the award of the bonus for this month? Explain, using the appropriate statistical measures to support your position.

3-78. The Rippon Investment company offers two different mutual funds. The stocks in the Growth Fund have generated an average return of 8% with a standard deviation of 2%. The stocks in the Specialized Fund have generated an average return of 18% with a standard deviation of 6%.
a. Based on the data provided, which of these funds has exhibited greater relative variability?

Use the proper statistical measure to make your determination.

b. Suppose an investor who is very risk-averse is interested in one of these two funds. Based strictly on relative variability, which fund would you recommend? Discuss.

c. Suppose the distributions for the two stock funds had a bell-shaped distribution with the means and standard deviations previously indicated. Which fund appears to be the best investment, assuming future returns will mimic past returns? Explain.

3-79. Since deregulation has taken place, the airline industry has undergone substantial changes with respect to ticket prices. Many discount fares are available if a customer knows how to obtain the discount. Many travelers complain that they get a different price every time they call. The American Consumer Institute recently priced tickets between Spokane, Washington, and St. Louis, Missouri. The passenger was to fly coach class, round-trip, staying seven days. Calls were made directly to airlines and to travel agents with the following results. Note that the data reflect round-trip airfare.

$229.00	$345.00	$599.00	$229.00	$429.00	$605.00
$339.00	$339.00	$229.00	$279.00	$344.00	$407.00

a. Compute the mean quoted airfare.

b. Compute the variance and standard deviation in airfares quoted. Treat the data as a sample.

3-80. The Smithfield Agricultural Company operates in the Midwest. The company owns and leases a total of 34,000 acres of prime farmland. Most of the crops are grain. Because of its size, the company can afford to do a great amount of testing to determine what seed types produce the greatest yields. Recently, the company tested three types of corn seed on test plots. The following values were observed after the first test year:

	Seed Type A	Seed Type B	Seed Type C
Mean Bushels/Acre	88	56	100
Standard Deviation	25	15	16

a. Based on the results of this testing, which seed seems to produce the greatest average yield per acre? Comment on the type of testing controls that should have been used to make this study valid.

b. Suppose the company is interested in consistency. Which seed type shows the least relative variability?

c. Assuming the Empirical Rule applies, describe the production distribution for each of the three seed types.

d. Suppose you were a farmer and had to obtain at least 135 bushels per acre to escape bankruptcy. Which seed type would you plant? Explain your choice.

e. Rework your answer to part d assuming the farmer needed 115 bushels per acre instead.

3-81. The manager of the Clark Fork Station Restaurant recently selected a random sample of 18 customers and kept track of how long the customers were required to wait from the time they arrived at the restaurant until they were actually served dinner. This study resulted from several complaints the manager had received from customers saying that their wait time was unduly long and that it appeared that the objective was to keep people waiting in the lounge for as long as possible to increase the lounge business. The following data were recorded, with time measured in minutes:

34	24	43	56	74	20	19	33	55
43	54	34	27	34	36	24	54	39

a. Compute the mean waiting time for this sample of customers.

b. Compute the median waiting time for this sample of customers.

c. Compute the variance and standard deviation of waiting time for this sample of customers.

d. Develop a frequency distribution using seven classes each with a class width of 10. Make the lower limit of the first class 15.

e. Develop a frequency histogram for the frequency distribution.

f. Construct a box and whisker plot of these data.

g. The manager is considering giving a complementary drink to customers whose waiting time is longer than the third quartile. Determine the minimum number of minutes a customer would have to wait in order to receive a complementary drink.

3-82. The Hillside Bowling Alley manager has selected a random sample of his league customers. He asked them to record the number of games they bowl during the month of December, including both league and open bowling. The reason for his interest in this data is that he is planning on offering a special discount to customers who bowl over a specified number of games each month. The sample of eight people produced the following data:

13	32	12	9	16	17	16	12

a. Compute the mean for these sample data.

b. Compute the median for these sample data.

c. Compute the mode for these sample data.

d. Calculate the variance and standard deviation for these sample data.

e. Note that one person in the sample bowled 32 games. What effect, if any, does this large value have on each of the three measures of location? Discuss.

f. For these sample data, which measure of location provides the best measure of the center of the data? Discuss.

g. Given this sample data, suppose the manager wishes to give discounts to bowlers in the top quartile. What should the minimum number of games bowled be in order to receive a discount?

3-83. Stock investors often look to beat the performance of the S&P 500 Index, which generally serves as a yardstick for the market as a whole. The following table shows a comparison of five-year cumulative total shareholder returns for Idaho Power Company Common Stock (NYSE Symbol: IDA), the S&P 500 Index, and the Edison Electric Institute (EEI) 100 Electric Utilities Index. The data assumes that $100 was invested on 12/31/1992, with returns compounded monthly. Construct appropriate statistical measures that illustrate the performance of the three investment options for the years 1992–1997. How well has Idaho Power Company performed during this period compared to the S&P 500? How well has it performed relative to its industry?

Year	Idaho Power	S&P 500	EEI 100 Electric Utilities
1992	$100.00	$100.00	$100.00
1993	117.38	110.08	111.15
1994	97.62	111.53	98.29
1995	134.11	153.45	128.78
1996	147.92	188.69	130.32
1997	189.73	251.63	166.00

3-84. Zagat Survey®, a leading provider of leisure-based survey results released (September 28,2005) its 2005 San Francisco Restaurants Survey. It marked the 25th year that Zagat Survey reported on diners and the 19th year that the company has covered San Franciso. The participants dined out an average of 3.2 times per week, with the average price per meal falling from the previous year from $34.07 to $33.75.

a. If the standard deviation of the price of meals in San Francisco was $10, determine the largest proportion of the 2005 meal prices that could be larger than $50.

b. If the check was paid in Chinese currency ($1 USD = 8.0916 Chinese yuan), determine the mean and standard deviation of meal prices in San Francisco. How would this change of currency affect your answer to part a?

Computer Database Exercises

3-85. According to the National Retail Federation (NRF), the NRF 2005 Halloween Consumer Intentions and

Actions Survey, conducted by BIGresearch, found that consumer spending ($3.29 billion) for 2005 was expected to be 5.4% above the amount for 2004. Much of the increase in spending was expected to come from young adults. Consumers in the 18–24 age group expected to spend an overall average of $50.75. On costumes alone they expect to spend an average of $22.00. A file entitled **Costumes** contains similar data.

a. Calculate the mean and standard deviation of these data.

b. Determine the following intervals for this data set: $\bar{x} \pm 1s, \bar{x} \pm 2s, \bar{x} \pm 3s$.

c. Suppose your responsibility as an assistant manager was to determine the price of costumes to be sold. The manager has informed you to set the price of one costume so that it was beyond the budget of only 2.5% of the customers. Assume that the data set has a bell-shaped distribution.

3-86. PayScale is a source of online compensation information, providing access to accurate compensation data for both employees and employers. PayScale allows users to obtain compensation information providing a snapshot of the job market. Recently, it published statistics for the salaries of MBA graduates. The file entitled **Payscale** contains data with the same characteristics as that obtained by PayScale for California and Florida.

a. Calculate the standard deviations of the salaries for both states' MBA graduates. Which state seems to have the widest spectrum of salaries for MBA graduates?

b. Calculate the average and median salary for each state's MBA graduates.

c. Examining the averages calculated in part b, determine which state's MBA graduates have the largest relative dispersion.

3-87. *Yahoo! Finance* makes available historical stock prices. It lists the opening, high, and low stock prices for each stock available on NYSE and NASDAQ. A file entitled **Gestock** gives this data for General Electric from July 5, 2005 to October 21, 2005.

a. Calculate the difference between the opening and closing stock prices for GE over this time period. Then calculate the mean, median, and standard deviation of these differences.

b. Indicate what the mean in part a indicates about the relative prices of the opening and closing stock prices for General Electric.

c. Compare the dispersion of the opening stock prices with the difference between the opening and closing stock prices.

3-88. The data in the file named **Fast100** was collected by D. L. Green & Associates, a regional investment management company that specializes in working with clients who wish to invest in smaller companies with high growth potential. To aid the investment firm in locating appropriate investments for its clients, Sandra Williams, an assistant client manager, put together a database on 100 fast-growing companies. The database consists of data on eight variables for each of the 100 companies. Note that in some cases data are not available. A code of -99 has been used to signify missing data. These data will have to be omitted from any calculations.

a. Select the variable Sales. Develop a frequency distribution and histogram for Sales.

b. Compute the mean, median, and standard deviation for the Sales variable.

c. Determine the interquartile range for the Sales variable.

d. Construct a box and whisker plot for the sales variable. Identify any outliers. Discard the outliers and recalculate the measures in part b.

e. Each year a goal is set for sales. Next year's goal will be to have average sales that are at this year's 65th percentile. Identify next year's sales goal.

3-89. The Environmental Protection Agency (EPA) tests all new cars and provides a mileage rating for both city and highway driving conditions. Thirty cars were tested and are contained in the data file **Automobiles**. The file contains data on several variables. In this problem, focus on the city and highway mileage data.

a. Calculate the sample mean mpg for both city and highway driving for the 30 cars. Also calculate the sample standard deviation for the two mileage variables. Do the data tend to support the premise that cars will get better mileage on the highway than around town? Discuss.

b. Referring to part a, what can the EPA conclude about the relative variability between car models for highway versus city driving? (*Hint*: Compute the appropriate measure to compare relative variability.)

c. Assume that mileage ratings are approximately bell-shaped. Approximately what proportion of cars gets at least as good mileage in city driving conditions as the mean mileage for highway driving for all cars?

3-90. Zepolle's Bakery makes a variety of bread types that it sells to supermarket chains in the area. One of Zepolle's problems is that the number of loaves of each type of bread sold each day by the chain stores varies considerably, making it difficult to know how many loaves to bake. A sample of daily demand data is contained in the file called **Bakery**.

a. Which bread type has the highest average daily demand?

b. Develop a frequency distribution for each bread type.

c. Which bread type has the highest standard deviation in demand?

d. Which bread type has the greatest relative variability? Which type has the lowest relative variability?

e. Assuming that these sample data are representative of demand during the year, determine how many loaves of each type of bread should be made such that demand would be met on at least 75% of the days during the year.

f. Create a new variable called Total Loaves Sold. On which day of the week is the average for total loaves sold the highest?

3-91. The Cozine Corporation operates a garbage hauling business. Up to this point, the company has been charged a flat fee for each of the garbage trucks that enters the county landfill. The flat fee is based on the assumed truck weight of 45,000 pounds. In two weeks, the company is required to appear before the county commissioners to discuss a rate adjustment. In preparation for this meeting, Cozine has hired an independent company to weigh a sample of Cozine's garbage trucks just prior to their entering the landfill. The data file **Cozine** contains the data the company has collected.

a. Based on the sample data, what percentile does the 45,000-pound weight fall closest to?

b. Compute appropriate measures of central location for the data.

c. Construct a frequency histogram based on the sample data. Use the $2^k \geq n$ guideline (see Chapter 2) to determine the number of classes. Also, construct a box and whisker plot for these data. Discuss the relative advantages of histograms and box and whisker plots for presenting these data.

d. Use the information determined in parts a–c to develop a presentation to the county commissioners. Make sure the presentation attempts to answer the question of whether Cozine deserves a rate reduction.

3-92. The Internal Revenue Service has come under a great deal of criticism in recent years for various actions it is purported to have taken against U.S. citizens related to collecting federal income taxes. The IRS is also criticized for the complexity of the tax code, although the tax laws are actually written by congressional staff and passed by Congress. For the past few years, one of the country's biggest tax-preparing companies has sponsored an event in which 50 certified public accountants from all sizes of CPA firms are asked to determine the tax owed for a fictitious citizen. The IRS is also asked to determine the "correct" tax owed. Last year, the "correct" figure stated by the IRS was $11,560. The file **Taxes** contains the data for the 50 accountants.

a. Compute a new variable that is the difference between the IRS number and the number determined by each accountant.

b. For this new variable computed in part a, develop a frequency distribution.

c. For the new variable computed in part a, determine the mean, median, and standard deviation.

d. Determine the percentile that would correspond to the "correct" tax figure if the IRS figure were one of the CPA firms' estimated tax figures. Describe what this implies about the agreement between the IRS and consultants' calculated tax.

VIDEO CASE 3

Drive-Thru Service Times @ McDonald's

When you're on the go and looking for a quick meal, where do you go? If you're like millions of people every day, you make a stop at McDonald's. Known as "quick service restaurants" in the industry (not "fast food"), companies such as McDonald's invest heavily to determine the most efficient and effective ways to provide fast, high quality service in all phases of their business.

Drive-thru operations play a vital role. It's not surprising that attention is focused on the drive-thru process. After all, over 60% of individual restaurant revenues in the United States come from the drive-thru experience. Yet understanding the process is more complex than just counting cars. Marla King, professor at the company's international training center, Hamburger University, got her start 25 years ago working at a McDonald's drive-thru. She now coaches new restaurant owners and managers. "Our stated drive-thru service time is 90 seconds or less. We train every manager and team member to understand that a quality customer experience at the drive-thru depends on them," says Marla. Some of the factors that affect a customers' ability to complete their purchases within 90 seconds include restaurant staffing, equipment layout in the restaurant, training, and efficiency of the grill team, and frequency of customer arrivals to name a few. Also, customer order patterns also play a role. Some customers will just order drinks, while others seem to need enough food to feed an entire soccer team. And then there are the special orders. Obviously, there is plenty of room for variability here.

Yet that doesn't stop the company from using statistical techniques to better understand the drive-thru action. In particular, McDonald's utilizes numerical measures of the center and spread in the data and to help transform the data into useful information. In order for restaurant managers to achieve the goal in their own restaurants, they need training in proper restaurant and drive-thru operations. Hamburger University, McDonald's training center located near Chicago, Illinois, satisfies that need. In the mock-up restaurant service lab, managers go through a "before and after" training scenario. In the "before" scenario," they run the restaurant for thirty minutes as if they were back in their home restaurants. Managers in the training class are assigned to be crew, customers, drive-thru

cars, special needs guests (such as hearing impaired, indecisive, or clumsy), or observers. Statistical data about the operations, revenues, and service times are collected and analyzed. Without the right training, the restaurant's operations usually start breaking down after 10–15 minutes. After debriefing and analyzing the data collected, the managers make suggestions for adjustments and head back to the service lab to try again. This time, the results usually come in well within standards. "When presented with the quantitative results, managers are pretty quick to make the connections between better operations, higher revenues, and happier customers," Marla states.

When managers return to their respective restaurants, the training results and techniques are shared with staff who are charged with implementing the ideas locally. The results of the training eventually are measured when McDonald's conducts a restaurant operations improvement process study, or ROIP. The goal is simple: improved operations. When the ROIP review is completed, statistical analyses are performed and managers are given their results. Depending on the results, decisions might be made that require additional financial resources, building construction, staff training, or reconfiguring layouts. Yet one thing is clear: statistics drive the decisions behind McDonald's drive-thru service operations.

Discussion Questions:

1. After returning from the training session at Hamburger University, a McDonald's store owner selected a random sample 362 of drive-thru customers and carefully measured the time it took from when a customer entered the McDonald's property until the customer had received the order at the drive-thru window. These data are in the file called **McDonald's Drive-Thru Waiting Times**. Note, the owner selected some customers during the breakfast period, others during lunch and others during dinner. For the overall sample, compute the key measures of central tendency. Based on these measures, what conclusion might the owner reach with respect to how well his store is doing in meeting the 90 second customer service goal? Discuss.

2. Referring to question 1, compute the key measures of central tendency for drive-thru times broken down by

breakfast, lunch, and dinner time periods. Based on these calculations, does it appear that the store is doing better at one of these time periods than the others in providing shorter drive-thru waiting times? Discuss.

3. Referring to questions 1 and 2, compute the range and standard deviation for drive-thru times for the overall sample and for the three different times of the day. Also calculate the appropriate measure of relative

variability for each time period. Discuss these measures of variability and what they might imply about what customers can expect at this McDonald's drive-thru.

4. Determine, the 1st and 3rd quartiles for drive-thru times and develop a box and whisker diagram for the overall sample data. Are there any outliers identified in these sample data? Discuss.

CASE 3.1

WGI—Human Resources

WGI is a large international construction company with operations in 43 countries. The company has been a major player in the reconstruction efforts in Iraq with a number of subcontracts under the major contractor, Haliburton, Inc. However, the company is also involved in many small projects both in the United States and around the world. One of these is a sewer line installation project in Madison, Wisconsin. The contract is what is called a "cost plus" contract, meaning that the city of Madison will pay for all direct costs, including materials and labor, of the project plus an additional fee to WGI. Roberta Bernhart is the human resource manager for the Madison project and is responsible for overseeing all aspects of employee compensation and HR issues.

WGI is required to produce a variety of reports to the Madison City Council on an annual basis. Recently, the council asked WGI to prepare a report showing the current hourly rates for the nonsalaried work crew on the project. Specifically, the council is interested in any proposed pay increases to the work crew that will ultimately be passed along to the city of Madison. In response to the city's request, Roberta put together a data file for all 19 nonsalaried work crew members, called **WGI**, which shows their currently hourly pay rate and the proposed increase to take place the first of next month. These data are as follows:

Name	Current Rate	New Rate
Jody	$20.55	$22.55
Tim	$22.15	$23.81
Thamas	$14.18	$15.60
Shari	$14.18	$15.60
Johnn	$18.80	$20.20
Jared	$18.98	$20.20
Loren	$25.24	$26.42
Mike	$18.36	$19.28

Name	Current Rate	New Rate
Patrick	$17.20	$18.06
Sharon	$16.99	$17.84
Sam	$16.45	$17.27
Susan	$18.90	$19.66
Chris	$18.30	$19.02
Steve F	$27.45	$28.12
Kevin	$16.00	$16.64
Larry	$17.47	$18.00
MaryAnn	$23.99	$24.47
Mark	$22.62	$23.08
Aaron	$15.00	$15.40

The city council expects the report to contain both graphic and numerical descriptive analyses. Roberta has outlined the following tasks and has asked you to help her.

Required Tasks:

1. Develop, and interpret, histograms showing the distributions of current hourly rates and proposed new hourly rates for the crew members.
2. Compute and interpret key measures of central tendency and variation for the current and new hourly rates. Determine the coefficient of variation for each.
3. Compute a new variable called pay increase that reflects the difference between the proposed new pay rate and the current rate. Develop a histogram for this variable, and then compute key measures of the center and variation for the new variable.
4. Compute a new variable that is the percentage increase in hourly pay rate. Prepare a graphical and numerical description of this new variable.
5. Prepare a report to the city council that contains the results from tasks 1–4.

CASE 3.2

National Call Center

Candice Worthy and Philip Hanson are day shift supervisors at National Call Center's Austin, Texas, facility. National provides contract call center services for a number of companies, including banks and major retail companies. Candice and Philip have both been with the company for slightly over five years, having joined National right after graduating with bachelor degrees from the University of Texas. As they walked down the hall together after the weekly staff meeting, the two friends were discussing the assignment they were just handed by Mark Gonzales, the division manager. The assignment came out of a discussion at the meeting in which one of National's clients wanted a report describing the calls being handled for them by National. Mark had asked Candice and Philip to describe the data in a file called **National Call Center** and produce a report that would both graphically and numerically analyze the data. The data are for a sample of 57 calls and for the following variables:

Account Number

Caller Gender

Account Holder Gender

Past Due Amount

Current Account Balance

Nature of Call (Billing Question or Other)

By the time they reached their office Candice and Philip had outlined some of the key tasks that they needed to do.

Required Tasks:

1. Develop bar charts showing the mean and median current account balance by gender of the caller.
2. Develop bar charts showing the mean and median current account balance by gender of the account holder.
3. Construct a scatter diagram showing current balance on the horizontal axis and past due amount on the vertical axis.
4. Compute the key descriptive statistics for the center and for the variation in current account balance broken down by gender of the caller, gender of the account holder, and by the nature of the call.
5. Repeat task 4 but compute the statistics for the past due balances.
6. Compute the coefficient of variation for current account balances for male and female account holders.
7. Develop frequency and relative frequency distributions for the gender of callers, gender of account holders, and nature of the calls.
8. Develop joint frequency and joint relative frequency distributions for the account holder gender by whether or not the account has a past due balance.
9. Write a report to National's client that contains the results for tasks 1–8 along with a discussion of these statistics and graphs.

CASE 3.3

Welco Lumber Company—Part B

Case 2.3 in Chapter 2 introduced you to the Welco Lumber Company and to Gene Denning, Welco Lumber Company's process improvement team leader. Welco Lumber makes cedar fencing materials at its Naples, Idaho, facility employing about 160 people.

In Case 2.3 you were asked to help Gene develop a graphical descriptive analysis for data collected from the head rig. The head rig is a large saw that breaks down the logs into slabs and cants. Refer to Case 2.3 for more details involving a study that Gene recently conducted in which he videotaped 365 logs being broken down by the head rig. All three operators, April, Sid and Jim, were involved. Each log was marked as to its true diameter.

Then Gene observed the way the log was broken down and the degree to which the cants were properly centered. He then determined the projected value of the finished product from each log given the way it was actually cut. In addition, he also determined what the value would have been had the log been cut in the optimal way. Data for this study is in a file called **Welco Lumber**.

In addition to the graphical analysis that you helped Gene perform in Case 2.3, you have been asked to assist Gene by analyzing these data using appropriate measures of the center and variation. He wishes to focus on the lost profit to the company and whether there are differences among the operators. Also, do the operators tend to perform better on small logs than on large logs? In general, he is hoping to learn as much as possible from this study and needs your help with the analysis.

CASE 3.4

AJ's Fitness Center

When A. J. Reeser signed papers to take ownership of the fitness center previously known as The Park Center Club, he realized that he had just taken the biggest financial step in his life. Every asset he could pull together had been pledged against the mortgage. If the new AJ's Fitness Center didn't succeed, he would be in really bad shape financially. But A. J. didn't plan on failing. After all, he had never failed at anything.

As a high school football All-American, A. J. had been heavily recruited by major colleges around the country. Although he loved football, he and his family had always put academics ahead of sports. Thus, he surprised almost everyone other than those who knew him best when he chose to attend an Ivy League university not particularly noted for its football success. Although he excelled at football and was a member of two winning teams, he also succeeded in the classroom and graduated in four years. He spent six years working for McKinsey & Company, a major consulting firm, in which he gained significant experience in a broad range of business situations.

He was hired away from McKinsey & Company by the Dryden Group, a management services company that specializes in running health and fitness operations and recreational resorts throughout the world. After eight years of leading the Fitness Center section at Dryden, A. J. found that earning a high salary and the perks associated with corporate life were not satisfying him. Besides, the travel was getting old now that he had married and had two young children. When the opportunity to purchase The Park Center Club came, he decided that the time was right to control his own destiny.

A key aspect of the deal was that AJ's Fitness Club would keep its existing clientele, consisting of 1,833 memberships. One of the things that A. J. was very concerned about was whether these members would stay with the club after the sale or move on to other fitness clubs in the area. He knew that keeping existing customers is a lot less expensive than attracting new customers.

Within days of assuming ownership, A. J. developed a survey that was mailed to all 1,833 members. The letter that accompanied the survey discussed A. J.'s philosophy and asked several key questions regarding the current level of satisfaction. Survey respondents were eligible to win a free lifetime membership in a drawing—an inducement that was no doubt responsible for the 1,214 usable responses.

To get help with the analysis of the survey data, A. J. approached the College of Business at a local university with the idea of having a senior student serve as an intern at AJ's Fitness Center. In addition to an hourly wage, the intern would get free use of the fitness facilities for the rest of the academic year.

The intern's first task was to key the data from the survey into a file that could be analyzed using a spreadsheet or a statistical software package. The survey contained eight questions that were keyed into eight columns, as follows:

Column 1: Satisfaction with the club's weight- and exercise-equipment facilities

Column 2: Satisfaction with the club's staff

Column 3: Satisfaction with the club's exercise programs (aerobics, etc.)

Column 4: Satisfaction with the club's overall service

Note, columns 1 through 4 were coded on an ordinal scale as follows:

1	2	3	4	5
Very Unsatisfied	Unsatisfied	Neutral	Satisfied	Very Satisfied

Column 5: Number of years that the respondent had been a member at this club

Column 6: Gender (1 = Male, 2 = Female)

Column 7: Typical number of visits to the club per week

Column 8: Age

The data, saved in the file **AJFitness**, were clearly too much for anyone to comprehend in raw form. At yesterday's meeting, A. J. asked the intern to "make some sense of the data." When the intern asked for some direction, A. J.'s response was, "That's what I'm paying you the big bucks for. I just want you to develop a descriptive analysis of these data. Use whatever charts, graphs, and tables that will help us understand our customers. Also, use any pertinent numerical measures that will help in the analysis. For right now, give me a report that discusses the data. Why don't we set a time to get together next week to review your report?"

References

Berenson, Mark L., and David M. Levine, *Basic Business Statistics: Concepts and Applications,* 10th ed. (Upper Saddle River, NJ: Prentice Hall, 2006).

Microsoft Excel 2007 (Redmond, WA: Microsoft Corp., 2007).

Minitab for Windows Version 15 (State College, PA: Minitab, 2007).

Siegel, Andrew F., *Practical Business Statistics*, 5th ed. (Burr Ridge, IL: Irwin, 2003).

Tukey, John W., *Exploratory Data Analysis* (Reading, MA: Addison-Wesley, 1977).

Special Review Section

Chapter 1 The Where, Why, and How of Data Collection
Chapter 2 Graphs, Charts, and Tables—Describing Your Data
Chapter 3 Describing Data Using Numerical Measures

This is the first of two special review sections in this text. The material in these sections, which is presented using block diagrams and flowcharts, is intended to help you tie together the material from several key chapters. These sections are not a substitute for reading and studying the chapters covered by the review. However, you can use this review material to add to your understanding of the individual topics in the chapters.

Chapters 1–3

Chapters 1 to 3 introduce data, data collection, and statistical tools for describing data. The steps needed to gather "good" statistical data, transform it to usable information, and present the information in a manner that allows good decisions are outlined in the following figures.

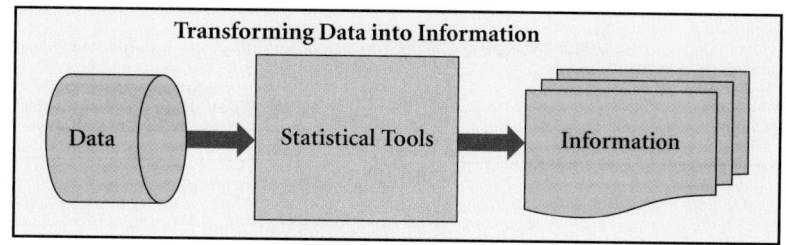

A Typical Application Sequence

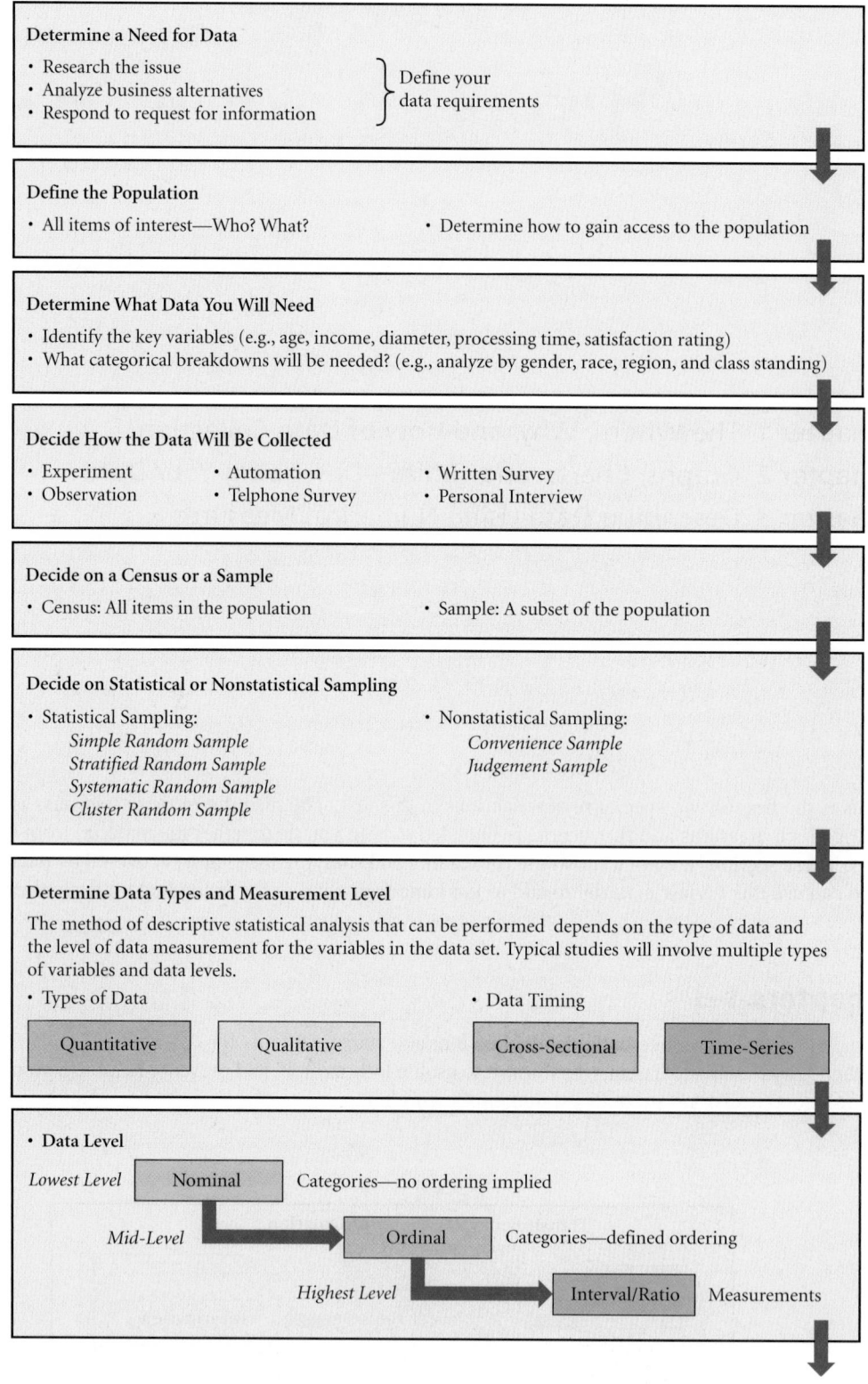

Determine a Need for Data

- Research the issue
- Analyze business alternatives
- Respond to request for information

} Define your data requirements

Define the Population

- All items of interest—Who? What?
- Determine how to gain access to the population

Determine What Data You Will Need

- Identify the key variables (e.g., age, income, diameter, processing time, satisfaction rating)
- What categorical breakdowns will be needed? (e.g., analyze by gender, race, region, and class standing)

Decide How the Data Will Be Collected

- Experiment
- Observation
- Automation
- Telphone Survey
- Written Survey
- Personal Interview

Decide on a Census or a Sample

- Census: All items in the population
- Sample: A subset of the population

Decide on Statistical or Nonstatistical Sampling

- Statistical Sampling:
  Simple Random Sample
  Stratified Random Sample
  Systematic Random Sample
  Cluster Random Sample

- Nonstatistical Sampling:
  Convenience Sample
  Judgement Sample

Determine Data Types and Measurement Level

The method of descriptive statistical analysis that can be performed depends on the type of data and the level of data measurement for the variables in the data set. Typical studies will involve multiple types of variables and data levels.

- Types of Data

  Quantitative   Qualitative

- Data Timing

  Cross-Sectional   Time-Series

- Data Level

Lowest Level   Nominal   Categories—no ordering implied

Mid-Level   Ordinal   Categories—defined ordering

Highest Level   Interval/Ratio   Measurements

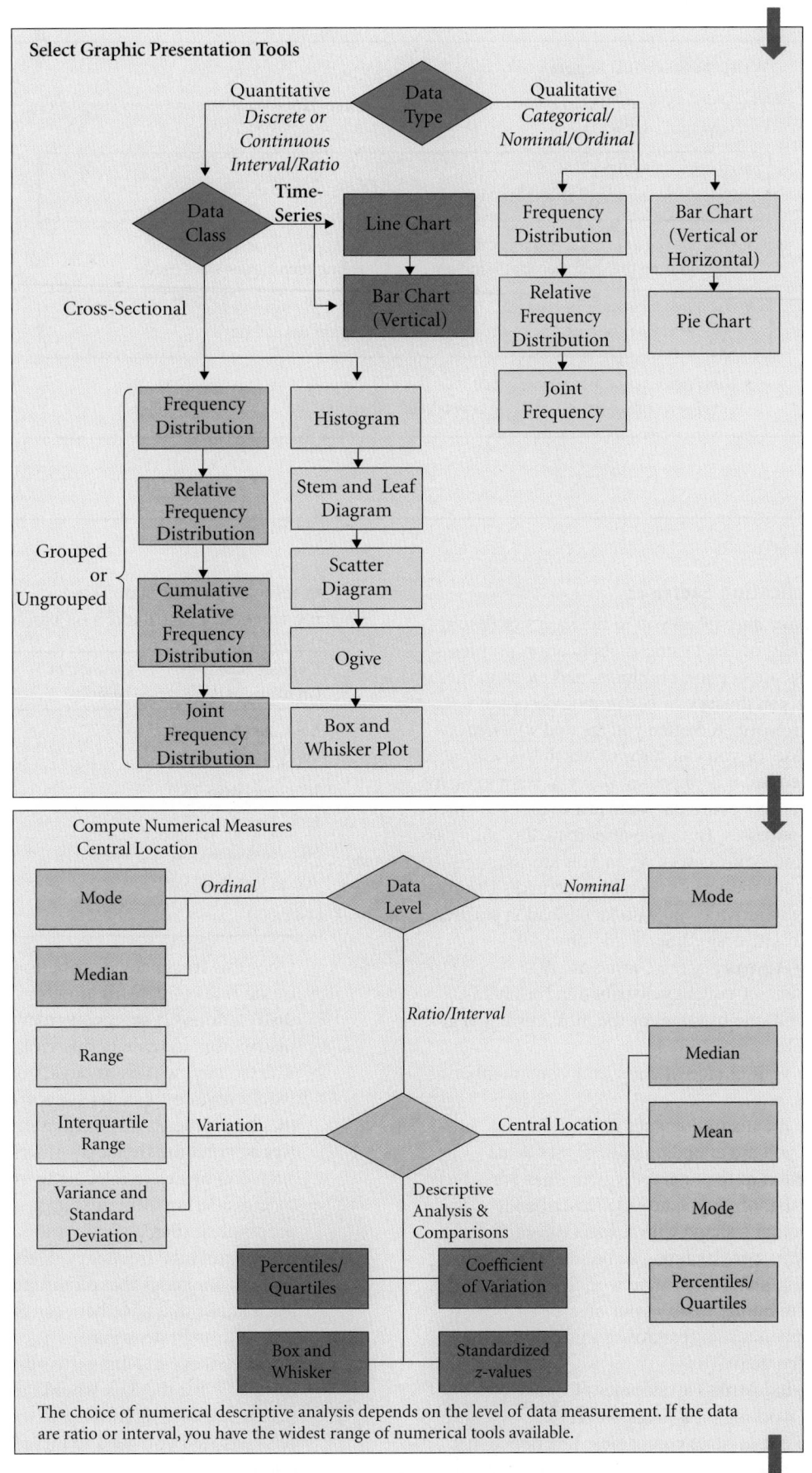

Select Graphic Presentation Tools

The choice of numerical descriptive analysis depends on the level of data measurement. If the data are ratio or interval, you have the widest range of numerical tools available.

Write the Statistical Report

There is no one set format for writing a statistical report. However, there are a few suggestions you may find useful.

- *Lay the foundation*:
  Provide background and motivation for the analysis.

- *Describe the data collection methodology*:
  Explain how the data were gathered and the sampling techniques were used.

- *Use a logical sequence*:
  Follow a systematic jplan for presenting your findings and analysis.

- *Label figures and tables by number*:
  Employ a consistent numbering and labeling format.

Exercises

Integrative Application Exercises

Chapters 1 to 3 have introduced you to the basics of descriptive statistics. Many of the business application problems, advanced business application problems, and cases in these chapters will give you practice in performing descriptive statistical analysis. However, too often you are told which procedure you should use, or you can surmise which to use by the location of the exercise. It is important that you learn to identify the appropriate procedure on your own in order to solve problems for test purposes. But more important, this ability is essential throughout your career when you are required to select procedures for the tasks you will undertake. The following exercises will provide you with identification practice.

SR.1. Go to your university library and obtain the *Statistical Abstract of the United States*.
a. Construct a frequency distribution for unemployment rate by state for the most current year available.
b. Justify your choice of class limits and number of classes.
c. Locate the unemployment rate for the state in which you are attending college. (1) What proportion of the unemployment rates are below that of your state? (2) Describe the distribution's shape with respect to symmetry. (3) If you were planning to build a new manufacturing plant, what state would you choose in which to build? Justify your answer. (4) Are there any unusual features of this distribution? Describe them.

SR.2. The State Industrial Development Council is presently working on a financial services brochure to send to out-of-state companies. It is hoped that the brochure will be helpful in attracting companies to relocate to your state. You are given the following frequency distribution on banks in your state:

Deposit Size (in millions)	Number of Banks	Total Deposits (in millions)
Less than 5	2	7.2
5 to less than 10	7	52.1
10 to less than 25	6	111.5
25 to less than 50	3	95.4
50 to less than 100	2	166.6
100 to less than 500	2	529.8
Over 500	2	1663.0

a. Does this frequency distribution violate any of the rules of construction for frequency distributions? If so, reconstruct the frequency distribution to remedy this violation.
b. The Council wishes to target companies that would require financial support from banks that have at least $25 million in deposits. Reconstruct the frequency distribution to attract such companies to relocate to your state. Do this by considering different classes that would accomplish such a goal.
c. Reconstruct the frequency distribution to attract companies that require financial support from banks that have between $5 million and $25 million in deposits.
d. Present an eye-catching, two-paragraph summary of what the data would mean to a company that is considering moving to the state. Your boss has said you need to include relative frequencies in this presentation.

SR.3. As an intern for Intel Corporation, suppose you have been asked to help the vice president prepare a newsletter to the shareholders. You have been given access to the data in a file called **Intel** that contains Intel Corporation financial data for the years 1987–1996. Go to the Internet or to Intel's annual report and update the file to include the same variables for the years 1997 to the present. Then, use graphs to effectively present the data in a format that would be usable for the vice president's newsletter. Write a short article that discusses the information shown in your graphs.

SR.4. The Woodmill Company makes windows and door trim products. The first step in the process is to rip dimension (2×8, 2×10, etc.) lumber into narrower pieces. Currently, the company uses a manual process in which an experienced operator quickly looks at a board and determines what rip widths to use. The decision is based on the knots and defects in the wood.

A company in Oregon has developed an optical scanner that can be used to determine the rip widths. The scanner is programmed to recognize defects and to determine rip widths that will "optimize" the value of the board. A test run of 100 boards was put through the scanner and the rip widths were identified. However, the boards were not actually ripped. A lumber grader determined the resulting values for each of the 100 boards assuming that the rips determined by the scanner had been made. Next, the same 100 boards were manually ripped using the normal process. The grader then determined the value for each board after the manual rip process was completed. The resulting data, in the file **Woodmill**, consist of manual rip values and scanner rip values for each of the 100 boards.

a. Develop a frequency distribution for the board values for the scanner and the manual process.

b. Compute appropriate descriptive statistics for both manual and scanner values. Use these data along with the frequency distribution developed in part a to prepare a written report that describes the results of the test. Be sure to include in your report a conclusion regarding whether the scanner outperforms the manual process.

c. Which process, scanner or manual, generated the most values that were more than 2 standard deviations from the mean?

d. Which of the two processes has the least relative variability?

SR.5. The commercial banking industry is undergoing rapid changes due to advances in technology and competitive pressures in the financial services sector. The data file **Banks** contains selected information tabulated by *Fortune* concerning the revenues, profitability, and number of employees for the 51 largest U.S. commercial banks in terms of revenues. Use the information in this file to complete the following:

a. Compute the mean, median, and standard deviation for the three variables revenues, profits, and number of employees.

b. Convert the data for each variable to a z-value. Consider Mellon Bank Corporation headquartered in Pittsburgh. How does it compare to the average bank in the study on the three variables? Discuss.

c. As you can see by examining the data and by looking at the statistics computed in part a, not all banks had the same revenue, same profit, or the same number of employees. Which variable had the greatest relative variation among the banks in the study?

d. Calculate a new variable: profits per employee. Develop a frequency distribution and a histogram for this new variable. Also compute the mean, median, and standard deviation for the new variable. Write a short report that describes the profits per employee for the banks.

e. Referring to part d, how many banks had a profit per employee ratio which exceeded 2 standard deviations from the mean?

Here is an integrative case study designed to give you more experience. In addition, we have included several term project assignments that require you to collect and analyze data.

REVIEW CASE 1

State Department of Insurance

This case study describes the efforts undertaken by the director of the Insurance Division to assess the magnitude of the uninsured motorist problem in a western state. The objective of the case study is to introduce you to a data collection application and show how one organization developed a database. The database on your data CD called **Liabins** is a subset of the data actually collected by the state department.

The impetus for the case came from the legislative transportation committee, which heard much testimony during the recent legislative session about the problems that occur when an uninsured motorist is involved in a traffic accident where damages to individuals and property occur. The state's law enforcement officers also testified that a large number of vehicles are not covered by liability insurance.

Because of both political pressure and a sense of duty to do what is right, the legislative committee spent many hours wrestling with what to do about drivers who do not carry the mandatory liability insurance. Because the actual magnitude of the problem was unknown, the committee finally arrived at a compromise plan, which required the state Insurance Division to perform random audits of vehicles to determine whether the vehicle was covered by liability insurance. The audits are to be performed on approximately 1% of the state's 1 million registered vehicles each month. If a vehicle is found not to have liability insurance, the vehicle license and the owner's driver's license will be revoked for three months and a $250 fine will be imposed.

However, before actually implementing the audit process, which is projected to cost $1.5 million per year, Herb Kriner, director of the Insurance Division, was told to conduct a preliminary study of the uninsured motorists problem in the state and to report back to the legislative committee in six months.

The Study

A random sample of 12 counties in the state was selected in a manner that gave the counties with higher numbers of registered vehicles proportionally higher chances of being selected. Two locations were selected in each county and the state police set up roadblocks on a randomly selected day. Vehicles with in-state license plates were stopped at random until approximately 100 vehicles had been stopped at each location. The target total was about 2,400 vehicles statewide.

The issue of primary interest was whether the vehicle was insured. This was determined by observing whether the vehicle was carrying the required certificate of insurance. If so, the officer took down the insurance company name and address and the policy number. If the certificate was not in the car, but the owner stated that insurance was carried, the owner was given a postcard to return within five days supplying the required information. A vehicle was determined to be uninsured if no postcard was returned or if, subsequently, the insurance company reported that the policy was not valid on the day of the survey.

In addition to the issue of insurance coverage, Herb Kriner wanted to collect other information about the vehicle and the owner. This was done using a personal interview during which the police officer asked a series of questions and observed certain things such as seat belt usage and driver's and vehicle license expiration status. Also, the owners' driving records were obtained through the Transportation Department's computer division and added to the information gathered by the state police.

The Data

The data are contained in the file **Liabins**. The sheet titled "Description" contains an explanation of the data set and the variables.

Issues to Address

Herb Kriner has two weeks before making a presentation to the legislative subcommittee that has been dealing with the liability insurance issue. As Herb's chief analyst, your job is to perform a comprehensive analysis of the data and to prepare the report that Herb will deliver to the legislature. Remember, this report will go a long way in determining whether the state should spend the $1.5 million to implement a full liability insurance audit system.

Term Project Assignments

For the project selected, you are to devise a sampling plan, collect appropriate data, and carry out a full descriptive analysis aimed at shedding light on the key issues for the project. The finished project will include a written report of a length and format specified by your professor.

Project A

Issue: Your College of Business and Economics seeks input from business majors regarding class scheduling. Some potential issues are

- Day or evening
- Morning or afternoon
- One-day, two-day, or three-day schedules
- Weekend
- Location (on or off campus)

Project B

Issue: Intercollegiate athletics is a part of most major universities. Revenue from attendance at major sporting events is one key to financing the athletic program. Investigate the drivers of attendance at your university's men's basketball and football games. Some potential issues:

- Game times
- Game days (basketball)
- Ticket prices
- Athletic booster club memberships
- Competition for entertainment dollars

Project C

Issue: The department of your major is interested in surveying department alumni. Some potential issues are

- Satisfaction with degree
- Employment status

- Job satisfaction
- Suggestions for improving course content

Project D

Project Objective

The objective of this business statistics capstone project is to provide you with an opportunity to integrate the statistical tools and concepts that you have learned thus far in your business statistics course. Like all real-world applications, completing this project will not require you to utilize every statistical technique covered in the first three chapters. Rather, an objective of the assignment is for you to determine which of the statistical tools and techniques are appropriate for the situation you have selected.

Project Description

Assume that you are working as an intern for a financial management company. Your employer has a large number of clients who trust the company managers to invest their funds. In your position, you are responsibile for producing reports for clients when they request information. Your company has two large data files with financial information for a large number of U.S. companies. The first is called **US Companies 2003**, which contains financial information for the companies' 2001 or 2002 fiscal year-end. The second file is called **US Companies 2005**, which has data for the fiscal 2003 or 2004 year-end. The 2003 file has data for 7,098 companies. The 2005 file has data for 6,992 companies. Thus, many companies are listed in both files but some are just in one or the other.

The two files have many of the same variables, but the 2003 file has a larger range of financial variables than the 2005 file. For some companies, the data for certain variables are not available and a code of NA is used to so indicate. The 2003 file has a special worksheet that contains the description of each variable. These descriptions apply to the 2005 data file as well.

You have been given access to these two data files for use in preparing your reports. Your role will be to perform certain statistical analyses that can be used to help convert these data into useful information in order to respond to the clients' questions.

This morning, one of the partners of your company received a call from a client who asked for a report that would compare companies in the financial services industry (SIC codes in the 6000s) to companies in production-oriented business (SIC codes in the 2000s and 3000s). There are no firm guidelines on what the report should entail, but the partner has suggested the following:

- Start with the 2005 data file. Pull the data for all companies with the desired SIC codes into a new worksheet.
- Prepare a complete descriptive analysis of key financial variables using appropriate charts and graphs to help compare the two types of businesses.
- Determine whether there are differences between the two classes of companies in terms of key financial measures.
- Using data from the 2003 file for companies that have these SIC codes and that are also in the 2005 file, develop a comparison that shows the changes over the time span both within SIC code grouping and between SIC code groupings.

Project Deliverables

To successfully complete this capstone project, you are required to deliver a management report that addresses the partner's requests (listed above) and also contains at least one other substantial type of analysis not mentioned by the partner. This latter work should be set off in a special section of the report.

The final report should be presented in a professional format using the style or format suggested by your instructor.

Chapter FOUR

Using Probability and Probability Distributions

CHAPTER OUTCOMES

After studying the material in Chapter 4, you should:

1. Understand the three approaches to assessing probabilities.
2. Be able to apply the Addition Rule.
3. Know how to use the Multiplication Rule.
4. Know how to use Bayes' Theorem for applications involving conditional probabilities.

PREPARING FOR CHAPTER FOUR

- Review the discussion of statistical sampling in Section 1.3.

- Examine recent business periodicals and newspapers looking for examples where probability concepts are discussed.

- Think about how you determine what decision to make in situations where you are uncertain about your choices.

WHY YOU NEED TO KNOW

A few years ago when states were determining whether to sanction statewide and multistate lotteries, a commercial opposing the lotteries aired on television. The commercial showed three teenagers walking home from school discussing what they were going to do when they left high school. One boy said that he was going to college to study engineering and that he planned to design airplanes. A girl said that she wanted to be a surgeon and was going to go to medical school. When the third boy was asked about his plans, he responded that he was going to win the Powerball Lottery and be a multimillionaire. The point was that if the state approved lotteries, some people would pin their future on outcomes that had only the slightest possibility of happening to them. Most people recognize when buying a ticket there is a small *probability* of winning the lottery and whether they win or lose is based on chance alone.

In business decision making, there are many instances where chance is involved in determining the outcome of a decision. For instance, when a tire manufacturer establishes a warranty on its tires, there is a certain probability that any given tire will last less than the warranty mileage and customers will have to be compensated. A food processor recognizes that there is a chance that one or more of its products will be substandard and dissatisfy the customer. Airlines overbook flights to make sure that the seats on the plane are as full as possible because they know there is a certain probability that customers will not show for their flight. Accountants perform audits on the financial statements of a client and sign off on the statements as accurate while realizing that there is a chance that problems exist that were not uncovered by the audit. Professional poker players base their decisions to fold or play a hand based on their assessment of the chances that their hand beats those of their opponents.

If we always knew what the result of our decisions would be, our life as decision makers would be a lot less stressful. However, in most instances uncertainty exists. To deal with this uncertainty, we need to know how to incorporate probability concepts into the decision process. Chapter 4 takes the first step in teaching you how to do this by introducing the basic concepts and rules of probability. You need to have a solid understanding of these basics before moving on to the more practical probability applications that you will encounter in business.

4.1 The Basics of Probability

Before we can apply *probability* to the decision-making process, we must understand what it means. The mathematical study of probability originated more than 300 years ago. The Chevalier de Méré, a French nobleman (who today would probably own a gaming house in Monte Carlo), began asking questions about games of chance. He was mostly interested in the probability of observing various outcomes when dice were repeatedly rolled. The French mathematician Blaise Pascal (you may remember studying Pascal's triangle in a mathematics class) with the help of his friend Pierre de Fermat was able to answer de Méré's questions. Of course, Pascal began asking more and more complicated questions of himself and his colleagues, and the formal study of probability began.

Important Probability Terms

Several explanations of what probability is have come out of this mathematical study. However, the definition of **probability** is quite basic.

Probability
The chance that a particular event will occur.

The probability value will be in the range 0 to 1. A value of 0 means the event will not occur. A probability of 1 means the event will occur. Anything between 0 and 1 reflects the uncertainty of the event occurring. The definition given is for a countable number of events.

For instance, if we look out the window and see rain, we can say the probability of rain today is 1 since we know for sure that it will rain. If an airplane has a top speed of 450 mph, and the distance between city A and city B is 900 miles, we can say the probability the plane will make the trip in 1.5 hours is zero—it can't happen. These examples involve situations where we are *certain* of the outcome and our 1 and 0 probabilities reflect this.

However, in most business situations, we do not have certainty, but instead are uncertain. For instance, if a local pizza company is given the right to sell pizzas at college football games, then knowing how many pizzas to have on hand so as not to run short or to have too many leftover pizzas involves uncertainty. The manager does not know for sure how many pizzas will be demanded. If he decides to stock 300 pizzas, he might say that the chance of needing more than 300 pizzas is 0.30. This value between 0 and 1 reflects his uncertainty about the demand for pizzas at the game.

Events and Sample Space As discussed in Chapter 1, data come in many forms and are gathered in many ways. In a business environment, when a sample is selected or a decision is made, there are generally many possible outcomes. In probability language, the process that produces the outcomes is an **experiment**. In business situations, the experiment can range from an investment decision to a personnel decision to a choice of warehouse location.

Experiment
A process that produces a single outcome whose result cannot be predicted with certainty.

For instance, a very simple experiment might involve flipping a coin one time. When this experiment is performed, two possible experimental outcomes can occur: head and tail. If the coin-tossing experiment is expanded to involve two flips of the coin, the experimental outcomes are

> Head on first flip and Head on second flip, denoted by (H,H)
>
> Head on first flip and tail on second flip, denoted by (H,T)
>
> Tail on first flip and Head on second flip, denoted by (T,H)
>
> Tail on first flip and Tail on second flip, denoted by (T,T)

Sample Space
The collection of all outcomes that can result from a selection, decision, or experiment.

The collection of possible experimental outcomes is called the **sample space**.

EXAMPLE 4-1 Defining the Sample Space

TRY PROBLEM 4.1

Able Accounting   A partner for Able Accounting, a large regional accounting firm, is analyzing the performance of her many audit teams. She is particularly interested in whether the audits are finished by the projected completion date. She is interested in determining the sample space (possible outcomes) for two randomly selected audits. To do this, she can use the following steps:

Step 1 Define the experiment.
The experiment is the audit. Of interest is the status of an audit completion.

Step 2 Define the outcomes for one trial of the experiment.
The partner can define the outcomes to be

$$e_1 = \text{Audit done early}$$
$$e_2 = \text{Audit done on time}$$
$$e_3 = \text{Audit done late}$$

Step 3 Define the sample space.
The sample space (SS) for an experiment involving a single audit is

$$SS = \{e_1, e_2, e_3\}$$

If the experiment is expanded to include two audits, the sample space is

$$SS = \{e_1, e_2, e_3, e_4, e_5, e_6, e_7, e_8, e_9\}$$

where the outcomes include what happens on both audits and are defined as

Outcome	Audit 1	Audit 2
e_1	early	early
e_2	early	on time
e_3	early	late
e_4	on time	early
e_5	on time	on time
e_6	on time	late
e_7	late	early
e_8	late	on time
e_9	late	late

TRY PROBLEM 4.1

EXAMPLE 4-2 Defining the Sample Space

Lincoln Marketing Research Recently, Lincoln Marketing Research in Lincoln, Nebraska, was retained to interview television viewers to determine whether they objected to having ads for hard liquor on TV. The analyst assigned to the project is interested in listing the sample space (possible outcomes). To do this, he can use the following steps:

Step 1 Define the experiment.
The experiment involves selecting three television viewers and posing the question: "Would you object to hard-liquor advertisements on television?"

Step 2 Determine the outcome for a single trial of the simple experiment.
The possible outcomes when one person is interviewed are

no
yes

Step 3 Define the sample space.
If three people are interviewed (3 trials), the sample space (possible outcomes) is

Outcome		Viewer 1	Viewer 2	Viewer 3
e_1	=	no	no	no
e_2	=	no	no	yes
e_3	=	no	yes	no
e_4	=	no	yes	yes
e_5	=	yes	no	no
e_6	=	yes	no	yes
e_7	=	yes	yes	no
e_8	=	yes	yes	yes

For instance, one possible experimental outcome is e_1, all three people say no. Thus this outcome is (no, no, no).

Using Tree Diagrams A tree diagram is often a useful way to define the sample space for an experiment that helps ensure that no outcomes are omitted. Example 4-3 illustrates how a tree diagram is used.

TRY PROBLEM 4.2

EXAMPLE 4-3 Using a Tree Diagram to Define the Sample Space

Lincoln Marketing Research In Example 4-2, Lincoln Marketing Research was involved in a project in which television viewers were asked whether they objected to hard-liquor advertisements being shown on television. The analyst is interested in listing the sample space, using a tree diagram as an aid, when three viewers are interviewed. The following steps can be used:

Step 1 Define the experiment.
Three people are interviewed and asked, "Would you object to hard-liquor advertisements on television?" Thus, the experiment consists of three trials.

Step 2 Define the outcomes for a single trial of the experiment.
The possible outcomes when one person is interviewed are

no
yes

Step 3 **Define the sample space for three trials using a tree diagram.**
Begin by determining the outcomes for a single trial. Illustrate these with tree branches beginning on the left side of the page:

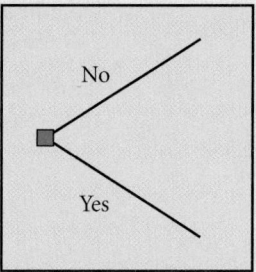

For each of these branches, add branches depicting the outcomes for a second trial. Continue until the tree has the number of sets of branches corresponding to the number of trials.

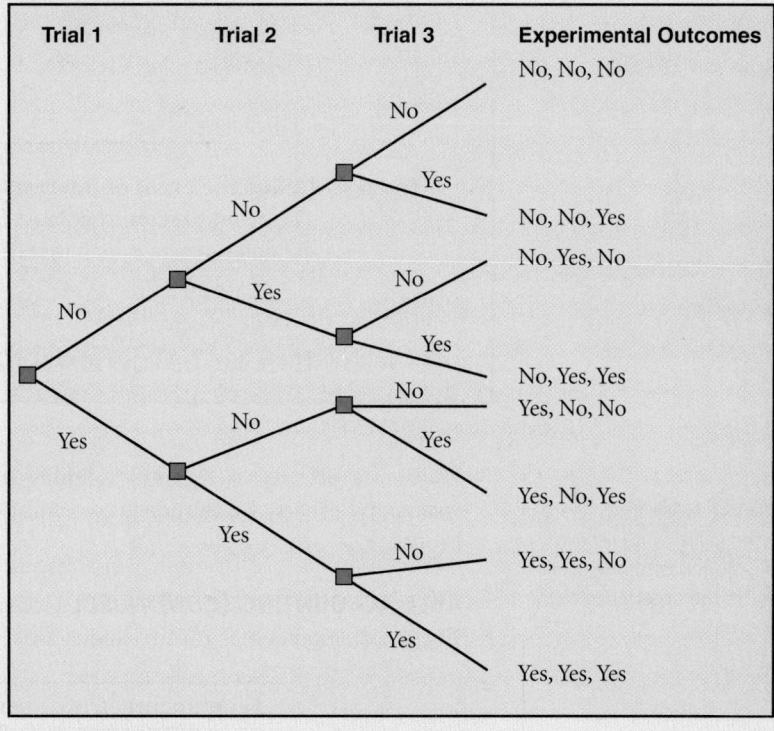

Event

A collection of experimental outcomes.

A collection of possible outcomes is called an **event**. An example will help clarify these terms.

EXAMPLE 4-4 Defining an Event of Interest

TRY PROBLEM 4.10

Able Accounting The Able Accounting firm in Example 4-1 is interested in the sample space for an audit experiment in which the outcome of interest is the audit's completion status. The sample space is the list of all possible outcomes from the experiment. The accounting firm is also interested in specifying the outcomes that make up an event of interest. This can be done using the following steps:

Step 1 **Define the experiment.**
The experiment consists of two randomly chosen audits.

Step 2 List the outcomes associated with one trial of the experiment.
For a single audit the following completion-status possibilities exist:

Audit done early
Audit done on time
Audit done late

Step 3 Define the sample space.
For two audits (two trials), we define the sample space:

Experimental Outcome		Audit 1	Audit 2
e_1	=	early	early
e_2	=	early	on time
e_3	=	early	late
e_4	=	on time	early
e_5	=	on time	on time
e_6	=	on time	late
e_7	=	late	early
e_8	=	late	on time
e_9	=	late	late

Step 4 Define the event of interest.
The event of interest at least one audit is completed late is composed of all the outcomes in which one or more audits are late. This event (E) is

$$E = \{e_3, e_6, e_7, e_8, e_9\}$$

There are five ways in which one or more audits are completed late.

Mutually Exclusive Events Keeping in mind the definitions for *experiment, sample space*, and *events*, we introduce two additional concepts. The first is **mutually exclusive events**.

Mutually Exclusive Events
Two events are mutually exclusive if the occurrence of one event precludes the occurrence of the other event.

ABLE ACCOUNTING (*CONTINUED*) Consider again the Able Accounting firm example. The possible outcomes for two audits are

Experimental Outcomes		Audit 1	Audit 2
e_1	=	early	early
e_2	=	early	on time
e_3	=	early	late
e_4	=	on time	early
e_5	=	on time	on time
e_6	=	on time	late
e_7	=	late	early
e_8	=	late	on time
e_9	=	late	late

Suppose we define one event as consisting of the outcomes in which at least one of the two audits is late.

$$E_1 = \{e_3, e_6, e_7, e_8, e_9\}$$

Further, suppose we define two more events as follows:

$$E_2 = \text{neither audit is late} = \{e_1, e_2, e_4, e_5\}$$
$$E_3 = \text{both audits are finished at the same time} = \{e_1, e_5, e_9\}$$

Events E_1 and E_2 are mutually exclusive: If E_1 occurs, E_2 cannot occur; if E_2 occurs, E_1 cannot occur. That is, if at least one audit is late, then it is not possible for neither audit to be late. We can verify this fact by observing that no outcomes in E_1 appear in E_2. This observation provides another way of defining mutually exclusive events: Two events are mutually exclusive if they have no common outcomes.

Independent and Dependent Events A second probability concept is that of **independent** versus **dependent** events.

Business Application

Independent Events
Two events are independent if the occurrence of one event in no way influences the probability of the occurrence of the other event.

Dependent Events
Two events are dependent if the occurrence of one event impacts the probability of the other event occurring.

MOBILE EXPLORATION Mobile Exploration is a subsidiary of the Mobile Corporation and is responsible for oil and natural gas exploration worldwide. During the exploration phase, seismic surveys are conducted that provide information about the earth's underground formations. Based on past history, the company knows that if the seismic readings are favorable, oil or gas more likely will be discovered than if the seismic readings are not favorable. However, the readings are not perfect indicators. Suppose the company currently is exploring in the eastern part of Australia. The possible outcomes for the seismic survey are defined as

$$e_1 = \text{favorable}$$
$$e_2 = \text{unfavorable}$$

If the company decides to drill, the outcomes are defined as

$$e_3 = \text{strike oil or gas}$$
$$e_4 = \text{dry hole}$$

If we let the event A be that the seismic survey is favorable and event B be that the hole is dry, we can say that the events A and B are not mutually exclusive, because if one event occurs, it does not preclude the other event from occurring. We can also say that the two events are dependent because the chance of a dry hole depends on whether the seismic survey is favorable or unfavorable.

EXAMPLE 4-5 Mutually Exclusive Events

TRY PROBLEM 4.8

Barcelona Assembly Barcelona Assembly, located in Barcelona, Spain, does contract assembly work for Hewlett-Packard. Each item produced on the assembly line can be thought of as an experimental trial. The managers at this facility can analyze their process to determine whether the events of interest are mutually exclusive using the following steps:

Step 1 Define the experiment.
The experiment is producing a part on an assembly line.

Step 2 Define the outcomes for a single trial of the experiment.
On each trial the outcome is either a *good* or a *defective* item.

Step 3 Define the sample space.
If two products are produced (two trials), the following sample space is defined:

Experimental Outcomes	
Product 1	Product 2
e_1 = good	good
e_2 = good	defective
e_3 = defective	good
e_4 = defective	defective

Step 4   Determine whether the events are mutually exclusive.
Let event E_1 be defined as both products produced are good, and let event E_2 be defined as at least one product is defective:

$$E_1 = \text{both good} = \{e_1\}$$
$$E_2 = \text{at least one defective} = \{e_2, e_3, e_4\}$$

Then events E_1 and E_2 are determined to be mutually exclusive because the two events have no outcomes in common. Having two good items and at the same time having at least one defective item is not possible.

CHAPTER OUTCOME #1

Methods of Assigning Probability

Part of the confusion surrounding probability may be due to the fact that probability can be assigned to outcomes in more than one way. There are three common ways to assign probability to outcomes: *classical probability assessment, relative frequency of occurrence,* and *subjective probability assessment.* The following notation is used when we refer to the probability of an event:

$$P(E_i) = \text{probability of event } E_i \text{ occurring}$$

Classical Probability Assessment   The first method of probability assessment involves **classical probability**, or *a priori* probability.

Classical Probability Assessment
The method of determining probability based on the ratio of the number of ways an outcome or event of interest can occur to the number of ways *any* outcome or event can occur when the individual outcomes are equally likely.

You are probably already familiar with classical probability. It had its beginning with games of chance and is still most often discussed in those terms.

Consider again the experiment of flipping a coin one time. There are two possible outcomes: head and tail. Each of these is equally likely. Thus, using the classical assessment method, the probability of a head is the ratio of the number of ways a head can occur (1 way) to the total number of ways any outcome can occur (2 ways). Thus we get

$$P(\text{head}) = \frac{1 \text{ way}}{2 \text{ ways}} = \frac{1}{2} = 0.50$$

The chance of a head occurring is 1 out of 2, or 0.50.

In those situations in which all possible outcomes are *equally likely,* the classical probability measurement is defined in Equation 4.1.

Classical Probability Assessment

$$P(E_i) = \frac{\text{Number of ways } E_i \text{ can occur}}{\text{Total number of possible outcomes}} \tag{4.1}$$

TRY PROBLEM 4.11

EXAMPLE 4-6   Classical Probability Assessment

Galaxy Furniture   The managers at Galaxy Furniture plan to hold a special promotion over Labor Day Weekend. Each customer making a purchase exceeding $100 will qualify to select an envelope from a large drum. Inside the envelope are coupons for percentage discounts off the purchase total. At the beginning of the weekend, there were 500 coupons. Four hundred of these were for 10% discount, 50 were for 20% discount, 45 were for 30%, and 5 were for 50% discount. Customers were interested in determining the probability of getting a particular discount amount. The probabilities can be determined using classical assessment with the following steps:

Step 1 Define the experiment.
An envelope is selected from a large drum.

Step 2 Determine whether the possible outcomes are equally likely.
In this case, the envelopes with the different discount amounts are unmarked from the outside and are thoroughly mixed in the drum. Thus, any one envelope has the same probability of being selected as any other envelope. The outcomes are equally likely.

Step 3 Determine the total number of outcomes.
There are 500 envelopes in the drum.

Step 4 Define the event of interest.
We might be interested in assessing the probability that the first customer will get a 20% discount.

Step 5 Determine the number of outcomes associated with the event of interest.
There are 50 coupons with a discount of 20% marked on them.

Step 6 Compute the classical probability using Equation 4.1:

$$P(E_i) = \frac{\text{Number of ways } E_i \text{ can occur}}{\text{Total number of possible outcomes}}$$

$$P(20\% \text{ Discount}) = \frac{\text{Number of ways 20\% can occur}}{\text{Total number of possible outcomes}} = \frac{50}{500} = 0.10$$

Note: After the first customer selects an envelope from the drum, the probability that the next customer will get a particular discount will change, because the values in the denominator and possibly the numerator will change.

As you can see, the classical approach to probability measurement is fairly straightforward. Many games of chance are based on classical probability assessment. However, classical probability assessment is difficult to apply to most business situations. Rarely are the individual outcomes equally likely. For instance, you might be thinking of starting a business. The sample space is

$$SS = \{\text{Succeed, Fail}\}$$

Would it be reasonable to use classical assessment to determine the probability that your business will succeed? If so, we would make the following assessment:

$$P(\text{Succeed}) = \frac{1}{2}$$

If this were true, then the chance of any business succeeding would be 0.50. Of course, this is not true. Too many factors go into determining the success or failure of a business. The possible outcomes (Succeed, Fail) are not equally likely. Instead, we need another method of assessment in these situations.

Relative Frequency Assessment The **relative frequency assessment** approach is based on actual observations.

Equation 4.2 shows how the relative frequency assessment method is used to assess probabilities.

Relative Frequency Assessment
The method that defines probability as the number of times an event occurs divided by the total number of times an experiment is performed in a large number of trials.

Relative Frequency

$$P(E_i) = \frac{\text{Number of times } E_i \text{ occurs}}{N} \qquad (4.2)$$

where:

$$E_i = \text{The event of interest}$$
$$N = \text{Number of trials}$$

Business Application

HATHAWAY HEATING & AIR CONDITIONING The sales manager at Hathaway Heating & Air Conditioning has recently developed the customer profile shown in Table 4.1. The profile is based on a random sample of 500 customers. As a promotion for the company, the sales manager plans to randomly select a customer once a month and perform a free service on the customer's system. What is the probability that the first customer selected is a residential customer? What is the probability that the first customer has a Hathaway heating system?

To determine the probability that the customer selected is residential, we determine from Table 4.1 the number of residential customers and divide by the total number of customers, both residential and commercial. We then apply Equation 4.2:

$$P(E_2) = P(\text{Residential}) = \frac{400}{500} = 0.80$$

Thus, there is an 80% chance the customer selected will be a residential customer.

The probability the customer selected has a Hathaway heating system is determined by the ratio of the number of customers with heating systems to the number of total customers.

$$P(E_3) = P(\text{Heating}) = \frac{200}{500} = 0.40$$

There is a 40% chance the randomly selected customer will have a Hathaway heating system.

The sales manager hopes the customer selected is a residential customer with a heating system. Because there are 145 customers in this category, the relative frequency method assesses the probability of this event occurring as follows:

$$P(E_2) \text{ with } (E_3) = P(\text{Residential with Heating}) = \frac{145}{500} = 0.29$$

There is a 29% chance the customer selected will be a residential customer with a heating system.

TABLE 4.1 Hathaway Heating & Air Conditioning Co.

		Customer Category		
		E_1 Commercial	E_2 Residential	Total
E_3	Heating Systems	55	145	200
E_4	Air-Conditioning Systems	45	255	300
	Total	100	400	500

EXAMPLE 4-7 Relative Frequency Probability Assessment

TRY PROBLEM 4.10

Thomas' Dairy Bar Thomas' Dairy Bar is located in a busy mall in Pittsburgh, Pennsylvania. Thomas' sells ice cream and frozen yogurt products. One of the difficulties in this business is knowing how much of a given product to prepare for the day. The manager is interested in determining the probability that a customer will select yogurt over ice cream. She has maintained records of customer purchases for the past three weeks. The probability can be assessed using relative frequency with the following steps:

Step 1 Define the experiment.
A randomly chosen customer will select between ice cream and yogurt.

Step 2 Define the events of interest.
The manager is interested in the event E_1 customer selects yogurt.

Step 3 Determine the total number of occurrences.
In this case, she has observed 2,250 sales of ice cream and yogurt in the past three weeks. Thus, $N = 2,250$.

Step 4 For the event of interest, determine the number of occurrences.
In the past three weeks, 1,570 sales were for yogurt.

Step 5 Use Equation 4.2 to determine the probability assessment.

$$P(E_1) = \frac{\text{Number of times } E_1 \text{ occurs}}{N} = \frac{1,570}{2,250} = 0.6978$$

Thus, based on past history, the chance that a customer will purchase yogurt is just under 0.70.

POTENTIAL ISSUES WITH THE RELATIVE FREQUENCY ASSESMENT METHOD There are a couple of concerns that you should be aware of before applying the relative frequency assessment method. First, in order for this method to be useful, all of the observed frequencies must be comparable. For instance, consider again the case where you are interested in starting a small business. Two outcomes can occur: business succeeds or business fails. If we are interested in the probability that the business will succeed, we might be tempted to study a sample of, say, 200 small businesses that have been started in the past and determine the number of those that have succeeded—say, 50. Using Equation 4.2 for the relative frequency method, we get

$$P(\text{Succeed}) = \frac{50}{200} = 0.25$$

However, before we can conclude the chance your small business will succeed is 0.25, you must be sure that the conditions of each of the 200 businesses match your conditions (that is, location, type of business, management expertise and experience, financial standing, and so on). If not, then the relative frequency method should not be used.

Another issue involves the size of the denominator in Equation 4.2. If the number of possible occurrences is quite small, the probability assessment may be unreliable. For instance, suppose a basketball player has taken five free throws during the season and missed them all. The relative frequency method would determine the probability that he will make the next free throw to be

$$P(\text{make}) = \frac{0 \text{ made}}{5 \text{ shots}} = \frac{0}{5} = 0.0$$

But do you think there is really no chance the next free throw will be made? No, even the notoriously poor free-throw shooter, Shaquille O'Neal of the NBA's Miami Heat, has some chance of making a free throw. The problem is that the base of five free throws is too small to provide a reliable probability assessment

Subjective Probability Assessment

The method that defines probability of an event as reflecting a decision maker's state of mind regarding the chances that the particular event will occur.

Subjective Probability Assessment   Unfortunately, even though managers may have some past experience to guide their decision making, there always will be new factors affecting each decision that make that experience only an approximate guide to the future. In other cases, managers may have little or no past experience and, therefore, may not be able to use a relative frequency as even a starting point in assessing the desired probability. When past experience is not available, decision makers must make a **subjective probability assessment**. A subjective probability is a measure of a personal conviction that an outcome will occur. Therefore, in this instance, probability represents a person's belief that an event will occur.

Business Application

HARRISON CONSTRUCTION   The Harrison Construction Company is preparing a bid for a road construction project. The company's engineers are very good at defining all the elements of the projects (labor, materials, and so on) and know the costs of these with a great deal of certainty. In finalizing the bid amount, the managers add a profit markup to the projected costs. The problem is how much markup to add. If they add too much, they won't be the low bidder and may lose the contract. If they don't mark it up enough, they may get the project and make less profit than they might have made had they used a higher markup. The managers are considering four possible markup values, stated as percentages of base costs:

10%   12%   15%   20%

To make their decision, the managers need to assess the probability of winning the contract at each of these markup levels. Because they have never done another project exactly like this one, they can't rely on relative frequency of occurrence. Instead, they must subjectively assess the probability based on whatever information they currently have available, such as who the other bidders are, the rapport Harrison has with the potential client, and so forth.

After considering these values, the Harrison managers make the following assessments:

$$P(\text{Win at } 10\%) = 0.30$$
$$P(\text{Win at } 12\%) = 0.25$$
$$P(\text{Win at } 15\%) = 0.15$$
$$P(\text{Win at } 20\%) = 0.05$$

These assessments indicate the managers' state of mind regarding the chances of winning the contract. If new information (for example, a competitor drops out of the bidding) becomes available before the bid is submitted, these assessments could change.

Each of the three methods by which probabilities are assessed has specific advantages and specific applications. Regardless of how decision makers arrive at a probability assessment, the rules by which people use these probabilities in decision making are the same. These rules will be introduced in Section 4.2.

4-1: Exercises

Skill Development

4-1. If two customers are asked to list their choice of ice cream flavor from among vanilla, chocolate, and strawberry, list the sample space showing the possible outcomes.

4-2. Customers at a video store are allowed to rent one, two, or three movies. Use a tree diagram to list the sample space for the number of movies rented by three customers (assuming that each one rents at least one movie.)

4-3. A special roulette wheel, which has only an even number of red and black spots, has come up red four times in a row. Assuming that the roulette wheel is fair, what concept allows a player to know that the probability the next spin of the wheel will come up black is 0.5?

4-4. In a survey, respondents were asked to indicate their favorite brand of cereal (Post or Kellogg's). They were allowed only one choice. What is the probability concept that implies it is not possible for a single respondent to state both Post and Kellogg's to be the favorite cereal?

4-5. In each of the following, indicate what method of probability assessment would most likely be used to assess the probability:
   a. What is the probability that a major earthquake will occur in California in the next three years?
   b. What is the probability that a customer will return a purchase for a refund?
   c. An inventory of appliances contains four white washers and one black washer. If a customer selects one at random, what is the probability that the black washer will be selected?

4-6. Pat and Tom are long-time friends living in Las Vegas. They agree on many things, but not the outcome of the American League pennant race and the World Series. Pat is originally from Boston and Tom is from New York. They have a steak dinner bet on next year's race, with Pat betting on the Red Sox and Tom on the Yankees. Both are convinced they will win.
   a. What probability assessment technique is being used by the two friends?
   b. Why would the relative frequency technique not be appropriate in this situation?

4-7. Students who live on-campus and purchase a meal plan are randomly assigned to one of three dining halls: the Commons, Northeast, and Frazier. What is the probability that the next student to purchase a meal plan will be assigned to the Commons?

4-8. The following data are for products produced by a company:

Model	Color		
	Blue	**Brown**	**White**
XB-50	302	105	200
YZ-99	40	205	130

   a. Based on the relative frequency assessment method, what is the probability that a manufactured item is brown?
   b. What is the probability that the product manufactured is a YZ-99?
   c. What is the joint probability that a product manufactured is a YZ-99 and brown?

   d. Suppose a product was chosen at random. Consider the two events: The event that model YZ-99 was chosen and the event that a white product was chosen. Are these two events mutually exclusive? Explain.

4-9. A large corporation in search of a CEO and a CFO has narrowed the fields for each position to a short list. The CEO candidates graduated, respectively, from Chicago (C) and three Ivy League universities: Harvard (H), Princeton (P), and Yale (Y). The three CFO candidates graduated, respectively, from MIT (M), Northwestern (N), and two Ivy League universities: Dartmouth (D) and Brown (B). One candidate from each of the respective lists is chosen to fill the positions. The event of interest is that both positions are filled with candidates from the Ivy League.
   a. Determine whether the outcomes are equally likely.
   b. Determine the number of equally likely outcomes.
   c. Define the event of interest.
   d. Determine the number of outcomes associated with the event of interest.
   e. Compute the classical probability of the event of interest using Equation 4.1.

4-10. The results of a census of 2,500 employees of a mid-sized company with 401(k) retirement accounts are as follows:

Account Balance (to nearest $)	Male	Female
<$25,000	635	495
$25,000–$49,999	185	210
$50,000–$99,999	515	260
>$100,000	155	45

Suppose researchers are going to sample employees from the company for further study.
   a. Based on the relative frequency assessment method, what is the probability that a randomly selected employee will be a female?
   b. Based on the relative frequency assessment method what is the probability that a randomly selected employee will have a 401(k) account balance of between $25,000 and $49,999?
   c. Compute the probability that a randomly selected employee will be a female with an account balance between $50,000 and $99,999?

4-11. Three consumers go to a specialty retailer of consumer electronics to examine HDTVs. Let B indicate that one of the consumers buys an HDTV. Let D be that the consumer doesn't buy an HDTV. Define the following events: (1) only two consumers buy an HDTV, (2) at most two consumers buy HDTVs, and (3) at least two consumers buy HDTVs. Assume these events are equally likely.

a. Determine whether the outcomes are equally likely.

b. Determine the number of equally likely events.

c. Define the events of interest in each of the events. To define the events of interest, list the possible outcomes in each of the following events:
  - only two consumers buy an HDTV (E_1)
  - at most two consumers buy HDTVs (E_2)
  - at least two consumers buy HDTVs (E_3)

d. Determine the number of outcomes associated with each of the events of interest. Use the classical probability assessment approach to assign probabilities to each of the possible outcomes and calculate the probabilities of the events in part.

e. Compute the classical probabilities of each of the events in part e by using Equation 4.1.

Business Applications

4-12. While recognizing that many new electronic products may not earn a profit, Mary Tangrin, the head of marketing for Plasco Optics, is enthusiastic about the new product coming out of the R&D lab. It will increase the megapixel capability of cell phone cameras to the 6+ range. She made a presentation to the company CEO stating the probability the company will earn a profit in excess of $20 million next year is 80%. Comment on this probability assessment.

4-13. The Carlisle Medical Clinic has five doctors on staff. The doctors have agreed to keep the office open on Saturdays, but with only three doctors. The office manager has decided to make up Saturday schedules in such a way that no set of three doctors will be in the office together more than once. How many weeks can be covered by this schedule? (*Hint*: Use a tree diagram to list the sample space.)

4-14. A study of the advertisements in the classified section of a local newspaper shows that 204 are help-wanted ads, 520 are real estate ads, and 306 are for other ads.

a. If the newspaper plans to select an ad at random each week to be published free, what is the probability that the ad for a specific week will be a help-wanted ad?

b. What method of probability assessment is used to determine the probability in part a?

c. Are the events that a help-wanted ad is chosen and that an ad for other types of products or services is chosen for this promotion on a specific week mutually exclusive? Explain.

4-15. Larry Miller, owner of the Utah Jazz basketball team of the NBA, owns several automobile dealerships in Utah and Idaho. One of his dealerships sells Buick, Cadillac, and Pontiac automobiles. It also sells used cars that it gets as trade-ins on new car purchases. Supposing two cars are sold on Tuesday by the dealership, what is the sample space for the type of cars that might be sold?

4-16. Blackburn Cedar, Inc. manufactures cedar fencing material in Marysville, Washington. The company's quality manager inspected 5,900 boards and found that 4,100 could be rated as a #1 grade.

a. If the manager wanted to assess the probability that a board being produced will be a #1 grade, what method of assessment would he likely use?

b. Referring to your answer in part a, what would you assess the probability of a #1 grade board to be?

4-17. At a recent meeting of the top managers for Nabisco, three marking managers were asked to assess the probability that sales for next year will be more than 15% higher than the current years. One manager stated that the probability of this happening was 0.40. The second manager assessed the probability to be 0.60, and the third manager stated the probability to be 0.90.

a. What method of probability assessment are the three managers using?

b. Which manager is expressing the least uncertainty in the probability assessment?

c. Why is it that the three managers did not provide the same probability assessment?

4-18. Flying Pie Pizzeria bakes and sells pizzas for three kinds of customers: dine-in, delivery, and pickup. Last year's pizza sales at the Flying Pie showed that 12,753 orders were for dine-in, 5,893 pizzas were delivery orders, and 3,122 orders were carry-out. Suppose an audit of last year's sales is being conducted.

a. If a customer order is selected at random, what is the probability it will be a carryout order?

b. What method of probability assessment was used to determine the probability in part a?

c. If two customer orders are selected at random, list the sample space indicating the type of order for both customers.

4-19. VERCOR provides merger and acquisition consultants to assist corporations when an owner decides to offer the business for sale. One of their news releases, "Tax Audit Frequency Is Rising," written by David L. Perkins, Jr., a VERCOR partner, originally appeared in *The Business Owner*. Perkins indicated that audits of the largest businesses, those corporations with assets of $10 million and over, climbed to 9,560 in 2004. That was up from a low of 7,125 in 2003. One in six large corporations was audited in fiscal 2004.

a. Designate the type of probability assessment method that Perkins used to assess the probability of large corporations being audited in fiscal 2004.

b. Determine the number of large corporations that filed tax returns for the 2004 fiscal year.

c. Determine the probability that a large corporation was not audited using the relative frequency probability assessment method.

4-20. The results of Fortune Personnel Consultants' survey of 405 workers was reported in *USA Today* (Snapshots, September 16, 2005). One of the questions in the survey asked, "Do you feel it's OK for your company to monitor your Internet use?" The possible responses were: (1) Only after informing me, (2) Does not need to inform me, (3) Only when company believes I am misusing, (4) Company does not have right, and (5) Only if I have previously misused. The following table contains the results for the 405 respondents:

Response	1	2	3	4	5
Number of Respondents	223	130	32	14	6

a. Calculate the probability that a randomly chosen respondent would indicate that there should be some restriction concerning the company's right to monitor Internet use.

b. Indicate the method of probability assessment used to determine the probability in part a.

c. Are the events that a randomly selected respondent chose response (1) and that another randomly selected respondent chose response (2) independent, mutually exclusive, or dependent events? Explain.

Computer Database Exercises

4-21. According to a September, 2005, article on the Womensenews.org Web site, "...Caesarean sections, in which a baby is delivered by abdominal surgery, have increased fivefold in the past 30 years, prompting concern among health advocates...." The data in the file called **Babies** indicate whether the past 50 babies delivered at a local hospital were delivered using the Caesarean method.

a. Based on these data, what is the probability that a baby born in this hospital will be born using the Caesarean method?

b. What concerns might you have about using these data to assess the probability of a Caesarean birth? Discuss.

4-22. Recently, a large state university conducted a survey of undergraduate students regarding their use of computers. The results of the survey are contained in the data file **ComputerUse**.

a. Based on the data from the survey, what is the probability that undergraduate students at this university will have a major that requires them to use a computer on a daily basis?

b. Based on the data from this survey, if a student is a business major, what is the probability of the student believing that the computer lab facilities are very adequate?

4-23. A company produces scooters used by small businesses, such as pizza parlors, that find them convenient for making short deliveries. The company is notified whenever a scooter breaks down, and the problem is classified as being either mechanical or electrical. The company then matches the scooter to the plant where it was assembled. The file **Scooters** contains a random sample of 200 breakdowns. Use the data in the file and the relative frequency assessment method to find the following probabilities:

a. What is the probability the scooter was assembled at the Tyler plant?

b. What is the probability that a scooter breakdown was due to a mechanical problem?

c. What is the probability that a scooter with an electrical problem was assembled at the Lincoln plant?

4-24. A Harris survey conducted in April of 2005 asked, in part, what was the most important reason that people give for never using a wireless phone exclusively. The responses were: (1) Like the safety of traditional phone, (2) Need line for Net access, (3) Pricing not attractive enough, (4) Weak or unreliable cell signal at home, (5) Coverage not good enough, and (6) Other. The file entitled **Wireless** contains the responses for the 1,088 respondents.

a. Calculate the probability that a randomly chosen respondent would not use a wireless phone exclusively because of some type of difficulty in placing and receiving calls with a wireless phone.

b. Calculate the probability that a randomly chosen person would not use a wireless phone exclusively because of some type of difficulty in placing and receiving calls with a wireless phone and is over the age of 55.

c. Determine the probability that a randomly chosen person would not use a wireless phone exclusively because of a perceived need for Net access and the safety of a traditional phone.

d. Of those respondents under 36, determine the probability that an individual in this age group would not use a wireless phone exclusively because of some type of difficulty in placing and receiving calls with a wireless phone.

4-25. CNN staff writer Pariia Bhatnagar reported ("Coke, Pepsi Losing the Fizz," March 8, 2005) that Atlanta-based Coke saw its domestic market share drop to 43.1% in 2004. New York-based PepsiCo has used its "Pepsi Challenge" advertising approach to increase its market share, that stood at 31.7% in 2004. A selection of soft-drink users is asked to taste the two disguised soft drinks and indicate which they prefer. The file entitled **Challenge** contains the results of a simulated Pepsi Challenge on a college campus.

a. Determine the probability that a randomly chosen student prefers Pepsi.

b. Determine the probability that one of the students prefers Pepsi and is less than 20 years old.

c. Of those students who are less than 20 years old, calculate the probability that a randomly chosen student prefers (1) Pepsi and (2) Coke.

d. Of those students who are at least 20 years old, calculate the probability that a randomly chosen student prefers (1) Pepsi and (2) Coke.

4.2 The Rules of Probability

Measuring Probabilities

The probability attached to an event represents the likelihood the event will occur on a specified trial of an experiment. This probability also measures the perceived uncertainty about whether the event will occur.

Possible Values and Sum If we are certain about the outcome of an event, we will assign the event a probability of 0 or 1, where $P(E_i) = 0$ indicates the event E_i will not occur, and $P(E_i) = 1$ means that E_i will definitely occur. If we are uncertain about the result of an experiment, we measure this uncertainty by assigning a probability between 0 and 1. Probability Rule 1 shows that the probability of an event occurring is always between 0 and 1.

Probability Rule 1

For any event E_i,

$$0 \le P(E_i) \le 1 \quad \text{for all } i \tag{4.3}$$

All possible outcomes associated with an experiment form the sample space. Therefore, the sum of the probabilities of all possible outcomes is 1, as shown by Probability Rule 2.

Probability Rule 2

$$\sum_{i=1}^{k} P(e_i) = 1 \tag{4.4}$$

where:

$$k = \text{Number of outcomes in the sample}$$
$$e_i = i\text{th outcome}$$

CHAPTER OUTCOME #2   **Addition Rule for Individual Outcomes** If a single event is composed of two or more individual outcomes, then the probability of the event is found by summing the probabilities of the individual outcomes. This is illustrated by Probability Rule 3.

Probability Rule 3: Addition Rule for Individual Outcomes

The probability of an event E_i is equal to the *sum* of the probabilities of the individual outcomes forming E_i. For example, if

$$E_i = \{e_1, e_2, e_3\}$$

then

$$P(E_i) = P(e_1) + P(e_2) + P(e_3) \tag{4.5}$$

Business Application

EDWARD'S CINEMAS Edward's Cinemas is considering opening a 20-screen complex in Lansing, Michigan, and has recently performed a resident survey as part of its decision-making process. One question of particular interest is how often a respondent goes to a movie during one month. Table 4.2 shows the results of the survey for this question.

The sample space for the experiment for each respondent is

$$SS = \{e_1, e_2, e_3, e_4\}$$

where the possible outcomes are

$$e_1 = \geq 10 \text{ movies}$$
$$e_2 = 3 \text{ to } 9 \text{ movies}$$
$$e_3 = 1 \text{ to } 2 \text{ movies}$$
$$e_4 = 0 \text{ movies}$$

Using the relative frequency assessment approach, we assign the following probabilities.

$$
\begin{aligned}
P(e_1) &= 400/5{,}000 = 0.08 \\
P(e_2) &= 1{,}900/5{,}000 = 0.38 \\
P(e_3) &= 1{,}500/5{,}000 = 0.30 \\
P(e_4) &= 1{,}200/5{,}000 = \underline{0.24} \\
&\phantom{= 1{,}200/5{,}000 =} \Sigma = \overline{1.00}
\end{aligned}
$$

Assume we are interested in the event "respondent attends 1 to 9 movies per month."

$$E = \text{Respondent attends 1 to 9 movies}$$

The outcomes that make up E are

$$E = e_2, e_3$$

We can find the probability, $P(E)$, by using Probability Rule 3 (Equation 4.5), as follows:

$$
\begin{aligned}
P(E) &= P(e_2) + P(e_3) \\
&= 0.38 + 0.30 \\
&= 0.68
\end{aligned}
$$

TABLE 4.2 Edward's Cinemas Survey Results

Movies Per Month	Frequency	Relative Frequency
≥ 10	400	0.08
3 to 9	1,900	0.38
1 to 2	1,500	0.30
0	1,200	0.24
Total	5,000	1.00

EXAMPLE 4-8 The Addition Rule for Individual Outcomes

TRY PROBLEM 4.26

KFI 640 Radio The KFI 640 radio station in Dover, Delaware, is a combination news/talk and "oldies" station. During a 24-hour day, a listener can tune in and hear any of the following four programs being broadcast:

"oldies" music

news stories

talk programming

commercials

Recently, the station has been having trouble with its transmitter. Each day, the station's signal goes dead for a few seconds; it seems that these outages are equally likely to occur at any time during the 24-hour broadcast day. There seems to be no pattern regarding what is playing at the time the transmitter problem occurs. The station manager is concerned about the probability that these problems will occur during either a news story or a talk show.

Step 1 Define the experiment.
The station conducts its broadcast starting at 12:00 midnight, extending until a transmitter outage is observed.

Step 2 Define the possible outcomes.
The possible outcomes are the type of programming that is playing when the transmitter outage occurs. There are four possible outcomes:

$$e_1 = \text{oldies} \quad e_2 = \text{news} \quad e_3 = \text{talk shows} \quad e_4 = \text{commercials}$$

Step 3 Determine the probability of each possible outcome.
The station manager has determined that out of the 1,440 minutes per day, 540 minutes are "oldies," 240 minutes are news, 540 minutes are talk, and 120 minutes are commercials. Therefore, the probability of each type of programming being on at the moment the outage occurs is assessed as follows:

Outcome = e_i	$P(e_i)$
e_1 = oldies	$P(e_1) = \dfrac{540}{1,440} = 0.375$
e_2 = news	$P(e_2) = \dfrac{240}{1,440} = 0.167$
e_3 = talk shows	$P(e_3) = \dfrac{540}{1,440} = 0.375$
e_4 = commercials	$P(e_4) = \dfrac{120}{1,440} = 0.083$
	$\Sigma = 1.000$

Note, based on Equation 4.4 (Probability Rule 2), the sum of the probabilities of the individual possible outcomes is 1.0.

Step 4 Define the event of interest.
The event of interest is a transmitter problem occurring during a news or talk program. This is

$$E = \{e_2, e_3\}$$

Step 5 Use Probability Rule 3 (Equation 4.5) to compute the desired probability.

$$P(E) = P(e_2) + P(e_3)$$
$$P(E) = 0.167 + 0.375$$
$$P(E) = 0.542$$

Thus, there is slightly more than a 0.5 probability that when a transmitter problem occurs it will happen during either a news or talk program.

Complement

The complement of an event *E* is the collection of all possible outcomes not contained in event *E*.

Complement Rule Closely connected with Probability Rules 1 and 2 is the **complement** of an event. The complement of event *E* is represented by $\bar{E}$. Thus, the Complement Rule is a corollary to Probability Rules 1 and 2.

Complement Rule

$$P(\bar{E}) = 1 - P(E) \tag{4.6}$$

That is, the probability of the complement of event *E* is 1 minus the probability of event *E*.

EXAMPLE 4-9 The Complement Rule

TRY PROBLEM 4.31

Haupert Machinery The sales manager for Haupert Machinery in Medford, Oregon, is preparing to call on a new customer, a building contractor. The sales manager wants to sell the contractor some equipment. Before making the presentation, the manager lists four possible outcomes and his subjectively assessed probabilities related to the sales prospect.

Outcomes (Sales)	P(Sales)
$ 0	0.70
$ 2,000	0.20
$15,000	0.07
$50,000	0.03
	$\Sigma = 1.00$

Note that each probability is between 0 and 1 and that the sum of the probabilities is 1, as required by Rules 1 and 2.

The owner is interested in knowing the probability of sales >$0. This can be found using the Complement Rule with the following steps:

Step 1 Determine the probabilities for the outcomes.

$$P(\$0) = 0.70$$
$$P(\$2,000) = 0.20$$
$$P(\$15,000) = 0.07$$
$$P(\$50,000) = 0.03$$

Step 2 Find the desired probability.

Let E be the event sales = \$0. The probability of not selling anything to the building contractor is

$$P(E) = 0.70$$

The complement, $\bar{E}$, is all sales >\$0. Using the Complement Rule, the probability of sales >\$0 is

$$P(\text{Sales} > \$0) = 1 - P(\text{sales} = \$0)$$
$$P(\text{Sales} > \$0) = 1 - 0.70$$
$$P(\text{Sales} > \$0) = 0.30$$

Based on his subjective assessment, there is a 30% chance the sales manager will sell something to the building contractor.

Addition Rule for Two Events

Business Application

CHAPTER OUTCOME #2

EDWARD'S CINEMAS (*CONTINUED*) Suppose the people who conducted the survey for Edward's Cinemas also asked questions about the respondents' ages. The company's managers consider age important in deciding on location because its theaters do better in areas with a younger population base. Table 4.3 shows the breakdown of the sample by age group and by the number of times a respondent goes to a movie per month.

Table 4.3 shows that there are seven events defined. For instance, E_1 is the event that respondent attends 10 or more movies per month. This event is composed of three individual outcomes associated with the three age categories. These are

$$E_1 = \{e_1, e_2, e_3\}$$

In another case, event E_5 corresponds to a respondent being less than 30 years of age. It is composed of four individual outcomes associated with the four levels of movie attendance. These are

$$E_5 = \{e_1, e_4, e_7, e_{10}\}$$

Table 4.3 illustrates two important concepts in data analysis: *joint frequencies* and *marginal frequencies*. Joint frequencies, which were discussed in Chapter 2, are the values inside the table. They provide information on age group and movie viewing jointly. Marginal frequencies are the row and column totals. These values give information on only the age group or only movie attendance.

TABLE 4.3 Edward's Cinemas

Movies per Month	Age Group			Total
	E_5 Less than 30	E_6 30 to 50	E_7 Over 50	
E_1 $\geq$ 10 Movies	e_1 200	e_2 100	e_3 100	400
E_2 3 to 9 Movies	e_4 600	e_5 900	e_6 400	1,900
E_3 1 to 2 Movies	e_7 400	e_8 600	e_9 500	1,500
E_4 0 Movies	e_{10} 700	e_{11} 500	e_{12} 0	1,200
Total	1,900	2,100	1,000	5,000

TABLE 4.4 Edward's Cinemas—Joint Probability Table

Movies per Month	Age Group			
	E_5 Less than 30	E_6 30 to 50	E_7 Over 50	Total
E_1 ≥10 Movies	e_1 200/5,000 = 0.04	e_2 100/5,000 = 0.02	e_3 100/5,000 = 0.02	400/5,000 = 0.08
E_2 3 to 9 Movies	e_4 600/5,000 = 0.12	e_5 900/5,000 = 0.18	e_6 400/5,000 = 0.08	1,900/5,000 = 0.38
E_3 1 to 2 Movies	e_7 400/5,000 = 0.08	e_8 600/5,000 = 0.12	e_9 500/5,000 = 0.10	1,500/5,000 = 0.30
E_4 0 Movies	e_{10} 700/5,000 = 0.14	e_{11} 500/5,000 = 0.10	e_{12} 0/5,000 = 0	1,200/5,000 = 0.24
Total	1,900/5,000 = 0.38	2,100/5,000 = 0.42	1,000/5,000 = 0.20	5,000/5,000 = 1

For example, 2,100 people in the survey are in the 30 to 50-year age group. This column total is a marginal frequency for the age group 30 to 50 years, which is represented by E_6. Now notice that 600 respondents are younger than 30 years old and attend a movie three to nine times a month. The 600 is a joint frequency whose outcome is represented by e_4. The joint frequencies are the number of times their associated outcomes occur.

Table 4.4 shows the relative frequencies for the data in Table 4.3. These values are the probabilities of the events and outcomes.

Suppose we wish to find the probability of E_4 (0 movies) **or** E_6 (being in the 30-to-50 age group). That is,

$$P(E_4 \text{ or } E_6) = ?$$

To find this probability, we must use Probability Rule 4.

Probability Rule 4: Addition Rule for Any Two Events, E_1 and E_2

$$P(E_1 \text{ or } E_2) = P(E_1) + P(E_2) - P(E_1 \text{ and } E_2) \qquad (4.7)$$

The key word in knowing when to use Rule 4 is *or*. The word *or* indicates addition. (You may have covered this concept as a *union* in a math class. $P(E_1 \text{ or } E_2) = P(E_1 \cup E_2)$.). Figure 4.1 is a Venn diagram that illustrates the application of the Addition Rule for Two Events. Notice that the probabilities of the outcomes in the overlap between the two events, E_1 and E_2, is double-counted when the probabilities of the outcomes in E_1 are added to those of E_2. Thus, the probabilities of the outcomes in the overlap, which is E_1 *and* E_2, needs to be subtracted to avoid the double counting.

FIGURE 4.1

**Venn Diagram—
Addition Rule for
Two Events**

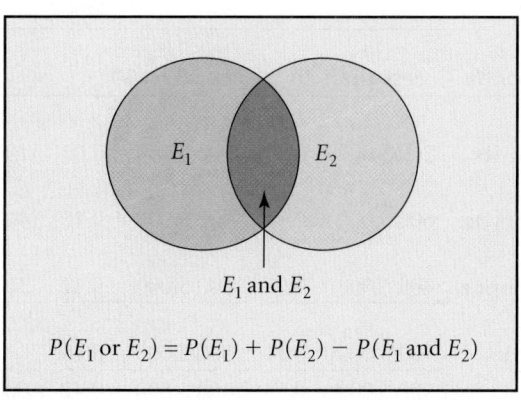

$$P(E_1 \text{ or } E_2) = P(E_1) + P(E_2) - P(E_1 \text{ and } E_2)$$

TABLE 4.5 Edward's Cinemas—Addition Rule Example

Movies per Month	E_5 Less than 30	E_6 30 to 50	E_7 Over 50	Total
	Age Group			
E_1 ≥10 Movies	e_1 200/5,000 = 0.04	e_2 100/5,000 = 0.02	e_3 100/5,000 = 0.02	400/5,000 = 0.08
E_2 3 to 9 Movies	e_4 600/5,000 = 0.12	e_5 900/5,000 = 0.18	e_6 400/5,000 = 0.08	1,900/5,000 = 0.38
E_3 1 to 2 Movies	e_7 400/5,000 = 0.08	e_8 600/5,000 = 0.12	e_9 500/5,000 = 0.10	1,500/5,000 = 0.30
E_4 0 Movies	e_{10} 700/5,000 = 0.14	e_{11} 500/5,000 = 0.10	e_{12} 0/5,000 = 0	1,200/5,000 = 0.24
Total	1,900/5,000 = 0.38	2,100/5,000 = 0.42	1,000/5,000 = 0.20	5,000/5,000 = 1

Referring to the Edward's Cinemas situation, the probability of E_4 (0 movies) *or* E_6 (being in the 30-to-50 age group) is:

$$P(E_4 \text{ or } E_6) = ?$$

Table 4.5 shows the relative frequencies with the events of interest shaded. The overlap corresponds to the *joint occurrence* (intersection) of attending 0 movies *and* being in the 30-to-50 age group. The probability of the outcomes in the overlap is represented by $P(E_4$ and $E_6)$ and must be subtracted. This is done to avoid double-counting the probabilities of the elementary events that are in both E_4 and E_6 when calculating the $P(E_4$ or $E_6)$. Thus,

$$P(E_4 \text{ or } E_6) = P(E_4) + P(E_6) - P(E_4 \text{ and } E_6)$$
$$= 0.24 + 0.42 - 0.10$$
$$= 0.56$$

Therefore, the probability that a respondent will either be in the 30-to-50 age group or attend zero movies during a month is 0.56.

What is the probability a respondent will go to 1–2 movies *or* be in the over-50 age group? Again, we can use Rule 4:

$$P(E_3 \text{ or } E_7) = P(E_3) + P(E_7) - P(E_3 \text{ and } E_7)$$

Table 4.6 shows the relative frequencies for these events. We have

$$P(E_3 \text{ or } E_7) = 0.30 + 0.20 - 0.10 = 0.40$$

Thus, there is a 0.40 chance that a respondent will go to 1–2 movies **or** be in the "over 50" age group.

TABLE 4.6 Edward's Cinemas—Addition Rule Example

Movies per Month	E_5 Less than 30	E_6 30 to 50	E_7 Over 50	Total
	Age Group			
E_1 ≤10 Movies	e_1 200/5,000 = 0.04	e_2 100/5,000 = 0.02	e_3 100/5,000 = 0.02	400/5,000 = 0.08
E_2 3 to 9 Movies	e_4 600/5,000 = 0.12	e_5 900/5,000 = 0.18	e_6 400/5,000 = 0.08	1,900/5,000 = 0.38
E_3 1 to 2 Movies	e_7 400/5,000 = 0.08	e_8 600/5,000 = 0.12	e_9 500/5,000 = 0.10	1,500/5,000 = 0.30
E_4 0 Movies	e_{10} 700/5,000 = 0.14	e_{11} 500/5,000 = 0.10	e_{12} 0/5,000 = 0	1,200/5,000 = 0.24
Total	1,900/5,000 = 0.38	2,100/5,000 = 0.42	1,000/5,000 = 0.20	5,000/5,000 = 1

EXAMPLE 4-10 Addition Rule for Two Events

TRY PROBLEM 4.26

Cranston Forest Products Cranston Forest Products manufactures lumber for large materials supply centers like Home Depot and Lowe's. A representative from Home Depot is due to arrive at the Cranston plant for a meeting to discuss lumber quality. When the Home Depot representative arrives, he will ask Cranston managers to randomly select one board from Cranston's finished goods inventory for a quality check. Boards of three dimensions and three lengths are in the inventory. The following chart shows the number of boards of each size and length.

| | Dimension | | | |
Length	E_4 2″ × 4″	E_5 2″ × 6″	E_6 2″ × 8″	Total
E_1 = 8 feet	1,400	1,500	1,100	4,000
E_2 = 10 feet	2,000	3,500	2,500	8,000
E_3 = 12 feet	1,600	2,000	2,400	6,000
Total	5,000	7,000	6,000	18,000

The Cranston manager will be selecting one board at random from the inventory to show the Home Depot representative. Suppose he is interested in the probability that the board selected will be 8 feet long or a 2″ × 6″. To find this probability, he can use the following steps:

Step 1 Define the experiment.
One board is selected from the inventory and its dimension is obtained.

Step 2 Define the events of interest.
The manager is interested in boards that are 8 feet long.

$$E_1 = \text{8-foot boards}$$

He is also interested in the 2″ × 6″ dimension, so

$$E_5 = 2″ × 6″ \text{ boards}$$

Step 3 Determine the probability for each event.
There are 18,000 boards in inventory, and 4,000 of these are 8 feet long, so

$$P(E_1) = \frac{4,000}{18,000} = 0.2222$$

Of the 18,000 boards, 7,000 are 2″ × 6″, so the probability is

$$P(E_5) = \frac{7,000}{18,000} = 0.3889$$

Step 4 Determine whether the two events overlap and if so, compute the joint probability.
Of the 18,000 total boards, 1,500 are 8 feet long and 2″ × 6″. Thus the joint probability is

$$P(E_1 \text{ and } E_5) = \frac{1,500}{18,000} = 0.0833$$

Step 5   Compute the desired probability using Probability Rule 4.

$$P(E_1 \text{ or } E_2) = P(E_1) + P(E_5) - P(E_1 \text{ and } E_5)$$
$$P(E_1 \text{ or } E_2) = 0.2222 + 0.3889 - 0.0833$$
$$= 0.5278$$

The chance of selecting an 8-foot board or a $2'' \times 6''$ is just under 0.53.

Addition Rule for Mutually Exclusive Events   We indicated previously that when two events are mutually exclusive, both events cannot occur at the same time. Thus, for mutually exclusive events,

$$P(E_1 \text{ and } E_2) = 0$$

Therefore, when you are dealing with mutually exclusive events, the Addition Rule assumes a different form, shown as Rule 5.

Probability Rule 5: Addition Rule for Mutually Exclusive Events

For two mutually exclusive events E_1 and E_2,

$$P(E_1 \text{ or } E_2) = P(E_1) + P(E_2) \tag{4.8}$$

Figure 4.2 is a Venn diagram illustrating the application of the Addition Rule for Mutually Exclusive Events.

Conditional Probability

In dealing with probabilities, you will often need to determine the chances of two or more events occurring either at the same time or in succession. For example, a quality control manager for a manufacturing company may be interested in the probability of selecting two successive defective products from an assembly line. If the probability of this event is low, the quality control manager will be surprised when it occurs and might readjust the production process. In other instances, the decision maker might know that an event has occurred and may then want to know the probability of a second event occurring. For instance, suppose that an oil company geologist who believes oil will be found at a certain drilling site makes a favorable report. Because oil is not always found at locations with a favorable report, the oil company's exploration vice president might well be interested in the probability of finding oil, given the favorable report.

Situations such as this refer to a probability concept known as **conditional probability**.

Probability Rule 6 offers a general rule for conditional probability. The notation $P(E_1 | E_2)$ reads "probability of event E_1 *given* event E_2 has occurred." Thus, the probability of one event is conditional upon a second event having occurred.

Conditional Probability
The probability that an event will occur *given* that some other event has already happened.

FIGURE 4.2

Venn Diagram—Addition Rule for Two Mutually Exclusive Events

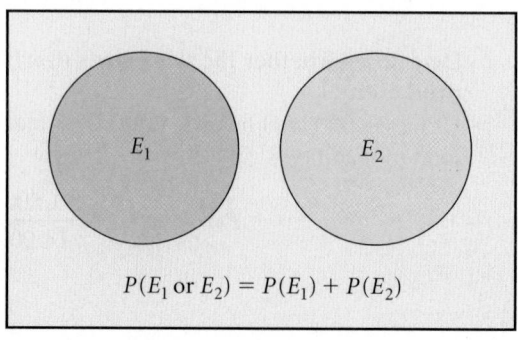

$$P(E_1 \text{ or } E_2) = P(E_1) + P(E_2)$$

Probability Rule 6: Conditional Probability for Any Two Events

For any two events E_1, E_2,

$$P(E_1|E_2) = \frac{P(E_1 \text{ and } E_2)}{P(E_2)}$$

(4.9)

where:

$$P(E_2) > 0$$

Rule 6 uses a *joint probability*, $P(E_1 \text{ and } E_2)$, and a *marginal probability*, $P(E_2)$, to calculate the conditional probability $P(E_1|E_2)$. Note that to find a conditional probability, we find the ratio of how frequently E_1 occurs to the total number of observations, given that we restrict our observations to only those cases in which E_2 has occurred.

Business Application

WEST.NET West.net, an Internet service provider, is in an increasingly competitive industry. The company has studied its customers' Internet habits. Among the information collected are the data shown in Table 4.7.

The company is focusing on high-volume users, and one of the factors that will influence West.net's marketing strategy is whether time spent using the Internet is related to a customer's gender. For example, suppose the company knows a user is female and wants to know the chances this woman will spend between 20 and 40 hours a month on the Internet. Let:

$$E_2 = \{e_3, e_4\} = \text{Event: Person uses services 20 to 40 hours per month}$$
$$E_4 = \{e_1, e_3, e_5\} = \text{Event: User is female}$$

A marketing analyst needs to know the probability of E_2 *given* E_4.

Table 4.8 shows the relative frequencies of interest. One way to find the desired probability is as follows:

1. We know E_4 has occurred (customer is female). There are 850 females in the survey.
2. Of the 850 females, 300 use Internet services 20 to 40 hours per month.
3. Then,

$$P(E_2|E_4) = \frac{300}{850}$$
$$= 0.35$$

However, we can also apply Rule 6, as follows:

$$P(E_2|E_4) = \frac{P(E_2 \text{ and } E_4)}{P(E_4)}$$

TABLE 4.7 Joint Frequency Distribution for West.net

	Gender		
Hours per Month	E_4 Female	E_5 Male	Total
E_1 <20	e_1 450	e_2 500	950
E_2 20 to 40	e_3 300	e_4 800	1,100
E_3 >40	e_5 100	e_6 350	450
Total	850	1,650	2,500

TABLE 4.8 Joint Relative Frequency Distribution for West.net

Hours per Month	Gender		Total
	E_4 Female	E_5 Male	
E_1 <20	e_1 450/2,500 = 0.18	e_2 500/2,500 = 0.20	950/2,500 = 0.38
E_2 20 to 40	e_3 300/2,500 = 0.12	e_4 800/2,500 = 0.32	1,100/2,500 = 0.44
E_3 >40	e_5 100/2,500 = 0.04	e_6 350/2,500 = 0.14	450/2,500 = 0.18
Total	850/2,500 = 0.34	1,650/2,500 = 0.66	2,500/2,500 = 1.00

From Table 4.8, we get the joint probability $P(E_2 \text{ and } E_4) = 0.12$ and

$$P(E_4) = 0.34$$

Then,

$$P(E_2 | E_4) = \frac{0.12}{0.34} = 0.35$$

EXAMPLE 4-11 Computing Conditional Probabilities

TRY PROBLEM 4.32

Retirement Planning   After the Enron Corporation collapse in late fall, 2001, in which thousands of Enron employees lost most or all of their retirement savings, many people began to take a closer look at how their own retirement money is invested. A recent survey conducted by a major financial publication yielded the following table, which shows the number of people in the study by age group and percentage of retirement funds in the stock market.

	Age of Investor	Percentage of Retirement Investments in the Stock Market					Total
		E_5 <5%	E_6 5 < 10%	E_7 10 < 30%	E_8 30 < 50%	E_9 50% or more	
E_1	<30 years	70	240	270	80	55	715
E_2	30 < 50 years	90	300	630	1,120	1,420	3,560
E_3	50 < 65 years	110	305	780	530	480	2,205
E_4	65+ years	200	170	370	260	65	1,065
	Total	470	1,015	2,050	1,990	2,020	7,545

The publication's editors are interested in knowing the probability that someone 65 or older will have 50% or more of retirement funds invested in the stock market. Assuming the data collected in this study reflect the population of investors, the editors can find this conditional probability using the following steps:

Step 1 Define the experiment.
A randomly selected person age 65 or older has his or her portfolio analyzed for percentage of retirement funds in the stock market.

Step 2 Define the events of interest.
In this case, we are interested in two events:

$$E_4 = 65+ \text{ years}$$
$$E_9 = 50\% \text{ or more in stocks}$$

Step 3 **Define the probability statement of interest.**

The editors are interested in

$$P(E_9|E_4) = \text{Probability of 50\% or more stocks } given \text{ 65+ years}$$

Step 4 **Convert the data to probabilities using the relative frequency assessment method.**

We begin with the event that is given to have occurred (E_4). A total of 1,065 people in the study were 65+ years of age. Of the 1,065 people, 65 had 50% or more of their retirement funds in the stock market.

$$P(E_9|E_4) = \frac{65}{1,065} = 0.061$$

Thus, the conditional probability that someone 65 or older will have 50% or more of retirement assets in the stock market is 0.061. This value can be found using Step 5 as well.

Step 5 **Use Probability Rule 6 to find the conditional probability.**

$$P(E_9|E_4) = \frac{P(E_9 \text{ and } E_4)}{P(E_4)}$$

The necessary probabilities are found using the relative frequency assessment method:

$$P(E_4) = \frac{1,065}{7,545} = 0.1412$$

and the joint probability is

$$P(E_9 \text{ and } E_4) = \frac{65}{7,545} = 0.0086$$

Then using Probability Rule 6 we get

$$P(E_9|E_4) = \frac{P(E_9 \text{ and } E_4)}{P(E_4)} = \frac{0.0086}{0.1412} = 0.061$$

Tree Diagrams Another way of organizing the events of an experiment that aids in the calculation of probabilities is the *tree diagram*.

Business Application

WEST.NET (*CONTINUED*) Figure 4.3 illustrates the tree diagram for West.net, the Internet service provider discussed earlier. Note that the branches at each node in the tree diagram represent mutually exclusive events. Moving from left to right, the first two branches indicate the two customer types (male and female—mutually exclusive events). Three branches grow from each of these original branches, representing the three possible categories for Internet use. The probabilities for the events male and female are shown on the first two branches. The probabilities shown on the right of the tree are the joint probabilities for each combination of gender and hours of use. These figures are found using Table 4.8, which was shown earlier. The probabilities on the branches following the male and female branches showing hours of use are conditional probabilities. For example, we can find the probability that a male customer (E_5) will spend more than 40 hours on the Internet (E_3) by

$$P(E_3|E_5) = \frac{P(E_3 \text{ and } E_5)}{P(E_5)} = \frac{0.14}{0.66} = 0.2121$$

FIGURE 4.3

Tree Diagram for West.net

Conditional Probability for Independent Events We earlier discussed that two events are independent if the occurrence of one event has no bearing on the probability that the second event occurs. Therefore, when two events are independent, the rule for conditional probability takes a different form, as indicated in Probability Rule 7.

Probability Rule 7: Conditional Probability for Independent Events

For independent events E_1, E_2,

$$P(E_1|E_2) = P(E_1) \qquad P(E_2) > 0 \qquad\qquad (4.10)$$

and

$$P(E_2|E_1) = P(E_2) \qquad P(E_1) > 0$$

As Rule 7 shows, the conditional probability of one event occurring, given a second independent event has already occurred, is simply the probability of the event occurring.

TRY PROBLEM 4.41

EXAMPLE 4-12 Checking for Independence

Cranston Forest Products In Example 4-10, the manager at the Cranston Forest Products Company reported the following data on the boards in inventory:

	Dimension			
Length	E_4 2″ × 4″	E_5 2″ × 6″	E_6 2″ × 8″	Total
E_1 = 8 feet	1,400	1,500	1,100	4,000
E_2 = 10 feet	2,000	3,500	2,500	8,000
E_3 = 12 feet	1,600	2,000	2,400	6,000
Total	5,000	7,000	6,000	18,000

He will be selecting one board at random from the inventory to show a visiting customer. Of interest is whether the length of the board is independent of the dimension. This can be determined using the following steps:

Step 1 Define the experiment.
A board is randomly selected and its dimensions determined.

Step 2 Define one event for length and one event for dimension.
Let E_2 = event that the board is 10 feet long and E_5 = event that the board is a $2'' \times 6''$ dimension.

Step 3 Determine the probability for each event.

$$P(E_2) = \frac{8{,}000}{18{,}000} = 0.4444 \quad \text{and} \quad P(E_5) = \frac{7{,}000}{18{,}000} = 0.3889$$

Step 4 Assess the joint probability of the two events occurring.

$$P(E_2 \text{ and } E_5) = \frac{3{,}500}{18{,}000} = 0.1944$$

Step 5 Compute the conditional probability of one event given the other using Probability Rule 6.

$$P(E_2 | E_5) = \frac{P(E_2 \text{ and } E_5)}{P(E_5)} = \frac{0.1944}{0.3889} = 0.50$$

Step 6 Check for independence using Probability Rule 7.
Because $P(E_2 | E_5) = 0.50 \neq P(E_2) = 0.4444$, the two events are not independent and, therefore, board length and board dimension are not independent.

CHAPTER OUTCOME #3

Multiplication Rules

We needed the joint probability of two events in the discussion on addition of two events and in the discussion on conditional probability. We were able to find $P(E_1 \text{ and } E_2)$ simply by examining the joint relative frequency tables. However, we often need to find $P(E_1 \text{ and } E_2)$ when we do not know the joint relative frequencies. When this is the case, we can use the multiplication rule for two events.

Multiplication Rule for Two Events

Probability Rule 8: Multiplication Rule for Any Two Events

For two events, E_1 and E_2,

$$P(E_1 \text{ and } E_2) = P(E_1)P(E_2 | E_1) \tag{4.11}$$

Business Application

REAL COMPUTER CO. To illustrate how to find a joint probability, consider an example involving the Real Computer Co., a manufacturer of personal computers, that uses two suppliers for CD-ROM drives. These parts are intermingled on the manufacturing-floor inventory rack. When a computer is assembled, the CD-ROM unit is pulled randomly from inventory without regard to which company made it. Recently, a customer ordered two personal computers. At the time of assembly, the CD-ROM inventory contained 30 MATX units and 50 Quinex units. What is the probability that both computers ordered by this customer will have MATX units?

To answer this question, we must recognize that two events are required to form the desired outcome. Therefore, let

$$E_1 = \text{Event: MATX CD-ROM in first computer}$$
$$E_2 = \text{Event: MATX CD-ROM in second computer}$$

The probability that both computers contain MATX units is written as $P(E_1 \text{ and } E_2)$. The key word here is *and*, as contrasted with the Addition Rule, in which the key word is *or*. The *and* signifies that we are interested in the joint probability of two events, as noted by $P(E_1 \text{ and } E_2)$. To find this probability, we employ Probability Rule 8.

$$P(E_1 \text{ and } E_2) = P(E_1)P(E_2|E_1)$$

We start by assuming that each CD-ROM in the inventory has the same chance of being selected for assembly. For the first computer,

$$P(E_1) = \frac{\text{Number of MATX units}}{\text{Number of CD-ROMs in inventory}}$$
$$= \frac{30}{80} = 0.375$$

Then, because we are not replacing the first CD-ROM, we find $P(E_2|E_1)$ by

$$P(E_2|E_1) = \frac{\text{Number of remaining MATX units}}{\text{Number of remaining CD-ROM units}}$$
$$= \frac{29}{79} = 0.3671$$

Now, by Rule 8,

$$P(E_1 \text{ and } E_2) = P(E_1)P(E_2|E_1) = (0.375)(0.3671)$$
$$= 0.1377$$

Therefore, there is a 13.77% chance the two personal computers will get MATX CD-ROMS.

Using a Tree Diagram

REAL COMPUTER (*CONTINUED*) A tree diagram can be used to display the situation facing Real Computer Co. The two branches on the left side of the tree in Figure 4.4 show the possible CD-ROM options for the first computer. The two branches coming from each of the first branches show the possible CD-ROM options for the second computer. The probabilities at the far right are the joint probabilities for the CD-ROM options for the two computers. As we determined previously, the probability that both computers will get a MATX unit is 0.1377, as shown on the top right on the tree diagram.

We can use the Multiplication Rule and the Addition Rule in one application when we determine the probability that two systems will have different CD-ROMs. Looking at Figure 4.4, we see there are two ways this can happen.

$$P[(\text{MATX } and \text{ Quinex}) \ or \ (\text{Quinex } and \text{ MATX})] = ?$$

If the first CD-ROM is a MATX and the second one is a Quinex, then the first cannot be a Quinex and the second a MATX. These two events are mutually exclusive and, therefore, Rule 6 can be used to calculate the required probability. The joint probabilities (generated from the Multiplication Rule) are shown on the right side of the tree. To find the desired probability, using Rule 6 we can add the two joint probabilities:

$$P[(\text{MATX } and \text{ Quinex}) \ or \ (\text{Quinex } and \text{ MATX})] =$$
$$0.2373 \quad + \quad 0.2373 \quad = 0.4746$$

The chance that a customer buying two computers will get two different CD-ROMs is 47.46%.

FIGURE 4.4

Tree Diagram for the CD-ROM Example

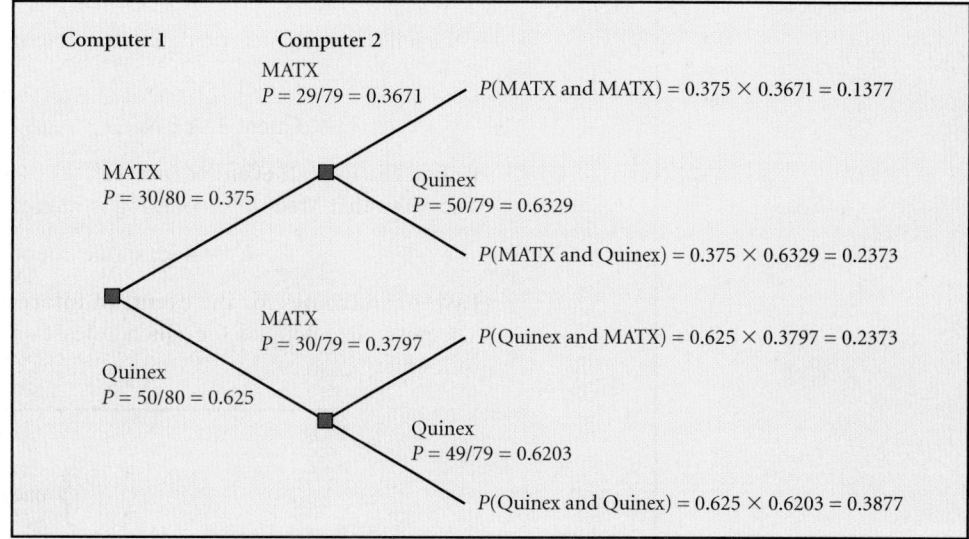

Multiplication Rule for Independent Events When we determined the probability that two computers would have a MATX CD-ROM unit, we used the general multiplication rule (Rule 8). The general multiplication rule requires that conditional probability be used because the probability associated with the second computer depends on the CD-ROM selected for the first computer. The chance of obtaining a MATX was lowered from 30/79 to 29/79, given the first CD-ROM was a MATX.

However, if the two events of interest are *independent*, the imposed condition does not alter the probability, and the Multiplication Rule takes the form shown in Probability Rule 9.

Probability Rule 9: Multiplication Rule for Independent Events

For independent events E_1, E_2,

$$P(E_1 \text{ and } E_2) = P(E_1)P(E_2) \qquad (4.12)$$

The joint probability of two independent events is simply the product of the probabilities of the two events. Rule 9 is the primary way that you can determine whether any two events are independent. If the product of the probabilities of the two events equals the joint probability, then the events are independent.

EXAMPLE 4-13   Using the Multiplication Rule and the Addition Rule

TRY PROBLEM 4.31

Medlin Accounting Medlin Accounting prepares tax returns for individuals and companies. Over the years, the firm has tracked its clients and has discovered that 12% of the individual returns have been selected for audit by the Internal Revenue Service. On one particular day, the firm signed two new individual tax clients. The firm is interested in the probability that at least one of these clients will be audited. This probability can be found using the following steps:

Step 1   Define the experiment.
The IRS randomly selects a tax return to audit.

Step 2   Define the possible outcomes.
For a single client, the following outcomes are defined:

$$A = \text{audit}$$
$$N = \text{no audit}$$

For each of the clients, we define the outcomes as

$$\text{Client 1: } A_1; N_1$$
$$\text{Client 2: } A_2; N_2$$

Step 3 **Define the overall event of interest.**
The event that Medlin Accounting is interested in is

$$E = \text{at least one client is audited}$$

Step 4 **List the outcomes for the events of interest.**
The possible outcomes for which at least one client will be audited are as follows:

E_1:	A_1	A_2	both are audited
E_2:	A_1	N_2	$\left.\begin{array}{c}\\\\\end{array}\right\}$ one client is audited
E_3:	N_1	A_2	

Step 5 **Compute the probabilities for the events of interest.**
Assuming the chances of the clients being audited are independent of each other, probabilities for the events are determined using Probability Rule 9 for independent events:

$$P(E_1) = P(A_1 \text{ and } A_2) = 0.12 \times 0.12 = 0.0144$$
$$P(E_2) = P(A_1 \text{ and } N_2) = 0.12 \times 0.88 = 0.1056$$
$$P(E_3) = P(N_1 \text{ and } A_2) = 0.88 \times 0.12 = 0.1056$$

Step 6 **Determine the probability for the overall event of interest.**
Because events E_1, E_2, and E_3 are mutually exclusive, compute the probability of at least one client being audited using Rule 5, the Addition Rule for Mutually Exclusive Events:

$$P(E_1 \text{ or } E_2 \text{ or } E_3) = P(E_1) + P(E_2) + P(E_3)$$
$$= 0.0144 + 0.1056 + 0.1056$$
$$= 0.2256$$

The chance of one or both of the clients being audited is 0.2256.

CHAPTER OUTCOME #4

Bayes' Theorem

As decision makers, you will often encounter situations that require you to assess probabilities for events of interest. Your assessment may be based on relative frequency or subjectivity. However, you may then come across new information that causes you to revise the probability assessment. For example, a human resource manager who has interviewed a person for a sales job might assess a low probability that the person will succeed in sales. However, after seeing the person's very high score on the company's sales aptitude test, the manager might revise her assessment upward. A medical doctor might assign an 80% chance that a patient has a particular disease. However, after seeing positive results from a lab test, he might increase his assessment to 95%.

In these situations, you will need a way to formally incorporate the new information. One very useful tool for doing this is called *Bayes' Theorem*, which is named for the Reverend Thomas Bayes, who developed the special application of conditional probability in the 1700s. Letting event B be an event that is given to have occurred, the conditional probability of event E_i occurring can be computed using Equation 4.9:

$$P(E_i | B) = \frac{P(E_i \text{ and } B)}{P(B)}$$

The numerator can be reformulated using the Multiplication Rule (Equation 4.11) as

$$P(E_i \text{ and } B) = P(E_i)P(B|E_i)$$

The conditional probability is then:

$$P(E_i|B) = \frac{P(E_i)P(B|E_i)}{P(B)}$$

The denominator, $P(B)$, can be found by adding the probability of the k possible ways that event B can occur. This is

$$P(B) = P(E_1)P(B|E_1) + P(E_2)P(B|E_2) + \cdots + P(E_k)P(BE_k)$$

Then Bayes' Theorem is formulated as Equation 4.13.

Bayes' Theorem

$$P(E_i|B) = \frac{P(E_i)P(B|E_i)}{P(E_1)P(B|E_1) + P(E_2)P(B|E_2) + \cdots + P(E_k)P(B|E_k)} \qquad (4.13)$$

where:

$$E_i = i\text{th event of interest of the } k \text{ possible events}$$
$$B = \text{Event that has occurred that might impact } P(E_i)$$

Events E_1 to E_k are mutually exclusive and collectively exhaustive.

Business Application

VARDEN SOAP CO. The Varden Soap Company has two production facilities, one in Ohio and one in Virginia. The company makes the same type of soap at both facilities. The Ohio plant makes 60% of the company's total soap output, and the Virginia plant 40%. All soap from the two facilities is sent to a central warehouse, where it is intermingled. After extensive study, the quality assurance manager has determined that 5% of the soap produced in Ohio and 10% of the soap produced in Virginia is unusable due to quality problems. When the company sells a defective product, it incurs not only the cost of replacing the item but also the loss of goodwill. The vice president for production would like to allocate these costs fairly between the two plants. To do so, he knows he must first determine the probability that a defective item was produced by a particular production line. Specifically, he needs to answer these questions:

1. What is the probability that the soap was produced at the Ohio plant, given that the soap is defective?
2. What is the probability that the soap was produced at the Virginia plant, given that the soap is defective?

In notation form, with D representing the event that an item is defective, what the manager wants to know is

$$P(\text{Ohio}|D) = ?$$
$$P(\text{Virginia}|D) = ?$$

We can use Bayes' Theorem (Equation 4.13) to determine these probabilities, as follows:

$$P(\text{Ohio}|D) = \frac{P(\text{Ohio})P(D|\text{Ohio})}{P(D)}$$

We know that event D (defective soap) can happen if it is made in either Ohio or Virginia. Thus,

$$P(D) = P(\text{Ohio and Defective}) + P(\text{Virginia and Defective})$$
$$P(D) = P(\text{Ohio})P(D|\text{Ohio}) + P(\text{Virginia})P(D|\text{Virginia})$$

We already know that 60% of the soap comes from Ohio and 40% from Virginia. So, $P(\text{Ohio}) = 0.60$ and $P(\text{Virginia}) = 0.40$. These are called the *prior* probabilities. Without Bayes' Theorem, we would likely allocate the total cost of defects in a 60/40 split between Ohio and Virginia, based on total production. However, the new information about the quality from each line is

$$P(D|\text{Ohio}) = 0.05 \quad \text{and} \quad P(D|\text{Virginia}) = 0.10$$

which can be used to properly allocate the cost of defects. This is done using Bayes' Theorem.

$$P(\text{Ohio}|D) = \frac{P(\text{Ohio})P(D|\text{Ohio})}{P(\text{Ohio})P(D|\text{Ohio}) + P(\text{Virginia})P(D|\text{Virginia})}$$

then,

$$P(\text{Ohio}|D) = \frac{(0.60)(0.05)}{(0.60)(0.05) + (0.40)(0.10)} = 0.4286$$

and

$$P(\text{Virginia}|D) = \frac{P(\text{Virginia})P(D|\text{Virginia})}{P(\text{Virginia})P(D|\text{Virginia}) + P(\text{Ohio})P(D|\text{Ohio})}$$

$$P(\text{Virginia}|D) = \frac{(0.40)(0.10)}{(0.40)(0.10) + (0.60)(0.05)} = 0.5714$$

These probabilities are called the *revised* probabilities. The prior probabilities have been revised given the new quality information. We now see that 42.86% of the cost of defects should be allocated to the Ohio plant, and 57.14% should be allocated to the Virginia plant.

Note, the denominator $P(D)$ is the overall probability of defective soap. This probability is

$$
\begin{aligned}
P(D) &= P(\text{Ohio})\,P(D|\text{Ohio}) + P(\text{Virginia})P(D|\text{Virginia}) \\
&= (0.60)(0.05) + (0.40)(0.10) \\
&= 0.03 + 0.04 \\
&= 0.07
\end{aligned}
$$

Thus, 7% of all the soap made by Varden is defective.

You might prefer to use a tabular approach like that shown in Table 4.9 when you apply Bayes' Theorem. Another alternative is to use a tree diagram, as illustrated in the following business application involving the IRS.

Bayes' Theorem Using a Tree Diagram

Business Application

IRS AUDIT This year experts project that 20% of all taxpayers will file an incorrect tax return. The Internal Revenue Service (IRS) itself is not perfect. IRS auditors claim there is an error when no problem exists about 10% of the time. The audits also indicate no error with a tax return when in fact there really is a problem about 30% of the time.

TABLE 4.9 Bayes' Theorem Calculations for Varden Soap

Events	Prior Probabilities	Conditional Probabilities	Joint Probabilities	Revised Probabilities
Ohio	0.60	0.05	(0.60)(0.05) = 0.03	0.03/0.07 = 0.4286
Virginia	0.40	0.10	(0.40)(0.10) = 0.04	0.04/0.07 = 0.5714
			0.07	1.0000

The IRS has just notified a taxpayer there is an error in his return. What is the probability that the return actually has an error? We use the following notation:

$$E = \text{The return actually contains an error}$$
$$NE = \text{The return contains no error}$$
$$AE = \text{Audit says an error exists}$$
$$ANE = \text{Audit says no error}$$

Then, we are interested in determining

$$P(E|AE) = ?$$

From the information provided, we know the following:

$P(E) = 0.20$	$P(ANE|E) = 0.30$	$P(AE|NE) = 0.10$
$P(NE) = 0.80$	$P(AE|E) = 0.70$	$P(ANE|NE) = 0.90$

We need to use Bayes' Theorem to determine the probability of interest. A tree diagram can be used to do this. Figure 4.5 shows the tree diagram and probabilities. Now,

$$P(E|AE) = \frac{P(E \text{ and } AE)}{P(AE)} = ?$$

From Figure 4.5 we see that $P(E \text{ and } AE) = 0.14$. To find $P(AE)$, we add the probabilities of the ways in which AE occurs (audit says an error occurred), because those two ways are mutually exclusive.

$$P(AE) = P(E \text{ and } AE) + P(NE \text{ and } AE) = 0.14 + 0.08 = 0.22$$

Then,

$$P(E|AE) = \frac{P(E \text{ and } AE)}{P(AE)} = \frac{0.14}{0.22} = 0.6364$$

The probability that the return contains an error, given that the IRS audit indicates an error exists, is 0.6364.

FIGURE 4.5

Tree Diagram for the IRS Audit Example

TRY PROBLEM 4.35

EXAMPLE 4-14 Bayes' Theorem

Techtronics Equipment Corporation The Techtronics Equipment Corporation has developed a new electronic device that it would like to sell to the U.S. military for use in fighter aircraft. The sales manager believes there is a 0.60 chance that the military will place an order. However, after making an initial sales presentation, military officials will often ask for a second presentation to other military decision makers. Historically, 70% of successful companies are asked to make a second presentation, whereas 50% of unsuccessful companies are asked back a second time. Suppose Techtronics Equipment has just been asked to make a second presentation; what is the revised probability that the company will make the sale? This probability can be determined using the following steps:

Step 1 **Define the events.**
In this case, there are two events:

$$S = \text{sale} \qquad N = \text{no sale}$$

Step 2 **Determine the prior probabilities for the events.**
The probability of the events prior to knowing whether a second presentation will be requested are

$$P(S) = 0.60 \qquad P(N) = 0.40$$

Step 3 **Define an event that if it occurs, could alter the prior probabilities.**
In this case, the altering event is the invitation to make a second presentation. We label this event as SP.

Step 4 **Determine the conditional probabilities.**
The conditional probabilities are associated with being invited to make a second presentation:

$$P(SP|S) = 0.70 \qquad P(SP|N) = 0.50$$

Step 5 **Use the tabular approach for Bayes' Theorem to determine the *revised probabilities*.**
These correspond to

$$P(S|SP) \quad \text{and} \quad P(N|SP)$$

Event	Prior Probability	Conditional Probabilities	Joint Probabilities	Revised Probabilities
S = sale	0.60	$P(SP|S) = 0.70$	$P(S)P(SP|S) = (0.60)(0.70) = 0.42$	$0.42/0.62 = 0.6774$
N = no sale	0.40	$P(SP|N) = 0.50$	$P(S)P(SP|S) = (0.40)(0.50) = 0.20$	$0.20/0.62 = 0.3226$
			0.62	1.0000

Thus, using Bayes' Theorem, if Techtronics Equipment gets a second presentation opportunity, the probability of making the sale is revised upward from 0.60 to 0.6774.

4-2: Exercises

Skill Development

4-26. Historically, on Christmas Day the weather in a certain Midwestern city has had the following distribution:

Event	Relative Frequency
Clear & dry	.20
Cloudy & dry	.30
Rain	.40
Snow	.10

a. Based on these data, what is the probability that next Christmas will be dry?

b. Based on the data, what is the probability that next Christmas will be rainy or cloudy and dry?

c. Supposing next Christmas is dry, determine the probability that it will also be cloudy.

4-27. A fast-food restaurant has determined that the chance a customer will order a soft drink is 0.90. The probability that a customer will order a hamburger is 0.60. The probability that a customer will order french fries is 0.50.

a. If a customer places an order, what is the probability that the order will include a soft drink and no fries if these two events are independent?

b. The restaurant has also determined that if a customer orders a hamburger, the probability the customer will also order fries is 0.80. Determine the probability that the order will include a hamburger and fries.

4-28. A basketball team has 10 players. Five are seniors, 2 are juniors, and 3 are sophomores. Two players are randomly selected to serve as captains for the next game. What is the probability that both players selected are seniors?

4-29. A paint store carries three brands of paint. A customer wants to buy another gallon of paint to match paint that she purchased at the store previously. She can't recall the brand name and does not wish to return home to find the old can of paint. So she selects two of the three brands of paint at random and buys them.

a. What is the probability that she matched the paint brand?

b. Her husband also goes to the paint store and fails to remember what brand to buy. So he also purchases two of the three brands of paint at random. Determine the probability that both the woman and her husband fail to get the correct brand of paint. (*Hint*: Are the husband's selections independent of his wife's selections?)

4-30. An event occurs with probability $P(E_1) = 0.35$, $P(E_2) = 0.15$, $P(E_3) = 0.40$. If the event B occurs, the probability becomes $P(E_1|B) = 0.25$, $P(B) = 0.30$.

a. Calculate $P(E_1 \text{ and } B)$.

b. Compute $P(E_1 \text{ or } B)$.

c. Assume that E_1, E_2, and E_3 are independent events. Calculate $P(E_1 \text{ and } E_2 \text{ and } E_3)$.

4-31. A construction company has submitted two bids, one to build a large hotel in London and the other to build a commercial office building in New York City. The company believes it has a 40% chance of winning the hotel bid and a 25% chance of winning the office building bid. The company also believes that winning the hotel bid is independent of winning the office building bid.

a. What is the probability the company will win both contracts?

b. What is the probability the company will win at least one contract?

c. What is the probability the company will lose both contracts?

4-32. A small manufacturing plant has sales offices located in four cities: Dallas, Seattle, Boston, and Los Angeles. An analysis of the plant's Accounts receivables reveals the number of overdue invoices by days, as shown here.

Days Overdue	Dallas	Seattle	Boston	Los Angeles
Under 30 days	137	122	198	287
30–60 days	85	46	76	109
61–90 days	33	27	55	48
Over 90 days	18	32	45	66

Assume the invoices are stored and managed from a central database.

a. What is the probability that a randomly selected invoice from the database is from the Boston sales office?

b. What is the probability that a randomly selected invoice from the database is between 30 and 90 days overdue?

c. What is the probability that a randomly selected invoice from the database is over 90 days old and from the Seattle office?

d. If a randomly selected invoice is from the Los Angeles office, what is the probability that it is 60 or fewer days overdue?

4-33. A quality manager for a major computer manufacturer has collected the following data on the quality status of disk drives by supplier. She inspected a total of 700 disk drives.

	Drive Status	
Supplier	**Working**	**Defective**
Company A	120	10
Company B	180	15
Company C	50	5
Company D	300	20

a. Based on these inspection data, what is the probability of randomly selecting a disk drive from company B?

b. What is the probability of a defective disk drive being received by the computer company?

c. What is the probability of a defect given that company B supplied the disk drive?

4-34. Three events occur with probabilities of $P(E_1) = 0.35$, $P(E_2) = 0.15$, $P(E_3) = 0.40$. Other probabilities are: $P(B \mid E_1) = 0.25$, $P(B \mid E_2) = 0.15$, $P(B \mid E_3) = 0.60$.

a. Compute $P(E_1 \mid B)$.

b. Compute $P(E_2 \mid B)$.

c. Compute $P(E_3 \mid B)$.

4-35. A Harris study conducted for Lincoln Mercury indicated (*USA Today* Snapshots, April 2005) that 42% of men and 61% of women would stop and ask for directions. The U.S. Census Bureau's 2004 census determined that for individuals 18 or over, 48.2% were men and 51.8% were women. This exercise addresses this age group.

a. A randomly chosen driver gets lost on a road trip. Determine the probability that the driver is a woman and stops to ask for directions.

b. Calculate the probability that the driver stops to ask for directions.

c. Given that a driver stops to ask for directions, determine the probability that the driver was a man.

Business Applications

4-36. A local photocopy shop has three black-and-white copy machines and two color copiers. Based on historical data, the chances that each black-and-white copier will be down for repairs is 0.10. The color copiers are more of a problem and are down 20% of the time each.

a. Based on this information, what is the probability that if a customer needs a color copy, both color machines will be down for repairs?

b. If a customer wants both a color copy and a black-and-white copy, what is the probability that the necessary machines will be available? (Assume that the color copier can also be used to make a black-and-white copy if needed.)

c. If the manager wants to have at least a 99% chance of being able to furnish a black-and-white copy upon demand, is the present configuration sufficient? (Assume that the color copier can also be used to make a black-and-white copy if needed.) Back up your answer with appropriate probability computations.

d. What is the probability that all five copiers will be up and running at the same time? Suppose the manager added a fourth black-and-white copier; how would the probability of all copiers being ready at any one time be affected?

4-37. Refer to Problem 4.36. The owners of the photocopy shop are going to open a new photocopy store. They wish to meet the increasing demand for color photocopies and to have more reliable service. As a goal, they would like to have at least a 99.9% chance of being able to furnish a black-and-white copy or a color copy upon demand. They also wish to purchase only four copiers. They have asked for your advice regarding the mix of black-and-white and color copiers. Supply them with your advice. Provide calculations and reasons to support your advice.

4-38. The Ace Construction Company has submitted a bid on a state government project in Delaware. The price of the bid was predetermined in the bid specifications. The contract is to be awarded on the basis of a blind drawing from those who have bid. Five other companies have also submitted bids.

a. What is the probability of the Ace Construction Company winning the bid?

b. Suppose that there are two contracts to be awarded by a blind draw. What is the probability of Ace winning both contracts? Assume sampling with replacement.

c. Referring to part b, what is the probability of Ace not winning either contract?

d. Referring to part b, what is the probability of Ace winning exactly one contract?

4-39. A manager of a gasoline filling station is thinking about a promotion that she hopes will bring in more business to the full-service island. She is considering the option that when a customer requests a fill-up, if the pump stops with the dollar amount at $9.99, the customer will get the gasoline free. Previous studies show that 70% of the customers require $10.00 or more when they fill up, so would not be eligible for the free gas. What is the probability that a customer will get free gas at this station if the promotion is implemented?

4-40. Referring to Problem 4.39, suppose the manager is concerned about alienating customers who buy $10.00 or more, since they would not be eligible to win the free gas under the original concept. To overcome this, she is thinking about changing the contest. The customer will get free gas if any of the following happens:

$9.99, $11.11, $12.22, $13.33, $14.44, $15.55
$16.66, $17.77, $18.88, $19.99

Past data show that only 5% of all customers require $20.00 or more. If one of these big-volume customers arrives, he will get to blind draw a ball from a box containing 100 balls (99 red, 1 white). If the white ball is picked, the customer gets his gas free. Considering this new promotion, what is the probability that a customer will get free gas?

4-41. For a number of years, the Seattle, Washington real estate market has been booming with prices skyrocketing. Recently, the Washington Real Estate Commission studied the sales patterns in Seattle for single-family homes. One chart presented in the commission's report is reproduced here. It shows the number of homes sold by price range and number of days the home was on the market.

Price Range ($000)	Days on the Market		
	1–7	**8–30**	**Over 30**
Under $200	125	15	30
$200–$500	200	150	100
$501–$1,000	400	525	175
Over $1,000	125	140	35

a. Using the relative frequency approach to probability assessment, what is the probability that a house will be on the market more than 7 days?

b. Is the event 1–7 days on the market independent of the price $200–$500?

c. Suppose a home has just sold in Seattle and was on the market less than 8 days, what is the most likely price range for that home?

4-42. A marketing research company has randomly surveyed 200 men who watch professional sports. The men were separated according to their educational level (college degree or not) and whether they preferred the NBA or the NFL. The results of the survey are shown here.

Sports Preference	College Degree	No College Degree
NBA	40	55
NFL	10	95

a. What is the probability that a randomly selected survey participant prefers the NFL?

b. What is the probability that a randomly selected survey participant has a college degree and prefers the NBA?

c. Suppose a survey participant is randomly selected and you are told that he has a college degree. What is the probability that this man prefers the NFL?

d. Is a survey participant's preference for the NBA independent of having a college degree?

4-43. A corporation has 11 manufacturing plants. Seven of the plants are domestic and 4 are outside the United States. Each year a performance evaluation is conducted for 4 randomly selected plants. What is the probability that a performance evaluation will include at least 1 plant outside the United States? (*Hint*: Begin by finding the probability that only domestic plants are selected.)

4-44. The Skiwell Manufacturing Company gets materials for its cross-country skis from two suppliers. Supplier A's materials make up 30% of what is used, with supplier B providing the rest. Past records indicate that 15% of supplier A's materials are defective and 10% of B's are defective. Since it is impossible to tell which supplier the materials came from once they are in inventory, the manager wants to know which supplier most likely supplied the defective materials the foreman has brought to his attention. Provide the manager this information.

4-45. Alpine Cannery is currently processing vegetables from the summer harvest. The manager has found a case of cans that has not been properly sealed. There are three lines that processed cans of this type, and the manager wants to know which line is most likely to be responsible for this mistake. Provide the manager this information.

Line	Contribution to Total	Proportion Defective
1	0.40	0.05
2	0.35	0.10
3	0.25	0.07

4-46. A major electronics manufacturers has determined that when one of its televisions is sold, there is 0.08 chance that the set will need service before the warranty period expires. It has also assessed a 0.05 chance that a DVD player will need service prior to the expiration of the warranty expireing.

a. Suppose a customer purchases one of the company's televisions and one of the DVD players. What is the probability that at least one of the products will require service prior to the warranty period expiring?

b. Suppose a retailer sells four televisions on a particular Saturday. What is the probability that none of the four will need service prior to the warranty expiring?

c. Suppose a retailer sells four televisions on a particular Saturday. What is the probability that at least one needs repair?

4-47. A distributor of Christmas tree lights has four suppliers from which she purchases lights. This past season she purchased 40% of the lights from Franklin Lighting, 30% from Wilson & Sons, 20% from Evergreen Supply, and the rest from

A. L. Scott. In prior years, 3% of Franklin's lights were defective, 6% of the Wilson's lights were defective, 2% of Evergreen's were defective, and 8% of the Scott lights were defective. When the lights arrive at the distributor, she puts them in inventory without identifying the supplier. Suppose that a light string has been pulled from inventory; what is the probability that it was supplied by Franklin Lighting?

4-48. *USA Today* reported ("Study finds better survival rates at 'high-volume' hospitals," July 25, 2005) that "high-volume" hospitals performed at least 77% of bladder removal surgeries; "low-volume" hospitals performed at most 23%. Assume the percentages are 77% and 23%. In the first two weeks after surgery, 3.1% of patients at low-volume centers died compared to 0.7% at the high-volume hospitals.

   a. Calculate the probability that a randomly chosen bladder-cancer patient had surgery at a high-volume hospital and survived the first two weeks after surgery.

   b. Calculate the probability that a randomly chosen bladder-cancer patient survived the first two weeks after surgery.

   c. If two bladder-cancer patients were chosen randomly, determine the probability that only one would survive the first two weeks after surgery.

   d. If two bladder-cancer patients were chosen randomly, determine the probability that at least one would survive the first two weeks after surgery.

4-49. The Committee for the Study of the American Electorate indicated that 60.7% of the voting-age voters cast ballots in the 2004 presidential election. They also indicated that 85.3% of registered voters voted in the election. The proportion of those who voted for President Bush was 50.8.

   a. Determine the proportion of voting-age voters who voted for President Bush.

   b. Determine the proportion of voting-age voters who were registered to vote.

Computer Database Exercises

4-50. A Courtyard Hotel by Marriott conducted a survey of its guests. Sixty-two surveys were completed. Based upon the data from the survey, found in the file **CourtyardSurvey**, determine the following probabilities using the relative frequency assessment method.

   a. Of two customers selected, what is the probability that both will be on a business trip?

   b. What is the probability that a customer will be on a business trip or experienced a hotel problem during a stay at the Courtyard?

   c. What is the probability that a customer on business has an in-state area code phone number?

   d. Based on the data in the survey, can the Courtyard manager conclude that a customer's rating regarding staff attentiveness is independent of whether he or she is traveling on business, pleasure, or both? Use the rules of probability to make this determination.

4-51. Continuing with the Marriott survey done by the managers of a Wisconsin Marriott Courtyard, based on the data from the survey, found in the file **CourtyardSurvey**, determine the following probabilities using the relative frequency assessment method.

   a. Of two customers selected, what is the probability that neither will be on a business trip?

   b. What is the probability that a customer will be on a business trip or did not experience a hotel problem during a stay at the Courtyard?

   c. What is the probability that a customer on a pleasure trip has an in-state area code phone number?

4-52. The data file **Colleges** contains data on over 1,300 colleges and universities in the United States. Suppose a company is planning to award a significant grant to a randomly selected college or university. Using the relative frequency method for assessing probabilities and the rules of probability, respond to the following. (If data are missing for a needed variable, reduce the number of colleges in the study appropriately.)

   a. What is the probability that the grant will go to a private college or university?

   b. What is the probability that the grant will go to a college or university that has a student/faculty ratio over 20?

   c. What is the probability that the grant will go to a college or university that is both private and has a student/faculty ratio over 20?

   d. If the company decides to split the grant into two grants, what is the probability that both grants will go to California colleges and universities? What might you conclude if this did happen?

4-53. A Harris survey conducted in April of 2005 asked, in part, what the most important reason was that people give for never using a wireless phone exclusively. The responses were: (1) Like the safety of traditional phone, (2) Need line for Net access, (3) Pricing not attractive enough, (4) Weak or unreliable cell signal at home, (5) Coverage not good enough, and (6) Other. The file entitled **Wireless** contains the responses for the 1,088 respondents.

   a. Of those respondents 36 or older, determine the probability that an individual in this age group would not use a wireless phone exclusively because of some type of difficulty in placing and receiving calls with a wireless phone.

b. Of those respondents younger than 36, determine the probability that an individual in this age group would not use a wireless phone exclusively because of some type of difficulty in placing and receiving calls with a wireless phone.

c. If three respondents were selected at random from those respondents younger than 36, calculate the probability that at least one of the respondents stated the most important reason for not using a wireless exclusively was that they need a line for Net access.

4-54. PricewaterhouseCoopers Saratoga in its 2005/2006 Human Capital Index Report indicated the average number of days it took for an American company to fill a job vacancy in 2004 was 48 days. Sample data similar to that used in the study is in a file entitled **Hired**. Categories for the days and hire cost are provided under the headings Time and Cost, respectively.

a. Calculate the probability that a company vacancy took at most 100 days or cost at most $4,000 to fill.

b. Of the vacancies that took at most 100 days to fill, calculate the probability that the cost was at most $4,000.

c. If three of the vacancies were chosen at random, calculate the probability that two of the vacancies cost at most $4,000 to fill.

4-55. A company produces scooters used by small businesses, such as pizza parlors, that find them convenient for making short deliveries. The company is notified whenever a scooter breaks down, and the problem is classified as being either mechanical or electrical. The company then matches the scooter to the plant where it was assembled. The file **Scooters** contains a random sample of 200 breakdowns. Use the data in the file to find the following probabilities.

a. If a scooter was assembled in the Tyler plant, what is the probability its breakdown was due to an electrical problem?

b. Is the probability of a scooter having a mechanical problem independent of the scooter being assembled at the Lincoln plant?

c. If mechanical problems are assigned a cost of $75 and electrical problems are assigned a cost of $100, how much cost would be budgeted for the Lincoln and Tyler plants next year if a total of 500 scooters were expected to be returned for repair?

4-56. *Ars Technia, LLD* published a news release (Eric Bangeman, "Dell still king of market share," January 18, 2005) that presented the results of a study concerning the world and domestic market share for the major manufacturers of personal computers. The file entitled **PCMarket** contains a sample that would produce the market shares alluded to in the article and the highest academic degrees achieved by the owners of those PCs.

a. Determine the probability that the person had achieved at least a bachelor's degree and owns a Dell PC.

b. If a randomly selected person owned a Dell PC, determine the probability that the person had achieved at least a bachelor's degree.

c. Consider these two events: (1) At least a bachelor's degree, and (2) Owns a Dell PC. Are these events independent, dependent, or mutually exclusive? Explain.

Summary and Conclusions

Probability provides decision makers a quantitative measure of the chance a particular outcome will occur. Probability allows decision makers to quantify uncertainty. The objectives of this chapter have been to discuss the various types of probability and to provide the basic rules that govern probability operations.

By understanding the basic rules of probability, you will be able to effectively measure the chances of events of interest occurring. If you need to combine probabilities, the Addition Rule and the Multiplication Rule are useful in specific instances. Bayes' Theorem helps when dealing with conditional probabilities in special circumstances and in revising prior probabilities based on new information. Table 4.10 presents a summary classification of several of the basic rules of probability.

Chapter 5 expands on the discussion of probability and introduces the concept of a probability distribution and several useful discrete probability distributions, including the binomial, Poisson and hypergeometric, which will be used throughout the remainder of the text.

Equations

Classical Probability Measurement

$$P(E_i) = \frac{\text{Number of ways } E_i \text{ can occur}}{\text{Total number of elementary events}} \quad \textbf{(4.1)}$$

Relative Frequency

$$P(E_i) = \frac{\text{Number of times } E_i \text{ occurs}}{N} \quad \textbf{(4.2)}$$

TABLE 4.10 Probability Rules Summary

Event Type	Keyword "OR" Addition Rule	Keyword "AND" Multiplication Rule	Keyword "GIVEN" Conditional Rule
Mutually Exclusive	$P(A \text{ or } B) = P(A) + P(B)$	$P(A \text{ and } B) = 0$	$P(A|B) = 0$
Independent	$P(A \text{ or } B) = P(A) + P(B) - P(A \text{ and } B)$	$P(A \text{ and } B) = P(A)P(B)$	$P(A|B) = P(A)$
Dependent	$P(A \text{ or } B) = P(A) + P(B) - P(A \text{ and } B)$	$P(A \text{ and } B) = P(A)P(B|A)$	$P(A|B) = \dfrac{P(A \text{ and } B)}{P(B)}$

Probability Rule 1

$$0 \le P(E_i) \le 1 \quad \text{for all } i \qquad \textbf{(4.3)}$$

Probability Rule 2

$$\sum_{i=1}^{k} P(e_i) = 1 \qquad \textbf{(4.4)}$$

Probability Rule 3
Addition rule for individual outcomes:
The probability of an event E_i is equal to the *sum* of the probabilities of the possible outcomes forming E_i. For example, if

$$E_i = \{e_1, e_2, e_3\}$$

then

$$P(E_i) = P(e_1) + P(e_2) + P(e_3) \qquad \textbf{(4.5)}$$

Complement Rule

$$P(\bar{E}) = 1 - P(E) \qquad \textbf{(4.6)}$$

Probability Rule 4
Addition rule for any two events E_1 and E_2:

$$P(E_1 \text{ or } E_2) = P(E_1) + P(E_2) - P(E_1 \text{ and } E_2) \qquad \textbf{(4.7)}$$

Probability Rule 5
Addition rule for mutually exclusive events E_1, E_2:

$$P(E_1 \text{ or } E_2) = P(E_1) + P(E_2) \qquad \textbf{(4.8)}$$

Probability Rule 6
Conditional probability for any two events E_1, E_2:

$$P(E_1|E_2) = \frac{P(E_1 \text{ and } E_2)}{P(E_2)} \qquad \textbf{(4.9)}$$

Probability Rule 7
Conditional probability for independent events E_1, E_2:

$$P(E_1|E_2) = P(E_1); \qquad P(E_2) > 0 \qquad \textbf{(4.10)}$$

and

$$P(E_2|E_1) = P(E_2); \qquad P(E_1) > 0$$

Probability Rule 8
Multiplication rule for two events, E_1 and E_2:

$$P(E_1 \text{ and } E_2) = P(E_1)P(E_2|E_1) \qquad \textbf{(4.11)}$$

Probability Rule 9
Multiplication rule for independent events E_1, E_2:

$$P(E_1 \text{ and } E_2) = P(E_1)P(E_2) \qquad \textbf{(4.12)}$$

Bayes' Theorem

$$P(E_i|B) = $$

$$\frac{P(E_i)P(B|E_i)}{P(E_1)P(B|E_1) + P(E_2)P(B|E_2) + \cdots + P(E_k)P(B|E_k)}$$

$$\textbf{(4.13)}$$

Key Terms

Classical probability
   assessment   164
Conditional probability   180
Dependent events   163
Event   161

Experiment   159
Independent events   163
Mutually exclusive events   162
Probability   158
Relative frequency assessment   165

Sample space   159
Subjective probability
   assessment   168

Chapter Exercises

Conceptual Questions

4-57. Discuss what is meant by the *relative frequency assessment approach* to probability assessment. Provide a business-related example, other than the one given in the text, where this method of probability assessment might be used.

4-58. Discuss what is meant by *subjective probability*. Provide a business-related example in which subjective probability assessment would likely be used. Also provide an example of when you have personally used subjective probability assessment.

4-59. Discuss what is meant by *classical probability assessment* and indicate why classical assessment is not often used in business applications.

4-60. Consider the following table:

	A	$\overline{A}$	Totals
B	800	200	1,000
$\overline{B}$	600	400	1,000
Totals	1,400	600	2,000

Explore the complements of conditional events:
a. Calculate the following probabilities: $P(A|B)$, $P(\overline{A}|\overline{B})$, $P(\overline{A}|B)$, $P(A|\overline{B})$.
b. Now determine which pair of events are complements of each other. (*Hint*: Use the probabilities calculated in part a and the Complement Rule.)

4-61. Examine the following table:

	A	$\overline{A}$	Totals
B	200	800	1,000
$\overline{B}$	300	700	1,000
Totals	500	1,500	2,000

a. Calculate the following probabilities: $P(A)$, $P(\overline{A})$, $P(A|B)$, $P(\overline{A}|B)$, $P(A|\overline{B})$, and $P(\overline{A}|\overline{B})$.
b. Show that (1) A and B, (2) A and $\overline{B}$, (3) $\overline{A}$ and B, (4) $\overline{A}$ and $\overline{B}$ are dependent events.
c. Reconstruct the preceeding table, keeping the same marginal totals, so that the pairs of events (1) A and B, (2) A and $\overline{B}$, (3) $\overline{A}$ and B, (4) $\overline{A}$ and $\overline{B}$ are independent, therefore showing if any pair of events are independent, so also are any combination of the two events and their complements.

4-62. Examine the relationship between independent, dependent, and mutually exclusive events. Consider two events A and B that are mutually exclusive such that $P(A) \neq 0$.
a. Calculate $P(A|B)$.

b. What does your answer to part a, say about whether two mutually exclusive events are dependent or independent?
c. Consider two events C and D such that $P(C) = 0.4$ and $P(C|D) = 0.15$. (1) Are events C and D mutually exclusive? (2) Are events C and D independent or dependent? Are dependent events necessarily mutually exclusive events?

Business Applications

4-63. Suppose you were given a three-question multiple-choice quiz in which each question had four optional answers.
a. What is the probability of getting a perfect score if you were forced to guess at each question?
b. Suppose it takes at least two correct answers out of three to pass the test. What is the probability of passing if you are forced to guess at each question? What does this indicate about studying for such an exam?
c. Suppose through some late-night studying you are able to correctly eliminate two answers on each question. Now answer parts a and b.

4-64. Simmons Market Research conducted a national consumer study of 13,787 respondents in the spring of 2005. A subset of the respondents was asked to indicate the primary source of the vitamins or mineral supplements they consume. More than 6 out of 10 U.S. adults take vitamins or mineral supplements. Of those who do, 58% indicated a multiple formula was their choice.
a. Calculate the probability that a randomly chosen U.S. adult takes a multiple formula as their primary source.
b. Calculate the probability that a randomly chosen U.S. adult does not take a multiple formula.
c. If three U.S. adults were chosen at random, compute the probability that two of them take a multiple formula as their primary source.

4-65. *USA Today* reported (Moneyline, November 4, 2005) that the IRS audited 1 in 63 wealthy individuals and families, about 1 of every 107 individuals, 20% of corporations in general, and 44% of the largest corporations with assets of at least $250 million.
a. Calculate the probability that at least 1 wealthy individual in a sample of 10 would be audited.
b. Compute the probability that at least 1 from a sample of 10 corporations with assets of at least $250 million would be audited.
c. Calculate the probability that a randomly chosen wealthy CEO of a corporation with assets of $300 million would be audited or that the corporation would be audited.

4-66. The National Association of Convenience Stores (NACS) released the result of a survey conducted during the first half of 2005. The survey indicated that 70% of gas purchases paid for at the pump were made with a credit or debit card.

a. Indicate the type of probability assessment method that NACS would use to assess this probability.

b. In one local store, 10 randomly chosen customers were observed. All 10 of these customers used a credit or a debit card. If the NACS statistic applies to this area, determine the probability that 10 out of 10 customers would use a credit or debit card.

c. If 90% of gas purchases paid for at the pump were made with a credit or debit card, determine the probability that 10 out of 10 customers would use a credit or debit card.

d. Based upon your answers to parts b and c, does it appear that a larger percentage of individuals use credit or debit cards than is true for the nation as a whole? Explain.

4-67. Cascade Paint mixes paint in three separate plants and then ships the unmarked cans to a central warehouse. Plant A supplies 50% of the paint and past records indicate that the paint is incorrectly mixed 10% of the time. Plant B contributes 30% with a defective rate of 5%. Plant C supplies 20% with paint mixed incorrectly 20% of the time. If Cascade guarantees its product and spent $10,000 replacing improperly mixed paint last year, how should the cost be distributed among the three plants?

4-68. A company is considering changing its starting hour from 8:00 A.M. to 7:30 A.M. A census of the company's 1,200 office and production workers shows 370 of its 450 production workers favor the change and a total of 715 office workers favor the change. To further assess worker opinion, the region manager decides to talk with random workers.

a. What is the probability a randomly selected worker will be in favor of the change?

b. What is the probability a randomly selected worker will be against the change *and* be an office worker?

c. Are the events job type and opinion, independent? Explain.

4-69. The Chocolate House specializes in hand-dipped chocolates for special occasions. Recently, several long-time customers have complained about the quality of the chocolates. It seems there are several partially covered chocolates in each box. The defective chocolates should have been caught when the boxes were packed. The manager is wondering which of the three packers is not doing the job

properly. Clerk 1 packs 40% of the boxes and usually has a 2% defective rate. Clerk 2 packs 30% with a 2.5% defective rate. Clerk 3 boxes 30% of the chocolates and her defective rate is 1.5%. Which clerk is most likely responsible for the boxes that raised the complaints?

4-70. Recreational developers are considering opening a skiing area near a western U.S. town. They are trying to decide whether to open an area catering to family skiers or to some other group. To help make their decision, they gather the following information. If

A_1 = Family will ski
A_2 = Family will not ski
B_1 = Family has children but none in the 8–16 age group
B_2 = Family has children in the 8–16 age group
B_3 = Family has no children

then, for this location,

$$P(A_1) = 0.40$$
$$P(B_2) = 0.35$$
$$P(B_1) = 0.25$$
$$P(A_1|B_2) = 0.70$$
$$P(A_1|B_1) = 0.30$$

a. Use the probabilities given to construct a joint probability distribution table.

b. What is the probability a family will ski *and* have children who are not in the 8–16 age group? How do you write this probability?

c. What is the probability a family with children in the 8–16 age group will not ski?

d. Are the categories "skiing" and "family composition" independent?

Computer Database Exercises

4-71. The ECCO company makes backup alarms for machinery like forklifts and commercial trucks. When a customer returns one of the alarms under warranty, the quality manager logs data on the product. From the data available in the file named **Ecco**, use relative frequency to find the following probabilities.

a. What is the probability the product was made at the Salt Lake City plant?

b. What is the probability the reason for the return was due to a wiring problem?

c. What is the joint probability the returned item was from the Salt Lake City plant and had a wiring-related problem?

d. What is the probability that a returned item was made on the day shift at the Salt Lake plant and had a cracked lens problem?

e. If an item was returned, what is the most likely profile for the item, including plant location, shift, and cause of problem?

4-72. Continuing with the ECCO company from Problem 4.71, when a customer returns one of the alarms under warranty, the quality manager logs data on the product. From the data available in the **Ecco** file, use relative frequency to find the following probabilities.

a. If a part was made in the Salt Lake plant, what is the probability the cause of the returned part was due to wiring?

b. If the company incurs a $30 cost for each returned alarm, what percentage of the cost should be assigned to each plant if it is known that 70% of all production is done in Boise, 20% in Salt Lake, and the rest is done in Toronto?

4-73. A survey of 150 CEOs was conducted in which the CEOs were to list their corporation's geographical location: Northeast (NE), Southeast (SE), Midwest (MW), Southwest (SW), and West (W). They were also requested to indicate their company's industrial type: Communication (C), Electronics (E), Finance (F), and Manufacturing (M). The file entitled **CEOInfo** contains sample data similar to that used in this study.

a. Determine the probability that a randomly chosen CEO would have a corporation in the West.

b. Compute the probability that a randomly chosen CEO would have a corporation in the West and headed an electronics corporation.

c. Calculate the probability that a randomly chosen CEO would have a corporation in the East or headed a communications corporation.

d. Of the corporations located in the East, calculate the probability that a randomly selected CEO would head a communications corporation.

4-74. The Employee Benefit Research Institute (EBRI) issued a news release ("Saving in America: Three Key Sets of Figures") on October 25, 2005. In 2005, about 69% of workers said they have saved for retirement. The file entitled **Retirement** contains sample data of the total savings and investments of those who saved for retirement similar to that used in this study.

a. Construct a frequency distribution of the total savings and investments using the intervals: (1) Less than $25,000, (2) $25,000–$49,999, (3) $50,000–$99,999, (4) $100,000–$249,999, and (5) $250,000 or more.

b. Determine the probability that an individual who has saved for retirement has saved less than $50,000. Use relative frequencies.

c. Determine the probability that a randomly chosen individual has saved less than $50,000 toward retirement.

d. Calculate the probability that at least two of four individuals have saved less than $50,000 toward retirement.

4-75. *USA Today* reported (Stephanie Armour, "Generation Y," November 7, 2005) on the impact of Generation Y on the workforce. The workforce is comprised of (1) Silent generation (born before 1946), 7.5%; (2) Baby boomers (1946–1964), 42%; (3) Generation X (1965–1976), 29.5%; and (4) Generation Y (1977 –1989), 21%. Even ways of communication are changing. Randstad Holding, an international supplier of services to businesses and institutions, examined the different methods of communication preferred by the different elements of the workforce. The file entitled **Communication** contains sample data similar to that used in this study.

a. Construct a frequency distribution for each of the generations. Use the communication categories (1) Gp Meeting, (2) Face-to-Face, (3) e-mail, and (4) Other.

b. Calculate the probability that a randomly chosen member of the workforce prefers communicating face-to-face.

c. Given that an individual in the workforce prefers to communicate face-to-face, determine the generation of which the individual is most likely a member.

CASE 4.1

Great Air Commuter Service

The Great Air Commuter Service Company started in 1984 to provide efficient and inexpensive commuter travel between Boston and New York City. People in the airline industry know Peter Wilson, the principal owner and operating manager of the company, as "a real promoter." Before founding Great Air, Peter operated a small regional airline in the Rocky Mountains with varying success. When Cascade Airlines offered to buy his company, Peter decided to sell and return to the East.

Peter arrived at his office near Fenway Park in Boston a little later than usual this morning. He had stopped to have a business breakfast with Aaron Little, his long-time friend and sometime partner in various business deals. Peter needed some advice and through the years has learned to rely on Aaron as a ready source, no matter what the subject.

Peter explained to Aaron that his commuter service needed a promotional gimmick to improve its visibility in the business communities in Boston and New York. Peter was thinking of running a contest on each flight and awarding the winner a prize. The idea would be that travelers who commute between Boston and New York might just as well have fun on the way and have a chance to win a nice prize.

As Aaron listened to Peter outlining his contest plans, his mind raced through contest ideas. Aaron thought that a large variety of contests would be needed, because many of the passengers would likely be repeat customers and might tire of the same old thing. In addition, some of the contests should be chance-type contests, whereas others should be skill-based.

"Well, what do you think?" asked Peter. Aaron finished his scrambled eggs before responding. When he did, it was completely in character. "I think it will fly," Aaron said, and proceeded to offer a variety of suggestions.

Peter felt good about the enthusiastic response Aaron had given to the idea and thought that the ideas discussed at breakfast presented a good basis for the promotional effort. Now back at the office, Peter does have some concerns with one part of the plan. Aaron thought that in addition to the regular in-flight contests for prizes (such as free flights, dictation equipment, and business periodical subscriptions), each month on a randomly selected day a major prize should be offered on all Great Air flights. This would encourage regular business fliers to fly Great Air all the time. Aaron proposed that the prize could be a trip to the Virgin Islands or somewhere similar, or the cash equivalent.

Great Air has three flights daily to New York and three flights returning to Boston, for a total of six flights. Peter is concerned that the cost of funding six prizes of this size each month plus six daily smaller prizes might be excessive. He also believes that it might be better to increase the size of the large prize to something such as a new car but use a contest that will not guarantee a winner.

But what kind of a contest can be used? Just as he is about to dial Aaron's number, Margaret Runyon, Great Air's marketing manager, enters Peter's office. He has been waiting for her to return from a meeting so he can run the contest idea past her and get her input.

Margaret's response is not as upbeat as Aaron's, but she does think the idea is worth exploring. She offers an idea for the large-prize contest that she thinks might be workable. She outlines the contest as follows.

On the first of each month she and Peter will randomly select a day for that month on which the major contest will be run. That date will not be disclosed to the public. Then on each flight that day, the flight attendant will have passengers write down their birthdays (month and day). If any two people on the plane have the same birthday, they will place their names in a hat and one name will be selected to receive the grand prize.

Margaret explains that because the capacity of each flight is 40 passengers plus the crew, there is a very low chance of a birthday match and, therefore, the chance of giving away a grand prize on any one flight is small. Peter likes the idea, but when he asks Margaret what the probability is that a match will occur, her response does not sound quite right. She believes the probability for a match will be 40/365 for a full plane and less than that when there are fewer than 40 passengers aboard.

After Margaret leaves, Peter decides that it would be useful to know the probability of one or more birthday matches on flights with 20, 30, and 40 passengers. Further, he wants to know what the chances are that he will end up awarding two or more major prizes during a given month, assuming that the six flights carry the same number of passengers (20, 30, or 40). He realizes that he will need some help from someone with a knowledge of statistics.

CASE 4.2

Let's Make a Deal

Quite a few years ago, a popular show called *Let's Make a Deal* appeared on network television. Contestants were selected from the audience. Each contestant would bring some silly item that they would trade for a cash prize or a prize behind one of three doors.

Suppose that you have been selected as a contestant on the show. You are given a choice of three doors. Behind one door is a new sports car. Behind the other doors are a pig and chicken—booby prizes to be sure! Let's suppose that you pick door number one. Before opening that door, the host, who knows what is behind each door, opens door two to show you the chicken. He then asks you, "Would you be willing to trade door one for door three?" What should you do?

References

Blyth, C. R., "Subjective vs. Objective Methods in Statistics." *American Statistician*, 26 (June 1972), pp. 20–22.

Hogg, R. V., and Elliot A. Tanis, *Probability and Statistical Inference*, 7th ed. (Upper Saddle River, NJ: Prentice Hall, 2005).

Marx, Morris L., and Richard J. Larsen, *An Introduction to Mathematical Statistics and Its Applications*, 4th ed. (Upper Saddle River, NJ: Prentice Hall, 2006).

Microsoft Excel 2007 (Redmond, WA: Microsoft Corp., 2007).

Minitab for Windows Version 15 (State College, PA: Minitab, 2007).

Raiffa, H., *Decision Analysis: Introductory Lectures on Choices Under Uncertainty* (Reading, MA: Addison-Wesley, 1968).

Siegel, Andrew F., *Practical Business Statistics*, 5th ed. (Burr Ridge, IL: Irwin, 2003).

Chapter FIVE

Discrete Probability Distributions

CHAPTER OUTCOMES

After studying the material in Chapter 5, you should:

1. Be able to calculate and interpret the expected value of a discrete random variable.
2. Be able to apply the binomial distribution to business decision-making situations.
3. Be able to compute probabilities for the Poisson and hypergeometric distributions and apply these distributions to decision-making situations.

PREPARING FOR CHAPTER FIVE

- Review the concepts of simple random sampling discussed in Chapter 1.
- Review the discussion of weighted averages in Chapter 3.
- Review the basic rules of probability in Chapter 4, including the Addition and Multiplication rules.

WHY YOU NEED TO KNOW

Each day, Dell, the computer manufacturer, receives component parts such as disk drives, motherboards, and internal modems from suppliers. When a batch of parts arrives, the quality assurance section randomly samples a fixed number of parts and tests them to see if any are defective. Suppose in one such test a sample of 20 parts is selected from a supplier whose contract calls for at most 5% defective parts. How many defective parts in the sample of 20 should Dell expect if the contract is being satisfied? What should be concluded if the sample contains 3 defects? Answers to these questions require calculations based on a probability distribution known as the *binomial distribution*.

How many teller stations should Pittsburg-based Mellon Bank construct in a new branch bank? If there are four teller stations, will customers have to wait too long or will there be excess capacity and wasted space? To help answer these questions, decision makers use a probability distribution known as the *Poisson distribution*.

A personnel manager has a chance to promote 3 people from 10 equally qualified candidates. Suppose none of six women are selected by the manager. Is this evidence of gender bias or would we expect to see this type of result? A distribution known as the *hypergeometric distribution* would be very helpful in addressing this issue.

The *binomial, Poisson,* and *hypergeometric* distributions are three *discrete* probability distributions used in business decision making. This chapter introduces discrete probability distributions and shows how they are used in business settings. As you learned in Chapter 4, probability is the way decision makers express their uncertainty about outcomes and events. Through the use of well-established discrete probability distributions like those introduced in Chapter 5, you will be better prepared for making decisions in an uncertain environment.

5.1 Introduction to Discrete Probability Distributions

Random Variables

As discussed in Chapter 4, when a random experiment is performed, some outcome must occur. When the experiment has a quantitative characteristic, we can associate a number with each outcome. For example, an inspector who examines three sheets of plywood can judge each sheet as "acceptable" or "unacceptable." The outcome of the experiment defines the specific number of acceptable sheets of plywood. The possible outcomes are

$$x = \{0, 1, 2, 3\}$$

Random Variable
A variable that takes on different numerical values based on chance.

The value, x, is called a **random variable** since the numerical values it takes on are random. Although the inspector knows these are the possible values for the variable before she samples, she does not know which value will occur in any given trial. Further, the value of the random variable may be different each time three plywood sheets are inspected.

Discrete Random Variable
A random variable that can only assume a finite number of values or an infinite sequence of values such as 0, 1, 2 . . . .

Two classes of random variables exist: **discrete random variables** and **continuous random variables**. For instance, if a bank auditor randomly examines 15 accounts to verify the accuracy of the balances, the number of inaccurate account balances can be represented by a discrete random variable with the following values:

$$x = \{0, 1, \ldots 15\}$$

Continuous Random Variables
Random variables that can assume any value in an interval.

In another situation, 10 employees were recently hired by a major electronics company. The number of females in that group can be described as a discrete random variable with possible values equal to

$$x = \{0, 1, 2, 3, \ldots 10\}$$

Notice that the value for a discrete random variable is often determined by counting. In the bank auditing example, the value of variable x is determined by counting the number of accounts with errors. In the hiring example, the value of variable x is determined by counting the number of females hired.

In other situations, the random variable is said to be continuous. For example, the exact time it takes a trainee to perform a job task may be any value between two points, say 1 minute to 10 minutes. If x is the time required, then x is continuous because, if measured precisely enough, the possible values, x, can be any value in the interval 1 to 10 minutes. Other examples of continuous variables include measures of distance and measures of weight when measured precisely. A continuous random variable is generally defined by measuring, which is contrasted with a discrete random variable, whose value is typically determined by counting. Chapter 6 focuses on some important probability distributions for continuous random variables.

Displaying Discrete Probability Distributions Graphically The probability distribution for a discrete random variable is composed of the values the variable can assume and the probabilities for each of the possible values. For example, if three parts are tested to determine if they are defective, the probability distribution for the number of defectives might be

x = Number of Defectives	$P(x)$
0	0.10
1	0.30
2	0.40
3	0.20
	$\Sigma = 1.00$

Graphically, the discrete probability distribution associated with these defectives can be represented by the areas of rectangles in which the base is one unit wide and the height corresponds to the probability. The areas of the rectangles sum to 1. Figure 5.1 illustrates two examples of discrete probability distributions. Figure 5.1(a) shows a discrete random variable with only three possible outcomes. Figure 5.1(b) shows the probability distribution for a discrete variable that has 21 possible outcomes. Note, as the number of possible outcomes increases, the distribution becomes smoother. In all cases, the sum of the probabilities is 1.

Discrete probability distributions have extensive applications in business decision-making situations. In the remainder of this section, we discuss several important issues that are of particular importance to discrete probability distributions.

Mean and Standard Deviation of Discrete Distributions

A probability distribution, like a frequency distribution, can be only partially described by a graph. To aid in a decision situation, you may need to calculate the distribution's *mean* and *standard deviation*. These values measure the central location and spread, respectively, of the probability distribution.

CHAPTER OUTCOME #1

Calculating the Mean The mean of a discrete probability distribution is also called the **expected value** of the output variable from an experiment. The expected value is actually a *weighted average* of the random variable values, in which the weights are the probabilities assigned to the values. The expected value is given in Equation 5.1.

Expected Value
The mean of a probability distribution. The average value when the experiment that generates values for the random variable is repeated over the long run.

Expected Value of a Discrete Probability Distribution

$$E(x) = \Sigma x P(x) \tag{5.1}$$

where:

$E(x)$ = Expected value of x
x = Values of the random variable
$P(x)$ = Probability of the random variable taking on the value x

---

FIGURE 5.1

**Discrete Probability
Distributions**

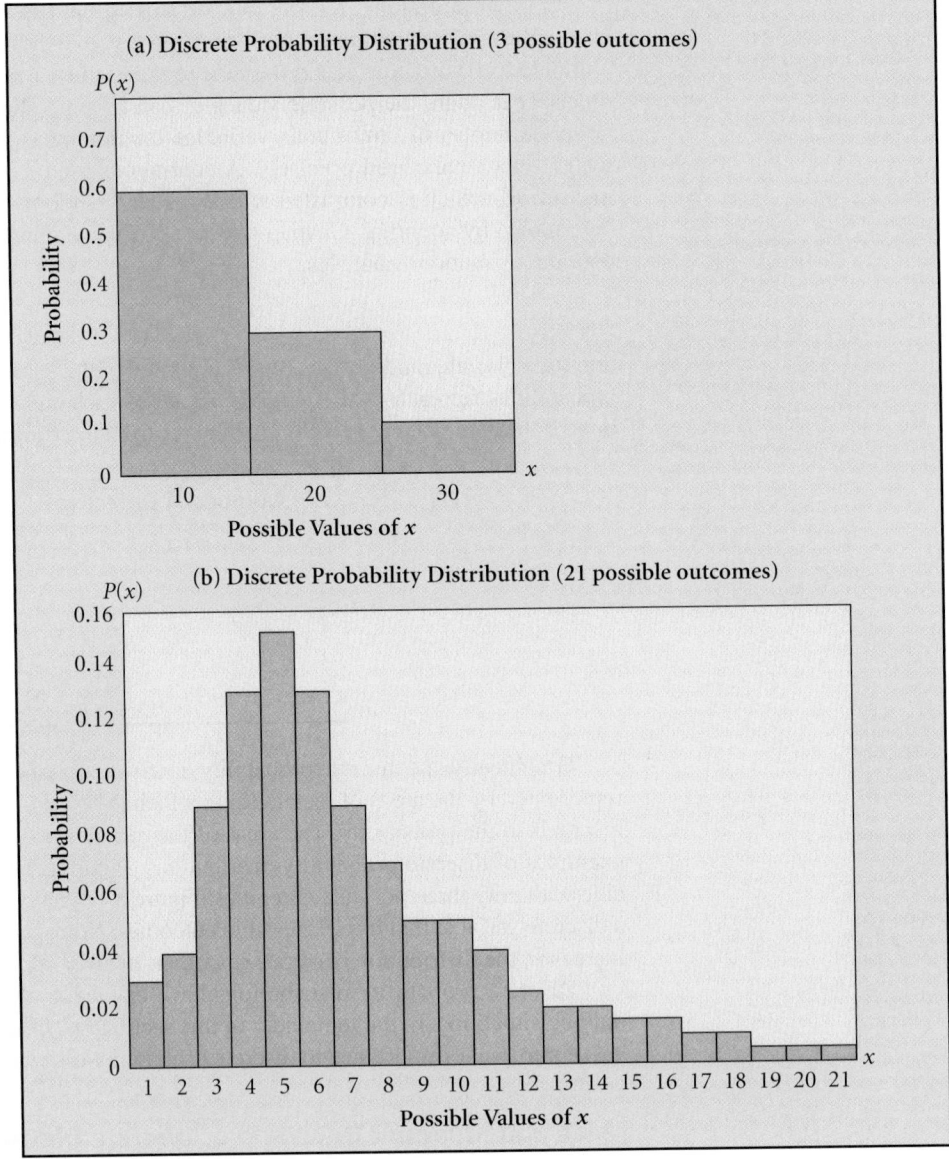

(a) Discrete Probability Distribution (3 possible outcomes)

(b) Discrete Probability Distribution (21 possible outcomes)

Calculating the Standard Deviation   The standard deviation measures the spread, or dispersion, in a set of data. The standard deviation also measures the spread in the values of a random variable. To calculate the standard deviation for a discrete probability distribution, use Equation 5.2.

Standard Deviation of a Discrete Probability Distribution

$$\sigma_x = \sqrt{\sum [x - E(x)]^2\, P(x)} \qquad (5.2)$$

where:

x = Values of the random variable
$E(x)$ = Expected value of x
$P(x)$ = Probability of the random variable taking on the value x

TRY PROBLEM 5.5

Wagner Investments Wagner Investments is located in Fairfax, West Virginia. The company manages assets for clients throughout the Southeast. Recently, the managing partner conducted a study of the firm's clients with respect to the number of their stock transactions during the past week. The discrete random variable, x, is the number of transactions per client, ranging from 0 to 3. The following frequency distribution was developed:

x	Frequency
0	150
1	110
2	50
3	90
	$\Sigma = 400$

Assuming that these data reflect the typical week, the manager wishes to develop a discrete probability distribution and compute the mean and standard deviation for the distribution. This can be done using the following steps:

Step 1 **Convert the frequency distribution into a probability distribution using the relative frequency assessment method.**

x	Frequency
0	150/400 = 0.375
1	110/400 = 0.275
2	50/400 = 0.125
3	90/400 = 0.225
	$\Sigma = 1.000$

Step 2 **Compute the expected value using Equation 5.1.**

$$E(x) = \Sigma\, xP(x)$$
$$E(x) = (0)(0.375) + (1)(0.275) + (2)(0.125) + (3)(0.225)$$
$$E(x) = 1.20$$

The expected value is 1.20 stock trades per week. Thus, assuming the distribution of the number of transactions is representative of that of each individual client, the long-run average number of trades per week for a client will be 1.20.

Step 3 **Compute the standard deviation using Equation 5.2.**

$$\sigma_x = \sqrt{\Sigma[x - E(x)]^2 P(x)}$$

x	$P(x)$	$[x - E(x)]$	$[x - E(x)]^2$	$[x - E(x)]^2 P(x)$
0	0.375	0 − 1.2 = −1.20	1.44	0.540
1	0.275	1 − 1.2 = −.20	0.04	0.011
2	0.125	2 − 1.2 = .80	0.64	0.080
3	0.225	3 − 1.2 = 1.80	3.24	0.729
				$\Sigma = 1.360$

$$\sigma_x = \sqrt{1.36} = 1.17$$

The standard deviation of the discrete probability distribution is 1.17 transactions per week.

TABLE 5.1 Probability Distribution—Defect Rate for Supplier B

Defect Rate x	Probability P(x)
0.01	0.3
0.05	0.4
0.10	0.2
0.15	0.1

Business Application

GUGLIANA & SONS Gugliana & Sons in New York imports Halloween masks from China and other Far East countries for distribution in the United States and Canada. For one particular product line, Gugliana currently has two suppliers. Both suppliers have a poor record when it comes to quality. Gugliana is planning to purchase 100,000 of a particular Halloween mask and wants to use the least-cost supplier for the entire purchase. Supplier A is less expensive by $0.10 per mask and has an ongoing record of supplying 10% defects. Supplier B is more expensive but may be a higher-quality supplier. Gugliana records indicate that the rate of defects from supplier B varies. Table 5.1 shows the probability distributions for the defect percentages for supplier B. Each defect is thought to cost the company $0.95.

Looking first at supplier A, at a defect rate of 0.10, out of 100,000 units the number of defects is expected to be 10,000. The cost of these is $0.95 × 10,000 = $9,500. For supplier B, the expected defect rate is found using Equation 5.1 as follows:

$$E(\text{defect rate}) = \Sigma\, xP(x)$$

$$E(\text{defect rate}) = (0.01)(0.3) + (0.05)(0.4) + (0.10)(0.2) + (0.15)(0.1)$$

$$E(\text{defect rate}) = 0.058$$

Thus, supplier B is expected to supply 5.8% defects, or 5,800 out of the 100,000 units ordered, for an expected cost of $0.95 × 5,800 = $5,510. Based on defect cost alone, supplier B is less expensive ($5,510 versus $9,500). However, recall that supplier B's product sells for $0.10 per unit more. Thus, on a 100,000-unit order, supplier B costs an extra $0.10 × 100,000 = $10,000 more than supplier A. The relative costs are

Supplier A = $9,500   Supplier B = $5,510 + $10,000 = $15,510

Therefore, based on expected costs, supplier A should be selected to supply the 100,000 Halloween masks.

5-1: Exercises

Skill Development

5-1. There are six questions on a multiple-choice quiz. Let x represent the number of questions a student answers correctly.
a. Is x a continuous or discrete random variable?
b. What are the possible values of x?

5-2. Suppose a health insurance company surveys its customers to determine the number of children under age 22 living in each household.
a. What is the random variable for this survey?
b. Is the random variable discrete or continuous?

5-3. Two numbers are randomly drawn with replacement from a list of five. If the five numbers are 2, 2, 4, 6, 8, what is the probability distribution of the sum of the two numbers selected? Show the probability distribution graphically.

5-4. Because of bad weather, the number of days next week that the captain of a charter fishing boat can leave port is uncertain. Let x = number of days that the boat is able to leave port per week. The following probability distribution for the variable, x, was determined based on historical data when the weather was poor:

x	P(x)
0	0.05
1	0.10
2	0.10
3	0.20
4	0.20
5	0.15
6	0.15
7	0.05

Based on the probability distribution, what is the expected number of days per week the captain can leave port?

5-5. Given the following discrete probability distribution,

x	P(x)
100	0.25
125	0.30
150	0.45

a. Calculate the expected value of x.
b. Calculate the variance of x.
c. Calculate the standard deviation of x.

5-6. Given the following discrete probability distribution,

x	P(x)
50	0.375
65	0.15
70	0.225
75	0.05
90	0.20

a. Calculate the expected value of x.
b. Calculate the variance of x.
c. Calculate the standard deviation of x.

5-7. The roll of a pair of dice has the following probability distribution, where the random variable x is the sum of the values produced by each die:

x	P(x)	x	P(x)
2	1/36	8	5/36
3	2/36	9	4/36
4	3/36	10	3/36
5	4/36	11	2/36
6	5/36	12	1/36
7	6/36		

a. Calculate the expected value of x.
b. Calculate the variance of x.
c. Calculate the standard deviation of x.

5-8. Consider the following discrete probability distribution:

x	P(x)
5	0.10
10	0.15
15	0.25
20	0.50

a. Calculate the expected value of the random variable.
b. Let $y = x + 5$. Calculate the expected value of the new random variable y.
c. Let $z = 5x$. Calculate the expected value of the new random variable z.
d. From your calculations in part a and part b, indicate the effect that adding a constant to a random variable has upon the expected value of the random variable.
e. From your calculations in part a and part c, indicate the effect that multiplying a random variable by a constant has upon the expected value of the random variable.

5-9. Consider the following discrete probability distribution:

x	P(x)
3	0.13
6	0.12
9	0.15
12	0.60

a. Calculate the variance and standard deviation of the random variable.
b. Let $y = x + 7$. Calculate the variance and standard deviation of the random variable y.
c. Let $z = 7x$. Calculate the variance and standard deviation of the random variable z.
d. From your calculations in part a and part b, indicate the effect that adding a constant to a random variable has upon its variance and standard deviation.
e. From your calculations in part a and part c, indicate the effect that multiplying a random variable with a constant has upon the variance and the standard deviation of the random variable.

5-10. Examine the following probability distribution:

x	5	10	15	20	25	30	35	40	45	50
P(x)	0.01	0.05	0.14	0.20	0.30	0.15	0.05	0.04	0.01	0.05

a. Calculate the expected value and standard deviation for this random variable.
b. Denote the expected value as μ. Calculate $\mu - \sigma$ and $\mu + \sigma$.
c. Determine the proportion of the distribution that is contained within the interval $\mu \pm \sigma$.
d. Repeat part c for (1) $\mu \pm 2\sigma$ and (2) $\mu \pm 3\sigma$.

Business Applications

5-11. The U.S. Census Bureau (2004 Annual Social & Economic Supplement) collects demographics concerning the number of people in families per household. Assume the distribution of the number of people per household is shown in the following table:

x	P(x)
2	0.27
3	0.25
4	0.28
5	0.13
6	0.04
7	0.03

a. Calculate the expected number of people in families per household in the United States.
b. Compute the variance and standard deviation of the number of people in families per household.

5-12. The manager of a computer repair center in Trenton, New Jersey, has read an advertisement from a local competitor that guarantees all computer repairs within four days. Based on his company's past experience, he wants to know if he can offer a similar guarantee. His past service records are used to determine the following probability distribution:

Number of Days	Probability
1	0.15
2	0.25
3	0.30
4	0.18
5	0.12

a. Calculate the mean number of days his customers wait for a computer repair.
b. Also calculate the variance and standard deviation.
c. Based on the calculations in parts a and b, what conclusion should the manager reach regarding his company's repair times?

5-13. The Bittercreek Grille in Denver, Colorado, has the capacity to seat 130 people at a time. The restaurant manger has been gathering data on the number of minutes a dinner party of four spends in the restaurant from the moment they are seated to when they pay the check. What is the mean number of minutes for a dinner party of four? What is the variance and standard deviation?

Number of Minutes	Probability
60	0.05
70	0.15
80	0.20
90	0.45
100	0.10
110	0.05

5-14. Barclay Brothers, Inc. sells lighting fixtures for commercial and residential applications. The company currently has only one supplier for a particular type of ceiling light fixture. Based on historical data that the company has maintained, it has assessed the following probability distribution for the proportion of defective lights that it receives from this supplier:

Proportion Defective	Probability
0.01	0.4
0.02	0.3
0.05	0.2
0.10	0.1

This supplier charges Barclay Brothers, Inc. $29.00 per unit for this light fixture. While the supplier will replace any defects free of charge, Barclay managers figure the cost of dealing with the defects is about $5.00 each.

a. Assuming that Barclay is planning to purchase 2,000 of these fixtures from the supplier, what is the total expected cost to Barclay for the deal?
b. Suppose that Barclay has an opportunity to buy the same light fixture from another supplier at a cost of $28.50 per unit. However, based on their investigations, Barclay managers have assessed

the following probability distribution for the proportion of defective fixtures that will be delivered by the new supplier:

Proportion Defective x	Probability $P(x)$
0.01	0.1
0.02	0.1
0.05	0.7
0.10	0.1

Assuming that the defect cost is still $5.00 each, based on total expected cost for an order of 2,000 light fixtures, should Barclay buy from the new supplier or stick with its original supplier?

5-15. A manufacturing firm located in the United States uses a component that is supplied by a company in Italy. The component is sent by air to the manufacturing firm after a replenishment order is received. The component is expensive to carry in inventory and consequently is not always available in stock when requested. Furthermore, shipping schedules are such that the lead time for transportation of the component is not a constant. Using historical records, the manufacturing firm has developed the following probability distribution for the product's lead time. The distribution is shown here, where the random variable x is the number of days between the placement of the replenishment order and the receipt of the item.

x	$P(x)$
2	0.15
3	0.45
4	0.30
5	0.075
6	0.025

a. What is the average lead time for the component?
b. What is the coefficient of variation for delivery lead time?
c. How might the manufacturing firm in the United States use this information?

5-16. A retail store keeps four alarm clock radios in stock. At the end of a week, the store restocks the item if it has fewer than four clock radios available. The amount that is restocked each week is the number of clock radios necessary to bring the in-stock level up to four. If weekly demand is greater than the four units in stock, the store

loses the sale. The radio sells for $25 and costs the store $15. The store estimates that the probability distribution of weekly demand for the radio is as follows:

x (Weekly Demand)	$P(x)$
0	0.05
1	0.05
2	0.10
3	0.20
4	0.40
5	0.10
6	0.05
7	0.05

a. What is the expected weekly demand for the alarm clock radio?
b. What is the probability that weekly demand will be greater than the number of available radios?
c. What is the expected weekly profit from the sale of the alarm clock radio? (Remember: There are only four clock radios available in any week to meet demand.)
d. On average, how much profit is lost each week because the radio is not available when demanded?

5-17. A large corporation in search of a CEO and a CFO has narrowed the fields for each position to a short list. The CEO candidates graduated, respectively, from Chicago (C) and three Ivy League universities: Harvard (H), Princeton (P), and Yale (Y). The four CFO candidates graduated, respectively, from MIT (M), Northwestern (N), and two Ivy League universities, Dartmouth (D) and Brown (B). The personnel director wishes to determine the distribution of the number of Ivy League graduates who could fill these positions.

a. Assume the selections were made randomly. Construct the probability distribution of the number of Ivy League graduates who fill these positions.
b. Would it be surprising if both positions were filled with Ivy League graduates?
c. Calculate the expected value and standard deviation of the number of Ivy League graduates who fill these positions.

5-18. Bicano Trading Co. is a manufacturer of a wide spectrum of footwear, including indoor slippers, children's shoes, and sandals, located in Fizhou, China. To keep up with increasing demand, it is considering three expansion plans: (1) a small factory with yearly costs of $150,000, that will increase the production of flip-flops by 400,000; (2) a mid-sized factory with yearly costs of $250,000, that will increase the production of flip-flops by 600,000; and (3) a large factory with yearly costs of $350,000, that will increase the production of flip-flops by 900,000. The profit per flip-flop is projected to be $0.75. The probability distribution of demand for flip-flops is considered to be

Demand	300,000	700,000	900,000
Probability	0.2	0.5	0.3

a. Compute the expected profit for each of the expansion plans.
b. Calculate the standard deviation for each of the expansion plans.
c. Which expansion plan would you suggest? Provide the statistical reasoning behind your selection.

Computer Database Exercises

5-19. Covercraft manufactures covers to protect automobile interiors and finishes. Its Block-It 200 Series fabric has a limited two-year warranty. Periodic testing is done to determine if the warranty policy should be changed. One such study may have examined those covers that became unserviceable while still under warranty. Data that could be produced by such a study is contained in the file entitled **Covers**. The data represent assessment the number of months a cover was used until it became unserviceable.
a. Produce a frequency distribution for these data. Convert the frequency distribution into a probability distribution using the relative frequency assessment method.
b. Calculate the expected value and standard deviation for the time until the covers became unserviceable.
c. The quality control department thinks that among those covers that do become unserviceable while still under warranty the majority last longer than 19 months. Produce the relevant statistic to verify this assumption.

5-20. Barnes & Noble made an agreement with a publisher to begin selling a magazine on a trial basis. The magazine retails for $3.95 in other stores. Barnes & Noble bought it for $1.95 and sold it for $3.49. During the trial period, it placed 10 copies of the magazine in each of 150 stores throughout the country. The file entitled **Sold** contains the number of magazines sold in each of the stores.
a. Produce a frequency distribution for these data. Convert the frequency distribution into a probability distribution using the relative frequency assessment method.
b. Calculate the expected profit from the sale of these ten magazines.
c. Barnes & Noble is negotiating returning all unsold magazines for a salvage price. Determine the salvage price Barnes & Noble will need to obtain to yield a positive expected profit from selling ten magazine.

5-21. Pfizer Inc. is the manufacturer of Revolution (Selamectin) a topical parasiticide used for the treatment, control, and prevention of flea infestation, heartworm, and ear mites for dogs and cats. One of its selling points is that it provides protection for an entire month. Such claims are made on the basis of research and statistical studies. The file entitled **Fleafree** contains data similar to that obtained in Pfizer's research. It presents the number of days Revolution could remain effective when applied to mature cats.
a. Produce a frequency distribution for these data. Convert the frequency distribution into a probability distribution using the relative frequency assessment method.
b. Calculate the expected value and standard deviation for the number of days Revolution could remain effective.
c. If the marketing department wished to advertise the number of days that 90% of the cats remain protected while using Revolution, what would this number of days be?

5.2 The Binomial Probability Distribution

In Section 5.1 you learned that random variables can be classified as either **discrete** or **continuous**. In most instances, the value of a discrete random variable is determined by counting. For instance, the number of customers who arrive at a store each day is a discrete variable. Its value is determined by counting the customers.

Several theoretical discrete distributions have extensive application in business decision making. A probability distribution is called *theoretical* when the mathematical properties of its random variable are used to produce its probabilities. Such distributions are different from the distributions that are obtained subjectively or from observation. Sections 5.2 and 5.3 focus on theoretical discrete probability distributions. Chapter 6 will introduce important theoretical continuous probability distributions.

The Binomial Distribution

Binomial Probability Distribution Characteristics
A distribution that gives the probability of *x* successes in *n* trials in a process that meets the following conditions:
1. A trial has only two possible outcomes: a success or a failure.
2. There is a fixed number, *n*, identical trials.
3. The trials of the experiment are independent of each other. This means that if one outcome is a success, this does not influence the chance of another outcome being a success.
4. The process must be consistent in generating successes and failures. That is, the probability, *p*, associated with a success remains constant from trial to trial.
5. If *p* represents the probability of a success, then $(1 - p) = q$ is the probability of a failure.

Business Application

The first theoretical probability distribution we will consider is the **binomial distribution** that describes processes whose trials have only two possible outcomes. The physical events described by this type of process are widespread. For instance, a quality control system in a manufacturing plant labels each tested item as either defective or acceptable. A firm bidding for a contract either will or will not get the contract. A marketing research firm may receive responses to a questionnaire in the form of "Yes, I will buy" or "No, I will not buy." The personnel manager in an organization is faced with two possible outcomes each time he offers a job—either the applicant accepts the offer or rejects it.

Characteristics of the Binomial Distribution

The binomial distribution requires that the experiment's trials be independent. This can be assured if the sampling is performed with replacement from a finite population. This means that an item is sampled from a population and returned to the population, after its characteristic(s) have been recorded, before the next item is sampled. However, sampling with replacement is the exception rather than the rule in business applications. Most often, the sampling is performed without replacement. Strictly speaking, when sampling is performed without replacement, the conditions for the binomial distribution cannot be satisfied. However, the conditions are approximately satisfied if the sample selected is quite small relative to the size of the population from which the sample is selected. A commonly used rule of thumb is that the binomial distribution can be applied if the sample size is at most 5% of the population size.

HOUSEHOLD SECURITY Household Security produces and installs 300 custom-made home security units every week. The units are priced to include one-day installation service by two technicians. A unit with either a design or production problem must be modified on-site and will require more than one day to install.

Household Security has completed an extensive study of its design and manufacturing systems. The information shows that if the company is operating at standard quality, 10% of the security units will have problems and will require more than one day to install. The binomial distribution applies to this situation because the following conditions exist.

1. There are only two possible outcomes when a unit is installed: It is good or it is defective (will take more than one day to install). Finding a defective unit in this application will be considered a success. A success occurs when we observe the outcome of interest.
2. Each unit is designed and made in the same way.
3. The outcome of a security unit (good or defective) is independent of whether the preceding system was good or defective.
4. The probability of a defective system, $p = 0.10$, remains constant from unit to unit.
5. The probability of a good system, $q = 1 - p = 0.90$, remains constant from unit to unit.

To determine the likely cause of defects—design or manufacturing—the quality assurance group at Household Security has developed a plan for dismantling a random sample of four security units each week. Because the sample size is small (4/300 = 0.0133 or 1.33%) relative to the size of the population (300 units per week), the conditions of independence and constant probability will be approximately satisfied because the sample is less than 5% of the population.

TABLE 5.2 Sample Space for Household Security

Results	No. of Defectives	No. of Ways
G,G,G,G	0	1
G,G,G,D	1	
G,G,D,G		
G,D,G,G,		4
D,G,G,G		
G,G,D,D	2	
G,D,G,D		
D,G,G,D		
G,D,D,G		6
D,G,D,G		
D,D,G,G		
D,D,D,G	3	
D,D,G,D		
D,G,D,D		4
G,D,D,D		
D,D,D,D	4	1

We let the number of defective units be the random variable of interest. The number of defectives is limited to discrete values, $x = 0, 1, 2, 3,$ or 4. We can determine the probability that the random variable will have any of the discrete values. One way is to list the sample space, as shown in Table 5.2. We can find the probability of zero defectives, for instance, by employing the Multiplication Rule for Independent Events.

$$P(x = 0 \text{ defectives}) = P(G \text{ and } G \text{ and } G \text{ and } G)$$

where:

$$G = \text{Unit is good (not defective)}$$

Here,

$$P(G) = 0.90$$

and we have assumed the units are independent. Using the Multiplication Rule for Independent Events introduced in Chapter 4 (Rule 9):

$$P(G \text{ and } G \text{ and } G \text{ and } G) = P(G)P(G)P(G)P(G) = (0.90)(0.90)(0.90)(0.90)$$
$$= 0.90^4$$
$$= 0.6561$$

We can also find the probability of exactly one defective in a sample of four. This is accomplished using both the Multiplication Rule for Independent Events and the Addition Rule for Mutually Exclusive Events, which was also introduced in Chapter 4 (Rule 5):

$$P(1 \text{ defective}) = P(G \text{ and } G \text{ and } G \text{ and } D) + P(G \text{ and } G \text{ and } D \text{ and } G)$$
$$+ P(G \text{ and } D \text{ and } G \text{ and } G) + P(D \text{ and } G \text{ and } G \text{ and } G)$$

where:

$$P(G \text{ and } G \text{ and } G \text{ and } D) = P(G)P(G)P(G)P(D) = (0.90)(0.90)(0.90)(0.10)$$
$$= (0.90^3)(0.10)$$

Likewise:

$$P(G \text{ and } G \text{ and } D \text{ and } G) = (0.90^3)(0.10)$$
$$P(G \text{ and } D \text{ and } G \text{ and } G) = (0.90^3)(0.10)$$
$$P(D \text{ and } G \text{ and } G \text{ and } G) = (0.90^3)(0.10)$$

Then:

$$P(1 \text{ defective}) = (0.90^3)(0.10) + (0.90^3)(0.10) + (0.90^3)(0.10) + (0.90^3)(0.10)$$
$$= (4)(0.90^3)(0.10)$$
$$= 0.2916$$

Note that each of the four possible ways of finding one defective unit has the same probability $[(0.90^3)(0.10)]$. We determine the probability of one of the ways to obtain one defective unit and multiply this value by the number of ways (four) of obtaining one defective unit. This produces the overall probability of one defective unit.

Combinations In this relatively simply application, we can fairly easily list the sample space and from that count the number of ways that each possible number of defectives can occur. However, for examples with larger sample sizes, this approach is inefficient. A more effective method exists for counting the number of ways binomial events can occur. This method is called the **counting rule for combinations**. This rule is used to find the number of outcomes from an experiment in which x objects are to be selected from a group of n objects. Equation 5.3 is used to find the combinations.

Counting Rule for Combinations

$$C_x^n = \frac{n!}{x!(n-x)!} \tag{5.3}$$

where:

$C_x^n = $ Number of combinations of x objects selected from n objects
$n! = n(n-1)(n-2) \ldots (2)(1)$
$0! = 1$ by definition

Using Equation 5.3, we find the number of ways that $x = 2$ defectives can occur in a sample of $n = 4$ as

$$C_x^n = \frac{n!}{x!(n-x)!} = \frac{4!}{2!(4-2)!} = \frac{(4)(3)(2)(1)}{(2)(1)(2)(1)} = \frac{24}{4} = 6 \text{ way}$$

Refer to Table 5.2 to see that this is the same value for 2 defects in a sample of 4 that was obtained by listing the sample space.

Now we can find the probabilities of two defectives.

$$P(2 \text{ defectives}) = (6)(0.90^2)(0.10^2)$$
$$= 0.0486$$

Use this method to verify the following:

$$P(3 \text{ defectives}) = (4)(0.90)(0.10^3)$$
$$= 0.0036$$
$$P(4 \text{ defectives}) = (1)(0.10^4)$$
$$= 0.0001$$

TABLE 5.3 Binomial Distribution for Household Security: $n = 4$, $p = 0.10$

x = # of Defects	$P(x)$
0	0.6561
1	0.2916
2	0.0486
3	0.0036
4	0.0001
	$\Sigma = 1.0000$

FIGURE 5.2

Binomial Distribution for Household Security

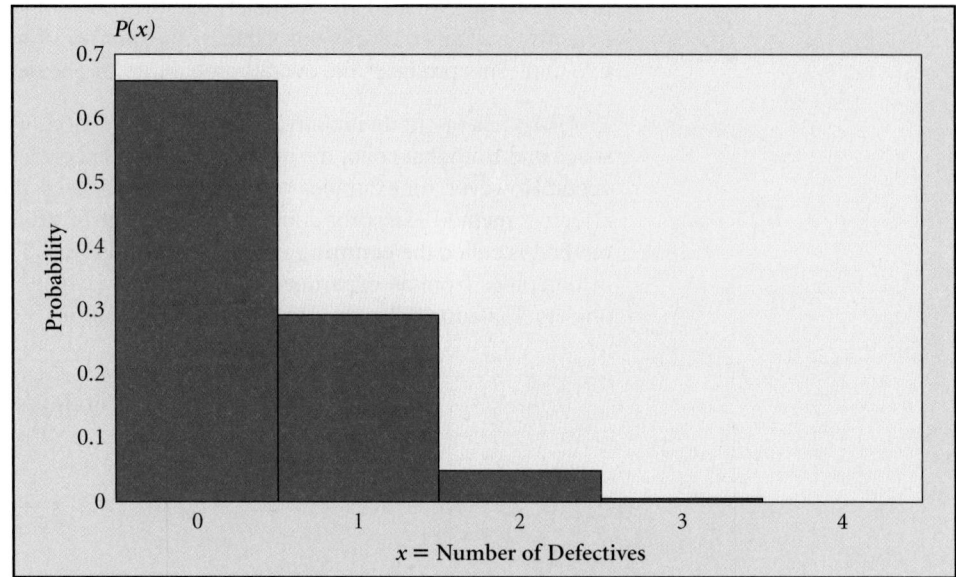

The key to developing the probability distribution for a binomial process is first to determine the probability of any one way the event of interest can occur and then to multiply this probability by the number of ways that event can occur. Table 5.3 shows the binomial probability distribution for the number of defective security units in a sample size of 4 when the probability of any individual unit being defective is 0.10. The probability distribution is graphed in Figure 5.2. Most samples would contain zero or one defective units when the production system is functioning as designed.

Binomial Formula The steps that we have taken to develop this binomial probability distribution can be summarized through a formula called the *binomial formula*, shown as Equation 5.4. Note, this formula is composed of two parts: the combinations of x items selected from n items and the probability of one of the ways that x items can occur.

Binomial Formula

$$P(x) = \frac{n!}{x!(n-x)!} p^x q^{n-x} \tag{5.4}$$

where:

n = Random sample size
x = Number of successes (when a success is defined as what we are looking for)
$n - x$ = Number of failures

p = Probability of a success
$q = 1 - p$ = Probability of a failure
$n! = n(n - 1)(n - 2)(n - 3) \ldots (2)(1)$
$0! = 1$ by definition

Applying Equation 5.4 to the security system example for $n = 4$, $p = 0.10$, and $x = 2$ defects, we get

$$P(x) = \frac{n!}{x!(n-x)!} p^x q^{n-x}$$

$$P(2) = \frac{4!}{2!2!}(0.10^2)(0.90^2) = 6(0.10^2)(0.90^2) = 0.0486$$

This is the same value we calculated earlier when we listed out the sample space on page 215.

TRY PROBLEM 5.22

EXAMPLE 5-2 Using the Binomial Formula

Hanson's Car Wash   Hanson's Car Wash offers a full refund to anyone who is not satisfied with the way the car looks after it is washed. The owners believe the wash results from car to car are independent and that the probability a customer will ask for a refund is 0.20. Suppose a random sample of six cars is observed. In four instances, the customer has asked for a refund. The owners might be interested in the probability of four refunds in six cars. If the binomial distribution applies, the probability can be found using the following steps:

Step 1   **Define the characteristics of the binomial distribution.**
In this case, the characteristics are

$$n = 6, \qquad p = 0.20, \qquad q = 1 - p = 0.80$$

Step 2   **Determine the probability of x successes in n trials using the binomial formula, Equation 5.4.**
In this case, $n = 6$, $p = 0.20$, $q = 0.80$, and we are interested in the probability of $x = 4$ successes.

$$P(x) = \frac{n!}{x!(n-x)!} p^x q^{n-x}$$

$$P(4) = \frac{6!}{4!(6-4)!}(0.20^4)(0.80^{6-4})$$

$$P(4) = 15(0.20^4)(0.80^2)$$

$$P(4) = 0.0154$$

There is only a 0.0154 chance that exactly four customers will want a refund in a sample of six if the chance that any one of the customers will want a refund is 0.20.

Using the Binomial Distribution Table   Using Equation 5.4 to develop the binomial distribution is not difficult, but it can be time-consuming. To make binomial probabilities easier to find, you can use the binomial table in Appendix B. This table is constructed to give individual probabilities for different sample sizes and probabilities of success. Each column is headed by a probability, p, which is the probability associated with a success. The column headings correspond to probabilities of success ranging from 0.01 to 0.50. Down the left side of the table are integer values that correspond to the number of

TABLE 5.4 Binomial Table ($n = 10$)

x	p = 0.01	p = 0.02	p = 0.03	p = 0.04	p = 0.05	p = 0.06	p = 0.07	p = 0.08	p = 0.09	p = 0.10	
					$n = 10$						
0	0.9044	0.8171	0.7374	0.6648	0.5987	0.5386	0.4840	0.4344	0.3894	0.3487	10
1	0.0914	0.1667	0.2281	0.2770	0.3151	0.3438	0.3643	0.3777	0.3851	0.3874	9
2	0.0042	0.0153	0.0317	0.0519	0.0746	0.0988	0.1234	0.1478	0.1714	0.1937	8
3	0.0001	0.0008	0.0026	0.0058	0.0105	0.0168	0.0248	0.0343	0.0452	0.0574	7
4	0.0000	0.0000	0.0001	0.0004	0.0010	0.0019	0.0033	0.0052	0.0078	0.0112	6
5	0.0000	0.0000	0.0000	0.0000	0.0001	0.0001	0.0003	0.0005	0.0009	0.0015	5
6	0.0000	0.0000	0.0000	0.0000	0.0000	0.0000	0.0000	0.0000	0.0001	0.0001	4
7	0.0000	0.0000	0.0000	0.0000	0.0000	0.0000	0.0000	0.0000	0.0000	0.0000	3
8	0.0000	0.0000	0.0000	0.0000	0.0000	0.0000	0.0000	0.0000	0.0000	0.0000	2
9	0.0000	0.0000	0.0000	0.0000	0.0000	0.0000	0.0000	0.0000	0.0000	0.0000	1
10	0.0000	0.0000	0.0000	0.0000	0.0000	0.0000	0.0000	0.0000	0.0000	0.0000	0
	p = 0.99	p = 0.98	p = 0.97	p = 0.96	p = 0.95	p = 0.94	p = 0.93	p = 0.92	p = 0.91	p = 0.90	x

successes, x, for the specified sample size, n. If we are dealing with probabilities ranging from 0.51 to 1.0, we use the values of p located at the bottom of the columns. The corresponding values of x are on the right side of the table, running from bottom to top.

Business Application

U.S. BIO U.S. Bio, a pharmaceutical company, has developed a drug to restore hair growth in men. Like most drugs, this product has potential side effects. One of these is increased blood pressure. The company is willing to market the drug if there are blood-pressure increases in 2% or fewer of the men using the drug.

The company plans to conduct a clinical test with 10 randomly selected men. The number of men with increased blood pressure will be $x = 0, 1, 2, \ldots 10$. We can use the binomial table in Appendix B to develop the probability distribution. Table 5.4 shows the portion of the binomial table we need for $p = 0.02$ and $n = 10$. Go to the column for $p = 0.02$. The values of x are listed down the left side of the table. For example, the probability of 3 occurrences is 0.0008. This means that it is extremely unlikely that 3 men, in a sample of 10, would exhibit increased blood pressure if the overall fraction having this side effect is 0.02. Note, in Table 5.4, the probabilities for all values of $x > 3$ are 0.0000. So, to four decimal places, the probability of 4 men experiencing increased blood pressure is zero. The true probability is not zero but is very small. Then;

$$P(x \geq 3) = 0.0008 + 0.0000 + 0.0000 + \cdots + 0.0000 = 0.0008$$

There are about 8 chances in 10,000 that we would find 3 or more men with increased blood pressure if the probability of it happening for any one person is $p = 0.02$. If the test did show that 3 men had elevated blood pressure after taking the new drug, the true rate of high blood pressure likely exceeds 2%, and the company should have serious doubts about marketing the drug.

EXAMPLE 5-3 Using the Binomial Table

TRY PROBLEM 5.25

Nielsen TV Ratings The Nielsen Company is the best-known television ratings company. On Tuesday after the 2002 Masters Golf Tournament in Augusta, Georgia, which Tiger Woods won, the company announced that slightly more than 9% of all televisions were tuned to the final round on Sunday. Assuming that the 9% rating is correct, what is the probability that in a random sample of 20 television sets, 2 or fewer would have been tuned to the Masters? This question can be answered, assuming that the binomial distribution applies, using the following steps:

Step 1 **Define the characteristics of the binomial distribution.**
In this case, the characteristics are

$$n = 20, \qquad p = 0.09, \qquad q = 1 - p = 0.91$$

Step 2 **Go to the binomial table in Appendix B. Locate the appropriate column for p and the appropriate section in the table for the sample size, n.**
In this case, we locate the section of the table corresponding to sample size equal to $n = 20$ and go to the column headed $p = 0.09$. The probabilities from the binomial table are

x	P(x)
0	0.1516
1	0.3000
2	0.2818
3	0.1672
4	0.0703
5	0.0222
6	0.0055
7	0.0011
8	0.0002

Step 3 **Define the event of interest and obtain the probabilities from the binomial table.**
We are interested in the probability of 2 or fewer sets tuned to the Masters. This is

$$P(x \le 2) = P(x = 0) + P(x = 1) + P(x = 2)$$

From the binomial table we get

$$P(x \le 2) = 0.1516 + 0.3000 + 0.2818$$
$$= 0.7334$$

Thus, there is a 0.7334 chance that 2 or fewer sets in a random sample of 20 were tuned to the Masters.

EXAMPLE 5-4 Using the Binomial Distribution

TRY PROBLEM 5.26

Naumann Research Naumann Research is a full-service marketing research consulting firm. Recently it was retained to do a project for a major U.S. airline. The airline was considering changing from an assigned-seating reservation system to one in which fliers would be able to take any seat they wished on a first-come, first-served basis. The airline believes that 80% of its fliers would like this change if it was accompanied with a reduction in ticket prices. Naumann Research will survey a large number of customers on this issue, but prior to conducting the full research, it has selected a random sample of 20 customers and determined that 12 like the proposed change. What is the probability of finding 12 or fewer who like the change if the probability is 0.80 that a customer will like the change?

If we assume the binomial distribution applies, we can use the following steps to answer this question:

Step 1 **Define the characteristics of the binomial distribution.**
In this case, the characteristics are

$$n = 20, \quad p = 0.80, \quad q = 1 - p = 0.20$$

Step 2 **Go to the binomial table in Appendix B. Locate the appropriate column for p and the appropriate section in the table for the sample size, n.**
First, locate the section of the table corresponding to sample size equal to $n = 20$. Then, because $p > 0.50$, we find the desired column by looking to the p-values at the bottom of each column. Locate the column for $p = 0.80$.

Step 3 **Define the event of interest.**
We are interested in knowing

$$P(x \leq 12) = P(12) + P(11) + \cdots + P(0)$$

Step 4 **Locate the desired probabilities in the binomial table and sum them.**
Since $p > 0.50$, the values of x are in the far right column of the binomial table. Go to the row corresponding to $x = 12$ and the column for $p = 0.80$ in the section of the table for $n = 20$ to get

$$P(12) = 0.0222$$

Repeat this for the values of x from 12 down to 0:

$$P(x \leq 12) = 0.0222 + 0.0074 + 0.0020 + 0.0005 + 0.0001$$
$$+ 0.0000 + \cdots + 0.0000$$
$$= 0.0322$$

Thus, it is quite unlikely that if 80% of customers like the new seating plan that 12 or fewer in a sample of 20 would like it. The airline may want to rethink its plan.

Mean and Standard Deviation of the Binomial Distribution

In Section 5.1 we stated the mean of a discrete probability distribution is also referred to as the *expected value*. The expected value of a discrete random variable, x, is found using Equation 5.1.

$$\mu_x = E(x) = \Sigma \, xP(x)$$

Mean of a Binomial Distribution This equation can be used with any discrete probability distribution, including the binomial. However, if we are working with a binomial distribution, the expected value can be found more easily by using Equation 5.5.

Expected Value of a Binomial Distribution

$$\mu_x = E(x) = np \tag{5.5}$$

where:

$$n = \text{Sample size}$$
$$p = \text{Probability of a success}$$

Business Application

Excel and Minitab Tutorial

CATALOG SALES Catalog sales have been a part of the U.S. economy for many years, and companies such as Lands' End, L.L. Bean, and Eddie Bauer have enjoyed increased business. One feature that has made mail-order buying so popular is the ease with which customers can return merchandise. Nevertheless, one mail-order catalog has the goal of no more than 11% of all purchased items returned.

The binomial distribution can describe the number of items returned. For instance, in a given hour the company shipped 300 items. If the probability of an item being returned is $p = 0.11$, the expected number of items (mean) to be returned is

$$\mu_x = E(x) = np$$
$$\mu_x = E(x) = (300)(0.11) = 33$$

Thus, the average number of returned items for each 300 items shipped is 33.

Suppose the company sales manager wants to know if the return rate is stable at 11%. To test this, she monitors a random sample of 300 items and finds that 44 have been returned. This return rate exceeds the mean of 33 units, which concerns her. However, before reaching a conclusion, she will be interested in the probability of observing 44 or more returns in a sample of 300.

$$P(x \geq 44) = 1 - P(x \leq 43)$$

The binomial table in Appendix B does not contain sample sizes of 300. Instead, we can use Excel's **BINOMDIST** function or the binomial tool in Minitab's **Calc— Probability Distribution** menu to find the probability. The Excel and Minitab output in Figure 5.3a and Figure 5.3b show the cumulative probability of 43 or fewer is equal to

$$P(x \leq 43) = 0.97$$

Then the probability of 44 or more returns is

$$P(x \geq 44) = 1 - 0.97 = 0.03$$

There is only a 3% chance of 44 or more items being returned if the 11% return rate is still in effect. This low probability suggests that the return rate may have increased above 11% because we would not expect to see 44 returned items. The probability is very small.

FIGURE 5.3A

Excel 2007 Output for Mail-Order Sales Returns

Excel 2007 Instructions:
1. Open a blank worksheet.
2. Select **Formulas**.
3. Click on *fx* (**Function wizard**).
4. Select the **Statistical category**.
5. Select the **BINOMDIST** function.
6. Fill in the requested information in the template.
7. **True** indicates cumulative probabilities.

FIGURE 5.3B

Minitab Output for Mail-Order Sales Returns

Minitab Instructions:
1. Choose **Calc > Probability Distribution > Binomial**.
2. Choose **Cumulative probability**.
3. In **Number of trials** enter sample size.
4. In **Probability of success** enter p.
5. In **Input constant** enter the number of successes: x.
6. Click **OK**.

TRY PROBLEM 5.33

EXAMPLE 5-5 Finding the Mean of the Binomial Distribution

Naumann Research   In Example 5-4, Naumann Research had been hired to do a study for a major airline that is planning to change from a designated-seat assignment plan to an open-seating system. The company believes that 80% of its customers approve of the idea. Naumann Research interviewed a sample of $n = 20$ and found 12 who like the proposed change. If the airline is correct in its assessment of the probability, what is the expected number of people in a sample of $n = 20$ who will like the change? We can find this using the following steps:

> **Step 1**   **Define the characteristics of the binomial distribution.**
> In this case, the characteristics are
> $$n = 20, \qquad p = 0.80, \qquad q = 1 - p = 0.20$$
> **Step 2**   **Use Equation 5.5 to find the expected value.**
> $$\mu_x = E(x) = np$$
> $$E(x) = 20(0.80) = 16$$

The average number who would say they like the proposed change is 16 in a sample of 20.

Standard Deviation of a Binomial Distribution The standard deviation for any discrete probability distribution can be calculated using Equation 5.2. We show this again as

$$\sigma_x = \sqrt{\sum [x - E(x)]^2 P(x)}$$

If a discrete probability distribution meets the binomial distribution conditions, the standard deviation is more easily computed by Equation 5.6.

Standard Deviation of the Binomial Distribution

$$\sigma = \sqrt{npq} \tag{5.6}$$

where:

$$n = \text{Sample size}$$
$$p = \text{Probability of a success}$$
$$q = 1 - p = \text{Probability of a failure}$$

TRY PROBLEM 5.33

EXAMPLE 5-6 Finding the Standard Deviation of a Binomial Distribution

Naumann Research Refer to Examples 5-4 and 5-5, in which Naumann Research surveyed a sample of $n = 20$ airline customers about changing the way seats are assigned on flights. The airline believes that 80% of its customers approve of the proposed change. Example 5-5 showed that if the airline is correct in its assessment, the expected number in a sample of 20 who would like the change is 16. However, there are other possible outcomes if 20 customers are surveyed. What is the standard deviation of the random variable, x, in this case? We can find the standard deviation for the binomial distribution using the following steps:

Step 1 **Define the characteristics of the binomial distribution.**
In this case, the characteristics are

$$n = 20, \quad p = 0.80, \quad q = 1 - p = 0.20$$

Step 2 **Use Equation 5.6 to calculate the standard deviation.**

$$\sigma = \sqrt{npq} = \sqrt{20(0.80)(0.20)} = 1.7889$$

Additional Information about the Binomial Distribution

At this point, several comments about the binomial distribution are worth making. If p, the probability of a success, is 0.50, the binomial distribution is *symmetrical* and bell-shaped, regardless of the sample size. This is illustrated in Figure 5.4, which shows frequency histograms for samples of $n = 5$, $n = 10$, and $n = 50$. Notice that all three distributions are centered at the expected value, $E(x) = np$.

When the value of p differs from 0.50 in either direction, the binomial distribution is skewed. The skewness will be most pronounced when n is small and p approaches 0 or 1. However, the binomial distribution becomes more bell-shaped as n increases. The frequency histograms shown in Figure 5.5 bear this out.

FIGURE 5.4

The Binomial Distribution with Varying Sample Sizes ($p = 0.50$)

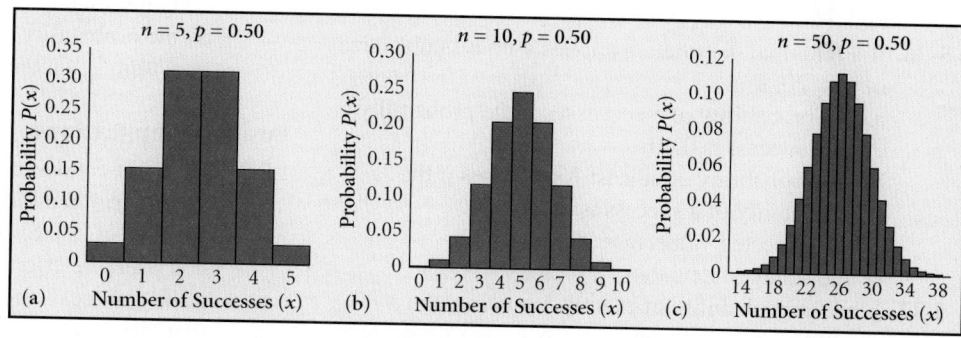

FIGURE 5.5

The Binomial Distribution with Varying Sample Sizes ($p = 0.05$)

5-2: Exercises

Skill Development

5-22. For a binomial distribution with a sample size equal to 10 and a probability of a success equal to 0.30, what is the probability that the sample will contain exactly three successes? Use the binomial formula to determine the probability.

5-23. A bank manager has recently examined the credit card account balances for the customers of her bank and found that 20% have an outstanding balance that is at the credit card limit. Suppose the manager randomly selects 15 customers and finds 4 that have balances at the limit. Assume that the properties of the binomial distribution apply.
  a. What is the probability of finding 4 customers in a sample of 15 who have "maxed out" their credit cards?
  b. What is the probability that 4 or fewer customers in the sample will have balances at the limit of the credit card?

5-24. Use the binomial formula to calculate the following probabilities for an experiment in which $n = 5$ and $p = 0.4$:
  a. the probability that x is at most 1
  b. the probability that x is at least 4
  c. the probability that x is less than 1

5-25. Studies indicate that 40% of all home buyers will do some remodeling to their home within the first five years of home ownership. If this is true, use the binomial distribution to determine the probability that in a random sample of 20 homeowners, two or fewer will remodel their homes. Use the binomial table.

5-26. If a binomial distribution applies with a sample size of $n = 20$, find
  a. the probability of 5 successes if the probability of a success is 0.40
  b. the probability of at least 7 successes if the probability of a success is 0.25
  c. the expected value, $n = 20$, $p = 0.20$
  d. the standard deviation, $n = 20$, $p = 0.20$

5-27. Find the probability of exactly 5 successes in a sample of $n = 10$ when the probability of a success is 0.70.

5-28. Assuming the binomial distribution applies with a sample size of $n = 15$, find
  a. the probability of 5 or more successes if the probability of a success is 0.30.
  b. the probability of fewer than 4 successes if the probability of a success is 0.75.
  c. the expected value of the random variable if the probability of success is 0.40.
  d. the standard deviation of the random variable if the probability of success is 0.40.

5-29. A random variable follows a binomial distribution with a probability of success equal to 0.45. For $n = 11$, find
  a. the probability of exactly 1 success.
  b. the probability of 4 or fewer successes.
  c. the probability of at least 8 successes.

5-30. Use the binomial distribution table to determine the following probabilities:
  a. $n = 6, p = 0.08$; find $P(x = 2)$.
  b. $n = 9, p = 0.80$; determine $P(x < 4)$.
  c. $n = 11, p = 0.65$; calculate $P(2 < x \leq 5)$.
  d. $n = 14, p = 0.95$; find $P(x \geq 13)$.
  e. $n = 20, p = 0.50$; compute $P(x > 3)$.

5-31. A random variable follows a binomial distribution with a probability of success equal to 0.65. For a sample size of $n = 7$, find
  a. the probability of exactly 3 successes.
  b. the probability of 4 or more successes.
  c. the probability of exactly 7 successes.
  d. the expected value of the random variable.

5-32. Use the binomial distribution in which $n = 6$ and $p = 0.3$ to calculate the following probabilities:
  a. x is at most 1.
  b. x is at least 2.
  c. x is more than 5.
  d. x is less than 6.

5-33. Given a binomial distribution with $n = 8$ and $p = 0.40$, obtain the following:
  a. the mean
  b. the standard deviation
  c. the probability that the number of successes is larger than the mean.
  d. the probability that the number of successes is within 2 standard deviations of the mean.

Business Applications

5-34. An audit conducted by the St. Aleanis Hospital has determined that 15% of all patient bills contain an error of one form or another. After spending considerable effort to improve the hospital's billing process, the administrators are convinced that things have improved. They believe that the new error rate is somewhere closer to 0.05.
  a. Suppose that recently the hospital randomly sampled 10 patient bills and conducted a thorough study to determine whether an error exists. It found 3 bills with errors. Assuming that managers are correct that they have improved the error rate to 0.05, what is the probability that they would find 3 or more errors in a sample of 10 bills?
  b. Referring to part a, what conclusion would you reach based on the probability of finding 3 or more errors in the sample of 10 bills?

5-35. The Committee for the Study of the American Electorate indicated that 60.7% of the voting-age voters cast ballots in the 2004 presidential election. It also indicated 30.8% of voting-age voters cast ballots for President Bush. A start-up company in San Jose, California, has 10 employees.

a. How many of the employees would you expect to have voted for President Bush?

b. All of the employees indicated that they voted in the 2004 presidential election. Determine the probability of this assuming they followed the national trend.

c. Eight of the employees voted for President Bush. Determine the probability that at least 8 of the employees would vote for President Bush if they followed the national trend.

d. Based upon your calculation in part c, do the employees reflect the national trend? Support your answer with statistical calculations and reasoning.

5-36. In his article entitled "Acceptance Sampling Solves Drilling Issues: A Case Study," published in *Woodworking Magazine* in 2002, author Ken Wong discusses a problem faced by furniture manufacturing companies dealing with the quality of the drilling of dowel holes. Wong states, "Incorrect sizing and distances with respect to dowel holes can cause many problems for the rest of the process especially when drilling is conducted early in the production process."

Consider the case of Dragon Wood Furniture in Bismarck, North Dakota, which believes that when the drilling process is operating at an acceptable rate, the upper limit on the percentage of incorrectly drilled dowel holes is 4%. To monitor its drilling process, Dragon Wood Furniture randomly samples 20 products each hour and determines if the dowel hole in each product is correctly drilled or not. If, in the sample of 20 holes, 1 or more incorrectly drilled holes is discovered, the production process is stopped and the drilling process is recalibrated.

a. If the process is really operating correctly ($p = 0.04$), what is the probability that the sampling effort will produce $x = 0$ defective holes and thus the process will properly be left to continue running?

b. Suppose the true defect rate has risen to 0.10, what is the probability the sample will produce results that properly tell the managers to halt production to recalibrate the drilling machine?

c. Prepare a short letter to the manufacturing manager at Dragon Wood Furniture discussing the effectiveness of the sampling process that her company is using. Base your response on the results to parts a and b.

5-37. McNeal Advertising in Chicago recently developed an advertising campaign for a major retail chain. McNeal executives believe that for an ad campaign to be successful, at least 80% of those seeing a television commercial must be able to recall the name of the company featured in the commercial one hour after viewing the commercial. Before distributing the ad campaign nationally, the company plans to show the commercial to a random sample of 20 people. It will also show the same people two additional commercials for different products or businesses.

a. Assuming that the advertisement will be successful (80% will be able to recall the name of the company in the ad), what is the expected number of people in the sample who will recall the company featured in the McNeal commercial one hour after viewing the three commercials?

b. Suppose that in the sample of 20 people, 11 were able to recall the name of the company in the McNeal commercial one hour after viewing. Based on the premise that the advertising campaign will be successful, what is the probability of 11 or fewer people being able to recall the company name?

c. Based on your responses to parts a and b, what conclusion might McNeal executives make about this particular advertising campaign?

5-38. Gateway 2000 Inc. receives large shipments of microprocessors from Intel Corp. It must try to ensure the proportion of microprocessors that are defective is small. Suppose Gateway decides to test 5 microprocessors out of a shipment of thousands of these microprocessors. Suppose that if at least 1 of the microprocessors is defective, the shipment is returned.

a. If Intel Corp.'s shipment contains 10% defective microprocessors, calculate the probability the entire shipment will be returned.

b. If Intel and Gateway agree that Intel will not provide more than 5% defective chips, calculate the probability that the entire shipment will be returned even though only 5% are defective.

c. Calculate the probability that the entire shipment will be kept by Gateway even though the shipment has 10% defective microprocessors.

5-39. A survey by KRC Research for *U.S. News* reported that 37% of people plan to spend more on eating out after they retire. If 8 people are randomly selected, then determine the

a. expected number of people who plan to spend more on eating out after they retire.

b. standard deviation of the individuals who plan to spend more on eating out after they retire.

c. probability that 2 or fewer in the sample indicate that they actually plan to spend more on eating out after retirement.

5-40. The Nielsen Company is the major media ratings company and conducts surveys on a weekly basis to determine what percentage of households are tuned to particular television programs. The following table shows the ratings data for network television programs for the week of September 7 to September 13, 2005:

Rank*	Program	Network	Household Rating**	Total Viewers***
1	*CSI*	CBS	18.2	29,546,000
2	*Desperate Housewives*	ABC	15.8	25,934,000
3	*NFL Monday Night Football*	ABC	14.3	21,860,000
4	*Without A Trace*	CBS	13.8	20,784,000
5	*Grey's Anatomy*	ABC	12.5	19,737,000
6	*CSI: Miami*	CBS	12.3	18,393,000
7	*CSI: NY*	CBS	12.3	19,225,000
8	*Lost*	ABC	12.0	20,012,000
9	*Cold Case*	CBS	11.1	17,424,000
10	*NCIS*	CBS	11.0	17,792,000
11	*Survivor: Guatemala*	CBS	11.0	18,981,000

*Rank is based on U.S. Household Rating % from Nielsen Media Research's National People Meter Sample.

**A household Rating is the estimate of the size of a television audience relative to the total universe, expressed as a percentage. As of September 26, 2005, there are an estimated 110.2 million television households in the U.S. A single national household ratings point represents 1%, or 1,102,000 households.

***Total viewers includes all persons over the age of two.

Source: www.nielsenmedia.com/ratings/ broadcast_programs.html

a. Suppose that immediately after the time slot that *Survivor* was playing during this week the producers of the show commissioned a study which called for the consultants to randomly call 25 people and interview those who said that they had just watched *Survivor*. Suppose the consultant submits a report saying that it had found no one in the sample of 25 homes who claimed to have watched the program and therefore did not do any surveys. What is the probability of this happening, assuming that the Nielsen ratings for the show are accurate?

b. Suppose the producers for *Desperate Housewives* planned to survey 1,000 people on the day following the broadcast of the program. The purpose of the survey was to determine what the reaction would be if one of the leading characters was murdered on the show. Based on the Nielsen ratings, what would be the expected number of people who would end up being included in the analysis, assuming that all 1,000 people could be reached?

5-41. A manufacturing firm produces a product that has a ceramic coating. The coating is baked onto the product and the baking process is known to produce 15% defective items (for example, cracked or chipped finishes). Every hour, 20 products from the thousands that are baked hourly are sampled from the ceramic-coating process and inspected.

a. What is the probability that 5 defective items will be found in the next sample of 20?

b. On average, how many defective items would be expected to occur in each sample of 20?

c. How likely is it that 15 or more nondefective (good) items would occur in a sample due to chance alone?

5-42. The Employee Benefit Research Institute reports that in 2005 69% of workers reported that they and/or their spouse had saved some money for retirement. (*Source*: Employee Benefit Research Institute and Matthew Greenwald and Associates, Inc. 1994–2005 Retirement Confidence Surveys.)

a. If a random sample of 30 workers is taken, what is the probability that fewer than 17 workers and/or their spouses have saved some money for retirement?

b. If a random sample of 50 workers is taken, what is the probability that more than 40 workers and/or their spouses have saved some money for retirement?

5-43. A small hotel in a popular resort area has 20 rooms. The hotel manager estimates that 15% of all confirmed reservations are "no-shows." Consequently, the hotel accepts confirmed reservations for as many as 25 rooms. If more confirmed reservations arrive than there are rooms, the overbooked guests are sent to another hotel and given a complementary dinner. If the hotel currently has 25 confirmed reservations, find:

a. the probability that no customers will be sent to another hotel.

b. the probability that exactly 2 guests will be sent to another hotel.

c. the probability that 3 or more guests will be sent to another hotel.

5-44. Radio frequency identification (RFID) is an electronic scanning technology that can be used to identify items in a number of ways. One advantage of RFID is that it can eliminate the need to manually count inventory, which can help to improve inventory management. The technology is not infallible, however, and sometimes errors occur when items are scanned. If the probability that a scanning error occurs is 0.0065, find:

a. the probability that exactly 20 items will be scanned incorrectly from the next 5,000 items scanned.

b. the probability that more than 20 items will be scanned incorrectly from the next 5,000 items scanned.

c. the probability that the number of items scanned incorrectly is between 10 and 25 from the next 5,000 items scanned.

d. What is the expected number of items scanned incorrectly from the next 5,000 items scanned?

5-45. Peter S. Kastner, director of the consulting firm Vericours Inc. reported (Brian Grow, *Business Week*, "The Great Rebate Runaround," December 5, 2005) that fully 40% of all rebates are not redeemed because consumers either fail to apply for them or their applications are rejected. TCA Fulfillment Services published its redemption rates: 50% for a $30 rebate for a $100 product, 10% for a $10 rebate on a $100 product, and 35% for a $50 rebate on a $200 product.

a. Calculate the weighted average proportion of redemption rates for TCA Fulfillment using the size of the rebate to establish the weights. Does it appear that TCA Fulfillment has a lower rebate rate than that indicated by Vericours? Explain.

b. To more accurately answer the question posed in part a, a random sample of 20 individuals who purchased an item accompanied by a rebate could be asked if they submitted their rebate. Suppose 4 of the questioned individuals said they did redeem their rebate. If Vericours' estimate of the redemption rate is correct, determine the expected number of rebates that would be redeemed. Does it appear that Vericours' estimate may too high?

c. Determine the likelihood that such an extreme sample result indicated in part b or something more extreme would occur if the weighted average proportion provides the actual rebate rate.

d. Repeat the calculations of part c assuming that Vericours' estimate of the redemption rate is correct.

e. Are you convinced that the redemption rate is smaller than indicated by Vericours? Explain.

5-46. *Business Week* reported (Amy Borrus, "Investors May Not Want This Hot Line," December 5, 2005) that business executives want to break down the obstacles that keep them from communicating directly with stock owners. Ms. Borrus reports that 80% of shareholders hold stock in "street names," which are registered with their bank or brokerage. If the brokerage doesn't furnish these names to the corporations, they cannot communicate with their shareholders. To determine if the percent reported by Ms. Borrus is correct, a sample of 20 shareholders was asked if they held their stock in "street names." Seventeen responded that they did.

a. Suppose the true proportion of shareholders that hold stock under street names is 0.80, calculate the probability that 17 or more of the sampled individuals hold their stock under street names.

b. Repeat the calculation in part a using proportions of 0.70 and 0.90.

c. Based upon your calculations in parts a and b, which proportion do you think is most likely true? Support your answer.

Computer Database Exercises

5-47. Tony Hsieh is CEO of e-tailer Zappos.com. His company sells shoes online. It differentiates itself by its selection of shoes and a devotion to customer service. It offers free shipping and free return shipping. An area where costs could be cut back is the shipping charges for return shipping, specifically those that result from the wrong size of shoes being sent. Zappos may try to keep the percentage of returns due to incorrect size to no more than 5%. The file entitled **Shoesize** contains a sample of 125 shoe sizes that were sent to customers and the sizes that were actually ordered.

a. Determine the number of pairs of wrong-size shoes that were delivered to customers.

b. Calculate the probability of obtaining at least that many pairs of wrong-sized shoes delivered to customers if the proportion of incorrect sizes is actually 0.05.

c. On the basis of your calculation, determine whether Zappos has kept the percentage of returns due to incorrect size to no more than 5%. Support your answer with statistical reasoning.

d. If Zappos sells 5 million pairs of shoes in one year and it costs an average of $4.75 a pair to return them, calculate the expected cost associated with wrong-sized shoes being returned using the probability calculated from the sample data.

5-48. International Data Corp. (IDC) has shown that the average return on business analytics projects was almost four-and-a-half times the initial investment. Analytics consists of tools and applications that present better metrics to the user and to the probable future outcome of an event. IDC looked at how long it takes a typical company to recoup its investment in analytics. It determined that 29% of the U.S. corporations that adopted analytics took six months or less to recoup their investment. The file entitled **Analytics** contains a sample of the time it might have taken 35 corporations to recoup their investment in analytics.

a. Determine the number of corporations that recovered their investment in analytics in six months or less.

b. Calculate the probability of obtaining at most the number of corporations that you determined in part a if the percent of those recovering their investment is as indicated by IDC.

c. Determine the 70th percentile of the number of the 35 corporations that recovered their investment in analytics in six months or less. (*Hint*: Recall and use the definition of percentiles from Section 3.1.)

5-49. *USA Today* has reported (Ginny Graves, "As women rise in society, many married couples still don't do 'equal,'" June 30, 2005) on the gender gap that exists between married spouses. One of the measures of the progress that has been made in that area is the number of women who outearn their husbands. According to the 2003 census conducted by the Bureau of Labor Statistics, 32.5% of female spouses outearn their male counterparts. The file entitled **Gendergap** contains the income of 150 married couples in Utah.

a. Determine the number of families in which the female outearns her husband.

b. Calculate the expected number of females who outearn their male counterparts in the sample of 150 married couples based on the B.L.S. study.

c. If the percentage of married females in Utah who outearn their male counterparts is the same as indicated by the Bureau of Labor Statistics, determine the probability that at least the number found in part a would occur.

d. Based on your calculation in part c, does the Bureau of Labor Statistics' percentage seem plausible is Utah different than the rest of the United States?

5.3 Other Discrete Probability Distributions

The binomial distribution is very useful in many business situations, as indicated by the examples and applications presented in the previous section. However, as we pointed out, there are several requirements that must hold before we can use the binomial distribution to determine probabilities. If those conditions are not satisfied, there may be other theoretical probability distributions that could be employed. In this section we introduce two other very useful discrete probability distributions: the Poisson distribution and the hypergeometric distribution.

The Poisson Distribution

CHAPTER OUTCOME #3

To use the binomial distribution, we must be able to count the number of successes and the number of failures. Although in many situations you may be able to count the number of successes, you often cannot count the number of failures. For example, suppose a company builds freeways in Vermont. The company could count the number of chuckholes that develop per mile (here a chuckhole is referred to as a success because it is what we are looking for), but how could it count the number of nonchuckholes? Or what about a hospital supplying emergency medical services in Los Angeles? It could easily count the number of emergencies its units respond to in one hour, but how could it determine how many calls it did not receive? Obviously, in these cases the number of possible outcomes (successes + failures) is difficult, if not impossible, to determine. If the total number of possible outcomes cannot be determined, the binomial distribution cannot be applied. In these cases you may be able to use the Poisson distribution.

Characteristics of the Poisson Distribution The Poisson distribution[1] describes a process that extends over time, space, on any well-defined unit of inspection. The outcomes of interest, such as emergency calls or chuckholes, occur at random, and we count the number of outcomes that occur in a given segment of time or space. We might count the number of emergency calls in a 1-hour period or the number of chuckholes in a two-mile stretch of freeway. As we did with the binomial distribution, we will call these outcomes *successes* even though (like chuckholes) they might be undesirable.

The possible counts are the integers 0, 1, 2, . . . , and we would like to know the probability of each of these values. For example, what is the chance of getting exactly 4 emergency calls in a particular hour? What is the chance that a chosen two-mile stretch of freeway will contain 0 chuckholes?

We can use the Poisson probability distribution to answer these questions if we make the following assumptions:

1. We know λ, the average number of successes in one segment. For example, we know that there is an average of 8 emergency calls per hour ($\lambda = 8$) or an average of 15 chuckholes per mile of freeway ($\lambda = 15$).
2. The probability of x successes in a segment is the same for all segments of the same size. For example, the probability distribution of emergency calls is the same for any one-hour period of time at the hospital.
3. What happens in one segment has no influence on any nonoverlapping segment. For example, the number of calls arriving between 9:30 P.M. and 10:30 P.M. has no influence on the number of calls between 11:00 P.M. and 12:00 midnight.
4. We imagine dividing time or space into tiny subsegments. Then the chance of *more* than one success in a subsegment is negligible and the chance of exactly one success in a tiny subsegment of length t is λt. For example, the chance of 2 emergency calls in the same second is essentially 0, and if $\lambda = 8$ calls per hour, the chance of a call in any given second is $(8)(1/3,600) \approx 0.0022$.

Once λ has been determined, we can calculate the average occurrence rate for any number of segments (t). This is λt. Note that λ and t must be in compatible units. If we have $\lambda = 20$ arrivals per hour, the segments must be in hours or fractional parts of an hour. That is, if we have $\lambda = 20$ per hour and we wish to work with half-hour time periods, the segment would be

$$t = \frac{1}{2}\,\text{hour}$$

not $t = 30$ minutes.

Although the Poisson distribution is often used to describe situations such as the number of customers who arrive at a hospital emergency room per hour or the number of calls the Hewlett-Packard LaserJet printer service center receives in a 30-minute period, the segments need not be time intervals. Poisson distributions are also used to describe such random variables as the number of knots in a sheet of plywood or the number of contaminants in a gallon of lake water. The segments would be the sheet of plywood and the gallon of water.

Another important point is that λt, the average number in t segments is not necessarily the number we will see if we observe the process for one segment. We might expect an average of 20 people to arrive at a checkout stand in any given hour, but we do not expect to find exactly that number arriving every hour. The actual arrivals will form a distribution with an expected value, or mean, equal to λt. So, for the Poisson distribution,

$$E[x] = \mu_x = \lambda t$$

---

[1] The Poisson distribution can be derived as the limiting distribution of the binomial distribution as the number of trials, n, tends to infinity. It serves as a good approximation to the binomial when n is large.

Once λ and t have been specified, the probability for any discrete value in the Poisson distribution can be found using Equation 5.7.

Poisson Probability Distribution

$$P(x) = \frac{(\lambda t)^x \, e^{-\lambda t}}{x!}$$

(5.7)

where:

t = Number of segments of interest
x = Number of successes in t segments
λ = Expected number of successes in one segment
e = Base of the natural logarithm system (2.71828 . . .)

Business Application

FIRST CITY BANK A study conducted at First City Bank shows that the average number of arrivals to the teller section of the bank per hour is 16. Further, the distribution for the number of arrivals is considered to be Poisson distributed. Figure 5.6 shows the shape of the Poisson distribution for $\lambda = 16$. The probability of each possible number of customers arriving can be computed using Equation 5.7. For example, we can find the probability of $x = 12$ customers in one hour ($t = 1$) as follows:

$$P(x = 12) = \frac{(\lambda t)^x \, e^{-\lambda t}}{x!} = \frac{16^{12} e^{-16}}{12!} = 0.0661$$

Poisson Probability Distribution Table As was the case with the binomial distribution, a table of probabilities exists for the Poisson distribution. (The full Poisson table appears in Appendix C.) The Poisson table shows the probabilities for different λt values. We can use the following business application to illustrate how to use the Poisson table.

Business Application

FIRST CITY BANK At First City Bank, customers are thought to arrive at the teller section according to a Poisson distribution with $\lambda = 16$ customers per hour. (See Figure 5.6.) Based on previous studies, the bank manager believes that the service time for each customer is quite constant at 15 minutes. Suppose, during each 15-minute time period, the bank has three tellers available. This means that three customers can be served during each 15-minute

---

FIGURE 5.6

Poisson Distribution for Bank Customer Arrivals with $\lambda = 16$

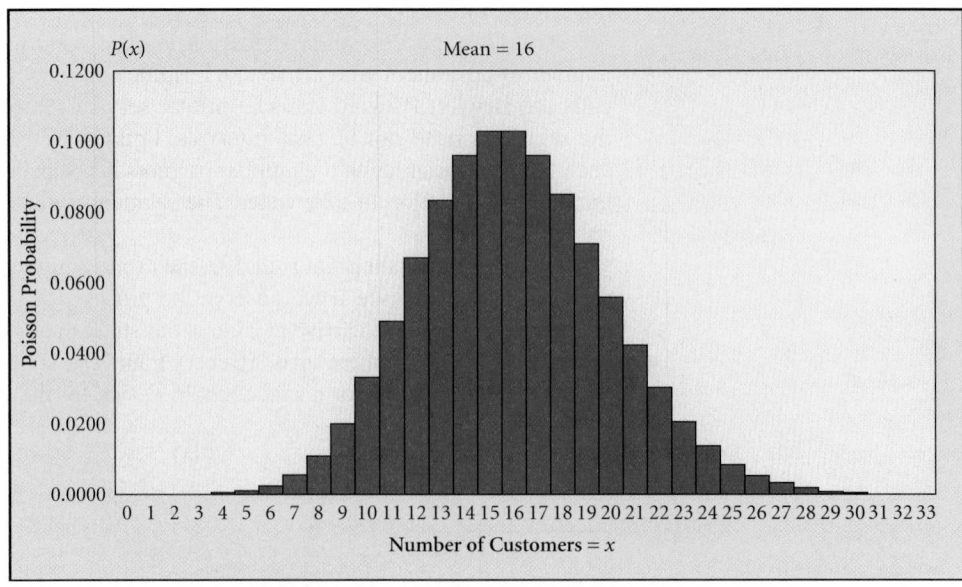

segment. The manager is interested in the probability that one or more customers will have to wait for service during the first 15 minutes the bank is open each morning.

To determine the probability the manager is interested in, you will need to convert the mean arrivals from $\lambda = 16$ customers per hour to a new average for a 15-minute segment. Fifteen minutes corresponds to 0.25 hours, so you will change the segment size, t, from $t = 1$ to $t = 0.25$. Then the mean number of arrivals in 15 minutes is $\lambda t = 16(0.25) = 4$ customers.

Now, because there are three tellers, any time four or more customers arrive in the first 15-minute period of the day, at least one customer will have to wait for service. Thus,

$$P(1 \text{ or more customers wait}) = P(4) + P(5) + P(6) + \cdots$$

or you can use the *Complement Rule*, discussed in Chapter 4, as follows:

$$P(1 \text{ or more customers wait}) = 1 - P(x \le 3)$$

The Poisson table in Appendix C can be used to find the necessary probabilities. A portion of the Poisson table is shown in Table 5.5. To use the table, first go across the top of the table until you find the desired value of λt. In this case, look for $\lambda t = 4.0$. Next, go down the left-hand side to find the value of x corresponding to the number of occurrences of interest. For example, consider $x = 3$ customer arrivals. The probability of $x = 3$ is given as 0.1954. Thus,

$$P(3) = 0.1954$$

Then to find $P(x \le 3)$, we get the following probabilities from the Poisson table:

$$P(x \le 3) = P(0) + P(1) + P(2) + P(3)$$
$$P(x \le 3) = 0.0183 + 0.0733 + 0.1465 + 0.1954$$
$$P(x \le 3) = 0.4335$$

Then the probability of one or more customers having to wait is

$$P(1 \text{ or more customers wait}) = 1 - P(x \le 3)$$
$$P(1 \text{ or more customers wait}) = 1 - 0.4335 = 0.5665$$

TABLE 5.5 Poisson Distribution Table

x	3.10	3.20	3.30	3.40	3.50	3.60	3.70	3.80	3.90	4.00
0	0.0450	0.0408	0.0369	0.0334	0.0302	0.0273	0.0247	0.0224	0.0202	0.0183
1	0.1397	0.1304	0.1217	0.1135	0.1057	0.0984	0.0915	0.0850	0.0789	0.0733
2	0.2165	0.2087	0.2008	0.1929	0.1850	0.1771	0.1692	0.1615	0.1539	0.1465
3	0.2237	0.2226	0.2209	0.2186	0.2158	0.2125	0.2087	0.2046	0.2001	0.1954
4	0.1733	0.1781	0.1823	0.1858	0.1888	0.1912	0.1931	0.1944	0.1951	0.1954
5	0.1075	0.1140	0.1203	0.1264	0.1322	0.1377	0.1429	0.1477	0.1522	0.1563
6	0.0555	0.0608	0.0662	0.0716	0.0771	0.0826	0.0881	0.0936	0.0989	0.1042
7	0.0246	0.0278	0.0312	0.0348	0.0385	0.0425	0.0466	0.0508	0.0551	0.0595
8	0.0095	0.0111	0.0129	0.0148	0.0169	0.0191	0.0215	0.0241	0.0269	0.0298
9	0.0033	0.0040	0.0047	0.0056	0.0066	0.0076	0.0089	0.0102	0.0116	0.0132
10	0.0010	0.0013	0.0016	0.0019	0.0023	0.0028	0.0033	0.0039	0.0045	0.0053
11	0.0003	0.0004	0.0005	0.0006	0.0007	0.0009	0.0011	0.0013	0.0016	0.0019
12	0.0001	0.0001	0.0001	0.0002	0.0002	0.0003	0.0003	0.0004	0.0005	0.0006
13	0.0000	0.0000	0.0000	0.0000	0.0001	0.0001	0.0001	0.0001	0.0002	0.0002
14	0.0000	0.0000	0.0000	0.0000	0.0000	0.0000	0.0000	0.0000	0.0000	0.0001

The probability of one or more customers having to wait in the first 15-minute period of the day is 0.5665.

Suppose that when the bank manager sees this probability, she is very concerned. She states that she wants enough tellers ready so that the chance of waiting does not exceed 0.10. To determine the appropriate number of tellers, you can use the Poisson table to find the following:

$$P(1 \text{ or more customers wait}) = 1 - P(x \leq ?) \leq 0.10$$

In other words, a customer will have to wait if more customers arrive than there are servers. As long as the number of arrivals, x, is less than or equal to the number of servers, no one will wait. Then what value of x will provide the following?

$$1 - P(x \leq ?) \leq 0.10$$

Therefore, you want

$$P(x \leq ?) \geq 0.90$$

You can go to the table for $\lambda t = 4.0$ and scan down the column summing probabilities starting with $P(x = 0) = 0.0183$ until the sum is 0.90 or higher. When you reach $x = 7$, the sum of the probabilities $P(x \leq 7) \geq 0.9489$. Then,

$$P(1 \text{ or more customers wait}) = 1 - P(x \leq 7) = 0.0511$$

Because 0.0511 is less than or equal to the 0.10 limit imposed by the manager, she would have to schedule seven tellers.

SUMMARY   Using the Poisson Distribution

The following steps are used to find probabilities using the Poisson Distribution:

1. Define the segment units.
The segment units are usually blocks of time, areas of space, or volume.

2. Determine the mean of the random variable.
The mean is the parameter that defines the Poisson distribution and is referred to as λ. It is the average number of successes in a segment of unit size.

3. Determine t, the number of the segments to be considered, and then calculate λt.

4. Define the event of interest and use the Poisson formula or the Poisson table to find the probability.

TRY PROBLEM 5.51

EXAMPLE 5-7   Using the Poisson Distribution

Grogan Fabrics   Grogan Fabrics, headquartered in Auckland, New Zealand, makes wool fabrics for export to many other countries around the world. Before shipping, fabric quality tests are performed. The industry standards call for the average number of defects per fabric bolt to not exceed 5. During a recent test, the inspector selected a 30-yard bolt at random and carefully examined the first 3 yards, finding 3 defects. To determine the probability of this event occurring if the fabric meets the industry standards, assuming that the Poisson distribution applies, the company can perform the following steps:

Step 1   Define the segment unit.
Because the mean was stated as 5 defects per fabric bolt, the segment unit in this case is one 30-yard fabric bolt.

Step 2   Determine the mean of the random variable.
In this case if the company meets the industry standards, the mean will be

$$\lambda = 5$$

Step 3 Determine the segment size t.

The company quality inspectors analyzed 3 yards from a 30-yard bolt, which is equal to 0.1 units. So $t = 0.1$. Then,

$$\lambda t = 5(0.1) = 0.50$$

When looking at 3 yards, the company would expect to find .5 defects if the industry standards are being met.

Step 4 Define the event of interest and use the Poisson formula or the Poisson tables to find the probability.

In this case, 3 defects were observed. Because 3 exceeds the expected number ($\lambda t = .5$) the company would want to find

$$P(x \geq 3) = P(x = 3) + P(x = 4) + \cdots$$

The Poisson table in Appendix C is used to determine these probabilities. Locate the desired probability under the column headed $\lambda t = 0.50$. Then find the values of x down the left-hand column.

$$P(x \geq 3) = 0.0126 + 0.0016 + 0.0002$$
$$= 0.0144$$

This low probability may cause the company some concern about whether it is actually meeting the quality standards.

The Mean and Standard Deviation of the Poisson Distribution The mean of the Poisson distribution is λt. This is the value we use to specify which Poisson distribution we are using. We must know the mean before we can find probabilities for a Poisson distribution.

Figure 5.6 illustrated that the outcome of a Poisson distributed variable is subject to variation. Like any other discrete probability distribution, the standard deviation for the Poisson can be computed using Equation 5.2:

$$\sigma_x = \sqrt{\sum [x - E(x)]^2 P(x)}$$

However, for a Poisson distribution, the standard deviation also can be found using Equation 5.8.

Standard Deviation of the Poisson Distribution

$$\sigma = \sqrt{\lambda t} \tag{5.8}$$

The standard deviation of the Poisson distribution is simply the square root of the mean. Therefore, if you are working with a Poisson process, reducing the mean can reduce the variability also.

Business Application

Excel and Minitab Tutorial

HERITAGE TILE To illustrate the importance of the relationship between the mean and standard deviation of the Poisson distribution, consider Heritage Tile in New York City. The company makes ceramic tile for kitchens and bathrooms. The quality standards call for the number of imperfections in a tile to average 3 or fewer. The distribution of imperfections is thought to be Poisson. Both Minitab and Excel generate Poisson probabilities in much the same way as for the binomial distribution, which was discussed earlier in Section 5.2. If we assume that the company is meeting the standard, Figure 5.7a and Figure 5.7b show the Poisson probability distribution generated using Excel and Minitab when $\lambda t = 3.0$. Even though the average number of defects is 3, the manager is concerned about the high

FIGURE 5.7A

Excel 2007 Output for Heritage Tile Example

Excel 2007 Instructions:
1. Open a blank worksheet.
2. Enter values for *x* ranging from 0 to 10.
3. Place the cursor in the first blank cell in the next column.
4. Click on *fx* (**Function wizard**) and then select the **Statistical** category.
5. Select the **Poisson** function.
6. Reference the cell with the desired *x*-value and enter the mean. Enter **False** to choose noncumulative probabilities.
7. Copy function down for all values of *x*.
8. Graph using **Insert > Column** and label axes and title appropriately.

FIGURE 5.7B

Minitab Output for Heritage Tile Example

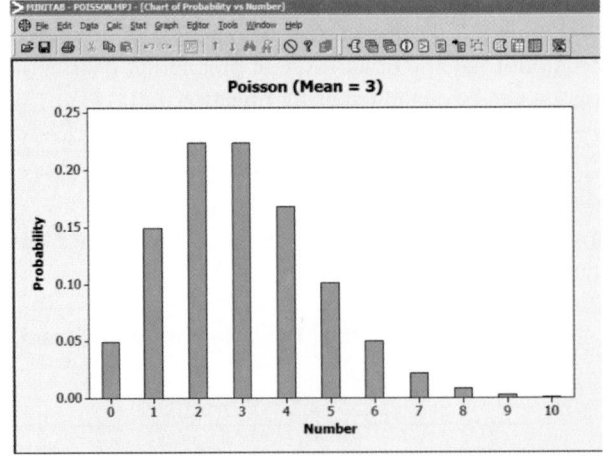

Minitab Instructions:
1. Create column *Number* with integers from 0 to 10.
2. Choose **Calc > Probability Distributions > Poisson**.
3. Select **Probability**.
4. In **Mean**, enter 3.
5. Select **Input column**.
6. In **Input column**, enter the column of integers.
7. In **Optional storage**, enter column *Probability*.
8. Click **OK**.
9. Choose **Graph > Bar Chart**.
10. In **Bars represent**, select **Values from a Table**, select **Simple**.
11. Click **OK**.
12. In **Graph variables**, Insert *Probability*.
13. In **Categorical variable**, insert *Number*.
14. Click **OK**.

probabilities associated with the number of imperfections equal to 4, 5, 6, or more on a tile. The variability is too great. Using Equation 5.5, the standard deviation for this distribution is

$$\sigma = \sqrt{3.0} = 1.732$$

This large standard deviation means that although some tiles will have few if any imperfections, others will have several, causing problems for installers and unhappy customers.

A quality improvement effort directed at reducing the average number of imperfections to 2.0 would also reduce the standard deviation to

$$\sigma = \sqrt{2.0} = 1.414$$

Further reductions in the average would also reduce variation in the number of imperfections between tiles. This would mean more consistency for installers and higher customer satisfaction.

The Hypergeometric Distribution

Although the binomial and Poisson distributions are very useful in many business decision-making situations, they both require that the trials be independent. For instance, in binomial applications the probability of a success on one trial must be the same as the probability of a success on any other trial. Although there are certainly times when this assumption can be satisfied, or at least approximated, in instances in which the population is fairly small and we are sampling without replacement, the condition of independence will not hold. In these cases, a discrete probability distribution referred to as the *hypergeometric distribution* can be useful.

Business Application

LINDELL CORPORATION The Lindell Corporation manufactures high-speed printers for computer systems. Lindell printers are compatible with most of the major computer vendors' hardware. Because of the intense competition in the marketplace for printers and other peripherals, Lindell has made every attempt to make a high-quality printer. However, a recent production run of 20 printers contained 2 printers that tested out as defective. The problem was traced to a shipment of defective cables that Lindell received shortly before the production run started.

The production manager ordered that the entire batch of 20 printers be isolated from other production output until further testing could be completed. Unfortunately, a new shipping clerk packaged 10 of these isolated printers and shipped them to the California State Purchasing Department to fill an order that was already overdue. By the time the production manager noticed what had happened, the printers were already in transit.

The immediate concern was whether one or more of the defectives had been included in the shipment. The new shipping clerk thought there was a good chance that no defectives were included. Short of reinspecting the remaining printers, how might the Lindell Corporation determine the probability that no defectives were actually shipped?

At first glance, it might seem that the question could be answered by employing the binomial distribution with $n = 10$, $p = 2/20 = 0.10$, and $x = 0$. Using the binomial distribution table in Appendix B, we get

$$P(x = 0) = 0.3487$$

There is a 0.3487 chance that no defectives were shipped, assuming the selection process satisfied the requirements of a binomial distribution. However, for the binomial distribution to be applicable, the trials must be independent, and the probability of a success, p, must remain constant from trial to trial. In order for this to occur when the sampling is from a "small," *finite* population, the sampling must be performed with *replacement*. This means that after each item is selected, it is returned to the population and, therefore, may be selected again later in the sampling.

In the Lindell example, the sampling was performed without replacement because each printer could only be shipped one time. Also, the population of printers is finite with size $N = 20$, which is a "small" population. Thus, p, the probability of a defective printer, does not remain equal to 0.10 on each trial. The value of p on any particular trial depends on what has already been selected on previous trials.

The event of interest is

$$G\ G\ G\ G\ G\ G\ G\ G\ G\ G$$

The probability that the first printer selected for shipment would be good would be 18/20, because there were 18 good printers in the batch of 20. Now, assuming the first printer selected was good, the probability the second printer was good is 17/19, because we then had only 19 printers to select from and 17 of those would be good. The probability that all 10 printers selected were good is

$$\frac{18}{20} \times \frac{17}{19} \times \frac{16}{18} \times \frac{15}{17} \times \frac{14}{16} \times \frac{13}{15} \times \frac{12}{14} \times \frac{11}{13} \times \frac{10}{12} \times \frac{9}{11} = 0.2368$$

This value is not the same as the 0.3847 probability we got when the binomial distribution was used. This demonstrates that when sampling is performed without replacement from finite populations, the binomial distribution produces inaccurate probabilities unless the sample is small relative to the size of the population. Under that circumstance, the value of p will not change very much as the sample is selected, and the binomial distribution will be a reasonable approximation to the actual probability distribution.

In those cases in which the sample is large relative to the size of the population, a discrete probability distribution, called the **hypergeometric distribution** is the correct distribution for computing probabilities for the random variable of interest.

$$C_x^n = \frac{n!}{x!(n-x)!}$$

Hypergeometric Distribution

The hypergeometric distribution is formed by the ratio of the number of ways an event of interest can occur over the total number of ways any event can occur.

We then use Equation 5.3 for counting combinations (see Section 5.2) to form the equation for computing probabilities for the hypergeometric distribution. When each trial has two possible outcomes (success and failure), hypergeometric probabilities are computed using Equation 5.9.

Hypergeometric Distribution (Two Possible Outcomes per Trial)

$$P(x) = \frac{C_{n-x}^{N-X} \cdot C_x^X}{C_n^N} \tag{5.9}$$

where:

N = Population size
X = Number of successes in the population
n = Sample size
x = Number of successes in the sample
$n - x$ = Number of failures in the sample

Notice that the numerator of Equation 5.9 is the product of the number of ways you can select x successes in a random sample out of the X successes in the population and the number of ways you can select $n - x$ failures in a sample from the $N - X$ failures in the population. The denominator in the equation is the number of ways the sample can be selected from the population.

In the Lindell example, the probability of zero defectives being shipped ($x = 0$) is

$$P(x = 0) = \frac{C_{10-0}^{20-2} \cdot C_0^2}{C_{10}^{20}}$$

$$P(x = 0) = \frac{C_{10}^{18} \cdot C_0^2}{C_{10}^{20}}$$

Carrying out the arithmetic, we get

$$P(x=0) = \frac{(43,758)(1)}{184,756} = 0.2368$$

As we found before, the probability that zero defectives were included in the shipment is 0.2368, or approximately 24%.

The probabilities of $x = 1$ and $x = 2$ defectives can also be found by using Equation 5.9, as follows:

$$P(x=1) = \frac{C_{10-1}^{20-2} \cdot C_1^2}{C_{10}^{20}} = 0.5264$$

and

$$P(x=2) = \frac{C_{10-2}^{20-2} \cdot C_2^2}{C_{10}^{20}} = 0.2368$$

Thus, the hypergeometric probability distribution for the number of defective printers in a random selection of 10 is

x	$P(x)$
0	0.2368
1	0.5264
2	0.2368
	$\Sigma = 1.0000$

Recall that when we introduced the hypergeometric distribution, we said that it is used in situations when we are sampling without replacement from a finite population. However, when the population size is large relative to the sample size, decision makers typically use the binomial distribution as an approximation of the hypergeometric. This eases the computational burden and provides useful approximations in those cases. Although there is no exact rule for when the binomial approximation can be used, we suggest that the sample should be less than 5% of the population size. Otherwise, use the hypergeometric distribution when sampling is done without replacement from the finite population.

EXAMPLE 5-8   The Hypergeometric Distribution (Two Outcomes Per Trial)

TRY PROBLEM 5.52

Gender Equity   One of the biggest changes in U.S. business practice in the past few decades has been the inclusion of women in the management ranks of companies. Tom Peters, management consultant and author of such books as *In Search of Excellence*, has stated that one of the reasons the Middle Eastern countries have suffered economically compared with countries such as the United States is that they have not included women in their economic system. However, there are still issues in U.S. business. Consider a situation in which a Maryland company needed to downsize one department having 30 people— 12 women and 18 men. Ten people were laid off, and upper management said the layoffs were done randomly. By chance, 40% (12/30) of the layoffs would be women. Of the

10 laid off, 8 were women. A labor attorney is interested in the probability of 8 or more women being laid off by chance alone. This can be determined using the following steps:

Step 1 **Determine the population size and the combined sample size.**

The population size and sample size are

$$N = 30 \quad \text{and} \quad n = 10$$

Step 2 **Define the event of interest.**

The attorney is interested in the event:

$$P(x \geq 8) = ?$$

What are the chances that 8 or more women would be selected?

Step 3 **Determine the number of successes in the population and the number of successes in the sample.**

In this situation, a success is the event that a woman is selected. There are $X = 12$ women in the population and $x \geq 8$ in the sample. We will break this down as $x = 8$, $x = 9$, $x = 10$.

Step 4 **Compute the desired probabilities using Equation 5.9.**

$$P(x) = \frac{C_{n-x}^{N-X} \cdot C_x^X}{C_n^N}$$

We want:[2]

$$P(x \geq 8) = P(x = 8) + P(x = 9) + P(x = 10)$$

$$P(x = 8) = \frac{C_{10-8}^{30-12} \cdot C_8^{12}}{C_{10}^{30}} = \frac{C_2^{18} \cdot C_8^{12}}{C_{10}^{30}} = 0.0025$$

$$P(x = 9) = \frac{C_1^{18} \cdot C_9^{12}}{C_{10}^{30}} = 0.0001$$

$$P(x = 10) = \frac{C_0^{18} \cdot C_{10}^{12}}{C_{10}^{30}} \approx 0.0000$$

Therefore, $P(x \geq 8) = 0.0025 + 0.0001 + 0.0000 = 0.0026$

The chances that 8 or more women would have been selected among the 10 people chosen for layoff strictly due to chance is 0.0026. The attorney will likely wish to challenge the layoffs based on this extremely low probability.

The Hypergeometric Distribution with More Than Two Possible Outcomes per Trial

Equation 5.9 assumes that on any given sample selection or trial only one of two possible outcomes will occur. However, the hypergeometric distribution can easily be extended to consider any number of possible categories of outcomes on a given trial by employing Equation 5.10.

---

[2] Note, you can use Excel's HYPGEOMDIST function to compute these probabilities.

Hypergeometric Distribution (k Possible Outcomes per Trial)

$$P(x_1, x_2, \ldots, x_k) = \frac{C_{x_1}^{X_1} \cdot C_{x_2}^{X_2} \cdot C_{x_3}^{X_3} \cdot \ldots \cdot C_{x_k}^{X_K}}{C_n^N} \qquad (5.10)$$

where:

$$\sum_{i=1}^{k} X_i = N$$

$$\sum_{i=1}^{k} x_i = n$$

N = Population size
n = Total sample size
X_i = Number of items in the population with outcome i
x_i = Number of items in the sample with outcome i

EXAMPLE 5-9 The Hypergeometric Distribution for Multiple Outcomes

TRY PROBLEM 5.53

Brand Preference Study Consider a marketing study that involves placing tooth-paste made by four different companies in a basket at the exit to a drugstore. A sign on the basket invites customers to take one tube free of charge. At the beginning of the study, the basket contains the following:

5 brand A tubes

4 brand B tubes

6 brand C tubes

4 brand D tubes

The researchers were interested in the brand selection patterns for customers who could select without regard to price. Suppose six customers were observed and three selected brand B, two selected brand D, and one selected brand C. No one selected brand A. The probability of this selection mix, assuming the customers were selecting entirely at random without replacement from a finite population, can be found using the following steps:

Step 1 **Determine the population size and the combined sample size.**

The population size and sample size are

$$N = 19 \quad \text{and} \quad n = 6$$

Step 2 **Define the event of interest.**

The event of interest is

$$P(x_1 = 0; x_2 = 3; x_3 = 1; x_4 = 2) = ?$$

Step 3 **Determine the number in each category in the population and the number in each category in the sample.**

$X_1 = 5$	(brand A)	$x_1 = 0$
$X_2 = 4$	(brand B)	$x_2 = 3$
$X_3 = 6$	(brand C)	$x_3 = 1$
$X_4 = 4$	(brand D)	$x_4 = 2$
$N = 19$		$n = 6$

Step 4 Compute the desired probability using Equation 5.10.

$$P(x_1, x_2, x_3, \ldots, x_k) = \frac{C_{x_1}^{X_1} \cdot C_{x_2}^{X_2} \cdot C_{x_3}^{X_3} \cdot \ldots \cdot C_{x_k}^{X_k}}{C_n^N}$$

$$P(0, 3, 1, 2) = \frac{C_0^5 \cdot C_3^4 \cdot C_1^6 \cdot C_2^4}{C_6^{19}}$$

$$= \frac{(1)(4)(6)(6)}{27,132} = \frac{144}{27,132}$$

$$= 0.0053$$

There are slightly more than 5 chances in 1,000 of this exact selection occurring by random chance.

5-3: Exercises

Skill Development

5-50. Arrivals to a bank ATM machine are distributed according to a Poisson distribution with a mean equal to three per 15 minutes.
a. Determine the probability that in a given 15-minute segment no customers will arrive at the ATM machine.
b. What is the probability that fewer than four customers will arrive in a 30-minute segment?

5-51. The mean number of typing errors per page made by a member of the typing pool for a large company is thought to be 1.5 and the number of errors is distributed according to a Poisson distribution. If three pages are examined, what is the probability that more than 3 errors will be observed?

5-52. A population of 10 items contains 3 that are red and 7 that are green. What is the probability that in a random sample of 3 items selected without replacement, 2 red and 1 green items are selected? Assume that sampling is performed without replacement.

5-53. Consider a situation in which a used-car lot contains five Fords, four GM cars, and five Toyotas. If five cars are selected at random to be placed on a special sale, what is the probability that three are Fords and two are GM cars?

5-54. If a random variable follows a Poisson distribution with $\lambda = 20$ and $t = \frac{1}{2}$, find the
a. expected value, variance, and standard deviation of this Poisson distribution.
b. probability of exactly 8 successes.

5-55. A corporation has 11 manufacturing plants. Seven of the plants are domestic and 4 are located outside the United States. Each year a performance evaluation is conducted for 4 randomly selected plants.

a. What is the probability that a performance evaluation will include exactly 1 plant outside the United States?
b. What is the probability that a performance evaluation will contain 3 plants from the United States?
c. What is the probability that a performance evaluation will include 2 or more plants from outside the United States?

5-56. A random variable, x, has a hypergeometric distribution with $N = 10$, $X = 7$, and $n = 4$. Calculate the following quantities:
a. $P(x = 3)$
b. $P(x = 5)$
c. $P(x \geq 4)$
d. Find the largest x' so that $P(x > x') > 0.25$.

5-57. Determine the following values associated with a Poisson distribution with λt equal to 3:
a. $P(x \leq 3)$
b. $P(x > 3)$
c. $P(2 < x \leq 5)$
d. Find the smallest x' so that $P(x \leq x') > 0.50$.

Business Applications

5-58. A new phone answering system installed by the Ohio Power Company is capable of handling five calls every 10 minutes. Prior to installing the new system, company analysts determined that the incoming calls to the system are Poisson distributed with a mean equal to two every 10 minutes. If this incoming call distribution is what the analysts think it is, what is the probability that in a 10-minute period more calls will arrive than the system can handle? Based on this probability, comment on the adequacy of the new answering system.

5-59. An Internet bank can process a maximum of 25 electronic transfers every minute during the busiest periods of the day. If it receives more transfer requests than this, then the bank's computer system will become so overburdened that it will slow to the point that no electronic transfers can be handled. If, during the busiest periods of the day, requests for electronic transfers arrive at the rate of 170 per 10-minute period on average, what is the probability that the system will be overwhelmed by requests? Assume that the process can be described using a Poisson distribution.

5-60. The Weyerhauser Lumber Company headquartered in Tacoma, Washington, is one of the largest timber and wood products companies in the world. Weyerhauser manufactures plywood at one of its Oregon plants. Plywood contains minor imperfections that can be repaired with small "plugs." One customer will accept plywood with a maximum of 3.5 plugs per sheet on average. Suppose a shipment was sent to this customer and when the customer inspected two sheets at random, 10 plugged defects were counted. What is the probability of observing 10 or more plugged defects if in fact the 3.5 average per sheet is being satisfied? Comment on what this probability implies about whether you think the company is meeting the 3.5 per sheet defect rate.

5-61. A stock portfolio contains 20 stocks. Of these stocks, 10 are considered "large-cap" stocks, 5 are "mid-cap" stocks, and 5 are "small cap." The portfolio manager has been asked by his client to develop a report that highlights 7 randomly selected stocks. When she presents her report to the client, all 7 of the stocks are "large-cap" stocks. The client is very suspicious that the manager has not randomly selected the stocks. She believes that the chances of all 7 of the stocks being "large cap" must be very low. Compute the probability of all 7 being "large cap" and comment on the concerns of the client.

5-62. A glass factory produces windshields for large commercial trucks. Assume that the process that produces the windshields can be described by a Poisson distribution with an average of 4.8 defects per windshield.
  a. What is the probability that a windshield will have fewer than 6 blemishes?
  b. What is the probability that six randomly sampled windshields from the production process will each have 7 or fewer blemishes?

5-63. East-West Translations publishes textbooks of ancient Oriental teachings for English-speaking universities. The company is currently testing a computer-based translation service. Since Oriental symbols are difficult to translate,

East-West assumes the computer program will make some errors, but then so do human translators. The computer service claims its error rate will average 3 per 400 words of translation. East-West randomly selects a 1,200-word passage. Assuming that the Poisson distribution applies, if the computer company's claim is accurate,
  a. determine the probability no errors will be found.
  b. calculate the probability more than 14 errors will be found.
  c. find the probability fewer than 9 errors will be found.
  d. If 15 errors are found in the 1,200-word passage, what would you conclude about the computer company's claim? Why?

5-64. The Farmhill Nursery sells trees and other yard and garden items. Currently, the nursery has 10 fruit trees, 8 pine trees, and 14 maple trees. It plans to give 4 trees away at next Saturday's lawn and garden show in the city park. The four winners can select which type of tree they want. Assume they select randomly.
  a. What is the probability that all 4 winners will select the same type of tree?
  b. What is the probability that 3 winners will select pine trees and the other tree will be a maple?
  c. What is the probability that no fruit trees and 2 of each of the others will be selected?

5-65. Fasteners used in a manufacturing process are shipped by the supplier to the manufacturer in boxes that contain 20 fasteners. Because the fasteners are critical to the production process, their failure will cause the product to fail. The manufacturing firm and the supplier have agreed that a random sample of 4 fasteners will be selected from every box and tested to see if the fasteners meet the manufacturer's specifications. The nature of the testing process is such that tested fasteners become unusable and must be discarded. The supplier and the manufacturer have agreed that if 2 or more fasteners fail the test, the entire box will be selected as being defective. Assume that a new box has just been received for inspection. If the box has 5 defective fasteners, what is the probability that a random sample of 4 will have 2 or more defective fasteners? What is the probability the box will be accepted?

5-66. Lucky Dogs sells spicy hot dogs from a pushcart. The owner of Lucky Dogs is open every day between 11:00 A.M. and 1:00 P.M. Assume the demand for spicy hot dogs follows a Poisson distribution with a mean of 50 per hour.
  a. What is the probability the owner will run out of spicy dogs over the two-hour period if he stocks his cart with 115 spicy dogs every day?

b. How many spicy hot dogs should the owner stock if he wants to limit the probability of being out of stock to less than 2.5%?

5-67. The Geek Squad is a 24-hour computer support task force. It provides in-home installation services as well as tech support to solve hardware, software, or computer peripheral crises. Geek Squad started 10 years ago as a small tech-support business in Minneapolis. It got such a positive response that Best Buy bought it. A shipment of 20 Intel® Pentium® 4 processors was sent to the Geek Squad. Four of them were defective. One of the Geek Squad technicians selected 5 of the processors to put in his parts inventory and went on three service calls.

a. Determine the probability that only 1 of the 5 processors is defective.

b. Determine the probability that 3 of the 5 processors are not defective.

c. Determine the probability that the technician will have enough processors to replace 3 defective processors at the repair sites.

5-68. According to an article ("401(k) balances rise," *Moneyline*, August 5, 2005) in *USA Today*, about one-third of eligible workers haven't enrolled in their employers' 401(k) plans. Costco has been contemplating new incentives to encourage more participation from its employees. Of the 12 employees in one of Costco's automotive departments, 5 have enrolled in Costco's 401(k) plan. The store manager has randomly selected 7 of the automotive department employees to receive investment training.

a. Calculate the probability that all of the employees who are currently enrolled in the 401(k) program are selected for the investment training.

b. Calculate the probability that none of the employees who are currently enrolled in the 401(k) program is selected for the investment training.

c. Compute the probability that more than half of the employees who are currently enrolled in the 401(k) are selected for the investment train.

5-69. The Small Business Administration's Center for Women's Business Research indicated (*USA Today*, "Small businesses cautiously plan to add staff," June 22, 2005) that 30% of private firms had female owners, 52% had male owners, and 18% had male and female co-owners. In one community, there are 50 privately owned firms. Ten privately owned firms are selected to receive assistance in marketing their products. Assume the percentages indicated by the Small Business Administration apply to this community.

a. Calculate the probability that one-half of the firms selected will be solely owned by a woman, 3 owned by men, and the rest co-owned by females and males.

b. Calculate the probability that all of the firms selected will be solely owned by women.

c. Calculate the probability that 6 will be owned by a woman and the rest co-owned.

Computer Database Exercises

5-70. The National Federation of Independent Business (NFIB) survey contacted 130 small firms. One of the many inquiries was to determine the number of employees the firms had. The file entitled **Employees** contains the responses by the firms. The number of employees was grouped into the following categories: (1) Fewer than 20; (2) 20–99; (3) 100–499; and (4) 500 or more.

a. Determine the number of firms in each of these categories.

b. If NFIB is to contact 25 of these firms to gather further information, determine the probability that it will choose the following number of firms in each category: (1) 22, (2) 2, (3) 1, and (4) 0.

c. Calculate the probability that it will choose all of the firms from those businesses with fewer than 20 workers.

5-71. Cliff Summey is the quality assurance engineer for Sticks and Stones Billiard Supply, a manufacturer of billiard supplies. One of the items that Sticks and Stones produces is sets of pocket billiard balls. Cliff has been monitoring the finish of the pocket billiard balls. He is concerned that sets of billiard balls have been shipped with an increasing number of scratches. The company's goal is to have no more than an average of one scratch per set of pocket billiard balls. A set contains 16 balls. Over the last week, Cliff has selected a sample of 48 billiard balls and inspected them to determine the number of scratches. The data collected by Cliff is displayed in the file called **Poolball**.

a. Determine the number of scratches in the sample.

b. Calculate the average number of scratches for 48 pocket billiard balls if Sticks and Stones has met its goal.

c. Determine the probability that there would be at least as many scratches observed per set of pocket billiard balls if Sticks and Stones has met its goal.

d. Based upon the sample evidence, does it appear that Sticks and Stones has met its goal? Provide statistical reasons for your conclusion.

Summary and Conclusions

Chapter 5 has introduced the concept of discrete probability distributions and has introduced several specific discrete probability distributions, including the binomial, Poisson, and hypergeometric. All of these distributions are used by decision makers. Figure 5.8 summarizes the different distributions introduced in this chapter.

The binomial distribution is useful when the value of a discrete random variable is based on independent trials and when on a given trial there are two possible outcomes and we can count the number of successes and failures. The Poisson distribution, also a discrete distribution, deals with situations in which the trials are independent but we are able to count only the successes. The final discrete distribution introduced in this chapter is the hypergeometric distribution. This distribution applies when the trials are dependent and the sample size is large relative to the size of the finite population.

Subsequent chapters will introduce continuous probability distributions. Among these will be the normal, uniform, exponential, and *t*, *chi-square*, and the *F distributions*. These additional distributions play important roles in statistical decision making.

EQUATIONS

Expected Value of Discrete Probability Distribution

$$E(x) = \sum x P(x) \qquad (5.1)$$

FIGURE 5.8

Probability Distribution Summary

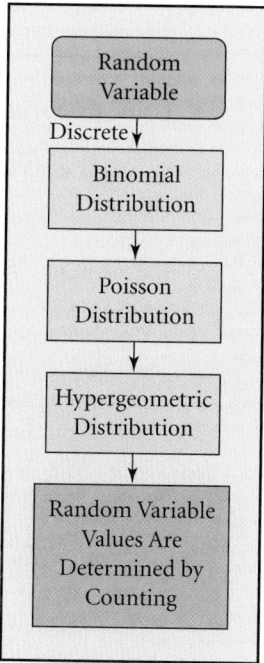

Standard Deviation of Discrete Probability Distribution

$$\sigma_x = \sqrt{\sum [x - E(x)]^2 P(x)} \qquad (5.2)$$

Counting Rule for Combinations

$$C_x^n = \frac{n!}{x!(n-x)!} \qquad (5.3)$$

Binomial Formula

$$P(x) = \frac{n!}{x!(n-x)!} p^x q^{n-x} \qquad (5.4)$$

Expected Value of a Binomial Distribution

$$\mu_x = E(x) = np \qquad (5.5)$$

Standard Deviation of the Binomial Distribution

$$\sigma = \sqrt{npq} \qquad (5.6)$$

Poisson Probability Distribution

$$P(x) = \frac{(\lambda t)^x e^{-\lambda t}}{x!} \qquad (5.7)$$

Standard Deviation of the Poisson Distribution

$$\sigma = \sqrt{\lambda t} \qquad (5.8)$$

Hypergeometric Distribution (Two Possible Outcomes per Trial)

$$P(x) = \frac{C_{n-x}^{N-X} \cdot C_x^X}{C_n^N} \qquad (5.9)$$

Hypergeometric Distribution (k Possible Outcomes per Trial)

$$P(x_1, x_2, x_3, \ldots, x_k) = \frac{C_{x_1}^{X_1} \cdot C_{x_2}^{X_2} \cdot C_{x_3}^{X_3} \cdot \ldots \cdot C_{x_k}^{X_k}}{C_n^N} \qquad (5.10)$$

Key Terms

Binomial distribution   213
Continuous random variable   204
Counting rule for combinations   215

Discrete random variable   204
Expected value   205
Poison distribution   228

Random variable   204
Hypergeometric distribution   236

Chapter Exercises

Conceptual Questions

5-72. How is the shape of the binomial distribution changed for a given value of p as the sample size is increased? Discuss.

5-73. Discuss the basic differences and similarities between the binomial distribution and the Poisson distribution.

5-74. Three discrete distributions were discussed in this chapter. Each was defined by a random variable that measured the number of successes. In order to apply these distributions, you must know which one to use. Describe the distinguishing characteristics for each distribution.

5-75. Beginning statistics students are often puzzled by two characteristics of distributions in this chapter: (1) the trials are independent, and (2) the probability of a success remains constant from trial to trial. Students often think these two characteristics are the same. The questions in this exercise points out the difference. Consider a hypergeometric distribution where $N = 3$, $X = 2$, and $n = 2$.

   a. Mathematically demonstrate that the trials for this experiment are dependent by calculating the probability of obtaining a success on the second trial if the first trial resulted in a success. Repeat this calculation if the first trial was a failure. Use these two probabilities to prove that the trials are dependent.

   b. Now calculate the probability that a success is obtained on each of the three respective trials and, therefore, demonstrate that the trials are dependent but that the probability of a success is constant from trial to trial.

5-76. Consider an experiment in which a sample of size $n = 5$ is taken from a binomial distribution.

   a. Calculate the probability of each value of the random variable for the probability of a success equal to (1) 0.1, (2) 0.25, (3) 0.50, (4) 0.75, and (5) 0.9.

   b. Which probabilities produced a right-skewed distribution? Why?

   c. Which probability of a success yielded a symmetric distribution? Why?

   d. Which probabilities produced a left-skewed distribution? Discuss why.

Business Applications

5-77. A food packaging business in California has a process that inserts tomato juice into 24-ounce containers. When the process is in control, half the cans actually contain more than 24 ounces and half contain less. Suppose a quality inspector has just randomly sampled nine cans and found that all nine had more than 24 ounces. Calculate the probability that this result would occur if the filling process was actually still in control. Based on this probability, what conclusion might be reached? Discuss.

5-78. The Harris Newspaper Company sometimes makes printing errors in its advertising and is forced to provide corrected advertising in the next issue of the paper. The managing editor has done a study of this problem and found the following data:

No. of Errors x	Relative Frequency
0	0.56
1	0.21
2	0.13
3	0.07
4	0.03

   a. Using the relative frequencies as probabilities, what is the expected number of errors? Interpret what this value means to the managing editor.

   b. Compute the variance and standard deviation for the number of errors and explain what these values measure.

5-79. The Ziteck Corporation buys parts from international suppliers. One part is currently being purchased from a Malaysian supplier under a contract that calls for at most 5% of the 10,000 parts to be defective. When a shipment arrives, Ziteck randomly samples 10 parts. If it finds 2 or fewer defectives in the sample, it keeps the shipment; otherwise, it returns the entire shipment to the supplier.

   a. Assuming that the conditions for the binomial distribution are satisfied, what is the probability that the sample will lead Ziteck to keep the shipment if the defect rate is actually 0.05?

b. Suppose the supplier is actually sending Ziteck 10% defects. What is the probability that the sample will lead Ziteck to accept the shipment anyway?

c. Comment on this sampling plan (sample size and accept/reject point). Do you think it favors either Ziteck or the supplier? Discuss.

5-80. Your company president has told you that the company experiences product returns at the rate of two per month with the number of product returns distributed as a Poisson random variable. Determine the probability that next month there will be

a. no returns.

b. one return.

c. two returns.

d. more than two returns.

e. In the last three months your company has had only one month in which the number of returns was at most two. Calculate the probability of this event occurring. What will you tell the president of your company concerning the return rate? Make sure you support your statement with something other than opinion.

5-81. The Defense Department has recently advertised for bids for producing a new night-vision binocular. Vista Optical has decided to submit a bid for the contract. The first step was to supply a sample of binoculars for the army to test at its Kentucky development grounds. Vista makes a superior night-vision binocular. However, the 4 sent to the army for testing were taken from a development lab project of 20 units that contained 4 defectives. The army has indicated it will reject any manufacturer that submits 1 or more defective binoculars. What is the probability that this mistake has cost Vista any chance for the contract?

5-82. VERCOR provides merger and acquisition consultants to assist corporations when owners decide to offer their business for sale. One of its news releases, "Tax Audit Frequency Is Rising," written by David L. Perkins, Jr., a VERCOR partner, which originally appeared in *The Business Owner,* indicated that the proportion of the largest businesses, those corporations with assets of $10 million and over, that were audited was 0.17.

a. One member of VERCOR's board of directors is on the board of directors of four other large corporations. Calculate the expected number of

these five corporations that should get audited assuming selection is random.

b. Three of the five corporations were actually audited. Determine the probability that at least three of the five corporations would be audited if 17% of large corporations are audited. (Assume random selection.)

c. The board member is concerned that the corporations have been singled out to be audited by the IRS. Respond to these thoughts using probability and statistical logic.

5-83. The Aims Photo Company sends photographers around to various department stores in the South to take pictures of children. The company charges only $0.99 for a sitting, which consists of six poses. The company then makes up three packages that are offered to the parents, who have a choice of buying 0, 1, 2, or all 3 of the packages. Based on his experience in the business, Samuel Aims has assessed the following probabilities of the number of packages that might be purchased by a parent:

No. of Packages x	$P(x)$
0	0.30
1	0.40
2	0.20
3	0.10

a. What is the expected number of packages to be purchased by each parent?

b. What is the standard deviation for the random variable, x?

c. Suppose all of the picture packages are to be priced at the same level. How much should they be priced if the Aims Company wants to break even? Assume that the production costs are $3.00 per package. Remember that the sitting charge is $0.99.

5-84. An Iverson Investment Company account manager recently gave a public seminar in which he discussed a number of issues, including investment risk analysis. In that seminar, he reminded people that the coefficient of variation often can be used as a measure of risk of an investment. (See Chapter 3 for a review of the coefficient of variation.) To demonstrate his point, he used two hypothetical stocks as examples. He let x equal the change in assets for a $1,000.00 investment in stock 1 and y reflect the change in assets for a $1,000.00 investment in stock 2. He showed the seminar participants the following probability distributions:

x	P(x)	y	P(y)
−$1,000.00	0.10	−$1,000.00	0.20
0.00	0.10	0.00	0.40
500.00	0.30	500.00	0.30
1,000.00	0.30	1,000.00	0.05
2,000.00	0.20	2,000.00	0.05

a. Compute the expected values for random variables x and y.
b. Compute the standard deviations for random variables x and y.
c. Recalling that the coefficient of variation is determined by the ratio of the standard deviation over the mean, compute the coefficient of variation for each random variable.
d. Referring to part c, suppose the seminar director said that the first stock was more risky since its standard deviation was greater than the standard deviation of the second stock. How would you respond? (*Hint*: What do the coefficients of variation imply?)

5-85. The Bentfield Electronics Company purchases parts from a variety of vendors. In each case the company is particularly concerned with the quality of the products it purchases. Part number 34-78D is used in the company's new laser printer. The parts are sensitive to dust and can easily be damaged in shipment even if they are acceptable when they leave the vendor's plant. In a shipment of four parts, the purchasing agent has assessed the following probability distribution for the number of defective products:

x	P(x)
0	0.20
1	0.20
2	0.20
3	0.20
4	0.20

a. What is the expected number of defectives in a shipment of four parts? Discuss what this value really means to Bentfield.
b. Compute and interpret the standard deviation of the number of defective parts in a shipment of four.
c. Examine the probabilities as assessed and indicate why this probability distribution is called a uniform distribution. Provide some

reasons why the probabilities might all be equal, as they are in this case.

5-86. Simmons Market Research conducted a national consumer study of 13,787 respondents in the spring of 2005. The respondents were asked to indicate the primary source of the vitamins or mineral supplements they consume. Thirty-five percent indicated a multiple formula was their choice. A subset of 20 respondents who used multiple vitamins may have been selected for further questioning. Half of them used a One A Day vitamin; the rest used generic brands. Four members of this subset were asked to fill out a more complete health survey.
a. Calculate the probability that the final selection of 4 members were all One A Day multiple vitamin users.
b. Compute the number of One A Day users expected to be selected.
c. Calculate the probability that fewer than half of the final selection were One A Day users.

5-87. The 700-room Westin Charlotte offers a premiere uptown location in the heart of the city's financial district. On a busy weekend, the hotel has 20 rooms that are not occupied. Suppose that smoking is allowed in 8 of the rooms. A small tour group arrives, which has four smokers and six nonsmokers. The desk clerk randomly selects 10 rooms and gives the keys to the tour guide to distribute to the travelers.
a. Compute the probability that the tour guide will have the correct mix of rooms so that all members of the tour group will receive a room that accommodates their smoking preferences.
b. Determine the probability that the tour guide will have to assign at least one nonsmoker to a smoking room.
c. Determine the probability that the tour guide will have to assign at least one smoker to a nonsmoking room.

Computer Database Exercises

5-88. A 23-mile stretch of a two-lane highway east of Paso Robles, California, was once considered a "death trap" by residents of San Luis Obispo County. Formerly known as "Blood Alley," Highway 46 gained notoriety for the number of fatalities (29) and crashes over a 240-week period. More than two-thirds involved head-on collisions. The file entitled **Crashes** contains the simulated number of fatal crashes during this time period.
a. Determine the average number of crashes in the 240-weeks.
b. Calculate the probability that at least 19 crashes would occur over the 240-week period if the average number of deaths per week was as calculated in part a.

c. Calculate the probability that at least 19 crashes would occur over a five-year period if the average number of deaths per week was as calculated in part a.

d. A coalition of state, local, and private organizations devised a coordinated and innovative approach to dramatically reduce deaths and injuries on this road. During the 16 months before and after completion of the project, fatal crashes were reduced to zero. Calculate the probability that there would be no fatal crashes if the mean number of fatal crashes was not changed by the coalition. Does it appear that the average number of fatal accidents has indeed decreased?

5-89. American Household, SM Inc. produces a wide array of home safety and security products. One of its products is the First Alert SA302 Dual Sensor Remote Control Smoke Alarm. As part of its quality control program, it constantly tests to assure that the alarms work. A change in the manufacturing process requires the company to determine the proportion of alarms that fail the quality control tests. Each day, 20 smoke alarms are taken from the production line and tested and the number of defectives is recorded. A file entitled **Smokeless** contains the possible results from the last 90 days of testing.

a. Compute the proportion of defective smoke alarms.

b. Calculate the expected number and the standard deviation of defectives for each day's testing. Assume the proportion of defectives is what was computed in part a. (*Hint*: Recall the formulas for the mean and the standard deviation for a binomial distribution.)

c. In order to make sure that the proportion of defectives does not change, the quality control manager wants to establish control limits that are 3 standard deviations above the mean and 3 standard deviations below the mean. Calculate these limits.

d. Determine the probability that a randomly chosen set of 20 smoke alarms would have a number of defectives that was beyond the control limits established in part c.

5-90. Covercraft manufactures covers to protect automobile interiors and finishes. Its Block-It 200 Series fabric has a limited two-year warranty. Periodic testing is done to determine if the warranty policy should be changed. One such study examined those covers that became unserviceable while still under warranty. Data that could be produced by such a study is contained in the file entitled **Covers**. The data represent the number of months a cover was used until it became unserviceable. Covercraft might want to examine more carefully the covers that became unserviceable while still under warranty. Specifically, it wants to examine those that became unserviceable before they had been in use less than one year.

a. Determine the number of covers that became unserviceable before they had been in use less than a year and a half.

b. If Covercraft quality control staff selects 20 of the covers at random, determine the probability that none of them will have failed before they had been in service less than a year and a half.

c. If Covercraft quality control staff needs to examine at least 5 of the failed covers, determine the probability that they will obtain this many.

CASE 5.1

SaveMor Pharmacies

A common practice now is for large retail pharmacies to buy the customer base from smaller, independent pharmacies. The way this works is that the buyer requests to see the customer list along with the buying history. The buyer then makes an offer based on its projection of how many of the seller's customers will move their business to the buyer's pharmacy and on how many dollars of new business will come to the buyer as a result of the purchase. Once the deal is made, the buyer and seller usually send out a joint letter to the seller's customers explaining the transaction and informing them that their prescription files have been transferred to the purchasing company.

The problem is that there is no guarantee regarding what proportion of the existing customers will make the switch to the buying company. That is the issue facing Heidi Fendenand, acquisitions manager for SaveMor Pharmacies. SaveMor has the opportunity to purchase the 6,780-person customer base from Hubbard Pharmacy in San Jose, California. Based on previous acquisitions, Heidi believes that if 70% or more of the customers will make the switch, then the deal is favorable to SaveMor. However, if 60% or less make the move to SaveMor, then the deal will be a bad one and she would recommend against it.

Quincy Kregthorpe, a research analyst who works for Heidi, has suggested that SaveMor take a new approach to this acquisition decision. He has suggested that SaveMor contact a random sample of 20 Hubbard customers telling them of the proposed sale and asking them if they will be willing to switch their business to SaveMor. Quincy has suggested that if 15 or more of the 20 customers indicate that they would make the switch, then SaveMor should go ahead with the purchase. Otherwise, it should decline the deal or negotiate a lower purchase price.

Heidi liked this idea and contacted Cal Hubbard, Hubbard's owner, to discuss the idea of surveying 20 randomly selected customers. Cal was agreeable as long as only these 20 customers would be told about the potential sale.

Before taking the next step, Heidi met with Quincy to discuss the plan one more time. She was concerned that the proposed sampling plan might have too high a probability of rejecting the purchase deal even if it was a positive one from SaveMor's viewpoint. On the other hand, she was concerned that the plan might also have a high probability of accepting the purchase deal when in fact it would be unfavorable to SaveMor. After discussing these concerns for over an hour, Quincy finally offered to perform an evaluation of the sampling plan.

Required Tasks:

1. Compute the probability that the sampling plan will provide a result that suggests that SaveMor should reject the deal even if the true proportion of all customers who would switch is actually 0.70.
2. Compute the probability that the sampling plan will provide a result that suggests that SaveMor should accept the deal even if the true proportion of all customers who would switch is actually only 0.60.
3. Write a short report to Heidi outlining the sampling plan, the assumptions on which the evaluation of the sampling plans has been based, and the conclusions regarding the potential effectiveness of the sampling plan. The report should make a recommendation about whether Heidi should go through with the idea of using the sampling plan.

CASE 5.2

Arrowmark Vending

Arrowmark Vending has the contract to supply pizza at all home football games for a university in the Big 12 athletic conference. It is a constant challenge at each game to determine how many pizzas to have available at the games. Tom Kealey, operations manager for Arrowmark, has determined that his fixed cost of providing pizzas, whether he sells 1 pizza or 4,000 pizzas, is $1,000. This cost includes hiring employees to work at the concession booths, hiring extra employees to cook the pizzas the day of the game, delivering them to the game, and advertising during the game. He believes that this cost should be equally allocated between two types of pizzas.

Tom has determined that he will supply only two types of pizzas: plain cheese and pepperoni and cheese combo. His cost to make a plain cheese pizza is $4.50 each, and his cost to make pepperoni and cheese combo is $5.00 each. Both pizzas will sell for $9.00 at the game. Unsold pizzas have no value and are donated to a local shelter for the homeless.

Past experience has shown the following demand distributions for the two types of pizza at home games:

Plain Cheese Demand	Probability	Pepperoni and Cheese Demand	Probability
200	0.10	300	0.10
300	0.15	400	0.20
400	0.15	500	0.25
500	0.20	600	0.25
600	0.20	700	0.15
700	0.10	800	0.05
800	0.05		
900	0.05		

Required Tasks:

1. For each type of pizza, determine the profit (or loss) associated with producing at each possible demand level. For instance, determine the profit if 200 plain cheese pizzas are produced and 200 are demanded. What is the profit if 200 plain cheese are produced but 300 were demanded, and so on?

2. Compute the expected profit associated with each possible production level (assuming Tom will only produce at one of the possible demand levels) for each type of pizza.
3. Prepare a short report to Tom that provides him with the information regarding how many of each type of pizza he should produce if he wants to achieve the highest expected profit from pizza sales at the game.

CASE 5.3

Boise Cascade Corporation

At the Boise Cascade Corporation, lumber mill logs arrive by truck and are scaled (measured to determine the number of board feet) before they are dumped into a log pond. Figure C-5.3 illustrates the basic flow. The mill manager must determine how many scale stations to have open during various times of the day. If he has too many stations open, the scalers will have excessive idle time and the cost of scaling will be unnecessarily high. On the other hand, if too few scale stations are open, some log trucks will have to wait.

The manager has studied the truck arrival patterns and has determined that during the first open hour (7:00–8:00 A.M.), the trucks randomly arrive at 12 per hour on average. Each scale station can scale 6 trucks per hour (10 minutes each). If the manager knew how many trucks would arrive during the hour, he would know how many scale stations to have open.

0 to 6 trucks:	open 1 scale station
7 to 12 trucks:	open 2 scale stations
etc.	

However, the number of trucks is a random variable and is uncertain. Your task is to provide guidance for the decision.

FIGURE C-5.3

Truck Flow for Boise Cascade Mill Example

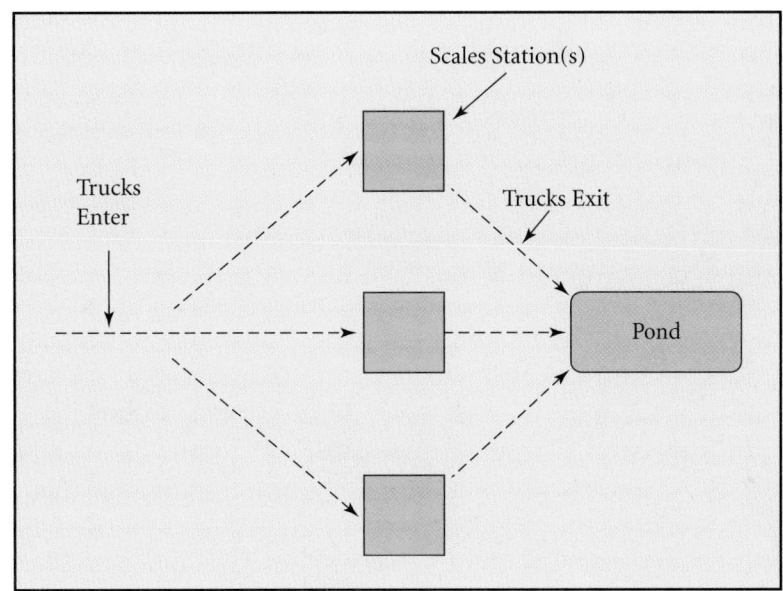

References

Hogg, R. V., and Elliot A. Tanis, *Probability and Statistical Inference*, 6th ed. (Upper Saddle River, NJ: Prentice Hall, 2001).

Larsen, Richard J., and Moriss L. Marx, *Introduction to Mathematical Statistics and Its Applications*, 4th ed. (Upper Saddle River, NJ: Prentice Hall, 2006).

Microsoft Excel 2007 (Redmond, WA: Microsoft Corp., 2007).

Minitab for Windows Version 15 (State College, PA: Minitab, 2007).

Siegel, Andrew F., *Practical Business Statistics*, 5th ed. (Burr Ridge, IL: Irwin, 2003).

Chapter SIX

Introduction to Continuous Probability Distributions

CHAPTER OUTCOMES

After studying the material in Chapter 6 you should be able to:

1. Convert a normal distribution to a standard normal distribution.
2. Determine probabilities using the normal distribution.
3. Calculate values of the random variable associated with specified probabilities from a normal distribution.
4. Calculate probabilities associated with a uniformly distributed random variable.
5. Determine probabilities for an exponential probability distribution.

PREPARING FOR CHAPTER SIX

- Review the methods for determining the probability for a discrete random variable in Chapter 5.

- Review the discussion of the mean and standard deviation in Sections 3.1 and 3.2.

- Review the concept of *z*-scores outlined in Section 3.3.

WHY YOU NEED TO KNOW

As shown in Chapter 5, you will encounter many business situations where the variable of interest is discrete and probability distributions such as the binomial, Poisson, or the hypergeometric will be useful for helping analyze decision situations. However, you will also deal with applications where the variable of interest is *continuous* rather than discrete. For instance, Toyota managers are interested in a measure called cycle time, which is the time between cars coming off the assembly line. Their factory may be designed to produce a car every 55 seconds and the operations managers would be interested in determining the probability the actual time between cars will exceed 60 seconds. A pharmaceutical company may be interested in the probability that a new drug will reduce blood pressure by more than 20 points for patients. The Kellogg company is interested in the probability that cereal boxes labeled as containing 16 ounces will actually contain at least that much cereal.

In each of these examples, the value of the variable of interest is determined by measuring (measuring the time between cars, measuring the blood pressure reading, measuring the weight of cereal in a box). In every instance, the number of possible values for the variable is limited only by the capacity of the measuring device. The constraints imposed by the measuring devices produce a finite number of outcomes. In these and similar situations, a continuous probability distribution can be used to approximate the distribution of possible outcomes for the random variables. The approximation is appropriate when the number of possible outcomes is large. Chapter 6 introduces three specific continuous probability distributions of particular importance for decision making and the study of business statistics. The first of these, the *normal distribution*, is by far the most important because a great many applications involve random variables that possess the characteristics of the normal distribution. In addition, many of the topics in the remaining chapters of this textbook dealing with statistical estimation and hypothesis testing are based on the normal distribution.

In addition to the normal distribution, you will be introduced to the uniform distribution and the exponential distribution. Both are important continuous probability distributions and have many applications in business decision making. You need to have a firm understanding and working knowledge of all three continuous probability distributions introduced in this chapter.

6.1 The Normal Probability Distribution

Chapter 5 introduced three important discrete probability distributions: the binomial distribution, the Poisson distribution, and the hypergeometric distribution. For each distribution, the random variable of interest is discrete and its value is determined by *counting*. For instance, a market researcher may be interested in the probability that a new product will receive favorable reviews by at least three-fourths of those sampling the product. The researcher might sample 100 people and then count the number of people who provide favorable reviews. The random variable could be values such as 65, 66, 67, . . . , 75, 76, 77, etc. The number of possible positive reviews could never be a fraction such as 76.80 or 79.25. The possible outcomes are limited to integer values between 0 and 100 in this case.

In other instances, you will encounter applications in which the value of the random variable is determined by *measuring* rather than by counting. In these cases, the random variable is said to be approximately *continuous* and can take on any value along some defined continuum. For instance, a Pepsi-Cola can that is supposed to contain 12 ounces might actually contain any amount between 11.90 and 12.10 ounces, such as 11.9853 ounces. When the variable of interest is approximately continuous, the probability distribution associated with the random variable is called a *continuous probability distribution*.

One important difference between discrete and continuous probability distributions involves the calculation of probabilities associated with specific values of the random variable. For instance, in the market research example in which 100 people were surveyed, we could use the binomial distribution to find the probability of any specific number of positive reviews, such as $P(x = 75)$ or $P(x = 76)$. While these individual probabilities may be small values, they can be computed because the random variable is discrete. However, if the random variable is continuous as in the Pepsi-Cola example, there are an uncountably infinite number of possible outcomes for the random variable. Theoretically, the probability of any one of these individual outcomes is zero. That is, $P(x = 11.92) = 0$ or $P(x = 12.05) = 0$. Thus, when you are working with continuous distributions, you will find the probability for a range of possible values such as $P(x \leq 11.92)$ or $P(11.92 \leq x \leq 12.0)$. Likewise, you can conclude that

$$P(x \leq 11.92) = P(x < 11.92)$$

because we assume that $P(x = 11.92) = 0$.

There are many different continuous probability distributions, but the most important of these is the *normal distribution*.

The Normal Distribution

You will encounter many business situations in which the random variable of interest will be treated as a continuous variable. There are several continuous distributions that are frequently used to describe physical situations. The most useful continuous probability distribution is the **normal distribution**.[1] The reason is that the output from a great many processes (both man-made and natural) are normally distributed.

Figure 6.1 illustrates a typical normal distribution and highlights the normal distribution's characteristics. All normal distributions have the same general shape as the one shown in Figure 6.1. However, they can differ in their mean value and their variation, depending on the situation being considered. The process being represented determines the scale of the horizontal axis. It may be pounds, inches, dollars, or any other attribute with a continuous measurement. Figure 6.2 shows several normal distributions with different centers and different spreads. Note that the total area (probability) under each normal curve equals 1.

The normal distribution is described by the rather-complicated-looking probability density function, shown in Equation 6.1.

Normal Distribution

The normal distribution is a bell-shaped distribution with the following properties:

1. It is *unimodal*; that is, the normal distribution peaks at a single value.
2. It is *symmetrical*; this means that the two areas under the curve between the mean and any two points equidistant on either side of the mean are identical. One side of the distribution is the mirror image of the other side.
3. The mean, median, and mode are equal.
4. The normal approaches the horizontal axis on either side of the mean toward plus and minus infinity (∞). In more formal terms, the normal distribution is *asymptotic* to the *x* axis.
5. The amount of variation in the random variable determines the height and spread of the normal distribution.

Normal Distribution Density Function

$$f(x) = \frac{1}{\sigma\sqrt{2\pi}} e^{-(x-\mu)^2/2\sigma^2}$$

(6.1)

where:

x = Any value of the continuous random variable

σ = Population standard deviation

π = 3.14159

e = Base of the natural log $\approx 2.71828\ldots$

μ = Population mean

FIGURE 6.1

Characteristics of the Normal Distribution

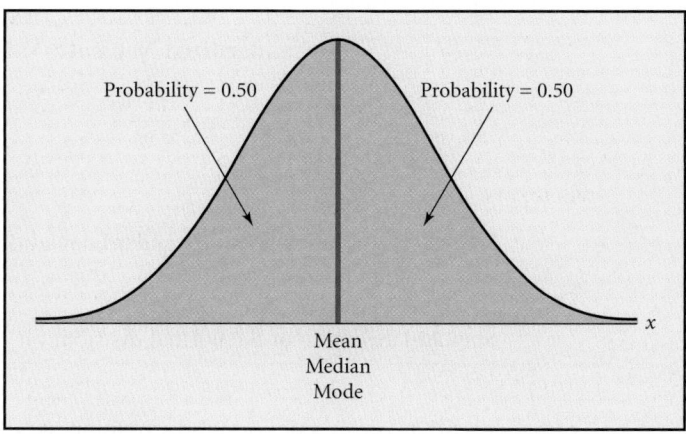

Probability = 0.50   Probability = 0.50

Mean
Median
Mode

x

---

[1] It is common to refer to the very large family of normal distributions as "*the* normal distribution." Keep in mind, however, that "the normal distribution" really is a very large family of distributions.

FIGURE 6.2

Difference Between Normal Distributions

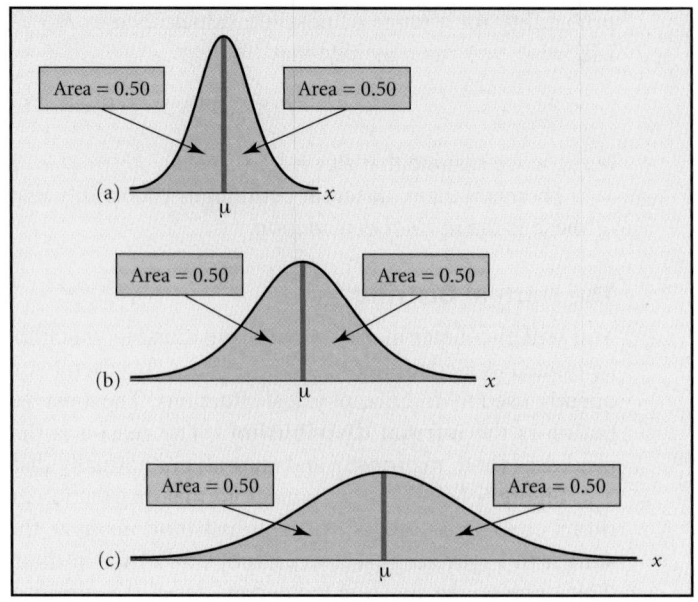

To graph the normal distribution, we need to know the mean, μ, and the standard deviation, σ. Placing μ, σ, and a value of the variable, x, into the probability density function, we can calculate a height, $f(x)$, of the density function. If we try enough x-values, we will get a curve like those shown in Figures 6.1 and 6.2.

The area under the normal curve corresponds to probability. The probability, $P(x)$, is equal to 0 for any particular x. However, we can find the probability for a range of values between x_1 and x_2 by finding the area under the curve between these two values. A special normal distribution called the *standard normal distribution* is used to find areas (probabilities) for a normal distribution.

CHAPTER OUTCOME #1

Standard Normal Distribution
A normal distribution that has a mean = 0.0 and a standard deviation = 1.0. The horizontal axis is scaled in z-values that measure the number of standard deviations a point is from the mean. Values above the mean have positive z-values. Values below the mean have negative z-values.

The Standard Normal Distribution

The trick to finding probabilities for a normal distribution is to convert the normal distribution to a **standard normal distribution**.

To convert a normal distribution to a standard normal distribution, the values (x) of the random variable are standardized as outlined previously in Chapter 3. The conversion formula is shown as Equation 6.2.

Standardized Normal z-Value

$$z = \frac{x - \mu}{\sigma} \tag{6.2}$$

where:

z = Scaled value (the number of standard deviations a point x is from the mean)
x = Any point on the horizontal axis
μ = Mean of the normal distribution
σ = Standard deviation of the normal distribution

Equation 6.2 *rescales* any normal distribution axis from its true units (time, weight, dollars, barrels, and so forth) to the standard measure referred to as a *z-value*. Thus, any value of the normally distributed continuous random variable can be represented by a unique *z*-value.

FIGURE 6.3

Distribution of Days Homes Stay on the Market Until They Sell

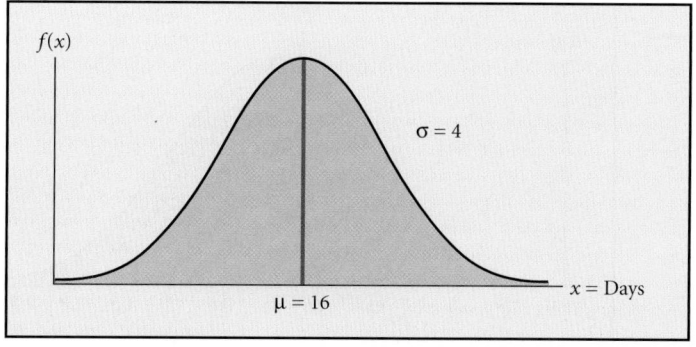

Business Application

REAL ESTATE SALES A July 25, 2005, article in the *Washington Post* by Kirstin Downey and Sandra Fleishman entitled "D.C. Area Housing Market Cools Off" stated that the average time that a home remained on the market before selling in Fairfax County is 16 days. Suppose that further analysis performed by Metropolitan Regional Information Systems Inc., which runs the local multiple-listing service, shows the distribution of days that homes stay on the market before selling is approximated by a normal distribution with a standard deviation of 4 days. Figure 6.3 shows this normal distribution with $\mu = 16$ and $\sigma = 4$.

Three homes that were sold in Fairfax County were selected from the multiple-listing inventory. The days that these homes spent on the market were

Home 1: $x = 16$ days

Home 2: $x = 18.5$ days

Home 3: $x = 9$ days

Equation 6.2 is used to convert these values from a normally distributed population with $\mu = 16$ and $\sigma = 4$ to corresponding z-values in a standard normal distribution. For Home 1, we get

$$z = \frac{x - \mu}{\sigma} = \frac{16 - 16}{4} = 0$$

Note, Home 1 was on the market 16 days, which happens to be equal to the population mean. The standardized z-value corresponding to the population mean is zero. This indicates that the population mean is 0 standard deviations from itself.

For Home 2, we get

$$z = \frac{x - \mu}{\sigma} = \frac{18.5 - 16}{4} = 0.63$$

Thus, for this population, a home that stays on the market 18 days is 0.63 standard deviations higher than the mean. The standardized z-value for Home 3 is

$$z = \frac{x - \mu}{\sigma} = \frac{9 - 16}{4} = -1.75$$

The z-value is -1.75. This means a home from this population that stays on the market for only 9 days has a value that is 1.75 standard deviations below the population mean. Note, a negative z-value always indicates the x-value is less than the mean, μ.

The z-value represents the number of standard deviations a point is above or below the population mean. Equation 6.2 can be used to convert any value of x from the population distribution to a corresponding z-value. If the population distribution is normally distributed as shown in Figure 6.3, then the distribution of z-values will also be normally distributed and is called the *standard normal distribution*. Figure 6.4 shows a standard normal distribution.

FIGURE 6.4

Standard Normal Distribution

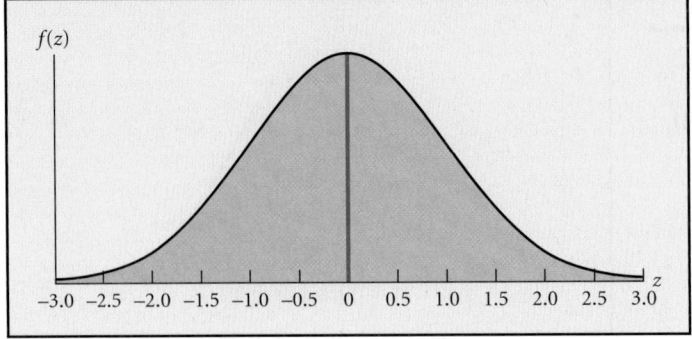

You can convert the normal distribution to a standard normal distribution and use the standard normal table to find the desired probability. Example 6-1 shows the steps required to do this.

CHAPTER OUTCOME #2

Using the Standard Normal Table The *standard normal table* in Appendix D provides probabilities (or areas under the normal curve) for many different *z*-values. The standard normal table is constructed so that the probabilities provided represent the chance of a value falling between the *z*-value and the population mean.

The standard normal table is also reproduced in Table 6.1. This table provides probabilities for *z*-values between $z = 0.00$ and $z = 3.09$.

SUMMARY Using the Normal Distribution

If a continuous random variable is distributed as a normal distribution, the distribution is symmetrically distributed around the mean, or expected value, and is described by the mean and standard deviation. To find probabilities associated with a normally distributed random variable, use the following steps:

1. Determine the mean, μ, and the standard deviation, σ.
2. Define the event of interest, such as $P(x \geq x_1)$.
3. Convert the normal distribution to the standard normal distribution using Equation 6.2:

$$z = \frac{x - \mu}{\sigma}$$

4. Use the standard normal distribution tables to find the probability associated with the calculated *z*-value. The table gives the probability between the *z*-value and the mean.
5. Determine the desired probability using the knowledge that the probability of a value being on either side of the mean is 0.50 and the total probability under the normal distribution is 1.0.

TRY PROBLEM 6.1

EXAMPLE 6-1 Using The Standard Normal Table

Employee Commute Time After completing a study, a company in Kansas City concluded the time its employees spend commuting to work each day is normally distributed with a mean equal to 15 minutes and a standard deviation equal to 3.5 minutes. One employee has indicated that she commutes 22 minutes per day. To find the probability that an employee would commute 22 or more minutes per day, you can use the following steps:

Step 1 Determine the mean and standard deviation for the random variable.
The parameters of the probability distribution are

$$\mu = 15 \quad \text{and} \quad \sigma = 3.5$$

Step 2 Define the event of interest.
The employee has a commute time of 22 minutes. We wish to find

$$P(x \geq 22) = ?$$

Step 3 **Convert the random variable to a standardized value using Equation 6.2.**

$$z = \frac{x - \mu}{\sigma} = \frac{22 - 15}{3.5} = 2.00$$

Step 4 **Find the probability associated with the z-value in the standard normal distribution table (Appendix D).**

To find the probability associated with $z = 2.00$, [i.e., $P(0 \le z \le 2.00)$], do the following:

1. Go down the left-hand column of the table to $z = 2.0$.
2. Go across the top row of the table to 0.00 for the second decimal place in $z = 2.00$.
3. Find the value where the row and column intersect.

The value, 0.4772, is the probability that a value in a normal distribution will lie between the mean and 2.00 standard deviations above the mean.

Step 5 **Determine the probability for the event of interest.**

$$P(x \ge 22) = ?$$

We know that the area on each side of the mean under the normal distribution is equal to 0.50. In Step 4 we computed the probability associated with $z = 2.00$ to be 0.4772, which is the probability of a value falling between the mean and 2.00 standard deviations above the mean. Then, the probability we are looking for is

$$P(x \ge 22) = P(z \ge 2.00) = 0.5000 - 0.4772 = 0.0228$$

Business Application

REAL ESTATE SALES (*CONTINUED*) Earlier, we discussed the situation involving real estate sales in Fairfax County near Washington D.C. in which a report showed that the mean days a home stays on the market before it sells is 16 days. We assumed the distribution for days on the market before a home sells was normally distributed with $\mu = 16$ and $\sigma = 4$. A local D.C. television station interviewed an individual whose home had recently sold after 14 days on the market. Contrary to what the reporter had anticipated, this homeowner was mildly disappointed in how long her home took to sell. She said she thought it should have sold quicker given the fast-paced real estate market, but the reporter countered that he thought the probability was quite high that a home would require 14 or more days to sell. Specifically, we want to find

$$P(x \ge 14) = ?$$

This probability corresponds to the area under a normal distribution to the right of $x = 14$ days. This will be the sum of the area between $x = 14$ and $\mu = 16$ plus the area to the right of $\mu = 16$. Refer to Figure 6.5.

To find this probability, you first convert $x = 14$ days to its corresponding z-value. This is equivalent to determining the number of standard deviations $x = 14$ is from the population mean of $\mu = 16$. Equation 6.2 is used to do this as follows:

$$z = \frac{x - \mu}{\sigma} = \frac{14 - 16}{4} = -0.50$$

Because the normal distribution is symmetrical, even though the z-value is negative 0.50, we find the desired probability by going to the standard normal distribution table for a

TABLE 6.1 Standard Normal Distribution Table

To illustrate: 19.85% of the area under a normal curve lies between the mean, μ, and a point 0.52 standard deviation units away.

0.1985

Example:
$z = 0.52$ (or -0.52)
$P(0 \leq z \leq 0.52) = 0.1985$, or 19.85%

z	.00	.01	.02	.03	.04	.05	.06	.07	.08	.09
0.0	.0000	.0040	.0080	.0120	.0160	.0199	.0239	.0279	.0319	.0359
0.1	.0398	.0438	.0478	.0517	.0557	.0596	.0636	.0675	.0714	.0753
0.2	.0793	.0832	.0871	.0910	.0948	.0987	.1026	.1064	.1103	.1141
0.3	.1179	.1217	.1255	.1293	.1331	.1368	.1406	.1443	.1480	.1517
0.4	.1554	.1591	.1628	.1664	.1700	.1736	.1772	.1808	.1844	.1879
0.5	.1915	.1950	.1985	.2019	.2054	.2088	.2123	.2157	.2190	.2224
0.6	.2257	.2291	.2324	.2357	.2389	.2422	.2454	.2486	.2517	.2549
0.7	.2580	.2611	.2642	.2673	.2704	.2734	.2764	.2794	.2823	.2852
0.8	.2881	.2910	.2939	.2967	.2995	.3023	.3051	.3078	.3106	.3133
0.9	.3159	.3186	.3212	.3238	.3264	.3289	.3315	.3340	.3365	.3389
1.0	.3413	.3438	.3461	.3485	.3508	.3531	.3554	.3577	.3599	.3621
1.1	.3643	.3665	.3686	.3708	.3729	.3749	.3770	.3790	.3810	.3830
1.2	.3849	.3869	.3888	.3907	.3925	.3944	.3962	.3980	.3997	.4015
1.3	.4032	.4049	.4066	.4082	.4099	.4115	.4131	.4147	.4162	.4177
1.4	.4192	.4207	.4222	.4236	.4251	.4265	.4279	.4292	.4306	.4319
1.5	.4332	.4345	.4357	.4370	.4382	.4394	.4406	.4418	.4429	.4441
1.6	.4452	.4463	.4474	.4484	.4495	.4505	.4515	.4525	.4535	.4545
1.7	.4554	.4564	.4573	.4582	.4591	.4599	.4608	.4616	.4625	.4633
1.8	.4641	.4649	.4656	.4664	.4671	.4678	.4686	.4693	.4699	.4706
1.9	.4713	.4719	.4726	.4732	.4738	.4744	.4750	.4756	.4761	.4767
2.0	.4772	.4778	.4783	.4788	.4793	.4798	.4803	.4808	.4812	.4817
2.1	.4821	.4826	.4830	.4834	.4838	.4842	.4846.	.4850	.4854	.4857
2.2	.4861	.4864	.4868	.4871	.4875	.4878	.4881	.4884	.4887	.4890
2.3	.4893	.4896	.4898	.4901	.4904	.4906	.4909	.4911	.4913	.4916
2.4	.4918	.4920	.4922	.4925	.4927	.4929	.4931	.4932	.4934	.4936
2.5	.4938	.4940	.4941	.4943	.4945	.4946	.4948	.4949	.4951	.4952
2.6	.4953	.4955	.4956	.4957	.4959	.4960	.4961	.4962	.4963	.4964
2.7	.4965	.4966	.4967	.4968	.4969	.4970	.4971	.4972	.4973	.4974
2.8	.4974	.4975	.4976	.4977	.4977	.4978	.4979	.4979	.4980	.4981
2.9	.4981	.4982	.4982	.4983	.4984	.4984	.4985	.4985	.4986	.4986
3.0	.4987	.4987	.4987	.4988	.4988	.4989	.4989	.4989	.4990	.4990

FIGURE 6.5

Probabilities from the Normal Curve for Fairfax Real Estate

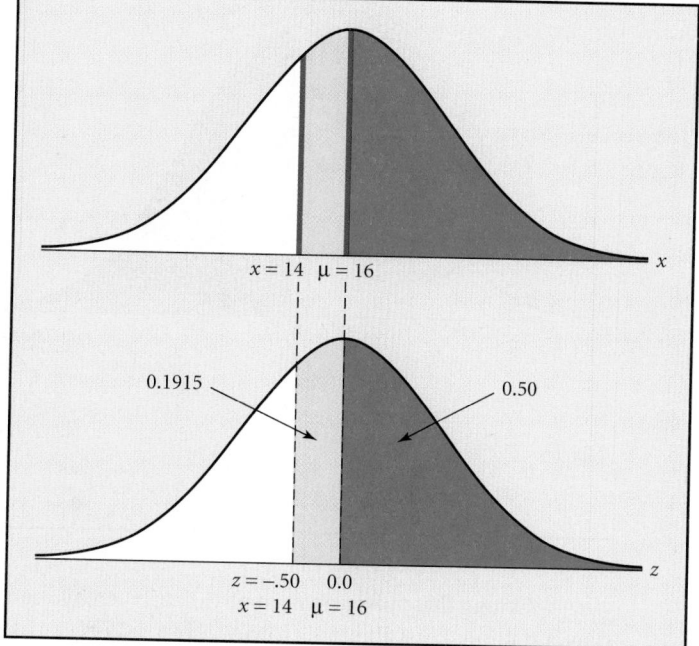

positive $z = 0.50$. The probability in the table for $z = 0.50$ corresponds to the probability of a z-value occurring between $z = 0.50$ and $z = 0.0$. This is the same as the probability of a z-value falling between $z = -0.50$ and $z = 0.00$. Thus, from the standard normal table (Table 6.1 or Appendix D), we get

$$P(-0.50 \le z \le 0.00) = 0.1915$$

This is the area between $x = 14$ and $\mu = 16$ in Figure 6.5. We now add 0.1915 to 0.5000, which is the probability of a value exceeding $\mu = 16$. Therefore, the probability that a home will require 14 or more days to sell is

$$P(x \ge 14) = 0.1915 + 0.5000 = 0.6915$$

This is illustrated in Figure 6.5. Thus, there is nearly a 70% chance that a home will require at least 14 days to sell.

Business Application   **LONGLIFE BATTERY COMPANY** Several states, including California, have passed legislation requiring automakers to sell a certain percentage of zero-emissions cars within their borders. One current alternative is battery-powered cars. The major problem with battery-operated cars is the limited time they can be driven before the batteries must be recharged. Longlife Battery, a start-up company, has developed a battery pack it claims will power a car at a sustained speed of 45 miles per hour for an average of 8 hours. But of course there will be variations: Some battery packs will last longer and some shorter than 8 hours. Current data indicate that the standard deviation of battery operation time before a charge is needed is 0.4 hours. Data show a normal distribution of uptime on these battery packs. Automakers are concerned that batteries may run short. For example, drivers might find an "8-hour" battery that lasts 7.5 hours or less unacceptable. What are the chances of this happening with the Longlife battery pack?

To calculate the probability the batteries will last 7.5 hours or less, find the appropriate area under the normal curve shown in Figure 6.6. There is approximately 1 chance in 10 that a battery will last 7.5 hours or less when the vehicle is driven at 45 miles per hour.

Suppose this level of reliability is unacceptable to the automakers. Instead of a 10% chance of an "8-hour" battery lasting 7.5 hours or less, the automakers will accept no more than a 2% chance. Longlife Battery asks the question, what would the mean uptime have to be to meet the 2% requirement?

FIGURE 6.6

Longlife Battery Company

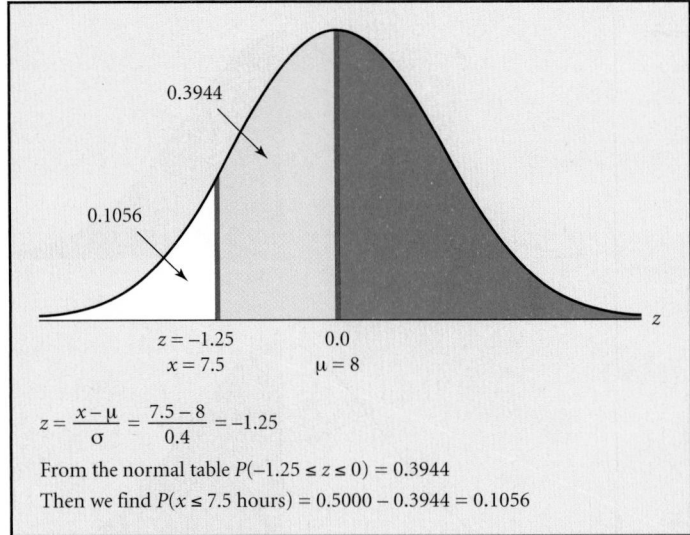

$$z = \frac{x - \mu}{\sigma} = \frac{7.5 - 8}{0.4} = -1.25$$

From the normal table $P(-1.25 \leq z \leq 0) = 0.3944$

Then we find $P(x \leq 7.5 \text{ hours}) = 0.5000 - 0.3944 = 0.1056$

Assuming that uptime is normally distributed, we can answer this question by using the standard normal distribution. However, instead of using the standard normal table to find a probability, we use it in reverse to find the z-value that corresponds to a known probability. Figure 6.7 shows the uptime distribution for the battery packs. Note, the 2% probability is shown in the left tail of the distribution. This is the allowable chance of a battery lasting 7.5 hours or less. We must solve for μ, the mean uptime that will meet this requirement.

1. Go to the body of the standard normal table, where the probabilities are located, and find the probability as close to 0.48 as possible. This is 0.4798.
2. Determine the z-value associated with 0.4798. This is $z = 2.05$. Because we are below the mean, the z is negative. Thus, $z = -2.05$.
3. The formula for z is

$$z = \frac{x - \mu}{\sigma}$$

4. Substituting the known values, we get

$$-2.05 = \frac{7.5 - \mu}{0.4}$$

FIGURE 6.7

Longlife Battery Company, Solving for the Mean

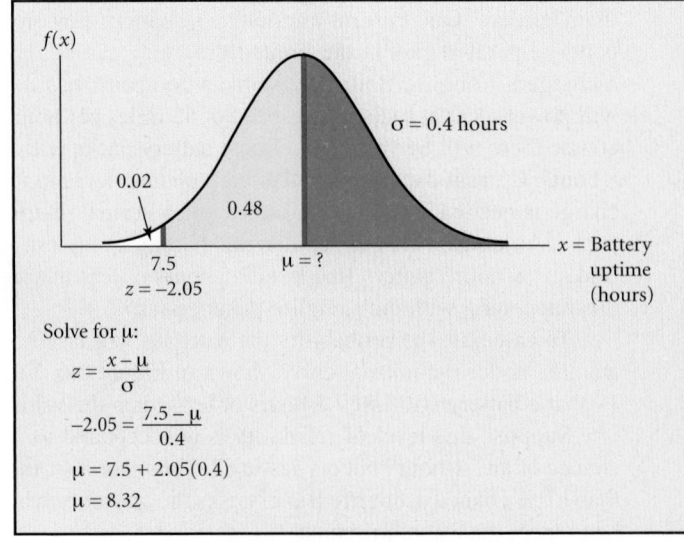

Solve for μ:

$$z = \frac{x - \mu}{\sigma}$$

$$-2.05 = \frac{7.5 - \mu}{0.4}$$

$$\mu = 7.5 + 2.05(0.4)$$

$$\mu = 8.32$$

FIGURE 6.8

Excel 2007 Output for State Bank and Trust Service Times

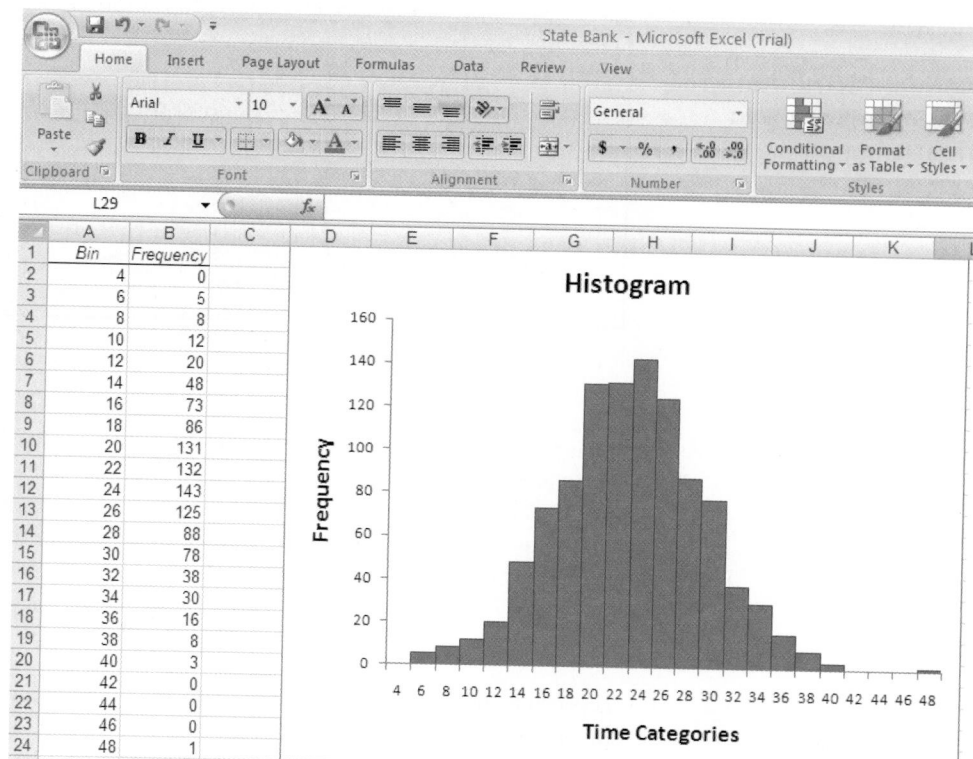

Bin	Frequency
4	0
6	5
8	8
10	12
12	20
14	48
16	73
18	86
20	131
22	132
24	143
26	125
28	88
30	78
32	38
34	30
36	16
38	8
40	3
42	0
44	0
46	0
48	1

Excel 2007 Instructions:
1. Open file: State Bank.xls.
2. Create bins (upper limit of each class).
3. Select **Data > Data Analysis**.
4. Select **Histogram**.
5. Define data and bin ranges.
6. Check **Chart Output**.
7. Define Output Location.
8. Select the chart and right click.
9. Click on **Format Data Series** and set gap width to zero.

Minitab Instructions (for similar results):
1. Open file: State Bank. MTW.
2. Choose **Graph > Histogram**.
3. Click **Simple**.
4. Click **OK**.
5. In **Graph Variables**, enter data column **Service Time**.
6. Click **OK**.

5. Solve for μ:

$$\mu = 7.5 + 2.05(0.4) = 8.32 \text{ hours}$$

Longlife Battery will need to increase the mean life of the battery pack to 8.32 hours to meet the automakers' requirement that no more than 2% of the batteries fail in 7.5 hours or less.

Excel and Minitab Tutorial

CHAPTER OUTCOME #3

STATE BANK AND TRUST The director of operations for the State Bank and Trust recently performed a study of the time bank customers spent from the time they walk into the bank until they complete their banking. The data file, **State Bank**, contains the data for a sample of 1,045 customers randomly observed over a four-week period. The customers in the survey were limited to those who were there for "basic bank business," such as making a deposit or a withdrawal, or cashing a check. The histogram in Figure 6.8 shows that the times appear to be distributed quite closely to a normal distribution.[2]

The mean service for the 1,045 customers was 22.14 minutes, with a standard deviation equal to 6.09 minutes. On the basis of these data, the manager assumes that the service times are normally distributed with $\mu = 22.14$ and $\sigma = 6.09$. Given these assumptions, the

---

[2] A statistical technique known as the chi-square goodness-of-fit test, introduced in Chapter 13, can be used to determine statistically whether the data follow a normal distribution.

FIGURE 6.9

Normal Distribution for the State Bank and Trust Example

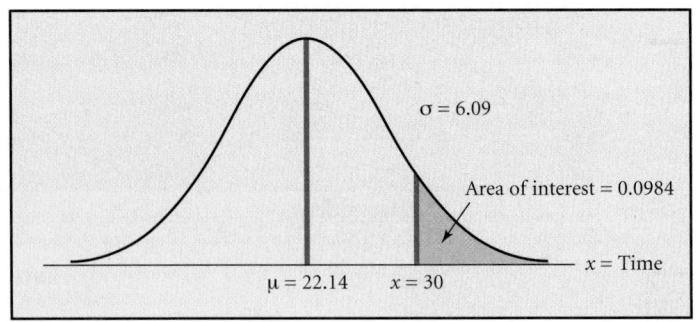

manager is considering providing a gift certificate to a local restaurant to any customer who is required to spend more than 30 minutes in the service process for basic bank business. Before doing this, she is interested in the probability of having to pay off on this offer.

Figure 6.9 shows the theoretical distribution, with the area of interest identified. The manager is interested in finding

$$P(x > 30 \text{ minutes})$$

This can be done manually or with Excel or Minitab. Figure 6.10A and Figure 6.10B show the output. The cumulative probability is

$$P(x \le 30) = 0.9016$$

Then to find the probability of interest, we subtract this value from 1.0, giving

$$P(x > 30 \text{ minutes}) = 1.0 - 0.9016 = 0.0984$$

FIGURE 6.10A

Excel 2007 Output for State Bank and Trust

Excel 2007 Instructions:
1. Open a blank worksheet.
2. Select **Formulas**.
3. Click on f_x (**Function Wizard**).
4. Select the **Statistical** category.
5. Select the **NORMDIST** function.
6. Fill in the requested information in the template.
7. **True** indicates cumulative probabilities.
8. Click **OK**.

FIGURE 6.10B

**Minitab Output for
State Bank and Trust**

Minitab Instructions:
1. Choose **Calc > Probability Distribution > Normal**.
2. Choose **Cumulative probability**.
3. In **Mean**, enter μ.
4. In **Standard deviation**, enter σ.
5. In **Input constant**, enter *x*.
6. Click **OK**.

Thus, there are just under 10 chances in 100 that the bank would have to give out a gift certificate. Suppose the manager believes this policy is too liberal. She wants to set the time limit so that the chance of giving out the gift is only 5%. You can use the standard normal table, the **Probability Distribution** command in Minitab, or the **NORMSINV** function in Excel to find the new limit.[3] To use the table, we first consider that the manager wants a 5% area in the upper tail of the normal distribution. This will leave

$$0.50 - 0.05 = 0.45$$

between the new time limit and the mean. Now go to the body of the standard normal table, where the probabilities are, and locate the value as close to 0.45 as possible (0.4495 or 0.4505). Next, determine the *z*-value that corresponds to this probability. Because 0.45 lies midway between 0.4495 and 0.4505, we interpolate halfway between $z = 1.64$ and $z = 1.65$ to get

$$z = 1.645$$

Now, we know

$$z = \frac{x - \mu}{\sigma}$$

We then substitute the known values and solve for *x*:

$$1.645 = \frac{x - 22.14}{6.09}$$
$$x = 22.14 + 1.645(6.09)$$
$$x = 32.158 \text{ minutes}$$

Therefore, any customer required to wait more than 32.158 (or 32) minutes will receive the gift. This should result in about 5% of the customers getting the restaurant certificate. Obviously, the bank will work to reduce the average service time or standard deviation so even fewer customers will have to be in the bank for more than 32 minutes.

---

[3] The function is =NORMSINV(.95) in Excel. This will return the *z*-value corresponding to the area to left of the upper tail equaling .05.

TRY PROBLEM 6.15

EXAMPLE 6-2 Using the Normal Distribution

Premier Technologies Premier Technologies has a contract to assemble components for radar systems to be used by the U.S. military. The time required to complete one part of the assembly is thought to be normally distributed, with a mean equal to 30 hours and a standard deviation equal to 4.7 hours. In order to keep the assembly flow moving on schedule, this assembly step needs to be completed in 26 to 35 hours. To determine the probability of this happening, use the following steps:

Step 1 Determine the mean, μ, and the standard deviation, σ.

The mean assembly time for this step in the process is thought to be 30 hours, and the standard deviation is thought to be 4.7 hours.

Step 2 Define the event of interest.

We are interested in determining the following:

$$P(26 \leq x \leq 35) = ?$$

Step 3 Convert values of the specified normal distribution to corresponding values of the standard normal distribution using Equation 6.2:

$$z = \frac{x - \mu}{\sigma}$$

We need to find the z-value corresponding to $x = 26$ and to $x = 35$.

$$z = \frac{x - \mu}{\sigma} = \frac{26 - 30}{4.7} = -0.85 \quad \text{and} \quad z = \frac{35 - 30}{4.7} = 1.06$$

Step 4 Use the standard normal table to find the probabilities associated with each z-value.

For $z = -0.85$, the probability is 0.3023.
For $z = 1.06$, the probability is 0.3554.

Step 5 Determine the desired probability for the event of interest.

$$P(26 \leq x \leq 35) = 0.3023 + 0.3554 = 0.6577$$

Thus, there is a 0.6577 chance that this step in the assembly process will stay on schedule.

Approximate Areas Under the Normal Curve In Chapter 3 we introduced the Empirical Rule for probabilities with bell-shaped distributions. For the normal distribution we can make this rule more precise. Knowing the area under the normal curve between $\pm 1\sigma$, $\pm 2\sigma$, and $\pm 3\sigma$ provides a useful benchmark for estimating probabilities and checking reasonableness of results. Figure 6.11 shows these benchmark areas for any normal distribution.

FIGURE 6.11

**Approximate Areas
Under the Normal Curve**

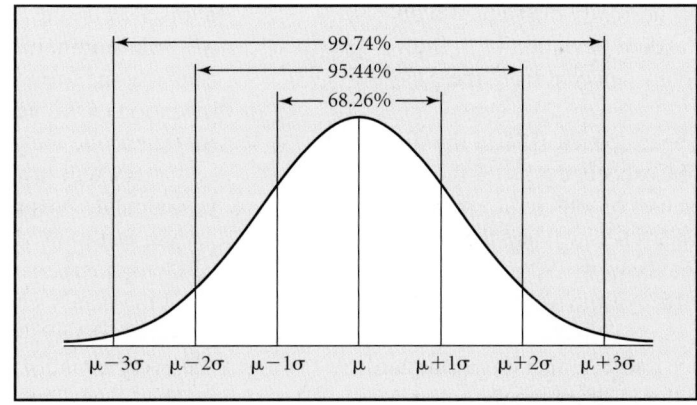

6-1: Exercises

Skill Development

6-1. A population is normally distributed with $\mu = 100$ and $\sigma = 20$.
  a. Find the probability that a value randomly selected from this population will have a value greater than 130.
  b. Find the probability that a value randomly selected from this population will have a value less than 90.
  c. Find the probability that a value randomly selected from this population will have a value between 90 and 130.

6-2. For a standardized normal distribution, calculate the following probabilities:
  a. $P(0.00 < z \le 2.33)$
  b. $P(-1.00 < z \le 1.00)$
  c. $P(1.78 < z < 2.34)$

6-3. For a normally distributed population with $\mu = 200$ and $\sigma = 20$, determine the standardized z-value for each of the following:
  a. $x = 225$
  b. $x = 190$
  c. $x = 240$

6-4. For a standardized normal distribution, calculate the following probabilities:
  a. $P(z < 1.5)$
  b. $P(z \ge 0.85)$
  c. $P(-1.28 < z < 1.75)$

6-5. A random variable is known to be normally distributed with the following parameters:

$$\mu = 5.5 \quad \text{and} \quad \sigma = .50$$

  a. Determine the value of x such that the probability of a value from this distribution exceeding x is at most 0.10.
  b. Referring to your answer in part a, what must the population mean be changed to if the

probability of exceeding the value of x found in part a is reduced from 0.10 to 0.05?

6-6. For a standardized normal distribution, determine a value, say z_0, so that
  a. $P(0 < z < z_0) = 0.4772$
  b. $P(-z_0 \le z < 0) = 0.45$
  c. $P(-z_0 \le z \le z_0) = 0.95$
  d. $P(z > z_0) = 0.025$
  e. $P(z \le z_0) = 0.01$

6-7. Assume that a random variable is normally distributed with a mean of 1,500 and a variance of 324.
  a. What is the probability that a randomly selected value will be greater than 1,550?
  b. What is the probability that a randomly selected value will be less than 1,485?
  c. What is the probability that a randomly selected value will be either less than 1,475 or greater than 1,535?

6-8. A randomly selected value from a normal distribution is found to be 2.1 standard deviations above its mean.
  a. What is the probability that a randomly selected value from the distribution will be greater than 2.1 standard deviations above the mean?
  b. What is the probability that a randomly selected value from the distribution will be less than 2.1 standard deviations from the mean?

6-9. A random variable is normally distributed with a mean of 60 and a standard deviation of 9.
  a. What is the probability that a randomly selected value from the distribution will be less than 46.5?
  b. What is the probability that a randomly selected value from the distribution will be greater than 78?
  c. What is the probability that a randomly selected value will be between 51 and 73.5?

6-10. A random variable is normally distributed with a mean of 25 and a standard deviation of 5. If an observation is randomly selected from the distribution:

   a. What value will be exceeded 10% of the time?

   b. What value will be exceeded 85% of the time?

   c. Determine two values of which the smallest has 25% of the values below it and the largest has 25% of the values above it.

   d. What value will 15% of the observations be below?

6-11. Consider a random variable, z, that has a standardized normal distribution. Determine the following probabilities:

   a. $P(0 < z < 1.96)$

   b. $P(z > 1.645)$

   c. $P(1.28 < z \le 2.33)$

   d. $P(-2 \le z \le 3)$

   e. $P(z > -1)$

6-12. For the following normal distributions with parameters as specified, calculate the required probabilities:

   a. $\mu = 5, \sigma = 2$; calculate $P(0 < x < 8)$.

   b. $\mu = 5, \sigma = 4$; calculate $P(0 < x < 8)$.

   c. $\mu = 3, \sigma = 2$; calculate $P(0 < x < 8)$.

   d. $\mu = 4, \sigma = 3$; calculate $P(x > 1)$.

   e. $\mu = 0, \sigma = 3$; calculate $P(x > 1)$.

6-13. A random variable, x, has a normal distribution with $\mu = 13.6$ and $\sigma = 2.90$. Determine a value, x_0, so that

   a. $P(x > x_0) = 0.05$.

   b. $P(x \le x_0) = 0.975$.

   c. $P(\mu - x_0 \le x \le \mu + x_0) = 0.95$.

Business Applications

6-14. The average number of acres burned by forest and range fires in a large New Mexico county is 4,300 acres per year, with a standard deviation of 750 acres. The distribution of the number of acres burned is normal.

   a. Compute the probability in any year that more than 5,000 acres will be burned.

   b. Determine the probability in any year that fewer then 4,000 acres will be burned.

   c. What is the probability that between 2,500 and 4,200 acres will be burned?

   d. In those years when more than 5,500 acres are burned, help is needed from eastern-region fire teams. Determine the probability help will be needed in any year.

6-15. In the National Weekly Edition of the *Washington Post* (December 19–25, 2005), firstStreet, Inc. advertised an atomic digital watch from LaCrosse Technology. It is radio-controlled and maintains its accuracy by reading a radio signal from a WWVB radio signal from Colorado. It neither loses nor gains a second in 20 million years. It is powered by a 3-volt lithium battery expected to last three years. Suppose the life of the battery has a standard deviation of 0.3 years and is normally distributed.

   a. Determine the probability that the watch's battery will last longer than $3\frac{1}{2}$ years.

   b. Calculate the probability that the watch's battery will last more than 2.75 years.

   c. Compute the length-of-life value for which 10% of the watch's batteries last longer.

6-16. A global financial institution transfers a large data file every evening from offices around the world to its New York City headquarters. Once the file is received, it must be cleaned and partitioned before being stored in the company's data warehouse. Each file is the same size and the time required to transfer, clean, and partition a file is normally distributed, with a mean of 1.5 hours and a standard deviation of 15 minutes.

   a. If one file is selected at random, what is the probability that it will take longer than 1 hour and 55 minutes to transfer, clean, and partition the file?

   b. If a manager must be present until 85% of the files are transferred, cleaned, and partitioned, how long will the manager need to be there?

   c. What percentage of the data files will take between 63 minutes and 110 minutes to be transferred, cleaned, and partitioned?

6-17. Bowser Bites Industries (BBI) sells large bags of dog food to warehouse clubs. BBI uses an automatic filling process to fill the bags. Weights of the filled bags are approximately normally distributed with a mean of 50 kilograms and a standard deviation of 1.25 kilograms.

   a. What is the probability that a filled bag will weigh less than 49.5 kilograms?

   b. What is the probability that a randomly sampled filled bag will weigh between 48.5 and 51 kilograms?

   c. What is the minimum weight a bag of dog food could be and remain in the top 15% of all bags filled?

   d. BBI is unable to adjust the mean of the filling process. However, it is able to adjust the standard deviation of the filling process. What would the standard deviation need to be so that no more than 2% of all filled bags weigh more than 52 kilograms?

6-18. T & S Industries manufactures a wash-down motor that is used in the food processing industry. The motor is marketed with a warranty that guarantees it will be replaced free of charge if it fails within the first 13,000 hours of operation. On the average, T & S wash-down motors operate for 15,000 hours with a standard deviation of 1,250 hours before failing. The number of operating hours before failure is approximately normally distributed.

   a. What is the probability that a wash-down motor will have to be replaced free of charge?

   b. What percentage of T & S wash-down motors can be expected to operate for more than 17,500 hours?

   c. If T & S wants to design a wash-down motor so that no more than 1% are replaced free of charge, what would the average hours of operation before failure have to be if the standard deviation remains at 1,250 hours?

6-19. An Internet retailer stocks a popular electronic toy at a central warehouse that supplies the eastern United States. Every week the retailer makes a decision about how many units of the toy to stock. Suppose that weekly demand for the toy is approximately normally distributed with a mean of 2,500 units and a standard deviation of 300 units.

   a. If the retailer wants to limit the probability of being out of stock of the electronic toy to no more than 2.5% in a week, how many units should the central warehouse stock?

   b. If the retailer has 2,750 units on hand at the start of the week, what is the probability that weekly demand will be greater than inventory?

   c. If the standard deviation of weekly demand for the toy increases from 300 units to 500 units, how many more toys would have to be stocked to ensure that the probability of weekly demand exceeding inventory is no more than 2.5%?

6-20. A private equity firm is evaluating two alternative investments. Although the returns are random, each investment's return can be described using a normal distribution. The first investment has a mean return of $2,000,000 with a standard deviation of $125,000. The second investment has a mean return of $2,275,000 with a standard deviation of $500,000.

   a. How likely is it that the first investment will return $1,900,000 or less?

   b. How likely is it that the second investment will return $1,900,000 or less?

   c. If the firm would like to limit the probability of a return being less than $1,750,000, which investment should it make?

6-21. A-1 Plumbing and Repair provides customers with firm quotes for a plumbing repair job before actually starting the job. In order to be able to do this, A-1 has been very careful to maintain time records over the years. For example, it has determined that the time it takes to remove a broken sink disposal and install a new unit is normally distributed with a mean equal to 47 minutes and a standard deviation equal to 12 minutes. The company bills at $75.00 for the first 30 minutes and $2.00 per minute for anything beyond 30 minutes.

   Suppose the going rate for this procedure by other plumbing shops in the area is $85.00, not including the cost of the new equipment. If A-1 bids the disposal job at $85, on what percentage of such jobs will the actual time required exceed the time for which it will be getting paid?

6-22. J.J. Kettering & Associates is a financial planning group in Fresno, California. The company specializes in doing financial planning for schoolteachers in the Fresno area. As such, it administers a 403(b) tax shelter annuity program in which public schoolteachers can participate. The teachers can contribute up to $20,000 per year on a pretax basis to the 403(b) account. Very few teachers have incomes sufficient to allow them to make the maximum contribution. The lead analyst at J.J. Kettering & Associates has recently analyzed the company's 403(b) clients and determined that the annual contribution is approximately normally distributed with a mean equal to $6,400. Further, he has determined that the probability a customer will contribute over $13,000 is 0.025. Based on this information, what is the standard deviation of contributions to the 403(b) program?

6-23. A senior loan officer for Wells Fargo Bank has recently studied the bank's real estate loan portfolio and found that the distribution of loan balances is approximately normally distributed with a mean of $155,600 and a standard deviation equal to $33,050. As part of an internal audit, bank auditors recently randomly selected 100 real estate loans from the portfolio of all loans and found that 80 of these loans had balances below $170,000. The senior loan officer is concerned that the sample selected by the auditors is not representative of the overall portfolio. In particular, he is interested in knowing the expected proportion of loans in the portfolio that would have balances below $170,000. You are asked to conduct an appropriate analysis and write a short report to the senior loan officers with your conclusion about the sample.

6-24. MP-3 players, and most notably the Apple iPod, have become an industry standard for people who want to have access to their favorite music and videos in a portable environment. The iPod can store massive numbers of songs and videos with its 60-GB hard drive. Although owners of the iPod have the potential to store lots of data, a recent study showed that the actual disk storage being used is normally distributed with a mean equal to 1.95 GB and a standard deviation of 0.48 GB. Suppose a competitor to Apple is thinking of entering the market with a low-cost iPod clone that has only 1.0 GB of storage. The marketing slogan will be "Why Pay for Storage Capacity that You Don't Need?"

Based on the data from the study of iPod owners, what percentage of owners, based on their current usage, would have enough capacity with the new 1-GB player?

6-25. According to *Business Week* (Pallavi Gogoi, "Pregnant with Possibility," December 26, 2005), Maternity Chic, a purveyor of designer maternity wear, sells dresses and pants priced around $150 each for an average total sale of $1,200. The total sale has a normal distribution with a standard deviation of $350.

a. Calculate the probability that a randomly selected customer will have a total sale of more than $1,500.

b. Compute the probability that the total sale will be within 2 standard deviations of the mean total sales.

c. Determine the median total sale.

6-26. *USA Today* reported (Sandra Block, "Costs rising, so tame credit card bills now," October 18, 2005) that the average credit card debt per U.S. household was $9,312 in 2004. Assume that the distribution of credit card debt per household has a normal distribution with a standard deviation of $3,000.

a. Determine the percentage of households that have a credit card debt of more than $15,000.

b. One household has a credit card debt that is at the 95th percentile. Determine its credit card debt.

c. If four households were selected at random, determine the probability that at least half of them would have credit card debt of more than $15,000.

6-27. The Aberdeen Coca-Cola Bottling located in Aberdeen, North Carolina, is the bottler and distributor for Coca-Cola products in the Aberdeen area. The company's product line includes 12-ounce cans of Coke products. The cans are filled by an automated filling process that can be adjusted to any mean fill volume and will fill cans according to a normal distribution. However, not all cans will contain the same volume due to variation in the filling process. Historical records show that regardless of what the mean is set at, the standard deviation in fill will be 0.035 ounces. Operations managers at the plant know that if they put too much Coke in a can, the company loses money. If too little is put in the can, customers are short-changed and the North Carolina Department of Weights and Measures may fine the company. The following diagram shows how soft drinks are made:

a. Suppose the industry standards for fill volume call for each 12-ounce can to contain between 11.98 and 12.02 ounces. Assuming that the Aberdeen manager sets the mean fill at 12 ounces, what is the probability that a can will contain a volume of Coke product that falls in the desired range?

b. Assume that the Aberdeen manager is focused on an upcoming audit by the North Carolina Department of Weights and Measures. She knows that their process is to select one Coke can at random and if it contains less than 11.97 ounces, the company will be reprimanded and potentially fined. Assuming that the manager wants at most a 5% chance of this happening, at

Source: Pall Corporation, January 2006.

what level should she set the mean fill level? Comment on the ramifications of this step, assuming that company fills tens of thousands of cans each week.

6-28. Georgia-Pacific is a major forest products company in the United States. In addition to timberlands, the company owns and operates numerous manufacturing plants that make lumber and paper products. At one of their plywood plants, the operations manager has been struggling to make sure that the plywood thickness meets quality standards. Specifically, all sheets of their $\frac{3}{4}$-inch plywood must fall within the range 0.747 to 0.753 inches in thickness. Studies have shown that the current process produces plywood that has thicknesses that are normally distributed with a mean of 0.751 inches and a standard deviation equal to 0.004 inches.

   a. Use either Excel or Minitab to determine the proportion of plywood sheets that will meet quality specifications (0.747 to 0.753), given how the current process is performing.

   b. Referring to part a, suppose the manager is unhappy with the proportion of product that is meeting specifications. Assuming that he can get the mean adjusted to 0.75 inches, what must the standard deviation be if he is going to have 98% of his product meet specifications?

Computer Database Exercises

6-29. An article in *USA Today* (Julie Appleby, "AARP: Drug prices zoom past inflation," November 2, 2005) indicated that the wholesale prices for the 200 brand-name drugs most commonly used by Americans over age 50 rose an average of 6.1% in the 12 months ended June, 2005. The report listed the 10 drugs with the largest increases in the first 6 months of 2005. Atrovent, a treatment for lung conditions such as emphysema, had the largest increase. The price per day, on average, rose from $2.12 to $2.51. The file entitled **Drug$** contains data similar to that obtained in AARP's research.

   a. Produce a relative frequency histogram for these data. Does it seem plausible the data were sampled from a population that was normally distributed?

   b. Compute the mean and standard deviation for the sample data in the file **Drug$**.

   c. Assuming the sample came from a normally distributed population and the sample standard deviation is a good approximation for the population standard deviation, determine the probability that a randomly chosen transaction would yield a price of $2.12 or smaller even though the population mean was still $2.51.

6-30. *USA Today*'s annual survey of public flagship universities (Arienne Thompson and Breanne Gilpatrick, "Double-digit hikes are down," October 5, 2005) indicates that the median increase in in-state tuition was 7% for the 2005–2006 academic year. A file entitled **Tuition** contains the percentage change for the 67 flagship universities.

   a. Produce a relative frequency histogram for these data. Does it seem plausible that the data is from a population which has a normal distribution?

   b. Suppose the decimal point of the three largest numbers had inadvertently been moved one place to the right in the data. Move the decimal point one place to the left and reconstruct the relative frequency histogram. Now does it seem plausible that the data have an approximate normal distribution?

   c. Use the normal distribution of part b to approximate the proportion of universities that raised their in-state tuition more than 10%. Use the appropriate parameters obtained from this population.

   d. Use the normal distribution of part b to approximate the fifth percentile for the percent of tuition increase.

6-31. The PricewaterhouseCoopers Saratoga release, 2005/2006 Human Capital Index Report, indicated that the average cost for an American company to fill a job vacancy during that time period was $3,270. Sample data similar to that used in the study is in a file entitled **Hired**.

   a. Produce a relative frequency histogram for these data. Does it seem plausible the data were sampled from a normally distributed population?

   b. Calculate the mean and standard deviation of the cost of filling a job vacancy.

   c. Determine the probability that the cost of filling a job vacancy would be between $2,000 and $3,000.

   d. Given that the cost of filling a job vacancy was between $2,000 and $3,000, determine the probability that it would be more than $2,500.

6.2 Other Continuous Probability Distributions

The normal distribution is the most frequently used continuous probability distribution in statistics. However, there are other continuous distributions that apply to business decision making. This section introduces two of these: the uniform distribution and the exponential distribution.

FIGURE 6.12

Uniform Distributions

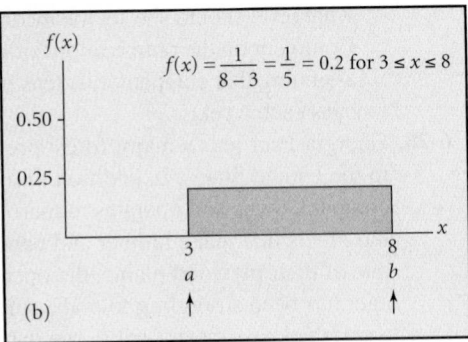

CHAPTER OUTCOME #4

Uniform Probability Distribution

The *uniform distribution* is sometimes referred to as the *distribution of little information*, because the probability over any interval of the continuous random variable is the same as for any other interval of the same width.

Equation 6.3 defines the *continuous uniform density function*.

Continuous Uniform Density Function

$$f(x) = \begin{cases} \dfrac{1}{b-a} & \text{if } a \le x \le b \\ 0 & \text{otherwise} \end{cases} \qquad (6.3)$$

where:

$f(x)$ = Value of the density function at any x-value
a = Lower limit of the interval from a to b
b = Upper limit of the interval from a to b

Figure 6.12 illustrates two examples of uniform probability distributions with different a to b intervals. Note the height of the probability density function is the same for all values of x between a and b for a given distribution. The graph of the uniform distribution is a rectangle.

EXAMPLE 6-3 Using the Uniform Distribution

TRY PROBLEM 6.32

Stern Manufacturing Company   The Stern Manufacturing Company makes seat-belt buckles for all types of vehicles. The inventory level for the spring mechanism used in producing the buckles is only enough to continue production for two more hours. The purchasing clerk estimates that the springs will be delivered one to four hours from the time they are ordered. Because the dispatcher offers no other information about the pending delivery schedule, the time it will take to replenish the inventory is said to be *uniformly distributed* over the interval of one to four hours. We are interested in the probability that the company will run out of parts due to the shipment taking more than two hours. The probability can be determined using the following steps:

Step 1 **Define the density function.**
The height of the probability rectangle, $f(x)$, for the delivery-time interval of one to four hours is determined using Equation 6.3, as follows:

$$f(x) = \frac{1}{b-a}$$

$$f(x) = \frac{1}{4-1} = \frac{1}{3} = 0.33$$

Step 2 Define the event of interest.

The production scheduler is specifically concerned that shipment will take longer than two hours to arrive. This event of interest is $x > 2.0$.

Step 3 Calculate the required probability.

We determine the probability as follows:

$$P(x > 2.0) = 1 - P(x \le 2.0)$$
$$= 1 - f(x)(2.0 - 1.0)$$
$$= 1 - 0.33(1.0)$$
$$= 1 - 0.33$$
$$= 0.67$$

Thus, there is a 67% chance that production will be delayed because the shipment is more than two hours late.

Like the normal distribution, the uniform distribution can be further described by specifying the mean and the standard deviation. These values are computed using Equations 6.4 and 6.5.

Mean and Standard Deviation of a Uniform Distribution

Mean (Expected Value):

$$E(x) = \mu = \frac{a+b}{2} \tag{6.4}$$

Standard Deviation:

$$\sigma = \sqrt{\frac{(b-a)^2}{12}} \tag{6.5}$$

where:

a = Lower limit of the interval from a to b
b = Upper limit of the interval from a to b

EXAMPLE 6-4 The Mean and Standard Deviation of a Uniform Distribution

TRY PROBLEM 6.33

Austrian Airlines   The service manager for Austrian Airlines is uncertain about the time needed for the ground crew to turn an airplane around from the time it lands until it is ready to take off. He has been given information from the operations supervisor indicating that the times seem to range between 15 and 45 minutes. Without any further information, the service manager will apply a uniform distribution to the turnaround.

Based on this, he can determine the mean and standard deviation for the airplane turn-around times using the following steps:

Step 1 Define the density function.

Equation 6.3 can be used to define the distribution:

$$f(x) = \frac{1}{b-a} = \frac{1}{45-15} = \frac{1}{30} = 0.0333$$

Step 2 Compute the mean of the probability distribution using Equation 6.4.

$$\mu = \frac{a+b}{2} = \frac{15+45}{2} = 30$$

Thus, the mean turnaround time is 30 minutes.

Step 3 Compute the standard deviation using Equation 6.5.

$$\sigma = \sqrt{\frac{(b-a)^2}{12}} = \sqrt{\frac{(45-15)^2}{12}} = \sqrt{75} = 8.66$$

The standard deviation is 8.66 minutes.

CHAPTER OUTCOME #5

The Exponential Probability Distribution

Another continuous probability distribution that is frequently used in business situations is the *exponential distribution*. The exponential distribution is used to measure the time that elapses between two occurrences of an event, such as the time between "hits" on an Internet home page. The exponential distribution might also be used to describe the time between arrivals of customers at a bank drive-in teller window or the time between failures of an electronic component. Equation 6.6 shows the probability density function for the exponential distribution.

Exponential Density Function

A continuous random variable that is exponentially distributed has the probability density function given by

$$f(x) = \lambda e^{-\lambda x}, \qquad x \geq 0 \qquad \textbf{(6.6)}$$

where:

$$e = 2.71828\ldots$$
$$1/\lambda = \text{the mean time between events } (\lambda > 0)$$

Note, the parameter that defines the exponential distribution is λ (lambda). You should recall from Chapter 5 that λ is the mean value for the Poisson distribution. If the number of occurrences per time period is known to be Poisson distributed with a mean of λ, then the time between occurrences will be exponentially distributed with a mean time of $1/\lambda$.

If we select a value for λ, we can graph the exponential distribution by substituting λ and different values for x into Equation 6.6. For instance, Figure 6.13 shows exponential density functions for $\lambda = 0.5$, $\lambda = 1.0$, $\lambda = 2.0$, and $\lambda = 3.0$. Note in Figure 6.13 that for any exponential density function, $f(x), f(0) = \lambda$, as x increases, $f(x)$ approaches zero. It can

FIGURE 6.13

**Exponential
Distributions**

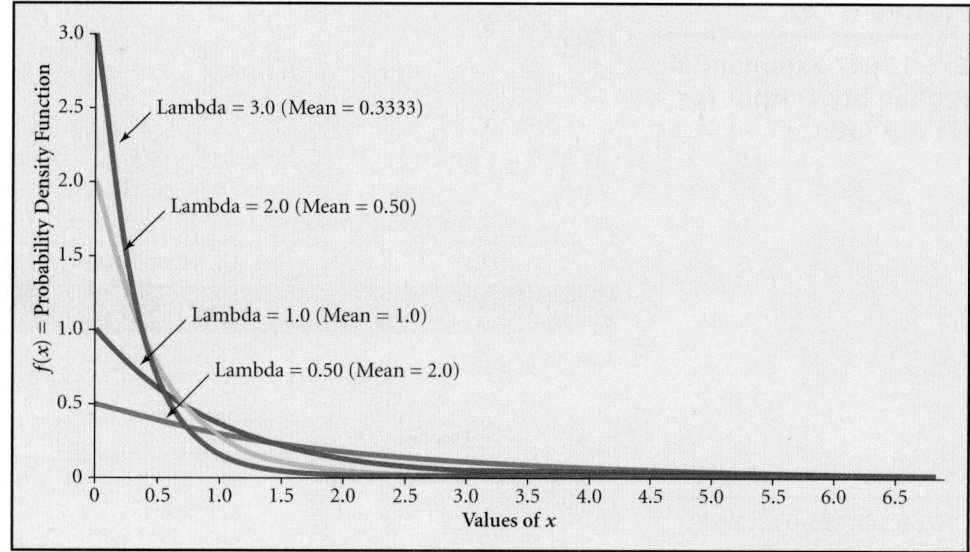

also be shown that *the standard deviation of any exponential distribution is equal to the mean, $1/\lambda$.*

As with any continuous probability distribution, the probability that a value will fall within an interval is the area under the graph between the two points defining the interval. Equation 6.7 is used to find the probability that a value will be equal to or less than a particular value for an exponential distribution.

Exponential Probability

$$P(0 \le x \le a) = 1 - e^{-\lambda a} \tag{6.7}$$

where:

a = the value of interest
$1/\lambda$ = mean
e = natural number = 2.71828

Appendix E contains a table of $e^{-\lambda a}$ values for different values of λa. You can use this table and Equation 6.7 to find the probabilities when the λa of interest is contained in the table. You can also use Minitab or Excel to find exponential probabilities, as the following application illustrates.

**Business
Application**

Excel and Minitab Tutorial

HAINES INTERNET SERVICES The Haines Internet Services Company has determined that the number of customers who attempt to connect to the Internet per hour is Poisson distributed with $\lambda = 30$ per hour. The time between connect requests is exponentially distributed with a mean time between calls of 2.0 minutes, computed as follows:

$$\lambda = 30 \text{ per } 60 \text{ minutes} = 0.50 \text{ per minute}$$

The mean time between calls, then, is

$$1/\lambda = \frac{1}{0.50} = 2.0 \text{ minutes}$$

Because of the system that Haines uses, if customer requests are too close together— 45 seconds (0.75 minutes) or less—some customers fail to connect. The managers at Haines are analyzing whether they should purchase new equipment that will eliminate this problem. They need to know the probability that a customer will fail to connect. Thus, they want

$$P(x \le 0.75 \text{ minutes}) = ?$$

FIGURE 6.14A

Excel 2007 Exponential Probability Output for Haines Internet Services

Inputs:
x = 0.75 minutes
= 45 seconds
Lambda = 0.50 per minute
True = output is the cumulative probability

Excel 2007 Instructions:
1. Open blank worksheet.
2. Select **Formulas** tab.
3. Select **More Functions**.
4. Select **Statistical > EXPONDIST**.
5. Enter values for *x*, lambda and "true" for cumulative.
6. Click **OK**.

FIGURE 6.14B

Minitab Exponential Probability Output for Haines Internet Services

Minitab Instructions:
1. Choose **Calc > Probability Distributions > Exponential**.
2. Choose **Cumulative probability**.
3. In **Scale**, enter μ.
4. In **Input constant**, enter value for *x*.
5. Click **OK**.

To find this probability using a calculator, we need to first determine λa. In this example, $\lambda = 0.50$ and $a = 0.75$. Then,

$$\lambda a = (0.50)(0.75) = 0.3750$$

We find that the desired probability is

$$1 - e^{-\lambda a} = 1 - e^{-0.3750}$$
$$= 0.3127$$

The managers can also use the **EXPONDIST** function in Excel or the **Probability Distribution** command in Minitab to compute the precise value for the desired probability.[4] Figure 6.14A and Figure 6.14B show that the chance of failing to connect is 0.3127. This means that nearly one-third of the customers will experience a problem with the current system.

---

[4] The Excel EXPONDIST function requires that λ be inputted rather than $1/\lambda$.

6-2: Exercises

Skill Development

6-32. A continuous random variable is uniformly distributed between 100 and 150.
   a. What is the probability a randomly selected value will be greater than 135?
   b. What is the probability a randomly selected value will be less than 115?
   c. What is the probability a randomly selected value will be between 115 and 135?

6-33. Suppose a random variable, x, has a uniform distribution with $a = 5$ and $b = 9$.
   a. Calculate $P(5.5 \leq x \leq 8)$.
   b. Determine $P(x > 7)$.
   c. Compute the mean, μ, and standard deviation, σ, of this random variable.
   d. Determine the probability that x is in the interval $(\mu \pm 2\sigma)$.

6-34. Let x be an exponential random variable with $\lambda = 0.5$. Calculate the following probabilities:
   a. $P(x < 5)$
   b. $P(x > 6)$
   c. $P(5 \leq x \leq 6)$
   d. $P(x \geq 2)$
   e. the probability that x is at most 6

6-35. The time between telephone calls to a cable television payment processing center follows an exponential distribution with a mean of 1.5 minutes.
   a. What is the probability that the time between the next two calls will be 45 seconds or less?
   b. What is the probability that the time between the next two calls will be greater than 112.5 seconds?

6-36. The useful life of an electrical component is exponentially distributed with a mean of 2,500 hours.
   a. What is the probability the circuit will last more than 3,000 hours?
   b. What is the probability the circuit will last between 2,500 and 2,750 hours?
   c. What is the probability the circuit will fail within the first 2,000 hours?

6-37. Determine the following:
   a. the probability that a uniform random variable whose range is between 10 and 30 assumes a value in the interval (10 to 20) or (15 to 25).
   b. the quartiles for a uniform random variable whose range is from 4 to 20.
   c. the mean time between events for an exponential random variable that has a median equal to 10.
   d. the 90th percentile for an exponential random variable that has the mean time between events equal to 0.4.

Business Applications

6-38. When only the value-added time is considered, the time it takes to build a laser printer is thought to be uniformly distributed between 8 and 15 hours.
   a. What are the chances that it will take more than 10 value-added hours to build a printer?
   b. How likely is it that a printer will require less than 9 value-added hours?
   c. Suppose a single customer orders two printers. Determine the probability that the first and second printer each will require less than 9 value-added hours to complete.

6-39. The time to failure for a power supply unit used in a particular brand of personal computer is thought to be exponentially distributed with a mean of 4,000 hours as per the contract between the vendor and the PC maker. The PC manufacturer has just had a warranty return from a customer who had the power supply fail after 2,100 hours of use.
   a. What is the probability that the power supply would fail at 2,100 hours or less? Based on this probability, do you feel the PC maker has a right to require that the power supply maker refund the money on this unit?
   b. Assuming that the PC maker has sold 100,000 computers with this power supply, approximately how many should be returned due to failure at 2,100 hours or less?

6-40. *USA Today* reported (Dennis Cauchon and Julie Appleby, "Hospitals go where the money is," January 3, 2006) that the average patient cost per stay in American hospitals was $8,166. Assume that this cost is exponentially distributed.
   a. Determine the probability that a randomly selected patient's stay in an American hospital will cost more than $10,000.
   b. Calculate the probability that a randomly selected patient's stay in an American hospital will cost less than $5,000.
   c. Compute the probability that a randomly selected patient's stay in an American hospital will cost between $8,000 and $12,000.

6-41. Suppose you are traveling on business to a foreign country for the first time. You do not have a bus schedule or a watch with you. However, you have been told that buses stop in front of your hotel every 20 minutes throughout the day. If you show up at the bus stop at a random moment during the day, what is the probability that
   a. you will have to wait for more than 10 minutes?
   b. you will only have to wait for 6 minutes or less?
   c. you will have to wait between 8 and 15 minutes?

6-42. A delicatessen located in the heart of the business district of a large city serves a variety of customers. The delicatessen is open 24 hours a day every day of the week. In an effort to speed up take-out orders, the deli accepts orders by fax. If, on the average, 20 orders are received by fax every two hours throughout the day, find the
   a. probability that a faxed order will arrive within the next 9 minutes.
   b. probability that the time between two faxed orders will be between and 3 and 6 minutes.
   c. probability that 12 or more minutes will elapse between faxed orders.

6-43. During the busiest time of the day customers arrive at the Daily Grind Coffee House on the average of 15 customers per 20-minute period.
   a. What is the probability that a customer will arrive within the next 3 minutes?
   b. What is the probability that the time between the arrivals of customers is 12 minutes or more?
   c. What is the probability that the next customer will arrive between 4 and 6 minutes?

6-44. The time required to prepare a dry cappuccino using whole milk at the Daily Grind Coffee House is uniformly distributed between 25 and 35 seconds. Assuming a customer has just ordered a whole-milk dry cappuccino,
   a. What is the probability that the preparation time will be more than 29 seconds?
   b. What is the probability that the preparation time will be between 28 and 33 seconds?
   c. What percentage of whole-milk dry cappuccinos will be prepared within 31 seconds?
   d. What is the standard deviation of preparation times for a dry cappuccino using whole milk at the Daily Grind Coffee House?

6-45. American Airlines states that the flight between Fort Lauderdale, Florida, and Los Angeles takes 5 hours and 37 minutes. Assume that the actual flight times are uniformly distributed between 5 hours and 20 minutes and 5 hours and 50 minutes.
   a. Determine the probability that the flight will be more than 10 minutes late.
   b. Calculate the probability that the flight will be more than 5 minutes early.
   c. Compute the average flight time between these two cities.
   d. Determine the variance in the flight times between these two cities.

6-46. A corrugated container company is testing whether a computer decision model will improve the uptime of its box production line. Currently, knives used in the production process are checked manually and replaced when the operator believes the knives are dull. Knives are expensive, so operators are encouraged not to change the knives early. Unfortunately, if knives are left running for too long, the cuts are not made properly, which can jam the machines and require that the entire process be shut down for unscheduled maintenance. Shutting down the entire line is costly in terms of lost production and repair work, so the company would like to reduce the number of shutdowns that occur daily. Currently, the company experiences an average of 0.75 knife-related shutdowns per shift, exponentially distributed. In testing, the computer decision model reduced the frequency of knife-related shutdowns to an average of 0.20 per shift, exponentially distributed. The decision model is expensive but the company will install it if it can help achieve the target of four consecutive shifts without a knife-related shutdown.
   a. Under the current system, what is the probability that the plant would run four or more consecutive shifts without a knife-related shutdown?
   b. Using the computer decision model, what is the probability that the plant could run four or more consecutive shifts without a knife-related shutdown? Has the decision model helped the company achieve its goal?
   c. What would be the maximum average number of shutdowns allowed per day such that the probability of experiencing four or more consecutive shifts without a knife-related shutdown is greater than or equal to 0.70?

6-47. The average amount spent on electronics each year in U.S. households is $1,250 according to an article in *USA Today* (Michelle Kessler, "Gadget makers make mad dash to market," January 4, 2006). Assume that the amount spent on electronics each year has an exponential distribution.
   a. Calculate the probability that a randomly chosen U.S. household would spend more than $5,000 on electronics.
   b. Compute the probability that a randomly chosen U.S. household would spend more than the average amount spent by U.S. households.
   c. Determine the probability that a randomly chosen U.S. household would spend more than 1 standard deviation below the average amount spent by U.S. households.

Computer Database Exercises

6-48. Rolls-Royce PLC provides forecasts for the business jet market and covers the regional and major aircraft markets. In a recent release, Rolls-Royce indicated that in both North America and Europe the number of delayed departures has declined since a peak in 1999/2000. This is partly due to a reduction in the number of flights at major airports and the younger aircraft fleets, but also results from improvements in Air Traffic Management (ATM) capacity, especially in Europe. Comparing January–April 2003 with the same period in 2001 (for similar traffic levels), the average en route delay per flight was reduced by 65%, from 2.2 minutes to 0.7 minutes. The file entitled **Delays** contains a possible sample of the en route delay times in minutes for 200 flights.

a. Produce a relative frequency histogram for this data. Does it seem plausible the data come from a population that has an exponential distribution?

b. Calculate the mean and standard deviation of the en route delays.

c. Determine the probability that this exponential random variable will be smaller than its mean.

d. Determine the median time in minutes for the en route delays assuming they have an exponential distribution with a mean equal to that obtained in part b.

e. Using only the information obtained in parts c and d, describe the shape of this distribution. Does this agree with the findings in part a?

6-49. The city of San Luis Obispo, California, Transit Program provides daily fixed-route transit service to the general public within the city limits and to Cal Poly State University's staff and students. The most heavily traveled route schedules a city bus to arrive at Cal Poly at 8:54 A.M. The file entitled **Late** lists plausible differences between the actual and scheduled time of arrival rounded to the nearest minute for this route.

a. Produce a relative frequency histogram for this data. Does it seem plausible the data came from a population that has a uniform distribution?

b. Provide the density for this uniform distribution.

c. Classes start 10 minutes after the hour and classes are a 5-minute walk from the drop-off point. Determine the probability that a randomly chosen bus on this route would cause the students on board to be late for class. Assume the differences form a continuous uniform distribution with a range the same as the sample.

d. Determine the median difference between the actual and scheduled arrival times.

6-50. *USA Today* has reported (Kathy Chu, "Banks rake in more in fees but don't share," December 1, 2005) that as of October, 2005 the average fee charged by banks to process a ATM transaction was $2.91. The file entitled **ATM Fees** contains a list of ATM fees that might be required by banks.

a. Produce a relative frequency histogram for this data. Does it seem plausible the data came from a population that has an exponential distribution?

b. Calculate the mean and standard deviation of the ATM fees.

c. Assume that the distribution of ATM fees is exponentially distributed with the same mean as that of the sample. Determine the probability that a randomly chosen bank's ATM fee would be greater than $3.00.

Summary and Conclusions

Chapter 6 has extended the discussion of probability distributions by introducing three continuous probability distributions: the normal, uniform, and exponential distributions. Although all three distributions have applications in business decision making, the normal distribution is by far the most important. As you will see in subsequent chapters, the normal distribution is used in many ways in both hypothesis testing and estimation.

In Chapter 6, we showed that the normal distribution, with its special properties, is used extensively in statistical decision making. You will encounter the normal distribution numerous times as you study the material in subsequent chapters. An important point is that any normal distribution can be transformed to the corresponding standard normal probability distribution. You can then use the standard normal distribution to find probabilities associated with the original normal distribution. We also

illustrated how Excel and Minitab can also be used to find probabilities associated with normal and exponential distributions.

The continuous distributions introduced in this chapter (normal, uniform, and exponential) combined with the discrete distributions (binomial, Poisson, and hypergeometric) introduced in Chapter 5 are the distributions that you will very frequently encounter in business decision-making situations. Figure 6.15 summarizes these discrete and continuous probability distributions.

Subsequent chapters will introduce other continuous probability distributions. Among these will be the *t-distribution*, the *chi-square distribution*, and the *F-distribution*. These additional distributions also play important roles in statistical decision making. The basic concept that the area under a continuous curve is equivalent to the probability is true for all continuous distributions.

FIGURE 6.15

Probability Distribution Summary

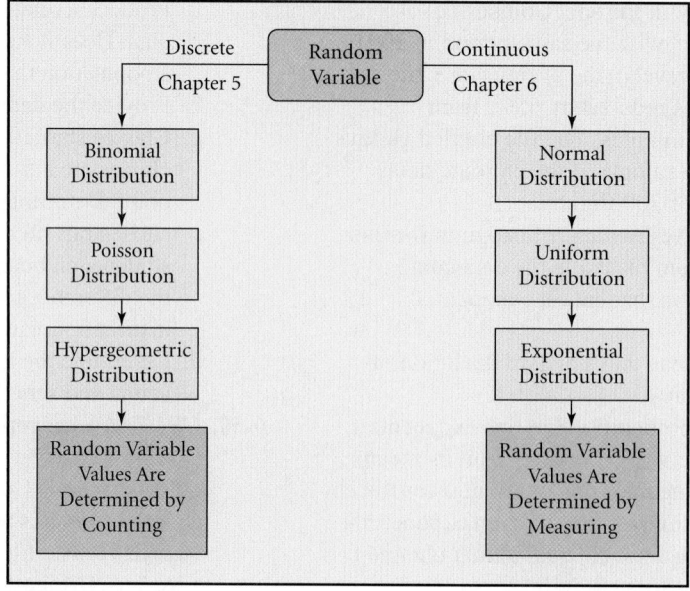

Equations

Normal Distribution Density Function

$$f(x) = \frac{1}{\sigma\sqrt{2\pi}} e^{-(x-\mu)^2/2\sigma^2}$$ **(6.1)**

Standardized Normal z-Value

$$z = \frac{x - \mu}{\sigma}$$ **(6.2)**

Continuous Uniform Density Function

$$f(x) = \begin{cases} \dfrac{1}{b-a} & \text{if } a \le x \le b \\ 0 & \text{otherwise} \end{cases}$$ **(6.3)**

Mean of the Uniform Distribution

$$E(x) = \mu = \frac{a+b}{2}$$ **(6.4)**

Standard Deviation of the Uniform Distribution

$$\sigma = \sqrt{\frac{(b-a)^2}{12}}$$ **(6.5)**

Exponential Density Function

$$f(x) = \lambda e^{-\lambda x}, \qquad x \ge 0$$ **(6.6)**

Exponential Probability

$$P(0 \le x \le a) = 1 - e^{-\lambda a}$$ **(6.7)**

Key Terms

Normal distribution   253
Standard normal distribution   254

Chapter Exercises

Conceptual Questions

6-51. The probability that a value from a normally distributed random variable will exceed the mean is 0.50. The same is true for the uniform distribution. Why is this not necessarily true for the exponential distribution? Discuss and show examples to illustrate your point.

6-52. Suppose you tell one of your fellow students that when working with a continuous distribution, it does not make sense to try to compute the probability of any specific value since it will be zero. She says that this can't be true, since when the experiment is performed some value must occur so the probability can't be zero. Your task is to respond to her statement and in doing so explain why it is appropriate to find the probability for specific ranges of values for a continuous distribution.

6-53. Discuss the difference between discrete and continuous probability distributions. Discuss two situations where a variable of interest may be considered either continuous or discrete.

6-54. Recall the Empirical Rule from Chapter 3. It stated that if the data distribution is bell-shaped, then the interval $\mu \pm \sigma$ contains approximately 68% of the values, $\mu \pm 2\sigma$ contains approximately 95%, and $\mu \pm 3\sigma$ contains virtually all of the data values. The "bell-shaped" distribution referenced is the normal distribution.

   a. Verify that a standard normal distribution contains approximately 68% of the values in the interval $\mu \pm \sigma$.

   b. Verify that a standard normal distribution contains approximately 95% of the values in the interval $\mu \pm 2\sigma$.

   c. Verify that a standard normal distribution contains virtually all of the data in the interval $\mu \pm 3\sigma$.

6-55. The exponential distribution has a characteristic that is called the "memoryless" property. This means $P(X > x) = P(X > x + x_0 | X \geq x_0)$. To illustrate this, consider the calls coming into 911. Suppose that the distribution of the time between occurrences has an exponential distribution with a mean of one half hour ($= 0.5$).

   a. Calculate the probability that no calls come in during the first hour.

   b. Now suppose that you are monitoring the call frequency and you note that a call does not come in during the first two hours, determine the probability that no calls will come in during the next hour.

6-56. Revisit Problem 6-55, but here, let's examine whether it would matter when you started monitoring the 911 calls if the time between occurrences had a uniform distribution with a mean of 2 and a range of 4.

   a. Calculate the probability that no call comes in during the first hour.

   b. Now suppose that you are monitoring the call frequency and you note that no call comes in during the first two hours. Determine the probability that no calls will arrive during the next hour.

Business Applications

6-57. Two automatic dispensing machines are being considered for use in a fast-food chain. The first dispenses an amount of liquid that has a normal distribution with a mean of 11.9 ounces and a standard deviation of 0.07 ounces. The second dispenses an amount of liquid that has a normal distribution with a mean of 12.0 ounces and a standard deviation of 0.05 ounces. Acceptable amounts of dispensed liquid are between 11.9 and 12.0 ounces. Calculate the relevant probabilities and determine which machine should be selected.

6-58. An online article (http://beauty.about.com) by Julyne Derrick, "Shelf Lives: How Long Can you Keep Makeup," suggests that eye shadow and eyeliner each have a shelf life of up to three years. Suppose the shelf lives of these two products are exponentially distributed with an average shelf life of one year.

   a. Calculate the probability that the shelf life of eye shadow will be longer than three years.

   b. Determine the probability that at least one of these products will have a shelf life of more than three years.

   c. Determine the probability that a purchased eyeliner that is useful after one year will be useful after three years.

6-59. One of the products of Pittsburg Plate Glass Industries (PPG) is laminated safety glass. It is made up of two pieces of glass 0.125 inch thick, with a thin layer of vinyl sandwiched between them. The average thickness of the laminated safety glass is 0.25 inch. The thickness of the glass does not vary from the mean by more than 0.10 inch. Assume the thickness of the glass has a uniform distribution.

   a. Provide the density for this uniform distribution.

   b. If the glass has a thickness that is more than 0.05 inch below the mean, it must be discarded for safety considerations. Determine the probability that a randomly selected automobile glass is discarded due to safety considerations.

   c. If the glass is more than 0.075 above the mean, it will create installation problems and must be discarded. Calculate the probability that a randomly selected automobile glass will be rejected due to installation concerns.

   d. Given that a randomly selected automobile glass is not rejected for safety considerations, determine the probability that it will be rejected for installation concerns.

6-60. The Sea Pines Golf Course is preparing for a major LPGA golf tournament. Since parking near the course is extremely limited (room for only 500 cars), the course officials have contracted with the local community to provide parking and a bus shuttle service. Sunday, the final day of the tournament, will have the largest crowd and the officials estimate there will be between 8,000 and 12,000 cars needing parking spaces, but think no value is more likely than another. The tournament committee is discussing how many parking spots to contract from the city. If they want to limit the chance of not having enough provided parking to 10%, how many spaces do they need from the city on Sunday?

6-61. The manager for Select-a-Seat, a company that sells tickets to athletic games, concerts, and other events, has determined that the number of people arriving at the Broadway location on a typical day is Poisson distributed with a mean of 12 per hour. It takes approximately four minutes to process a ticket request. Thus, if customers arrive in intervals that are less than four minutes, they will have to wait. Assuming that a customer has just arrived and the ticket agent is starting to serve that customer, what is the probability that the next customer who arrives will have to wait in line?

6-62. The personnel manager for a large company is interested in the distribution of sick-leave hours for employees of her company. A recent study revealed the distribution to be approximately normal, with a mean of 58 hours per year and a standard deviation of 14 hours.

An office manager in one division has reason to believe that during the past year, two of his employees have taken excessive sick leave relative to everyone else. The first employee used 74 hours of sick leave, and the second used 90 hours. What would you conclude about the office manager's claim and why?

6-63. The Bryce Brothers Lumber Company is considering buying a machine that planes lumber to the correct thickness. The machine is advertised to produce "6-inch lumber" having a thickness that is normally distributed, with a mean of 6 inches and a standard deviation of 0.1 inch.
a. If building standards in the industry require a 99% chance of a board being between 5.85 and 6.15 inches, should Bryce Brothers purchase this machine? Why or why not?
b. To what level would the company that manufactures the machine have to reduce the standard deviation for the machine to conform to industry standards?

6-64. A small private ambulance service in Oklahoma has determined that the time between emergency calls is exponentially distributed with a mean of 41 minutes. When a unit goes on call, it is out of service for 60 minutes. If a unit is busy when an emergency call is received, the call is immediately routed to another service. The company is considering buying a second ambulance. However, before doing so, the owners are interested in determining the probability that a call will come in before the ambulance is back in service. Without knowing the costs involved in this situation, does this probability tend to support the need for a second ambulance? Discuss.

6-65. The St. Maries plywood plant is part of the Potlatch Corporation's Northwest Division. The plywood superintendent organized a study of the tree diameters that are being shipped to the mill. After collecting a large amount of data on diameters, he concluded that the distribution is approximately normally distributed with a mean of 14.25 inches and a standard deviation of 2.92 inches. Because of the way plywood is made, there is a certain amount of waste on each log because the peeling process leaves a core that is approximately 3 inches thick. For this reason, he feels that any log less than 10 inches in diameter is not profitable for making plywood.
a. Based on the data he has collected, what is the probability that a log will be unprofitable?
b. An alternative is to peel the log and then sell the core as "peeler logs." These peeler logs are sold as fence posts and for various landscape projects. There is not as much profit in these peeler logs, however. The superintendent has determined that he can make a profit if the peeler log's diameter is not more than 32% of the diameter of the log. Using this additional information, calculate the proportion of logs that will be unprofitable.

Computer Database Exercises

6-66. Continental Fan Manufacturing Inc. was established in 1986 as a manufacturer and distributor of quality ventilation equipment. Continental Fan's products include the AXC range hood exhaust fans. The file entitled **Fan Life** contains the length of life of 125 randomly chosen AXC fans that were used in an accelerated life-testing experiment.
a. Produce a relative frequency histogram for the data. Does it seem plausible the data came from a population that has an exponential distribution?
b. Calculate the mean and standard deviation of the fans' length of life.
c. Calculate the median length of life of the fans.
d. Determine the probability that a randomly chosen fan will have a life of more than 25,000 hours.

6-67. Team Marketing Report (TMR) produces the Fan Cost Index™ (FCI) survey, now in its 13th year, that tracks the cost of attendance for a family of four at NFL football games. The FCI includes four average-price tickets, four small soft drinks, two small beers, four hot dogs, two game programs, parking, and two adult-size caps. The league's average FCI in 2005 was $329.82. The file entitled **NFL Price** is a sample of 175 randomly chosen fans' FCIs.
a. Produce a relative frequency histogram for these data. Does it seem plausible the data were

sampled from a population that was normally distributed?

b. Calculate the mean and standard deviation of the league's FCI.

c. Calculate the 90th percentile of the leagues fans' FCI.

d. The San Francisco 49ers had an FCI of $347. Determine the percentile of the FCI of a randomly chosen family whose FCI is the same as that of the 49ers average FCI.

6-68. Championship Billiards, owned by D & R Industries, Lincolnwood, Illinois, provides some of the finest billiard fabrics, cushion rubber, and component parts in the industry. It sells billiard cloth in bolts and half-bolts. A half-bolt of billiard cloth has an average length of 35 yards with widths of either 62 or 66 inches. The file entitled **Half Bolts** contains the lengths of 120 randomly selected half-bolts.

a. Produce a relative frequency histogram for this data. Does it seem plausible the data came from a population that has a uniform distribution?

b. Provide the density, $f(x)$, for this uniform distribution.

c. A billiard retailer, Sticks & Stones Billiard Supply, is going to recover the pool tables in the local college pool hall, which has eight tables. It takes approximately 3.8 yards per table. If Championship ships a randomly chosen half-bolt, determine the probability that it will contain enough cloth to recover the eight tables.

6-69. The Hydronics Company is in the business of developing health supplements. Recently, the company's R&D department came up with two weight-loss plans that included products produced by Hydronics. To determine whether these products are effective, the company has conducted a test. A total of 300 people who were 30 pounds or more overweight were recruited to participate in the study. Of these, 100 people were given a placebo supplement, 100 people were given plan 1, and 100 people were given plan 2. As might be expected, some people dropped out of the study before the four-week study period was completed. The weight loss (or gain) for each individual is listed in the data file called **Hydronics**. Note, positive values indicate that the individual actually gained weight during the study period.

a. Develop a frequency histogram for the weight loss (or gain) for those people on plan 1. Does it appear from this graph that weight loss is approximately normally distributed?

b. Referring to part a, assuming that a normal distribution does apply, compute the mean and standard deviation weight loss for the plan 1 subjects.

c. Referring to parts a and b, assume that the weight-change distribution for plan 1 users is

normally distributed and that the sample mean and standard deviation are used to directly represent the population mean and standard deviation. Then, what is the probability that a plan 1 user will lose over 12 pounds in a four-week period?

d. Referring to your answer in part c, would it be appropriate for the company to claim that plan 1 users can expect to lose as much as 12 pounds in four weeks? Discuss.

6-70. The Future-Vision Cable TV Company recently surveyed its customers. A total of 548 responses were received. Among other things, the respondents were asked to indicate their household income. The data from the survey are found in a file named **Future-Vision**.

a. Develop a frequency histogram for the income variable. Does it appear from the graph that income is approximately normally distributed? Discuss.

b. Compute the mean and standard deviation for the income variable.

c. Referring to parts a and b and assuming that income is normally distributed and the sample mean and standard deviation are good substitutes for the population values, what is the probability that a Future-Vision customer will have an income exceeding $40,000?

d. Suppose that Future-Vision managers are thinking about offering a monthly discount to customers who have a household income below a certain level. If the management wants to grant discounts to no more than 7% of the customers, what income level should be used for the cutoff?

6-71. The Cozine Corporation runs the landfill operation outside Little Rock, Arkansas. Each day, each of the company's trucks makes several trips from the city to the landfill. On each entry the truck is weighed. The data file **Cozine** contains a sample of 200 truck weights. Determine the mean and standard deviation for the garbage truck weights. Assuming that these sample values are representative of the population of all Cozine garbage trucks, and assuming that the distribution is normally distributed,

a. determine the probability that a truck will arrive at the landfill weighing in excess of 46,000 pounds.

b. compare the probability in a to the proportion of trucks in the sample that weighed over 46,000 pounds. What does this imply to you?

c. Suppose the managers are concerned that trucks are returning to the landfill before they are fully loaded. If they have set a minimum weight of 38,000 pounds before the truck returns to the landfill, what is the probability that a truck will fail to meet the minimum standard?

CASE 6.1

State Entitlement Programs

Franklin Joiner, director of health, education and welfare, had just left a meeting with the state's newly elected governor and several of the other recently appointed department heads. One of the governor's campaign promises was to try to halt the rising cost of a certain state entitlement program. In several speeches, the governor indicated the state of Idaho should allocate funds only to those individuals ranked in the bottom 10% of the state's income distribution. Now the governor wants to know how much one could earn before being disqualified from the program and he also wants to know the range of incomes for the middle 95% of the state's income distribution.

Frank had mentioned in the meeting that he thought incomes in the state could be approximated by a normal distribution and that mean per capita income was about $33,000 with a standard deviation of nearly $9,000. The Governor was expecting a memo in his office by 3:00 P.M. that afternoon with answers to his questions.

CASE 6.2

Credit Data, Inc.

Credit Data, Inc. has been monitoring the amount of time its bill collectors spend on calls that produce contacts with consumers. Management is interested in the distribution of time a collector spends on each call in which they initiate contact, inform a consumer about an outstanding debt, discuss a payment plan, and receive payments by phone. Credit Data is mostly interested in how quickly a collector can initiate and end a conversation to move on to the next call. For employees of Credit Data, time is money in the sense that one account may require one call and 2 minutes to collect, while another account may take five calls and 10 minutes per call to collect. The company has discovered that the time that collectors spend talking to consumers about accounts is approximated by a normal distribution with a mean of 8 minutes and a standard deviation of 2.5 minutes. The managers believe that the mean is too high and should be reduced by more efficient phone call methods. Specifically, they wish to have no more than 10% of all calls require more than 10.5 minutes.

Required Tasks:

1. Assuming that training can affect the average time but not the standard deviation, the managers are interested in knowing to what level the mean call time needs to be reduced in order to meet the 10% requirement.
2. Assuming that the standard deviation can be affected by training but the mean time will remain at 8 minutes, to what level must the standard deviation be reduced in order to meet the 10% requirement?
3. If nothing is done, what percent of all calls can be expected to require more than 10.5 minutes?

CASE 6.3

American Oil Company

Chad Williams, field geologist for the American Oil Company, settled into his first-class seat on the Sun-Air flight between Los Angeles and Oakland, California. Earlier that afternoon, he had attended a meeting with the design engineering group at the Los Angeles New Product Division. He was now on his way to the home office in Oakland. He was looking forward to the one-hour flight because it would give him a chance to reflect on a problem that surfaced during the meeting. It would also give him a chance to think about the exciting opportunities that lay ahead in Australia.

Chad works with a small group of highly trained people at American Oil who literally walk the earth looking for new sources of oil. They make use of the latest in electronic equipment to take a wide range of measurements from many thousands of feet below the earth's surface. It is one of these electronic machines that is the source of Chad's current problem. Engineers in Los Angeles have designed a sophisticated enhancement that will greatly improve the equipment's ability to detect oil. The enhancement requires 800 capacitors, which must operate within ±0.50 microns from the specified standard of 12 microns.

The problem is that the supplier can provide capacitors that operate according to a normal distribution, with a mean of 12 microns and a standard deviation of 1 micron. Thus, Chad knows that not all capacitors will meet the specifications required by the new piece of exploration equipment. This will mean that in order to have at least 800 usable capacitors, American Oil will have to order more than 800 from the supplier. However, these items are very expensive, so he wants to order as few as possible to meet their needs. At the meeting, the group agreed that they wanted a 98% chance that any order of capacitors would contain the sufficient number of usable items. If the project is to remain on schedule, Chad must place the order by tomorrow. He wants the new equipment ready to go by the time he leaves for an exploration trip in Australia. As he reclined in his seat, sipping a cool lemonade, he wondered whether a basic statistical technique could be used to help determine how many capacitors to order.

References

Albright, Christian S., Wayne L. Winston, and Christopher Zappe, *Data Analysis for Managers with Microsoft Excel* (Pacific Grove, CA: Duxbury, 2003).

Hogg, R. V., and Elliot A. Tanis, *Probability and Statistical Inference*, 5th ed. (Upper Saddle River, NJ: Prentice Hall, 1997).

Marx, Morris L., and Richard J. Larsen, *Mathematical Statistics and Its Applications*, 3rd ed. (Upper Saddle River, NJ: Prentice Hall, 2000).

Microsoft Excel 2007 (Redmond, WA: Microsoft Corp., 2007).

Minitab for Windows Version 15 (State College, PA: Minitab, 2007).

Siegel, Andrew F., *Practical Business Statistics*, 4th ed. (Burr Ridge, IL: Irwin, 2000).

Introduction to Sampling Distributions

CHAPTER OUTCOMES

After studying the material in Chapter 7, you should be able to:

1. Understand the concept of sampling error.
2. Determine the mean and standard deviation for the sampling distribution of $\bar{x}$.
3. Understand the importance of the Central Limit Theorem.
4. Determine the mean and standard deviation for the sampling distribution of the sample proportion, p.
5. Apply sampling distributions for both $\bar{x}$ and p.

PREPARING FOR CHAPTER SEVEN

- Review the discussion of random sampling in Chapter 1.

- Review the steps for computing means and standard deviations in Chapter 3.

- Make sure you are familiar with the normal distribution and how to compute standardized z-values introduced in Chapter 6.

- Review the concepts associated with finding probabilities with a standard normal distribution discussed in Chapter 6.

WHY YOU NEED TO KNOW

A marketing research executive receives a summary report from her analyst that indicates the mean dollars spent by adults on winter-sports recreation activities per year is $302.45. As she reads further, she learns that the mean value is based on a statistical sample of 540 adults in Vermont. The $302.45 is a *statistic*, not a *parameter*, because it is based on a sample rather than an entire population. If you were this marketing executive, you might have several questions:

- Is the actual population mean equal to $302.45?
- If the population mean is not $302.45, how close is $302.45 to the true population mean?
- Is a sample of 540 taken from a population of several million sufficient to provide a "good" estimate of the population mean?

A major manufacturer of personal computers selects a random sample of computers boxed and ready for shipment to customers. These computers are unboxed and inspected to see whether what is in the box matches exactly what the customer order specifies. This past week, 233 systems were sampled and 18 had one or more discrepancies. This is a 7.7% defect rate. Should the quality engineer conclude that exactly 7.7% of the 13,300 computers made this week reached the customer with one or more order discrepancies? Is the actual percentage higher or lower than 7.7%, and by how much? Should the quality engineer request that more computers be sampled?

The questions facing the marketing executive and the quality engineer are common to those faced by people in business everywhere. If you haven't already, you will almost assuredly find yourself in a similar situation many times in the future. To help answer these questions, you need to have an understanding of *sampling distributions*. Whenever decisions are based on samples rather than an entire population, questions about the sample results exist. Anytime we sample from a population, there are many, many possible samples that could have been selected. Each sample will contain different items. Because of this, the sample means for each possible sample can be different, or the sample percentages can be different. The sampling distribution describes the distribution of possible sample outcomes. If you know what this distribution looks like, it will help you understand the specific result you have obtained from the one sample you have selected.

This chapter introduces you to the important concepts of sampling error and sampling distributions and discusses how you can use this knowledge to help answer the questions facing the marketing executive and the quality engineer. The information presented here provides an essential building block to understanding statistical estimation and hypothesis testing, which will be covered in upcoming chapters.

7.1 Sampling Error: What It Is and Why It Happens

As discussed in previous chapters, you will encounter many situations in business in which a sample will be taken from a population and you will be required to analyze the sample data. Chapter 1 introduced several different statistical sampling techniques. Chapters 2 and 3 introduced a variety of descriptive tools that are useful in analyzing sample data. The objective of random sampling is to gather data that mirror a population. Then when analysis is performed on the sample data, the results will be as though we had worked with all the population data. However, we very rarely know if our objective has been achieved. To be able to determine if a sample replicates the population, we must know the entire population, and if that is the case, we do not need to sample. We can just census the population. Because we do not know the population, we require that our sample be random so that bias is not introduced into an already difficult task.

CHAPTER OUTCOME #1

Calculating Sampling Error

Sampling Error
The difference between a measure computed from a sample (a statistic) and the corresponding measure computed from the population (a parameter).

Regardless of how careful we are in using random sampling methods, the sample may not be a perfect reflection of the population. For example a *statistic* such as $\bar{x}$ might be computed for sample data. Unless the sample is a replication of the population, the statistic will likely not equal the *parameter*, μ. In this case, the difference between the sample mean and the population mean is called **sampling error**. In the case in which we are interested in the mean value, the sampling error is computed using Equation 7.1.

Sampling Error of the Sample Mean

$$\text{Sampling error} = \bar{x} - \mu \qquad (7.1)$$

where:

$$\bar{x} = \text{sample mean}$$
$$\mu = \text{population mean}$$

Business Application

KORNFIELD, HARRINGTON & SANDMEYER The architectural firm of Kornfield, Harrington & Sandmeyer (KH&S) has designed 12 shopping centers. Table 7.1 shows a list of the 12 projects and the total square footage of each project.

Because these 12 projects are all the shopping centers the company has worked on, the square-feet area for all 12 projects, shown in Table 7.1, is a population. Equation 7.2 is used to compute the mean square feet in the population of projects.

Population Mean

$$\mu = \frac{\sum x}{N} \qquad (7.2)$$

where:

$$\mu = \text{Population mean}$$
$$x = \text{Values in the population}$$
$$N = \text{Population size}$$

Parameter
A measure computed from the entire population.

Simple Random Sample
A sample selected in such a manner that each possible sample of a given size has an equal chance of being selected.

The mean square feet for the 12 shopping centers is

$$\mu = \frac{114,560 + 202,300 + \cdots + 125,200 + 156,900}{12}$$
$$\mu = 158,972 \text{ square feet}$$

The averaged square footage of the shopping centers designed by the firm is 158,972 square feet. This value is a **parameter**. No matter how many times we compute the value, assuming no arithmetic mistakes, we will get the same value for the population mean.

KH&S is a finalist to be the architectural firm for a new shopping center in Orlando, Florida. The developers who will hire the firm plan to select a **simple random sample** of $n = 5$ projects from those that the finalists have completed. The developers will travel to these shopping centers and examine the designs and interview owners and shoppers. (You may want to refer to Chapter 1 to review the material on simple random samples.)

Refer to the shopping center data in Table 7.1, and suppose the developers randomly select the following five KH&S projects from the population:

TABLE 7.1 Square Feet for Shopping Center Projects

Project	Square Feet
1	114,560
2	202,300
3	78,600
4	156,700
5	134,600
6	88,200
7	177,300
8	155,300
9	214,200
10	303,800
11	125,200
12	156,900

Project	Square Feet
5	134,600
4	156,700
1	114,560
8	155,300
9	214,200

Key in the selection process is the finalists' past performance on large projects, so the developers might be interested in the mean size of the shopping centers that the finalists have designed. Equation 7.3 is used to compute the sample mean.

Sample Mean

$$\bar{x} = \frac{\sum x}{n} \tag{7.3}$$

where:

$\bar{x}$ = Sample mean
x = Sample values selected from the population
n = Sample size

The sample mean is

$$\bar{x} = \frac{134,600 + 156,700 + 114,560 + 155,300 + 214,200}{5} = \frac{775,360}{5} = 155,072$$

The average number of square feet in the random sample of five shopping centers selected by the developers is 155,072. This value is a *statistic* based on the sample.

Recall the mean for the population:

$$\mu = 158,972 \text{ square feet}$$

The sample mean is

$$\bar{x} = 155,072 \text{ square feet}$$

As you can see, the sample mean does not equal the population mean. This difference is called *sampling error*. Using Equation 7.1, we compute the sampling error as follows.

$$\text{Sampling error} = \bar{x} - \mu$$
$$= 155,072 - 158,972 = -3,900 \text{ square feet}$$

The sample mean for the random sample of $n = 5$ shopping centers is 3,900 square feet less than the population mean. Regardless of how carefully you construct your sampling plan, you can expect to see sampling error. A random sample will almost never be a perfect image of its population. The sample value and the population value will most likely be different.

Suppose the developer who selected the random sample throws these five projects back into the stack and selects a second random sample of five as follows:

Project	Square Feet
9	214,200
6	88,200
5	134,600
12	156,900
10	303,800

The mean for this sample is

$$\bar{x} = \frac{214,200 + 88,200 + 134,600 + 156,900 + 303,800}{5} = \frac{897,700}{5} = 179,540 \text{ square feet}$$

This time, the sample mean is larger than the population mean. This time the sampling error is

$$\bar{x} - \mu = 179,540 - 158,972$$
$$= 20,568 \text{ square feet}$$

This illustrates some useful fundamental concepts.

- The size of the sampling error depends on which sample is selected.
- The sampling error may be positive or negative.
- There is potentially a different $\bar{x}$ for each possible sample.

If the developers wanted to use the sample mean to estimate the population mean, in one case they would be 3,900 square feet too small and in the other, they would be 20,568 square feet too large.

TRY PROBLEM 7.1

EXAMPLE 7-1   Computing the Sampling Error

Jim's Appliances   Jim's Appliances is a discount appliance dealer that specializes in kitchen appliances. On Saturday morning, the store's inventory included 10 electric ranges. The retail price, in dollars, for these 10 ranges were

| $479 | $569 | $599 | $649 | $649 | $699 | $699 | $749 | $799 | $799 |

Suppose the manager wished to do a quick analysis of the electric range inventory and randomly sampled $n = 4$ ranges. The selected ranges had retail prices of

| $569 | $649 | $799 | $799 |

The sampling error can be computed using the following steps:

Step 1   Determine the population mean using Equation 7.2.

$$\mu = \frac{\Sigma x}{N} = \frac{479 + 569 + 599 + \cdots + 799 + 799}{10} = \frac{6,690}{10} = \$669$$

Step 2   Compute the sample mean using Equation 7.3.

$$\bar{x} = \frac{\Sigma x}{n} = \frac{569 + 649 + 799 + 799}{4} = \frac{2,816}{4} = \$704$$

Step 3 Compute the sampling error using Equation 7.1.

$$\bar{x} - \mu = 704 - 669 = \$35$$

This sample of four has a sampling error of $35. The sample of electric ranges has a slightly larger mean retail price than the population as a whole.

The Role of Sample Size in Sampling Error

Business Application

KORNFIELD, HARRINGTON & SANDMEYER (*CONTINUED*) Previously, we selected random samples of size 5 and computed the resulting sampling error. There are actually 792 possible samples of size 5 taken from 12 projects. This value is found using the counting rule for combinations, which was discussed in Chapter 6.[1]

In actual situations, only one sample is selected, and the decision maker uses the sample measure to estimate the population measure. A "small" sampling error may be acceptable. However, if the sampling error is "too large," conclusions about the population could be misleading.

We can look at the extremes on either end to evaluate the potential for extreme sampling error. The population of square feet for the 12 projects is

Project	Square Feet
1	114,560
2	202,300
3	78,600
4	156,700
5	134,600
6	88,200
7	177,300
8	155,300
9	214,200
10	303,800
11	125,200
12	156,900

Suppose, by chance, the developers ended up with the five smallest shopping centers in their sample. These would be

Project	Square Feet
3	78,600
6	88,200
1	114,560
11	125,200
5	134,600

The mean of this sample is

$$\bar{x} = 108,232 \text{ square feet}$$

---

[1] The number of combinations of x items from a sample of n is $\dfrac{n!}{(x)!\,(n-x)!}$.

Of all the possible random samples, this one provides the smallest sample mean. The sampling error is

$$\bar{x} - \mu = 108,232 - 158,972 = -50,740 \text{ square feet}$$

Thus, if this sample is selected, the sampling error would be $-50,740$ square feet.

On the other extreme, suppose the sample contained the five largest shopping centers, as follows.

Project	Square Feet
10	303,800
9	214,200
2	202,300
7	177,300
12	156,900

The mean for this sample is $\bar{x} = 210,900$. This is the largest possible sample mean from all the possible samples. The sampling error in this case would be

$$\bar{x} - \mu = 210,900 - 158,972 = 51,928 \text{ square feet}$$

The potential for extreme sampling error ranges from

$$-50,740 \text{ to } +51,928 \text{ square feet}$$

The remaining possible random samples will provide sampling errors between these limits.

What happens if the sample size is larger or smaller? Suppose the developers scale back their sample size to $n = 3$ shopping centers. Table 7.2 shows the extremes. By reducing the sample size from 5 to 3, the range of potential sampling error has increased from

$$(-50,740 \text{ to } +51,928 \text{ square feet})$$

to

$$(-65,185.33 \text{ to } +81,128 \text{ square feet})$$

This illustrates that the potential for extreme sampling error is greater when smaller-sized samples are used.

Although larger sample sizes reduce the potential for extreme sampling error, there is no guarantee that the larger sample size will always give the smallest sampling error.

TABLE 7.2 Shopping Center Example for $n = 3$ (Extreme Samples)

Smallest Shopping Centers		Largest Shopping Centers	
Project	Square Feet	Project	Square Feet
3	78,600	10	303,800
6	88,200	9	214,200
1	114,560	2	202,300
$\bar{x} = 93,786.67$ sq. feet		$\bar{x} = 240,100$ sq. feet	
Sampling Error:		Sampling Error:	
$93,786.67 - 158,972 = -65,185.33$ square feet		$240,100 - 158,972 = 81,128$ square feet	

TABLE 7.3 Shopping Center Example with Different Sample Sizes

	n = 5			n = 3	
Project	Square Feet		Project	Square Feet	
4	156,700		12	156,900	
1	114,560		8	155,300	
7	177,300		4	156,700	
11	125,200				
10	303,800				

$\bar{x} = 175,512$ sq. feet $\bar{x} = 156,300$ sq. feet

Sampling Error: Sampling Error:
$175,512 - 158,972 = 16,540$ square feet $156,300 - 158,972 = -2,672$ square feet

For example, Table 7.3 shows two further applications of the shopping center data. As illustrated, this random sample of 3 had a sampling error of $-2,672$ square feet, whereas this random sample of 5 had a sampling error of 16,540 square feet. In this case, the smaller sample was "better" than the larger sample. However, in Section 7-2, you will learn that, on average, the sampling error produced by large samples will be less than the sampling error from small samples.

7-1: Exercises

Skill Development

7-1. The following population is provided:

17	15	8	12	9	7	9	11
12	14	16	9	5	10	14	13
12	12	11	9	14	8	14	12

Further, a simple random sample from this population gives the following values:

12	9	5	10	14	11

Compute the sampling error for the sample mean in this situation.

7-2. The following data are the 16 values in a population:

10	5	19	20	10	8	10	2
14	18	7	8	14	2	3	10

a. Compute the population mean.
b. Suppose a simple random sample of 5 values from the population is selected with the following results:

5	10	20	2	3

Compute the mean of this sample.

c. Based on the results for parts a and b, compute the sampling error for the sample mean.

7-3. A population has a mean of 125. If a random sample of 8 items from the population results in the following sampled values, what is the sampling error for the sample?

103	123	99	107	121	100	100	99

7-4. Assume that the following represent a population of $N = 16$ values.

25	12	21	13	19	17	15	18
23	16	18	15	22	14	23	17

a. Compute the population mean.
b. If a random sample of $n = 9$ includes the following values:

12	18	13	17	23	14	16	25	15

compute the sample mean and calculate the sampling error for this sample.
c. Determine the range of extreme sampling error for a sample of size $n = 4$. (*Hint*: Calculate the

lowest possible sample mean and highest possible sample mean.)

7-5. Consider the following population:

18	26	32	17	34	17	17	22
29	24	24	35	13	29	38	

The following sample was drawn from this population:

35	18	24	17	24	32	17	29

a. Determine the sampling error for the sample mean.
b. Determine the largest possible sampling error for this sample of $n = 8$.
c. Determine the smallest possible sampling error for this sample of $n = 8$.

7-6. Consider the following population:

3	6	9

a. Calculate the population mean.
b. Select, with replacement, and list each possible sample of size 2. Also, calculate the sample mean for each sample.
c. Calculate the sampling error associated with each sample mean.
d. Assuming that each sample is equally likely, produce the distribution of the sampling errors.

7-7. Assume that the following represent a population of $N = 24$ values:

10	14	32	9	34	19	31	24
33	11	14	30	6	27	33	32
28	30	10	31	19	13	6	35

a. If a random sample of $n = 10$ items includes the following values, compute the sampling error for the sample mean:

32	19	6	11	10
19	28	9	13	33

b. For a sample of size $n = 6$, compute the range for the possible sampling error. (*Hint*: Find the sampling error for the 6 smallest sample values and the 6 largest sample values.)
c. For a sample of size $n = 12$, compute the range for the possible sampling error. How does sample size affect the potential for extreme sampling error?

Business Applications

7-8. An Internet Service Provider states that the average number of hours its customers are online each day is 3.75. Suppose a random sample of 14 of the company's customers is selected and the average number of hours that they are online each day is measured. The sample results are

3.11	1.97	3.52	4.56	7.19	3.89	7.71
2.12	4.68	6.78	5.02	4.28	3.23	1.29

Based on the sample of 14 customers, how much sampling error exists? Would you expect the sampling error to increase or decrease if the sample size was increased to 40?

7-9. A computer lab at a small college has 25 computers. Twice during the day a full scan for viruses is performed on each computer. Because of differences in the configuration of the computers, the times required to complete the scan are different for each machine. Records for the scans are kept and indicate that the time (in seconds) required to perform the scan for each machine is as shown here.

Time in Seconds to Complete Scan

1,500	1,347	1,552	1,453	1,371
1,362	1,447	1,362	1,216	1,378
1,647	1,093	1,350	1,834	1,480
1,522	1,410	1,446	1,291	1,601
1,365	1,575	1,134	1,532	1,534

a. What is the mean time required to scan all 25 computers?
b. Suppose a random sample of 5 computers is taken and the scan times for each are as follows: 1,534, 1,447, 1,371, 1,410, and 1,834. If these 5 randomly sampled computers are used to estimate the mean scan time for all 25 computers, what would the sampling error be?
c. What is the range of possible sampling error if a random sample size of 7 computers is taken to estimate the mean scan time for all 25 machines?

7-10. The Patterson Real Estate Company has 20 listings for homes in Fresno, California. The number of days that each house has been on the market without selling is as follows:

26	45	16	77	33	50	19	23	55	107
88	15	7	19	30	60	80	66	31	17

a. Considering these 20 values to be the population of interest, what is the mean of the population?
b. The company is making a sales brochure and wishes to feature 5 homes selected at random from the list. The number of days the 5 sampled homes have been on the market is

77	60	15	31	23

If these 5 houses were used to estimate the mean for all 20, what would the sampling error be?
c. What is the range of possible sampling error if 5 homes are selected at random from the population?

7-11. Holland Management Services manages apartment complexes in Tucson, Arizona. They currently have 30 units available for rent. The monthly rental prices for this population of 30 units are

$455	690	450	495	550	780	800	395	500	405
675	550	490	495	700	995	650	550	400	750
600	780	650	905	415	600	600	780	575	750

a. What is the range of possible sampling error if a random sample of size $n = 6$ is selected from the population?
b. What is the range of possible sampling error if a random sample of size $n = 10$ is selected? Compare your answers to parts a and b and explain why the difference exists.

7-12. The administrator at Saint Frances Hospital is concerned about the amount of overtime that the nursing staff is incurring and wonders whether so much overtime is really necessary. The hospital employs 60 nurses. Following is the number of hours of overtime reported by each nurse last week. These data are the population of interest.

Nurse	OT	Nurse	OT	Nurse	OT
1	2	21	4	41	3
2	1	22	2	42	3
3	7	23	3	43	2
4	0	24	5	44	1
5	4	25	5	45	3
6	2	26	6	46	3
7	6	27	2	47	3
8	4	28	2	48	3
9	2	29	7	49	4
10	5	30	4	50	6
11	5	31	4	51	0
12	4	32	3	52	3
13	5	33	3	53	4
14	0	34	4	54	6
15	6	35	5	55	0
16	0	36	5	56	3
17	2	37	0	57	3
18	4	38	0	58	7
19	2	39	4	59	5
20	5	40	3	60	7

Using the random numbers table in Appendix A with a starting point in column (digit) 14 and row 10, select a random sample of 6 nurses. Go down the table from the starting point. Determine the mean hours of overtime for these 6 nurses and calculate the sampling error associated with this particular sample mean.

7-13. A new report ("Morbitity and Mortality Weekly Report," July 1, 2005) from The Centers for Disease Control (CDC) indicates that smokers, on average, miss 6.16 days of work per year due to sickness (including smoking-related acute and chronic conditions). Nonsmokers miss an average of 3.86 days of work per year. If the CDC believes that the average days of work missed by smokers is the same in 2007 as it was in 2005, it may wish to confirm this by sampling. The sample to support the supposition might be

13	4	4	5	12	8	9	11	1	5
6	9	14	6	3	5	10	7	0	14
6	15	0	2	5	3	10	8	6	7
0	0	15	14	6	2	2	1	4	15
10	12	3	0	14	10	0	1	9	14

Determine the sampling error of this sample assuming that the CDC supposition is correct.

7-14. Princess Cruises recently offered a 16-day voyage from Beijing to Bangkok during the time period from May to August. The announced price, excluding airfare, for a room with an ocean view or a balcony was listed as $3,475. Cruise fares usually are quite variable due to discounting by the cruise line and travel agents. A sample of 20 passengers who purchased this cruise paid the following amounts:

3,559	3,005	3,389	3,505	3,605	3,545	3,529	3,709	3,229	3,419
3,439	3,375	3,349	3,559	3,419	3,569	3,559	3,575	3,449	3,119

a. Calculate the sample mean cruise fare.
b. Determine the sampling error for this sample.
c. Would the results obtained in part b indicate that the average cruise fare during this period for this cruise is different from the listed price? Explain your answer from a statistical point of view.

7-15. An investment advisor has worked with 24 clients for the past five years. Following are the percentage rates of average five-year returns that these 24 clients have experienced over this time frame on their investments:

| 11.2 | 11.2 | 15.9 | 2.7 | 4.6 | 7.6 | 15.6 | 1.3 | 3.3 | 4.8 | 12.8 | 14.9 |
| 10.1 | 10.9 | 4.9 | −2.1 | 12.5 | 3.7 | 7.6 | 4.9 | 10.2 | 0.4 | 9.6 | −0.5 |

This investment advisor plans to introduce a new investment program to a sample of his customers this year. Because this is experimental, he plans to randomly select 5 of the customers to be part of the program. However, he would like those selected to have a mean return rate close to the population mean for the 24 clients. Suppose the following five values represent the average five-year annual return for the clients that were selected in the random sample:

| 11.2 | −2.1 | 12.5 | 1.3 | 3.3 |

Calculate the sampling error associated with the mean of this random sample. What would you tell this advisor regarding the sample he has selected?

Computer Database Exercises

7-16. Maher, Barney, and White LLC is a legal firm with 40 employees. All of the firm's employees are eligible to participate in the company's 401(k) plan and the firm is proud of its 100% participation rate. The file **MBW 401** contains the most recent year-end 401(k) account balance for each of the firm's 40 employees.
a. Compute the population mean and population standard deviation for the most recent year-end 401(k) account balances at Maher, Barney, and White.
b. Suppose that an audit of the firm's 401(k) plan is being conducted and 12 randomly selected employee account balances are to be examined. If the following employees (indicated by employee number) are randomly selected to be included in the study, what is the estimate for the most recent year-end mean 401(k) account balance? How much sampling error is present in this estimate?

| **Employee #** | | | | | | | | | | | |
| 26 | 8 | 31 | 3 | 38 | 30 | 17 | 9 | 21 | 39 | 18 | 11 |

c. Calculate the range of possible sampling error if a random sample of 15 employees is used to estimate the most recent year-end mean 410(k) account balance.

7-17. The Dow-Jones Industrial Index is a well-known stock index and its value is reported on the nightly news all across the country. People everywhere are interested in ". . . what the Dow did today." The index was originally developed in 1884 and has been in place ever since as a gauge of how the U.S. stock market is doing. Currently, it is computed as the sum of the stock prices of 30 large industrial companies. Some of the companies included in the Dow-Jones Industrials are 3M Corporation, Alcoa, American Express, Boeing, ExxonMobil, GE, GM, HP, IBM, Microsoft, and Wal-Mart. For a complete listing and other information about the Dow-Jones Industrials Index, you can go to the Web site: http://invest-faq.com/articles/stock-index-djia.html

The file **Dow Jones 2000–2005** contains the opening, closing, daily high, and daily low values for the Dow for every day between January 2, 2000 and May 10, 2005.
a. Assuming that the data in this file constitute the population of interest, what is the population mean closing value of the Dow?
b. Using Excel or Minitab, select a simple random sample of 50 closing prices (make sure not to include any duplicate days) and calculate the sample mean and the sampling error for the sample.
c. Repeat part b but this time increase the sample size to 100 days.
d. Repeat parts b and c but this time use a sample size of 10 days.
e. Write a short statement discussing your results. Were they as expected? Explain.

7-18. The file entitled **Clothing** contains the monthly retail sales ($millions) of U.S. women's clothing stores from January 2000 to October 2005. A sample taken from this population to estimate the average sales in this time period follows:

2,942	2,574	2,760	2,939	2,642	2,905	2,568
2,677	2,572	3,119	2,697	2,884	2,632	2,742
2,671	2,884	2,946	2,825	2,987	2,729	2,676
2,846	3,112	2,924	2,676			

a. Calculate the population mean.
b. Calculate the sample mean.
c. How much sampling error is present in this sample?
d. Determine the range of possible sampling error if 25 sales figures are sampled at random from this population.

7-19. The Badke Foundation was set up by the Fred Badke family following his death in 2001. Fred had been a very successful heart surgeon and real estate investor in San Diego, and the family wanted to set up an organization that could be used to help less fortunate people. However, one of the concepts behind the Badke Foundation was to use the Badke money as seed money to be used to gather contributions from middle-class families. To help in the solicitation of contributions, the foundation was considering the idea of hiring a consulting company that specialized in this activity. Leaders of the consulting company maintained in their presentation that the mean contribution from families who actually contributed after receiving a specially prepared letter would be $20.00.

Before actually hiring the company, the Badke Foundation sent out the letter and request materials to many people in the San Diego area. They received back contributions from 166 families. The contribution amounts are in the data file called **Badke**.

a. Assuming that these data reflect a random sample of the population of contributions that would be received, compute the sampling error based on the claim made by the consulting firm.

b. Comment on any issues you have with the assumption that the data represent a random sample. Does the calculation of the sampling error matter if the sample is not a random sample? Discuss.

7-20. The United States Senate is one of the two houses of the Congress of the United States. Each state is represented in the Senate by two senators. The total number of senators is currently fixed at 100, each of whom serve six-year terms. The salaries for the senators of the 109th Congress are presented in the file entitled **Senator**.

a. Calculate the average salary of the senators of the 109th Congress.

b. Determine the smallest and largest possible sampling error in estimating the average salary of the senators for a sample of size 10.

c. Repeat the calculation in called for in part b for samples of size 5 and 2.

d. What effect does a change in the sample size seem to have on the dispersion of the sampling errors?

7-21. Welco Lumber Company is based in Shelton, Washington, and is a privately held company that makes cedar siding, cedar lumber, and cedar fencing products for sale and distribution throughout North America. The major cost of production is the cedar logs that are the raw material necessary to make the finished cedar products. Thus, it is very important to the company to get the maximum yield from each log. Of course, the dollar value to be achieved from a log depends initially on the diameter of the log. Each log is 8 feet long when it reaches the mill. The file called **Welco** contains a random sample of logs of various diameters and the potential value of the finished products that could be developed from the log if it was to be made into fence boards.

a. Calculate the sample mean potential value for each diameter of logs in the sample.

b. Discuss whether there is a way to determine how much sampling error exists for a given diameter log based on the sample. Can you determine whether the sampling error will be positive or negative? Discuss.

7.2 Sampling Distribution of the Mean

Section 7.1 introduced the fundamental concepts of sampling error. A random sample selected from a population will not perfectly match the population. Thus the sample statistic likely will not equal the population parameter. If this difference arises because the random sample is not a perfect representation of the population, it is called sampling error.

In business applications, decision makers select a single random sample from a population. They compute a sample measure and use it to make decisions about the entire population. For example, the Nielsen Company takes a single random sample of television viewers to determine the percentage of the population who are watching a particular program during a particular week. Of course, the sample selected is only one of many possible samples that could have been selected from the same population. The sampling error will differ depending on which sample is selected. If, in theory, you were to select all possible random samples of a given size and compute the sample means for each one, these means would vary above and below the true population mean. If we graphed these values as a histogram, the graph would be the **sampling distribution**.

In this section, we introduce the basic concepts of sampling distributions. We will use an Excel tool to select repeated samples from the same population for demonstration purposes only. The same thing can be done using Minitab.

Simulating the Sampling Distribution for $\bar{x}$

AIMS INVESTMENT COMPANY Aims Investment Company handles employee retirement funds, primarily for small companies. The CD-ROM file called **AIMS** contains data on the number of mutual funds in each client's portfolio. The file contains data for all 200 Aims customers, so it is considered a population. Figure 7.1 shows a histogram and important numerical measures for the population.

The mean number of mutual funds in a portfolio is 2.505 funds. The standard deviation is 1.507 funds. The graph in Figure 7.1 indicates that the population is spread between 0 and 6 funds, with more customers owning 2 funds than any other number.

Suppose the controller at Aims plans to select a random sample of 10 accounts. In Excel, we can use the *Sampling* tool to generate the random sample.[2] Figure 7.2 shows the number of mutual funds owned for a random sample of 10 clients. The sample mean of 1.8 is also shown. To illustrate the concept of a sampling distribution, we repeat this process 500 times, generating 500 different random samples of size 10. For each sample, we compute the sample mean. Figure 7.3 shows the frequency histogram for these sample means. Note that the horizontal axis represents the $\bar{x}$-values. The graph in Figure 7.3 is not a complete sampling distribution because it is based on only 500 samples out of the many possible samples that could be selected. However, this simulation gives us an idea of what the sampling distribution looks like.

Look again at the population distribution in Figure 7.1 and compare it with the shape of the frequency histogram in Figure 7.3. Although the population distribution is somewhat skewed, the distribution of sample means is taking the shape of a normal distribution.

Sampling Distribution
The distribution of all possible values of a statistic for a given sample size that has been randomly selected from a population.

Business Application

Excel and Minitab Tutorial

CHAPTER OUTCOME #2

FIGURE 7.1

Distribution of Mutual Funds for the Aims Investment Company

Population mean $\mu = 2.505$ funds

Population standard
  deviation $\sigma = 1.507$ funds

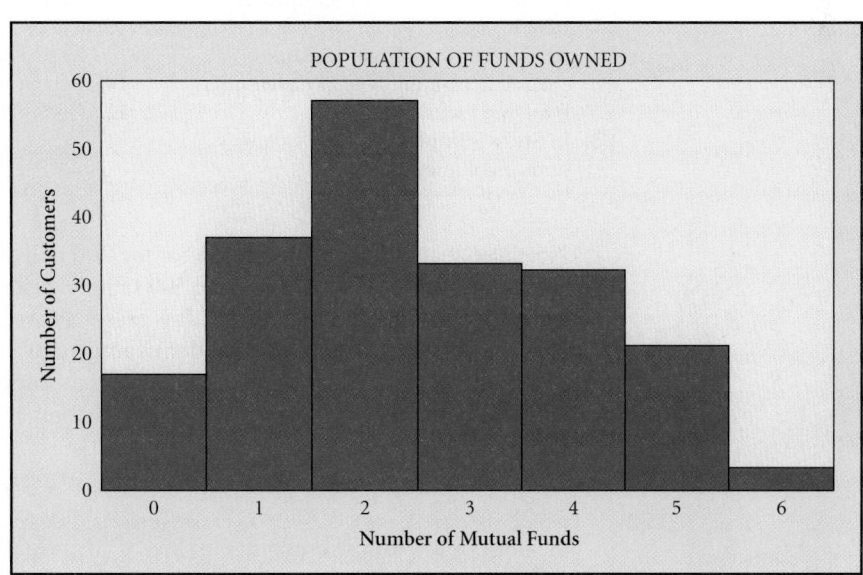

---

[2] The same thing can be achieved in Minitab by using the **Sample from Columns** option under the **Calc-Random Data** command.

FIGURE 7.2

Excel 2007 Output for the Aims Investment Company First Sample Size *n* = 10

Excel 2007 Instructions:
1. Open File: AIMS.xls.
2. Select **Data tab**.
3. Select **Data Analysis**.
4. Select **Sampling**.
5. Define the population data range [B2:B201].
6. Select **Random Sampling**.
7. Select **Output Option**.
8. Compute sample mean using Excel Equation = average (d2d11).

Minitab Instructions (for similar results):
1. Open file: AIMS.MTW.
2. Choose **Calc > Random Data > Sample From Columns**.
3. In **Number of rows to Sample**, enter the sample size.
4. In box following **From column(s)**, enter data column: *Number of Mutual Fund Accounts*.
5. In **Store Samples in**, enter sample's storage column.

6. Click **OK**.
7. Choose **Calc > Calculator**.
8. In **Store Result in Variable** enter column to store mean.
9. Choose **Mean** from **Functions**. **Expression: Mean (Sample Column)**.
10. Repeat steps 3–10 to form sample.
11. Click **OK**.

Note also that the population mean for the 200 individual customers in the population is 2.505 mutual funds. If we average the 500 sample means in Figure 7.3, we get 2.41. This value is the *mean of the sample means*. It is reasonably close to the population mean.

Had we selected all possible random samples of size 10 from the population and computed all possible sample means, the average sample mean would be equal to the population mean. This concept is expressed as Theorem 1.

Theorem 1

For any population, the average value of all possible sample means computed from all possible random samples of a given size from the population will equal the population mean. This is expressed as

$$\mu_{\bar{x}} = \mu$$

FIGURE 7.3

Aims Investment Company, Histogram of 500 Sample Means from Sample Size *n* = 10

Unbiased Estimator

A characteristic of certain statistics in which the average of all possible values of the sample statistic equals a parameter.

When the average of all possible values of the sample statistic equals the corresponding parameter, we call that statistic an **unbiased estimator** of the parameter.

Also, the population standard deviation is 1.507 mutual funds. This measures the variation in the number of mutual funds between individual customers. When we compute the standard deviation of the 500 sample means, we get 0.421, which is considerably smaller than the population standard deviation. If all possible random samples of size *n* are selected from the population, the distribution of possible sample means will have a standard deviation that is equal to the population standard deviation divided by the square root of the sample size, as Theorem 2 states.

Theorem 2
For any population, the standard deviation of the possible sample means computed from all possible random samples of size *n* is equal to the population standard deviation divided by the square root of the sample size. This is shown as

$$\sigma_{\bar{x}} = \frac{\sigma}{\sqrt{n}}$$

Recall the population standard deviation is $\sigma = 1.507$. Then, based on Theorem 2, had we selected all possible random samples of size $n = 10$ rather than only 500 samples, the standard deviation for the possible sample means would be

$$\sigma_{\bar{x}} = \frac{\sigma}{\sqrt{n}} = \frac{1.507}{\sqrt{10}} = 0.477$$

Our simulated value of 0.421 is fairly close to 0.477.

The standard deviation of the sampling distribution will be less than the population standard deviation. To further illustrate, suppose we increased the sample size from $n = 10$ to $n = 20$ and selected 500 new samples of size 20. Figure 7.4 shows the distribution of the 500 different sample means.

The distribution in Figure 7.4 is even closer to a normal distribution than what we observed in Figure 7.3. As sample size increases, the distribution of sample means will become shaped more like a normal distribution. The average sample mean for these 500 samples is

FIGURE 7.4

Aims Investment
Company, Histogram of
Sample Means from
Sample Size $n = 20$

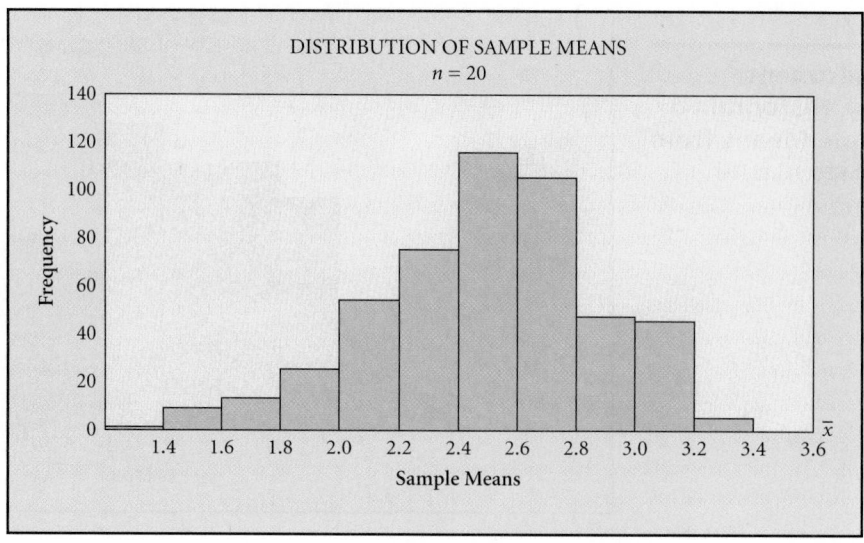

2.53, and the standard deviation of the different sample means is 0.376. Based on Theorems 1 and 2, for a sample size of 20, we would expect the following:

$$\mu_{\bar{x}} = \mu = 2.505 \quad \text{and} \quad \sigma_{\bar{x}} = \frac{\sigma}{\sqrt{n}} = \frac{1.507}{\sqrt{20}} = 0.337$$

Thus, our simulated values are quite close to the theoretical values we would expect had we selected all possible random samples of size 20.

Sampling from Normal Populations The previous discussion began with the population of mutual funds shown in Figure 7.1. The population was not normally distributed, but as we increased the sample size, the sampling distribution of possible sample means began to approach a normal distribution. We will return to this situation shortly, but what happens if the population itself is normally distributed? To help answer this question, we can again use Excel to generate a normally distributed population.[3]

Figure 7.5 shows a simulated population that is approximately normally distributed with a mean equal to 1,000 and a standard deviation equal to 200. The data range is from 250 to 1,800.

Next, we simulate the selection of 2,000 random samples of size 10 from the population and compute the sample mean for each sample. These sample means can then be graphed as a frequency histogram, as shown in Figure 7.6. This histogram represents the sampling distribution. Note that it, too, is approximately normally distributed.

We next compute the average of the 2,000 sample means and use it to approximate $\mu_{\bar{x}}$, as follows:

$$\mu_{\bar{x}} \approx \frac{\sum \bar{x}}{2,000} = \frac{2,000,178}{2,000} \approx 1,000$$

The mean of these sample means is approximately 1,000. This is the same value as the population mean.

We also approximate the standard deviation of the sample means as follows:

$$\sigma_{\bar{x}} \approx \sqrt{\frac{\sum (\bar{x} - \mu_{\bar{x}})^2}{2,000}} = 62.10$$

---

[3] The same task can be performed in Minitab using the **Calc** > **Random Data** command. However, you will have to generate each sample individually, which will take time.

FIGURE 7.5

Simulated Normal Population Distribution

FIGURE 7.6

Approximated Sampling Distribution (*n* = 10)

We see the standard deviation of the sample means is 62.10. This is much smaller than the population standard deviation, which is 200. The largest sample mean was just more than 1,212, and the smallest sample mean was just less than 775. Recall, however, that the population ranged from 250 to 1,800. The variation in the sample means always will be less than the variation for the population as a whole. Using Theorem 2, we would expect the sample means to have a standard deviation equal to

$$\sigma_{\bar{x}} = \frac{\sigma}{\sqrt{n}} = \frac{200}{\sqrt{10}} = 63.25$$

Our simulated standard deviation of 62.10 is fairly close to the theoretical value of 63.25.

We have used this simulated example to illustrate how a sampling distribution is developed. However, in actual practice we only select one random sample from the population, and we know this sample is subject to sampling error. The sample mean may be either larger or smaller than the population mean. In the example, we assumed the population is normally distributed. Because the population forms a continuous distribution and has an uncountable number of values, we could not possibly obtain all possible random samples from this population. As a result, we would be unable to construct the true sampling distribution. Figure 7.6 is an approximation based on 2,000 samples. Fortunately, an important statistical theorem exists that overcomes this obstacle:

Theorem 3

If a population is normally distributed, with mean μ and a standard deviation σ, the sampling distribution of the sample mean $\bar{x}$ is also normally distributed with a mean equal to the population mean ($\mu_{\bar{x}} = \mu$) and a standard deviation equal to the population standard deviation divided by the square root of the sample size ($\sigma_{\bar{x}} = \sigma/\sqrt{n}$).

In Theorem 3, the quantity $\sigma_{\bar{x}} = \sigma/\sqrt{n}$ is the *standard deviation of the sampling distribution*. Another term that is given to this is the *standard error of $\bar{x}$*, because it is the measure of the standard deviation of the potential sampling error.

Suppose we again use the simulated population shown in Figure 7.5, with $\mu = 1,000$ and $\sigma = 200$. We are interested in seeing what the sampling distribution will look like for different size samples. For a sample size of 5, Theorem 3 indicates that the sampling distribution will be normally distributed and have a mean equal to 1,000 and a standard deviation equal to

$$\sigma_{\bar{x}} = \frac{200}{\sqrt{5}} = 89.44$$

If we were to take a random sample of 10 (as simulated earlier), Theorem 3 indicates the sampling distribution would be normal, with a mean equal to 1,000 and a standard deviation equal to

$$\sigma_{\bar{x}} = \frac{200}{\sqrt{10}} = 63.25$$

For a sample size of 20, the sampling distribution will be centered at $\mu_{\bar{x}} = 1,000$, with a standard deviation equal to

$$\sigma_{\bar{x}} = \frac{200}{\sqrt{20}} = 44.72$$

Notice, as the sample size is increased, the standard deviation of the sampling distribution is reduced. This means the potential for extreme sampling error is reduced when larger sample sizes are used. Figure 7.7 shows sampling distributions for sample sizes of 5, 10, and 20. When the population is normally distributed, the sampling distribution of $\bar{x}$ will always be normal and centered at the population mean. Only the spread in the distribution will change as the sample size changes.

This illustrates a very important statistical concept referred to as **consistency**. Earlier we defined a statistic as *unbiased* if the average value of the statistic equals the parameter to be estimated. Theorem 1 asserted that the sample mean is an *unbiased* estimator of the population mean. However, just because a statistic is unbiased does not tell us whether the statistic will be close in value to the parameter. But if as the sample size is increased, we can expect the value of the statistic to become closer to the parameter, then we say that the statistic is a **consistent estimator** of the parameter. Figure 7.7 illustrates that the sample mean is a consistent estimator of the population mean.

The sampling distribution is composed of all possible sample means. Half the sample means will lie above the center of the sampling distribution and half will lie below. The relative distance that a given sample mean is from the center can be determined by *standardizing* the sampling distribution. As discussed in Chapter 6, a standardized value is determined by

Consistent Estimator
An unbiased estimator is said to be a consistent estimator if the difference between the estimator and the parameter tends to become smaller as the sample size becomes larger.

FIGURE 7.7

Theorem 3 Examples

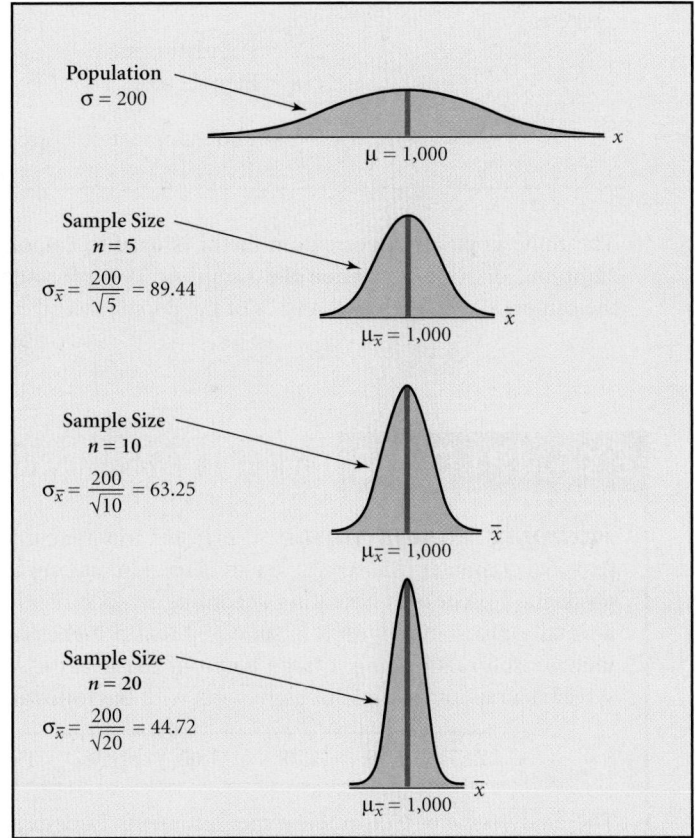

converting the value from its original units into a z-value. A z-value measures the number of standard deviations a value is from the mean. This same concept can be used when working with a sampling distribution. Equation 7.4 shows how the z-values are computed.

---

z-Value for Sampling Distribution of $\bar{x}$

$$z = \frac{\bar{x} - \mu}{\frac{\sigma}{\sqrt{n}}}$$

(7.4)

where:

$\bar{x}$ = Sample mean
μ = Population mean
σ = Population standard deviation
n = Sample size

Note, if the sample that is being selected is large relative to the size of the population (greater than 5% of the population size), and the sampling is being done without replacement, we need to modify how we compute the standard deviation of the sampling distribution and z-value using what is known as the *finite population correction factor* as shown in Equation 7.5.

---

z-Value Adjusted for the Finite Population Correction Factor

$$z = \frac{\bar{x} - \mu}{\frac{\sigma}{\sqrt{n}} \sqrt{\frac{N - n}{N - 1}}}$$

(7.5)

where:

$$N = \text{Population size}$$
$$n = \text{Sample size}$$
$$\sqrt{\frac{N-n}{N-1}} = \text{Finite population correction factor}$$

The finite population correction factor is used to calculate the standard deviation of the sampling distribution when the sampling is performed without replacement or when the sample size is greater than 5% of the population size.

EXAMPLE 7-2 Finding the Probability that $\bar{x}$ is in a Given Range

TRY PROBLEM 7.23

Vextronix Manufacturing Vextronix Manufacturing makes precision parts for the personal computer industry. One part is used in making the motor unit for PCs. When the production process is operating according to specifications, the diameter of the parts is normally distributed with a mean equal to 1.5 inches and a standard deviation of 0.05 inches. Before shipping a large batch of these parts, Vextronix quality analysts have selected a random sample of eight parts with the following diameters:

1.57	1.59	1.48	1.60	1.59	1.62	1.55	1.52

The analysts want to use these measurements to determine if the process is no longer operating within the specifications. The following steps can be used:

Step 1 Determine the mean for this sample.

$$\bar{x} = \frac{\sum x}{n} = \frac{12.52}{8} = 1.565 \text{ inches}$$

Step 2 Define the sampling distribution for $\bar{x}$ using Theorem 3.
Theorem 3 indicates that if the population is normally distributed, the sampling distribution for $\bar{x}$ will also be normally distributed, with

$$\mu_{\bar{x}} = \mu \quad \text{and} \quad \sigma_{\bar{x}} = \frac{\sigma}{\sqrt{n}}$$

Thus, in this case, the mean of the sampling distribution should be 1.50 inches, and the standard deviation should be $0.05/\sqrt{8} = 0.0177$ inches.

Step 3 Define the probability statement of interest.
Because the sample mean is $\bar{x} = 1.565$, which is greater than the mean of the sampling distribution, we want to find

$$P(\bar{x} \geq 1.565 \text{ inches}) = ?$$

Step 4 Convert the sample mean to a standardized z-value, using Equation 7.4.

$$z = \frac{\bar{x} - \mu}{\frac{\sigma}{\sqrt{n}}} = \frac{1.565 - 1.50}{\frac{0.05}{\sqrt{8}}} = \frac{0.065}{0.0177} = 3.67$$

Step 5 Use the standard normal distribution table to determine the desired probability.

$$P(z \geq 3.67) = ?$$

> The standard normal distribution table in Appendix D does not show z-values as high as 3.67. This implies that $P(z \geq 3.67) \approx 0.00$. So, if the production process is working properly, there is virtually no chance that a random sample of eight items will have a mean diameter of 1.565 inches or greater. Because the analysts at Vextronix did find this sample result, there is a very good chance that something is wrong with the process.

CHAPTER OUTCOME #3

The Central Limit Theorem

Theorem 3 applies when the population is normally distributed. Although there are many situations in business when this will be the case, there are also many situations when the population is not normal. For example, incomes in a region tend to be right skewed. Some distributions, such as people's weight, are bimodal (a peak weight group for males and another peak weight group for females).

What does the sampling distribution of $\bar{x}$ look like when a population is not normally distributed? The answer is . . . it depends. It depends on what the shape of the population is and what size sample is selected. To illustrate, suppose we have a U-shaped population, such as the one in Figure 7.8, with mean = 14.00 and standard deviation equal to 3.00. Now, we select 3,000 simple random samples of size 3 and compute the mean for each sample. These $\bar{x}$-values are graphed in the histogram shown in Figure 7.9.

FIGURE 7.8

Simulated Nonnormal Population

$\mu = 14.00$
$\sigma = 3.00$

x -Values

FIGURE 7.9

Frequency Histogram of $\bar{x}$ ($n = 3$)

14.02 = Average of sample means
 1.82 = Standard deviation of sample means

Sample Means
($\bar{x}$)

The number of all possible random samples of size 3 obtained from the population is, of course, considerably larger than 3,000. Therefore, we would not expect that these samples would produce exactly the same results as if we had actually taken all the possible random samples of size 3. However, the results would be reasonably close to the value that would be obtained for the average of all the possible means. The average of these 3,000 sample means is

$$\frac{\sum \bar{x}}{3,000} \approx \mu_{\bar{x}} = 14.02$$

Notice this value is approximately equal to the population mean of 14.00, as Theorem 1 would suggest. Next we compute the standard deviation as

$$\sigma_{\bar{x}} \approx \sqrt{\frac{\sum (\bar{x} - \mu_{\bar{x}})^2}{3,000}} = 1.82$$

The standard deviation of the sampling distribution is less than the standard deviation for the population, which was 3.00. This will always be the case.

The frequency histogram of $\bar{x}$-values for the 3,000 samples of 3 looks different than the population distribution, which is U-shaped. Suppose we increase the sample size to 10 and take 3,000 samples from the same U-shaped population. The resulting frequency histogram of $\bar{x}$-values is shown in Figure 7.10. Now the frequency distribution looks much like a normal distribution. The average of the sample means is still equal to 14.02, which is virtually equal to the population mean. The standard deviation for this sampling distribution is now reduced to 0.97.

This example is not a special case. Instead, it illustrates a very important statistical concept called the **Central Limit Theorem**.

Theorem 4: The Central Limit Theorem

For simple random samples of n observations taken from a population with mean μ and standard deviation σ, regardless of the population's distribution, provided the sample size is sufficiently large, the distribution of the sample means, $\bar{x}$, will be approximately normal with a mean equal to the population mean ($\mu_{\bar{x}} = \mu$) and a standard deviation equal to the population standard deviation divided by the square root of the sample size ($\sigma_{\bar{x}} = \sigma/\sqrt{n}$). The larger the sample size, the better the approximation to the normal distribution.

FIGURE 7.10

Frequency Histogram of $\bar{x}$ ($n = 10$)

14.02 = Average of sample means
0.97 = Standard deviation of sample means

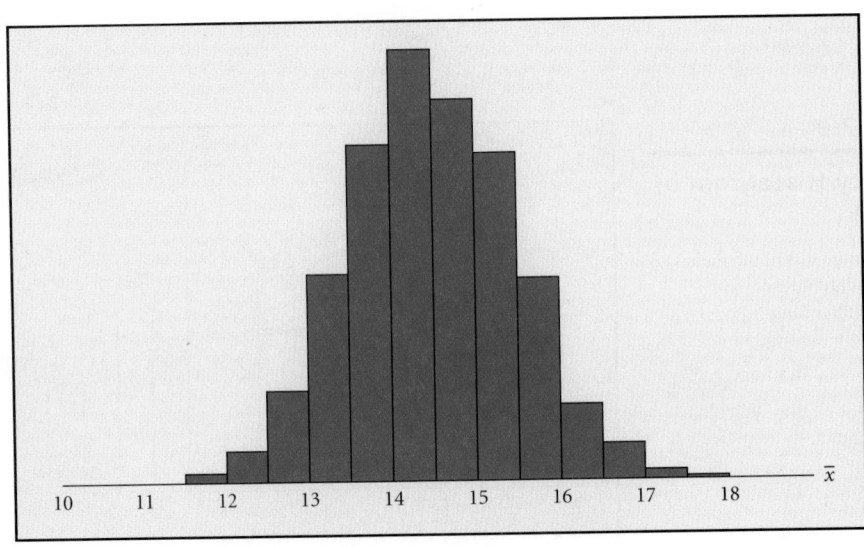

The Central Limit Theorem is very important because with it we know the shape of the sampling distribution even though we may not know the shape of the population distribution. The one catch is that the sample size must be "sufficiently large." What is a sufficiently large sample size?

The answer depends on the shape of the population. If the population is quite symmetric, then sample sizes as small as 2 or 3 will provide a normally distributed sampling distribution. If the population is highly skewed or otherwise irregularly shaped, the required sample size will be larger. Recall the example of the U-shaped population. The frequency distribution obtained from samples of 3 was shaped differently than the population, but not like a normal distribution. However, for samples of 10, the frequency distribution was a very close approximation to a normal distribution. Figures 7.11, 7.12, and 7.13 show some examples of the Central Limit Theorem concept. Simulation studies indicate that even for very strange-looking populations, samples of 25 to 30 produce sampling distributions that are approximately normal. Thus, *a conservative definition of a sufficiently large sample size is n ≥ 30*. The Central Limit Theorem is illustrated in the following example.

SUMMARY Sampling Distribution of $\bar{x}$

To find probabilities associated with a sampling distribution of $\bar{x}$ for samples of size n from a population with mean μ and standard deviation σ, use the following steps.

1. Compute the sample mean using

$$\bar{x} = \frac{\sum x}{n}$$

2. Define the sampling distribution.
   If the population is normally distributed, the sampling distribution also will be normally distributed for any size sample. If the population is not normally distributed but the sample size is sufficiently large, the sampling distribution will be approximately normal. In either case, the sampling distribution will have

$$\mu_{\bar{x}} = \mu \quad \text{and} \quad \sigma_{\bar{x}} = \frac{\sigma}{\sqrt{n}}$$

3. Define the probability statement of interest.
   We are interested in finding the probability of some range of sample means, such as

$$P(\bar{x} \geq 25) =$$

4. Use the standard normal distribution to find the probability of interest, using Equation 7.4 or 7.5 to convert the sample mean to a corresponding z-value.

$$z = \frac{\bar{x} - \mu}{\dfrac{\sigma}{\sqrt{n}}} \quad \text{or} \quad z = \frac{\bar{x} - \mu}{\dfrac{\sigma}{\sqrt{n}} \sqrt{\dfrac{N-n}{N-1}}}$$

Then use the standard normal table to find the probability associated with the calculated z-value.

EXAMPLE 7-3 Finding the Probability that $\bar{x}$ is in a Given Range

CHAPTER OUTCOME #5

Fairway Stores, Inc.   Past sales records indicate that sales at the store are right skewed, with a population mean of $12.50 per customer and a standard deviation of $5.50. The store manager has selected a random sample of 100 sales receipts. She is interested in determining the probability of getting a sample mean between $12.25 and $13.00 from this population. To find this probability, she can use the following steps.

Step 1 Determine the sample mean.
In this case, two sample means are being considered:

$$\bar{x} = \$12.25 \quad \text{and} \quad \bar{x} = \$13.00$$

Step 2 Define the sampling distribution.
The Central Limit Theorem can be used because the sample size is large enough ($n = 100$) to determine that the sampling distribution will be approximately normal (even though the population is right skewed), with

$$\mu_{\bar{x}} = \$12.50 \quad \text{and} \quad \sigma_{\bar{x}} = \frac{\$5.50}{\sqrt{100}} = \$0.55$$

Step 3 Define the probability statement of interest.
The manager is interested in

$$P(\$12.25 \leq \bar{x} \leq \$13.00) = ?$$

Step 4 Use the standard normal distribution to find the probability of interest.
Assuming the population of sales records is quite large, we use Equation 7.4 to convert the sample means to corresponding z-values.

$$z = \frac{\bar{x} - \mu}{\dfrac{\sigma}{\sqrt{n}}} = \frac{12.25 - 12.50}{\dfrac{5.50}{\sqrt{100}}} = -0.46 \quad \text{and} \quad z = \frac{\bar{x} - \mu}{\dfrac{\sigma}{\sqrt{n}}} = \frac{13.00 - 12.50}{\dfrac{5.50}{\sqrt{100}}} = 0.91$$

From the standard normal table in Appendix D, the probability associated with $z = -0.46$ is 0.1772, and the probability for $z = 0.91$ is 0.3186. Therefore,

$$P(\$12.25 \leq \bar{x} \leq \$13.00) = P(-0.46 \leq z \leq 0.91) = 0.1772 + 0.3186 = 0.4958$$

There is nearly a 0.50 chance that the sample mean will fall in the range $12.25 to $13.00.

FIGURE 7.11

Central Limit Theorem with Uniform Population Distribution

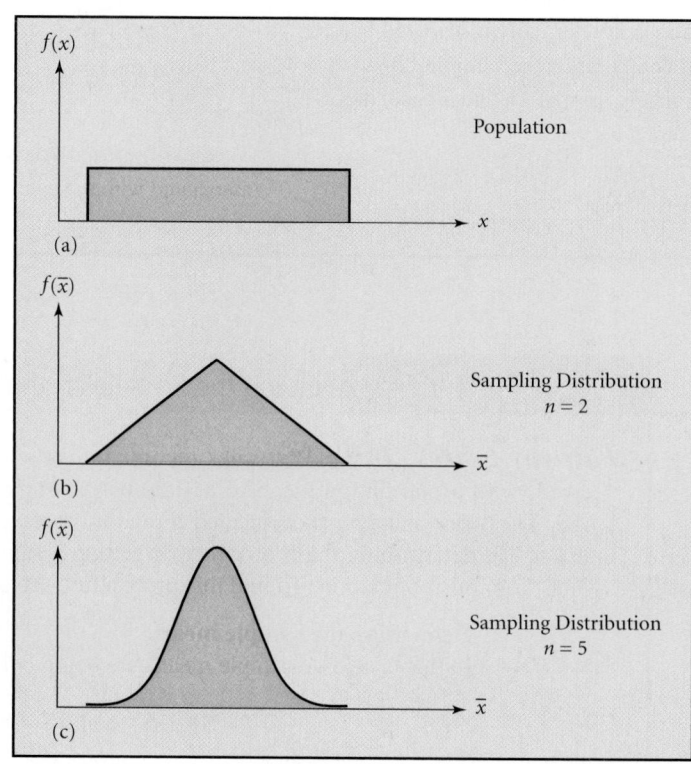

FIGURE 7.12

Central Limit Theorem with Triangular Population

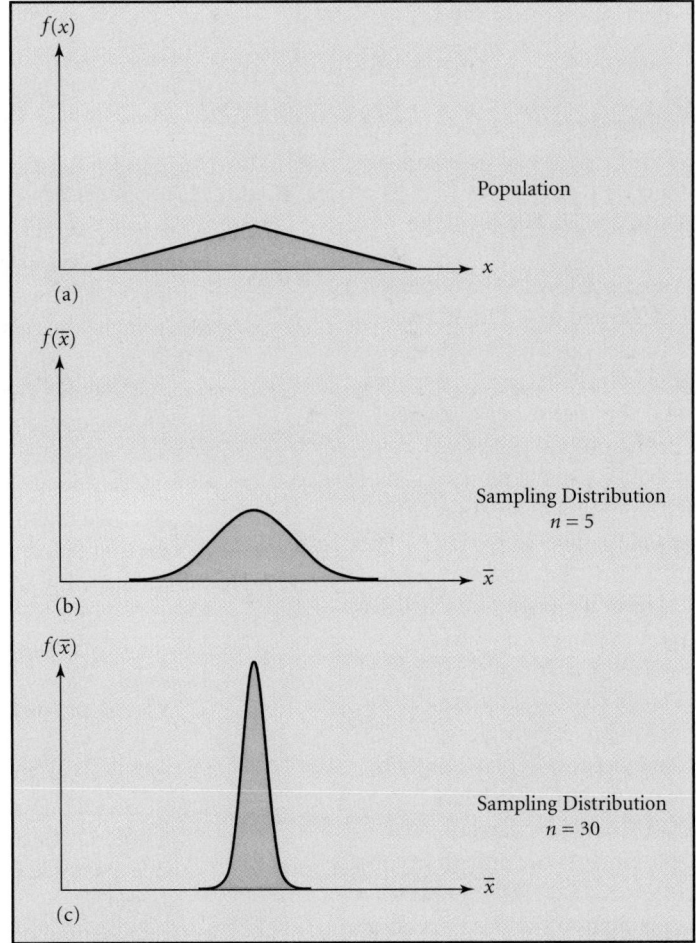

FIGURE 7.13

Central Limit Theorem with a Skewed Population

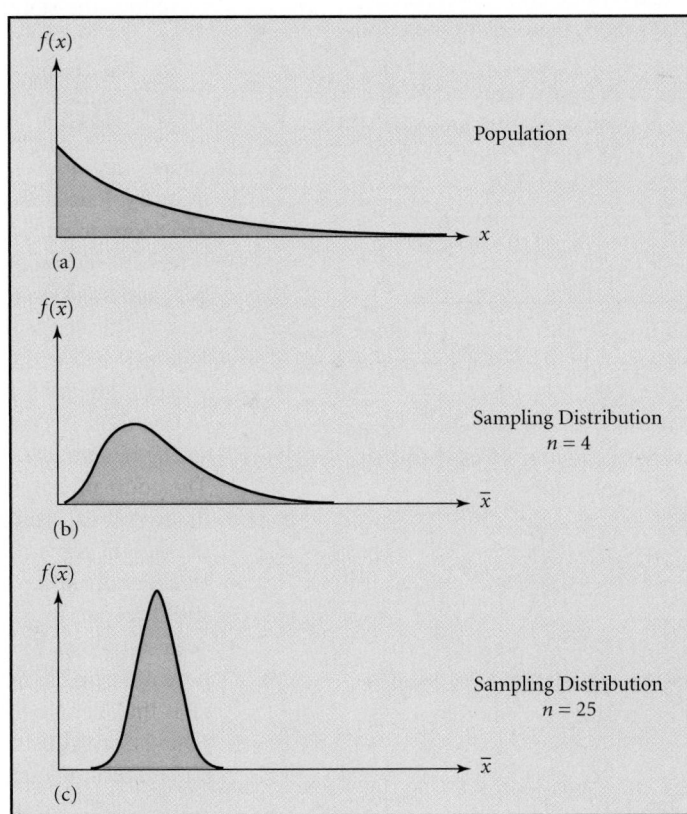

7-2: Exercises

Skill Development

7-22. If a population is known to be normally distributed with $\mu = 250$ and $\sigma = 40$, what will be the characteristics of the sampling distribution for $\bar{x}$ based on a random sample of size 25 selected from the population?

7-23. Suppose that a population is known to be normally distributed with $\mu = 2,000$ and $\sigma = 230$. If a random sample of size $n = 8$ is selected, calculate the probability that the sample mean will exceed 2,100.

7-24. A normally distributed population has a mean of 500 and a standard deviation of 60.
  a. Determine the probability that a random sample of size 16 selected from this population will have a sample mean less than 475.
  b. Determine the probability that a random sample of size 25 selected from the population will have a sample mean greater than or equal to 515.

7-25. A population with a mean of 1,250 and a standard deviation of 400 is known to be highly skewed to the right. If a random sample of 64 items is selected from the population, what is the probability that the sample mean will be less than 1,325?

7-26. A random sample of 100 items is selected from a population of size 350. What is the probability that the sample mean will exceed 200 if the population mean is 195 and the population standard deviation equals 20? (*Hint*: Use the finite correction factor since the sample size is more than 5% of the population size.)

7-27. Suppose nine items are randomly sampled from a normally distributed population with a mean of 100 and a standard deviation of 20. The nine randomly sampled values are

125	95	66	116	99
91	102	51	110	

Calculate the probability of getting a sample mean that is smaller than the sample mean for these nine sampled values.

7-28. Consider a normal distribution with mean = 12 and standard deviation = 90. Calculate $P(\bar{x} > 36)$ for each of the following sample sizes:
  a. $n = 1$
  b. $n = 9$
  c. $n = 16$
  d. $n = 25$

7-29. Given a distribution that has a mean of 40 and a standard deviation of 13, calculate the probability that a sample of 49 has a sample mean that is
  a. greater than 37.
  b. at most 43.
  c. between 37 and 43.
  d. between 43 and 45.
  e. no more than 35.

Business Applications

7-30. Armstrong Windows makes windows for use in homes and commercial buildings. The standards for glass thickness call for the glass to average 0.375 inches with a standard deviation equal to 0.050 inches. Suppose a random sample of $n = 50$ windows yields a sample mean of 0.392 inches.
  a. What is the probability of $\bar{x} \geq 0.392$ if the windows meet the standards?
  b. Based on your answer to part a, what would you conclude about the population of windows? Is it meeting the standards?

7-31. Suppose the life of a particular brand of calculator battery is approximately normally distributed with a mean of 75 hours and a standard deviation of 10 hours.
  a. What is the probability that a single battery randomly selected from the population will have a life between 70 and 80 hours?
  b. What is the probability that 16 randomly sampled batteries from the population will have a sample mean life of between 70 and 80 hours?
  c. If the manufacturer of the battery is able to reduce the standard deviation of battery life from 10 to 9 hours, what would be the probability that 16 batteries randomly sampled from the population will have a sample mean life of between 70 and 80 hours?

7-32. Draper, Inc. makes particleboard for the building industry. Particleboard is built by mixing wood chips and resins together, forming the mix into a 4-feet by 8-feet sheets, and pressing the sheets under extreme heat and pressure to form a 4×8 sheet that is used as a substitute for plywood. The strength of the particleboards is tied to the board's weight. Boards that are too light are brittle and do not meet the quality standard for strength. Boards that are too heavy are strong but are difficult for customers to work with. The company knows that there will be variation in the boards' weight. Product specifications call for the weight per sheet to average 10 pounds with a standard deviation of 1.75 pounds. During each shift, Draper, Inc. employees select and weigh a random sample of 25 boards. The boards are thought to have a normally distributed weight distribution.

If the average of the sample slips below 9.60 pounds, an adjustment is made to the process to add more moisture and resins to increase the weight (and, Draper hopes, the strength).

a. Assuming that the process is operating correctly according to specifications, what is the probability that a sample will indicate that an adjustment is needed?

b. Assume the population mean weight per sheet slips to 9 pounds. Determine the probability that the sample will indicate an adjustment is not needed.

c. Assuming that 10 pounds is the mean weight, what should the cutoff be if the company wants no more than a 5% chance that a sample of 25 boards will have an average weight less than 9.6 lbs?

7-33. Many Happy Returns is a tax preparation service with offices located throughout the western United States. Suppose the average number of returns processed by employees of Many Happy Returns during tax season is 12 per day with a standard deviation of 3 per day. A random sample of 36 employees taken during tax season revealed the following number of returns processed daily:

11	17	13	9	13	13	13	12	15
15	13	15	10	15	13	13	15	13
9	9	9	15	13	14	9	14	11
11	17	16	9	8	10	15	12	11

a. What is the probability of having a sample mean equal to or smaller than the sample mean for this sample if the population mean is 12 processed returns daily with a standard deviation of 3 returns per day?

b. What is the probability of having a sample mean larger than the one obtained from this sample if the population mean is 12 processed returns daily with a standard deviation of 3 returns per day?

c. Explain how it is possible to answer parts a and b when the population distribution of daily tax returns at Many Happy Returns is not known.

7-34. SeaFair Fashions relies on its salesforce of 220 to do an initial screening of all new fashions. The company is currently bringing out a new line of swimwear and has invited 40 salespeople to its Orlando home office. An issue of constant concern to the SeaFair sales office is the volume of orders generated by each salesperson. Last year, the overall company average was $417,330 with a standard deviation of $45,285. (*Hint*: The finite population correction factor, Equation 7.5, is required.)

a. Determine the probability the sample of 40 will have a sales average less than $400,000.

b. What shape do you think the distribution of all possible sample means of 40 will have? Discuss.

c. Determine the value of the standard deviation of the distribution of the sample mean of all possible samples of size 40.

d. How would the answers to parts a, b, and c change if the home office brought 60 salespeople to Orlando? Provide the respective answers for this sample size.

e. Each year SeaFair invites the sales personnel with sales above the 85th percentile to enjoy a complementary vacation in Hawaii. Determine the smallest average salary for the sales personnel that were in Hawaii last year. (Assume the distribution of sales was normally distributed last year.)

7-35. The branch manager for American Savings and Loan in Topeka, Kansas has worked with his employees in an effort to reduce the waiting time for customers at the bank. Recently, she and the team concluded that average waiting time is now down to 3.5 minutes with a standard deviation equal to 1.0 minute. However, before making a statement at a managers' meeting, this branch manager wanted to double-check that the process was working as thought. To make this check, she randomly sampled 25 customers and recorded the time they had to wait. She discovered that mean wait time for this sample of customers was 4.2 minutes. Based on the team's claims about waiting time, what is the probability that a sample mean for $n = 25$ people would be as large or larger than 4.2 minutes? What should the manager conclude based on these data?

7-36. Airlines have recently toughened their standards for the weight of checked baggage, limiting the weight of a bag to 50 pounds on domestic U.S. flights. Heavier bags will be carried but at a substantial fee. Suppose that one major airline has stated in an internal memo to employees that the mean weight for bags checked last year on the airline was 34.3 pounds with a standard deviation of 5.7 pounds. Further, it stated that the distribution of weights was approximately normally distributed. This memo was leaked to a consumers group in Atlanta. This group had selected and weighed a random sample of 14 bags to be checked on a flight departing from Atlanta. The following data (pounds) were recorded:

29	27	40	34	30	30	35
44	33	28	36	33	30	40

What is the probability that a sample mean as small or smaller than the one for this sample would occur if the airline's claims about the population of baggage weight is accurate? Comment on the results.

7-37. In an article entitled "Fuel economy calculations to be altered," (*USA Today*, January 11, 2006), James R. Healey indicated that the government planned to change how it calculates fuel economy for new cars and trucks. This is the first modification since 1985. It is expected to lower average mileage for city driving in conventional cars from 10 to 20%. AAA has forecast that the 2008 Ford F-150 would achieve 15.7 mile per gallon. The 2005 Ford F-150 was tested by AAA members driving the vehicle themselves and was found to have an average of 14.3 mpg.

a. Assume that the mean obtained by AAA members is the true mean for the population of 2008 Ford F-150 trucks and that the population standard deviation is 5 mpg. Suppose 100 AAA members were to test the 2008 F-150. Determine the probability that the average mpg would be at least 15.7.

b. The current method of calculating the mpg forecasts that the 2008 F-150 will average 16.8 mpg. Determine the probability that these same 100 AAA members would average more that 16.8 mpg while testing the 2008 F-150.

c. The new method is expected to lower the average mileage by somewhere between 10 and 20%. Calculate the probability that the average obtained by the 100 AAA members will be somewhere between 10 and 20% smaller than the 14.3 mpg obtained during the 2005 trials even if the new method is not employed.

7-38. ACNielsen is a New York-based corporation and a member of the modern marketing research industry. One of the items that ACNielsen tracks is the expenditure on over-the-counter (OTC) cough medicines. In *USA Today* (Rita Rubin, "Cough syrup left out in the cold," January 10, 2006), ACNielsen was quoted as indicating that $620 million was spent on OTC cough medicines in the United States in 2005. The article also indicated that nearly 30 million visits for coughs were made to doctors' offices in the United States.

a. Determine the average cost of OTC cough medicines per doctor's office visit based on 30 million purchases.

b. Assuming that the average cost indicated in part a is the true average cost of OTC cough medicines per doctor's visit and the standard deviation is $10, determine the probability that the average cost for a random selection of 30 individuals will result in an average expenditure of more than $25 in OTC cough medicines.

c. Determine 90th percentile for the average cost of OTC cough medicines for a sample of 36 individuals, all of whom have visited a doctor's office for cough symptoms.

Computer Database Exercises

7-39. Acee Bottling and Distributing bottles and markets Pepsi-Cola products in southwestern Montana. The average fill volume for Pepsi cans is supposed to be 12 ounces. The filling machine has a known standard deviation of 0.05 ounces. Each week, the company selects a simple random sample of 60 cans and carefully measures the volume in each can. The results of the latest sample are shown in the file called **Acee Bottling**. Based on the data in the sample, what would you conclude about whether the filling process is working as expected? Base your answer on the probability of observing the sample mean you compute for these sample data.

7-40. The highly respected financial magazine *Forbes* publishes data on CEO salaries each year. At the end of 2005, *Forbes* posted CEO compensation data to its Web site (www.forbes.com/2005/04/20/05ceoland.html). These data reflect the total compensation for CEOs for the 496 of the nation's 500 largest companies and are listed on your CD in a file called **CEO Compensation**.

a. Treating the data in the file as the population of interest, compute the population mean and standard deviation for CEO compensation.

b. Use either Excel of Minitab to select a simple random sample of $n = 100$ executive compensation amounts. Compute the sample mean for this sample. Find the probability of getting a sample mean as extreme or more extreme than the one you got. (*Hint*: Use the finite population correction factor because the sample is large relative to the size of the population.)

7-41. The data file called **CEO Compensation** contains data for the CEOs of 496 of the nation's top 500 companies in 2005. These data are published by the Forbes organization and are available on its Web site (www.forbes.com/2005/04/20/05ceoland .html).

a. Treating these data as the population of interest, compute the population mean and standard deviation for CEO age.

b. Select a random sample of $n = 12$ CEOs and calculate the sample mean age for this sample. Also compute the sampling error.

c. Based on your result in part b, compute the probability of getting a sample mean as large or larger than the one you obtained.

7-42. The file **Salaries** contains the annual salary for all faculty at a small state college in the Midwest. Assume that these faculty salaries represent the population of interest.

a. Compute the population mean and population standard deviation.

b. Develop a frequency distribution of these data using 10 classes. Do the population data appear to be normally distributed?

c. What is the probability that a random sample of 16 faculty selected from the population would have a sample mean annual salary greater than or equal to $56,650?

d. Suppose the following 25 faculty were randomly sampled from the population and used to estimate the population mean annual salary:

Faculty ID Number				
137	040	054	005	064
134	013	199	168	027
095	065	193	059	192
084	176	029	143	182
009	033	152	068	044

What would the sampling error be?

e. Referring to part d, what is the probability of obtaining a sample mean smaller than the one obtained from this sample?

7-43. Bruce Leichtman is president of Leichtman Research Group, Inc. (LRG), which specializes in research and consulting on broadband, media, and entertainment industries. In a recent survey, the company determined the cost of extra high-definition (HD) gear needed to watch television in HD. The costs ranged from $5 a month for a set-top box to $200 for a new satellite. The file entitled **HDCosts** contains a sample of the cost of the extras whose purchase was required to watch television in HD. Assume that the population average cost is $150 and the standard deviation is $50.

a. Create a box and whisker plot and use it and the sample average to determine if the population

from which this sample was obtained could be normally distributed.

b. Determine the probability that the mean of a random sample of size 150 costs for HD extras would be more than $5 away from the mean of the sample described above.

c. Given your response to part a, do you believe the results obtained in part b are valid? Explain.

7-44. The NPD Group released its annual 2005 U.S. Video Game Industry Retail Sales Report on January 17, 2006. It contained the company's selection of the top 10 video games based upon units sold in 2005. The top-selling video game was *Madden NFL 06* published by Electronic Arts. The average retail price for this video game was $46. The file entitled **Madden** contains a random sample of the retail prices paid for *Madden NFL 06* in 2006.

a. Calculate the sample mean and standard deviation of retail prices paid for *Madden NFL 06* in 2006.

b. To assist in determining if the average retail price has fallen, calculate the probability that a sample of size 200 would result in a sample mean no larger than the one calculated in part a. Assume that the sample standard deviation is representative of the population standard deviation.

c. In part b you used $46 as the population mean. Calculate the probability required in part b, assuming that the population mean is $45.75.

d. On the basis of your calculations in parts b and c, does it seem likely that the average retail price for *Madden NFL 06* has decreased in 2006? Explain.

7.3 Sampling Distribution of a Proportion

Working with Proportions

In many instances, the objective of sampling is to estimate a population proportion. For instance, an accountant may be interested in determining the proportion of accounts payable balances that are correct. A production supervisor may wish to determine the percentage of product that is defect-free. A marketing research department might want to know the proportion of potential customers who will purchase a particular product. In all these instances, the decision makers could select a sample, compute the sample proportion, and make their decision based on the sample results.

Sample proportions are subject to sampling error, just as are sample means. The concept of sampling distributions provides us a way to assess the potential magnitude of the sampling error for proportions in given situations.

Business Application   **LINCOLN RESEARCH** Consider Lincoln Research, a market research firm that surveyed every customer in a certain region who purchased a specific brand of tires during the first week of March last year. The key question in the survey was: "Are you satisfied with the service received at this tire store?"

Population Proportion
The fraction of values in a population that have a specific attribute.

The population size was 80 customers. The number of customers who answered "Yes" to the question was 72. The value of interest in this example is the **population proportion**. Equation 7.6 is used to compute a population proportion.

Population Proportion

$$\pi = \frac{X}{N} \tag{7.6}$$

where:

π = Population proportion
X = Number of items in the population having the attribute of interest
N = Population size

The proportion of customers in the population who are satisfied with the tires and service is

$$\pi = \frac{72}{80} = 0.90$$

Therefore, 90% of the population responded "Yes" to the survey question. This is the *parameter*. It is a measurement taken from the population. It is the "true value."

Now, suppose that the market research firm wishes to do a follow-up survey for a simple random sample of $n = 20$ of the customers. What fraction of this sample will be people who had previously responded "Yes" to the satisfaction question?

The answer depends on which sample is selected. There are many possible random samples of 20 that could be selected from 80 people. However, the marketing research firm will select only one of these possible samples. At one extreme, suppose the 20 people selected for the sample included all 8 who answered "No" to the satisfaction question and 12 others who answered "Yes." The **sample proportion** is computed using Equation 7.7.

Sample Proportion
The fraction of items in a sample that have the attribute of interest.

Sample Proportion

$$p = \frac{x}{n} \tag{7.7}$$

where:

p = Sample proportion
x = Number of items in the sample with the attribute of interest
n = Sample size

For the tire store example, the sample proportion of "Yes" responses is

$$p = \frac{12}{20} = 0.60$$

The sample proportion of "Yes" responses is 0.60, whereas the population proportion is 0.90. The difference between the sampling value and the population value is sampling error. Equation 7.8 is used to compute the sampling error involving a single proportion.

CHAPTER OUTCOME #1

Single-Proportion Sampling Error

$$\text{Sampling error} = p - \pi \tag{7.8}$$

where:

π = Population proportion
p = Sample proportion

Then for this extreme situation we get

$$\text{Sampling error} = 0.60 - 0.90 = -0.30$$

If a sample on the other extreme had been selected and all 20 people came from the original list of 72 who had responded "Yes" the sample proportion would be

$$p = \frac{20}{20} = 1.00$$

For this sample, the sampling error is

$$\text{Sampling error} = 1.00 - 0.90 = 0.10$$

Thus, the range of sampling error in this example is from -0.30 to 0.10. As with any sampling situation, you can expect some sampling error. The sample proportion will probably not equal the population proportion because the sample selected will not be a perfect replica of the population.

EXAMPLE 7-4 Sampling Error for a Proportion

TRY PROBLEM 7.49

Hewlett-Packard–Compaq Merger In 2002 a proxy fight took place between the management of Hewlett-Packard (HP) and Walter Hewlett, the son of one of HP's founders, over whether the merger between HP and Compaq should be approved. Each outstanding share of common stock was allocated one vote. After the vote in March 2002, the initial tally showed that the proportion of shares in the approval column was 0.51. After the vote, a lawsuit was filed by a group led by Walter Hewlett, which claimed improprieties by the HP management team. Suppose the attorneys for the Hewlett faction randomly selected 40 shares from the millions of total shares outstanding. The intent was to interview the owners of these shares to determine whether they had voted for the merger. Of the shares in the sample, 26 carried an "Approval" vote. The attorneys can use the following steps to assess the sampling error:

Step 1 Determine the population proportion.
In this case, the proportion of votes cast in favor of the merger is

$$\pi = 0.51$$

This is the number of approval votes divided by the total number of shares.

Step 2 Compute the sample proportion using Equation 7.7.
The sample proportion is

$$p = \frac{x}{n} = \frac{26}{40} = 0.65$$

Step 3 Compute the sampling error using Equation 7.8.

$$\text{Sampling error} = p - \pi = 0.65 - 0.51 = 0.14$$

The proportion of "Approval" votes from the shares in this sample exceeds the population proportion by 0.14.

CHAPTER OUTCOME #4

Sampling Distribution of *p*

In many applications you will be interested in determining the proportion (π) of all items that possess a particular attribute. The best estimate of this population proportion will be p, the sample proportion. However, any inference about how close your estimate is to the true population value will be based on the distribution of this sample proportion, p, whose underlying distribution is the binomial. However, if the sample size is sufficiently large such that

$$n\pi \geq 5 \quad \text{and} \quad n(1-\pi) \geq 5$$

then the normal distribution can be used as a reasonable approximation to the discrete binomial distribution.[4] Providing we have a large enough sample size, the distribution of all possible sample proportions will be approximately normally distributed. In addition to being normally distributed, the sampling distribution will have a mean and standard error as indicated in Equations 7.9 and 7.10.

Mean and Standard Error of the Sampling Distribution of p

$$\text{Mean} = \mu_p = \pi \tag{7.9}$$

and

$$\text{Standard error} = \sigma_p = \sqrt{\frac{\pi(1-\pi)}{n}} \tag{7.10}$$

where:

$$\pi = \text{Population proportion}$$
$$n = \text{Sample size}$$
$$p = \text{Sample proportion}$$

In Section 7.2, we introduced Theorem 4: The Central Limit Theorem, which indicated that regardless of the shape of the population distribution, the distribution of possible sample means would be approximately normal as long as the sample size is sufficiently large. Theorem 5 is similar but pertains to the sampling distribution for the sample proportion.

Theorem 5: Sampling Distribution of p

Regardless of the value of the population proportion, π, the sampling distribution for the sample proportion, p, will be approximately normally distributed with $\mu_p = \pi$ and

$$\sigma_p = \sqrt{\frac{\pi(1-\pi)}{n}},$$

providing $n\pi \geq 5$ and $n(1 - \pi) \geq 5$. The approximation to the normal distribution improves as the sample size increases and π approaches 0.50.

Business Application

HEATON MANUFACTURING Heaton Manufacturing makes Christmas ornaments that it ships to retailers throughout the United States. Heaton executives have observed that 15% of the ornaments, even when specially packed, are damaged before reaching the retailer. There appears to be no particular pattern to the damage. Whether one ornament breaks seems independent of whether any other ornament breaks.

---

[4] An application of the Central Limit Theorem provides the nationale for this statement. Recall that $p = x/n$, where x is the sum of random variables (x_i) whose values are 0 and 1. Thus, $x/n = \Sigma x_i/n$. Therefore, p is in reality just a sample mean. Each of these x_i can be thought of as binomial random variables from a sample of size $n = 1$. Thus, they each have a mean of $\mu = n\pi = \pi$ and a variance of $\sigma^2 = n\pi(1 - \pi) = \pi(1 - \pi)$. As we have seen from the Central Limit Theorem, the sample mean has an expected value of μ and a variance of σ^2/n. Thus, the sample proportion has an expected value of $\mu = \pi$ and a variance of $\sigma^2 = \pi(1 - \pi)/n$.

Suppose that Heaton heard from a retail customer who claimed that 18% of the 500 ornaments she purchased were damaged. Assume the general damage rate of

$$\pi = 0.15$$

holds for the population of all ornaments. How likely is it that a sample of

$$n = 500$$

units will contain 18% or more broken items? To answer this question, we first check to determine if the sample size is sufficiently large. Because both

$$n(\pi) = 500(0.15) = 75 \geq 5 \quad \text{and} \quad n(1 - \pi) = 500(0.85) = 425 \geq 5$$

we can safely conclude that the sampling distribution of sample proportions will be approximately normal. Using Equations 7.9 and 7.10, we can compute the mean and standard error for the sampling distribution as follows:

$$\mu_p = 0.15$$

and

$$\sigma_p = \sqrt{\frac{(0.15)(0.85)}{500}} = 0.016$$

Equation 7.11 is used to convert the sample proportion to a standardized z-value.

---

z-Value for Sampling Distribution of p

$$z = \frac{p - \pi}{\sigma_p} \tag{7.11}$$

where:

z = Number of standard errors p is from π

p = Sample proportion

$\sigma_p = \sqrt{\dfrac{\pi(1 - \pi)}{n}}$ = Standard error of the sampling distribution[5]

π = Population proportion

From Equation 7.11, we get

$$z = \frac{p - \pi}{\sigma_p} = \frac{0.18 - 0.15}{\sqrt{\dfrac{(0.15)(0.85)}{500}}} = 1.88$$

Therefore, the 0.18 damage rate reported by the customer is 1.88 standard errors above the population mean of 0.15. Figure 7.14 illustrates that the chances of a damage rate of 0.18 or more is

$$P(p \geq 0.18) = 0.0301$$

Because this is a very low probability, the Heaton managers might want to see if there was something unusual about how this shipment was packed.

---

[5] If the sample size n is greater than 5% of the population size, the standard error of the sampling distribution should be computed using the finite population correction factor as $\sigma_p = \sqrt{\pi(1 - \pi)/n}\sqrt{(N - n)/(N - 1)}$.

FIGURE 7.14

Standard Normal Distribution for Heaton Manufacturing

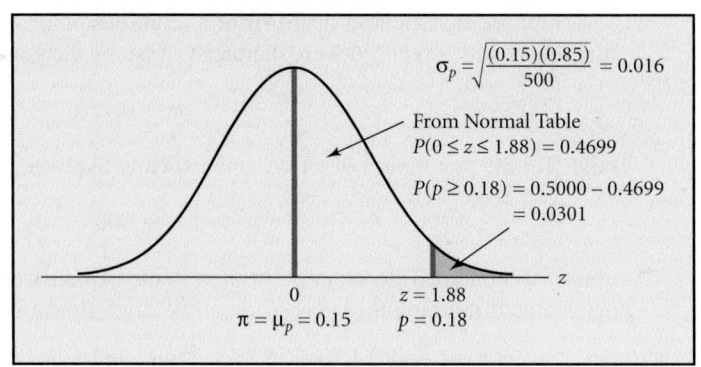

$$\sigma_p = \sqrt{\frac{(0.15)(0.85)}{500}} = 0.016$$

From Normal Table
$P(0 \le z \le 1.88) = 0.4699$

$P(p \ge 0.18) = 0.5000 - 0.4699$
$\qquad\qquad\quad = 0.0301$

$z = 1.88$
$p = 0.18$

$\pi = \mu_p = 0.15$

SUMMARY | Sampling Distribution of p

To find probabilities associated with a sampling distribution for a single-population proportion, the following steps can be used.

1. Determine the population proportion, π, using

$$\pi = \frac{X}{N}$$

2. Calculate the sample proportion using

$$p = \frac{x}{n}$$

3. Determine the mean and standard deviation of the sampling distribution using

$$\mu_p = \pi \quad \text{and} \quad \sigma_p = \sqrt{\frac{\pi(1-\pi)}{n}}$$

4. Define the event of interest. For example:

$$P(p \ge 0.30) = ?$$

5. If $n\pi$ and $n(1 - \pi)$ are both ≥ 5, then convert p to a standardized z-value using

$$z = \frac{p - \pi}{\sigma_p}$$

6. Use the standard normal distribution table in Appendix D to determine the required probability.

TRY PROBLEM 7.53

CHAPTER OUTCOME #5

EXAMPLE 7-5 | Finding the Probability that p is in a Given Range

The Daily Statesman The classified-advertisement manager for the *Daily Statesman* newspaper believes that the proportion of "apartment for rent" ads placed in the paper that result in a rental within two weeks is 0.80 or higher. She would like to make this claim as part of the paper's promotion of its classified section. Before doing this, she has selected a simple random sample of 100 "apartment for rent" ads. Of these, 73 resulted in a rental within the two-week period. To determine the probability of this result or something more extreme, she can use the following steps:

Step 1 **Determine the population proportion, π.**
The population proportion is believed to be $\pi = 0.80$, based upon the manager's experience.

Step 2 **Calculate the sample proportion.**
In this case, a random sample of $n = 100$ ads was selected, with 73 having the attribute of interest. Thus,

$$p = \frac{x}{n} = \frac{73}{100} = 0.73$$

Step 3 **Determine the mean and standard deviation of the sampling distribution.**

The mean of the sampling distribution is equal to p, the population proportion. So

$$\mu_p = \pi = 0.80$$

The standard deviation of the sampling distribution for p is computed using

$$\sigma_p = \sqrt{\frac{\pi(1-\pi)}{n}} = \sqrt{\frac{0.80(1-0.80)}{100}} = 0.04$$

Step 4 **Define the event of interest.**

In this case, because 0.73 is less than 0.80, we are interested in

$$P(p \leq 0.73) = ?$$

Step 5 **If πp and $n(1 - \pi)$ are both ≥ 5, then convert p to a standardized z-value.**

Checking, we get

$$n\pi = 100(0.80) = 80 \geq 5 \quad \text{and} \quad n(1 - \pi) = 100(0.20) = 20 \geq 5$$

Then we convert to a standardized z-value using

$$z = \frac{p - \pi}{\sigma_p} = \frac{0.73 - 0.80}{\sqrt{\dfrac{0.80(1-0.80)}{100}}} = -1.75$$

Step 6 **Use the standard normal distribution table in Appendix D to determine the probability for the event of interest.**

We want

$$P(p \leq 0.73) \quad \text{or} \quad P(z \leq -1.75)$$

From the normal distribution table for $z = -1.75$, we get 0.4599, which corresponds to the probability of a z-value between -1.75 and 0.0. To get the probability of interest, we subtract 0.4599 from 0.5000, giving 0.0401. There is only a 4% chance that a random sample of $n = 100$ would produce a sample proportion of $p \leq 0.73$ if the population proportion is 0.80. She might want to use caution before making this claim.

7-3: Exercises

Skill Development

7-45. If a random sample of 200 items is taken from a population in which the proportion of items having a desired attribute is $\pi = 0.30$, what is the probability that the proportion of successes in the sample will be less than or equal to 0.27?

7-46. Given a population where the proportion of items with a desired attribute is $\pi = 0.25$, if a sample of 400 is taken,

a. what is the standard deviation of the sampling distribution of p?

b. what is the probability the proportion of successes in the sample will be greater than 0.22?

7-47. Given a population in which the probability of success is $\pi = 0.20$. If a sample of 500 items is taken, then

a. calculate the probability the proportion of successes in the sample will be between 0.18 and 0.23.

b. calculate the probability the proportion of successes in the sample will be between 0.18 and 0.23 if the sample size is 200.

7-48. Given a population where the proportion of items with a desired attribute is $\pi = 0.50$, if a sample of 200 is taken,

   a. find the probability the proportion of successes in the sample will be between 0.47 and 0.51.

   b. referring to part a, what would the probability be if the sample size were 100?

7-49. The proportion of items in a population that possess a specific attribute is known to be 0.70.

   a. If a simple random sample of size $n = 100$ is selected and the proportion of items in the sample that contain the attribute of interest is 0.65, what is the sampling error?

   b. Referring to part a, what is the probability that a sample of size 100 would have a sample proportion of 0.65 or less if the population proportion is 0.70?

7-50. Given a population where the probability of a success is $\pi = 0.40$, if a sample of 1,000 is taken,

   a. calculate the probability the proportion of successes in the sample will be less than 0.42.

   b. what is the probability the proportion of successes in the sample will be greater than 0.44?

7-51. A survey is conducted from a population of people of whom 40% have a college degree. The following sample data were recorded for a question asked each person sampled, "Do you have a college degree?"

YES	NO	NO	YES	YES
YES	YES	YES	YES	YES
YES	NO	NO	NO	YES
NO	YES	YES	NO	NO
NO	YES	YES	YES	NO
YES	NO	YES	NO	NO
YES	NO	NO	NO	YES
YES	NO	NO	NO	NO
NO	NO	YES	NO	NO
NO	YES	NO	YES	YES
NO	NO	NO	YES	NO
NO	NO	NO	YES	YES

   a. Calculate the sample proportion of respondents who have a college degree.

   b. What is the probability of getting a sample proportion as extreme or more extreme than the one observed in part a if the population has 40% with college degrees?

7-52. A random sample of size 100 is to be taken from a population that has a proportion equal to 0.35. The sample proportion will be used to estimate the population proportion.

   a. Calculate the probability that the sample proportion will be within ± 0.05 of the population proportion.

   b. Calculate the probability that the sample proportion will be within ± 1 standard error of the population proportion.

   c. Calculate the probability that the sample proportion will be within ± 0.10 of the population proportion.

7-53. A population has a proportion equal to 0.30. Calculate the following probabilities with $n = 100$:

   a. $P(p \leq 0.35)$

   b. $P(p > 0.40)$

   c. $P(0.25 < p \leq 0.40)$

   d. $P(p \geq 0.27)$.

Business Applications

7-54. According to the Labor Department, in 2004, 14% of architects and engineers were women (*Idaho Statesman*, January 22, 2006). Suppose a random sample of 50 architects and engineers is selected.

   a. How likely is it that the random sample of 50 architects and engineers will contain 11 or more women in these positions?

   b. How likely is it that the random sample will contain fewer than 5 women in these positions?

   c. If the random sample included 200 architects and engineers, how would this change your answer to part b?

7-55. United Manufacturing and Supply makes sprinkler valves for use in residential sprinkler systems. United supplies these valves to major companies such as Rain Bird and Nelson, who in turn sell sprinkler products to retailers. United recently entered into a contract to supply 40,000 sprinkler valves. The contract called for at least 97% of the valves to be free of defects. Before shipping the valves, United managers tested 200 randomly selected valves and found 190 defect-free valves in the sample. The managers wish to know the probability of finding 190 or fewer defect-free valves if in fact the population of 40,000 valves is 97% defect-free. Discuss how they could use this information to determine whether to ship the valves to the customer.

7-56. The J R Simplot Company is one of the world's largest privately held agricultural companies, employing over 10,000 people in the United States, Canada, China, Mexico, and Australia. More information can be found at the company's Web site: www.Simplot.com. One of its major products is french fries that are sold primarily on the commercial market to customers such as McDonald's and Burger King. French fries have numerous quality attributes that are important to customers. One of these is called "dark ends," which are the dark-colored ends that can occur when the fries are cooked. Suppose a major customer will accept 0.06 of the fries having "dark ends."

Recently, the customer called the Simplot Company saying that a recent random sample of 300 fries was tested from a shipment and 27 fries had "dark ends." Assuming that the population does meet the 0.06 standard, what is the probability of getting a sample of 300 with 27 or more dark ends? Comment on this result.

7-57. The National Association of Realtors released a survey indicating that a surprising 43% of first-time home buyers purchased their homes with no-money-down loans during 2005. The fear is that house prices will decline and leave homeowners owing more than their home is worth. PMI Mortgage Insurance estimates that there existed a 50% risk that prices will decline within two years in major metro areas such as San Diego, Boston, Long Island, N.Y., Los Angeles, and San Francisco.

  a. A survey taken by realtors in the San Francisco area found that 12 out of the 20 first-time home buyers sampled purchased their home with no-money-down loans. Calculate the probability that at least 12 in a sample of 20 first-time buyers, would take out no-money-down loans if San Francisco's proportion is the same as the nationwide proportion of no-money-down loans.

  b. Determine the probability requested in part a if the nationwide proportion is 0.43.

  c. Determine the probability that between 8 and 12 of a sample of 20 first-time home buyers would take out no-money-down loans.

7-58. Airgistics provides air consolidation and freight-forwarding services for companies that ship their products internationally. As a part of its commitment to continuous process improvement, Airgistics monitors the performance of its partner carriers to ensure that high standards of on-time delivery are met. Airgistics currently believes that it achieves a 96% on-time performance for its customers. Recently, a random sample of 200 customer shipments was selected for study, and 188 of them were found to have met the on-time delivery promise.

  a. What is the probability that a random sample of 200 customer shipments would contain 188 or fewer on-time deliveries if the true population of on-time deliveries is 96%?

  b. Would you be surprised if the random sample of 200 customer shipments had 197 on-time deliveries?

  c. Suppose the random sample of 200 customer shipments revealed that 178 were on-time. Would such a finding cause you to question Airgistics' claim that its on-time performance is 96%? Support your answer with a probability calculation.

7-59. TransUnion is a leading global provider of business intelligence services. TransUnion enables businesses to manage financial risk and capitalize on market opportunities using credit decisioning and fraud prevention tools, advanced target-marketing products, risk and profitability models, and portfolio management. Transunion reported that 33% of the mortgages in 2005 were adjustable-rate mortgages (ARMs).

  a. In samples of mortgages of size 75, what proportion of the samples would you expect to produce sample proportions equal to or larger than 0.25?

  b. If a sample of size 75 produced a sample proportion of 0.45, what would you infer that the population proportion of mortgages with ARMs really is?

  c. In a sample of 90 mortgages, what would the probability be that the number of mortgages with ARMS would be between 25 and 35?

Computer Database Exercises

7-60. A study conducted by Watson Wyatt Worldwide, a human resources consulting firm, revealed that 13% of Fortune 1000 companies either terminated or froze their defined-benefit pension plans in 2005 (*Idaho Statesman*, January 8, 2006). As part of a study to evaluate how well its benefits package compares to other Fortune 1000 companies, a retail firm randomly samples 36 Fortune 1000 companies in odd-numbered years and asks them to complete a benefits questionnaire. One question that is asked is whether the company has changed its defined-benefits pension plan by either freezing it or terminating it during the survey year. The results of the 2005 survey are contained in the file **Pension Survey**.

  a. Open the file **Pension Survey**. Create a new variable that has a value equal to 1 if the firm has either terminated or frozen its defined-benefits pension plan during 2005, and equal to 0 if the firm has not significantly altered its pension plan.

  b. Determine the sample proportion of companies that either terminated or froze their defined-benefits pension plan during 2005.

  c. How likely is it that a sample proportion greater than or equal to the one found in the survey would occur if the true population of firms who have terminated or frozen their defined-benefits pension plan in 2005 is as reported by Watson Wyatt Worldwide?

7-61. *Driven*, a recently released magazine targeted to young professionals, states that 65% of its subscribers have an annual income greater than $100,000. The sales staff at *Driven* uses this high proportion of subscribers earning more than $100,000 as a selling point when trying to get companies to place advertisements with the magazine. *Driven* is currently trying to sell a large amount of advertising to Meuscher, an upscale chocolatier, for a special year-end issue on fine foods and wines. Before committing to advertise in *Driven*, Meuscher's market research staff has decided to randomly sample 201 of *Driven's* subscribers to verify Driven's claim that 65% of its subscribers earn more then $100,000 annually.

   a. The file **Driven** contains the responses of 201 randomly sampled subscribers of the magazine. The responses are coded "Yes" if the subscriber earns over $100,000 annually and "No" if the subscriber does not earn over $100,000 annually. Open the file **Driven** and create a new variable that has a value of 1 for "yes" and 0 for "no."

   b. Calculate the sample proportion of subscribers who have annual incomes greater than $100,000.

   c. How likely is it that a sample proportion greater than the one calculated in part b would be obtained if the population proportion of subscribers earning over $100,000 annually is 65%?

   d. Based on the probability you calculated in part c, should Meuscher advertise in *Driven*?

7-62. The Bureau of Labor Statistics, U.S. Office of Personnel Management, indicated that the 2005 average hourly compensation (salary plus benefits) for federal workers (not including military or postal service employees) was $44.82. The rates for private industry and state and local government workers are believed to be considerably less than that. The file entitled **Paychecks** contains a random sample of the hourly amounts paid to state and local government workers.

   a. If the hourly compensation for federal workers was normally distributed, determine the median hourly compensation.

   b. Calculate the sample proportion of the state and local government workers whose hourly compensation is less than $44.82.

   c. If a sample of size 150 was obtained from a population whose population proportion was equal to your answer to part a, determine the probability that the sample proportion would be equal to or greater than the answer obtained in part b.

   d. On the basis of your work in parts a, b, and c, would you conclude that the proportion of state and local workers whose hourly compensation is less than $44.82 is the same as that of the federal workers? Explain.

7-63. Procter & Gamble merged with Gillette in 2005. One of the concerns the new, larger company has is the increasing burden of retirement expenditures. An effort is being made to encourage employees to participate in 401(k) accounts. Nationwide, 66% of eligible workers participate in these accounts. The file entitled **Gillette** contains responses of 200 Procter & Gamble workers when asked if they were currently participating in a 401(k) account.

   a. Determine the sample proportion of P&G workers who participate in 401(k) accounts.

   b. Determine the sampling error if in reality P&G workers have the same proportion of participants in 401(k) accounts as does the rest of the nation.

   c. Determine the probability that a sample proportion at least as large as that obtained in the sample would be obtained if P&G workers have the same proportion of participants in 401(k) accounts as does the rest of the nation.

   d. Does it appear that a larger proportion of P&G workers participate in 401(k) accounts than do the workers of the nation as a whole? Support your response.

7-64. The Bureau of Transportation Statistics releases information concerning the monthly percentage of U.S. airline flights that land no later than 15 minutes after scheduled arrival. The average of these percentages for the 12 months in 2004 was 78.08%. This data become available as soon as feasible. However, the airlines can provide preliminary results by obtaining a sample. The file entitled **Ontime** contains the sample data indicating the number of minutes after scheduled arrival time that the aircraft arrived. Note that a negative entry indicates the minutes before the scheduled arrival time that the aircraft arrived.

   a. Calculate the proportion of sampled airline flights that landed within 15 minutes of scheduled arrival.

   b. Calculate the probability that a sample proportion of "on-time" flights would be within ± 0.06 of a population proportion = 0.7808.

   c. If the airlines' goal was to attain the same proportion of on-time arrivals as in 2004, do the preliminary results indicate that they have met this goal? Support your assertions.

Summary and Conclusions

When a manager selects a sample, it is only one of many samples that could have been selected. Consequently, the sample mean, $\bar{x}$, is only one of the many possible sample means that could have been found. There is no reason to believe that the single $\bar{x}$-value will equal the population mean, μ. The difference between $\bar{x}$ and μ is called sampling error. Because sampling error exists, decision makers must be aware of how the sample means are distributed in order to discuss the potential for extreme sampling error. The same issues hold for proportions.

This chapter introduced several important theorems. These theorems describe the distribution of sample means and proportions taken from any population. The more important of these theorems is the Central Limit Theorem. The concepts of estimation and hypothesis testing (Chapters 8–12) depend heavily on the Central Limit Theorem. The important aspect of the Central Limit Theorem is that no matter how the population is distributed, if the sample size is large enough, the sampling distribution will be approximately normal.

The chapter also presented several new statistical terms, which are listed in the Key Terms section. Be sure you understand these concepts and how they apply to the material in this chapter. You will encounter these terms many times as you continue in this text.

Equations

Sampling Error of the Sample Mean

$$\text{Sampling error} = \bar{x} - \mu \tag{7.1}$$

Population Mean

$$\mu = \frac{\sum x}{N} \tag{7.2}$$

Sample Mean

$$\bar{x} = \frac{\sum x}{n} \tag{7.3}$$

z-Value for Sampling Distribution of $\bar{x}$

$$z = \frac{\bar{x} - \mu}{\dfrac{\sigma}{\sqrt{n}}} \tag{7.4}$$

z-Value Adjusted for the Finite Population Correction Factor

$$z = \frac{\bar{x} - \mu}{\dfrac{\sigma}{\sqrt{n}} \sqrt{\dfrac{N-n}{N-1}}} \tag{7.5}$$

Population Proportion

$$\pi = \frac{X}{N} \tag{7.6}$$

Sample Proportion

$$p = \frac{x}{n} \tag{7.7}$$

Single-Proportion Sampling Error

$$\text{Sampling error} = p - \pi \tag{7.8}$$

Mean of the Sampling Distribution of p

$$\text{Mean} = \mu_p = \pi \tag{7.9}$$

Standard Deviation of the Sampling Distribution of p

$$\sigma_p = \sqrt{\frac{\pi(1-\pi)}{n}} \tag{7.10}$$

z-Value for Sampling Distribution of p

$$z = \frac{p - \pi}{\sigma_p} \tag{7.11}$$

Key Terms

Chapter Exercises

Conceptual Questions

7-65. Discuss why the sampling distribution will be less variable than the population distribution. Give a short example to illustrate your answer.

7-66. A sample of size 30 is obtained from a population that has a proportion of 0.34. Determine the range of sampling errors possible when the sample proportion is used to estimate the population proportion. (*Hint*: Review the Empirical Rule.)

7-67. Under what conditions should the finite population correction factor be used in determining the standard error of a sampling distribution?

7-68. A researcher has collected all possible samples of a size of 150 from a population and listed the sample means for each of these samples.
   a. If the average of the sample means is 450.55, what would be the numerical value of the true population mean? Discuss.
   b. If the standard deviation of the sample means is 12.25, determine the standard deviation of the model from which the samples came. To perform this calculation, assume the population has a size of 1,250.

7-69. Discuss the similarities and differences between a standard deviation and a standard error.

7-70. Suppose we are told the sampling distribution developed from a sample of size 400 has a mean of 56.78 and a standard error of 9.6. If the population is known to be normally distributed, what are the population mean and population standard deviation? Discuss how these values relate to the values for the sampling distribution.

7-71. If a population is known to be normally distributed, what size sample is required to ensure that the sampling distribution of $\bar{x}$ is normally distributed?

7-72. Consider the standard error of a sample proportion obtained from a sample of size 100.
   a. Determine the standard error obtained from a population with $\pi = 0.1$.
   b. Repeat part a for a population proportion equal to (1) 0.5 and (2) 0.9.
   c. Which population proportion results in the largest standard error?
   d. Given your responses to parts a, b, and c, which value of a population proportion would produce the largest sampling error?

Business Applications

7-73. Suppose at your university some administrators believe that the proportion of students preferring to take classes at night exceeds 0.30. The president is skeptical and so has an assistant take a simple random sample of 200 students. Of these, 66 indicate that they prefer night classes. What is the probability of finding a sample proportion equal to or greater than that found if the president's skepticism is justified? Assume $n \leq 5$ percent of N.

7-74. The time it takes a mechanic to tune an engine is known to be normally distributed with a mean of 45 minutes and a standard deviation of 14 minutes.
   a. Determine the mean and standard error of a sampling distribution for a sample size of 20 tune-ups. Draw a picture of the sampling distribution.
   b. Calculate the largest sampling error you would expect to make in estimating the population mean with the sample size of 20 tune-ups.

7-75. A year-old study found the service time for all drive-through customers at the Stardust Coffee Shop is uniformly distributed between 3 and 6 minutes. Assuming the service time distribution has not changed, a random sample of 49 customers is taken and the service time for each is recorded.
   a. Calculate the mean and standard deviation of service times for all drive-through customers at the Stardust Coffee Shop. (*Hint*: Review the uniform distribution from Chapter 6.)
   b. What is the probability that a sample of 49 customers would have a sample mean of 4.25 minutes or more if the true population mean and standard deviation for service times are as calculated in part a?
   c. How can the probability in part b be determined when the population of service times is not normally distributed?

7-76. Frito-Lay is one of the world's largest makers of snack foods. One of the final steps in making products like Cheetos and Doritos is to package the product in sacks or other containers. Suppose Frito-Lay managers set the fill volume on Cheetos to an average volume of 16 ounces. The filling machine is know to fill with a standard deviation of 0.25 ounces with a normal distribution around the mean fill level.
   a. What is the probability that a single bag of Cheetos will have a fill volume that exceeds 16.10 ounces?
   b. What is the probability that a random sample of 12 bags of Cheetos will have a mean fill volume that exceeds 16.10 ounces?
   c. Compare your answers to parts a and b and discuss why they are different.

7-77. MPC makes personal computers that are then sold directly over the phone and over the Internet. One of the most critical factors in the success of PC makers is how fast they can turn their inventory of parts. Faster inventory turns means lower average inventory cost. Recently at a meeting, the VP of manufacturing said that there is no reason to continue offering hard disk drives that have less than a 40.0-GB storage capacity since only 10% of MPC customers ask for the smaller hard disks. After much discussion and debate about the accuracy of the VP's figure, it was decided to sample 100 orders from the past week's sales. This sample revealed 14 requests for drives with less than 40.0-GB capacity.

a. Determine the probability of finding 14 or more requests like this if the VP's assertion is correct. Do you believe that the proportion of customers requesting hard drives with storage capacity is as small as 0.10? Explain.

b. Suppose a second sample of 100 customers was selected. This sample again yielded 14 requests for a hard drive with less than 40.0 GB of storage. Combining this sample information with that found in part a, what conclusion would you now reach regarding the VP's 10% claim. Base your answer on probability.

7-78. One of the major video rental chains recently made a change in its rental policies. One change is to allow the movie to be rented for three nights instead of one. The marketing team that made this decision reasoned that at least 70% of the customers would return the movie by the second night anyway. A sample of 500 customers found 68% returned the movie prior to the third night.

a. Given the marketing team's estimate, what would be the probability of a sample result with 68% or fewer returns prior to the third night?

b. Based on your calculations, would you recommend the adoption of the new rental policy? Support your answer with statistical reasoning and calculations.

7-79. When its ovens are working properly, the time required to bake fruit pies at Ellardo Bakeries is normally distributed with a mean of 45 minutes and a standard deviation of 5 minutes. Yesterday, a random sample of 16 pies had an average baking time of 50 minutes.

a. If Ellardo's ovens are working correctly, how likely is it that a sample of 16 pies would have an average baking time of 50 minutes or more?

b. Would you recommend that Ellardo inspect its ovens to see if they are working properly? Justify your answer.

7-80. The Baily Hill Bicycle Shop sells mountain bikes and offers a maintenance program to its customers. The manager has found the average repair bill during the maintenance program's first year to be $15.30 with a standard deviation of $7.00.

a. What is the probability a random sample of 40 customers will have a mean repair cost exceeding $16.00?

b. What is the probability the mean repair cost for a sample of 100 customers will be between $15.10 and $15.80?

c. The manager has decided to offer a spring special. He is aware of the mean and standard deviation for repair bills last year. Therefore, he has decided to randomly select and repair the first 50 bicycles for $14 each. He notes this is not even 1 standard deviation below the mean price to make such repairs. He asks your advice. Is this a risky thing to do? Based upon the probability of a repair bill being $14.00 or less, what would you recommend? Discuss.

7-81. The Bendbo Corporation has a total of 300 employees in its two manufacturing locations and the headquarters office. A study conducted five years ago showed the average commuting distance to work for Bendbo employees was 6.2 miles with a standard deviation of 3 miles. Recently, a follow-up study based on a random sample of 100 employees indicated an average travel distance of 5.9 miles.

a. Assuming that the mean and standard deviation of the original study hold, what is the probability of obtaining a sample mean of 5.9 miles or less?

b. Based on this probability, do you think the average travel distance may have decreased?

c. A second random sample of 40 was selected. This sample produced a mean travel distance of 5.9 miles. If the mean for all employees is 6.2 miles and the standard deviation is 3 miles, what is the probability of observing a sample mean of 5.9 miles or less?

d. Discuss why the probabilities differ even though the sample results were the same in each case.

7-82. *USA Today* reported (Mindy Fetterman, "Facing cash woes in retirement," January 13, 2006) on an analysis performed by Hewitt Associates, which indicated that the median amount saved in a 401(k) plan by people 50 to 59 years old is $53,440. The average saved is $115,260 for that age group. Assume the standard deviation is $75,000.

a. Examining these statements, would it be possible to use a normal distribution to determine the proportion of workers who have saved more than $115,260? Support your assertions.

b. If it is possible to determine the probability that a sample of size 5 has an average amount saved in a 401(k) plan that is more than $115,260, do so. If not, explain why you are unable to do so.

c. Repeat the instructions in part b with a sample size of 35.

7-83. Dave Wilson, president of the Graduate Management Admissions Council (GMAC) reported (Del Jones, *USA Today*, "New MBAs finding education pays off big time," January 19, 2006) the results of a GMAC survey of 5,829 graduates. The average annual base salary in 2005 increased to $88,626. The high annual base salary was set in 2001 at approximately $92,500 after adjusting for inflation.

a. Assuming that the standard deviation of the salary and bonus for new MBAs was $40,000, calculate the probability that a randomly selected sample of size 5,829 graduates would yield a sample mean of at most $88,626 if the population mean equaled $92,500.

b. Is it plausible that the average annual base salaries for both 2001 and 2005 were actually the same? Support your assertions.

c. Determine the probability that at least half of 5 MBA students who graduated in 2001 would get annual base salaries of at least $92,500.

7-84. Frank N. Magid Associates conducted a telephone survey of 1,109 consumers to obtain the number of cell phones in houses. The survey obtained the following results:

Cell phones	0	1	2	3	≥ 4
Percent	19	26	33	13	9

a. Determine the sample proportion of households that own two or more cell phones.

b. If the proportion of households that own two or more cell phones is equal to 0.50, determine the probability that in a sample of 1,109 consumers at least 599 would own two or more cell phones.

c. The margin of error of the survey was ±3 percentage points. This means that the sample proportion would be within 3 percentage points of the population proportion. If the population proportion of households that had two or more cell phones was 0.50, determine the probability that the margin of error would be ±3 percentage points.

Computer Database Exercises

7-85. The file **High Desert Banking** contains information regarding consumer, real estate, and small commercial loans made last year by the bank. Use your computer software to do the following:

a. Construct a frequency histogram using eight classes for dollar value of loans made last year. Does the population distribution appear to be normally distributed?

b. Compute the population mean for all loans made last year.

c. Compute the population standard deviation for all loans made last year.

d. Select a simple random sample of 36 loans. Compute the sample mean. By how much does the sample mean differ from the population mean? Use the Central Limit Theorem to determine the probability that you would have a sample mean this small or smaller and the probability that you would have a sample mean this large or larger.

7-86. Airline analysts indicated that the airline industry was nearing recovery at the beginning of 2006. One of the key indicators was the strength of the business sector's travel. The average fare paid for business travel rose during the third quarter of 2005 to $219, up from $200 in the third quarter of 2004. The file entitled **Busfares** contains sample prices paid by business travelers in the first quarter of 2006.

a. Determine the sample average fare for business travelers in 2006.

b. Determine the sampling error.

c. If this data were normally distributed, determine the probability that the sample mean would be as far away from the population mean or more so.

d. Does it appear that the average business traveler's fare has risen since 2005's third quarter? Explain.

7-87. The **Patients** file on your CD-ROM contains information for a random sample of geriatric patients. During a meeting, one hospital administrator indicated that 70% of the geriatric patients are males.

a. Based on the data contained in the **Patients** file, would you conclude the administrator's assertion concerning the proportion of male geriatric patients is correct? Justify your answer.

b. The administrator also believes 80% of all geriatric patients are covered by Medicare (Code = CARE). Again, based on the data contained in the file, what conclusion should the hospital administrator reach concerning the proportion of geriatric patients covered by Medicare? Discuss.

7-88. The data file **Trucks** contains data on a sample of 200 trucks that were weighed on two scales. The WIM (weigh-in-motion) scale weighs the trucks as they drive down the highway. The POE scale weighs the trucks while they are stopped at the port-of-entry station. The maker of the WIM scale believes that its scale will weigh heavier than the POW scale 60% of the time when gross weight is considered.

a. Create a new variable that has a value = 1 when the WIM gross weight > POE gross weight, and 0 otherwise.

b. Determine the sample proportion of times the WIM gross weight exceeds POE gross weight.

c. Based on this sample, what is the probability of finding a proportion less than that found in part b? For this calculation, assume the WIM maker's assertion is correct.

d. Based on the probability found in part c, what should the WIM maker conclude? Is his 60% figure reasonable?

7-89. *USA Today* reported (Snapshots, "Adults jump online," July 29, 2005) the results of a survey conducted by HarrisInteractive to determine the percentage of adults who use a computer to access the Internet (from work, home, or other locations). The newspaper indicated the survey revealed that 74% of adults use a computer to access the Internet. The file entitled **Online** produces a representative sample of the data collected by *USA Today*.

a. Calculate the sample proportion of adults who connect to the Internet using a computer.

b. If the Harris poll's estimate of the proportion of adults using the Internet is correct, determine the sampling error for the sample in the **Online** file.

c. Determine the probability that a sample proportion would be at most as far away as the **Online**'s if the Harris poll's estimate was correct.

d. The Harris poll indicated that its sample had a margin of error of $\pm 2\%$. The sample size used by the Harris poll was 2,022. Calculate the probability that the sample proportion from a sample size of 2,022 would be at most as far away from the population proportion as suggested by the margin of error.

7-90. Covercraft manufactures covers to protect automobile interiors and finishes. Its Block-It 200 Series fabric has a limited two-year warranty. Periodic testing is done to determine if the warranty policy should be changed. One such study may have examined those covers that became unserviceable while still under warranty. Data that could be produced by such a study is contained in the file entitled **Covers**. The data represent the number of months a cover was used until it became unserviceable. Covercraft might want to examine more carefully the covers that became unserviceable while still under warranty. Specifically, it wants to examine those that became unserviceable before they had been in use less than one year.

a. Covercraft has begun to think that it should lower its warranty period to perhaps 20 months. It believes that in doing this, 20% of the covers that now fail before the warranty is up will have surpassed the 20-month warranty rate. Calculate the proportion of the sample that became unserviceable after 20 months of service.

b. Determine the probability of obtaining a sample proportion at least as large as that calculated in part a if the true proportion was equal to 0.20.

c. Based upon you calculation in part b, should Covercraft lower its warranty period to 20 months? Support your answer.

CASE 7.1

Carpita Bottling Company

Don Carpita owns and operates Carpita Bottling Company in Lakeland, Wisconsin. The company bottles soda pop and beer and distributes the products in the counties surrounding Lakeland.

The company has four bottling machines, which can be adjusted to fill bottles at any mean fill level between 2 ounces and 72 ounces. The machines exhibit some variation in actual fill from the mean setting. For instance, if the mean setting is 16 ounces, the actual fill may be slightly more or less than that amount.

Three of the four filling machines are relatively new, and their fill variation is not as great as that of the older machine. Don has observed that the standard deviation in fill for the three new machines is about 1% of the mean fill level when the mean fill is set at 16 ounces or less, and it is 0.5% of the mean at settings exceeding 16 ounces. The older machine has a standard deviation of about 1.5% of the mean setting regardless of the mean fill setting. However, the older machine tends to underfill bottles more than overfill, so the older machine is set at a mean fill slightly in excess of the desired mean to compensate for the propensity to underfill. For example, when 16-ounce bottles are to be filled, the machine is set at a mean fill level of 16.05 ounces.

The company can simultaneously fill bottles with two brands of soda pop using two machines, and it can use the other two machines to bottle beer. Although each filling machine has its own warehouse and the products are loaded from the warehouse directly on a truck, products from two or more filling machines may be loaded on the same truck. However, an individual store almost always receives bottles on a particular day from just one machine.

On Saturday morning Don received a call at home from the J. R. Summers Grocery store manager. She was very upset because the shipment of 16-ounce bottles of beer received yesterday contained several bottles that were not adequately filled. The manager wanted Don to replace the entire shipment at once.

Don gulped down his coffee and prepared to head to the store to check out the problem. He started thinking how he could determine which machine was responsible for the problem. If he could at least determine whether it was the old machine or one of the new ones, he could save his maintenance people a lot of time and effort checking all the machines.

His plan was to select a sample of 64 bottles of beer from the store and measure the contents. Don figures that he might be able to determine, on the basis of the average contents, whether it is more likely that the beer was bottled by a new machine or by the old one.

The results of the sampling showed an average of 15.993 ounces. Now Don needs some help in determining whether a sample mean of 15.993 ounces or less is more likely to come from the new machines or the older machine.

CASE 7.2

Truck Safety Inspection

The Idaho Department of Law Enforcement, in conjunction with the federal government, recently began a truck inspection program in Idaho. The current inspection effort is limited to an inspection of only those trucks that visually appear to have some defect when they stop at one of the weigh stations in the state. The proposed inspection program will not be limited to the trucks with visible defects, but it will potentially subject all trucks to a comprehensive safety inspection.

Jane Lund of the Department of Law Enforcement is in charge of the new program. She has stated that the ultimate objective of the new truck inspection program is to reduce the number of trucks with safety defects operating in Idaho. Ideally, all trucks passing through, or operating within Idaho would be inspected once a month, and substantial penalties would be applied to operators if safety defects were discovered. Ms. Lund is confident that such an inspection program would, without fail, reduce the number of defective trucks operating on Idaho's highways. However, each safety inspection takes about an hour, and because of limited money to hire inspectors, she realizes that all trucks cannot be inspected. She also knows it is unrealistic to have trucks wait to be inspected until trucks ahead of them have been checked. Such delays would cause problems with the drivers.

In meetings with her staff, Jane has suggested that before the inspection program begins, the number of defective trucks currently operating in Idaho should be estimated. This estimate can be compared with later estimates to see if the inspection program has been effective. To arrive at this initial estimate, Jane thinks that some sort of sampling plan to select representative trucks from the population for all trucks in the state must be developed. She has suggested that this sampling be done at the eight weigh stations near Idaho's borders, but she is unsure how to establish a statistically sound sampling plan that is practical to implement.

References

Berenson, Mark L., and David M. Levine, *Basic Business Statistics: Concepts and Applications*, 10th ed. (Upper Saddle River, NJ: Prentice Hall, 2006).

Cochran, William G., *Sampling Techniques*, 3rd ed. (New York: Wiley, 1977).

Hogg, R. V., and Elliot A. Tanis, *Probability and Statistical Inference*, 6th ed. (Upper Saddle River, NJ: Prentice Hall, 2001).

Johnson, Richard A., and Dean W. Wichern, *Business Statistics: Decision Making with Data* (New York: Wiley, 1997).

Larsen, Richard J., and Moriss L. Marx, *Introduction to Mathematical Statistics and Its Applications*, 4th ed. (Upper Saddle River, NJ: Prentice Hall, 2006).

Microsoft Excel 2007 (Redmond, WA: Microsoft Corp., 2007).

Minitab for Windows Version 15 (State College, PA: Minitab, 2007).

Chapter EIGHT

Estimating Single Population Parameters

8.1 Point and Confidence Interval Estimates for a Population Mean

8.2 Determining the Required Sample Size for Estimating a Population Mean

8.3 Estimating a Population Proportion

CHAPTER OUTCOMES

After studying the material in Chapter 8, you should be able to:

1. Distinguish between a point estimate and a confidence interval estimate.
2. Construct and interpret a confidence interval estimate for a single population mean using both the standard normal and t distributions.
3. Determine the required sample size for estimating a single population mean.
4. Establish and interpret a confidence interval estimate for a single population proportion.
5. Determine the required sample size for estimating a single population proportion.

PREPARING FOR CHAPTER EIGHT

- Review material on calculating and interpreting sample means and standard deviations in Chapter 3.

- Review the normal distribution in Section 6.1.

- Make sure you understand the concepts associated with sampling distributions for $\bar{x}$ and p by reviewing Sections 7.1, 7.2, and 7.3.

WHY YOU NEED TO KNOW

Wherever you find yourself working, you may need to know population values (*parameters*) to help you make decisions. An accountant needs to know the percentage of accounts with correct balances. A marketing manager needs to know the average income in her target-market area. A manufacturing manager needs to know the average machine downtime in his plant. The programming manager at a major television network needs to know the percentage of people watching each of his shows so he can cancel the poor performers. A restaurant manager needs to know the percentage of customers who will order the daily special so she will know how many orders to have available.

In these cases and many others like them, decision makers need to know a population parameter. However, gaining access to an entire population is extremely expensive and time-consuming and, in many cases, infeasible. Therefore, an alternative approach is to select a sample from the population. The sample data are used to compute a desired statistic that forms an estimate of the corresponding population parameter.

Chapter 1 discussed various sampling techniques, including statistical and nonstatistical methods. Chapter 7 introduced the concepts of sampling error and sampling distributions. Chapter 8 builds on these concepts and introduces the steps needed to develop and interpret statistical estimations of various population values. The concepts introduced here will be very useful. You will undoubtedly need to estimate population parameters as a regular part of your managerial decision-making activities. In addition, you will receive estimates that other people have developed that you will need to evaluate before relying on them as inputs to your decision-making process. Was the sample size large enough to provide valid estimates of the population parameter? How confident can you be that the estimate matches the population parameter of interest? These and similar questions can all be answered using the concepts and tools presented in this chapter.

8.1 Point and Confidence Interval Estimates for a Population Mean

CHAPTER OUTCOME #1

Point Estimates and Confidence Intervals

You, no doubt, have either been a respondent to, or have seen the results of, a political poll taken during an election year. These polls attempt to determine the percentage of voters who will favor a particular candidate or a particular issue. For example, suppose a poll indicates that 62% of the people older than 18 in your state favor limiting property taxes to 1% of the market value of the property. The pollsters have not contacted every person in the state, rather they have sampled only a relatively few people to arrive at the 62% figure. In statistical terminology, the 62% is the **point estimate** for the true population percentage of people who favor the property-tax limitation.

The Environmental Protection Agency (EPA) tests the mileage of automobiles sold in the United States. The resulting EPA mileage rating is actually a point estimate for the true average mileage of all cars of a given model.

Cost accountants study their company's production processes to determine product costs. Often the accountants select a sample of items and follow each sampled item through a complete production process. The costs at each step in the process are measured and summed to determine the total cost. They then divide the sum by the sample size to get the mean cost. This figure is the point estimate for the true mean cost of all the items produced. The point estimate is used in assigning a selling price to the finished product.

Which point estimator the decision maker uses depends on the population characteristic the decision maker wishes to estimate. However, regardless of the population value being estimated, we always expect **sampling error**.

Chapter 7 discussed sampling error. We cannot eliminate sampling error, but we can deal with it in our decision process. For example, when cost accountants use $\bar{x}$, the average cost of a sample of items, to establish the average cost of production, the point estimate, $\bar{x}$, will most likely not equal the population mean, μ. In fact, the probability of $\bar{x} = \mu$ is essentially zero. With $\bar{x}$ as their only information, the cost accountants will have no way of determining exactly how far $\bar{x}$ is from μ.

Point Estimate

A single statistic, determined from a sample, that is used to estimate the corresponding population parameter.

Sampling Error

The difference between a measure (a statistic) computed from a sample and the corresponding measure (a parameter) computed from the population.

To overcome this problem with point estimates, the most common procedure is to calculate an interval estimate known as a **confidence interval**.

An application will help to make this definition clear.

Excel and Minitab Tutorial

Business Application

NAGEL BEVERAGE COMPANY The Nagel Beverage Company has recently installed a new soft-drink filling machine that allows the operator to adjust the mean fill quantity. However, no matter what the mean setting, the actual volume of the liquid in each soft-drink can will vary. The machine has been carefully tested and is known to fill cans with a standard deviation of $\sigma = 0.2$ ounce.

The filling machine has been adjusted to fill cans at an average of 12 ounces. After running the machine for several hours, a simple random sample of 100 cans is selected and the volume of soda in each can is measured in the company's quality lab. Figure 8.1 shows the frequency histogram of the sample data. (The data are in a file on your CD-ROM called **Nagel-Beverage**.) Notice that the distribution seems to be centered at a point larger than 12 ounces. The manager wishes to use the sample data to estimate the mean fill amount for all cans filled by this machine.

The sample mean computed from 100 cans is $\bar{x} = 12.09$ ounces. This is the *point estimate* of the population mean, μ. Because of the potential for sampling error, the manager should not expect a particular $\bar{x}$ to equal μ. However, as discussed in Chapter 7, the Central Limit Theorem indicates that the distribution of all possible sample means will be approximately normally distributed around the population mean with its spread measured by $\sigma/\sqrt{n}$, as illustrated in Figure 8.2.

Although the sample mean is 12.09 ounces, the manager knows the true population mean may be higher or lower than this number. To account for the potential for sampling error, the manager can develop a *confidence interval estimate* for μ. This estimate will take the form:

Confidence Interval

An interval developed from sample values such that if all possible intervals of a given width were constructed, a percentage of these intervals, known as the confidence level, would include the true population parameter.

Lower confidence limit — Point estimate — Upper confidence limit

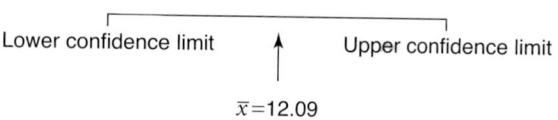

Lower confidence limit   Upper confidence limit

$\bar{x} = 12.09$

FIGURE 8.1

Excel 2007 Histogram for Nagel Beverage

Excel 2007 Instructions:
1. Open File: Nagel Beverage.xls.
2. Create bins (upper limit of each class).
3. Select **Data > Data Analysis**.
4. Select **Histogram**.
5. Define data and bin ranges.
6. Check **Chart Output**.
7. Modify bin definitions.
8. Select chart and right click.
9. Click on **Format Data Series** and close gap width to zero.
10. Label Axes using **Layout > Axis Titles**.

Bin	Frequency
11.51 - 11.6	1
11.61 - 11.7	2
11.71 - 11.8	7
11.81 - 11.9	9
11.91 - 12	16
12.01 - 12.1	18
12.11 - 12.2	14
12.21 - 12.3	16
12.31 - 12.4	9
12.41 - 12.5	5
12.51 - 12.6	3

Minitab Instructions (for similar results):
1. **Open file:** Nagel Beverage MTW.
2. Choose **Graph > Histogram**.
3. Click **Simple**.
4. Click **OK**.
5. In **Graph** variables, enter data Column: *Ounces*.
6. Click **OK**.

FIGURE 8.2

Sampling Distribution of $\bar{x}$

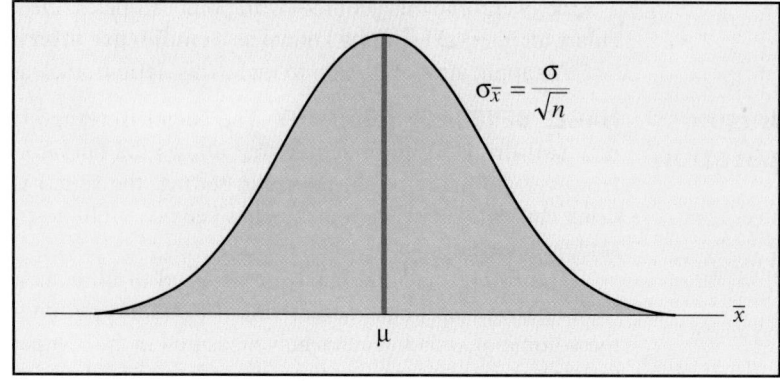

The key now is to determine the upper and lower limits of the interval. The specific method for computing these values depends on whether the population standard deviation, σ, is known or unknown. We first take up the case in which σ is known.

Confidence Interval Estimate for the Population Mean, σ Known

Standard Error

A value which measures the spread of the sample means around the population mean. The standard error is reduced when the sample size is increased.

There are two cases that must be considered. In the case in which the simple random sample is drawn from a normal distribution with a mean of μ and a standard deviation of σ, the sampling distribution of the sample mean is a normal distribution with a mean of μ and a standard deviation (or **standard error**) of $\sigma/\sqrt{n}$. This is true for any sample size.

The second case is that in which the population does not have a normal distribution. Chapter 7 addressed these specific circumstances. Recall that in such cases the Central Limit Theorem can be invoked if the sample size is sufficiently large ($n \geq 30$). In such cases, the sampling distribution is also a normal distribution, with a mean of μ and a standard deviation of $\sigma/\sqrt{n}$. The standard deviation, $\sigma/\sqrt{n}$ is known as the *standard error* of the sample mean.

In both these cases, the sampling distribution for $\bar{x}$ is assumed to be normally distributed. Looking at the sampling distribution in Figure 8.2, it is apparent that the probability that $\bar{x}$ will exceed μ is the same as the probability that $\bar{x}$ will be less than μ. We also know from our discussion in Chapter 7 that we can calculate the percentage of sample means in the interval formed by a specified distance above and below μ. This percentage corresponds to the probability that the sample mean will be in the specified interval. For example, the probability of obtaining a value for $\bar{x}$ that is within 1.96 standard errors either side of μ is 0.95. To verify this, recall from Chapter 7 that the standardized z-value measures the number of standard errors $\bar{x}$ is from μ. The probability from the standard normal distribution table corresponding to $z = 1.96$ is 0.4750. Likewise, the probability corresponding to $z = -1.96$ is equal to 0.4750. Therefore,

$$P(-1.96 \leq z \leq 1.96) = 0.4750 + 0.4750 = 0.95$$

This is illustrated in Figure 8.3.

Because the standard error is $\sigma/\sqrt{n}$, then 95% of all sample means will fall in the range

$$\mu - 1.96\frac{\sigma}{\sqrt{n}} \text{----------} \mu + 1.96\frac{\sigma}{\sqrt{n}}$$

This is illustrated in Figure 8.4.

FIGURE 8.3

Critical Value for a 95% Confidence Interval

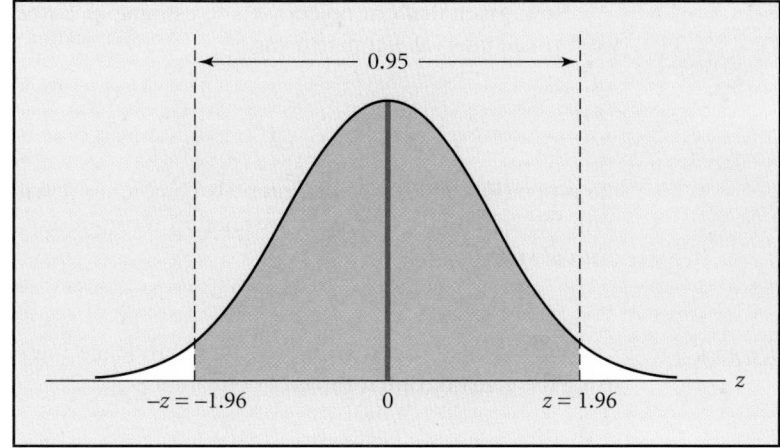

In a like manner, we can determine that 80% of all sample means will fall in the range

$$\mu - 1.28\frac{\sigma}{\sqrt{n}} \text{ -------------- } \mu + 1.28\frac{\sigma}{\sqrt{n}}$$

Also, we can determine that 90% of all sample means will fall in the range

$$\mu - 1.645\frac{\sigma}{\sqrt{n}} \text{ -------------- } \mu + 1.645\frac{\sigma}{\sqrt{n}}$$

This concept can be generalized to any probability by substituting the appropriate z-value from the standard normal distribution.

FIGURE 8.4

95% Confidence Intervals from Selected Random Samples

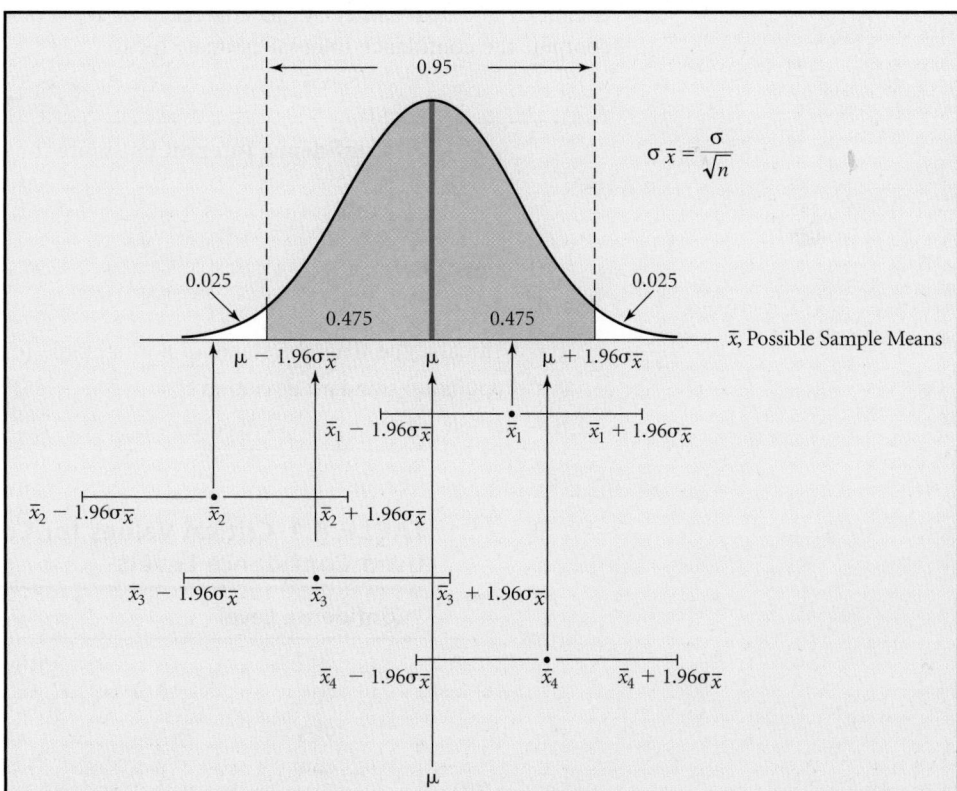

Note: Most intervals include μ and some do not. Those intervals that do not contain the population mean are developed from sample means that fall in either tail of the sampling distribution. If enough intervals, developed from a given sample size, were constructed, 95% would include μ.

Now, given that our objective is to estimate μ based on a random sample of size n, if we form an interval estimate using

$$\bar{x} \pm z \frac{\sigma}{\sqrt{n}}$$

the proportion of all possible intervals containing μ will equal the probability associated with the specified z-value. In estimation terminology, the z-value is referred to as the *critical value*.

CHAPTER OUTCOME # 2

Confidence Interval Calculation Confidence interval estimates can be constructed using the general format shown in Equation 8.1.

Confidence Interval General Format

Point Estimate $\pm$ (Critical Value)(Standard Error) **(8.1)**

Confidence Level

The percentage of all possible confidence intervals that will contain the true population parameter.

The first step in developing a confidence interval estimate is to specify the **confidence level** that is needed to determine the critical value.

Once you decide on the confidence level, the next step is to determine the critical value. If the population standard deviation is known, and the population is normally distributed, or if the sample size is large enough to comply with the Central Limit Theorem requirements, the critical value is a z-value from the standard normal table. Table 8.1 shows several of the most frequently used critical values.

The next step is to compute the standard error for the sampling distribution, shown in Chapter 7 and also earlier in this chapter to be $\sigma_{\bar{x}} = \sigma/\sqrt{n}$. Then, Equation 8.2 is used to compute the confidence interval estimate for μ.

Confidence Interval Estimate for μ, σ Known

$$\bar{x} \pm z \frac{\sigma}{\sqrt{n}}$$ **(8.2)**

where:

z = Critical value from the standard normal table for a specified confidence level

σ = Population standard deviation

n = Sample size

TABLE 8.1 Critical Values for Commonly Used Confidence Levels

Confidence Level	Critical Value
80%	$z = 1.28$
90%	$z = 1.645$
95%	$z = 1.96$
99%	$z = 2.575$

Note: Instead of using the standard normal table, you can also find the critical z-value using Excel's **NORMSINV** function or Minitab's **Calc > Probability Distribution** command.

Business
Application

NAGEL BEVERAGE COMPANY (CONTINUED) Recall that the sample of 100 cans produced a sample mean of $\bar{x} = 12.09$ ounces and the Nagel manager knows that $\sigma = 0.2$ ounce. Thus, the 95% confidence interval estimate for the population mean is

$$\bar{x} \pm z \frac{\sigma}{\sqrt{n}}$$

$$12.09 \pm 1.96 \frac{0.2}{\sqrt{100}}$$

$$12.09 \pm 0.039$$

12.051 ounces -------------- 12.129 ounces

Based on this sample information, the Nagel manager believes that the true mean fill for all cans is within the following interval:

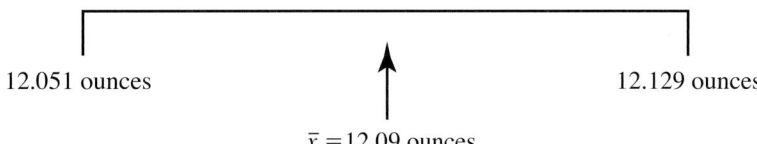

12.051 ounces   12.129 ounces

$\bar{x} = 12.09$ ounces

Because this interval does not contain the target mean of 12 ounces, the manager should conclude that the filling equipment is out of adjustment and is putting in too much soda, on average.

SUMMARY Confidence Interval Estimate for μ with σ Known

Use the following steps to compute a confidence interval estimate for the population mean when the population standard deviation is assumed known and either the population distribution is normal or the sample size *n* is ≥ 30.

1. Define the population of interest and select a simple random sample of size *n*.

2. Specify the confidence level.

3. Compute the sample mean using

$$\bar{x} = \frac{\sum x}{n}$$

4. Determine the standard error of the sampling distribution using

$$\sigma_{\bar{x}} = \frac{\sigma}{\sqrt{n}}$$

5. Determine the critical value, *z*, from the standard normal table.

6. Compute the confidence interval estimate using

$$\bar{x} \pm z \frac{\sigma}{\sqrt{n}}$$

EXAMPLE 8-1 Confidence Interval Estimate for μ, σ Known

TRY PROBLEM 8.1

Saint Regis Hospital   Administrators at Saint Regis Hospital wish to know the mean dollars spent on medical expenses for the patients who were admitted to the hospital during the previous year. To do this, they could use the following steps:

Step 1 Define the population of interest and select a simple random sample of size *n*.
The population is all patients who were admitted to the hospital during the previous year. A simple random sample of 200 patients will be selected.

Step 2 Specify the confidence level.
The administrators want to develop a 90% confidence interval estimate. Thus, 90% of all possible intervals will contain the population mean.

Step 3 Compute the sample mean.

After the sample has been selected and the dollars spent on medical care last year have been recorded for each of the 200 people sampled, the sample mean is computed using

$$\bar{x} = \frac{\sum x}{n}$$

Assume the sample mean is $5,230.

Step 4 Determine the standard error of the sampling distribution.

Suppose past studies have indicated that the population standard deviation is

$$\sigma = \$500$$

Then the standard error of the sampling distribution is computed using

$$\sigma_{\bar{x}} = \frac{\sigma}{\sqrt{n}} = \frac{\$500}{\sqrt{200}} = \$35.36$$

Step 5 Determine the critical value, z, from the standard normal table.

Because the sample size is large, the Central Limit Theorem applies. The sampling distribution will be normally distributed, and the critical value will be a z-value from the standard normal distribution. The administrators want 90% confidence, so the z-value is 1.645.

Step 6 Compute the confidence interval estimate.

The 90% confidence interval estimate for the population mean is

$$\bar{x} \pm z \frac{\sigma}{\sqrt{n}}$$

$$\$5,230 \pm 1.645 \frac{500}{\sqrt{200}}$$

$$\$5,230 \pm \$58.16$$

$$\$5,171.84 \text{ ———— } \$5,288.16$$

Thus, based on the sample results, with 90% confidence, the administrators at Saint Regis Hospital believe that the true population mean for dollars spent on medical care last year is between $5,171.84 and $5,288.16.

Special Message About Interpreting Confidence Intervals

There is a subtle distinction to be made here. Beginning students often wonder if it is permissible to say, "There is a 0.90 probability that the population mean is between $5,171.84 and $5,288.16." This may seem to be the logical consequence of constructing a confidence interval. However, we must be very careful to attribute probability only to random events or variables. Because the population mean is a fixed value, there can be no probability statement about the population mean. The confidence interval we have computed will either contain the population mean or it will not. If you were to produce all the possible confidence intervals using the mean of each possible sample of a given size from the population, 90% of these intervals would contain the population mean.

Impact of the Confidence Level on the Interval Estimate

Business Application

NAGEL BEVERAGE (*CONTINUED*) In the Nagel Beverage example, the manager specified a 95% confidence level. The resulting confidence interval estimate for the population mean was

$$\bar{x} \pm z\frac{\sigma}{\sqrt{n}}$$
$$12.09 \pm 1.96\frac{0.2}{\sqrt{100}}$$
$$12.09 \pm 0.04$$
$$12.05 \text{ ounces} \text{-----------} 12.13 \text{ ounces}$$

Margin of Error
The amount that is added and subtracted to the point estimate to determine the endpoints of the confidence interval. Also, a measure of how close we expect the point estimate to be to the population parameter with the specified level of confidence.

The quantity, 0.04, on the right of the $\pm$ sign above is called the **margin of error**. This is illustrated in Equation 8.3. The margin of error defines the relationship between the sample mean and the population mean.

Margin of Error for Estimating μ, σ Known

$$e = z\frac{\sigma}{\sqrt{n}} \tag{8.3}$$

where:

e = Margin of error
z = Critical value
$\dfrac{\sigma}{\sqrt{n}}$ = Standard error of the sampling distribution

---

Now suppose the manager at Nagel is willing to settle for 80% confidence. This will impact the critical value. To determine the new value, divide 0.80 by 2, giving 0.40. Go to the standard normal table and locate a probability value (area under the curve) that is as close to 0.40 as possible. The corresponding z-value is 1.28.[1] The 80% confidence interval estimate is

$$\bar{x} \pm z\frac{\sigma}{\sqrt{n}}$$
$$12.09 \pm (1.28)\frac{0.2}{\sqrt{100}}$$
$$12.09 \pm 0.03$$
$$12.06 \text{ ounces} \text{---------} 12.12 \text{ ounces}$$

Based on this sample information and the 80% confidence interval, we believe that the true average fill level is between 12.06 ounces and 12.12 ounces.

By lowering the confidence level, the method used to produce the interval is less likely to contain the population mean. However, on the positive side, the margin of error has been reduced from ± 0.04 ounces to ± 0.03 ounces. For equivalent samples from a population:

1. If the confidence level is decreased, the margin of error is reduced.
2. If the confidence level is increased, the margin of error is increased.

The Nagel manager will need to decide which is more important, a higher confidence level or a lower margin of error.

---
[1] You can also use Excel's **NORMSINV** function = **NORMSINV**(.90) = 1.281.

EXAMPLE 8-2 Impact of Changing the Confidence Level

TRY PROBLEM 8.5

DuVall Services DuVall Services operates a garbage hauling company in a south Florida city. Each year, the company must apply for a new contract with the city. The contract is in part based on the pounds of garbage hauled. Part of the analysis that goes into contract development is an estimate of the mean pounds of garbage put out by each customer in the city. The city has asked for both 99% and 90% confidence interval estimates for the mean. If, after the contract has been signed, the actual mean pounds deviates from the estimate over time, an adjustment will be made (up or down) in the amount DuVall receives. The steps used to generate these estimates follow.

Step 1 **Define the population of interest and select a simple random sample of size *n*.**
The population is the collection of all of Duvall's customers, and a simple random sample of $n = 100$ customers is selected.

Step 2 **Specify the confidence level.**
The city requires 99% and 90% confidence interval estimates.

Step 3 **Compute the sample mean.**
After the sample has been selected and the pounds of garbage have been determined for each of the 100 customers sampled, the sample mean is computed using

$$\bar{x} = \frac{\sum x}{n}$$

Suppose the sample mean is 40.78 pounds.

Step 4 **Determine the standard error of the sampling distribution.**
Suppose, from past years, the population standard deviation is known to be $\sigma = 12.6$ pounds. Then the standard error of the sampling distribution is computed using

$$\sigma_{\bar{x}} = \frac{\sigma}{\sqrt{n}} = \frac{12.6}{\sqrt{100}} = 1.26 \text{ pounds}$$

Step 5 **Determine the critical value, *z*, from the standard normal table.**
First, the city wants a 99% confidence interval estimate so the *z*-value is determined by finding a probability in Appendix D corresponding to $0.99/2 = 0.495$. The correct *z*-value is between $z = 2.57$ and $z = 2.58$. We split the difference to get the critical value: $z = 2.575$. For 90% confidence, the critical *z* is determined to be 1.645.

Step 6 **Compute the confidence interval estimate.**
The 99% confidence interval estimate for the population mean is

$$\bar{x} \pm z\frac{\sigma}{\sqrt{n}}$$

$$40.78 \pm 2.575\frac{12.6}{\sqrt{100}}$$

$$40.78 \pm 3.24$$

$$37.54 \text{ pounds} \text{ --------------- } 44.02 \text{ pounds}$$

The margin of error at 99% confidence is ± 3.24 pounds.

The 90% confidence interval estimate for the population mean is

$$\bar{x} \pm z \frac{\sigma}{\sqrt{n}}$$

$$40.78 \pm 1.645 \frac{12.6}{\sqrt{100}}$$

$$40.78 \pm 2.07$$

38.71 pounds -------------- 42.85 pounds

The margin of error is only 2.07 pounds when the confidence level is reduced from 99% to 90%. The margin of error will be smaller when the confidence level is smaller.

Lowering the confidence level is one way to reduce the margin of error. However, by examining Equation 8.3, you will note there are two other values that affect the margin of error. One of these is the population standard deviation. The more the population's standard deviation, σ, can be reduced, the smaller the margin of error will be. In a business environment, large standard deviations for measurements related to the quality of a product are not desired. In fact, corporations spend considerable effort to decrease the variation in their products either by changing their process or by controlling variables that cause the variation. Typically, all avenues for reducing the standard deviation should be pursued before thoughts of reducing the confidence level are entertained.

Unfortunately, there are many situations in which reducing the population standard deviation is not possible. In these cases, another step that can be taken to reduce the margin of error is to increase the sample size. As you learned in Chapter 7, an increase in sample size reduces the standard error of the sampling distribution. This can be the most direct way of reducing the margin of error as long as obtaining an increased sample is not prohibitively costly or unattainable for other reasons.

Impact of the Sample Size on the Interval Estimate

Business Application

NAGEL BEVERAGE (*CONTINUED*) Suppose the Nagel Beverage Company production manager decided to increase the sample to 400 cans. This is a four-fold increase over the original sample size. We learned in Chapter 7 that an increase in sample size reduces the standard error of the sampling distribution because the standard error is computed as $\sigma/\sqrt{n}$. Thus, without adversely affecting his confidence level, the manager can reduce the margin of error by increasing his sample size.

Assume that the sample mean for the larger sample size also happens to be $\bar{x} = 12.09$ ounces. The new 95% confidence interval estimate is

$$12.09 \pm 1.96 \frac{0.2}{\sqrt{400}}$$

$$12.09 \pm 0.02$$

12.07 ounces -------------- 12.11 ounces

Notice that by increasing the sample size to 400 cans, the margin of error is reduced from the original 0.04 ounces to 0.02 ounces. The production manager now believes that his sample mean is within ± 0.02 ounces of the true population mean.

He was able to reduce the margin of error without reducing the confidence level. However, the downside is that a sample of 400 cans instead of 100 cans will cost more money and take more time. That's the trade-off. Absent the possibility of reducing the population standard deviation, if he wants to reduce the margin of error, he must either reduce the confidence level or increase the sample size, or some combination of each. If he is unwilling to do so, he will have to accept the larger margin of error.

Confidence Interval Estimates for the Population Mean, σ Unknown

In the Nagel Beverage Company example, the manager was dealing with a filling machine that had a known standard deviation in fill volume. You may encounter situations in which the standard deviation is known. However, in most cases, if you do not know the population mean, you also will not know the population standard deviation. When this occurs, you need to make a minor, but important, modification to the confidence interval estimation process.

Student's *t*-Distribution

When the population standard deviation is known, the sampling distribution of the mean has only one unknown parameter: its mean, μ. This is estimated by $\bar{x}$. However, when the population standard deviation is unknown, there are two unknown parameters, μ and σ, which can be estimated by $\bar{x}$ and s, respectively. This estimation doesn't affect the general format for a confidence interval, as shown earlier in Equation 8.1:

$$\text{Point Estimate} \pm (\text{Critical Value})(\text{Standard Error})$$

However, not knowing the population standard deviation does affect the critical value. Recall that when σ is known and the population is normally distributed or the Central Limit Theorem applies, the critical value is a *z*-value taken from the standard normal table. But when σ is not known, the critical value is a *t*-value taken from a family of distributions called the **Student's *t*-distributions**.

Student's *t*-Distributions
A family of distributions that is bell-shaped and symmetric like the standard normal distribution but with greater area in the tails. Each distribution in the *t*-family is defined by its degrees of freedom. As the degrees of freedom increase, the *t*-distribution approaches the normal distribution.

Because the specific *t*-distribution chosen is based upon its *degrees of freedom*, it is important to understand what degrees of freedom means. Recall that the sample standard deviation is an estimate of the population's standard deviation and is defined as

$$s = \sqrt{\frac{\sum(x - \bar{x})^2}{n - 1}}$$

Therefore, if we wish to estimate the population standard deviation, we must first calculate the sample mean. The sample mean is itself an estimator of a parameter, namely, the population mean. The sample mean is obtained from a sample of n randomly an independently chosen data values. Once the sample mean has been obtained, there are only $n - 1$ independent pieces of data information left in the sample.

To illustrate, examine a sample of size $n = 3$ in which the sample mean is calculated to be 12. This implies that the sum of the three data values equals 36 (3×12). If you know that the first two data values are 10 and 8, respectively, then the third data value is determined to be 18. Similarly, if you know that the first two data values are 18 and 7, respectively, the third data value must be 11. You are free to choose any two of the three data values. In general, if you must estimate k parameters before you are able to estimate the population's standard deviation from a sample of n data values, you have the freedom to choose any $n - k$ data values before the remaining k-values are determined. This value, $n - k$, is called the **degrees of freedom**.

Degrees of Freedom
The number of independent data values available to estimate the population's standard deviation. If k parameters must be estimated before the population's standard deviation can be calculated from a sample of size n, the degrees of freedom are equal to $n - k$.

When the population is normally distributed, the *t*-value represents the number of standard errors $\bar{x}$ is from μ, as shown in Equation 8.4. Appendix F contains a table of standardized *t*-values that correspond to specified tail areas and different degrees of freedom. The *t*-table is used to determine the critical value when we do not know the population standard deviation. The *t*-table is reproduced in the inside front cover of your text and also in Table 8.2. Note, in Equation 8.4 on page 342, we use the sample standard deviation, s, to estimate the population standard deviation, σ. The fact that we are estimating σ is the reason the *t*-distribution is more spread out (i.e., has a larger standard deviation) than the normal distribution (see Figure 8.5). By estimating σ, we are introducing more uncertainty into the estimation process; therefore, to achieve the same level of confidence requires a larger number of standard deviations. As the sample size increases, our estimate of σ becomes better and the *t*-distribution converges to the *z*-distribution.

TABLE 8.2 Values of *t* for Selected Probabilities

	Probabilities (or Areas Under t-Distribution Curve)								
Conf. Level	0.1	0.3	0.5	0.7	0.8	0.9	0.95	0.98	0.99
One Tail	0.45	0.35	0.25	0.15	0.1	0.05	0.025	0.01	0.005
Two Tails	0.9	0.7	0.5	0.3	0.2	0.1	0.05	0.02	0.01
d.f.					*Values of* t				
1	0.1584	0.5095	1.0000	1.9626	3.0777	6.3137	12.7062	31.8210	63.6559
2	0.1421	0.4447	0.8165	1.3862	1.8856	2.9200	4.3027	6.9645	9.9250
3	0.1366	0.4242	0.7649	1.2498	1.6377	2.3534	3.1824	4.5407	5.8408
4	0.1338	0.4142	0.7407	1.1896	1.5332	2.1318	2.7765	3.7469	4.6041
5	0.1322	0.4082	0.7267	1.1558	1.4759	2.0150	2.5706	3.3649	4.0321
6	0.1311	0.4043	0.7176	1.1342	1.4398	1.9432	2.4469	3.1427	3.7074
7	0.1303	0.4015	0.7111	1.1192	1.4149	1.8946	2.3646	2.9979	3.4995
8	0.1297	0.3995	0.7064	1.1081	1.3968	1.8595	2.3060	2.8965	3.3554
9	0.1293	0.3979	0.7027	1.0997	1.3830	1.8331	2.2622	2.8214	3.2498
10	0.1289	0.3966	0.6998	1.0931	1.3722	1.8125	2.2281	2.7638	3.1693
11	0.1286	0.3956	0.6974	1.0877	1.3634	1.7959	2.2010	2.7181	3.1058
12	0.1283	0.3947	0.6955	1.0832	1.3562	1.7823	2.1788	2.6810	3.0545
13	0.1281	0.3940	0.6938	1.0795	1.3502	1.7709	2.1604	2.6503	3.0123
14	0.1280	0.3933	0.6924	1.0763	1.3450	1.7613	2.1448	2.6245	2.9768
15	0.1278	0.3928	0.6912	1.0735	1.3406	1.7531	2.1315	2.6025	2.9467
16	0.1277	0.3923	0.6901	1.0711	1.3368	1.7459	2.1199	2.5835	2.9208
17	0.1276	0.3919	0.6892	1.0690	1.3334	1.7396	2.1098	2.5669	2.8982
18	0.1274	0.3915	0.6884	1.0672	1.3304	1.7341	2.1009	2.5524	2.8784
19	0.1274	0.3912	0.6876	1.0655	1.3277	1.7291	2.0930	2.5395	2.8609
20	0.1273	0.3909	0.6870	1.0640	1.3253	1.7247	2.0860	2.5280	2.8453
21	0.1272	0.3906	0.6864	1.0627	1.3232	1.7207	2.0796	2.5176	2.8314
22	0.1271	0.3904	0.6858	1.0614	1.3212	1.7171	2.0739	2.5083	2.8188
23	0.1271	0.3902	0.6853	1.0603	1.3195	1.7139	2.0687	2.4999	2.8073
24	0.1270	0.3900	0.6848	1.0593	1.3178	1.7109	2.0639	2.4922	2.7970
25	0.1269	0.3898	0.6844	1.0584	1.3163	1.7081	2.0595	2.4851	2.7874
26	0.1269	0.3896	0.6840	1.0575	1.3150	1.7056	2.0555	2.4786	2.7787
27	0.1268	0.3894	0.6837	1.0567	1.3137	1.7033	2.0518	2.4727	2.7707
28	0.1268	0.3893	0.6834	1.0560	1.3125	1.7011	2.0484	2.4671	2.7633
29	0.1268	0.3892	0.6830	1.0553	1.3114	1.6991	2.0452	2.4620	2.7564
30	0.1267	0.3890	0.6828	1.0547	1.3104	1.6973	2.0423	2.4573	2.7500
40	0.1265	0.3881	0.6807	1.0500	1.3031	1.6839	2.0211	2.4233	2.7045
50	0.1263	0.3875	0.6794	1.0473	1.2987	1.6759	2.0086	2.4033	2.6778
60	0.1262	0.3872	0.6786	1.0455	1.2958	1.6706	2.0003	2.3901	2.6603
70	0.1261	0.3869	0.6780	1.0442	1.2938	1.6669	1.9944	2.3808	2.6479
80	0.1261	0.3867	0.6776	1.0432	1.2922	1.6641	1.9901	2.3739	2.6387
90	0.1260	0.3866	0.6772	1.0424	1.2910	1.6620	1.9867	2.3685	2.6316
100	0.1260	0.3864	0.6770	1.0418	1.2901	1.6602	1.9840	2.3642	2.6259
250	0.1258	0.3858	0.6755	1.0386	1.2849	1.6510	1.9695	2.3414	2.5956
500	0.1257	0.3855	0.6750	1.0375	1.2832	1.6479	1.9647	2.3338	2.5857
∞					See Normal Distribution				

FIGURE 8.5

t-**Distribution and Normal Distribution**

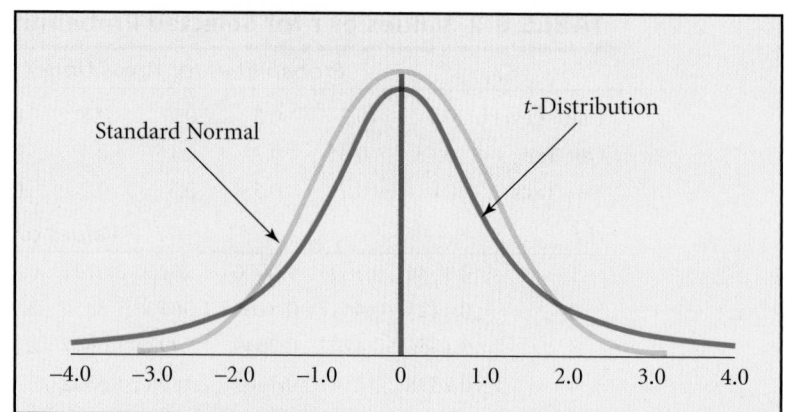

$$t\text{-Value for }\bar{x}$$

$$t = \frac{\bar{x} - \mu}{\frac{s}{\sqrt{n}}}$$ (8.4)

where:

$\bar{x}$ = Sample mean
μ = Population mean
s = Sample standard deviation
n = Sample size

A s s u m p t i o n

We should emphasize that the *t*-distribution is based on the assumption that the population is normally distributed. Although beyond the scope of this text, it can be shown that as long as the population is reasonably symmetric, the *t*-distribution can be used.

Business Application

Excel and Minitab Tutorial

HERITAGE SOFTWARE Heritage Software, a maker of educational and business software, operates a service center in Tulsa, Oklahoma, where employees respond to customer calls about questions and problems with the company's software packages. Recently, a team of Heritage employees was asked to study the average length of time service representatives spend with customers. The team decided that a simple random sample of 25 calls would be collected and the population mean call time would be estimated based on the sample data. Not only did the team not know the average length of time, μ, but it also didn't know the standard deviation of length of service time, σ.

Table 8.3 shows the sample data for 25 calls. (These data are on your CD-ROM in a file called **Heritage**.) The managers at Heritage Software are willing to assume the population of call times is approximately normal.[2]

Heritage's sample mean and standard deviation are

$$\bar{x} = 7.088 \text{ minute}$$
$$s = 4.64 \text{ minute}$$

If the managers need a single-valued estimate of the population mean, they would use the point estimate, $\bar{x} = 7.088$ minutes. However, they should realize that this point estimate is

---

[2] Chapter 13 introduces a statistical technique called the goodness-of-fit test that can be used to test whether the sample data could have come from a normally distributed population. PHStat and Minitab contain box and whisker plot features, and you could also use Excel or Minitab to construct a histogram.

TABLE 8.3 Sample Call Times for Heritage Software

7.1	11.6	12.4	8.5	0.4
13.6	1.7	11.0	6.1	11.0
1.4	16.9	3.7	3.3	0.8
3.6	2.6	14.6	6.1	6.4
1.9	7.7	8.8	6.9	9.1

subject to sampling error. To take the sampling error into account, the managers can construct a confidence interval estimate. Equation 8.5 shows the formula for the confidence interval estimate for the population mean when the population standard deviation is unknown.

CHAPTER OUTCOME # 2

Confidence Interval Estimate for μ, σ Unknown

$$\bar{x} \pm t\frac{s}{\sqrt{n}} \tag{8.5}$$

where:

$\bar{x} =$ Sample mean
$t =$ Critical value from the t-distribution with $n - 1$ degrees of freedom for the desired confidence level
$s =$ Sample standard deviation
$n =$ Sample size

The first step is to specify the desired confidence level. For example, suppose the Heritage team specifies a 95% confidence level. To get the critical t-value from the t-table in Appendix F, go to the top of the table to the row labeled *Conf. Level*. Locate the column headed 0.95. Next, go to the row corresponding to

$$n - 1 = 25 - 1 = 24 \text{ degrees of freedom}$$

The critical t-value for 95% confidence and 24 degrees of freedom is

$$t = 2.0639^*$$

The Heritage team can now compute the 95% confidence interval estimate using Equation 8.5 as follows:

$$\bar{x} \pm t\frac{s}{\sqrt{n}}$$

$$7.088 \pm 2.0639\frac{4.64}{\sqrt{25}}$$

$$7.088 \pm 1.915$$

5.173 min. $----------------$ 9.003 min.

Therefore, based on the random sample of 25 calls and the 95% confidence interval, the Heritage Software team has estimated the true average time per call to be between 5.173 minutes and 9.003 minutes.

---

* You can get the t critical value by using Excel's **TINV** function. For this example, enter **TINV**(0.05,24) to get 2.0639. (*Note*: The **TINV** function requires that $1 -$ confidence level $= 0.95$ be used, whereas the **NORMSINV** function requires 0.025.) You can also insert the cumulative probability 0.975 into Minitab's **Calc > Probability Distribution > t** command.

FIGURE 8.6

Excel 2007 Output for the Heritage Example

Excel 2007 Instructions:
1. Open file: Heritage.xls.
2. Select **Data** tab.
3. Select **Data Analysis**.
4. Select **Descriptive Statistics**.
5. Specify data range for the data.
6. Define **Output Location**.
7. Check **Summary Statistics**.
8. Click **OK**.

	A	B
1	Column1	
2		
3	Mean	7.088
4	Standard Error	0.9281
5	Median	6.9
6	Mode	11
7	Standard Deviation	4.6404
8	Sample Variance	21.5336
9	Kurtosis	-0.7565
10	Skewness	0.3473
11	Range	16.5
12	Minimum	0.4
13	Maximum	16.9
14	Sum	177.2
15	Count	25
16	Confidence Level(95.0%)	1.9155
17		

$\bar{x} = 7.088$

Confidence Interval
7.088 ± 1.915
5.173 -------------- 9.003

Margin of Error

FIGURE 8.7

Minitab Output for the Heritage Example

MINITAB - Heritage.MPJ

Session

One-Sample T: Data

95% Confidence Interval Estimate
5.173 min ----------------9.003 min

Variable	N	Mean	StDev	SE Mean	95% CI
Data	25	7.08800	4.64043	0.92809	(5.17252, 9.00348)

Minitab Instructions:
1. Open file: Heritage.MTW.
2. Choose **Stat > Basic Statistics > 1–sample t.**
3. In **Samples in column**, enter data column.
4. Click **Options**.
5. In **Confidence level**, enter confidence level.
6. Click **OK. OK.**

Excel and Minitab have procedures for computing the confidence interval estimate of the population mean. The Excel output is shown in Figure 8.6. Note, the margin of error is printed. You will have to use it and the sample mean to compute the upper and lower limits. Figure 8.7 shows the results when Minitab is used to compute the 95% confidence interval estimate for the Heritage Company.

TRY PROBLEM 8.8

EXAMPLE 8-3 Confidence Interval Estimate for μ, σ Unknown

Medlin & Associates Medlin & Associates is a regional CPA firm located near Minneapolis. Recently, a team conducted an audit for a discount chain. One part of the audit involved developing an estimate for the mean dollar error in total charges that occur during the checkout process. The firm wishes to develop a 90% confidence interval estimate for the population mean. To do so, it can use the following steps:

Step 1 **Define the population and select a simple random sample of size n from the population.**

In this case, the population consists of errors made in all customers' bills at the discount chain store in a given week. A simple random sample of $n = 20$ is selected, with the following data. (*Note*: Positive values indicate that the customer was overcharged.)

$0.00	$1.20	$0.43	$1.00	$1.47	$0.83	$0.50	$3.34	$1.58	$1.46
−$0.36	−$1.10	$2.60	$0.00	$0.00	−$1.70	$0.83	$1.99	$0.00	$1.34

Step 2 **Specify the confidence level.**

A 90% confidence interval estimate is desired.

Step 3 **Compute the sample mean and sample standard deviation.**

After the sample has been selected and the billing errors have been determined for each of the 20 customers sampled, the sample mean is computed using

$$\bar{x} = \frac{\sum x}{n} = \frac{\$15.41}{20} = \$0.77$$

The sample standard deviation is computed using

$$s = \sqrt{\frac{\sum(x-\bar{x})^2}{n-1}} = \sqrt{\frac{(0.00-0.77)^2 + (1.20-0.77)^2 + \cdots + (1.34-0.77)^2}{20-1}} = \$1.19$$

Step 4 **Determine the standard error of the sampling distribution.**

Because the population standard deviation is unknown, the standard error of the sampling distribution is estimated using

$$\sigma_{\bar{x}} = \frac{s}{\sqrt{n}} = \frac{\$1.19}{\sqrt{20}} = \$0.27$$

Step 5 **Determine the critical value for the desired level of confidence.**

Because we do not know the population standard deviation and the sample size is reasonably small, the critical value will come from the t-distribution, providing we can assume that the population is normally distributed. A box and whisker plot can give some insight about how the population might look.

Minimum	−1.7
First Quartile	0
Median	0.83
Third Quartile	1.47
Maximum	3.34

This diagram does not indicate that there is any serious skewness or other abnormality in the data, so we will continue with the normal distribution assumption.

The critical value for 90% confidence and $20 - 1 = 19$ degrees of freedom is found in the t-distribution table as $t = 1.7291$.

Step 6 Compute the confidence interval estimate.
The 90% confidence interval estimate for the population mean is

$$\bar{x} \pm t \frac{s}{\sqrt{n}}$$

$$0.77 \pm 1.7291 \frac{1.19}{\sqrt{20}}$$

$$0.77 \pm 0.46$$

$$\$0.31 \text{ -------------- } \$1.23$$

Thus, based upon the sample data, with 90% confidence, the auditors can conclude that the population mean dollar error at the checkout is between $0.31 and $1.23. Since both limits are positive, the auditors should conclude that the clerks overcharge customers on average.

Estimation with Larger Sample Sizes We saw earlier that a change in sample size can affect the margin of error in a statistical estimation situation when the population standard deviation is known. This is also true in applications in which the standard deviation is not known. In fact, the effect of a change is compounded because the change in sample size affects both the calculation of the standard error and the critical value from the *t*-distribution.

The *t*-distribution table in Appendix F shows degrees of freedom up to 30 and then incrementally to 500. Observe that for any confidence level, as the degrees of freedom increase, the *t*-value gets smaller as it approaches a limit equal to the *z*-value from the standard normal table in Appendix D for the same confidence level. If you need to estimate the population mean with a sample size that is not listed in the *t*-table, you can use the Excel **TINV** function or Minitab's **Calc > Probability Distribution > *t*** command to get the critical *t*-value for any specified degrees of freedom and then use Equation 8.5.

You should have noticed that the format for confidence interval estimates for μ is essentially the same, regardless of whether the population standard deviation is known. The basic format is

Point Estimate ± (Critical Value)(Standard Error)

Later in this chapter, we introduce estimation examples in which the population value of interest is π, the population proportion. The same confidence interval format is used. In addition, the trade-offs between margin of error, confidence level, and sample size that were discussed in this section also apply to every other estimation situation.

SUMMARY Confidence Interval Estimates for a Single Population Mean

A confidence interval estimate for a single population mean can be developed using the following steps.

1. Define the population of interest and the variable for which you wish to estimate the population mean.
2. Determine the sample size and select a simple random sample.
3. Compute the confidence interval as follows, depending on the conditions that exist:

■ If σ is known, and the population is normally distributed, use

$$\bar{x} \pm z \frac{\sigma}{\sqrt{n}}$$

■ If σ is unknown and we can assume that the population distribution is approximately normal, use

$$\bar{x} \pm t \frac{s}{\sqrt{n}}$$

8-1: Exercises

Skill Development

8-1. Construct a 95% confidence interval estimate for the population mean given the following values:

$$\bar{x} = 300 \quad \sigma = 55 \quad n = 250$$

8-2. Construct a 98% confidence interval estimate for the population mean given the following values:

$$\bar{x} = 120 \quad \sigma = 20 \quad n = 50$$

8-3. Construct a 90% confidence interval estimate for the population mean given the following values:

$$\bar{x} = 70 \quad \sigma = 15 \quad n = 65$$

8-4. Assuming the population of interest is approximately normally distributed, construct a 95% confidence interval estimate for the population mean given the following values:

$$\bar{x} = 18.4 \quad s = 4.2 \quad n = 13$$

8-5. The following sample data have been collected based on a simple random sample from a normally distributed population:

2	8	0	2	3
5	3	1	4	2

a. Compute a 90% confidence interval estimate for the population mean.

b. Show what the impact would be if the confidence level is increased to 95%. Discuss why this occurs.

8-6. Determine the margin of error for a confidence interval estimate for the population mean of a normal distribution given the following information:

a. confidence level = 0.98, $n = 13$, $s = 15.68$

b. confidence level = 0.99, $n = 25$, $\sigma = 3.47$

c. confidence level = 0.98, standard error = 2.356

8-7. Determine the 90% confidence interval estimate for the population mean of a normal distribution given $n = 100$, $\sigma = 121$, and $\bar{x} = 1,200$.

8-8. A random sample of $n = 12$ values taken from a normally distributed population resulted in the following sample values:

107	109	99	91	103	105
105	94	107	94	97	113

Use the sample information to construct a 95% confidence interval estimate for the population mean.

8-9. A random sample of $n = 9$ values taken from a normally distributed population with a population variance of 25 resulted in the following sample values:

53	46	55	45	44	52	46	60	49

Use the sample values to construct a 90% confidence interval estimate for the population mean.

8-10. A random sample of size 20 yields $\bar{x} = 3.13$ and $s^2 = 1.45$. Calculate a confidence interval for the population mean whose confidence level is as follows:

a. 0.99

b. 0.98

c. 0.95

d. 0.90

e. 0.80

f. What assumptions were necessary to establish the validity of the confidence intervals calculated in parts a through e?

8-11. A random sample was selected from a population having a normal distribution. Calculate a 90% confidence interval estimate for μ for each of the following situations:

a. $\Sigma x = 134$, $n = 10$, $s = 3.1$

b. $\Sigma x = 3,744$, $n = 120$, $s = 8.2$

c. $\Sigma x = 40.5$, $n = 9$, $\sigma = 2.9$

d. $\Sigma x = 585.9$, $\Sigma x^2 = 15,472.37$, $n = 27$ (*Hint*: Refer to Equation 3.13)

Business Applications

8-12. A 2005 article written by Will Lester of the Associated Press reported on a poll in which 80% of those surveyed say that Americans who currently own a SUV (sport utility vehicle) should switch to a more fuel-efficient vehicle to ease America's dependency on foreign oil. This study was conducted by the Pew Research Center for the People & The Press and was conducted in September 2005. As a follow-up to this report, a consumer group conducted a study of SUV owners to estimate the mean mileage for their vehicles. A simple random sample of 91 SUV owners was selected and the owners were asked to report their highway mileage. The following results were summarized from the sample data:

$$\bar{x} = 18.2 \text{ mpg}$$
$$s = 6.3 \text{ mpg}$$

Based on these sample data, compute and interpret a 90% confidence interval estimate for the mean highway mileage for SUVs.

8-13. Presto Pizza delivers pizzas throughout its local market area at no charge to the customer. However, customers often tip the driver. The owner is interested in estimating the mean tip income per delivery. To do this, she has selected a simple random sample of 12 deliveries and has recorded the tips that were received by the drivers. These data are

$2.25	$2.50	$2.25	$2.00	$2.00	$1.50
$0.00	$2.00	$1.50	$2.00	$3.00	$1.50

a. Based on these sample data, what is the best point estimate to use as an estimate of the true mean tip per delivery?

b. Suppose the owner is interested in developing a 90% confidence interval estimate. Given the fact that the population standard deviation is unknown, what distribution will be used to obtain the critical value?

c. Referring to part b, what assumption is required to use the specified distribution to obtain the critical value? Develop a box and whisker plot to illustrate whether this assumption seems to be reasonably satisfied.

d. Referring to parts b and c, construct and interpret the 90% confidence interval estimate for the population mean.

8-14. The Evergreen Company operates retail pharmacies in 10 eastern states. Recently, the company's internal audit department selected a random sample of 300 prescriptions issued throughout the system. The objective of the sampling was to estimate the average dollar value of all prescriptions issued by the company. The following data were collected:

$$\bar{x} = \$14.23$$
$$s = 3.00$$

a. Determine the 90% confidence interval estimate for the true average sales value for prescriptions issued by the company. Interpret the interval estimate.

b. One of its retail outlets recently reported that it had monthly revenue of $7,392 from 528 prescriptions. Are such results to be expected? Do you believe that the retail outlet should be audited? Support your answer with calculations and logic.

8-15. According to *USA Today* (Chris Woodyard, "More autos getting that touch of personality," February 3, 2006), customers are not settling for automobiles straight off the production lines. As an example, those who purchase a $355,000 Rolls-Royce "typically" add $25,000 in accessories. One of the affordable automobiles to receive additions is BMW's Mini Cooper. A sample of 179 recent Mini purchasers yielded a sample mean of $5,000 above the $17,500 base sticker price. Suppose the cost of accessories purchased for all Mini Coopers has a standard deviation of $1,500.

a. Calculate a 95% confidence interval for the average cost of accessories on Mini Coopers.

b. Determine the margin of error in estimating the average cost of accessories on Mini Coopers.

c. What sample size would be required to reduce the margin of error by 50%?

8-16. A regional U.S. commercial bank issues both Visa credit cards and MasterCard credit cards. As a part of its annual review of the profitability of each type of credit card, the bank randomly samples 36 customers to measure the average annual charges per card. It has completed its analysis of the Visa card accounts and is now focused on its MasterCard customers. A random sample of 36 MasterCard accounts shows the following annual spending per account (rounded to the nearest dollar):

$2,869	$3,770	$2,854	$2,750	$2,574	$2,972
$2,549	$3,267	$3,013	$2,707	$2,794	$1,189
$2,230	$2,178	$3,032	$3,485	$2,679	$2,010
$1,994	$2,768	$3,853	$2,064	$3,244	$2,738
$2,807	$2,395	$3,405	$3,006	$3,368	$2,691
$1,996	$3,008	$2,730	$2,518	$2,710	$3,719

a. Based on these randomly sampled accounts, what is the best point estimate of the true mean annual spending for MasterCard account holders?

b. If the bank is interested in developing a 95% confidence interval estimate of mean annual spending, what distribution will be used to determine the critical value?

c. Determine the standard error of the sampling distribution.

d. Construct the 95% confidence interval estimate for the population mean of annual MasterCard spending for the bank's customers.

e. If the bank desires to have a higher level of confidence in its interval estimate, what will happen to the margin of error?

8-17. A *USA Today* article in July 2005 reported on a study that was conducted by American Express in which corporate clients were surveyed to determine the extent to which hotel room rates quoted by central reservation systems differ from the rates negotiated by the companies. In 2004, it is thought that 1.4 million rooms per night were booked for corporate business. The American Express study found that the mean overcharge by hotels was $11.35 per night. Suppose a follow-up study was done in which a random sample of 30 corporate hotel bookings was analyzed. Only those cases where an error occurred were included in the study. The following data show the amounts by which the quoted rate differs from the negotiated rate. Positive values indicate an overcharge and negative values indicate an undercharge.

$15.45	$5.23	−$5.72	$30.86	$6.31	$14.00	$2.09	$18.91	$20.73	$12.72
−$17.34	$23.60	$12.48	$6.02	$15.84	$3.48	$0.93	$5.72	$8.29	$3.00
$6.64	$24.81	$4.57	$11.61	$9.25	−$4.85	$25.60	−$4.56	$7.14	$12.45

a. Compute a 95% confidence interval estimate for the mean error in hotel charges. Interpret the confidence interval estimate.

b. Based on the interval computed in part a, do these sample data tend to support the results of the American Express study? Explain.

8-18. XtraNet, an Internet service provider (ISP), has experienced rapid growth in the past five years. As a part of its marketing strategy, XtraNet promises fast connections and dependable service. To achieve its objectives, XtraNet constantly evaluates the capacity of its servers. One component of its evaluation is an analysis of the average amount of time a customer is connected and using the Internet daily. A random sample of 12 customer records shows the following daily usage times, in minutes:

268	336	296	311	306	335
301	278	290	393	373	329

a. Using the sample data, compute the best point estimate of the population mean for daily usage times for XtraNet's customers.

b. The managers of Xtranet's marketing department would like to develop a 99% confidence interval estimate for the population mean daily customer usage time. Because the population standard deviation of daily customer usage time is unknown and the sample size is small, what assumption must the marketing managers make concerning the population of daily customer usage times?

c. Construct and interpret a 99% confidence interval for the mean daily usage time for XtraNet's customers.

d. Assume that before the sample was taken, Xtranet's marketing staff believed that mean daily usage for its customers was 267 minutes. Does their assumption concerning mean daily usage seem reasonable based on the confidence interval developed in part c?

8-19. The concession managers for the Arkansas Travelers (a minor league baseball team located in Little Rock) are interested in estimating the average amount spent on food by fans attending the team's Friday night home games. Suppose a random sample of 36 receipts for food orders was taken from last year's receipts for Friday night home games with the following food expenditures recorded:

$30.50	$10.63	$3.77	$21.90	$21.95	$9.65
$14.31	$11.39	$25.36	$15.79	$30.88	$12.20
$8.48	$20.70	$28.54	$9.13	$15.54	$14.95
$11.96	$11.91	$8.28	$12.87	$24.26	$21.04
$20.08	$10.08	$25.37	$12.02	$11.61	$11.22
$25.36	$28.07	$17.71	$23.00	$31.79	$17.70

a. Based on the sampled receipts, what is the best point estimate for the mean food expenditures for Friday night home games?

b. Use the sample information to construct a 95% confidence interval estimate for the true mean expenditures for Friday night home games.

c. Before the sample was taken, the food concessions manager stated that mean food expenditures were about $19.00 per order. Does his statement seem consistent with the results obtained in part b?

8-20. Nielsen Media Research reported that the average American home watched more television in 2005 than in any previous season. From September 2004 to September 2005 (the official start and end of TV season in the United States), the average time spent by U.S. households tuned into television was 8 hours and 11 minutes per day. This is 2.7% higher than the previous season, 12.5% higher than 10 years ago, and the highest levels ever reported since television viewing was first measured by Nielsen Media Research in the 1950s. In order to determine if television viewing has changed in 2006, a sample (in minutes) similar to the following would be used:

494	533	597	530	577	514	466	416	403	625
562	448	592	567	564	537	370	627	416	511
750	661	570	579	494	533	549	583	610	423

a. Calculate the sample standard deviation and mean number of minutes spent viewing television.

b. Calculate a 95% confidence interval for the average number of minutes spent viewing television in 2006.

c. Would the results obtained in part b indicate that households viewed more television in 2006 than in 2005?

Computer Database Exercises

8-21. The manager at a new tire and repair shop in Hartford, Connecticut, wants to establish guidelines for the time it should take to put new brakes on vehicles. In particular, he is interested in estimating the mean installation time for brakes for passenger cars and SUVs made by three different manufacturers. To help with this process, he set up an experiment in his shop in which five brake jobs were performed for each manufacturer and each class of vehicle. He recorded the number of minutes that it took to complete the jobs. These data are in a file called **Brake-test** and are also shown as follows:

	Manufacturer		
	Company A	Company B	Company C
Passenger Car	55	68	80
	58	49	67
	66	78	70
	44	60	77
	78	72	90
Vehicle Model			
SUV	102	89	119
	89	90	102
	127	88	98
	78	95	80
	90	101	106

a. Use software such as Excel or Minitab to compute the point estimate for the population mean installation time for each category.

b. Use software such as Excel or Minitab to compute the necessary sample statistics needed to construct 95% confidence interval estimates for the population mean installation times. What assumption is required?

c. Based on the results from part b, what conclusions might you reach about the three companies in terms of the time it takes to install their brakes for passenger cars and for SUVs? Discuss.

8-22. One of the reasons for multiple car accidents on highways is thought to be poor visibility. Recently, the National Transportation Agency (NTA) of the federal government sponsored a study of one rural section of highway in Idaho that had been the scene of several multiple car accidents. Two visibility sensors were located near the site for the purposes of recording the number of miles of visibility each time the visibility reading is performed by the sensors. The two visibility sensors are made by different companies, Scorpion and Vanguard. The NTA would like to develop 95% confidence interval estimates of the mean visibility at this location as recorded by both visibility sensors. The random sample data are in a file called **Visibility**. Also,

comment on whether there appears to be a difference between the two sensors in terms of average visibility readings.

8-23. Suppose a study of 196 randomly sampled privately-insured adults with incomes over 200% of the 2005 poverty level is to be used to measure out-of-pocket medical expenses for prescription drugs for this income class in 2005. The sample data are in the file **Drug Expenses**.

a. Based on the sample data, construct a 95% confidence interval estimate for the mean annual out-of-pocket expenditures on prescription drugs for this income class in 2005. Interpret this interval.

b. The study's authors hope to use the information to make recommendations concerning insurance reimbursement guidelines and patient copayment recommendations. If the margin of error calculated in part a is considered to be too large for this purpose, what options are available to the study's authors?

8-24. The file **German Coffee** contains a random sample of 144 German coffee drinkers and measures the annual coffee consumption in kilograms for each sampled coffee drinker. A marketing research firm wants to use this information to develop an advertising campaign to increase German coffee consumption.

a. Based on the sample's results, what is the best point estimate of average annual coffee consumption for German coffee drinkers?

b. Develop and interpret a 90% confidence interval estimate for the mean annual coffee consumption of German coffee drinkers.

8-25. The per capita consumption of chicken has risen from 28 pounds in 1960 to 86.7 pounds in 2005 according to the U.S. Department of Agriculture. That constitutes an average increase of approximately 1.30 pounds per capita per year. To determine if this trend has continued, in 2006 a random sample of 200 individuals was selected to determine the amount of chicken they consumed in 2006. A file entitled **Chickwt** contains the data.

a. Calculate the mean and standard deviation of the amount of chicken consumed by the individuals in the sample.

b. Calculate a 99% confidence interval for the 2006 per capita consumption of chicken in the United States.

c. Based upon your calculation in part b, determine if the specified trend has continued.

8-26. The Transportation Security Administration (TSA) has examined the possibility of a Registered Traveler program. This program is intended to be a way to shorten security lines for "trusted travelers." USA TODAY (Thomas Frank, "Faster checks of fliers to start," January 20, 2006) reported on a study run in 2005 at Orlando International Airport. 13,000 people paid an annual $80 fee to participate in the program. They spent an average of four seconds in security lines at Orlando according to Verified Identity Pass, the company that ran the program. For comparison purposes, a sample was obtained of the time it took the other passengers to pass through security at Orlando. The file entitled **PASSTIME** contains this data. Assume the distribution of time required to pass through security at Orlando International Airport for those flyers in the Registered Traveler program is normally distributed.

a. Calculate a 95% confidence interval for the average time required to pass through security at Orlando International Airport for those flyers not in the Registered Traveler program.

b. Produce a 95% confidence interval for the average time required to pass through security at Orlando International Airport for those flyers in the Registered Traveler program.

c. Is it plausible to conclude that the average time to pass through security for those who are not Registered Travelers would take as much as 65 times or longer than for those in the Registered Travelers program? Support your assertions.

CHAPTER OUTCOME #3

8.2 Determining the Required Sample Size for Estimating a Population Mean

We have discussed the basic trade-offs that are present in all statistical estimations: the desire to have a high confidence level, a low margin of error, and a small sample size. The problem is these three objectives conflict. For a given sample size, a high confidence level will tend to generate a large margin of error. For a given confidence level, a small sample size will result in an increased margin of error. Reducing the margin of error requires either reducing the confidence level or increasing the sample size or both.

A common question from business decision makers who are planning an estimation application is, "How large a sample size do I really need?" To answer this question, we usually begin by asking a couple of questions of our own:

1. How much money do you have budgeted to do the sampling?
2. How much will it cost to select each item in the sample?

The answers to these questions provide the upper limit on the sample size that can be selected. For instance, if the decision maker indicates that she has a $2,000 budget for selecting the sample and the cost will be about $10 per unit to collect the sample, the sample size's upper limit is $2,000 ÷ $10 = 200 units.

Keeping in mind the estimation trade-offs discussed earlier, the issue should be fully discussed with the decision maker. For instance, is a sample of 200 sufficient to give the desired margin of error at a specified confidence level? Is 200 more than is needed to achieve the desired margin of error?

Therefore, before we can give a definite answer about what sample size is needed, the decision maker must specify her confidence level and a desired margin of error. Then the required sample size can be computed.

Determining the Required Sample Size for Estimating μ, σ Known

Business Application

MISSION VALLEY POWER COMPANY Consider the Mission Valley Power Company (MVP) in northwest Michigan, which has more than 6,000 residential customers. In response to a request by the Michigan Public Utility Commission, MVP needs to estimate the average kilowatts of electricity used by customers on February 1. The only way to get this number is to select a random sample of customers and take a meter reading after 5:00 P.M. on January 31 and again after 5:00 P.M. on February 1. The commission has specified that any estimate presented in the utility's report must be based on a 95% confidence level. Further, the margin of error must not exceed ±30 kilowatts. Given these requirements, what size sample is needed?

To answer this question, if the population standard deviation is known, we start with Equation 8.3, the equation for calculating the margin of error.

$$e = z \frac{\sigma}{\sqrt{n}}$$

We next substitute into this equation the values we know. For example, the margin of error was specified to be

$$e = 30 \text{ kilowatts}$$

The confidence level was specified to be 95%. The z-value for 95% is 1.96. (Refer to the standard normal table in Appendix D.) This gives us

$$30 = 1.96 \frac{\sigma}{\sqrt{n}}$$

We need to know the population standard deviation. MVP might know this value from other studies that it has conducted in the past or from similar studies done by other utility companies. Assume for this example that σ, the population standard deviation, is 200 kilowatts. We can now substitute

$$\sigma = 200$$

into the equation for e, as follows:

$$30 = 1.96 \frac{200}{\sqrt{n}}$$

We now have a single equation with one unknown, n, the sample size. Doing the algebra to solve for n, we get

$$n = \left(\frac{1.96(200)}{30} \right)^2 = 170.73 \approx 171 \text{ customers}$$

Thus, to meet the requirements of the utility commission, a sample of $n = 171$ customers should be selected. Equation 8.6 is used to determine the required sample size for estimating a single population mean when σ is known.

Sample Size Requirement for Estimating μ, σ Known

$$n = \left(\frac{z\sigma}{e} \right)^2 = \frac{z^2\sigma^2}{e^2} \qquad \textbf{(8.6)}$$

where:

z = Critical value for the specified confidence level

e = Desired margin of error

σ = Population standard deviation

If MVP feels that the cost of sampling 171 customers will be too high, it might appeal to the commission to allow for a higher margin of error or a lower confidence level. For example, if the confidence level is lowered to 90%, the z-value is lowered to 1.645, as found in the standard normal table.[3]

---

[3] You can also use the Excel function, **NORMSINV**, to determine the z-value or Minitab's **Calc > Probability Distributions > Normal** command.

We can now use Equation 8.6 to determine the revised sample-size requirement.

$$n = \frac{1.645^2 \, (200)^2}{30^2} = 120.27 = 121$$

MVP will need to sample only 121 (120.27 rounded up) customers for a confidence level of 90% rather than 95%.

EXAMPLE 8-4 Determining the Required Sample Size, σ Known

TRY PROBLEM 8.27

Gordon's Self-Service Gasoline   The general manager for Gordon's Self-Service Gasoline is interested in estimating the mean number of gallons of gasoline that are purchased by customers at his Kansas City location. He would like his estimate to be within plus or minus 0.50 gallons, and he would like the estimate to be at the 99% confidence level. Past studies have shown that the standard deviation for purchase amount is 4.0 gallons. To determine the required sample size, he can use the following steps:

Step 1 Specify the desired margin of error.
The manager wishes to have his estimate be within ±0.50 gallons, so the margin of error is

$$e = 0.50 \text{ gallons}$$

Step 2 Determine the population standard deviation.
Based on other studies, the manager is willing to conclude that the population standard deviation is known. Thus,

$$\sigma = 4.0$$

Step 3 Determine the critical value for the desired level of confidence.
The critical value will be a *z*-value from the standard normal table for 99% confidence. This is

$$z = 2.575$$

Step 4 Compute the required sample size using Equation 8.6.
The required sample size is

$$n = \frac{z^2 \sigma^2}{e^2} = \frac{2.575^2 4.0^2}{0.50^2} = 424.36 \approx 425 \text{ customers}$$

Note: The sample size is always rounded up to the next integer value.

Determining the Required Sample Size for Estimating μ, σ Unknown

Equation 8.6 assumes that you know the population standard deviation. Although this may be the case in some situations, most likely we won't know the population standard deviation. To get around this problem, we can use three approaches. One is to use a value for σ that is considered to be at least as large as the true σ. This will provide a conservatively large sample size.

Pilot Sample
A sample taken from the population of interest of a size smaller than the anticipated sample size that is used to provide an estimate for the population standard deviation.

The second option is to select a **pilot sample**, a sample from the population that is used explicitly to estimate σ.

The third option is to use the range of the population to estimate the population's standard deviation. Recall the Empirical Rule in Chapter 3 and the examination in Chapter 6 of the normal distribution. Both sources suggest that μ ± 3σ contains virtually all of the data values of a normal distribution. If this were the case, then μ − 3σ would be approximately the smallest number and μ + 3σ would be approximately the largest number.

Remember that the Range $= R =$ Maximum Value – Minimum Value. So, $R \approx (\mu + 3\sigma) - (\mu - 3\sigma) = 6\sigma$. We can, therefore, obtain an estimate of the standard deviation as

$$\sigma \approx \frac{R}{6}$$

We can also use a procedure that produces a larger estimate of the standard deviation, which will lead to a larger, more conservative sample size. This involves dividing the range by 4 instead of 6.

We seldom know the standard deviation of the population. However, very often we have a very good idea about the largest and smallest value of the population. Therefore, this third method can be used in many instances in which you do not wish to, or cannot, obtain a pilot sample or you are unable to offer a conjecture concerning a conservatively large value of the standard deviation.

EXAMPLE 8-5 Determining the Required Sample Size, σ Unknown

TRY PROBLEM 8.32

Georgia Lumber Mill Consider a Georgia lumber mill manager who wishes to know the average diameter of logs the mill cuts. Not only does she not know μ, she also does not know the population standard deviation. She wants a 90% confidence level and is willing to have a margin of error of 0.50 inch in estimating the true mean diameter. The required sample size can be determined using the following steps:

Step 1 Specify the desired margin of error.
The manager wants the estimate to be within ± 0.50 inch of the true mean. Thus,

$$e = 0.50$$

Step 2 Determine an estimate for the population standard deviation.
The manager will select a pilot sample of $n = 20$ logs and measure the diameter of each. These values are

18.9	22.4	24.6	25.7	26.3	28.4	21.7	31.0	19.0	31.7
17.4	25.5	20.1	34.3	25.9	20.3	21.6	25.8	31.6	28.8

The estimate for the population standard deviation is the sample standard deviation for the pilot sample. This is computed using

$$s = \sqrt{\frac{\Sigma(x - \bar{x})^2}{n-1}} = \sqrt{\frac{(18.9 - 25.05)^2 + (22.4 - 25.05)^2 + \cdots + (28.8 - 25.05)^2}{20 - 1}} = 4.85$$

We will use

$$\sigma \approx 4.85$$

Step 3 Determine the critical value for the desired level of confidence.
The critical value will be a z-value from the standard normal table. The 90% confidence level gives

$$z = 1.645$$

Step 4 Calculate the required sample size using Equation 8.6.
Using the pilot sample's standard deviation the required sample size is

$$n = \frac{z^2\sigma^2}{e^2} = \frac{(1.645^2)(4.85^2)}{0.50^2} = 254.61 = 255$$

The required sample size is 255, but we can use the pilot sample as part of this total. Thus, the net required sample size in this case is $255 - 20 = 235$.

8-2: Exercises

Skill Development

8-27. A manager wishes to estimate a population mean using a 95% confidence interval estimate that has a margin of error of ±44.0. If the population standard deviation is thought to be 680, what is the required sample size?

8-28. A sample size must be determined for estimating a population mean given that the confidence level is to be 90%, and the desired margin of error is 0.30. The largest value in the population is thought to be 15 and the smallest value is thought to be 5.
  a. Calculate the sample size required to estimate the population using a generously large sample size. (*Hint*: Use the range/4 option.)
  b. If a conservatively small sample size is desired, calculate the required sample size. (*Hint*: Use the range/6 option.) Discuss why the answers in parts a and b are different.

8-29. An advertising company wishes to estimate the mean household income for all single working professionals who own a foreign automobile. If the advertising company wants a 90% confidence interval estimate with a margin of error of ±$2,500, what sample size is needed if the population standard deviation is known to be $27,500?

8-30. Suppose a study estimated the population mean for a variable of interest using a 99% confidence interval. If the width of the estimated confidence interval (the difference between the upper limit and the lower limit) is 600 and the sample size used in estimating the mean is 1,000, what is the population standard deviation?

8-31. What sample size is needed to estimate a population mean within ±50 of the true mean value using a confidence level of 95%, if the true population variance is known to be 122,500?

8-32. A decision maker is interested in estimating the mean of a population based on a random sample. She wants the confidence level to be 90% and the margin of error to be ±0.30. She does not know what the population standard deviation is, so she has selected the following pilot sample:

8.80	4.89	10.98	15.11	14.79
16.93	1.27	9.06	14.38	5.65
7.24	3.24	2.61	6.09	6.91

Based on this pilot sample, how many more items must be sampled so that the decision

maker can make the desired confidence interval estimate?

8-33. Calculate the smallest sample size required to estimate the population mean under the following specifications:
  a. confidence level 95%, $\sigma = 16$, and $e = 4$
  b. confidence level 90%, $\sigma = 23$, and $e = 0.5$
  c. confidence level 99%, $\sigma = 0.5$, and $e = 1$
  d. confidence level 98%, $\sigma = 1.5$, and $e = 0.2$
  e. confidence level 95%, $\sigma = 16$, and $e = 4$

8-34. Determine the smallest sample size required to estimate the population mean under the following specifications:
  a. $e = 2.4$, confidence level = 80%, data between 50 and 150
  b. $e = 2.4$, confidence level = 90%, data between 50 and 150
  c. $e = 1.2$, confidence level = 90%, data between 50 and 150
  d. $e = 1.2$ confidence level = 90%, data between 25 and 175

Business Applications

8-35. A public policy research group is conducting a study of health care plans and would like to estimate the average dollars contributed annually to health savings accounts by participating employees. A pilot study conducted a few months earlier indicated that the standard deviation of annual contributions to such plans was $1,225. The research group wants the study's findings to be within $100 of the true mean with a confidence level of 90%. What sample size is required?

8-36. A production process that fills 12-ounce cereal boxes is known to have a population standard deviation of 0.009 ounce. If a consumer protection agency would like to estimate the mean fill, in ounces, for 12-ounce cereal boxes with a confidence level of 92% and a margin of error of 0.001, what size sample must be used?

8-37. With the high cost of fuel and the intense competition driving ticket prices down, the major airline companies have had a very difficult time financially in recent years. One major carrier is considering lowering the weight of check-in luggage allowed from the current 50 pounds. However, before making any changes, the airline wishes to estimate the mean weight per bag checked by passengers. It wants the estimate to be within ±0.25 pounds of the true population mean. A pilot sample of bags checked gives the following results:

35	33	37	33	36	40	34	40	39	40
39	41	35	42	43	46	34	41	38	44

a. What size sample should the airline use if it wants to have 95% confidence?

b. Suppose the airline managers do not want to take as large a sample as the one you determined in part a, what general options do they have to lower the required sample size?

8-38. The Longmont Computer Leasing Company leases computers and peripherals like laser printers. The printers have a counter that keeps track of the number of pages printed. The company wishes to estimate the mean number of pages that will be printed in a month on its leased printers. The plan is to select a random sample of printers and record the number on each printer's counter at the beginning of May. Then, at the end of May, the number on the counter will be recorded again and the difference will be the number of copies on that printer for the month. The company wants the estimate to be within ±100 pages of the true mean with a 95% confidence level.

a. The standard deviation in pages printed is thought to be about 1,400 pages. How many printers should be sampled?

b. Suppose that the conjecture concerning the size of the standard deviation is off (plus or minus) by as much as 10%. What percentage change in the required sample size would this produce?

8-39. An Associated Press article in July 2005 by Eileen Alt Powell discussed the changes that banks are making to the way they calculate the minimum payment due on credit card balances. The changes are being pushed by federal regulators. In the past, minimum payments were set at about 2% of the outstanding balance. Each credit card issuer is making its own changes. For example, Bank of America Corporation in Charlotte, North Carolina, went from a minimum of 2.2% of the balance to a flat amount of $10 plus all fees and interest due.

Suppose that a large California-based bank is in the process of considering what changes to make. It wishes to survey its customers to estimate the mean percent payment on their outstanding balance that customers would like to see. The bank wants to construct a 99% confidence interval estimate with a margin of error of ±0.2 percent. A pilot sample of $n = 50$ customers showed a sample standard deviation of 1.4%.

How many more customers does the bank need to survey in order to construct the interval estimate?

8-40. The Northwest Pacific Phone Company wishes to estimate the average number of minutes its customers spend on long-distance calls per month. The company wants the estimate made with 99% confidence and a margin of error of no more than 5 minutes.

a. A previous study indicated that the standard deviation for long-distance calls is 21 minutes per month. What should the sample size be?

b. Determine the required sample size if the confidence level were changed from 99% to 90%.

c. What would the required sample size be if the confidence level was 95% and the margin of error was 8 minutes?

8-41. A regional chain of fast-food restaurants would like to estimate the mean time required to serve its drive-thru customers. Because speed of service is a critical factor in the success of its restaurants, the chain wants to have as accurate an estimate of the mean service time as possible.

a. If the population standard deviation of service times is known to be 30 seconds, how large a sample must be used to estimate the mean service time for drive-thru customers if a margin of error of no more than ±10 seconds of the true mean with a 99% level of confidence is required?

b. Suppose the manager believes that a margin of error of ±10 seconds is too high and has decided it should be cut in half to a margin of error of ±5 seconds. He is of the opinion that by cutting the margin of error in half, the required sample size will double over what was required for a margin of error of ±10. Is the manager correct concerning the sample-size requirement for the reduced margin of error? (Provide supporting calculations.)

8-42. *Business Week* reports (Jack Ewing, "Bulgarian Back Lot, Hollywood Dreams," January 23, 2006) that film production companies are gravitating toward Eastern Europe. There studios have a reputation of skilled technical work at a relatively low cost. But Bulgaria is even cheaper, with costs below those of Hollywood. As an example, weekly soundstage rental prices are quoted as $3.77 per square meter in Bulgaria and $16.50 for their U.S. counterparts. To verify these figures, a sample of 50 rentals was taken producing the average quoted for Bulgaria.

a. Determine the standard deviation of the weekly rental prices if the margin of error associated with the estimate was $2 using a 95% confidence level.

b. How much would the sample size have to be increased to decrease the margin of error by $1?

c. Calculate the change in the standard deviation that would have to be realized to produce the same decrease in the margin of error as realized in part b.

8-43. The Federal Communications Commission released a report (Leslie Cauley, *USA Today*, "Study: A la carte cable would be cheaper," February 10, 2006) refuting an earlier report released in 2004 by the FCC under the prior chairman, Michael Powell. The 2006 report indicates that cable subscribers would save as much as 13% on their cable TV bills. The average monthly cable prices were estimated to be $41.04. Typically, such reports announce a margin of error of say, $1.25 and a confidence level of 95%. Suppose the standard deviation of the monthly cost of cable TV bills was $10.00.

a. Determine the sample size of the study released by the FCC in 2006.

b. Calculate the sample size required to decrease the margin of error by a dollar.

c. A typical sample size used in national surveys is 1,500 to 2,000. Determine a range for the margin of error corresponding to this range of sample sizes.

Computer Database Exercises

8-44. Suppose a random sample of 137 households in Detroit was selected to determine the average annual household spending on food at home for Detroit residents. The sample results are contained in the file **Detroit Eats**.

a. Using the sample standard deviation as an estimate for the population standard deviation, calculate the sample size required to estimate the true population mean to within ±$25 with 95% confidence. How many additional samples must be taken?

b. Using the sample standard deviation as an estimate for the population standard deviation, calculate the sample size required to estimate the true population mean to within ±$25 with 90% confidence. How many additional samples must be taken?

8-45. Phone Solutions, Inc. specializes in providing call center services for companies who wish to outsource their call center activities. There are two main ways that Phone Solutions, Inc. has historically billed its clients: by the call or by the minute. Phone Solutions is currently negotiating with a new client who wants to be billed for the number of minutes that Phone Solutions is on the phone with customers. Before a contract is written, Phone

Solutions plans to receive a random sample of calls and keep track of the minutes spent on the phone with the customer. From this it plans to estimate the mean call time. It wishes to develop a 95% confidence interval estimate for the population mean call time and wants this estimate to be within ±0.15 minutes. The question is, how many calls should Phone Solutions use in its sample?

Since the population standard deviation is unknown, a pilot sample was taken by having three call centers operated by Phone Solutions, Inc. each take 50 calls for a total pilot sample of 150 calls. The minutes for each of these calls are listed in the file called **PhoneSolutions**.

a. How many additional calls will be needed to compute the desired confidence interval estimate for the population mean?

b. In the event that the managers at Phone Solutions, Inc. want a smaller sample size, what options do they have? Discuss in general terms.

8-46. Bruce Leichtman is president of Leichtman Research Group, Inc. (LRG), which specializes in research and consulting on broadband, media, and entertainment industries. In a recent survey, the company determined the cost of extra high-definition (HD) gear needed to watch television in HD. The costs ranged from $5 a month for a set-top box to $200 for a new satellite receiver. The file entitled **HDcosts** contains a sample of the cost of the extras whose purchase was required to watch television in HD.

a. Produce a 95% confidence interval for the population mean cost of the extras whose purchase would be required to watch television in HD.

b. Calculate the margin of error for this experiment.

c. If you were to view the sample used in part a to be a pilot sample, how many additional data values would be required to produce a margin of error of 5? Assume the population standard deviation is 50.353.

8-47. The Bureau of Labor Statistics, U.S. Office of Personnel Management, indicated that the 2005 average hourly compensation (salary plus benefits) for federal workers (not including military or postal service employees) was $44.82. The rates for private industry and state and local government workers are believed to be considerably less than that. The file entitled **Paychecks** contains a random sample of the hourly amounts paid to state and local government workers.

a. Generate the margin of error for estimating the average hourly amounts paid to state and local government workers with a 98%

confidence level if the population standard deviation is 6.

b. Determine the sample size required to produce a margin of error equal to 1.40. Assume the population standard deviation equals 6.22.

c. Does it appear that state and local government workers have a smaller average hourly compensation than federal workers? Support your opinion.

8.3 Estimating a Population Proportion

The previous sections have illustrated the methods for developing confidence interval estimates when the population value of interest is the mean. However, you will encounter many situations in which the value of interest is the proportion of items in the population that possess a particular attribute. For example, you may wish to estimate the proportion of customers who are satisfied with the service provided by your company. The notation for the *population proportion* is π. The point estimate for π is the *sample proportion, p*, which is computed using Equation 8.7.

Sample Proportion

$$p = \frac{x}{n} \tag{8.7}$$

where:

x = Number of occurrences

n = Sample size

In Chapter 7, we introduced the sampling distribution for proportions. We indicated then that when the sample size is sufficiently large [$n\pi \geq 5$ and $n(1 - \pi) \geq 5$], the sampling distribution can be approximated by a normal distribution centered at π, with a standard error for p computed using Equation 8.8.

Standard Error for p

$$\sigma_p = \sqrt{\frac{\pi(1 - \pi)}{n}} \tag{8.8}$$

where:

π = Population proportion

n = Sample size

Notice that in Equation 8.8, the population proportion, π, is required. But if we already knew the value for π, we would not need to determine its estimate. If π is unknown, we can estimate the value for the standard error by substituting p for π, as shown in Equation 8.9, providing that $np \geq 5$ and $n(1 - p) \geq 5$.

Estimate for the Standard Error of p

$$\sigma_p \approx \sqrt{\frac{p(1 - p)}{n}} \tag{8.9}$$

where:

p = Sample proportion

n = Sample size

Figure 8.8 illustrates the sampling distribution for p.

FIGURE 8.8

Sample Distribution for p

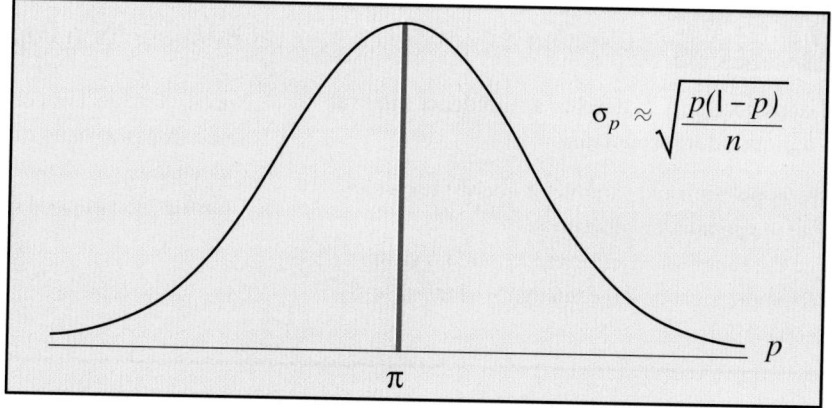

$$\sigma_p \approx \sqrt{\frac{p(1-p)}{n}}$$

CHAPTER OUTCOME # 4

Confidence Interval Estimate for a Population Proportion

The confidence interval estimate for a population proportion is formed using the same general format that we used to estimate a population mean. This was shown originally as Equation 8.1:

$$\text{Point Estimate} \pm (\text{Critical Value})(\text{Standard Error})$$

Equation 8.10 shows the specific format for *confidence intervals involving population proportions*.

Confidence Interval Estimate for π

$$p \pm z\sqrt{\frac{p(1-p)}{n}} \tag{8.10}$$

where:

      p = Sample proportion

      n = Sample size

      z = Critical value from the standard normal distribution for the desired confidence level

---

The critical value for a confidence interval estimate of a population proportion will always be a z-value from the standard normal distribution. Recall from Table 8.1, the most commonly used critical values are

Critical Value	Confidence Level
$z = 1.28$	80%
$z = 1.645$	90%
$z = 1.96$	95%
$z = 2.575$	99%

For other confidence levels, you can find the critical z-value in the standard normal distribution table in Appendix D.

SUMMARY Developing a Confidence Interval Estimate for a Population Proportion

Here are the steps necessary to develop a confidence interval estimate for a population proportion.

1. Define the population and variable of interest for which to estimate the population proportion.
2. Determine the sample size and select a random sample. Note, the sample must be large enough so that $n\pi \geq 5$ and $n(1 - \pi) \geq 5$.
3. Specify the level of confidence and obtain the critical value from the standard normal distribution table.
4. Calculate p, the sample proportion.
5. Construct the interval estimate using Equation 8.10.

$$p \pm z_2 \sqrt{\frac{p(1 - p)}{n}}$$

TRY PROBLEM 8.48

EXAMPLE 8-6 Confidence Interval for a Population Proportion

Quick Lube The Quick Lube Company operates a chain of oil-change outlets in several states. When a customer comes in for service, the date of service and the mileage on the car are recorded. A computer program tracks the customers, and when three months have almost passed, a reminder card is sent to the customer.

The marketing manager is interested in estimating the *proportion* of customers who return after getting a card. Of a simple random sample of 100 customers, 62 returned within one month after the card was mailed. A confidence interval estimate for the true population proportion is found using the following steps:

Step 1 Define the population and the variable of interest.
The population is all customers who have their oil changed at Quick Lube, and the variable of interest is the number who respond to a reminder card that is mailed to them.

Step 2 Determine the sample size.
A simple random sample of $n = 100$ customers receive cards. (Note, as long as $\pi \geq 0.05$ and $\pi \leq 0.95$, a sample size of 100 will meet the requirements that $n\pi \geq 5$ and $n(1 - \pi) \geq 5$.

Step 3 Specify the desired level of confidence and determine the critical value.
Assuming that a 95% confidence level is desired, the critical value from the standard normal distribution table (Appendix D) will be $z = 1.96$.

Step 4 Compute the point estimate based on the sample data.
Equation 8.7 is used to compute the sample proportion.

$$p = \frac{x}{n} = \frac{62}{100} = 0.62$$

Step 5 Compute the confidence interval using Equation 8.10.
The 95% confidence interval estimate is

$$p + z \sqrt{\frac{p(1 - p)}{n}}$$

$$0.62 \pm 1.96 \sqrt{\frac{0.62(1 - 0.62)}{100}}$$

$$0.62 \pm 0.095$$
$$0.525 \text{ -------------- } 0.715$$

Using the sample of 100 customers and a 95% confidence interval, the manager estimates that the true percentage of customers who will respond to the reminder card will be between 52.5% and 71.5%.

Determining the Required Sample Size for Estimating a Population Proportion

CHAPTER OUTCOME #5

Changing the confidence level affects the interval width. Likewise, changing the sample size will affect the interval width. An increase in sample size will reduce the standard error and reduce the interval width. A decrease in the sample size will have the opposite effect. For many applications, decision makers would like to determine a required sample size before doing the sampling. As was the case for estimating the population mean, the required sample size in a proportion application is based on the desired margin of error, the desired confidence level, and the variation in the population. The **margin of error**, e, is computed using Equation 8.11.

Margin of Error for Estimating π

$$e = z\sqrt{\frac{\pi(1-\pi)}{n}}$$

(8.11)

where:

π = Population proportion

z = Critical value from standard normal distribution for the desired confidence level

n = Sample size

Equation 8.12 is used to determine the required sample size for a given confidence level and margin of error.

Sample Size for Estimating π

$$n = \frac{z^2\pi(1-\pi)}{e^2}$$

(8.12)

where:

π = Value used to represent the population proportion

e = Desired margin of error

z = Critical value from standard normal distribution for the desired confidence level

---

Business Application

QUICK LUBE (*CONTINUED*) Referring to Example 8-6, recall that the marketing manager developed a confidence interval estimate for the proportion of customers who would respond to a reminder card. This interval was

$$0.62 \pm 1.96\sqrt{\frac{0.62(1-0.62)}{100}}$$

$$0.62 \pm 0.095$$

$$0.525 \text{ -------------- } 0.715$$

The calculated margin of error in this situation is 0.095. Suppose the marketing manager wants the margin of error reduced to $e = \pm0.04$ at a 95% confidence level. This will require an increase in sample size. To apply Equation 8.12, the margin of error and the confidence level are specified by the decision maker. However, the population proportion, π, is not something you can control. In fact, if you already knew the value for π, you wouldn't need to estimate it and the sample-size issue wouldn't come up.

Two methods overcome this problem. First, you can select a *pilot sample* and compute the sample proportion, p, and substitute p for π. Then, once the sample size is computed, the pilot sample can be used as part of the overall required sample.

Second, you can select a conservative value for π. The closer π is to 0.50, the greater is the variation because $\pi(1-\pi)$ is greatest when $\pi = 0.50$. For example, if the manager has reason to believe that the population proportion, π, will be about 0.60, he could use a value for π a little closer to 0.50—say, 0.55. If he doesn't have a good idea of what π is, he could conservatively use $\pi = 0.50$, which will give a sample size at least large enough to meet requirements.

Suppose the Quick Lube manager selects a pilot sample of $n = 100$ customers and sends these people cards. Further, suppose $x = 62$ of these customers respond to the mailing. Then,

$$p = \frac{62}{100} = 0.62$$

is substituted for π in Equation 8.12. For a 95% confidence level, the z-value is

$$z = 1.96$$

and the margin of error is equal to

$$e = 0.04$$

Substitute these values into Equation 8.12 and solve for the required sample size.

$$n = \frac{1.96^2 (0.62)(1 - 0.62)}{0.04^2} = 565.676 = 566$$

Because the pilot sample of 100 can be included, the Quick Lube manager needs to send out an additional 466 cards to randomly selected customers. If this is more than the company can afford or wishes to include in the sample, the margin of error can be increased or the confidence level can be reduced.

EXAMPLE 8-7 Sample Size Determination for Estimating π

TRY PROBLEM 8.50

The Newsday Times The managing editor for the *The Newsday Times* paper is interested in estimating the proportion of the paper's customers who like the new design for the sports page. She wishes to develop a 90% confidence interval estimate and would like to have the estimate be within ± 0.05 of the true population proportion. To determine the required sample size, she can use the following steps:

Step 1 Define the population and variable of interest.
The population is all customers of the newspaper. The variable of interest is the number of customers who like the new sports page.

Step 2 Determine the level of confidence and find the critical z-value using the standard normal distribution table.
The desired confidence level is 90%. The z-value for 90% confidence is 1.645.

Step 3 Determine the desired margin of error.
The editor wishes the margin of error to be 0.05.

Step 4 Arrive at a value to use for π.
Two options can be used to obtain a value for π:

1. Use a pilot sample and compute p, the sample proportion. Use p to represent π.
2. Select a value for π that is closer to 0.50 than you actually believe the value to be. If you have no idea what π might be, use $\pi = 0.50$ to give a generously large sample size.

In this case, suppose the editor has no idea what π is but wants to make sure that her sample is sufficiently large to meet her estimation requirements. Then she will use $\pi = 0.50$.

Step 5 Use Equation 8.12 to determine the sample size.
$$n = \frac{z^2 \pi(1 - \pi)}{e^2} = \frac{1.645^2 (0.50)(1 - 0.50)}{0.05^2} = 270.0625 = 271$$

The editor should randomly survey 271 customers. (Always round up.)

8-3: Exercises

Skill Development

8-48. A decision maker is interested in estimating a population proportion. A sample of size $n = 150$ yields 115 successes. Based on these sample data, construct a 90% confidence interval estimate for the true population proportion.

8-49. At issue is the proportion of people in a particular county who do not have health care insurance coverage. A simple random sample of 240 people were asked if they have insurance coverage and 66 replied that they did not have coverage. Based on these sample data, determine the 95% confidence interval estimate for the population proportion.

8-50. A magazine company is planning to survey customers to determine the proportion who will renew their subscription for the coming year. The magazine wants to estimate the population proportion with 95% confidence and a margin of error equal to ± 0.02. What sample size is required?

8-51. Compute the 90% confidence interval estimate for the population proportion, π, based on a sample size of 100 when the sample proportion, p, is equal to 0.40.

8-52. A pilot sample of 75 items was taken and the number of items with the attribute of interest was found to be 15. How many more items must be sampled to construct a 99% confidence interval estimate for π with a 0.025 margin of error?

8-53. A random sample of 200 items reveals that 144 of the items have the attribute of interest.
a. What is the point estimate for the population proportion for all items having this attribute?
b. Use the information from the random sample to develop a 95% confidence interval estimate for the population proportion, π, of all items having this attribute of interest.

8-54. A random sample of size 150 taken from a population yields a proportion equal to 0.35.
a. Determine if the sample size is large enough so that the sampling distribution can be approximated by a normal distribution.
b. Construct a 90% confidence interval for the population proportion.
c. Interpret the confidence interval calculated in part b.
d. Produce the margin of error associated with this confidence interval.

8-55. A random sample of 40 television viewers was asked if they had watched the current week's *Lost* episode. The following data represent their responses:

no	no	no	yes	no	no	no	yes	no	yes
no	no	no	yes	no	no	no	no	yes	no
yes	no	no	no	no	yes	no	no	no	no
no	no	no	no	no	no	no	no	no	no

a. Calculate the proportion of viewers in the sample who indicated they watched the current week's episode of *Lost*.
b. Compute a 95% confidence for the proportion of viewers in the sample who indicated they watched the current week's episode of *Lost*.
c. Calculate the smallest sample size that would produce a margin of error of 0.025 if the population proportion is well represented by the sample proportion in part a.

Business Applications

8-56. The television landscape has certainly been changing in recent years as satellite and cable TV providers compete for old-line TV networks' viewers. In fact, prior to 2005, the networks had lost viewers in the 18–49 age group for over 10 consecutive years according to a May 2005 article in the *Wall Street Journal* by Brooks Barnes. However, according to the article, in 2005 the networks will post their first gain in viewers. Suppose that CBS plans to conduct interviews with television viewers in an attempt to estimate the proportion of viewers in the 18–49 age group who watch "most" of their television on network TV as opposed to cable or satellite. It wishes to have 95% confidence and a margin of error in its estimate of ± 0.03. A pilot sample of size 50 was selected and the sample proportion was 0.61. In order to achieve these results with a simple random sample, how many additional viewers should be sampled?

8-57. As the automobile accident rate increases, insurers are forced to increase their premium rates. Companies such as All-State have recently been running a campaign they hope will result in fewer accidents by their policyholders. For each six-month period that a customer goes without an accident, All-State will reduce the customer's premium rate by a certain percentage. Companies like All-State have reason to be concerned about driving habits, based on a survey conducted by Drive for Life, a safety group sponsored by Volvo of North America, in which 1,100 drivers were surveyed. Among those surveyed, 74% said that careless or aggressive driving was the biggest threat on the road. One-third of the respondents said that cell phone usage by other drivers was the driving behavior that annoyed them the most. (*Source*: Knight Ridder Newspapers, June 2005.)

Based on these data, assuming that the sample was a simple random sample, construct and interpret a 95% confidence interval estimate for the true proportion in the population of all drivers who are annoyed by cell phone users.

8-58. A survey of 499 women for the American Orthopedic Foot and Ankle Society revealed that 38% wear flats to work.

  a. Use this sample information to develop a 99% confidence interval for the population proportion of women who wear flats to work.

  b. Suppose the society also wished to estimate the proportion of women who wear athletic shoes to work with a margin of error of 0.01 with 95% confidence. Determine the sample size required.

8-59. An Associated Press article in the summer of 2005 written by Rukmini Callimachi pointed out that Nike, the world's largest maker of athletic shoes, has started to feature female models who are not the traditional rail-thin women who have graced billboards and magazine covers for the last 20–25 years. These new models, called "real people," may be larger than the former models, but they are still very athletic and represent what Nike spokeswoman Caren Ball calls "what is real" as opposed to "what is ideal." The article also reports on a survey of 1,000 women conducted by *Allure* magazine in which 91% of the respondents said that they were satisfied with what they see in the mirror. Nike managers would like to use these data to develop a 90% confidence interval estimate for the true proportion of all women who are satisfied with their bodies. Develop and interpret the 90% confidence interval estimate.

8-60. Most major airlines allow passengers to carry two pieces of luggage (of a certain maximum size) onto the plane. However, their studies show that the more carry-on baggage passengers have, the longer it takes the plane to unload and load passengers. One regional airline is considering changing its policy to allow only one carry-on per passenger. Before doing so, it decided to collect some data. Specifically, a random sample of 1,000 passengers was selected. The passengers were observed and the number of bags carried on the plane was noted. Out of the 1,000 passengers, 345 had more than one bag.

  a. Based on this sample, develop and interpret a 95% confidence interval estimate for the proportion of the traveling population that would have been impacted had the "one-bag" limit been in effect. Discuss your result.

  b. The domestic version of Boeing's 747 has a capacity for 568 passengers. Determine an interval estimate of the number of passengers that you would expect to carry more than one piece of luggage on the plane. Assume the plane is at its passenger capacity.

  c. Suppose the airline also noted whether the passenger was male or female. Out of the 1,000 passengers observed, 690 were males. Of this group, 280 had more than one bag. Using this data, obtain and interpret a 95% confidence interval estimate for the proportion of male passengers in the population who would have been affected by the "one-bag" limit. Discuss.

  d. Suppose the airline decides to conduct a survey of its customers to determine their opinion of the proposed "one-bag" limit. The plan calls for a random sample of customers on different flights to be given a short written survey to complete during the flight. One key question on the survey will be: "Do you approve of limiting the number of carry-on bags to a maximum of one bag?" Airline managers expect that only about 15% will say yes. Based on this assumption, what size sample should the airline take if it wants to develop a 95% confidence interval estimate for the population proportion who will say "yes" with a margin of error of ±0.02?

8-61. Suppose the Albuquerque Chamber of Commerce has decided to conduct a survey to estimate the proportion of adults between the ages of 25 and 35 living in the metropolitan area who have a college degree in a high-technology field. The chamber hopes to use the survey's results to attract more high-technology firms to the region. The chamber wants the survey to estimate the population proportion within a margin of error of 0.03 percentage points with a level of confidence of 95%.

  a. If the chamber has no information concerning the proportion of adults between the ages of 25 and 35 who have a college degree in a high-technology field before the survey is taken, how large a sample size must be used?

  b. Suppose the chamber conducted a pilot study of 200 adults between the ages of 25 and 35 that indicated 28 with the desired attribute. How large a sample would be needed for the survey to estimate the population proportion within a margin of error of ±0.03 with a 95% level of confidence?

8-62. In 2005, a survey of 777 teenagers between the ages of 13 and 18 conducted by JA Worldwide/Deloitte & Touche USA LLP found that 69% agree that people who practice good business ethics are more successful than those who do not. (*Source*: *Idaho Statesman*, January 8, 2005.)

a. Calculate the 90% confidence interval estimate for the true population proportion, π, given the survey information.

b. What is the largest possible sample size needed to estimate the true population proportion, π, within a margin of error of ± 0.02 with a confidence level of 95% if there was no prior knowledge concerning the proportion of respondents who would agree with the survey's question?

c. If the survey in part a had a margin of error of ± 0.04 percentage points, determine the level of confidence that was used in estimating the population proportion if there was no prior knowledge concerning the percentage of teenagers who would respond as they did.

8-63. A multinational corporation employing several thousand workers at its campus in a large city in the southwestern United States would like to estimate the proportion of its employees who commute to work by any means other than an automobile. The company hopes to use the information to develop a proposal to encourage more employees to forgo their automobiles as a part of their commute. A pilot study of 100 randomly sampled employees found that 14 commute to work by means other than an automobile.

a. How many more employees must the company randomly sample in order to be able to estimate the true population of employees who commute to work by means other than an automobile with a margin of error of ± 0.03 and a level of confidence of 90%?

b. Suppose that after the full sample is taken it was found that 50 employees commute to work by means other than an automobile. Construct a 90% confidence interval estimate for the true population of employees who commute to work using means other than an automobile. (*Hint*: Your sample size will be the total sample size required for part a.)

8-64. A report released by the College Board asserted (Mary Beth Marklein, *USA Today*, "Advanced Placement on upswing," February 8, 2006) that the percentage of students who took and passed Advanced Placement courses in all subjects has increased in every state and the District of Columbia since 2000. Among public school students, 14.1% in the class of 2005 earned a passing grade on at least one AP exam, the report indicated. In an attempt to determine if the proportion of those passing the math and science AP Exams is equal to the 14.1% success rate, a random sample of 300 students enrolled in AP math and science classes has been selected.

a. If 35 of the students in the sample passed at least one AP math or science class, calculate the

proportion of those students who passed at least one AP math or science exam. Does this statistic indicate that the proportion of students who are passing at least one AP math or science class is less than that of those taking AP exams as a whole? Support your assertions.

b. Calculate the probability that a sample proportion equal to or less than that calculated in part a would occur if the population proportion was actually 0.141. Answer the question posed in part a using this probability.

c. Calculate a 98% confidence interval for the proportion of those students who passed at least one AP math or science class. Answer the question posed in part a using this confidence interval. Does this answer correspond to that of part b? Support your assertions.

8-65. The MainStay Investments of New York Life Investment Management survey of respondents between the ages of 26 to 82 indicated that 66% of Seniors, 61% of Baby Boomers, and 58% of Generation X expect IRAs to be their primary source of income in retirement. The margin of error was given as ± 5 percentage points.

a. Calculate a 95% confidence interval for the proportion of Seniors who expect IRAs to be their primary source of income in retirement.

b. Although the sample size for the entire survey was listed, the sample size for each of the three generations was not given. Assuming the confidence level was 95%, determine the sample size for each of the three generations.

Computer Database Exercises

8-66. Neverslip, Inc. produces belts for industrial use. As part of its continuous process improvement program, Neverslip has decided to monitor on-time shipments of its products. Suppose a random sample of 140 shipments was taken from shipping records for the last quarter and the shipment was recorded as being either "on-time" or "late." The results of the sample are contained in the file **Neverslip**.

a. Using the randomly sampled data, calculate a 90% confidence interval estimate for the true population proportion, π, for on-time shipments for Neverslip.

b. What is the margin of error for the confidence interval calculated in part a?

c. One of Neverslip's commitments to its customers is that 95% of all shipments will arrive on time. Based on the confidence interval calculated in part a, is Neverslip meeting its on-time commitment?

8-67. According to the Employee Benefit Research Institute (www.ebri.org) 34% of workers between the ages of 35 and 44 owned a 401(k)-type retirement plan in 2002. Suppose a recent survey was conducted by the Atlanta Chamber of Commerce to determine the participation rate of 35–44-year-old working adults in the Atlanta metropolitan area in 401(k)-type retirement plans. The Atlanta survey randomly sampled 144 working adults in Atlanta between the ages of 35 and 44. The results of the survey can be found in the file **Atlanta Retirement**.

a. Use the information in the file **Atlanta Retirement** to compute a 95% confidence interval estimate for the true population proportion of working adults in Atlanta between the ages of 35 and 44 in 401(k)-type retirement plans in 2002.

b. Based on the confidence interval calculated in part a, can the Atlanta Chamber of Commerce advertise that a greater percentage of working adults in Atlanta between the ages of 35 and 44 have 401(k) plans than in the nation as a whole for the same age group? Support your answer with the confidence level you calculated above.

8-68. A study by the Investment Company Institute (ICI) in 2004, which randomly surveyed 3,500 households and drew upon information from the Internal Revenue Service, found that 72% of households have conducted at least one IRA rollover from an employer-sponsored retirement plan (www.financial-planning.com). Suppose a recent random sample of 90 households in the greater Miami area was taken and respondents were asked whether they had ever funded an IRA account with a rollover from an employer-sponsored retirement plan. The results are in the file **Miami Rollover**.

a. Based on the random sample of Miami households, what is the best point estimate for the proportion of all Miami households that have ever funded an IRA account with a rollover from an employer-sponsored retirement plan?

b. Construct a 99% confidence interval estimate for the true population proportion of Miami households that had ever funded an IRA account with a rollover from an employer-sponsored retirement plan.

c. If the sponsors of the Miami study found that the margin of error was too high, what could they do to reduce it if they were not willing to change the level of confidence?

8-69. The 2005 Emerging Workforce Study conducted by Harris Interactive on behalf of Spherion, a leader in providing value-added staffing, recruiting, and workforce solutions, utilized a random sample of 502 senior human resources executives. The survey asked which methods the executives felt led them to find their best candidates. The file entitled **Referrals** contains the responses indicating those that chose "referrals" as their best method.

a. Determine the margin of error that would accrue with a confidence level of 95%.

b. Calculate a 95% confidence interval for the proportion of executives who chose "referrals" as their best method.

c. Determine the sample size required to decrease the margin of error by 25%.

8-70. A survey by Frank N. Magid Associates Inc. concluded that men, of any age, are twice as likely as women to play console video games. The survey was based on a sample of males and females ages 12 and older. A file entitled **Gameboys** contains responses that would result in the findings obtained by Magid Associates for the 18–34-year-old age group.

a. Calculate a 99% confidence interval for both the male and female responses.

b. Using the confidence intervals in part a, provide the minimum and maximum ratio of the population proportions.

c. Does your analysis in parts a and b substantiate the statement that men in this age group are twice as likely to play console video games? Support your assertions.

Summary and Conclusions

By the time you have reached this point, you may be wondering how you are ever going to keep all these different estimation processes straight. If you try to memorize them, you probably won't be able to do it. However, if you develop an understanding of the basic logic of estimation, it is very manageable.

Remember, your first objective is to estimate a population value based on information from a sample. There are two types of estimates: point estimates and interval estimates. Point estimates are subject to potential sampling error. Point estimates are almost always different from the population value. A confidence interval estimate takes into account the potential for sampling error and provides a range within which we believe the true population value falls. There is a common format for all confidence interval estimates:

$$\text{Point Estimate} \pm (\text{Critical Value})(\text{Standard Error})$$

The point estimate is at the center of the interval. The amount that we add and subtract to the point estimate is called the margin of error.

Although this format is always used, there are slightly different formulas that we use depending on what population value we are estimating and certain other conditions. You shouldn't try to memorize these formulas. Instead, you should focus on sorting out the characteristics of the situation at hand. Once you do that, you can locate the appropriate formula to determine the interval estimate. The key will be on correctly interpreting the results and applying these results to your decision situation.

Figure 8.9 contains a diagram that you should find useful as you work the problems and cases at the end of this chapter and later on when you encounter estimation applications in your work.

Equations

Confidence Interval General Format

$$\text{Point Estimate} \pm (\text{Critical Value})(\text{Standard Error}) \quad \textbf{(8.1)}$$

Confidence Interval Estimate for μ, σ Known

$$\bar{x} \pm z \frac{\sigma}{\sqrt{n}} \quad \textbf{(8.2)}$$

Margin of Error for Estimating μ, σ Known

$$e = z \frac{\sigma}{\sqrt{n}} \quad \textbf{(8.3)}$$

t-Value for $\bar{x}$

$$t = \frac{\bar{x} - \mu}{\frac{s}{\sqrt{n}}} \quad \textbf{(8.4)}$$

Confidence Interval Estimate for μ, σ Unknown

$$\bar{x} \pm t \frac{s}{\sqrt{n}} \quad \textbf{(8.5)}$$

Sample Size Requirement for Estimating μ, σ Known

$$n = \left(\frac{z\sigma}{e} \right)^2 = \frac{z^2 \sigma^2}{e^2} \quad \textbf{(8.6)}$$

Sample Proportion

$$p = \frac{x}{n} \quad \textbf{(8.7)}$$

Standard Error for p

$$\sigma_p = \sqrt{\frac{\pi(1 - \pi)}{n}} \quad \textbf{(8.8)}$$

Estimate for the standard error of p

$$\sigma_p \approx \sqrt{\frac{p(1 - p)}{n}} \quad \textbf{(8.9)}$$

Confidence Interval Estimate for π

$$p \pm z \sqrt{\frac{p(1 - p)}{n}} \quad \textbf{(8.10)}$$

Margin of Error for Estimating π

$$e = z \sqrt{\frac{\pi(1 - \pi)}{n}} \quad \textbf{(8.11)}$$

Sample Size for Estimating π

$$n = \frac{z^2 \pi(1 - \pi)}{e^2} \quad \textbf{(8.12)}$$

FIGURE 8.9

Flow Diagram for Confidence Interval Estimation Alternatives

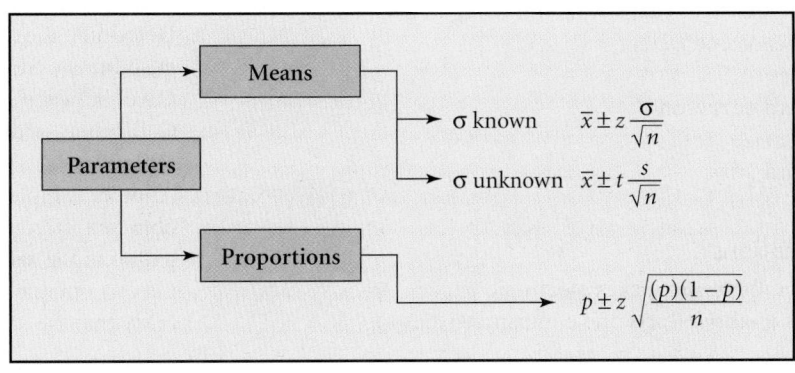

Key Terms

Chapter Exercises

Conceptual Questions

8-71. When we need to estimate the population mean, and the population standard deviation is unknown, we are hit with a "double whammy" when it comes to the margin of error. Explain what the "double whammy" is and why it occurs. (*Hint*: Consider the sources of variation in the margin of error.)

8-72. Explain why the critical value for a given confidence level when the population variance is not known is always greater than the critical value for the same confidence level when the population variance is known.

8-73. An insurance company in Iowa recently conducted a survey of its automobile policy customers to estimate the mean miles these customers commute to work each day. The result based on a random sample of 300 policyholders indicated the population mean was between 3.5 and 6.7 miles. This interval estimate was constructed using 95% confidence.

After receiving this result, one of the managers was overheard telling a colleague that 95% of all customers commute between 3.5 and 6.7 miles to work each day. How would you respond to this statement? Is it correct? Why or why not? Discuss.

8-74. Examine the equation for the margin of error when estimating a population mean

$$e = \frac{z\sigma}{\sqrt{n}}$$

Indicate the effect on the margin of error resulting from an increase in each of the following items:
a. confidence coefficient
b. *z*-value
c. standard deviation
d. sample size
e. standard error

Business Applications

8-75. Arco Manufacturing makes electronic pagers. As part of its quality efforts, the company wishes to estimate the mean number of days the pager is used before repair is needed. A pilot sample of 40 pagers indicates a sample standard deviation of 200 days. The company wishes its estimate to have a margin of error of no more than 50 days and the confidence level must be 95%.
a. Given this information, how many additional pagers should be sampled?
b. The pilot study was initiated because of the costs involved in sampling. Each sampled observation costs approximately $10 to obtain. Originally, it was thought that the population's standard deviation might be as large as 300. Determine the amount of money saved by obtaining the pilot sample. (*Hint*: Determine the total cost of obtaining the required samples for both methods.)

8-76. A random sample of 25 sports utility vehicles (SUVs) of the same year and model revealed the following miles per gallon (mpg) values:

12.4	13.0	12.6	12.1	13.1
13.0	12.0	13.1	11.4	12.6
9.5	13.25	12.4	10.7	11.7
10.0	14.0	10.9	9.9	10.2
11.0	11.9	9.9	12.0	11.3

Assume that the population for mpg for this model year is normally distributed.
a. Use the sample results to develop a 95% confidence interval estimate for the population mean miles per gallon.
b. Determine the average number of gallons of gasoline the SUVs described here would use to travel between Los Angeles and San Francisco, California—a distance of approximately 400 miles.
c. Another sample of the same size is to be obtained. If you know that the average miles per gallon in the second sample will be larger than the one obtained in part a, determine the probability that the sample mean will be larger than

the upper confidence limit of the confidence interval you calculated.

8-77. A random sample of 441 shoppers revealed that 76% made at least one purchase at a discount store last month.

    a. Based on this sample information, what is the 90% confidence interval for the population proportion of shoppers who made at least one discount store purchase last month?

    b. The city of San Luis Obispo has a population of 35,000 people. Referring to part a, determine a 90% confidence interval for the number of shoppers who made at least one discount store purchase last month.

8-78. According to an investigative reporter (Jim Drinkard, "Legislators want to ground 'fact-finding' trips," *USA Today*, January 19, 2006), members of Congress are coming under more scrutiny for "fact-finding" trips. Since 2000, members of Congress have made 6,666 trips paid for by private interests. The trips were worth about $19.6 million.

    a. Calculate the average cost of these "fact-finding" trips.

    b. If the cost of the trips could be considered to have a normal distribution, determine the standard deviation of the cost of the trips. (*Hint*: Recall the Empirical Rule.)

    c. Choose a reasonable confidence level and calculate a confidence interval for the average cost of congressional "fact-finding" trips from the year 2000 until January 19, 2006.

8-79. In an article entitled "Airport screeners' strains, sprains highest among workers" (*USA Today*, January 11, 2006), Thomas Frank reported that the injury rate for airport screeners was 29%, far exceeding the 4.5% injury rate for the rest of the federal workforce. The 48,000 full- and part-time screeners were reported to have missed nearly a quarter million days because of injuries in the recent fiscal year.

    a. Calculate the average number of days missed by airport screeners.

    b. If one were to estimate the average number of days missed to within 1 hour in 2006 with a confidence level of 90%, determine the smallest sample size that would be required. Assume the standard deviation of the number of days missed is 1.5 days and that a work day consists of 8 hours.

    c. How close could the estimate get if a sample of size 100 was used?

Computer Database Exercises

8-80. The quality manager for a major automobile manufacturer is interested in estimating the mean number of paint defects in cars produced by the company. She wishes to have her estimate be within ±0.10 of the true mean and wants 98% confidence in the estimate. The data in the files called **CarPaint** on the CD-ROM contains a pilot sample that was conducted for the purpose of determining a value to use for the population standard deviation. How many additional cars need to be sampled to provide the estimate required by the quality manager?

8-81. The Jordeen Bottling Company recently did an extensive sampling of its soft-drink inventory in which 5,000 cans were sampled. Employees weighed each can and used these weights to determine the fluid ounces in the cans. The data are in a file on your CD-ROM called **Jordeen**. Based on this sample data, should the company conclude that the mean volume is 12 ounces? Base your conclusion on a 95% confidence interval estimate and discuss.

8-82. On its first day on the stock market, the Chinese Internet search engine, Baidu, increased its share price from $27.00 to $122.54, an increase of 354%. This was larger than any other Chinese IPO and the second biggest for a foreign IPO. However, of the nine other biggest foreign IPOs with the largest first-day gains, all are trading below their IPO prices by an average of 88%. To determine the relationship between the IPOs with the largest first-day gains and the other IPOs, a sample might be taken to determine the average percentage decrease in the share prices of those IPOs not in the group of the nine IPOs with the largest first-day gains. A file entitled **BigIPO$** contains such a sample. Note that an increase in share prices is represented as a negative decrease.

    a. Calculate a 95% confidence interval for the average percentage decrease after the first-day offering in the share of those IPOs not in the ten IPOs with the largest first-day gains.

    b. Does it appear that there is a difference in the average percentage decrease in the share prices of the two groups? Support your assertions.

8-83. The Future-Vision Company is considering applying for a franchise to market satellite television dish systems in a Florida market area. As part of the company's research into this opportunity, staff in the new acquisitions department conducted a survey of 548 homes selected at random in the market area. They asked a number of questions on the survey. The data for some of the variables are in a file called **Future-Vision**. One key question asked whether the household was currently connected to cable TV.

a. Using the sample information, what is the 95% confidence interval estimate for the true proportion of households in the market area that subscribe to cable television?

b. Based on the sample data, develop a 95% confidence interval estimate for the mean income and interpret this estimate.

8-84. The NPD Group released its annual 2005 U.S. Video Game Industry Retail Sales Report on January 17, 2006. It contained their selection of the top 10 video games based upon units sold in 2005. The top-selling video game was *Madden NFL 06*, published by Electronic Arts. The average retail price for this video game was $46. The file entitled **Madden** contains a sample of the retail prices paid for *Madden NFL 06* in 2006.

a. Calculate a 95% confidence interval for the average retail price paid for *Madden NFL 06* in 2006.

b. On the basis of the confidence interval constructed in part a, does it seem likely that the average retail price for *Madden NFL 06* has decreased in 2006? Explain.

c. What sample size would be required to generate a margin of error of $1?

8-85. Paper-R-Us is a national distributor of printer and copier paper for commercial use. The data file called **Sales** contains the annual, year-to-date sales values for each of the company's customers. Suppose the internal audit department has decided to audit a sample of these accounts. Specifically,

they have decided to sample 36 accounts. However, before they actually conduct the in-depth audit (a process that involves tracking all transactions for each sampled account), they want to be sure that the sample they have selected is representative of the population.

a. Compute the population mean.

b. Use all the data in the population to develop a frequency distribution and histogram.

c. Calculate the proportion of accounts for customers in each region of the country.

d. Select a random sample of accounts. Develop a frequency distribution for this sample data. Compare this distribution to that of the population. (*Hint*: You might want to consider using relative frequencies for comparison purposes.)

e. Construct a 95% confidence interval estimate for the population mean sales per customer. Discuss how you would use this interval estimate to help determine whether the sample is a good representation of the population. (*Hint*: You may want to use the finite population correction factor since the sample is large relative to the size of the population.)

f. Use the information developed in parts a–e to draw a conclusion about whether the sample is a representative sample of the population. What other information would be desirable? Discuss.

VIDEO CASE 4

New Product Introductions @ McDonald's

New product ideas are a staple of our culture. Just take a look around you–how many billboards or television commercials can you count with new products or services? So, where do those ideas come from? If you're a company like McDonald's, the ideas don't come out of thin air. Instead, they're the result of careful monitoring of consumer preferences, trends, and tastes.

McDonald's menu is a good example of how consumer preferences have affected change in food offerings. What used to be a fairly limited lunch and dinner menu consisting of burgers, shakes, and fries has now become incredibly diverse. The Big Mac came along in 1968, and Happy Meals were introduced in 1979. Breakfast now accounts for nearly 30% of business in the US, and chicken offerings comprise 30% of menu choices. Healthy offerings such as apple dippers, milk jugs and fruit and yogurt parfaits are huge sellers. The

company now rolls out at least three new products a year. Wade Thoma, VP US Menu Management, leads the team behind most of today's menu options. He meets regularly with Chef Dan, the company's executive chef, to give the Chef's team some idea anchor points with which to play.

When the chef's team is through playing with the concept, Wade's Menu Management team holds what they call a "rally." At a rally, numerous food concepts developed by Chef Dan's team are presented, tasted, discussed and voted on. The winners move on to focus group testing. The focus groups are a huge source of external data that helps the Menu Management team with its decision on whether to introduce a product. If a product scores 8 out of 10 on a variety of rankings, the idea moves forward.

The real test begins in the field. Wade and his team need to determine if the new product idea can actually be executed consistently in the restaurants. Data collected from the company's partnership with its owner/operators and suppliers is key. If a product takes 5 seconds too long to make, or the equipment doesn't fit into existing kitchen configurations, its chances of implementation are low, even though consumer focus groups indicated a high probability of success.

Throughout the idea development process, various statistical methods are used to analyze the data collected. The data are handed over to the company's US Consumer and Business Insights team for conversion into meaningful information the menu management team can use. At each step along the way, the statistical analyses are used to decide whether to move to the next step. The recent introduction of the new Asian chicken salad is a good example of a recent new product offering that made it all the way to market. Analysis was performed on data collected in focus groups and eventually revealed the Asian salad met all the statistical hurdles for the salad to move forward.

Data collection and statistical analysis don't stop when the new products hit the market. Wade Thoma's team and the McDonald's US Consumer and Business Insights group continue to forecast and monitor sales, the ingredient supply chain, customer preferences, competitive reactions, and more. As for the new Asian salad, time will tell just how successful it will become. But you can be sure statistical techniques such as multiple regression will be used to analyze it!

Discussion Questions:

1. During the past year, McDonald's introduced a new dessert product into their European market area. This product had already passed all the internal hurdles described in this case including the focus group analysis and the operations analysis. The next step was to see how well the product would be received in the marketplace. In particular McDonald's managers are interested in estimating the mean number of orders for this dessert per 1,000 customer transactions. A random sample of 142 stores throughout Europe was selected. Store managers tracked the number of dessert orders per 1,000 transactions during a two week trial period. These sample data are in the data file called **McDonald's New Product Introduction**. Based upon these sample data, construct and interpret a 95 percent confidence interval estimate for mean number of dessert orders per 1,000 orders.

2. Referring to question 1, suppose that Wade Thoma and his group are not happy with the margin of error associated with the confidence interval estimate and want the margin of error to be no greater than ±3 dessert orders per 1,000 customer orders. To meet this objective, how many more stores should be included in the sample? Alternatively, if the managers don't wish to increase the sample size, what other option is available to reduce the margin of error? Discuss the pros and cons of both approaches.

CASE 8.1

Management Solutions, Inc.

The round-trip to the "site" was just under 360 miles, which gave Fred Kitchener and Mike Kyte plenty of time to discuss the next steps in the project. The site is a rural stretch of highway in Idaho where two visibility sensors are located. The project is part of a contract Fred's company, Management Solutions, Inc., has with the state of Idaho and the Federal Highway Administration. Under the contract, among other things, Management Solutions is charged with evaluating the performance of a new technology for measuring visibility. The larger study involves determining whether visibility sensors can be effectively tied to electronic message signs that would warn motorists of upcoming visibility problems in rural areas.

Mike Kyte, a transportation engineer and professor at the University of Idaho, has been involved with the project as a consultant to Fred's company since the initial proposal. Mike is very knowledgeable about visibility sensors and traffic systems. Fred's expertise is in managing projects like this one, in which it is important to get people from multiple organizations to work together effectively.

As the pair headed back toward Boise from the site, Mike was more excited than Fred had seen him in a long time. Fred

reasoned that the source of excitement was that they had finally been successful in getting solid data to compare the two visibility sensors in a period of low visibility. The previous day at the site had been very foggy. The Scorpion Sensor is a tested technology that Mike has worked with for some time in urban applications. However, it has never before been installed in such a remote location as this stretch of highway I-84, which connects Idaho and Utah. The other sensor produced by the Vanguard Company measures visibility in a totally new way using laser technology.

The data that had excited Mike so much were collected by the two sensors and fed back to a computer system at the port of entry near the test site. The measurements were collected every 5 minutes for the 24-hour day. As Fred took advantage of the 75 mph speed limit through southern Idaho, Mike kept glancing at the data on the printout he had made of the first few 5-minute time periods. The Scorpion system had not only provided visibility readings but it also had provided other weather-related data, such as temperature, wind speed, wind direction, and humidity.

Mike's eyes went directly to the two visibility columns. Ideally, the visibility readings for the two sensors would be the same at any 5-minute period, but they weren't. After a few exclamations of surprise from Mike, Fred suggested that they come up with an outline for the report they would have to make from these data for the project team meeting next week. Both agreed that a full descriptive analysis of all the data, including graphs and numerical measures, was necessary. In addition, Fred wanted to use these early data to provide an estimate for the mean visibility provided by the two sensors. They agreed that estimates were needed for the day as a whole and also for only those periods when the Scorpion system showed visibility under 1.0 mile. They also felt that the analysis should look at the other weather factors, too, but they weren't sure just what was needed.

As the lights in the Boise Valley became visible, Mike agreed to work up a draft of the report, including a narrative based on the data in the CD-ROM file called **Visibility**. Fred said that he would set up the project team meeting agenda, and Mike could make the presentation. Both men agreed that the data were strictly a sample and that more low-visibility data would be collected when conditions occurred.

CASE 8.2

Federal Aviation Administration

In January 2003, the FAA ordered that passengers be weighed before boarding 10–19-seat passenger planes. The order was instituted in response to a crash that occurred on January 8, 2003 in Charlotte, North Carolina, in which all 21 passengers, including the pilot and co-pilot, of a 19-seat Beech 1900 turbo-prop died. One possible cause of the crash was that the plane may have been carrying too much weight.

The airlines were asked to weigh adult passengers and carry-on bags randomly over a one-month period in order to estimate the mean weight per passenger (including luggage). A total of 426 people and their luggage were weighed, and the sample data are contained in a data file called **FAA**.

Required Tasks:

1. Prepare a descriptive analysis of the data using charts, graphs, and numerical measures.
2. Construct and interpret a 95% confidence interval estimate for the mean weight for male passengers.
3. Construct and interpret a 95% confidence interval estimate for the mean weight for female passengers.
4. Construct and interpret a 95% confidence interval estimate for the mean weight for all passengers.
5. Indicate what sample size would be required if the margin of error in the estimate for the mean of all passengers is to be reduced by half.

CASE 8.3

Cell Phone Use

Helen Hutchins and Greg Haglund took the elevator together to the fourth-floor meeting room where they were scheduled to meet the rest of the market research team at the Franklin Company. On the way up, Helen mentioned that she had terminated her contract for the land-line telephone in her apartment and was going to be using her cell phone exclusively to save money. "I rarely use my house phone anymore and about the only calls I get are from organizations wanting donations or doing surveys," she said. Greg said that he and his wife were thinking about doing the same thing.

As Helen and Greg walked toward the meeting room, Helen suddenly stopped. "If everyone did what I am doing, wouldn't that affect our marketing research telephone surveys?" she asked. "I mean, when we make calls the numbers are all to land-line phones. Won't we be missing out on some people we should be talking to when we do our surveys?" Helen continued. Greg indicated that it could be a problem if very many people were using cell phones exclusively like Helen. "Maybe we need to discuss this at the meeting today," Greg said.

When Helen and Greg brought up the subject to the market research team, several others indicated that they had been having similar concerns. It was decided that a special study was needed among the Franklin customer base to estimate the proportion of customers who were now using only a cell phone for telephone service. It was decided to randomly sample customers using personal interviews at their business outlets, but no one had any idea of how many customers they needed to interview. One team member mentioned that he had read an Associated Press article recently that said that about 8% of all households have only a cell phone. Greg mentioned that any estimate that they came up with should have a margin of error of ±0.03, and the others at the meeting agreed.

Required Tasks:

1. Assuming that the group wishes to develop a 95% confidence interval estimate, determine the required sample size if the population proportion of cell-phone-only users is 8%.
2. Supposing the group is unwilling to use the 8% baseline proportion and wants to have their sample size be conservatively large enough to provide a margin of error of no greater than ±0.03 with 95% confidence, determine the sample size that will be needed.

References

Berenson, Mark L., and David M. Levine, *Basic Business Statistics Concepts and Applications*, 10th ed. (Upper Saddle River, NJ: Prentice Hall, 2006).

Hogg, Robert V., and Elliot A. Tanis, *Probability and Statistical Inference*, 6th ed. (Upper Saddle River, NJ: Prentice Hall, 2001).

Larsen, Richard J., and Moriss L. Marx, *Introduction to Mathematical Statistics and Its Applications*, 4th ed. (Upper Saddle River, NJ: Prentice Hall, 2006).

Microsoft Excel 2007 (Redmond, WA: Microsoft Corp., 2007).

Minitab for Windows Version 15 (State College, PA: Minitab, 2007).

Siegel, Andrew F., *Practical Business Statistics*, 5th ed. (Burr Ridge, IL: Irwin, 2003).

Introduction to Hypothesis Testing

CHAPTER OUTCOMES

After studying the material in Chapter 9, you should be able to:

1. Formulate null and alternative hypotheses for applications involving a single population mean or proportion.
2. Know what Type I and Type II errors are.
3. Correctly formulate a decision rule for testing a null hypothesis.
4. Know how to use the test statistic, critical value, and *p*-value approaches to test the null hypothesis.
5. Compute the probability of a Type II error.

PREPARING FOR CHAPTER NINE

- Review the concepts associated with the Central Limit Theorem in Section 7.2.

- Examine Section 7.3 on the sampling distribution for proportions.

- Familiarize yourself with Student's *t*-distributions in Section 8.1.

- Review the standard normal distribution and the Student's *t*-distribution tables, making sure you know how to find critical values in both tables.

Why You Need To Know

As a business decision maker, you will encounter many applications that will require you to *estimate* a population parameter. Chapter 8 introduced statistical estimation and included many examples. Estimating a population parameter based on a sample statistic is a component of business statistics called *statistical inference*. An important component of statistical inference is *hypothesis testing*. In hypothesis testing, we begin with some belief regarding what the value of a population parameter is, or should be. We then use sample data to either refute or support the initial belief.

For example, suppose the Coca-Cola plant in Tampa, Florida, produces approximately 400,000 cans of Coke products daily. Each can is supposed to contain 12 fluid ounces. However, like all processes, the automated filling machine is subject to variation and each can will contain either slightly more or less than the 12-ounce target. The important thing is that the mean fill is 12 fluid ounces. Every two hours, the plant quality manager selects a random sample of cans and computes the sample mean. His initial belief is that the filling process is providing an average fill of 12 ounces. This is his *hypothesis*. If the sample mean is "close" to 12 ounces, then the sample data would tend to support the hypothesis and the machine would be allowed to continue filling cans. However, if the sample mean is "significantly" higher or lower than 12 ounces,

the data would refute the hypothesis and the machine would be stopped and adjusted.

Hypothesis testing is performed regularly in many industries. Companies in the pharmaceutical industry must perform many hypothesis tests on new drug products before they are deemed to be safe and effective by the federal Food and Drug Administration (FDA). In these instances, the drug is hypothesized to be both unsafe and ineffective. Then, if the sample results from the studies performed provide "significant" evidence to the contrary, the FDA will allow the company to market the drug.

Hypothesis testing is the basis of the legal system in which judges and juries hear evidence in court cases. In a criminal case, the hypothesis in the American legal system is that the defendant is innocent. Based upon the totality of the evidence presented in the trial, if the jury concludes that "beyond a reasonable doubt" the defendant committed the crime, the hypothesis of innocence will be rejected and the defendant will be found guilty. If the evidence is not strong enough, the defendant will be judged not guilty.

Hypothesis testing is a major part of business statistics. Chapter 9 introduces the fundamentals involved in conducting hypothesis tests. Many of the remaining chapters in this text will introduce additional hypothesis-testing techniques, so you need to gain a solid understanding of concepts presented in this chapter.

9.1 Hypothesis Tests for Means

By now you know that information contained in a sample is subject to sampling error. The sample mean will almost certainly not equal the population mean. Therefore, in situations in which you need to test a claim about a population mean by using the sample mean, you can't simply compare the sample mean to the claim and reject the claim if $\bar{x}$ and the claim are different. Instead, you need a testing procedure that incorporates the potential for sampling error.

Statistical hypothesis testing provides managers with a structured analytical method for making decisions of this type. It lets them make decisions in such a way that the probability of decision errors can be controlled, or at least measured. Even though statistical hypothesis testing does not eliminate the uncertainty in the managerial environment, the techniques involved often allow managers to identify and control the level of uncertainty.

The techniques presented in this chapter assume the data are selected using an appropriate statistical sampling process and that the data are interval or ratio level. In short, we assume we are working with good data.

Formulating the Hypotheses

Null Hypothesis
The statement about the population parameter that will be tested. The null hypothesis will be rejected only if the sample data provide substantial contradictory evidence.

Alternative Hypothesis
The hypothesis that includes all population values not included in the null hypothesis. The alternative hypothesis is deemed to be true if the null hypothesis is rejected.

Null and Alternative Hypotheses   In hypothesis testing, two hypotheses are formulated. One is the **null hypothesis**. The null hypothesis is represented by H_0 and contains an equality sign, such as "=," "≤," or "≥." The second hypothesis is the **alternative hypothesis** (represented by H_A). Based on the sample data, we either reject H_0 or we do not reject H_0.

Correctly specifying the null and alternative hypotheses is important. If done incorrectly, the results obtained from the hypothesis test may be misleading. Unfortunately, how you should formulate the null and alternative hypotheses is not always obvious. As you gain experience with hypothesis-testing applications, the process becomes easier. To help you get started, we have developed some guidelines for specifying the null and alternative hypotheses. The major point to remember is the "benefit of the doubt" goes to the null hypothesis. Only significant differences will lead to rejecting the null hypothesis.

Testing the Status Quo In many cases, you will be interested in whether a situation has changed. We refer to this as testing the status quo, and this is a common application of hypothesis testing. For example, the Kellogg Company makes many food products, including a variety of breakfast cereals. At the company's Battle Creek, Michigan, plant, Frosted Mini-Wheats are produced and packaged for distribution around the world. If the packaging process is working properly, the mean fill per box is 16 ounces. Every hour quality analysts at the plant select a random sample of filled boxes and measure their contents. They use the sample data to test the following null and alternative hypotheses:

$$H_0: \mu = 16 \text{ ounces (status quo)}$$
$$H_A: \mu \neq 16 \text{ ounces}$$

The null hypothesis is reasonable because the line supervisor would assume the process is operating correctly before starting production. As long as the sample mean is "reasonably" close to 16 ounces, the analysts will assume the filling process is working properly. Only when the sample mean is seen to be too large or too small will the analysts reject the null hypothesis (the status quo) and take action to identify and fix the problem.

As another example, the Transportation Security Administration (TSA), which is responsible for screening passengers at U.S. airports, publishes on its Web site the average waiting times for customers to pass through security. For example, on Mondays between 9:00 and 10:00 A.M., the average waiting time at Atlanta's Hartsfield International Airport is supposed to be 15 minutes or less. Periodically, TSA staff will select a random sample of passengers during this time slot and measure their actual wait times. These sample data will be used to test the following null and alternative hypotheses:

$$H_0: \mu \leq 15 \text{ minutes (status quo)}$$
$$H_A: \mu > 15 \text{ minutes}$$

Only if the sample mean wait time is "substantially" greater than 15 minutes will TSA employees reject the null hypothesis and conclude there is a problem with staffing levels. Otherwise, they will assume that the 15-minute standard (the status quo) is being met and no action will be taken.

Testing a Research Hypothesis Many business and scientific applications involve research applications. For example, companies such as Intel, Procter & Gamble, Dell Computers, Pfizer, and 3M continually introduce new and improved products. However, before introducing a new product, the companies want to be sure that the new product is superior to the original. In the case of drug companies like Pfizer, the government requires them to show their product is both safe and effective. Because statistical evidence is needed to indicate that the new product is effective, the default position (or null hypothesis) is it is no better than the original (or in the case of a drug, it is unsafe and ineffective.) The burden of proof is placed on the new product and the alternative hypothesis is formulated as the **research hypothesis**.

Research Hypothesis
The hypothesis the decision maker attempts to demonstrate to be true. Because this is the hypothesis deemed to be the most important to the decision maker, it will be declared true only if the sample data strongly indicates that it is true.

For example, suppose the Goodyear Tire and Rubber Company has a new tread design that its engineers claim will outlast its competitor's leading tire. The competitor's tire has been demonstrated to provide an average of 60,000 miles of use. Thus the research hypothesis for Goodyear is that its tire is superior, meaning that it will last *more than* 60,000 miles. The research hypothesis becomes the alternative hypothesis:

$$H_0: \mu \leq 60,000$$
$$H_A: \mu > 60,000 \text{ (research hypothesis)}$$

The burden of proof is on Goodyear. Only if the sample data show a sample mean that is "substantially" larger than 60,000 miles will the null hypothesis be rejected and Goodyear's position be affirmed.

In another example, suppose the Agri-Seed Company has developed a new fertilizer for commercial farming. Agri-Seed would introduce this product on the market only if it provides yields superior to its current fertilizer product. Experience shows that when the current fertilizer is used to grow sugar beets, a mean yield of 30 tons per acre is expected. To test the new fertilizer, Agri-Seed researchers will set up the following null and alternative hypotheses:

$$H_0: \mu \leq 30 \text{ tons}$$
$$H_A: \mu > 30 \text{ tons (research hypothesis)}$$

The alternative hypothesis is the research hypothesis. If the null hypothesis is rejected, then Agri-Seed will have statistical evidence to show that the new fertilizer is superior to the existing product.

Testing a Claim About the Population Analyzing claims using hypothesis tests can be complicated because the benefit of the doubt goes to the null hypothesis. Sometimes you will want to give the benefit of the doubt to the claim, but in other instances you will be skeptical about the claim and will want to place the burden of proof on the claim. For consistency purposes, the rule adopted in this text is that if the claim contains the equality, the claim goes in the null. If the claim does not contain the equality, it goes in the alternative.

A recent radio commercial has stated the average waiting time at a medical clinic is less than 15 minutes. A claim like this can be tested using hypothesis testing. The null and alternative hypotheses should be formulated such that one contains the claim and the other reflects the opposite position. Since the claim does not contain the equality ($\mu < 15$), the claim should be the alternative hypothesis. The appropriate null and alternative hypotheses are, then, as follows:

$$H_0: \mu \geq 15$$
$$H_A: \mu < 15 \text{ (claim)}$$

In cases like this where the claim corresponds to the alternative hypothesis, the *burden of proof* is on the medical clinic. If the sample mean is "substantially" less than 15 minutes, the null hypothesis would be rejected and the alternative hypothesis (and the claim) would be accepted. Otherwise, the null hypothesis would not be rejected and the claim could not be accepted.

SUMMARY Formulating the Null and Alternative Hypotheses

1. The null and alternative hypotheses must be stated in terms of the population of interest (e.g., μ, π, or σ).

2. If the application involves a test of the status quo, the status quo forms the null hypothesis and the burden of proof is to show that the status quo has changed.

3. If the application involves a research issue, the research hypothesis forms the alternative hypothesis.

4. If a claim has been made about the population parameter, the decision maker must determine if he or she is inclined to agree with the claim before gathering any data. If so, the claim establishes the null hypothesis; otherwise, it forms the alternative hypothesis.

EXAMPLE 9-1 Formulating the Null and Alternative Hypotheses

CHAPTER OUTCOME #1

TRY PROBLEM 9.13

Student Work Hours In today's economy, university students often work many hours to help pay for the high costs of a college education. Suppose a university in the Midwest is considering changing its class schedule to accommodate students working long hours. The registrar has stated a change is needed because the mean number of hours worked by undergraduate students at the university is more than 20 per week. The following steps can be taken to establish the appropriate null and alternative hypotheses:

Step 1 **Determine the population parameter of interest.**
In this case, the population parameter of interest is the mean hours worked, μ. The null and alternative hypotheses must be stated in terms of the population parameter.

Step 2 **Determine whether the application involves a test of the status quo, a research application, or a claim about the population parameter.**
In this case, the registrar has made a claim stating that the mean hours worked "is more than 20" per week. Because changing the class scheduling system would be expensive and time-consuming, the assumption is made that the number of hours worked is less than or equal to 20. Thus, the burden of proof is placed on the registrar to justify her claim that the mean is greater than 20 hours.

Step 3 **Formulate the null and alternative hypotheses.**
Keep in mind that the equality goes in the null hypothesis.

$$H_0: \mu \leq 20 \text{ hours}$$
$$H_A: \mu > 20 \text{ hours (claim)}$$

Example 9-2 illustrates another example of how the null and alternative hypotheses are formulated.

EXAMPLE 9-2 Formulating the Null and Alternative Hypotheses

TRY PROBLEM 9.14

Boulder Potato Company   The Boulder Potato Company produces several snack and food products that are sold in food stores throughout Colorado and Arizona. The company uses an automatic filling machine to fill the sacks with the desired weight. For instance, when the company is running potato chips on the fill line, the machine is set to fill the sacks with 20 ounces. Thus, if the machine is working properly, the mean fill will be 20 ounces. Each hour, a sample of sacks is collected and weighed, and the technicians determine whether the machine is still operating correctly or whether it needs adjustment. The following steps can be used to establish the null and alternative hypotheses to be tested.

Step 1 **Determine the population parameter of interest.**
In this case, the population parameter of interest is the mean weight per sack, μ.

Step 2 **Determine whether the application involves a claim about the population parameter, a research application, or a test of the status quo.**
The status quo is that the machine is filling the sacks with the proper amount, which is $\mu = 20$ ounces. We will believe this to be true unless we find evidence to suggest otherwise. If such evidence exists, then the filling process needs to be adjusted.

Step 3 **Formulate the null and alternative hypotheses.**
Keep in mind that the equality goes in the null hypothesis.
The null and alternative hypotheses are

$$H_0: \mu = 20 \text{ ounces (status quo)}$$
$$H_A: \mu \neq 20 \text{ ounces}$$

FIGURE 9.1

The Relationship Between Decisions and States of Nature

		State of Nature	
		Null Hypothesis True	Null Hypothesis False
Decision	Conclude Null True (Don't reject H_0)	Correct Decision	Type II Error
	Conclude Null False (Reject H_0)	Type I Error	Correct Decision

Type I Error

Rejecting the null hypothesis when it is, in fact, true.

Type II Error

Failing to reject the null hypothesis when it is, in fact, false.

CHAPTER OUTCOME #2

Types of Statistical Errors Because of the potential for extreme sampling error, two possible errors can occur when a hypothesis is tested: **Type I** and **Type II errors**. These errors show the relationship between what actually exists (a state of nature) and the decision made based on the sample information.

Figure 9.1 shows the possible actions and states of nature associated with any hypothesis-testing application. As you can see, there are three possible outcomes: no error (correct decision), Type I error, and Type II error. *Only one of these outcomes will occur for a hypothesis test.* From Figure 9.1, if the null hypothesis is true and an error is made, it must be a Type I error. On the other hand, if the null hypothesis is false and an error is made, it must be a Type II error.

Many statisticians argue that you should never use the phrase "accept the null hypothesis." Instead you should use "*do not reject* the null hypothesis." Thus, the only two hypothesis-testing decisions would be *reject H_0* or "*do not reject H_0.*" This is why in a jury verdict to acquit a defendant, the verdict is "not guilty" rather than innocent. Just because the evidence is insufficient to convict does not necessarily mean that the defendant is innocent.

This thinking is appropriate when hypothesis testing is employed in situations in which some future action is not dependent on the results of the hypothesis test. However, in most business applications, the purpose of the hypothesis test is to direct the decision maker to take one action or another, based on the test results. So, in this text, when hypothesis testing is applied to decision-making situations, *not rejecting* the null hypothesis is essentially the same as *accepting it*.[1]

Business Application

MORGAN LANE REAL ESTATE COMPANY The Morgan Lane Real Estate Company has offices in and around the Napa Valley in the northern California wine country. The real estate market in this area has been "hot" for a number of years and homes commonly sell above the asking price very quickly. Once a buyer and seller agree to terms on a home, the closing process (appraisal, inspection, loan application, etc.) begins. The standard time for closings in the Napa area is no more than 25 days. The managing partner at Morgan Lane wishes to test whether her agency's closings are meeting this standard. Treating the 25 days as the status quo, the null and alternative hypotheses to be tested are

$$H_0: \mu \leq 25 \text{ days (status quo)}$$
$$H_A: \mu > 25 \text{ days}$$

She will select a random sample of home sales closed by Morgan Lane agents. In this application, a Type I error would occur if the sample data lead the manager to conclude that the mean closing time exceeds 25 days (H_0 is rejected) when in fact $\mu \leq 25$ days. If a Type I error occurred, the manager would needlessly spend time and resources trying to speed up a process that already meets the industry standards.

Alternatively, a Type II error would occur if the sample evidence leads the manager to incorrectly conclude that $\mu \leq 25$ days (H_0 is not rejected) when the mean closing time

---

[1] Whichever language you use, you should make an effort to understand both arguments and make an informed choice. If your instructor requests that you reference the action in a particular way, it would behoove you to follow the instructions. Having gone through this process ourselves, we prefer to state the choice as "don't reject the null hypothesis." This terminology will be used throughout this text.

exceeds 25 days. Now the manager would take no action to improve closing times at Morgan Lane when changes are needed to improve customer service.

Significance Level and Critical Value

The objective of a hypothesis test is to use sample information to decide whether to reject the null hypothesis about a population parameter. How do decision makers determine whether the sample information supports or refutes the null hypothesis? The answer to this question is the key to understanding statistical hypothesis testing.

In hypotheses tests for a single population mean, the sample mean, $\bar{x}$, is used to test the hypotheses under consideration. Depending on how the null and alternative hypotheses are formulated, certain values of $\bar{x}$ will tend to support the null hypothesis, whereas other values will appear to contradict it. In the Morgan Lane example, the null and alternative hypotheses were formulated as

$$H_0: \mu \leq 25 \text{ days}$$
$$H_A: \mu > 25 \text{ days}$$

Values of $\bar{x}$ less than or equal to 25 days would tend to support the null hypothesis. By contrast, values of $\bar{x}$ greater than 25 days would tend to refute the null hypothesis. The larger the value of $\bar{x}$, the greater the evidence that the null hypothesis should be rejected. However, because we expect some sampling error, do we want to reject H_0 for any value of $\bar{x}$ that is greater than 25 days? Probably not. But should we reject H_0 if $\bar{x} = 26$ days, or $\bar{x} = 30$ days, or $\bar{x} = 35$ days? At what point do we stop attributing the result to sampling error?

In order to perform the hypothesis test, we need to select a *cutoff* point that is the demarcation between rejecting and not rejecting the null hypothesis. Our *decision rule* for the Morgan Lane application is then

If $\bar{x} >$ cutoff, reject H_0.
If $\bar{x} \leq$ cutoff, do not reject H_0.

If $\bar{x}$ is greater than the cutoff, we will reject H_0 and conclude that the average closing time *does* exceed 25 days. If $\bar{x}$ is less than or equal to the cutoff, we will not reject H_0; in this case our test does not give sufficient evidence that the closing time exceeds 25 days.

Recall from the Central Limit Theorem (see Chapter 7) that, for large samples, the distribution of the possible sample means is approximately normal, with a center at the population mean μ. The null hypothesis in our example is $\mu \leq 25$ days. Figure 9.2 shows the sampling distribution for $\bar{x}$ assuming that $\mu = 25$. The shaded region on the right is called the *rejection region*. The area of the rejection region gives the probability of getting an $\bar{x}$ larger than the cutoff when μ is really 25, so it is the probability of making a Type I statistical error. This probability is called the **significance level** of the test and is given the symbol α (alpha).

Significance Level

The maximum allowable probability of committing a Type I statistical error. The probability is denoted by the symbol α.

FIGURE 9.2

Sampling Distribution of $\bar{x}$ for Morgan Lane

The decision maker carrying out the test specifies the significance level, α. The value of α is determined based on the costs involved in committing a Type I error. If making a Type I error is costly, we will want the probability of a Type I error to be small. If a Type I error is less costly, then we can allow a higher probability of a Type I error.

However, in determining α, we must also take into account the probability of making a Type II error, which is given the symbol β (beta). The two error probabilities, α and β, are inversely related.[2] That is, if we reduce α, then β will increase. Thus, in setting α, you must consider both sides of the issue.

Calculating the specific dollar costs associated with making Type I and Type II errors is often difficult and may require a subjective management decision. Therefore, any two managers might well arrive at different alpha levels. However, in the end, the choice for alpha must reflect the decision maker's best estimate of the costs of these two errors.[3]

Having chosen a significance level α, the decision maker then must calculate the corresponding cutoff point, which is called a **critical value**.

Critical Value
The value corresponding to a significance level that determines those test statistics that lead to rejecting the null hypothesis and those that lead to a decision not to reject the null hypothesis.

CHAPTER OUTCOME #4

Hypothesis Test for μ, σ Known

Calculating Critical Values To calculate critical values corresponding to a chosen α, we need to know the sampling distribution of the sample mean $\bar{x}$. If our sampling conditions satisfy the Central Limit Theorem requirements or if the population is normally distributed and we know the population standard deviation σ, then the sampling distribution of $\bar{x}$ is normal with mean equal to the population mean μ and standard deviation $\sigma/\sqrt{n}$.[4] With this information we can calculate a critical z-value, called z_α, or a critical $\bar{x}$-value, called $\bar{x}_\alpha$. We illustrate both calculations in the Morgan Lane Real Estate example.

Business Application

MORGAN LANE REAL ESTATE (*CONTINUED*) Suppose the managing partners decide they are willing to incur a 0.10 probability of committing a Type I error. Assume also that the population standard deviation, σ, for closing is 3 days and the sample size is 64 homes. Given that the sample size is large ($n \geq 30$) and that the population standard deviation is known ($\sigma = 3$ days), we can state the critical value in two ways. First, we can establish the critical value as a z-value.

Figure 9.3 shows that if the rejection region on the upper end of the sampling distribution has an area of 0.10, the z-value from the standard normal table (or by using Excel's **NORMSINV** function or Minitab's **Calc > Probability Distributions** command) corresponding to the critical value is 1.28. Thus, $z_{0.10} = 1.28$. If the sample mean lies more than 1.28 standard deviations above $\mu = 25$ days, H_0 should be rejected; otherwise we will not reject H_0.

FIGURE 9.3

Determining the Critical Value as a *z*-Value

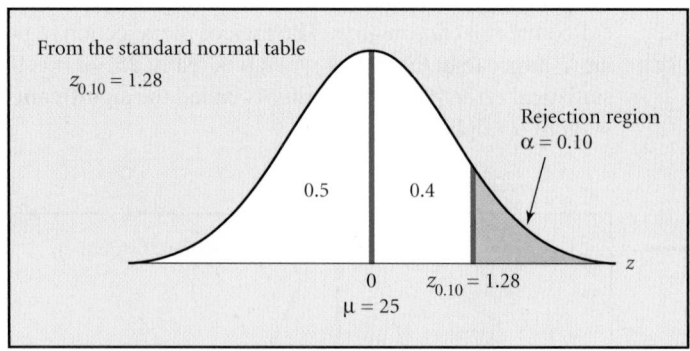

---

[2] The sum of alpha and beta may coincidently equal 1. However, in general, the sum of these two error probabilities does not equal 1.

[3] We will discuss Type II errors more fully later in this chapter. Contrary to the Type I situation in which we specify the desired alpha level, beta is computed based on certain assumptions. Methods for computing beta are shown in Section 9.3.

[4] For many population distributions, the Central Limit Theorem applies for sample sizes as small as 4 or 5. Sample sizes $n \geq 30$ assure us that the sampling distribution will be approximately normal regardless of population distribution.

FIGURE 9.4

Determining the Critical Value as an $\bar{x}$-Value, Morgan Lane Example

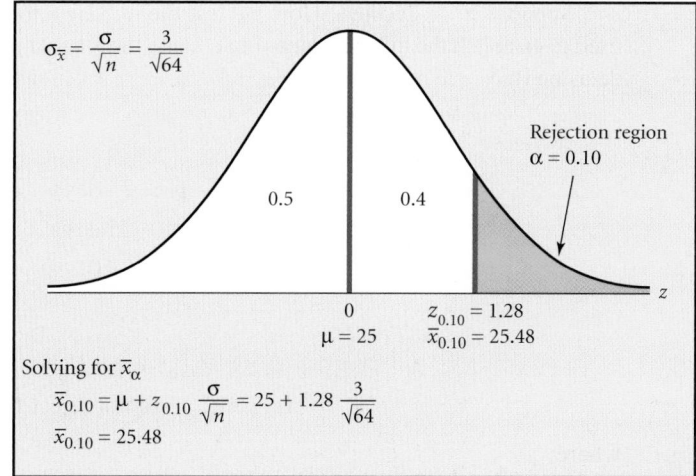

We can also express the critical value in the same units as the sample mean. In the Morgan Lane example, we can calculate a critical $\bar{x}$ value, $\bar{x}_\alpha$, so that if $\bar{x}$ is greater than the critical value, we should reject H_0. If $\bar{x}$ is less than or equal to $\bar{x}_\alpha$, we should not reject H_0. Equation 9.1 shows how $\bar{x}_\alpha$ is computed. Figure 9.4 illustrates the use of Equation 9.1 for computing the critical value, $\bar{x}_\alpha$.

$\bar{x}_\alpha$ for Hypothesis Tests, σ Known

$$\bar{x}_\alpha = \mu + z_\alpha \frac{\sigma}{\sqrt{n}} \tag{9.1}$$

where:

μ = Hypothesized value for the population mean
z_α = Critical value from the standard normal distribution
σ = Population standard deviation
n = Sample size

Applying Equation 9.1, we determine the value for $\bar{x}_\alpha$ as follows:

$$\bar{x}_\alpha = \mu + z_\alpha \frac{\sigma}{\sqrt{n}}$$

$$\bar{x}_{0.10} = 25 + 1.28 \frac{3}{\sqrt{64}}$$

$$\bar{x}_{0.10} = 25.48 \text{ days}$$

Also refer to Figure 9.4 for a graphical illustration showing how $\bar{x}_\alpha$ is determined.

If $\bar{x} > 25.48$ days, H_0 should be rejected and changes made in the process; otherwise, H_0 should not be rejected and the process should not be changed. Any sample mean between 25.48 and 25 days would be attributed to sampling error, and the null hypothesis would not be rejected. A sample mean of 25.48 or fewer days will support the null hypothesis.

Decision Rules and Test Statistics To conduct a hypothesis test, you can use three equivalent approaches. You can calculate a z-value and compare it to the critical value, z_α. Alternatively, you can calculate the sample mean, $\bar{x}$, and compare it to the critical value, $\bar{x}_\alpha$. Finally, you can use a method called the p-value approach, to be discussed later in this section. It makes no difference which approach you use, each method yields the same conclusion.

Suppose $\bar{x} = 26$ days. How we test the null hypothesis depends on the procedure we used to establish the critical value. First, using the z-value method, we establish the following decision rule:

Hypotheses

$$H_0: \mu \leq 25 \text{ days}$$
$$H_A: \mu > 25 \text{ days}$$
$$\alpha = 0.10$$

Decision Rule

If $z > z_{0.10}$, reject H_0.

If $z \leq z_{0.10}$, do not reject H_0.

where:

$$z_{0.10} = 1.28$$

Recall that the number of homes sampled is 64 and the population standard deviation is assumed known at 3 days. The calculated z-value is called the **test statistic.**

The z-test statistic is computed using Equation 9.2.

Test Statistic

A function of the sampled observations that provides a basis for testing a statistical hypothesis.

---

z-Test Statistic for Hypothesis Tests for μ, σ Known

$$z = \frac{\bar{x} - \mu}{\frac{\sigma}{\sqrt{n}}}$$

(9.2)

where:

$\bar{x} = $ Sample mean
$\mu = $ Hypothesized value for the population mean
$\sigma = $ Population standard deviation
$n = $ Sample size

Given that $\bar{x} = 26$ days, applying Equation 9.2 we get

$$z = \frac{\bar{x} - \mu}{\frac{\sigma}{\sqrt{n}}} = \frac{26 - 25}{\frac{3}{\sqrt{64}}} = 2.67$$

Thus, $\bar{x} = 26$ is 2.67 standard deviations above the hypothesized mean. Because z is greater than the critical value,

$$z = 2.67 > z_{0.10} = 1.28, \text{ reject } H_0.$$

Now we use the second approach, which established (see Figure 9.4) a decision rule, as follows:

Decision Rule

If $\bar{x} > \bar{x}_{0.10}$, reject H_0;
Otherwise, do not reject H_0.

Then,

If $\bar{x} > 25.48$ days, reject H_0;
Otherwise, do not reject H_0.

Then, because

$$\bar{x} = 26 > \bar{x}_{0.10} = 25.48, \text{ reject } H_0.$$

Note that the two approaches yield the same conclusion, as they always will if you perform the calculations correctly. We have found that academic applications of hypothesis testing tend to use the z-value method, whereas organizational applications of hypothesis testing often use the $\bar{x}$ approach.

You will often come across a different language used to express the outcome of a hypothesis test. For instance, a statement for the hypothesis test just presented would be "The hypothesis test was significant at an α (or significance level) of 0.10." This simply means that the null hypothesis was rejected using a significance level of 0.10.

SUMMARY   One-Tailed Test for a Hypothesis About a Population Mean, σ Known

To test the hypothesis, perform the following steps:

1. Specify the population parameter of interest.

2. Formulate the null hypothesis and the alternative hypothesis in terms of the population mean, μ.

3. Specify the desired significance level (α).

4. Construct the rejection region. (We strongly suggest you draw a picture showing where in the distribution the rejection region is located.)

5. Compute the test statistic.

$$\bar{x} = \frac{\sum x}{n} \quad \text{or} \quad z = \frac{\bar{x} - \mu}{\dfrac{\sigma}{\sqrt{n}}}$$

6. Reach a decision. Compare the test statistic with $\bar{x}_\alpha$ or z_α.

7. Draw a conclusion regarding the null hypothesis.

TRY PROBLEM 9.3

EXAMPLE 9-3   One-Tailed Hypothesis Test for μ, σ Known

Providence Heart Institute   The Providence Heart Institute in Columbia, South Carolina, performs many open-heart surgery procedures. Recently, research physicians at Providence have developed a new heart bypass surgery procedure that they believe will reduce the average recovery time. The hospital board will not recommend the new procedure unless there is substantial evidence to suggest that it is better than the existing procedure. Records indicate that the current mean recovery rate for the standard procedure is 42 days, with a standard deviation of 5 days. To test whether the new procedure actually results in a lower mean recovery time, the procedure was performed on a random sample of 36 patients.

Step 1   Specify the population parameter of interest.
We are interested in the mean recovery time, μ.

Step 2   Formulate the null and alternative hypotheses.

$$H_0: \mu \geq 42 \text{ (status quo)}$$
$$H_A: \mu < 42$$

Step 3   Specify the desired significance level (α).
The researchers wish to test the hypothesis using a 0.05 level of significance.

Step 4   Construct the rejection region.
This will be a one-tailed test, with the rejection region in the lower (left-hand) tail of the sampling distribution. The critical

FIGURE 9.5

Providence Heart Institute Hypothesis Test

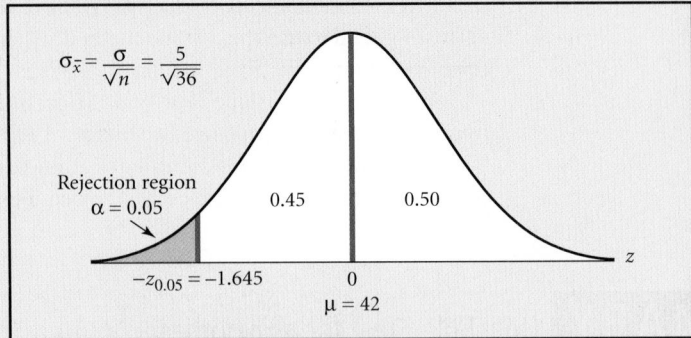

value is $-z_{0.05} = -1.645$. Therefore, the decision rule becomes

If $z < -1.645$, reject H_0; otherwise, do not reject H_0.

Step 5   Compute the test statistic.
For this example we will use z. Assume the sample mean, computed using $\bar{x} = \dfrac{\sum x}{n}$, is 40.2 days. Then,

$$z = \frac{\bar{x} - \mu}{\dfrac{\sigma}{\sqrt{n}}} = \frac{40.2 - 42}{\dfrac{5}{\sqrt{36}}} = -2.16$$

Step 6   Reach a decision. (See Figure 9.5.)
The decision rule is

If $z < -1.645$, reject H_0
Otherwise, do not reject.

Because $-2.16 < -1.645$, reject H_0.

Step 7   Draw a conclusion.
There is sufficient evidence to conclude that the new bypass procedure does result in a shorter average recovery period.

TRY PROBLEM 9.5

EXAMPLE 9-4   Hypothesis Test for μ, σ Known

Employee Commute Time   A study in southern California claimed that the mean commute time for all employees working in Orange County exceeds 40 minutes. This figure is higher than what has been assumed in the past. The plan is to test this claim using an alpha level equal to 0.05 and a sample size of $n = 100$ commuters. Based on previous studies, suppose that the population standard deviation is known to be $\sigma = 8$ minutes. The hypothesis test can be conducted using the following steps:

Step 1   Specify the population parameter of interest.
The population parameter of interest is the mean commute time, μ.

Step 2   **Formulate the null and alternative hypotheses.**
The new claim is that $\mu > 40$. Because this is different from past studies, it will become the alternative hypothesis. Thus, the null and alternative hypotheses are

$$H_0: \mu \le 40 \text{ minutes}$$
$$H_A: \mu > 40 \text{ minutes (claim)}$$

Step 3   **Specify the significance level.**
The alpha level is specified to be 0.05.

Step 4   **Construct the rejection region.**
Alpha is the area under the standard normal distribution to the right of the critical value. Because the population standard deviation is known, the critical z-value, $z_{0.05}$, is found by locating the z-value that corresponds to an area equal to $0.50 - 0.05 = 0.45$. The critical z-value from the standard normal table is 1.645.

Step 5   **Compute the critical value.**
Suppose that the sample of 100 commuters showed a sample mean of 43.5 minutes. We can calculate $\bar{x}_\alpha = \bar{x}_{0.05}$ using Equation 9.1 as follows:

$$\bar{x}_\alpha = \mu + z_\alpha \frac{\sigma}{\sqrt{n}}$$
$$\bar{x}_{0.05} = 40 + 1.645 \left(\frac{8}{\sqrt{100}} \right)$$
$$\bar{x}_{0.05} = 41.32$$

Step 6   **Reach a decision.**
The decision rule is

If $\bar{x} > 41.32$, reject H_0;
Otherwise, do not reject.

Because $\bar{x} = 43.5 > 41.32$, we reject H_0.

Step 7   **Draw a conclusion.**
There is sufficient evidence to conclude that the mean commute time exceeds 40 minutes.

p-value

The probability (assuming the null hypothesis is true) of obtaining a test statistic at least as extreme as the test statistic we calculated from the sample. The *p*-value is also known as the *observed significance level*.

p-value Approach   In addition to the two hypothesis-testing approaches discussed previously, a third approach for conducting hypothesis tests also exists. This third approach uses a *p*-value instead of a critical value.

If the calculated *p*-value is smaller than the probability in the rejection region (α), then the null hypothesis is rejected. If the calculated *p*-value is greater than or equal to α, then the hypothesis will not be rejected. The *p*-value approach is popular today because *p*-values are usually computed by statistical software packages, including Excel and Minitab. The advantage to reporting test results using a *p*-value is that it provides more information than simply stating whether the null hypothesis is rejected. The decision maker is presented with a measure of the degree of significance of the result (i.e., the *p*-value). This allows the reader the opportunity to evaluate the *extent* to which the data disagree with the null hypothesis, not just whether they disagree.

TRY PROBLEM 9.9

EXAMPLE 9-5 Hypothesis Test Using p-values, σ Known

OmniFitness Club The manager at the Omni Fitness Club in Muskegon, Michigan, believes that the recent remodeling project has greatly improved the club's appeal for members and that they now stay longer at the club per visit than before the remodeling. Studies show that the previous mean time per visit was 36 minutes, with a standard deviation equal to 11 minutes. A simple random sample of $n = 200$ visits is selected, and the current sample mean is 36.8 minutes. To test the manager's claim, and partially justify the remodeling project, using an alpha $= 0.05$ level, the following steps can be used:

Step 1 Specify the population parameter of interest.
The manager is interested in the mean time per visit, μ.

Step 2 Formulate the null and alternative hypotheses.
Based on the manager's claim that the current mean stay is longer than before the remodeling, the null and alternative hypotheses are

$$H_0: \mu \leq 36 \text{ minutes}$$
$$H_A: \mu > 36 \text{ minutes (claim)}$$

Step 3 Specify the significance level.
The alpha level specified for this test is $\alpha = 0.05$.

Step 4 Compute the test statistic.
Because the sample size is large and the population standard deviation is assumed known, the test statistic will be a z-value, which is computed as follows:

$$z = \frac{\bar{x} - \mu}{\frac{\sigma}{\sqrt{n}}} = \frac{36.8 - 36}{\frac{11}{\sqrt{200}}} = 1.0285 = 1.03$$

Step 5 Calculate the p-value.
In this example, the p-value is the probability of a z-value from the standard normal distribution being at least as large as 1.03. This is stated as

$$p\text{-value} = P(z \geq 1.03)$$

From the standard normal distribution table in Appendix D,

$$p(z \geq 1.03) = 0.5000 - 0.3485 = 0.1515$$

Step 6 Reach a decision.
The decision rule is

If p-value $< \alpha = 0.05$, reject H_0;

Otherwise, do not reject H_0.

Because the p-value $= 0.1515 > \alpha = 0.05$, do not reject the null hypothesis.

Step 7 Draw a conclusion.
The difference between the sample mean and the hypothesized population mean is not large enough to attribute the difference to anything but sampling error.

Why do we need three methods to test the same hypothesis when they all give the same result? The answer is that we don't. However, you need to be aware of all three methods because you will encounter each in business situations. The p-value approach is especially important because many statistical software packages provide a p-value that you can use to test a hypothesis quite easily, and a p-value provides a measure of the degree of significance associated with the hypothesis test. This text will use both test-statistic approaches, as well as the *p*-value approach to hypothesis testing.

Types of Hypothesis Tests

Hypothesis tests are formulated as either **one-tailed tests** or **two-tailed tests** depending on how the null and alternative hypotheses are presented.

For instance, in the Morgan Lane application, the null and alternative hypotheses are

Null hypothesis	H_0: $\mu \leq 25$ days
Alternative hypothesis	H_A: $\mu > 25$ days

This hypothesis test is one-tailed because the entire rejection region is located in the upper tail and the null hypothesis will be rejected only when the sample mean falls in the extreme upper tail of the sampling distribution (see Figure 9.4). In this application, it will take a sample mean substantially larger than 25 days in order to reject the null hypothesis.

In Example 9.2 involving the Boulder Potato Company, the null and alternative hypotheses involving the mean fill of potato chip sacks is

$$H_0: \mu = 20 \text{ ounces (status quo)}$$
$$H_A: \mu \neq 20 \text{ ounces}$$

In this two-tailed hypotheses test, the null hypothesis will be rejected if the sample mean is extremely large (upper tail) or extremely small (lower tail). The alpha level would be split evenly between the two tails.

p-Value for Two-Tailed Tests

In the previous *p*-value example, the rejection region was located in one tail of the sampling distribution. In those cases, the null hypothesis was of the ≥ or ≤ format. However, sometimes the null hypothesis will be stated as a direct equality. The following application involving the Golden Peanut Company shows how to use the *p*-value approach for a two-tailed test.

GOLDEN PEANUT COMPANY Consider the Golden Peanut Company in Alpharetta, Georgia which packages salted and unsalted, unshelled peanuts in 16-ounce sacks. The company's filling process strives for an average fill amount equal to 16 ounces. Therefore, Golden would test the following null and alternative hypotheses:

$$H_0: \mu = 16 \text{ ounces (status quo)}$$
$$H_A: \mu \neq 16 \text{ ounces}$$

The null hypothesis will be rejected if the test statistic falls in either tail of the sampling distribution. The size of the rejection region is determined by α. Each tail has an area equal to α/2.

The *p*-value for the two-tailed test is computed in a manner similar to that for a one-tailed test. First, determine the *z*-test statistic as follows:

$$z = \frac{\bar{x} - \mu}{\frac{\sigma}{\sqrt{n}}}$$

Suppose for this situation, Golden managers calculated a $z = 3.32$. Next, find $P(z > 3.32)$ using either the standard normal table in Appendix D, Excel's **NORMSDIST** function, or Minitab's **Calc > Probability Distributions** command. In this case, because $z = 3.32$ exceeds the table values, we will use Excel or Minitab to obtain

$$P(z \leq 3.32) = 0.9995$$

Then

$$P(z > 3.32) = 1 - 0.9995 = 0.0005$$

One-Tailed Test
A hypothesis test in which the entire rejection region is located in one tail of the sampling distribution. In a one-tailed test, the entire alpha level is located in one tail of the distribution.

Two-Tailed Test
A hypothesis test in which the entire rejection region is split into the two tails of the sampling distribution. In a two-tailed test, the alpha level is split evenly between the two tails.

Business Application

FIGURE 9.6

Two-Tailed Test—Golden Peanut Example

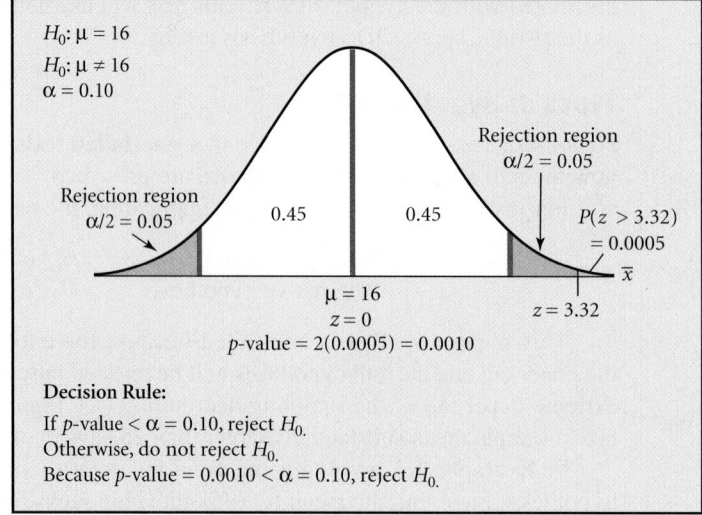

Decision Rule:
If p-value $< \alpha = 0.10$, reject H_0.
Otherwise, do not reject H_0.
Because p-value $= 0.0010 < \alpha = 0.10$, reject H_0.

However, because this is a two-tailed hypothesis test, the p-value is found by multiplying the 0.0005 value by 2 (to account for the chance that our sample result could have been on either side of the distribution). Thus

$$p\text{-value} = 2(0.0005) = 0.0010$$

Assuming an alpha $= 0.10$ level, then because the

$$p\text{-value} = 0.0010 < \alpha = 0.10, \text{ we reject } H_0.$$

Figure 9.6 illustrates the two-tailed test for the Golden Peanut Company example.

SUMMARY   Two-Tailed Test for a Hypothesis About a Population Mean, σ Known

To conduct a two-tailed hypothesis test when the population standard deviation is known, you can perform the following steps.

1. Specify the population parameter of interest.
2. Formulate the null and alternative hypotheses in terms of the population mean, μ.
3. Specify the desired significance level, α.
4. Construct the rejection region.
   Determine the critical values for each tail, $z_{\alpha/2}$ and $-z_{\alpha/2}$ from the standard normal table. If needed, calculate $\bar{x}_{(\alpha/2)L}$ and $\bar{x}_{(\alpha/2)U}$

Define the two-tailed decision rule using one of the following:

- If $z > z_{\alpha/2}$, or if $z < -z_{\alpha/2}$ reject H_0; otherwise, do not reject H_0.
- If $\bar{x} < \bar{x}_{(\alpha/2)L}$ or $\bar{x} > \bar{x}_{(\alpha/2)U}$ reject H_0; otherwise, do not reject H_0.
- If p-value $< \alpha$, reject H_0; otherwise, do not reject H_0.

5. Compute the test statistic, $z = (\bar{x} - \mu)/(\sigma/\sqrt{n})$, or find the p-value.
6. Reach a decision.
7. Draw a conclusion.

TRY PROBLEM 9.2

EXAMPLE 9-6   Two-Tailed Hypothesis Test for μ, σ Known

The Wilson Glass Company   The Wilson Glass Company has a contract to supply plate glass for home and commercial windows. The contract specifies that the mean thickness of the glass must be 0.375 inches. The standard deviation, σ, is known to be 0.05 inch. Before sending the first shipment, Wilson managers wish to test whether they are meeting the requirements by selecting a random sample of $n = 100$ thickness measurements.

Step 1 Specify the population parameter of interest.
The mean thickness of glass is of interest.

Step 2 Formulate the null and the alternative hypotheses.
The null and alternative hypotheses are

$$H_0: \mu = 0.375 \text{ inch (status quo)}$$
$$H_A: \mu \neq 0.375 \text{ inch}$$

Note, the test is two-tailed because the company is concerned that the glass could be too thick or too thin.

Step 3 Specify the desired significance level (α).
The managers wish to test the hypothesis using an $\alpha = 0.05$.

Step 4 Construct the rejection region.
This is a two-tailed test. The critical z values for the upper and lower tails are found in the standard normal table. These are

$$-z_{\alpha/2} = -z_{0.05/2} = -z_{0.025} = -1.96$$

and

$$z_{\alpha/2} = z_{0.05/2} = z_{0.025} = 1.96$$

Define the two-tailed decision rule:

If $z > 1.96$, or if $z < -1.96$, reject H_0; otherwise, do not reject H_0.

Step 5 Compute the test statistic.
Select the random sample and calculate the sample mean.
Suppose that the sample mean for the random sample of 100 measurements is

$$\bar{x} = \frac{\sum x}{n} = 0.378 \text{ inch}$$

The z test statistic is

$$z = \frac{\bar{x} - \mu}{\frac{\sigma}{\sqrt{n}}} = \frac{0.378 - 0.375}{\frac{0.05}{\sqrt{100}}} = 0.60$$

Step 6 Reach a decision.
Because $-1.96 < z = 0.60 < 1.96$, do not reject the null hypothesis.

Step 7 Draw a conclusion.
The Wilson Company does not have sufficient evidence to conclude that it is not meeting the contract.

Hypothesis Test for μ, σ Unknown

In Chapter 8, we introduced situations where the objective was to estimate a population mean when the population standard deviation was not known. In those cases, the critical value is a t-value from the t-distribution rather than a z-value from the standard normal distribution. The same logic is used in hypothesis testing when σ is unknown (which will usually be the case). Equation 9.3 is used to compute the test statistic for testing hypotheses about a population mean when the population standard deviation is unknown.

---

t-Test Statistic for Hypothesis Test for u, σ Unknown

$$t = \frac{\bar{x} - \mu}{\frac{s}{\sqrt{n}}} \tag{9.3}$$

where:

$\bar{x}$ = Sample mean

μ = Hypothesized value for the population mean

s = Sample standard deviation, $s = \sqrt{\dfrac{\Sigma(x - \bar{x})^2}{n-1}}$

n = Sample size

In order to employ the *t*-distribution, we must make the following assumption:

Assumption

The population is normally distributed.

If the population from which the simple random sample is selected is approximately normal, the *t*-test statistic computed using Equation 9.3 will be distributed according to a *t*-distribution with $n - 1$ degrees of freedom.

SUMMARY One- or Two-Tailed Tests for μ, σ Unknown

1. Specify the population parameter of interest, μ.
2. Formulate the null hypothesis and the alternative hypothesis.
3. Specify the desired significance level (α).
4. Construct the rejection region.

   If it is a two-tailed test, determine the critical values for each tail, $t_{\alpha/2}$ and $-t_{\alpha/2}$, from the *t*-distribution table. If the test is a one-tailed test, find either t_α or $-t_\alpha$, depending on the tail of the rejection region. Degrees of freedom are $n - 1$. If desired, the critical *t*-values can be used to find the appropriate $\bar{x}_\alpha$ or the $\bar{x}_{\alpha/2L}$ and $\bar{x}_{\alpha/2U}$ Values.

   Define the decision rule.
   a. If the test statistic falls into the rejection region, reject H_0; otherwise, do not reject H_0.
   b. If the *p*-value is less than α, reject H_0; otherwise, do not reject H_0.

5. Assuming that the population is approximately normal, compute the test statistic.

   Select the random sample and calculate the sample mean, $\bar{x} = \Sigma x/n$, and the sample standard deviation,

   $s = \sqrt{\dfrac{\Sigma(x - \bar{x})^2}{n-1}}$. Then calculate

   $$t = \frac{\bar{x} - \mu}{\dfrac{s}{\sqrt{n}}} \text{ or } p\text{-value}$$

6. Reach a decision.
7. Draw a conclusion.

TRY PROBLEM 9.15

EXAMPLE 9-7 Hypothesis Test for μ, σ Unknown

Dairy Fresh Ice Cream The Dairy Fresh Ice Cream plant in Greensboro, Alabama, uses a filling machine for its 64-ounce cartons. There is some variation in the actual amount of ice cream that goes into the carton. The machine can go out of adjustment and put a mean amount either less or more than 64 ounces in the cartons. To monitor the filling process, the production manager selects a simple random sample of 16 filled ice cream cartons each day. He can test whether the machine is still in adjustment using the following steps:

   Step 1 Specify the population parameter of interest.
   The manager is interested in the mean amount of ice cream.

Step 2   **Formulate the appropriate null and alternative hypotheses.**
The status quo is that the machine continues to fill ice cream cartons with a mean equal to 64 ounces. Thus, the null and alternative hypotheses are

H_0: μ = 64 ounces (Machine is in adjustment.)
H_A: $\mu \neq$ 64 ounces (Machine is out of adjustment.)

Step 3   **Specify the desired level of significance.**
The test will be conducted using an alpha level equal to 0.05.

Step 4   **Construct the rejection region.**
We first produce a box and whisker plot for a rough check on the normality assumption.

The sample data are

62.7	64.7	64.0	64.5	64.6	65.0	64.4	64.2
64.6	65.5	63.6	64.7	64.0	64.2	63.0	63.6

The box and whisker plot is

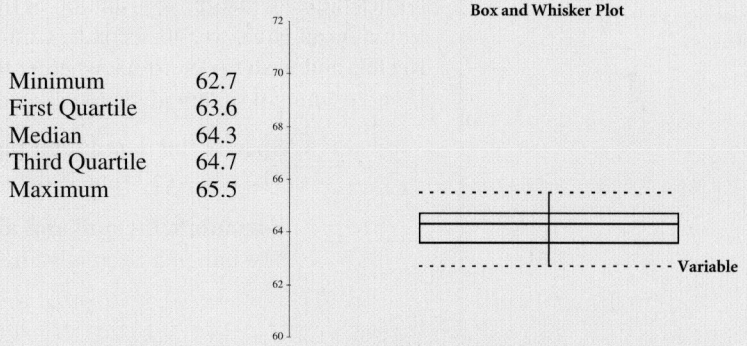

Minimum	62.7
First Quartile	63.6
Median	64.3
Third Quartile	64.7
Maximum	65.5

Box and Whisker Plot

The box and whisker diagram does not indicate that the population distribution is unduly skewed. Thus, the normal distribution assumption is reasonable based on these sample data.

Now we determine the critical values from the t-distribution.

Based on the null and alternative hypotheses, this test is two-tailed. Thus, we will split the alpha into two tails and determine the critical value from the t-distribution with $n - 1$ degrees of freedom. Using Appendix F, the critical t for $\alpha/2 = 0.025$, and $16 - 1 = 15$ degrees of freedom is $t = \pm 2.1315$.

The decision rule for this two-tailed test is

If $t < -2.1315$ or $t > 2.1315$, reject H_0;
Otherwise, do not reject H_0.

Step 5   **Compute the t-test statistic using Equation 9.3.**
The sample mean is

$$\bar{x} = \frac{\sum x}{n} = \frac{1,027.3}{16} = 64.2$$

The sample standard deviation is

$$s = \sqrt{\frac{\sum(x - \bar{x})^2}{n-1}} = 0.72$$

The t-test statistic is

$$t = \frac{\bar{x} - \mu}{\frac{s}{\sqrt{n}}} = \frac{64.2 - 64}{\frac{0.72}{\sqrt{16}}} = 1.11$$

Step 6   Reach a decision.
Because $t = 1.11$ is not less than -2.1315 and not greater than 2.1315, we do not reject the null hypothesis.

Step 7   Draw a conclusion.
Based on these sample data, the company does not have sufficient evidence to conclude that the filling machine is out of adjustment.

EXAMPLE 9-8 Testing the Hypothesis for μ, σ Unknown

TRY PROBLEM 9.16

The Qwest Company   The Qwest Company operates service centers in various cities where customers can call to get answers to questions about their bills. Previous studies indicate that the distribution of time required for each call is normally distributed, with a mean equal to 540 seconds. Company officials have selected a random sample of 16 calls and wish to determine whether the mean call time is now fewer than 540 seconds after a training program given to call center employees.

Step 1   Specify the population parameter of interest.
The mean call time is the population parameter of interest.

Step 2   Formulate the null and alternative hypotheses.
The null and alternative hypotheses are

$$H_0: \mu \geq 540 \text{ seconds (status quo)}$$
$$H_A: \mu < 540 \text{ seconds}$$

Step 3   Specify the significance level.
The test will be conducted at the 0.01 level of significance. Thus, $\alpha = 0.01$.

Step 4   Construct the rejection region.
Because this is a one-tailed test and the rejection region is in the lower tail, the critical value from the t-distribution with $16 - 1 = 15$ degrees of freedom is $-t_\alpha = -t_{0.01} = -2.6025$.

Step 5   Compute the test statistic.
The sample mean for the random sample of 16 calls is $\bar{x} = \sum x/n = 510$

seconds, and the sample standard deviation is $s = \sqrt{\dfrac{\sum(x - x)^2}{n - 1}} = 45$ seconds.

Assuming that the population distribution is approximately normal, the test statistic is

$$t = \frac{\bar{x} - \mu}{\frac{s}{\sqrt{n}}} = \frac{510 - 540}{\frac{45}{\sqrt{16}}} = -2.67$$

Step 6   Reach a decision.
Because $t = -2.67 < -2.6025$, the null hypothesis is rejected.

Step 7   Draw a conclusion.
There is sufficient evidence to conclude that the mean call time for service calls has been reduced below 540 seconds.

Business Application

Excel and Minitab Tutorial

FRANKLIN TIRE AND RUBBER COMPANY The Franklin Tire and Rubber Company recently conducted a test on a new tire design to determine whether the company could make the claim that the mean tire mileage would exceed 60,000 miles. The test was conducted in Alaska. A simple random sample of 100 tires was tested, and the number of miles each tire lasted until it no longer met the federal government minimum tread thickness was recorded. The data (shown in thousands of dollars) are in the CD-ROM file called **Franklin**.

The null and alternative hypotheses to be tested are

$$H_0: \mu \leq 60$$
$$H_A: \mu > 60 \text{ (research hypothesis)}$$
$$\alpha = 0.05$$

Excel does not have a special procedure for testing hypotheses for single population means. However, the Excel add-ins software called PHStat on the CD-ROM that accompanies this text has the necessary hypothesis-testing tools. Figure 9.7a and Figure 9.7b show the Excel PHStat and the Minitab outputs.[5]

We denote the critical value of an upper- or lower-tail test with a significance level of α as t_α or $-t_\alpha$. The critical value for $\alpha = 0.05$ and 99 degrees of freedom is $t_{0.05} = 1.6604$. Using the critical value approach, the decision rule is

If the t test statistic > $1.6604 = t_{0.05}$, reject H_0; otherwise, do not reject H_0.

FIGURE 9.7A

Excel 2007 (PHStat) Output for Franklin Tire Hypothesis Test Results

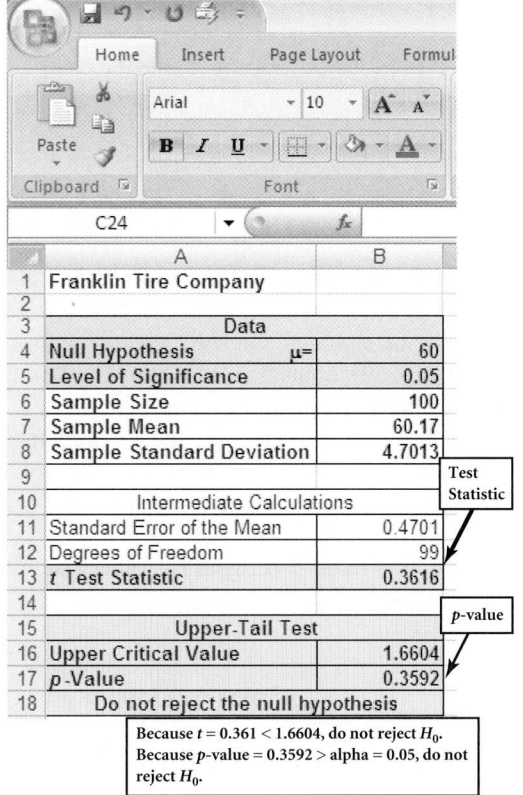

Excel 2007 (PHStat) Instructions:
1. Open file Franklin.xls.
2. Click on **PHStat** tab.
3. Select **One Sample Test**, *t*-test for **Mean, Sigma Unknown**.
4. Enter Hypothesized Mean.
5. Check **"Sample Statistics Unknown"**.
6. Check **Test Option > Upper Tail** Test.

---

[5] This test can be done in Excel without the benefit of the PHStat add-ins by using Excel equations. Please refer to the Excel tutorial on your CD-ROM for the specifics.

FIGURE 9.7B

Minitab Output for Franklin Tire Hypothesis Test Results

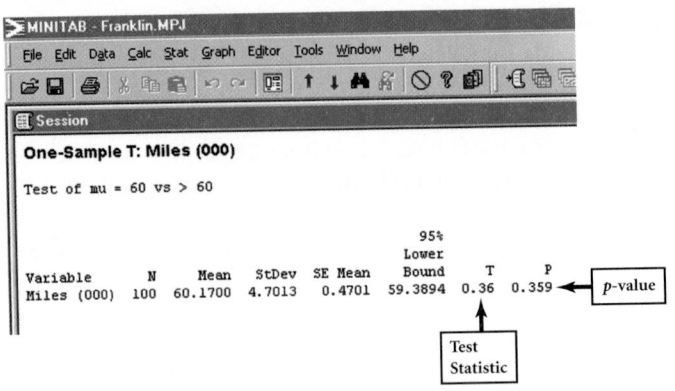

Minitab Instructions:
1. Open file: Franklin.MTW.
2. Choose **Stat > Basic Statistics > 1-sample *t*.**
3. In **Samples in columns**, enter data column.

4. Select **Perform hypothesis test** and enter hypothesized mean.
5. Select **Options**, in **Confidence level** insert confidence level.
6. In **Alternative**, select hypothesis direction.
7. Click **OK.**

The sample mean, based on a sample of 100 tires is $\bar{x} = 60.17$ (60,170 miles), and the sample standard deviation is $s = 4.701$ (4,701 miles). The *t* test statistics shown in Figure 9.7a and 9.7b are computed as follows:

$$t = \frac{\bar{x} - \mu}{\frac{s}{\sqrt{n}}} = \frac{60.17 - 60}{\frac{4.701}{\sqrt{100}}} = 0.3616$$

Because

$$t = 0.3616 < t_{0.05} = 1.6604, \text{ do not reject the null hypothesis.}$$

Thus, based upon the sample data, the evidence is insufficient to conclude that the new tires have an average life exceeding 60,000 miles. Based on this test, the company would not be justified in making the claim.

Franklin managers could also use the *p*-value approach to test the null hypothesis because the output shown in Figures 9.7a and 9.7b provides the *p*-value. In this case, the *p*-value = 0.3592. The decision rule for a test is

If *p*-value $< \alpha$ reject H_0; otherwise, do not reject H_0.

Because

$$p\text{-value} = 0.3592 > \alpha = 0.05$$

we do not reject the null hypothesis. This is the same conclusion we reached using the *t* test statistic approach.

This section has introduced the basic concepts of hypothesis testing. There are several ways to test a null hypothesis. Each method will yield the same result; however, computer software such as Minitab and Excel show the *p*-values automatically. Therefore, decision makers increasingly use the *p*-value approach.

9-1: Exercises

Skill Development

9-1. Determine the appropriate critical value(s) for each of the following tests concerning the population mean:
a. upper-tailed test: $\alpha = 0.025$; $n = 25$; $\sigma = 3.0$
b. lower-tailed test: $\alpha = 0.05$; $n = 30$; $s = 9.0$
c. two-tailed test: $\alpha = 0.02$; $n = 51$; $s = 6.5$
d. two-tailed test: $\alpha = 0.10$; $n = 36$; $\sigma = 3.8$

9-2. For the following hypothesis test:

$$H_0: \mu = 200$$
$$H_A: \mu \neq 200$$
$$\alpha = 0.01$$

with $n = 64$, $\sigma = 9$, and $\bar{x} = 196.5$, state
a. the decision rule in terms of the critical value of the test statistic.
b. the calculated value of the test statistic.
c. the conclusion.

9-3. For the following hypothesis test:

$$H_0: \mu \geq 23$$
$$H_A: \mu < 23$$
$$\alpha = 0.025$$

with $n = 25$, $s = 8$, and $\bar{x} = 20$, state
a. the decision rule in terms of the critical value of the test statistic.
b. the calculated value of the test statistic.
c. the conclusion.

9-4. For the following hypothesis test:

$$H_0: \mu \leq 45$$
$$H_A: \mu > 45$$
$$\alpha = 0.02$$

with $n = 80$, $\sigma = 9$, and $\bar{x} = 47.1$, state
a. the decision rule in terms of the critical value of the test statistic.
b. the calculated value of the test statistic.
c. the appropriate p-value.
d. the conclusion.

9-5. For the following hypothesis test:

$$H_0: \mu = 60.5$$
$$H_A: \mu \neq 60.5$$
$$\alpha = 0.05$$

with $n = 15$, $s = 7.5$, and $\bar{x} = 62.2$, state
a. the decision rule in terms of the critical value of the test statistic.
b. the calculated value of the test statistic.
c. the conclusion.

9-6. For the following hypothesis:

$$H_0: \mu \leq 70$$
$$H_A: \mu > 70$$

with $n = 20$, $\bar{x} = 71.2$, $s = 6.9$, and $\alpha = 0.1$, state

a. the decision rule in terms of the critical value of the test statistic.
b. the calculated value of the test statistic.
c. the conclusion.

9-7. For each of the following z-test statistics, compute the p-value assuming that the hypothesis test is a one-tailed test:
a. $z = 1.34$
b. $z = 2.09$
c. $z = -1.55$

9-8. For each of the following pairs of hypotheses, determine whether each pair represents valid hypotheses for a hypothesis test. Explain reasons for any pair that is indicated to be invalid.
a. $H_0: \mu = 15$, $H_A: \mu > 15$
b. $H_0: \mu = 20$, $H_A: \mu \neq 20$
c. $H_0: \mu < 30$, $H_A: \mu > 30$
d. $H_0: \mu \leq 40$, $H_A: \mu \geq 40$
e. $H_0: \bar{x} \leq 45$, $H_A: \bar{x} > 45$
f. $H_0: \mu \leq 50$, $H_A: \mu > 55$

9-9. A sample taken from a population yields a sample mean of 58.4. Calculate the p-value for each of the following circumstances:
a. $H_A: \mu > 58$, $n = 16$, $\sigma = 0.8$
b. $H_A: \mu \neq 45$, $n = 41$, $s = 35.407$
c. $H_A: \mu \neq 45$, $n = 41$, $\sigma = 35.407$
d. $H_A: \mu < 69$; data: 60.1, 54.3, 57.1, 53.1, 67.4

9-10. Provide the relevant critical value for each of the following circumstances:
a. $H_A: \mu > 13$, $n = 15$, $\sigma = 10.3$, $\alpha = 0.05$
b. $H_A: \mu \neq 21$, $n = 23$, $s = 35.40$, $\alpha = 0.02$
c. $H_A: \mu \neq 35$, $n = 41$, $\sigma = 35.407$, $\alpha = 0.01$
d. $H_A: \mu < 49$; data: 12.5, 15.8, 44.3, 22.6, 18.4; $\alpha = 0.10$
e. $H_A: \mu > 15$, $n = 27$, $\sigma = 12.4$

9-11. For each of the following scenarios, indicate which type of statistical error could have been committed or, alternatively, that no statistical error was made. When warranted, provide a definition for the indicated statistical error.
a. Unknown to the statistical analyst, the null hypothesis is actually true.
b. The statistical analyst fails to reject the null hypothesis.
c. The statistical analyst rejects the null hypothesis.
d. Unknown to the statistical analyst, the null hypothesis is actually true and the analyst fails to reject the null hypothesis.
e. Unknown to the statistical analyst, the null hypothesis is actually false.
f. Unknown to the statistical analyst, the null hypothesis is actually false and the analyst rejects the null hypothesis.

Business Applications

9-12. A mail-order business prides itself in its ability to fill customers' orders in six calendar days or less on the average. Periodically, the operations manager selects a random sample of customer orders and determines the number of days required to fill the orders. Based upon this sample information, he decides whether the desired standard is being met. He will assume that the average number of days to fill customers' orders is six or less unless the data suggest strongly otherwise.

    a. Establish the appropriate null and alternative hypotheses.

    b. On one occasion where a sample of 40 customers was selected, the average number of days was 6.65, with a sample standard deviation of 1.5 days. Can the operations manager conclude that his mail-order business is achieving its goal? Use a significance level of 0.025 to answer this question.

    c. Calculate the p-value for this test. Conduct the test using this p-value.

    d. The operations manager wishes to monitor the efficiency of his mail-order service often. Therefore, he does not wish to repeatedly calculate z-values to conduct the hypothesis tests. Obtain the critical value, $\bar{x}_\alpha$, so that the manager can simply compare the sample mean to this value to conduct the test. Use $\bar{x}$ as the test statistic to conduct the test.

9-13. The National Club Association reported that the average initiation fee for full membership in U.S. country clubs was $33,757 in 2004 (Natlclub.org). Suppose a recent random sample of nine U.S. country clubs revealed the following initiation fees:

Full Membership Initiation Fees ($)				
34,121	36,472	30,054	36,005	41,295
37,771	31,205	38,299	30,602	

Based on the sample information, can you conclude that initiation fees for U.S. country club memberships have increased over the 2004 amount? Conduct your test at the $\alpha = 0.05$ level of significance.

9-14. The director of a state agency believes that the average starting salary for clerical employees in the state is less than $30,000 per year. To test her hypothesis, she has collected a simple random sample of 100 starting clerical salaries from across the state and found that the sample mean is $29,750.

    a. State the appropriate null and alternative hypotheses.

    b. Assuming the population standard deviation is known to be $2,500 and the significance level for the test is to be 0.05, what is the critical value (stated in dollars)?

    c. Referring to your answer in part b, what conclusion should be reached with respect to the null hypothesis?

    d. Referring to your answer in part c, which of the two statistical errors might have been made in this case? Explain.

9-15. The makers of Mini-Oats Cereal have an automated packaging machine that can be set at any targeted fill level between 12 and 32 ounces. Every box of cereal is not expected to contain exactly the targeted weight, but the average of all boxes filled should. At the end of every shift (eight hours), 16 boxes are selected at random and the mean and standard deviation of the sample are computed. Based on these sample results, the production control manager determines whether the filling machine needs to be readjusted or whether it remains all right to operate. Use $\alpha = 0.05$.

    a. Establish the appropriate null and alternative hypotheses to be tested for boxes that are supposed to have an average of 24 ounces.

    b. At the end of a particular shift during which the machine was filling 24-ounce boxes of Mini-Oats, the sample mean of 16 boxes was 24.32 ounces, with a standard deviation of 0.70 ounce. Assist the production control manager in determining if the machine is achieving its targeted average.

    c. Why do you suppose the production control manager would prefer to make this hypothesis test a two-tailed test? Discuss.

    d. Conduct the test using a p-value. (*Hint*: Use Excel's **TINV** function.)

    e. Considering the result of the test, which of the two types of errors in hypothesis testing could you have made?

9-16. A recent internal report issued by the marketing manager for a national oil-change franchise indicated that the mean number of miles between oil changes for franchise customers is at least 3,600 miles. One Texas franchise owner conducted a study to determine whether the marketing manager's statement was accurate for his franchise's customers. He selected a simple random sample of 10 customers and determined the number of miles each had driven the car between oil changes. The following sample data were obtained:

3,655	4,204	1,946	2,789	3,555
3,734	3,208	3,311	3,920	3,902

a. State the appropriate null and alternative hypotheses.

b. Use the test statistic approach with $\alpha = 0.05$ to test the null hypothesis.

9-17. On May 25, 2005, *The Wall Street Journal* carried a feature story titled "Millionaire Ranks Hit New High." The article discussed the results of a survey conducted by the Boston Consulting Group, which showed that the number of individuals in the United States with net worth exceeding $20,000,000 had increased by 3,000 per year since 1999. Suppose a second group has claimed that the average age of a millionaire is now under 55 years. To test this, a random sample of 30 millionaires, was selected; the following sample data reflect the ages of the sampled individuals:

40	55	78	27	55	33
51	76	54	67	40	31
60	61	50	42	78	80
25	38	74	46	48	57
30	65	80	26	46	49

a. State the appropriate null and alternative hypotheses.

b. Use the test statistic approach to test the null hypothesis with $\alpha = 0.01$.

Computer Database Exercises

9-18. The Center on Budget and Policy Priorities (www.cbpp.org) reported that average out-of-pocket medical expenses for prescription drugs for privately insured adults with incomes over 200% of the poverty level was $173 in 2002. Suppose an investigation was conducted to determine whether the increased availability of generic drugs, Internet drug purchases, and cost controls has reduced out-of-pocket drug expenses. A random sample of 196 privately insured adults with incomes over 200% of the poverty level was recently taken, and their 2005 out-of-pocket medical expenses for prescription drugs were collected. The data are in the file **Drug Expenses**. Based on the sample data, can you provide statistical support to conclude that 2005 out-of-pocket prescription drug expenses are lower than the 2002 average? Use a level of significance of 0.01 to conduct your analysis.

9-19. At a recent meeting, the manager of a national call center for a major Internet bank made the statement that the average past-due amount for customers who have been called previously about their bill is now no larger than $20.00. Other bank managers at the meeting suggested that this statement may be

in error and that it might be worthwhile to conduct a test to see if there is statistical support for the call center manager's statement. The file called **Bank Call Center** contains data for a random sample of 67 customers from the call center population. Assuming that the population standard deviation for past due amounts is known to be $60.00, what should be concluded based on the sample data? Test using $\alpha = 0.10$.

9-20. The U.S. Census Bureau Consumer Expenditure Survey reported that the average annual household spending on food at home for 2002–2003 in the Midwest was $2,918 (www.census.gov). Suppose a sample was taken of 137 households in Detroit to determine whether the average annual household spending of food at home for Detroit residents was greater than the Midwest average. The sample results are contained in the file **Detroit Eats**. Based on the sample data, can you conclude at the 0.02 level of significance that average household spending for food at home in Detroit is higher than the Midwest average?

9-21. Hono Golf is a professional R&D manufacturer for golf products in Taiwan and China. One of the golf accessories it produces at its plant in Tainan Hsing, Taiwan, is plastic golf tees. The injector molder produces golf tees that are designed to have an average height of 66 mm. To determine if this specification is met, random samples are taken from the production floor. One sample is contained in the CD-ROM file labeled **THeight**.

a. Determine if the process is not producing the tees to specification. Use a significance level of 0.01.

b. If the hypothesis test determines the specification is not being met, the production process will be shut down while causes and remedies are determined. At times this occurs even though the process is functioning to specification. What type of statistical error would this be?

9-22. A key factor in the world's economic condition is the population growth of the countries in the world. The file called **Countries** contains data for 74 countries in alphabetic order. Consider these 74 countries to be the population of all countries in the world.

a. From this population, suppose a systematic random sample of every fifth country is selected starting with the fifth country on the list. From this sample, test the null hypothesis that the mean population growth percentage between the years 1990 and 2000 is equal to 1.5%. Test using $\alpha = 0.05$.

b. Now compute the average population growth rate for all 74 countries. After examining the result of the hypothesis test in part a, what type of statistical error, if any, was committed? Explain your answer.

9.2 Hypothesis Tests for Proportions

So far, this chapter has focused on hypothesis tests about a single population mean. Although many decision problems involve a test of a population mean, there are also cases in which the parameter of interest is the population proportion. For example, a production manager might consider the proportion of defective items produced on an assembly line in order to determine whether the line should be restructured. Likewise, a life insurance salesperson's performance assessment might include the proportion of existing clients who renew their policies.

Testing a Hypothesis About a Single Population Proportion

The basic concepts of hypothesis testing for proportions are the same as for means.

1. The null and alternative hypotheses are stated in terms of a population parameter, now π instead of μ, and the sample statistic becomes p instead of $\bar{x}$.
2. The null hypothesis should be a statement concerning the parameter that includes the equality.
3. The significance level of the hypothesis determines the size of the rejection region.
4. The test can be one- or two-tailed, depending on how the alternative hypothesis is formulated.

Business Application

FIRST AMERICAN BANK AND TITLE The internal auditors at First American Bank and Title Company routinely test the bank's system of internal controls. Recently, the audit manager examined the documentation on the bank's 22,500 outstanding automobile loans. The bank's procedures require that the file on each auto loan account contain certain specific documentation, such as a list of applicant assets, statement of monthly income, list of liabilities, and certificate of automobile insurance. If an account contains all the required documentation, then it complies with bank procedures.

The audit manager has established a 1% noncompliance rate as the bank's standard. If more than 1% of the 22,500 loans do not have appropriate documentation, then the internal controls are not effective and the bank needs to improve the situation. The audit staff does not have enough time to examine all 22,500 files to determine the true population noncompliance rate. As a result, the audit staff selects a random sample of 600 files, examines them, and determines the number of files not in compliance with bank documentation requirements. The sample findings will tell the manager if the bank is exceeding the 1% noncompliance rate for the population of all 22,500 loan files. The manager will not act unless the noncompliance rate exceeds 1%. The default position is that the internal controls are effective. Thus, the null and alternative hypotheses are

$$H_0: \pi \leq 0.01 \text{ (Internal controls are effective.)}$$
$$H_A: \pi > 0.01 \text{ (Internal controls are not effective.)}$$

Suppose the sample of 600 accounts uncovered 9 files with inadequate loan documentation. The question is whether 9 out of 600 is sufficient to conclude that the bank has a problem. To answer this question statistically, we need to recall a lesson from Chapter 7.

Requirement

> The sample size, n, is large such that $n\pi \geq 5$ and $n(1 - \pi) \geq 5$.[6]

If this requirement is satisfied, the sampling distribution is approximately normal with mean $= \pi$ and standard deviation $= \sqrt{\pi(1 - \pi)/n}$.

The bank's auditors have a general policy of performing these tests with a significance level of

$$\alpha = 0.02$$

---

[6] A paper published in *Statistical Science* by L. Brown et. al. entitled "Interval Estimation for a Binomial Proportion" in 2001, pp. 101–133, suggests that the requirement should be $n\pi \geq 15$ and $n(1 - \pi) \geq 15$. However, most sources still use the 5 limit.

They are willing to reject a true null hypothesis 2% of the time. In this case, if a Type I statistical error is committed, the internal controls will be considered ineffective when, in fact, they are working as intended.

Once the null and alternative hypotheses and the significance level have been specified, we can formulate the decision rule for this test. Figure 9.8 shows how the decision rule is developed. Notice the critical value, $p_{0.02}$, is 2.05 standard deviations above $\pi = 0.01$. Thus, the decision rule is:

$$\text{If } p > p_{0.02} = 0.0182, \text{ reject } H_0.$$

Because there were 9 deficient files in the sample of 600 files, this means that

$$p = 9/600 = 0.015$$

Because

$$p = 0.015 < p_{0.02} = 0.0182, \text{ do not reject } H_0.$$

The null hypothesis H_0 should not be rejected, based on these sample data. Therefore, the auditors will conclude the system of internal controls is working effectively.

Alternatively, we could have based the test on a test statistic (z) with a standard normal distribution. This test statistic is calculated using Equation 9.4.

---

z-Test Statistic for Proportions

$$z = \frac{p - \pi}{\sqrt{\dfrac{\pi(1-\pi)}{n}}} \tag{9.4}$$

where:

$$p = \text{Sample proportion}$$
$$\pi = \text{Hypothesized population proportion}$$
$$n = \text{Sample size}$$

FIGURE 9.8

Decision Rule for First American Bank and Title Example

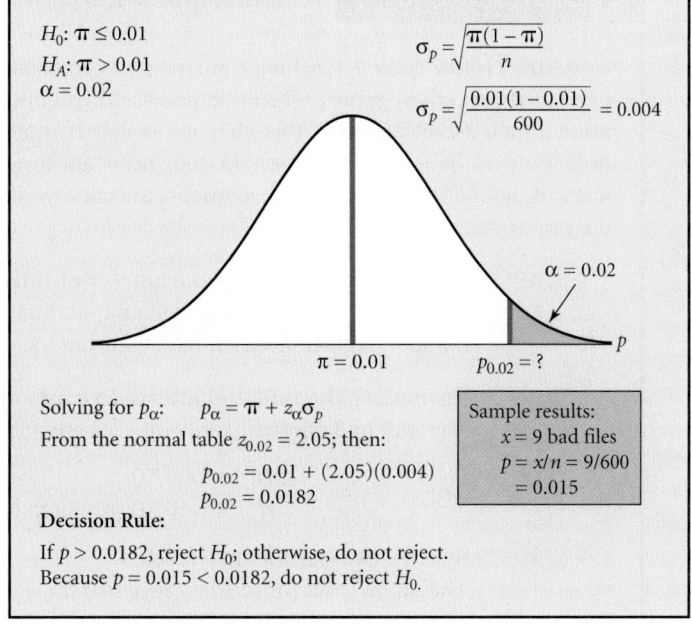

H_0: $\pi \leq 0.01$
H_A: $\pi > 0.01$
$\alpha = 0.02$

$\sigma_p = \sqrt{\dfrac{\pi(1-\pi)}{n}}$

$\sigma_p = \sqrt{\dfrac{0.01(1-0.01)}{600}} = 0.004$

$\alpha = 0.02$

$\pi = 0.01$ $p_{0.02} = ?$

Solving for p_α: $p_\alpha = \pi + z_\alpha \sigma_p$
From the normal table $z_{0.02} = 2.05$; then:

$p_{0.02} = 0.01 + (2.05)(0.004)$
$p_{0.02} = 0.0182$

Sample results:
$x = 9$ bad files
$p = x/n = 9/600$
$= 0.015$

Decision Rule:
If $p > 0.0182$, reject H_0; otherwise, do not reject.
Because $p = 0.015 < 0.0182$, do not reject H_0.

The z-value for this test statistic is

$$z = \frac{0.015 - 0.01}{0.004} = 1.25$$

As was established in Figure 9.8, the critical value is

$$z_{0.02} = 2.05$$

We reject the null hypothesis only if $z > z_{0.02}$. Because

$$z = 1.25 < 2.05$$

we don't reject the null hypothesis. This, of course, was the same conclusion we reached when we used p as the test statistic. Both test statistics must yield the same decision.

SUMMARY Testing Hypotheses About a Single Population Proportion

1. Specify the population parameter of interest.
2. Formulate the null and alternative hypotheses.
3. Specify the significance level for testing the null hypothesis.
4. Construct the rejection region.
     For a one-tail test, determine the critical value, z_α, from the standard normal distribution table or

$$p_\alpha = \pi + z_\alpha \sqrt{\frac{\pi(1-\pi)}{n}}$$

For a two-tail test, determine the critical values

$z_{(\alpha/2)L}$ and $z_{(\alpha/2)U}$ from the standard normal table or $p_{(\alpha/2)L}$ and $p_{(\alpha/2)U}$

5. Compute the test statistic, $p = \dfrac{x}{n}$ or $z = \dfrac{p - \pi}{\sqrt{\pi(1-\pi)/n}}$

6. Reach a decision by comparing z to z_α or p to p_α or by comparing the p-value to α.

7. Draw a conclusion.

TRY PROBLEM 9.27

EXAMPLE 9-9 Testing Hypotheses for a Single Population Proportion

Season Ticket Sales   A major university is considering increasing the season ticket prices for basketball games. The athletic director is concerned that some people will terminate their ticket orders if this change occurs. If more than 10% of the season ticket orders would be terminated, the AD does not want to implement the price increase. To test this, a random sample of ticket holders are surveyed and asked what they would do if the prices were increased.

Step 1 Specify the population parameter of interest.
       The parameter of interest is the population proportion of season ticket holders who would terminate their orders.

Step 2 Formulate the null and alternative hypotheses.
       The null and alternative hypotheses are

$$H_0: \pi \leq 0.10$$
$$H_A: \pi > 0.10 \text{ (research hypothesis)}$$

Step 3 Specify the significance level.
       The alpha level for this test is $\alpha = 0.05$.

Step 4 Construct the rejection region.

The critical value from the standard normal table for this upper-tailed test is $z_\alpha = z_{0.05} = 1.645$.

The decision rule is

If $z > 1.645$, reject H_0; otherwise, do not reject.

Step 5 Compute the test statistic.

The random sample of $n = 100$ season ticket holders showed that 14 would cancel their ticket orders if the price change were implemented. The sample proportion is

$$p = \frac{x}{n} = \frac{14}{100} = 0.14$$

$$z = \frac{p - \pi}{\sqrt{\dfrac{\pi(1 - \pi)}{n}}} = \frac{0.14 - 0.10}{\sqrt{\dfrac{0.10(1 - 0.10)}{100}}} = 1.33$$

Step 6 Reach a decision.

The decision rule is

If $z > z_{0.05}$, reject H_0.

Because $z = 1.33 < 1.645$, do not reject H_0.

As you learned in Section 9.1, there are alternative approaches to testing a hypothesis. In addition to the z-test statistic approach, you could compute the critical value, p_α, and compare $p = 0.14$ to p_α. The critical value is computed as follows:

$$p_\alpha = \pi + z_\alpha \sqrt{\frac{\pi(1 - \pi)}{n}}$$

$$p_{0.05} = 0.10 + 1.645 \sqrt{\frac{0.10(1 - 0.10)}{100}} = 0.149$$

The decision rule is

If $p > p_{0.05}$, reject H_0.

Because $0.14 < 0.149$, do not reject H_0. This is the same decision we reached using the z-test statistic approach.

The hypothesis can also be tested using the p-value approach. To find the p-value for a one-tailed test, we use the calculated z-value shown previously in step 5 to be $z = 1.33$. Then,

p-value $= P(z > 1.33)$

From the standard normal table, the probability associated with $z = 1.33$ is 0.4082. Then,

p-value $= 0.5 - 0.4082 = 0.0918$

The decision rule is

If p-value $< \alpha$, reject H_0.

Because p-value $= 0.0918 > 0.05$, do not reject H_0.

All three hypothesis testing approaches provide the same decision.

> **Step 7   Draw a conclusion.**
> Based on the sample data, the athletic director does not have sufficient evidence to conclude that more than 10% of the season ticket holders will cancel their ticket orders.

9-2: Exercises

Skill Development

9-23. Determine the appropriate critical value(s) for each of the following tests concerning the population proportion:
   a. upper-tailed test: $\alpha = 0.025$, $n = 48$
   b. lower-tailed test: $\alpha = 0.05$, $n = 30$
   c. two-tailed test: $\alpha = 0.02$, $n = 129$
   d. two-tailed test; $\alpha = 0.10$, $n = 36$

9-24. For the following hypothesis test:

$$H_0: \pi = 0.40$$
$$H_A: \pi \neq 0.40$$
$$\alpha = 0.01$$

with $n = 64$ and $p = 0.42$, state
   a. the decision rule in terms of the critical value of the test statistic.
   b. the calculated value of the test statistic.
   c. the conclusion.

9-25. For the following hypothesis test:

$$H_0: \pi \geq 0.75$$
$$H_A: \pi < 0.75$$
$$\alpha = 0.025$$

with $n = 100$ and $p = 0.66$, state
   a. the decision rule in terms of the critical value of the test statistic.
   b. the calculated value of the test statistic.
   c. the conclusion.

9-26. Calculate the z-test statistic for a hypothesis test in which the null hypothesis states that the population proportion, π, equals 0.40 if the following sample information is present:

$$n = 150, x = 30$$

9-27. Given the following null and alternative hypotheses:

$$H_0: \pi \geq 0.60$$
$$H_A: \pi < 0.60$$

test the hypothesis using $\alpha = 0.01$ assuming that a sample of $n = 200$ yielded $x = 105$ items with the desired attribute.

9-28. A test of hypothesis has the following hypotheses:

$$H_0: \pi \leq 0.45$$
$$H_A: \pi > 0.45$$

For a sample size of 30, and a sample proportion of 0.55,
   a. for an $\alpha = 0.025$, determine the critical value.
   b. calculate the numerical value of the test statistic.
   c. state the test's conclusion.
   d. determine the p-value.

9-29. A sample of size 25 was obtained to test the hypotheses

$$H_0: \pi = 0.30$$
$$H_A: \pi \neq 0.30$$

Calculate the p-value for each of the following sample results:
   a. $p = 0.12$
   b. $p = 0.35$
   c. $p = 0.42$
   d. $p = 0.5$

Business Applications

9-30. A major issue facing many states is whether to legalize casino gambling. Suppose the governor of one state believes that more than 55% of the state's registered voters would favor some form of legal casino gambling. However, before backing a proposal to allow such gambling, the governor has instructed his aides to conduct a statistical test on the issue. To do this, the aides have hired a consulting firm to survey a simple random sample of 300 voters in the state. Of these 300 voters, 175 actually favored legalized gambling.
   a. State the appropriate null and alternative hypotheses.
   b. Assuming that a significance level of 0.05 is used, what conclusion should the governor reach based upon these sample data? Discuss.

9-31. An issue that faces individuals investing for retirement is allocating assets among different investment choices. Suppose a study conducted 10 years ago showed that 65% of investors preferred stocks to real estate as an investment. In a recent random sample of 900 investors, 360 preferred real estate to stocks. Is this new data sufficient to allow you to conclude that the proportion of investors preferring stocks to real estate has declined from 10 years ago? Conduct your analysis at the $\alpha = 0.02$ level of significance.

9-32. A Washington Post–ABC News poll taken in March 2005 found that 72% of people are concerned about the possibility that their personal records could be stolen over the Internet (*Salina Journal*, June 13, 2005). If a random sample of 300 college students at a Midwestern university were taken and 228 of them were concerned about the possibility that their personal records could be stolen over the Internet, could you conclude at the 0.025 level of significance that a higher proportion of the university's college students are concerned about Internet theft than the public at large? Report the *p*-value for this test.

9-33. An April 2004 article published by the *Detroit Free Press* entitled "Assistance: IRS Help Centers Give the Wrong Information" discusses the propensity of IRS staff employees to give wrong tax information to taxpayers who call with questions. IRS Inspector General Pamela Gardiner told a Senate subcommittee that ". . . the IRS employees at 400 taxpayer assistance centers nationwide encountered 8.5 million taxpayers face-to-face last year. The problem: When inspector general auditors posing as taxpayers asked them to answer tax questions, the answers were right 69% of the time" (see www.freep.com/money/business/taxhel12_20040412.htm).

Suppose an independent commission was formed to test whether the 0.69 accuracy rate is correct or whether it is actually higher or lower. The commission has randomly selected $n = 180$ tax returns that were completed by IRS assistance employees and found that 105 of the returns were accurately completed.
a. State the appropriate null and alternative hypotheses.
b. Using an $\alpha = 0.05$ level, based on the sample data, what conclusion should be reached about the IRS rate of correct tax returns? Discuss your results.

9-34. A July 13, 2005 article on the front page of *The Wall Street Journal* entitled "As Identity Theft Moves Online, Crime Rings Mimic Big Business" states that 39% of the consumer scam complaints by American consumers is about identity theft. Suppose a random sample of 90 complaints is obtained. Of these complaints, 40 were regarding identity theft. Based on these sample data, what conclusion should be reached about the statement made in *The Wall Street Journal*? (Test using $\alpha = 0.10$.)

9-35. In July 2005, an Associated Press article written by Eileen Powell entitled "Credit Card Payments Going Up" described a recent change in credit card policies. Under pressure from federal regulators, credit card issuers have started to raise the minimum payment that consumers are required to pay on outstanding credit card balances. Suppose a claim is made that more than 40% of all credit card holders pay the minimum payment. To test this claim, a random sample of payments made by credit card customers was collected. The sample contained data for 400 customers, of which 174 paid the minimum payment.
a. State the appropriate null and alternative hypotheses.
b. Based on the sample data, test the null hypothesis using an alpha level equal to 0.05. Discuss the results of the test.

9-36. The practice of "phishing," or using the Internet to pilfer personal information, has become an increasing concern, not only for individual computer users but also for online retailers and financial institutions. *The Wall Street Journal* (June 23, 2005) reported 28% of people who bank online have cut back on their Internet use. The North Central Educators Credit Union instituted an extensive online security and educational program six months ago in an effort to combat phishing before the problem became extreme. The credit union's managers are certain that while Internet use may be down, it is much less than 28% of its customers. In fact, they are convinced that at most 10% of their customers have reduced their Internet banking transactions.

The credit union's IT department analyzed 200 randomly selected accounts and determined that 24 indicated Internet banking had either been reduced or stopped entirely.
a. State the appropriate null and alternative hypotheses for this situation.
b. Using $\alpha = 0.05$ and the *p*-value approach, indicate whether the sample data support the managers' contention.

9-37. CEO Chris Foreman of Pacific Theaters Exhibition Corp. is taking steps to reverse the decline in movie attendance. Moviegoers' comfort is one of the issues facing theaters. Pacific Theaters has begun offering assigned seating, no in-theater advertising, and a live announcer who introduces films and warns patrons to turn off cell phones. Despite such efforts, an Associated Press/America Online News poll of 1,000 adults (*USA Today*, "Movie maladies," June 23, 2005) discovered that 730 of those surveyed preferred seeing movies in their homes.
a. Using a significance level of 0.025, conduct a statistical procedure to determine if the Associated Press/America Online News poll indicates that more than 70% of adults prefer seeing movies in their homes. Use a *p*-value approach.

b. Express a Type II error in the context of this exercise's scenario.

9-38. Harris Interactive Inc., the 15th largest market research firm in the world, is a Rochester, New York-based company. In 2005, one of their surveys indicated that 26% of women have had experience with a Global Positioning System device. The survey (*USA Today*, Snapshots, July 12, 2005) indicated that 36% of the men surveyed used a Global Positioning System device.

a. If the survey was based upon a sample size of 290 men, does this data indicate that the proportion of men is the same as the proportion of women who have had experience with a Global Positioning System device? Use a significance level of 0.05.

b. Obtain the *p*-value for the test indicated in part a.

9-39. A large number of complaints have been received in the past six months regarding airlines losing fliers' baggage. The airlines claim the problem is nowhere near as great as the newspaper articles have indicated. In fact, one airline spokesman claimed that less than 1% of all bags fail to arrive at the destination with the passenger. To test this claim, 800 bags were randomly selected at various airports in the United States when they were checked with this airline. Of these, 6 failed to reach the destination when the passenger (owner) arrived.

a. Is this sufficient evidence to support the airline spokesman's claim? Test using a significance level of 0.05. Discuss.

b. Estimate the proportion of bags that fail to arrive at the proper destination using a technique for which 95% confidence applies.

Computer Database Exercises

9-40. According to the Employee Benefit Research Institute (www.ebri.org), 34% of workers between the ages of 35 and 44 owned a 401(k)-type retirement plan in 2002. Suppose a recent survey was conducted by the Atlanta Chamber of Commerce to determine the participation rate of 35–44-year-old working adults in the Atlanta metropolitan area who owned 401(k)-type retirement plans. The results of the survey can be found in the file **Atlanta Retirement**. Based on the survey results, can the Atlanta Chamber of Commerce conclude that the participation rate for 35–44-year-old working adults in Atlanta is higher than the 2002 national rate? Conduct your analysis at the 0.025 level of significance.

9-41. A survey by the Pew Internet & American Life Project conducted between January 13 and February 9, 2005 (http://www.pewinternet.org/pdfs/PIP_Spam_Ap05.pdf) found that 21% of workers with an e-mail account at work say that they are getting more spam than a year ago.

Suppose a large multinational company, after implementing a policy to combat spam, asked 198 randomly selected employees with e-mail accounts at work whether they are receiving more spam today than they did a year ago. The results of the survey are in the file **Spam**. At the 0.025 level of significance, can the company conclude that a smaller percentage of its employees is receiving more spam than a year ago than that found by the Pew study?

9-42. A study by the Investment Company Institute (ICI) in 2004, which randomly surveyed 3,500 households and drew upon information from the Internal Revenue Service, found that 72% of households have conducted at least one IRA rollover from an employer-sponsored retirement plan (www.financial-planning.com). Suppose a recent random sample of 90 households in the greater Miami area was taken and respondents were asked whether they had ever funded an IRA account with a rollover from an employer-sponsored retirement plan. The results are in the file **Miami Rollover**. Based on the sample data, can you conclude at the 0.10 level of significance that the proportion of households in the greater Miami area that have funded an IRA with a rollover is different from the proportion for all households reported in the ICI study?

9-43. Cell phones are becoming an integral part of our daily lives. Commissioned by Motorola, a new behavioral study took researchers to nine cities worldwide from New York to London. Using a combination of personal interviews, field studies, and observation, the study identified a variety of behaviors that demonstrate the dramatic impact cell phones are having on the way people interact. The study found cell phones give people a newfound personal power, enabling unprecedented mobility and allowing them to conduct their business on the go. Interesting enough, gender differences can be found in phone use. Women see their cell phone as a means of expression and social communication, while males tend to use it as an interactive toy. A cell phone industry spokesman stated that half of all cell phones in use are registered to females.

a. State the appropriate null and alternative hypotheses for testing the industry claim.

b. Based on a random sample of cell phone owners shown in the data file called **Cell Phone Survey**, test the null hypothesis. (Use $\alpha = 0.05$.)

9-44. The Electronic Controls Company (ECCO) is one of the largest makers of backup alarms in the world. Backup alarms are the safety devices that emit a high-pitched beeping sound when a truck, forklift, or other equipment is operated in reverse. ECCO is well known in the industry for its high quality and excellent customer service, but some products are returned under warranty due to quality problems. ECCO's operations manager recently stated that less than half of the warranty returns are wiring-related problems. To verify if she is correct, a company intern was asked to select a random sample of warranty returns and determine the proportion that were returned due to wiring problems. The data the intern collected are shown in the data file called **ECCO**.

a. State the appropriate null and alternative hypotheses.

b. Conduct the hypothesis test using $\alpha = 0.02$ and provide an interpretation of the result of the hypothesis test in terms of the operation manager's claim.

9-45. Joseph-Armand Bombardier founded the company in the 1930s that is now known as Seadoo in Canada. His initial invention of the snowmobile in 1937 led the way to what is now a 7,600-employee, worldwide company specializing in both snow and water sports vehicles. The company stresses high quality in both manufacturing and dealer service. Suppose that the company standard for customer satisfaction is 95% "highly satisfied." Company managers recently completed a customer survey of 700 customers from around the world. The responses to the question, "What is your overall level of satisfaction with Seadoo?" are provided in the file called **Seadoo**.

a. State the appropriate null and alternative hypotheses to be tested.

b. Using an alpha level of 0.05, conduct the hypothesis test and discuss the conclusions.

9.3 Type II Errors

Sections 9.1 and 9.2 provided several examples that illustrated how hypotheses and decision rules for tests of the population mean or population proportion are formulated. In these examples, we determined the critical values by first specifying the significance level, alpha: the maximum allowable probability of committing a Type I error. As we indicated, if the cost of committing a Type I error is high, the decision maker will want to specify a small significance level.

This logic provides a basis for establishing the critical value for the hypothesis test. However, it ignores the possibility of committing a Type II error. Recall that a Type II error occurs if a false null hypothesis is "accepted." The probability of a Type II error is given by the symbol β, the Greek letter beta. We discussed in Section 9.1 that α and β are inversely related. That is, if we make α smaller, β will increase. However, the two are not proportional. A case in point: Cutting α in half will not necessarily double β.

CHAPTER OUTCOME #5

Calculating Beta

Once α has been specified for a hypothesis test involving a particular sample size, β cannot also be specified. Rather, the β value is fixed, and all the decision maker can do is calculate it. However, β is not a single value. Because a Type II error occurs when a false null hypothesis is "accepted" (refer to Figure 9.1), there is a β value for each possible population value for which the null hypothesis is false. To calculate beta, we must first specify a "what-if" value for the true population parameter. Then, β is computed conditional on that parameter being true. Keep in mind that β is computed before the sample is taken, so its value is not dependent on the sample outcome.

For instance, if the null hypothesis is that the mean income for a population is equal to or greater than $30,000, then β could be calculated for any value of μ less than $30,000. We would get a different β for each value of μ. An application will help clarify this concept.

Business Application

AMERICAN LIGHTING COMPANY The American Lighting Company has developed a new light bulb to last more than 700 hours on average. If a hypothesis test could confirm this, the company would use the "greater than 700 hour" statement in its advertising. The null and alternative hypotheses are

$$H_0: \mu \le 700 \text{ hours}$$
$$H_A: \mu > 700 \text{ hours (research hypothesis)}$$

The null hypothesis is false for all possible values of $\mu > 700$ hours. Thus, for each of the infinite number of possibilities, a value of β can be determined. (*Note:* σ is assumed to be a known value of 15 hours.)

Figure 9.9 shows how β is calculated if the true value of μ is 701 hours. By specifying the significance level to be 0.05 and a sample size of 100 bulbs, the chance of committing a Type II error is approximately 0.8365. This means that if the true population mean is 701 hours, there is nearly an 84% chance that the sampling plan American Lighting is using will not reject the assumption that the mean is 700 hours or less.

Figure 9.10 shows that if the "what-if" mean value ($\mu = 704$) is farther from the hypothesized mean ($\mu = 700$), beta becomes smaller. The greater the difference between the mean specified in H_0 and the mean selected from H_A, the easier it is to tell the two apart, and the less likely we are to not reject the null hypothesis when it is actually false. Of course the opposite is also true. As the mean selected from H_A moves increasingly closer to the mean specified in H_0, the harder it is for the hypothesis test to distinguish between the two.

Controlling Alpha and Beta

Ideally, we want both alpha and beta to be as small as possible. Although we can set alpha at any desired level, for a specified sample size and standard deviation, the calculated value of beta depends on the population mean chosen from the alternative hypothesis and the significance level. For a specified sample size, reducing alpha will increase beta. However, we

FIGURE 9.9

Beta Calculation for True $\mu = 701$

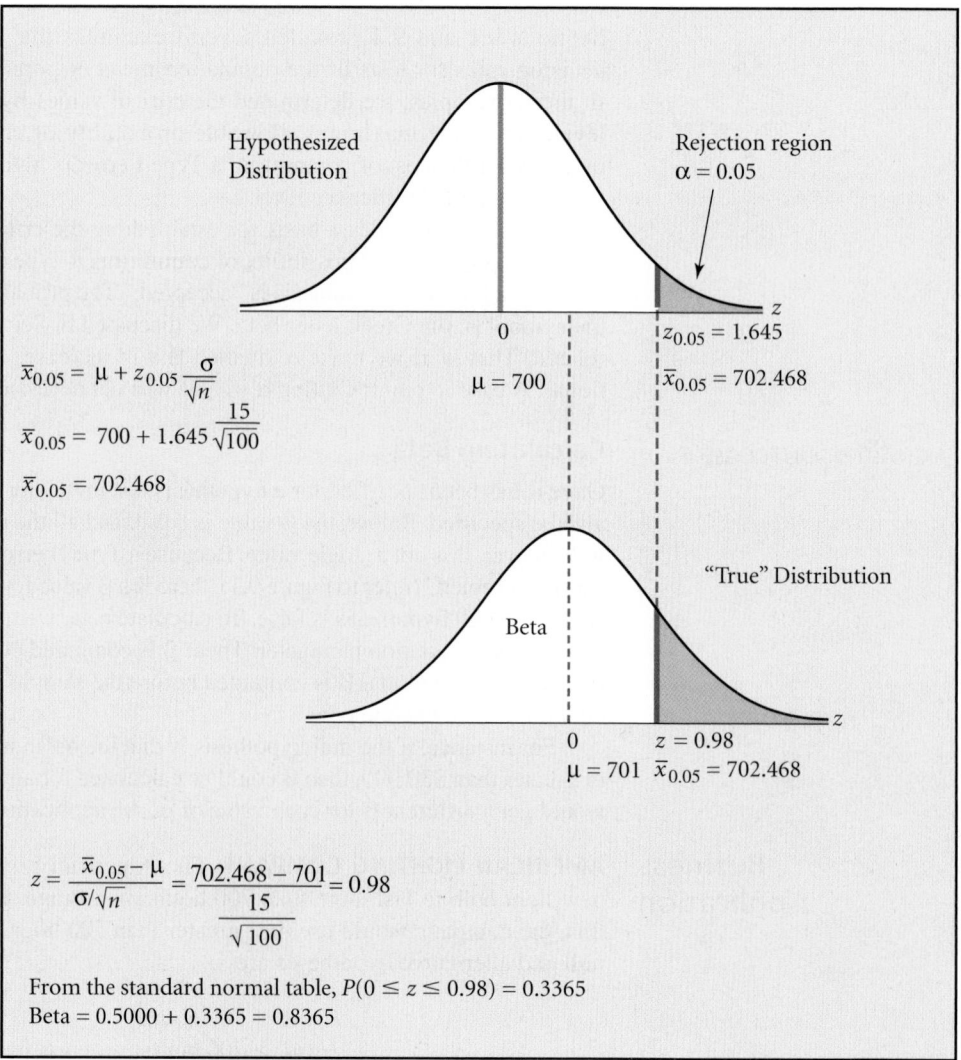

$$\bar{x}_{0.05} = \mu + z_{0.05}\frac{\sigma}{\sqrt{n}}$$

$$\bar{x}_{0.05} = 700 + 1.645\frac{15}{\sqrt{100}}$$

$$\bar{x}_{0.05} = 702.468$$

$$z = \frac{\bar{x}_{0.05} - \mu}{\sigma/\sqrt{n}} = \frac{702.468 - 701}{\dfrac{15}{\sqrt{100}}} = 0.98$$

From the standard normal table, $P(0 \le z \le 0.98) = 0.3365$
Beta $= 0.5000 + 0.3365 = 0.8365$

FIGURE 9.10

Beta Calculation for True $\mu = 704$

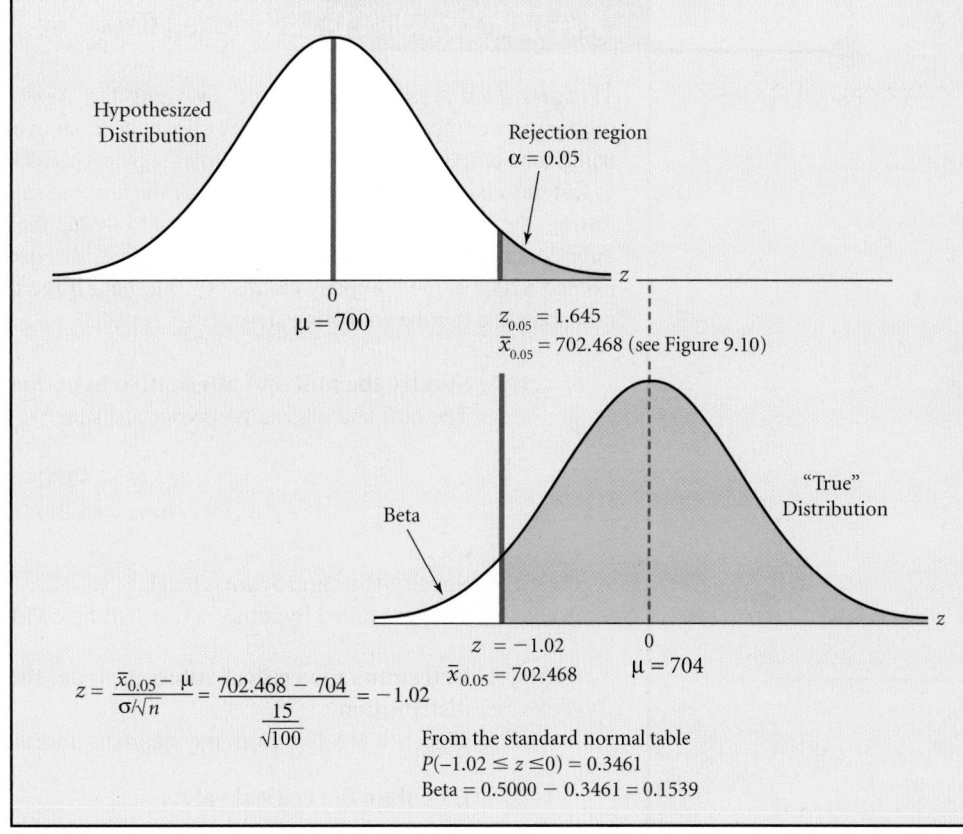

$$z = \frac{\bar{x}_{0.05} - \mu}{\sigma/\sqrt{n}} = \frac{702.468 - 704}{\frac{15}{\sqrt{100}}} = -1.02$$

From the standard normal table
$P(-1.02 \le z \le 0) = 0.3461$
Beta $= 0.5000 - 0.3461 = 0.1539$

can simultaneously control the size of both alpha and beta if we are willing to increase the sample size.

The American Lighting Company planned to take a sample of 100 light bulbs. In Figure 9.9, we showed that beta $= 0.8365$ when the "true" population mean was 701 hours. This is a very large probability and would be unacceptable to the company. However, if the company is willing to incur the cost associated with a sample size of 500 bulbs, the probability of a Type II error could be reduced to 0.5596, as shown in Figure 9.11. This is a big improvement and is due to the fact that the standard error ($\sigma/\sqrt{n}$) is reduced because of the increased sample size.

SUMMARY Calculating Beta

The probability of committing a Type II error can be calculated using the following steps.

1. Formulate the null and alternative hypotheses.
2. Specify the significance level. (*Hint*: Draw a picture of the hypothesized sampling distribution showing the rejection region(s) and the acceptance region found by specifying the significance level.)
3. Determine the critical value, z_α, from the standard normal distribution.
4. Determine the critical value, $\bar{x}_\alpha = \mu + z_\alpha \sigma/\sqrt{n}$ for an upper-tail test, or $\bar{x}_\alpha = \mu - z_\alpha \sigma/\sqrt{n}$ for a lower-tail test.

5. Specify the stipulated value for μ, the "true" population mean for which you wish to compute β. (*Hint*: Draw the "true" distribution immediately below the hypothesized distribution.)
6. Compute the z-value based on the stipulated population mean as

$$z = \frac{\bar{x}_\alpha - \mu}{\frac{\sigma}{\sqrt{n}}}$$

7. Use the standard normal table to find β, the probability associated with "accepting" the null hypothesis when it is false.

TRY PROBLEM 9.52

EXAMPLE 9-10 Computing Beta

Wright Tax Assistance, Inc. Wright Tax Assistance, Inc., a major income tax preparation company, has claimed its clients save an average of more than $200 each by using the company's services. A consumer's group plans to randomly sample 64 customers to test this claim. The standard deviation of the amount saved is assumed to be $100. Before testing, the consumer's group is interested in knowing the probability that they will mistakenly conclude that the mean savings is less than or equal to $200 when, in fact, it does exceed $200, as the company claims. To find beta if the true population mean is $210, the company can use the following steps.

Step 1 **Specify the null and alternative hypotheses.**
The null and alternative hypotheses are

$$H_0: \mu \leq \$200$$
$$H_A: \mu > \$200 \text{ (claim)}$$

Step 2 **Specify the significance level.**
The one-tailed hypothesis test will be conducted using $\alpha = 0.05$.

Step 3 **Determine the critical value, z_α, from the standard normal distribution.**
The critical value from the standard normal is $z_\alpha = z_{0.05} = 1.645$.

Step 4 **Calculate the critical value.**

$$\bar{x}_{0.05} = \mu + z_{0.05}\frac{\sigma}{\sqrt{n}} = 200 + 1.645\frac{100}{\sqrt{64}} = 220.56$$

Thus, the null hypothesis will be rejected if $\bar{x} > 220.56$.

Step 5 **Specify the stipulated value for μ.**
The null hypothesis is false for all values greater than $200. What is beta if the stipulated mean is $210?

Step 6 **Compute the z-value based on the stipulated population mean.**
The **z-value** based on stipulated population mean is

$$z = \frac{\bar{x}_{0.05} - \mu}{\frac{\sigma}{\sqrt{n}}} = \frac{220.56 - 210}{\frac{100}{\sqrt{64}}} = 0.84$$

Step 7 **Determine beta.**
From the standard normal table, the probability associated with $z = 0.84$ is 0.2995. Then $\beta = 0.5000 + 0.2995 = 0.7995$. There is a 0.7995 probability that the hypothesis test will lead the consumer agency to mistakenly believe that the mean tax savings is less than or equal to $200 when, in fact, the mean savings is $210.

FIGURE 9.11

American Lighting Company, Beta Calculation for "True" μ = 701 and n = 500

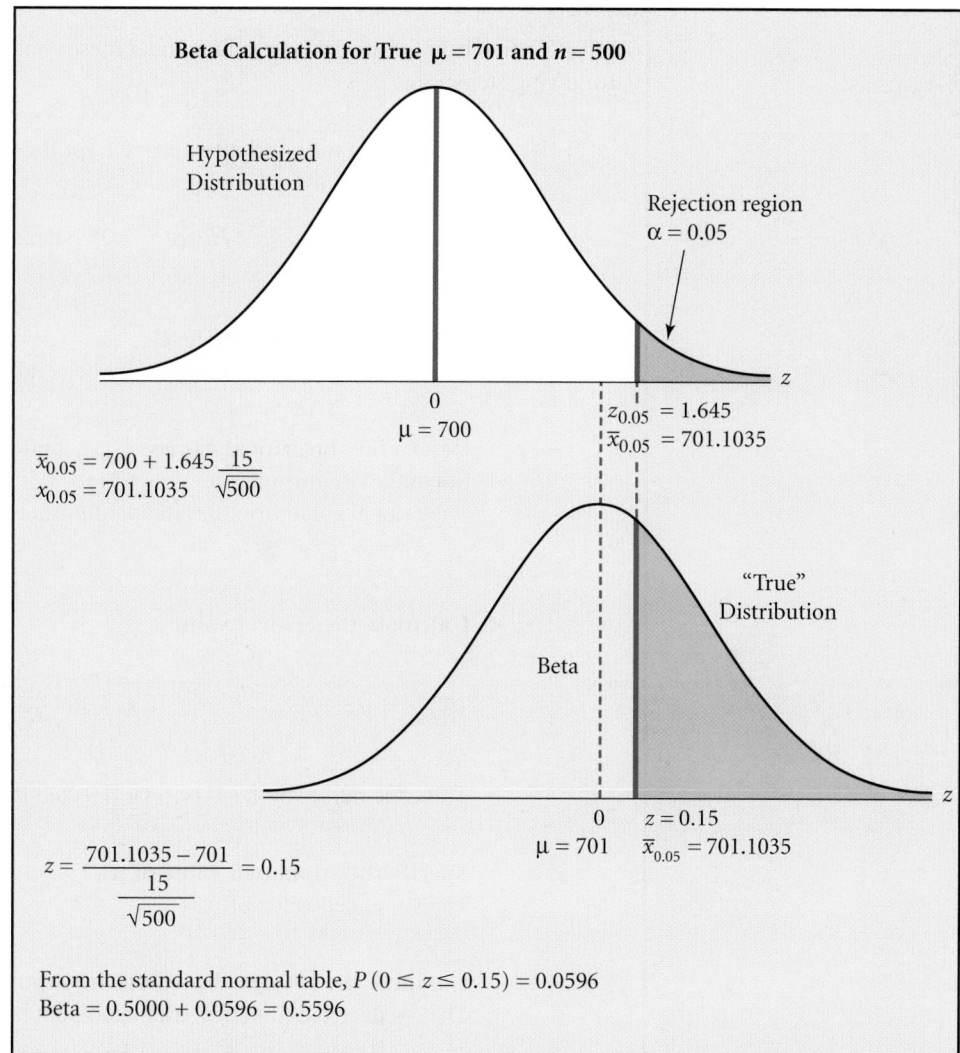

Beta Calculation for True μ = 701 and n = 500

Hypothesized Distribution

Rejection region
α = 0.05

0
μ = 700

$z_{0.05} = 1.645$
$\bar{x}_{0.05} = 701.1035$

$\bar{x}_{0.05} = 700 + 1.645 \dfrac{15}{\sqrt{500}}$
$x_{0.05} = 701.1035$

"True" Distribution

Beta

0   z = 0.15
μ = 701 $\bar{x}_{0.05} = 701.1035$

$z = \dfrac{701.1035 - 701}{\dfrac{15}{\sqrt{500}}} = 0.15$

From the standard normal table, $P\,(0 \le z \le 0.15) = 0.0596$
Beta $= 0.5000 + 0.0596 = 0.5596$

EXAMPLE 9-11 Calculating Beta for a Two-Tailed Test

TRY PROBLEM 9.54

Saluc, a Belgium-based manufacturer of billiard balls, produces and distributes billiard balls under the registered trademark Aramith in more than 85 countries and has a market share of 80% worldwide. High-technology machinery and computerized equipment allow the company to produce balls that require tight dimensional tolerances. Perhaps the most important dimension is the diameter of the balls. They must have a diameter that is 2.25 inches wide for the American market. If the diameter is too large or small, it affects the playing characteristics of the balls. Therefore, each hour the quality control engineers select a random sample of 20 balls from the production line and measure the diameter of each ball. The standard deviation is tightly controlled as well. Assume σ = 0.005 inches. Experience might show that as the production machinery ages, the diameter of the balls tends to increase. Suppose that the quality engineers are interested in how likely the test procedure they use will conclude that the mean diameter is equal to 2.25 inches when, in fact, the mean equals 2.255 inches. They want to know the probability of a Type II error. To find beta for this test procedure under these conditions, the engineers can use the following steps:

Step 1   Specify the null and alternative hypotheses.
The null and alternative hypotheses are

$$H_0: \mu = 2.25 \text{ (status quo)}$$
$$H_A: \mu \neq 2.25$$

Step 2   Specify the significance level.
The two-tailed hypothesis test will be conducted using $\alpha = 0.05$.

Step 3   Determine the critical values, $z_{(\alpha/2)L}$ and $z_{(\alpha/2)U}$, from the standard normal distribution.
The critical value from the standard normal is $z_{(\alpha/2)L}$ and $z_{(\alpha/2)U} = \pm z_{0.025} = \pm 1.96$.

Step 4   Calculate the critical values.

$$\bar{x}_{L,U} = \mu \pm z_{0.025} \frac{\sigma}{\sqrt{n}} = 2.25 \pm 1.96 \frac{0.005}{\sqrt{20}} \rightarrow \bar{x}_L = 2.2478; \bar{x}_U = 2.2522$$

Thus, the null hypothesis will be rejected if $\bar{x} < 2.2478$ or $\bar{x} > 2.2522$.

Step 5   Specify the stipulated value of μ.
The stipulated value of μ is 2.255.

Step 6   Compute the z-values based on the stipulated population mean.
The z-values based on the stipulated population mean is

$$z = \frac{\bar{x}_L - \mu}{\frac{\sigma}{\sqrt{n}}} = \frac{2.2478 - 2.255}{\frac{0.005}{\sqrt{20}}} = -6.44 \quad \text{and} \quad z = \frac{\bar{x}_U - \mu}{\frac{\sigma}{\sqrt{n}}} = \frac{2.2522 - 2.255}{\frac{0.005}{\sqrt{20}}} = -2.50$$

Step 7   Determine beta and reach a conclusion.
Beta is the probability from the standard normal distribution between $z = -6.44$ and $z = -2.50$. From the standard normal table, we get

$$(0.5000 - 0.5000) + (0.5000 - 0.4938) = 0.0062$$

Thus, beta = 0.0062. There is a very small chance (only 0.0062) that this hypothesis test will fail to detect that the mean diameter has shifted to 2.255 inches from desired mean of 2.25 inches. This low beta will give the engineers confidence that their test can detect problems when they occur.

As shown in Section 9.2, many business applications will involve hypotheses tests about population proportions rather than population means. Example 9-12 illustrates the steps needed to compute the beta for a hypothesis test involving proportions.

EXAMPLE 9-12   Calculating Beta for a Test of a Population Proportion

TRY PROBLEM 9.56

The National Federation of Independent Business (NFIB) has offices in Washington, D.C., and all 50 state capitals. NFIB is the nation's largest small-business lobbying group. Its research foundation provides policymakers, small-business owners, and other interested parties empirically based information on small businesses. NFIB often initiates surveys to provide this information. In 2004, a speech by a senior Republican administration official claimed that at least 30% of all small businesses were owned, or operated, by women. NFIB internal analyses had the number at closer to 25%. As a result, the NFIB analysts planned to conduct a test of the Republican claim but were interested in the probability (beta) of accepting the claim if in fact the true percentage was 25%. A simple random sample of 500 small businesses will be selected.

Step 1 Specify the population parameter of interest.
NFIB is interested in the proportion of female-owned small businesses, π.

Step 2 Specify the null and alternative hypotheses.

$$H_0: \pi \geq 0.30 \text{ (claim)}$$
$$H_A: \pi < 0.30$$

Step 3 Specify the significance level.
The one-tailed hypothesis test will be conducted using $\alpha = 0.025$.

Step 4 Determine the critical value, z_α, from the standard normal distribution.
The critical value from the standard normal is $z_\alpha = z_{0.025} = -1.96$.

Step 5 Calculate the critical value.

$$p_{0.025} = \pi - z_{0.025}\sqrt{\frac{\pi(1-\pi)}{n}} = 0.30 - 1.96\sqrt{\frac{0.30(1-0.70)}{500}} = 0.2598$$

Therefore, the null hypothesis will be rejected if $p > 0.2598$.

Step 6 Specify the stipulated value for the "true" π.
The stipulated value is 0.25.

Step 7 Compute the z-value based on the stipulated population proportion.
The z-value is

$$z = \frac{p_\alpha - \pi}{\sqrt{\dfrac{\pi(1-\pi)}{n}}} = \frac{0.2598 - 0.25}{\sqrt{\dfrac{0.25(1-0.25)}{500}}} = 0.51$$

Step 8 Determine beta.
From the standard normal table, the probability associated with $z = 0.51$ is 0.1950. Then $\beta = 0.5000 - 0.1950 = 0.3050$. Thus, there is a 0.3050 chance that the hypothesis test will "accept" the null hypothesis that the percentage of women-owned or operated small businesses is 30% if in fact the true percentage is only 25%. The NFIB may wish to increase the sample size to improve beta.

As you now know, hypothesis tests are subject to error. The two potential statistical errors are

Type I (rejecting a true null hypothesis)

Type II ("accepting" a false null hypothesis)

In most business applications, there are adverse consequences associated with each type of error. In some cases, the errors can mean dollar costs to a company. For instance, suppose a health insurance company is planning to set its premium rates based on a hypothesized mean annual claims amount per participant as follows:

$$H_0: \mu \leq \$1,700$$
$$H_A: \mu > \$1,700$$

If the company tests the hypothesis and "accepts" the null, it will institute the planned premium rate structure. However, if a Type II error is committed, the actual average claim will exceed $1,700 and the company will incur unexpected payouts and will suffer reduced profits. On the other hand, if the company rejects the null hypothesis, it will probably increase its premium rates. But if a Type I error is committed, there would be no justification for the rate increase and the company may not be competitive in the marketplace and could lose customers.

In other cases, the costs associated with either a Type I or a Type II error may be even more serious. If a drug company's hypothesis tests for a new drug incorrectly conclude that the drug is safe when in fact it is not (Type I error), the company's customers may become ill or even die as a result. You might refer to recent reports dealing with pain medications such as Vicodin. On the other hand, a Type II error would mean that a potentially useful and safe drug would most likely not be made available to people who need it if the hypothesis tests incorrectly determined that the drug was not safe.

In the U.S. legal system where a defendant is hypothesized to be innocent, a Type I error by a jury would result in a conviction of an innocent person. DNA evidence has recently resulted in a number of convicted people being set free. A case in point is Hubert Geralds, who was convicted of killing Rhonda King in 1994 in the state of Illinois. However, Type II errors in our court system result in guilty people being set free to potentially commit other crimes.

The bottom line is that as a decision maker using hypothesis testing, you need to be aware of the potential costs associated with both Type I and Type II statistical errors and conduct your tests accordingly.

Power of the Test

Power

The probability that the hypothesis test will reject the null hypothesis when the null hypothesis is false.

In the previous examples, we have been concerned about the chance of making a Type II error. We would like beta to be as small as possible. If the null hypothesis is false, we want to reject it. Another way to look at this is that we would like the hypothesis test to have a high probability of rejecting a false null hypothesis. This concept is expressed by what is called the **power** of the test. When the alternative hypothesis is true, the power of the test is computed using Equation 9.5.

Power
Power $= 1 - \beta$ **(9.5)**

Refer again to the business application involving the American Lighting Company. Beta calculations were presented in Figure 9.9, 9.10, and 9.11. For example, in Figure 9.9, the company was interested in the probability of a Type II error if the "true" population mean was 701 hours instead of the hypothesized mean of 700 hours. This probability, called beta, was shown to be 0.8365. Then for this same test,

$$Power = 1 - B$$
$$Power = 1 - 0.8365 = 0.1635$$

Thus, in this situation, there is only a 0.1635 chance that the hypothesis test will correctly reject the null hypothesis that the mean is 700 or fewer hours when in fact it really is 701 hours.

In Figure 9.10, when a "true" mean of 704 hours was considered, the value of beta dropped to 0.1539. Likewise, power is increased:

$$Power = 1 - 0.1539 = 0.8461$$

So the probability of correctly rejecting the null hypothesis increases to 0.8461 when the "true" mean is 704 hours.

We also saw in Figure 9.11 that an increase in sample size resulted in a decreased beta value. For a "true" mean of 701 but with a sample size increase from 100 to 500, the value of beta dropped from 0.8365 to 0.5596. That means that power is increased from 0.1635 to 0.4404 due to the increased size of the sample.

A graph called a **power curve** can be created to show the power of a hypothesis test for various levels of the "true" population parameter. Figure 9.12 shows the power curve for the American Lighting Company application for a sample size of $n = 100$.

Power Curve

A graph showing the probability that the hypothesis test will correctly reject a false null hypothesis for a range of possible "true" values for the population parameter.

FIGURE 9.12

Power Curve—American Lighting Company

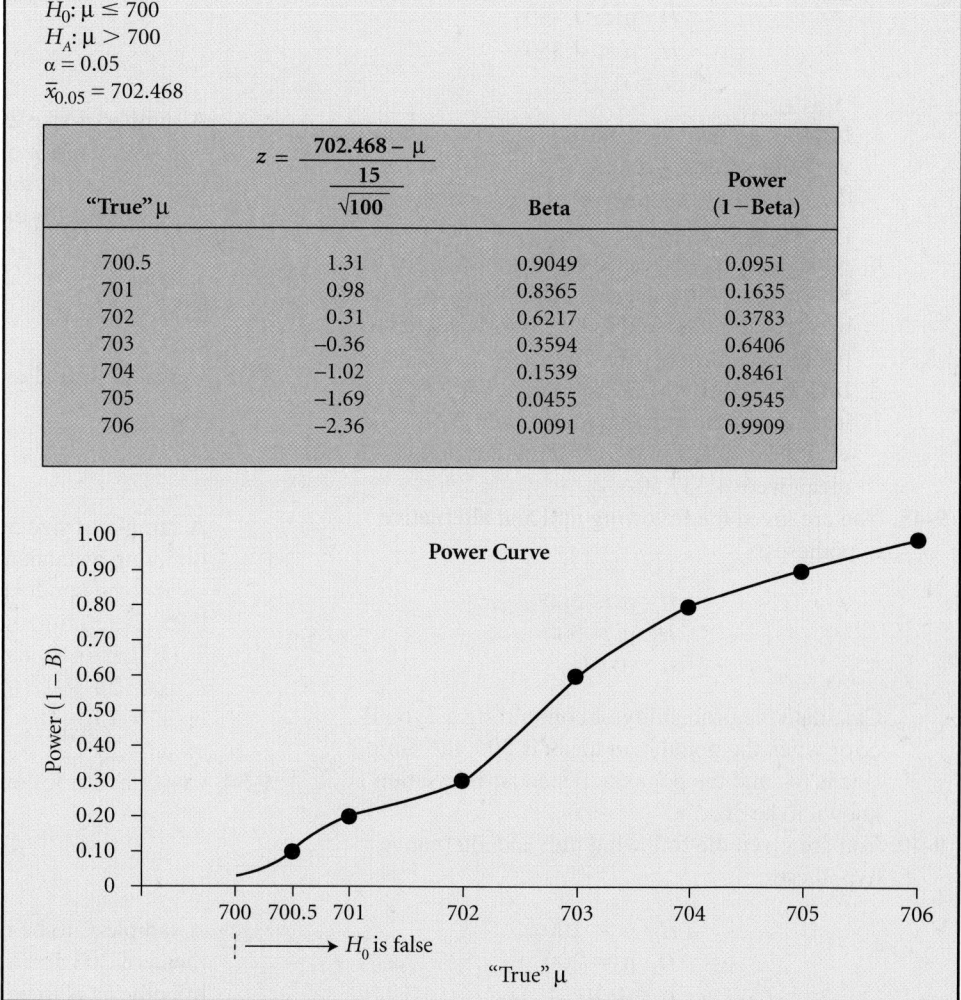

$H_0: \mu \leq 700$
$H_A: \mu > 700$
$\alpha = 0.05$
$\bar{x}_{0.05} = 702.468$

"True" μ	$z = \dfrac{702.468 - \mu}{\dfrac{15}{\sqrt{100}}}$	Beta	Power $(1 - \text{Beta})$
700.5	1.31	0.9049	0.0951
701	0.98	0.8365	0.1635
702	0.31	0.6217	0.3783
703	−0.36	0.3594	0.6406
704	−1.02	0.1539	0.8461
705	−1.69	0.0455	0.9545
706	−2.36	0.0091	0.9909

9-3: Exercises

Skill Development

9-46. You are given the following null and alternative hypotheses:

$$H_0: \mu = 1.20$$
$$H_A: \mu \neq 1.20$$
$$\alpha = 0.10$$

a. If the true population mean is 1.25, determine the value of beta. Assume the population standard deviation is known to be 0.50 and the sample size is 60.
b. Referring to part a, calculate the power of the test.
c. Referring to parts a and b, what could be done to increase power and reduce beta when the true population mean is 1.25? Discuss.
d. Indicate clearly the decision rule that would be used to test the null hypothesis, and determine what decision should be made if the sample mean were 1.23.

9-47. You are given the following null and alternative hypotheses:

$$H_0: \mu \geq 4{,}350$$
$$H_A: \mu < 4{,}350$$
$$\alpha = 0.05$$

a. If the true population mean is 4,345, determine the value of beta. Assume the population standard deviation is known to be 200 and the sample size is 100.
b. Referring to part a, calculate the power of the test.
c. Referring to parts a and b, what could be done to increase power and reduce beta when the true population mean is 4,345? Discuss.
d. Indicate clearly the decision rule that would be used to test the null hypothesis, and determine what decision should be made if the sample mean were 4,337.50.

9-48. You are given the following null and alternative hypotheses:

$$H_0: \mu \leq 500$$
$$H_A: \mu > 500$$
$$\alpha = 0.01$$

Calculate the probability of committing a Type II error when the population mean is 505, the sample size is 64, and the population standard deviation is known to be 36.

9-49. You are given the following null and alternative hypotheses:

$$H_0: \mu = 200$$
$$H_A: \mu \neq 200$$
$$\alpha = 0.10$$

Calculate the probability of committing a Type II error when the population mean is 197, the sample size is 36, and the population standard deviation is known to be 24.

9-50. For each of the following situations, indicate what the general impact on the Type II error probability will be:
a. The alpha level is increased.
b. The "true" population mean is moved farther from the hypothesized population mean.
c. The alpha level is decreased.
d. The sample size is increased.

9-51. Solve for beta when the "true" population mean is 103 and the following information is given:

$$H_0: \mu \leq 100$$
$$H_A: \mu > 100$$
$$\alpha = 0.05$$
$$\sigma = 10$$
$$n = 49$$

9-52. Consider the following hypotheses:

$$H_0: \mu \geq 103$$
$$H_A: \mu < 103$$

A sample of size 20 is to be taken from a population with a mean of 100 and a standard deviation of 4. Determine the probability of committing a Type II error for each of the following significance levels:
a. $\alpha = 0.01$
b. $\alpha = 0.025$
c. $\alpha = 0.05$

9-53. Consider the following hypotheses:

$$H_0: \mu = 30$$
$$H_A: \mu \neq 30$$

A sample of size 50 is to be taken from a population with a standard deviation of 13. The hypothesis is to be conducted using a significance level of 0.05. Determine the probability of committing a Type II error when
a. $\mu = 22$
b. $\mu = 25$
c. $\mu = 29$

9-54. Consider the following hypotheses:

$$H_0: \mu \leq 201$$
$$H_A: \mu > 201$$

A sample is to be taken from a population with a mean of 203 and a standard deviation of 3. The hypothesis is to be conducted using a significance level of 0.05. Determine the probability of committing a Type II error when

a. $n = 10$
b. $n = 20$
c. $n = 50$

9-55. The following hypotheses are to be tested:

$$H_0: \pi \geq 0.35$$
$$H_A: \pi < 0.35$$

A random sample of 400 is taken. Using each set of information following, compute the power of the test.

a. $\alpha = 0.01$, true $\pi = 0.32$
b. $\alpha = 0.025$, true $\pi = 0.33$
c. $\alpha = 0.05$, true $\pi = 0.34$

9-56. The following hypotheses are to be tested:

$$H_0: \pi \leq 0.65$$
$$H_A: \pi > 0.65$$

A random sample of 500 is taken. Using each set of information following, compute the power of the test.

a. $\alpha = 0.01$, true $\pi = 0.68$
b. $\alpha = 0.025$, true $\pi = 0.67$
c. $\alpha = 0.05$, true $\pi = 0.66$

Business Applications

9-57. Waiters at Finegold's Restaurant and Lounge earn most of their income from tips. Each waiter is required to "tip-out" a portion of tips to the table bussers and hostesses. The manager has based the "tip-out" rate on the assumption that the mean tip is at least 15% of the customer bill. To make sure that this is the correct assumption, he has decided to conduct a test by randomly sampling 60 bills and recording the actual tips.

a. State the appropriate null and alternative hypotheses.
b. Calculate the probability of a Type II error if the true mean is 14%. Assume that the population standard deviation is known to be 2% and a significance level equal of 0.01 will be used to conduct the hypothesis test.

9-58. According to data from the Environmental Protection Agency, the average daily water consumption for a household of four people in the United States is approximately 243 gallons. (*Source*: http://www.catskillcenter.org/programs/csp/H20/Lesson3/house3.htm) Suppose a state agency plans to test this claim using an alpha level equal to 0.05 and a random sample of 100 households with four people.

a. State the appropriate null and alternative hypotheses.
b. Calculate the probability of committing a Type II error if the true population mean is 230 gallons. Assume that the population standard deviation is known to be 40 gallons.

9-59. According to JobWeb®, a Web site of career development and job-search information for college students and new college graduates, owned and sponsored by the National Association of Colleges and Employers (NACE), the average starting salary for accounting graduates in 2004 exceeded $41,000. Suppose that the American Society for Certified Public Accountants planned to test this claim by randomly sampling 200 accountants who graduated in 2004.

a. State the appropriate null and alternative hypotheses.
b. Compute the power of the hypothesis test to reject the null hypothesis if the true population mean starting salary is only $40,000. Assume that the population standard deviation is known to be $4,600 and the test is to be conducted using an alpha level equal to 0.01.

9-60. Swift is the holding company for Swift Transportation Co., Inc., a truckload carrier headquartered in Phoenix, Arizona. Swift operates the largest truckload fleet in the United States. Before Swift switched to its current computer-based billing system, the average payment time from customers was approximately 40 days. Suppose before purchasing the present billing system, it performed a test by examining a random sample of 24 invoices to see if the system would reduce the average billing time. The sample indicates that the average payment time is 38.7 days.

a. The company that created the billing system indicates that it would reduce the average billing time to less than 40 days. Conduct a hypothesis test to determine if the new computer-based billing system would reduce the average billing time to less than 40 days. Assume the standard deviation is known to be 6 days. Use a significance level of 0.025.
b. If the billing system actually reduced the average billing time to 36 days, determine the probability that a wrong decision was made in part a.

9-61. Nationwide Mutual Insurance, based in Columbus, Ohio, is one of the largest diversified insurance and financial services organizations in the world, with more than $157 billion in assets. Nationwide ranked #99 on the Fortune 100 list in 2005. The company provides a full range of insurance and financial services. In a July 26, 2005 news release ("ID Theft Victims Struggle to Achieve Resolution"), Nationwide reported the results of a new survey of 1,097 identity theft victims. The survey shows victims spend an average of 81 hours trying to resolve their case. If the true average time spent was 81 hours, determine the probability that a test of hypothesis designed to test that the average was less than 85 hours would select the research hypothesis. Use $\alpha = 0.05$ and a standard deviation of 50.

9-62. The union negotiations between labor and management at the Stone Container paper mill in Minnesota hit a snag when management asked labor to take a cut in health insurance coverage. As part of its justification, management claimed that the average amount of insurance claims filed by union employees did not exceed $250 per employee. The union's chief negotiator requested that a sample of 100 employees' records be selected and that this claim be tested statistically. The claim would be accepted if the sample data did not strongly suggest otherwise. The significance level for the test was set at 0.10.

a. State the null and alternative hypotheses.

b. Before the sample was selected, the negotiator was interested in knowing the power of the null hypothesis if the mean amount of insurance claims were $260. (Assume the standard deviation in claims is $70.00, as determined in a similar study at another plant location.) Calculate this probability for the negotiator.

c. Referring to part b, how would the power of the test change if $\alpha = 0.05$ is used?

d. Suppose alpha is left at 0.10, but the standard deviation of the population is $50.00 rather than $70.00. What will be the power of the test? State the generalization that explains the relationship between the answers to part b and d.

e. Referring to part d, based on the probability computed, if you were the negotiator, would you be satisfied with the sampling plan in this situation? Explain why or why not. What steps could be taken to improve the sampling plan?

9-63. *BusinessWeek* indicated in an article (Robert Barker, "Brew at Bargain Prices," August 8, 2005) that per capita U. S. beer consumption in 2004 was 21.6 gallons. A survey is designed to determine if the per capita consumption has changed in the current year. A hypothesis test is to be conducted using a sample size of 1,500, a significance level of 0.01, and a standard deviation of 40. Determine the probability that the test will be able to correctly detect that the per capita consumption has changed if it has declined by 10%.

9-64. Runzheimer International, a management consulting firm specializing in transportation reimbursement, released the results of a survey on July 28, 2005. It indicated that it costs more to own a car in Detroit, an amazing $11,844 a year for a mid-sized sedan, than in any other city in the country. The survey revealed that insurance, at $5,162 annually for liability, collision, and comprehensive coverage, is the biggest single reason that maintaining a car

in the Motor City is so expensive. A sample size of 100 car owners in Los Angeles was used to determine if the cost of owning a car was more than 10% less than in Detroit. A hypothesis test with a significance level of 0.01 and a standard deviation of $750 is used. Determine the probability that the test will conclude that the cost of owning a car in Los Angeles is not more than 10% less than in Detroit when in fact the average cost is $10,361.

Computer Database Exercises

9-65. In an article in *BusinessWeek* ("Living on the Edge at American Apparel," June 27, 2005), Dov Chaney, the CEO of American Apparel, indicated that the apparel store industry's average sales were $1,800/7 (= $257.14) a square foot. A hypothesis test was requested to determine if the data supported the statement made by the American Apparel CEO using an $\alpha = 0.05$ and the sample size of 41. Produce the probability that the data will indicate that American Apparel stores produce an average of seven times the apparel industry average when in fact they only produce an average six times the apparel industry average with a standard deviation of 100. The CD-ROM file called **Apparel** contains data for a random sample of several competitors' sales per square foot. Use $\alpha = 0.05$.

9-66. *USA Today* reports (Gary Stoller, "Hotel bill mistakes mean many pay too much," July 12, 2005) that George Hansen, CEO of Wichita-based Corporate Lodging Consultants, conducted a recent review of hotel bills over a 12-month period. The review indicated that, on average, errors in hotel bills resulted in overpayment of $11.35 per night. To determine if such mistakes are being made at a major hotel chain, the CEO might direct a survey yielding the following data:

9.99	9.87	11.53	12.40	12.36	11.68	12.52	9.34	13.13	10.78
9.76	10.88	10.61	10.29	10.23	9.29	8.82	8.70	8.22	11.01
12.40	9.55	11.30	10.21	8.19	10.56	8.49	7.99	8.03	10.53

The CD-ROM file **OverPay** contains this data.

a. Conduct a hypothesis test with $\alpha = 0.05$ to determine if the average overpayment is smaller than that indicated by Corporate Lodging Consultants.

b. If the actual average overpayment at the hotel chain was $11 with an actual standard deviation of $1.50, determine the probability that the hypothesis test would correctly indicate that the actual average is less than $11.35.

Summary and Conclusions

This chapter has introduced the fundamentals of hypothesis testing. The concepts presented here provide decision makers with tools for using sample information to decide whether a given null hypothesis should be rejected.

In this chapter we have concentrated on examples of hypothesis tests involving a single population mean and a single population proportion. In subsequent chapters you will see that the hypothesis-testing methodology is basically the same for all situations. The central issue is always to determine whether the sample information tends to support or refute the null hypothesis.

We have emphasized the importance of recognizing that when a hypothesis is tested, an error might occur. Type I and Type II statistical errors have been discussed. We have shown how to determine the probability of committing each type of error for applications involving a single population mean.

You have probably noticed that the statistical estimation techniques discussed in Chapter 8 and hypothesis testing have much in common. Both estimation and hypothesis testing are used extensively by business decision makers. Estimation procedures are most useful when decision makers

FIGURE 9.13

Deciding Which Hypothesis Testing Procedure to Use

TABLE 9.1 Statistical Inference Tools—One Sample Situations

	Population Mean μ	Population Proportion π
Statistic	$\bar{x} = \dfrac{\sum x}{n}$	$p = \dfrac{x}{n}$
Confidence Interval	σ **known:** $\bar{x} \pm z \dfrac{\sigma}{\sqrt{n}}$ σ **unknown:** $\bar{x} \pm t \dfrac{s}{\sqrt{n}}$	$p \pm z \sqrt{\dfrac{p(1-p)}{n}}$
Hypotheses	**Example** $H_0: \mu \leq 200$ $H_A: \mu > 200$	**Example** $H_0: \pi \geq 0.60$ $H_A: \pi < 0.60$
Test Statistic	σ **known:** $z = \dfrac{\bar{x} - \mu}{\dfrac{\sigma}{\sqrt{n}}}$ σ **unknown:** $t = \dfrac{\bar{x} - \mu}{\dfrac{s}{\sqrt{n}}}$	$z = \dfrac{p - \pi}{\sqrt{\dfrac{\pi(1-\pi)}{n}}}$

have little or no idea of the value of a population parameter and are primarily interested in determining these values. On the other hand, hypothesis testing is used when a claim about a population parameter needs to be tested. Estimation and hypothesis testing are the central components of statistical inference and will be used throughout the remaining chapters of this text. Figure 9.13 on the previous page is a flow diagram that should help you determine which hypothesis-testing procedure to use in various situations. *Note*: Figure 9.13 assumes a right-tailed hypothesis test. Table 9.1 provides a matrix format to help you determine which statistical tools to apply in specific situations.

Equations

$\bar{x}_\alpha$ *for Hypothesis Tests, σ Known*

$$\bar{x}_\alpha = \mu + z_\alpha \frac{\sigma}{\sqrt{n}} \tag{9.1}$$

z-Test Statistic for Hypothesis Tests for μ, σ *Known*

$$z = \frac{\bar{x} - \mu}{\dfrac{\sigma}{\sqrt{n}}} \tag{9.2}$$

t-Test Statistic for Hypothesis Tests for μ, σ *Unknown*

$$t = \frac{\bar{x} - \mu}{\dfrac{s}{\sqrt{n}}} \tag{9.3}$$

z-Test Statistic for Proportions

$$z = \frac{p - \pi}{\sqrt{\dfrac{\pi(1-\pi)}{n}}} \tag{9.4}$$

Power

$$\text{Power} = 1 - \beta \tag{9.5}$$

Key Terms

Alternative hypothesis	376	Power	414	Test statistic	384
Critical value	382	Power curve	415	Type I error	380
Null hypothesis	376	Research hypothesis	377	Type II error	380
One-tailed test	389	Significance level	381		
p-value	387	Two-tailed test	389		

Chapter Exercises

Conceptual Questions

9-67. Discuss the two types of statistical errors that can occur when a hypothesis is tested. Illustrate what you mean by using a business example for each.

9-68. Discuss the issues a decision maker should consider when determining the significance level to use in a hypothesis test.

9-69. What is meant by the term *critical value* in a hypothesis-testing situation? Illustrate what you mean with a business example.

9-70. Discuss why it is necessary to use an estimate of the standard error for a confidence interval and not for a hypothesis test concerning a population proportion.

9-71. What is the maximum probability of committing a Type I error called? How is this probability determined? Discuss.

9-72. Recall that the power of the test is the probability the null hypothesis is rejected when H_0 is false. Explain whether power is definable if the given parameter is the value specified in the null hypothesis.

9-73. Examine the test statistic used in testing a population proportion. Why is it impossible to test the hypothesis that the population proportion equals zero using such a test statistic? Try to determine a way that such a test could be conducted.

9-74. The Oasis Chemical Company develops and manufactures pharmaceutical drugs for distribution and sale in the United States. The pharmaceutical business can be very lucrative when useful and safe drugs are introduced into the market. Whenever the Oasis research lab considers putting a drug into production, the company must actually establish the following sets of null and alternative hypotheses:

Set 1	Set 2
H_0: The drug is safe.	H_0: The drug is effective.
H_A: The drug is not safe.	H_A: The drug is not effective.

Take each set of hypotheses separately.
  a. Discuss the considerations that should be made in establishing alpha and beta.
  b. For each set of hypotheses, describe what circumstances would suggest that a Type I error would be of more concern.
  c. For each set of hypotheses, describe what circumstances would suggest that a Type II error would be of more concern.

9-75. For each of the following scenarios, indicate which test statistic would be used or which test could not be conducted using the materials from this chapter:
  a. Testing a mean when σ is known and the population sampled from has a normal distribution.
  b. Testing a mean when σ is unknown and the population sampled from has a normal distribution.
  c. Testing a proportion in which $n\pi = 12$ and $n(1 - \pi) = 4$.
  d. Testing a mean when s is obtained from a small sample and the population sampled from has a skewed distribution.

9-76. In a hypothesis test, indicate the type of statistical error that can be made if
  a. the null hypothesis is rejected.
  b. the null hypothesis is not rejected.
  c. the null hypothesis is true.
  d. the null hypothesis is not true.

9-77. While conducting a hypothesis test, indicate the effect on
  a. β when α is decreased while the sample size remains constant.
  b. β when α is held constant and the sample size is increased.
  c. the power when α is held constant and the sample size is increased.
  d. the power when α is decreased and the sample size is held constant.

Business Applications

9-78. Peterson Automotive is the local dealership selling Honda automobiles. It recently stated in an advertisement that Honda owners average more than 85,000 miles before trading in or selling their Honda. To test this, an independent agency selected a simple random sample of 80 Honda owners who have either traded or sold their Honda and determined the number of miles on the car when the owner parted with the car. They plan to test Peterson's claim at the alpha = 0.05 level.
  a. State the appropriate null and alternative hypotheses.
  b. If the sample mean is 86,200 miles and the sample standard deviation is 12,000 miles, what conclusion should be reached about the claim?

9-79. The Ohio State Tax Commission attempts to set up payroll-tax withholding tables such that by the end of the year, an employee's income tax withholding is about $100 below his actual income tax owed to the state. The commission director claims that when all the Ohio tax returns are in, the average additional payment will be less than $100.

A random sample of 50 accounts revealed an average additional payment of $114 with a sample standard deviation of $50.

a. Testing at a significance level of 0.10, do the sample data refute the director's claim?

b. Determine the largest sample mean (with the same sample size and standard deviation) that would fail to refute the director's claim.

9-80. Bowman Electronics sells electronic components for car stereos. It claims that the average life of a component exceeds 4,000 hours. To test this claim, it has selected a random sample of $n = 12$ of the components and traced the life between installation and failure. The following data were obtained:

| 1,973 | 4,838 | 3,805 | 4,494 | 4,738 | 5,249 |
| 4,459 | 4,098 | 4,722 | 5,894 | 3,322 | 4,800 |

a. State the appropriate null and alternative hypotheses.

b. Assuming that the test is to be conducted using a 0.05 level of significance, what conclusion should be reached based on these sample data? Be sure to examine the required normality assumption.

9-81. The college of business at a state university has a computer literacy requirement for all graduates: Students must show proficiency with a computer spreadsheet software package and with a word-processing software package. To assess whether students are computer literate, a test is given at the end of each semester. The test is designed so that at least 70% of all students who have taken a special microcomputer course will pass. Suppose that, in a random sample of 100 students who have recently finished the microcomputer course, 63 pass the proficiency test.

a. Using a significance level of 0.05, what conclusions should the administrators make regarding the difficulty of the test?

b. Describe a Type II error in the context of this problem.

9-82. In a March 2002 article, *Golf Digest* reported on a survey conducted involving 300 golfers in which the respondents were asked their views about the impact of new technologies on the game of golf. Before the study, a group of United States Golf Association officials believed that less than 50% of golfers believed that professional golfers should have different equipment rules than amateurs. The survey conducted by the *Golf Digest* found 67% did not favor different equipment rules.

a. If the claim made by the USGA is to be tested, what should the null and alternative hypotheses be?

b. Based on the sample data, and an alpha level equal to 0.05, use the *p*-value approach to conduct the hypothesis test.

9-83. *USA Today* reports (Darryl Haralson, "It's all about Overstock.com," July 25, 2005) on an ad for Overstock.com which sells discounted merchandize on its Web site. To evaluate the effectiveness of the ads, Harris Interactive conducted a nationwide poll of 883 adults. Of the 883 adults, 168 thought the ads were very effective. This was compared to the Harris Ad Track average of 21%.

a. Determine if the sample size is large enough for the test in part b to warrant approximating the sample proportion's distribution with a normal distribution.

b. Does the Harris poll provide evidence to contend that the proportion of adults who find Overstock.com's ads to be very effective is smaller than the Harris Ad Track average? Use a significance level of 0.05.

9-84. ACNielsen is a New York-based leading global provider of marketing research information services, analytical systems and tools, and professional client service. A recent issue of its magazine (Todd Hale, "Winning Retail Strategies Start with High Value Consumers," *Consumer Insight*, Spring 2005) addressed, in part, consumers attitudes to self-checkout lines. Of the 17,346 EDLP (every day low price) shoppers, only 3,470 indicated an interest in this service. If Wal-Mart's CEO, Lee Scott, had decided not to install self-checkout lines unless consumer interest was more than 17.5%, would he order the installation?

a. Determine if the sample size for the test indicated is large enough to warrant approximating the sample proportion's distribution with a normal distribution.

b. Use a significance level of 0.05 and the *p*-value approach to answer the question put forward above.

9-85. The Arrow Tire and Rubber Company plans to warranty its new mountain bike tire for 12 months. However, before it does this, the company wants to be sure that the mean lifetime of the tires is at least 18 months under normal operations. It will put the warranty in place unless the sample data strongly suggest that the mean lifetime of the tires is less than 18 months. The company plans to test this statistically using a random sample of tires. The test will be conducted using an alpha level of 0.03.

a. If the population mean is actually 16.5 months, determine the probability the hypothesis test will lead to incorrectly accepting the null hypothesis. Assume that the population standard deviation is known to be 2.4 months and the sample size is 60.

b. If the population mean is actually 17.3, calculate the chance of committing a Type II error. This is a specific example of a generalization relating the probability of committing a Type II error and the parameter being tested. State this generalization.

c. Without calculating the probability, state whether the probability of a Type II error would be larger or smaller than that calculated in part b if you were to calculate it for a hypothesized mean of 15 months. Justify your answer.

d. Suppose the company decides to increase the sample size from 60 to 100 tires. What can you expect to happen to the probabilities calculated in part a?

9-86. The makers of Mini-Oats Cereal have an automated packaging machine that can be set at any targeted fill level between 12 and 32 ounces. At the end of every shift (eight hours), 16 boxes are selected at random and the mean and standard deviation of the sample are computed. Based on these sample results, the production control manager determines whether the filling machine needs to be readjusted or whether it remains all right to operate. Previous data suggest the fill level has a normal distribution with a standard deviation of 0.65 ounces. Use $\alpha = 0.05$. The test is a two-sided test to determine if the mean fill level was equal to 24 ounces.

a. Calculate the probability that the test procedure will detect that the average fill level is not equal to 24 ounces when in fact it equals 24.5 ounces.

b. On the basis of your calculation in part a, would you suggest a change in the test procedure? Explain what change you would make and the reasons you would make this change.

9-87. The Lazer Company has a contract to produce a part for Boeing Corporation that must have an average diameter of 6 inches and a standard deviation of 0.10 inch. The Lazer Company has developed the process that will meet the specifications with respect to the standard deviation, but it is still trying to meet the mean specifications. A test run (considered a random sample) of parts was produced and the company wishes to determine whether this latest process that produced the sample will produce parts meeting the requirement of an average diameter equal to 6 inches.

a. Specify the appropriate research, null, and alternative hypotheses.

b. Develop the decision rule assuming that the sample size is 200 parts and the significance level is 0.01.

c. What should the Lazer Company conclude if the sample mean diameter for the 200 parts is 6.03 inches? Discuss.

9-88. The personnel manager for a large airline has claimed that, on average, workers are asked to work no more than 3 hours overtime per week. Past studies show the standard deviation in overtime hours per worker to be 1.2 hours.

Suppose the union negotiators wish to test this claim by sampling payroll records for 250 employees. They believe that the personnel manager's claim is untrue but want to base their conclusion on the sample results.

a. State the research, null, and alternative hypotheses and discuss the meaning of Type I and Type II errors in the context of this case.

b. Establish the appropriate decision rule if the union wishes to have no more than a 0.01 chance of a Type I error.

c. The payroll records produced a sample mean of 3.15 hours. Do the union negotiators have a basis for a grievance against the airline? Support your answer with a relevant statistical procedure.

9-89. About 74% of Freddie Mac-owned loans were refinanced in the second quarter of 2005 (*USA Today*, Lifeline, August 3, 2005), resulting in new mortgages carrying loan amounts at least 5% above the original mortgage balance. The median loan refinanced in the second quarter was 2.6 years old. If a sample size of 2,500 was used to obtain this information,

a. determine if the sample size for the test in part b is large enough to warrant approximating the sample proportion's distribution with a normal distribution.

b. use this information to determine if less than 75% of new mortgages had a loan amount at least 5% above the original mortgage balance. Use a test statistic approach with $\alpha = 0.025$.

9-90. Cisco Systems, Inc. is the leading maker of networking gear that connects computers to the Internet. Company managers are concerned with the productivity of their workers as well as their job satisfaction. Kate D'Camp is the senior vice president for human resources. She often initiates surveys concerning Cisco's personnel. A typical survey asked, "Do you feel it's OK for your company to monitor your Internet use?" Two hundred and twenty-three of the 405 respondents chose "Only after informing me." Cisco would consider monitoring if more than 50% of its workers wouldn't mind if informed beforehand that the company was going to monitor their Internet usage.

a. D'Camp may have read the *USA Today* issue (Snapshots, August 2, 2005) that indicated 55% of American workers wouldn't object after being informed. So she might desire that the test indicate with a high probability that more than 50% of Cisco workers wouldn't object when in fact her workers reflect the opinion of all

American workers. Calculate the probability that this would be the case. (*Hint*: Review the procedure concerning the sample mean and perform the analogous procedure for a proportion.)

b. Conduct the procedure to determine if the proportion of workers who wouldn't object to the company monitoring their Internet use after they were informed is more than 50%. Use a significance level of 0.05.

9-91. General Motors Corp., the world's largest automaker, has been the global industry sales leader since 1931. Founded in 1908, GM today employs about 317,000 people around the world. As do most large corporations, it offers an extensive retirement program. According to *USA Today* (Moneyline, August 5, 2005), during 2004 the average balance in workers 401(k) accounts rose 10%, to $61,000. To determine if GM's workers are keeping pace with the rest of the nation's workforce, a sample of 55 might be obtained and produce a sample average of $61,834.12.

a. If the standard deviation for the amount in workers' accounts is $1,734.23, determine if GM's workers' average balance in 401(k) accounts is keeping pace. Use a significance level of 0.025.

b. Determine the largest plausible average balance in the GM workers' 401(k) accounts in which you could have 90% confidence.

Computer Database Exercises

9-92. The Haines Lumber Company makes plywood for the furniture industry. One product it makes is $\frac{3}{4}$-inch oak veneer panels. It is very important that the panels conform to specifications. One specification calls for the panels to be made to an average thickness of 0.75 inch. Each hour, 5 panels are selected at random and measured. After 20 hours a total of 100 panels have been measured. The thickness measures are in a file called **Haines**.

a. Formulate the appropriate null and alternative hypotheses relative to the thickness specification.

b. Based on the sample data, what should the company conclude about the status of its product meeting the thickness specification? Test at a significance level of 0.01. Discuss your results in a report to the production manager.

9-93. The Wilson Company uses a great deal of water in the process of making industrial milling equipment. To comply with the federal clean water laws, it has a water purification system that all wastewater goes through before being discharged into a settling pond on the company's property. To determine whether the company is complying with the federal requirements, sample measures are taken every so often. One requirement is that the average pH level

not exceed 7.4. A sample of 95 pH measures has been taken. The data for these measures are shown in a file called **Wilson Water**.

a. Considering the requirement for pH level, state the appropriate null and alternative hypotheses. Discuss why it is appropriate to form the hypotheses with the federal standard as the alternative hypothesis.

b. Based on the sample data of pH level, what should the company conclude about its current status on meeting the federal requirement? Test the hypothesis at the 0.05 level. Discuss your results in a memo to the company's environmental relations manager.

9-94. The AJ Fitness Center has surveyed 1,214 of its customers. Of particular interest is whether over 60% of the customers who express overall service satisfaction with the club (represented by codes 4 or 5) are female. If this is not the case, the promotions director feels she must initiate new exercise programs that are designed specifically for women. Should the promotions director initiate the new exercise programs? Support your answer with the relevant hypothesis test utilizing a *p*-value to perform the test. The data are found in a data file called **AJ Fitness** ($\alpha = 0.05$).

9-95. At the annual meeting of the Golf Equipment Manufacturer's Association, a speaker made the claim that over 30% of all golf clubs being used by nonprofessional United States Golf Association members are "knock-offs." These "knock-offs" are clubs that look very much like the more expensive originals, such as Big Bertha drivers, but are actually nonauthorized copies that are sold at a very reduced rate. This claim prompted the association to conduct a study to see if the problem was as big as the speaker said. A random sample of 400 golfers was selected from the USGA membership ranks. The players were called and asked to indicate the brand of clubs that they used and several other questions. Out of the 400 golfers, data were collected from 294 of them. Based on the response to club brand, a determination was made whether the club was "original" or a "copy." The data are in a file called **Golf Survey**.

a. Based on the sample data, what conclusion should be reached if the hypothesis is tested at a significance level of 0.05? Show the decision rule.

b. Determine whether a Type I or Type II error for this hypothesis test would be more severe. Given your determination, would you advocate raising or lowering the significance level for this test? Explain your reasoning.

c. Confirm that the sample proportion's distribution can be approximated by a normal distribution.

d. Based on the sample data, what should the USGA conclude about the use of "knock-off" clubs by the high-handicap golfers? Is the official's statement justified?

9-96. The Inland Empire Food Store Company has stated in its advertising that the average shopper will save more than $5.00 per week by shopping at Inland stores. A consumer group has decided to test this assertion by sampling 50 shoppers who currently shop at other stores. It selects the customers and then notes each item purchased at their regular store. These same items are then priced at the Inland store and the total bill is compared. The data in the file **Inland Foods** reflect savings at Inland for the 50 shoppers. Note that those cases where the bill was higher at Inland are marked with a minus sign.

a. Set up the appropriate null and alternative hypotheses to test Inland's claim.

b. Using a significance level of 0.05, develop the decision rule and test the hypothesis. Can Inland Empire support its advertising claim?

c. Which type of hypothesis error would the consumer group be most interested in controlling? Which type of hypothesis error would the company be most interested in controlling? Explain your reasoning.

9-97. The Cell Tone Company sells cellular phones and airtime in several northwestern states. At a recent meeting, the marketing manager stated that the average age of its customers is under 40. This came up in conjunction with a proposed advertising plan that is to be directed toward a young audience. Before actually completing the advertising plan, Cell Tone decided to randomly sample customers. Among the questions asked in the survey of 50 customers in the Jacksonville, Florida, area was the customer's age. The data are available in a data file called **Cell Phone Survey**.

a. Based on the statement made by the marketing manager, formulate the appropriate null and alternative hypotheses.

b. The marketing manager must support his statement concerning average customer age in an upcoming board meeting. Using a significance level of 0.10, provide this support for the marketing manager.

c. Consider the result of the hypothesis test you conducted in part b. Which of the two types of hypothesis test errors could you have committed? How could you discover if you had, indeed, made this error?

d. Calculate the critical value, $\bar{x}_\alpha$.

e. Use the critical value, $\bar{x}_\alpha$, to determine the p-value and conduct the test using the p-value approach.

f. Note that the sample data list the customer's age to the nearest year. (1) If we denote a randomly selected customer's age (to the nearest year) as x_i, is x_i a continuous or discrete random variable? (2) Is it possible that x_i has a normal distribution? Consider your answers to (1) and (2) and the fact that $\bar{x}$ must have a normal distribution to facilitate the calculation in part b. Does this mean that the calculation you have performed in part b is inappropriate? Explain your answer.

9-98. MBNA offers personal and business credit cards, loans, and savings products. It was bought by Bank of America in June 2005. One of the selling points for MBNA was its position relative to the rest of the credit card industry. MBNA's customers' average annual spending per active account before the purchase was $6,920. To demonstrate its relative position in the industry, MBNA's CFO, H. Vernon Wright, might authorize a survey producing the following data on the annual spending, to the nearest dollar, of accounts in the industry:

3,680	6,255	6,777	7,412	4,902	5,522	5,190	7,976	4,116	3,949
6,814	2,264	4,991	5,353	5,914	5,828	6,059	6,354	6,193	5,648
6,117	7,315	6,458	4,973	6,554	1,926	4,395	5,341	4,921	6,268
4,061	4,777	5,876	5,984	3,381	5,441	4,268	7,657	6,449	4,821

This sample is contained in the CD-ROM file labeled **ASpending**.

a. Conduct a hypothesis test to determine if MBNA has larger average annual spending per active account than the rest of the credit card industry. Use a p-value approach and a significance level of 0.025.

b. If the industry's annual spending per active account was normally distributed with a mean of $5,560 and a standard deviation of $1,140, determine the probability that a randomly chosen account would have an annual spending larger than MBNA's.

9-99. TOMRA Systems ASA is a Norwegian company that manufactures reverse vending machines (RVMs). In most cases, RVMs are used in markets that have deposits on beverage containers, offering an efficient and convenient method of identifying the deposit amount of each container returned and providing a refund to the customer. Prices for such machines range from about $9,000 for single-container machines to about $35,000 for higher-volume, multi-container (can, plastic, glass) machines. To pay for a single-container machine in one year, an average monthly income would have to be at least $750. The following sample was obtained to determine if that goal could be reached:

765.37	748.21	813.77	633.21	714.74	802.96	696.06	880.65
701.80	696.16	905.01	688.51	922.43	753.97	728.60	690.06
839.48	1010.56	789.13	754.35	749.97	802.31	809.15	775.27

This sample is contained in the CD-ROM file labeled **RVMIncome**.

a. Conduct a hypothesis test to determine if the goal can be reached. Use a significance level of 0.05 and the *p*-value approach.
b. There are 10 sites in which an RVM could be placed. Unknown to the vendor, only 4 of the sites will allow the vendor to meet the goal of paying for the machine in one year. If he installs four of the RVMs, determine the probability that at least two of them will be paid off in a year.

VIDEO CASE 4

New Product Introductions @ McDonald's

New product ideas are a staple of our culture. Just take a look around you—how many billboards or television commercials can you count with new products or services? So, where do those ideas come from? If you're a company like McDonald's, the ideas don't come out of thin air. Instead, they're the result of careful monitoring of consumer preferences, trends, and tastes.

McDonald's menu is a good example of how consumer preferences have affected change in food offerings. What used to be a fairly limited lunch and dinner menu consisting of burgers, shakes, and fries has now become incredibly diverse. The Big Mac came along in 1968, and Happy Meals were introduced in 1979. Breakfast now accounts for nearly 30% of business in the US, and chicken offerings comprise 30% of menu choices. Healthy offerings such as apple dippers, milk jugs and fruit and yogurt parfaits are huge sellers. The company now rolls out at least three new products a year. Wade Thoma, VP US Menu Management, leads the team behind most of today's menu options. He meets regularly with Chef Dan, the company's executive chef, to give the Chef's team some idea anchor points to play with.

When the chef's team is through playing with the concept, Wade's Menu Management team holds what they call a "rally." At a rally, numerous food concepts developed by Chef Dan's team are presented, tasted, discussed and voted on. The winners move on to focus group testing. The focus groups are a huge source of external data that helps the Menu Management team with its decision on whether to introduce a product. If a product scores 8 out of 10 on a variety of rankings, the idea moves forward.

The real test begins in the field. Wade and his team need to determine if the new product idea can actually be executed consistently in the restaurants. Data collected from the company's partnership with its owner/operators and suppliers is key. If a product takes 5 seconds too long to make, or the equipment doesn't fit into existing kitchen configurations, its chances of implementation are low, even though consumer focus groups indicated a high probability of success.

Throughout the idea development process, various statistical methods are used to analyze the data collected. The data are handed over to the company's US Consumer and Business Insights team for conversion into meaningful information the menu management team can use. At each step along the way, the statistical analyses are used to decide whether to move to the next step. The recent introduction of the new Asian chicken salad is a good example of a recent new product offering that made it all the way to market. Analysis was performed on data collected in focus groups and eventually revealed the Asian salad met all the statistical hurdles for the salad to move forward.

Data collection and statistical analysis don't stop when the new products hit the market. Wade Thoma's team and the McDonald's US Consumer and Business Insights group continue to forecast and monitor sales, the ingredient supply chain, customer preferences, competitive reactions, and more. As for the new Asian salad, time will tell just how successful it will become. But you can be sure statistical techniques such as multiple regression will be used to analyze it!

Discussion Questions:

1. During the past year, McDonald's introduced a new dessert product into their European market area. This product had already passed all the internal hurdles described in this case including the focus group analysis and the operations analysis. The next step was to see how well the product would be received in the marketplace. The hurdle rate that has been set for this product is a mean equal to 160 orders per 1,000 transactions. If the mean exceeds 160, the product will be introduced on a permanent basis. A random sample of 142 stores through-out Europe was selected. Store managers tracked the number of dessert orders per 1,000 transactions during a two week trial period. These sample data are in the data file called **McDonald's New Product Introduction**. Using a significance level equal to 0.05, conduct the appropriate hypothesis test. Be sure to state the null and alternative hypothesis and show the results of the test. Write a short report that summarizes the hypothesis test and indicate what conclusion Wade Thoma and his group should reach about this new dessert product.

2. Referring to question 1, suppose a second hurdle is to be used in this case in determining whether the new dessert product should be introduced. This hurdle involves the proportion of every 1,000 transactions that the number of dessert orders exceeds 200. Wade Thoma has indicated that this proportion must exceed 0.15. Based on the sample data, using a significance level equal to 0.05, what conclusion should be reached. Write a short report that specifies the null and alternative hypotheses and shows the test results. Indicate what conclusion should be reached based on this hypothesis test.

CASE 9.1

Campbell Brewery, Inc., Part 1

Don Campbell and his younger brother, Edward, purchased Campbell Brewery from their father in 1983. The brewery makes and bottles beer under two labels and distributes it throughout the Southwest. Since purchasing the brewery, Don has been instrumental in modernizing operations.

One of the latest acquisitions is a filling machine that can be adjusted to fill at any average fill level desired. Because the bottles and cans filled by the brewery are exclusively the 12-ounce size, when they received the machine Don set the fill level to 12 ounces and left it that way. According to the manufacturer's specifications, the machine will fill bottles or cans around the average, with a standard deviation of 0.15 ounce.

Don just returned from a brewery convention in which he attended a panel discussion related to problems with filling machines. One brewery representative discussed a problem her company had. It failed to learn that its machine's average fill went out of adjustment until several months later, when its cost accounting department reported some problems with beer production in bulk not matching output in bottles and cans. It turns out that the machine's average fill had increased from 12 ounces to 12.07 ounces. With large volumes of production, this deviation meant a substantial loss in profits.

Another brewery reported the same type of problem, but in the opposite direction. Its machine began filling bottles with slightly less than 12 ounces on the average. Although the consumers could not detect the shortage in a given bottle, the state and federal agencies responsible for checking the accuracy of packaged products discovered the problem in their testing and substantially fined the brewery for the underfill.

These problems were a surprise to Don Campbell. He had not considered the possibility that the machine might go out of adjustment and pose these types of problems. In fact, he became very concerned because the problems of losing profits and potentially being fined by the government were ones that he wished to avoid, if possible. After the convention, Don and Ed decided to hire a consulting firm with expertise in these matters to assist them in setting up a procedure for monitoring the performance of the filling machine.

The consultant suggested that they set up a sampling plan in which once a month they would sample some number of bottles and measure their volumes precisely. If the average of the sample deviated too much from 12 ounces, they would shut the machine down and make the necessary adjustments. Otherwise, they would let the filling process continue. The consultant identified two types of problems that could occur from this sort of sampling plan:

1. They might incorrectly decide to adjust the machine when it was not really necessary to do so.
2. They might incorrectly decide to allow the filling process to continue when, in fact, the true average had deviated from 12 ounces.

After carefully considering what the consultant told them, Don indicated that he wanted no more than a 0.02 chance of the first problem occurring because of the costs involved. He also decided that if the true average fill had slipped to 11.99 ounces, he wanted no more than a 0.05 chance of not detecting this with his sampling plan. He wanted to avoid problems with state and federal agencies. Finally, if the true average fill had actually risen to 12.007 ounces, he wanted to be able to detect this 98% of the time with his sampling plan. Thus, he wanted to avoid the lost profits that would result from such a problem.

In addition, Don needs to determine how large a sample size is necessary to meet his requirements.

CASE 9.2

Wings of Fire

Following his graduation from college, Tony Smith wanted to continue to live and work in Oxford. However, the community was small and there were not a lot of readily available opportunities for a new college graduate. Fortunately, Tony had some experience working in the food service industry gained in the summers and throughout high school at his uncle's restaurant in Buffalo. When Tony decided to leverage his experience into a small delivery and take-out restaurant located close to the university, he thought he had hit upon a great idea. Tony would offer a limited fare consisting of the Buffalo Wings his uncle had perfected at his restaurant. Tony called his restaurant Wings of Fire. While success came slowly, the uniqueness of Tony's offering coupled with the growth of the university community made Wings of Fire a success.

Tony's business was pretty simple. Tony purchased wings locally. The wings were then seasoned and prepared in Tony's restaurant. Once an order was received, Tony cooked the wings, which were then delivered or picked up by the customer. Tony's establishment was small and there was no place for customers to dine in the restaurant. However, his wings proved so popular that over time Tony hired several employees, including three delivery drivers. Business was steady and predictable during the week with the biggest days being home football Saturdays.

A little over a year ago, Oxford really began to grow and expand. Tony noticed that his business was beginning to suffer when other fast-food delivery restaurants opened around campus. Some of these restaurants were offering guarantees such as "30 minutes or its free." Tony's Wings of Fire now had to compete with fish tacos, specialty pizzas, and gourmet burgers. Most of these new restaurants, however, were dine-in establishments that provided carry-out and delivery as a customer convenience. However, Tony was certain that he would need to offer a delivery guarantee in order to remain competitive with the newer establishments.

Tony was certain that a delivery guarantee of "30 minutes or it's free" could easily be accomplished every day except on football Saturdays. Tony thought that if he could offer a 30-minute guarantee on his busiest day, he would be able to hold onto and perhaps even recover market share

from the competition. However, before he was willing to commit to such a guarantee, Tony wanted to ensure that it was possible to meet the 30-minute promise.

Tony knew it would be no problem for customers to pick up orders within 30 minutes of phoning them in. However, he was less confident about delivering orders to customers in 30 minutes or less. Not only would the wings need to be cooked and packaged but the delivery time might be affected by the availability of drivers. Tony decided that he needed to analyze the opportunity further.

As a part of his analysis, Tony decided to take a random sample of deliveries over five different football weekends. Cooking time and packaging time were not considered in his analysis because wings were not cooked for individual orders. Rather, large numbers of wings were cooked at a single time and then packaged in boxes of 12. Tony therefore decided to focus his analysis on the time required to deliver cooked and packaged wings. He collected information on the amount of time an order had to wait for a driver (the pick-up time) as well as the amount of time required to transport the wings to the customer (the drive time). The sampled information is in the file **Wings of Fire**. Tony is not willing to offer the guarantee on football Saturdays unless he can be reasonably sure that the total time to deliver a customer's order is less than 30 minutes, on average. Tony would also like to have an estimate of the actual time required to deliver a customer's order on football Saturdays. Finally, Tony would like to know how likely it is that the total time to make a delivery would take more than 30 minutes. Based on the sampled data, should Tony offer the guarantee? What percent of the Saturday deliveries would result in a customer receiving a free order? What recommendations might help Tony improve his Saturday delivery times?

References

Berenson, Mark L., Timothy C. Krehbiel, and David M. Levine, *Basic Business Statistics*: *Concepts and Applications and CD Package*, 10th ed. (Upper Saddle River, NJ: Prentice Hall, 2006).

Brown, L., et al., "Interval Estimation for a Binomial Proportion," *Statistical Science*, 2001, pp. 101–133.

Hogg, Robert V., and Elliot A. Tanis, *Probability and Statistical Inference*, 7th ed. (Upper Saddle River, NJ: Prentice Hall, 2005).

Larsen, Richard J., and Morris L. Marx, *An Introduction to Mathematical Statistics and Its Applications*, 3rd ed. (Upper Saddle River, NJ, Prentice Hall, 2001).

Microsoft Excel 2007 (Redmond, WA: Microsoft Corp., 2007).

Minitab Release 15 Statistical Software for Windows (State College, PA: Minitab, 2007).

Siegel, Andrew F., *Practical Business Statistics with Student CD ROM*, 5th ed. (Burr Ridge, IL: Irwin, 2003).

Chapter TEN

Estimation and Hypothesis Testing for Two Population Parameters

CHAPTER OUTCOMES

After studying the material in Chapter 10, you should be able to:

1. Discuss the logic behind, and demonstrate the techniques for, using sample data to test hypotheses and develop interval estimates about the difference between two population means for independent samples.

2. Develop confidence interval estimates and conduct hypothesis tests for the difference between two population means for paired samples.

3. Carry out hypothesis tests and establish interval estimates, using sample data, for the difference between two population proportions.

PREPARING FOR CHAPTER TEN

- Review material on calculating and interpreting sample means and standard deviations in Chapter 3.

- Review the normal distribution in Section 6.1.

- Make sure you understand the concepts associated with sampling distributions for $\bar{x}$ and p by reviewing Sections 7.1, 7.2, and 7.3.

- Review the steps for developing confidence interval estimates for a single population mean and a single population proportion in Sections 8.1 and 8.3.

- Review the methods for testing hypotheses about single population means and single population proportions in Chapter 9.

WHY YOU NEED TO KNOW

Chapter 9 introduced the concepts of hypothesis testing and illustrated its application through examples involving a single population parameter. However, in many business decision-making situations, managers must decide between two or more alternatives. For example, farmers must decide which of several brands and types of wheat to plant. Fleet managers in large companies must decide which model and make of car to purchase next year. Airlines must decide whether to purchase replacement planes from Boeing or Airbus. When deciding on a new advertising campaign, a company may need to evaluate proposals from competing advertising agencies. Hiring decisions may require a personnel director to select one employee from a list of applicants. Production managers are often confronted with decisions concerning whether to change a production process or leave it alone. Each day

consumers purchase a product from among several competing brands.

The difficulty in such situations is that the decision maker must make the decision based on limited (sample) information. Fortunately, there are statistical tools that can help decision makers use sample information to compare different populations (alternative choices). In this chapter, we introduce these tools and techniques by discussing methods that can be used to make statistical comparisons between two populations. Later, we will discuss some methods to extend this comparison to more than two populations. Whether we are discussing cases involving two populations or those with more than two populations, the techniques we present are all extensions of the statistical tools involving a single population parameter introduced in Chapters 8 and 9.

10.1 Estimation for Two Population Means Using Independent Samples

In this section, we build on the concepts introduced in Chapters 8 and 9 and examine situations in which we are interested in the difference between two population means. We look first at the case where the samples from the two populations are **independent**.

We will introduce techniques for estimating the difference between the means of two normally distributed populations in the following situations:

Independent Samples
Samples selected from two or more populations in such a way that the occurrence of values in one sample has no influence on the probability of the occurrence of values in the other sample(s).

1. The population standard deviations are known and the samples are independent.
2. The population standard deviations are unknown and the samples are independent.
3. The samples are not independent.

Estimating the Difference Between Two Population Means when σ_1 and σ_2 Are Known, Using Independent Samples

Recall that in our Chapter 8 discussion of estimation involving a single population mean we introduced procedures that applied when the population standard deviation was assumed to be known. The standard normal distribution z-values were used in establishing the critical value and developing the interval estimate when the populations are normally distributed.[1] The general format for a confidence interval estimate is shown in Equation 10.1. This same format applies when we are interested in estimating the difference between two population means.

Confidence Interval, General Format

Point Estimate $\pm$ (Critical Value)(Standard Error) **(10.1)**

You will often be interested in estimating the difference between two population means. For instance, you may wish to estimate the difference in mean starting salaries between males and females, the difference in mean production in union and nonunion

---

[1] If the samples from the two populations are large ($n \geq 30$) the normal distribution assumption is not required.

factories, or the difference in mean service times at two different fast-food businesses. In these situations, the best point estimate for $\mu_1 - \mu_2$ is

$$\text{Point Estimate} = \bar{x}_1 - \bar{x}_2$$

In situations when you know the population standard deviations, σ_1, and σ_2, and when the samples selected from the two populations are independent, an extension of the Central Limit Theorem tells us that the sampling distribution for all possible differences between $\bar{x}_1$ and $\bar{x}_2$ will be approximately normally distributed with a standard error computed as shown in Equation 10.2. Further, the critical value for determining the confidence interval will be a z-value from the standard normal distribution. In these circumstances, the confidence interval estimate for $\mu_1 - \mu_2$ is found by using Equation 10.3.

Standard Error of $\bar{x}_1 - \bar{x}_2$ When σ_1 and σ_2 Are Known

$$\sigma_{\bar{x}_1 - \bar{x}_2} = \sqrt{\frac{\sigma_1^2}{n_1} + \frac{\sigma_2^2}{n_2}} \qquad (10.2)$$

where:

$$\sigma_1^2 = \text{variance of population 1}$$
$$\sigma_2^2 = \text{variance of population 2}$$
$$n_1 \text{ and } n_2 = \text{sample sizes from populations 1 and 2}$$

CHAPTER OUTCOME #1

Confidence Interval Estimate for $\mu_1 - \mu_2$ When σ_1 and σ_2 Are Known, Independent Samples

$$(\bar{x}_1 - \bar{x}_2) \pm z \sqrt{\frac{\sigma_1^2}{n_1} + \frac{\sigma_2^2}{n_2}} \qquad (10.3)$$

The z-values for several of the most commonly used confidence levels are

CONFIDENCE LEVEL	CRITICAL z-VALUE
80%	$z = 1.28$
90%	$z = 1.645$
95%	$z = 1.96$
99%	$z = 2.575$

EXAMPLE 10-1 — Confidence Interval Estimate for $\mu_1 - \mu_2$ When σ_1 and σ_2 Are Known, Using Independent Samples

TRY PROBLEM 10.3

Crawford & Associates Crawford & Associates was recently retained to survey customers of one of the nation's largest food chains to estimate the difference in mean time spent in the store per visit between men and women shoppers. Previous studies indicate that the standard deviation is 11 minutes for males and 16 minutes for females. To develop a 95% confidence interval estimate, the following steps are taken:

Step 1 Define the population parameter of interest.
In this case, the company is interested in estimating the difference in mean time spent in the store between males and females. The measure of interest is $\mu_1 - \mu_2$.

Step 2 Specify the desired confidence level and determine the critical value.
The interval estimate will be developed using a 95% confidence interval. Because the population standard deviations are known, the critical value is a z-value from the standard normal table. The critical value is

$$z = 1.96$$

Step 3 Select independent samples from the two populations and compute the point estimate.
The company has selected simple random samples of 100 males and 100 females at different times in different stores owned by the food chain. The resulting sample means are

Males: $\bar{x}_1 = 34.5$ minutes   Females: $\bar{x}_2 = 42.4$ minutes

The point estimate is

$$\bar{x}_1 - \bar{x}_2 = 34.5 - 42.4 = -7.9 \text{ minutes}$$

Women in the sample spent an average of 7.9 minutes longer shopping at the stores.

Step 4 Develop the confidence interval estimate using Equation 10.3.

$$(\bar{x}_1 - \bar{x}_2) \pm z\sqrt{\frac{\sigma_1^2}{n_1} + \frac{\sigma_2^2}{n_2}}$$

$$-7.9 \pm 1.96\sqrt{\frac{11^2}{100} + \frac{16^2}{100}}$$

$$-7.9 \pm 3.8056$$

The 95% confidence interval estimate for the difference in mean time spent in the chain's food stores between men and women is

$$-11.7056 \leq (\mu_1 - \mu_2) \leq -4.0944$$

Thus, based on the sample data, women spend on average between 4.09 and 11.71 minutes longer at the food stores.

Estimating the Difference Between Two Means When σ_1 and σ_2 Are Unknown, Using Independent Samples

CHAPTER OUTCOME #1

In Chapter 8, you learned that when estimating a single population mean when the population standard deviation is unknown and the sample sizes are small, the critical value is a t-value from the t-distribution. This is also the case when you are interested in estimating the difference between two population means, if the following assumptions hold:

Assumptions

■ The populations are normally distributed.
■ The populations have equal variances.
■ The samples are independent.

The following application illustrates how a confidence interval estimate is developed using the t-distribution.

Business Application

RETIREMENT INVESTING A major political issue for the past decade has focused on the long-term future of the U.S. Social Security system. Many people who have entered the workforce in the past 20 years believe the system will not be solvent when they retire, so they are actively investing in their own retirement accounts. One investment alternative is a tax-sheltered annuity (TSA) marketed by life insurance companies. Certain people, depending on occupation, qualify to invest part of their paychecks in a TSA and pay no federal income tax on this money until it is withdrawn. While the money is invested, the insurance companies invest it in either stock or bond portfolios. A second alternative open to many people is a plan known as a 401(k), in which employees contribute a portion of their paychecks to purchase stocks, bonds, or mutual funds. In some cases, employers match all or part of the employee contributions. In many 401(k) systems, the employees can control how their funds are invested.

A recent study in North Carolina was interested in estimating the difference in mean annual contributions for individuals covered by the two plans [TSA or 401(k)]. A simple random sample of 15 people from the population of adults who are eligible for a TSA investment was selected. A second sample of 15 people was selected from the population of adults in North Carolina who have 401(k) plans. The variable of interest is the dollar amount of money invested in the retirement plan during the previous year. Specifically, we are interested in estimating $\mu_1 - \mu_2$ using a 95% confidence interval estimate where:

μ_1 = Mean dollars invested by the TSA-eligible population during the past year
μ_2 = Mean dollars invested by the 401(k)-eligible population during the past year

The sample results are

TSA-Eligible	401(k)-Eligible
$n_1 = 15$	$n_2 = 15$
$\bar{x}_1 = \$2,119.70$	$\bar{x}_2 = \$1,777.70$
$s_1 = \$709.70$	$s_2 = \$593.90$

Before applying the t-distribution, we need to determine whether the assumptions are likely to be satisfied. First, the samples are considered independent because the amount invested by one group should have no influence on the amount invested by the other.

Next, Figure 10.1 shows the sample data and the box and whisker plots for the two samples. These plots exhibit characteristics that are reasonably consistent with those associated with normal distributions and approximately equal variances. Although using a box and whisker plot to check the t-distribution assumptions may seem to be imprecise, fortunately studies have shown the t-distribution to be applicable even when

FIGURE 10.1

Investment Study—Sample Information

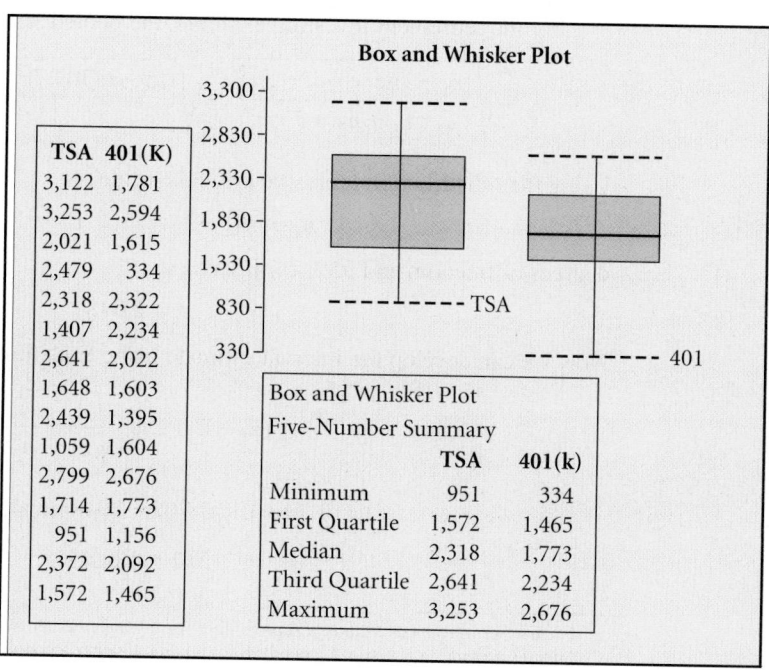

there are small violations of the assumptions. This is particularly the case when the sample sizes are approximately equal.[2]

Equation 10.4 can be used to develop the confidence interval estimate for the difference between two population means when you have small independent samples.

Confidence Interval Estimate for $\mu_1 - \mu_2$ When σ_1 and σ_2 Are Unknown, Independent Samples

$$(\bar{x}_1 - \bar{x}_2) \pm t s_p \sqrt{\frac{1}{n_1} + \frac{1}{n_2}} \tag{10.4}$$

where:

$$s_p = \sqrt{\frac{(n_1 - 1)s_1^2 + (n_2 - 1)s_2^2}{n_1 + n_2 - 2}} = \text{pooled standard deviation}$$

t = critical t-value from the t-distribution, with degrees of freedom equal to $n_1 + n_2 - 2$

To use Equation 10.4, we must compute the pooled standard deviation, s_p. If the equal-variance assumption holds, then both s_1^2 and s_2^2 are estimators of the same population variance, σ^2. To use only one of these, say s_1^2, to estimate σ^2 would be disregarding the information obtained from the other sample. To use the average of s_1^2 and s_2^2, if the sample sizes were different, would ignore the fact that more information about σ^2 is obtained from the sample having the larger sample size. We, therefore, use a weighted average of s_1^2 and s_2^2, denoted as s_p^2 to estimate σ^2, where the weights are the degrees of freedom associated with each sample. The square root of s_p^2 is known as the *pooled standard deviation* and is computed using

$$s_p = \sqrt{\frac{(n_1 - 1)s_1^2 + (n_2 - 1)s_2^2}{n_1 + n_2 - 2}}$$

Notice that the sample size we have available to estimate σ^2 is $n_1 + n_2$. However, to produce s_p, we must first calculate s_1^2 and s_2^2. This requires that we estimate μ_1 and μ_2 using $\bar{x}_1$ and $\bar{x}_2$, respectively. The degrees of freedom are equal to the sample size minus the parameters estimated before the variance estimate is obtained. Therefore, our degrees of freedom must equal $n_1 + n_2 - 2$.

For the retirement investing example, the pooled standard deviation is

$$s_p = \sqrt{\frac{(n_1 - 1)s_1^2 + (n_2 - 1)s_2^2}{n_1 + n_2 - 2}} = \sqrt{\frac{(15 - 1)(709.7)^2 + (15 - 1)(593.9)^2}{15 + 15 - 2}} = 654.37$$

Using the t-distribution table, the critical t-value for

$$n_1 + n_2 - 2 = 15 + 15 - 2 = 28$$

degrees of freedom and 95% confidence is

$$t = 2.0484$$

Now we can develop the interval estimate using Equation 10.4

$$(\bar{x}_1 - \bar{x}_2) \pm t s_p \sqrt{\frac{1}{n_1} + \frac{1}{n_2}}$$

$$(2{,}119.70 - 1{,}777.70) \pm 2.0484(654.37)\sqrt{\frac{1}{15} + \frac{1}{15}}$$

$$342 \pm 489.45$$

---

[2] Chapter 11 introduces a statistical procedure for testing whether two populations have equal variances. Chapter 13 provides a statistical procedure for testing whether a population is normally distributed.

Thus, the 95% confidence interval estimate for the difference in mean dollars for people who invest in a TSA versus those who invest in a 401(k) is

$$-\$147.45 \leq (\mu_1 - \mu_2) \leq \$831.45$$

This confidence interval estimate crosses zero and therefore indicates there may be no difference between the mean contributions to TSA accounts or to 401(k) accounts by adults in North Carolina. The implication of this result is that the average amount invested by those individuals who invest in pre-tax TSA programs is no more or no less than that invested by those participating in after-tax 401(k) programs. Based on this result, there may be an opportunity to encourage the TSA investors to increase deposits because they should be able to invest more dollars without impacting take-home pay.

EXAMPLE 10-2 Confidence Interval Estimate for $\mu_1 - \mu_2$ When σ_1 and σ_2 Are Unknown, Using Independent Samples

TRY PROBLEM 10.1

Sneva Pharmaceutical Research The head of research and development at Sneva Pharmaceutical Research is interested in estimating the difference between males and females with respect to the mean time from when a patient takes a new medication until the medication can be detected in the blood. Once she estimates the difference, if a difference does exist, the company can use this information to guide doctors in how to advise their male and female patients to use this medication. A simple random sample of six males and eight females participated in the study. The estimate can be developed using the following steps:

Step 1 Define the population parameter of interest.
The objective here is to estimate the difference in mean time between males and females with respect to the speed at which the medication reaches the blood. The parameter of interest is $\mu_1 - \mu_2$.

Step 2 Select independent samples from the two populations.
The research lab has selected simple random samples of six males and eight females. Because the impact of the medication in one person does not influence the impact in another person, the samples are independent. The resulting sample means and sample standard deviations are

Males: $\bar{x}_1 = 13.6$ minutes   Females: $\bar{x}_2 = 11.2$ minutes
$s_1 = 3.1$ minutes $s_2 = 5.0$ minutes
$n_1 = 6$ $n_2 = 8$

Step 3 Compute the point estimate.
The point estimate is

$$\bar{x}_1 - \bar{x}_2 = 13.6 - 11.2 = 2.4 \text{ minutes}$$

Step 4 Specify the desired confidence level and determine the critical value.
The research manager wishes to have a 95% confidence interval estimate. Because the population standard deviations are unknown, the critical value will be a t-value from the t-distribution as long as the population variances are equal and the populations are assumed to be normally distributed.
The critical t for 95% confidence and $6 + 8 - 2 = 12$ degrees of freedom is

$$t = 2.1788$$

Step 5 Develop a confidence interval using Equation 10.4.

$$(\bar{x}_1 - \bar{x}_2) \pm t s_p \sqrt{\frac{1}{n_1} + \frac{1}{n_2}}$$

where:

$$s_p = \sqrt{\frac{(n_1 - 1)s_1^2 + (n_2 - 1)s_2^2}{n_1 + n_2 - 2}} = \sqrt{\frac{(6-1)3.1^2 + (8-1)5^2}{6+8-2}} = 4.31$$

Then the interval estimate is

$$2.4 \pm 2.1788(4.31)\sqrt{\frac{1}{6} + \frac{1}{8}}$$

$$2.4 \pm 5.0715$$

$$-2.6715 \le (\mu_1 - \mu_2) \le 7.4715$$

Because the interval crosses zero, the research manager cannot conclude that a difference exists between males and females with respect to the mean time needed for the medication to be detected in the blood. Thus, with respect to this factor, it does not seem to matter whether the patient is male or female, so no advice for doctors is warranted.

What If the Population Variances Are Not Equal? If you have reason to believe that the population variances are substantially different, Equation 10.4 is not appropriate for computing the confidence interval. Instead of computing the pooled standard deviation as part of the confidence interval formula, we use Equations 10.5 and 10.6.

Confidence Interval for the Difference Between Two Means When σ_1 and σ_2 Are Unknown and Not Equal, Independent Samples

$$(\bar{x}_1 - \bar{x}_2) \pm t\sqrt{\frac{s_1^2}{n_1} + \frac{s_2^2}{n_2}} \tag{10.5}$$

where:

t is from the t-distribution with degrees of freedom computed using:

$$df = \frac{(s_1^2/n_1 + s_2^2/n_2)^2}{\left(\dfrac{(s_1^2/n_1)^2}{n_1 - 1} + \dfrac{(s_2^2/n_2)^2}{n_2 - 1}\right)} \tag{10.6}$$

EXAMPLE 10-3 Estimating $\mu_1 - \mu_2$ When the Population Variances Are Not Equal

TRY PROBLEM 10.5

Capital One Credit Cards The marketing managers at Capital One Credit Cards are planning to roll out a new marketing campaign addressed at increasing bank card use. As one part of the campaign, the company will be offering a low interest rate incentive to induce people to spend more money using its charge cards. However, the company is concerned whether this plan will have a different impact on married card holders than on unmarried card holders. So, prior to starting the marketing campaign nationwide, the company tests it on a random sample of 30 unmarried and 25 married customers. The managers wish to estimate the difference in mean credit card spending for unmarried versus married for a two-week period immediately after being exposed to the marketing campaign. Based on past data, the managers have reason to believe the spending distributions for unmarried and married will be approximately normally distributed, but they are unwilling to conclude the population variances for spending are equal for the two populations.

A 95% confidence interval estimate for the difference in population means can be developed using the following steps:

Step 1 **Define the population parameter of interest.**

The parameter of interest is the difference between the mean dollars spent on credit cards by unmarried versus married customers in the two-week period after being exposed to Capital One's new marketing program.

Step 2 **Select independent samples from the two populations.**

Independent samples of 30 unmarried and 25 married were taken and the credit card spending for each sampled customer during the two-week period was recorded. The following sample results were observed:

	Unmarried	Married
Mean	$455.10	$268.90
St. Dev.	$102.40	$ 77.25

Step 3 **Compute the point estimate.**

The point estimate is the difference between the two sample means:

$$\text{Point Estimate} = \bar{x}_1 - \bar{x}_2 = 455.10 - 268.90 = 186.20$$

Step 4 **Specify the desired confidence level and determine the critical value.**

The desired confidence level is 95%. Because we are unable to assume the population variances are equal, we must first use Equation 10.6 to calculate the degrees of freedom for the t-distribution. This is done as follows:

$$df = \frac{(s_1^2/n_1 + s_2^2/n_2)^2}{\left(\dfrac{(s_1^2/n_1)^2}{n_1 - 1} + \dfrac{(s_2^2/n_2)^2}{n_2 - 1}\right)}$$

$$= \frac{(102.40^2/30 + 77.25^2/25)^2}{\left(\dfrac{(102.40^2/30)^2}{29} + \dfrac{(77.25^2/25)^2}{24}\right)} = \frac{346,011.98}{6,586.81} = 52.53$$

Thus, the degrees of freedom (rounded down) will be 52. At the 95% confidence level, using the t-distribution table, the approximate t-value is 2.0086. Note, since there is no entry for 52 degrees of freedom in the table, we have selected the t-value associated with 95% confidence and 50 degrees of freedom which provides a slightly larger t-value than would have been the case for 52 degrees of freedom. Thus, the interval estimate will be generously wide.

Step 5 **Develop the confidence interval estimate using Equation 10.5.**

The confidence interval estimate is computed using

$$(\bar{x}_1 - \bar{x}_2) \pm t\sqrt{\frac{s_1^2}{n_1} + \frac{s_2^2}{n_2}}$$

Then the interval estimate is

$$(\$455.10 - \$268.90) \pm 2.0086\sqrt{\frac{102.40^2}{30} + \frac{77.25^2}{25}}$$

$$\$186.20 \pm \$48.72$$

$$\$137.48 \leq (\mu_1 - \mu_2) \leq \$234.92$$

$$\$137.48 \text{------------------------} \$234.92$$

The test provides evidence to conclude unmarried customers, after being introduced to the marketing program, spend more than married customers, on average, by anywhere from \$137.48 to \$234.92 in the two weeks following the marketing campaign. But before concluding that the campaign is more effective for unmarried than married customers the managers would want to compare these results with data from customer accounts prior to the marketing campaign.

10-1: Exercises

Skill Development

10-1. The following information is based on independent random samples taken from two normally distributed populations having equal variances:

$$n_1 = 24 \qquad n_2 = 28$$
$$\bar{x}_1 = 130 \qquad \bar{x}_2 = 125$$
$$s_1 = 19 \qquad s_2 = 17.5$$

Based on the sample information, determine the 95% confidence interval estimate for the difference between the two population means.

10-2. The following information is based on independent random samples taken from two normally distributed populations having equal variances:

$$n_1 = 15 \qquad n_2 = 13$$
$$\bar{x}_1 = 50 \qquad \bar{x}_2 = 53$$
$$s_1 = 5 \qquad s_2 = 6$$

Based on the sample information, determine the 90% confidence interval estimate for the difference between the two population means.

10-3. Construct a 95% confidence interval estimate for the difference between two population means based on the following information:

Population 1	Population 2
$\bar{x}_1 = 355$	$\bar{x}_2 = 330$
$\sigma_1 = 34$	$\sigma_2 = 40$
$n_1 = 50$	$n_2 = 80$

10-4. Construct a 90% confidence interval estimate for the difference between two population means given the following sample data selected from two normally distributed populations with equal variances:

Sample 1			Sample 2		
29	25	31	42	39	38
35	35	37	42	40	43
21	29	34	46	39	35

10-5. Construct a 95% percent confidence interval for the difference between two population means using the following sample data that have been selected from normally distributed populations with different population variances:

Sample 1				Sample 2			
473	386	406	379	349	359	346	395
346	438	391	328	398	401	411	384
388	388	456	429	363	437	388	273

10-6. Two random samples were selected independently from populations having normal distributions. The following statistics were extracted from the samples:

$$\bar{x}_1 = 42.3 \qquad \bar{x}_2 = 32.4$$

a. If $\sigma_1 = 3$ and $\sigma_2 = 2$ and the sample sizes are $n_1 = 50$, $n_2 = 50$, calculate a 95% confidence interval for the difference between the two population means.

b. If $\sigma_1 = \sigma_2$, $s_1 = 3$, and $s_2 = 2$, and the sample sizes are $n_1 = 10$, $n_2 = 10$, calculate a 95% confidence interval for the difference between the two population means.

c. If $\sigma_1 \neq \sigma_2$, $s_1 = 3$, and $s_2 = 2$, and the sample sizes are $n_1 = 10$, $n_2 = 10$, calculate a 95% confidence interval for the difference between the two population means.

Business Applications

10-7. A pet food producer manufactures and then fills 25-pound bags of dog food on two different production lines located in separate cities. In an effort to determine whether differences exist between the average fill rates for the two lines, a random sample of 19 bags from line 1 and a random sample of

23 bags from line 2 were recently selected. Each bag's weight was measured and the following summary measures from the samples are reported:

	Production Line 1	Production Line 2
Sample Size, n	19	23
Sample Mean, $\bar{x}$	24.96	25.01
Sample Standard Deviation, s	0.07	0.08

Management believes that the fill rates of the two lines are normally distributed with equal variances.
   a. What is the point estimate for the difference between the population means of the two lines?
   b. Develop a 95% confidence interval estimate of the true mean difference between the two lines.
   c. Based on the 95% confidence interval estimate calculated in part b, what can the managers of the production lines conclude about the differences between the average fill rates for the two lines?

10-8. A credit card company operates two customer service centers: one in Boise and one in Richmond. Callers to the service centers dial a single number and a computer program routs callers to the center having the fewest calls waiting. As part of a customer service review program, the credit card center would like to determine whether the average length of a call (not including hold time) is different for the two centers. The managers of the customer service centers are willing to assume that the populations of interest are normally distributed with equal variances. Suppose a random sample of phone calls to the two centers is selected and the following results are reported:

	Boise	Richmond
Sample Size	120	135
Sample Mean (seconds)	195	216
Sample St. Dev. (seconds)	35.10	37.80

   a. Using the sample results, develop a 90% confidence interval estimate for the difference between the two population means.
   b. Based on the confidence interval constructed in part a, what can be said about the difference between the average call time at the two centers?

10-9. Amax Industries operates two manufacturing facilities that specialize in doing custom manufacturing work for the semiconductor industry. The facility in Denton, Texas, is highly automated, whereas the

facility in Lincoln, Nebraska, has more manual functions. For the past few months, both facilities have been working on a large order for a specialized product. The vice president of operations is interested in estimating the difference in mean time it takes to complete a part on the two lines. To do this, he has requested that a random sample of 15 parts at each facility be tracked through from start to finish and the time required be recorded. The following sample data were recorded:

Denton, Texas	Lincoln, Nebraska
$\bar{x}_1 = 56.7$ hours	$\bar{x}_2 = 70.4$ hours
$s_1 = 7.1$ hours	$s_1 = 8.3$ hours

Assuming that the populations are normally distributed with equal population variances, construct and interpret a 95% confidence interval estimate.

10-10. Wilson Construction and Concrete Company is known as a very progressive company that is willing to try new ideas to improve its products and service. One of the key factors of importance in concrete work is the time it takes for the concrete to "set up." The company is considering a new additive that can be put in the concrete mix to help reduce the setup time. Before going ahead with the additive, the company plans to test it against the current additive. To do this, 14 batches of concrete are mixed using each of the additives. The following results were observed:

Old Additive	New Additive
$\bar{x} = 17.2$ hours	$\bar{x} = 15.9$ hours
$s = 2.5$ hours	$s = 1.8$ hours

   a. Use these sample data to construct a 90% confidence interval estimate for the difference in mean setup time for the two concrete additives. On the basis of the confidence interval produced, do you agree that the new additive helps reduce the setup time for cement? Explain your answer.
   b. Assuming that the new additive is slightly more expensive than the old additive, do the data support switching to the new additive if the managers of the company are primarily interested in reducing average setup time?

10-11. Two companies that manufacture batteries for electronics products have submitted their products to an independent testing agency. The agency tested 200 of each company's batteries and recorded the length of time the batteries lasted before failure. The following results were determined:

Company A	Company B
$\bar{x} = 41.5$ hours	$\bar{x} = 39.0$ hours
$s = 3.6$	$s = 5.0$

a. Based on these data, determine the 95% confidence interval to estimate the difference in average life of the batteries for the two companies. Do these data indicate that one company's batteries will outlast the other company's batteries on average? Explain.

b. Suppose the manufacturers of each of these batteries wished to warranty their batteries. One small company to which they both ship batteries receives shipments of 200 batteries weekly. If the average length of time to failure of the batteries is less than a specified number, the manufacturer will refund the company's purchase price of that set of batteries. What value should each manufacturer set if they wish to refund money on at most 5% of the shipments?

10-12. A working paper (Mark Aguiar and Erik Hurst, "Measuring Trends in Leisure: The Allocation of Time Over Five Decades," 2006) for the Federal Reserve Bank of Boston concluded that average leisure time spent per week by women in 2003 was 33.80 hours and 37.56 hours for men. The sample standard deviations were 40 and 70, respectively. These results were obtained from samples of women and men of size 8,492 and 6,752, respectively. In this study, "leisure" refers to the time individuals spent socializing, in passive leisure, in active leisure, volunteering, in pet care, gardening, and recreational child care. Assume that the amount of leisure time spent by men and women has a normal distribution.

a. Determine the pooled estimate of the common populations' standard deviation.

b. Produce the margin of error to estimate the difference of the two population means with a confidence level of 95%.

c. Calculate a 95% confidence interval for the difference in the average leisure time between women and men.

d. Do your results in part c indicate that the average amount of men's leisure time was larger than that of women's in 2003? Support your assertions.

10-13. The Graduate Management Admission Council reports a shift in the job-hunting strategies among second-year MBA candidates. Even though their prospective base salary has increased from $81,900 to $93,770 from 2002 to 2005, it appears that MBA candidates are submitting fewer job applications. Data obtained from online surveys of 1,442 MBA candidates at 30 business school programs indicate that in 2002 the average number of job applications

per candidate was 38.9 and 2.0 in 2005. The sample variances were 64 and 0.32, respectively.

a. Examine the sample variances. Conjecture whether this sample evidence indicates that the two population variances are equal to each other. Support your assertion.

b. On the basis of your answer in part a, construct a 99% confidence interval for the difference in the average number of job applications submitted by master's degree candidates between 2002 and 2005.

c. Using your result in part b, is it plausible that the difference in the average number of job applications submitted is 36.5? Is it plausible that the difference in the average number of job applications submitted is 37? Are your answers to these two questions contradictory? Explain.

Computer Database Exercises

10-14. The owner of the A.J. Fitness Center is interested in estimating the difference in mean years that female members have been with the club compared to male members. He wishes to develop a 95% confidence interval estimate. Sample data are in the file called **AJ Fitness**. Assuming that the sample data are approximately normal and that the two populations have equal variances, develop and interpret the confidence interval estimate. Discuss the result.

10-15. Logston Enterprises operates a variety of businesses in and around the St. Paul, Minnesota, area. Recently, the company was notified by the law firm representing several female employees that a lawsuit was going to be filed claiming that males were given preferential treatment when it came to pay raises by the company. The Logston human resources manager has requested that an estimate be made of the difference between mean percentage raises granted to males versus females. Sample data are contained in the file **Logston Enterprises**. She wants you to develop, and interpret, a 95% confidence interval estimate. She further states that the distribution of percentage raises can be assumed approximately normal and she expects the population variances to be about equal.

10-16. Platinum Billiards, Inc., based in Jacksonville, Florida, is a retailer of billiard supplies. It stands out among billiard suppliers because of the research it does to assure its products are top-notch. One experiment was conducted to measure the speed attained by a cue ball struck by various weighted pool cues. The conjecture is that a light cue generates faster speeds while breaking the balls at the beginning of a game of pool. Anecdotal experience has indicated that a billiard cue weighing less than 19 ounces generates faster speeds. Platinum used a robotic arm to investigate this claim. The research generated the data given in the file entitled **Breakcue**.

a. Calculate the sample standard deviation and mean speed produced by cues in the two weight categories: (1) under 19 ounces and (2) at or above 19 ounces.

b. Calculate a 95% confidence interval for the difference in the average speed of a cue ball generated by each of the weight categories.

c. Is the anecdotal evidence correct? Support your assertion.

d. What assumptions are required so that your results in part b would be valid?

10-17. The Federal Reserve reported in its comprehensive Survey of Consumer Finances, released every three years, that the average income of families in the United States declined from 2001 to 2004. This was the first decline since 1989–1992. A sample of incomes was taken in 2001 and repeated in 2004. After adjusting for inflation, the data that arise from these samples are given in a file entitled **Incomes**.

a. Determine the percentage decline indicated by the two samples.

b. Using these samples, produce a 90% confidence interval for the difference in the average family income between 2001 and 2004.

c. Is it plausible that there has been no decline in the average income of U.S. families? Support your assertion.

d. How large an error could you have made by using the difference in the sample means to estimate the difference in the population means?

10.2 Hypothesis Tests for Two Population Means Using Independent Samples

CHAPTER OUTCOME #1

You will encounter many business situations such as those illustrated in Section 10.1, in which you will be interested in estimating the difference between two population means. However, you will also encounter many other situations that will require you to test whether two populations have equal means, or whether one population mean is larger (smaller) than another. These hypothesis-testing applications are just an extension of the hypothesis-testing process introduced in Chapter 9 for a single population mean. They also build directly on the estimation process introduced in Section 10.1.

In this section, we will introduce hypothesis-testing techniques for the difference between the means of two normally distributed populations in the following situations:

1. The population standard deviations are known and the samples are independent.
2. The population standard deviations are unknown and the samples are independent.

The logic of all hypothesis tests is that if the sample statistic is "substantially" different from the hypothesized population parameter, the null hypothesis should be rejected. If

SUMMARY   The Hypothesis-Testing Process for Two Population Means

The hypothesis-testing process for tests involving two population means introduced in this section is essentially the same as for a single population mean. The process is composed of the following steps:

1. Specify the population parameter of interest.
2. Formulate the appropriate null and alternative hypotheses. The null hypothesis should contain the equality. Possible formats for testing whether two populations have equal means are

$H_0: \mu_1 - \mu_2 = 0.0$ $H_0: \mu_1 - \mu_2 \le 0.0$ $H_0: \mu_1 - \mu_2 \ge 0.0$
$H_A: \mu_1 - \mu_2 \neq 0.0$ $H_A: \mu_1 - \mu_2 > 0.0$ $H_A: \mu_1 - \mu_2 < 0.0$
two-tailed test   one-tailed test   one-tailed test

3. Specify the significance level (α) for testing the hypothesis. Alpha is the maximum allowable probability of committing a Type I statistical error.
4. Compute the test statistic or the *p*-value. Of course, you must first select simple random samples from each population and compute the sample means.
5. Construct the rejection region and develop the decision rule.
6. Reach a decision. Apply the decision rule to determine whether to reject the null hypothesis.
7. Draw a conclusion.

the sample statistics are consistent with the hypothesized population parameter, the null hypothesis will not be rejected. Two possible errors can occur:

Type I Error: Rejecting H_0 when it is true (alpha error).
Type II Error: Not rejecting H_0 when it is false (beta error).

The probability of a Type I error is controlled by the decision maker by the choice of α. Recall from Section 9-3 that α and β are inversely related. If we reduce α, then β is increased, assuming everything else remains constant.

The remainder of this section presents examples of hypothesis tests under different situations.

Testing for $\mu_1 - \mu_2$ When σ_1 and σ_2 Are Known, Using Independent Samples

In Section 10.1, we said that *independent samples* occur when the samples from the two populations are taken in such a way that the occurrence of values in one sample has no influence on the probability of occurrence of the values in the second sample. In special cases in which the population standard deviations are known and the samples are independent, the test statistic is a *z*-value computed using Equation 10.7.

---

z-Test Statistic for $\mu_1 - \mu_2$ When σ_1 and σ_2 Are Known, Independent Samples

$$z = \frac{(\bar{x}_1 - \bar{x}_2) - (\mu_1 - \mu_2)}{\sqrt{\dfrac{\sigma_1^2}{n_1} + \dfrac{\sigma_2^2}{n_2}}} \qquad (10.7)$$

where

$$(\mu_1 - \mu_2) = \text{hypothesized difference in population means}$$

If the calculated *z*-value using Equation 10.7 exceeds the critical *z*-value from the standard normal distribution, the null hypothesis is rejected. Example 10-4 illustrates the use of this test statistic.

| **EXAMPLE 10-4** | Hypothesis Test for $\mu_1 - \mu_2$ When σ_1 and σ_2 Are Known, Independent Samples |

TRY PROBLEM 10.19

Phillips Systems   Phillips Systems is an Ohio-based company that makes parts for the automotive industry. One part is a bolt used in the engine manifold system. The company has two machines that make these bolts. It is well established that the standard deviation for bolts made by machine 1 is 0.025 inches and the standard deviation for machine 2 is 0.034 inches. At question is whether machine 2 also provides bolts with higher average diameters. If the test determines that machine 2 has a larger average diameter than machine 1, the managers will have maintenance attempt to adjust the diameters downward or they will replace the machine. To test this, you can use these steps:

Step 1 Specify the population parameter of interest.
This is $\mu_1 - \mu_2$, the difference in the two population means.

Step 2 Formulate the appropriate null and alternative hypotheses.
We are interested in determining whether the mean diameter for machine 2 exceeds that for machine 1. The following null and alternative hypotheses are specified:

$$\begin{array}{ccc} H_0: \mu_1 - \mu_2 \geq 0.0 & & H_0: \mu_1 \geq \mu_2 \\ H_A: \mu_1 - \mu_2 < 0.0 & \text{or} & H_A: \mu_1 < \mu_2 \end{array}$$

Step 3 **Specify the significance level for the test.**
The test will be conducted using $\alpha = 0.05$.

Step 4 **Compute the test statistic.**
Select simple random samples from the two populations and compute the sample means. A simple random sample of 100 bolts is selected from machine 1's production, and another simple random sample of 100 bolts is selected from machine 2's production. The samples are independent because the diameters of bolts made by one machine can in no way influence the diameter of bolts made by the other machine. The means computed from the samples are

$$\bar{x}_1 = 0.501 \text{ inches} \quad \text{and} \quad \bar{x}_2 = 0.509 \text{ inches}$$

The test statistic is obtained using Equation 10.7.

$$z = \frac{(\bar{x}_1 - \bar{x}_2) - (\mu_1 - \mu_2)}{\sqrt{\dfrac{\sigma_1^2}{n_1} + \dfrac{\sigma_2^2}{n_2}}}$$

$$z = \frac{(0.501 - 0.509) - 0}{\sqrt{\dfrac{0.025^2}{100} + \dfrac{0.034^2}{100}}} = -1.90$$

Step 5 **Determine the rejection region and state the decision rule.**
Because the population standard deviations are assumed to be known, the critical value is a z-value from the standard normal distribution. This test is a one-tailed lower-tail test, with $\alpha = 0.05$. From the standard normal distribution, the critical z-value is

$$-z_{0.05} = -1.645$$

The decision rule compares the test statistic from Step 4 to the critical z-value.

If $z < -1.645$, reject the null hypothesis;
Otherwise, do not reject the null hypothesis.

Alternatively, you can state the decision rule in terms of a p-value, as follows:

If p-value $< \alpha = 0.05$, reject the null hypothesis;
Otherwise, do not reject the null hypothesis.

Step 6 **Reach a decision.**
The critical $-z_{0.05} = -1.645$ and the test statistic value was computed to be $z = -1.90$. Applying the decision rule,

Because $z = -1.90 < -1.645$, reject the null hypothesis.

Figure 10.2 illustrates this hypothesis test.

Step 7 **Draw a conclusion.**
There is statistical evidence to conclude that the bolts made by machine 2 have a larger mean diameter than those made by machine 1. Thus, action must be taken to modify the mean diameters from machine 2 or replace it.

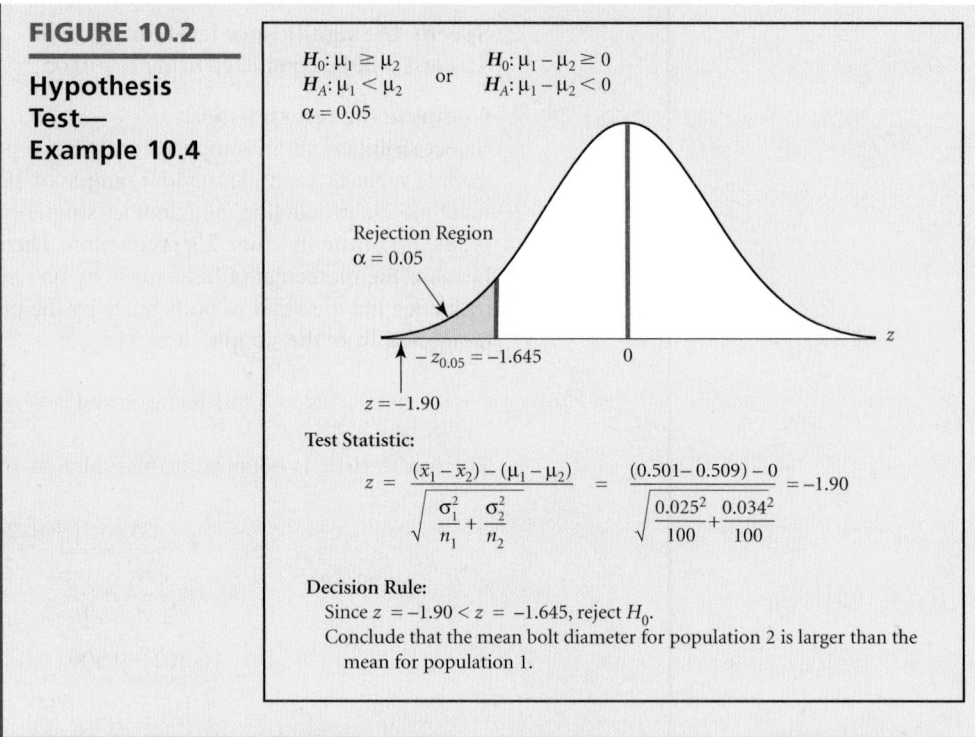

FIGURE 10.2

Hypothesis Test—Example 10.4

$H_0: \mu_1 \geq \mu_2$
$H_A: \mu_1 < \mu_2$ or $H_0: \mu_1 - \mu_2 \geq 0$
$H_A: \mu_1 - \mu_2 < 0$
$\alpha = 0.05$

Rejection Region
$\alpha = 0.05$

$-z_{0.05} = -1.645$ 0 z

$z = -1.90$

Test Statistic:

$$z = \frac{(\bar{x}_1 - \bar{x}_2) - (\mu_1 - \mu_2)}{\sqrt{\dfrac{\sigma_1^2}{n_1} + \dfrac{\sigma_2^2}{n_2}}} = \frac{(0.501 - 0.509) - 0}{\sqrt{\dfrac{0.025^2}{100} + \dfrac{0.034^2}{100}}} = -1.90$$

Decision Rule:
Since $z = -1.90 < z = -1.645$, reject H_0.
Conclude that the mean bolt diameter for population 2 is larger than the mean for population 1.

Using p-values The *z*-test statistic computed in Example 10-4 indicates the difference in sample means is 1.90 standard errors below the hypothesized difference of zero. Because this falls below the z critical level of -1.645, the null hypothesis was rejected. You could have also tested this hypothesis using the *p*-value approach introduced in Chapter 9. The *p*-value for this one-tailed test is the probability of a *z*-value in a standard normal distribution being less than -1.90. From the standard normal table, the probability associated with $z = -1.90$ is 0.4713. Then the *p*-value is

$$p\text{-value} = 0.5000 - 0.4713 = 0.0287$$

The decision rule to use with *p*-values is

If *p*-value $< \alpha$, reject the null hypothesis;
Otherwise, do not reject the null hypothesis.

Because

$$p\text{-value} = 0.0287 < \alpha = 0.05$$

reject the null hypothesis and conclude that the mean bolt diameter for machine 2 is larger than the mean for machine 1.

Testing $\mu_1 - \mu_2$ When σ_1 and σ_2 Are Unknown, Using Independent Samples

In Section 10.1 we showed that to develop a confidence interval estimate for the difference between two population means when the standard deviations are unknown, we used the *t*-distribution to obtain the critical value. As you might suspect, this same approach is taken for hypothesis-testing situations. Equation 10.8 shows the *t*-test statistic that will be used when σ_1 and σ_2 are unknown.

_t_-Test Statistic for $\mu_1 - \mu_2$ When σ_1 and σ_2 Are Unknown and Assumed Equal, Independent Samples

$$t = \frac{(\bar{x}_1 - \bar{x}_2) - (\mu_1 - \mu_2)}{s_p \sqrt{\dfrac{1}{n_1} + \dfrac{1}{n_2}}}, \qquad df = n_1 + n_2 - 2 \tag{10.8}$$

where:

$$\bar{x}_1 \text{ and } \bar{x}_2 = \text{Sample means from populations 1 and 2}$$
$$\mu_1 - \mu_2 = \text{Hypothesized difference between population means}$$
$$n_1 \text{ and } n_2 = \text{Sample sizes from the two populations}$$
$$s_p = \text{Pooled standard deviation (see Equation 10.4)}$$

The test statistic in Equation 10.8 is based on three assumptions:

Assumptions

■ Each population has a normal distribution.[3]
■ The two population variances, σ_1^2 and σ_2^2, are equal.
■ The samples are independent.

Notice that in Equation 10.8 we are using the pooled estimate for the common population standard deviation that we developed in Section 10.1.

Business Application

RETIREMENT INVESTING Recall the earlier example discussing a study in North Carolina involving retirement investing. The leaders of the study are interested in determining whether there is a difference in mean annual contributions for individuals covered by tax-sheltered annuities (TSA) and those with 401(k) retirement programs. A simple random sample of 15 people from the population of adults who are eligible for a TSA investment was selected. A second sample of 15 people was selected from the population of adults in North Carolina who have 401(k) plans. The variables of interest are the dollars invested in the two retirement plans during the previous year.

Specifically, we are interested in testing the following null and alternative hypotheses:

$$\begin{array}{ccc} H_0: \mu_1 - \mu_2 = 0.0 & & H_0: \mu_1 = \mu_2 \\ H_A: \mu_1 - \mu_2 \neq 0.0 & \text{or} & H_A: \mu_1 \neq \mu_2 \end{array}$$

μ_1 = Mean dollars invested by the TSA-eligible population during the past year
μ_2 = Mean dollars invested by the 401(k)-eligible population during the past year

The leaders of the study select a significance level of $\alpha = 0.05$. The sample results are

TSA-Eligible	401(k)-Eligible
$n_1 = 15$	$n_2 = 15$
$\bar{x}_1 = \$2,119.70$	$\bar{x}_2 = \$1,777.70$
$s_1 = \$709.70$	$s_2 = \$593.90$

Because the investments by individuals with TSA accounts is in no way influenced by investments by individuals with 401(k) accounts, the samples are considered independent. The box and whisker plots shown earlier in Figure 10.1 are consistent with what might be expected if the populations have equal variances and are approximately normally distributed.

We are now in a position to complete the hypothesis test to determine whether the mean dollar amount invested by TSA employees is different from the mean amount

---

[3] In Chapter 13 we will introduce a technique called the goodness-of-fit test, which we can use to test whether the sample data come from a population that is normally distributed.

invested by 401(k) employees. We first determine the critical value from the t-distribution table in Appendix F with degrees of freedom equal to

$$n_1 + n_2 - 2 = 15 + 15 - 2 = 28$$

and $\alpha = 0.05$ for the two-tailed test.[4] The appropriate t-value is

$$t_{0.025} = 2.0484 = \text{critical value}$$

To continue the hypothesis test, we compute the pooled standard deviation.

$$s_p = \sqrt{\frac{(n_1 - 1)s_1^2 + (n_2 - 1)s_2^2}{n_1 + n_2 - 2}} = \sqrt{\frac{(15-1)(709.7)^2 + (15-1)(593.9)^2}{15 + 15 - 2}} = 654.37$$

Note that the pooled standard deviation is partway between the two sample standard deviations. Now, keeping in mind that the hypothesized difference between μ_1 and μ_2 is zero, we compute the t-test statistic using Equation 10.8, as follows:

$$t = \frac{(\bar{x}_1 - \bar{x}_2) - (\mu_1 - \mu_2)}{s_p \sqrt{\frac{1}{n_1} + \frac{1}{n_2}}} = \frac{(2,119.70 - 1,777.70) - 0.0}{654.37 \sqrt{\frac{1}{15} + \frac{1}{15}}} = 1.4313$$

FIGURE 10.3

Hypothesis Test for the Equality of the Two Population Means for the North Carolina Investment Study

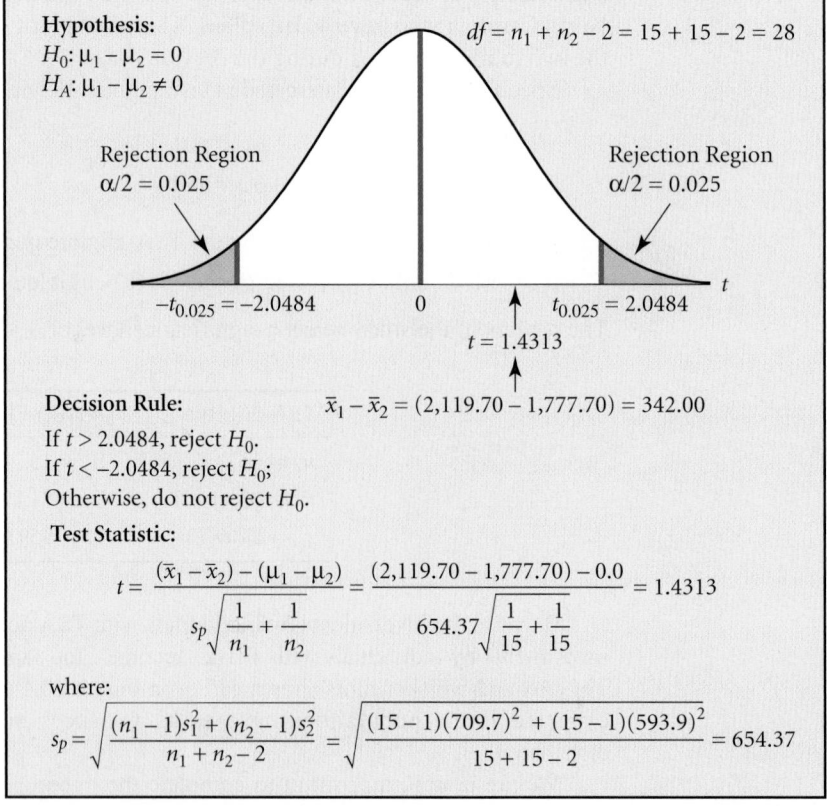

Hypothesis:
$H_0: \mu_1 - \mu_2 = 0$
$H_A: \mu_1 - \mu_2 \neq 0$

$df = n_1 + n_2 - 2 = 15 + 15 - 2 = 28$

Rejection Region
$\alpha/2 = 0.025$

Rejection Region
$\alpha/2 = 0.025$

$-t_{0.025} = -2.0484$ 0 $t_{0.025} = 2.0484$

$t = 1.4313$

$\bar{x}_1 - \bar{x}_2 = (2,119.70 - 1,777.70) = 342.00$

Decision Rule:
If $t > 2.0484$, reject H_0.
If $t < -2.0484$, reject H_0;
Otherwise, do not reject H_0.

Test Statistic:

$$t = \frac{(\bar{x}_1 - \bar{x}_2) - (\mu_1 - \mu_2)}{s_p \sqrt{\frac{1}{n_1} + \frac{1}{n_2}}} = \frac{(2,119.70 - 1,777.70) - 0.0}{654.37 \sqrt{\frac{1}{15} + \frac{1}{15}}} = 1.4313$$

where:

$$s_p = \sqrt{\frac{(n_1 - 1)s_1^2 + (n_2 - 1)s_2^2}{n_1 + n_2 - 2}} = \sqrt{\frac{(15-1)(709.7)^2 + (15-1)(593.9)^2}{15 + 15 - 2}} = 654.37$$

---

[4] You can also use Excel's **TINV** function or Minitab's **Calc > Probability Distributions** command.

This indicates that the difference in sample means is 1.4313 standard errors above the hypothesized difference of zero. Because

$$t = 1.4313 < t_{0.025} = 2.0484$$

the null hypothesis should not be rejected.

The difference in sample means is attributed to sampling error. Figure 10.3 summarizes this hypothesis test. Based on the sample data, there is no statistical justification to believe that the mean annual investment by individuals who are eligible for the tax-sheltered annuity option is different than for those individuals who are eligible for the 401(k) plan.

Business Application

Excel and Minitab Tutorial

SUV VEHICLE MILEAGE Both Excel and Minitab have procedures for performing the necessary calculations to test hypotheses involving two population means. Consider a national car rental company that is interested in testing to determine whether there is a difference in mean mileage for sport utility vehicles (SUVs) driven in town versus those driven on the highway. Based on its experience with regular automobiles, the company believes the mean highway mileage will exceed the mean city mileage.

To test this belief, the company has randomly selected 25 SUV rentals driven only on the highway and another random sample of 25 SUV rentals driven only in the city. The vehicles were filled with 14 gallons of gasoline. The company then asked each customer to drive their car until it ran out of gasoline. At that point, the elapsed miles were noted and the miles per gallon (mpg) were recorded. For their trouble, the customers received free use of the SUV and a coupon valid for one week's free rental. The results of the experiment are contained in the CD-ROM file **Mileage**.

Both Excel and Minitab contain procedures for performing the calculations we will need to determine whether the manager's belief about SUV highway mileage can be justified. We first formulate the null and alternative hypotheses to be tested.

$$H_0: \mu_1 - \mu_2 \leq 0.0 \qquad H_0: \mu_1 \leq \mu_2$$
$$H_A: \mu_1 - \mu_2 > 0.0 \qquad \text{or} \qquad H_A: \mu_1 > \mu_2$$

FIGURE 10.4

Excel 2007 Output—SUV Mileage Descriptive Statistics

Excel 2007 Instructions:
1. Open file: Mileage.xls.
2. Select **Data > Data Analysis**.
3. Select **Descriptive Statistics**.
4. Define the data range for all variables to be analyzed.
5. Select **Summary Statistics**.
6. Specify output location.
7. Click **OK**.

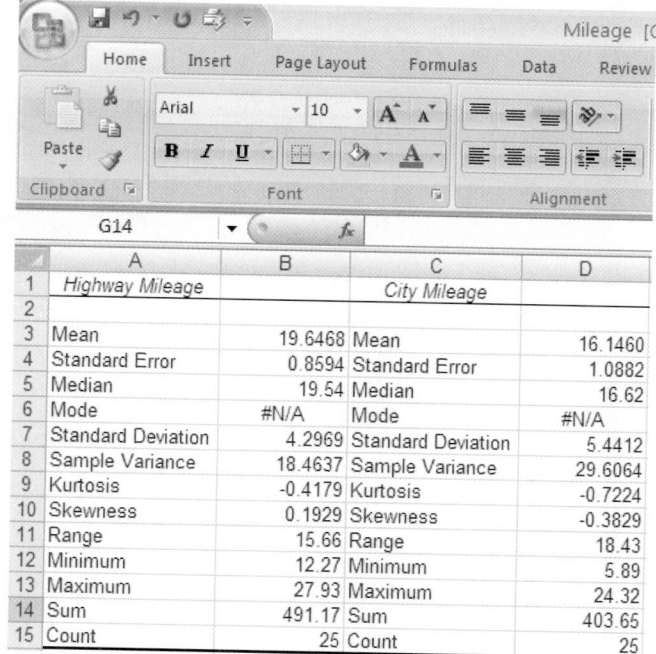

	A	B	C	D
1	Highway Mileage		City Mileage	
2				
3	Mean	19.6468	Mean	16.1460
4	Standard Error	0.8594	Standard Error	1.0882
5	Median	19.54	Median	16.62
6	Mode	#N/A	Mode	#N/A
7	Standard Deviation	4.2969	Standard Deviation	5.4412
8	Sample Variance	18.4637	Sample Variance	29.6064
9	Kurtosis	-0.4179	Kurtosis	-0.7224
10	Skewness	0.1929	Skewness	-0.3829
11	Range	15.66	Range	18.43
12	Minimum	12.27	Minimum	5.89
13	Maximum	27.93	Maximum	24.32
14	Sum	491.17	Sum	403.65
15	Count	25	Count	25

Population 1 represents highway mileage, and Population 2 represents city mileage. The test is conducted using a significance level of $0.05 = \alpha$.

Figure 10.4 shows the descriptive statistics for the two independent samples.

Figure 10.5a and Figure 10.5b display the Excel and Minitab box and whisker plots for the two samples. Based on these plots, the normal distribution and equal variance assumptions appear reasonable. We will proceed with the test of means assuming normal distributions and equal variances.

FIGURE 10.5A

Excel 2007 Output (PHStat Add-in) Box and Whisker Plot— SUV Mileage Test

Excel 2007 Instructions:
1. Open file Mileage.xls.
2. Click on **Add-Ins** (make sure PHStat is installed).
3. Select **Data > PHStat**.
4. Select **Descriptive Statistics**.
5. Select **Box and Whisker Plot**.
6. Select data (both columns including headings).
7. Check **Multiple Groups– Unstacked**.
8. Click **OK**.

FIGURE 10.5B

Minitab Output Box and Whisker Plot—SUV Mileage Test

Minitab Instructions:
1. Open file Mileage MTW.
2. Choose **Graph > Boxplot**.
3. Under **Multiple Ys**. select **Simple**.
4. Click **OK**.
5. In **Graph variables**, enter data columns.
6. Click **OK**.

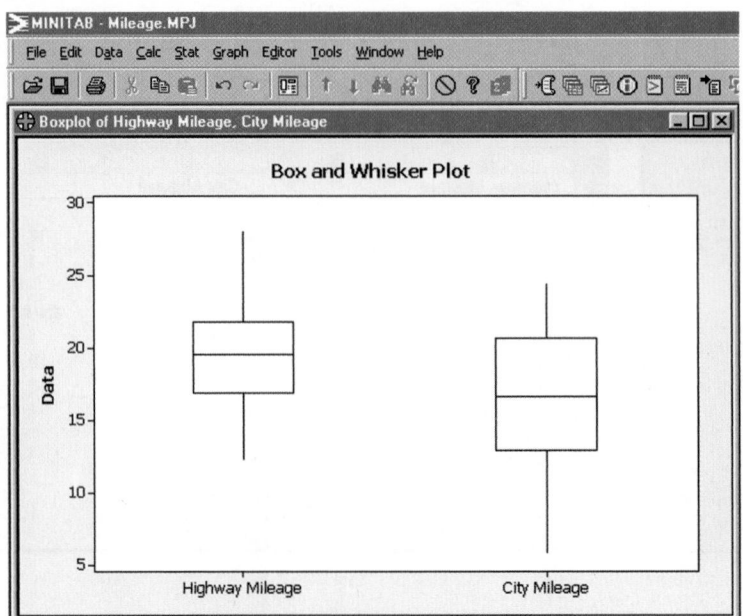

FIGURE 10.6A

Excel 2007 Output—
SUV Mileage *t*-Test for
Two Population Means

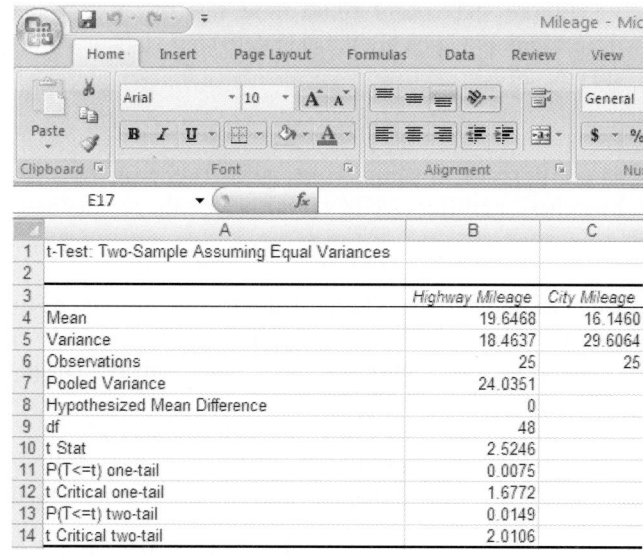

Excel 2007 Instructions:
1. Open file: Mileage.xls.
2. Select **Data > Data Analysis**.
3. Select *t*-test: **Two-Sample Assuming Equal Variances**.
4. Define data ranges for each of the two variables of interest.
5. Set **Hypothesized Difference** equal to 0.0
6. Set **Alpha** at 0.05.
7. Specify output location.
8. Click **OK**.
9. Click on **Home** and adjust decimal places in output.

FIGURE 10.6B

Minitab Output—SUV
Mileage *t*-Test for Two
Population Means

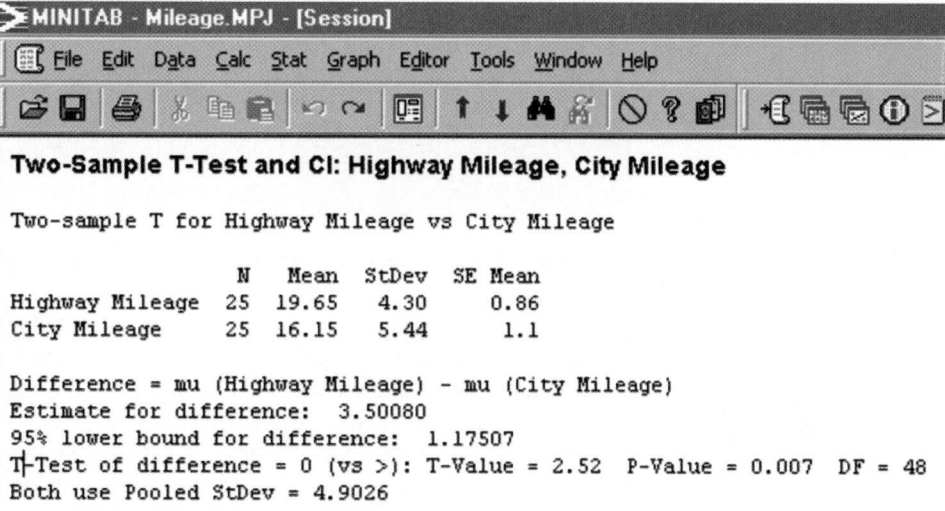

Minitab Instructions:
1. Open file: Mileage.MTW
2. Choose **Stat > Basic Statistics > 2-Sample *t***.
3. Choose **Samples in different columns**.
4. In **First**, enter the first data column.
5. In **Second**, enter the other data column.
6. Check **Assume equal variances**.
7. Click **Options** and enter $1 - \alpha$ in **Confidence level**.
8. In **Alternative** choose *greater than*.
9. Click **OK. OK**.

Figure 10.6a and Figure 10.6b show the outputs from these procedures. The mean highway mileage is 19.6468 mpg, whereas the mean for city driving is 16.146. At issue is whether this difference in sample means (19.6468 − 16.146 = 3.5008 mpg) is sufficient to conclude the mean highway mileage exceeds the mean city mileage. The one-tail *t* critical value for $\alpha = 0.05$ is shown in Figure 10.6a to be

$$t_{0.05} = 1.6772$$

Figures 10.6a and 10.6b show that the "*t*-Stat" value from Excel and the *t*-value from Minitab, which are the calculated test statistics (or *t*-values, based on Equation 10.8), are equal to

$$t = 2.52$$

The difference in sample means (3.5008 mpg) is 2.52 standard errors larger than the hypothesized difference of zero. Because the test statistic

$$t = 2.52 > t_{0.05} = 1.6772$$

we reject the null hypothesis. Thus, the sample data do provide sufficient evidence to conclude that mean SUV highway mileage exceeds mean SUV city mileage, and this study confirms the expectations of the rental company managers. This will factor into the company's fuel pricing.

The outputs shown in Figures 10.6a and 10.6b also provide the *p*-value for the one-tailed test, which can also be used to test the null hypothesis. Recall, if the calculated *p*-value is less than alpha, the null hypothesis should be rejected. The decision rule is

If *p*-value < 0.05, reject H_0;
Otherwise, do not reject H_0.

The *p*-value for the one-tailed test is 0.0075. Because $0.0075 < 0.05$, the null hypothesis is rejected. This is the same conclusion as the one we reached using the test statistic approach.

EXAMPLE 10-5	Hypothesis Test for $\mu_1 - \mu_2$ When σ_1 and σ_2 Are Unknown, Using Independent Samples

TRY PROBLEM 10.21

Color Printer Ink Cartridges   An Associated Press news story out of Brussels, Belgium, on May 16, 2002, indicated the European Union was considering a probe of computer makers after consumers complained that they were being overcharged for ink cartridges. Companies such as Cannon, Hewlett-Packard, and Epson are the printer market leaders and make most of their printer-related profits by selling replacement ink cartridges. Suppose an independent test agency wishes to conduct a test to determine whether name-brand ink cartridges generate more color pages on average than competing generic ink cartridges. The test can be conducted using the following steps:

Step 1   Specify the population parameter of interest.
We are interested in determining whether the mean number of pages printed by name-brand cartridges (population 1) exceeds the mean pages printed by generic cartridges (population 2).

Step 2   Formulate the appropriate null and alternative hypotheses.
The following null and alternative hypotheses are specified:

$$H_0: \mu_1 - \mu_2 \leq 0.0 \qquad\qquad H_0: \mu_1 \leq \mu_2$$
$$H_A: \mu_1 - \mu_2 > 0.0 \quad \text{or} \quad H_A: \mu_1 > \mu_2$$

Step 3   Specify the significance level for the test.
The test will be conducted using $\alpha = 0.05$.

When the populations have standard deviations that are unknown, the critical value is a *t*-value from the *t*-distribution if the populations are assumed to be normally distributed and the population variances are assumed to be equal.

A simple random sample of 10 users was selected, and the users were given a name-brand cartridge. A second sample of 8 users was given generic cartridges. Both groups used their printers until the ink ran out. The number of pages printed was recorded. The samples are independent because the pages printed by users in one group did not in any way influence the pages printed by users in the second group. The means computed from the samples are

$$\bar{x}_1 = 322.5 \text{ pages} \quad \text{and} \quad \bar{x}_2 = 298.3 \text{ pages}$$

Because we do not know the population standard deviations, these values are computed from the sample data and are

$$s_1 = 48.3 \text{ pages} \quad \text{and} \quad s_2 = 53.3 \text{ pages}$$

Suppose previous studies have shown that the number of pages printed by both types of cartridge tend to be approximately normal with equal variances.

Step 4   Compute the test statistic using Equation 10.8.

$$t = \frac{(\bar{x}_1 - \bar{x}_2) - (\mu_1 - \mu_2)}{s_p \sqrt{\dfrac{1}{n_1} + \dfrac{1}{n_2}}}$$

The pooled standard deviation is

$$s_p = \sqrt{\frac{(n_1 - 1)s_1^2 + (n_2 - 1)s_2^2}{n_1 + n_2 - 2}} = \sqrt{\frac{(10 - 1)48.3^2 + (8 - 1)53.3^2}{10 + 8 - 2}} = 50.55$$

Then the t-test statistic is

$$t = \frac{(322.5 - 298.3) - 0.0}{50.55\sqrt{\dfrac{1}{10} + \dfrac{1}{8}}} = 1.0093$$

Step 5   Construct the rejection region.
Based on a one-tailed test with $\alpha = 0.05$, the critical value is a t-value from the t-distribution with $10 + 8 - 2 = 16$ degrees of freedom. From the t-table, the critical t-value is

$$t_{0.05} = 1.7459 = \text{critical value}$$

The calculated test statistic from Step 4 is compared to the critical t-value to form the decision rule. The decision rule is

If $t > 1.7459$, reject the null hypothesis;
Otherwise, do not reject the null hypothesis.

Step 6   Reach a decision.
Because

$$t = 1.0093 < t_{0.05} = 1.7459$$

do not reject the null hypothesis.
Figure 10.7 illustrates the hypothesis test.

Step 7   Draw a conclusion.
Based on these sample data, there is insufficient evidence to conclude that the mean number of pages produced by name-brand ink cartridges exceeds the mean for generic cartridges.

FIGURE 10.7

Example 10-5 Hypothesis Test

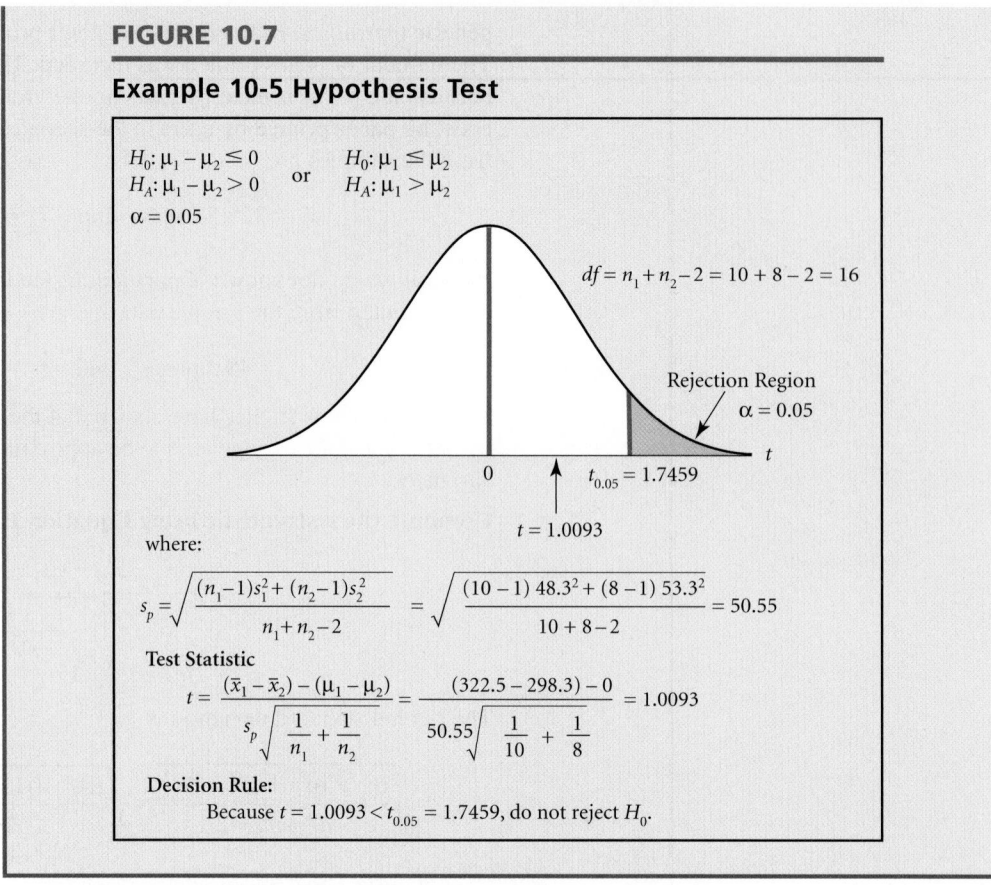

$H_0: \mu_1 - \mu_2 \leq 0$ or $H_0: \mu_1 \leq \mu_2$
$H_A: \mu_1 - \mu_2 > 0$ or $H_A: \mu_1 > \mu_2$
$\alpha = 0.05$

$df = n_1 + n_2 - 2 = 10 + 8 - 2 = 16$

Rejection Region
$\alpha = 0.05$

0 $t_{0.05} = 1.7459$

$t = 1.0093$

where:

$$s_p = \sqrt{\frac{(n_1-1)s_1^2 + (n_2-1)s_2^2}{n_1 + n_2 - 2}} = \sqrt{\frac{(10-1)\,48.3^2 + (8-1)\,53.3^2}{10 + 8 - 2}} = 50.55$$

Test Statistic

$$t = \frac{(\bar{x}_1 - \bar{x}_2) - (\mu_1 - \mu_2)}{s_p\sqrt{\dfrac{1}{n_1} + \dfrac{1}{n_2}}} = \frac{(322.5 - 298.3) - 0}{50.55\sqrt{\dfrac{1}{10} + \dfrac{1}{8}}} = 1.0093$$

Decision Rule:
  Because $t = 1.0093 < t_{0.05} = 1.7459$, do not reject H_0.

What If the Population Variances Are Not Equal? In the previous examples, we assumed that the population variances were equal, and we carried out the hypothesis test for two population means using Equation 10.8. Even in cases where the population variances are not equal, the t-test as specified in Equation 10.8 is generally considered to be appropriate as long as the sample sizes are equal.[5] However, if the sample sizes are not equal and if the sample data lead us to suspect that the variances are not equal, the t-test statistic must be approximated using Equation 10.9. In cases where the variances are not equal, the degrees of freedom are computed using Equation 10.10.[6]

---

t-Test Statistic for $\mu_1 - \mu_2$ When Population Variances Are Unknown and Not Assumed Equal

$$t = \frac{(\bar{x}_1 - \bar{x}_2) - (\mu_1 - \mu_2)}{\sqrt{\dfrac{s_1^2}{n_1} + \dfrac{s_2^2}{n_2}}} \qquad (10.9)$$

Degrees of Freedom for t-Test Statistic When Population Variances Are Not Equal

$$df = \frac{(s_1^2/n_1 + s_2^2/n_2)^2}{\left(\dfrac{(s_1^2/n_1)^2}{n_1 - 1} + \dfrac{(s_2^2/n_2)^2}{n_2 - 1}\right)} \qquad (10.10)$$

---

[5] Studies show that when the sample sizes are equal or almost equal, the t distribution is appropriate even when one population variance is twice the size of the other.

[6] Chapter 11 introduces a statistical procedure for testing whether two populations have equal variances.

10-2: Exercises

Skill Development

10-18. Given the following null and alternative hypotheses:

$$H_0: \mu_1 \geq \mu_2$$
$$H_A: \mu_1 < \mu_2$$

together with the following sample information:

Sample 1	Sample 2
$n_1 = 14$	$n_2 = 18$
$\bar{x}_1 = 565$	$\bar{x}_2 = 578$
$s_1 = 28.9$	$s_2 = 26.3$

a. assuming that the populations are normally distributed with equal variances, test at the 0.10 level of significance whether you would reject the null hypothesis based on the sample information. Use the test statistic approach.

b. assuming that the populations are normally distributed with equal variances, test at the 0.05 level of significance whether you would reject the null hypothesis based on the sample information. Use the test statistic approach.

10-19. Given the following null and alternative hypotheses, conduct a hypothesis test using an alpha equal to 0.05. (*Note*: The population standard deviations are assumed to be known.)

$$H_0: \mu_1 \leq \mu_2$$
$$H_A: \mu_1 > \mu_2$$

The sample means for the two populations are shown as follows:

$$\bar{x}_1 = 144 \qquad \bar{x}_2 = 129$$
$$\sigma_1 = 11 \qquad \sigma_2 = 16$$
$$n_1 = 40 \qquad n_2 = 50$$

10-20. A decision maker wishes to test the following null and alternative hypotheses using an alpha level equal to 0.05:

$$H_0: \mu_1 - \mu_2 = 0$$
$$H_A: \mu_1 - \mu_2 \neq 0$$

The population standard deviations are assumed to be known. After collecting the sample data, the test statistics is computed to be

$$z = 1.78$$

a. Using the test statistic approach, what conclusion should be reached about the null hypothesis?

b. Using the *p*-value approach, what decision should be reached about the null hypothesis?

c. Will the two approaches (test statistic and *p*-value) ever provide different conclusions based on the same sample data? Explain.

10-21. The following null and alternative hypotheses have been stated:

$$H_0: \mu_1 - \mu_2 = 0$$
$$H_A: \mu_1 - \mu_2 \neq 0$$

To test the null hypothesis, random samples have been selected from the two normally distributed populations with equal variances. The following sample data were observed:

Sample from Population 1			Sample from Population 2		
33	29	35	46	43	42
39	39	41	46	44	47
25	33	38	50	43	39

Test the null hypothesis using an alpha level equal to 0.05.

10-22. Given the following null and alternative hypotheses:

$$H_0: \mu_1 - \mu_2 = 0$$
$$H_A: \mu_1 - \mu_2 \neq 0$$

and the following sample information:

Sample 1	Sample 2
$n_1 = 125$	$n_2 = 120$
$s_1 = 31$	$s_2 = 38$
$\bar{x}_1 = 130$	$\bar{x}_2 = 105$

a. develop the appropriate decision rule, assuming a significance level of 0.05 is to be used.

b. test the null hypothesis and indicate whether the sample information leads you to reject or fail to reject the null hypothesis. Use the test statistic approach.

10-23. The following statistics were obtained from independent samples from populations that have normal distributions:

Sample	1	2
n_i	41	51
$\bar{x}_i$	25.4	33.2
s_i	5.6	7.4

a. Use the following statistics to conduct a test of hypothesis if the alternative hypothesis is $\mu_1 - \mu_2 < -4$. Use a significance level of 0.01.

b. Determine the *p*-value for the test described in part a.

c. Describe the type of statistical error that could have been made as a result of your hypothesis test.

10-24. Consider the following two independently chosen samples whose population variances are not equal to each other.

Sample 1	Sample 2
12.1	10.5
13.4	9.5
11.7	8.2
10.7	7.8
14.0	11.1

a. Using a significance level of 0.025, test the null hypothesis that $\mu_1 - \mu_2 \leq 0$.
b. Calculate the p-value.

Business Applications

10-25. The management of the Shadow Pines Golf Club regularly monitors the golfers on its course for speed of play. Suppose a random sample of golfers was taken in 2005 and another random sample of golfers was selected in 2006. The results of the two samples as follows:

2005	2006
$\bar{x}_1 = 225$	$\bar{x}_2 = 219$
$s_1 = 20.25$	$s_2 = 21.70$
$n_1 = 36$	$n_2 = 31$

Based on the sample results, can the management of the Shadow Pines Golf Club conclude that average speed of play is different in 2006 than in 2005? Conduct the appropriate hypothesis test at the 0.10 level of significance. Assume that the management of the club is willing to accept the assumption that the populations of playing times for each year are approximately normally distributed with equal variances.

10-26. Alta, Inc. produces a variety of climbing and mountaineering equipment. One of its products is a traditional three-strand climbing rope. An important characteristic of any climbing rope is its tensile strength. Alta produces the three-strand rope on two separate production lines: one in Bozeman and the other in Challis. The Bozeman line has recently installed new production equipment. Alta regularly tests the tensile strength of its ropes by randomly selecting ropes from production and subjecting them to various tests. The most recent random sample of ropes, taken after the new equipment was installed at the Bozeman plant, revealed the following:

Bozeman	Challis
$\bar{x}_1 = 7,200$ lb	$\bar{x}_2 = 7,087$ lb
$s_1 = 425$	$s_2 = 415$
$n_1 = 25$	$n_2 = 20$

Alta's production managers are willing to assume that the population of tensile strengths for each plant is approximately normally distributed with equal variances. Based on the sample results, can Alta's managers conclude that there is a difference between the mean tensile strengths of ropes produced in Bozeman and Challis? Conduct the appropriate hypothesis test at the 0.05 level of significance.

10-27. Sherwin-Williams is a major paint manufacturer. Recently, the R&D department came out with a new paint product designed to be used in areas that are particularly prone to periodic moisture and hot sun. They believe that this new paint will be superior to anything that Sherwin-Williams or its competitors currently offer. However, they are concerned about the coverage area that a gallon of the new paint will provide compared to their current products. The R&D department set up a test in which two random samples of paint were selected. The first sample consisted of 25 one-gallon containers of the company's best-selling paint and the second sample consisted of 15 one-gallon containers of the new paint under consideration. The following statistics were computed from each sample and refer to the number of square feet that each gallon will cover:

Best-Selling Paint	New Paint Product
$\bar{x}_1 = 423$ sq. feet	$\bar{x}_2 = 406$ sq. feet
$s_1 = 22.4$ sq. feet	$s_2 = 16.8$ sq. feet
$n_1 = 25$	$n_2 = 15$

The R&D managers are concerned the average area covered per gallon will be less for the new paint than for the existing product. Based on the sample data, what should they conclude if they base their conclusion on a significance level equal to 0.01?

10-28. The marketing manager for a major retail grocery chain is wondering about the location of the stores' dairy products. She believes that the mean amount spent by customers on dairy products per visit is higher in stores where the dairy section is in the central part of the store compared with stores that have the dairy section at the rear of the store. To consider relocating the dairy products, the manager feels that the increase in the mean amount spent by customers must be at least 25 cents. To determine whether relocation is justified, her staff selected a random sample of 25 customers at stores where the dairy section is central in the store. A second sample of 25 customers was selected in stores with the dairy section at the rear of the store. The following sample results were observed:

Central Dairy	Rear Dairy
$\bar{x}_1 = \$3.74$	$\bar{x}_2 = \$3.26$
$s_1 = \$0.87$	$s_2 = \$0.79$

a. Conduct a hypothesis test with a significance level of 0.05 to determine if the manager should relocate the dairy products in those stores displaying their dairy products in the rear of the store.

b. If a statistical error associated with hypothesis testing was made in this hypothesis test, what error could it have been? Explain.

10-29. Albertsons has been one of the largest grocery chains in the United States for some time with over 1,100 grocery stores, but in the early 2000s the company began to feel the competitive pinch from companies like Wal-Mart and Costco. In January 2006, the company announced that it would be sold to SuperValu, Inc. headquartered in Minneapolis. Prior to the sale, Albertsons had attempted to lower prices and regain its competitive edge. In an effort to maintain its profit margins, Albertsons took several steps to lower costs. One was to replace some of the traditional checkout stands with auto-mated self-checkout facilities. After making the change in some test stores, the company performed a study to determine whether the average purchase through a self-checkout facility was less than the average purchase at the traditional checkout stand.

To conduct the test, a random sample of 125 customer transactions at the self-checkout was obtained and a second random sample of 125 trans-actions from customers using the traditional checkout process was obtained. The following statistics were computed from each sample:

Self-Checkout	Traditional Checkout
$\bar{x}_1 = \$45.68$	$\bar{x}_2 = \$78.49$
$s_1 = \$58.20$	$s_2 = \$62.45$
$n_1 = 125$	$n_2 = 125$

Based on these sample data, what should be concluded with respect to the average transaction amount for the two checkout processes? Test using an $\alpha = 0.05$ level.

10-30. The *Washington Post Weekly Edition* (Robert J. Samuelson, "Homes as Hummers," July 18–24, 2005) quoted an Urban Institute study that stated that about 80% of the estimated $200 billion of federal housing subsidies consisted of tax breaks (mainly deductions for mortgage interest payments). Samples indicated that the federal housing benefits average was $8,268 for those with incomes between $200,000 and $500,000

and only $365 for those with incomes of $40,000 to $50,000. The respective standard deviations were 2,100 and 150. They were obtained from sample sizes of 150.

a. Examine the sample standard deviations. What do these suggest is the relationship between the two population standard deviations? Support your assertion.

b. Conduct a hypothesis test to determine if the average federal housing benefits are at least $7,750 more for those in the $200,000 to $500,000 income range. Use a 0.05 significance level.

c. Having reached your decision in part b, state the type of statistical error that could have been made by you.

d. Is there any way to determine whether you were in error in the hypothesis selection you made in part b? Support your answer.

10-31. The College Board's *2005 Trends in Student Aid* addresses, among other topics, the difference in the average college debt accumulated by undergraduate bachelor of arts degree recipients by type of college for the 2003–2004 academic year. Samples might have been used to determine this difference in which the private, for-profit colleges' average was $24,200 and the public college average was $10,600. Suppose the respective standard deviations were 2,050 and 2,084. The sample sizes were 75 and 205, respectively.

a. Examine the sample standard deviations. What do these suggest is the relationship between the two population standard deviations? Support your assertion.

b. Conduct a hypothesis test to determine if the average college debt for bachelor of arts degree recipients is at least $12,500 more for graduates from private colleges than from public colleges. Use a 0.01 significance level and a *p*-value approach for this hypothesis test.

Computer Database Exercises

10-32. Suppose a professional job-placement firm that monitors salaries in professional fields is interested in determining if the increased price of oil and the outsourcing of computer-related jobs have had an effect on the starting salaries of chemical and elec-trical engineering graduates. Specifically, the job-placement firm would like to know if the 2005 average starting salary for chemical engineering majors is higher than the 2005 average starting salary for electrical engineering majors. To conduct its test, the job-placement firm has selected a ran-dom sample of 124 electrical engineering majors and 110 chemical engineering majors who gradu-ated and received jobs in 2005. Each graduate was asked to report their starting salary. The results of the survey are contained in the file **Starting Salaries**.

a. Conduct a hypothesis test to determine whether the mean starting salary for 2005 graduates in chemical engineering is higher than the mean starting salary for 2005 graduates in electrical engineering. Conduct the test at the 0.05 level of significance. Be sure to state a conclusion. (Assume that the firm believes the two populations from which the samples were taken are approximately normally distributed with equal variances.)

b. Suppose the job-placement firm is unwilling to assume that the two populations are normally distributed with equal variances. Conduct the appropriate hypothesis test to determine whether a difference exists between the mean starting salaries for the two groups. Use a level of significance of 0.05. What conclusion should the job-placement firm reach based on the hypothesis test?

10-33. The Marriott Corporation operates the largest chain of hotel and motel properties in the world. The Fairfield Inn and the Residence Inn are just two of the hotel brands that Marriott owns. At a recent managers meeting, a question was posed regarding whether the average length of stay was different at these two properties in the United States. A summer intern was assigned the task of testing to see if there is a difference. She started by selecting a simple random sample of 100 hotel reservations from Fairfield Inn. Next, she selected a simple random sample of 100 hotel reservations from the Residence Inn. In both cases, she recorded the number of nights' stay for each reservation. The resulting data are in the file called **Marriott**.

a. State the appropriate null and alternative hypotheses.

b. Based on these sample data and a 0.05 level of significance, what conclusion should be made about the average length of stay at these two hotel chains?

10-34. A *USA Today* editorial (Alejandro Gonzalez, "CEO Dough," January 20, 2006) addressed the growth of compensation for corporate CEOs. Quoting a study made by *BusinessWeek*, *USA Today* indicated that the pay packages for CEOs have increased almost sevenfold on average over the past decade. The file entitled **CEODough** contains the salaries of CEOs in 1994 and in 2004, adjusted for inflation.

a. Determine the ratio of the average salary for 1994 and 2004. Does it appear that *BusinessWeek* was correct? Explain your answer.

b. Examine the sample standard deviations. What do these suggest is the relationship between the two population standard deviations? Support your assertion.

c. Based upon your response to part b, conduct a test of hypothesis to determine if the difference in the average CEO salary between 1994 and 2004 is more than $9.8 million. Use a *p*-value approach with a significance level of 0.025.

10-35. JetBlue is the fastest-growing U.S. airline. It was launched in February 2000 and its initial public offering was in 2002. In 2005, it experienced its first quarterly loss and finished $20.3 million in the red. CEO David Neeleman's top priority was to get an average of an additional $5 to $10 per trip out of JetBlue customers' pocketbooks. To determine his success, surveys could provide this information. The file entitled **Jetblue** contains results of samples gathered for 2005 and 2006.

a. Produce a 95% confidence interval for the difference in the average fares paid by JetBlue passengers from 2005 and 2006. Based on the confidence interval, is it possible that Neeleman has been able to increase the average fare by at least $10? Explain your response.

b. Conduct a test of hypothesis to answer the question posed in part a. Use a significance level of 0.025.

c. Did you reach the same conclusion in both parts a and b? Is this a coincidence or will it always be so? Explain your response.

10.3 Interval Estimation and Hypothesis Tests for Paired Samples

Paired Samples

Samples that are selected in such a way that values in one sample are matched with the values in the second sample for the purpose of controlling for extraneous factors. Another term for paired samples is *dependent samples*.

Sections 10.1 and 10.2 introduced the methods by which decision makers can estimate and test the hypotheses for the difference between the means for two populations when the two samples are independent. In each example, the samples were independent because the sample values from one population did not have the potential to influence the probability that values would be selected from the second population. However, there are instances in business in which you would want to use **paired samples** to control for sources of variation that might otherwise distort the conclusions of a study.

Why Use Paired Samples?

There are many situations in business where using paired samples should be considered. For instance, a paint manufacturer might be interested in comparing the area that a new paint mix will cover per gallon with an existing paint mixture. One approach would be to have one random sample of painters apply a gallon of the new paint mixture. A second sample of painters would be given the existing mix. In both cases, the number of square feet that was covered by the gallon of paint would be recorded. In this case, the samples would be independent because the area covered by painters using the new mixture would not be in any way affected by the area covered by painters using the existing mixture.

This would be a fine way to do the study unless the painters themselves could influence the area that the paint will cover. For instance, suppose some painters, because of their technique or experience, are able to cover more area from a gallon of paint than other painters. Then, if by chance most of these "good" painters happened to get assigned to the new mix, the results might show that the new mix covers more area, not because it is a better paint, but because the painters that used it during the test were better.

To combat this potential problem, the company might want to use paired samples. To do this, one group of painters would be selected and each painter would use 1 gallon of each paint mix. Doing this controls for the effect of the painter's ability or technique. The following application involving engine-oil testing is one in which paired samples would most likely be warranted.

Business Application

TESTING ENGINE OIL A major oil company wanted to estimate the difference in average mileage for cars using a regular engine oil compared with cars using a synthetic-oil product. The company used a paired-sample approach to control for any variation in mileage arising because of different cars and drivers. A random sample of 10 motorists (and their cars) was selected. Each car was filled with gasoline, the oil was drained, and new, regular oil was added. The car was driven 200 miles on a specified route. The car then was filled with gasoline and the miles per gallon were computed. After the 10 cars completed this process, the same steps were performed using synthetic oil. Because the same cars and drivers tested both types of oil, the miles-per-gallon measurements for synthetic oil and regular engine oil will most likely be related. The two samples are not independent, but are instead considered paired samples. Thus, we will compute the *paired difference* between the values from each sample, using Equation 10.11.

CHAPTER OUTCOME #2

	A	B	C
1	Synthetic	Original	d
2	19.8	20.7	-0.9
3	28.8	25.8	3
4	20.4	27.8	-7.4
5	18.7	14.9	3.8
6	23.4	21.6	1.8
7	27.1	21.1	6
8	28.4	28	0.4
9	21.4	13	8.4
10	26.4	24.4	2
11	19.9	14.3	5.6

Excel 2007 Instructions:
1. Open file: Engine Oil.xls.

FIGURE 10.8

Excel 2007 Worksheet for Engine Oil Study

Paired Difference

$$d = x_1 - x_2 \tag{10.11}$$

where:

d = Paired difference
x_1 and x_2 = Values from sample 1 and 2, respectively

Figure 10.8 shows the Excel spreadsheet for this engine oil study with the paired differences computed. The data are in the file on your CD-ROM called **Engine-Oil.**

The first step to develop the interval estimate is to compute the *mean paired difference*, $\bar{d}$, using Equation 10.12. This value is the best point estimate for the population mean paired difference, μ_d.

Point Estimate for the Population Mean Paired Difference, μ_d

$$\bar{d} = \frac{\sum_{i=1}^{n} d_i}{n} \tag{10.12}$$

where:

d_i = ith paired difference value
n = Number of paired differences

Using Equation 10.12, we determine $\bar{d}$ as follows:

$$\bar{d} = \frac{\Sigma d}{n} = \frac{22.7}{10} = 2.27$$

The next step is to compute the *sample standard deviation for the paired differences* using Equation 10.13.

Sample Standard Deviation for Paired Differences

$$s_d = \sqrt{\frac{\sum_{i=1}^{n}(d_i - \bar{d})^2}{n-1}}$$ (10.13)

where:

d_i = ith paired difference

$\bar{d}$ = Mean paired difference

The sample standard deviation for the paired differences is

$$s_d = \sqrt{\frac{\Sigma(d - \bar{d})^2}{n-1}} = \sqrt{\frac{172.8}{10-1}} = 4.38$$

Assuming that the population of paired differences is normally distributed, the confidence interval estimate for the population mean paired difference is computed using Equation 10.14.

Confidence Interval Estimate for Population Mean Paired Difference, μ_d

$$\bar{d} \pm t \frac{s_d}{\sqrt{n}}$$ (10.14)

where:

t = Critical t value from t-distribution with $n-1$ degrees of freedom

$\bar{d}$ = Sample mean paired difference

s_d = Sample standard deviation of paired differences

n = Number of paired differences (sample size)

For a 95% confidence interval with $10 - 1 = 9$ degrees of freedom, we use a critical t from the t-distribution of

$$t = 2.2622$$

The interval estimate obtained from Equation 10.14 is

$$\bar{d} \pm t \frac{s_d}{\sqrt{n}}$$

$$2.27 \pm 2.2622 \frac{4.38}{\sqrt{10}}$$

$$2.27 \pm 3.13$$

$$-0.86 \text{ mpg} \text{ ----------------- } 5.40 \text{ mpg}$$

EXAMPLE 10-6	Confidence Interval Estimate for the Difference Between Population Means, Paired Samples

TRY PROBLEM 10.38

Golf Ball Testing   Technology has done more to change golf than possibly any other sport in recent years. Titanium woods and irons and new golf ball designs have impacted professional and amateur golfers alike. A maker of golf balls has developed a new ball technology and is interested in estimating the mean difference in driving distance for this new ball versus its existing best-seller. To conduct the test, the developers selected six professional golfers and had each golfer hit each ball one time. Here are the steps necessary to develop a confidence interval estimate for the difference in population means for paired samples.

Step 1 **Define the population parameter of interest.**
Because the same golfers hit each golf ball, the company is controlling for the variation in the golfers' ability to hit a golf ball. The samples are paired, and the population value of interest is μ_d, the mean paired difference in distance. We assume that the population of paired differences is normally distributed.

Step 2 **Specify the desired confidence level and determine the appropriate critical value.**
For a 95% confidence interval, the critical value is a t-value from the t-distribution with $n - 1 = 5$ degrees of freedom. From the t-table, we get

$$t = 2.5706$$

Step 3 **Collect the sample data and compute the point estimate, $\bar{d}$, and the standard deviation, s_d.**
The sample data, paired differences, are shown as follows.

Golfer	Existing Ball	New Ball	d
1	278	285	−7
2	299	301	−2
3	280	276	4
4	295	300	−5
5	268	273	−5
6	301	299	2

The point estimate is computed using Equation 10.12.

$$\bar{d} = \frac{\Sigma d}{n} = \frac{-13}{6} = -2.17 \text{ yards}$$

The standard deviation for the paired differences is computed using Equation 10.13.

$$s_d = \sqrt{\frac{\Sigma(d - \bar{d})^2}{n - 1}} = 4.36 \text{ yards}$$

Step 4 **Compute the confidence interval estimate using Equation 10.14.**

$$\bar{d} \pm t \frac{s_d}{\sqrt{n}}$$

$$-2.17 \pm 2.5706 \frac{4.36}{\sqrt{6}}$$

$$-2.17 \pm 4.58$$

$$-6.75 \text{ yards} \text{ ---------------------- } 2.41 \text{ yards}$$

> Based upon these sample data and the confidence interval estimate which contains zero, the company must conclude that the new ball's average distance may not be any longer than that of the existing best-seller. This may affect whether the company will continue to make the new ball.

The key in deciding whether to use paired samples is to determine whether a factor exists that might adversely influence the results of the estimation. In the engine-oil test example, we controlled for potential outside influence by using the same cars to test both oils. In Example 10-6, we controlled for golfer ability by having the same golfers hit both golf balls. If you determine that there is no need to control for an outside source of variation, then independent samples should be used, as discussed earlier in this section.

Hypothesis Testing for Paired Samples

CHAPTER OUTCOME #2   As we just illustrated, there will be instances when paired samples can be used to control for an outside source of variation. For instance in Example 10-5 involving the ink cartridges, the original test of whether name-brand cartridges yield a higher mean number of printed pages than generic cartridges involved different users for the two types of cartridges, so the samples were independent. However, different users may use more or less ink as a rule; therefore, we could control for that source of variation by having a sample of people use both types of cartridges in a paired test format.

If a paired-sample experiment is used, the test statistic is computed using Equation 10.15.

---

t-Test Statistic for Paired-Sample Test

$$t = \frac{\bar{d} - \mu_d}{\dfrac{s_d}{\sqrt{n}}}, \qquad df = (n - 1) \tag{10.15}$$

where:

$$\bar{d} = \text{Mean paired difference} = \frac{\sum d}{n}$$

μ_d = Hypothesized population mean paired difference

$$s_d = \text{Sample standard deviation for paired differences} = \sqrt{\frac{\sum(d - \bar{d})^2}{n - 1}}$$

n = Number of paired values in the sample

EXAMPLE 10-7   Hypothesis Test for μ_d, Paired Samples

TRY PROBLEM 10.39

Color Printer Ink Cartridges   Referring to Example 10-5, suppose the experiment regarding ink cartridges is conducted differently. Instead of having different samples of people use name-brand and generic cartridges, the test is done using paired samples. This means that the same people will use both types of cartridges, and the pages printed in each case will be recorded. The test under this paired-sample scenario can be conducted using the following steps. Six randomly selected people have agreed to participate.

> **Step 1   Specify the population value of interest.**
> In this case we will form paired differences by subtracting the generic pages from the name-brand pages. We are interested in determining

whether name-brand cartridges produce more printed pages, on average, than generic cartridges, so we would expect the paired difference to be positive. We assume that the paired differences are normally distributed.

Step 2 Formulate the null and alternative hypotheses.
The null and alternative hypotheses are

$$H_0: \mu_d \leq 0.0$$
$$H_A: \mu_d > 0.0$$

Step 3 Specify the significance level for the test.
The test will be conducted using $\alpha = 0.01$.

Step 4 Construct the rejection region.
The critical value is a t-value from the t-distribution, with $\alpha = 0.01$ and $6 - 1 = 5$ degrees of freedom. The critical value is

$$t_{0.01} = 3.3649$$

The decision rule is

If $t > 3.3649$, reject the null hypothesis;
Otherwise, do not reject the null hypothesis.

Step 5 Compute the test statistic.
Select the random sample and compute the mean and standard deviation for the paired differences.

In this case a random sample of six people tests each type of cartridge. The following data and paired differences were observed:

Printer User	Name-Brand	Generic	d
1	306	300	6
2	256	260	−4
3	402	357	45
4	299	286	13
5	306	290	16
6	257	260	−3

The mean paired difference is

$$\bar{d} = \frac{\Sigma d}{n} = \frac{73}{6} = 12.17$$

The standard deviation for the paired differences is

$$s_d = \sqrt{\frac{\Sigma(d - \bar{d})^2}{n-1}} = 18.02$$

The test statistic is calculated using Equation 10.15.

$$t = \frac{\bar{d} - \mu_d}{\frac{s_d}{\sqrt{n}}} = \frac{12.17 - 0.0}{\frac{18.02}{\sqrt{6}}} = 1.6543$$

Step 6 Reach a decision.
Because $t = 1.6543 < t_{0.01} = 3.3649$, do not reject the null hypothesis.

Step 7 Draw a conclusion.
Based on these sample data, there is insufficient evidence to conclude that name-brand ink cartridges produce more pages on average than generic brands.

10-3: Exercises

Skill Development

10-36. The following sample data have been collected from a paired sample from two populations. The claim is that the first population mean will be at least as large as the mean of the second population. This claim will be assumed to be true unless the data strongly suggest otherwise.

Sample 1	Sample 2
4.4	3.7
2.7	3.5
1.0	4.0
3.5	4.9
2.8	3.1
2.6	4.2
2.4	5.2
2.0	4.4
2.8	4.3

a. State the appropriate null and alternative hypotheses.
b. Based on the sample data, what should you conclude about the null hypothesis? Test using $\alpha = 0.10$.
c. Calculate a 90% confidence interval for the difference in the population means. Are the results from the confidence interval consistent with the outcome of your hypothesis test? Explain why.

10-37. The following dependent samples were randomly selected. Use the sample data to construct a 95% confidence interval estimate for the population mean paired difference.

Sample 1	Sample 2
22	31
25	24
27	25
26	32
22	25
21	27
23	31
25	27
28	31
27	31
23	26

10-38. You are given the following results of a paired-difference test:

$$\bar{d} = -4.6$$
$$s_d = 0.25$$
$$n = 16$$

a. Construct and interpret a 99% confidence interval estimate for the paired difference in mean values.
b. Construct and interpret a 90% confidence interval estimate for the paired difference in mean values.

10-39. A paired sample study has been conducted to determine whether two populations have equal means. Twenty paired samples were obtained with the following sample results:

$$\bar{d} = 12.45 \qquad s_d = 11.0$$

Based on these sample data and a significance level of 0.05, what conclusion should be made about the population means?

10-40. The following paired samples have been obtained from normally distributed populations. Construct a 90% confidence interval estimate for the mean paired difference between the two population means.

Sample #	Sample 1	Sample 2
1	3,693	4,635
2	3,679	4,262
3	3,921	4,293
4	4,106	4,197
5	3,808	4,536
6	4,394	4,494
7	3,878	4,094

10-41. The following samples are observations taken from the same elements at two different times:

Unit	Sample 1	Sample 2
1	15.1	4.8
2	12.3	5.7
3	14.9	6.2
4	17.5	9.4
5	18.1	2.3
6	18.4	4.7

a. Assume that the populations are normally distributed and construct a 90% confidence interval for the difference in the means of the distribution at the times in which the samples were taken.

b. Perform a test of hypothesis to determine if the difference in the means of the distribution at the first time period is 10 units larger than at the second time period. Use a level of significance equal to 0.10.

10-42. Consider the following set of samples obtained from two normally distributed populations whose variances are equal:

Sample 1:	11.2	11.2	7.4	8.7	8.5	13.5	4.5	11.9
Sample 2:	11.7	9.5	15.6	16.5	11.3	17.6	17.0	8.5

a. Suppose that the samples were independent. Perform a test of hypothesis to determine if there is a difference in the two population means. Use a significance level of 0.05.

b. Now suppose that the samples were paired samples. Perform a test of hypothesis to determine if there is a difference in the two population means.

c. How do you account for the difference in the outcomes of part a and part b? Support your assertions with a statistical rationale.

Business Applications

10-43. Production engineers at Corbatron believe that a modified layout on its assembly lines might increase average worker productivity (measured in the number of units produced per hour). However, before the engineers are ready to install the revised layout officially across the entire firm's production lines, they would like to study the modified line's effects on output. The following data represent the average hourly production output of 12 randomly sampled employees before and after the line was modified:

Employee	*1*	*2*	*3*	*4*	*5*	*6*	*7*	*8*	*9*	*10*	*11*	*12*
Before	49	45	43	44	48	42	46	46	49	42	46	44
After	49	46	48	50	46	50	45	46	47	51	51	49

At the 0.05 level of significance, can the production engineers conclude that the modified (after) layout has increased average worker productivity?

10-44. The United Way raises money for community charity activities. Recently, in one community, the fund-raising committee was concerned about whether there is a difference in the proportion of employees who give to United Way, depending on whether the employer is a private business or a government agency. A random sample of people who had been contacted about contributing last year was selected. Of those contacted, 70 worked for a private business and 50 worked for a government agency. For the 70 private-sector employees, the mean contribution was $230.25 with a standard deviation equal to $55.52. For the 50 government employees in the sample the mean and standard deviation was $309.45 and $61.75 respectively.

a. Based on these sample data and $\alpha = 0.05$, what should be concluded? Be sure to show the decision rule.

b. Construct a 95% confidence interval for the difference between the mean contributions of private business and government agency employees who contribute to United Way. Do the hypothesis test and the confidence interval produce compatible results? Explain and give reasons for your answer.

10-45. An article on the PureEnergySystems.com Web site written by Louis LaPoint discusses a product called Acetone. The article stated that "acetone (CH_3COCH_3) is a product that can be purchased inexpensively in most locations around the world, such as in common hardware, auto parts, or drug stores. Added to the fuel tank in tiny amounts, acetone aids in the vaporization of the gasoline or diesel, increasing fuel efficiency, engine longevity, and performance—as well as reducing hydrocarbon emissions." To test whether this product actually does increase fuel efficiency in passenger cars, a consumer group has randomly selected 10 people to participate in the study. The following procedure was used:

1. People are to bring their cars into a specified gasoline station and have the car filled with regular, unleaded gasoline at a particular pump. Nothing extra is added to the gasoline at this fill-up. The car's odometer is recorded at the time of fill-up.

2. When the tank is nearly empty, the person is to bring the car to the same gasoline station and pump and have it refilled with gasoline. The odometer is read again and the miles per gallon are recorded. This time, a rescribed quantity of acetone is added to the fuel.

3. When the tank is nearly empty, the person is to bring the car back to the same station and pump to have it filled. The miles per gallon will be recorded.

Each person is provided with free tanks of gasoline and asked to drive their car normally.

The following miles per gallon were recorded:

Driver	MPG: No Additive	MPG: Acetone Added
1	18.4	19.0
2	23.5	22.8
3	31.4	30.9
4	26.5	26.9
5	27.2	28.4
6	16.3	18.2
7	19.4	19.2
8	20.1	21.4
9	14.2	16.1
10	22.1	21.5

a. Discuss the appropriateness of the way this study was designed and conducted. Why didn't they select two samples with different drivers in each and have one group use the acetone and the other group not use it? Discuss.

b. Using a significance level of 0.05, what conclusion should be reached based on these sample data? Discuss.

10-46. One of the advances that has helped to diminish carpal tunnel syndrome is ergonomic keyboards. The ergonomic keyboards may also increase typing speed. Ten administrative assistants were chosen to type on both standard and ergonomic keyboards. The resulting typing speeds follow:

Ergonomic:	69	80	60	71	73	64	63	70	63	74
Standard:	70	68	54	56	58	64	62	51	64	53

a. Were the two samples obtained independently? Support your assertion.

b. Conduct a hypothesis test to determine if the ergonomic keyboards increase the average words per minute attained while typing. Use a p-value approach with a significance level of 0.01.

10-47. An article in *The American Statistician* (M. L. R. Ernst, et al., "Scatterplots for unordered pairs," 50 (1996), pp. 260–265. Reports on the difference in the measurements by two evaluators of the cardiac output of 23 patients by using Doppler echocardiography. Both observers took measurements from the same patients. The measured outcomes were as follows:

Patient	1	2	3	4	5	6	7	8	9	10	11	12
Evaluator 1	4.8	5.6	6.0	6.4	6.5	6.6	6.8	7.0	7.0	7.2	7.4	7.6
Evaluator 2	5.8	6.1	7.7	7.8	7.6	8.1	8.0	8.21	6.6	8.1	9.5	9.6

Patient	13	14	15	16	17	18	19	20	21	22	23
Evaluator 1	7.7	7.7	8.2	8.2	8.3	8.5	9.3	10.2	10.4	10.6	11.4
Evaluator 2	8.5	9.5	9.1	10.0	9.1	10.8	11.5	11.5	11.2	11.5	12.0

a. Conduct a hypothesis test to determine if the average cardiac outputs measured by the two evaluators differ. Use a significance level of 0.02.

b. Calculate the standard error of the difference between the two average outputs assuming that the sampling was done independently. Compare this with the standard error obtained in part a.

Computer Database Exercises

10-48. A treadmill manufacturer has developed a new machine with softer tread and better fans than its current model. The manufacturer believes these new features will enable runners to run for longer times than they can on its current machines. To determine whether the desired result is achieved, the manufacturer randomly sampled 35 runners. Each runner was measured for one week on the current machine and for one week on the new machine. The weekly total number of minutes for each runner on the two types of machines was collected. The results are contained in the file **Treadmill**. At the 0.02 level of significance, can the treadmill manufacturer conclude that the new machine has the desired result?

10-49. The National Association of Home Builders published an article ("Housing Facts, Figures, and Trends," August 2005) summarizing characteristics of the housing market in the United States. Data are listed for the average and median selling prices for houses during the period 1995 to 2004 and also January to July of 2005. The file entitled **House** contains these data. Assume the data can be viewed as samples of the relevant populations.

a. Discuss whether the two samples are independent or dependent.

b. Based upon your answer to part a, calculate a 90% confidence interval for the difference between the means of the average and median selling prices for houses during the period 1995 to 2004.

c. Noting your answer to part b, would it be plausible to assert that the mean of the average selling prices for houses during the period 1995 to 2004 is more than the average of the median selling prices during this period? Support your assertions.

d. Using a *p*-value approach and a significance level of 0.05, conduct a hypothesis test to determine if the mean of the average selling prices for houses during the period 1995 to 2004 is more than $30,000 larger than the mean of the median selling prices during this period.

10-50. As the number of air travelers with time on their hands increases, it would seem that spending on retail purchases in airports would increase as well. A study by *Airport Revenue News* addressed the per person spending at selected airports for merchandise, excluding food, gifts, and news items. A file entitled **Revenues** contains sample data selected from airport retailers in 2001 and again in 2004.

a. Conduct a hypothesis test to determine if the average amount of retail spending by air travelers has increased as least as much as approximately 10 cents a year from 2001 to 2004. Use a significance level of 0.025.

b. Using the appropriate analysis (that of part a or other appropriate methodology), substantiate the statement that average retail purchases in airports increased over the time period between 2001 and 2004. Support your assertions.

c. Parts a and b give what seems to be a mixed message. Is there a way to determine what values are plausible for the difference between the average revenue in 2001 and 2004? If so, conduct the appropriate procedure.

10.4 Estimation and Hypothesis Tests for Two Population Proportions

The previous sections illustrated the methods for estimating and testing hypotheses involving two population means. There are many business situations in which these methods can be applied. However, there are other instances involving two populations in which the measures of interest are not the population means. For example, Chapter 9 introduced the methodology for testing hypotheses involving a single population proportion. This section extends that methodology to tests involving hypotheses about the difference between two population proportions. First, we will look at a confidence interval estimation involving two population proportions.

Estimating the Difference Between Two Population Proportions

Business Application

CHAPTER OUTCOME #3

V. C. ELROY AGENCY Advertising agencies spend a significant amount of time determining whether proposed advertisements will appeal to different market segments before the ads run on national media. Recently, the V. C. Elroy Agency in Chicago developed an advertising campaign for a national fast-food chain. Among the many issues the ad managers were interested in was the difference in how appealing males and females would find the ads.

Obviously, there was no way to gauge the attitudes of the entire population of men and women who would eventually see or hear the ads. Instead, the Elroy agency showed the ad campaign to a random sample of 425 men and 370 women. In the results that follow, the variable *x* indicates the number in the sample who said they liked the campaign.

Men	Women
$n_1 = 425$	$n_2 = 370$
$x_1 = 240$	$x_2 = 196$

Based on these sample data, the sample proportions are

$$p_1 = \frac{240}{425} = 0.565 \quad \text{and} \quad p_2 = \frac{196}{370} = 0.530$$

The point estimate for the difference in population proportions is

$$p_1 - p_2 = 0.565 - 0.530 = 0.035$$

So, the single best estimate for the difference in the proportion of men versus women who liked the ad campaign is 0.035. However, all point estimates are subject to sampling error. A confidence interval estimate for the difference in population proportions can be developed using Equation 10.16, providing the sample sizes are sufficiently large. A rule of thumb for "sufficiently large" is that np and $n(1 - p)$ are greater than or equal to 5 for both samples.

Confidence Interval Estimate for $\pi_1 - \pi_2$

$$(p_1 - p_2) \pm z \sqrt{\frac{p_1(1 - p_1)}{n_1} + \frac{p_2(1 - p_2)}{n_2}} \qquad \text{(10.16)}$$

where:

p_1 = Sample proportion from population 1
p_2 = Sample proportion from population 2
z = Critical value from the standard normal table

The Elroy managers can substitute the sample results into Equation 10.16 to establish a 95% confidence interval estimate, as follows:

$$(0.565 - 0.530) \pm 1.96 \sqrt{\frac{0.565(1 - 0.565)}{425} + \frac{0.530(1 - 0.530)}{370}}$$

$$0.035 \pm 0.069$$

$$-0.034 \leq (\pi_1 - \pi_2) \leq 0.104$$

Thus, based on the sample data and using a 95% confidence interval, the managers estimate that the true difference in proportion of males versus females who like the ad campaign is between −0.034 and 0.104. At one extreme, 3.4% more females like the ad than males. At the other extreme, 10.4% more males like the ad than females. Because zero is included in the interval, there may be no difference between males and females based on these data. Consequently, the managers are not able to conclude that one group or the other has a stronger preference for the fast-food ad campaign.

Hypothesis Tests for the Difference Between Two Population Proportions

Business Application

Excel and Minitab Tutorial

POMONA FABRICATIONS Pomona Fabrications, Inc., produces handheld hair dryers that several major retailers sell as in-house brands. A critical component of a handheld hair dryer is the motor-heater unit, which accounts for most of the dryer's cost and also for most of the product's reliability problems. Product reliability is important to Pomona because the company offers a one-year warranty. Of course, Pomona is also interested in reducing production costs.

Ponoma's research and development department has recently created a new motor-heater unit with fewer parts than the current unit, which would lead to a 15% cost savings per hair dryer. However, the company's vice president of product development is unwilling to authorize the new component unless it is more reliable than the current motor-heater.

The research and development department has decided to test samples of both units to see which motor-heater is more reliable. Two hundred fifty units of each type will be tested under conditions that simulate one year's use, and the proportion of each type that fails within that time will be recorded. This leads to the formulation of the following null and alternative hypotheses:

$$H_0: \pi_1 - \pi_2 \geq 0.0 \qquad \text{or} \qquad H_0: \pi_1 \geq \pi_2$$
$$H_A: \pi_1 - \pi_2 < 0.0 \qquad \qquad H_A: \pi_1 < \pi_2$$

where:

π_1 = Population proportion of new dryer type that fails in simulated one-year period
π_2 = Population proportion of existing dryer type that fails in simulated one-year period

The null hypothesis states that the new motor-heater is no better than the old, or current, motor-heater. The alternative states that the new unit has a smaller proportion of failures within one year than the current unit. In other words, the alternative states that the new unit is more reliable. The company wants clear evidence before changing units. If the null hypothesis is rejected, the company will conclude that the new motor-heater unit is more reliable than the old unit and should be used in producing the hair dryers. To test the null hypothesis, we can use the test statistic approach.

The test statistic is based on the sampling distribution of $p_1 - p_2$. In Chapter 7 we showed that when $n\pi \geq 5$ and $n(1 - \pi) \geq 5$, the sampling distribution of the sample proportion is approximately normally distributed, with a mean equal to π and a variance equal to $\pi(1-\pi)/n$.

Likewise, in the two-sample case, the sampling distribution of $p_1 - p_2$ will also be approximately normal if

Assumptions

$$n_1\pi_1 \geq 5, n_1(1 - \pi_1) \geq 5, \quad \text{and} \quad n_2\pi_2 \geq 5, n_2(1 - \pi_2) \geq 5$$

Because π_1 and π_2 are unknown, we substitute the sample proportions, p_1 and p_2, to determine whether the sample size requirements are satisfied.

The mean of the sampling distribution of $p_1 - p_2$ is the difference of the population proportions, $\pi_1 - \pi_2$. The variance is, however, the sum of the variances, $\pi_1(1-\pi_1)/n_1 + \pi_2(1-\pi_2)/n_2$. Because the test is conducted using the assumption that the null hypothesis is true, we assume that $\pi_1 = \pi_2 = \pi$ and estimate their common value, π, using a pooled estimate, as shown in Equation 10.17. The z-test statistic for the difference between two proportions is given as Equation 10.18.

Pooled Estimator for Overall Proportion

$$\bar{p} = \frac{n_1 p_1 + n_2 p_2}{n_1 + n_2} = \frac{x_1 + x_2}{n_1 + n_2} \tag{10.17}$$

where:

x_1 and x_2 = Number from samples 1 and 2 with the characteristic of interest

z-Test Statistic for Difference Between Population Proportions

$$z = \frac{(p_1 - p_2) - (\pi_1 - \pi_2)}{\sqrt{\bar{p}(1-\bar{p})\left(\frac{1}{n_1} + \frac{1}{n_2}\right)}} \tag{10.18}$$

where:

$(\pi_1 - \pi_2)$ = Hypothesized difference in proportions from populations 1 and 2, respectively
p_1 and p_2 = Sample proportions for samples selected from populations 1 and 2, respectively
$\bar{p}$ = Pooled estimator for the overall proportion for both populations combined

The reason for taking a weighted average in Equation 10.17 is to give more weight to the larger sample. Note that the numerator is the total number of items with the characteristic of interest in the two samples, and the denominator is the total sample size. Again, the pooled estimator, p is used when the null hypothesis is that there is no difference between the population proportions.

Assume that Pomona is willing to use a significance level of 0.05 and that 55 of the new motor-heaters and 75 of the originals failed the one-year test. Figure 10.9 illustrates the decision-rule development and the hypothesis test. As you can see, Pomona should reject the null hypothesis based on the sample data. Thus, the firm should conclude that the new motor-heater is more reliable than the old one. Because the new one is also less costly, the company should now use the new unit in the production of hair dryers.

The p-value approach to hypothesis testing could also have been used to test Pomona's hypothesis. In this case, the calculated value of the test statistic, $z = -2.04$, results in a p-value of 0.0207 ($0.5 - 0.4793$) from the standard normal table. Because this p-value is smaller than the significance level of 0.05, we would reject the null hypothesis. Remember, whenever your p-value is smaller than the alpha value, your sample contains evidence to reject the null hypothesis.

Both Minitab and the PHStat add-ins to Excel contain procedures for performing hypothesis tests involving two population proportions. Figures 10.10a and 10.10b show the PHStat output and the Minitab output for the Pomona example. The output contains both the z-test statistic and the p-value. As we observed from our manual calculations, the difference in sample proportions is sufficient to reject the null hypothesis that there is no difference in population proportions.

FIGURE 10.9

Hypothesis Test of Two Population Proportions for Pomona Fabrications

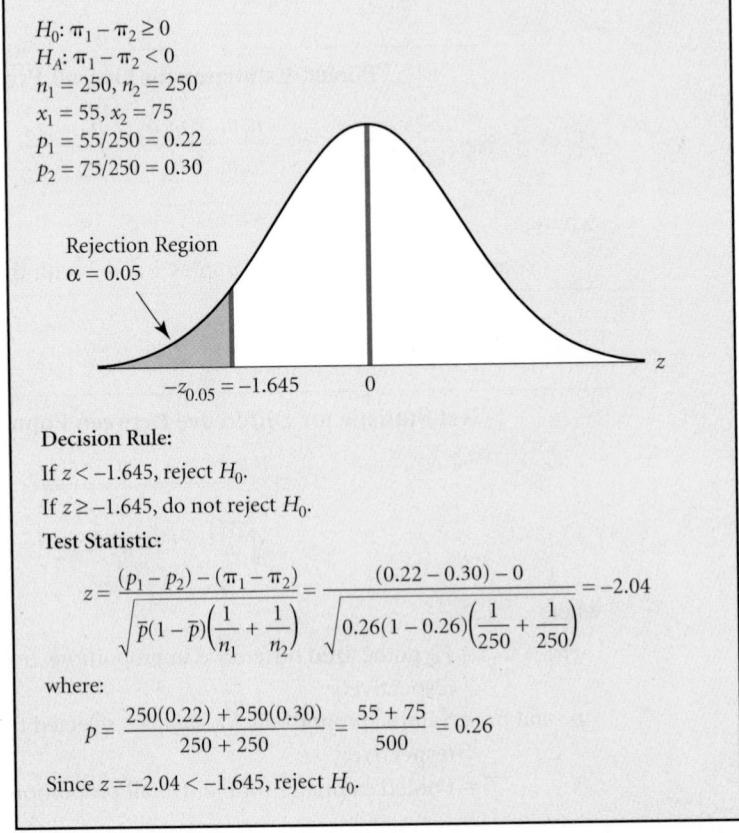

$H_0: \pi_1 - \pi_2 \geq 0$
$H_A: \pi_1 - \pi_2 < 0$
$n_1 = 250, n_2 = 250$
$x_1 = 55, x_2 = 75$
$p_1 = 55/250 = 0.22$
$p_2 = 75/250 = 0.30$

Rejection Region
$\alpha = 0.05$

$-z_{0.05} = -1.645$ 0 z

Decision Rule:

If $z < -1.645$, reject H_0.

If $z \geq -1.645$, do not reject H_0.

Test Statistic:

$$z = \frac{(p_1 - p_2) - (\pi_1 - \pi_2)}{\sqrt{\bar{p}(1-\bar{p})\left(\frac{1}{n_1} + \frac{1}{n_2}\right)}} = \frac{(0.22 - 0.30) - 0}{\sqrt{0.26(1 - 0.26)\left(\frac{1}{250} + \frac{1}{250}\right)}} = -2.04$$

where:

$$p = \frac{250(0.22) + 250(0.30)}{250 + 250} = \frac{55 + 75}{500} = 0.26$$

Since $z = -2.04 < -1.645$, reject H_0.

FIGURE 10.10A

Excel 2007 (PHStat) Output of the Two Proportions Test for Pomona Fabrications

Excel 2007 (PHStat) Instructions:
1. Open blank worksheet.
2. Click on Add-Ins (Make sure PHStat is installed).
3. Select **PHStat**.
4. Select **Two Sample Test**.
5. Select **Z test for Differences in Two Proportions**.
6. Enter samples sizes and number of occurrences.
7. Specify **Alpha** equal to 0.05.
8. Indicate **Lower-tail test** option.
9. Click **OK**.

	A	B	C	D	E	F
4	Hypothesized Difference	0				
5	Level of Significance	0.05				
6	Group 1					
7	Number of Successes	55				
8	Sample Size	250				
9	Group 2					
10	Number of Successes	75				
11	Sample Size	250				
12						
13	Intermediate Calculations					
14	Group 1 Proportion	0.22				
15	Group 2 Proportion	0.3				
16	Difference in Two Proportions	-0.08				
17	Average Proportion	0.26				
18	Z Test Statistic	-2.039				
19						
20	Lower-Tail Test					
21	Lower Critical Value	-1.645				
22	p-Value	0.021				
23	Reject the null hypothesis					

FIGURE 10.10B

Minitab Output of the Two Proportions Test for Pomona Fabrications

Test and CI for Two Proportions

```
Sample   X    N   Sample p
1        55  250  0.220000
2        75  250  0.300000
```

$z = -2.04 < -1.645$
Reject the null hypothesis.

```
Difference = p (1) - p (2)
Estimate for difference:  -0.08
95% upper bound for difference:  -0.0157369
Test for difference = 0 (vs < 0):  Z = -2.04  P-Value = 0.021
```

Excel Instructions:
1. Choose **Stat > Basic Statistics > 2 Proportions**.
2. Choose **Summerized data**.
3. In **First** enter **Trials** and Events for sample 1. (e.g., 250 and 55).
4. In **Second** enter **Trials** and Events for sample 2. (e.g., 250 and 75).
5. Select **Options**, Insert $1 - \alpha$ in **Confidence level**.
6. In **Alternative** select *less than*.
7. Check **Use pooled estimate of p for test**.
8. Click **OK. OK**.

| EXAMPLE 10-8 | Hypothesis Test for the Difference Between Two Population Proportions |

TRY PROBLEM 10.51

Gregston Ticketing Gregston Ticketing is evaluating two suppliers of a scanning system it is considering purchasing. Both scanners are designed to detect forged tickets for sporting events. High-quality scanners and printers and home computers have made forged tickets an increasing industry problem. The company is interested in determining whether there is a difference in the proportion of forged tickets detected by the two suppliers. To conduct this test, use the following steps:

Step 1 **Specify the population parameter of interest.**
In this case, the population parameter of interest is the population proportion of detected forged tickets. At issue is whether there is a difference between the two suppliers in terms of the proportion of forged tickets detected.

Step 2 **Formulate the appropriate null and alternative hypotheses.**
The null and alternative hypotheses are

$$H_0: \pi_1 - \pi_2 = 0.0$$
$$H_A: \pi_1 - \pi_2 \neq 0.0$$

Step 3 **Specify the significance level.**
The test will be conducted using an $\alpha = 0.02$.

Step 4 **Compute the z-test statistic using Equation 10.18 and apply it to the decision rule.**
Two hundred known forged tickets will be randomly selected and scanned by systems from each supplier. For supplier one, 186 forgeries are detected, and for supplier two, 168 are detected. The sample proportions are

$$p_1 = \frac{x_1}{n_1} = \frac{186}{200} = 0.93 \qquad p_2 = \frac{x_2}{n_2} = \frac{168}{200} = 0.84$$

The test statistic is then calculated using Equation 10.18.

$$z = \frac{(p_1 - p_2) - (\pi_1 - \pi_2)}{\sqrt{\bar{p}(1-\bar{p})\left(\frac{1}{n_1} + \frac{1}{n_2}\right)}}$$

where:

$$\bar{p} = \frac{n_1 p_1 + n_2 p_2}{n_1 + n_2} = \frac{200(0.93) + 200(0.84)}{200 + 200} = 0.885 \qquad \text{(see Equation 10.17)}$$

Then:

$$z = \frac{(0.93 - 0.84) - 0.0}{\sqrt{0.885(1 - 0.885)\left(\frac{1}{200} + \frac{1}{200}\right)}} = 2.8211$$

Step 5 **Construct the rejection region.**
For a two-tailed test, the critical values for each side of the distribution are

$$-z_{0.01} = -2.33 \text{ and } z_{0.01} = 2.33$$

The decision rule based on the z-test statistic is

If $z < -2.33$ or $z > 2.33$, reject the null hypothesis;
Otherwise, do not reject the null hypothesis.

Step 6 **Reach a decision.**
Because $z = 2.8211 > z_{0.01} = 2.33$, reject the null hypothesis.

Step 7 **Draw a conclusion.**
The difference between the two sample proportions does provide sufficient evidence to allow us to conclude a difference exists between the two suppliers.

10-4: Exercises

Skill Development

10-51. Given the following null and alternative hypotheses and level of significance:

$$H_0: \pi_1 = \pi_2$$
$$H_A: \pi_1 \neq \pi_2$$
$$\alpha = 0.10$$

together with the sample information:

Sample 1	Sample 2
$n_1 = 120$	$n_2 = 150$
$x_1 = 42$	$x_2 = 57$

conduct the appropriate hypothesis test using the p-value approach. What conclusion would be reached concerning the null hypothesis?

10-52. Given the following null and alternative hypotheses:

$$H_0: \pi_1 - \pi_2 \leq 0.0$$
$$H_A: \pi_1 - \pi_2 > 0.0$$

and the following sample information:

Sample 1	Sample 2
$n_1 = 60$	$n_2 = 80$
$x_1 = 30$	$x_2 = 24$

a. Based on $\alpha = 0.02$ and the sample information, what should be concluded with respect to the null and alternative hypotheses? Be sure to clearly show the decision rule.

b. Calculate the p-value for this hypothesis test. Based on the p-value, would the null hypothesis be rejected? Support your answer with calculations and/or reasons.

10-53. Given the following sample information randomly selected from two populations:

Sample 1	Sample 2
$n_1 = 200$	$n_2 = 150$
$x_1 = 40$	$x_2 = 27$

a. Determine if the sample sizes are large enough so that the sampling distribution for the difference between the sample proportions is approximately normally distributed.

b. Calculate a 95% confidence interval for the difference between the two population proportions.

10-54. In each of the following cases, determine if the sample sizes are large enough so that the sampling distribution of the differences in the sample proportions can be approximated with a normal distribution:

a. $n_1 = 15$, $n_2 = 20$, $x_1 = 6$, and $x_2 = 16$
b. $n_1 = 10$, $n_2 = 30$, $p_1 = 0.6$, and $x_2 = 19$
c. $n_1 = 25$, $n_2 = 16$, $x_1 = 6$, and $p_2 = 0.40$
d. $n_1 = 100$, $n_2 = 75$, $p_1 = 0.05$, and $p_2 = 0.05$

10-55. Independent random samples of size 50 and 75 are selected. The sampling results in 35 and 35 successes, respectively. Test the following hypotheses:

a. $H_0: \pi_1 - \pi_2 = 0$ vs. $H_A: \pi_1 - \pi_2 \neq 0$. Use $\alpha = 0.05$.
b. $H_0: \pi_1 - \pi_2 \geq 0$ vs. $H_A: \pi_1 - \pi_2 < 0$. Use $\alpha = 0.05$.
c. $H_0: \pi_1 - \pi_2 \leq 0$ vs. $H_A: \pi_1 - \pi_2 > 0$. Use $\alpha = 0.025$.
d. $H_0: \pi_1 - \pi_2 = 0.05$ vs. $H_A: \pi_1 - \pi_2 \neq 0.05$. Use $\alpha = 0.02$.

Business Applications

10-56. Suppose a random sample of 100 U.S. companies taken in 2005 showed that 21 offered high-deductible health insurance plans to their workers. A separate random sample of 120 firms taken in 2006 showed that 30 offered high-deductible health insurance plans to their workers. Based on the sample results, can you conclude that there is a higher proportion of U.S. companies offering high-deductible health insurance plans to their workers in 2006 than in 2005? Conduct your hypothesis test at a level of significance $\alpha = 0.05$.

10-57. Suppose as part of a national study of economic competitiveness a marketing research firm randomly sampled 200 adults between the ages of 27 and 35 living in metropolitan Seattle and 180 adults between the ages of 27 and 35 living in metropolitan Minneapolis. Each adult selected in the sample was asked, among other things, whether or not they had a college degree. Sixty-six (66) adults from the Seattle sample answered yes and sixty-three (63) adults from the Minneapolis sample answered yes when asked if they had a college degree. Based on the sample data, can we conclude that there is a difference between the population proportions of adults between the ages of 27 and 35 in the two cities with college degrees? Use a level of significance of 0.01 to conduct the appropriate hypothesis test.

10-58. In an article entitled "Childhood pastimes are increasingly moving indoors," Dennis Cauchon (*USA Today*, July, 12, 2005) asserts that there have been huge declines in spontaneous outdoor activities such as bike riding, swimming, and touch football. Separate studies by the national Sporting Goods Association and American Sports Data indicate that bike riding alone is down 31% since 1995. According to the surveys, 68% of 7- to 11-year-olds rode a bike at least six times in 1995 and only 47% did in 2004. Assume the sample sizes were 1,500 and 2,000, respectively.

  a. Calculate a 95% confidence interval to estimate the proportion of 7- to 11-year-olds who rode their bike at least six times in 2004. Does this suggest that it is plausible to believe the proportion of 7- to 11-year-olds who rode their bike at least six times in 2004 is the same as in 1995?

  b. Conduct a test of hypothesis to answer the question posed in part a. Are the results of parts a and b contradictory? Explain.

10-59. The American College Health Association produced the National College Health Assessment (Andy Gardiner, "Surfacing from depression," February 6, 2006). The assessment indicates that the percentage of U.S. college students who report having been diagnosed with depression has risen from 2000. The assessment surveyed 47,202 students at 74 campuses. They discovered that 10.3% and 14.9% of students indicated that they had been diagnosed with depression in 2000 and 2004, respectively. Assume that half of the students surveyed were surveyed in 2004.

  a. Conduct a hypothesis test to determine if there has been more than a 0.04 increase in the proportion of students who indicate they have been diagnosed with depression. Use a significance level of 0.05 and a *p*-value approach to this test.

  b. Indicate the margin of error for estimating $\pi_1 - \pi_2$ with $p_1 - p_2$.

  c. Determine the smallest difference between the two proportions of students who indicate that they had been diagnosed with depression in 2000 and 2004 that the test in part a would be able to detect.

Computer Database Exercises

10-60. A marketing research firm is interested in determining whether there is a difference between the proportion of households in Chicago and the proportion of households in Milwaukee who purchase groceries online. The research firm decided to randomly sample households earning over $50,000 a year in the two cities and ask them if they purchased any groceries online last year. The random sample involved 150 Chicago households and 135 Milwaukee households. The results of the sample can be found in the file **On-line Groceries**.

  a. Construct a 95% confidence interval estimate for the difference between the two population proportions.

  b. At the 0.10 level of significance, can the marketing research firm conclude that a greater proportion of households in Chicago earning over $50,000 annually buys more groceries on-line than do similar households in Milwaukee? Support your answer with the appropriate hypothesis test.

10-61. As part of a nationwide study on home Internet use, researchers randomly sampled 150 urban households and 150 rural households. Among the questions asked of the sampled households was whether they used the Internet to download computer games. The survey results for this question are contained in the file **Internet Games**. Based on the sample results, can the researchers conclude that there is a difference between the proportion of urban households and rural households that use the Internet to download computer games? Conduct your test using a level of significance $\alpha = 0.01$.

10-62. The Boston Consulting Group released its 2005 ITC Study of 940 executives representing 68 countries. One of the questions on the survey examined if the executives ranked innovation as the top priority for the coming year. The responses from 400 executives in the United States and 300 in Asia are given in the file entitled **Priority**.

  a. Determine if the sample sizes are large enough to provide assurance that the sampling distribution of the difference in the sample proportion of executives who feel innovation is their top priority is normally distributed.

  b. Determine if the same proportion of U.S. and Asian executives feel that innovation is their top priority for the coming year. Use a significance value of 0.05 and the *p*-value approach.

10-63. *USA Today* notes (Mary Beth Marklein, "College gender gap widens: 57% are women," October 20, 2005) that there are more men than women ages 18–24 in the United States—15 million versus 14.2 million. The male/female ratio in colleges today is 42.6/57.4. However, there is a discrepancy in the percentage of males dependent upon their parents' income. The file entitled **Diversity** contains the gender of undergrads (18–24) whose parents income is in two categories: (1) low income— less than $30,000, and (2) upper income—$70,000 or more.

a. Determine if the sample sizes are large enough so that the sampling distribution of the difference between the sample proportions of male undergraduates in the two income categories can be approximated by a normal distribution.

b. Perform a test of hypothesis to determine that the proportion of male undergraduates in the upper income category is more than 1% greater than that of the low income category. Use a significance level of 0.01.

c. Calculate the difference between the two sample proportions. Given the magnitude of this difference, explain the results of part b.

Summary and Conclusions

Using sample information to reach conclusions about the population from which the sample was selected is common in business decision making. This inferential analysis takes on two forms: estimation and hypothesis testing. Chapter 8 introduced the fundamentals of statistical estimation. There we discussed how to formulate and interpret confidence interval estimates involving a single population parameter.

Chapter 9 introduced hypothesis testing in which we were interested in a single population parameter. It presented the basic concepts and discussed the types of statistical errors that can be made when a hypothesis is tested using sample information. In Chapter 10, we have extended the discussion of estimation and hypothesis testing to situations involving two populations. In some instances, the samples from the two populations are considered independent. In other cases, to control for potential sources of variation, we paired the samples and used a paired-sample test to determine whether the population means were different.

In addition to tests about population means, this chapter introduced estimating and hypothesis testing for two population proportions.

You may have difficulty in determining which procedure to use in a given situation. Figure 10.11 shows a flow diagram that you might find useful. As you work the problems at the end of the chapter, you might use this diagram to help you sort through the options.

Equations

Confidence Interval Format

Point Estimate $\pm$ (CriticalValue)(Standard Error) **(10.1)**

Standard Error of $\bar{x}_1 - \bar{x}_2$ When σ_1 and σ_2 Are Known

$$\sigma_{\bar{x}_1 - \bar{x}_2} = \sqrt{\frac{\sigma_1^2}{n_1} + \frac{\sigma_2^2}{n_2}} \qquad \textbf{(10.2)}$$

Confidence Interval Estimate for $\mu_1 - \mu_2$ When σ_1 and σ_2 Are Known, Independent Samples

$$(\bar{x}_1 - \bar{x}_2) \pm z \sqrt{\frac{\sigma_1^2}{n_1} + \frac{\sigma_2^2}{n_2}} \qquad \textbf{(10.3)}$$

Confidence Interval Estimate for $\mu_1 - \mu_2$ When σ_1 and σ_2 Are Unknown, Independent Samples

$$(\bar{x}_1 - \bar{x}_2) \pm ts_p \sqrt{\frac{1}{n_1} + \frac{1}{n_2}} \qquad \textbf{(10.4)}$$

Confidence Interval Estimate for $\mu_1 - \mu_2$ When σ_1 and σ_2 Are Unknown and Not Equal, Independent Samples

$$(\bar{x}_1 - \bar{x}_2) \pm t \sqrt{\frac{s_1^2}{n_1} + \frac{s_2^2}{n_2}} \qquad \textbf{(10.5)}$$

Degrees of Freedom for Estimating Difference Between Population Means When σ_1 and σ_2 Are Not Equal

$$df = \frac{(s_1^2/n_1)^2 + (s_2^2/n_2)^2}{\left(\dfrac{(s_1^2/n_1)^2}{n_1 - 1} + \dfrac{(s_2^2/n_2)^2}{n_2 - 1} \right)} \qquad \textbf{(10.6)}$$

FIGURE 10.11

Estimation and Hypothesis Testing Flow Diagram

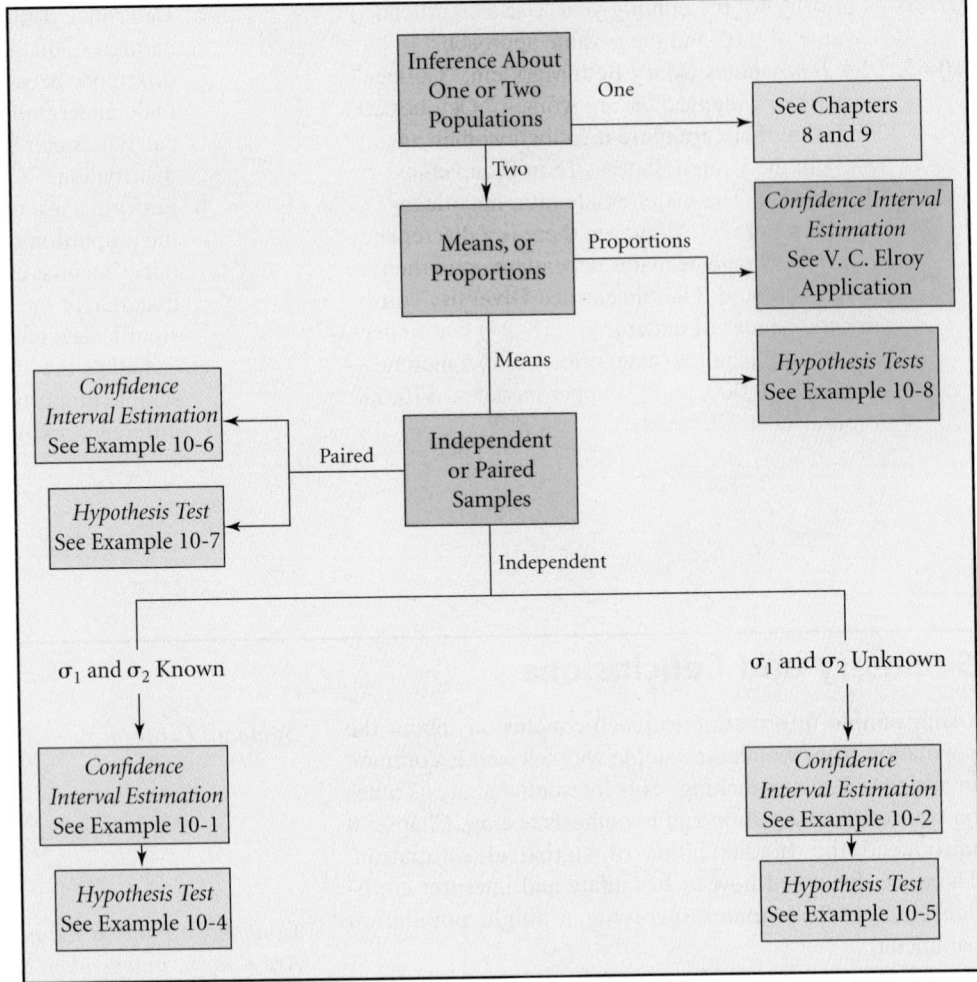

---

z-Test Statistic for $\mu_1 - \mu_2$ When σ_1 and σ_2 Are Known and Assumed Equal, Independent Samples

$$z = \frac{(\bar{x}_1 - \bar{x}_2) - (\mu_1 - \mu_2)}{\sqrt{\dfrac{\sigma_1^2}{n_1} + \dfrac{\sigma_2^2}{n_2}}} \qquad \textbf{(10.7)}$$

t-Test Statistic for $\mu_1 - \mu_2$ When σ_1 and σ_2 Are Unknown and Assumed Equal, Independent Samples

$$t = \frac{(\bar{x}_1 - \bar{x}_2) - (\mu_1 - \mu_2)}{s_p\sqrt{\dfrac{1}{n_1} + \dfrac{1}{n_2}}}, \quad df = n_1 + n_2 - 2 \quad \textbf{(10.8)}$$

t-Test Statistic for $\mu_1 - \mu_2$ When Population Variances Are Unknown and Not Assumed Equal

$$t = \frac{(\bar{x}_1 - \bar{x}_2) - (\mu_1 - \mu_2)}{\sqrt{\dfrac{s_1^2}{n_1} + \dfrac{s_2^2}{n_2}}} \qquad \textbf{(10.9)}$$

Degrees of Freedom for t-Test Statistic When Population Variances Are Not Equal

$$df = \frac{(s_1^2/n_1 + s_2^2/n_2)^2}{\left(\dfrac{(s_1^2/n_1)^2}{n_1 - 1} + \dfrac{(s_2^2/n_2)^2}{n_2 - 1}\right)} \qquad \textbf{(10.10)}$$

Paired Difference

$$d = x_1 - x_2 \qquad \textbf{(10.11)}$$

Point Estimate for the Population Mean Paired Difference, μ_d

$$\bar{d} = \frac{\displaystyle\sum_{i=1}^{n} d_i}{n} \qquad \textbf{(10.12)}$$

Sample Standard Deviation for Paired Differences

$$s_d = \sqrt{\frac{\displaystyle\sum_{i=1}^{n} (d_i - \bar{d})^2}{n - 1}} \qquad \textbf{(10.13)}$$

Confidence Interval Estimate for Population Mean Paired Difference, μ_d

$$\bar{d} \pm t \frac{s_d}{\sqrt{n}} \qquad \textbf{(10.14)}$$

t-Test Statistic for Paired-Sample Test

$$t = \frac{\bar{x}_d - \mu_d}{\frac{s_d}{\sqrt{n}}}, \qquad df = (n-1) \qquad \textbf{(10.15)}$$

Confidence Interval Estimate for $\pi_1 - \pi_2$

$$(p_1 - p_2) \pm z \sqrt{\frac{p_1(1-p_1)}{n_1} + \frac{p_2(1-p_2)}{n_2}} \qquad \textbf{(10.16)}$$

Pooled Estimator for Overall Proportion

$$\bar{p} = \frac{n_1 p_1 + n_2 p_2}{n_1 + n_2} = \frac{x_1 + x_2}{n_1 + n_2} \qquad \textbf{(10.17)}$$

z-Test Statistic for Difference Between Population Proportions

$$z = \frac{(p_1 - p_2) - (\pi_1 - \pi_2)}{\sqrt{\bar{p}(1-\bar{p})\left(\frac{1}{n_1} + \frac{1}{n_2}\right)}} \qquad \textbf{(10.18)}$$

Key Terms

Independent samples	430	Paired samples	456

Chapter Exercises

Conceptual Questions

10-64. Explain, in nontechnical terms, why pairing observations, if possible, is often a more effective tool than is taking independent samples.

10-65. Why, when dealing with two independent samples where you cannot assume the population variances are equal, should the degrees of freedom be adjusted?

10-66. Consider the following set of samples obtained from two normally distributed populations whose variances are equal:

Sample 1:	11.2	11.2	7.4	8.7	8.5	13.5	4.5	11.9
Sample 2:	11.7	9.5	15.6	16.5	11.3	17.6	17.0	8.5

a. Suppose that the samples were independent. Perform a test of hypothesis to determine if there is a difference in the two population means. Use a significance level of 0.05.

b. Now suppose that the samples were paired samples. Perform a test of hypothesis to determine if there is a difference in the two population means.

c. How do you account for the difference in the outcomes of part a and part b? Support your assertions with a statistical rationale.

10-67. Examine the following information:

	Sample 1	Sample 2
n_i	15	10
$\bar{x}_i$	12	7
s_i	3	4

a. Construct a 95% confidence interval for $\mu_1 - \mu_2$.

b. Calculate the test statistic that would be used to determine if $\mu_1 - \mu_2 =$ the upper confidence limit. Given this, what would be the result of the test be if you wish to test $\mu_1 - \mu_2 =$ (any value larger than the upper confidence limit)?

c. Calculate the test statistic that would be used to determine if $\mu_1 - \mu_2 =$ the lower confidence limit. Given this, what would be the result of the test be if you wish to test $\mu_1 - \mu_2 =$ (any value smaller than the lower confidence limit)?

d. Given your answers to parts b and c, how could you use the confidence interval to conduct a two-tailed hypothesis test?

Business Applications

10-68. The Wilcox Company sells breakable china through a mail-order system that has been very profitable. One of its major problems is freight damage. It insures the items at shipping, but the inconvenience to the customer when a piece gets broken can cause the customer not to place another order in the future. Thus, packaging is important to the Wilcox Company.

In the past, the company has purchased two different packaging materials from two suppliers. The assumption was that there would be no difference in the proportion of damaged shipments resulting from use of either packaging material. The sales manager recently decided a study of this issue should be done. Therefore, a random sample of 300 orders using shipping material 1 and a random sample of 250 orders using material 2 were pulled from the files. The number of damaged parcels, x, was recorded for each material as follows:

Material 1	Material 2
$n_1 = 300$	$n_2 = 250$
$x_1 = 19$	$x_2 = 12$

a. Is the normal distribution a good approximation for the distribution of the difference between the sample proportions? Provide support for your answer.
b. Based on the sample information and $\alpha = 0.03$, what should the Wilcox Company conclude?

10-69. Allstate Insurance is one of the major automobile insurance companies in the country. Recently, the western region claims manager instructed an intern in her department to develop a confidence interval estimate of the difference between the mean years that male customers have been insured by Allstate versus female customers. The intern randomly selected 13 male and 13 female customers from the account records and recorded the number of years that the customer had been insured by Allstate. These data (rounded to the nearest year) are as follows:

Males				Females			
14	9	9	16	3	10	4	7
14	8	12	11	10	5	4	1
6	9	10	7	4	4	6	9
3				2			

Based on these data, construct and interpret a 90% confidence interval estimate for the difference between the mean years for male and female customers.

10-70. Bach Photographs is a photography business with studios in two locations. The owner is interested in monitoring business activity closely at the two locations. Among the factors in which he is interested is whether the mean customer orders per day for the two locations is the same. A random sample of 11 days' orders for the two locations showed the following data:

Location A			Location B		
$444	$478	$501	$233	$127	$230
200	400	350	299	250	300
167	250	300	800	340	400
300	600		780	370	

The owner wishes to know the difference between the average amount in customer orders per day for the two locations. He has no idea what this difference might be. What procedure would you use under these circumstances? Explain your reasoning.

10-71. A student group is conducting a study to determine whether there is a difference between textbook prices for new textbooks sold by the on-campus bookstore at a university located in the Midwest and an Internet retailer. A random sample of 10 textbooks was taken and the campus price and the Internet retailer's price for each textbook were collected. At the 0.01 level of significance, can the student group conclude that there is a difference in average textbook prices for new textbooks sold on campus and over the Internet?

Textbook	Physics	Chemistry	Spanish	Accounting	Calculus
Campus	108	114	114	110	118
Internet	124	120	107	112	122

Textbook	Economics	Art	Biology	History	English
Campus	108	119	115	119	114
Internet	123	125	108	117	119

10-72. Turbo-Tax and Tax-Cut are the two of the best-selling tax preparation software packages. Recently, a consumer group conducted a test to estimate the difference in the mean time it would take an individual to complete their federal income tax using these two products. To run the test, they selected a random sample of 16 people. All 16 people used both software packages to complete their taxes. Half of the people were assigned Turbo-Tax first followed by Tax-Cut. The other half used the products in the opposite order. The following values represent the time in minutes that it took to complete the returns:

Individual	Turbo-Tax	Tax-Cut
1	70	88
2	56	71
3	79	89
4	94	66
5	93	78
6	101	64
7	42	74
8	71	99
9	91	79
10	59	68
11	65	93
12	50	93
13	47	86
14	60	86
15	63	81
16	43	83

Based on these sample data, construct and interpret a 95% confidence interval estimate for the difference between the two population means.

10-73. The National Association of Realtors 2005 profile of home buyers and sellers indicates that the percentage of home buyers who are single women has more than doubled since 1981, while the percentages of home buyers who are single men has declined. This despite evidence indicating that women's salaries still lag those of men. The association's profile states that the median income for men and women home buyers was $58,939 and $47,315, respectively. Assume the respective standard deviations and sample sizes were $10,000 and $9,000 and 200 and 302.

a. Conduct a hypothesis test to determine if the median income for men buying homes is more than $10,000 larger than that of women. Use a significance level of 0.05.

b. Describe any additional assumptions required to validate the results of the hypothesis test in part a.

10-74. In an article entitled "Airport screeners' strains, sprains highest among workers" (*USA Today*, January 11, 2006), Thomas Frank reported that the injury rate for airport screeners was 29%, far exceeding the 4.5% injury rate for the rest of the federal workforce. Assume the sample sizes required to obtain these percentages were 75 and 125, respectively.

a. Determine if the sample sizes were large enough to allow the distribution of the difference of the sample proportions to be approximated with a normal distribution.

b. Conduct a hypothesis test to determine if the injury rate of airport screeners is more than 10%

larger than that of the rest of the federal workforce. Use a significance level of 0.05.

Computer Database Exercises

10-75. One of the statistics that the College Board monitors is the rising tuition at private and public four-year colleges. The tuition and fees for private and public four-year colleges for the 1980–81 academic year in 2005 dollars were $8,180 and $1,818, respectively. The file entitled **College$** contains data that yields the same average tuition and fees (adjusted for inflation) for colleges in private and public four-year colleges obtained by the College Board for 2005–2006.

a. Do the data indicate that the gap between tuition and fees at private and public colleges has more than doubled in the 2005–2006 academic year as compared to that of the 1980–81 academic year? Use a significance level of 0.01. Assume the population variances are equal.

b. What statistical error could have been made if one were made based on the decision reached in part a? Provide an explanation.

10-76. Reviewers from the Oregon Evidence-based Practice Center at the Oregon Health and Science University investigated the effectiveness of prescription drugs in assisting people to fall asleep and stay asleep. The Oregon reviewers, led by Susan Carson, M.P.H., concluded that Sonata was better than Ambien at putting people to sleep quickly, while patients on Ambien slept longer and reported having a better quality sleep than those taking Sonata. Samples taken by Carson and her associates are contained in a file entitled **Shuteye**. The samples reflect an experiment in which individuals were randomly given the two brands of pills on separate evenings. Their time spent sleeping was recorded for each of the brands of sleeping pills.

a. Does the experiment seem to have dependent or independent samples? Explain your reasoning.

b. Do the data indicate that the researchers were correct? Conduct a statistical procedure to determine this.

c. Conduct a procedure to determine the plausible differences in the average number of hours slept by those taking Ambien and Sonata.

10-77. As part of a study on student loan debt, a national agency that underwrites student loans is examining the differences in student loan debt for undergraduate students. One question that the agency would like to address specifically is whether the mean undergraduate debt of Hispanic students graduating in 2005 is less than the mean undergraduate debt of Asian-American students graduating in 2005. To conduct the study, a random sample of 92

Hispanic students and a random sample 110 Asian-American students who completed an undergraduate degree in 2005 was taken. The undergraduate debt incurred for financing college for each sampled student was collected. The sample results can be found in the file **Student Debt**.

a. Assume that the agency believes the two populations from which the samples were taken are approximately normally distributed with equal variances. Conduct a hypothesis test at the 0.01 level of significance to determine whether the mean undergraduate debt for Hispanic students is less than the mean undergraduate debt for Asian-American students.

b. For what values of alpha would your decision in part a change?

c. Suppose the agency is unwilling to assume the two populations from which the samples are taken are approximately normally distributed with equal variances. Conduct the appropriate test to determine whether the mean undergraduate debt for Hispanic students is less than the mean undergraduate debt for Asian-American students. Use the *p*-value approach to conduct the test. State a conclusion.

10-78. Vintner Mortgage Company in Chicago, Illinois, markets residential and commercial loans to customers in the region. Recently, the company's board of directors asked whether the company had experienced a difference in the proportion of loan defaults between residential and commercial customers. To prepare an answer to this question, company officials selected a random sample of 200 residential loans and 105 commercial loans that had been issued prior to 1995. The loans were analyzed to determine their status. A loan that is still being paid was labeled "Active" and a default loan was labeled "Default." The resulting data are in a file called **Vintner**.

a. Based on the sample data and a significance level equal to 0.05, does there appear to be a difference in the proportion of loan defaults between residential and commercial customers?

b. Prepare a short response to the Vintner board of directors. Include in your report a graph of the data that supports your statistical analysis.

c. Consider the outcome of the hypothesis test in part a. In the last five audits, 10 residential and 10 commercial customers were selected. In three of the audits, there were more residential than commercial loan defaults. Determine the probability of such an occurrence.

CASE 10.1

Motive Power Company—Part 1

Cregg Hart is manufacturing manager for Motive Power Company, a locomotive engine and rail car manufacturer. The company has been very successful in recent years, and in July 2006 signed two major contracts totaling nearly $200 million. A key to the company's success has been its focus on quality. Customers from around the world have been very pleased with the attention to detail put forth by Motive Power.

One of the things Cregg has been adamant about is that Motive Power's suppliers also provide high quality. As a result, when the company finds good suppliers, it stays with them and tries to establish a long-term relationship. However, Cregg must also factor in the costs of parts and materials and has instructed his purchasing staff to be on the lookout for "better deals."

Recently, Sheryl Carleson, purchasing manager at Motive Power, identified a new rivet supplier in Europe that claims its rivets are as good or better quality than Motive Power's current supplier's but at a much lower cost. One key quality factor is the rivet diameter. When Sheryl approached Cregg about the possibility of going with the new supplier for rivets, he suggested that they conduct a test

to determine if there is any difference in the average diameter of the rivets from the two companies. Sheryl requested that the new company send 100 rivets and she pulled a random sample of 100 rivets from her inventory of rivets from the original supplier. She then asked an intern to measure the diameters to three decimal places using a micrometer. The resulting data from both suppliers is given in the CD-ROM file called **Motive Power**.

Required Tasks:

1. Develop histograms showing the distribution of rivet diameters from the two suppliers.
2. Compute the sample means and standard deviations for the two sets of data.
3. Comment on whether it appears the assumptions required for testing if the two populations have equal mean diameters are satisfied.
4. Select a level of significance for testing whether the two suppliers have rivets with equal mean diameters. Discuss the factors you used in arriving at the level of significance you have selected.
5. Perform the appropriate null and alternative hypothesis test. Discuss the results.
6. Prepare a short report outlining your recommendation.

CASE 10.2

Hamilton Marketing Services

Alex Hamilton founded Hamilton Marketing Services in 1999 after leaving a major marketing consulting firm in Chicago. Hamilton Marketing Services focuses on small- to medium-sized retail firms and has been quite successful in providing a wide range of marketing and advertising services.

A few weeks ago, a relatively new customer that Alex himself has been working with for the past several months called with an idea. This customer, a pet grooming company, is interested in changing the way it prices its full-service dog grooming service. The customer is considering two options: (1) a flat $40.00 per visit price and (2) a $30.00 per visit price if the dog owner signs up for a series of four groomings. However, the pet grooming service is unsure how these options would be received by its customers. The owner was hoping there was some type of study Alex could have his company do that would provide information on what the difference in response rate would be for the two pricing options. He was interested in determining if one option would bring in more revenue than the other.

At the time, Alex suggested that a flier with an attached coupon be sent to a random sample of potential customers. One sample of customers would receive the coupon listing the $40.00 price. A second sample of customers would receive the coupon listing the $30.00 price and the requirement for signing up for a series of four visits. Each coupon would have an expiration date of one month from the date of issue. Then the pet grooming store owner could track the responses to these coupon offers and bring the data back to Alex for analysis.

Yesterday, the pet store owner e-mailed an Excel file called **Grooming Price Test** to Alex. Alex has now asked you to assist with the analysis. He has mentioned using a 95% confidence interval and wants a short report describing the data and summarizing which pricing strategy is preferred both from a proportion-response standpoint and from a revenue-producing standpoint.

CASE 10.3

Green Valley Assembly Company

The Green Valley Assembly Company assembles consumer electronics products for manufacturers that need temporary extra production capacity. As such, it has periodic product changes. Because the products Green Valley assembles are marketed under the label of well-known manufacturers, high quality is a must.

Tom Bradley of the Green Valley personnel department has been very impressed by recent research concerning job-enrichment programs. In particular, he has been impressed with the increases in quality that seem to be associated with these programs. However, some studies have shown no significant increase in quality, and they imply that the money spent on such programs has not been worthwhile.

Tom has talked to Sandra Hansen, the production manager, about instituting a job-enrichment program in the assembly operation at Green Valley. Sandra was somewhat pessimistic about the potential, but she agreed to introduce the program. The plan was to implement the program in one wing of the plant and continue with the current method in the other wing. The procedure was to be in effect for six months. After that period, a test would be made to determine the effectiveness of the job-enrichment program.

After the six-month trial period, a random sample of employees from each wing produced the following output measures:

Old	Job-Enriched
$n_1 = 50$	$n_2 = 50$
$\bar{x}_1 = 11/hr$	$\bar{x}_2 = 9.7/hr$
$s_1 = 1.2/hr$	$s_2 = 0.9/hr$

Both Sandra and Tom wonder whether the job-enrichment program has affected production output. They would like to use these sample results to determine whether the average output has changed and to determine whether the employees' consistency has been affected by the new program.

A second sample from each wing was selected. The measure was the quality of the products assembled. In the "old" wing, 79 products were tested and 12% were found to be defectively assembled. In the "job-enriched" wing, 123 products were examined and 9% were judged defectively assembled.

With all these data, Sandra and Tom are beginning to get a little confused. However, they realize that there must be some way to use the information in order to make a judgment about the effectiveness of the job-enrichment program.

CASE 10.4

U-Need-It Rental Agency

Richard Fundt has operated the U-Need-It rental agency in a northern Wisconsin city for the past five years. One of the biggest rental items has always been chainsaws; lately, the demand for these saws has increased dramatically. Richard buys chainsaws at a special industrial rate and then rents them for $10 per day. The chainsaws are used an average of 50 to 60 days per year. Although Richard makes money on any chainsaw, he obviously makes more on those saws that last the longest.

Richard worked for a time as a repairperson and can make most repairs on the equipment he rents, including chainsaws. However, he would also like to limit the time he spends making repairs. U-Need-It is currently stocking two types of saws: North Woods and Accu-Cut. Richard has an impression that one of the models, Accu-Cut, does not seem to break down as much as the other. Richard currently has 8 North Woods saws and 11 Accu-Cut saws. He decides to keep track of the number of hours each is used between major repairs. He finds the following values, in hours:

Accu-Cut		North Woods	
48	46	48	78
39	88	44	94
84	29	72	59
76	52	19	52
41	57		
24			

The North Woods sales representative has stated that the company may be raising the price of its saws in the near future. This will make them slightly more expensive than the Accu-Cut models. However, the prices have tended to move with each other in the past.

References

Berenson, Mark L., and David M. Levine, *Basic Business Statistics Concepts and Applications*, 10th ed. (Upper Saddle River, NJ: Prentice Hall, 2006).

Cryer, Jonathan D., and Robert B. Miller, *Statistics for Business: Data Analysis and Modeling*, 2nd ed. (Belmont, CA: Duxbury Press, 1994).

Johnson, Richard A. and Dean W. Wichern, *Business Statistics: Decision Making with Data* (New York: John Wiley & Sons, 1997).

Larsen, Richard J., Morris L. Marx, and Bruce Cooil, *Statistics for Applied Problem Solving and Decision Making* (Pacific Grove, CA: Duxbury Press, 1997).

Microsoft Excel 2007 (Redmond, WA: Microsoft Corp., 2007).

Minitab for Windows Version 15 (State College, PA: Minitab, 2007).

Siegel, Andrew F., *Practical Business Statistics*, 5th ed. (Burr Ridge, IL: Irwin, 2003).

Chapter ELEVEN

Hypothesis Tests and Estimation for Population Variances

11.1 Hypothesis Tests and Estimation for a Single Population Variance

11.2 Hypothesis Tests for Two Population Variances

CHAPTER OUTCOMES

After studying the material in Chapter 11, you should be able to:

1. Formulate and carry out hypothesis tests for a single population variance.
2. Develop and interpret confidence interval estimates for a population variance.
3. Formulate and carry out hypothesis tests for the difference between two population variances.

PREPARING FOR CHAPTER ELEVEN

- Review material on calculating and interpreting sample means and variances in Chapter 3.

- Examine Section 9.1 on formulating null and alternative hypotheses.

- Make sure you understand the concepts of Type I and Type II error discussed in Chapter 9.

WHY YOU NEED TO KNOW

Chapters 9 and 10 introduced the concepts of hypothesis testing for one and two population means and proportions. There are also business situations where decision makers must reach a conclusion about the value of a single population variance, or about the relationship between two population variances. For example, knowing that a machine fills soda bottles with a specific average fill rate may not be enough. The manager must also be concerned about the variability in the fill rate. If the machine is too variable, then some bottles may be underfilled and will cause problems with consumers who believe they have been cheated. If the machine overfills the bottles, then soda is wasted and unnecessary costs are incurred in the bottling process. The manager in this case must monitor both the average fill and the variation in the fill of the bottling process. A manager may also be required to decide if there is a difference in the variability of sales between two different sales territories, or if the output of one production process is more or less variable than another. Just as we have tools and techniques involving population means and proportions, we also have tools and techniques for a single population variance and two population variances. In this chapter we discuss methods that can be used to make inferences concerning one and two population variances. The techniques presented in this chapter will also introduce new distributions that will be used in later chapters. When reading this chapter, keep in mind that the techniques discussed here are extensions of the estimation and hypothesis-testing concepts introduced in Chapters 8, 9 and 10.

11.1 Hypothesis Tests and Estimation for a Single Population Variance

In the previous three chapters, we concentrated on examples involving population means and proportions. However, in many cases you may also be as interested in the spread of a population as in its central location. For instance, military planes designed to penetrate enemy defenses have a ground-following radar system. The radar tells the pilot exactly how far the plane is above the ground. A radar unit that is correct *on the average* is useless if the readings are distributed widely around the average value. Many airport shuttle systems have stopping sensors to deposit passengers at the correct spot in a terminal. A sensor that, *on the average*, lets passengers off at the correct point could leave many irritated people long distances up and down the track. Therefore, many product specifications involve both an average value and some limit on the dispersion that the individual values can have. For example, the specification for a steel push pin may be an average length of 1.78 inches plus or minus 0.01 inch. A company using these pins would be interested in both the average length and how much these pins vary in length.

Business applications in which the population variance is important will use one of two statistical procedures: hypothesis tests or confidence interval estimates. In hypothesis-testing applications, a null hypothesis will be formulated in terms of σ^2. For example, a wood products company might hypothesize that the population variance in tree growth per year, σ^2, is no greater than 14.0 feet squared (remember, variance is in squared units). Then, based on sample data from the population of trees owned by the company, the null hypothesis will either be rejected or not rejected.

In other cases, the application might require the population variance be estimated. For instance, a marketing manager is planning to conduct a survey of restaurant customers to determine how many times per month they dine out. Before conducting the survey, she needs to determine the required sample size. One key factor in determining the sample size (see Chapter 9) is the value of the population variance. Thus, before she can determine the required sample size, she will need to estimate the population variance by taking a *pilot sample* and constructing a confidence interval estimate for σ^2.

Section 11.1 introduces the methods for testing hypotheses and for constructing confidence interval estimates for a single population variance.

Business Application

Chi-Square Test for One Population Variance

Usually when we think of measuring variation, the standard deviation is used as the measure because it is measured in the same units as the mean. Ideally, in the ground-following radar example, we would want to test to see whether the standard deviation exceeds a certain level, as determined by the product specifications. Unfortunately, there is no statistical test that directly tests the standard deviation. However, there is a procedure called the chi-square test that can be used to test the population variance. We can convert any standard deviation hypothesis test into one involving the variance, as shown in the following example.

Business Application

CHAPTER OUTCOME #1

H & L MACHINES H & L Machines services copy machines. Looking at past records and manufacturer recommendations, the company determined the mean service time for a properly trained staff working on a Kodak Image Source 85 should be 2 hours, with a standard deviation not to exceed 0.5 hour. Past data indicate that the 2-hour average is being achieved. However, variability may be excessive. The service schedule is built around the assumptions of $\mu = 2$ hours and $\sigma = 0.5$ hour. If the service-time standard deviation exceeds 0.5 hour, the service schedule gets disrupted.

The service manager has decided to select a random sample of service calls and use the sample data to determine whether the service-time standard deviation exceeds 0.5 hour. The methodology for conducting such a test is generally the same as for testing a population mean or proportion.

Ideally, the manager would like to test the following null and alternative hypotheses:

$$H_0: \sigma \leq 0.5$$
$$H_A: \sigma > 0.5$$

Because there is no statistical technique for directly testing hypotheses about a population standard deviation, she will use a test for a population variance. We first convert the standard deviation to a variance by squaring the standard deviation and then restate the null and alternative hypotheses as follows:

$$H_0: \sigma^2 \leq 0.25$$
$$H_A: \sigma^2 > 0.25$$

As with all hypothesis tests, the decision to reject or accept the null hypothesis will be based on the statistic computed from the sample. In testing hypotheses about a single population variance, the appropriate sample statistic is s^2, the *sample variance*.

To test a null hypothesis about a population variance, we compare s^2 with the hypothesized population variance, σ^2. To do this, we need to standardize the distribution of the sample variance in much the same way as we used the z-distribution and the t-distribution when testing hypotheses about the population mean.

Assumption

> If the random sample is from a normally distributed population, the distribution for the standardized sample variance is a *chi-square distribution*.

The chi-square distribution is a continuous distribution of a standardized random variable, computed by using Equation 11.1.

Chi-Square Test for a Single Population Variance

$$\chi^2 = \frac{(n-1)s^2}{\sigma^2} \tag{11.1}$$

where:

χ^2 = Standardized chi-square variable
n = Sample size
s^2 = Sample variance
σ^2 = Hypothesized variance

Examining Equation 11.1, you will note that this test statistic can be rewritten as

$$\chi^2 = \frac{(n-1)s^2}{\sigma^2} = \frac{(n-1)\dfrac{\Sigma(x-\bar{x})^2}{n-1}}{\sigma^2} = \frac{\Sigma(x-\bar{x})^2}{\sigma^2} = \Sigma\left(\frac{x-\bar{x}}{\sigma}\right)^2$$

If the sample is obtained from a normal distribution, the last expression inside the parentheses is essentially a z-value. Recall that $z = (x-\mu)/\sigma$. Therefore, χ^2 is the sum of squared z-values. When a z-value from a normal distribution is squared, it produces a chi-squared variable with 1 degree of freedom. The sum of n independent chi-squared variables is also a chi-squared random variable with n degrees of freedom. Here, however, we must estimate the population mean using the sample mean (because μ is unknown) before we estimate the population variance using s^2. You may recall from the discussion concerning degrees of freedom in Chapter 8 that this reduces the degrees of freedom by 1. Therefore, the distribution of χ^2 is a chi-squared distribution with $n-1$ degrees of freedom.

The central location and shape of the chi-square distribution depends only on the degrees of freedom, $n-1$. Figure 11.1 illustrates chi-square distributions for various degrees of freedom. Note that as the degrees of freedom increase, the chi-square distribution comes closer to being symmetrical.

Business Application

H & L MACHINES (*CONTINUED*) Returning to the H & L Machines example, suppose the dispatch manager took a random sample of 20 service calls and found a variance of 0.33 hour squared. Figure 11.2 illustrates the hypothesis test at a significance level of 0.10.

Appendix G contains a table of upper-tail chi-square critical values for various probabilities and degrees of freedom. The use of the chi-square table is similar to the use of the t-distribution table. For example, to find the critical value, $\chi^2_{0.10}$, for the H & L Machines example, determine the degrees of freedom, $n-1 = 20-1 = 19$, and the desired significance level, 0.10. Because this is an upper-tail, one-tail test, go to the chi-square table under the column headed 0.10 and find the χ^2 value in this column that intersects the row corresponding to the appropriate degrees of freedom. You should find the critical value of $\chi^2_{0.10} = 27.2036$.

As you can see in Figure 11.2, the chi-square test statistic, calculated using Equation 11.1, is

$$\chi^2 = \frac{(n-1)s^2}{\sigma^2} = \frac{(19)(0.33)}{0.25} = 25.08$$

This falls to the left of the rejection region, meaning the manager should not reject the null hypothesis based on these sample data. Thus, based on these results, there is insufficient evidence to conclude that the service representatives complete their service calls with a standard deviation of more than 0.5 hour.

FIGURE 11.1

Chi-Square Distributions

FIGURE 11.2

Chi-square Test for One Population Variance for the H & L Machines Example

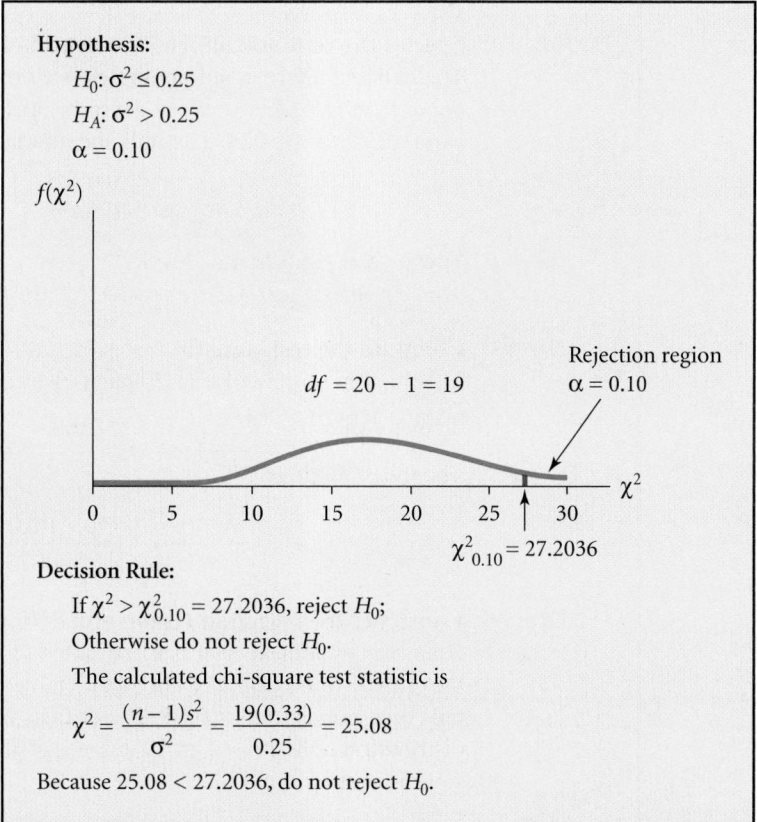

Hypothesis:

$H_0: \sigma^2 \le 0.25$

$H_A: \sigma^2 > 0.25$

$\alpha = 0.10$

$f(\chi^2)$

$df = 20 - 1 = 19$

Rejection region $\alpha = 0.10$

χ^2

$\chi^2_{0.10} = 27.2036$

Decision Rule:

If $\chi^2 > \chi^2_{0.10} = 27.2036$, reject H_0;

Otherwise do not reject H_0.

The calculated chi-square test statistic is

$$\chi^2 = \frac{(n-1)s^2}{\sigma^2} = \frac{19(0.33)}{0.25} = 25.08$$

Because 25.08 < 27.2036, do not reject H_0.

SUMMARY   Hypotheses Tests for a Single Population Variance

To conduct a hypothesis for a single population variance, you can use the following steps:

1. Specify the population parameter of interest.
2. Formulate the null and alternative hypotheses in terms of σ^2, the population variance.
3. Specify the level of significance for the hypothesis test.
4. Compute the test statistic.
   Select a random sample and compute the sample variance, $s^2 = \dfrac{\sum(x - \bar{x})^2}{n-1}$. Based on the sample variance, $\chi^2 = \dfrac{(n-1)s^2}{\sigma^2}$.

5. Construct the rejection region and define the decision rule. Obtain the critical value, χ^2_σ, from the chi-square distribution table.
6. Reach a decision.
7. Draw a conclusion.

TRY PROBLEM 11.1

EXAMPLE 11-1   One-Tailed Hypotheses Tests for a Population Variance

Abo Manufacturing Company   One specification listed in the contract between the Abo Manufacturing Company and its customers concerns the variability in the diameter of the part being supplied. Before shipping a batch of parts, Abo employees take a random sample of 20 parts from the batch and test to see whether the standard deviation exceeds the 0.05-inch specification. This can be done using the following steps:

Step 1   Specify the population parameter of interest.
   The standard deviation for the diameter of a part is the parameter of interest.

Step 2 Specify the null and alternative hypotheses.
The null and alternative hypotheses must be stated in terms of the population variance, so we convert the specification, $\sigma = 0.05$, to the variance, $\sigma^2 = 0.0025$. The null and alternative hypotheses are

$$H_0: \sigma^2 \le 0.0025$$
$$H_A: \sigma^2 > 0.0025$$

Step 3 Specify the significance level.
The hypothesis test will be conducted using $\alpha = 0.05$.

Step 4 Compute the test statistic.
The random sample of $n = 20$ parts gives a sample variance for part diameter of $s^2 = \dfrac{\sum(x - \bar{x})^2}{n - 1} = 0.0108$.
The test statistic is

$$\chi^2 = \frac{(n-1)s^2}{\sigma^2} = \frac{(20-1)0.0108}{0.0025} = 82.08$$

Step 5 Construct the rejection region and define the decision rule.
Note, this hypothesis test is a one-tailed, upper-tail test. Thus we obtain the critical value from the chi-square table where the area in the upper tail corresponds to $\alpha = 0.05$. The critical value from the chi-square distribution with $20 - 1 = 19$ degrees of freedom and 0.05 level of significance is

$$\chi_\alpha^2 = \chi_{0.05}^2 = 30.1435.$$

The decision rule is stated as

If $\chi^2 > \chi_{0.05}^2 = 30.1435$, reject H_0; otherwise, do not reject.

Step 6 Reach a decision.
Because $\chi^2 = 82.08 > 30.1435$, reject the null hypothesis.

Step 7 Draw a conclusion.
Conclude that the variance of the population does exceed the 0.0025 limit. The company appears to have a problem with its product variation.

EXAMPLE 11-2 | Two-Tailed Hypotheses Tests for a Population Variance

TRY PROBLEM 11.2

Smithfield Agriculture Company The operations manager for the Smithfield Agriculture Company headquartered in Omaha, Nebraska, has spent the past several years overseeing a major project in which the company has been experimenting with different combinations of wheat hybrids and fertilizer in an effort to increase average bushels per acre yield while reducing the variability in per acre yield. Consistent yield is desirable so that the company can more accurately project its total harvest. Based on studies completed prior to the 2006 growing season, the manager had determined that for a particular wheat variety and type of fertilizer, the average yield per acre was 88 bushels with a standard deviation of 6 bushels per acre. During the 2006 season, the manager conducted another test in which he used this same combination of wheat and fertilizer but modified the volume of fertilizer applied. He was interested in determining whether this change has impacted the standard deviation either up or down. The test was conducted on a random sample of 12 one-acre plots. The following data were recorded:

89	85	91	95
95	97	81	89
94	86	87	83

He can analyze this data using the following steps:

Step 1 **Specify the population parameter of interest.**
The manager is interested in the standard deviation of the yield per acre if this combination of wheat and fertilizer is used.

Step 2 **Specify the null and alternative hypotheses.**
The null and alternative hypotheses are stated in terms of the population variance since there is no test that deals specifically with the population standard deviation. Thus, we must convert the population standard deviation, $\sigma = 6$, to a variance, $\sigma^2 = 36$. Because the manager is interested in whether there has been a change (up or down), the test will be a two-tailed test with the null and alternative hypotheses formulated as follows:

$$H_0: \sigma^2 = 36$$
$$H_A: \sigma^2 \neq 36$$

Step 3 **Specify the significance level.**
The hypothesis test will be conducted using an $\alpha = 0.10$.

Step 4 **Compute the test statistic.**
The random sample of $n = 12$ acres gives a sample standard variance computed as

$$s^2 = \frac{\sum (x - \bar{x})^2}{n-1} = 26.6$$

Then the test statistic is

$$\chi^2 = \frac{(n-1)s^2}{\sigma^2} = \frac{(12-1)26.6}{36} = 8.13$$

Step 5 **Construct the rejection region and define the decision rule.**
Because this is a two-tail test, two critical values from the chi-square distribution in Appendix G are required, one for the upper (right) tail and one for the lower (left) tail. The alpha will be split evenly between the two tails with $\alpha/2 = 0.05$ in each tail. The degrees of freedom for the chi-square distribution is $n - 1 = 12 - 1 = 11$. The upper-tail critical value is found by locating the column headed 0.05 and going to the row for 11 degrees of freedom. This gives $\chi^2_{0.05} = 19.6752$. The lower critical value is found by going to the column headed 0.95 and to the row for 11 degrees of freedom. (Refer to Figure 11.3.) This gives $\chi^2_{0.95} = 4.5748$. Thus, the decision rule is

If $\chi^2 > \chi^2_{0.05} = 19.6752$, or if
$\chi^2 < \chi^2_{0.95} = 4.5748$, reject the null hypothesis;
Otherwise, do not reject the null hypothesis.

Step 6 **Reach a decision.**
Because $\chi^2 = 8.13 > \chi^2_{0.95} = 4.5748$ and $\chi^2 = 8.13 < \chi^2_{0.05} = 19.6752$, do not reject the null hypothesis based on these sample data.

FIGURE 11.3

Chi-square Rejection Regions for Two-Tailed Test of One Population Variance

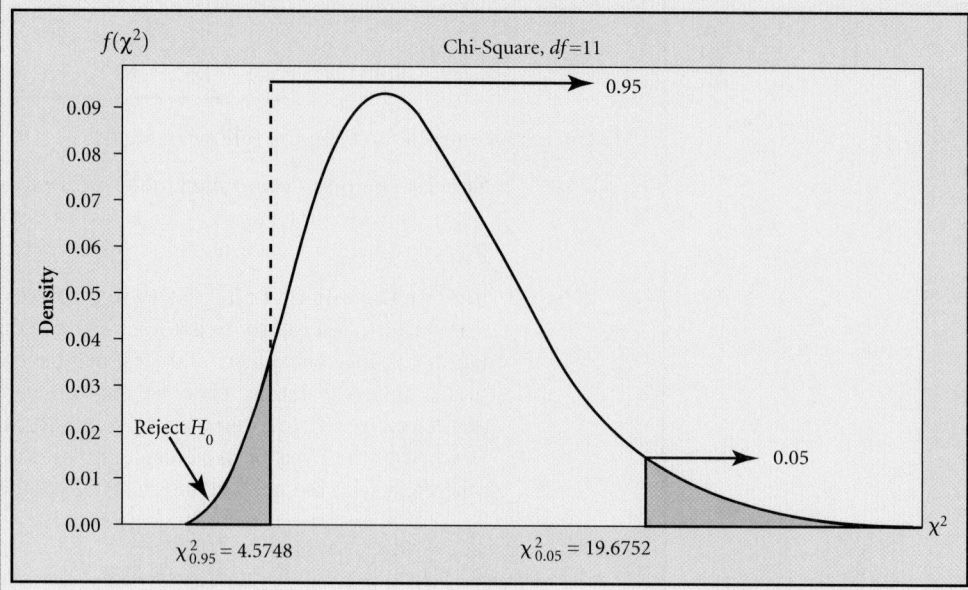

Step 7 **Draw a conclusion.**

After conducting this test, the operations manager for the Smithfield Agriculture Company can state there is insufficient evidence to conclude that changing the fertilizer volume has had any affect on the variability of yield from acre to acre.

Interval Estimation for a Population Variance

CHAPTER OUTCOME #2

Chapter 8 introduced confidence interval estimation for a single population mean and a single population proportion. We now extend those concepts to situations in which we are interested in estimating a population variance. Although the basic concepts are the same when we interpret a confidence interval estimate for a variance, the methodology for computing the interval estimate is slightly different. Equation 11.2 is used to construct the interval estimate.

Confidence Interval Estimate for σ^2

$$\frac{(n-1)s^2}{\chi_U^2} \le \sigma^2 \le \frac{(n-1)s^2}{\chi_L^2} \qquad (11.2)$$

where

$$s^2 = \text{Sample variance}$$
$$n = \text{Sample size}$$
$$\chi_L^2 = \text{Lower critical value}$$
$$\chi_U^2 = \text{Upper critical value}$$

The logic of Equation 11.2 is best demonstrated using Figure 11.4. In a similar manner to the discussion associated with Figure 8.4 in Chapter 8 for estimating a population mean, when estimating a population variance, for a 95% confidence interval estimate, 95% of the area in the distribution will be between the lower and upper critical values. But since

FIGURE 11.4

Critical χ^2 Values for Estimating σ^2

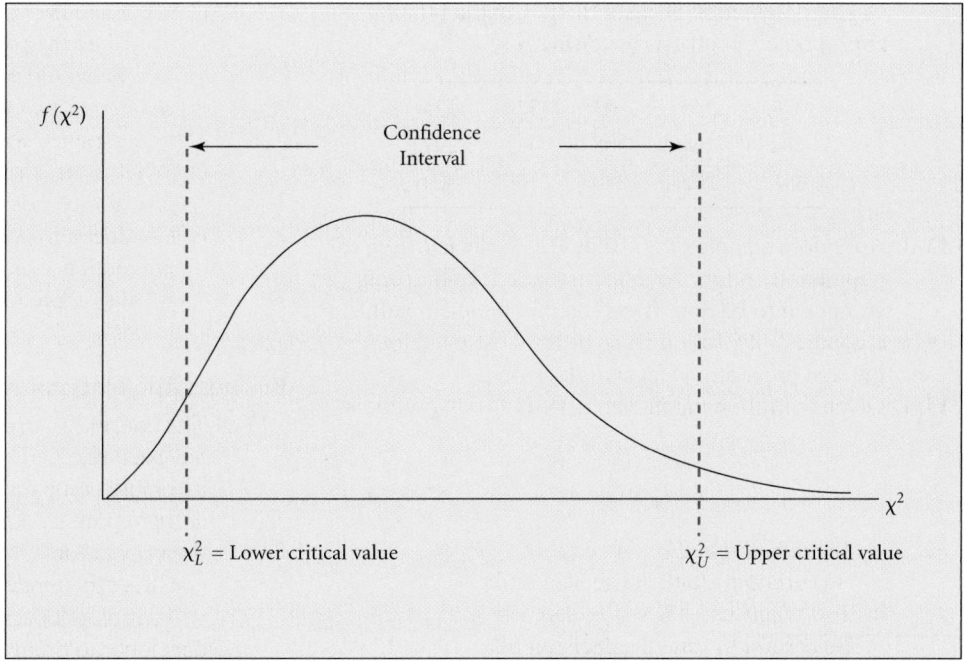

the chi-square distribution is not symmetrical and contains only positive numbers, two values must be found from the table in Appendix G.

In Equation 11.2, the denominators come from the chi-square distribution with $n - 1$ degrees of freedom. For example, in an application in which the sample size is $n = 10$ and the desired confidence level is 95%, there is 0.025 in both the lower and upper tails of the distribution. Then from the chi-square table in Appendix G we get the critical value

$$\chi_U^2 = \chi_{0.025}^2 = 19.0228$$

Likewise, we get

$$\chi_L^2 = \chi_{0.975}^2 = 2.7004$$

Now suppose that the sample variance computed from the sample of $n = 10$ values is $s^2 = 44$. Then using Equation 11.2, we construct the 95% confidence interval as follows:

$$\frac{(10-1)44}{19.0228} \leq \sigma^2 \leq \frac{(10-1)44}{2.7004}$$
$$20.82 \leq \sigma^2 \leq 146.64$$

Thus, at the 95% confidence level, we conclude that the population variance is in the range 20.82 to 146.64. By taking the square root, you can convert the interval estimate to one for the population standard deviation:

$$4.56 \leq \sigma \leq 12.11$$

11-1: Exercises

Skill Development

11-1. A manager is interested in determining if the population standard deviation has dropped below 130. Based on a sample of $n = 20$ items selected randomly from the population, conduct the appropriate hypothesis test at a 0.05 significance level. The sample standard deviation is 105.

11-2. The following sample data have been collected for the purpose of testing whether a population standard deviation is equal to 40. Conduct the appropriate hypothesis test using $\alpha = 0.05$.

318	255	323	325	334
354	266	308	321	297
316	272	346	266	309

11-3. A random sample of 20 values was selected from a population and the sample standard deviation was computed to be 360. Based on this sample result, compute a 95% confidence interval estimate for the true population standard deviation.

11-4. Given the following null and alternative hypotheses:

$$H_0: \sigma^2 = 100$$
$$H_A: \sigma^2 \neq 100$$

a. Test when $n = 27$, $s = 9$, and $\alpha = 0.10$. Be certain to state the decision rule.
b. Test when $n = 17$, $s = 6$, and $\alpha = 0.05$. Be certain to state the decision rule.

11-5. Given the following null and alternative hypotheses:

$$H_0: \sigma^2 = 50$$
$$H_A: \sigma^2 \neq 50$$

a. Test when $n = 12$, $s = 9$, and $\alpha = 0.10$. Be certain to state the decision rule.
b. Test when $n = 19$, $s = 6$, and $\alpha = 0.05$. Be certain to state the decision rule.

11-6. Suppose a random sample of 22 items produces a sample standard deviation of 16.
a. Use the sample results to develop a 90% confidence interval estimate for the population variance.
b. Use the sample results to develop a 95% confidence interval estimate for the population variance.

11-7. Historical data indicate that the standard deviation of a process is 6.3. A recent sample
a. of size 28 produced a variance of 66.2. Test to determine if the variance has increased using a significance level of 0.05. Use the p-value approach.
b. of size 8 produced a variance of 9.02. Test to determine if the variance has decreased using a significance level of 0.025. Use the test statistic approach.
c. of size 18 produced a variance of 62.9. Test to determine if the variance has changed using a significance level of 0.10. Use a p-value approach.

11-8. Examine the sample obtained from a normally distributed population

Sample:	5.2	10.4	5.1	2.1	4.8	15.5	10.2
	8.7	2.8	4.9	4.7	13.4	15.6	14.5

a. Calculate the variance.
b. Calculate the probability that a randomly chosen sample would produce a sample variance at least as large as that produced in part a if the population variance was equal to 20.
c. What is the statistical term used to describe the probability calculated in part b?
d. Conduct a hypothesis test to determine if the population variance is larger than 15.3. Use the p-value approach and a significance level equal to 0.05.

Business Applications

11-9. The consulting firm of Winston & Associates has been retained by an electronic component assembly company in Phoenix, Arizona, to design and program a computer simulation model of their operations. Winston & Associates plan to construct the model using ProModel software (see www.Promodel.com). This software allows the developer to program into the model probability distributions for things like machine downtime, defect rates, daily demand, and so forth. The closer the distributions specified in the computer model match those that actually occur in the assembly plant, the better the simulation model will perform. For one machine center, Winston consultants have assumed that when the center goes down for repairs, the time that it will be down will be normally distributed with an average of 30 minutes and a standard deviation equal to 10 minutes. Before finalizing the model, the consultants will collect a random sample of downtimes and test whether their downtime assumptions are valid. The following sample data reflect 10 randomly selected downtimes at this machine center from records over the past four weeks:

25	11	34	49	48
56	2	26	46	14

a. Using $\alpha = 0.05$, conduct the appropriate test for the mean downtime at this machine center.
b. Using $\alpha = 0.05$, conduct the appropriate test for the standard deviation in downtime.
c. Based on the hypothesis tests in parts a and b, what conclusions should the consulting company reach? Discuss.

11-10. The manager for City Transit Services in Portland, Oregon, is interested in estimating the standard deviation for the time it takes a bus to travel between the Portland rose garden and the Portland airport. To develop an estimate for the standard deviation, he has collected a random sample of the times required for 15 trips. The sample standard deviation is 6.2 minutes. Based on these data, what is the 90% confidence interval estimate for the true population standard deviation?

11-11. The Flicks is a small, independent theater that shows foreign and limited-release films. One attraction of the Flicks is that it sells beer and wine as well as premium coffee and pastries at its snack bar. Friday and Saturday nights are the busiest nights at the Flicks, and the owners of the theater are interested in estimating the variance in sales at the snack bar on Friday nights. Suppose a random sample of 14 Friday evenings is selected and the snack bar sales for each evening are recorded. The results of the sample in dollars are as follows:

279.66	329.91	314.99	358.08	341.14	303.28	325.88
369.29	336.90	316.54	356.57	313.49	351.04	295.36

Use the random sample of sales to develop a 95% confidence interval estimate of the variance of Friday night snack bar sales at the Flicks.

11-12. Airlines face the challenging task of keeping their planes on schedule. One key measure is the number of minutes a plane deviates from the targeted arrival time. Ideally, the measure for each arrival will be zero minutes, indicating that the plane arrived exactly on time. However, experience indicates that even under the best of circumstances there will be inherent variability. Suppose one major airline has set standards that require the planes to arrive, on average, on time, with a standard deviation not to exceed 2 minutes. To determine whether these standards are being met, each month the airline selects a random sample of 12 airplane arrivals and determines the number of minutes early or late the flight is. For last month, the times, rounded to the nearest minute, are:

3	−7	4	2	−2	5	11	−3	4	6	−4	1

a. State the appropriate null and alternative hypothesis for testing the standard regarding the mean value. Test the hypothesis using a significance level equal to 0.05. What assumption will be required?

b. State the appropriate null and alternative hypotheses regarding the standard deviation. Use the sample data to conduct the hypothesis test with $\alpha = 0.05$.

c. Discuss the results of both tests. What should the airline conclude regarding its arrival standards? What factors could influence the arrival times of flights?

11-13. A software design firm has recently developed a prototype educational computer game for children. One of the important factors in the success of a game like this is the time it takes the child to play the game. Two factors are important: the mean time it takes to play, and the variability in time required from child to child. Experience indicates that the mean time should be 10 minutes or less and the standard deviation should not exceed 4 minutes. The company has decided to test this prototype with 10 children selected at random from the local school district. The following values represent the time (rounded to the nearest minute) each child spent until completing the game:

9	14	11	8	13	15	11	10	7	12

a. The developers of the software will assume the mean time to completion of the game is 10 minutes or less unless the data strongly suggest otherwise. State the appropriate null and alternative hypotheses for testing the requirement regarding the mean value.

b. Referring to part a, test the hypotheses using a significance level equal to 0.10. What assumption will be required?

c. The developers of the software will assume the standard deviation of the time to completion of the game does not exceed 4 minutes unless the data strongly suggest otherwise. State the appropriate null and alternative hypotheses regarding the standard deviation. Use the sample data to conduct the hypothesis test with a significance level = 0.10.

11-14. A corporation makes CV joints for automobiles. An integral part of CV joints is the bearings that allow the joints to rotate differentially. One application utilizes six bearings in a CV joint that have an average diameter of 2.5 centimeters. The consistency of the diameters is vital to the operation of the joint. The specifications require that the variance of these diameters be no more than 0.0015 cm^2. The diameter is continually monitored by the quality control team. Twenty subsamples of size 10 are obtained every day. One of these subsamples produced bearings that had a variance of 0.00317 cm^2.

a. Calculate the probability that a subsample of size 10 would produce a sample variance that would be at least 0.00317 cm^2 if the population variance was 0.0015 cm^2.

b. On the basis of your calculation in part a, conduct a hypothesis test to determine if the quality control team should advise management to stop production and search for causes of the inconsistency of the bearing diameters. Use a significance level of 0.05.

11-15. *BusinessWeek* reported ("UPFront," January 16, 2006) that the average wage for construction workers was about $19 an hour. These data were obtained from the National Compensation Survey of the Bureau of Labor Statistics. The survey suggests that construction wages can vary widely. Hartford, Connecticut, wages are approximately 38% larger and Brownsville, Texas, is about 30% lower than the national average. A sample of 25 construction workers in San Antonio, Texas, yielded an average wage of $13.87 and a standard deviation of $1.46.

a. Estimate the standard deviation of the nation's construction wages. (*Hint:* Recall the relationship between the standard deviation and the range of a normal distribution used in the sample-size calculations in the confidence interval for a population mean.)

b. Does it appear that both the average and the standard deviation of the construction workers' wages in San Antonio are smaller than those of the nation as a whole? Use hypotheses tests and a significance level of 0.05 to make your determination.

Computer Database Exercises

11-16. Canidae Corporation, based in San Luis Obispo, California, is a producer of pet food. One of its products is Felidae cat food. The Chicken and Rice Cat and Kitten Formula is a dry cat food that comes in various sizes. Canidae guarantees that 32% of this cat food is crude protein. In the 6.6-pound (3-kilogram) size, this would indicate that 2.11 pounds would be crude protein. Of course, these figures are averages. The amount of crude protein varies with each sack of cat food. The file entitled **Catfood** contains the amounts of crude protein found in sacks randomly sampled from the production line. Assume the amount of crude protein in the 6.6-pound size is normally distributed.

a. If Canidae wishes to have the weight of crude protein sacks rounded off to 2.11 pounds, determine the standard deviation of the weight of crude protein. (*Hint:* Recall the relationship between the standard deviation and the range of a normal distribution used in the sample-size calculations in the confidence interval for a population mean.)

b. Using your result in part a, conduct a hypothesis test to determine if the standard deviation of the weight of crude protein in the 6.6-pound sack of

Felidae cat food is too large to meet Canidae's wishes. Use a significance level of 0.01.

11-17. Due to the sharp rise in oil prices, the cost of heating a home rose sharply in the winter of 2006. The average cost was $1,044, which was an increase of 33% above that in 2005. In addition to concern over the increase in average heating costs was the possibility of a sharp increase in the variability in heating costs. This would signal that lower-income families were simply not heating their homes as much, while those in higher income brackets were heating their homes as required. The file entitled **Homeheat** contains a sample of heating costs that accrued during the winter of 2006. Historical data indicate that heating costs have had a standard deviation of about $100.

a. Conduct a test of hypothesis to see if the variability in heating costs in the winter of 2006 was larger than that indicated by historical data. Use both the test statistic and the *p*-value approach and a significance level of 0.025.

b. Construct a box and whisker plot and indicate whether it indicates that the hypothesis test of part a is valid.

11-18. The Fillmore Institute has established a service designed to help charities increase the amount of money they collect from their direct-mail solicitations. Its consulting is aimed at increasing the mean dollar amount returned from each giver and also reducing the variation in amount contributed from giver to giver. The Badke Foundation collects money for heart disease research. Over the last eight years, records show that the average contribution per returned envelope is $14.25 with a standard deviation of $6.44. The Badke Foundation directors decided to try the Fillmore services on a test basis. They used the recommended letters and other request materials and sent out 1,000 requests. From these, 166 were returned. The data showing the dollars returned per giver are in the file called **Badke**.

Based on the sample data, what conclusions should the Badke Foundation reach regarding the Fillmore consulting services? Use appropriate hypothesis tests with an significance level = 0.05 to reach your conclusions. (*Hint:* Use Excel's **ChiInv** function or Minitab's **Calc > Probability Distributions** command to obtain the critical value for the the chi-square distribution.)

11.2 Hypothesis Tests for Two Population Variances

CHAPTER OUTCOME #3

F-Test for Two Population Variances

The previous section introduced a method for testing hypotheses involving a single population standard deviation. Recall that in order to conduct the test, we had to first convert the standard deviation to the variance. Then we used the chi-square distribution to determine whether the sample variance led us to reject the null hypothesis. However, decision makers are often faced with decision problems involving two population standard deviations. Although there is no hypothesis test that directly tests standard deviations, there is a procedure that can be used to test whether two populations have equal variances. We typically formulate null and alternative hypotheses of the following forms:

Two-Tailed Test	Upper One-Tailed Test	Lower One-Tailed Test
$H_0: \sigma_1^2 = \sigma_2^2$	$H_0: \sigma_1^2 \leq \sigma_2^2$	$H_0: \sigma_1^2 \geq \sigma_2^2$
$H_A: \sigma_1^2 \neq \sigma_2^2$	$H_A: \sigma_1^2 > \sigma_2^2$	$H_A: \sigma_1^2 < \sigma_2^2$

In order to test a hypothesis involving two population variances, we first compute the sample variances. We then compute the test statistic shown as Equation 11.3.

F-Test Statistic for Testing Whether Two Populations Have Equal Variances

$$F = \frac{s_i^2}{s_j^2} \qquad (df: D_1 = n_i - 1 \quad \text{and} \quad D_2 = n_j - 1) \qquad \textbf{(11.3)}$$

where:

$$n_i = \text{Sample size } i\text{th population}$$
$$n_j = \text{Sample size from } j\text{th population}$$
$$s_i^2 = \text{Sample variance from the } i\text{th population}$$
$$s_j^2 = \text{Sample variance from the } j\text{th population}$$

Analyzing this test statistic requires that we introduce the F-distribution. Although it is beyond the scope of this book, statistical theory shows the F-distribution is equal to the ratio of two independent chi-square distributions. Like the chi-square and the t-distributions, the appropriate F-distribution is determined by its degrees of freedom. However, the F-distribution has two degrees of freedom, D_1 and D_2, that depend on the sample sizes for the variances in the numerator and denominator, respectively, in Equation 11.3.

In order to apply the F-distribution to test whether two population variances are equal, the following assumptions must be made:

Assumptions

- The populations are normally distributed.
- The samples are randomly and independently selected.

Independent Samples
Samples selected from two or more populations in such a way that the occurrence of values in one sample has no influence on the probability of the occurrence of values in the other sample(s).

Independent samples will occur when the sample data are obtained in such a way that the values in one sample are in no way influenced by the values in the second sample.

The test statistic shown in Equation 11.3 is formed as the ratio of two sample variances. There are two key points to remember when formulating this ratio.

1. To use the F distribution table in this text, for a two-tailed test, always place the larger sample variance in the numerator. This will make the calculated F-value greater than 1.0 and push the F-value toward the upper tail of the F-distribution.
2. For the one-tailed test, examine the alternative hypothesis. For the population that is *predicted* (based on the alternative hypothesis) to have the larger variance, place that sample variance in the numerator.

The following applications and examples will illustrate the specific methods used for testing for a difference between two population variances.

Business Application

***E. COLI* BACTERIA TESTING** Recent years have seen several national scares involving contaminated meat carrying *E. coli* bacteria. The recommended preventative measure is to cook the meat at a required temperature. However, different meat patties cooked for the same amount of time will have different final internal temperatures because of variations in the patties and variations in burner temperatures. A regional hamburger chain will replace its current burners with one of two new digitally controlled models.

The chain's purchasing agents have arranged to randomly sample 11 patties of meat cooked by burner model 1 and 13 meat patties cooked by burner model 2 to learn if there is a difference in temperature variation between the two models. If a difference exists, the chain's managers have decided to select the model that provides the smaller variation in final internal meat temperature. Ideally, they would like a test that compares standard deviations, but no such test exists. Instead, they must convert the standard deviations to variances. The hypotheses are

$$H_0: \sigma_1^2 = \sigma_2^2$$
$$H_A: \sigma_1^2 \neq \sigma_2^2$$

The null and alternative hypotheses are formulated for a two-tailed test. Intuitively, you might reason that if the two population variances are actually equal, the sample variances should be approximately equal also. That would mean that the ratio of the two sample variances should be approximately 1. We will reject the null hypothesis if one sample variance is significantly larger than the other and if the ratio of sample variances is significantly greater than 1. The managers will use a significance level of $\alpha = 0.10$.

The next step is to collect the sample data. Figure 11.5 shows the sample data and the box and whisker plot. The assumption of independence is met because the two burners were used to cook different meat patties and the temperature measures are not related. The box and whisker plots provide no evidence to suggest that the distributions are highly skewed, so the assumption that the populations are normally distributed may hold.

The sample variances are computed using Equation 11.4.

Sample Variance

$$s^2 = \frac{\sum(x - \overline{x})^2}{n - 1}$$

(11.4)

where:

$$\overline{x} = \frac{\sum x}{n} = \text{Sample mean}$$

$$n = \text{Sample size}$$

FIGURE 11.5

E. Coli **Bacteria Testing Sample Data**

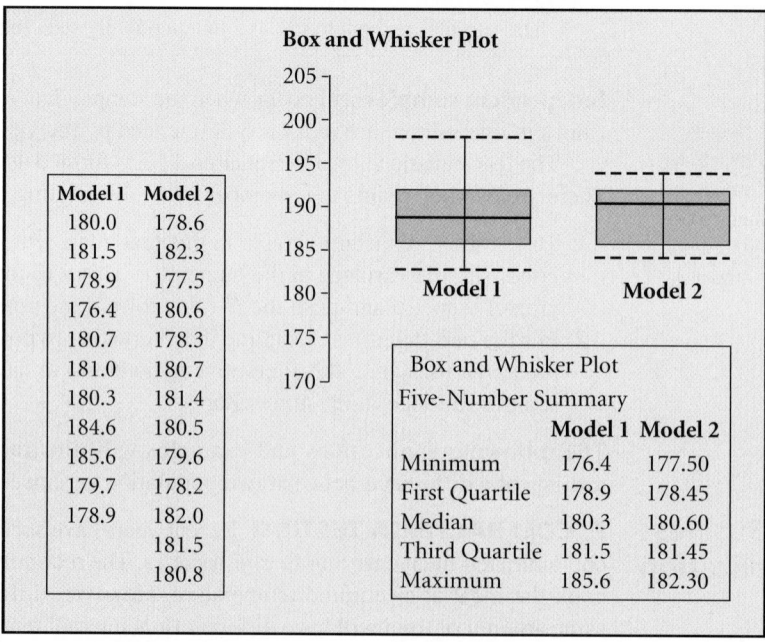

Based on the sample data shown in Figure 11.5, the sample variances are

$$s_1^2 = 6.7 \quad \text{and} \quad s_2^2 = 2.5$$

The null hypothesis is that the two population variances are equal, making this a two-tailed test. Thus, we form the test statistic using Equation 11.3 by placing the larger sample variance in the numerator. The calculated F-value is

$$F = \frac{s_1^2}{s_2^2} = \frac{6.7}{2.5} = 2.68$$

If the calculated F-value exceeds the critical value, then the null hypothesis is rejected. The critical F-value is determined by locating the appropriate F-distribution table for the desired alpha level and the correct degrees of freedom. This requires the following thought process:

1. If the test is two-tailed, use the table corresponding to $\alpha/2$. For example, if $\alpha = 0.10$ for a two-tailed test, the appropriate F table is the one with the upper tail equal to 0.05.
2. If the test is one-tailed, use the F table corresponding to the significance level. If $\alpha = 0.05$ for a one-tailed test, use the table with the upper-tail area equal to 0.05.

In this example, the test is two-tailed and α is 0.10. Thus, we go to the F-distribution table in Appendix H for the upper-tail area equal to 0.05.

The next step is to determine the appropriate degrees of freedom. In Chapter 8 we showed that the degrees of freedom of any test statistic are equal to the number of independent data values available to estimate the population variance. We lose 1 degree of freedom for each parameter we are required to estimate. For both the numerator and denominator in Equation 11.3, we must estimate the population mean using $\bar{x}$ before we calculate s^2. In each case, we lose 1 degree of freedom. Therefore, we have two distinct degrees of freedom, D_1 and D_2, where D_1 is equal to $n - 1$ for the variance in the numerator of the F-test statistic and D_2 is equal to $n - 1$ for the variance in the denominator. Recall that for a two-tailed test, the larger sample variance is placed in the numerator. In this example, model 1 has the larger sample variance, so model 1 is placed in the numerator with a sample size of 11, so $D_1 = 11 - 1 = 10$ and $D_2 = 13 - 1 = 12$.

Locate the page of the F table corresponding to the desired upper-tail area. In this text we have three options (0.05, 0.025, and 0.01). The F table is arranged in columns and rows. The columns correspond to the D_1 degrees of freedom and the rows correspond to the D_2 degrees of freedom. For this example, the critical F-value at the intersection of $D_1 = 10$ and $D_2 = 12$ degrees of freedom is 2.753.[1]

Figure 11.6 summarizes the hypothesis test. Note that the decision rule is

If calculated $F > 2.753$, reject H_0;

Otherwise, do not reject H_0.

Because $F = 2.68 < 2.753$, the conclusion is that the null hypothesis is not rejected based on these sample data; that is, we cannot conclude that there is a difference in the population variances.

---

[1] If you prefer, you can use Excel's **FINV** function or Minitab's **Calc > Probability Distributions** command to determine the critical F-value. The **FINV** function is $= FINV(.05,10,12) = 2.753$.

FIGURE 11.6

**F-Test for the *E. Coli*
Example**

Hypothesis:

$H_0: \sigma_1^2 = \sigma_2^2$

$H_A: \sigma_1^2 \neq \sigma_2^2$

$\alpha = 0.10$

$f(F)$

df: $D_1 = 10, D_2 = 12$

Rejection region
$\alpha/2 = 0.05$

$F_{0.05} = 2.753$

F

Decision Rule:

If $F > 2.753$, reject H_0;

Otherwise, do not reject H_0.

The F-test is

$$F = \frac{s_1^2}{s_2^2} = \frac{6.7}{2.5} = 2.68$$

Because $F = 2.68 \leq F_{0.05} = 2.753$, do not reject H_0.

Note: The right-hand tail of the F-distribution always contains an
area of $\alpha/2$ if the hypothesis is two-tailed.

EXAMPLE 11-3 Two-Tailed Test for Two Population Variances

TRY PROBLEM 11.20

Airport Security   Since the September 11 tragedy in New York City, Washington D.C.
and Pennsylvania, airport security has been tightened substantially around the world. The
federal government has taken over the management of airport security in U.S. airports,
and private security companies have been replaced by federal employees. Suppose that
the security manager at O'Hare airport in Chicago is concerned about the waiting time
for passengers required to pass through security checks before being admitted to the
departure gates. Of particular interest is whether there is a difference in the standard
deviation of waiting time at concourses A and B. The following steps can be used to test
whether there is a difference in population variances:

Step 1 Specify the population parameter of interest.

The population parameter of interest is the standard deviation in waiting
times at the two concourses.

Step 2 Formulate the appropriate null and alternative hypotheses.

Because we are interested in determining if a difference exists in standard
deviation and because neither concourse is predicted to have a higher variance, the test will be two-tailed, and the hypotheses are established as

$$H_0: \sigma_A^2 = \sigma_B^2$$
$$H_A: \sigma_A^2 \neq \sigma_B^2$$

Note: The hypotheses are stated in terms of the population variances.

Step 3 Specify the level of significance.

The test will be conducted using an $\alpha = 0.02$.

Step 4 Compute the test statistic.

The test statistic is formed by the ratio of the two sample variances. Because this is a two-tailed test, the larger sample variance is placed in the numerator.

Select random samples from each population of interest, determine whether the assumptions have been satisfied, and compute the test statistic.

Random samples of 25 passengers from Concourse A and 31 passengers from Concourse B were selected and the waiting time for each passenger was recorded. There is no connection between the two samples, so the assumption of independence is satisfied. The stem and leaf diagrams do not dispute the assumption of normality.

	Stem and Leaf Display for Concourse A Stem unit: 1		Stem and Leaf Display for Concourse B Stem unit: 1
Statistics	8 | 9	**Statistics**	4 | 7
Sample Size 25	9 | 0	Sample Size 31	5 |
Mean 14.58	10 | 2 3 7 9	Mean 16.25	6 | 3
Median 14.16	11 | 9	Median 15.77	7 |
Std. Deviation 3.77	12 | 2 4	Std. Deviation 4.79	8 |
Minimum 8.89	13 | 2	Minimum 4.70	9 |
Maximum 22.16	14 | 0 0 2 2	Maximum 24.38	10 | 8
	15 | 5 6 9		11 | 1 4 7
	16 | 2		12 | 2 4
	17 | 0 4		13 |
	18 | 2 4		14 | 2 2 2 8
	19 |		15 | 1 3 7 8
	20 | 8		16 |
	21 | 5		17 | 0 5
	22 | 2		18 | 3 6
			19 | 0 1 3 3
			20 | 4
			21 | 8 8
			22 | 1 4 9
			23 |
			24 | 4

$$F = \frac{4.79^2}{3.77^2} = 1.614$$

Step 5 Construct the rejection region.

To determine the critical value from the F-distribution, we can use either Excel's **FINV** function, Minitab's **Calc > Probability Distributions** command, or the F table in Appendix H. The degrees of freedom are D_1 = numerator sample size − 1, and D_2 = denominator sample size − 1. As shown in the statistics section of the stem and leaf display, Concourse B has the larger standard deviation, thus we get

$$D_1 = n_B - 1 = 31 - 1 = 30 \quad \text{and} \quad D_2 = n_A - 1 = 25 - 1 = 24$$

Then for $\alpha/2 = 0.01$, we get a critical $F_{0.01} = 2.577$. The null hypothesis is rejected if $F > F_{0.01} = 2.577$. Otherwise, do not reject the null hypothesis.

Step 6 Reach a decision.
Compare the test statistic to the critical value and reach a conclusion with respect to the null hypothesis.

Because $F = 1.614 < F_{0.01} = 2.577$, do not reject the null hypothesis.

Step 7 Draw a conclusion.
There is no reason to conclude that there is a difference in the variability of waiting time at Concourses A and B.

Business Application

Excel and Minitab Tutorial

BANK ATM MACHINES One-tailed tests on two population variances are performed much like two-tailed tests. Consider the systems development group for a midwestern bank, which has developed a new software algorithm for its ATM machines. Although reducing average transaction time is an objective, the systems programmers also want to reduce the variability in transaction speed. They believe the standard deviation for transaction time will be less with the new software (population 2) than it was with the old algorithm (population 1). For their analysis, the programmers have performed 7 test runs using the original software and 11 test runs using the new system. Although the managers want to determine the standard deviation of transaction time, they must perform the test as a test of variances because no method exists for testing standard deviations directly. Thus, the null and alternative hypotheses are

$$H_0: \sigma_1^2 \le \sigma_2^2 \quad \text{or} \quad \sigma_1^2 - \sigma_2^2 \le 0$$
$$H_A: \sigma_1^2 > \sigma_2^2 \quad \text{or} \quad \sigma_1^2 - \sigma_2^2 > 0$$

The hypothesis is to be tested using a significance level of $\alpha = 0.01$.

In order to use the F-test to test whether these sample variances come from populations with equal variances, we need to make sure that the sample variances are independent and the populations are approximately normally distributed. Because the test runs using the two algorithms were unique, the variances are independent. The following box and whisker plots give no reason to indicate that, based on these small samples, the populations are not approximately normal.

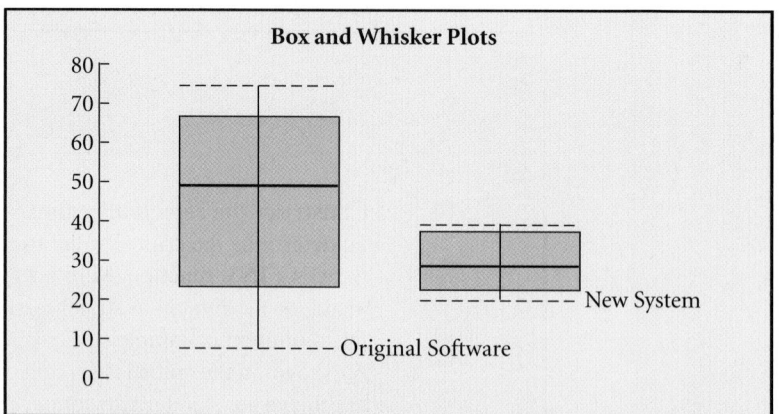

Figure 11.7a and Figure 11.7b illustrate the one-tailed hypothesis test for this situation using a significance level of 0.01. Recall that in a two-tailed test, placing the larger sample variance in the numerator and the smaller variance in the denominator forms the F-ratio. In a one-tailed test, we look to the alternative hypothesis to determine which sample variance should go in the numerator. In this example, population 1 (the original software) is thought to have the larger variance. Then the sample variance from population 1 forms the

FIGURE 11.7A

**Excel 2007 Output
F-Test Example of ATM
Transaction Time**

Excel 2007 Instructions:
1. Open file: ATM.xls.
2. Select **Data > Data Analysis**.
3. Select **F-Test Two-Sample for Variances**.
4. Define the data range for the two variables.
5. Specify **Alpha** equal to 0.01.
6. Specify output location.
7. Click **OK**.
8. Click on **Home** tab and adjust decimals places in output.

numerator, regardless of the size of the sample variances. Excel and Minitab correctly compute the calculated *F*-ratio.

If you are performing the test manually, the *F*-ratio needs to be formed correctly for two reasons. First, the correct *F*-ratio will be computed. Second, the correct degrees of freedom will be used to determine the critical value to test the null hypothesis. In this one-tailed example, the numerator represents population 1 and the denominator represents population 2. This means that the degrees of freedom are

$$D_1 = n_1 - 1 = 7 - 1 = 6 \quad \text{and} \quad D_2 = n_2 - 1 = 11 - 1 = 10$$

Using the *F*-distribution table in Appendix H, Minitab's **Calc > Probability Distributions** command, or Excel's **FINV** function, you can determine

$$F_{0.01} = 5.39$$

for this one-tailed test with a $\alpha = 0.01$.

FIGURE 11.7B

Minitab Output *F*-Test Example of ATM Transaction Time

Minitab Instructions:
1. Open file: ATM. MTW.
2. Choose **Stat > Basic Statistics > 2 Variances**.
3. Select **Samples in different columns**, enter one data column in First and another in **Second**.
4. Click on **Options**.
5. In **Confidence Level**, enter $1 - \alpha$.
6. Click **OK. OK.**

```
MINITAB - ATM.MPJ - [Session]

File  Edit  Data  Calc  Stat  Graph  Editor  Tools  Window  Help

Test for Equal Variances: Original Software, New System

99% Bonferroni confidence intervals for standard deviations

                     N    Lower    StDev    Upper
Original Software    7  13.4736  24.7523  83.5533
      New System    11   4.3581   7.1759  16.7866


F-Test (normal distribution)
Test statistic = 11.90, p-value = 0.001
```

The sample data for the test runs are in a CD-ROM file called **ATM**. The sample variances are

$$s_1^2 = 612.68$$
$$s_2^2 = 51.49$$

Thus, the calculated F-ratio is

$$F = \frac{612.68}{51.49} = 11.898$$

As shown in Figure 11.7a, the calculated $F = 11.898 > F_{0.01} = 5.39$, so the null hypothesis, H_0, is rejected. Based on the sample data, the systems programmers have evidence to support their claim that the new ATM algorithm will result in reduced transaction-time variability.

There are many business decision-making applications in which you will need to test whether two populations have equal variances.

TRY PROBLEM 11.21

EXAMPLE 11-4   One-Tailed Test for Two Population Variances

Thomas Supply   Thomas Supply has a contract to assemble component parts that will be used by a leading maker of personal computers. One critical part is available from two suppliers. Thomas currently buys from supplier 1 because of its parts are less expensive. However, Thomas will purchase from supplier 2, if the standard deviation in thickness is less than that for supplier 1. The following steps can be used to conduct a test for the two suppliers:

Step 1   Specify the population parameter of interest.
Thomas Supply is concerned with the standard deviation in thickness. Therefore, the population parameter of interest is the standard deviation, σ.

Step 2   Formulate the appropriate null and alternative hypotheses.
Because Thomas managers are concerned with whether supplier 1's standard deviation will exceed that of supplier 2, the test will be one-tailed, and the null and alternative hypotheses are formed as follows:

$$H_0: \sigma_1^2 \leq \sigma_2^2$$
$$H_A: \sigma_1^2 > \sigma_2^2$$

Note: The hypotheses must be stated in terms of the population variances.

Step 3   Specify the significance level.
The test will be conducted using an alpha level equal to 0.05.

Step 4   Compute the test statistic.
A simple random sample of 11 parts was selected from each supplier with the sample variances of

$$s_1^2 = 0.799 \quad \text{and} \quad s_2^2 = 0.547$$

The assumptions of independence and normal populations are believed to be satisfied in this case.

The test statistic is an F-ratio formed by placing the variance that is predicted to be larger (as shown in the alternative hypothesis) in the numerator. Supplier 1 is predicted to have the larger variance in the alternative hypothesis. Thus the test statistic is

$$F = \frac{0.799}{0.547} = 1.4607$$

Step 5 Construct the rejection region.
Based on sample sizes of 11 parts from each supplier, the critical value for a one-tailed test with $\alpha = 0.05$ and $D_1 = 10$ and $D_2 = 10$ degrees of freedom is 2.978. The null hypothesis is rejected if $F > F_{0.05} = 2.978$. Otherwise, do not reject the null hypothesis.

Step 6 Reach a decision.
Because $F = 1.4607 < F_{0.05} = 2.978$, do not reject the null hypothesis.

Step 7 Draw a conclusion.
Based on the sample data, there is insufficient evidence to conclude that the variance of part thickness from supplier 1 is greater than that for supplier 2. Therefore, Thomas will continue to purchase from supplier 1.

Additional F-test Considerations Recall that in Chapter 10, the t-test for the difference between two population means with independent samples assumed that the two populations have equal variances. Oftentimes, decision makers use the F-test introduced in this section to test whether the assumption of equal variances is satisfied. However, studies have shown that the F-test may not be particularly effective in detecting certain differences in population variances that can adversely affect the t-test. Therefore, other tests for equality of variances, such as the Aspen-Welch test, may be preferred as preliminary tests to the t-test for two population means. (See the Markowski reference at the end of this chapter.)

11-2: Exercises

Skill Development

11-19. Find the appropriate critical F-value, from the F-distribution table for each of the following:
a. $D_1 = 16$, $D_2 = 14$, $\alpha = 0.01$
b. $D_1 = 5$, $D_2 = 12$, $\alpha = 0.05$
c. $D_1 = 16$, $D_2 = 20$, $\alpha = 0.01$

11-20. Given the following null and alternative hypotheses:

$$H_0: \sigma_1^2 = \sigma_2^2$$
$$H_A: \sigma_1^2 \neq \sigma_2^2$$

and the following sample information:

Sample 1	Sample 2
$n_1 = 11$	$n_2 = 21$
$s_1 = 15$	$s_2 = 33$

a. if $\alpha = 0.02$, state the decision rule for the hypothesis.
b. test the hypothesis and indicate whether the null hypothesis should be rejected.

11-21. Given the following null and alternative hypotheses:

$$H_0: \sigma_1^2 \leq \sigma_2^2$$
$$H_A: \sigma_1^2 > \sigma_2^2$$

and the following sample information:

Sample 1	Sample 2
$n_1 = 13$	$n_2 = 21$
$s_1^2 = 1,450$	$s_2^2 = 1,320$

a. if $\alpha = 0.05$, state the decision rule for the hypothesis.
b. test the hypothesis and indicate whether the null hypothesis should be rejected.

11-22. Given the following null and alternative hypotheses:

$$H_0: \sigma_1^2 \leq \sigma_2^2$$
$$H_A: \sigma_1^2 > \sigma_2^2$$

and the following sample information:

Sample 1	Sample 2
$n_1 = 21$	$n_2 = 12$
$s_1^2 = 345.7$	$s_2^2 = 745.2$

a. if $\alpha = 0.01$, state the decision rule for the hypothesis. (Be careful to pay attention to the alternative hypothesis to construct this decision rule.)

b. test the hypothesis and indicate whether the null hypothesis should be rejected.

11-23. Consider the following two independently chosen samples:

Sample 1	Sample 2
12.1	10.5
13.4	9.5
11.7	8.2
10.7	7.8
14.0	11.1

a. Use a significance level of 0.05 for testing the hypothesis that $\sigma_1^2 \leq \sigma_2^2$.

b. Calculate the p-value.

c. Interpret the p-value.

11-24. You are given two random samples with the following information:

Item	Sample 1	Sample 2
1	19.6	21.3
2	22.1	17.4
3	19.5	19.0
4	20.0	21.2
5	21.5	20.1
6	20.2	23.5
7	17.9	18.9
8	23.0	22.4
9	12.5	14.3
10	19.0	17.8

a. Based on these samples, test at $\alpha = 0.10$ whether the true difference in population variances is equal to zero.

b. If you are able to obtain it from suitable computer software, determine the p-value for this hypothesis test. Otherwise, place a bound on the p-value using Appendix H.

Business Applications

11-25. A national TV telethon committee is interested in determining whether males' donations have greater variability in amount than do those of females. To test this, random samples of 25 males and 25 females were selected from people who donated during last year's telethon. The following statistics were computed from the sample data:

Males	Females
$\bar{x} = \$12.40$	$\bar{x} = \$8.92$
$s = \$2.50$	$s = \$1.34$

Based on a significance level of 0.05, does it appear that males' donations have greater variability in amount than do those of females?

11-26. As purchasing agent for the Horner-Williams Company, you have primary responsibility for securing high-quality raw materials at the best possible price. One particular material that the Horner-Williams Company uses a great deal is aluminum. After careful study, you have been able to reduce the prospective vendors to two. It is unclear whether these two vendors produce aluminum that is equally durable.

To compare durability, the recommended procedure is to put pressure on the aluminum until it cracks. The vendor whose aluminum requires the greatest average pressure will be judged to be the one that provides the most durable product.

To carry out this test, 14 pieces from vendor 1 and 14 pieces from vendor 2 are selected at random. The following results in pounds per square inch were noted:

Vendor I	Vendor 2
$n_1 = 14$	$n_2 = 14$
$\bar{x}_1 = 2,345\,\text{psi}$	$\bar{x}_2 = 2,411\,\text{psi}$
$s_1 = 300$	$s_2 = 250$

Before testing the hypothesis about difference in population means, suppose the purchasing agent for the company was concerned about whether the assumption of equal population variances was satisfied.

a. Based on the sample data, what would you tell him if you tested at the significance level of 0.10?

b. Would your conclusion differ if you tested at the significance level of 0.02? Discuss.

c. What would be the largest significance level that would cause the null hypothesis to be rejected?

11-27. The production control manager at Ashmore Manufacturing is interested in determining whether there is a difference in standard deviation of product diameter for part #XC-343 for units made at the Trenton, New Jersey, plant versus those made at the Atlanta, Georgia, plant. The Trenton plant is highly automated and thought to provide better quality control. Thus, the parts produced there should be less variable than those made in Atlanta.

A random sample of 15 parts was selected from those produced last week at Trenton. The standard deviation for these parts was 0.14 inch. A sample of 13 parts was selected from those made in

Atlanta. The sample standard deviation for these parts was 0.202 inch.

a. Based on these sample data, is there sufficient evidence to conclude that the Trenton plant produces parts that are less variable than those of the Atlanta plant? Test using $\alpha = 0.05$.

b. Consider the scenario that the Trenton plant is discovered to have a smaller variability than the Atlanta plant. Management, on this basis, decides that they must expend a large amount of money to upgrade the machinery in Atlanta. Suppose also that, in reality, the difference in the observed variability between the two plants is a result of sampling error. Specify the type of error associated with hypothesis testing that was made. How would you modify the hypothesis procedure to guard against such an error?

11-28. The *Washington Post Weekly Edition* (Robert J. Samuelson, "Homes as Hummers," July 18–24, 2005) quoted an Urban Institute study that stated that about 80% of the estimated $200 billion of federal housing subsidies consisted of tax breaks (mainly deductions for mortgage interest payments). Samples indicated that federal housing benefits average $8,268 for those with incomes between $200,000 and $500,000 and only $365 for those with incomes of $40,000 to $50,000. The respective standard deviations were 2,100 and 150. They were, obtained from samples sizes of 150.

To determine the appropriate hypothesis test concerning the average federal housing benefits of the two income groups it is necessary to determine if the population variances are equal. Conduct a test of hypothesis to this effect using a significance level of 0.02.

11-29. CNNMoney.com (Jeanne Sahadi, "Lucrative degrees for college grads," April 19, 2005) displayed the average starting salaries for college graduates in various majors. For business majors, the highest was in accounting with an average salary of $43,809. In business administration, the average was $39,448. However, average salaries supply only part of the information in career selection. For those not at the top of their class, large variances might mean salaries considerably below the anticipated values. To determine the relative variances in these two areas, samples of size 20 produced standard deviations of 2,636 and 1,513, respectively.

a. Conduct a test of hypothesis to determine if the standard deviation of the starting salary in accounting is larger than that in business administration. Use a significance level of 0.05.

b. Calculate the probability that a randomly selected college student would pursue an accounting degree and end up with a salary smaller than the average starting salary in business administration. Assume the sample standard deviation of the accounting starting salaries is a sufficiently good approximation to the population's standard deviation.

Computer Database Exercises

11-30. The First Night Stage Company operates a small, nonprofit theater group in Milwaukee, Wisconsin. Each year the company solicits donations to help fund its operations. This year, it obtained the help of a marketing research company in the city. This company's representatives proposed two different solicitation brochures. They are interested in determining whether there is a difference in the standard deviation of dollars returned between the two brochures. To test this, a random sample of 20 people was selected to receive brochure A and another random sample of 20 people was selected to receive brochure B. The data are contained in the file called **First-Night**. Based on these sample data, what should the First Night Company conclude about the two brochures with respect to their variability? Test using a significance level of 0.02.

11-31. The Celltone company is in the business of providing cellular phone coverage. Recently, it conducted a study of its customers who have purchased either the "Basic Plan" or the "Business Plan" service. At issue is the number of minutes of use by the customers during the midnight to 7:00 A.M. time period Monday through Friday over a four-week period. The belief of Celltone managers is that the standard deviation in minutes used by Business Plan customers will be less than that for the Basic Plan customers. Data for this study are in a file called **Celltone**. Assume that the managers wish to test this using a 0.05 level of significance.

Determine if the standard deviation in minutes used by Business Plan customers is less than that for the Basic Plan customers using an alpha level equal to 0.05.

11-32. The *Boston Globe* ("College graduation rates below national average," January 29, 2006) examined the graduation rates at community colleges in Massachusetts. Overall, 16.4% of full-time community college students in Massachusetts earn a degree or certificate within three years. This appears to be well below the national average of 24.7. To determine this, random samples were taken in both Massachusetts and in the nation as a whole. A file entitled **Masspass** contains outcomes of this sampling. Assume the populations have normal distributions.

a. Determine if there is a difference in the variances of the percent of community college students who earn a degree or certificate within three years in both Massachusetts and in the rest of the nation. Use the *p*-value approach with a significance level of 0.05.

b. On the basis of the results of part a, select the appropriate procedure to determine if there is a significant difference between the average graduation rates for Massachusetts and for the remainder of the nation.

11-33. A *USA Today* editorial (Alejandro Gonzalez, "CEO Dough," January 20, 2006) addressed the growth of compensation for corporate CEOs. Quoting a study made by *BusinessWeek*, *USA Today* indicated that the pay packages have increased almost sevenfold on average over the past decade. The file entitled **CEODough** contains the salaries of CEOs in 1994 and in 2004, adjusted for inflation. Assume the populations are normally distributed.

a. Determine if there is a difference in the standard deviations of the salaries of CEOs in 1994 and 2004. Use a significance level of 0.02.

b. Calculate the proportion of CEO salaries for 2004 that are larger than the average salaries for CEOs in 1994. Assume the sample statistics are sufficiently good approximations to the populations' parameters.

Summary and Conclusions

There are many business situations where the decision maker must reach a conclusion about a single population variance or about the relationship between two population variances. Chapter 11 introduced a confidence interval estimate for a single population variance and two hypothesis tests, the first using the chi-square distribution for testing a single population variance and the second using the *F*-distribution for testing the relationship between two population variances. Together, these procedures provide the decision maker with powerful tools for making inferences concerning one and two population variances. Combining the techniques presented in Chapter 11 with the hypothesis-testing procedures in Chapters 9 and 10 gives the decision maker useful techniques for testing population parameters for one and two populations. Furthermore, Chapter 11 introduced two probability distributions, the chi-square distribution and the *F*-distribution. The chi-square distribution will again be used in Chapter 13, where goodness-of-fit and contingency analysis are discussed. The *F*-distribution will be used extensively in the analysis of variance and regression analysis chapters.

Equations

Chi-Square Test for a Single Population Variance

$$\chi^2 = \frac{(n-1)s^2}{\sigma^2} \qquad (11.1)$$

Confidence Interval Estimate for a Population Variance

$$\frac{(n-1)s^2}{\chi_U^2} \le \sigma^2 \le \frac{(n-1)s^2}{\chi_L^2} \qquad (11.2)$$

F-Test Statistic for Testing Whether Two Populations Have Equal Variances

$$F = \frac{s_i^2}{s_j^2} \quad (df: D_1 = n_i - 1 \quad \text{and} \quad D_2 = n_j - 1) \qquad (11.3)$$

Sample Variance

$$s^2 = \frac{\Sigma(x - \overline{x})^2}{n-1} \qquad (11.4)$$

Key Term

Independent samples   493

Chapter Exercises

Conceptual Questions

11-34. Much of the emphasis of modern quality control efforts involves identifying sources of variation in the processes associated with service or manufacturing operations. Discuss why variation in a process may impact quality.

11-35. Identify three situations where organizations would be interested in limiting the standard deviation of a process.

11-36. Identify three situations where the measured output of a process has a small variation and three situations where the variation is larger (for instance, the time for a phone call to ring the other phone versus the time to speak to a person when making a service call).

11-37. In a journal related to your declared major, locate an article where a hypothesis about one or two population variances is tested. Discuss why population variation was an important issue in the article, how the hypothesis was formulated, and the results of the test.

11-38. Consider testing the hypothesis H_A: $\sigma_1^2 > \sigma_2^2$ using samples of respective sizes 6 and 11. Note that we could represent this hypothesis as H_A: $\sigma_1^2/\sigma_2^2 > 1$. The samples yield $s_1^2 = 42.2$ and $s_2^2 = 1.1$. It hardly seems worth the time to conduct this test since the test statistic will obviously be very large, leading us to reject the null hypothesis. However, we might wish to test a hypothesis such as H_A: $\sigma_1^2/\sigma_2^2 > 10$. The test is conducted exactly the same way as the F-test of this chapter except that you use the test statistic $F = (s_1^2/s_2^2) (1/k)$, where $k = 10$ for this hypothesis. Conduct the indicated test using a significance level of 0.05.

Business Applications

11-39. Maher Saddles, Inc. produces bicycle seats. Among the many seats produced is one for the high-end mountain bicycle market. Maher's operation manager has recently made a change in the production process for this high-end seat and is scheduled to report on measures associated with the new process at the next staff meeting. After waiting for the process to become stable, he took a random sample of 25 assembly times and found a standard deviation of 47 seconds. He recognizes this is only a point estimate of the variation in completion times and so wants to report both a 90% and a 95% confidence interval estimate for the population variance.

11-40. A medical research group is investigating what differences might exist between two pain-killing drugs, Azerleive and Zynumbic. The researchers have already established there is no difference between the two drugs in terms of the average amount of time required before they take effect. However, they are also interested in knowing if there is any difference between the variability of time until pain relief occurs. A random sample of 24 patients using Azerleive and 32 patients using Zynumbic yielded the following results:

Azerlieve	Zynumbic
$n_A = 24$	$n_Z = 32$
$s_A = 37.5$ seconds	$s_Z = 41.3$ seconds

Based on these sample data, can the researchers conclude a difference exists between the two drugs?

11-41. In the production of its Nutty Toffee, Cordum Candies must carefully control the temperature of its cooking process. However, in response to customer surveys, the company has recently increased the size of the chopped nuts used in the process. The marketing manager is concerned that this change will effect the variability in the cooking temperature and compromise the taste and consistency of the toffee. The head cook finds this concern strange since the change was requested by the marketing department, but yesterday he took a random sample of 27 batches of toffee and found the standard deviation of the temperature to be 1.15°F. Realizing this is only a point estimate, the marketing manager has requested a 98% confidence interval estimate for the population variance in the cooking temperature.

11-42. Belden Inc. (NYSE: BWC) and Cable Design Technologies Corp. (NYSE: CDT) merged on Thursday, July 15, 2004. The new company, Belden CDT Inc., is one of the largest U.S.-based manufacturers of high-speed electronic cables and focuses on products for the specialty electronics and data networking markets, including connectivity. One of its products is a fiber-optic cable (TrayOptic). It is designed to have an overall diameter of 0.440 inch. A standard deviation greater than 0.05 inch would be unacceptable. A sample of size 20 was taken from the production line and yielded a standard deviation of 0.070.
   a. Determine if the standard deviation does not meet specifications using a significance level of 0.01.
   b. Express a Type II error in the context of this exercise.

11-43. Coca-Cola Bottling Co. Consolidated (CCBCC), headquartered in Charlotte, North Carolina, uses quality control techniques to assure that the average amount of Coke in the cans is 12 ounces. It maintains a small standard deviation of 0.05 ounce is acceptable. Any significant deviation in this standard deviation would negate any of the quality control measures concerning the average amount of Coke in its 12 ounce cans. A sample of size 20 indicated that the standard deviation was 0.070.
   a. Determine if the standard deviation of the amount of Coke in the cans differs from the standard deviation specified by the quality control division. Use a significance level of 0.10.
   b. The quality control sampling occurs several times a day. In one day, seven samples were taken and three indicated that the standard deviation was not 0.05. If the seven samples were taken at a time in which the standard deviation met specifications, determine the probability of having at least three out of seven samples say the specification was not being met.

11-44. The College Board's *2005 Trends in Student Aid* addresses, among other topics, the difference in the average college debt accumulated by undergraduate bachelor of arts degree recipients by type of college for the 2003–2004 academic year. Samples were used to determine this difference, in which the private, for-profit college average was $24,200 and the public college average was $10,600. Suppose the respective standard deviations were 2,050 and 2,084. The sample sizes were 75 and 205, respectively.

   a. In order to determine which hypothesis test procedure needs be used to determine if a difference exists in the average undergraduate debt between private and public colleges, one of the verifications that must be performed is whether the population variances are equal. Perform this test using a significance level of 0.10.

   b. Indicate the appropriate test that should be used to determine if a difference exists in the average undergraduate debt between private and public colleges.

11-45. A March 2006 Tillinghast-Towers-Perrin (TTP) study estimated the cost of the U.S. tort system to be $260 billion in 2004. This is approximately $886 per U.S. citizen. A response by the Economic Policy Institute (EPI) indicated that approximately half of the costs ($113 billion) were not costs in any real economic sense. It indicated they are transfer payments from wrongdoers to victims. To settle these points of contention, two samples of size 51 were obtained and produced sample standard deviations of $295 and $151.

   a. Determine if a two-sample *t*-distribution can be used to determine if at most half of the tort costs ($113 billion) were not costs in any real economic sense, i.e., the mean tort cost is ≤$886/2.

   b. What other requirement must be met before the test indicated in part a can be utilized?

Computer Database Exercises

11-46. The California State Highway Patrol recently conducted a study on a stretch of interstate highway south of San Francisco to determine what differences, if any, existed in driving speeds of cars licensed in California and cars licensed in Nevada. One of the issues to be examined was whether there was a diffrence in the variability of driving speeds between cars licensed in the two states. The data file **Speed-Test** contains speeds of 140 randomly selected California cars and 75 randomly selected Nevada cars. Based on these sample results, can you conclude at the 0.05 level of significance there is a difference between the variations in driving speeds for cars licensed in the two states?

11-47. The operations manager for Cozine Corporation is concerned with variation in the number of pounds of garbage collected per truck. If this variation is too high, the manager will change the truck pickup routes to try to better balance the loads. The manager believes the current truck routing system provides for consistent garbage pickup per truck and is unwilling to reroute the trucks unless the variability, measured by the standard deviation in pounds per truck, is greater than 3,900 pounds. The data file **Cozine** contains 200 truck weights. Assuming the data represent a random sample of 200 trucks selected from Cozine's daily operations, is there evidence the manager needs to change the routes to better balance the loads? Conduct your analysis using a 0.10 level of significance. Be sure to state your conclusion in terms of the operations manager's decision.

11-48. The X-John Company makes batteries specifically designed for cellular telephones. Recently, the R&D department has developed a new battery it believes will be less expensive to produce. The R&D engineers are concerned, however, about the consistency in the lasting power of the battery. If there is too much variability in battery life, cellular phone users will be unwilling to buy X-John batteries even if they are less expensive. Engineers have specified the standard deviation of battery life must be less than 5 hours. Treat the measurements in the file **X-John** as a random sample of 100 of the new batteries. Based on this sample, is there evidence the standard deviation of battery life is less than 5 hours? Conduct the appropriate hypothesis test using a level of significance of 0.01. Report the *p*-value for this test and be sure to state a conclusion in business terms.

11-49. Freedom Hospital is in the midst of contract negotiations with its resident physicians. There has been a lot of discussion about the hospital's ability to pay and the way patients are charged. The doctors' negotiator recently mentioned the geriatric charge system does not make sense. The negotiator is concerned there is a greater variability in the total charges for males than in the total charges for females. To investigate this issue, the hospital has collected a random sample of data for 138 patients. The data are contained in the file **Patients**. Using the data for total charges, conduct the appropriate test to respond to the negotiator's concern. Use a significance level of 0.05. State your conclusion in terms that address the issue raised by the negotiator.

11-50. The Transportation Security Administration (TSA) has examined the possibility of a Registered Traveler program. This program is intended to be a way to shorten security lines for "trusted travelers."

USA Today reported (Thomas Frank, "Faster checks of fliers to start," January 20, 2006) on a study run in 2005 at Orlando International Airport. Thirteen thousand people paid an annual $80 fee to participate in the program. They spent an average of four seconds in security lines at Orlando according to Verified Identity Pass, the company that ran the program. For comparison purposes, a sample of the time it took the other passengers to pass through security at Orlando was obtained. The file entitled **Passtime** contains these data.

a. Although the average time to pass through security is of importance, the standard deviation is also important. Conduct a hypothesis test to determine if the standard deviation is larger than $1\frac{1}{2}$ minutes (i.e., 90 seconds). Use a significance level of 0.01.

b. Considering the results of your hypothesis tests in part a, determine and define the type of statistical error that could have been made.

11-51. The Federal Reserve reported in its comprehensive Survey of Consumer Finances, released every three years, that the average income of families in the United States declined from 2001 to 2004. This was the first decline since 1989–1992. A sample of incomes was taken in 2001 and repeated in 2004. After adjusting for inflation, the data that arise from these samples are given in a file entitled **Incomes**.

a. Determine if the income of families in the United States in 2001 to 2004 had different standard deviations. Use a significance level of 0.05.

b. Would it be valid to use a two-sample *t*-test to determine if the average of incomes of U.S. families was different between 2001 and 2004? Explain.

11-52. Phone Solutions provides assistance to users of a personal finance software package. Users of the software call with their questions and trained consultants provide answers and information. One concern that Phone Solutions must deal with is the staffing of its call centers. As part of the staffing issue, it seeks to reduce the average variability in the time each consultant spends with each caller. A study of this issue is currently underway at the company's three call centers. Each call center manager has randomly sampled 50 days of calls, and the collected times, in minutes, are in the file **Phone Solutions**.

a. Call Center 1 has set the goal that the variation in phone calls, measured by the standard deviation of length of calls in minutes, should be less than 3.5 minutes. Using the data in the file, can the operations manager of Call Center 1 conclude her consultants are meeting the goal? Use a 0.10 level of significance.

b. Can the manager conclude there is greater variability in the average length of phone calls for Call Center 3 than for Call Center 2? Again, use a 0.10 level of significance to conduct the appropriate test.

CASE 11.1

Motive Power Company— Part 2

Cregg Hart is manufacturing manager for Motive Power Company, a locomotive engine and rail car manufacturer (see Case 10.1). The company has been very successful in recent years and in July 2006 signed two major contracts totaling nearly $200 million. A key to the company's success has been its focus on quality. Customers from around the world have been very pleased with the attention to detail put forth by Motive Power.

In Case 10.1, Sheryl Carleson came to Cregg with a new supplier of rivets that would provide a substantial price advantage for Motive Power over the current supplier. Cregg asked Sheryl to conduct a study in which samples of rivets were selected from both suppliers. (Data are in the called **Motive Power**.) In Case 10.1 the focus was on the mean diameter and a test to determine whether the population means were the same for the two suppliers. However, Cregg reminds Sheryl that not only is the mean diameter important,

so too is the variation in diameter. Too much variation in rivet diameter adversely affects quality. Cregg showed Sheryl the following table to emphasize what he meant:

Diameter		
Company A		Company B
0.375		0.375
0.376		0.400
0.374		0.350
0.375		0.325
0.375		0.425
0.376		0.340
0.374		0.410
0.375	Mean	0.375
0.00082	St. Dev.	0.03808

As Sheryl examined this example that Cregg had prepared, she was quickly convinced that looking at the mean diameters would not be enough to fully compare the rivet suppliers. She told Cregg that she would also ask her intern to perform the following tasks.

Required Tasks:

1. Review results from Case 10.1.
2. Conduct the appropriate hypothesis test to determine whether the two suppliers have equal standard deviations. (Test using a significance level equal to 0.05.)
3. Prepare a short report that ties together the results from Cases 10.1 and 11.1 to present to Cregg along with a conclusion as to whether the new supplier seems viable based on rivet diameters.

References

Berenson, Mark L., and David M. Levine, *Basic Business Statistics Concepts and Applications*, 10th ed. (Upper Saddle River, NJ: Prentice Hall, 2006).

Cryer, Jonathan D., and Robert B. Miller, *Statistics for Business: Data Analysis and Modeling*, 2nd ed. (Belmont, CA: Duxbury Press, 1994).

Duncan, Acheson, J., *Quality Control and Industrial Statistics*, 5th ed. (Burr Ridge, IL: Irwin, 1986).

Johnson, Richard A., and Dean W. Wichern, *Business Statistics: Decision Making with Data* (New York: John Wiley & Sons, 1997).

Larsen, Richard J., Morris L. Marx, and Bruce Cooil, *Statistics for Applied Problem Solving and Decision Making* (Pacific Grove, CA: Duxbury Press, 1997).

Markowski, Carol, and Edmund Markowski, Conditions for the Effectiveness of a Preliminary Test of Variance, *The American Statistician*, November 1990, no. 4, pp. 322–326.

Microsoft Excel 2007 (Redmond, WA: Microsoft Corp., 2007).

Minitab for Windows Version 15 (State College, PA: Minitab, 2007).

Siegel, Andrew F., *Practical Business Statistics*, 5th ed. (Burr Ridge, IL: Irwin, 2003).

Analysis of Variance

CHAPTER OUTCOMES

After studying the material in Chapter 12, you should be able to:

1. Understand the basic logic of analysis of variance.
2. Perform a single-factor hypothesis test using analysis of variance manually and with the aid of Excel or Minitab software.
3. Conduct and interpret post-analysis of variance pairwise comparisons procedures.
4. Recognize when randomized block analysis of variance is useful and be able to perform randomized block analysis.
5. Perform two-factor analysis of variance tests with replications using Excel or Minitab and interpret the output.

PREPARING FOR CHAPTER TWELVE

- Review the computational methods for the sample mean and the sample variance in Chapter 3.

- Review the basics of hypothesis testing discussed in Section 9.1.

- Reexamine the material on hypothesis testing for the difference between two population variances in Section 11.2.

WHY YOU NEED TO KNOW

Chapters 9, 10, and 11 introduced the basics of hypothesis testing. By now you should understand that, regardless of the population parameter in question, hypothesis-testing steps are basically the same.

1. Specify the population parameter of interest.
2. Formulate the null and alternative hypotheses,
3. Specify the level of significance.
4. Determine a decision rule defining the rejection and "acceptance" regions.
5. Select a random sample of data from the population(s). Compute the appropriate sample statistic(s). Finally, calculate the test statistic.
6. Reach a decision. Reject the null hypothesis, H_0, if the sample statistic falls in the rejection region; otherwise, do not reject the null hypothesis. If the test is conducted using the p-value approach, H_0 is rejected whenever the p-value is smaller than the significance level; otherwise H_0 is not rejected.
7. Draw a conclusion. State the result of your hypothesis test in the context of the exercise or analysis of interest.

Chapter 9 focused on hypothesis tests involving a single population. Chapters 10 and 11 expanded the hypothesis-testing process to include applications in which differences between two populations are involved. However, you will encounter many instances involving more than two populations. For example, the vice president of operations at Farber Rubber, Inc. oversees production at Farber's six different U.S. manufacturing plants. Because each plant uses slightly different manufacturing processes, the vice president needs to know if there are any differences in average strength of the products produced at the different plants.

Similarly, *Golf Digest*, a major publisher of articles about golf, might wish to determine which of five major brands of golf balls have the highest mean distance off the tee. The Environmental Protection Agency (EPA) might conduct a test to determine if there is a difference in the average miles-per-gallon performance of cars manufactured by the Big Three U.S. automobile producers. In each of these cases, testing a hypothesis involving more than two population means could be required.

This chapter introduces a tool called analysis of variance (ANOVA), which can be used to test whether there are differences among three or more population means. There are several ANOVA procedures, depending on the type of test that is being conducted. Our aim in this chapter is to introduce you to the basics of ANOVA and to illustrate how to use Microsoft Excel and Minitab to help conduct hypothesis tests involving three or more population parameters. You will almost certainly need either to apply ANOVA in future decision-making situations or to interpret the results of an ANOVA study performed by someone else. Thus, you need to be familiar with this powerful statistical tool.

12.1 One-Way Analysis of Variance

One-Way Analysis of Variance

An analysis of variance design in which independent samples are obtained from two or more levels of a single factor for the purpose of testing whether the levels have equal means.

In Chapter 10 we introduced the t-test for testing whether two populations have equal means when the samples from the two populations are independent. However, you will often encounter situations in which you are interested in determining whether three or more populations have equal means. To conduct this test, you will need a new tool called *analysis of variance* (*ANOVA*). There are many different analysis of variance designs to fit different situations. The simplest ANOVA design is **one-way analysis of variance**.

The Logic Behind One-Way ANOVA

Business Application

CHAPTER OUTCOME #1

BAYHILL MARKETING COMPANY The Bayhill Marketing Company is a full-service marketing and advertising firm in San Francisco, California. Although Bayhill provides many different marketing services, one of its most lucrative is coupon design. Companies that wish to increase sales often mail coupons to potential customers in their marketing areas. These companies hope that people will redeem the coupons and overall sales will increase. Bayhill's account managers help client companies design their coupons for maximum effectiveness. Of course, some coupon designs are more effective than others.

For example, a major greeting card company wants to work with Bayhill in developing a coupon offer for its "Special Events" card set. The card company has negotiated a deal with the American Express credit card company to include its coupon in every American Express cardholder's monthly statement. Now the company must decide what the coupon should offer and how it will look to maximize its effectiveness. Coupon effectiveness can be determined by the percentage of coupons redeemed or by the dollar value of the greeting card sets purchased with a redeemed coupon.

Through a series of meetings with the client and focus-group sessions with potential customers, Bayhill has developed four coupon designs. Bayhill has arranged with American Express to test these designs by sending out 200 of each coupon type to randomly selected cardholders. Bayhill will then select a random sample from redeemed coupons and determine the dollar value of greeting card sets purchased with each coupon. Table 12.1 shows the data for a sample of eight redemptions for each design. The values in the table are the dollar values of greeting-card sets ordered by each customer.

In this example, we are interested in whether the different coupon designs result in different mean order sizes. In other words, we are trying to determine if "coupon designs" are one of the possible causes of the variation in the dollar value of the card sets ordered (the response variable). In this case, coupon design is called a **factor**.

The *single factor* of interest is coupon design. This factor has four categories, measurements, or strata, called **levels**. These four levels are the four designs: 1, 2, 3, and 4. Because we are using only one factor here, each dollar value of card sets ordered is associated with only one level (that is, with coupon design—type 1, 2, 3, or 4), as you can see in Table 12.1. Each level is a population of interest.

The null and alternative hypotheses to be tested are

$$H_0: \mu_1 = \mu_2 = \mu_3 = \mu_4 \text{ (mean order sizes are equal)}$$
$$H_A: \text{At least two of the population means are different.}$$

The experimental design producing the data for this experiment is called a **completely randomized design**. The appropriate statistical tool for conducting the hypothesis test related to this experimental design is analysis of variance. Because this ANOVA addresses an experiment with only one factor, it is a one-way ANOVA, or a one-factor ANOVA. Because the sample size for each coupon design (level) is the same, the experiment has a **balanced design**.

ANOVA tests the null hypothesis that three or more populations have the same mean. The test is based on three assumptions:

Factor

A quantity under examination in an experiment as a possible cause of variation in the response variable.

Levels

The categories, measurements, or strata of a factor of interest in the current experiment.

Completely Randomized Design

An experiment is completely randomized if it consists of the independent random selection of observations representing each level of one factor.

Balanced Design

An experiment has a balanced design if the factor levels have equal sample sizes.

Assumptions

1. All populations are normally distributed.
2. The population variances are equal.
3. The observations are independent—that is, the occurrence of any one individual value does not affect the probability that any other observation will occur.
4. The data are interval or ratio level.

TABLE 12.1 Bayhill Marketing Company Coupon Order Data

| Customer | Coupon Design | | | |
	1	2	3	4
1	$ 4.10	$ 6.90	$ 4.60	$12.50
2	5.90	9.10	11.40	7.50
3	10.45	13.00	6.15	6.25
4	11.55	7.90	7.85	8.75
5	5.25	9.10	4.30	11.15
6	7.75	13.40	8.70	10.25
7	4.78	7.60	10.20	6.40
8	6.22	5.00	10.80	9.20

Grand Mean

Mean $\bar{x}_1 = \$7.00$ $\bar{x}_2 = \$9.00$ $\bar{x}_3 = \$8.00$ $\bar{x}_4 = \$9.00$ $\bar{\bar{x}} = \$8.25$

Variance $s_1^2 = 7.341$ $s_2^2 = 8.423$ $s_3^2 = 7.632$ $s_4^2 = 5.016$

Note: Data are dollar value of card sets ordered with each coupon.

If the null hypothesis is true, the populations have identical distributions. If so, the sample means for random samples from each population should be close in value. The basic logic of ANOVA is the same as the two-sample t-test introduced in Chapter 10. The null hypothesis should be rejected only if the sample means are substantially different.

You may be surprised to learn that the hypothesis test for equality of the population means is in fact an F-test involving two variances. To show you what we mean, consider that in Chapter 7 we showed that the distribution of sample means for a sample of size n taken from a normally distributed population has a standard deviation $\sigma_{\bar{x}} = \sigma/\sqrt{n}$. From this, the variance of the $\bar{x}$ values is $\sigma_{\bar{x}}^2 = \sigma^2/n$.

Figure 12.1 illustrates what the sampling distribution of $\bar{x}$ values would look like. If the null hypothesis is true, the sample means from each population can be thought of as values coming from the sampling distribution in Figure 12.1. The average value of the sample means would be an estimate for μ, the mean of the sampling distribution. Likewise, the variation in the sample means would be the estimate for the variance of the sampling distribution, $\sigma_{\bar{x}}^2$.

If, as assumed, the populations have the same variance, σ^2, we can solve for σ^2 as

$$n\sigma_{\bar{x}}^2 = \sigma^2$$

where n is the common sample size from each population. Consider the data in Table 12.1. The sample means are shown for sample sizes of eight. Also shown is the average of the sample means, $\bar{\bar{x}} = 8.25$. Then the estimate for $\sigma_{\bar{x}}^2$ is

$$s_{\bar{x}}^2 = \frac{(7-8.25)^2 + (9-8.25)^2 + (8-8.25)^2 + (9-8.25)^2}{4-1} = 0.917$$

It follows that an estimate of σ^2 is

$$n\left(s_{\bar{x}}^2\right) = 8(0.917) = 7.336$$

This value is referred to as the *between-levels (or treatments) estimate of σ^2*, and it is based on the premise that the null hypothesis is true and the means of the respective populations are equal.

Another approach to estimating the common variance, σ^2, is to use a pooled estimate. Because we assume that all k populations have the same variance, the average of the population variances is equal to the common population variance:

$$\sigma^2 = \frac{\sigma_1^2 + \sigma_2^2 + \cdots + \sigma_k^2}{k} = \frac{\sigma^2 + \sigma^2 + \cdots + \sigma^2}{k} = \frac{k\sigma^2}{k}$$

FIGURE 12.1

Sampling Distribution of $\bar{x}$

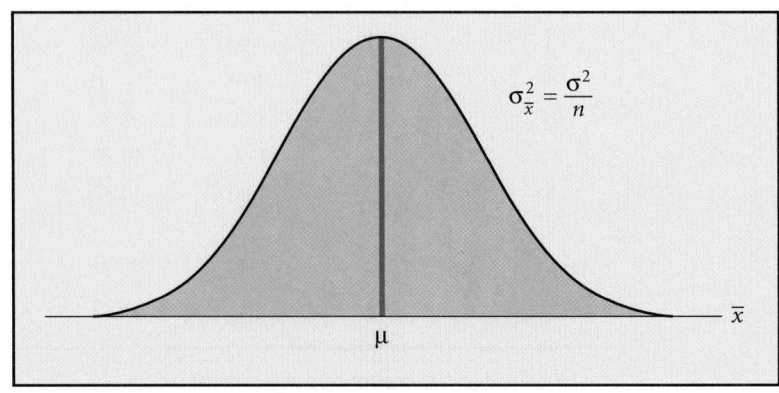

FIGURE 12.2

Variation in Sample Means

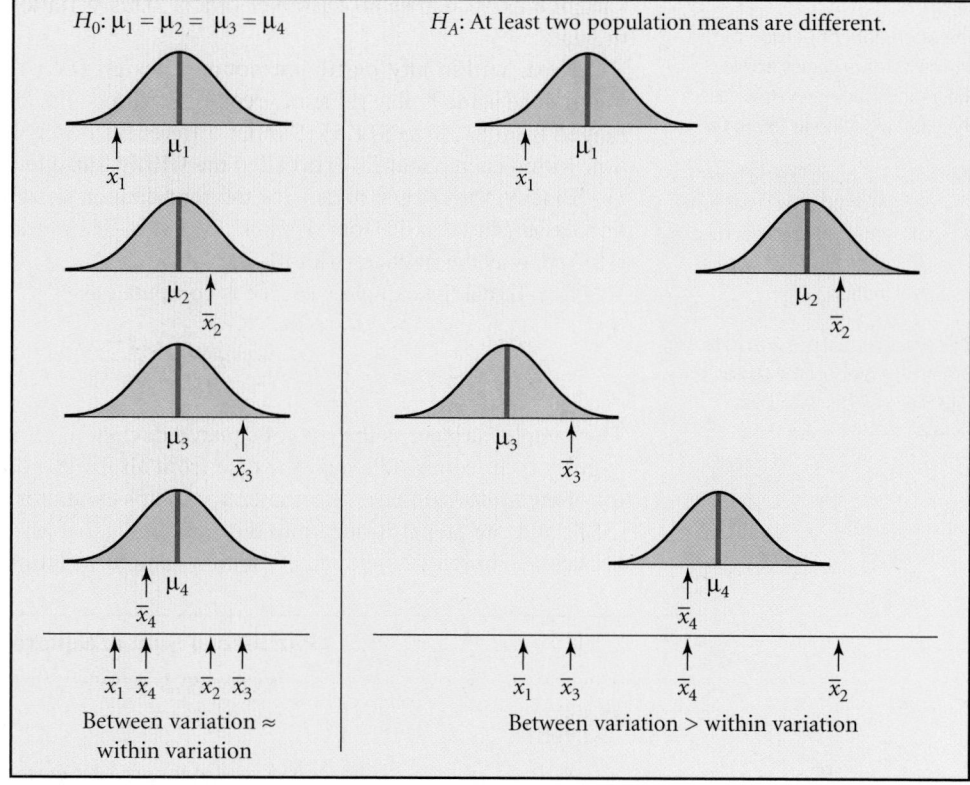

However, each population variance is a measure of the variation within that specific population and is not dependent on whether the means of the populations are equal. Thus, given equal sample sizes from each population, the *within-levels estimate of* σ^2 is

$$s^2 = \frac{s_1^2 + s_2^2 + \cdots + s_k^2}{k}$$

Based on the data in Table 12.1 for the Bayhill Marketing Company, the within-levels estimate for σ^2 is

$$s^2 = \frac{7.341 + 8.423 + 7.632 + 5.016}{4} = 7.103$$

Now, we have two estimates for the same population variance. The two estimates should have approximately the same value if the null hypothesis of equal means is true. However, if the populations have unequal means, the *between-levels estimate* for σ^2 will be greater than the *within-levels estimate* because the sample means will tend to differ substantially from one another. This is illustrated in Figure 12.2.

Thus, to test whether the population means are equal, you actually compare these two variance estimates. As you learned in Chapter 11, the *F*-distribution is used to test whether two variances are equal. As we will illustrate shortly, in ANOVA, the *F*-ratio is formed by taking the ratio of the between-level estimate over the within-level estimate. If this *F*-ratio gets too large, the null hypothesis of equal means is rejected.

Partitioning the Sum of Squares

Refer again to the sample data in Table 12.1. In order to understand the logic of ANOVA, you should note several things about the data. First, the dollar values of the orders are different throughout the data table. Some values are higher; others are lower. Thus,

Total Variation
The aggregate dispersion of the individual data values across the various factor levels is called the *total variation* in the data.

Within-Sample Variation
The dispersion that exists among the data values within a particular factor level is called the *within-sample variation*.

Between-sample Variation
Dispersion among the factor sample means is called the *between-sample variation*.

variation exists across all customer orders. This variation is called the **total variation** in the data.

Next, within any particular coupon design (i.e., factor levels), not all customers ordered the same dollar value of greeting-card sets. For instance, within level 1, order size ranged from $4.10 to $11.55. Similar differences occur within the other levels. The variation within each factor level is called the **within-sample variation**.

Finally, the sample means for the four coupon designs are not all equal. Thus, variation exists between the four designs' averages. This variation between the factor levels is referred to as the **between-sample variation**.

Recall that the sample variance is computed as

$$s^2 = \frac{\sum(x - \bar{x})^2}{n - 1}$$

The sample variance is the sum of squared deviations from the sample mean divided by its degrees of freedom. When all the data from all the samples are included, s^2 is the estimator of the *total variation*. The numerator of this estimator is called the *total sum of squares* (*SST*) and can be partitioned into the sum of squares associated with the estimators of the between-sample variation and the within-sample variation, as shown in Equation 12.1.

Partitioned Sum of Squares

$$SST = SSB + SSW \tag{12.1}$$

where:

SST = Total sum of squares
SSB = Sum of squares between
SSW = Sum of squares within

After separating the sum of squares, they are divided by their degrees of freedom to produce the respective variance estimators previously discussed. If the between-sample portion of the total variation is large relative to the within-sample variation, the ANOVA procedure will lead us to reject the null hypothesis and conclude the population means are different. The question is: How can we determine at what point any difference is statistically significant?

The ANOVA Assumptions

Business Application

BAYHILL MARKETING COMPANY (*CONTINUED*) Recall that Bayhill is testing whether the four coupon designs generate orders of equal average dollar value. The null and alternative hypotheses are

$$H_0: \mu_1 = \mu_2 = \mu_3 = \mu_4$$
$$H_A: \text{At least two population means are different.}$$

Before we jump into the ANOVA calculations, recall the four basic assumptions of ANOVA:

1. All populations are normally distributed.
2. The population variances are equal.
3. The sampled observations are independent.
4. The data are interval or ratio level.

Figure 12.3 demonstrates the first two assumptions. The populations are normally distributed and the spread (variance) is the same for each population. However, in this case, the populations have different means—and the null hypothesis is false. Figure 12.4 demonstrates the same assumptions but in a case in which the population means are equal; therefore, the null hypothesis is true.

FIGURE 12.3

Normal Populations with Equal Variances and Unequal Means

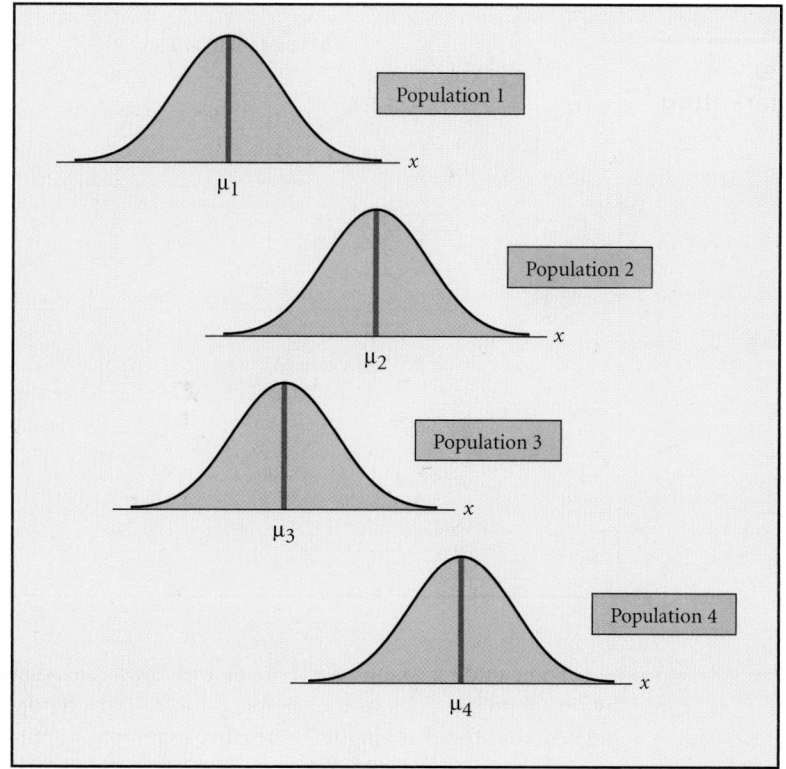

FIGURE 12.4

Normal Populations with Equal Variances and Equal Means

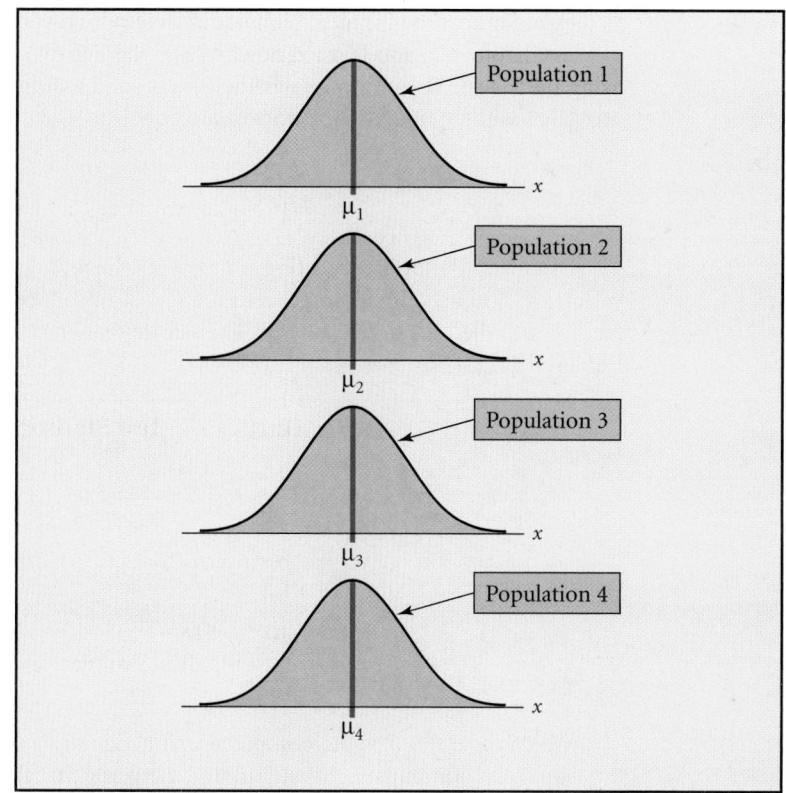

FIGURE 12.5

Box and Whisker Plot—Bayhill Marketing Company

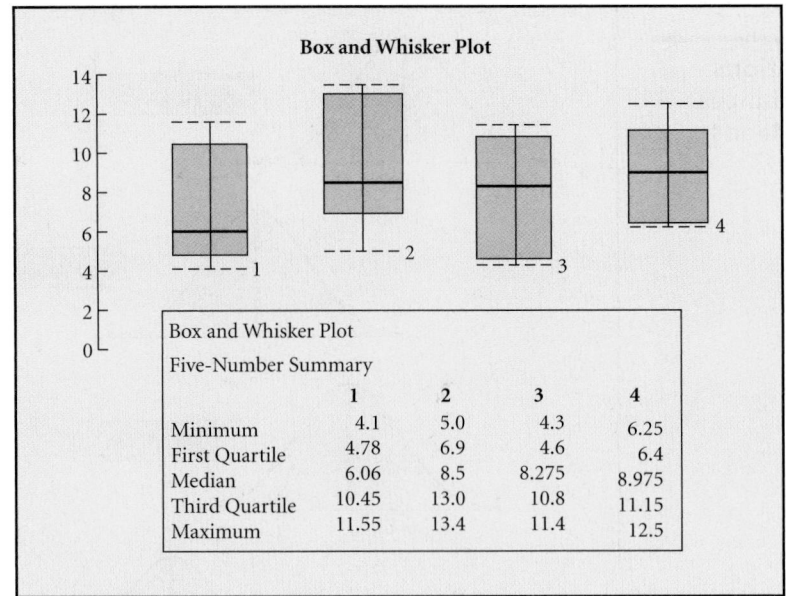

You can do a rough check to determine whether the normality assumption is satisfied by developing graphs of the sample data from each population. Histograms are probably the best tool for checking the normality assumption, but they require a fairly large sample size. The stem and leaf and box and whisker plots are alternatives when sample sizes are smaller. If the graphical tools show plots that are consistent with a normal distribution, then that evidence suggests the normality assumption is satisfied.[1] Figure 12.5 illustrates the box and whisker plot for the Bayhill data. Note, when the sample sizes are very small, as they are here, the graphical techniques may not be very effective.

In Chapter 11, you learned how to test whether two populations have equal variances using the F-test. To determine whether the second assumption is satisfied, we can hypothesize that all the population variances are equal:

$$H_0: \sigma_1^2 = \sigma_2^2 = \cdots = \sigma_k^2$$

H_A: Not all variances are equal.

Because you are now testing a null hypothesis involving more than two population variances, you need an alternative to the F-test introduced in Chapter 11. This alternative method is called *Hartley's F max*. The Hartley's F-test statistic is computed as shown in Equation 12.2.

Hartley's F-Test Statistic

$$F_{\max} = \frac{s_{\max}^2}{s_{\min}^2} \tag{12.2}$$

where:

$s_{\max}^2$ = Largest sample variance
$s_{\min}^2$ = Smallest sample variance

We can use the F-value computed using Equation 12.2 to test whether the variances are equal by comparing the calculated F to a critical value from the *Hartley's F*$_{\max}$

---

[1] Chapter 13 introduces a goodness-of-fit approach to testing whether sample data come from a normally distributed population.

distribution, which appears in Appendix I.[2] For the Bayhill example, the computed variance for each of the four samples is

$$s_1^2 = 7.341 \qquad s_2^2 = 8.423 \qquad s_3^2 = 7.632 \qquad s_4^2 = 5.016$$

Using Equation 12.2, we compute the F_{max} value as

$$F_{max} = \frac{8.423}{5.016} = 1.679$$

This value is now compared to the critical F_α from the table in Appendix I for $\alpha = 0.05$, with $k = 4$ and $\bar{n} - 1 = 7$ degrees of freedom. The value, k, is the number of populations ($k = 4$). The value $\bar{n}$ is the average sample size, which equals 8 in this example. If $\bar{n}$ is not an integer value, then set $\bar{n}$ equal to the integer portion of the computed $\bar{n}$. If $F_{max} > F_\alpha$, reject the null hypothesis of equal variances. If $F_{max} \leq F_\alpha$, do not reject the null hypothesis and conclude the population variances are equal. From the Hartley's F_{max} distribution table, the critical $F_{0.05} = 8.44$. Because $F_{max} = 1.679 \leq 8.44$, the null hypothesis of equal variances is not rejected.[3]

Examining your sample data to see whether you are meeting the basic assumptions is always a good idea, but you should be aware that the analysis of variance procedures discussed in this chapter are *robust*, in the sense that the analysis of variance test is relatively unperturbed when the equal-variance assumption is not met. This is especially so when all samples are the same size, as in the Bayhill Marketing Company example. Hence, for one-way analysis of variance, or any other ANOVA design, try to ensure all samples are the same size. Recall, we earlier referred to an analysis of variance design with equal sample sizes as a *balanced design*. If for some reason you are unable to use a balanced design, the rule of thumb is that the ratio of the largest sample size to the smallest sample size should not exceed 1.5.

When the samples are the same size (or meet the 1.5 ratio rule), the analysis of variance is also robust with respect to the assumption that the populations are normally distributed. So, in brief, the one-way ANOVA for independent samples can be applied to virtually any set of interval- or ratio-level data.

Finally, if the data are not interval or ratio level, or if they do not satisfy the normal distribution assumption, Chapter 17 introduces an ANOVA procedure called the Kruskal-Wallis One-Way ANOVA, which does not require these assumptions.

Applying One-Way ANOVA

Although the previous discussion covers the essence of ANOVA, to determine whether the null hypothesis should be rejected requires that we actually determine values of the estimators for the total variation, between-sample variation, and within-sample variation. Most ANOVA tests are done using a computer, but we will illustrate the manual computational approach once. Because software such as Excel and Minitab can be used to perform all calculations, future examples will be done using the computer. The software packages will do all the computations while we focus on interpreting the results.

Business Application

CHAPTER OUTCOME #2

BAYHILL MARKETING COMPANY (*CONTINUED*) Now we are ready to perform the necessary one-way ANOVA computations for the Bayhill example. Recall from Equation 12.1 that we can partition the total sum of squares into two components:

$$SST = SSB + SSW$$

---

[2] Other tests for equal variances exist. For example, Minitab has a procedure that uses Bartlett and Levine's test.

[3] Hartley's F_{max} test is very dependent on the populations being normally distributed and should not be used if the populations' distributions are skewed. Note also in Hartley's F_{max} table, $c = k$ and $v = \bar{n} - 1$.

The *total sum of squares* is computed as shown in Equation 12.3.

Total Sum of Squares

$$SST = \sum_{i=1}^{k} \sum_{j=1}^{n_i} (x_{ij} - \overline{\overline{x}})^2 \tag{12.3}$$

where:

SST = Total sum of squares
k = Number of populations (treatments)
n_i = Sample size from population i
x_{ij} = jth measurement from population i
$\overline{\overline{x}}$ = Grand mean (mean of all the data values)

Equation 12.3 is not as complicated as it appears. Manually applying Equation 12.3 to the Bayhill data shown in Table 12.1 on page 511 (grand mean $= \overline{\overline{x}} = 8.25$), we can compute SST as follows:

$$SST = (4.10 - 8.25)^2 + (5.90 - 8.25)^2 + (10.45 - 8.25)^2 + \cdots + (9.20 - 8.25)^2$$
$$SST = 220.88$$

Thus, the sum of the squared deviations of all values from the grand mean is 220.88. Equation 12.3 can also be restated as

$$SST = \sum_{i=1}^{k} \sum_{j=1}^{n_i} (x_{ij} - \overline{\overline{x}})^2 = (n_T - 1)s^2$$

where s^2 is the sample variance for all data combined, and n_T is the sum of the combined sample sizes.

We now need to determine how much of this total sum of squares is due to between-sample sum of squares and how much is due to within-sample sum of squares. The between-sample portion is called the *sum of squares between* and is found using Equation 12.4.

Sum of Squares Between

$$SSB = \sum_{i=1}^{k} n_i (\overline{x}_i - \overline{\overline{x}})^2 \tag{12.4}$$

where:

SSB = Sum of squares between samples
k = Number of populations
n_i = Sample size from population i
$\overline{x}_i$ = Sample mean from population i
$\overline{\overline{x}}$ = Grand mean

We can use Equation 12.4 to manually compute the sum of squares between for the Bayhill data, as follows.

$$SSB = 8(7 - 8.25)^2 + 8(9 - 8.25)^2 + 8(8 - 8.25)^2 + 8(9 - 8.25)^2$$
$$SSB = 22$$

Once both the SST and SSB have been computed, the *sum of squares within* (also called the sum of squares error, SSE) is easily computed using Equation 12.5. The sum of squares within can also be computed directly using Equation 12.6.

Sum of Squares Within

$$SSW = SST - SSB \tag{12.5}$$

or

Sum of Squares Within

$$SSW = \sum_{i=1}^{k} \sum_{j=1}^{n_i} (x_{ij} - \bar{x}_i)^2 \tag{12.6}$$

where:

SSW = Sum of squares within samples
k = Number of populations
n_i = Sample size from population i
$\bar{x}_i$ = Sample mean from population i
x_{ij} = jth measurement from population i

For the Bayhill example, the SSW is

$$SSW = 220.88 - 22.00$$
$$= 198.88$$

These computations are the essential first steps in performing the ANOVA test to determine whether the population means are equal. Table 12.2 illustrates the ANOVA table format that is used to conduct the test. The format shown in Table 12.2 is the standard ANOVA table layout. For the Bayhill example, we substitute the numerical values for SSB, SSW, and SST, and complete the ANOVA table, as shown in Table 12.3. The mean square column contains the MSB (mean square between samples) and the MSW (mean square within samples).[4] These values are computed by dividing the sum of squares by their respective degrees of freedom, as shown in Table 12.3.

Restating the null and alternative hypotheses for the Bayhill example:

H_0: $\mu_1 = \mu_2 = \mu_3 = \mu_4$
H_A: At least two population means are different.

TABLE 12.2 One-Way ANOVA Table: The Basic Format

Source of Variation	SS	df	MS	F-Ratio
Between samples	SSB	$k - 1$	MSB	$\dfrac{MSB}{MSW}$
Within samples	SSW	$n_T - k$	MSW	
Total	SST	$n_T - 1$		

where:

k = Number of populations
n_T = Sum of the sample sizes from all populations
df = Degrees of freedom

$$MSB = \text{Mean square between} = \frac{SSB}{k-1}$$

$$MSW = \text{Mean square within} = \frac{SSW}{n_T - k}$$

---

[4] MSW is also known as the *mean square for error (MSE)*.

TABLE 12.3 One-Way ANOVA Table for the Bayhill Marketing Co.

Source of Variation	SS	df	MS	F-Ratio
Between samples	22.00	3	7.33	$\dfrac{7.33}{7.10} = 1.03$
Within samples	198.88	28	7.10	
Total	220.88	31		

where:

$$MSB = \text{Mean square between} = \frac{SSB}{k-1} = \frac{22}{3} = 7.33$$

$$MSW = \text{Mean square within} = \frac{SSW}{n_T - k} = \frac{198.88}{28} = 7.10$$

Glance back at Figures 12.3 and 12.4. If the null hypothesis is true (that is, all the means are equal—Figure 12.4), MSW and MSB will be equal, except for the presence of sampling error. However, the more the sample means differ (Figure 12.3), the larger the MSB becomes. As the MSB increases, it will tend to get larger than the MSW. When this difference gets too large, we will conclude that the population means must not be equal, and the null hypothesis will be rejected. But how do we determine what "too large" is? How do we know when the difference is due to more than just sampling error?

To answer these questions, recall from Chapter 11 and from the development in "The Logic Behind the One-Way ANOVA" that the F-distribution is used to test whether two populations have the same variance. In the ANOVA test, if the null hypothesis is true, the ratio of MSB over MSW forms an F-distribution with $D_1 = k - 1$ and $D_2 = n_T - k$ degrees of freedom. If the calculated F-ratio in Table 12.3 gets too large, the null hypothesis is rejected.

Figure 12.6 illustrates the hypothesis test for a significance level of 0.05. Because the calculated F-ratio = 1.03 is less than the critical $F_{0.05} = 2.95$ (found using Excel's **FINV** function) with 3 and 28 degrees of freedom, the null hypothesis cannot be rejected. The F-ratio indicates that the between-levels estimate and the within-levels estimate are not different enough to conclude that the population means are different. This means there is insufficient statistical evidence to conclude that any one of the four coupon designs will generate higher average dollar values of orders than any of the other designs. Therefore, the choice of which coupon design to use can be based on other factors, such as printing cost.

FIGURE 12.6

Bayhill Company Hypothesis Test

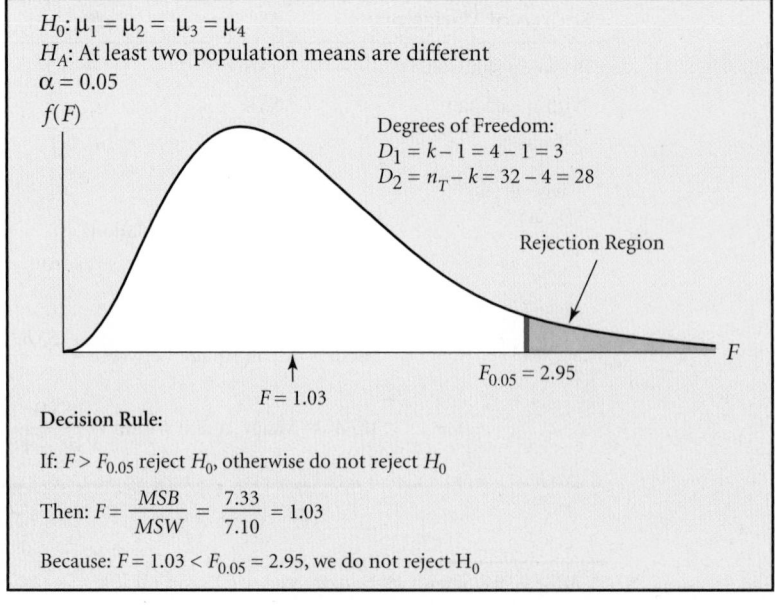

$H_0: \mu_1 = \mu_2 = \mu_3 = \mu_4$
$H_A:$ At least two population means are different
$\alpha = 0.05$

$f(F)$

Degrees of Freedom:
$D_1 = k - 1 = 4 - 1 = 3$
$D_2 = n_T - k = 32 - 4 = 28$

Rejection Region

$F_{0.05} = 2.95$

F

$F = 1.03$

Decision Rule:

If: $F > F_{0.05}$ reject H_0, otherwise do not reject H_0

Then: $F = \dfrac{MSB}{MSW} = \dfrac{7.33}{7.10} = 1.03$

Because: $F = 1.03 < F_{0.05} = 2.95$, we do not reject H_0

CHAPTER OUTCOME #2

TRY PROBLEM 12.6

EXAMPLE 12-1 One-Way Analysis of Variance

Westfall Relocation Company   The Westfall Relocation Company, located in Denver, Colorado, contracts with major corporations forced to lay off employees. Westfall provides a variety of services, including job searches, specialized training, and resume development. Westfall then bills the corporation for the services. It currently operates in three regions: the West, Southwest, and Northwest. Recently, Westfall's general manager questioned whether the company's mean billing amount differed by region. To determine this, the following steps can be performed:

Step 1 Specify the parameter(s) of interest.
The parameter of interest is the mean dollars billed in each region.

Step 2 Formulate the null and alternative hypotheses.
The appropriate null and alternative hypotheses are

$$H_0: \mu_W = \mu_{SW} = \mu_{NW}$$
$$H_A: \text{At least two populations have different means.}$$

Step 3 Specify the significance level (α) for testing the hypothesis.
The test will be conducted using an $\alpha = 0.05$.

Step 4 Select independent simple random samples from each population, and compute the sample means and the grand mean.
There are three regions. Simple random samples of employees served in these regions have been selected: 10 in the West, 8 in the Southwest, and 12 in the Northwest. Note, even though the sample sizes are not equal, the largest sample is not more than 1.5 times as large as the smallest sample size. The following sample data were collected:

West	Southwest	Northwest
$3,700	$3,300	$2,900
2,900	2,100	4,300
4,100	2,600	5,200
4,900	2,100	3,300
4,900	3,600	3,600
5,300	2,700	3,300
2,200	4,500	3,700
3,700	2,400	2,400
4,800		4,400
3,000		3,300
		4,400
		3,200

The sample means are

$$\bar{x}_W = \frac{\Sigma x}{n} = \frac{\$39,500}{10} = \$3,950$$

$$\bar{x}_{SW} = \frac{\$23,300}{8} = \$2,912.50$$

$$\bar{x}_{NW} = \frac{\$44,000}{12} = \$3,666.67$$

and the grand mean is the mean of the data from all samples:

$$\bar{\bar{x}} = \frac{\sum\sum x}{n_T} = \frac{\$3,700 + \$2,900 + \cdots + \$3,200}{30}$$

$$= \frac{\$106,800}{30}$$

$$= \$3,560$$

Step 5 **Check to see that the normality and equal variance assumptions have been satisfied.**

As long as we assume that the populations are normally distributed, Hartley's $F_{\max}$ test can be used to test whether the three populations have equal variances. The test statistic is

$$F_{\max} = \frac{s^2_{\max}}{s^2_{\min}}$$

The three variances are computed using

$$s^2_W = \frac{\sum(x - \bar{x}_w)^2}{n-1} = 1,062,777.8 \qquad s^2_{SW} = 695,535.7$$

$$s^2_{NW} = 604,242.4$$

Hartley's $F_{\max} = \dfrac{1,062,777.8}{604,242.4} = 1.76$

From the $F_{\max}$ table in Appendix I, the critical value for $\alpha = 0.05$, $c = 3$ ($c = k$), and $v = 9$ ($v = \bar{n} - 1$) is 5.34. Because $1.76 \leq 5.34$, we do not reject the null hypothesis of equal variances.

Step 6 **Determine the decision rule.**

The F-critical value from the F-distribution table in Appendix H for $D_1 = 2$ and $D_2 = 27$ degrees of freedom is a value between 3.316 and 3.403. The exact value $F_{0.05} = 3.354$ can be found using Excel's **FINV** function or Minitab's **Calc > Probability Distributions** command.

The decision rule is

If $F > 3.354$, reject the null hypothesis;
Otherwise, do not reject the null hypothesis.

Step 7 **Create the ANOVA table.**

Compute the total sum of squares, sum of squares between, and sum of squares within, and complete the ANOVA table.

Total Sum of Squares

$$SST = \sum_{i=1}^{k}\sum_{j=1}^{n_i}(x_{ij} - \bar{\bar{x}})^2$$

$$= (3,700 - 3,560)^2 + (2,900 - 3,560)^2 + \cdots + (3,200 - 3,560)^2$$

$$= 26,092,000$$

Sum of Squares Between

$$SSB = \sum_{i=1}^{k}n_i(\bar{x}_i - \bar{\bar{x}})^2$$

$$= 10(3,950 - 3,560)^2 + 8(2,912.50 - 3,560)^2 + 12(3,666.67 - 3,560)^2$$

$$= 5,011,583$$

Sum of Squares Within
$$SSW = SST - SSB = 26{,}092{,}000 - 5{,}011{,}583 = 21{,}080{,}417$$

The ANOVA table is

Source of Variation	SS	df	MS	F-Ratio
Between samples	5,011,583	2	2,505,792	$\dfrac{2{,}505{,}792}{780{,}756} = 3.209$
Within samples	21,080,417	27	780,756	
Total	26,092,000	29		

Step 8 Reach a decision.
Because the F-test statistic $= 3.209 < F_{0.05} = 3.354$, we do not reject the null hypothesis based on these sample data.

Step 9 Draw a conclusion.
We are not able to detect a difference in the mean billing per customer by region.

Business Application

Excel and Minitab Tutorial

HYDRONICS CORPORATION The Hydronics Corporation makes and distributes health products. Currently, the company's research department is experimenting with two new herb-based weight-loss-enhancing products. To gauge their effectiveness, researchers at the company conducted a test using 300 human subjects over a six-week period. All the people in the study were between 30 and 40 pounds overweight.

One-third of the subjects were randomly selected to receive a placebo—in this case, a pill containing only vitamin C. One-third of the subjects were randomly selected and given Product 1. The remaining 100 people received Product 2. The subjects did not know which pill they had been assigned. Each person was asked to take the pill regularly for six weeks and otherwise observe his or her normal routine. At the end of six weeks, the subjects' weight loss was recorded. The company was hoping to find statistical evidence that at least one of the products is an effective weight-loss aid.

The CD-ROM file **Hydronics** shows the study data. Positive values indicate that the subject lost weight, whereas negative values indicate that the subject gained weight during the six-week study period. As often happens in studies involving human subjects, people drop out. Thus, at the end of six weeks, only 89 placebo subjects, 91 Product 1 subjects, and 83 Product 2 subjects with valid data remained. Consequently, this experiment resulted in an unbalanced design. Although the sample sizes are not equal, they are close to being the same size and do not violate the 1.5 ratio rule of thumb mentioned earlier.

The null and alternative hypotheses to be tested using a significance level of 0.05 are

$$H_0: \mu_1 = \mu_2 = \mu_3$$
$$H_A: \text{At least two population means are different.}$$

The experimental design is completely randomized. The factor is diet supplement, which has three levels: placebo, Product 1, and Product 2. We will use a significance level of $\alpha = 0.05$.

Figure 12.7a and Figure 12.7b show the Excel and Minitab analysis of variance results. The top section of the Excel ANOVA and the bottom section of the Minitab ANOVA output provide descriptive information for the three levels. The ANOVA table is shown in the other section of the output. These tables look like the one we generated manually in the Bayhill example. However, Excel and Minitab also compute the p-value. In addition, Excel displays the critical value, F-critical, from the F-distribution table. Thus, you can test the null hypothesis by comparing the calculated F to the F-critical or by comparing the p-value to the significance level.

FIGURE 12.7A

Excel 2007 Output: Hydronics Weight Loss ANOVA Results

Excel 2007 Instructions:
1. Open file: Hydronics.xls.
2. On the **Data** tab, click **Data Analysis**.
3. Select **ANOVA: Single Factor**.
4. Define data range (columns B, C and D).
5. Specify alpha level = 0.05.
6. Indicate output location.
7. Click **OK**.

FIGURE 12.7B

Minitab Output: Hydronics Weight Loss ANOVA Results

Minitab Instructions:
1. Open file: Hydronics. MTW.
2. Chapter **Stat > ANOVA > One way**.
3. In **Response**, enter data column, *Loss*.
4. In **Factor**, enter factor level column, *Program*.
5. Click **OK**.

The decision rule is

$$\text{If } F > F_{0.05} = 3.03, \text{ reject } H_0;$$
$$\text{Otherwise, do not reject } H_0.$$

or

$$\text{If } p\text{-value} < \alpha = 0.05, \text{ reject } H_0;$$
$$\text{Otherwise, do not reject } H_0.$$

Because

$$F = 20.48 > F_{0.05} = 3.03 \text{ (or because } p\text{-value} \approx 0.0000 < \alpha = 0.05\text{)}$$

we reject the null hypothesis and conclude there is a difference in the mean weight loss for people on the three treatments. At least two of the populations have different means. The top portion of Figure 12.7a shows the descriptive measures for the sample data. For example, the subjects who took the placebo actually gained an average of 1.75 pounds. Subjects on Product 1 lost an average of 2.45 pounds, and subjects on Product 2 lost an average of 2.58 pounds.

CHAPTER OUTCOME #3

The Tukey-Kramer Procedure for Multiple Comparisons What does this conclusion imply about which treatment results in greater weight loss? One approach to answering this question is to use confidence interval estimates for all possible pairs of population means, based on the pooling of the two relevant sample variances, as introduced in Chapter 10.

$$s_p = \sqrt{\frac{(n_1 - 1)s_1^2 + (n_2 - 1)s_2^2}{n_1 + n_2 - 2}}$$

These confidence intervals are constructed using the formula also given in Chapter 10

$$(\bar{x}_1 - \bar{x}_2) \pm t s_p \sqrt{\frac{1}{n_1} + \frac{1}{n_2}}$$

It uses a weighted average of only the two sample variances corresponding to the two sample means in the confidence interval. However, in the Hydronics example, we have three samples, and thus three variances involved. If we were to use the pooled standard deviation, s_p shown here, we would be disregarding one-third of the information available to estimate the common population variance. Instead, we use confidence intervals based on the pooled standard deviation obtained from the square root of *MSW*. This is the square root of the weighted average of all (three in this example) sample variances. This is preferred to the interval estimate shown here because we are assuming that each of the three sample variances is an estimate of the common population variance.

A better method for testing which populations have different means after the one-way ANOVA has led us to reject the null hypothesis is called the *Tukey-Kramer procedure for multiple comparisons*.[5] To understand why the Tukey-Kramer procedure is superior, we introduce the concept of an **experiment-wide error rate**.

Experiment-Wide Error Rate
The proportion of experiments in which at least one of the set of confidence intervals constructed does not contain the true value of the population parameter being estimated.

The Tukey-Kramer procedure is based on the simultaneous construction of confidence intervals for all differences of pairs of treatment means. In this example, there are three different pairs of means ($\mu_1 - \mu_2, \mu_1 - \mu_3, \mu_2 - \mu_3$). The Tukey-Kramer procedure simultaneously constructs three different confidence intervals for a specified confidence level, say 95%. Intervals that do not contain zero imply that a difference exists between the associated population means.

Suppose we repeat the study a large number of times. Each time, we construct the Tukey-Kramer 95% confidence intervals. The Tukey-Kramer method assures us that in 95% of these experiments, the three confidence intervals constructed will include the true difference between the population means, $\mu_i - \mu_j$. In 5% of the experiments, at least one of the confidence intervals will not contain the true difference between the population means. Thus in 5% of the situations, we would make at least one mistake in our conclusions about

---

[5] There are other methods for making these comparisons. Statisticians disagree over which method to use. Later, we introduce alternative methods.

which populations have different means. This proportion of errors (0.05) is known as the experiment-wide error rate.

For a 95% confidence interval, the Tukey-Kramer procedure controls the experiment-wide error to a 0.05 level. However, because we are concerned with only this one experiment (with one set of sample data), the error rate associated with any one of the three confidence intervals is actually less than 0.05.

The Tukey-Kramer procedure allows us to simultaneously examine all pairs of populations *after* the ANOVA test has been completed without increasing the true alpha level. Because these comparisons are made after the ANOVA *F*-test, the procedure is called a post-test procedure.

The first step in using the Tukey-Kramer procedure is to compute the absolute differences between each pair of sample means. Using the results shown in Figure 12.7a, we get the following absolute differences.

$$|\bar{x}_1 - \bar{x}_2| = |-1.75 - 2.45| = 4.20$$
$$|\bar{x}_1 - \bar{x}_3| = |-1.75 - 2.58| = 4.33$$
$$|\bar{x}_2 - \bar{x}_3| = |2.45 - 2.58| = 0.13$$

The Tukey-Kramer procedure requires us to compare these absolute differences to the *critical range* that is computed using Equation 12.7.

Tukey-Kramer Critical Range

$$\text{Critical Range} = q_{1-\alpha} \sqrt{\frac{MSW}{2}\left(\frac{1}{n_i} + \frac{1}{n_j}\right)}$$
  (12.7)

where:

$q_{1-\alpha}$ = Value from studentized range table (Appendix J), with $D_1 = k$ and $D_2 = n_T - k$ degrees of freedom for the desired level of $1 - \alpha$ [k = number of groups or factor levels, and n_T = total number of data values from all populations (levels) combined]

MSW = Mean square within

n_i and n_j = Sample sizes from populations (levels) i and j, respectively

---

A critical range is computed for each pairwise comparison, but if the samples sizes are equal, only one critical-range calculation is necessary because the quantity under the radical in Equation 12.7 will be the same for all comparisons. If the calculated pairwise comparison value is greater than the critical range, we conclude the difference is significant.

The q value from the studentized range table in Appendix J for a significance level equal to

$$\alpha = 0.05$$

and

$$k = 3 \text{ and } n_T - k = 260 \text{ degrees of freedom}$$

For $D_2 = n_T - k = 260$ degrees of freedom, we use the row labeled ∞. The studentized range value for $1 - 0.05 = 0.95$ is approximately

$$q_{0.95} = 3.31$$

Then, for the placebo versus Product 1 comparison,

$$n_1 = 89 \quad \text{and} \quad n_2 = 91$$

TABLE 12.4 Hydronics Pairwise Comparisons—Tukey-Kramer Test

	$\lvert \bar{x}_i - \bar{x}_j \rvert$	Critical Range	Significant?
Placebo vs. Product 1	4.20	1.785	Yes
Placebo vs. Product 2	4.33	1.827	Yes
Product 1 vs. Product 2	0.13	1.818	No

we use Equation 12.7 to compute the critical range, as follows:

$$\text{Critical Range} = q_\alpha \sqrt{\frac{MSW}{2}\left(\frac{1}{n_i} + \frac{1}{n_j}\right)}$$

$$\text{Critical Range} = 3.31 \sqrt{\frac{26.18}{2}\left(\frac{1}{89} + \frac{1}{91}\right)} = 1.785$$

Because

$$\lvert \bar{x}_1 - \bar{x}_2 \rvert = 4.20 > 1.785$$

we conclude that

$$\mu_1 \neq \mu_2$$

The mean weight loss for the placebo group is not equal to the mean weight loss for the Product 1 group. Table 12.4 summarizes the results for the three pairwise comparisons. From the table we see that Product 1 and Product 2 both offer significantly higher average weight loss than the placebo. However, the sample data do not indicate a difference in the average weight loss between Product 1 and Product 2. Thus, the company can conclude that both Product 1 and Product 2 are superior to doing nothing.

Excel and Minitab Tutorial

CHAPTER OUTCOME #3

TRY PROBLEM 12.3

EXAMPLE 12-2 The Tukey-Kramer Procedure for Multiple Comparison

Digitron, Inc. Digitron, Inc., makes disc brakes for automobiles. Digitron's R&D department recently tested four brake systems to determine if there is a difference in the average stopping distance among them. Forty identical mid-sized cars were driven on a test track. Ten cars were fitted with Brake A, 10 with Brake B, and so forth. An electronic, remote switch was used to apply the brakes at exactly the same point on the road. The number of feet required to bring the car to a full stop was recorded. The data are in the CD-ROM file **Digitron**. Because we care to determine only whether the four brake systems have the same or different mean stopping distances, the test is a one-way (single-factor) test with four levels and can be completed using the following steps:

Step 1 Specify the parameter(s) of interest.
The parameter of interest is the mean stopping distance for each brake type. The company is interested in knowing whether a difference exists in mean stopping distance for the four brake types.

Step 2 Formulate the appropriate null and alternative hypotheses.
The appropriate null and alternative hypotheses are

$$H_0: \mu_1 = \mu_2 = \mu_3 = \mu_4$$
$$H_A: \text{At least two population means are different.}$$

Step 3   **Specify the significance level for the test.**
The test will be conducted using $\alpha = 0.05$.

Step 4   **Select independent simple random samples from each population.**

Step 5   **Check to see that the normality and equal-variance assumptions have been satisfied.**
Because of the small sample size, the box and whisker plot is used.

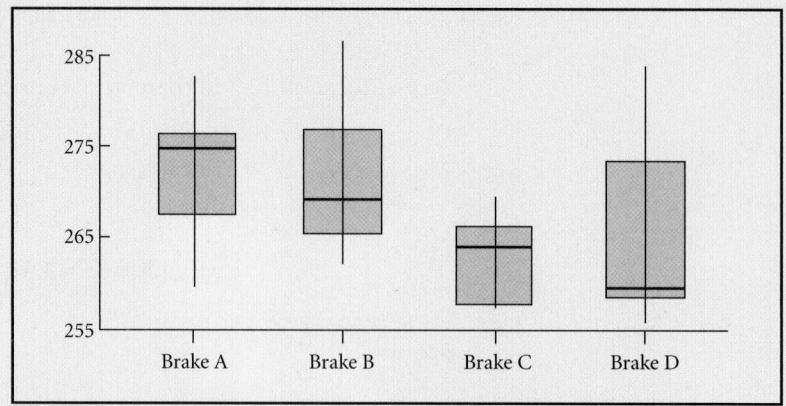

The box plots indicate some skewness in the samples and question the assumption of equality of variances. However, if we assume that the populations are approximately normally distributed, Hartley's F_{max} test can be used to test whether the four populations have equal variances. The test statistic is

$$F_{max} = \frac{s^2_{max}}{s^2_{min}}$$

The four variances are computed using $s^2 = \dfrac{\Sigma(x-\bar{x})^2}{n-1}$

$$s_1^2 = 49.9001 \quad s_2^2 = 61.8557 \quad s_3^2 = 21.7356 \quad s_4^2 = 106.4385$$

$$\text{Hartley's } F_{max} = \frac{106.4385}{21.7356} = 4.8970$$

From the F_{max} table in Appendix I, the critical value for $\alpha = 0.05$, $k = 4$, and $\bar{n} - 1 = 9$ is $F_{0.05} = 6.31$. Because $4.8970 < 6.31$, we conclude that the population variances could be equal. However, recalling our earlier discussion stating that when the sample sizes are equal, as they are in this example, the ANOVA test is robust in regards to both the equal variance and normality assumptions.

Step 6   **Determine the decision rule.**
Because $k - 1 = 3$ and $n_T - k = 36$, from Excel or Minitab $F_{0.05} = 2.8663$. The decision rule is

If the calculated $F > F_{0.05} = 2.8663$, reject H_0, or
If the p-value $< \alpha = 0.05$, reject H_0;
Otherwise, do not reject H_0.

Step 7   **Use Excel or Minitab to construct the ANOVA table.**
Figure 12.8 shows the Excel output for the ANOVA.

FIGURE 12.8

Excel 2007 One-Way ANOVA Output for the Digitron Example

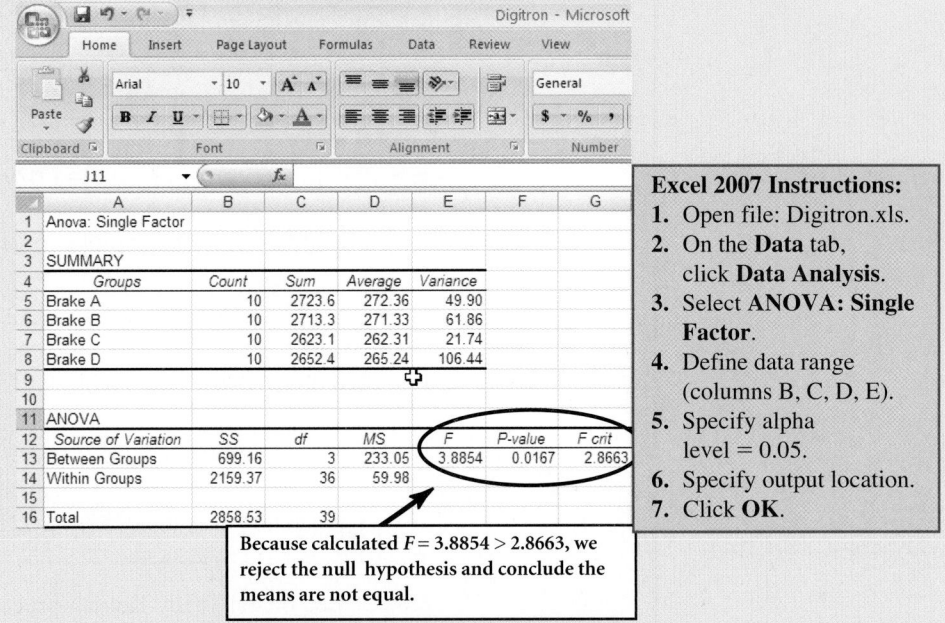

Excel 2007 Instructions:
1. Open file: Digitron.xls.
2. On the **Data** tab, click **Data Analysis**.
3. Select **ANOVA: Single Factor**.
4. Define data range (columns B, C, D, E).
5. Specify alpha level = 0.05.
6. Specify output location.
7. Click **OK**.

Because calculated $F = 3.8854 > 2.8663$, we reject the null hypothesis and conclude the means are not equal.

Minitab Instructions (for similar results):
1. Open file: Digitron.MTW.
2. Choose **Stat > ANOVA > One-way**.
3. In **Response**, enter data column, *Distance*.
4. In **Factor**, enter factor level column, *Brake*.
5. Click **OK**.

Step 8   Reach a decision.

From Figure 12.8, we see that

$$F = 3.89 > F_{0.05} = 2.8663, \text{ and}$$
$$p\text{-value} = 0.0167 < 0.05$$

We reject the null hypothesis.

Step 9   Draw a conclusion.

We conclude that not all population means are equal. But which systems are different? Is one system superior to all the others?

Step 10   Use the Tukey-Kramer test to determine which populations have different means.

Because we have rejected the null hypothesis of equal means, we need to perform a post-ANOVA multiple comparisons test. Using Equation 12.7 to construct the critical range to compare to the absolute differences in all possible pairs of sample means, the critical range is[6]

$$\text{Critical Range} = q_{1-\alpha}\sqrt{\frac{MSW}{2}\left(\frac{1}{n_i}+\frac{1}{n_j}\right)} = 3.79\sqrt{\frac{59.98}{2}\left(\frac{1}{10}+\frac{1}{10}\right)}$$

$$\text{Critical Range} = 9.282$$

---

[6] The *q*-value from the studentized range table with $\alpha = 0.05$ and degrees of freedom equal to $k = 4$ and $n_T - k = 36$ must be approximated using degrees of freedom 4 and 40 because the table does not show degrees of freedom of 4 and 36. This value is 3.79.

Only one critical range is necessary because the sample sizes are equal. If any pair of sample means has an absolute difference, $|\bar{x}_i - \bar{x}_j|$, greater than the critical range, we can infer that a difference exists in those population means. The possible pairwise comparisons (part of a family of comparisons called *contrasts*) are

Contrast	Significant Difference
$|\bar{x}_1 - \bar{x}_2| = |272.3590 - 271.3299| = 1.0291 < 9.282$	No
$|\bar{x}_1 - \bar{x}_3| = |272.3590 - 262.3140| = 10.0450 > 9.282$	Yes
$|\bar{x}_1 - \bar{x}_4| = |272.3590 - 265.2357| = 7.1233 < 9.282$	No
$|\bar{x}_2 - \bar{x}_3| = |271.3299 - 262.3140| = 9.0159 < 9.282$	No
$|\bar{x}_2 - \bar{x}_4| = |271.3299 - 265.2357| = 6.0942 < 9.282$	No
$|\bar{x}_3 - \bar{x}_4| = |262.3140 - 265.2357| = 2.9217 < 9.282$	No

Therefore, based on the Tukey-Kramer procedure, we can infer that population 1 (brake system A) and population 3 (brake system C) have different mean stopping distances. Because short stopping distances are preferred, system C would be preferred over system A, but no other differences are supported by these sample data. For the other contrasts, the difference between the two sample means is insufficient to conclude that a difference in population means exists.

Fixed Effects Versus Random Effects in Analysis of Variance

In the Digitron brake example, the company was testing four brake systems. These were the only brake systems under consideration. The ANOVA was intended to determine whether there was a difference in these four brake systems only. In the Hydronics weight-loss example, the company was interested in determining whether there was a difference in mean weight loss for two supplements and the placebo. In the Bayhill example involving coupon designs, the company narrowed its choices to four different designs, and the ANOVA test was used to determine whether there was a difference in means for these four designs only. Thus, in each of these examples, the inferences extend only to the factor levels being analyzed, and the levels are assumed to be the only levels of interest. This type of test is called a *fixed effects analysis of variance test*.

Suppose in the Bayhill coupon example that instead of paring the list of possible coupons to a final four, the company had simply selected a random sample of four coupon designs from all possible coupon designs being considered. In that case, the factor levels included in the test would be a random sample of the possible levels. Then, if the ANOVA leads to rejecting the null hypothesis, the conclusion applies to all possible coupon designs. The assumption is the possible levels have a normal distribution and the tested levels are a random sample from this distribution. When the factor levels are selected through random sampling, the analysis of variance test is called a *random effects test*.

12-1: Exercises

Skill Development

12-1. An advertising firm is interested in determining whether household incomes are different for subscribers to three different magazines. A random sample of 25 subscribers to each of the three magazines was taken and the annual household income for each subscriber was recorded. The partially completed ANOVA table for the analysis is shown here:

ANOVA

Source of Variation	SS	df	MS	F
Between Groups	2,949,085,157			
Within Groups				
Total	9,271,678,090			

a. Complete the ANOVA table by filling in the missing sums of squares, the degrees of freedom for each source, the mean square, and the calculated F-test statistic.

b. Based on the sample results, can the advertising firm conclude that there is a difference in household incomes for subscribers to the three magazines? You may assume normal distributions and equal variances. Conduct your test at the $\alpha = 0.10$ level of significance. Be sure to state a critical F-statistic, a decision rule, and a conclusion.

12-2. A manager is interested in testing whether three populations of interest have equal population means. Simple random samples of size 10 were selected from each population. The following ANOVA table and related statistics were computed:

ANOVA: Single Factor

Summary

Groups	Count	Sum	Average	Variance
Sample 1	10	507.18	50.72	35.06
Sample 2	10	405.79	40.58	30.08
Sample 3	10	487.64	48.76	23.13

ANOVA

Source	SS	df	MS	F	p-value	F-crit
Between Groups	578.78	2	289.39	9.84	0.0006	3.354
Within Groups	794.36	27	29.42			
Total	1,373.14	29				

a. State the appropriate null and alternative hypotheses.

b. Conduct the appropriate test of the null hypothesis assuming that the populations have equal variances and the populations are normally distributed. Use a 0.05 level of significance.

c. If warranted, use the Turkey-Kramer procedure for multiple comparisons to determine which populations have different means. (Assume $\alpha = 0.05$.)

12-3. An analyst is interested in testing whether four populations have equal means. The following sample data have been collected from populations that are assumed to be normally distributed with equal variances:

Sample 1	Sample 2	Sample 3	Sample 4
9	12	8	17
6	16	8	15
11	16	12	17
14	12	7	16
14	9	10	13

Conduct the appropriate hypothesis test using a significance level equal to 0.05.

12-4. Respond to each of the following questions using this partially completed one-way ANOVA table:

Source of Variation	SS	df	MS	F-ratio
Between Samples	1,745			
Within Samples		240		
Total	6,504	246		

a. How many different populations are being considered in this analysis?

b. Fill in the ANOVA table with the missing values.

c. State the appropriate null and alternative hypotheses.

d. Based on the analysis of variance F-test, what conclusion should be reached regarding the null hypothesis? Test using a significance level of 0.01.

12-5. Respond to each of the following questions using this partially completed one-way ANOVA table:

Source of Variation	SS	df	MS	F-ratio
Between Samples		3		
Within Samples	405			
Total	888	31		

a. How many different populations are being considered in this analysis?

b. Fill in the ANOVA table with the missing values.

c. State the appropriate null and alternative hypotheses.

d. Based on the analysis of variance F-test, what conclusion should be reached regarding the null hypothesis? Test using an $\alpha = 0.05$ level.

12-6. Given the following sample data:

Item	Group 1	Group 2	Group 3	Group 4
1	20.9	28.2	17.8	21.2
2	27.2	26.2	15.9	23.9
3	26.6	21.6	18.4	19.5
4	22.1	29.7	20.2	17.4
5	25.3	30.3	14.1	
6	30.1	25.9		
7	23.8			

a. Based on the computations for the within- and between-sample variation, develop the ANOVA table and test the appropriate null hypothesis using an $\alpha = 0.05$. Use the p-value approach.

b. If warranted, use the Tukey-Kramer procedure to determine which populations have different means. Use $\alpha = 0.05$.

12-7. Examine the three samples obtained independently from three populations:

Item	Group 1	Group 2	Group 3
1	14	17	17
2	13	16	14
3	12	16	15
4	15	18	16
5	16		14
6			16

a. Conduct a one-way analysis of variance on the data. Use alpha = 0.05.

b. If warranted, use the Tukey-Kramer procedure to determine which populations have different means. Use an experiment-wide error rate of 0.05.

Business Applications

12-8. HSBC Bank is a large, London-based, international banking company. One of the items it monitors is the credit balance of credit card customers. One possible analysis would be to determine if the average credit card balance depends upon the type of credit card used. Under consideration are Visa, MasterCard, Discover, and American Express. The sample sizes to be used for each level are 25, 25, 26, and 23, respectively.

a. Describe the parameter of interest for this analysis.

b. Determine the factor associated with this experiment.

c. Describe the levels of the factor associated with this analysis.

d. State the number of degrees of freedom available for determining the between-samples variation.

e. State the number of degrees of freedom available for determining the within-samples variation.

f. State the number of degrees of freedom available for determining the total variation.

12-9. ESSROC Cement Corporation is a leading North American cement producer with over 6.5 million metric tons of annual capacity. With headquarters in Nazareth, Pennsylvania, ESSROC operates production facilities strategically located throughout the United States, Canada, and Puerto Rico. One of its products is Portland cement. A Portland cement's properties and performance standards are defined by its type designation. Each type is designated by a Roman numeral. Ninety-two percent of the Portland cement produced in North America is Type I, II, or I/II, One characteristic of the type of cement is its compressive strength. Sample data for the compressive strength (psi) is shown as follows:

Type	Compressive Strength			
I	4,972	4,983	4,889	5,063
II	3,216	3,399	3,267	3,357
I/II	4,073	3,949	3,936	3,925

a. Develop the appropriate ANOVA table to determine if there is a difference in the average compressive strength among the three types of Portland cement. Use a significance level of 0.01.

b. If warranted, use the Tukey-Kramer procedure to determine which populations have different mean compressive strengths. Use an experiment-wide error rate of 0.01.

12-10. EverRun Incorporated produces treadmills for use in exercise clubs and recreation centers. EverRun assembles, sells, and services its treadmills, but it does not manufacture the treadmill motors. Rather, treadmill motors are purchased from an outside vendor. Currently, EverRun is considering which motor to include in its new ER1500 series. Three potential suppliers have been identified: Venetti, Madison, and Edison; however, only one supplier will be used. The motors produced by these three suppliers are identical in terms of noise and cost. Consequently, EverRun has decided to make its decision based on how long a motor operates at a high level of speed and incline before it fails. A random sample of 10 motors of each type is selected and each motor is tested to determine how many minutes (rounded to the nearest minute) it operates before it needs to be repaired. The sample information for each motor is as follows:

Venetti	Madison	Edison
14,722	13,649	13,296
14,699	13,592	13,262
12,627	11,788	11,552
13,010	12,623	11,036
13,570	14,552	12,978
14,217	13,441	12,170
13,687	13,404	12,674
13,465	13,427	11,851
14,786	12,049	12,342
12,494	11,672	11,557

a. At the $\alpha = 0.01$ level of significance, is there a difference in the average time before failure for the three different supplier motors?

b. Is it possible for EverRun to decide on a single motor supplier based on the analysis of the sample results? Support your answer by conducting the appropriate post-test analysis.

12-11. The Weidmann Group Companies, with headquarters in Rapperswil, Switzerland, are worldwide leaders in insulation systems technology for power and distribution transformers. One facet of its expertise is the development of dielectric fluids in electrical equipment. Mineral oil-based dielectric fluids have been used more extensively than other dielectric fluids. Their only shortcoming is their relatively low flash and fire point. One study examined the fire point of mineral oil, high-molecular-weight hydrocarbon (HMWH), and silicone. The fire points for each of these fluids were

Fluid	Fire Points (°C)				
Mineral Oil	162	151	168	165	169
HMWH	312	310	300	311	308
Silicone	343	337	345	345	337

a. Develop the appropriate ANOVA table to determine if there is a difference in the average fire points among the types of dielectric fluids. Use a significance level of 0.05.

b. If warranted, use the Tukey-Kramer procedure to determine which populations have different mean fire points. Use an experiment-wide error rate of 0.05.

12-12. The manager at the Hillsberg Savings and Loan is interested in determining whether there is a difference in the mean time that customers spend completing their transactions depending on which of four tellers they use. To conduct the test, the manager has selected simple random samples of 15 customers for each of the tellers and has timed them (in seconds) from the moment they start their transaction to the time the transaction is completed and they leave the teller station. The manager then asked one of her assistants to perform the appropriate statistical test. The assistant returned with the following, partially completed ANOVA table.

Summary

Groups	Count	Sum	Average	Variance
Teller 1	15	3,043.9		827.4
Teller 2	15	3,615.5		472.2
Teller 3	15	3,427.7		445.6
Teller 4	15	4,072.4		619.4

ANOVA

Source of Variation	SS	df	MS	F-ratio	p-value	F-crit
Between Groups	36,530.6				4.03E−09	2.7694
Within Groups						
Total	69,633.7	59				

a. State the appropriate null and alternative hypotheses.

b. Test to determine whether the population variances are equal. Use a significance level equal to 0.05

c. Fill in the missing parts of the ANOVA table and perform the statistical hypothesis test using an $\alpha = 0.05$ level.

d. Based on the result of the test in part c, if warranted, use the Tukey-Kramer method with $\alpha = 0.05$ to determine which tellers require the most time on average to complete a customer's transaction.

12-13. Suppose as part of your job you are responsible for installing emergency lighting in a series of state office buildings. Bids have been received from four manufacturers of battery-operated emergency lights. The costs are about equal, so the decision will be based on the length of time the lights last before failing. A sample of four lights from each manufacturer has been tested with the following values (time in hours) recorded for each manufacturer:

Type A	Type B	Type C	Type D
1,024	1,270	1,121	923
1,121	1,325	1,201	983
1,250	1,426	1,190	1,087
1,022	1,322	1,122	1,121

a. Using a significance level equal to 0.01, what conclusion should you reach about the four manufacturers' battery-operated emergency lights? Explain.

b. If the test conducted in part a reveals that the null hypothesis should be rejected, what manufacturer should be used to supply the lights? Can you eliminate one or more manufacturers based on these data? Use the appropriate test and $\alpha = 0.01$ for multiple comparisons. Discuss.

Computer Database Exercises

12-14. The Lottaburger restaurant chain in central New Mexico is conducting an analysis of its restaurants, which take pride in serving burgers and fries to go faster than the competition. As a part of its analysis, Lottaburger wants to determine if its speed of service is different across its four outlets. Orders at Lottaburger restaurants are tracked electronically and the chain is able to determine the speed with which every order is filled. The chain decided to randomly sample 20 orders from each of the four restaurants it operates. The speed of service for each randomly sampled order was noted and is contained in the file **Lottaburger**.

a. At the $\alpha = 0.05$ level of service, can Lottaburger conclude that the speed of service is different across the four restaurants in the chain?

b. If the chain concludes that there is a difference in speed of service, is there a particular restaurant the chain should focus its attention on? Use the appropriate test for multiple comparisons to support your decision. Use $\alpha = 0.05$.

12-15. A large metropolitan police force is considering changing from full-size cars to intermediates. The police force sampled cars from each of three manufacturers. The number sampled represents the number the manufacturer was able to provide for the test. Each car was driven for 5,000 miles, and the operating cost per mile computed. The operating costs, in cents per mile, for the 12 cars are provided in the data file called **Police**:

Car 1	Car 2	Car 3
13.3	12.4	13.9
14.3	13.4	15.5
13.6	13.1	15.2
12.8		14.5
14.0		

a. Perform an analysis of variance on these data. Assume a significance level of 0.05. Do the experimental data provide evidence that the average operating costs per mile for the three types of police cars are different? Use a p-value approach.

b. Referring to part a, based on the sample data and the appropriate test for multiple comparisons, what conclusions should be reached

concerning which type of car the police force should adopt? Discuss and prepare a report to the police chief. Use $\alpha = 0.05$.

c. Provide an estimate of the maximum and minimum difference in average savings per year if the police chief chooses the "best" versus the "worst" car using operating costs as a criterion. Assume that police cars are driven 30,000 miles a year. Use a 90% confidence interval.

12-16. Damage to homes caused by burst piping can be expensive to repair. By the time the leak is discovered, hundreds of gallons of water may have already flooded the home. Automatic shutoff valves can prevent extensive water damage from plumbing failures. The valves contain sensors that cut off water flow in the event of a leak, thereby preventing flooding. One important characteristic is the time (in milliseconds) required for the sensor to detect the water leak. Sample data obtained for four different shutoff valves are contained in the file entitled **Waterflow**.

a. Produce the relevant ANOVA table and conduct a hypothesis test to determine if the mean detection time differs among the four shutoff valve models. Use a significance level of 0.05.

b. Use the Tukey-Kramer multiple comparison technique to discover any differences in the average detection time. Use a significance level of 0.05.

c. Which of the four shutoff valves would you recommend? State your criterion for your selection.

12-17. Most auto batteries are made by just three manufacturers—Delphi, Exide, and Johnson Controls Industries. Each makes batteries sold under several different brand names. Delphi makes ACDelco and some EverStart (Wal-Mart) models. Exide makes Champion, Exide, Napa, and some EverStart batteries. Johnson Controls makes Diehard (Sears), Duralast (AutoZone), Interstate, Kirkland (Costco), Motorcraft (Ford), and some EverStarts. To determine if who makes the auto batteries affects the average length of life of the battery, the samples in the file entitled **Start** were obtained. The data represent the length of life (months) for batteries of the same specifications for each of the three manufacturers.

a. Determine if the average length of battery life is different among the batteries produced by the three manufacturers. Use a significance level of 0.05.

b. Which manufacturer produces the battery with the longest average length of life? If warranted conduct the Tukey-Kramer procedure to determine this. Use a significance level of 0.05. (*Note:* You will need to manipulate the data columns to obtain the appropriate factor levels).

CHAPTER OUTCOME #4

12.2 Randomized Complete Block Analysis of Variance

Section 12.1 introduced one-way ANOVA for testing hypotheses involving three or more population means. This ANOVA method is appropriate as long as we are interested in analyzing one factor at a time and we select independent random samples from the populations. For instance, Example 12-2 involving brake assembly systems at the Digitron Corporation (Figure 12.8) illustrated a situation in which we were interested in only one factor: type of brake assembly system. The measurement of interest was the stopping distance with each brake system. To test the hypothesis that the four brake systems were equal with respect to average stopping distance, four groups of the same make and model cars were assigned to each brake system independently. Thus, the one-way ANOVA design was appropriate.

There are, however, situations in which another factor may affect the observed response in a one-way design. Often this additional factor is unknown. This is the reason for randomization within the experiment. However, there are also situations in which we know the factor that is impinging on the response variable of interest. Chapter 10 introduced the concept of paired samples and indicated that there are instances when you will want to test for differences in two population means by controlling for sources of variation that might adversely affect the analysis. For instance, in the Digitron example, we might be concerned that, even though we used the same make and model of car in the study, the cars themselves may interject a source of variability that could affect the result. To control for this, we could use the concept of *paired samples* by using the same 10 cars for each of the four brake systems. When an additional factor with two or more levels is involved, a design technique called *blocking* can be used to eliminate its effect on the statistical analysis of the main factor of interest.

Randomized Complete Block ANOVA

Business Application

Excel and Minitab Tutorial

CITIZEN'S STATE BANK At Citizen's State Bank, homeowners can borrow money against the equity they have in their homes. To determine equity, the bank determines the home's value and subtracts the mortgage balance. The maximum loan is 90% of the equity.

The bank outsources the home appraisals to three companies: Allen & Associates, Heist Appraisal, and Appraisal International. The bank managers know that appraisals are not exact. Some appraisal companies may overvalue homes on average, whereas others might undervalue homes.

Bank managers wish to test the hypothesis that there is no difference in the average house appraisal among the three different companies. The managers could select a random sample of homes for Allen & Associates to appraise, a second sample of homes for Heist Appraisal to work on, and a third sample of homes for Appraisal International. One-way ANOVA would be used to compare the sample means. Obviously a problem could occur if, by chance, one company received larger, higher-quality homes located in better neighborhoods than the other companies. This company's appraisals would naturally be higher on average, not because it tended to appraise higher, but because the homes were simply more expensive.

Citizen's State Bank officers need to control for the variation in size, quality, and location of homes to fairly test that the three companies' appraisals are equal on the average. To do this, they select a random sample of properties and have each company appraise the same properties. In this case, the properties are called *blocks*, and the test design is called a *randomized complete block design*.

The data in Table 12.5 were obtained when each appraisal company was asked to appraise the same five properties. The bank managers wish to test the following hypothesis:

H_0: $\mu_1 = \mu_2 = \mu_3$
H_A: At least two populations have different means.

TABLE 12.5 Citizen's State Bank Property Appraisals (in thousands of dollars)

Property (Block)	Appraisal Company			Block Mean
	Allen & Associates	Heist Appraisal	Appraisal International	
1	78	82	79	79.67
2	102	102	99	101.00
3	68	74	70	70.67
4	83	88	86	85.67
5	95	99	92	95.33
Factor-Level Mean	$\bar{x}_1 = 85.2$	$\bar{x}_2 = 89$	$\bar{x}_3 = 85.2$	$\bar{\bar{x}} = 86.47 =$ Grand Mean

The randomized block design requires the following assumptions:

Assumptions

1. The populations are normally distributed.
2. The populations have equal variances.
3. The observations within samples are independent.
4. The data measurement must be interval or ratio level.

Because the managers have chosen to have the same properties appraised by each company (block on property), the samples are not independent, and a method known as *randomized complete block ANOVA* must be employed to test the hypothesis. This method is similar to the one-way ANOVA in Section 12.1. However, there is one more source of variation to be accounted for, the block variation. As was the case in Section 12.1, we must find estimators for each source of variation. Identifying the appropriate sums of squares and then dividing each by its degrees of freedom does this. As was the case in the one-way ANOVA, the sums of squares are obtained by partitioning the total sum of squares (*SST*). However, in this case the *SST* is divided into three components instead of two, as shown in Equation 12.8.

Sum of Squares Partitioning for Randomized Complete Block Design

$$SST = SSB + SSBL + SSW \qquad (12.8)$$

where:

$SST =$ Total sum of squares
$SSB =$ Sum of squares between factor levels
$SSBL =$ Sum of squares between blocks
$SSW =$ Sum of squares within levels

Both *SST* and *SSB* are computed just as we did with one-way ANOVA, using Equations 12.3 and 12.4. The *sum of squares for blocking (SSBL)* is computed using Equation 12.9.

Sum of Squares for Blocking

$$SSBL = \sum_{j=1}^{b} k(\bar{x}_j - \bar{\bar{x}})^2 \qquad (12.9)$$

where:

$$k = \text{Number of levels for the factor}$$
$$b = \text{Number of blocks}$$
$$\bar{x}_j = \text{The mean of the } j\text{th block}$$
$$\bar{\bar{x}} = \text{Grand mean}$$

Finally, the *sum of squares within (SSW)* is computed using Equation 12.10. This sum of squares is what remains (the residual) after the variation for all known factors has been removed. This residual sum of squares may be due to the inherent variability of the data, measurement error, or other unidentified sources of variation. Therefore, the sum of squares within is also known as the sum of squares of error, *SSE*.

Sum of Squares Within

$$SSW = SST - (SSB + SSBL) \tag{12.10}$$

The effect of computing *SSBL* and subtracting it from *SST* in Equation 12.10 is that *SSW* is reduced. Also, if the corresponding variation in the blocks is significant, the variation within the factor levels will be significantly reduced. This can make it easier to detect a difference in the population means if such a difference actually exists. If it does, the estimator for the within variability will in all likelihood be reduced and, thus, the denominator for the *F*-test statistic will be smaller. This will produce a larger *F*-test statistic, which will more likely lead to rejecting the null hypothesis. This will depend, of course, on the relative size of *SSBL* and the respective changes in the degrees of freedom.

Table 12.6 shows the completely randomized block ANOVA table format and equations for degrees of freedom, mean squares, and *F*-ratios. As you can see, we now have two *F*-ratios. The reason for this is that we test not only to determine whether the population means are equal but also to obtain an indication of whether the blocking was necessary by examining the ratio of the mean square for blocks to the mean square within.

Although you could manually compute the necessary values for the randomized block design, both Excel and Minitab contain a procedure that will do all the computations

TABLE 12.6 Basic Format for the Randomized Block ANOVA Table

Source of Variation	SS	df	MS	F-ratio
Between blocks	SSBL	$b - 1$	MSBL	$\dfrac{MSBL}{MSW}$
Between samples	SSB	$k - 1$	MSB	$\dfrac{MSB}{MSW}$
Within samples	SSW	$(k-1)(b-1)$	MSW	
Total	SST	$n_T - 1$		

where:

$$k = \text{Number of levels}$$
$$b = \text{Number of blocks}$$
$$df = \text{Degrees of freedom}$$
$$n_T = \text{Combined sample size}$$

$$MSBL = \text{Mean square blocking} = \frac{SSBL}{b-1}$$

$$MSB = \text{Mean square between} = \frac{SSB}{k-1}$$

$$MSW = \text{Mean square within} = \frac{SSW}{(k-1)(b-1)}$$

Note: Some randomized block ANOVA tables put *SSB* first, followed by *SSBL* and build the ANOVA table. The Citizen's State Bank appraisal data are included in your CD-Rom in the file **Citizens**. (Note that the first column contains labels for each block.)

Figures 12.9a and 12.9b show the ANOVA output. Using Excel or Minitab to perform the computations frees the decision maker to focus on interpreting the results. Note that Excel refers to the randomized block ANOVA as Two-Factor ANOVA without replication. Minitab refers to randomized block ANOVA as Two-Way ANOVA.

The main issue is to determine whether the three appraisal companies differ in average appraisal values. The primary test is

$$H_0: \mu_1 = \mu_2 = \mu_3$$
$$H_A: \text{At least two populations have different means.}$$
$$\alpha = 0.05$$

Using the output presented in Figures 12.9a and 12.9b, you can test this hypothesis two ways. First, we can use the F-distribution approach. Figure 12.10 shows the results of this test. Based on the sample data, we reject the null hypothesis and conclude that the three appraisal companies do not provide equal average values for properties.

The second approach to testing the null hypothesis is the p-value approach. The decision rule in an ANOVA application for p-values is

$$\text{If } p\text{-value} < \alpha \text{ reject } H_0;$$
$$\text{Otherwise, do not reject } H_0.$$

In this case, $\alpha = 0.05$ and the p-value in Figures 12.9a is 0.0103. Because p-value $= 0.0103 < \alpha = 0.05$ we reject the null hypothesis.

Both the F-distribution approach and the p-value approach give the same result, as they must.

Was Blocking Necessary? Before we take up the issue of determining which company provides the highest mean property values, we need to discuss one other issue. Recall that the bank managers chose to control for variation between properties by having each

FIGURE 12.9A

Excel 2007 Output: Citizen's State Bank Analysis of Variance

Excel 2007 Instructions:
1. Open file: Citizens.xls.
2. On the **Data** tab, click **Data Analysis**.
3. Select **ANOVA: Two-Factor Without Replication**.
4. Define data range (include column A).
5. Specify alpha level $= 0.05$.
6. Indicate output location.
7. Click **OK**.

Anova: Two-Factor Without Replication

SUMMARY	Count	Sum	Average	Variance
1	3	239	79.67	4.33
2	3	303	101.00	3.00
3	3	212	70.67	9.33
4	3	257	85.67	6.33
5	3	286	95.33	12.33
Allen & Associates	5	426	85.20	182.70
Heist Appraisal	5	445	89.00	136.00
Appraisal International	5	426	85.20	126.70

ANOVA

Source of Variation	SS	df	MS	F	P-value	F crit
Rows	1759.07	4	439.77	156.13	1.27E-07	3.838
Columns	48.13	2	24.07	8.54	0.0103	4.459
Error	22.53	8	2.82			
Total	1829.73	14				

Blocks

Within

Blocking Test
Main Factor Test

FIGURE 12.9B

Minitab Output: Citizen's State Bank Analysis of Variance

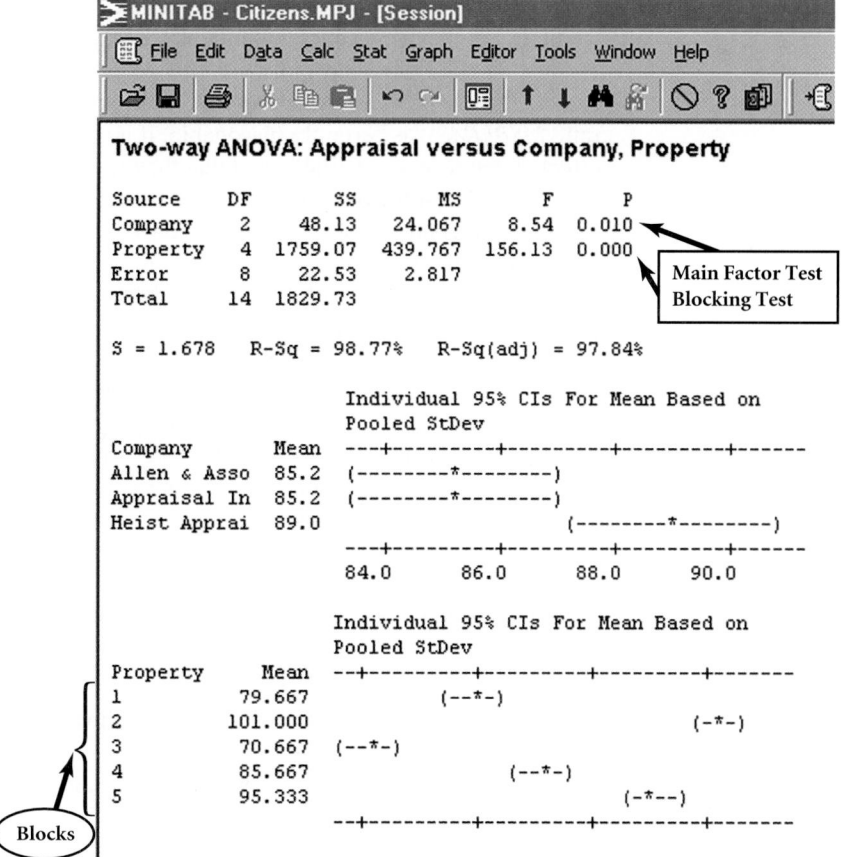

Minitab Instructions:
1. Open file: Citizens.MTW
2. Choose **Stat > ANOVA > Two-way**.
3. In **Response**, enter the data column (*Appraisal*).
4. In **Row Factor**, enter main factor indicator column (*Company*) and select **Display Means**.
5. In **Column Factor**, enter the block indicator column (*Property*) and select **Display Means**.
6. Choose **Fit additive model**.
7. Click **OK**.

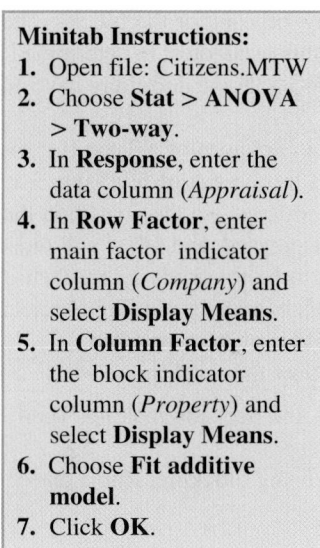

appraisal company evaluate the same five properties. This restriction is called blocking, and the properties are the blocks. The ANOVA output in Figure 12.9a contains information that allows us to test whether blocking was necessary.

If blocking was necessary, it would mean that appraisal values are in fact influenced by the particular property being appraised. The blocks then form a second factor of interest, and we formulate a secondary hypothesis test for this factor, as follows:

$$H_0: \mu_{b1} = \mu_{b2} = \mu_{b3} = \mu_{b4} = \mu_{b5}$$
$$H_A: \text{Not all block means are equal.}$$

Note that we are using μ_{bj} to represent the mean of the *j*th block.

FIGURE 12.10

Appraisal Company Hypothesis Test for Citizens State Bank

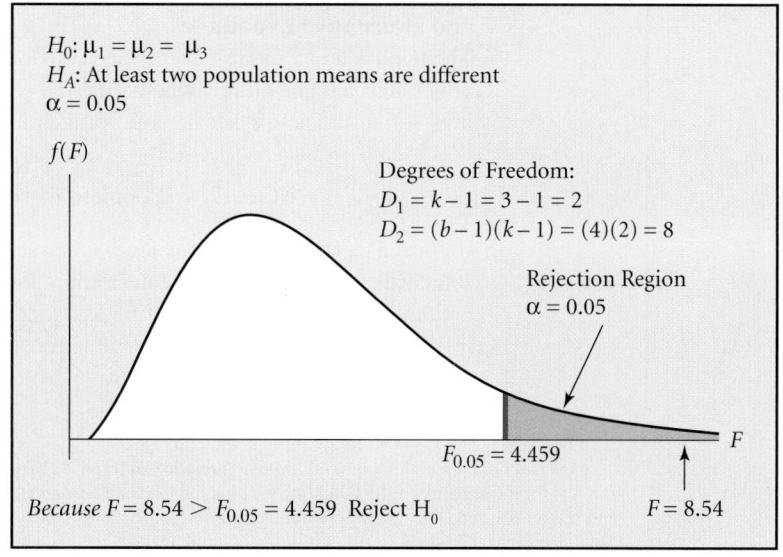

$H_0: \mu_1 = \mu_2 = \mu_3$
H_A: At least two population means are different
$\alpha = 0.05$

$f(F)$

Degrees of Freedom:
$D_1 = k - 1 = 3 - 1 = 2$
$D_2 = (b - 1)(k - 1) = (4)(2) = 8$

Rejection Region
$\alpha = 0.05$

$F_{0.05} = 4.459$

$F = 8.54$

F

Because $F = 8.54 > F_{0.05} = 4.459$ Reject H$_0$

It seems only natural to use a test statistic that consists of the ratio of the mean square for blocks to the mean square within. However, certain (randomization) restrictions placed on the complete block design make this proposed test statistic invalid from a theoretical statistics point of view. As an approximate procedure, however, the examination of the ratio $MSBL/MSW$ is certainly reasonable. If it is large, it implies that the blocks had a large effect on the response variable and that they were probably helpful in improving the precision of the F-test for the primary factor's means.[7] In performing the analysis of variance, we may also conduct a pseudotest to see whether the average appraisals for each property are equal. If the null hypothesis is "rejected," we have an indication that the blocking is necessary and the randomized block design is justified. However, we should be careful to present this only as an indication and not a precise test of hypothesis for the blocks. The output in Figures 12.9a provides the F-value and p-value for this pseudotest to determine if the blocking was a necessity. Because $F = 156.13 > F_{0.05} = 3.838$, we definitely have an indication that the blocking design was necessary.

If a hypothesis test indicates blocking is not necessary, the chance of a Type II error for the primary hypothesis has been unnecessarily increased by the use of blocking. The reason is that by blocking we not only partition the sum of squares, we also partition the degrees of freedom. Therefore, the denominator of MSW is decreased, and MSW will most likely increase. If blocking isn't needed, the MSW will tend to be relatively larger than if we had run a one-way design with independent samples. This can lead to failing to reject the null hypothesis for the primary test when it actually should have been rejected.

Therefore, if blocking is indicated to be unnecessary, follow these rules:

1. If the primary H_0 is rejected, proceed with your analysis and decision making. There is no concern.
2. If the primary H_0 is not rejected, redo the study without using blocking. Run a one-way ANOVA with independent samples.

EXAMPLE 12-3 Performing a Randomized Block Analysis of Variance

CHAPTER OUTCOME #4

TRY PROBLEM 12.21

Salsa O'le Inc. Salsa O'le is a new Mexican fast-food chain with three outlets in Utah. The franchise owner is interested in determining if the service quality at the three is the same. She has developed a test in which she selected 14 people who were asked to eat at each of the three fast-food outlets. The order of visits to the three outlets was randomized, but each customer visited each outlet one time. After each visit, each customer rated the service on a scale of 1 to 1,000, with 1,000 being the highest rating. A randomized block analysis of variance test can be performed using the following steps:

Step 1 **Specify the parameter of interest and formulate the appropriate null and alternative hypotheses.**

The parameter of interest is the mean customer-service rating for each outlet, and the question is whether there is a difference among the mean ratings at the three outlets. The appropriate null and alternative hypotheses are

H_0: $\mu_1 = \mu_2 = \mu_3$
H_A: At least two populations have different means.

In this case, the franchise owner wants to control for variation in customer standards by having the same customers visit each outlet. The ratings will be independent because the rating assigned by one customer does not influence the ratings assigned by other customers. Here, the customers are the blocks.

---

[7] Many authors argue that the randomization restriction imposed by using blocks means that the F-ratio really is a test for the equality of the block means plus the randomization restriction. For a summary of this argument and references, see D. C. Montgomery, *Design and Analysis of Experiments*, 4th ed. (New York: John Wiley & Sons, 1997) pp. 175–176.

Step 2 **Select simple random samples from each population, check the normality and equal-variance assumptions, and compute treatment means, block means, and the grand mean.**

The following sample data were observed:

Customer	Outlet 1	Outlet 2	Outlet 3	Block Means
1	830	647	630	702.33
2	743	840	786	789.67
3	652	747	730	709.67
4	885	639	617	713.67
5	814	943	632	796.33
6	733	916	410	686.33
7	770	923	727	806.67
8	829	903	726	819.33
9	847	760	648	751.67
10	878	856	668	800.67
11	728	878	670	758.67
12	693	990	825	836.00
13	807	871	564	747.33
14	901	980	719	866.67
Treatment Means	793.57	849.50	668.00	770.36 = Grand Mean

Step 3 **Compute the sums of squares and complete the ANOVA table.**

Four sums of squares are required:

Total Sum of Squares (Equation 12.3)

$$SST = \sum_{i=1}^{k} \sum_{j=1}^{n_i} (x_{ij} - \overline{\overline{x}})^2 = 614{,}641.6$$

Sum of Squares Between (Equation 12.4)

$$SSB = \sum_{i=1}^{k} n_i (\overline{x}_i - \overline{\overline{x}})^2 = 241{,}912.7$$

Sum of Squares Blocking (Equation 12.9)

$$SSBL = \sum_{j=1}^{b} k(\overline{x}_j - \overline{\overline{x}})^2 = 116{,}605.0$$

Sum of Squares Within (Equation 12.10)

$$SSW = SST - (SSB + SSBL) = 256{,}123.9$$

The ANOVA table is (see Table 12.6 format)

Source	SS	df	MS	F-Ratio
Between blocks	116,605.0	13	8,969.6	0.9105
Between samples	241,912.7	2	120,956.4	12.2787
Within samples	256,123.9	26	9,850.9	
Total	614,641.6	41		

Step 4 **Specify the level of significance for conducting the tests.**

The tests will be conducted using an $\alpha = 0.05$.

Step 5 **Test to determine whether blocking is effective.**

Fourteen people were used to evaluate and rate customer service. These constitute the blocks, so if blocking is effective, the mean rating across the three fast-food outlets will not be the same for all 14 customers. The null and alternative hypotheses are

$$H_0: \mu_{b1} = \mu_{b2} = \mu_{b3} = \ldots = \mu_{b14}$$
$$H_A: \text{Not all means are equal (blocking is effective).}$$

As shown in Step 3, the F-test statistic to test this null hypothesis is formed by

$$F = \frac{MSBL}{MSW} = \frac{8,969.6}{9,850.9} = 0.9105$$

The F-critical from the F-distribution, with $\alpha = 0.05$ and $D_1 = 13$ and $D_2 = 26$ degrees of freedom, can be approximated using the F-distribution table in Appendix H as

$$F_{\alpha=0.05} \approx 2.15$$

The exact F-critical can be found using the **FINV** function in Excel or the **Calc > Probability Distributions** command in Minitab as $F_{0.05} = 2.119$. Then, because

$$F = 0.9105 < F_{\alpha=0.05} = 2.119, \text{ do not reject the null hypothesis.}$$

This means that based on these sample data we cannot conclude that blocking was effective.

Step 6 **Conduct the main hypothesis test to determine whether the populations have equal means.**

We have three outlet locations. At issue is whether the mean service rating is equal for the three outlets. The appropriate null and alternative hypotheses are

$$H_0: \mu_1 = \mu_2 = \mu_3$$
$$H_A: \text{At least two populations have different means.}$$

As shown in the ANOVA table in Step 3, the F-test statistic for this null hypothesis is formed by

$$F = \frac{MSB}{MSW} = \frac{120,956.4}{9,850.9} = 12.2787$$

The F-critical from the F-distribution, with $\alpha = 0.05$ and $D_1 = 2$ and $D_2 = 26$ degrees of freedom, can be approximated using the F-distribution table in Appendix H as

$$F_{\alpha=0.05} \approx 3.40$$

The exact F-critical can be found using the **FINV** function in Excel or the **Calc > Probability Distributions** command in Minitab as $F = 3.369$. Then, because

$$F = 12.2787 > F_{\alpha=0.05} = 3.369, \text{ reject the null hypothesis.}$$

Even though in Step 5 we concluded that blocking was not effective, the sample data still lead us to reject the primary null hypothesis and conclude that the three outlets do not all have the same mean service rating. The owner will now be interested in looking into the issue in more detail to determine which outlets are providing better or worse service than the other. (See example 12.4.)

Fisher's Least Significant Difference Test

An analysis of variance test can be used to test whether the populations of interest have different means. However, even if the null hypothesis of equal population means is rejected, the ANOVA does not specify which population means are different. In Section 12.1, we showed how the Tukey-Kramer multiple comparisons procedure is used to determine where the population differences occur for a one-way ANOVA design. Likewise, *Fisher's least significant difference test* is one test for multiple comparisons that we can use for a randomized block ANOVA design.

If the primary null hypothesis has been rejected, then we can compare the absolute differences in sample means from any two populations to the *least significant difference (LSD)*, as computed using Equation 12.11.

Fisher's Least Significant Difference

$$LSD = t_{\alpha/2}\sqrt{MSW}\sqrt{\frac{2}{b}}$$

(12.11)

where:

$$\begin{aligned}
t_{\alpha/2} &= \text{One-tailed value from student's } t\text{-distribution for } \alpha/2 \\
&\quad \text{and } (k-1)(b-1) \text{ degrees of freedom} \\
MSW &= \text{Mean square within from ANOVA table} \\
b &= \text{Number of blocks} \\
k &= \text{Number of levels of the main factor}
\end{aligned}$$

EXAMPLE 12-4 Applying Fisher's Least Significant Difference Test

TRY PROBLEM 12.22

Salsa O'le Recall that in Example 12-3 the franchise operators for the three Salsa O'le fast-food outlets used a randomized block ANOVA design to conclude that the three outlets do not all have the same mean customer-service rating. To determine which populations have different means, you can use the following steps:

Step 1 Compute the *LSD* statistic using Equation 12.11.

$$LSD = t_{\alpha/2}\sqrt{MSW}\sqrt{\frac{2}{b}}$$

Using a significance level equal to 0.05, the *t*-critical for $(3-1)(14-1) = 26$ degrees of freedom is

$$t_{0.05/2} = 2.0555$$

The mean square within from the ANOVA table (see Example 12-3, Step 3) is

$$MSW = 9{,}850.9$$

The *LSD* is

$$LSD = t_{\alpha/2}\sqrt{MSW}\sqrt{\frac{2}{b}} = 2.0555\sqrt{9{,}850.9}\sqrt{\frac{2}{14}} = 77.11$$

Step 2 Compute the sample means from each population.

$$\bar{x}_1 = \frac{\sum x}{n} = 793.57 \qquad \bar{x}_2 = \frac{\sum x}{n} = 849.50 \qquad \bar{x}_3 = \frac{\sum x}{n} = 668$$

Step 3 Form all possible contrasts by finding the absolute differences between all pairs of sample means. Compare these to the *LSD* value.

Absolute Difference	Comparison	Significant Difference
$\|\bar{x}_1 - \bar{x}_2\| = \|793.57 - 849.50\| = 55.93$	$55.93 < 77.11$	No
$\|\bar{x}_1 - \bar{x}_3\| = \|793.57 - 668\| = 125.57$	$125.57 > 77.11$	Yes
$\|\bar{x}_2 - \bar{x}_3\| = \|849.50 - 668\| = 181.50$	$181.50 > 77.11$	Yes

We infer, based on the sample data, that the mean customer-service rating for outlet 1 exceeds the mean for outlet 3, and the mean for outlet 2 exceeds the mean for outlet 3. Now the manager may wish to study the processes at outlet 3 to see why the ratings are lower there than at the other two outlets. No difference's defected between outlets and 1 and 2.

12-2: Exercises

Skill Development

12-18. The following data were collected for a randomized block analysis of variance design with four populations and eight blocks:

	Group 1	Group 2	Group 3	Group 4
Block 1	56	44	57	84
Block 2	34	30	38	50
Block 3	50	41	48	52
Block 4	19	17	21	30
Block 5	33	30	35	38
Block 6	74	72	78	79
Block 7	33	24	27	33
Block 8	56	44	56	71

a. State the appropriate null and alternative hypotheses for the treatments and to determine whether blocking is necessary.

b. Construct the appropriate ANOVA table.

c. Using a significance level equal to 0.05, can you conclude that blocking was necessary in this case? Use a test-statistic approach.

d. Based on the data and a significance level equal to 0.05, is there a difference in population means for the four groups? Use a *p*-value approach.

e. If you found that a difference exists in part d, use the *LSD* approach to determine which populations have different means.

12-19. A study was conducted to determine if differences in new textbook prices exist between on-campus bookstores, off-campus bookstores, and Internet bookstores. To control for differences in textbook prices that might exist across disciplines, the study randomly selected 12 textbooks and recorded the price of each of the 12 books at each of the three retailers. You may assume normality and equal-variance assumptions have been met. The partially completed ANOVA table based on the study's findings is shown here:

ANOVA

Source of Variation	SS	df	MS	F
Textbooks	16,624			
Retailer	2.4			
Error				
Total	17,477.6			

a. Complete the ANOVA table by filling in the missing sums of squares, the degrees of freedom for each source, the mean square, and the calculated F-test statistic for each possible hypothesis test.

b. Based on the study's findings, was it correct to block for differences in textbooks? Conduct the appropriate test at the $\alpha = 0.10$ level of significance.

c. Based on the study's findings, can it be concluded that there is a difference in the average price of textbooks across the three retail outlets? Conduct the appropriate hypothesis test at the $\alpha = 0.10$ level of significance.

12-20. The following ANOVA table and accompanying information is the result of a randomized block ANOVA test.

Summary	Count	Sum	Average	Variance
1	4	443	110.8	468.9
2	4	275	68.8	72.9
3	4	1,030	257.5	1891.7
4	4	300	75.0	433.3
5	4	603	150.8	468.9
6	4	435	108.8	72.9
7	4	1,190	297.5	1891.7
8	4	460	115.0	433.3
Sample 1	8	1,120	140.0	7142.9
Sample 2	8	1,236	154.5	8866.6
Sample 3	8	1,400	175.0	9000.0
Sample 4	8	980	122.5	4307.1

ANOVA

Source of Variation	SS	df	MS	F	p-value	F-crit
Rows	199899	7	28557.0	112.8	0.0000	2.488
Columns	11884	3	3961.3	15.7	0.0000	3.073
Error	5317	21	253.2			
Total	217100	31				

a. How many blocks were used in this study?

b. How many populations are involved in this test?

c. Test to determine whether blocking is effective using an alpha level equal to 0.05

d. Test the main hypothesis of interest using $\alpha = 0.05$.

e. If warranted, conduct a LSD test with $\alpha = 0.05$ to determine which population means are different.

12-21. The following sample data were recently collected in the course of conducting a randomized block analysis of variance. Based on these sample data, what conclusions should be reached about blocking effectiveness and about the means of the three populations involved? Test using a significance level equal to 0.05.

Block	Sample 1	Sample 2	Sample 3
1	30	40	40
2	50	70	50
3	60	40	70
4	40	40	30
5	80	70	90
6	20	10	10

12-22. A randomized complete block design is carried out, resulting in the following statistics:

	$\bar{x}_1$	$\bar{x}_2$	$\bar{x}_3$	$\bar{x}_4$
Primary Factor	237.15	315.15	414.01	612.52
Block	363.57	382.22	438.33	

$SST = 364,428$

a. Determine if blocking was effective for this design.

b. Using a significance level of 0.05, produce the relevant ANOVA and determine if the average responses of the factor levels are equal to each other.

c. If you discovered that there were differences among the average responses of the factor levels, use the LSD approach to determine which populations have different means.

Business Applications

12-23. The California Lettuce Research Board was originally formed as the Iceberg Lettuce Advisory Board in 1973. The primary function of the board is to fund research on iceberg and leaf lettuce. The California Lettuce Research Board *Annual Report 2004–2005* published research (M. Cahn and H. Ajwa, "Salinity Effects on Quality and Yield of Drip Irrigated Lettuce") concerning the effect of varying levels of sodium absorption ratios (SAR) on the yield of head lettuce. The trials followed a randomized complete block design where variety of lettuce (Salinas and Sniper) was the main factor and salinity levels were the blocks. The measurements (the number of lettuce heads from each plot) of the kind observed were

SAR	Salinas	Sniper
3	104	109
5	160	163
7	142	146
10	133	156

a. Determine if blocking was effective for this design.
b. Using a significance level of 0.05, produce the relevant ANOVA and determine if the average number of lettuce heads among the SARs are equal to each other.
c. If you discovered that there were differences among the average number of lettuce heads among the SARs, use the *LSD* approach to determine which populations have different means.

12-24. CB Industries operates three shifts every day of the week. Each shift includes full-time hourly workers, nonsupervisory salaried employees, and supervisors/ managers. CB Industries would like to know if there is a difference among the shifts in terms of the number of hours of work missed due to employee illness. To control for differences that might exist across employee groups, CB Industries randomly selects one employee from each employee group and shift and records the number of hours missed for one year. The results of the study are shown here:

	Shift 1	Shift 2	Shift 3
Hourly	48	54	60
Nonsupervisory	31	36	55
Supervisors/Managers	25	33	40

a. Develop the appropriate test to determine whether blocking is effective or not. Conduct the test at the $\alpha = 0.05$ level of significance.
b. Develop the appropriate test to determine whether there are differences in the average number of hours missed due to illness across the three shifts. Conduct the test at the $\alpha = 0.05$ level of significance.
c. If it is determined that a difference in the average hours of work missed due to illness is not the same for the three shifts, use the *LSD* approach to determine which shifts have different means.

12-25. C & C Industries manufactures four different products that it ships to customers throughout the

United States. Delivery times are not a driving factor in C & C's decision as to which type of carrier to use (rail, plane, or truck) to deliver the product. However, breakage cost is very expensive and C & C would like to select a mode of delivery that reduces the amount of product breakage. To help it reach a decision, the managers of C & C have decided to examine the dollar amount of breakage incurred by the three alternative modes of transportation under consideration. Because each product's fragility is different, C & C's study wishes to control for differences due to type of product. C & C randomly assigns each product to each carrier and monitors the dollar breakage that occurs over the course of 100 shipments. The dollar breakage per shipment (to the nearest dollar) is as follows:

	Rail	Plane	Truck
Product 1	$7,960	$8,053	$8,818
Product 2	$8,399	$7,764	$9,432
Product 3	$9,429	$9,196	$9,260
Product 4	$6,022	$5,821	$5,676

a. Was C & C correct in its decision to block for type of product? Conduct the appropriate hypothesis test using a level of significance of 0.01.
b. Is there a difference due to carrier type? Conduct the appropriate hypothesis test using a level of significance of 0.01.

12-26. Grant Thornton LLP is the U.S. member firm of Grant Thornton International, one of the six global accounting, tax, and business advisory organizations. It provides firmwide auditing training for its employees in three different auditing methods. Auditors were grouped into four blocks according to the education they had received: (1) high school, (2) bachelor's, (3) master's, (4) doctorate. Three auditors at each education level were used— one assigned to each method. They were given a posttraining examination consisting of complicated auditing scenarios. The scores for the 12 auditors were

	Method 1	Method 2	Method 3
Doctorate	83	81	82
Master's	77	75	79
Bachelor's	74	73	75
H.S.	72	70	69

a. Indicate why blocking was employed in this design.
b. Determine if blocking was effective for this design by producing the relevant ANOVA.

c. Using a significance level of 0.05, determine if the average posttraining examination scores among the auditing methods are equal to each other.

d. If you discovered that there were differences among the average posttraining examination scores among the auditing methods, use the *LSD* approach to determine which populations have different means.

Chapter Database Exercises

12-27. In a local community there are three grocery chain stores. The three have been carrying out a spirited advertising campaign in which each claims to have the lowest prices. A local news station recently sent a reporter to the three stores to check prices on several items. She found that for certain items each store had the lowest price. This survey didn't really answer the question for consumers. Thus, the station set up a test in which 20 shoppers were given different lists of grocery items and were sent to each of the three chain stores. The sales receipts from each of the three stores were recorded in the data file **Groceries**.

a. Why should this price test be conducted using the design that the television station used? What was it attempting to achieve by having the same shopping lists used at each of the three grocery stores?

b. Based on a significance level of 0.05 and these sample data, test to determine whether blocking was necessary in this example. State the null and alternative hypotheses. Use a test-statistic approach.

c. Based on these sample data, can you conclude the three grocery stores have different sample means? Test using a significance level of 0.05. State the appropriate null and alternative hypotheses. Use a *p*-value approach.

d. Based on the sample data, which store has the highest average prices? Use Fisher's *LSD* test if appropriate.

12-28. The Cordage Institute based in Wayne, Pennsylvania, is an international association of manufacturers, producers, and resellers of cordage, rope, and twine. It is a not-for-profit corporation that reports on research concerning these products. Although natural fibers like manila, sisal, and cotton were once the predominant rope materials, industrial synthetic fibers dominate the marketplace today, with most ropes made of nylon, polyester, or polypropylene. One of the principal traits of rope material is its breaking strength. A research project generated data given in the file entitled **Knots**. The data listed were gathered on 10 different days from one-half-inch-diameter ropes.

a. Test to determine if inserting the day on which the testing was done was necessary. Use a significance level of 0.05.

b. Based on the data gathered by the Cordage Institute, can it be concluded that there is a difference in the average breaking strength of nylon, polyester, and polypropylene?

c. If you did conclude that there was a difference in the average breaking strength of the rope material, use Fisher's *LSD* approach to determine which material has the highest breaking strength.

12-29. Applebee's International, Inc. is a U.S. company that develops, franchises, and operates the Applebee's Neighborhood Grill and Bar restaurant chain. It is the largest chain of casual dining restaurants in the country, with over 1,500 restaurants across the United States. The headquarters is located in Overland Park, Kansas. The company is interested in determining if mean weekly revenue differs among three restaurants in a particular city. The file entitled **Applebees** contains revenue data for a sample of weeks for each of the three locations.

a. Test to determine if blocking the week on which the testing was done was necessary. Use a significance level of 0.05.

b. Based on the data gathered by Applebee's, can it be concluded that there is a difference in the average revenue among the three restaurants?

c. If you did conclude that there was a difference in the average revenue, use Fisher's *LSD* approach to determine which restaurant has the lowest mean sales.

12-30. When the world's largest retailer, Wal-Mart, decided to enter the grocery marketplace in a big way with its "Super Stores," it changed the retail grocery landscape in a major way. The other major chains such as Albertsons have struggled to stay competitive. In addition, regional discounters such as WINCO in the western United States have made it difficult for the traditional grocery chains. Recently, a study was conducted in which a "market basket" of products was selected at random from those items offered in three stores in Boise, Idaho: Wal-Mart, Winco, and Albertsons. At issue was whether the mean prices at the three stores are equal or whether there is a difference in prices. The sample data are in a the data file called **Food Price Comparisons**. Using an alpha level equal to 0.05, test to determine whether the three stores have equal population mean prices. If you conclude that there are differences in the mean prices, perform the appropriate posttest to determine which stores have different means.

12.3 Two-Factor Analysis of Variance with Replication

CHAPTER OUTCOME #5

Section 12.2 introduced an ANOVA procedure called the randomized complete block ANOVA. This method is used when we are interested in testing whether the means for the populations (levels) for a factor of interest are equal and we want to control for potential variation due to a second factor. The second factor is called the blocking factor. Consider again the Citizens State Bank property appraisal application, in which the bank was interested in determining whether the mean property valuation was the same for three different appraisal companies. The company used the same five properties to test each appraisal company in an attempt to reduce any variability that might exist due to the properties involved in the test. The properties were the blocks in that example, but we were not really interested in knowing whether the mean appraisal was the same for all properties. The single factor of interest was the appraisal companies.

However, you will encounter many situations in which there are actually two or more factors of interest in the same study. In this section, we limit our discussion to situations involving only two factors. The technique that is used when we wish to analyze two factors is called *two-factor ANOVA with replications*.

Two-Factor ANOVA with Replications

Business Application

Excel and Minitab Tutorial

FLY HIGH AIRLINES Like other major U.S. airlines, Fly High Airlines is concerned because many of its frequent flier program members have accumulated large quantities of free miles.[8] The airline worries that at some point in the future there will be a big influx of customers wanting to use their miles, and the airline will have difficulty satisfying all the requests at once. Thus, Fly High recently conducted an experiment in which each of three methods for redeeming frequent flier miles were offered to a sample of 16 customers. Each customer had accumulated more than 100,000 frequent flier miles. The customers were equally divided into four age groups. The variable of interest was the number of miles redeemed by the customers during the six-week trial. Table 12.7 shows the number of miles redeemed for each person in the study. These data are also contained in the **Fly High** file on your CD-ROM.

TABLE 12.7 Fly High Airlines Frequent Flier Miles Data

	Cash Option	Vacation	Shopping
Under 25 years	30,000	40,000	25,000
	0	25,000	25,000
	25,000	0	75,000
	0	0	5,000
25 to 40 years	60,000	40,000	30,000
	0	25,000	25,000
	0	5,000	50,000
	25,000	25,000	0
41 to 60 years	40,000	25,000	25,000
	25,000	50,000	50,000
	25,000	0	0
	0	25,000	0
Over 60 years	0	45,000	30,000
	5,000	25,000	25,000
	25,000	0	25,000
	50,000	50,000	50,000

---

[8] Name changed at request of the airline.

Method 1 offered cash inducements to use miles. Method 2 offered discount vacation options, and method 3 offered access to a discount-shopping program through the Internet. The airline wants to know if the mean number of miles redeemed under the three redemption methods is equal and whether the mean miles redeemed is the same across the four age groups.

A *two-factor ANOVA* design is the appropriate method in this case because the airline has two factors of interest. Factor A is the redemption offer type with three levels. Factor B is the age group of each customer with four levels. As shown in Table 12.7, there are $3 \times 4 = 12$ cells in the study and four customers in each cell. The measurements are called *replications* because we get four measurements (miles redeemed) at each combination of redemption offer level (Factor A) and age level (Factor B).

Two-factor ANOVA follows the same logic as all other ANOVA designs. Each factor of interest introduces variability into the experiment. As was the case in Sections 12.1 and 12.2, we must find estimators for each source of variation. Identifying the appropriate sums of squares and then dividing each by its degrees of freedom does this. As in the one-way ANOVA, the total sum of squares (*SST*) can be partitioned. The SST is partitioned into four parts as follows:

1. One part is due to differences in the levels of Factor A (SS_A).
2. Another part is due to the levels of Factor B (SS_B).
3. Another part is due to the *interaction* between Factor A and Factor B (SS_{AB}). (We will discuss the concept of interaction between factors later.)
4. The final component making up the total sum of squares is the sum of squares due to the inherent random variation in the data (*SSE*).

Figure 12.11 illustrates this partitioning concept. The variations due to each of these components will be estimated using the respective *mean squares* obtained by dividing the sums of squares by their degrees of freedom. If the variation accounted for by Factor A and Factor B is large relative to the error variation, we will tend to conclude that the factor levels have different means.

Table 12.8 illustrates the format of the two-factor ANOVA. Three different hypotheses can be tested from the information in this ANOVA table. First, for Factor A (redemption options), we have

$$H_0: \mu_{A1} = \mu_{A2} = \mu_{A3}$$
$$H_A: \text{Not all Factor A means are equal.}$$

FIGURE 12.11

Two-Factor ANOVA—Partitioning of Total Sums of Squares

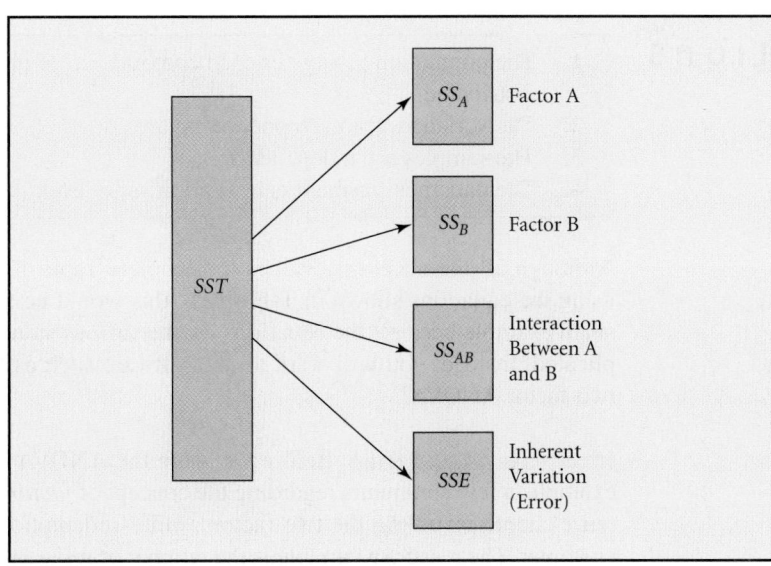

TABLE 12.8 Basic Format of the Two-Factor ANOVA Table

Source of Variation	SS	df	MS	F-Ratio
Factor A	SS_A	$a-1$	MS_A	$\dfrac{MS_A}{MSE}$
Factor B	SS_B	$b-1$	MS_B	$\dfrac{MS_B}{MSE}$
AB interaction	SS_{AB}	$(a-1)(b-1)$	MS_{AB}	$\dfrac{MS_{AB}}{MSE}$
Error	SSE	$n_T - ab$	MSE	
Total	SST	$n_T - 1$		

where:

$$a = \text{Number of levels of factor A}$$
$$b = \text{Number of levels of factor B}$$
$$n_T = \text{Total number of observation in all cells}$$

$$MS_A = \text{Mean square factor A} = \frac{SS_A}{a-1}$$

$$MS_B = \text{Mean square factor B} = \frac{SS_B}{b-1}$$

$$MS_{AB} = \text{Mean square interaction} = \frac{SS_{AB}}{(a-1)(b-1)}$$

$$MSE = \text{Mean square error} = \frac{SSE}{n_T - ab}$$

For Factor B (age levels):

$$H_0: \mu_{B1} = \mu_{B2} = \mu_{B3} = \mu_{B4}$$
$$H_A: \text{Not all Factor B means are equal.}$$

Test to determine whether interaction exists between the two factors:

H_0: Factors A and B do not interact to affect the mean response.
H_A: Factors A and B do interact.

Here are the necessary assumptions for the two-factor ANOVA:

Assumptions

1. The population values for each combination of pairwise factor levels are normally distributed.
2. The variances for each population are equal.
3. The samples are independent.
4. The data measurement is interval or ratio level.

Although all the necessary values to complete Table 12.8 could be computed manually using the equations shown in Table 12.9, this would be a time-consuming task for even a small example because the equations for the various sum-of-squares values are quite complicated. Instead, you will want to use software such as Excel or Minitab to perform the two-factor ANOVA.

Interaction Explained Before we share the ANOVA results for the Fly High Airlines example, a few comments regarding the concept of *factor interaction* are needed. Consider our example involving the two factors: miles-redemption-offer type and age category of customer. The response variable is the number of miles redeemed in the six weeks after the

TABLE 12.9 Two-Factor ANOVA Equations

Total Sum of Squares

$$SST = \sum_{i=1}^{a}\sum_{j=1}^{b}\sum_{k=1}^{n}(x_{ijk} - \bar{\bar{x}})^2 \qquad (12.12)$$

Sum of Squares Factor A

$$SS_A = bn\sum_{i=1}^{a}(\bar{x}_{i..} - \bar{\bar{x}})^2 \qquad (12.13)$$

Sum of Squares Factor B

$$SS_B = an\sum_{j=1}^{b}(\bar{x}_{.j.} - \bar{\bar{x}})^2 \qquad (12.14)$$

Sum of Squares Interaction Between Factors A and B

$$SS_{AB} = n\sum_{i=1}^{a}\sum_{j=1}^{b}(\bar{x}_{ij.} - \bar{x}_{i..} - \bar{x}_{.j.} + \bar{\bar{x}})^2 \qquad (12.15)$$

Sum of Squares Error

$$SSE = \sum_{i=1}^{a}\sum_{j=1}^{b}\sum_{k=1}^{n}(x_{ijk} - \bar{x}_{ij.})^2 \qquad (12.16)$$

where:

$$\bar{\bar{x}} = \frac{\displaystyle\sum_{i=1}^{a}\sum_{j=1}^{b}\sum_{k=1}^{n}x_{ijk}}{abn} = \text{Grand mean}$$

$$\bar{x}_{i..} = \frac{\displaystyle\sum_{j=1}^{b}\sum_{k=1}^{n}x_{ijk}}{bn} = \text{Mean of each level of Factor A}$$

$$\bar{x}_{.j.} = \frac{\displaystyle\sum_{i=1}^{a}\sum_{k=1}^{n}x_{ijk}}{an} = \text{Mean of each level of Factor B}$$

$$\bar{x}_{ij.} = \sum_{k=1}^{n}\frac{x_{ijk}}{n} = \text{Mean of each cell}$$

a = Number of levels of Factor A
b = Number of levels of Factor B
n = Number of replications in each cell

offer. Suppose one redemption-offer type is really better and results in a higher average miles being redeemed. If there is no interaction between age and offer type, then customers of all ages will have uniformly higher average miles redeemed for this offer type compared with the other offer types. If another offer type yields lower average miles, then if there is no interaction, all age groups receiving this offer type will redeem uniformly lower miles on average than the other offer types. Figure 12.12 illustrates a situation with no interaction between the two factors.

FIGURE 12.12

Differences Between Factor-Level Mean Values: No Interaction

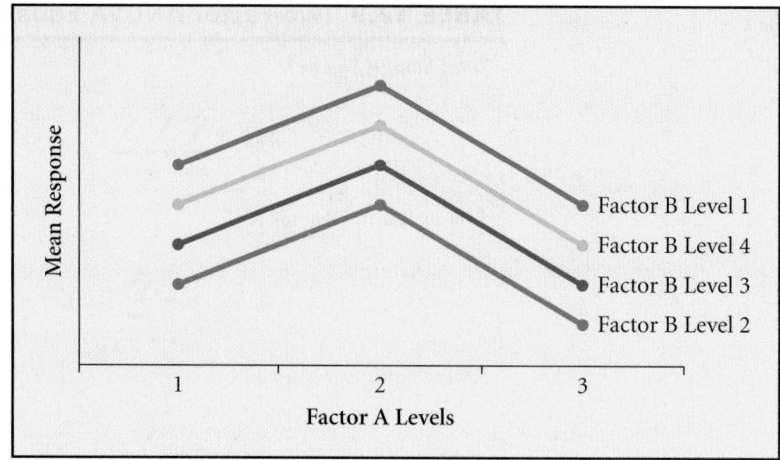

However, if interaction exists between the factors, we would see a graph similar to the one shown in Figure 12.13. Interaction would be indicated if one age group redeemed higher average miles than the other age groups with one program but lower average miles than the other age groups on the other mileage-redemption programs. In general, interaction occurs if the differences in the averages of the response variable for the various levels of one factor—say, Factor A—are not the same for each level of the other factor—say, Factor B. The general idea is that interaction between two factors means that the effect due to one of them is not uniform across all levels of the other factor.

Another example in which potential interaction might exist occurs in plywood manufacturing, where thin layers of wood called veneer are glued together to form plywood. One of the important quality attributes of plywood is its strength. However, plywood is made from different species of wood (pine, fir, hemlock, etc.), and different types of glue are available. If some species of wood work better (stronger plywood) with certain glues, whereas other species work better with different glues, we say that the wood species and the glue type interact.

If interaction is suspected, it should be accounted for by subtracting the interaction term (SS_{AB}) from the total sum-of-squares term in the ANOVA. From a strictly arithmetic point of view, the effect of computing SS_{AB} and subtracting it from SST is that SSE is reduced. Also, if the corresponding variation due to interaction is significant, the variation within the factor levels (error) will be significantly reduced. This can make it easier to detect a difference in the population means if such a difference actually exists. If so, MSE will most likely be reduced. This will produce a larger F-test statistic, which will more likely lead to correctly rejecting the null hypothesis. Thus by considering potential

FIGURE 12.13

Differences Between Factor-Level Mean Values: Interaction Present

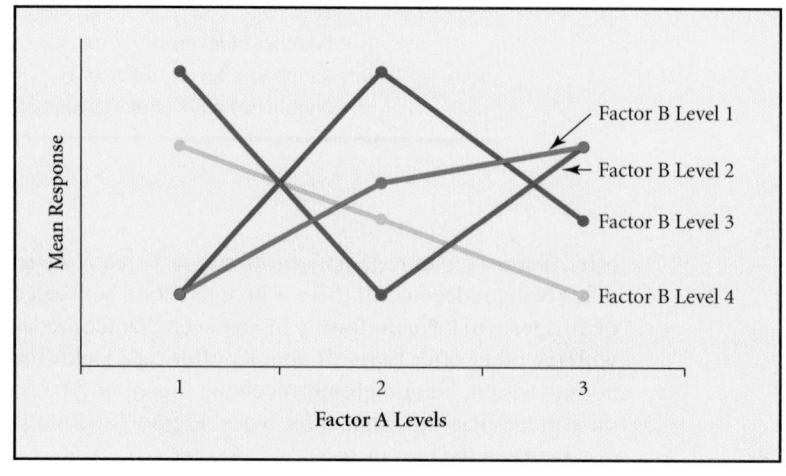

interaction, your chances of finding a difference in the Factor A and Factor B mean values, if such a difference exists is improved. This will depend, of course, on the relative size of SS_{AB} and the respective changes in the degrees of freedom. We will comment later on the appropriateness of testing the factor hypotheses if interaction is present. *Note that in order to measure the interaction effect, the sample size for each combination of Factor A and Factor B must be 2 or greater.*

Excel and Minitab contain a data analysis tool for performing two-factor ANOVA with replications. They can be used to compute the different sums of squares and complete the ANOVA table. However, Excel requires that the data be organized in a special way, as shown in Figure 12.14.[9] (Note, the first row must contain the names for each level of Factor A. Also, column 1 contains the Factor B level names. These must be in the row corresponding to the first sample item for each Factor B level.)

The Excel two-factor ANOVA output for this example is actually too big to fit on one screen. The top portion of the printout shows summary information for each cell, including means and variances (see Figure 12.15). At the bottom of the output (scroll down) is the ANOVA table shown in Figure 12.16a. Figure 12.16b shows the Minitab output. Excel changes a few labels. For example, Factor A (the miles redemption options) is now referred to as *Columns*. Factor B (age groups) is referred to as *Sample*. In Figures 12.16a and 12.16b, we see all the information necessary to test whether the three redemption offers (Factor A) result in different mean miles redeemed.

$$H_0: \mu_{A1} = \mu_{A2} = \mu_{A3}$$
$$H_A: \text{Not all means are equal.}$$
$$\alpha = 0.05$$

Both the p-value and F-distribution approaches can be used. Because

$$p\text{-value (columns)} = 0.5614 > \alpha = 0.05$$

the null hypothesis H_0 is not rejected. (Also, $F = 0.59 < F_{0.05} = 3.259$; the null hypothesis is not rejected.) This means the test data do not indicate that a difference exists between the average amount of mileage redeemed for the three types of offers. None seems superior to the others.

FIGURE 12.14

Excel 2007 Data Format for Two-Factor ANOVA—Fly High Airlines

Excel 2007 Instructions:
1. Open file: Fly High.xls.

Factor A Names

Factor B Names

---

[9] Minitab uses the same data input format for two-factor ANOVA as for randomized block ANOVA (see Section 12.2).

FIGURE 12.15

Excel 2007 Output (Part 1) for Two-Factor ANOVA—Fly High Airlines Example

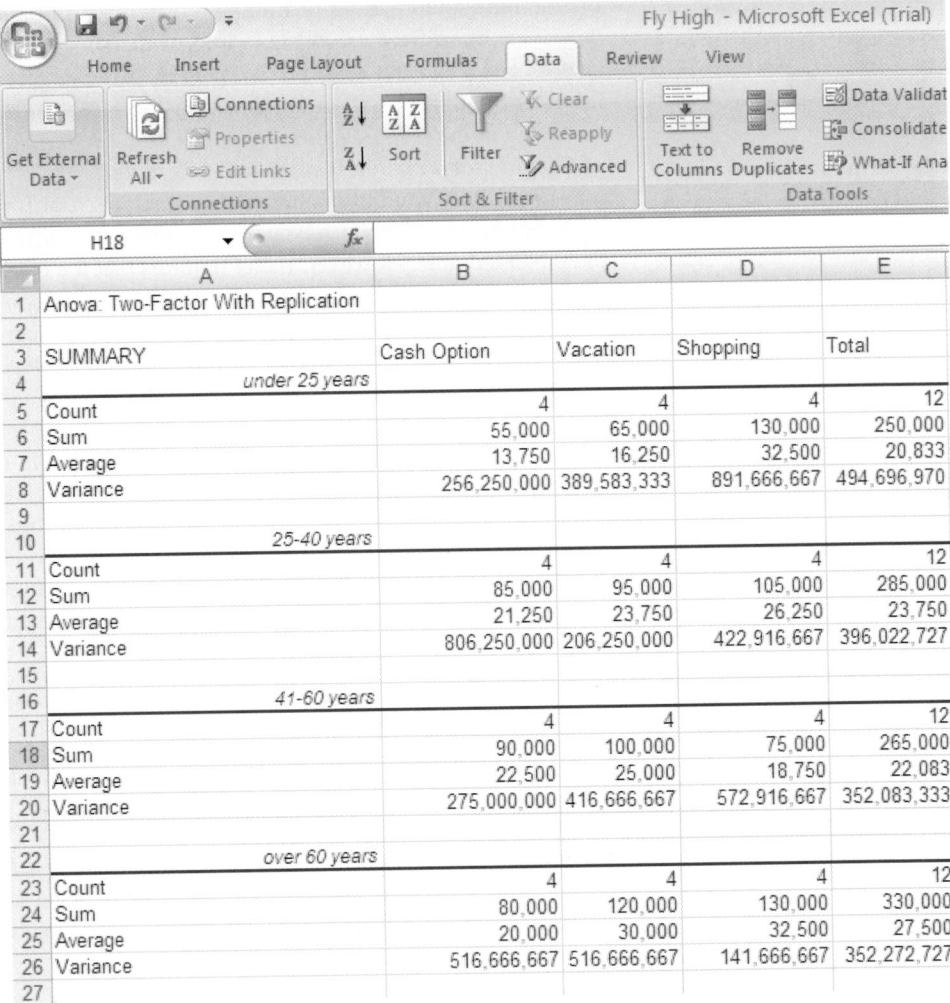

Excel 2007 Instructions:
1. Open file: Fly High.xls.
2. On the **Data** tab, click **Data Analysis**.
3. Select **ANOVA: Two Factor with Replication**.
4. Define data range (include factor A and B labels).
5. Specify the number of **rows per sample**.
6. Specify alpha level.

FIGURE 12.16A

Excel 2007 Output (Part 2) for Two-Factor ANOVA—Fly High Airlines Example

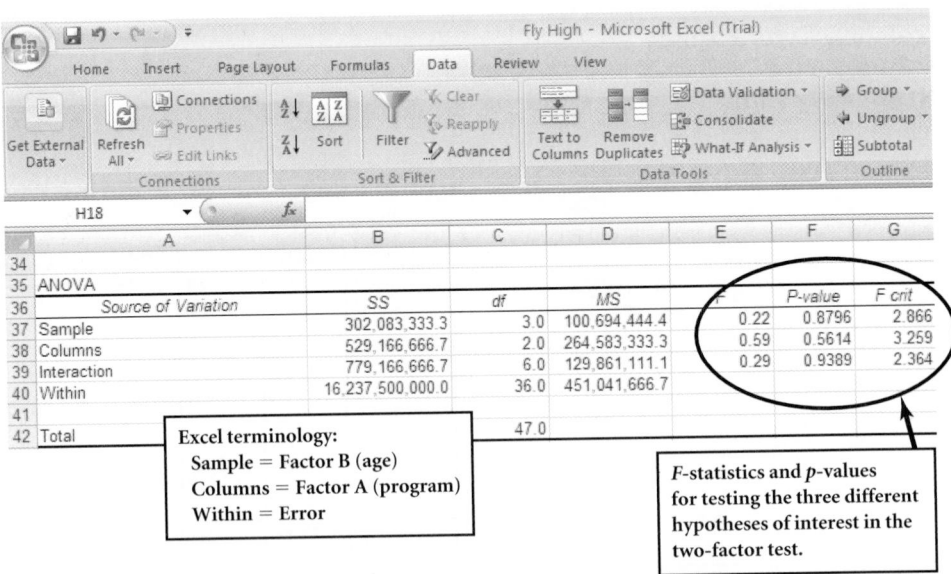

We can also test to determine if age level makes a difference in frequent flier miles redeemed.

$$H_0: \mu_{B1} = \mu_{B2} = \mu_{B3} = \mu_{B4}$$
$$H_A: \text{Not all Factor B means are equal.}$$
$$\alpha = 0.05$$

FIGURE 12.16B

Minitab Output for Two-Factor ANOVA—Fly High Airlines Example

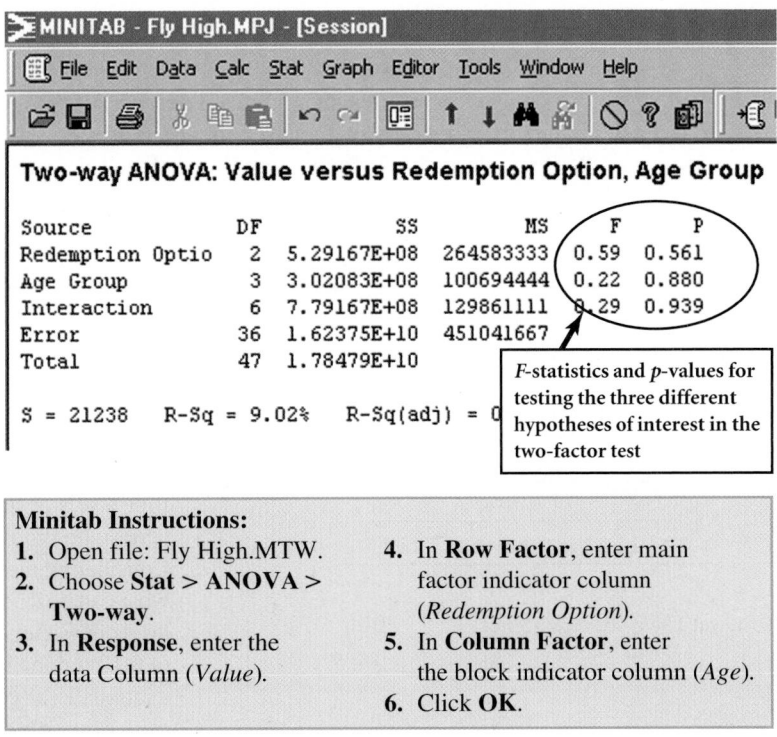

MINITAB - Fly High.MPJ - [Session]

File Edit Data Calc Stat Graph Editor Tools Window Help

Two-way ANOVA: Value versus Redemption Option, Age Group

Source	DF	SS	MS	F	P
Redemption Optio	2	5.29167E+08	264583333	0.59	0.561
Age Group	3	3.02083E+08	100694444	0.22	0.880
Interaction	6	7.79167E+08	129861111	0.29	0.939
Error	36	1.62375E+10	451041667		
Total	47	1.78479E+10			

$S = 21238$ R-Sq = 9.02%   R-Sq(adj) = 0

F-statistics and *p*-values for testing the three different hypotheses of interest in the two-factor test

Minitab Instructions:
1. Open file: Fly High.MTW.
2. Choose **Stat > ANOVA > Two-way**.
3. In **Response**, enter the data Column (*Value*).
4. In **Row Factor**, enter main factor indicator column (*Redemption Option*).
5. In **Column Factor**, enter the block indicator column (*Age*).
6. Click **OK**.

In Figure 12.16a, we see that the

$$p\text{-value} = 0.8796 > \alpha = 0.05$$
$$(\text{Also, } F = 0.22 < F_{0.05} = 2.866)$$

Thus, the null hypothesis is not rejected. The test data do not indicate that customer age significantly influences the average number of frequent flier miles that will be redeemed.

Finally, we can also test for interaction. The null hypothesis is that no interaction exists. The alternative is that interaction does exist between the two factors. The ANOVA table in Figure 12.16b shows a *p*-value of 0.939, which is greater than $\alpha = 0.05$. Based on these data, interaction between the two factors does not appear to exist. This would indicate that the differences in the average mileage redeemed between the various age categories are the same for each redemption-offer type.

A Caution About Interaction

In this example, the sample data indicate that no interaction between Factors A and B is present. Based on the sample data, we were unable to conclude that the three redemption offers resulted in different average frequent flier miles redeemed. Finally, we were unable to conclude that a difference in average miles redeemed occurred over the four different age groups.

The appropriate approach is to begin by testing for interaction. If the interaction null hypothesis is not rejected, proceed to test Factor A and Factor B hypotheses. However, if we conclude that interaction is present between the two factors, hypothesis tests for Factors A and B generally *should not* be performed. The reason is that findings of significance for either factor might be due only to interactive effects when the two factors are combined, and not to the fact that the levels of the factor differ significantly. It is also possible that interactive effects might mask differences between means of one of the factors for at least some of the levels of the other factor. If significant interaction is present, the experimenter may conduct a one-way ANOVA to test the levels of one of the factors, for example, Factor A, using only one level of the other factor, Factor B.

Thus, when conducting hypothesis tests for a two-factor ANOVA:

1. Test for interaction.
2. If interaction is present, conduct a one-way ANOVA to test the levels of one of the factors using only one level of the other factor.[10]
3. If no interaction is found, test Factor A and Factor B.

12.3: Exercises

Skill Development

12-31. Consider the following data for a two-factor experiment:

		Factor A		
		Level 1	Level 2	Level 3
Factor B	Level 1	33	30	21
		31	42	30
		35	36	30
	Level 2	23	30	21
		32	27	33
		27	25	18

a. Based on the sample data, do Factors A and B have significant interaction? State the appropriate null and alternative hypotheses and test using a significance level of 0.05.
b. Based on these sample data, can you conclude that the levels of Factor A have equal means? Test using a significance level of 0.05.
c. Do the data indicate that the levels of Factor B have different means? Test using a significance level equal to 0.05.

12-32. Consider the following partially completed two-factor analysis of variance table, which is an outgrowth of a study in which Factor A has four levels and Factor B has three levels. The number of replications was 11 in each cell.

Source of Variation	SS	df	MS	F-Ratio
Factor A	345.1			
Factor B				
AB interaction	1,123.2			
Error	256.7			
Total	1,987.3			

a. Complete the analysis of variance table.
b. Based on the sample data, can you conclude that the two factors have significant

interaction? Test using a significance level equal to 0.05.
c. Based on the sample data, should you conclude that the means for Factor A differ across the four levels or the means for Factor B differ across the three levels? Discuss.
d. Considering the outcome of part b, determine what can be said concerning the differences of the levels of Factors A and B. Use a significance level of 0.10 for any hypothesis tests required. Provide a rationale for your response to this question.

12-33. Consider the following data from a two-factor experiment:

	Factor A		
Factor B	Level 1	Level 2	Level 3
Level 1	43	25	37
	49	26	45
Level 2	50	27	46
	53	31	48

a. Determine if there is interaction between Factor A and Factor B. Use the p-value approach and a significance level of 0.05.
b. Does the average response vary among the levels of Factor A? Use the test-statistic approach and a significance level of 0.05.
c. Determine if there are differences in the average response between the levels of Factor B. Use the p-value approach and a significance level of 0.05.

12-34. Examine the following two-factor analysis of variance table:

Source	SS	df	MS	F-Ratio
Factor A	162.79	4		
Factor B			28.12	
AB Interaction	262.31	12		
Error				
Total	1,298.74	84		

---

[10] There are, however, some instances in which the effects of the factors provide important and meaningful information even though interaction is present. See D. R. Cox, *Planning of Experiments* (New York: John Wiley and Sons, 1992) pp. 107–108.

a. Complete the analysis of variance table.
b. Determine if interaction exists between Factor A and Factor B. Use $\alpha = 0.05$.
c. Determine if the levels of Factor A have equal means. Use a significance level of 0.05.
d. Does the ANOVA table indicate that the levels of Factor B have equal means? Use a significance level of 0.05.

12-35. A two-factor experiment yielded the following data:

Factor B	Factor A Level 1	Level 2	Level 3
Level 1	375	402	395
	390	396	390
Level 2	335	336	320
	342	338	331
Level 3	302	485	351
	324	455	346

a. Determine if there is interaction between Factor A and Factor B. Use the *p*-value approach and a significance level of 0.05.
b. Given your findings in part a, determine any significant differences among the response means of the levels of Factor A for Level 1 of Factor B.
c. Repeat part b at Levels 2 and 3 of Factor B, respectively.

Business Applications

12-36. A manufacturing firm produces a single product on three production lines. Because the lines were developed at different points in the firm's history, they use different equipment. The firm is considering changing the layouts of the lines and would like to know what effects different layouts would have on production output. A study was conducted to determine the average output for each line over four randomly selected weeks using each of the three layouts under consideration. The output (in hundreds of units produced) was measured for each line for each of the four weeks for each layout being evaluated. The results of the study are as follows

	Line 1	Line 2	Line 3
Layout 1	12	12	11
	10	14	10
	12	10	14
	12	11	12
Layout 2	17	16	18
	18	15	18
	15	16	17
	17	17	18
Layout 3	12	10	11
	12	11	11
	11	11	10
	11	11	12

a. Based on the sample data, can the firm conclude that there is an interaction effect between the type of layout and the production line? Conduct the appropriate test at the 0.05 level of significance.
b. At the 0.05 level of significance, can the firm conclude that there is a difference in mean output across the three production lines?
c. At the 0.05 level of significance, can the firm conclude that there is a difference in mean output due to the type of layout used?

12-37. A popular consumer staple was displayed in different locations in the same aisle of a grocery store to determine what, if any, effect different placement might have on its sales. The product was placed at one of three heights on the aisle—low, medium, and high—and at one of three locations in the store—at the front of the store, at the middle of the store, or at the rear of the store. The number of units sold of the product at the various height and distance combinations was recorded each week for five weeks. The following results were obtained:

	Front	Middle	Rear
Low	125	195	126
	143	150	136
	150	160	129
	138	195	136
	149	162	147
Medium	141	186	128
	137	161	133
	145	157	148
	150	165	145
	130	194	141
High	129	157	149
	141	152	137
	148	186	138
	130	164	126
	137	176	138

a. At the 0.10 level of significance, is there an interaction effect?
b. At the 0.10 level of significance, does the height of the product's placement have an effect on the product's mean sales?
c. At the 0.10 level of significance, does the location in the store have an effect on the product's mean sales?

12-38. A PEW Research Center survey was reported in *USA Today* (Nanci Hellmich, "Dieters are setting ambitious goals," April 26, 2006). It investigated how many pounds heavier the respondents were than their perceived ideal weight. They investigated whether these perceptions differed among different regions of the country and gender of the respondents. The following data (pounds) reflect the survey results:

Gender	Region			
	West	Midwest	South	Northeast
Men	14	18	15	16
	13	16	15	14
Women	16	20	17	17
	13	18	17	13

a. Determine if there is interaction between Region and Gender. Use the *p*-value approach and a significance level of 0.05.
b. Given your findings in part a, determine any significant differences among the discrepancy between the average existing and desired weights in the regions.
c. Repeat part b for the Gender factor.

Computer Database Exercises

12-39. A psychologist is conducting a study to determine whether there are differences between the ability of history majors and mathematics majors to solve various types of puzzles. Five mathematic majors and five history majors were randomly selected from the students at a liberal arts college in Maine. Each student was given five different puzzles to complete: a crossword puzzle, a cryptogram, a logic problem, a maze, and a cross sums. The time in minutes (rounded to the nearest minute) was recorded for each student in the study. If a student could not complete a puzzle in the maximum time allowed, or completed a puzzle incorrectly, then a penalty of 10 minutes was added to their time. The results are shown in the file **Puzzle**.
   a. Plot the mean time to complete a puzzle for each puzzle type by major. What conclusion would you reach about the interaction between major and puzzle type?
   b. At the 0.05 level of significance, is there an interaction effect?
   c. If interaction is present, conduct a one-way ANOVA to test whether the mean time to complete a puzzle for history majors depends on the type of puzzle. Does the mean time to complete a puzzle for mathematics majors depend on the type of puzzle? Conduct the one-way ANOVA tests at a level of significance of 0.05.

12-40. Mt. Jumbo Plywood Company makes plywood for use in furniture production. The first major step in the plywood process is the peeling of the logs into thin layers of veneer. A lathe that rotates the logs through a knife that peels the log into layers 3/8″ thick conducts the peeling process. Ideally, when a

log is reduced to a 4-inch core diameter, the lathe releases the core and a new log is loaded onto the lathe. However, a problem called "spinouts" occurs if the lathe kicks out a core that has more than 4 inches left. This wastes wood and costs the company money.

Before going to the lathe, the logs are conditioned in a water-filled vat that is heated to warm the logs. The company is concerned that improper log conditioning may lead to excessive spinouts. Two factors are believed to effect the core diameter: the vat temperature and the time the logs spend in the vat prior to peeling. The lathe supervisor has recently conducted a test during which logs were peeled at each combination of temperature and time. The sample data for this experiment are in the data file called **Mt Jumbo**. The data are the core diameters in inches.
   a. Based on the sample data, is there an interaction between water temperature and vat hours? Test using a significance level of 0.01. Discuss what interaction would mean in this situation. Use a *p*-value approach.
   b. Based on the sample data, is there a difference in mean core diameter at the three water temperatures? Test using a significance level of 0.01.
   c. Do the sample data indicate a difference in mean core diameter across the three vat times analyzed in this study? Use a significance level of 0.10 and a *p*-value approach.

12-41. The Iams Company sells Eukanuba and Iams premium dog and cat foods (dry and canned) in 70 countries. Iams makes dry dog and cat food at plants in Lewisburg, Ohio; Aurora, Nebraska; Henderson, North Carolina; Leipsic, Ohio; and Coevorden, The Netherlands. Its Eukanuba brand dry dog foods come in five formulas. One of the ingredients is of particular importance: crude fat. To discover if there is a difference in the average percent of crude fat among the five formulas and among the production sites, the sample data found in the file entitled **Eukanuba** is obtained.
   a. Determine if there is interaction between the Eukanuba formulas and plant site where they are produced. Use the *p*-value approach and a significance level of 0.025.
   b. Given your findings in part a, determine if there is a difference in the average percentage of crude fat in the Eukanuba formulas. Use a test-statistic approach with a significance level of 0.025.
   c. Repeat part b for the plant sites in which the formulas are produced.
   d. One important finding will be whether the average percent of crude fat for the "Reduced Fat"

formula is equal to the advertised 9%. Conduct a relevant hypothesis test to determine this using a significance level of 0.05.

12-42. The amount of sodium in food has been of increasing concern due to its health implications. Beers from various producers have been analyzed for their sodium content. The file entitled **Sodium** contains the amount of sodium (mg) discovered in 12 fluid ounces of beer produced by the four major producers: Anheuser-Busch Inc., Miller Brewing Co., Coors Brewing Co., and Pabst Brewing Co.

The types of beer (ales, lager, and specialty beers) were also scrutinized in the analysis.

a. Determine if there is interaction between the producer and the type of beer. Use a significance level of 0.05.

b. Given your findings in part a, determine if there is a difference in the average amount of sodium in 12 ounces of beer among the producers of the beer. Use a significance level of 0.05.

c. Repeat part b for the types of beer. Use a significance level of 0.05.

Summary and Conclusions

Chapter 12 has illustrated through a wide variety of examples that there are many instances in business in which we are interested in testing to determine whether three or more populations have equal means. The technique for performing such tests is called analysis of variance. ANOVA is an extension of the two-sample t-test procedure introduced in Chapter 10. The basic logic is that if the sample means tend to be substantially different, then the hypothesis of equal means is rejected.

Depending upon the experimental design employed, there are different hypothesis tests that must be performed. The most elementary of these experimental designs is the one-way design, which is used to test whether three or more populations have equal mean values when the samples from the populations are considered to be independent. If we need to control for an outside source of variation (analogous to forming paired samples in Chapter 10), we can use the randomized complete block design. If there are two factors of interest and we wish to test to see whether the levels of each separate factor have equal means, then a two-factor design with replications is used.

Regardless of which method is used, if the null hypothesis of equal means is rejected, methods exist to determine which pairs of populations have different means. Methods such as the Tukey-Kramer and Fisher's *LSD* method allow us to examine all possible contrasts without expanding the experiment-wide significance level.

Analysis of variance is actually an array of statistical techniques used to test hypotheses related to these (and many other) experimental designs. By completing this chapter, you will have been introduced to some of the most popular ANOVA techniques.

Equations

Partitioned Sum of Squares

$$SST = SSB + SSW \tag{12.1}$$

Hartley's F-Test Statistic

$$F_{max} = \frac{s_{max}^2}{s_{min}^2} \tag{12.2}$$

Total Sum of Squares

$$SST = \sum_{i=1}^{k} \sum_{j=1}^{n_i} (x_{ij} - \bar{\bar{x}})^2 \tag{12.3}$$

Sum of Squares Between

$$SSB = \sum_{i=1}^{k} n_i (\bar{x}_i - \bar{\bar{x}})^2 \tag{12.4}$$

Sum of Squares Within

$$SSW = SST - SSB \tag{12.5}$$

or

$$SSW = \sum_{i=1}^{k} \sum_{j=1}^{n_i} (x_{ij} - \bar{x}_i)^2 \tag{12-6}$$

Tukey-Kramer Critical Range

$$\text{Critical Range} = q_{1-\alpha} \sqrt{\frac{MSW}{2}\left(\frac{1}{n_i} + \frac{1}{n_j}\right)} \tag{12.7}$$

Sum of Squares Partitioning for Randomized Complete Block Design

$$SST = SSB + SSBL + SSW \tag{12.8}$$

Sum of Squares for Blocking

$$SSBL = \sum_{j=1}^{b} k(\bar{x}_j - \bar{\bar{x}})^2 \tag{12.9}$$

Sum of Squares Within

$$SSW = SST - (SSB + SSBL) \quad \textbf{(12.10)}$$

Fisher's Least Significant Difference

$$LSD = t_{\alpha/2} \sqrt{MSW} \sqrt{\frac{2}{b}} \quad \textbf{(12.11)}$$

Total Sum of Squares

$$SST = \sum_{i=1}^{a} \sum_{j=1}^{b} \sum_{k=1}^{n} (x_{ijk} - \bar{\bar{x}})^2 \quad \textbf{(12.12)}$$

Sum of Squares Factor A

$$SS_A = bn \sum_{i=1}^{a} (\bar{x}_{i..} - \bar{\bar{x}})^2 \quad \textbf{(12.13)}$$

Sum of Squares Factor B

$$SS_B = an \sum_{j=1}^{b} (\bar{x}_{.j.} - \bar{\bar{x}})^2 \quad \textbf{(12.14)}$$

Sum of Squares Interaction Between Factors A and B

$$SS_{AB} = n \sum_{i=1}^{a} \sum_{j=1}^{b} (\bar{x}_{ij.} - \bar{x}_{i..} - \bar{x}_{.j.} + \bar{\bar{x}})^2 \quad \textbf{(12.15)}$$

Sum of Squares Error

$$SSE = \sum_{i=1}^{a} \sum_{j=1}^{b} \sum_{k=1}^{n} (x_{ijk} - \bar{x}_{ij.})^2 \quad \textbf{(12.16)}$$

Key Terms

Balanced design   511
Between-sample variation   514
Completely randomized
   design   511

Experiment-wide error rate   525
Factor   511
Levels   511
One-way analysis of variance   510

Total variation   514
Within-sample variation   514

Chapter Exercises

Conceptual Questions

12-43. In journals related to your major locate two articles where tests of three or more population means were important. Discuss the issue being addressed, how the data were collected, the results of the statistical test, and any conclusions drawn based on the analysis.

12-44. Discuss why in some circumstances it is appropriate to use the randomized complete block design. Give an example other than those discussed in the text where this design could be used.

12-45. A one-way analysis of variance has just been performed. The conclusion reached is that the null hypothesis stating that the population means are equal has not been rejected. What would you expect the Tukey-Kramer procedure for multiple comparisons to show if it were performed for all pairwise comparisons? Discuss.

12-46. A two-way analysis of variance experiment is to be conducted to examine CEO salaries ($K) as a function of the number of years the CEO has been with the company and the size of the company's sales. The years spent with the company are categorized into 0–3, 4–6, 7–9, and > 9 years. The size of the

company is categorized using sales ($million) per year into three categories: 0–50, 51–100, and >100.

a. Describe the factors associated with this experiment.

b. List the levels of each of the factors identified in part a.

c. List the treatment combinations of the experiment.

d. Indicate the components of the ANOVA table that will be used to explain the variation in the CEOs' salaries.

e. Determine the degrees of freedom for each of the components in the ANOVA if two replications are used.

12-47. In any of the multiple comparison techniques (Tukey-Kramer, *LSD*), the estimate of the within-sample variance uses data from the entire experiment. However, if one were to do a two-sample *t*-test to determine if there were a difference between any two means, the estimate of the population variances would only include data from the two specific samples under consideration. Explain this seeming discrepancy.

Business Applications

12-48. Recent news stories have highlighted errors national companies such as H & R Block have made in preparing taxes. However, many people rely on local accountants to handle their tax work. A local television station, which prides itself in doing investigative reporting, decided to determine whether similar preparation problems occur in its market area.

The station selected eight people to have their taxes figured at each of three accounting offices in its market area. The following data shows the tax bills as figured by each of the three accounting offices:

Return	Office 1	Office 2	Office 3
1	4,376.20	5,100.10	4,988.03
2	5,678.45	6,234.23	5,489.23
3	2,341.78	2,242.60	2,121.90
4	9,875.33	10,300.30	9,845.60
5	7,650.20	8,002.90	7,590.88
6	1,324.80	1,450.90	1,356.89
7	2,345.90	2,356.90	2,345.90
8	15,468.75	16,080.70	15,376.70

a. Discuss why this test was conducted as a randomized block design. Why did the station think it important to have all three offices do the returns for each of the eight people?
b. Test to determine whether blocking was necessary in this situation. Use a significance level of 0.01. State the null and alternative hypotheses.
c. Based on the sample data, can the station report statistical evidence that there is a difference in the mean taxes due on tax returns? Test using a significance level of 0.01. State the appropriate null and alternative hypotheses.
d. Referring to part c, if you did conclude that a difference exists, use the appropriate test to determine which office has the highest mean tax due.

12-49. The development of the Internet has made many things possible in addition to downloading music. In particular, it allows an increasing number of people to telecommute, or work from home. While this has many advantages, it has required some companies to provide employees with the necessary equipment, which has made your job as office manager more difficult. Your company provides computers, printers, and Internet service to a number of engineers and programmers, and while the cost of hardware has decreased, the cost of supplies, in this case printer cartridges, has not. Because of the cost of name-brand printer replacement cartridges, several companies have entered the secondary market. You are presently considering offers from four companies. The prices are

equivalent, so you will make your decision based on length of service, specifically number of pages printed. You have given samples of four cartridges to 16 programmers and engineers and have received the following values:

Supplier A	Supplier B	Supplier C	Supplier D
424	650	521	323
521	725	601	383
650	826	590	487
422	722	522	521

a. Using a significance level equal to 0.01, what conclusion should you reach about the four manufacturers' printer cartridges? Explain.
b. If the test conducted in part a reveals that the null hypothesis should be rejected, which supplier should be used? Is there one or more you can eliminate based on these data? Use the appropriate test for multiple comparisons. Discuss.

12-50. The W. Atlee Burpee Co. was founded in Philadelphia in 1876 by an 18-year-old with a passion for plants and animals and a mother willing to lend him $1,000 of "seed money" to get started in business. Today, it is owned by George Ball, Jr. One of Burpee's most demanded seeds is corn. It continues to increase production to meet the growing demand. To this end, an experiment such as presented here is used to determine the combination of fertilizer and seed type that produces the largest number of kernels per ear.

	Fert. 1	Fert. 2	Fert. 3	Fert. 4
Seed A	807	995	894	903
	800	909	907	904
Seed B	1,010	1,098	1,000	1,008
	912	987	801	912
Seed C	1,294	1,286	1,298	1,199
	1,097	1,099	1,099	1,201

a. Determine if there is interaction between the type of seed and the type of fertilizer. Use a significance level of 0.05.
b. Given your findings in part a, determine if there is a difference in the average number of kernels per ear among the seeds.
c. Repeat part b for the types of fertilizer. Use a significance level of 0.05.

12-51. A senior analyst working for Ameritrade has reviewed purchases his customers have made over the last six months. He has categorized the mutual funds purchased into eight categories: (1) Aggressive Growth (AG), (2) Growth (G), (3) Growth-Income (G-I), (4) Income Funds (IF),

(5) International (I), (6) Asset Allocation (AA), (7) Precious Metal (PM), and (8) Bond (B). The percentage gains accrued by 3 randomly selected customers in each group are:

Mutual Fund	AG	G	G-1	IF	I	AA	PM	B
	6	7	5	1	14	−3	5	−1
	7	−2	6	0	13	7	7	3
	12	0	2	6	10	7	5	2

a. Develop the appropriate ANOVA table to determine if there is a difference in the average percentage gains accrued by his customers among the mutual fund types. Use a significance level of 0.05.

b. Use the Tukey-Kramer procedure to determine which mutual fund type has the highest average percentage gain. Use an experiment-wide error rate of 0.05.

12-52. Anyone who has gone into a supermarket or discount store has walked by displays at the end of aisles. These are referred to as endcaps and often prized because they increase the visibility of products. A manufacturer of tortilla chips has recently developed a new product, a blue corn tortilla chip. The manufacturer has arranged with a regional supermarket chain to display the chips on endcaps at four different locations in stores that have had similar weekly sales in snack foods. The dollar volumes of sales for the last six weeks in the four stores are

Week	Store 1	2	3	4
1	$1,430	$980	$1,780	$2,300
2	$2,200	$1,400	$2,890	$2,680
3	$1,140	$1,200	$1,500	$2,000
4	$880	$1,300	$1,470	$1,900
5	$1,670	$1,300	$2,400	$2,540
6	$990	$550	$1,600	$1,900

a. If the assumptions of a one-way ANOVA design are satisfied in this case, what should be concluded about the average sales at the four stores? Use a significance level of 0.05.

b. Discuss whether you think the assumptions of a one-way ANOVA are satisfied in this case and indicate why or why not. If they are not, what design is appropriate? Discuss.

c. Perform a randomized block analysis of variance test using a significance level of 0.05 to determine whether the mean sales for the four stores are different.

d. Comment on any differences between the means in parts b and c.

e. Suppose blocking was necessary and the researcher chooses not to use blocks. Discuss what impact this could have on the results of the analysis of variance.

f. Use Fisher's least significant difference procedure to determine which, if any, stores have different true average weekly sales.

Computer Database Exercises

12-53. The use of high-technology materials and design has dramatically impacted the game of golf. Not only are the professionals hitting the balls farther but so too are the average players. This has led to a rush to design new and better equipment.

Gordon Manufacturing produces golf balls. Recently, Gordon developed a golf ball made from a space-age material. This new golf ball promises greater distance off the tee. To test Gordon Manufacturing's claim, a test was set up to measure the average distance of four different golf balls (the New Gordon, Competitor 1, Competitor 2, Competitor 3) hit by a driving machine using three different types of drivers (Driver 1, Driver 2, Driver 3). The results (rounded to the nearest yard) are listed in the data file called **Gordon**. Conduct a test to determine if there are significant differences due to type of golf ball.

a. Does there appear to be interaction between type of golf ball and type of driver?

b. Conduct a test to determine if there is a significant effect due to the type of driver used.

c. How could the results of the tests be used by Gordon Manufacturing?

12-54. Maynards, a regional home improvement store chain located in the Intermountain West, is considering upgrading to a new series of scanning systems for its automatic checkout lanes. Although scanners can save customers a great deal of time, scanners will sometimes misread an item's price code. Before investing in one of three new systems, Maynards would like to determine if there is a difference in scanner accuracy. To investigate possible differences in scanner accuracy, 30 shopping carts were randomly selected from customers at the Golden, Colorado, store. The 30 carts differed from each other in both the number and types of items each contained. The items in each cart were then scanned by the three new scanning systems under consideration as well as by the current scanner used in all stores at a specially designed test facility for the purposes of the analysis. Each item was also checked manually, and a count was kept of the number of scanning errors made by each scanner for each basket. Each of the scannings was repeated 30 times, and the average number of scanning errors was determined. The sample data are in the data file called **GroBros**.

a. What type of experimental design did Maynards use to test for differences among scanning systems? Why was this type of design selected?

b. State the primary hypotheses of interest for this test.

c. At the 0.01 level of significance, is there a difference in the average number of errors among the four different scanners?

d. (1) Is there a difference in the average number of errors by cart? (2) Was Maynards correct in blocking by cart?

e. If you determined that there is a difference in the average number of errors among the four different scanners, identify where those differences exist.

f. Do you think that Maynards should upgrade from its existing scanner to Scanner A, Scanner B, or Scanner C? What other factors may it want to consider before making a decision?

12-55. PhoneEx provides call center services for many different companies. A large increase in its business has made it necessary to establish a new call center. Four cities are being considered—Little Rock, Wichita, Tulsa, and Memphis. The new center will employ approximately 1,500 workers and PhoneEx will transfer 75 people from its Omaha center to the new location. One concern in the choice of where to locate the new center is the cost of housing for the employees who will be moving there. To help determine whether significant housing cost differences exist across the competing sites, PhoneEx has asked a real estate broker in each city to randomly select a list of 33 homes between 5 and 15 years old and ranging in size between 1,975 and 2,235 square feet. The prices (in dollars) that were recorded for each city are contained in the file called **PhoneEx**.

a. At the 0.05 level of significance, is there evidence to conclude that the average price of houses between 5 and 15 years old and ranging in size between 1,975 and 2,235 square feet is not the same in the four cities? Use the p-value approach.

b. At the 0.05 level of significance, is there a difference in average housing price between

Wichita and Little Rock? Between Little Rock and Tulsa? Between Tulsa and Memphis?

c. Determine the sample size required to estimate the average housing price in Wichita to within $500 with a 95% confidence level. Assume the required parameters' estimates are sufficient for this calculation.

12-56. A *USA Today* editorial (Alejandro Gonzalez, "CEO Dough," January 20, 2006) addressed the growth of compensation for corporate CEOs. Quoting a study made by *BusinessWeek*, *USA Today* indicated that the pay packages for CEOs have increased almost sevenfold on average over the past decade. The file entitled **CEODough** contains the salaries of CEOs in 1994 and in 2004, adjusted for inflation.

a. Use analysis of variance to determine if there is a difference in the CEOs average salaries between 1994 and 2004, adjusted for inflation.

b. Determine if there is a difference in the CEOs average salaries between 1994 and 2004 using the two-sample t-test procedure.

c. What is the relationship between the two test statistics and the critical values, respectively, that were used in parts a and b?

12-57. An investigation into the effects of various levels of nitrogren (M. L. Vitosh, *Tri-State Fertilizer Recommendations for Corn, Soybeans, Wheat and Alfalfa*, Bulletin E-2567) at Ohio State University addressed the pounds/acre of nitrogen required to produce certain yield levels of corn on fields that had previously had other crops planted in them. The file entitled **Nitrogen** indicates the amount of nitrogen required to produce given quantities of corn planted.

a. Determine if there is interaction between the yield levels of corn and the crop that had been previously planted in the field. Use a significance level of 0.05.

b. Given your findings in part a, determine any significant differences among the average pounds/acre of nitrogen required to produce yield levels of corn on fields that had had corn as the previous crop.

c. Repeat part b for soybeans and grass sod, respectively.

VIDEO CASE 3
Drive-Thru Service Times @ McDonald's

When you're on the go and looking for a quick meal, where do you go? If you're like millions of people every day, you make a stop at McDonald's. Known as "quick service restaurants" in the industry (not "fast food"), companies such as McDonald's invest heavily to determine the most

efficient and effective ways to provide fast, high quality service in all phases of their business.

Drive-thru operations play a vital role. It's not surprising that attention is focused on the drive-thru process. After all, over 60% of individual restaurant revenues in the United States come from the drive-thru experience. Yet understanding the process is more complex than just counting cars. Marla King, professor at the company's international training center, Hamburger University, got her start 25 years ago working at a McDonald's drive-thru. She now coaches new restaurant owners and managers. "Our stated drive-thru service time is 90 seconds or less. We train every manager and team member to understand that a quality customer experience at the drive-thru depends on them," says Marla. Some of the factors that affect a customer's ability to complete their purchases within 90 seconds include restaurant staffing, equipment layout in the restaurant, training, and efficiency of the grill team, and frequency of customer arrivals to name a few. Also, customer order patterns also play a role. Some customers will just order drinks, while others seem to need enough food to feed an entire soccer team. And then there are the special orders. Obviously, there is plenty of room for variability here.

Yet that doesn't stop the company from using statistical techniques to better understand the drive-thru action. In particular, McDonald's utilizes statistical techniques to display data and to help transform the data into useful information. In order for restaurant managers to achieve the goal in their own restaurants, they need training in proper restaurant and drive-thru operations. Hamburger University, McDonald's training center located near Chicago, Illinois, satisfies that need. In the mock-up restaurant service lab, managers go through a "before and after" training scenario. In the "before" scenario," they run the restaurant for thirty minutes as if they were back in their home restaurants. Managers in the training class are assigned to be crew, customers, drive-thru cars, special needs guests (such as hearing impaired, indecisive, or clumsy), or observers. Statistical data about the operations, revenues, and service times are collected and analyzed. Without the right training, the restaurant's operations usually start breaking down after 10-15 minutes. After debriefing and analyzing the data

collected, the managers make suggestions for adjustments and head back to the service lab to try again. This time, the results usually come in well within standards. "When presented with the quantitative results, managers are pretty quick to make the connections between better operations, higher revenues, and happier customers," Marla states.

When managers return to their respective restaurants, the training results and techniques are shared with staff who are charged with implementing the ideas locally. The results of the training eventually are measured when McDonald's conducts a restaurant operations improvement process study, or ROIP. The goal is simple: improved operations. When the ROIP review is completed, statistical analyses are performed and managers are given their results. Depending on the results, decisions might be made that require additional financial resources, building construction, staff training, or reconfiguring layouts. Yet one thing is clear: statistics drive the decisions behind McDonald's drive-thru service operations.

Discussion Questions:

1. After returning from the training session at Hamburger University, a McDonald's store owner selected a random sample of 362 drive-thru customers and carefully measured the time it took from when a customer entered the McDonald's property until the customer had received the order at the drive-thru window. These data are in the file called **McDonald's Drive-Thru Waiting Times**. Note, the owner selected some customers during the breakfast period, others during lunch and others during dinner. Test, using an alpha level equal to 0.05 to determine whether the mean drive-thru time is equal during the three dining periods (breakfast, lunch and dinner.)

2. Referring to question 1, write a short report discussing the results of the test conducted. Make sure to include a discussion of any ramifications the results of this test might have regarding the efforts that the manager will need to take to reduce drive-thru times?

CASE 12.1

Agency for New Americans

Denise Walker collapsed at home after her first outing as a volunteer for the Agency for New Americans in Raleigh, North Carolina. Diane had a fairly good career going with various federal agencies after graduating with a degree in accounting. She decided, as many women have, to stay at home after she and her husband started a family. Now that their youngest was in high school, Denise decided she needed something more to do than manage the household. She decided on volunteer work and joined the Agency for New Americans.

The purpose of the Agency for New Americans is to help new arrivals become comfortable with the basic activities necessary to function in American society. One of the major activities, of course, is shopping for food and other necessities. Denise had just returned from her first outing to a supermarket with a recently arrived Somali Bantu family. It was their first time also, and they were astonished by both the variety and selection. Since the family was on a very limited budget, Diane spent much time talking about comparison shopping, and for someone working with a new currency this was hard. She didn't even want to tell them the store they were in was only one of four possible chains within a mile of their apartment. Diane realized the store she started with would be the one they would automatically return to when on their own.

Next week Diane and the family were scheduled to go to a discount store. Diane typically goes to a national chain close to her house but hasn't felt the need to be primarily a value shopper for some time. Since she feels the Somali family will automatically return to the store she picks, and she has her choice of two national chains and one regional

chain, she decides to not automatically take them to "her" store. Because each store advertises low prices and meeting all competitors' prices, she also doesn't want to base her decision on what she hears on commercials. Instead, she picks a random selection of items and finds the prices in each store. The items and prices are shown here and are also in the file **New Americans**. In looking at the data, Diane sees there are differences in some prices but wonders if there is any way to determine which store to take the family to.

Item	Regional	National 1	National 2
Men's 6 Pair Socks	4.49	6.99	4.27
L'eggs 4 pair pantyhose	5.00	5.99	5.00
Hanes 2 pair boxerbriefs	6.99	6.49	6.87
Hanes 3 pack white undershirts	6.99	6.99	5.96
Franklin soccer ball	11.99	15.99	10.88
Wilson NFL football	12.77	19.99	16.84
Spaulding infusion basketball	27.77	39.99	27.77
Top Flite XL 2000 15 ct golf balls	16.88	14.99	13.88
Rubbermaid 18 gal tote	4.49	4.99	3.94
Folgers coffee 34.5 oz	5.97	6.79	4.74
Charmin 12 double roll	6.79	6.29	5.74
Papermate 10 pack pens	1.24	1.39	1.04
Crayola 64 ct. crayons	2.99	3.24	2.84
The Mummy Returns DVD	19.99	22.99	19.95
Penzoil SAE 40 motor oil	1.79	1.79	1.66
Monopoly board game	10.99	12.99	9.74
Clue board game	13.98	14.99	13.78
Single hot wheels car	0.93	0.99	0.88
14 oz plain M&M's	2.27	2.44	2.44
Old Spice HE deodorant	2.78	2.99	2.99
1 L. Scope mouthwash	3.99	3.99	3.97
Pert Plus shampoo 2-in-1	4.99	5.99	4.46
Jergens lotion soothing aloe 24 fl oz	4.99	5.99	3.64
Venus razor	7.37	7.49	6.97
Gillette razor	6.99	7.49	5.54
Johnsons & Johnsons Baby Shampoo (15 oz.)	2.87	2.89	2.79
Infants Tylenol (1/2 fl. oz., grape)	3.59	4.49	4.49

CASE 12.2

McLaughlin Salmon Works

John McLaughlin's father correctly predicted that a combination of declining wild populations of salmon and an increase in demand for fish in general would create a growing market for salmon grown in "fish farms." Over recent years, an increasing percentage of salmon, trout, and catfish, for example, come from commercial opera-

tions. At first, operating a fish farm consisted of finding an appropriate location, installing the pens, putting in smelt, and feeding the fish until they grew to the appropriate size. However, as the number of competitors increased, successful operations were required to take a more scientific approach to raising fish.

Over the past year, John has been looking at the relationship between food intake and weight gain. Since food is a major cost of the operation, the higher the weight gain for a given amount of food, the more cost-effective the food. John's most recent effort involved trying to determine the relationship between four component mixes and three size progressions for the food pellets. Since smaller fish require smaller food pellets but larger pellets contain more food, one question John was addressing is at what rate to move from smaller to larger pellets. Also, since fish are harder to individually identify than livestock, the study involved constructing small individual pens and giving fish in each pen a

different combination of pellet mix and size progression. This involved a reasonable cost but a major commitment of time, and John's father wasn't sure the cost and time were justified. John had just gathered his first set of data and has started to analyze it. The data are shown here and are also in the file called **McLaughlin Salmon Works**. He is not only interested in whether one component mix, or one pellet size progression, seemed to lead to maximum weight gain but would really like to find one combination of mix and size progression that proved to be superior.

	Size Progression 1	Size Progression 2	Size Progression 3
Mix A	0.713	0.549	0.730
	0.639	0.631	0.639
	0.697	0.574	0.721
	0.680	0.516	0.508
	0.754	0.475	0.754
Mix B	0.451	0.492	0.574
	0.549	0.451	0.549
	0.492	0.393	0.672
	0.500	0.426	0.615
	0.525	0.475	0.631
Mix C	0.728	0.738	0.882
	0.803	0.713	0.902
	0.730	0.763	0.873
	0.745	0.754	0.861
	0.761	0.779	0.868
Mix D	0.549	0.443	0.639
	0.713	0.549	0.664
	0.574	0.459	0.648
	0.590	0.566	0.656
	0.533	0.492	0.631

CASE 12.3

NW Pulp and Paper

Cassie Coughlin had less than a week to finish her presentation to the CEO of NW Pulp and Paper. Cassie had inherited a project started by her predecessor as head of the new-product development section of the company, and by the nature of the business, dealing with wood products, projects tended to have long lifetimes. Her predecessor had successfully predicted the consequences of a series of events that, in fact, had occurred:

1. The western United States, where NW Pulp and Paper had its operations, was running out of water caused by a combination of population growth and increased irrigation. The situation had currently been made worse by

several years of drought. This meant many farming operations were becoming unprofitable.
2. The amount of timber harvesting from national forests continued to be limited.
3. At least some of the land that had been irrigated would become less productive due to alkaline deposits caused by taking water from rivers.

Based on these three factors, Cassie's predecessor had convinced the company to purchase a 2,000-acre farm that had four types of soil commonly found in the West and also had senior water rights. Water rights in the West are given by the state and senior rights are those that will continue to be able to get irrigation water after those with junior rights are cut off. His idea had been to plant three types of genetically modified poplar trees (these are generally fast-growing trees) on the four types of soil and assess growth rates. His contention was it might be economically feasible for the company to purchase more farms that were becoming less productive and become self-sufficient in its supply of raw material for making paper.

The project had been started 15 years ago, and since her predecessor had since retired, Cassie was now in charge of the project. The primary focus of the 15-year review was tree growth. Growth in this case did not refer to height but wood volume. Volume is assessed by measuring the girth of the tree three feet above the ground. She had just received data from the foresters who had been managing the experiment. They had taken a random sample of measurements from each of the tree types. The data are shown here and also can be found in the file **NW Pulp and Paper**. Cassie knew the CEO would at least be interested in whether one type of tree was generally superior and whether there was some unique combination of soil type and tree type that stood out.

	Tree Type 1	Tree Type 2	Tree Type 3
Soil Type 1	57	37	59
	48	47	47
	62	28	62
	53	41	55
Soil Type 2	25	30	40
	37	25	37
	30	28	52
	31	27	44
Soil Type 3	71	60	74
	68	57	80
	59	68	68
	63	55	76
Soil Type 4	37	24	48
	57	37	51
	40	26	49
	45	31	46

CASE 12.4

Quinn Restoration

Last week John Quinn sat back in the chair with his feet on his deck and nodded at his wife, Kate. They had just finished a conversation that would likely influence the direction their lives took for the next several years or longer.

John retired a little less than a year ago after 25 years in the Lake Oswego police department. He had steadily moved up the ranks and retired as a captain. While his career had, in his mind, gone excellently, he had been working much more than he had been home. Initially upon retiring he had reveled in the ability to spend time doing things he was never able to do while working: complete repairs around the house, travel with his wife, spend time with the children still at home, and visit those who had moved out. He was even able to knock five strokes off his golf handicap. However, he had become increasingly restless, and both he and Kate agreed he needed something to do, but that something did not involve a full-time job.

John had, over the years, bought, restored, and sold a series of older Corvettes. Although this had been entirely a hobby, it also had been a profitable one. The discussion John and Kate just concluded had involved expanding this hobby, not into a full-time job, but into a part-time business. John would handle the actual restoration, which he enjoyed, and Kate would cover the paperwork, ordering parts, keeping track of expenses, and billing clients, which John did not like. The last part of their conversation involved ordering parts.

In the past John had ordered parts for old Corvettes from one of three possible sources: Weckler's, American Auto Parts, or Corvette Central. Kate, however, didn't want to call all three any time John needed a part but instead wanted to set up an account with one of the three and be able to order parts over the Internet. The question was which company, if any, would be the appropriate choice. John agreed to develop a list of common parts. Kate would then call each of the companies asking for their prices, and, based on this information, determine with which company to establish the account. Kate spent time over the last week on the phone developing the data shown here and also located in the data file called **Quinn Restoration**. The question he now faced is whether the prices he found could lead him to conclude one company will be less expensive, on average, than the other two.

Part Name	American	Wecklers	Corvette Central
Air filter	9.95	10.95	11.95
Alternator	189.95	289.95	399.95
Battery	78.95	80.95	129.95
Carburetor	299.95	249.95	269.00

continued

Part Name	American	Wecklers	Corvette Central
Coil	28.95	26.95	23.85
Distributor	489.95	465.95	499.95
Exhaust	269.00	279.95	316.00
Front brakes	29.90	29.95	24.95
Gas tank	229.00	342.95	199.00
Headlight	11.95	11.95	8.95
Headers	170.95	168.95	141.95
Hood emblem	89.95	69.95	99.95
Intake manifold	204.95	204.95	475.00
Mufflers	199.00	187.95	174.00
Oil filter	9.95	9.95	10.95
Oil pump	34.95	34.95	39.00
Plug wires	26.95	26.95	49.95
Racing tires	229.00	184.95	168.00
Radiator	259.00	259.95	279.00
Rear brakes	48.95	52.95	46.95
Rims	479.95	419.95	280.00
Shocks (ea.)	29.95	28.95	39.95
Spark plugs (ea.)	3.44	2.95	4.50
Starter	119.00	123.95	189.65
Tachometer cable	13.95	20.95	15.95
Thermostat	10.95	10.50	16.45
Transmission	1,209.95	1,460.95	890.95
Valve covers	89.95	85.95	199.95
Water pump	169.00	184.95	189.00
Steering box	300.00	220.00	309.00

BUSINESS STATISTICS CAPSTONE PROJECT

Theme: Analysis of Variance

Project Objective:

The objective of this business statistics capstone project is to provide you with an opportunity to integrate the statistical tools and concepts that you have learned in your business statistics course. As in all real-world applications, it is not expected through the completion of this project that you will have utilized every statistical technique you have been taught in this course. Rather, an objective of the assignment will be for you to determine which of the statistical tools and techniques are appropriate to employ for the situation you have selected.

Project Description:

You are to identify a business or organizational issue that is appropriately addressed using analysis of variance or experimental design. You will need to specify one or more sets of null and alternative hypotheses to be tested in order to reach conclusions pertaining to the business or organizational issue you have selected. You are responsible for designing and carrying out an "experiment" or otherwise collecting appropriate data required to test the hypotheses using one or more of the analysis of variance designs introduced in your text and statistics course.

There is no minimum sample size. The sample size should depend on the design you choose and the cost and difficulty in obtaining the data. You are responsible for making sure that the data are accurate. All methods (or sources) for data collection should be fully documented.

Project Deliverables:

To successfully complete this capstone project, you are required to deliver, at a minimum, the following items in the context of a management report:

- A complete description of the central issue of your project and of the background of the company or organization you have selected as the basis for the project.

- A clear and concise explanation of the data collection method used. Included should be a discussion of your rationale for selecting the analysis of variance technique(s) used in your analysis.
- A complete descriptive analysis of all variables in the data set, including both numerical and graphical analysis. You should demonstrate the extent to which the basic assumptions of the analysis of variance designs have been satisfied.
- Provide a clear and concise review of the hypotheses tests that formed the objective of your project. Show any post-ANOVA multiple comparison tests where appropriate.
- Offer a summary and conclusion section that relates back to the central issue(s) of your project and discusses the results of the hypothesis tests.
- All pertinent appendix materials.

The final report should be presented in a professional format using the style or format suggested by your instructor.

References

Berenson, Mark L., and David M. Levine, *Basic Business Statistics: Concepts and Applications*, 10th ed. (Upper Saddle River, NJ: Prentice Hall, 2006).

Bowerman, Bruce L., and Richard T. O'Connell, *Linear Statistical Models: An Applied Approach*, 2nd ed. (Belmont, CA: Duxbury Press, 1990).

Cox, D. R., *Planning of Experiments* (New York: John Wiley & Sons, 1992).

Cryer, Jonathan D., and Robert B. Miller, *Statistics for Business: Data Analysis and Modeling*, 2nd ed. (Belmont, CA: Duxbury Press, 1994).

Microsoft Excel 2007 (Redmond, WA: Microsoft Corp., 2007).

Minitab for Windows Version 15 (State College, PA: Minitab, 2007).

Montgomery, D. C., *Design and Analysis of Experiments*, 4th ed. (New York: John Wiley & Sons, 1997).

Kutner, Michael H. Christopher J. Nachtsheim, John Neter, William Li, *Applied Linear Statistical Models*, 5th ed. (New York, McGraw-Hill Irwin, 2005).

Searle, S. R., and R. F. Fawcett, "Expected Mean Squares in Variance Component Models Having Finite Populations." *Biometrics*, 26 (1970), pp. 243–254.

Special Review Section

This review section, which is presented using block diagrams and flowcharts, is intended to help you tie together the material from several key chapters. This section is not a substitute for reading and studying the chapters covered by the review. However, you can use this review material to add to your understanding of the individual topics in the chapters.

Chapters 8 to 12

Statistical inference is the process of reaching conclusions about a population based on a random sample selected from the population. Chapters 8 to 12 introduced the fundamental concepts of statistical inference involving two major categories of inference, *estimation and hypothesis testing*. These chapters have covered a fairly wide range of different situations that for beginning students can sometimes seem overwhelming. The following diagrams will, we hope, help you better identify which specific estimation or hypothesis-testing technique to use in a given situation. These diagrams form something resembling a decision support system that you should be able to use as a guide through the estimation and hypothesis-testing processes.

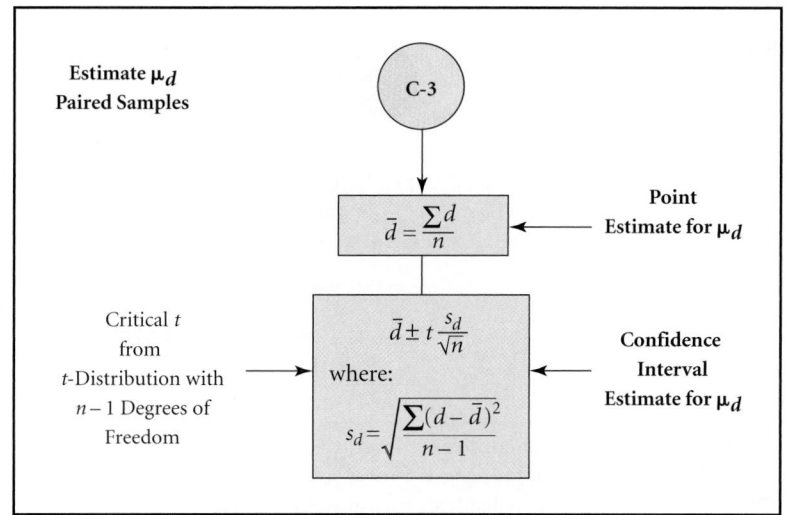

Estimate μ_d
Paired Samples

C-3

$$\bar{d} = \frac{\sum d}{n}$$

Point
Estimate for μ_d

Critical t
from
t-Distribution with
$n-1$ Degrees of
Freedom

$$\bar{d} \pm t\frac{s_d}{\sqrt{n}}$$
where:
$$s_d = \sqrt{\frac{\sum(d-\bar{d})^2}{n-1}}$$

Confidence
Interval
Estimate for μ_d

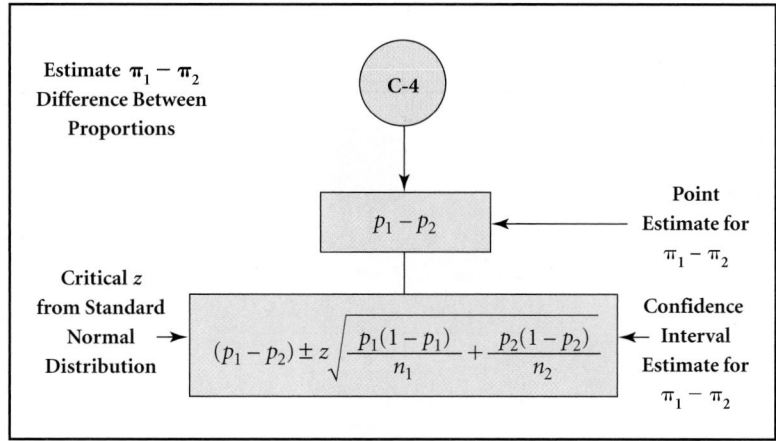

Estimate $\pi_1 - \pi_2$
Difference Between
Proportions

C-4

$$p_1 - p_2$$

Point
Estimate for
$\pi_1 - \pi_2$

Critical z
from Standard
Normal
Distribution

$$(p_1 - p_2) \pm z\sqrt{\frac{p_1(1-p_1)}{n_1} + \frac{p_2(1-p_2)}{n_2}}$$

Confidence
Interval
Estimate for
$\pi_1 - \pi_2$

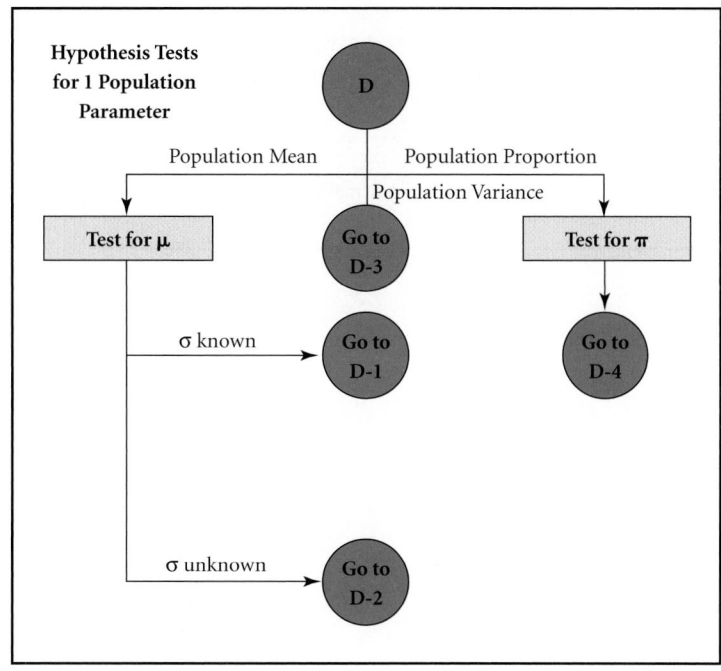

Hypothesis Tests
for 1 Population
Parameter

D

Population Mean

Population Proportion

Population Variance

Test for μ

Go to
D-3

Test for π

σ known

Go to
D-1

Go to
D-4

σ unknown

Go to
D-2

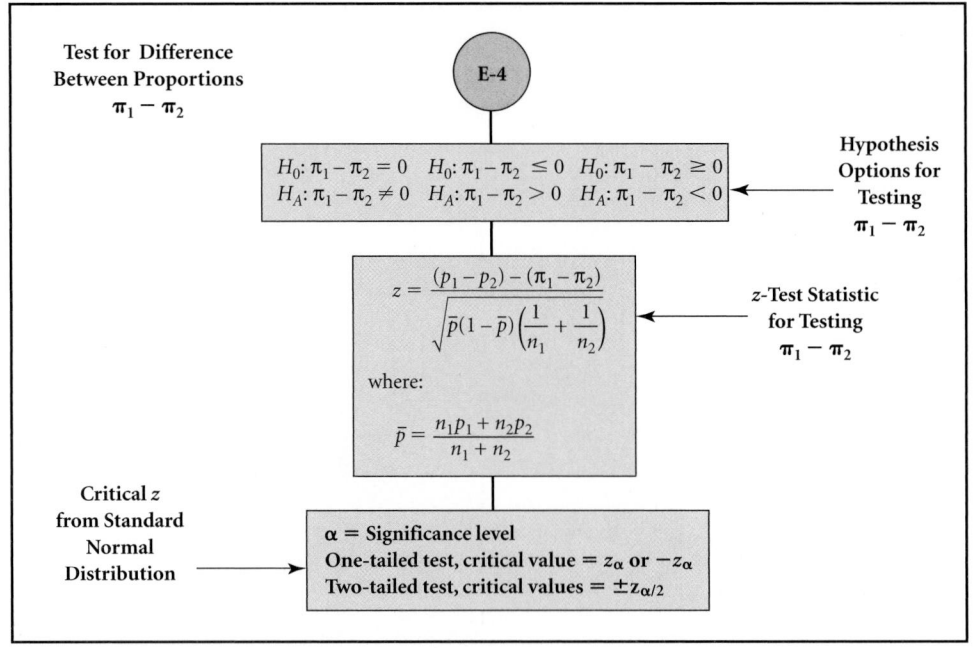

Test for Difference Between Proportions
$\pi_1 - \pi_2$

E-4

$H_0: \pi_1 - \pi_2 = 0 \quad H_0: \pi_1 - \pi_2 \leq 0 \quad H_0: \pi_1 - \pi_2 \geq 0$
$H_A: \pi_1 - \pi_2 \neq 0 \quad H_A: \pi_1 - \pi_2 > 0 \quad H_A: \pi_1 - \pi_2 < 0$

Hypothesis Options for Testing $\pi_1 - \pi_2$

$$z = \frac{(p_1 - p_2) - (\pi_1 - \pi_2)}{\sqrt{\bar{p}(1 - \bar{p})\left(\frac{1}{n_1} + \frac{1}{n_2}\right)}}$$

where:

$$\bar{p} = \frac{n_1 p_1 + n_2 p_2}{n_1 + n_2}$$

z-Test Statistic for Testing $\pi_1 - \pi_2$

Critical z from Standard Normal Distribution

α = **Significance level**
One-tailed test, critical value = z_α or $-z_\alpha$
Two-tailed test, critical values = $\pm z_{\alpha/2}$

Test for Difference Between Population Variances
$\sigma_1^2 - \sigma_2^2$

E-5

$H_0: \sigma_1^2 = \sigma_2^2 \quad H_0: \sigma_1^2 \leq \sigma_2^2 \quad H_0: \sigma_1^2 \geq \sigma_2^2$
$H_A: \sigma_1^2 \neq \sigma_2^2 \quad H_A: \sigma_1^2 > \sigma_2^2 \quad H_A: \sigma_1^2 < \sigma_2^2$

Hypothesis Options for Testing $\sigma_1^2 - \sigma_2^2$

For two-tailed test put larger sample variance in numerator
$df = D_1 = n_1 - 1$ and $D_2 = n_2 - 1$

$$F = \frac{s_1^2}{s_2^2}$$

F-Test Statistic for Testing $\sigma_1^2 - \sigma_2^2$

α = **Significance level**
One-tailed test, critical value = F_α
Two-tailed test, critical value = $F_{\alpha/2}$

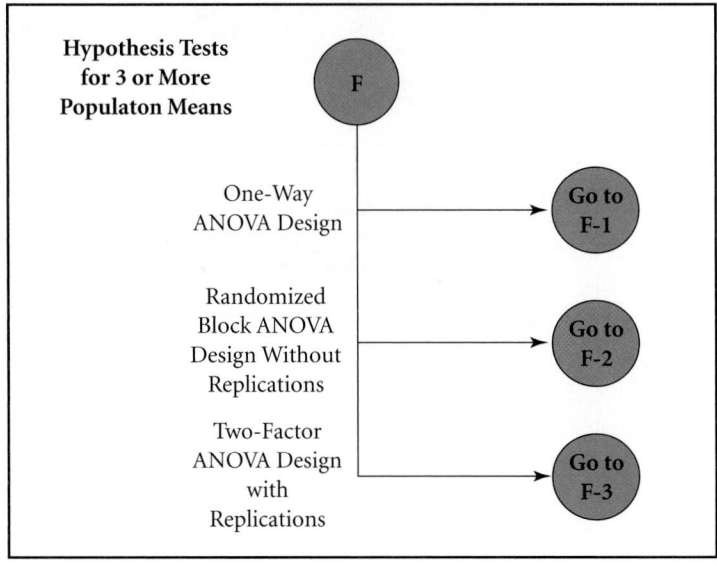

Hypothesis Tests for 3 or More Populaton Means

F

One-Way ANOVA Design → Go to F-1

Randomized Block ANOVA Design Without Replications → Go to F-2

Two-Factor ANOVA Design with Replications → Go to F-3

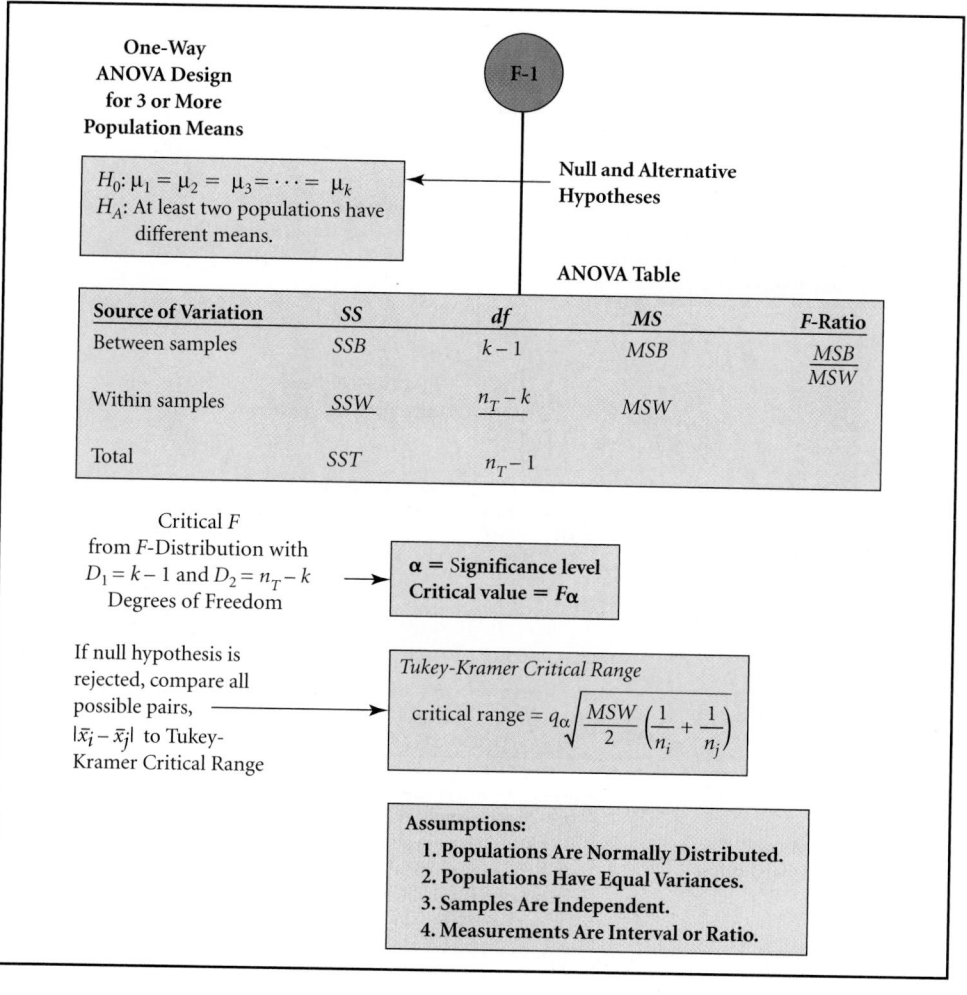

One-Way ANOVA Design for 3 or More Population Means

F-1

$H_0: \mu_1 = \mu_2 = \mu_3 = \cdots = \mu_k$
H_A: At least two populations have different means.

Null and Alternative Hypotheses

ANOVA Table

Source of Variation	SS	df	MS	F-Ratio
Between samples	SSB	$k-1$	MSB	$\dfrac{MSB}{MSW}$
Within samples	SSW	$n_T - k$	MSW	
Total	SST	$n_T - 1$		

Critical F from F-Distribution with $D_1 = k - 1$ and $D_2 = n_T - k$ Degrees of Freedom

α = Significance level
Critical value = $F\alpha$

If null hypothesis is rejected, compare all possible pairs, $|\bar{x}_i - \bar{x}_j|$ to Tukey-Kramer Critical Range

Tukey-Kramer Critical Range

$$\text{critical range} = q_\alpha \sqrt{\frac{MSW}{2}\left(\frac{1}{n_i} + \frac{1}{n_j}\right)}$$

Assumptions:
1. Populations Are Normally Distributed.
2. Populations Have Equal Variances.
3. Samples Are Independent.
4. Measurements Are Interval or Ratio.

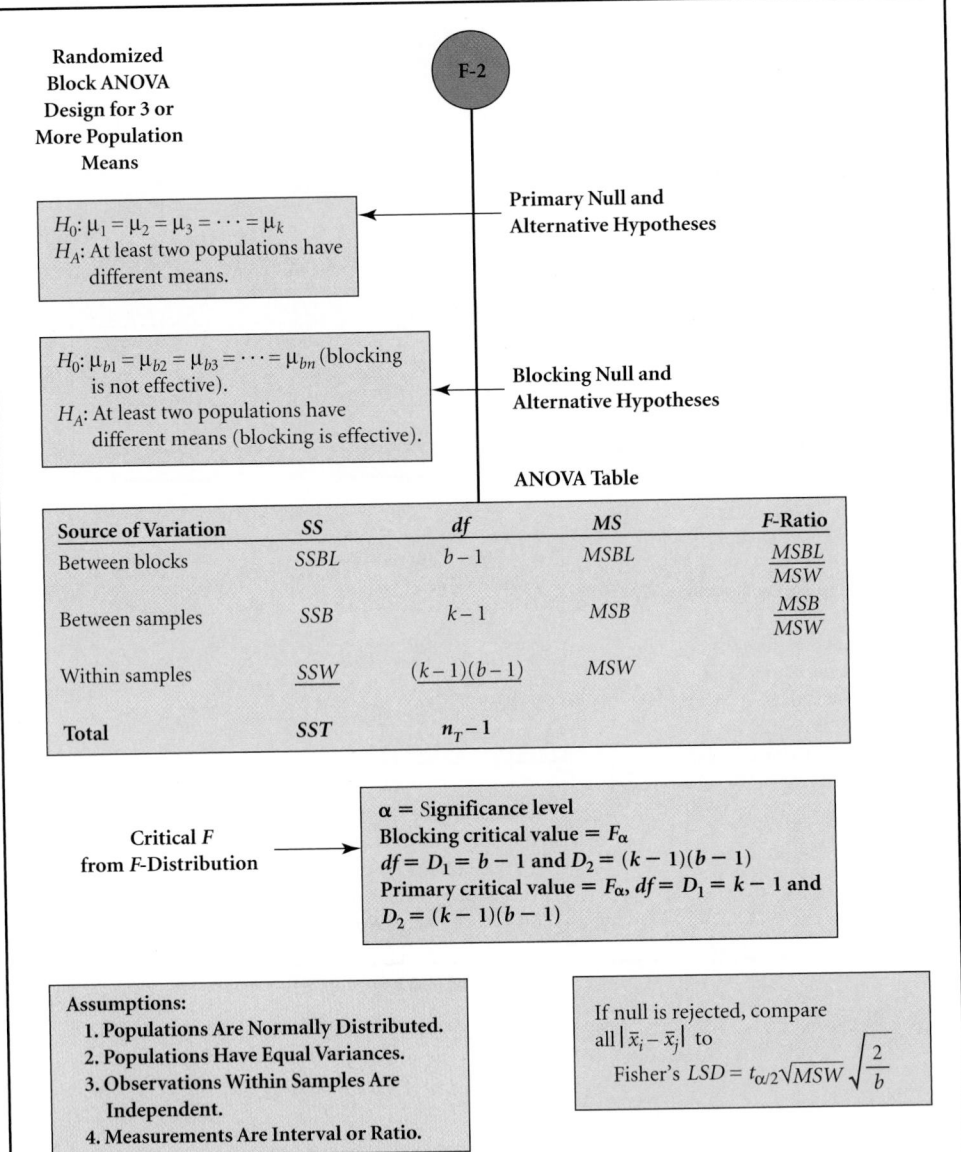

Randomized Block ANOVA Design for 3 or More Population Means

F-2

$H_0: \mu_1 = \mu_2 = \mu_3 = \cdots = \mu_k$
H_A: At least two populations have different means.

Primary Null and Alternative Hypotheses

$H_0: \mu_{b1} = \mu_{b2} = \mu_{b3} = \cdots = \mu_{bn}$ (blocking is not effective).
H_A: At least two populations have different means (blocking is effective).

Blocking Null and Alternative Hypotheses

ANOVA Table

Source of Variation	SS	df	MS	F-Ratio
Between blocks	SSBL	$b-1$	MSBL	$\dfrac{MSBL}{MSW}$
Between samples	SSB	$k-1$	MSB	$\dfrac{MSB}{MSW}$
Within samples	$\underline{SSW}$	$(k-1)(b-1)$	MSW	
Total	SST	$n_T - 1$		

Critical F from F-Distribution

α = Significance level
Blocking critical value = F_α
$df = D_1 = b - 1$ and $D_2 = (k-1)(b-1)$
Primary critical value = F_α, $df = D_1 = k - 1$ and $D_2 = (k-1)(b-1)$

Assumptions:
1. Populations Are Normally Distributed.
2. Populations Have Equal Variances.
3. Observations Within Samples Are Independent.
4. Measurements Are Interval or Ratio.

If null is rejected, compare all $|\bar{x}_i - \bar{x}_j|$ to
Fisher's $LSD = t_{\alpha/2}\sqrt{MSW}\sqrt{\dfrac{2}{b}}$

Two-Factor
ANOVA Design
with Replications

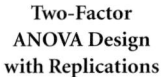

**Factor A Null and
Alternative Hypotheses**

$H_0: \mu_{A1} = \mu_{A1} = \mu_{A3} = \cdots = \mu_{Ak}$
H_A: Not all Factor A means are equal.

**Factor B Null and
Alternative Hypotheses**

$H_0: \mu_{B1} = \mu_{B2} = \mu_{B3} = \cdots = \mu_{Bn}$
H_A: Not all Factor B means are equal.

H_0: Factors A and B do not interact
to affect the mean response.
H_A: Factors A and B do interact.

Null and alternative hypotheses
for testing whether the two
factors interact

ANOVA Table

Source of Variation	SS	df	MS	F-Ratio
Factor A	SS_A	$a-1$	MS_A	$\dfrac{MS_A}{MSE}$
Factor B	SS_B	$b-1$	MS_B	$\dfrac{MS_B}{MSE}$
AB Interaction	SS_{AB}	$(a-1)(b-1)$	MS_{AB}	$\dfrac{MS_{AB}}{MSE}$
Error	$\underline{SSE}$	$\underline{n_T - ab}$	MSE	
Total	SST	$n_T - 1$		

α = Significance level
Factor A critical value = F_α, $df = D_1 = a - 1$ and $D_2 = n_T - ab$
Factor B critical value = F_α, $df = D_1 = b - 1$ and $D_2 = n_T - ab$
Interaction critical value = F_α, $df = D_1 = (a-1)(b-1)$ and $D_2 = n_T - ab$

Assumptions:
 1. The Population Values for Each Combination of Pairwise Factor Levels
    Are Normally Distributed.
 2. The Variances for Each Population Are Equal.
 3. The Samples Are Independent.
 4. Measurements Are Interval or Ratio.

Using the Flow Diagrams

Example Problem: A travel agent in Florida is interested in determining whether there is a difference in the mean out-of-pocket costs incurred by customers on two major cruise lines. To test this, she has selected a simple random sample of 20 customers who have taken cruise line I and has asked these people to track their costs over and above the fixed price of the cruise. She did the same for a second simple random sample of 15 people who took cruise line II.

You can use the flow diagrams to direct you to the appropriate statistical tool.

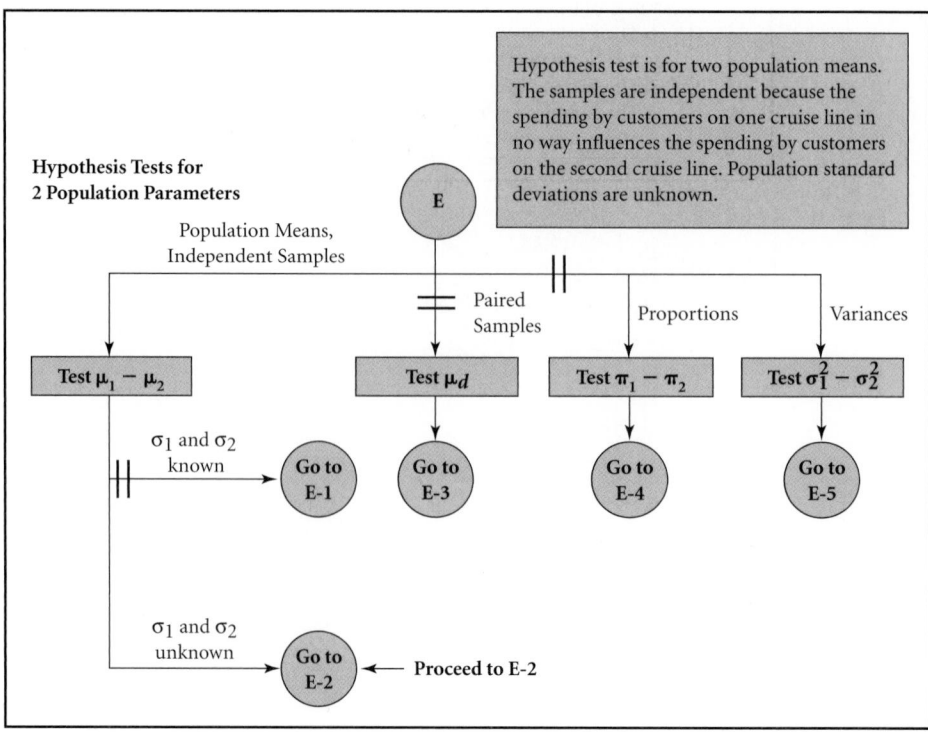

At E-2, we determine the null hypothesis to be

$$H_0: \mu_1 - \mu_2 = 0$$
$$H_A: \mu_1 - \mu_2 \neq 0$$

Next, we establish the test statistic as

$$t = \frac{(\bar{x}_1 - \bar{x}_2) - (\mu_1 - \mu_2)}{s_p \sqrt{\dfrac{1}{n_1} + \dfrac{1}{n_2}}}$$

where:

$$s_p = \sqrt{\frac{(n_1 - 1)s_1^2 + (n_2 - 1)s_2^2}{n_1 + n_2 - 2}}$$

Finally, the critical value is a t-value from the t-distribution with $20 + 15 - 2 = 33$ degrees of freedom. Note, if the degrees of freedom are not shown in the t table, use Excel's **TINV** or use Minitab to determine the t-value.

Thus, by using the flow diagrams and answering a series of basic questions, you should be successful in identifying the statistical tools required to address any problem or application covered in Chapters 8 to 12. You are encouraged to apply this process to the application problems and projects listed here.

Exercises

Integrative Application Problems

SR.1 Brandon Outdoor Advertising supplies neon signs to retail stores. A major complaint from its clients is that letters in the signs can burn out and leave the signs looking silly, depending on which letters stop working. The primary cause of neon letters not working is the failure of the starter unit attached to each letter. Starter units fail primarily based on turn-on/turn-off cycles. The present unit bought by Brandon averages 1,000 cycles before failure. A new manufacturer has approached Brandon claiming to have a model that is superior to the current unit. Brandon is skeptical but agrees to sample 50 starter units. It says it will buy from the new supplier if the sample results indicated the new unit is better. The sample of 50 gives the following values:

> Sample mean = 1,010 cycles
> Sample standard deviation = 48 cycles

Would you recommend changing suppliers?

SR.2 PestFree Chemicals has developed a new fungus preventative that may have a significant market among potato growers. Unfortunately, the actual extent of the fungus problem in any year depends on rainfall, temperature, and many other factors. To test the new chemical, PestFree has used it on 500 acres of potatoes and has used the leading competitor on an additional 500 acres. At the end of the season, 120 acres treated by the new chemical show significant levels of fungus infestation, whereas 160 of the acres treated by the leading chemical show significant infestation.

Do these data provide statistical proof that the new product is superior to the leading competitor?

SR.3 Last year Tucker Electronics decided to try to do something about turnover among assembly-line workers at its plants. It implemented two trial personnel policies, one based on an improved hiring policy and the other based on increasing worker responsibility. These policies were put into effect at two different plants, with the following results:

	Plant 1 Improved Hiring	Plant 2 Increased Responsibility
Workers in trial group	800	900
Turnover proportion	0.05	0.09

Do these data provide evidence that there is a difference between the turnover rates for the two trial policies?

SR.4 A Big 10 University has been approached by Wilson Sporting Goods. Wilson has developed a football designed specifically for practice sessions. Wilson would like to claim the ball will last for 500 practice hours before it needs to be replaced. Wilson has supplied six balls for use during spring and fall practice. The following data have been gathered on the time used before the ball must be replaced.

Hours	
551	511
479	435
440	466

Do you see anything wrong with Wilson claiming the ball will last 500 hours?

SR.5 The management of a chain of movie theaters believes the average weekend attendance at its downtown theater is greater than at its suburban theater. The following sample results were found from their accounting data.

	Downtown	Suburban
Number of weekends	11	10
Average attendance	855	750
Sample variance	1,684	1,439

Do these data provide sufficient evidence to indicate there is a difference in average attendance? The company is also interested in whether there is a significant difference in the variability of attendance.

SR.6 A large mail-order company has placed an order for 5,000 thermal-powered fans to sit on wood-burning stoves from a supplier in Canada, with the stipulation that no more than 2% of the units will be defective. To check the shipment, the company tests a random sample of 400 fans and finds 11 defective. Should this sample evidence lead the company to conclude the supplier has violated the terms of the contract?

SR.7 A manufacturer of automobile shock absorbers is interested in comparing the durability of its shocks with that of its two biggest competitors. To make the comparison, a set of one each of the manufacturer's and of the competitor's shocks were randomly selected and installed on the rear wheels of each of six randomly selected cars of the same type. After the cars had been driven 20,000 miles, the strength of each test shock was measured, coded, and recorded.

Car number	Manufacturer's	Competitor 1	Competitor 2
1	8.8	9.3	8.6
2	10.5	9.0	13.7
3	12.5	8.4	11.2
4	9.7	13.0	9.7
5	9.6	12.0	12.2
6	13.2	10.1	8.9

Do these data present sufficient evidence to conclude there is a difference in the mean strength of the three types of shocks after 20,000 miles?

SR.8 AstraZeneca is the maker of the stomach medicine Prilosec, which is the second-best-selling drug in the world. Recently, the company has come under close scrutiny concerning the cost of its medicines. The company's internal audit department selected a random sample of 300 purchases for Prilosec. They wished to characterize how much is being spent on this medicine. In the sample, the mean price per 20-milligram tablet of Prilosec was $2.70. The sample had a standard deviation of $0.30. Determine an estimate that will characterize the average range of values charged for a tablet of Prilosec.

SR.9 A manufacturer of PC monitors is interested in the effects that the type of glass and the type of phosphor used in the manufacturing process have on the brightness of the monitors. The director of research and development has received anecdotal evidence that the type of glass does not affect the brightness of the monitor as long as phosphor type 2 is used. However, the evidence seems to indicate that the type of glass does make a difference if two other phosphor types are used. Here are data to validate this anecdotal evidence.

	Phosphor Type		
Glass Type	1	2	3
1	279	307	287
	254	313	290
	297	294	285
2	243	253	252
	245	232	236
	267	223	278

Conduct a procedure to verify or repudiate the anecdotal evidence.

SR.10 The Vilmore Corporation is considering two word processing programs for its PCs. One factor that will influence its decision is the ease of use in preparing a business report. Consequently, Jody Vilmore selected a random sample of nine typists from the clerical pool and asked them to type a typical report using both word processors. The typists then were timed (in seconds) to determine how quickly they could type one of the frequently used forms. The results were as follows.

Typist	Processor 1	Processor 2
1	82	75
2	76	80
3	90	70
4	55	58
5	49	53
6	82	75
7	90	80
8	45	45
9	70	80

Jody wishes to have an estimate of the smallest and biggest differences that might exist in the average time required for typing the business form using the two programs. Provide this information.

SR.11 The research department of an appliance manufacturing firm has developed a solid-state switch for its blender that the department claims will reduce the percentage of appliances being returned under the one-year full warranty by a range of 3% to 6%. To determine if the claim can be supported, the testing department selects a group of the blenders manufactured with the new switch and the old switch and subjects them to a normal year's worth of wear. Out of 250 blenders tested with the new switch, 9 would have been returned. Sixteen would have been returned out of the 250 blenders with the old switch. Use a statistical procedure to verify or refute the department's claim.

SR.12 ◎ The Ecco Company makes electronics products for distribution throughout the world. As a member of the quality department, you are interested in the warranty claims that are made by customers who have experienced problems with Ecco products. The file on your CD-ROM called **Ecco** contains data for a random sample of warranty claims. Large warranty claims not only cost the company money but also provide adverse publicity. The quality manager has asked you to provide her with a range of values that would represent the percentage of warranty claims filed for more than $300. Provide this information for your quality manager.

Term Project Assignments

Investigate whether there are differences in grocery prices for three or more stores in your city.

a. Specify the type of testing procedure you will use.
b. What type of experimental design will be used? Why?
c. Develop a "typical" market basket of at least 10 items that you will price-check. Collect price data on these items at three or more different stores that sell groceries.

d. Analyze your price data using the testing procedure and experimental design you specified in parts a and b.
e. Present your findings in a report. Did you find differences in average prices of the "market basket" across the different grocery stores?

Business Statistics Capstone Project

Theme: Financial Data Analysis
Project Objective:

The objective of this business statistics capstone project is to provide you with an opportunity to integrate the statistical tools and concepts that you have learned in your business statistics course. Like all real-world applications, it is not expected that through the completion of this project you will have utilized every statistical technique you have been taught in this course. Rather, an objective of the assignment will be for you to determine which of the statistical tools and techniques are appropriate to apply for the situation you have selected.

Project Description:

Assume that you are working as an intern for a financial management company. Your employer has a large number of clients who trust the company managers to invest their funds. In your position, you have the responsibility for producing reports for clients when they request information. Your company has two large data files with financial information for a large number of U.S. companies. The first is called **US Companies 2003**, which contains financial information for the companies' 2001 or 2002 fiscal-year end. The second file is called **US Companies 2005**, which has data for the fiscal 2003 or 2004 year-end. The 2003 file has data for 7,441 companies. The 2005 file has data for 6,992 companies. Thus, many companies are listed in both files but some are just in one or the other.

The two files have many of the same variables, but the 2003 file has a larger range of financial variables than the 2005 file. For some companies, the data for certain variables are not available and a code of NA is used to so indicate. The 2003 file has a special worksheet containing the description of each variable. These descriptions apply to the 2005 data file as well.

You have been given access to these two data files for use in preparing your reports. Your role will be to perform certain statistical analyses that can be used to help convert these data into useful information in order to respond to the clients' questions.

This morning, one of the partners of your company received a call from a client who asked for a report that would compare companies in the financial services industry (SIC codes in the 6000's) to companies in production-oriented industries (SIC codes in the 2000's and 3000's)

There are no firm guidelines on what the report should entail, but the partner has suggested the following:

- Start with the 2005 data file. Pull the data for all companies with the desired SIC codes into a new worksheet.
- Prepare a complete descriptive analysis of key financial variables using appropriate charts and graphs to help compare the two types of businesses.
- Determine whether there are statistical differences between the two classes of companies in terms of key financial measures.
- Using data from the 2003 file for companies that have these SIC codes and which are also in the 2005 file, develop a comparison that shows the changes over the time span both within SIC code grouping and between SIC code grouping.

Project Deliverables:

To successfully complete this capstone project, you are required to deliver a management report that addresses the partner's requests (listed above) and also contains at least one other substantial type of analysis not mentioned by the partner. This latter work should be set off in a special section of the report.

The final report should be presented in a professional format using the style or format suggested by your instructor.

Chapter THIRTEEN

Goodness-of-Fit Tests and Contingency Analysis

CHAPTER OUTCOMES

After studying the material in Chapter 13, you should be able to:

1. Utilize the chi-square goodness-of-fit test to determine whether data from a process fit a specified distribution.

2. Set up a contingency analysis table and perform a chi-square test of independence.

PREPARING FOR CHAPTER THIRTEEN

- Review the logic involved in testing a null hypothesis discussed in Chapter 9.

- Review the characteristics of probability distributions such as the binomial, Poisson, uniform, and normal distributions in Chapters 5 and 6.

- Review the definitions of Type I and Type II errors in Chapter 9.

◆WHY YOU NEED TO KNOW

The previous 12 chapters have introduced a wide variety of statistical techniques that are frequently used in business decision making. We have discussed numerous descriptive tools and techniques, as well as estimation and hypothesis tests for one and two populations, hypothesis tests using the *t*-distribution, and analysis of variance. However, as we have often mentioned, these statistical tools are limited to use under those conditions for which they were originally developed. For example, the tests based on the standard normal distribution assume that the data can be measured at least at the interval level. The tests that employ the *t*-distribution assume that the sampled populations are normally distributed.

In those situations in which the conditions just mentioned are not satisfied, we suggest using nonparametric statistics. Several of the more widely used nonparametric techniques will be discussed in Chapter 17. These procedures will be shown to be generally the nonparametric equivalent of the classical procedures discussed in Chapters 8–12. The obvious questions when faced with a realistic decision-making situation are "Which test do I use? Should I consider a nonparametric test?" These questions are generally followed by a second question: "Do the data come from a normal distribution?" But recall that we have also described situations involving data from

Poisson or binomial distributions. How do we know which distribution applies to our situation? Fortunately, a statistical technique called *goodness-of-fit* exists that can help us answer this question. Using goodness-of-fit tests, we can decide whether a set of data comes from a specific hypothesized distribution.

You will also encounter many business situations in which the level of data measurement for the variable of interest is either nominal or ordinal, not interval or ratio. For example, a bank may use a code to indicate whether a customer is a good or poor credit risk. The bank may also have data for these customers that indicate, by a code, whether each person is buying or renting a home. The loan officer may be interested in determining whether credit-risk status is independent of home ownership. Because both credit risk and home ownership are qualitative, or categorical, variables, their measurement level is nominal and the statistical techniques introduced in Chapters 8–12 cannot be used to analyze this problem. We, therefore, need a new statistical tool to assist the manager in reaching an inference about the customer population. That statistical tool is contingency analysis. Contingency analysis is a widely used tool for analyzing the relationship between qualitative variables, one that decision makers in all business areas find helpful for data analysis.

13.1 Introduction to Goodness-of-Fit Tests

CHAPTER OUTCOME #1

Many of the statistical procedures introduced in earlier chapters require that the sample data come from populations that are normally distributed. For example, when we use the *t*-distribution in confidence interval estimation or hypothesis testing about one or two population means, the population(s) of interest is (are) assumed to be normally distributed. The *F*-test introduced in Chapters 11 and 12 is based on the assumption that the populations are normally distributed. But how can you determine whether these assumptions are satisfied? In other instances, you may wish to employ a particular probability distribution to help solve a problem related to an actual business process. In order to solve the problem, you may find it necessary to know whether the actual data from the process fit the probability distribution being considered. In such instances, a statistical technique known as a *goodness-of-fit test* can be used.

The term *goodness-of-fit* aptly describes the technique. Suppose a major retail department store believes that the proportion of customers who use each of the four entrances to the store is the same. This would mean that customer arrivals are *uniformly* distributed across the four entrances. Suppose a sample of 1,000 customers is observed entering the store and the entrance (A, B, C, or D) selected by each customer is recorded. Table 13.1 shows the results of the sample. If the manager's assumption about the entrances being used uniformly holds and if there was no sampling error involved, we would expect one-fourth of the customers, or 250, to enter through each door. When we allow for the potential of sampling error, we would still expect close to 250 customers entering through each entrance. The question is, how "good is the fit" between the sample data in Table 13.1 and the expected number of 250 people at each entrance? At what point do we no longer believe that the differences between what is actually observed at each entrance and what we expected

TABLE 13.1 Customer Door Entrance Data

Entrance	Number of Customers
A	260
B	290
C	230
D	220

can be attributed to sampling error? If these differences get too big, we will reject the uniformity assumption and conclude that customers prefer some entrances to others.

Chi-Square Goodness-of-Fit Test

The *chi-square goodness-of-fit test* can be used to determine whether the sample data come from any hypothesized distribution. Consider the following application.

Business Application

VISTA HEALTH GUARD Vista Health Guard, a Pennsylvania health clinic with 25 offices, is open seven days a week. The operations manager was recently hired from a similar position at a smaller chain of clinics in Florida. She is naturally concerned that the level of staffing—physicians, nurses, and other support personnel—be balanced with patient demand.

Currently, the staffing level is balanced Monday through Friday, with reduced staffing on Saturday and Sunday. Her predecessor explained that patient demand is fairly level throughout the week and about 25% less on weekends, but the new manager suspects that the staff members want to have weekends free. Although she was willing to operate with this schedule for a while, she has decided to study patient demand to see whether the assumed demand pattern still applies.

The operations manager requested a random sample of 20 days for each day of the week that showed the number of patients on each of the sample days. A portion of those data follows:

Day	Patient Count
Monday, May 6	325
Monday, October 7	379
Tuesday, July 2	456
Monday, July 15	323
Wednesday, April 3	467
etc.	etc.

For the 140 days observed, the total count was 56,000 patients. The total patient counts for each day of the week are shown in Table 13.2 and are graphed in Figure 13.1.

TABLE 13.2 Patient Count Data for the Vista Health Guard Example

Day	Total Patient Count
Sunday	4,502
Monday	6,623
Tuesday	8,308
Wednesday	10,420
Thursday	11,032
Friday	10,754
Saturday	4,361
Total	56,000

FIGURE 13.1

Graph of Actual Frequencies for Vista Health Guard

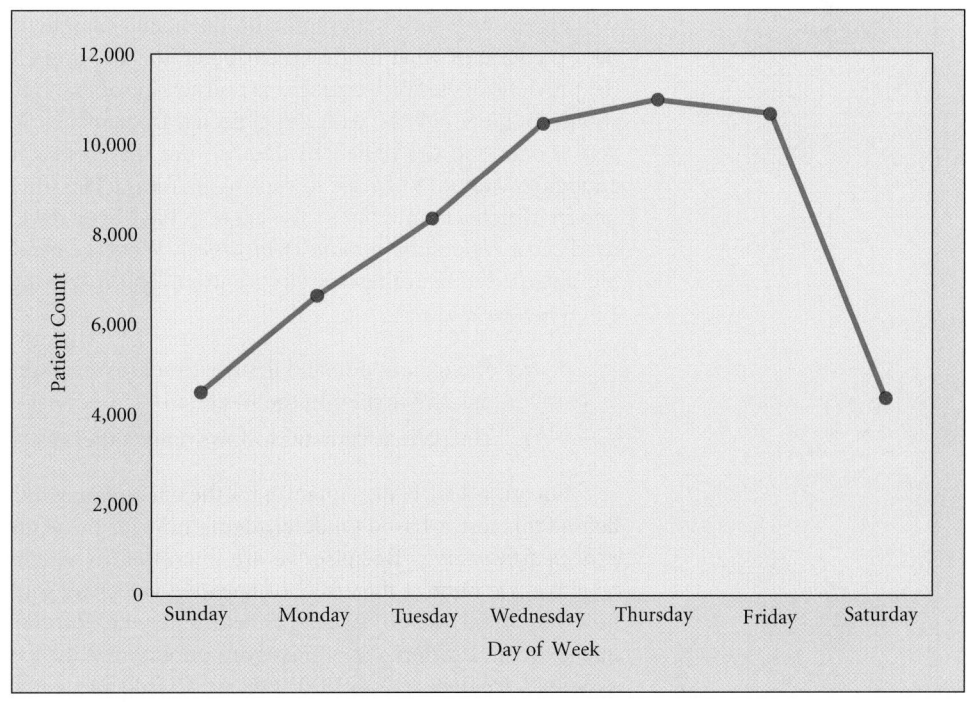

FIGURE 13.2

Actual and Expected Frequencies for Vista Health Guard

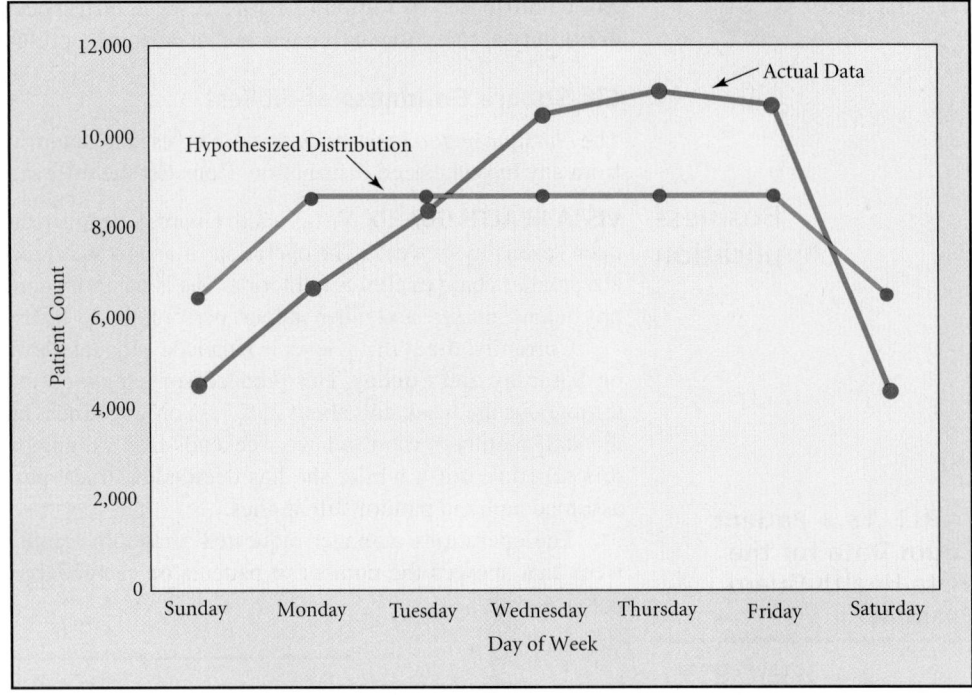

Recall that the previous operations manager at Vista Health Guard based his staffing on the premise that from Monday to Friday the patient count remained essentially the same and on Saturdays and Sundays it went down 25%. If this is so, how many of the 56,000 patients would we expect on Monday? How many on Tuesday, and so forth? To figure out this demand, we determine weighting factors by allocating four units each to days Monday through Friday and three units each (representing the 25% reduction) to Saturday and Sunday. The total number of units is then $(5 \times 4) + (2 \times 3) = 26$. The proportion of total patients expected on each weekday is 4/26 and the proportion expected on a weekend day is 3/26. The expected number of patients on a weekday is $(4/26) \times 56,000 = 8,615.38$, and the expected number on each weekend day is $(3/26) \times 56,000 = 6,461.54$.

Figure 13.2 shows a graph with the actual sample data and the expected values. With the exception of what might be attributed to sampling error, if the distribution claimed by the previous operations manager is correct, the actual frequencies for each day of the week should fit quite closely with the expected frequencies. As you can see in Figure 13.2, the actual data and the expected data do not match perfectly. However, is the difference enough to warrant a change in staffing patterns? The situation facing Vista Health Guard is one for which a number of statistical tests have been developed. One of the most frequently used is the *chi-square goodness-of-fit test*. What we need to examine is how well the sample data fit the hypothesized distribution. The following null and alternative hypotheses can represent this:

H_0: The patient demand distribution is evenly spread through the weekdays and 25% lower on the weekend.

H_A: The patient demand follows some other distribution.

Equation 13.1 is the equation for the chi-square goodness-of-fit test statistic. The logic behind this test is based on determining how far the actual *observed frequency* is from the *expected frequency*. Because we are interested in whether a difference exists, positive or negative, we remove the effect of negative values by squaring the differences. In addition, how important this difference is really depends on the magnitude of the expected frequency (e.g., a difference of 5 is more important if the expected frequency is 10 than if the expected frequency is 1,000), so we divide the squared difference by the expected

FIGURE 13.3

Chi-Square Goodness-of-Fit Test for Vista Health Guard

Hypotheses:

H_0: Patient demand is evenly spread through the weekdays and is 25% lower on weekends.
H_A: Patient demand follows some other distribution.
$\alpha = 0.05$

Day	Total Patient Count Observed o_i	Expected e_i
Sunday	4,502	6,461.54
Monday	6,623	8,615.38
Tuesday	8,308	8,615.38
Wednesday	10,420	8,615.38
Thursday	11,032	8,615.38
Friday	10,754	8,615.38
Saturday	4,361	6,461.54
Total	56,000	56,000

Test Statistic:

$$\chi^2 = \sum \frac{(o-e)^2}{e} = \frac{(4{,}502 - 6{,}461.54)^2}{6{,}461.54} + \frac{(6{,}623 - 8{,}615.38)^2}{8{,}615.38} + \cdots + \frac{(4{,}361 - 6{,}461.54)^2}{6{,}461.54}$$

$$\chi^2 = 594.2 + 460.8 + \cdots + 682.9$$

$$\chi^2 = 3{,}335.6$$

$df = k - 1 = 7 - 1 = 6$

Rejection Region

$\alpha = 0.05$

$\chi^2_{0.05} = 12.5916$

Decision Rule:

If $\chi^2 > 12.5916$, reject H_0;
Otherwise, do not reject H_0.
Because $3{,}335.6 > 12.5916$, not reject H_0.
Based on the sample data, we can conclude that the patient distribution is not the same as previously indicated.

frequency. Finally, we sum these difference ratios for all days. This sum is a statistic that has an approximate chi-square distribution.

Chi-Square Goodness-of-Fit Test Statistic

$$\chi^2 = \sum_{i=1}^{k} \frac{(o_i - e_i)^2}{e_i} \tag{13.1}$$

where:

o_i = Observed frequency for category i

e_i = Expected frequency for category i

k = Number of categories

The χ^2 statistic is distributed approximately as a chi-square only if the sample size is large.

Special Note

> A sample size of at least 30 is sufficient in most cases provided that none of the expected frequencies is too small.

This issue of expected cell frequencies will be expanded upon later. If the calculated chi-square statistic gets large, this is evidence to suggest the fit of the actual data to the hypothesized distribution is not good, and the null hypothesis should be rejected.

Figure 13.3 shows the hypothesis-test process and results for this chi-square goodness-of-fit test. Note that the degrees of freedom for the chi-square test are equal to $k - 1$, where k is the number of categories or observed cell frequencies. In this example, we have 7 categories corresponding to the days of the week, so the degrees of freedom are $7 - 1 = 6$. The critical value of 12.592 is found in Appendix G for an upper-tail test with 6 degrees of freedom and a significance level of 0.05.

As Figure 13.3 indicates, $\chi^2 = 3{,}335.6 > 12.5916$, so the null hypothesis is rejected and we should conclude that the demand pattern does not match the previously defined distribution. The data in Figure 13.3 indicate that demand is heavier than expected Wednesday through Friday and less than expected on the other days. The operations manager may now wish to increase staffing on Wednesday, Thursday, and Friday to more closely approximate current demand patterns.

EXAMPLE 13-1 Chi-Square Goodness-of-Fit Test

TRY PROBLEM 13.1

California Port of Entry When entering California, motorists are required to pass through a port-of-entry inspection station, where their vehicles are inspected to see whether fruit is being brought into the state. The state is concerned about fruit that might be infested with fruit flies and other insects. Full inspections are done on a random basis. One port of entry has five vehicle lanes. The manager wants to do a full inspection on the same number of vehicles in each lane each week. A goodness-of-fit test can be conducted to determine whether this objective is being met using the following steps:

Step 1 Formulate the appropriate null and alternative hypotheses.
Because the number of inspections is supposed to be the same across the five inspection lanes, the following null and alternative hypotheses are formed:

H_0: Distribution of inspections is uniform across the five lanes.
H_A: Distribution of inspections is not uniform.

Step 2 Specify the significance level.
The test will be conducted using $\alpha = 0.05$.

Step 3 Collect the sample data and compute the chi-square test statistic.
The manager collected data for a random sample of five weeks. The following data represent the number of inspections that were performed in each lane:

Lane	1	2	3	4	5
Inspections	358	402	577	403	380

A total of 2,120 inspections were performed during the sampled weeks. Under the hypothesis of a uniform distribution, 20% of this total (rounded to 424) should be performed at each lane. This is the expected cell frequency.

Equation 13.1 is used to form the test statistic based on these sample data.

$$\chi^2 = \sum \frac{(o-e)^2}{e} = \frac{(358-424)^2}{424} + \frac{(402-424)^2}{424}$$
$$+ \frac{(577-424)^2}{424} + \frac{(403-424)^2}{424} + \frac{(380-424)^2}{424}$$
$$= 72.231$$

Step 4 Determine the critical value.
The critical value for the goodness-of-fit test is a chi-square value from the chi-square distribution, with $k - 1 = 5 - 1 = 4$ degrees of freedom, and $\alpha = 0.05$ is 9.4877.

Step 5 Reach a decision.
The decision rule is

If $\chi^2 > 9.4877$, reject H_0;
Otherwise, do not reject H_0.

Because $\chi^2 = 72.231 > 9.4877$, reject the null hypothesis.

Step 6 Draw a conclusion.
We conclude that the inspections are not occurring equally across the five lanes. The manager will now be interested in determining why different lanes tend to receive more inspections than other lanes.

Business Application

Excel and Minitab Tutorial

WOODTRIM PRODUCTS, INC. Woodtrim Products, Inc. makes wood moldings, door frames, and window frames. It purchases lumber from mills throughout New England and eastern Canada. The first step in the production process is to rip the lumber into narrower strips. Different widths are used for different products. For example, wider pieces with no imperfections are used to make door and window frames. Once an operator decides on the appropriate width, that information is locked into a computer and a ripsaw automatically cuts the board to the desired size. The manufacturer of the saw claims that the ripsaw cuts an average deviation of zero from target and that the differences from target will be normally distributed, with a standard deviation of 0.01 inch.

Woodtrim has recently become concerned that the ripsaw may not be cutting to the manufacturer's specifications because operators at other machines downstream in the production process are finding excessive numbers of ripped pieces that are too wide or too narrow.

A quality improvement team (QIT) has started to investigate the problem. Team members selected a random sample of 300 boards just as they came off the ripsaw. To provide a measure of control, the only pieces sampled in the initial study had stated widths of $2\frac{7}{8}$ (2.875) inches. Each piece's width was measured halfway from its end. A portion of the data and the differences between the target 2.875 inches and the actual measured width are

FIGURE 13.4

Woodtrim Products Test Data

Excel 2007 Instructions:
1. Open file: Woodtrim.xls.

Sample	Actual Width	Target Width	Difference
1	2.870	2.875	-0.005
2	2.863	2.875	-0.012
3	2.885	2.875	0.010
4	2.872	2.875	-0.003
5	2.891	2.875	0.016
6	2.893	2.875	0.018
7	2.868	2.875	-0.007
8	2.861	2.875	-0.014

shown in Figure 13.4. The full data set is contained in the CD-ROM file **Woodtrim**. The team can use these data and the chi-square goodness-of-fit testing procedure to test the following null and alternative hypotheses:

H_0: The differences are normally distributed, with $\mu = 0$ and $\sigma = 0.01$.
H_A: The differences are not normally distributed, with $\mu = 0$ and $\sigma = 0.01$.

This example differs slightly from the previous examples because the hypothesized distribution is continuous rather than discrete. Thus, we organize the data into a grouped-data frequency distribution (see Chapter 2), as shown in Figure 13.5. Our choice of classes requires careful consideration. The chi-square goodness-of-fit test compares the actual cell frequencies with the expected cell frequencies. The test statistic from Equation 13.1,

$$\chi^2 = \Sigma \frac{(o-e)^2}{e}$$

is approximately chi-square distributed if the expected cell frequencies are large. Because the expected cell frequencies are used in computing the test statistic, the general recommendation is that the goodness-of-fit test be performed only when all expected cell frequencies are at least 5. If any of the cells have expected frequencies less than 5, the cells should be combined in a meaningful way such that the expected frequencies are at least 5. We have chosen to use $k = 6$ classes. The number of classes is your choice. Although Excel and Minitab do not have a tool for performing a chi-square goodness-of-fit test directly, we can perform the test using Excel functions and formulas and Minitab commands. (Both the Excel and Minitab tutorials on the CD-ROM take you through the specific steps required to complete this example.) Figure 13.5 shows the normal distribution probabilities, expected cell frequencies, and the chi-square calculation. The calculated chi-square statistic is $\chi^2 = 26.432$. The p-value associated with $\chi^2 = 26.432$ and $6 - 1 = 5$ degrees of freedom is 0.0001. Therefore, because p-value $= 0.0001$ is less than any reasonable level of significance, we reject the null hypothesis and conclude the ripsaw is not currently meeting the manufacturer's specification. The saw errors are not normally distributed with mean equal to 0 and a standard deviation equal to 0.01.

FIGURE 13.5

Excel 2007 Results—Goodness-of-Fit Test for the Woodtrim Example

Classes	o Observed Frequencies	Normal Distribution Probability	e Expected Frequency	$(o - e)^2/e$
less than -0.02	0	0.02275	6.83	6.825
-0.02 and under -0.01	42	0.13591	40.77	0.037
-0.01 and under 0.00	133	0.34134	102.40	9.142
0.00 and umder 0.01	75	0.34134	102.40	7.333
0.01 and unfder 0.02	47	0.13591	40.77	0.951
0.02 and over	3	0.02275	6.83	2.144
Total	300			
			Total =	26.432
			p-value =	0.0001

Excel 2007 Instructions:

1. Open file: Woodtrim.xls (see Figure 13.4).
2. Define Classes (column J).
3. Determine observed frequencies [(i.e. cell K4 formula is =COUNTIF($D$2: $D$301,"<0.0")-SUM($K$2:K3)].
4. Determine normal distribution probabilities, assuming the mean = 0.0 and st.dev = 0.01 [i.e., cell L4 formula is =NORMDIST(0,0,0.01,TURE)-SUM ($L$2:L3)].

5. Determine expected frequencies by multiplying normal probability by the same size $(n = 300)$.
6. Compute values for chi-square in column N (cell N5 formula is =[K5-M5]^2/M5].
7. Sum column N to get chi-square statistic.
8. Find p-value using **CHITEST** function [cell N10 formula is =**CHITEST(K2:K7, M2:M7)**].

Special Note

Note that in this case, because the null hypothesis specified both the mean and the standard deviation, the normal distribution probabilities were computed using these values. However, if either or both had not been specified, the sample values would be used in the probability computation. You would lose 1 additional degree of freedom for each parameter that was estimated from the sample data. This is true any time sample statistics are specified in place of population parameters in the hypothesis.

Minitab has a procedure for performing a goodness-of-fit test for a normal distribution. In fact, it offers three different approaches, none of which are exactly the chi-square approach just outlined. Figure 13.6 shows the Minitab results for the Woodtrim example. Consistent with our other Minitab and Excel results, this output illustrates that the null hypothesis should be rejected because the p-value < 0.01.

FIGURE 13.6

Minitab Output—Test of Normal-Distributed Ripsaw Cuts for the Woodtrim Example

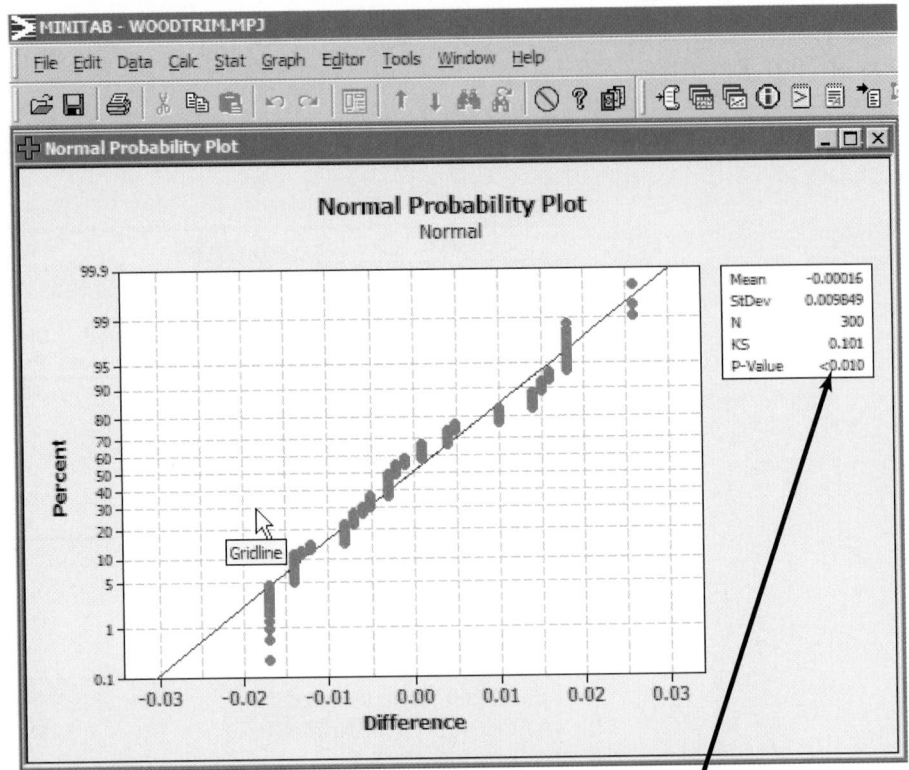

Minitab Instructions:
1. Open file: Woodtrim.MTW.
2. Choose **Stat > Basic Statistics > Normality Test**.
3. In **Variable**, enter data column (*Difference*).
4. Under Normality test, select **Kolmogorov-Smirnov**.
5. Click **OK**.

Because π-value < 0.01 is less than any reasonable level of significance, reject the null hypothesis of normality.

EXAMPLE 13-2 Goodness-of-Fit Test

TRY PROBLEM 13.3

Cushing Supply Cushing Supply makes component parts used in the automobile industry. For some time, shipping workers have been inspecting 10 parts from every day's production before shipping. If two or more of the parts are defective, they do a complete inspection on the day's parts to sort the defective from the good parts. If they find one or fewer, they go ahead and ship the parts without further analysis. The contract calls for at most 10% of the parts to be defective. At issue is whether Cushing managers can evaluate this sampling plan using a binomial distribution with $n = 10$ and $\pi = 0.10$. To test this, a goodness-of-fit test can be performed using the following steps:

Step 1 State the appropriate null and alternative hypotheses.
In this case, the null and alternative hypotheses are

H_0: Distribution of defects is binomial, with $n = 10$ and $\pi = 0.10$.
H_A: Distribution is not binomial, with $n = 10$ and $\pi = 0.10$.

Step 2 Specify the level of significance.
The test will be conducted using $\alpha = 0.025$.

Step 3 Collect the sample data and compute the chi-square test statistic using Equation 13.1.
The company selected a simple random sample of 100 days from past production records and recorded the number of defects for each day when

the sample of 10 items was inspected. The following table shows the computations for the chi-square statistic.

Defects	o Observed Defects	Binomial Probability $n = 10$, $\pi = 0.10$	e Expected Frequency	$\dfrac{(o_i - e_i)^2}{e_i}$
0	30	0.3487	34.87	0.6812
1	40	0.3874	38.74	0.0410
2	20	0.1937	19.37	0.0205
3 and over	10	0.0702	7.02	1.2650
Total	100			2.0067

The calculated chi-square test statistic is $\chi^2 = 2.0067$.

Step 4   Determine the critical value.
The critical value depends on the number of degrees of freedom and the level of significance. The degrees of freedom will be equal to $k - 1$, where k is the number of categories for which observed and expected frequencies will be recorded. In this case, the managers have set up the following groups:

Defects: 0   1   2   3 and over

Therefore, $k = 4$, and the degrees of freedom are $4 - 1 = 3$. The critical chi-square value for $\alpha = 0.025$ found in Appendix G is 9.3484.

Step 5   Reach a decision.
Because $\chi^2 = 2.0067$ is less than the critical value of 9.3484, we do not reject the null hypothesis.

Step 6   Draw a conclusion.
The binomial distribution may be the appropriate distribution to describe the company's sampling plan.

EXAMPLE 13-3   University Internet Service

TRY PROBLEM 13.2

Students in a computer information systems class at a major university have established an Internet service provider (ISP) company for the university's students, faculty, and staff. Customers of this ISP connect via a wireless signal available throughout the campus and surrounding business area. Capacity is always an issue for an ISP, and the students had to estimate the capacity demands for their service. Before opening for business, the students conducted a survey of likely customers. Based on this survey, they estimated that demand during the late afternoon and evening hours is Poisson distributed (refer to Chapter 5) with a mean equal to 10 users per hour. Based on this assumption, the students developed the ISP with the capacity to handle 20 users simultaneously. However, they have lately been receiving complaints from customers saying they have been denied access to the system because 20 users are already online. The students are now interested in determining whether the demand distribution may no longer be Poisson distributed with a mean equal to 10 per hour. To test this, they have collected data on the number of user requests for ISP access for 225 randomly selected time periods during the heavy-use hours. The following steps can be used to conduct the statistical test:

Step 1 State the appropriate null and alternative hypotheses.
The null and alternative hypotheses are

H_0: Demand distribution is Poisson distributed with mean equal to 10 users per time period.

H_A: The demand distribution is not distributed as a Poisson distribution with mean equal to 10 per period.

Step 2 Specify the level of significance.
The hypothesis test will be conducted using $\alpha = 0.05$.

Step 3 Collect the sample data and compute the chi-square test statistic using Equation 13.1.
A random sample of 225 time periods was selected and the number of users requesting access to the ISP at each time period was recorded. The observed frequencies based on the sample data are as follows:

Number of Requests	Observed Frequency
0	0
1	2
2	1
3	3
4	4
5	3
6	8
7	6
8	11
9	7
10	18
11	14
12	17
13	18
14	25
15	28
16	23
17	17
18	9
19 and over	11
Total	225

To compute the chi-square test statistic you must determine the expected frequencies. Start by determining the probability for each number of user requests based on the hypothesized distribution. (Poisson with $\lambda t = 10$.) The expected frequencies are calculated by multiplying the probability by the total observed frequency of 225. These results are as follows:

Number of Requests	Observed Frequency	Poisson Probability $\lambda t = 10$	Expected Frequency
0	0	0.0000	0.00
1	2	0.0005	0.11
2	1	0.0023	0.52
3	3	0.0076	1.71

(Continued)

Number of Requests	Observed Frequency	Poisson Probability $\lambda t = 10$	Expected Frequency
4	4	0.0189	4.25
5	3	0.0378	8.51
6	8	0.0631	14.20
7	6	0.0901	20.27
8	11	0.1126	25.34
9	7	0.1251	28.15
10	18	0.1251	28.15
11	14	0.1137	25.58
12	17	0.0948	21.33
13	18	0.0729	16.40
14	25	0.0521	11.72
15	28	0.0347	7.81
16	23	0.0217	4.88
17	17	0.0128	2.88
18	9	0.0071	1.60
19 and over	11	0.0072	1.62
Total	225	1	225

Now you need to check if any of the expected cell frequencies are less than 5. In this case, we see there are several instances where this is so. To deal with this, collapse categories so that all expected frequencies are at least 5. Doing this gives the following:

Number of Requests	Observed Frequency	Poisson Probability $\lambda t = 10$	Expected Frequency
4 or fewer	10	0.0293	6.58
5	3	0.0378	8.51
6	8	0.0631	14.20
7	6	0.0901	20.27
8	11	0.1126	25.34
9	7	0.1251	28.15
10	18	0.1251	28.15
11	14	0.1137	25.58
12	17	0.0948	21.33
13	18	0.0729	16.40
14	25	0.0521	11.72
15	28	0.0347	7.81
16 or more	60	0.0488	10.98
Total	225	1	225

Now we can compute the chi-square test statistic using Equation 13.1 as follows:

$$\chi^2 = \Sigma \frac{(o-e)^2}{e}$$

$$= \frac{(10-6.59)^2}{6.59} + \frac{(3-8.51)^2}{8.51} + \cdots + \frac{(60-10.98)^2}{10.98}$$

$$= 338.1$$

Step 4 **Determine the critical value.**
The critical value depends on the level of significance and the number of degrees of freedom. The degrees of freedom is equal to $k - 1$, where k is the number of categories. In this case, after collapsing the categories to get the expected frequencies to be at least 5, we have 13 categories. Thus, the degrees of freedom for the chi-square critical value is $13 - 1 = 12$. For this degree of freedom and a level of significance equal to 0.05, from Appendix G we find a critical value of $\chi^2 = 21.0261$. Thus the decision rule is

If $\chi^2 > 21.0261$, reject the null hypothesis;
Otherwise, do not reject.

Step 5 **Reach a decision.**
Because $\chi^2 = 338.1 > 21.0261$, reject the null hypothesis.

Step 6 **Draw a conclusion.**
The demand distribution is not Poisson distributed with a mean of 10. The students should conclude that either the mean demand per period has increased from 10 or the distribution is not Poisson or both. They may need to add more capacity to the ISP business.

13-1: Exercises

Skill Development

13-1. The following frequency distribution shows the number of times an outcome was observed from the toss of a die. Based on the frequencies that were observed from 2,400 tosses of the die, can it be concluded at the 0.05 level of significance that the die is fair?

Outcome	Frequency
1	352
2	418
3	434
4	480
5	341
6	375

13-2. Based on the sample data in the following frequency distribution, conduct a test to determine whether the population from which the sample data were selected is Poisson distributed with mean equal to 6. Test using $\alpha = 0.05$.

x	Frequency	x	Frequency
2 or less	7	9	53
3	29	10	35
4	26	11	28
5	52	12	18
6	77	13	13
7	77	14 or more	13
8	72	Total	500

13-3. A large retailer receives shipments of batteries for consumer electronic products in packages of 50 batteries. The packages are held at a distribution center and are shipped to retail stores as requested. Because some packages may contain defective batteries, the retailer randomly samples 400 packages from its distribution center and tests to determine whether the batteries are defective or not. The most recent sample of 400 packages revealed the following observed frequencies for defective batteries per package:

# of Defective Batteries per Package	Frequency of Occurrence
0	165
1	133
2	65
3	28
4 or more	9

The retailer's managers would like to know if they can evaluate this sampling plan using a binomial distribution with $n = 50$ and $\pi = 0.02$. Test at the $\alpha = 0.01$ level of significance.

13-4. A chi-square goodness-of-fit test is to be conducted to test whether a population is normally distributed. No statement has been made regarding the value of the population mean and standard deviation. A frequency distribution has been formed based on a random sample of 1,000 values. The frequency distribution has $k = 8$ classes. Assuming that the test is to be conducted at the $\alpha = 0.10$ level, determine the correct decision rule to be used.

13-5. An experiment that is claimed to have a binomial distribution with $\pi = 0.15$ and $n = 18$ and the number of successes is recorded. The experiment is conducted 200 times with the following results:

Number of Successes	0	1	2	3	4	5
Observed Frequency	80	75	39	6	0	0

Using a significance level of 0.01, is there sufficient evidence to conclude that the distribution is binomially distributed with $\pi = 0.15$ and $n = 18$?

13-6. Data collected from a hospital emergency room reflected the number of patients per day that visited the emergency room due to cardiac-related symptoms. It is believed that the distribution of the number of cardiac patients entering the emergency room per day over a two-month period has a Poisson distribution with a mean of 8 per day.

6	7	9	7	5	6	7	7	5	10
9	9	7	2	8	5	7	10	6	7
12	12	10	8	8	14	7	9	10	7
4	9	6	4	11	9	10	7	5	10
8	8	10	7	9	2	10	12	10	9
8	11	7	9	11	7	16	7	9	10

Use a chi-square goodness-of-fit test to determine if the data come from a Poisson distribution with mean of 8. Test using a significance level of 0.01.

Business Applications

13-7. Managers of a major book publisher believe that the occurrence of typographical errors in the books that the company publishes is Poisson distributed with a mean of 0.2 per page. Because of some customer quality complaints, the managers have arranged for a test to be conducted to determine if the error distribution still holds. A total of 400 pages were randomly selected and the number of errors per page was counted. These data are summarized in the following frequency distribution:

Errors	Frequency
0	335
1	56
2	7
3	2
Total	400

Conduct the appropriate hypothesis test using a significance level equal to 0.01. Discuss the results.

13-8. The Baltimore Steel and Pipe Company recently developed a new pipe product for a customer. According to specifications, the pipe is supposed to have an average outside diameter of 2.00 inches with a standard deviation equal to 0.10 inch and the distribution of outside diameters is to be normally distributed. Before going into full-scale production, the company selected a random sample of 30 sections of pipe from the initial test run. The following data were recorded:

Pipe Section	Diameter (inches)	Pipe Section	Diameter (inches)
1	2.04	16	1.96
2	2.13	17	1.89
3	2.07	18	1.99
4	1.99	19	2.13
5	1.90	20	1.90
6	2.06	21	1.91
7	2.19	22	1.95
8	2.01	23	2.18
9	2.05	24	1.94
10	1.98	25	1.93
11	1.95	26	2.08
12	1.90	27	1.82
13	2.10	28	1.94
14	2.02	29	1.96
15	2.11	30	1.81

a. Using a significance level of 0.01, perform the appropriate test.

b. Based on these data, should the company conclude that it is meeting the product specifications? Explain your reasoning.

13-9. HSBC Bank is a large, London-based, international banking company. One of its most important sources of income is home loans. A component of its effort to maintain and increase its customer base is excellent service. The loan manager at one of its branches in New York keeps track of the number of loan applicants who visit his branch's loan department per week. Having enough loan officers available is one of the ways of providing excellent service. Over the last year, the loan manager accumulated the following data:

Number of Customers	0	1	2	3	4	5	≥6
Frequencies	1	2	9	11	14	6	9

From previous years, the manager believes that the distribution of the number of customer arrivals has a Poisson distribution with an average of 3.5 loan applicants per week. Determine if the loan officer's belief is correct using a significance level of 0.025.

13-10. Quality control managers work in every type of production environment possible, from producing dictionaries to dowel cutting for boat plugs. The Cincinnati Dowel & Wood Products Co., located in Mount Orab, Ohio, manufactures wood dowels and wood turnings. Four-inch-diameter boat plugs are one of its products. The quality control procedures aimed at maintaining the 4-inch diameter are only valid if the diameters have a normal distribution. The quality control manager recently obtained the following summary diameters taken from randomly selected boat plugs on the production line:

Interval	Frequency	Interval	Frequency
<3.872	4	4.001–4.025	8
3.872–3.916	6	4.026–4.052	2
3.917–3.948	11	4.053–4.084	4
3.949–3.975	9	4.085–4.128	0
3.976–4.000	5	>4.128	1

The boat plug diameters are specified to have a normal distribution with a mean of 4 inches and a standard deviation of 0.10. Determine if the present distribution of the 4-inch boat plugs is currently adhering to specification. Use a chi-square goodness-of-fit test and a significance level of 0.05.

Computer Database Exercises

13-11. Executives at The Walt Disney Company are interested in estimating the mean spending per capita for people who visit Disney World in Orlando, Florida. Since they do not know the population standard deviation, they plan to use the *t*-distribution (see Chapter 9) to conduct the test. However, they realize that the *t*-distribution requires that the population be normally distributed. Six hundred customers were randomly surveyed and the amount spent by each one during their stay at Disney World was recorded. These data are in the file

called **Disney**. Before using these sample data to estimate the population mean, the managers wish to test to determine whether the population is normally distributed.
  a. State the appropriate null and alternative hypotheses.
  b. Organize the data into six classes and form the grouped data frequency distribution (refer to Chapter 2).
  c. Using the sample mean and sample standard deviation, calculate the expected frequencies, assuming that the null hypothesis is true.
  d. Conduct the test statistic and compare it to the appropriate critical value for a significance level equal to 0.05. What conclusion should be reached? Discuss.

13-12. The owners of Clair's Deli are considering remodeling their facility to include a drive-through window. There is room for three cars in the drive-through line if they build it. However, they are concerned that the capacity may be too low during their busy hours between 11:00 A.M. and 1:30 P.M. One of the factors they need to know is the distribution of the length of time it takes to fill an order for cars coming to the drive-through. In order to collect information on this, the owners have received permission from another deli in a nearby town to collect some data at that deli's drive-through. The data in the file called **Clair's Deli** reflect the service time per car.

  Based on these sample data, is there sufficient evidence to conclude that the distribution of service time is not normally distributed? Test using the chi-square distribution and α = 0.05.

13-13. Again, working with the Clair's Deli data in Problem 13-12, the number of cars that arrive in each 10-minute period is another factor that will determine whether the deli will have the capacity to handle the drive-through business. In addition to studying the service times, the owners also counted the number of cars that arrived at the deli in the nearby town in a sample of 10-minute time periods. These data are as follows:

3	2	0
2	3	3
3	3	3
0	2	3
0	3	3
1	1	0
2	4	9
1	2	4
2	1	1
4	1	3

Based on these data, is there evidence to conclude that the arrivals are not Poisson distributed? State the appropriate null and alternative hypotheses and test using a significance level of 0.025.

13-14. Damage to homes caused by burst piping can be expensive to repair. By the time the leak is discovered, hundreds of gallons of water may have already flooded the home. Automatic shutoff valves can prevent extensive water damage from plumbing failures. The valves contain sensors that cut off water flow in the event of a leak, thereby preventing flooding. One important characteristic is the time (in milliseconds) required for the sensor to detect the water flow. The data obtained for four different shutoff valves are contained in the file entitled **Waterflow**. The differences between the observed time for the sensor to detect the water flow and the predicted time (termed *residuals*) are listed and are assumed to be normally distributed. Using the four sets of residuals given in the data file, determine if the residuals have a normal distribution. Use a chi-square goodness-of-fit test and a significance level of 0.05. Use five groups of equal width to conduct the test.

13-15. An article in the *San Francisco Chronicle* (Michael Cabanatuan, "Most lanes on bridges to be for FasTrak," March 2, 2006) indicated that just 38% of drivers crossing the San Francisco Bay Area's seven state-owned bridges pay their tolls electronically, compared with rates nearing 80% at systems elsewhere in the nation. Albert Yee, director of highway and arterial operations for the regional Metropolitan Transportation Commission, indicated that the commission is eager to drive up the percentage of tolls paid electronically. In an attempt to see if its efforts are producing the required results, 15 vehicles each day are tracked through the toll lanes of the Bay Area bridges. The number of drivers using electronic payment to pay their toll for a period of three months appears in the file entitled **Fastrak**.

a. Determine if the distribution of the number of FasTrak users could be described as a binomial distribution with a population proportion equal to 0.50. Use a chi-square goodness-of-fit test and a significance level of 0.05.

b. Conduct a test of hypothesis to determine if the percent of tolls paid electronically has increased to more than 70% since March 2006.

13.2 Introduction to Contingency Analysis

CHAPTER OUTCOME #2

In Chapter 9 and 10 you were introduced to hypothesis tests involving one and two population proportions. Although these techniques are useful in many cases, you will also encounter many situations involving multiple population proportions. For example, a major mutual fund company offers six different mutual funds. The president of the company may wish to determine if the proportion of customers selecting each mutual fund is related to the four sales regions in which the customers reside. A hospital administrator who collects service-satisfaction data from patients might be interested in determining whether there is a significant difference in patient rating by hospital department. A personnel manager for a large corporation might be interested in determining whether there is a relationship between level of employee job satisfaction and job classification. In each of these cases, the proportions relate to characteristic categories of the variable of interest. The six mutual funds, four sales regions, hospital departments, and job classifications are all specific categories.

These situations involving categorical data call for a new statistical tool known as *contingency analysis* to help make decisions when multiple proportions are involved. Contingency analysis can be used when a level of data measurement is either nominal or ordinal and the values are determined by counting the number of occurrences in each category.

2 × 2 Contingency Tables

Business Application

DALGARNO PHOTO, INC.—Dalgarno Photo, Inc. gets much of its business from taking photographs for college yearbooks. Dalgarno hired a first-year MBA student to develop the survey it mailed to 850 yearbook representatives at the colleges and universities in its market area. The representatives were unaware that Dalgarno Photo had developed the survey.

The survey asked about the photography and publishing activities associated with yearbook development. For instance, what photographer and publisher services did the schools use, and what factors were most important in selecting services? The survey instrument contained 30 questions, which were coded into 137 separate variables.

Among his many interests in this study, Dalgarno's marketing manager questioned whether funding source and gender of the yearbook editor were related in some manner. To analyze this issue, we examine these two variables more closely. Source of university funding is a categorical variable, coded as follows:

$$1 = \text{Private funding}$$
$$2 = \text{State-funded}$$

Of the 221 respondents who provided data for this variable, 155 came from privately funded colleges or universities and 66 were from publicly funded institutions.

The second variable, gender of the yearbook editor, is also a categorical variable, with two response categories, coded as follows:

$$1 = \text{Male}$$
$$2 = \text{Female}$$

Of the 221 responses to the survey, 164 were from females and 57 were from males.

In cases in which the variables of interest are both categorical and the decision maker is interested in determining whether a relationship exists between the two, a statistical technique known as contingency analysis is useful. We first set up a two-dimensional table called a **contingency table**. The contingency table for these two variables is shown in Table 13.3.

Table 13.3 shows that 14 of the respondents were males from schools that are privately funded. The numbers at the extreme right and along the bottom are called the *marginal frequencies*. For example, 57 respondents were males, and 155 respondents were from privately funded institutions.

The issue of whether there is a relationship between responses to these two variables is formally addressed through a hypothesis test, in which the null and alternative hypotheses are stated as follows:

H_0: Gender of yearbook editor is independent of the college's funding source.
H_A: Gender of yearbook editor *is not* independent of the college's funding source.

If the null hypothesis is true, the population proportion of yearbook editors from private institutions who are males should be equal to the proportion of male editors from state-funded institutions. These two proportions should also equal the population proportion of male editors without regard to a school's funding source. To illustrate, we can use the sample data to determine the sample proportion of male editors as follows:

$$P_M = \frac{\text{Number of Male Editors}}{\text{Number of Respondents}} = \frac{57}{221} = 0.2579$$

Then, if the null hypothesis is true, we would expect 25.79% of the 155 privately funded schools, or 39.98 schools, to have a male yearbook editor. We would also expect 25.79% of the 66 state-funded schools, or 17.02, to have male yearbook editors. (Note that the expected numbers need not be integer values. Note also that the sum of expected frequencies in any column or row add up to the marginal frequency.) We can use this reasoning to determine the expected number of respondents in each cell of the contingency table, as shown in Table 13.4.

Contingency Table
A table used to classify sample observations according to two or more identifiable characteristics. It is also called a *crosstabulation table*.

TABLE 13.3
Contingency Table for Dalgarno Photo

	Source of Funding	
Gender	Private	State	
Male	14	43	57
Female	141	23	164
	155	66	221

TABLE 13.4 Contingency Table for Dalgarno Photo

Gender	Source of Funding		
	Private	State	
Male	$o_{11} = 14$	$o_{12} = 43$	57
	$e_{11} = 39.98$	$e_{12} = 17.02$	
Female	$o_{21} = 141$	$o_{22} = 23$	164
	$e_{21} = 115.02$	$e_{22} = 48.98$	
	155	66	221

You can simplify the calculations needed to produce the expected values for each cell. Note that the first cell's expected value, 39.98, was obtained by the following calculation:

$$e_{11} = 0.2579(155) = 39.98$$

However, because the probability, 0.2579, is calculated by dividing the row total, 57, by the grand total, 221, the calculation can also be represented as

$$e_{11} = \frac{(\text{Row Total})(\text{Column Total})}{\text{Grand Total}} = \frac{(57)(155)}{221} = 39.98$$

As a further example, we can calculate the expected value for the next cell in the same row. The expected number of male yearbook editors in state-funded schools is

$$e_{12} = \frac{(\text{Row Total})(\text{Column Total})}{\text{Grand Total}} = \frac{(57)(66)}{221} = 17.02$$

Keep in mind that the row and column totals (the marginal frequencies) must be the same for the expected values as for the observed values. Therefore, when there is only one cell left in a row or a column for which you must calculate an expected value, you can obtain it by subtraction. So, as an example, the expected value e_{12} could have been calculated as

$$e_{12} = 57 - 39.98 = 17.02$$

Allowing for sampling error, we would expect the actual frequencies in each cell to approximately match the corresponding expected cell frequencies when the null hypothesis is true. The greater the difference between the actual and the expected frequencies, the more likely the null hypothesis of independence is false and should be rejected. The statistical test to determine whether the sample data support or refute the null hypothesis is given by Equation 13.2. Do not be confused by the double summation in Equation 13.2; it merely indicates that all rows and columns must be used in calculating χ^2. As was the case in the goodness-of-fit tests, the degrees of freedom are the number of independent data values obtained from the experiment. In any given row, once you know $c - 1$ of the data values, the remaining data value is determined. For instance, once you know that 14 of the 57 male editors were from privately funded institutions, you know that 43 were from state-funded institutions.

Chi-Square Contingency Test Statistic

$$\chi^2 = \sum_{i=1}^{r} \sum_{j=1}^{c} \frac{(o_{ij} - e_{ij})^2}{e_{ij}} \qquad \text{with } df = (r-1)(c-1) \qquad \textbf{(13.2)}$$

where:

$$o_{ij} = \text{Observed frequency in cell } (i, j)$$
$$e_{ij} = \text{Expected frequency in cell } (i, j)$$
$$r = \text{Number of rows}$$
$$c = \text{Number of columns}$$

FIGURE 13.7

Chi-Square Contingency Analysis Test for Dalgarno Photo

Hypotheses:

H_0: Gender of yearbook editor is independent of college's funding source.
H_A: Gender of yearbook editor is not independent of college's funding source.
$\alpha = 0.05$

	Private	State
Male	$o_{11} = 14$ $e_{11} = 39.98$	$o_{12} = 43$ $e_{12} = 17.02$
Female	$o_{21} = 141$ $e_{21} = 115.02$	$o_{22} = 23$ $e_{22} = 48.98$

Test Statistic:

$$\chi^2 = \sum_{i=1}^{r} \sum_{i=1}^{c} \frac{(o_{ij} - e_{ij})^2}{e_{ij}} = \frac{(14 - 39.98)^2}{39.98} + \frac{(43 - 17.02)^2}{17.02}$$
$$+ \frac{(141 - 115.02)^2}{115.02} + \frac{(23 - 48.98)^2}{48.98} = 76.19$$

$f(\chi^2)$

$df = (r-1)(c-1) = (1)(1) = 1$

$\chi^2_{0.05} = 3.8415$

χ^2

Decision Rule:

If $\chi^2 > 3.8415$, reject H_0;
Otherwise, do not reject H_0.
Because $76.19 > 3.8415$, reject H_0. Thus, the gender of the yearbook editor and the school's source of funding are not independent.

Similarly, once $r - 1$ data values in a column are known, the remaining data value is determined. Therefore, the degrees of freedom are obtained by the expression $(r - 1)(c - 1)$.

Figure 13.7 presents the hypotheses and test results for this example. As was the case in the goodness-of-fit tests, the test statistic has a distribution that can be approximated by the chi-square distribution if the expected values are larger than 5. Note that the calculated chi-square statistic is compared to the tabled value of chi-square for an $\alpha = 0.05$ and degrees of freedom $= (2 - 1)(2 - 1) = 1$. Because $\chi^2 = 76.19 > 3.8415$, the null hypothesis of independence should be rejected. Dalgarno Photo representatives should conclude that the gender of the yearbook editor and each school's source of funding are not independent. By examining the data in Figure 13.7, you can see that private schools are more likely to have female editors, whereas state schools are more likely to have male yearbook editors.

EXAMPLE 13-4 | 2×2 Contingency Analysis

TRY PROBLEM 13.18

Barger Advertising Before releasing a major advertising campaign to the media, Barger Advertising runs a test on the material. Recently, it randomly called 100 people and asked them to listen to a commercial that was slated to run nationwide on the radio. At the end of the commercial, the respondents were asked to name the company that was in the ad. The company is interested in determining whether there is a relationship between gender and a person's ability to recall the company name. To test this, the following steps can be used:

Step 1 **Specify the null and alternative hypotheses.**
The company is interested in testing whether a relationship exists between gender and recall ability. Here are the appropriate null and alternative hypotheses.

H_0: Ability to correctly recall the company name is independent of gender.

H_A: Recall ability and gender are not independent.

Step 2 **Determine the significance level.**
The test will be conducted using a 0.01 level of significance.

Step 3 **Collect the sample data and compute the chi-square test statistic using Equation 13.2.**
The following contingency table shows the results of the sampling:

	Female	Male	Total
Correct Recall	33	25	58
Incorrect Recall	22	20	42
Total	55	45	100

The expected cell frequencies are determined by multiplying the row total by the column total and dividing by the overall sample size. For example, for the cell corresponding to female and correct recall, we get

$$\text{Expected} = \frac{58 \times 55}{100} = 31.90$$

The expected cell values for all cells are

	Female	Male	Total
Correct Recall	$o = 33$	$o = 25$	58
	$e = 31.90$	$e = 26.10$	
Incorrect Recall	$o = 22$	$o = 20$	42
	$e = 23.10$	$e = 18.90$	
Total	55	45	100

After checking to make sure all the expected cell frequencies > 5, the test statistic is computed using Equation 13.2.

$$\chi^2 = \sum_{i=1}^{r} \sum_{j=1}^{c} \frac{(o_{ij} - e_{ij})^2}{e_{ij}}$$

$$= \frac{(33 - 31.90)^2}{31.90} + \frac{(25 - 26.10)^2}{26.10} + \frac{(22 - 23.10)^2}{23.10} + \frac{(20 - 18.90)^2}{18.90} = 0.20$$

Step 4 Determine the critical value.
The critical value for this test will be the chi-square value, with $(r - 1)(c - 1) = (2 - 1)(2 - 1) = 1$ degree of freedom with an $\alpha = 0.01$. From Appendix G, the critical value is 6.6349.

Step 5 Reach a decision.
Because $\chi^2 = 0.20 < 6.6349$, do not reject the null hypothesis.

Step 6 Draw a conclusion.
Based on the sample data, there is no reason to believe that being able to recall the name of the company in the ad is related to gender.

$r \times c$ Contingency Tables

Business Application

Excel and Minitab Tutorial

BENTON INDUSTRIES Benton Industries manufactures carpets and draperies in the Atlanta area. It pays market wages, provides competitive benefits, and offers attractive options for employees in an effort to create a satisfied workforce and reduce turnover. Recently, however, several supervisors have complained that employee absenteeism is becoming a problem. In response to these complaints, the human resources manager studied a random sample of 500 employees. One aim of this study was to determine whether there is a relationship between absenteeism and marital status. Absenteeism during the past year was broken down into three levels:

1. 0 absences
2. 1 to 5 absences
3. over 5 absences

Marital status was divided into four categories:

1. single   2. married
3. divorced   4. widowed

Table 13.5 shows the contingency table for the sample of 500 employees. The table is also shown in the CD-ROM file **Benton**. The null and alternative hypotheses to be tested are

H_0: Absentee behavior is independent of marital status.
H_A: Absentee behavior is not independent of marital status.

TABLE 13.5 Contingency Table for Benton Industries

Marital Status	Absentee Rate 0	1–5	Over 5	Row Totals
Single	84	82	34	200
Married	50	64	36	150
Divorced	50	34	16	100
Widowed	16	20	14	50
Column Total	200	200	100	500

As with 2×2 contingency analysis, the test for independence can be made using the chi-square test, where the expected cell frequencies are compared to the actual cell frequencies and the test statistic shown as Equation 13.2 is used. The logic of the test says that if the actual and expected frequencies closely match, then the null hypothesis of independence is not rejected. However, if the actual and expected cell frequencies are substantially different overall, the null hypothesis of independence is rejected. The calculated chi-square statistic is compared to a table χ^2 critical value for the desired significance and degrees of freedom equal to $(r-1)(c-1)$.

The expected cell frequencies are determined assuming that the row and column variables are independent. This means, for example, that the probability of a married person being absent more than 5 days during the year is the same as the probability of any employee being absent more than 5 days. An easy way to compute the expected cell frequencies, e_{ij}, is given by Equation 13.3.

Expected Cell Frequencies

$$e_{ij} = \frac{(i\text{th Row Total})(j\text{th Column Total})}{\text{Total Sample Size}}$$

(13.3)

For example, the expected cell frequency for row 1, column 1 is

$$e_{11} = \frac{(200)(200)}{500} = 80$$

and the expected cell frequency for row 2, column 3 is

$$e_{23} = \frac{(150)(100)}{500} = 30$$

Figures 13.8a and 13.8b show the completed contingency table with the actual and expected cell frequencies that were developed using Excel and Minitab. The calculated chi-square test value is computed as follows:

$$\chi^2 = \sum_{i=1}^{r}\sum_{j=1}^{c} \frac{(o_{ij} - e_{ij})^2}{e_{ij}}$$

$$= \frac{(84-80)^2}{80} + \frac{(82-80)^2}{80} + \cdots + \frac{(20-20)^2}{20} + \frac{(14-10)^2}{10}$$

$$= 10.88$$

The degrees of freedom are $(r-1)(c-1) = (4-1)(3-1) = 6$. You can use the chi-square table in Appendix G to get the chi-square critical value for $\alpha = 0.05$ and 6 degrees of freedom, or you can use Minitab's **Probability Distributions** command or Excel's **CHIINV** function (CHIINV(0.05,6) = 12.5916). Because the calculated chi-square value

FIGURE 13.8A

Excel 2007 Output—
Benton Industries
Contingency Analysis
Test

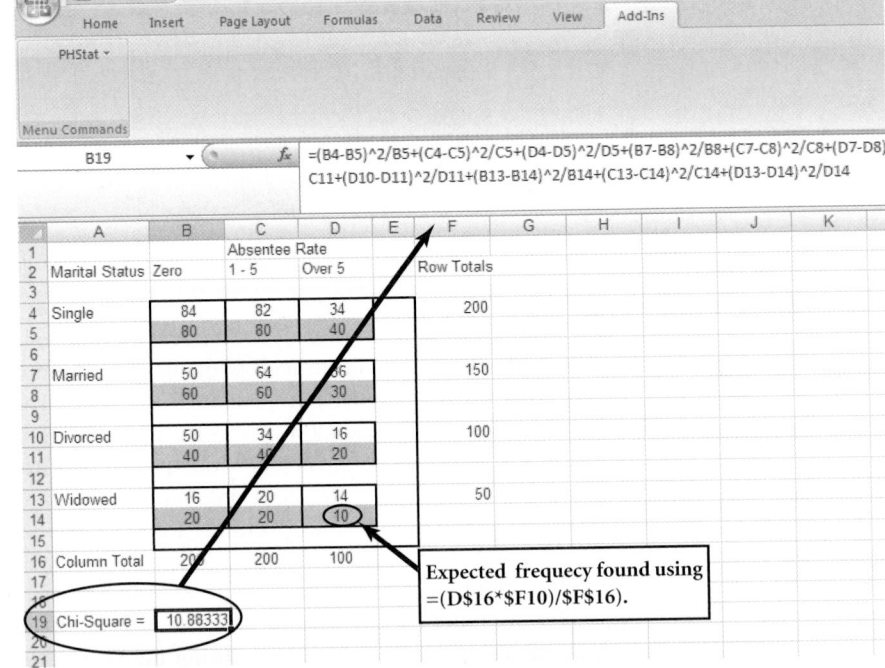

Excel 2007 Instructions:
1. Open file: Benton.xls.
2. Computed expected cell frequencies using Excel formula.
3. Compute chi-square statistics using Excel formula.

FIGURE 13.8B

Minitab Output—
Benton Industries
Contingency
Analysis Test

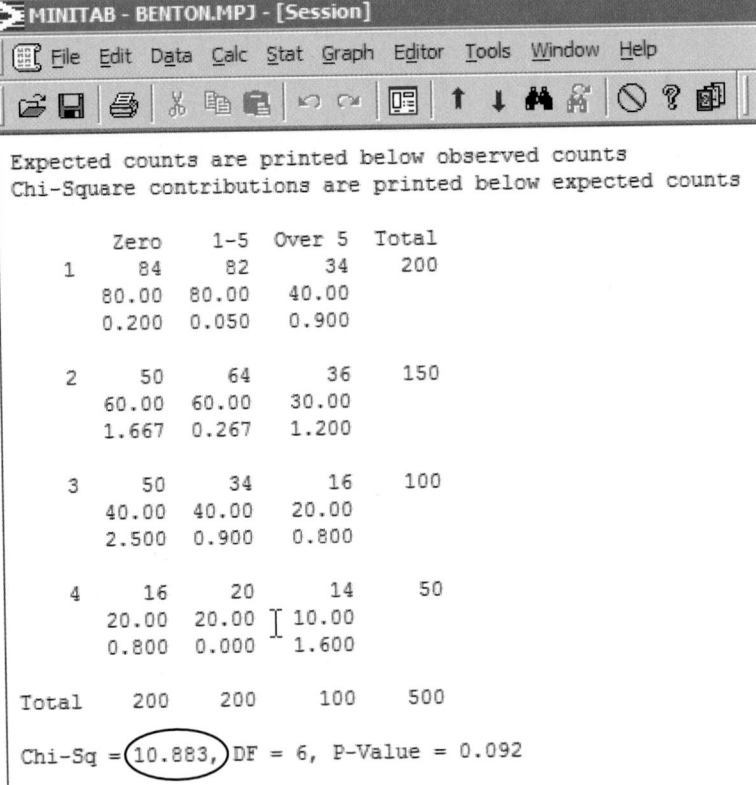

Minitab Instructions:
1. Open file: Benton.MTW.
2. Choose **Stat > Tables > Chi-Square Test**.
3. In Columns containing the table, enter data columns.
4. Click **OK**.

(10.883) shown in Figures 13.8a and 13.8b is less than 12.5916, we cannot reject the null hypothesis. Based on these sample data, there is *insufficient evidence* to conclude that absenteeism and marital status are not independent.

Chi-Square Test Limitations

The chi-square distribution is only an approximation for the true distribution for contingency analysis. We use the chi-square approximation because the true distribution is impractical to compute in most instances. However, the approximation (and, therefore, the conclusion reached) is quite good when all expected cell frequencies are at least 5.0. When expected cell frequencies drop below 5.0, the calculated chi-square value tends to be inflated and may inflate the true probability of a Type I error beyond the stated significance level. As a rule, if the null hypothesis is not rejected, you do not need to worry when the expected cell frequencies drop below 5.0.

There are two alternatives that can be used to overcome the small expected-cell-frequency problem. The first is to increase the sample size. This may increase the marginal frequencies in each row and column enough to increase the expected cell frequencies. The second option is to combine the categories of the row and/or column variables. If you do decide to group categories together, there should be some logic behind the resulting categories. You don't want to lose the meaning of the results through poor groupings. You will need to examine each situation individually to determine whether the option of grouping classes to increase expected cell frequencies makes sense.

13-2: Exercises

Skill Development

13-16. Utilize the following contingency table to answer the questions listed below.

	C_1	C_2
R_1	51	207
R_2	146	185
R_3	240	157

a. State the relevant null and alternative hypotheses.
b. Calculate the expected values for each of the cells.
c. Compute the chi-square test statistic for the hypothesis test.
d. Determine the appropriate critical value and reach a decision for the hypothesis test. Use a significance level of 0.05.
e. Obtain the p-value for this hypothesis test.

13-17. The billing department of a national cable service company is conducting a study of how customers pay their monthly cable bills. The cable company accepts payment in one of four ways: in person at a local office, by mail, by credit card, or by electronic funds transfer from a bank account. The cable company randomly sampled 400 customers to determine if there is a relationship between the customer's age and the payment method used. The following sample results were obtained:

Payment Method	Age of Customer			
	20–30	31–40	41–50	Over 50
In Person	8	12	11	13
By Mail	29	67	72	50
By Credit Card	26	19	5	7
By Funds Transfer	23	35	17	6

Based on the sample data, can the cable company conclude that there is a relationship between the age of the customer and the payment method used? Conduct the appropriate test at the $\alpha = 0.01$ level of significance.

13-18. A contingency analysis table has been constructed from data obtained in a phone survey of customers in a market area in which respondents were asked to indicate whether they owned a domestic or foreign car and whether they were a member of a union or not. The following contingency table is provided.

	Union	
Car	Yes	No
Domestic	155	470
Foreign	40	325

a. Use the chi-square approach to test whether type of car owned (domestic or foreign) is independent of union membership. Test using an $\alpha = 0.05$ level.
b. Calculate the p-value for this hypothesis test.

13-19. A marketing research firm is conducting a study to determine if there is a relationship between an individual's age and the individual's preferred source of news. The research firm asked 1,000 individuals to list their preferred source for news: newspaper, radio and television, or the Internet. The following results were obtained:

Preferred News Source	Age of Respondent			
	20–30	31–40	41–50	Over 50
Newspaper	19	62	95	147
Radio/TV	27	125	168	88
Internet	104	113	37	15

At the 0.01 level of significance, can the marketing research firm conclude that there is a relationship between the age of the individual and the individual's preferred source for news?

13-20. A loan officer wished to determine if the marital status of loan applicants was independent of the approval of loans. The following table presents the result of her survey:

	Approved	Rejected
Single	213	189
Married	374	231
Divorced	358	252

a. Conduct the appropriate hypothesis test that will provide an answer to the loan officer. Use a significance level of 0.01.

b. Calculate the p-value for the hypothesis test in part a.

13-21. An instructor in a large accounting class is interested in determining whether the grades that students get is related to how close to the front of the room the students sit. He has categorized the room seating as "Front," "Middle," and "Back." The following data were collected over two sections with 400 total students. Based on the sample data, can you conclude that there is a dependency relationship between seating location and grade using a significance level equal to 0.05?

	A	B	C	D	F	Total
Front	18	55	30	3	0	106
Middle	7	42	95	11	1	156
Back	3	15	104	14	2	138
Total	28	112	229	28	3	400

Business Applications

13-22. The following table classifies a stock's price change as up, down, or no change for both today's and yesterday's prices. Price changes were examined for 100 days. A financial theory states that stock prices follow what is called a "random walk." This means, in part, that the price change today for a stock must be independent of yesterday's price change. Test the hypothesis that daily stock price changes for this stock are independent. Let $\alpha = 0.05$.

		Price Change Previous Day		
		Up	No Change	Down
Price Change	Up	14	16	12
Today	No Change	6	8	6
	Down	16	14	8

13-23. A local appliance retailer handles four washing machine models for a major manufacturer: standard, deluxe, superior, and XLT. The marketing manager has recently conducted a study on the purchasers of the washing machines. The study recorded the model of appliance purchased and the credit account balance of the customer at the time of purchase. The sample data are in the following table. Based on these data, is there evidence of a relationship between the account balance and the model of washer purchased? Use a significance level of 0.025. Conduct the test using a p-value approach.

		Washer Model Purchased			
		Standard	Deluxe	Superior	XLT
Credit	Under $200	10	16	40	5
Balance	$200–$800	8	12	24	15
	Over $800	16	12	16	30

13-24. A random sample of 980 heads of households was taken from the customer list for State Bank and Trust. Those sampled were asked to classify their own attitudes and their parents' attitudes toward borrowing money as follows:

A: Borrow only for real estate and car purchases.

B: Borrow for short-term purchases such as appliances and furniture.

C: Never borrow money.

The following table indicates the responses from those in the study.

		Respondent		
		A	B	C
	A	240	80	20
Parent	B	180	120	40
	C	180	80	40

Test the hypothesis that the respondents' borrowing habits are independent from what they believe their parents' attitudes to be. Let $\alpha = 0.01$.

13-25. The California Lettuce Research board was originally formed as the Iceberg Lettuce Advisory Board in 1973. The primary function of the board is to fund research on iceberg and leaf lettuce. California Lettuce Research Board Annual Report 2004–2005 published research (M. Cahn and H. Ajwa, "Salinity Effects on Quality and Yield of Drip Irrigated Lettuce") concerning the effect of varying levels of sodium absorption ratios (SAR) on the yield of head lettuce. The measurements (the number of lettuce heads from each plot) of the kind observed were

		Salinas	Sniper
	3	104	109
SAR	**5**	160	163
	7	142	146
	10	133	156

a. Determine if the number of lettuce heads harvested for the two lettuce types is independent of the levels of sodium absorption ratios (SAR). Use a significance level of 0.025 and a *p*-value approach.

b. Which type of lettuce would you recommend?

13-26. In its ninth year, the Barclaycard Business Travel Survey has become an information source for business travelers not only in the UK but internationally as well. Each year, as a result of the research, Barclaycard Business has been able to predict and comment on trends within the industry for the business traveler. One question asked in the 2003/4 and 2004/5 surveys was, "Have you considered reducing hours spent away from home to increase quality of life?" The following table represents the responses:

	2003/4	2004/5	Total
Yes—have reduced	400	384	784
Yes—not been able to	400	300	700
No—not certain	400	516	916
Total	1200	1200	2400

a. Determine if the response to the survey question was independent of the year in which the question was asked. Use a significance level of 0.05.

b. Determine if there is a significant difference between the proportion of travelers who say they have reduced hours spent away from home between 2003/4 and the 2004/5 years.

Computer Database Exercises

13-27. The Marriott Company owns and operates a number of different hotel chains including the Courtyard chain. Recently, a survey was mailed to a random sample of 400 Courtyard customers. A total of 62 customers responded to the survey. The customers were asked a number of questions related to their satisfaction with the chain as well as several demographic questions. Among the issues of interest was whether there is a relationship between the likelihood that they will stay at the chain again and whether or not this was the customer's first stay at the Courtyard. The following

contingency table has been developed from the data set contained in the file called **CourtyardSurvey**:

		First Stay?		
		Yes	No	Total
	Definitely Will	9	12	21
	Probably Will	18	2	20
Stay Again?	**Maybe**	15	3	18
	Probably Not	2	1	3
	Total	44	18	62

Using a significance level equal to 0.05, test to see whether these sample data imply a relationship between the two variables. Discuss the results.

13-28. *Gift of the Gauche*, a left-handedness information Web site (www.left-handedness.info), provides information concerning left-handed activities, products, and demography. It indicates that about 10%–11% of the population of Europe and North America are left-handed. It also reports on demographic surveys. It cites an American study (1992) in which over 1 million magazine respondents found that 12.6% of the males were left-handed and 9.9% of the females, although this was not a random sample. The data obtained by a British survey of over 8,000 randomly selected men and women, published in Issue 37 of *The Graphologist* in 1992, is furnished in a file entitled **Lefties**. Based on this data, determine if the "handedness" of an individual is independent of their gender. Use a significance level of 0.01 and a *p*-value approach.

13-29. Daniel Vinson of the University of Missouri–Columbia (*USA Today*, "Study: Angry people more likely to be severely hurt," February 6, 2006) led a team of researchers investigating the increased risk of serious injuries in the workplace requiring emergency medical care when people are angry. The file entitled **Angry** contains the data collected by the team of researchers. It displays the emotions reported by patients just before they were injured.

a. Use the data in the file entitled **Angry** to construct a contingency table.

b. Determine if the type of emotion felt by patients just before they were injured is independent of the severity of that emotion. Use a contingency analysis and a significance level of 0.05.

13-30. ECCO (Electronic Controls Company) makes backup alarms that are used on such equipment as forklifts and delivery trucks. The quality manager recently performed a study involving a random sample of 110 warranty claims. One of the questions the manager wanted to answer was whether there is a relationship between the type of warranty complaint and the plant at which the alarm was made. The data are in the file called **ECCO**.

a. Calculate the expected values for the cells in this analysis. Suggest a way in which cells can be combined to assure that the expected value of each cell is at least 5 so that as many level combinations of the two variables as possible are retained.

b. Using a significance level of 0.01, conduct a relevant hypothesis test and provide an answer to the manager's question.

13-31. Referring to Problem 13-30, can the quality control manager conclude that the type of warranty problem is independent of the shift on which the alarm was manufactured? Test using a significance level of 0.05. Discuss your results.

Summary and Conclusions

This chapter has introduced two very useful statistical tools: goodness-of-fit tests and contingency analysis. Goodness-of-fit testing is used when a decision maker wishes to determine whether sample data come from a population having specific characteristics. The goodness-of-fit procedure that was introduced in this chapter is the chi-square goodness-of-fit test. This test relies on the idea that if the distribution of the sample data is substantially different from the hypothesized population distribution, then the population distribution from which these sample data came must not be what was hypothesized. For continuous data, the chi-square goodness-of-fit test is most effective when the sample data have been organized into a grouped frequency distribution.

Contingency analysis is a frequently used statistical tool that allows the decision maker to test whether responses to two variables are independent. Market researchers, for example, use contingency analysis on survey research data when at least one of the variables of interest is categorical. For instance, marketers may be interested in determining whether attitude about the quality of their company's product is independent of the gender of a customer. By using contingency analysis and the chi-square contingency test, they can make this determination based on a sample of customers. If either or both of the variables are continuous in nature, they must be recoded before contingency analysis can be performed. Most software can facilitate this recoding process.

Equations

Chi-Square Goodness-of-Fit Test Statistic

$$\chi^2 = \sum_{i=1}^{k} \frac{(o_i - e_i)^2}{e_i} \qquad (13.1)$$

Chi-Square Contingency Test Statistic

$$\chi^2 = \sum_{i=1}^{r} \sum_{j=1}^{c} \frac{(o_{ij} - e_{ij})^2}{e_{ij}} \qquad \text{with } df = (r-1)(c-1) \ (13.2)$$

Expected Cell Frequencies

$$e_{ij} = \frac{(i\text{th Row Total})(j\text{th Column Total})}{\text{Total Sample Size}} \qquad (13.3)$$

Key Term

Contingency table   606

Chapter Exercises

Conceptual Questions

13-32. Locate a journal article using either contingency analysis or a goodness-of-fit test. Discuss the article, paying particular attention to the reasoning behind using the particular statistical test.

13-33. Find a marketing research book (or borrow one from a friend). Does it discuss either of the tests considered in this chapter? If yes, outline the discussion. If no, determine where in the text such a discussion would be appropriate.

13-34. One of the topics in Chapter 10 was hypothesis testing for the difference between two population proportions. In order for the test to have validity, there were conditions set on the sample sizes with respect to the sample proportions. A 2 × 2 contingency table may also be utilized to test the difference between proportions of two independent populations. This procedure has conditions placed on the expected value of each cell. Discuss the relationship between these two conditions.

13-35. A 2 × 2 contingency table and a hypothesis test of the difference between two population proportions can be used to analyze the same data set. However, besides all their similarities, the hypothesis test of the difference between two proportions has two advantages. Identify these advantages.

Business Applications

13-36. Linda Stevens, the manager of Arlington Super Discount, always keeps four checkout stands open. However, she frequently notices lines for registers 1 and 2. She is not sure whether the layout of the store channels customers into these registers or whether the checkout clerks in these lines are simply slower than the other two.

Linda kept a record of which stands 2,000 shoppers chose for checkout. The shoppers checked out of the four stands according to the following pattern:

Stand 1	Stand 2	Stand 3	Stand 4
677	550	402	371

a. Based on these data, can Linda conclude that the proportion of shoppers using the four checkout stands is equal? (Use an $\alpha = 0.05$.)

b. A friend suggested that you could just as well conduct four hypothesis tests that the proportion of customers visiting each stand is equal to $\pi = 0.25$. Discuss the merits of this suggestion.

13-37. Cooper Manufacturing, Inc. of Dallas, Texas, has a contract with the U.S. Air Force to produce a part for a new fighter plane being manufactured. The part is a bolt that has specifications requiring that the length be normally distributed with a mean of 3.05 inches and a standard deviation of 0.015 inch. As part of the company's quality control efforts, each day Cooper's engineers select a random sample of 100 bolts produced that day and carefully measure the bolts to determine whether the production is within specifications. The following data were collected yesterday:

Length (inches)	Frequency
Under 3.030	5
3.030 and under 3.035	16
3.035 and under 3.040	7
3.040 and under 3.050	20
3.050 and under 3.060	36
3.060 and under 3.065	8
3.065 and over	8

Based on these sample data, what should Cooper's engineers conclude about the production output if they test using an $\alpha = 0.01$? Discuss.

13-38. The Cooper Company discussed in Problem 13-37 has a second contract with a private firm for which it makes fuses for an electronic instrument. The quality control department at Cooper periodically selects a random sample of five fuses and tests each fuse to determine whether it is defective. Based on these findings, the production process is either shut down (if too many defectives are observed) or allowed to run. The quality control department believes that the sampling process follows a binomial distribution and it has been using the binomial distribution to compute the probabilities associated with the sampling outcomes.

The contract allows for at most 5% defectives. The head of quality control recently compiled a list of the sampling results for the past 300 days in which five fuses were tested, with the following frequency distribution for the number of defectives observed. She is concerned that the binomial distribution with a sample size of 5 and a probability of defectives of 0.05 may not be appropriate.

Number of Defectives	Frequency
0	209
1	33
2	43
3	10
4	5
5	0

a. Calculate the expected values for the cells in this analysis. Suggest a way in which cells can be combined to assure that the expected value of each cell is at least 5.

b. Using a significance level of 0.10, what should the quality control manager conclude based on these sample data? Discuss.

13-39. A regional cancer treatment center has had success treating localized cancers with a linear accelerator. While admissions for further treatment nationally average 2.1 per patient per year, the center's director thinks that re-admissions with the new treatment are Poisson distributed, with a mean of 1.2 per patients per year. He has collected the following data on a random sample of 300 patients:

Re-admissions Last Year	Patients
0	139
1	87
2	48
3	14
4	8
5	1
6	1
7	0
8	2
	300

a. Adjust the data so that you can test the director's claim using a test statistic whose sampling distribution can be approximated by a chi-square distribution.

b. Assume the Type I error rate is to be controlled at 0.05. Do you agree with the director's claim? Why? Conduct a statistical procedure to support your opinion.

13-40. A survey performed by Simmons Market Research investigated the percentage of individuals in various age groups who indicated they were willing to pay more for environmentally friendly products. The results were presented in *USA Today* Snapshots (July 21, 2005). The survey had approximately 3,240 respondents in each age group. Results of the survey follow:

Age Group	18–24	25–34	35–44	45–54	55–64	65 and over
Percentage	11	17	19	20	14	19

Conduct a goodness-of-fit test analysis to determine if the proportions of individuals willing to pay more for environmentally friendly products in the various age groups are equal. Use a significance level of 0.01.

13-41. An article published in *USA Today* (Dennis Cauchon, "Childhood pastimes are increasingly moving indoors," July 12, 2005) asserts that many children are abandoning outdoor for indoor activities. The National Sporting Goods Association annual survey for 2004 (the latest data available) compared activity levels in 1995 versus 2004. A random selection of children (7- to 11-year-olds) indicating their favorite outdoor activity is given in the following table:

	Bicycling	Swimming	Baseball	Fishing	Touch football
1995	68	60	29	25	16
2004	47	42	22	18	10

Construct a contingency analysis to determine if the type of preferred outdoor activity is dependent on the year in this survey. Use a significance level of 0.05 and the *p*-value approach.

Computer Database Exercises

13-42. The airport manager at the Sacramento, California, airport recently conducted a study of passengers departing from the airport. A random sample of 100 passengers was selected. The data are in the file called **Airline Passengers**. An earlier study showed the following usage by airline:

Delta	20 %
Horizon	10 %
Northwest	10 %
Skywest	3 %
Southwest	25 %
United	32 %

a. If the manager wishes to determine whether the airline usage pattern has changed from that reported in the earlier study, state the appropriate null and alternative hypotheses.

b. Based on the sample data, what should be concluded? Test using a significance level of 0.01.

13-43. A pharmaceutical company is planning to market a drug that is supposed to help reduce blood pressure. The company claims that if the drug is taken properly, the amount of blood pressure loss will be normally distributed with a mean equal to 10 points on the diastolic reading and a standard deviation equal to 4.0. One hundred patients were administered the drug and data were collected showing the reduction in blood pressure at the end of the test period. The data are located in the file labeled **Blood Pressure**.

a. Using a goodness-of-fit test and a significance level equal to 0.05, what conclusion should be reached with respect to the distribution of diastolic blood pressure reduction? Discuss.

b. Conduct a hypothesis test to determine if the standard deviation for this population could be considered to be 4.0. Use a significance level of 0.10.

c. Given the results of the two tests in parts a and b, is it appropriate to construct a confidence interval based upon a normal distribution with a population standard deviation of 4.0? Explain your answer.

d. If appropriate, construct a 99% confidence interval for the mean reduction in blood pressure. Based upon this confidence interval, does an average diastolic loss of 10 seem reasonable for this procedure? Explain your reasoning.

13-44. The Employee Benefit Research Institute (EBRI) issued a news release "Saving in America: Three Key Sets of Figures," on October 25, 2005. In 2005, about 69% of workers said they and/or their spouses have saved for retirement. The file entitled **Retirement** contains the total savings and investments indicated. Use a contingency analysis to determine if the amount of total savings and investments is dependent upon the age of the worker.

13-45. An Ariel Capital Management and Charles Schwab survey was reported in *USA Today* (Snapshots, September 13, 2005). It addressed the proportion of African-Americans and White Americans who have money invested in the stock market. Suppose the file entitled **Stockrace** contains data obtained in the surveys. The survey asked 500 African-American and 500 White respondents if they personally had money invested in the stock market.

a. Create a contingency table using the data in the file **Stockrace**.

b. Conduct a contingency analysis to determine if the proportion of African-Americans differs from the proportion of White Americans who invest in stocks. Use a significance level of 0.05.

13-46. The state transportation department recently conducted a study of motorists in Idaho. Two main factors of interest were whether the vehicle was insured with liability insurance and whether the driver was wearing a seat belt. A random sample of 100 cars were stopped at various locations throughout the state. The data are in the file called **Liabins**. The investigators were interested in determining whether seat belt status is independent of insurance status. Conduct the appropriate hypothesis test using a 0.05 level of significance and discuss your results.

CASE 13.1

American Oil Company

Chad Williams sat back in his airline seat to enjoy the hour flight between Los Angeles and Oakland, California. The hour would give him time to reflect on his upcoming trip to Australia and the work he had been doing the past week in Los Angeles.

Chad is one man on a six-man crew employed by the American Oil Company to literally walk the earth searching for oil. His college degrees in geology and petroleum engineering landed him the job with American, but he never dreamed he would be doing the exciting work he now does. Chad and his crew spend several months in special locations around the world using highly sensitive electronic equipment for oil exploration.

The upcoming trip to Australia is one that Chad has been looking forward to since it was announced that his crew would be going there to search the Outback for oil. In preparation for the trip, the crew has been in Los Angeles at American's engineering research facility working on some new equipment that will be used in Australia.

Chad's thoughts centered on the problem he was having with a particular component part on the new equipment. The specifications called for 200 of the components, with each having a diameter of between 0.15 and 0.18 inch. The only available supplier of the component manufactures the components in New Jersey to specifications calling for normally distributed output, with a mean of 0.16 inch and a standard deviation of 0.02 inch.

Chad faces two problems. First, he is unsure that the supplier actually does produce parts with means of 0.16 inch and standard deviations of 0.02 inch according to a normal distribution. Second, if the parts are made to specifications, he needs to determine how many components to purchase if enough acceptable components are to be received to make two oil exploration devices.

The supplier has sent Chad the following data for 330 randomly selected components. Chad believes that the supplier is honest and that he can rely on the data.

Diameter (Inch)	Frequency
Under 0.14	5
0.14 and under 0.15	70
0.15 and under 0.16	90
0.16 and under 0.17	105
0.17 and under 0.18	50
Over 0.18	10
Total	330

Chad needs to have a report ready for Monday indicating whether he believes the supplier delivers at its stated specifications and, if so, how many of the components American should order to have enough acceptable components to outfit two oil exploration devices.

CASE 13.2

Bentford Electronics, Part 1

On Saturday morning, Jennifer Bentford received a call at her home from the production supervisor at Bentford Electronics Plant 1. The supervisor indicated that she and the supervisors from Plants 2, 3, and 4 had agreed that something must be done to improve company morale and, thereby, increase the production output of their plants. Jennifer Bentford, president of Bentford Electronics, agreed to set up a Monday morning meeting with the supervisors to see if they could arrive at a plan for accomplishing these objectives.

By Monday each supervisor had compiled a list of several ideas, including a four-day work week and inter-plant competitions of various kinds. A second meeting was set for Wednesday to discuss the issue further.

Following the Wednesday afternoon meeting, Jennifer Bentford and her plant supervisors agreed to implement a weekly contest called the NBE Game of the Week. The plant producing the most each week would be considered the NBE Game of the Week winner and would receive 10 points. The second-place plant would receive 7 points, and the third- and fourth-place plants would receive 3 points and 1 point, respectively. The contest would last 26 weeks. At the end of that period, a $200,000 bonus would be divided among the employees in the four plants proportional to the total points accumulated by each plant.

The announcement of the contest created a lot of excitement and enthusiasm at the four plants. No one complained about the rules because the four plants were designed and staffed to produce equally.

At the close of the contest, Jennifer Bentford called the supervisors into a meeting, at which time she asked for data to determine whether the contest had significantly improved productivity. She indicated that she had to know this before she could authorize a second contest. The supervisors, expecting this response, had put together the following data:

Units Produced (4 Plants Combined)	Before-Contest Frequency	During-Contest Frequency
0–2,500	11	0
2,501–8,000	23	20
8,001–15,000	56	83
15,001–20,000	15	52
	105 days	155 days

Jennifer examined the data and indicated that it looked like the contest was a success, but she wanted to base her decision to continue the contest on more than just an observation of the data. "Surely there must be some way to statistically test the worthiness of this contest," Jennifer stated. "I have to see the results before I will authorize the second contest."

References

Berenson, Mark L., and David M. Levine, *Basic Business Statistics: Concepts and Applications*, 10th ed. (Upper Saddle River, NJ: Prentice Hall, 2006).

Conover, W. J., *Practical Nonparametric Statistics*, 3rd ed. (New York: Wiley, 1999).

Higgins, James J., *Introduction to Modern Nonparametric Statistics*, 1st ed. (Pacific Grove, CA: Duxbury, 2004).

Marasculio, Leonard, and M. McSweeney, *Nonparametric and Distribution Free Methods for the Social Sciences* (Monterey, CA: Brooks/Cole, 1977).

Microsoft Excel 2007 (Redmond, WA: Microsoft Corp. 2007).

Minitab for Windows Version 15 (State College, PA: Minitab, Inc., 2007).

Chapter FOURTEEN

Introduction to Linear Regression and Correlation Analysis

CHAPTER OUTCOMES

After studying the material in Chapter 14, you should be able to:

1. Calculate and interpret the correlation between two variables.
2. Determine whether the correlation is significant.
3. Calculate the simple linear regression equation for a set of data and know the basic assumptions behind regression analysis.
4. Determine whether a regression model is significant.
5. Recognize regression analysis applications for purposes of prediction and description.
6. Calculate and interpret confidence intervals for the regression analysis.
7. Recognize some potential problems if regression analysis is used incorrectly.

PREPARING FOR CHAPTER FOURTEEN

- Review the methods for testing a null hypothesis using the *t*-distribution in Chapter 9.

- Review confidence intervals discussed in Chapter 8.

- Make sure you review the discussion about scatter plots in Chapter 2.

- Review the concepts associated with selecting a simple random sample in Chapter 1.

- Review the *F*-distribution and the approach for finding critical values from the *F*-table as discussed in Chapters 11 and 12.

◆WHY YOU NEED TO KNOW

Although some business situations involve only one variable, others require decision makers to consider the relationship between two or more variables. For example, an investment broker might be interested in the relationship between stock prices and the dividends issued by a publicly traded company. A marketing manager would be interested in examining the relationship between product sales and the amount of money spent on advertising. Finally, consider a real estate appraiser who is interested in determining the fair market value of a home or business. He would begin by collecting data on a sample of "comparable properties" that have sold recently. In addition to the selling price, he would collect data on other factors, such as the size and age of the property. He might then analyze the relationship between the price and the other variables and use this relationship to determine an appraised price for the property in question.

Simple linear regression and correlation analysis, which are introduced in this chapter, are statistical techniques the broker, marketing director, and appraiser will need in their analysis. These techniques are important to decision makers who need to determine the relationship between two variables. In Chapter 15, we will extend the discussion to include three or more variables. Regression analysis and correlation analysis are two of the most often applied statistical tools for business decision making.

14.1 Scatter Plots and Correlation

Scatter Plot

A two-dimensional plot showing the values for the joint occurrence of two quantitative variables. The scatter plot may be used to graphically represent the relationship between two variables. It is also known as a scatter diagram.

In those situations in which you are interested in analyzing the relationship between two quantitative variables, the **scatter plot**, or *scatter diagram*, introduced in Chapter 2 is very useful.

Figure 14.1 shows scatter plots that depict several potential relationships between values of a dependent variable, y, and an independent variable, x. A *dependent* (or *response*) *variable* is the variable whose variation we wish to explain. An *independent* (or *explanatory*) *variable* is a variable used to explain variation in the dependent variable. In Figure 14.1, (a) and (b) are examples of strong *linear* relationships between x and y. This means that for each unit change in the independent variable, x, the corresponding change in the dependent variable, y, will tend to be a fairly consistent amount. Note that this

FIGURE 14.1

Two-Variable Relationships

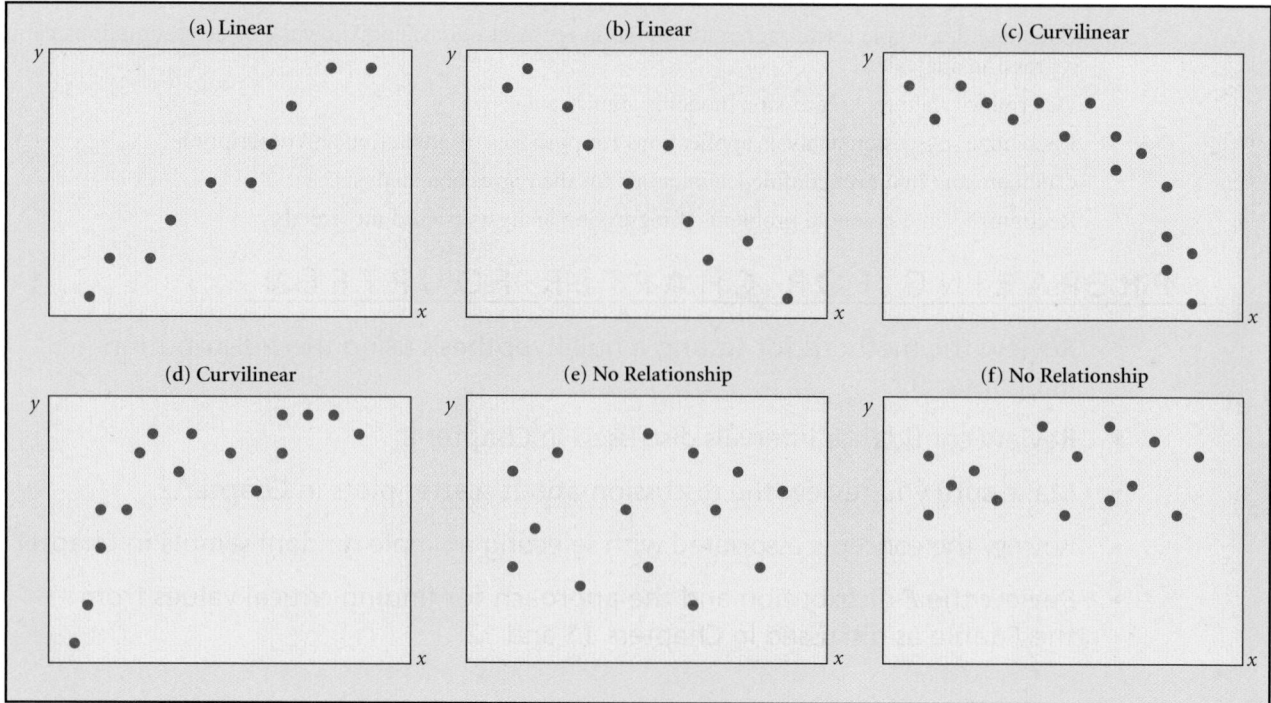

systematic change in y can be positive (y increases as x increases) or negative (y decreases as x increases). The degree of linearity exhibited depends on the degree of consistency in the change of the y variable when the independent variable, x, changes.

Figures 14.1 (c) and (d) illustrate situations in which the relationship between the x and y variable is nonlinear. There are many possible nonlinear relationships that can occur. The scatter plot is very useful for visually identifying the nature of the relationship.

Figures 14.1 (e) and (f) show examples in which there is no identifiable relationship between the two variables. This means that as x increases, y sometimes increases and sometimes decreases but with no particular pattern.

Correlation Versus Regression

In analyzing the relationship between two variables, there are two basic models that we can use, depending on the conditions under which the data are collected. These models are the subjects of this chapter. One model is referred to as the *regression model*, in which the relationship between x and y assumes that the x variable takes on known values specifically selected from all the possible values for x. The y variable is a random variable observed at the different levels of x.

A second model is referred to as the *correlation model* and is used in applications in which both the x and the y variables are considered to be random variables. These two models, regression versus correlation, arise in practice by the way in which the data are obtained. Consider models that might apply to the relationship between the amount of daily sunscreen sold, y, as a function of the day's high temperature, x. We could select a random sample of 36 days and record the amount of sunscreen sold and the day's maximum temperature. In this case, the measurements obtained for both variables are observations from a joint distribution of x and y. An analysis of these data would be done using the correlation model approach.

Suppose instead that we decide to collect data for days with maximum temperatures of 75, 80, 85, 90, 95, and 100. We would measure the amount of daily sunscreen sold (y) for several randomly chosen days in which the maximum temperature is at each of these pre-elected temperatures. That is, we might pick six days at random from a population of days that have a maximum temperature of 75 degrees and observe the amount of sunscreen sold, and so on. Now each observation of y is from the distribution of y for a fixed x value. The analysis of these data would be done using the regression model approach.

We stress the two types of sampling because there are important differences in what can be estimated using these two methods. As we will illustrate later in this chapter, when the data have been collected at specific levels of the x variable, as was suggested in the second situation, our estimates for the y variable will be conditional on the value of x we are using.[1]

Correlation Coefficient A quantitative measure of the strength of the linear relationship between two variables. The correlation ranges from -1.0 to $+1.0$. A correlation of ± 1.0 indicates a perfect linear relationship, whereas a correlation of 0 indicates no linear relationship.	

The Correlation Coefficient

In addition to analyzing the relationship between two variables graphically, we can also measure the strength of the linear relationship between two variables using a measure called the **correlation coefficient**.

The correlation coefficient for two variables can be estimated from sample data using Equation 14.1 or the algebraic equivalent, Equation 14.2.

CHAPTER OUTCOME #1

Sample Correlation Coefficient

$$r = \frac{\Sigma(x - \bar{x})(y - \bar{y})}{\sqrt{[\Sigma(x - \bar{x})^2][\Sigma(y - \bar{y})^2]}} \qquad\qquad (14.1)$$

---

[1] See Kutner et al., *Applied Linear Statistical Models*, 4th ed., p. 78, and N. R. Draper, and H. Smith, *Applied Regression Analysis*, 3rd ed., p. 89, for more discussion on this subject.

or the algebraic equivalent:

$$r = \frac{n\sum xy - \sum x \sum y}{\sqrt{[n(\sum x^2) - (\sum x)^2][n(\sum y^2) - (\sum y)^2]}}$$

(14.2)

where:

r = Sample correlation coefficient
n = Sample size
x = Value of the independent variable
y = Value of the dependent variable

The sample correlation coefficient computed using Equations 14.1 and 14.2 is called the *Pearson Product Moment Correlation*. The sample correlation coefficient, r, can range from a perfect positive correlation, $+1.0$, to a perfect negative correlation, -1.0. A perfect correlation is one in which a given change in the value of the x variable is accompanied by a specific uniform amount of change in the y variable. Graphically, the x, y points will plot on a straight line. If two variables have no linear relationship, the correlation between them is 0 and there is no linear relationship between the change in x and y. Consequently, the more the correlation differs from 0.0, the stronger the linear relationship between the two variables. The sign of the correlation coefficient indicates the direction of the relationship, but it does not aid in determining the strength.

Figure 14.2 illustrates some examples of correlation between two variables. Note for the correlation coefficient to equal plus or minus 1.0, all the (x, y) points form a perfectly straight line. The more the points depart from a straight line, the weaker (closer to 0.0) the correlation is between the two variables.

Business Application

MIDWEST DISTRIBUTION COMPANY Consider the application involving Midwest Distribution which supplies soft drinks and snack foods to convenience stores in Michigan, Illinois, and Iowa. Although Midwest Distribution has been profitable, the director of

FIGURE 14.2

Correlation Between Two Variables

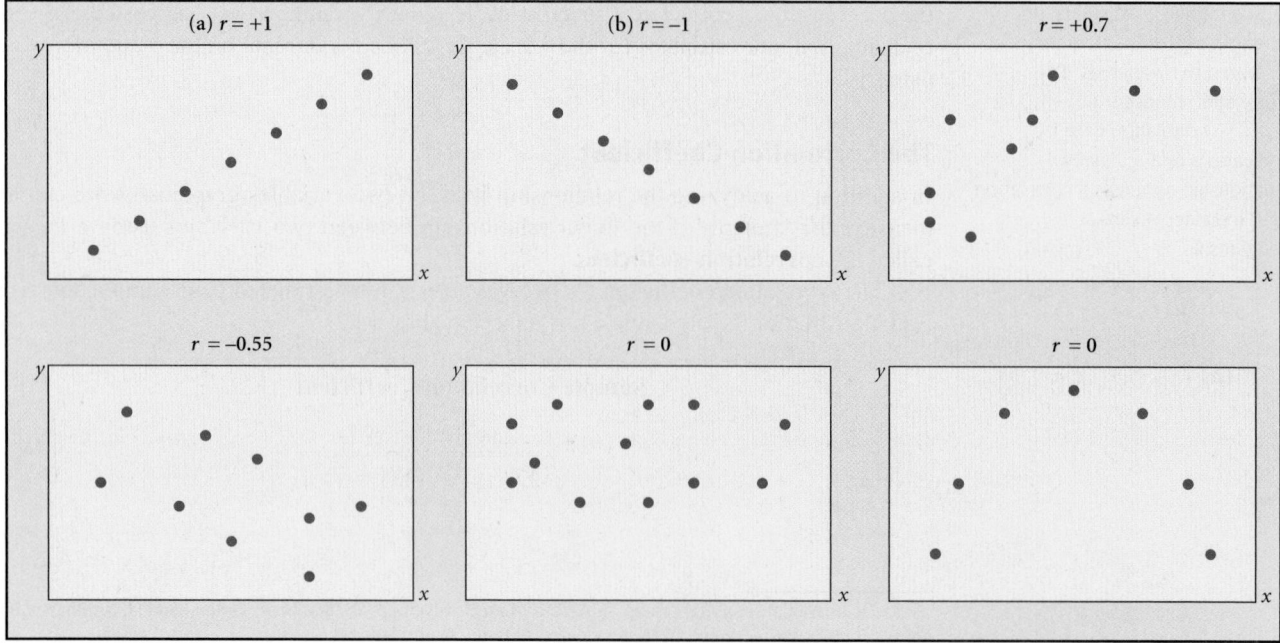

FIGURE 14.3

Excel 2007 Scatter Plot of Sales vs. Years with Midwest Distribution

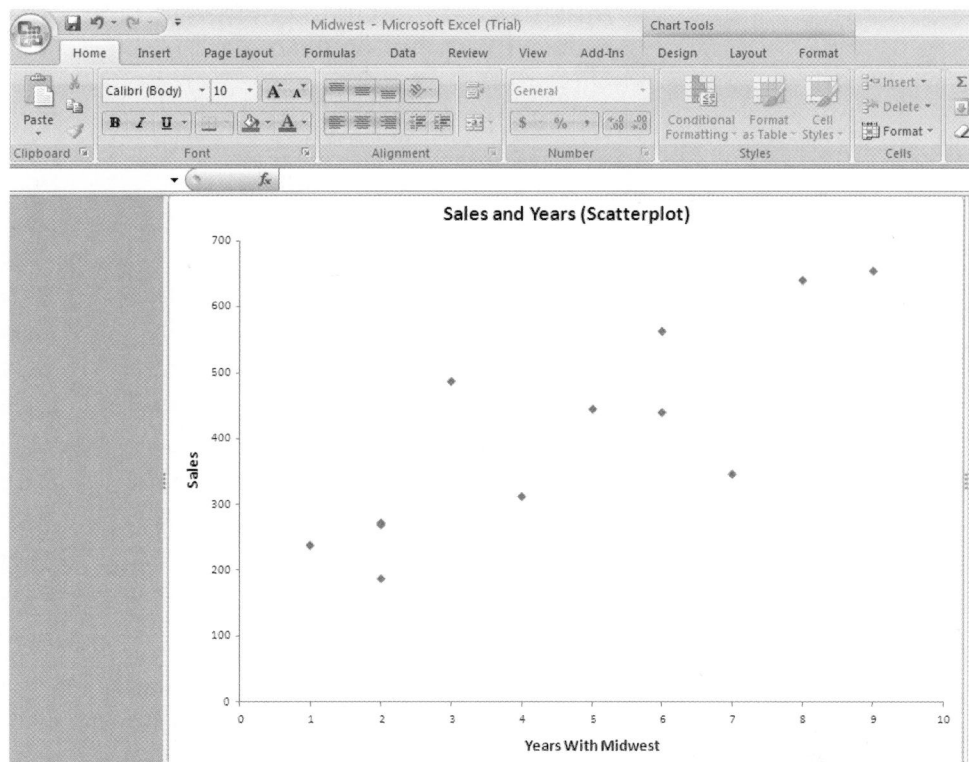

Excel 2007 Instructions:
1. Open file: Midwest.xls.
2. Move the *Sales* column to the *right* of *Years with midwest* column.
3. Select data for chart.
4. On **Insert tab**, click **XY (Scatter)**, and then click the **Scatter with only Markers** Option.
5. Use the **Layout** tab of the **Chart Tools** to add titles and remove grid lines.
6. Use the **Design** tab of the **Chart Tools** to move the chart to a new worksheet.

Minitab Instructions (for similar result):
1. Open file: Midwest MTW.
2. Choose **Graph > Scatterplot.**
3. Under **Scatterplot**, choose **Simple OK.**
4. Under **Y variable**, enter *y* column.
5. In **X variable**, enter *x* column.
6. Click **OK**.

Excel and Minitab Tutorial

marketing has been concerned about the rapid turnover in her salesforce. In the course of exit interviews, she discovered a major concern with the compensation structure.

Midwest Distribution has a two-part wage structure: a base salary and a commission computed on monthly sales. Typically, about half of the total wages paid comes from the base salary, which increases with longevity with the company. This portion of the wage structure is not an issue. The concern expressed by departing employees is that new employees tend to be given parts of the sales territory previously covered by existing employees and are assigned prime customers as a recruiting inducement.

At issue, then, is the relationship between sales (on which commissions are paid) and number of years with the company. The data for a random sample of 12 sales representatives are in the file called **Midwest** on your CD-ROM. The first step is to develop a scatter plot of the data. Both Excel and Minitab have procedures for constructing a scatter plot and computing the correlation coefficient.

The scatter plot for the Midwest data is shown in Figure 14.3. Based on this plot, total sales and years with the company appear to be linearly related. However, the strength of this relationship is uncertain. That is, how close do the points come to falling on a straight line? To answer this question, we need a quantitative measure of the strength of the linear relationship between the two variables. That measure is the correlation coefficient.

Equation 14.1 is used to determine the correlation between sales and years with the company. Table 14.1 shows the manual calculations that were used to determine this correlation coefficient of 0.8325. However, because the calculations are rather tedious and long, we almost always use computer software to perform the computation, as shown in Figure 14.4. The $r = 0.8325$ indicates that there is a fairly strong, positive correlation between these two variables for the sample data.

TABLE 14.1 Correlation Coefficient Calculations for the Midwest Distribution Example

Sales	Years					
y	x	$x - \bar{x}$	$y - \bar{y}$	$(x - \bar{x})(y - \bar{y})$	$(x - \bar{x})^2$	$(y - \bar{y})^2$
487	3	−1.58	82.42	−130.22	2.50	6,793.06
445	5	0.42	40.42	16.98	0.18	1,633.78
272	2	−2.58	−132.58	342.06	6.66	17,577.46
641	8	3.42	236.42	808.56	11.70	55,894.42
187	2	−2.58	−217.58	561.36	6.66	47,341.06
440	6	1.42	35.42	50.30	2.02	1,254.58
346	7	2.42	−58.58	−141.76	5.86	3,431.62
238	1	−3.58	−166.58	596.36	12.82	27,748.90
312	4	−0.58	−92.58	53.70	0.34	8,571.06
269	2	−2.58	−135.58	349.80	6.66	18,381.94
655	9	4.42	250.42	1,106.86	19.54	62,710.18
563	6	1.42	158.42	224.96	2.02	25,096.90
$\Sigma = 4{,}855$	$\Sigma = 55$			$\Sigma = 3{,}838.92$	$\Sigma = 76.92$	$\Sigma = 276{,}434.92$

$$\bar{y} = \frac{\Sigma y}{n} = \frac{4{,}855}{12} = 404.58 \qquad \bar{x} = \frac{\Sigma x}{n} = \frac{55}{12} = 4.58$$

Using Equation 14.1,

$$r = \frac{\Sigma (x - \bar{x})(y - \bar{y})}{\sqrt{\Sigma (x - \bar{x})^2 \, \Sigma (y - \bar{y})^2}} = \frac{3{,}838.92}{\sqrt{(76.92)(276{,}434.92)}} = 0.8325$$

FIGURE 14.4

Excel 2007 Correlation Output for Midwest Distribution

Excel 2007 Instructions:
1. Open file: Midwest.xls.
2. On the **Data** tab, click **Data Analysis**.
3. Select **Correlation**.
4. Define Data Range.
5. Click on **Labels in First Row**.
6. Specify output location.
7. Click **OK**.

Minitab Instructions (for similar results):
1. Open file: Midwest MTW.
2. Choose **Stat > Basic Statistics > Correlation**.
3. In **Variables**, enter *Y* and *X* columns.
4. Click **OK**.

Significance Test for the Correlation Although a correlation coefficient of 0.8325 seems quite high (relative to 0), you should remember that this value is based on a sample of 12 data points and is subject to sampling error. Therefore, a formal hypothesis-testing procedure is needed to determine whether the linear relationship between sales and years with the company is significant.

The null and alternative hypotheses to be tested are

$$H_0: \rho = 0 \quad \text{(no correlation)}$$
$$H_A: \rho \neq 0 \quad \text{(correlation exists)}$$

where the Greek symbol, ρ (rho) represents the population correlation coefficient.

We must test whether the sample data support or refute the null hypothesis. The test procedure utilizes the t-test statistic in Equation 14.3.

CHAPTER OUTCOME #2

Test Statistic for Correlation

$$t = \frac{r}{\sqrt{\dfrac{1 - r^2}{n - 2}}} \qquad df = n - 2 \qquad\qquad \textbf{(14.3)}$$

where:

$$t = \text{Number of standard errors } r \text{ is from } 0$$
$$r = \text{Sample correlation coefficient}$$
$$n = \text{Sample size}$$

The degrees of freedom for this test are $n - 2$, because we lose 1 degree of freedom for each of the two sample means that are used to estimate the population means for the two variables.

Figure 14.5 shows the hypothesis test for the Midwest Distribution example using an alpha level of 0.05. Recall that the sample correlation coefficient was $r = 0.8325$. Based on

FIGURE 14.5

Correlation Significance Test for the Midwest Distribution Example

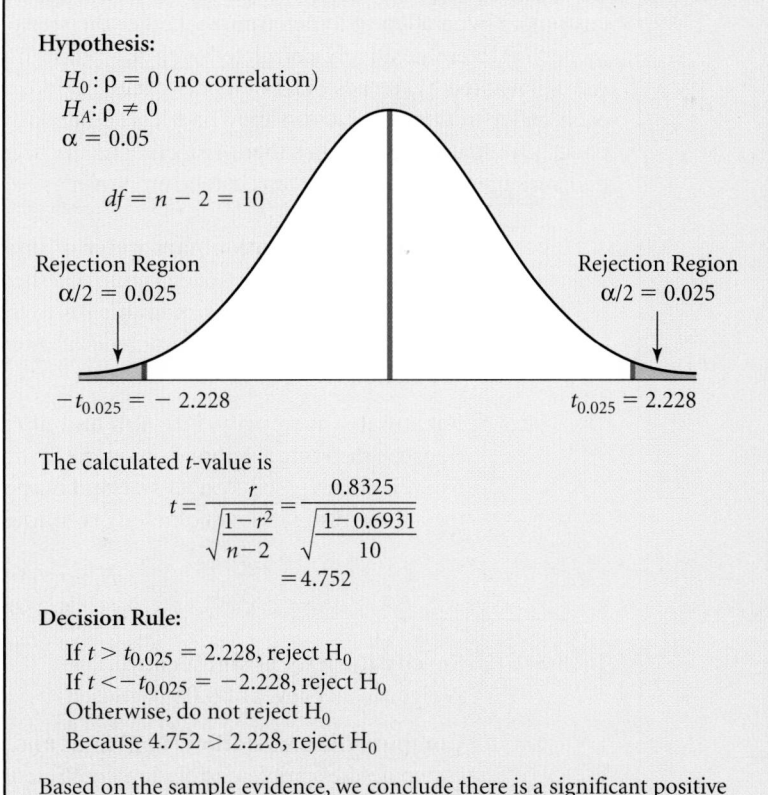

Hypothesis:

$H_0: \rho = 0$ (no correlation)
$H_A: \rho \neq 0$
$\alpha = 0.05$

$df = n - 2 = 10$

Rejection Region
$\alpha/2 = 0.025$

Rejection Region
$\alpha/2 = 0.025$

$-t_{0.025} = -2.228$

$t_{0.025} = 2.228$

The calculated t-value is

$$t = \frac{r}{\sqrt{\dfrac{1 - r^2}{n - 2}}} = \frac{0.8325}{\sqrt{\dfrac{1 - 0.6931}{10}}} = 4.752$$

Decision Rule:

If $t > t_{0.025} = 2.228$, reject H_0
If $t < -t_{0.025} = -2.228$, reject H_0
Otherwise, do not reject H_0
Because $4.752 > 2.228$, reject H_0

Based on the sample evidence, we conclude there is a significant positive linear relationship between years with the company and sales volume.

these sample data, we should conclude there is a significant, positive linear relationship in the population between years of experience and total sales for Midwest Distribution sales representatives. The implication is that the more years an employee has been with the company, the more sales that employee generates. This runs counter to the claims made by some of the departing employees. The manager will probably want to look further into the situation to see whether a problem might exist in certain regions.

The *t*-test for determining whether the population correlation is significantly different from 0 requires the following assumptions:

Assumptions

1. The data are interval- or ratio-level.
2. The two variables (*y* and *x*) are distributed as a *bivariate normal* distribution.

Although the formal mathematical representation is beyond the scope of this text, *two variables are bivariate normal if their joint distribution is normally distributed*. Although the *t*-test assumes a bivariate normal distribution, it is robust—that is, correct inferences can be reached even with slight departures from the normal-distribution assumption. (See Kutner et al., *Applied Linear Statistical Models* for further discussion of bivariate normal distributions.)

EXAMPLE 14-1 Correlation Analysis

TRY PROBLEM 14.1

Yellow Page Advertising Recently a publisher of a regional telephone book surveyed a simple random sample of 10 of its commercial yellow-page advertising customers in an attempt to determine whether the size of their advertisements, in square inches (*x*), were positively correlated with the proportion of calls to the businesses that were generated by the ads (*y*). For a one-month period, each commercial customer asked each caller to their business if they had learned about the business through the yellow pages. To determine whether there is a statistically significant correlation between the two variables, the following steps can be employed:

Step 1 Specify the population parameter of interest.
The publisher wishes to determine whether the size of an ad is positively correlated with the proportion of calls to the business that were generated by the ad. The parameter of interest is, therefore, the population correlation, ρ.

Step 2 Formulate the appropriate null and alternative hypotheses.
Because the regional phone company is interested in establishing a positive relationship between ad size and proportion of calls generated from the ad, the test will be one-tailed, as follows:

$$H_0: \rho \le 0$$
$$H_A: \rho > 0$$

Step 3 Specify the level of significance.
A significance level of 0.05 is chosen.

Step 4 Compute the correlation coefficient and the test statistic.
Compute the sample correlation coefficient using Equation 14.1 or 14.2, or by using software such as Excel or Minitab.

The following sample data were obtained:

Square Inches	Proportion of Calls Generated by Ad
9	0.13
16	0.16
25	0.21
16	0.18
20	0.18
16	0.19
20	0.15
20	0.17
16	0.13
9	0.11

Using Equation 14.1, we get

$$r = \frac{\sum(x - \bar{x})(y - \bar{y})}{\sqrt{[\sum(x - \bar{x})^2][\sum(y - \bar{y})^2]}} = 0.7796$$

Compute the t-test statistic using Equation 14.3.

$$t = \frac{r}{\sqrt{\dfrac{1 - r^2}{n - 2}}} = \frac{0.7796}{\sqrt{\dfrac{1 - 0.7796^2}{10 - 2}}} = 3.52$$

Step 5 Construct the rejection region and decision rule.
For an alpha level equal to 0.05, the one-tailed, upper-tail, critical value for $n - 2 = 10 - 2 = 8$ degrees of freedom is $t_{0.05} = 1.8595$. The decision rule is

> If $t > 1.8595$, reject the null hypothesis:
> Otherwise, do not reject the null hypothesis.

Step 6 Reach a decision.
Because

$$t = 3.52 > 1.8595, \text{ reject the null hypothesis.}$$

Step 7 Draw a conclusion.
Because the null hypothesis is rejected, the sample data do support the contention that there is a positive linear relationship between ad size and the proportion of calls that were generated by the ad.

Cause-and-Effect Interpretations Care must be used when interpreting the correlation results. For example, even though we found a significant linear relationship between years of experience and sales for the Midwest Distribution salesforce, the correlation does not imply cause and effect. Although an increase in experience may, in fact, cause sales to change, simply because the two variables are correlated does not guarantee a cause-and-effect situation. Two seemingly unconnected variables may be highly correlated. For example, over a period of time, teachers' salaries in North Dakota might be highly correlated with the price of grapes in Spain. Yet, we doubt that a change in grape prices will *cause* a corresponding change in salaries for teachers in North Dakota, or vice versa. When a correlation exists between two seemingly unrelated variables, the correlation is said to be a *spurious correlation*. You should take great care to avoid basing conclusions on spurious correlations.

The Midwest Distribution marketing director has a logical reason to believe that years of experience with the company and total sales are related. That is, sales theory and customer feedback hold that product knowledge is a major component in successfully marketing a product. However, a statistically significant correlation alone does not prove that this cause-and-effect relationship exists. When two seemingly unrelated variables are correlated, they may both be responding to changes in some third variable. For example, the observed correlation could be the effect of a company policy of giving better sales territories to more senior salespeople.

14-1: Exercises

Skill Development

14-1. A random sample of two variables, x and y, produced the following observations:

x	y
19	7
13	9
17	8
9	11
12	9
25	6
20	7
17	8

a. Develop a scatter plot for the two variables and describe what relationship, if any, exists.
b. Compute the correlation coefficient for these sample data.
c. Test to determine whether the population correlation coefficient is negative. Use a significance level of 0.05 for the hypothesis test.

14-2. The following data for the dependent variable, y, and the independent variable, x, have been collected using simple random sampling:

x	y
10	120
14	130
16	170
12	150
20	200
18	180
16	190
14	150
16	160
18	200

a. Construct a scatter plot for these data. Based on the scatter plot, how would you describe the relationship between the two variables?
b. Compute the correlation coefficient.

14-3. An industry study was recently conducted in which the sample correlation between units sold and marketing expenses was 0.57. The sample size for the study included 15 companies. Based on the sample results, test to determine whether there is a significant positive correlation between these two variables. Use an $\alpha = 0.05$.

14-4. You are given the following data for variables x and y:

x	y
3.0	1.5
2.0	0.5
2.5	1.0
3.0	1.8
2.5	1.2
4.0	2.2
1.5	0.4
1.0	0.3
2.0	1.3
2.5	1.0

a. Plot these variables in scatter plot format. Based on this plot, what type of relationship appears to exist between the two variables?
b. Compute the correlation coefficient for these sample data. Indicate what the correlation coefficient measures.
c. Test to determine whether the population correlation coefficient is positive. Use the $\alpha = 0.01$ level to conduct the test. Be sure to state the null and alternative hypotheses and show the test and decision rule clearly.

14-5. A random sample of the following two variables was obtained:

x	29	48	28	22	28	42	33	26	48	44
y	16	46	34	26	49	11	41	13	47	16

   a. Calculate the correlation between these two variables.

   b. Conduct a test of hypothesis to determine if there exists a correlation between the two variables in the population. Use a significance level of 0.10.

14-6. For each of the following circumstances, perform the indicated hypothesis tests:

   a. $H_A: \rho > 0$, $r = 0.53$, and $n = 30$ with $\alpha = 0.01$, using a test-statistic approach.

   b. $H_A: \rho \neq 0$, $r = -0.48$, and $n = 20$ with $\alpha = 0.05$, using a p-value approach.

   c. $H_A: \rho \neq 0$, $r = 0.39$, and $n = 45$ with $\alpha = 0.02$, using a test-statistic approach.

   d. $H_A: \rho < 0$, $r = 0.34$, and $n = 25$ with $\alpha = 0.05$, using a test-statistic approach.

Business Applications

14-7. A random sample of 50 high school students from a Seattle high school is selected and each student's scores on a standardized mathematics examination and a standardized English examination are recorded. Suppose the correlation coefficient for the two examination scores is 0.75.

   a. Provide an explanation of the sample correlation coefficient in this context.

   b. Using a level of significance of $\alpha = 0.01$, test to determine whether there is a positive linear relationship between mathematics scores and English scores for high school students at the Seattle high school.

14-8. A random sample of 50 bank accounts was selected from a local branch bank. The account balance and the number of deposits and withdrawals during the past month were the two variables recorded. The correlation coefficient for the two variables was -0.23.

   a. Discuss what the $r = -0.23$ measures. Make sure to frame your discussion in terms of the two variables mentioned here.

   b. Using an $\alpha = 0.10$ level, test to determine whether there is a significant linear relationship between account balance and the number of transactions in the account during the past month. State the null and alternative hypotheses and show the decision rule.

   c. Consider the decision you reached in part b. Describe the type of error you could have made in the context of this problem.

14-9. Farmers National Bank issues MasterCard credit cards to its customers. A main factor in determining whether a credit card will be profitable to the bank is the average monthly balance that the customer will maintain on the card that will be subject to finance charges. Bank analysts wish to determine whether there is a relationship between the average monthly credit card balance and the income stated on the original credit card application form. The following sample data have been collected from existing credit card customers:

Income	Credit Balance
$43,000	$345
$35,000	$1,370
$47,000	$1,140
$55,000	$201
$55,000	$56
$59,000	$908
$28,000	$2,345
$43,000	$104
$54,000	$0
$36,000	$1,290
$39,000	$130
$31,000	$459
$30,000	$0
$37,000	$1,950
$39,000	$240

   a. Indicate which variable is to be the independent variable and which is to be the dependent variable in the bank's analysis and indicate why.

   b. Construct a scatter plot for these data and describe what, if any, relationship appears to exists between these two variables.

   c. Calculate the correlation coefficient for these two variables and test to determine whether there is a significant correlation at the $\alpha = 0.05$ level.

14-10. Amazon.com has become one of the most successful online merchants. Two measures of its success are sales and net income/loss figures. In an article entitled "Amazon CEO takes long view," *USA Today* (Byron Acohido, July 6, 2005) presented these figures (in $million) for the period 1995 to 2004:

Net Income/Loss	-0.3	-5.7	-27.5	-124.5	-719.9
Sales	0.5	15.7	147.7	609.8	1,639.8
Net Income/Loss	-1,411.2	-567.3	-149.1	35.3	588.5
Sales	2,761.9	3,122.9	3,932.9	5,263.7	6,921.1

a. Produce a scatter plot for Amazon's net income/loss and sales figures for the period 1995 to 2004. Does there appear to be a linear relationship between these two variables? Explain your response.

b. Calculate the correlation coefficient between Amazon's net income/loss and sales figures for the period 1995 to 2004.

c. Conduct a hypothesis test to determine if a positive correlation exists between Amazon's net income/loss and sales figures. Use a significance level of 0.05 and assume that these figures form a random sample.

14-11. Complaints concerning excessive commercials seem to grow as the amount of "clutter," including commercials and advertisements for other television shows, steadily increases on network and cable TV. The analysis by Nielsen Monitor-Plus (Gary Levin, "Ad glut turns off viewers," *USA Today*, October 12, 2005) compares the average nonprogram minutes in an hour of prime time for both network and cable television.

Year	1996	1999	2001	2004
Network	9.88	14.00	14.65	15.80
Cable	12.77	13.88	14.50	14.92

a. Calculate the correlation coefficient for the average nonprogram minutes in an hour of prime time between network and cable television.

b. Conduct a hypothesis test to determine if a positive correlation exists between the average nonprogram minutes in an hour of prime time between network and cable television. Use a significance level of 0.05 and assume that these figures form a random sample.

Computer Database Exercises

14-12. Customers who made online purchases last quarter from an Internet retailer were randomly sampled from the retailer's database. The dollar value of each customer's quarterly purchases along with the time the customer spent shopping the company's online catalog that quarter were recorded. The sample results are contained in the file **Online**.

a. Create a scatter plot of the variables Time (x) and Purchases (y). What relationship, if any, appears to exist between the two variables?

b. Compute the correlation coefficient for these sample data. What does the correlation coefficient measure?

c. Conduct a hypothesis test to determine if there is a positive relationship between time viewing the retailer's catalog and dollar amount purchased. Use a level of significance equal to 0.025. Provide a managerial explanation of your results.

14-13. A regional accreditation board for colleges and universities is interested in determining whether a relationship exists between college student applicant verbal SAT scores and the in-state tuition costs at the university. Data have been collected on a sample of colleges and universities and are in the data file called **Colleges and Universities**.

a. Develop a scatter plot for these two variables and discuss what, if any, relationship you see between the two variables based on the scatter plot.

b. Compute the sample correlation coefficient.

c. Based on the correlation coefficient computed in part b, test to determine whether the population correlation coefficient is positive for these two variables. That is, can we expect schools that charge higher in-state tuition will attract students with higher average verbal SAT scores? Test using a 0.05 significance level.

14-14. Platinum Billiards, Inc. is a Jacksonville, Florida-based retailer of billiard supplies. It stands out among billiard suppliers because of the research it does to assure its products are top-notch. One experiment was conducted to measure the speed attained by a cue ball struck by various weighted pool cues. The conjecture is that a light cue generates faster speeds while breaking the balls at the beginning of a game of pool. Anecdotal experience has indicated that a billiard cue weighing less than 19 ounces generates faster speeds. Platinum used a robotic arm to investigate this claim. Its research generated the data given in the file entitled **Breakcue**.

a. To determine if there is a negative relationship between the weight of the pool cue and the speed attained by the cue ball, calculate a correlation coefficient.

b. Conduct a test of hypothesis to determine if there is a negative relationship between the weight of the pool cue and the speed attained by the cue ball. Use a significance level of 0.025 and a *p*-value approach.

14-15. As the number of air travelers with time on their hands increases, logic would indicate spending on retail purchases in airports would increase as well. A study by *Airport Revenue News* addressed the per person spending at select airports for merchandise excluding food, gifts, and news items. A file entitled **Revenues** contains sample data selected from airport retailers in 2001 and again in 2004.

a. Produce a scatter plot for the per person spending at selected airports for merchandise excluding food, gifts, and news items for the years 2001 and 2004. Does there appear to be a linear relationship between spending in 2001 and spending in 2004? Explain your response.

b. Calculate the correlation coefficient between the per person spending in 2001 and the per-person spending in 2004. Does it appear that an increase in per person spending in 2001 would be associated with an increase in spending in 2004? Support your assertion.

c. Conduct a hypothesis test to determine if a positive correlation exists between the per person spending in 2001 and that in 2004. Use a significance level of 0.05 and assume that these figures form a random sample.

14.2 Simple Linear Regression Analysis

In the Midwest Distribution application, we determined that the relationship between years of experience and total sales is linear and statistically significant, based on the correlation analysis performed in the previous section. Because hiring and training costs have been increasing, we would like to use this relationship to help formulate a more acceptable wage package for the salesforce.

The statistical method we will use to analyze the relationship between years of experience and total sales is *regression analysis*. When we have only two variables—a dependent variable, such as sales, and an independent variable, such as years with the company—the technique is referred to as *simple regression analysis*. When the relationship between the dependent variable and the independent variable is linear, the technique is **simple linear regression**.

Simple Linear Regression
The method of regression analysis in which a single independent variable is used to predict the dependent variable.

The Regression Model and Assumptions

The objective of simple linear regression (which we shall call *regression analysis*) is to represent the relationship between values of x and y with a model of the form shown in Equation 14.4.

Simple Linear Regression Model (Population Model)

$$y = \beta_0 + \beta_1 x + \varepsilon \qquad (14.4)$$

where:

y = Value of the dependent variable
x = Value of the independent variable
β_0 = Population's y intercept
β_1 = Slope of the population regression line
ε = Error term, or residual (i.e., the difference between the actual
y-value and the value of y predicted by the population model)

The simple linear regression population model described in Equation 14.4 has four assumptions:

Assumptions

1. Individual values of the error terms, ε, are statistically independent of one another, and these values represent a random sample from the population of possible ε-values at each level of x.
2. For a given value of x, there can exist many values of y and therefore many values of ε. Further, the distribution of possible ε-values for any x-value is normal.
3. The distributions of possible ε-values have equal variances for all values of x.
4. The means of the dependent variable, y, for all specified values of the independent variable, $(\mu_{y|x})$, can be connected by a straight line called the population regression model.

Figure 14.6 illustrates assumptions 2, 3, and 4. The regression model (straight line) connects the average of the y-values for each level of the independent variable, x. The

FIGURE 14.6

Graphical Display of Linear Regression Assumptions

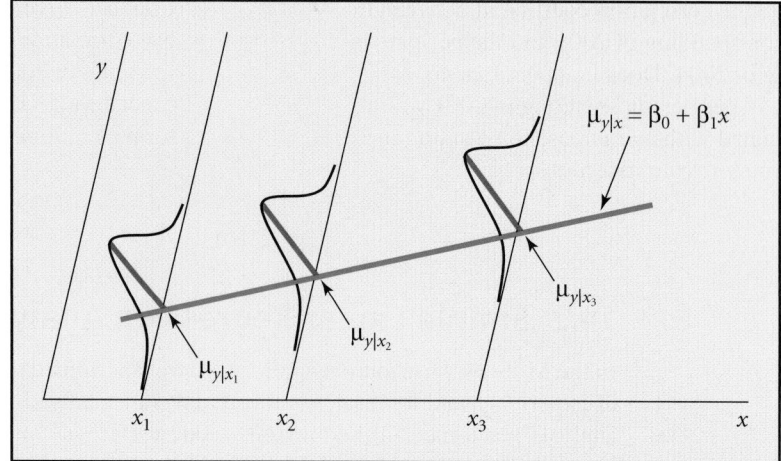

actual y-values for each level of x are normally distributed around the mean of y. Finally, observe that the spread of possible y-values is the same regardless of the level of x. The population regression line is determined by two values, β_0 and β_1. These values are known as the population *regression coefficients*. Value β_0 identifies the y intercept and β_1 the slope of the regression line. Under the regression assumptions, the coefficients define the true population model. For each observation, the actual value of the dependent variable, y, for any x is the sum of two components:

$$y = \underset{\text{Linear Component}}{\beta_0 + \beta_1 x} + \underset{\text{Random Error Component}}{\varepsilon}$$

The random error component, ε, may be positive, zero, or negative, depending on whether a single value of y for a given x falls above, on, or below the population regression line. Section 15.5 in Chapter 15 discusses how to check whether assumptions have been violated and the possible courses of action if the violations occur.

Meaning of the Regression Coefficients

Regression Slope Coefficient

The average change in the dependent variable for a unit change in the independent variable. The slope coefficient may be positive or negative, depending on the relationship between the two variables.

Coefficient β_1, the **regression slope coefficient** of the population regression line, measures the average change in the value of the dependent variable, y, for each unit change in x. The regression slope can be either positive, zero, or negative, depending on the relationship between x and y. For example, a positive population slope of 12 ($\beta_1 = 12$) means that for a 1-unit increase in x, we can expect an average 12-unit increase in y. Correspondingly, if the population slope is negative 12 ($\beta_1 = -12$), we can expect an average decrease of 12 units in y for a 1-unit increase in x.

The population's y intercept, β_0, indicates the mean value of y when x is 0. However, this interpretation holds only if the population could have x values equal to 0. When this cannot occur, β_0 does not have a meaningful interpretation in the regression model.

Business Application

MIDWEST DISTRIBUTION (*CONTINUED*) The Midwest Distribution marketing manager has data for a sample of 12 sales representatives. In Section 14.1, she has established that a significant linear relationship exists between years of experience and total sales using correlation analysis. (Recall that the sample correlation between the two variables was $r = 0.8325$.) Now she would like to estimate the regression equation that defines the *true* linear relationship (that is, the population's linear relationship) between years of experience and sales. Figure 14.3 shows the scatter plot for two variables: years with the company and sales. We need to use the sample data to estimate β_0 and β_1, the true intercept and slope of the line representing the relationship between two variables. The *regression line* through the sample data is the best estimate of the population regression line. However, there are an infinite number of possible regression lines for a set of points. For example, Figure 14.7 shows three of the possible different lines that pass through the Midwest Distribution data. Which line should be used to estimate the true regression model?

FIGURE 14.7

Possible Regression Lines

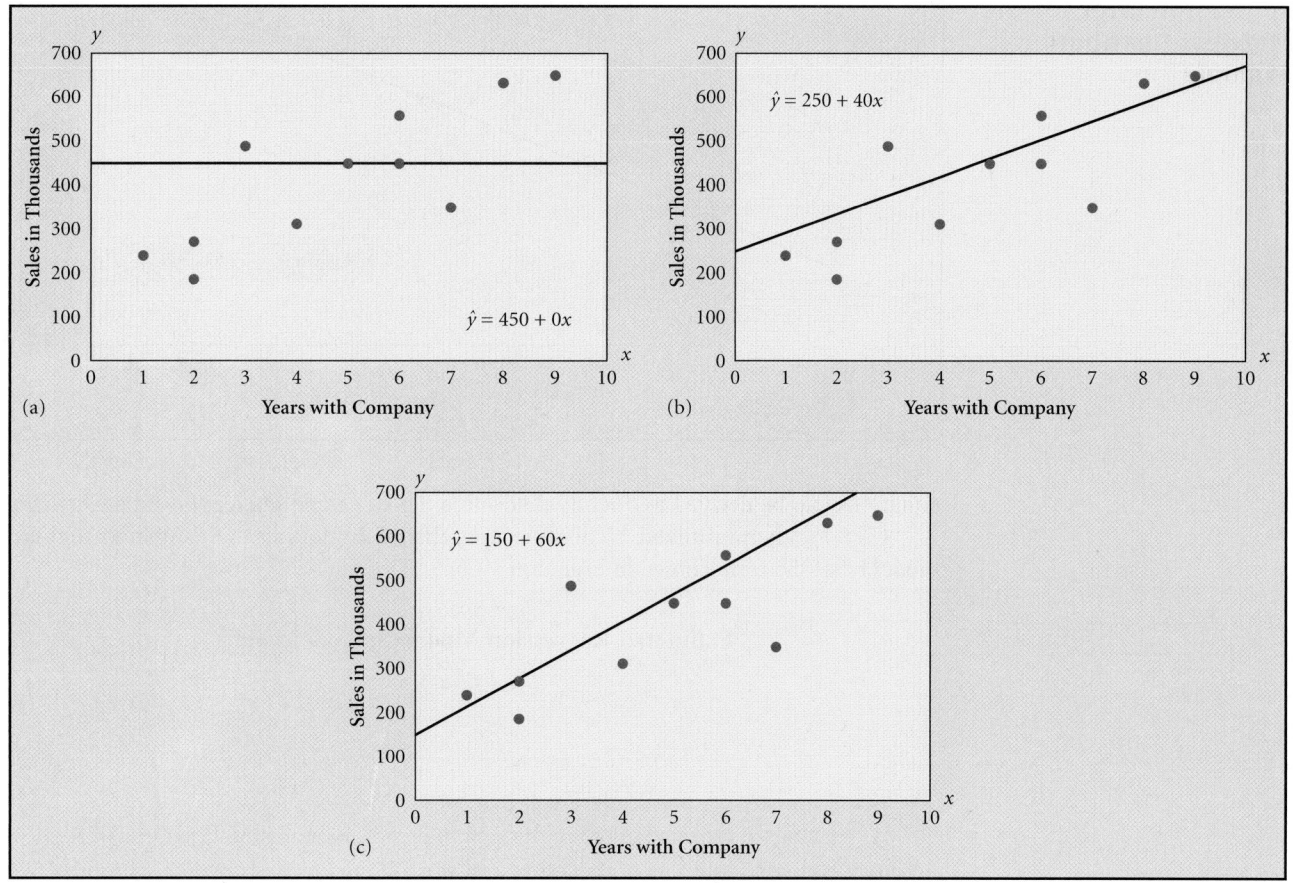

Least Squares Criterion
The criterion for determining a regression line that minimizes the sum of squared prediction errors.

Residual
The difference between the actual value of y and the predicted value $\hat{y}$ for a given level of the independent variable, x.

We must establish a criterion for selecting the best line. The criterion used is the **least squares criterion**.[2] To understand the least squares criterion, you need to know about prediction error, or **residual**, which is the distance between the actual y coordinate of an (x, y) point and the predicted value of that y coordinate produced by the regression line. Figure 14.8 shows how the prediction error is calculated for the employee who was with Midwest for four years ($x = 4$) using one possible regression line: $\hat{y} = 150 + 60x$ (where $\hat{y}$ is the predicted sales value). The predicted sales value is

$$\hat{y} = 150 + 60(4) = 390$$

However, the actual sales (y) for this employee were 312 (see Table 14.2). Thus, when $x = 4$, the difference between the observed value, $y = 312$, and the predicted value, $\hat{y} = 390$, is $312 - 390 = -78$. The residual (or prediction error) for this case when $x = 4$ is -78. Table 14.2 shows the calculated prediction errors and sum of squared errors for each of the three regression lines shown in Figure 14.7. Of these three potential regression models, the line with the equation $\hat{y} = 150 + 60x$ has the smallest sum of squared errors. However, is this line the best of all possible lines? That is, would $\sum_{i=1}^{n}(y_i - \hat{y}_i)^2$ be smaller than for any other line? One way to determine this is to calculate the sum of squared errors for all other regression lines. However, because there are an infinite number of these lines, this approach is not feasible. Fortunately, through the use of calculus,

---

[2] The reason we are using the sum of the squared residuals is that the sum of the residuals will be zero for the best regression line (the positive values will balance the negative values).

FIGURE 14.8

Computation of Regression Error for the Midwest Distribution Example

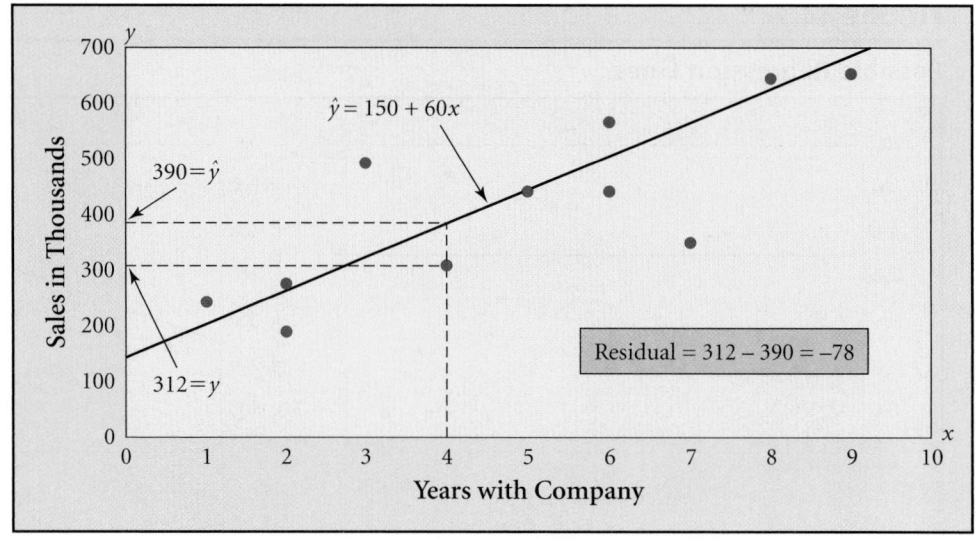

equations can be derived to directly determine the slope and intercept estimates such that $\sum_{i=1}^{n}(y_i - \hat{y}_i)^2$ is minimized.[3] This is accomplished by letting the estimated regression model be of the form shown in Equation 14.5.

CHAPTER OUTCOME 3

Estimated Regression Model (Sample Model)

$$\hat{y} = b_0 + b_1 x \tag{14.5}$$

where:

$\hat{y}$ = Estimated, or predicted, y-value

b_0 = Unbiased estimate of the regression intercept, found using Equation 14.8

b_1 = Unbiased estimate of the regression slope, found using Equation 14.6 or 14.7

x = Value of the independent variable

Equations 14.6 and 14.8 are referred to as the *least squares equations* because they provide the slope and intercept that minimize the sum of squared errors. Equation 14.7 is the algebraic equivalent of Equation 14.6 and may be easier to use when the computation is performed using a calculator.

Least Squares Equations

$$b_1 = \frac{\sum(x - \overline{x})(y - \overline{y})}{\sum(x - \overline{x})^2} \tag{14.6}$$

algebraic equivalent:

$$b_1 = \frac{\sum xy - \dfrac{\sum x \sum y}{n}}{\sum x^2 - \dfrac{(\sum x)^2}{n}} \tag{14.7}$$

and

$$b_0 = \overline{y} - b_1 \overline{x} \tag{14.8}$$

---

[3] The calculus derivation of the least squares equations is contained in the Kutner, et al. reference shown at the end of this chapter.

TABLE 14.2 Sum of Squared Errors for Three Linear Equations for Midwest Distribution

From Figure 14.7(a):
$\hat{y} = 450 + 0x$

			Residual	
x	$\hat{y}$	y	$y - \hat{y}$	$(y - \hat{y})^2$
3	450	487	37	1,369
5	450	445	−5	25
2	450	272	−178	31,684
8	450	641	191	36,481
2	450	187	−263	69,169
6	450	440	−10	100
7	450	346	−104	10,816
1	450	238	−212	44,944
4	450	312	−138	19,044
2	450	269	−181	32,761
9	450	655	205	42,025
6	450	563	113	12,769
				$\Sigma = 301{,}187$

From Figure 14.7(b):
$\hat{y} = 250 + 40x$

			Residual	
x	$\hat{y}$	y	$y - \hat{y}$	$(y - \hat{y})^2$
3	370	487	117	13,689
5	450	445	−5	25
2	330	272	−58	3,364
8	570	641	71	5,041
2	330	187	−143	20,449
6	490	440	−50	2,500
7	530	346	−184	33,856
1	290	238	−52	2,704
4	410	312	−98	9,604
2	330	269	−61	3,721
9	610	655	45	2,025
6	490	563	73	5,329
				$\Sigma = 102{,}307$

From Figure 14.7(c):
$\hat{y} = 150 + 60x$

			Residual	
x	$\hat{y}$	y	$y - \hat{y}$	$(y - \hat{y})^2$
3	330	487	157	24,649
5	450	445	−5	25
2	270	272	2	4
8	630	641	11	121
2	270	187	−83	6,889
6	510	440	−70	4,900
7	570	346	−224	50,176
1	210	238	28	784
4	390	312	−78	6,084
2	270	269	−1	1
9	690	655	−35	1,225
6	510	563	53	2,809
				$\Sigma = 97{,}667$

TABLE 14.3 Manual Calculations for Least Squares Regression Coefficients for the Midwest Distribution Example

y	x	xy	x^2	y^2
487	3	1,461	9	237,169
445	5	2,225	25	198,025
272	2	544	4	73,984
641	8	5,128	64	410,881
187	2	374	4	34,969
440	6	2,640	36	193,600
346	7	2,422	49	119,716
238	1	238	1	56,644
312	4	1,248	16	97,344
269	2	538	4	72,361
655	9	5,895	81	429,025
563	6	3,378	36	316,969
$\Sigma y = 4{,}855$	$\Sigma x = 55$	$\Sigma xy = 26{,}091$	$\Sigma x^2 = 329$	$\Sigma y^2 = 2{,}240{,}687$

$$\bar{y} = \frac{\Sigma y}{n} = \frac{4{,}855}{12} = 404.58 \qquad \bar{x} = \frac{\Sigma x}{n} = \frac{55}{12} = 4.58$$

$$b_1 = \frac{\Sigma xy - \dfrac{\Sigma x \Sigma y}{n}}{\Sigma x^2 - \dfrac{(\Sigma x)^2}{n}} = \frac{26{,}091 - \dfrac{55(4{,}855)}{12}}{329 - \dfrac{(55)^2}{12}}$$

$$= 49.91$$

Then,

$$b_0 = \bar{y} - b_1 \bar{x} = 404.58 - 49.91(4.58) = 175.99$$

The least squares regression line is, therefore,

$$\hat{y} = 175.99 + 49.91(x)$$

There is a slight difference between the manual calculation and the computer result due to rounding.

Table 14.3 shows the manual calculations, which are subject to rounding, for the least squares estimates for the Midwest Distribution example. However, you will almost always use a software package such as Excel or Minitab to perform these computations. (Figures 14.9a and 14.9b show the Excel and Minitab output.) In this case, the "best" regression line, given the least squares criterion, is $\hat{y} = 175.8288 + 49.9101(x)$. Figure 14.10 shows the predicted sales values along with the prediction errors and squared errors associated with this best simple linear regression line. Keep in mind that the prediction errors are also referred to as residuals. From Figure 14.10, the sum of the squared errors is 84,834.29. This is the smallest sum of squared residuals possible for this set of sample data. No other simple linear regression line through these 12 (x, y) points will produce a smaller sum of squared errors. Equation 14.9 presents a formula that can be used to calculate the sum of squared errors manually.

Sum of Squared Errors

$$SSE = \Sigma y^2 - b_0 \Sigma y - b_1 \Sigma xy \tag{14.9}$$

FIGURE 14.9A

Excel 2007 Midwest Distribution Regression Results

Excel 2007 Instructions:
1. Open file: Midwest.xls.
2. On the **Data** tab, click **Data Analysis**.
3. Select **Regression Analysis**.
4. Define x (Years with Midwest) and y (Sales) variable data range.
5. Select output location.
6. Check **Labels**.
7. Click **Residuals**.
8. Click **OK**.

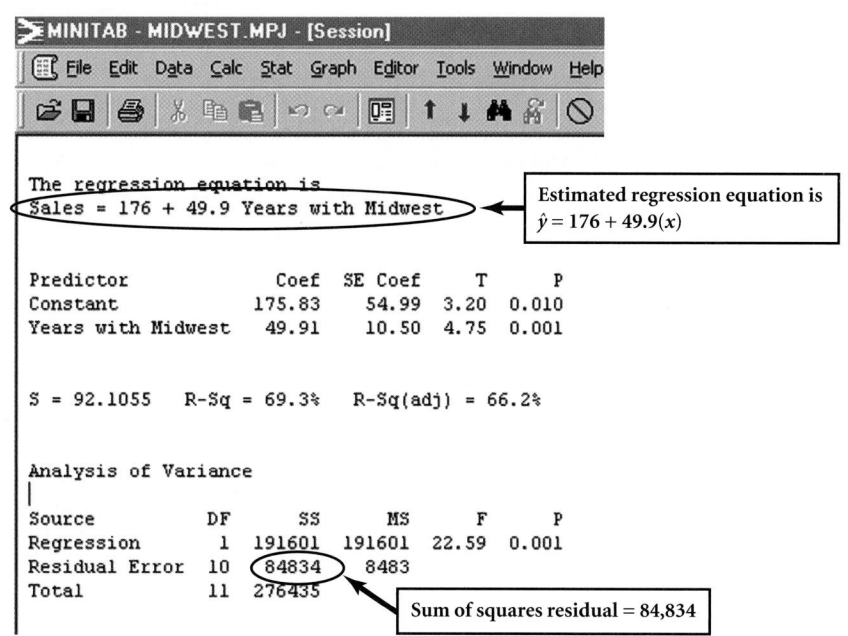

FIGURE 14.9B

Minitab Midwest Distribution Regression Results

Minitab Instructions:
1. Open file: Midwest. MTW.
2. Choose **Stat > Regression > Regression**.
3. In **Response,** enter the Y variable column.
4. In **Predictors**, enter the X variable column.
5. Click **Storage**; under **Diagnostic Measures** select **Residuals**.
6. Click **OK. OK.**

Figure 14.11 shows the scatter plot of sales and years of experience and the least squares regression line for Midwest Distribution. This line is the *best fit* for these sample data. The regression line passes through the point corresponding to $(\bar{x}, \bar{y})$. This will always be the case.

FIGURE 14.10

Residuals and Squared Residuals for the Midwest Distribution Example

Excel 2007 Instructions:
1. Create Squared Residuals using Excel formula (i.e. for cell d25, use = c25^2).
2. Sum the residuals and squared residuals columns.

Minitab Instructions (for similar results):
1. Choose **Calc > Column Statistics**.
2. Under **Statistics**, Choose **Sum**.
3. In **Input variable**, enter residual column.
4. Click **OK**.
5. Choose **Calc > Column Statistics**.
6. Under **Statistic**, choose **Sum of Squares**.
7. In **Input variable**, enter residual column.
8. Click **OK**.

D25 f_x =C25^2

	A	B	C	D
20				
21				
22	RESIDUAL OUTPUT			
23				
24	Observation	Predicted Sales	Residuals	Squared Residuals
25	1	325.5590466	161.4410	26063.1814
26	2	425.3791983	19.6208	384.9759
27	3	275.6489707	-3.6490	13.3150
28	4	575.1094258	65.8906	4341.5678
29	5	275.6489707	-88.6490	7858.6400
30	6	475.2892741	-35.2893	1245.3329
31	7	525.1993499	-179.1993	32112.4070
32	8	225.7388949	12.2611	150.3347
33	9	375.4691224	-63.4691	
34	10	275.6489707	-6.6490	
35	11	625.0195016	29.9805	
36	12	475.2892741	87.7107	7693.1714
37				
38		Sum =	0.0000	84834.2947
39				

Sum of residuals equal zero.
$SSE = 84,834.2947$

Least Squares Regression Properties

Figure 14.10 illustrates several important properties of least squares regression. These are:

1. The sum of the residuals from the least squares regression line is 0 (Equation 14.10). The total underprediction by the regression model is exactly offset by the total overprediction.

Sum of Residuals

$$\sum_{i=1}^{n} (y_i - \hat{y}_i) = 0 \qquad \textbf{(14.10)}$$

2. The sum of the squared residuals is the minimum (Equation 14.11).

Sum of Squared Residuals (Errors)

$$SSE = \sum_{i=1}^{n} (y_i - \hat{y}_i)^2 \qquad \textbf{(14.11)}$$

This property provided the basis for developing the equations for b_0 and b_1.

3. The simple regression line always passes through the mean of the y variable, $\bar{y}$, and the mean of the x variable, $\bar{x}$. So, to manually draw any simple linear regression line, all you need to do is to draw a line connecting the least squares y intercept with the $(\bar{x}, \bar{y})$ point.

4. The least squares coefficients are unbiased estimates of β_0 and β_1. Thus, the expected values of b_0 and b_1 equal β_0 and β_1, respectively.

FIGURE 14.11

Least Squares Regression Line for Midwest Distribution

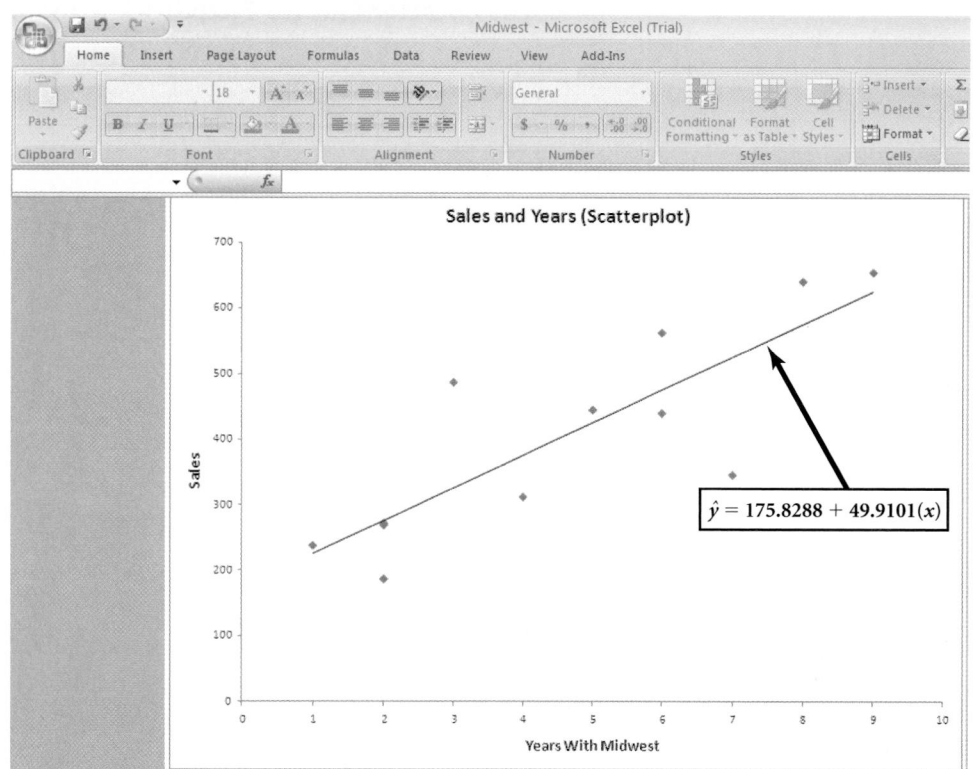

Excel 2007 Instructions:
1. Open file: Midwest.xls.
2. Move the *Sales* column to the right of *Years with Midwest* column.
3. Select data for chart.
4. On **Insert** tab, click **XY (Scatter)**, and then click **Scatter with only Markers** option.
5. Use the **Layout** tab of the **Chart Tools** to add titles and remove grid lines.
6. Use the **Design** tab of the **Chart Tools** to move the chart to a new worksheet.
7. Click on a chart point.
8. Right click and select **Add Trendline**.
9. Select **Linear**.

$$\hat{y} = 175.8288 + 49.9101(x)$$

TRY PROBLEM 14.20

Excel and Minitab Tutorial

EXAMPLE 14-2 Simple Linear Regression and Correlation

Fitzpatrick & Associates The investment firm Fitzpatrick & Associates wants to manage the pension fund of a major Chicago retailer. For their presentation to the retailer, the Fitzpatrick analysts want to use simple linear regression to model the relationship between profits and numbers of employees for 50 Fortune 500 companies in the firm's portfolio. The data for the analysis is contained in the CD-ROM file **Fortune 50**. This analysis can be done using the following steps:

Step 1 **Specify the independent and dependent variables.**
The object in this example is to model the linear relationship between number of employees (the independent variable) and each company's profits (the dependent variable).

Step 2 **Develop a scatter plot to graphically display the relationship between the independent and dependent variables.**
Figure 14.12 shows the scatter plot, where the dependent variable, y, is company profits and the independent variable, x, is number of employees. There appears to be a slight positive linear relationship between the two variables.

Step 3 **Calculate the correlation coefficient and the linear regression equation.**
Do either manually using Equations 14.1, 14.6, and 14.8, respectively, or by using Excel or Minitab software. Figure 14.13 shows the regression results. The sample correlation coefficient (called multiple R in Excel) is

$$r = 0.3638$$

FIGURE 14.12

Excel 2007 Scatter Plot for Fitzpatrick & Associates

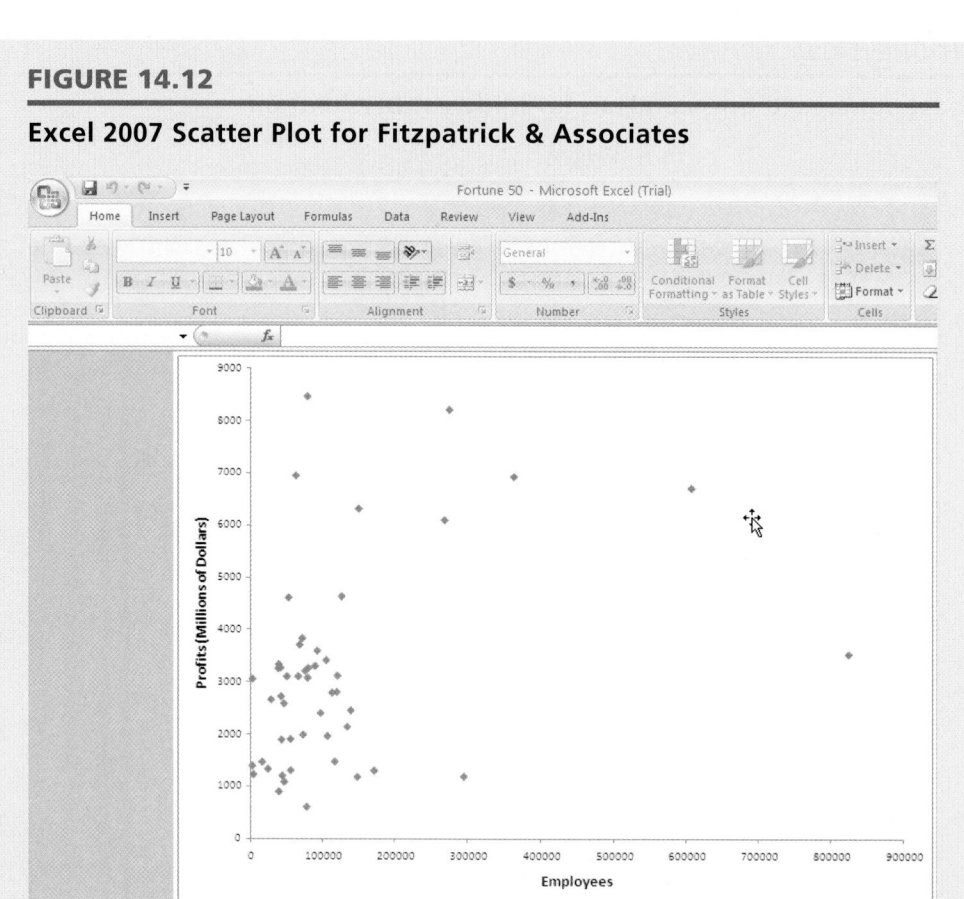

Excel 2007 Instructions:
1. Open file: Fortune 50.xls.
2. Copy the *Profits* column to the immediate right of *Employees* column.
3. Select data for chart (*Employees and Profits*).
4. On **Insert** tab, click **XY (Scatter)**, and then click the **Scatter with only Markers** option.
5. Use the **Layout** tab of the **Chart Tools** to add titles and remove grid lines.
6. Use the **Design** tab of the **Chart Tools** to move the chart to a new worksheet.

Minitab Instructions (for similar result):
1. Open file: Fortune 50.MTW.
2. Choose **Graph > Character Graphs > Scatterplot**.
3. In **Y variable**, enter y column.
4. In **X variable**, enter x column.
5. Click **OK**.

The regression equation is

$$\hat{y} = 2{,}556.88 + 0.0048x$$

The regression slope is estimated to be 0.0048, which means that for each additional employee, the average increase in company profit is 0.0048 million dollars, or $4,800. The intercept can only be interpreted when a value equal to zero for the x variable (employees) is plausible. Clearly, no company has zero employees, so the intercept in this case has no meaning other than it locates the height of the regression line for $x = 0$.

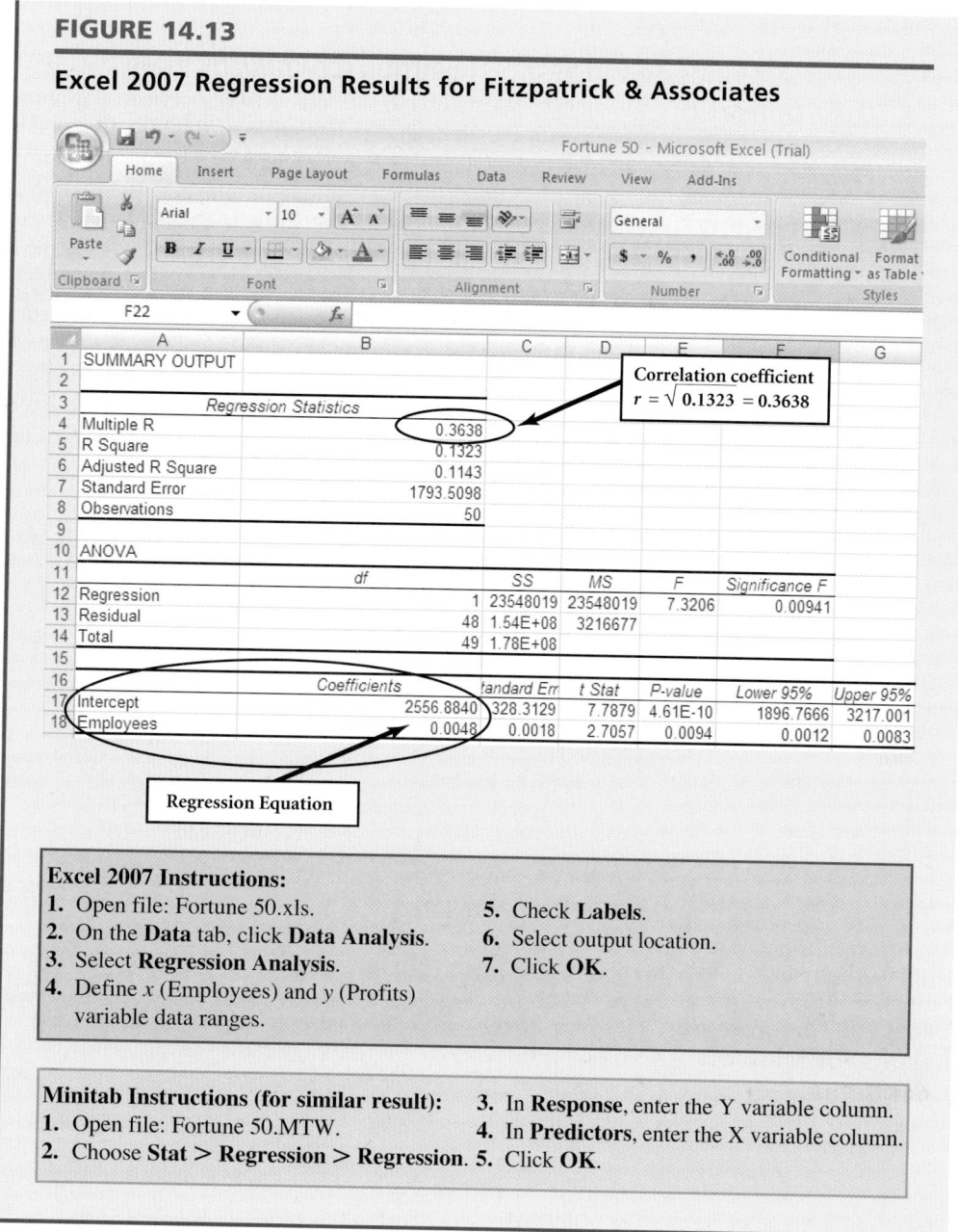

FIGURE 14.13

Excel 2007 Regression Results for Fitzpatrick & Associates

Excel 2007 Instructions:
1. Open file: Fortune 50.xls.
2. On the **Data** tab, click **Data Analysis**.
3. Select **Regression Analysis**.
4. Define *x* (Employees) and *y* (Profits) variable data ranges.
5. Check **Labels**.
6. Select output location.
7. Click **OK**.

Minitab Instructions (for similar result):
1. Open file: Fortune 50.MTW.
2. Choose **Stat > Regression > Regression**.
3. In **Response**, enter the Y variable column.
4. In **Predictors**, enter the X variable column.
5. Click **OK**.

CHAPTER OUTCOME #4

Significance Tests in Regression Analysis

In Section 14.1, we pointed out that the correlation coefficient computed from sample data is a point estimate of the population correlation coefficient and is subject to sampling error. We also introduced a test of significance for the correlation coefficient. Likewise, the regression coefficients developed from a sample of data are also point estimates of the true regression coefficients for the population. The regression coefficients are subject to sampling error. For example, due to sampling error the estimated slope coefficient may be positive or negative while the population slope is really 0. Therefore, we need a test procedure to determine whether the regression slope coefficient is statistically significant. As you will see in this section, the test for the simple linear regression slope coefficient is equivalent to the test for the correlation coefficient. That is, if the correlation between two variables is found to be significant, then the regression slope coefficient will also be significant.

The Coefficient of Determination, R^2

**Business
Application**

MIDWEST DISTRIBUTION (*CONTINUED*) Recall that the Midwest Distribution marketing manager was analyzing the relationship between the number of years an employee had been with the company (independent variable) and the sales generated by the employee (dependent variable). We note when looking at the sample data for 12 employees (see Table 14.3) that sales vary among employees. Regression analysis aims to determine the extent to which an independent variable can explain this variation. In this case, does number of years with the company help explain the variation in sales from employee to employee?

The *SST* (total sum of squares) can be used in measuring the variation in the dependent variable. *SST* is computed using Equation 14.12. For Midwest Distribution, the total sum of squares for sales is provided in the output generated by Excel or Minitab, as shown in Figure 14.14a and Figure 14.14b. As you can see, the total sum of squares in sales that needs to be explained is 276,434.92. Note that the *SST* value is in squared units and has no particular meaning.

Total Sum of Squares

$$SST = \sum_{i=1}^{n}(y_i - \overline{y})^2 \qquad (14.12)$$

where:

SST = Total sum of squares
n = Sample size
y_i = ith value of the dependent variable
$\overline{y}$ = Average value of the dependent variable

FIGURE 14.14A

Excel 2007 Regression Results for Midwest Distribution

Excel 2007 Instructions:
1. Open file: Midwest.xls.
2. On the **Data** tab, click **Data Analysis**.
3. Select **Regression Analysis**.
4. Define x (Years with Midwest) and y (Sales) variable data range.
5. Click on **Labels**.
6. Specify output location.
7. Click **OK**.

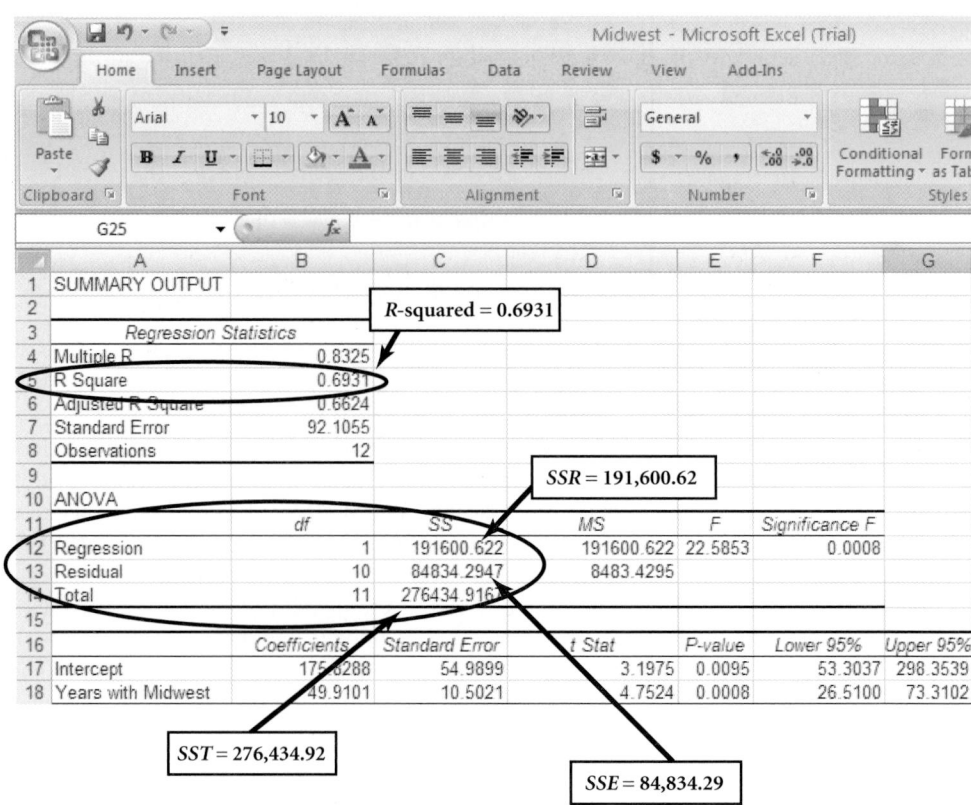

FIGURE 14.14B

Minitab Regression Results for Midwest Distribution

Minitab Instructions:
1. Open file: Midwest.MTW.
2. Choose **Stat > Regression > Regression**.
3. In **Response**, enter the *y* variable column.
4. In **Predictors**, enter the *x* variable column.
5. Click **OK**.

The least squares regression line is computed so that the sum of squared residuals is minimized (recall the discussion of the least squares equations). The sum of squares residuals is also called the *sum of squares error (SSE)* and is defined by Equation 14.13.

Sum of Squares Error

$$SSE = \sum_{i=1}^{n} (y_i - \hat{y}_i)^2 \qquad (14.13)$$

where:

n = Sample size
y_i = ith value of the dependent variable
$\hat{y}_i$ = ith predicted value of y given the ith value of x

SSE represents the amount of the total sum of squares in the dependent variable that *is not explained* by the least squares regression line. Excel refers to *SSE* as *sum of squares residual* and Minitab refers to SSE as *residual error*. This value is contained in the regression output shown in Figure 14.14a and Figure 14.14b.

$$SSE = \Sigma(y - \hat{y})^2 = 84,834.29$$

Thus, of the total sum of squares (*SST* = 276,434.92), the regression model leaves *SSE* = 84,834.29 unexplained. Then, the portion of the total sum of squares that *is explained* by the regression line is called the *sum of squares regression (SSR)* and is calculated by Equation 14.14.

Sum of Squares Regression

$$SSR = \sum_{i=1}^{n} (\hat{y}_i - \bar{y})^2 \tag{14.14}$$

where:

$\hat{y}_i$ = Estimated value of y for each value of x.

$\bar{y}$ = Average value of the y variable

The sum of squares regression ($SSR = 191,600.62$) is also provided in the regression output shown in Figure 14.14a and Figure 14.14b. You should also note that the following holds:

$$SST = SSR + SSE$$

For the Midwest Distribution example, in the Minitab output we get

$$276,435 = 191,601 + 84,834$$

Coefficient of Determination
The portion of the total variation in the dependent variable that is explained by its relationship with the independent variable. The coefficient of determination is also called R-squared and is denoted as R^2.

We can use these calculations to compute an important measure in regression analysis called the **coefficient of determination**. The coefficient of determination is calculated using Equation 14.15.

Coefficient of Determination, R^2

$$R^2 = \frac{SSR}{SST} \tag{14.15}$$

Then, for the Midwest Distribution example, the proportion of variation in sales that can be explained by its linear relationship with the years of salesforce experience is

$$R^2 = \frac{SSR}{SST} = \frac{191,600.62}{276,434.92} = 0.6931$$

This means that 69.31% of the variation in the sales data for this sample can be explained by the linear relationship between sales and years of experience. Notice that R-squared is part of the regression output in Figures 14.14a and 14.14b.

R^2 can be a value between 0 and 1.0. If there is a perfect linear relationship between two variables, then the coefficient of determination, R^2, will be 1.0. This would correspond to a situation in which the least squares regression line would pass through each of the points in the scatter plot. R^2 is the measure used by many decision makers to indicate how well the linear regression line fits the (x, y) data points. The better the fit, the closer R^2 will be to 1.0. R^2 will be close to 0 when there is a weak linear relationship.

Finally, when you are employing *simple linear regression* (a linear relationship between a single independent variable and the dependent variable), there is an alternative way of computing R^2, as shown in Equation 14.16.

Coefficient of Determination, Single Independent Variable Case

$$R^2 = r^2 \tag{14.16}$$

where:

R^2 = Coefficient of determination

r = Sample correlation coefficient

Therefore, by squaring the correlation coefficient, we can get R^2 for the simple regression model. Figure 14.14a shows the correlation, $r = 0.8325$, which is referred to as Multiple R in Excel. Then, using Equation 14.16, we get R^2.

$$R^2 = r^2$$
$$= 0.8325^2$$
$$= 0.6931$$

Keep in mind that $R^2 = 0.6931$ is based on the random sample of size 12 and is subject to sampling error. Thus, just because $R^2 = 0.6931$ for the sample data does not mean that knowing the number of years an employee has worked for the company will explain 69.31% of the variation in sales for the population of all employees with the company. Likewise, just because $R^2 > 0.0$ for the sample data does not mean that the population coefficient of determination, noted as ρ^2 (rho-squared), is greater than zero.

However, a statistical test exists for testing the following null and alternative hypotheses:

$$H_0: \rho^2 = 0$$
$$H_A: \rho^2 > 0$$

The test statistic is an F-test with the test statistic defined as shown in Equation 14.17.

Test Statistic for Significance of the Coefficient of Determination

$$F = \frac{\dfrac{SSR}{1}}{\dfrac{SSE}{(n-2)}} \quad df = (D_1 = 1, D_2 = n - 2)$$

(14.17)

where:

$$SSR = \text{Sum of squares regression}$$
$$SSE = \text{Sum of squares error}$$

For the Midwest Distribution example, the test statistic is computed using Equation 14.17 as follows:

$$F = \frac{\dfrac{191,600.62}{1}}{\dfrac{84,834.29}{(12-2)}} = 22.58$$

The critical value from the F-distribution table in Appendix H for $\alpha = 0.05$ and for 1 and 10 degrees of freedom is 4.965. This gives the following decision rule:

If $F > 4.965$, reject the null hypothesis;
Otherwise, do not reject the null hypothesis.

Because $F = 22.58 > 4.965$, we reject the null hypothesis and conclude the population coefficient of determination (ρ^2) is greater than zero. This means the independent variable explains a significant proportion of the variation in the dependent variable.

For a simple regression model (a regression model with a single independent variable), the test for ρ^2 is equivalent to the test shown earlier for the population correlation coefficient, ρ. Refer to Figure 14.5 to see that the t-test statistic for the correlation coefficient was $t = 4.752$. If we square this t-value we get

$$t^2 = 4.752^2 = F = 22.58$$

Thus, the tests are equivalent. They will provide the same conclusions about the relationship between the x and y variables.

Significance of the Slope Coefficient   For a simple linear regression model (one independent variable), there are three equivalent statistical tests.

1. Test for significance of the correlation between x and y.
2. Test for significance of the coefficient of determination.
3. Test for significance of the regression slope coefficient.

We have already introduced the first two of these tests. The third one deals specifically with the significance of the regression slope coefficient. The null and alternative hypotheses to be tested are

$$H_0: \beta_1 = 0$$
$$H_A: \beta_1 \neq 0$$

To test the significance of the simple linear regression slope coefficient, we are interested in determining whether the population regression slope coefficient is 0. A slope of 0 would imply that there is no linear relationship between x and y variables and the x variable, in its linear form is of no use in explaining the variation in y. If the linear relationship is useful, then we should reject the hypothesis that the regression slope is 0. However, because the estimated regression slope coefficient, b_1, is calculated from sample data, it is subject to sampling error. Therefore, even though b_1 is not 0, we must determine whether its difference from 0 is greater than would generally be attributed to sampling error.

If we selected several samples from the same population and for each sample determined the least squares regression line, we would likely get regression lines with different slopes and different y intercepts. This is analogous to getting different sample means from different samples. Just as the distribution of possible sample means has a standard error, the possible regression slopes have a standard error, which is given in Equation 14.18.

Simple Regression Standard Error of the Slope Coefficient (Population)

$$\sigma_{b_1} = \frac{\sigma_\varepsilon}{\sqrt{\sum(x - \bar{x})^2}} \qquad \textbf{(14.18)}$$

where:

σ_{b_1} = Standard deviation of the regression slope
(called the *standard error of the slope*)

σ_ε = Population standard error of the estimate

Equation 14.18 requires that we know the *standard error of the estimate*. It measures the dispersion of the dependent variable about its mean value at each value of the dependent variable in the original units of the dependent variable. However, because we are sampling from the population, we can estimate σ_ε as shown in Equation 14.19.

Simple Regression Estimator for the Standard Error of the Estimate

$$s_\varepsilon = \sqrt{\frac{SSE}{n - 2}} \qquad \textbf{(14.19)}$$

where:

SSE = Sum of squares error
n = Sample size

Equation 14.18, the standard error of the regression slope, applies when we are dealing with a population. However, in most cases, such as the Midwest Distribution example, we are dealing with a sample from the population. Thus, we need to estimate the regression slope's standard error using Equation 14.20.

Simple Regression Estimator for the Standard Deviation of the Slope

$$s_{b_1} = \frac{s_\varepsilon}{\sqrt{\sum(x - \bar{x})^2}} \qquad (14.20)$$

where:

s_{b_1} = Estimate of the standard error of the least squares slope

$s_\varepsilon = \sqrt{\dfrac{SSE}{n-2}}$ = Sample standard error of the estimate (the measure of deviation of the actual y-values around the regression line)

Business Application

MIDWEST DISTRIBUTION (*CONTINUED*) For Midwest Distribution, the regression outputs in Figures 14.15a and Figure 14.15b show $b_1 = 49.91$. The question is whether this value is different enough from 0 to have not been caused by sampling error. We find the answer by looking at the value of the estimate of the standard error of the slope, calculated using Equation 14.20, which is also shown in Figure 14.15a. The standard error of the slope coefficient is 10.50.

If the standard error of the slope σ_{b_1} is large, then the value of b_1 will be quite variable from sample to sample. Conversely, if σ_{b_1} is small, the slope values will be less variable. However, regardless of the standard error of the slope, the average value of b_1 will equal β_1, the true regression slope, if the assumptions of the regression analysis are satisfied. Figure 14.16 illustrates what this means. Notice that when the standard error of the slope is large, the sample slope can take on values *much* different from the true population slope. As Figure 14.16(a) shows, a sample slope and the true population slope can even have different signs. However, when σ_{b_1} is small, the sample regression lines will cluster closely around the true population line [Figure 14.16(b)].

FIGURE 14.15A

Excel 2007 Regression Results for Midwest Distribution

Excel 2007 Instructions:
1. Open file: Midwest.xls.
2. On the **Data** tab, click **Data Analysis**.
3. Select **Regression Analysis**.
4. Define x (Years with Midwest) and y (Sales) variable data range.
5. Click on **Labels**.
6. Specify output location.
7. Click **OK**.

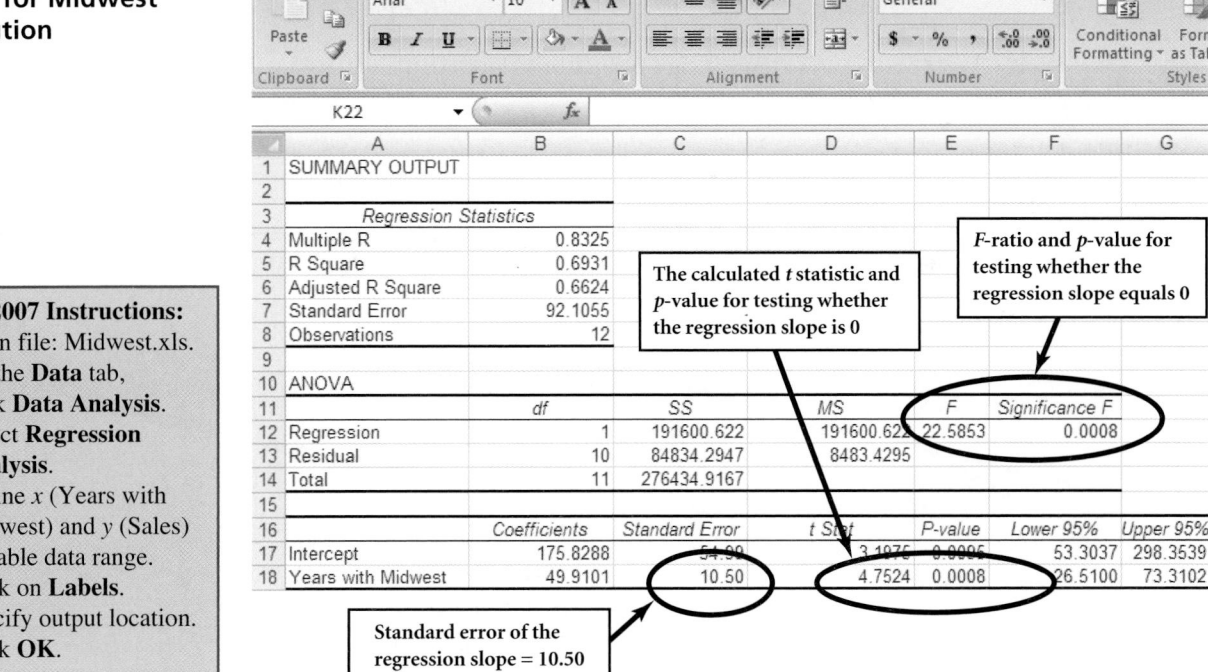

The calculated t statistic and p-value for testing whether the regression slope is 0

F-ratio and p-value for testing whether the regression slope equals 0

Standard error of the regression slope = 10.50

	A	B	C	D	E	F	G
1	SUMMARY OUTPUT						
2							
3	*Regression Statistics*						
4	Multiple R	0.8325					
5	R Square	0.6931					
6	Adjusted R Square	0.6624					
7	Standard Error	92.1055					
8	Observations	12					
9							
10	ANOVA						
11		*df*	*SS*	*MS*	*F*	*Significance F*	
12	Regression	1	191600.622	191600.622	22.5853	0.0008	
13	Residual	10	84834.2947	8483.4295			
14	Total	11	276434.9167				
15							
16		*Coefficients*	*Standard Error*	*t Stat*	*P-value*	*Lower 95%*	*Upper 95%*
17	Intercept	175.8288	54.90	3.1975	0.0095	53.3037	298.3539
18	Years with Midwest	49.9101	10.50	4.7524	0.0008	26.5100	73.3102

FIGURE 14.15B

Minitab Regression Results for Midwest Distribution

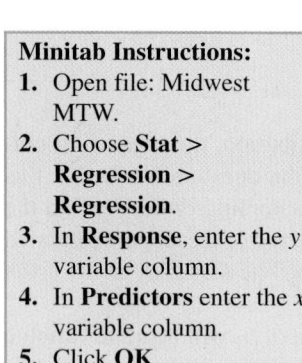

Minitab Instructions:
1. Open file: Midwest MTW.
2. Choose **Stat > Regression > Regression**.
3. In **Response**, enter the y variable column.
4. In **Predictors** enter the x variable column.
5. Click **OK**.

Because the sample regression slope will most likely not equal the true population slope, we must test to determine whether the true slope could possibly be 0. A slope of 0 in the linear model means that the independent variable will not explain any variation in the dependent variable, nor will it be useful in predicting the dependent variable. The null and alternative hypotheses to be tested at the 0.05 level of significance are

$$H_0: \beta_1 = 0$$
$$H_A: \beta_1 \neq 0$$

To test the significance of a slope coefficient, we use the t-test value in Equation 14.21.

FIGURE 14.16

Standard Error of the Slope

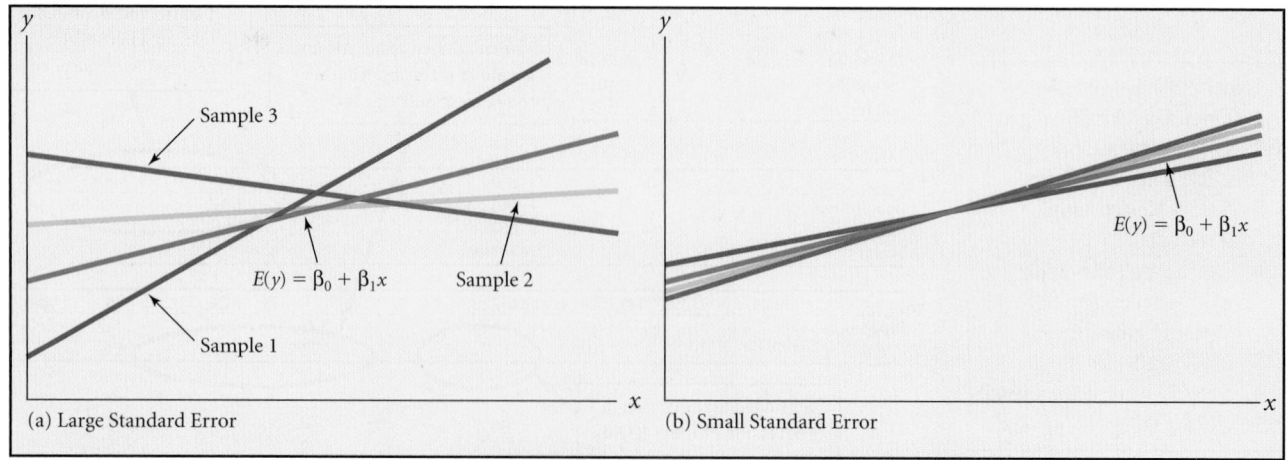

(a) Large Standard Error

(b) Small Standard Error

CHAPTER OUTCOME #4

Simple Linear Regression Test Statistic for Test of the Significance of the Slope

$$t = \frac{b_1 - \beta_1}{s_{b_1}} \qquad df = n - 2 \qquad \textbf{(14.21)}$$

where:

b_1 = Sample regression slope coefficient

β_1 = Hypothesized slope (usually $\beta_1 = 0$)

s_{b_1} = Estimator of the standard error of the slope

Figure 14.17 illustrates this test for the Midwest Distribution example. The calculated t-value of 4.752 exceeds the critical value from the t-distribution with 10 degrees of freedom and $\alpha/2 = 0.025$. This indicates that we should reject the hypothesis that the true regression slope is 0. Thus, years of experience can be used to help explain the variation in an individual representative's sales. (Note that the calculated t is the same value that we found in Figure 14.6 for the test of the correlation coefficient. Thus, this test is equivalent to the tests for ρ and ρ^2 presented earlier.

The output shown in Figures 14.15a and 14.15b also contains the calculated t statistic. The p-value for the calculated t statistic is also provided. As with other situations involving two-tailed hypothesis tests, if the p-value is less than α, the null hypothesis is rejected. In this case, because p-value $= 0.0008 < 0.05$, we reject the null hypothesis.

FIGURE 14.17

Significance Test of the Regression Slope for Midwest Distribution

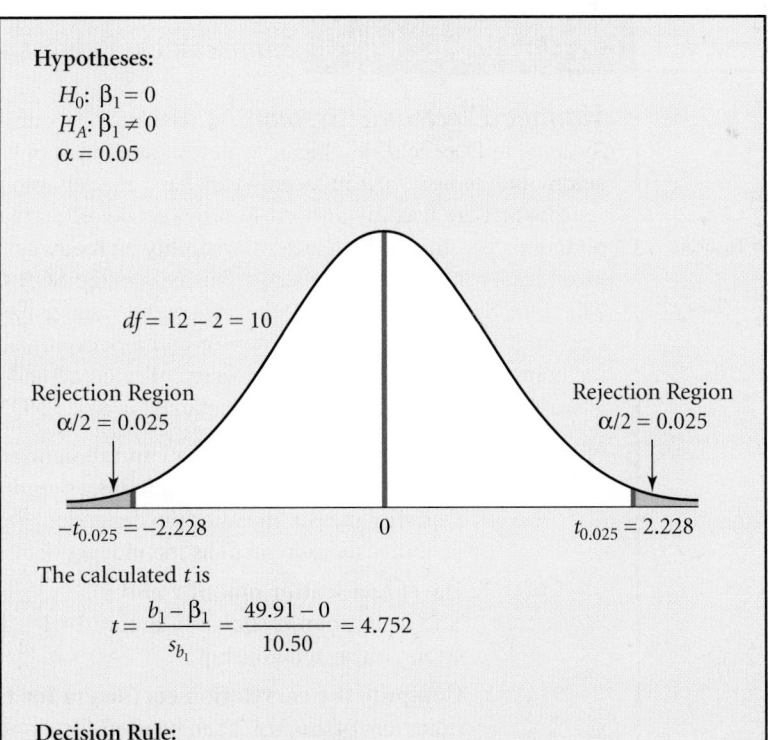

Hypotheses:

H_0: $\beta_1 = 0$
H_A: $\beta_1 \neq 0$
$\alpha = 0.05$

$df = 12 - 2 = 10$

Rejection Region
$\alpha/2 = 0.025$

Rejection Region
$\alpha/2 = 0.025$

$-t_{0.025} = -2.228$ 0 $t_{0.025} = 2.228$

The calculated t is

$$t = \frac{b_1 - \beta_1}{s_{b_1}} = \frac{49.91 - 0}{10.50} = 4.752$$

Decision Rule:

If $t > t_{0.025} = 2.228$, reject H_0.
If $t < -t_{0.025} = -2.228$, reject H_0.
Otherwise, do not reject H_0.
Because $4.752 > 2.228$, we should reject the null hypothesis and conclude that the true slope is not 0. Thus, the simple linear relationship that utilizes the independent variable, years with the company, is useful in explaining the variation in the dependent variable, sales volume.

SUMMARY   Simple Linear Regression Analysis

The following steps outline the process that can be used in developing a simple linear regression model and the various hypotheses tests used to determine the significance of a simple linear regression model.

1. Define the independent (x) and dependent (y) variables and select a simple random sample of pairs of (x, y) values.
2. Develop a scatter plot of y and x. You are looking for a linear relationship between the two variables.
3. Compute the correlation coefficient for the sample data.
4. Calculate the least squares regression line for the sample data and the coefficient of determination, R^2. The coefficient of determination measures the proportion of variation in the dependent variable explained by the independent variable.
5. Conduct any of the following tests for determining whether the regression model is statistically significant.

a. Test to determine whether the true regression slope is 0. The test statistic with $df = n - 2$ is

$$t = \frac{b_1 - \beta_1}{s_{b_1}} = \frac{b_1 - 0}{s_{b_1}}$$

b. Test to see whether ρ is significantly different from 0. The test statistic is

$$t = \frac{r}{\sqrt{\dfrac{1 - r^2}{n - 2}}}$$

c. Test to see whether ρ^2 is significantly greater than 0. The test statistic is

$$F = \frac{\dfrac{SSR}{1}}{\dfrac{SSE}{(n - 2)}}$$

6. Reach a decision.
7. Draw a conclusion.

EXAMPLE 14-3   Simple Linear Regression Analysis

Excel and Minitab Tutorial

TRY PROBLEM 14.17

Vantage Electronic Systems   Consider the example involving Vantage Electronic Systems in Deerfield, Michigan, which started out supplying electronic equipment for the automobile industry but in recent years has ventured into other areas. One area is visibility sensors that are used by airports to provide takeoff and landing information and by transportation departments to detect low visibility on roadways during fog and snow. The recognized leader in the visibility sensor business is the SCR Company, which makes a sensor called the Scorpion. The R&D department at Vantage has recently performed a test on its new unit by locating a Vantage sensor and a Scorpion sensor side-by-side. Various data, including visibility measurements, were collected at randomly selected points in time over a two-week period. These data are contained in a CD-ROM file called **Vantage**.

Step 1   Define the independent (x) and dependent (y) variables.
The analysis included a simple linear regression using the Scorpion visibility measurement as the dependent variable, y, and the Vantage visibility measurement as the independent variable, x.

Step 2   Develop a scatter plot of y and x.
The scatter plot is shown in Figure 14.18. There does not appear to be a strong linear relationship.

Step 3   Compute the correlation coefficient for the sample data.
Equation 14.1 or 14.2 can be used for manual computation, or we can use Excel or Minitab. The sample correlation coefficient is

$$r = 0.5778$$

Step 4   Calculate the least squares regression line for the sample data and the coefficient of determination, R^2.
Equations 14.7 and 14.8 can be used to manually compute the regression slope coefficient and intercept, respectively, and Equation 14.15 or 14.16

FIGURE 14.18

Scatter Plot—Example 14-3

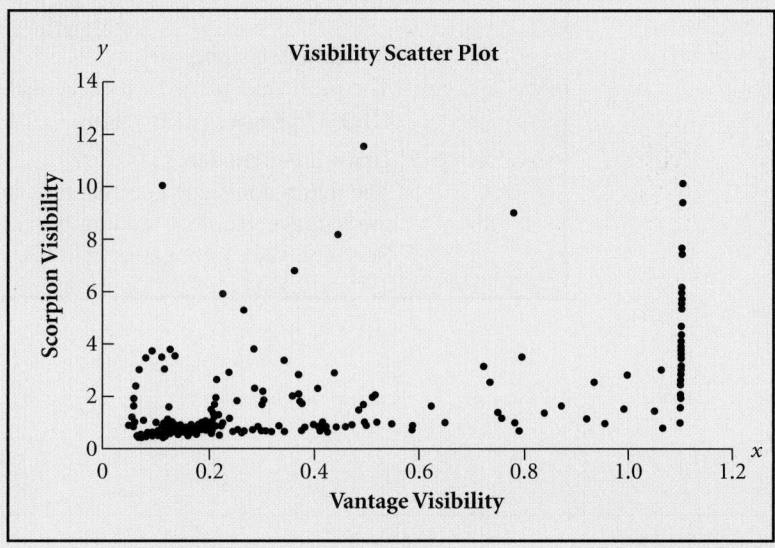

can be used to manually compute R^2. Excel and Minitab can also be used to eliminate the computational burden. The coefficient of determination is

$$R^2 = r^2 = 0.5778^2 = 0.3339$$

Thus, approximately 33% of the variation in the Scorpion visibility measures is explained by knowing the corresponding Vantage system visibility measure. The least squares regression equation is

$$\hat{y} = 0.586 + 3.017x$$

Step 5 **Conduct a test to determine whether the regression model is statistically significant (or whether the population correlation is equal to 0).**
The null and alternative hypotheses to test the correlation coefficient are

$$H_0: \rho = 0$$
$$H_A: \rho \neq 0$$

The t-test statistic using Equation 14.3 is

$$t = \frac{r}{\sqrt{\dfrac{1-r^2}{n-2}}} = \frac{0.5778}{\sqrt{\dfrac{1-0.5778^2}{280-2}}} = 11.8$$

The $t = 11.8$ exceeds the critical t for any reasonable level of α for 278 degrees of freedom, so the null hypothesis is rejected and we conclude that there is a statistically significant linear relationship between visibility measures for the two visibility sensors.

Alternatively, the null and alternative hypotheses to test the regression slope coefficient are

$$H_0: \beta_1 = 0$$
$$H_A: \beta_1 \neq 0$$

The *t*-test statistic is

$$t = \frac{b_1 - \beta_1}{s_{b_1}} = \frac{3.017 - 0}{0.2557} = 11.8$$

Step 6 Reach a decision.
The *t*-test statistic of 11.8 exceeds the *t*-critical for any reasonable level of α for 278 degrees of freedom.

Step 7 Draw a conclusion.
The regression slope coefficient is not equal to 0. This means that knowing the Vantage visibility reading provides useful help in knowing what the Scorpion visibility reading will be.

14-2: Exercises

Skill Development

14-16. You are given the following sample data for variables *x* and *y*:

x (independent)	y (dependent)
1	16
7	50
3	22
8	59
11	63
5	46
4	43

a. Construct a scatter plot for these data and describe what, if any, relationship appears to exist.

b. Compute the regression equation based on these sample data and interpret the regression coefficients.

c. Based on the sample data, what percentage of the total variation in the dependent variable can be explained by the independent variable?

d. Test the significance of the overall regression model using a significance level of 0.01.

e. Test to determine whether the true regression slope coefficient is equal to 0. Use a significance level of 0.01.

14-17. The following data for the dependent variable, *y*, and the independent variable, *x*, have been collected using simple random sampling:

x	y
10	120
14	130
16	170
12	150
20	200
18	180
16	190
14	150
16	160
18	200

a. Develop a simple linear regression equation for these data.

b. Calculate the sum of squared residuals, the total sum of squares, and the coefficient of determination.

c. Calculate the standard error of the estimate.

d. Calculate the standard deviation for the regression slope.

e. Conduct the hypothesis test to determine whether the regression slope coefficient is equal to 0. Test using α = 0.02.

14-18. You are given the following sample data for variables *y* and *x*:

y	140.1	120.3	80.8	100.7	130.2	90.6	110.5	120.2	130.4	130.3	100.1
x	5	3	2	4	5	4	4	5	6	5	4

a. Develop a scatter plot for these data and describe what, if any, relationship exists.

b. (1) Compute the correlation coefficient.
(2) Test to determine whether the correlation is significant at the significance level of 0.05. Conduct this hypothesis test using the p-value approach. (3) Compute the regression equation based on these sample data and interpret the regression coefficients.

c. Use the F-test approach to test the significance of the overall regression model using significance level equal to 0.05.

14-19. Consider the following sample data for the variables y and x:

x	30.3	4.8	15.2	24.9	8.6	20.1	9.3	11.2
y	14.6	27.9	17.6	15.3	19.8	13.2	25.6	19.4

a. Calculate the linear regression equation for these data.
b. Determine the predicted y-value when $x = 10$.
c. Estimate the change in the y variable resulting from the increase in the x variable of 10 units.
d. Conduct a hypothesis test to determine if an increase of 1 unit in the x variable will result in the decrease of the average value of the y variable. Use a significance of 0.025.

14-20. Examine the following sample data for the variables y and x:

x	1	2	3	4	5
y	4	2	5	8	9

a. Construct a scatter plot of these data. Describe the relationship between x and y.
b. Calculate the sum of squares error for the following equations: (1) $\hat{y} = 0.8 + 1.60x$, (2) $\hat{y} = 1 + 1.50x$, and (3) $\hat{y} = 0.7 + 1.60x$.
c. Which of these equations provides the "best" fit of these data? Describe the criterion you used to determine "best" fit.
d. Determine the regression line that minimizes the sum of squares error.

Business Applications

14-21. A shipping company believes that the variation in the cost of a customer's shipment can be explained by differences in the weight of the package being shipped. In order to investigate whether this relationship is useful, a random sample of 20 customer shipments was selected and the weight (in lb) and the cost (in dollars, rounded to the nearest dollar) for each shipment were recorded. The following results were obtained:

Weight (x)	Cost (y)
8	11
6	8
5	11
7	11
12	17
9	11
17	27
13	16
8	9
18	25
17	21
17	24
10	16
20	24
9	21
5	10
13	21
6	16
6	11
12	20

a. Construct a scatter plot for these data. What, if any, relationship appears to exist between the two variables?
b. Compute the linear regression model based on the sample data. Interpret the slope and intercept coefficients.
c. Test the significance of the overall regression model using a significance level equal to 0.05.
d. What percentage of the total variation in shipping cost can be explained by the regression model you developed in part b?

14-22. The Skelton Manufacturing Company recently did a study of its customers. A random sample of 50 customer accounts was pulled from the computer records. Two variables were observed:

y = Total dollar volume of business this year
x = Miles customer is from corporate headquarters

The following statistics were computed:

$$\hat{y} = 2{,}140.23 - 10.12x$$
$$s_{b_1} = 3.12$$

a. Interpret the regression slope coefficient.
b. Using a significance level of 0.01, test to determine whether it is true that the further a customer is from the corporate headquarters, the smaller is the total dollar volume of business.

14-23. College tuition has risen at a pace faster than inflation for more than two decades according to an article in *USA Today* (Andriene Lewis, "Tuition outstrips inflation," January 5, 2004). The following data indicate the average college tuition (in 2003 dollars) for private and public colleges:

Period	1983–84	1988–89	1993–94	1998–99	2003–04
Private	9,202	12,146	13,844	16,454	19,710
Public	2,074	2,395	3,188	3,632	4,694

a. Conduct a simple linear regression analysis of these data in which the average tuition for private colleges is predicted by the average public college tuition. Test the significance of the model using an $\alpha = 0.10$.

b. How much does the average private college tuition increase when the average public college tuition increases by $100?

c. When the average public college tuition reaches $7,500, how much would you expect the average private college tuition to be?

Computer Database Exercises

14-24. The consumer price index (CPI) is a measure of the average change in prices over time in a fixed market basket of goods and services typically purchased by consumers. The CPI for all urban consumers covers about 80% of the total population. It is prepared and published by the Bureau of Labor Statistics of the Department of Labor, which measures average changes in prices of goods and services. The Consumer Price Index is one way the government measures the general level of inflation. The annual percentage change in the value of this index is one way of measuring the annual inflation rate. The file entitled **CPI** contains the monthly CPI and inflation rate for the period 2000–2005.

a. Construct a scatter plot of the CPI versus inflation for the period 2000–2005. Describe the relationship that appears to exist between these two variables.

b. Conduct a hypothesis test to confirm your preconception of the relationship between the CPI and the inflation rate. Use $\alpha = 0.05$.

c. Does it appear that the CPI and the inflation rate are measuring the same component of our economy? Support your assertion with statistical reasoning.

14-25. The National Football League is arguably the most successful professional sports league in the United States. Following the 2005 season, the NFL commissioner's office staff performed an analysis in which a simple linear regression model was developed with average home attendance used as the dependent variable and the total number of games won during the season as the independent variable. The staff was interested in determining whether

games won could be used as a predictor for average attendance. Develop the simple linear regression model. (*Data source*: http://sports.espn.go.com.) The data are in the file called **NFL-2005**.

a. What percentage of total variation in average home attendance is explained by knowing the number of games the team won?

b. What is the standard error of the estimate for this regression model?

c. Using $\alpha = 0.05$, test to determine whether the regression slope coefficient is significantly different from 0.

d. After examining the regression analysis results, what should the NFL staff conclude about how the average attendance is related to the number of games the team won during the 2005 season?

14-26. The file **Online** contains a random sample of 48 customers who made purchases last quarter from an online retailer. The file contains information related to the time each customer spent viewing the online catalog and the dollar amount of purchases made. The retailer would like to analyze the sample data to determine whether a relationship exists between the time spent viewing the online catalog and the dollar amount of purchases.

a. Compute the regression equation based on these sample data and interpret the regression coefficients.

b. Compute the coefficient of determination and interpret its meaning.

c. Test the significance of the overall regression model using a significance level of 0.01.

d. Test to determine whether the true regression slope coefficient is equal to 0. Use a significance level of 0.01 to conduct the hypothesis test.

14-27. In a press release entitled "College Board Offers Glimpse of New SAT with Writing for Upcoming Class of '06," August 30, 2005, the College Board announced SAT scores for students in the class of 2005, the last to take the former version of the SAT featuring math and verbal sections. The board indicated that for the class of 2005, the average SAT math scores continued their strong upward trend, increasing from 518 in 2004 to 520 this year, 14 points above 10 years ago and an all-time high. The file entitled **MathSAT** contains the math SAT scores for the interval 1967 to 2005.

a. Produce a scatter plot of the average SAT math scores versus the year they were taken for all students (male and female) during the last 10 years (1996–2005).

b. Construct a regression equation to predict the average math scores with the year as the predictor.

c. Use regression to determine if the College Board's assertion concerning the improvement in SAT average math test scores over the last 10 years is overly optimistic.

14-28. One of the editors of a major automobile publication has collected data on 30 of the best-selling cars in the United States. The data are in a file called **Automobiles**. The editor is particularly interested in the relationship between highway mileage and curb weight of the vehicles.

a. Develop a scatter plot for these data. Discuss what the plot implies about the relationship between the two variables. Assume that you wish to predict highway mileage by using vehicle curb weight.

b. Compute the correlation coefficient for the two variables and test to determine whether there is a linear relationship between the curb weight and the highway mileage of automobiles.

c. (1) Compute the linear regression equation based on the sample data. (2) Cadillac's 1999 Sedan DeVille weighs approximately 4,012

pounds. Provide an estimate of the average highway mileage you would expect to obtain from this model.

14-29. *The Insider View of Las Vegas* Web site (www.insidervlv.com) furnishes information and facts concerning Las Vegas. A set of data published by them provides the amount of gaming revenue for various portions of Clark County, Nevada. The file entitled **VEGAS** provides the gaming revenue for the year 2005.

a. Compute the linear regression equation to predict the gaming revenue for Clark County based on the gaming revenue of the Las Vegas Strip.

b. Conduct a hypothesis test to determine if the gaming revenue from the Las Vegas Strip can be used to predict the gaming revenue for all of Clark County.

c. Estimate the increased gaming revenue that would accrue to all of Clark County if the gaming revenue on the Las Vegas Strip were to increase by a million dollars.

14.3 Uses for Regression Analysis

CHAPTER OUTCOME #5

Regression analysis is a statistical tool that is used for two main purposes: description and prediction. This section discusses these two applications.

Regression Analysis for Description

Business Application

Excel and Minitab Tutorial

CAR MILEAGE In the summer of 2006, gasoline prices soared to record levels in the United States, heightening motor vehicle customers' concern for fuel economy. Analysts at a major automobile company collected data on a variety of variables for a sample of 30 different cars and small trucks. Included among those data were the EPA highway mileage rating and the horsepower of each vehicle. The analysts were interested with the relationship between horsepower (x) and highway mileage (y). The data are contained in the file **Automobiles** on the CD-ROM.

A simple linear regression model can be developed using Excel or Minitab. The Excel output is shown in Figure 14.19. For these sample data, the coefficient of determination, $R^2 = 0.3016$, indicates that knowing the horsepower of the vehicle explains 30.16% of the variation in the highway mileage. The estimated regression equation is

$$\hat{y} = 31.1658 - 0.0286x$$

Before the analysts attempt to describe the relationship between horsepower and highway mileage, they first need to test whether there is a statistically significant linear relationship between the two variables. To do this, they can apply the *t*-test described in Section 14.2 to test the following null and alternative hypotheses:

$$H_0: \beta_1 = 0$$
$$H_A: \beta_1 \neq 0$$

at the significance level

$$\alpha = 0.05$$

FIGURE 14.19

Excel 2007 Regression Results for the Automobile Mileage Study

Excel 2007 Instructions:
1. Open file: Automobiles.xls.
2. Click on **Data** tab.
3. Select **Data Analysis > Regression**.
4. Define y variable range (Highway Mileage) and x variable range (Horse Power).
5. Check **Labels**.
6. Specify Output Location.
7. Click **OK**.

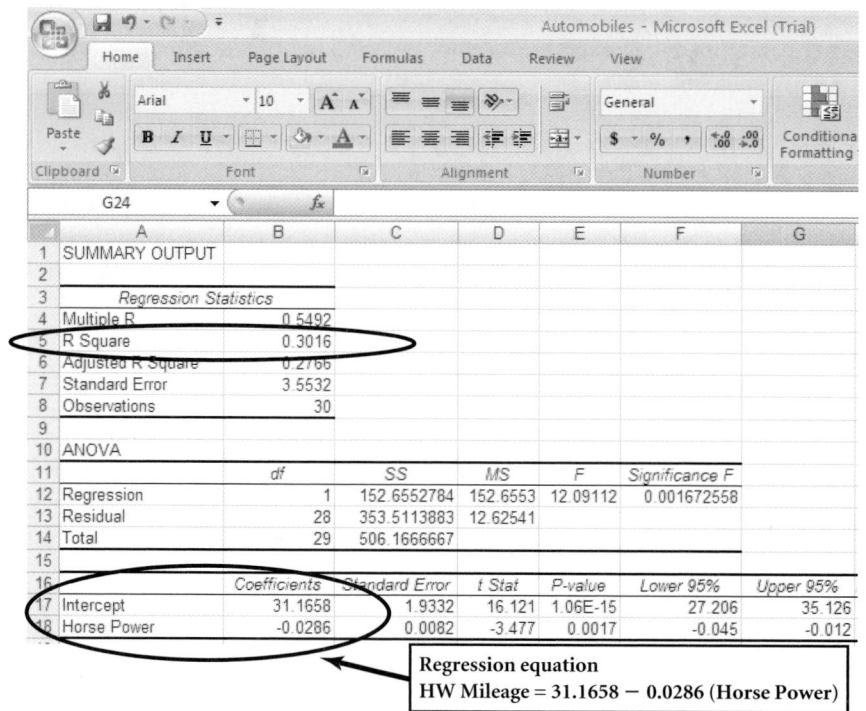

Regression equation
HW Mileage = 31.1658 − 0.0286 (Horse Power)

Minitab Instructions (for similar results):
1. Open file: Automobiles.MTW.
2. Choose **Stat > Regression > Regression.**
3. In **Response**, enter the y variable column.
4. In **Predictors**, enter the x variable column.
5. Click **OK**.

The calculated t statistic and the corresponding p-value are shown in Figure 14.19. Because the

$$p\text{-value (Significance F)} = 0.0017 < 0.05$$

the null hypothesis, H_0, is rejected and the analysts can conclude that the population regression slope is not equal to 0.

The sample slope, b_1, equals -0.0286. This means that for each 1-unit increase in horsepower, the highway mileage decreases by an average of 0.0286 miles per gallon. However, b_1 is subject to sampling error and is considered a *point estimate* for the true regression slope coefficient. From earlier discussions about point estimates in Chapters 8 and 10, we expect that $b_1 \neq \beta_1$. Therefore, to fully describe the relationship between the independent variable, horsepower, and the dependent variable, highway miles per gallon, we need to develop a *confidence interval estimate* for β_1. Equation 14.22 is used to do this.

CHAPTER OUTCOME #6

Confidence Interval Estimate for the Regression Slope, Simple Linear Regression

$$b_1 \pm t s_{b_1} \tag{14.22}$$

or equivalently,

$$b_1 \pm t \frac{s_\varepsilon}{\sqrt{\sum(x - \bar{x})^2}} \qquad df = n - 2$$

where:

s_{b_1} = Standard error of the regression slope coefficient

s_ε = Standard error of the estimate

The regression output shown in Figure 14.19 contains the 95% confidence interval estimate for the slope coefficient, which is

$$-0.045 \text{ ----------------- } -0.012$$

Thus, at the 95% confidence level, based on the sample data, the analysts for the car company can conclude that a 1-unit increase in horsepower will result in a drop in mileage by an average amount between 0.012 and 0.045 miles per gallon.

There are many other situations in which the prime purpose of regression analysis is description. Economists use regression analysis for descriptive purposes as they search for a way of explaining the economy. Market researchers also use regression analysis, among other techniques, in an effort to describe the factors that influence the demand for products.

EXAMPLE 14-4 Developing a Confidence Interval Estimate for the Regression Slope

TRY PROBLEM 14.31

Home Prices Home values are determined by a variety of factors. One factor is the size of the house (square feet). Recently, a study was conducted by First City Real Estate aimed at estimating the average value of each additional square foot of space in a house. A simple random sample of 319 homes that were sold within the past year was collected. The data are in a file called **First-City** on the CD-ROM. Here are the steps required to compute a confidence interval estimate for the regression slope coefficient:

Step 1 **Define the *y* (dependent) and *x* (independent) variables.**
The dependent variable is sales price, and the independent variable is square feet.

Step 2 **Obtain the sample data.**
The study consists of sales prices and corresponding square feet for a random sample of 319 homes.

Step 3 **Compute the regression equation and the standard error of the slope coefficient.**
These computations can be performed manually using Equations 14.7 and 14.8 for the regression model and Equation 14.20 for the standard error of the slope. Alternatively, we can use Excel or Minitab to obtain these values.

	Coefficients	Standard Error
Intercept (b_0)	39,838.48	7,304.95
Square Feet (b_1)	75.70	3.78

The point estimate for the regression slope coefficient is $75.70. Thus, for a 1-square-foot increase in the size of a house, house prices increase by an average of $75.70. This is a point estimate and is subject to sampling error.

Step 4 **Construct and interpret the confidence interval estimate for the regression slope using Equation 14.22.**
The confidence interval estimate is

$$b_1 \pm t s_{b_1}$$

where the degrees of freedom for the critical *t* is $319 - 2 = 317$. The critical *t* for a 95% confidence interval estimate is approximately 1.96, and the interval estimate is

$$\$75.70 \pm 1.96(\$3.78)$$
$$\$75.70 \pm \$7.41$$
$$\$68.29 \text{ ----------------- } \$83.11$$

So, for a 1-square-foot increase in house size, at the 95% confidence level, homes increase in price by an average of between $68.29 and $83.11.

Regression Analysis for Prediction

Business Application

CHAPTER OUTCOME #5

FREEDOM HOSPITAL One of the main uses of regression analysis is *prediction*. You may need to predict the value of the dependent variable based on the value of the independent variable. Consider the administrator for Freedom Hospital, who has been asked by the hospital's board of directors to develop a model to predict the total charges for a geriatric patient. The CD-ROM file **Patients** contains the data that the administrator has collected.

Although the Regression tool in Excel works well for generating the simple linear regression equation and other useful information, it does not provide predicted values for the dependent variable. However, both Minitab and the PHStat add-ins do provide predictions. We will illustrate the Minitab output, which is formatted somewhat differently from the Excel output but contains the same basic information.

The administrator is attempting to construct a simple linear regression model, with total charges as the dependent (y) variable and length of stay as the independent (x) variable. Figure 14.20 shows the Minitab regression output. The least squares regression equation is

$$\hat{y} = 528 + 1{,}353x$$

As shown in the figure, the regression slope coefficient is significantly different from 0 ($t = 14.17$; p-value $= 0.000$). The model explains 59.6% of the variation in the total charges (R-squared $= 59.6\%$). Notice in Figure 14.20 that Minitab has rounded the regression coefficient. The more precise values are provided in the column headed "Coef" and are

$$\hat{y} = 527.6 + 1{,}352.80x$$

The administrator could use this equation to predict total charges by substituting the length of stay into the regression equation for x. For example, suppose a patient has a five-day stay. The predicted total charges are

$$\hat{y} = 527.6 + 1{,}352.80(5)$$
$$\hat{y} = \$7{,}291.60$$

FIGURE 14.20

Minitab Regression Output for Freedom Hospital

Minitab Instructions:
1. Open file: Patients.MTW.
2. Choose **Stat > Regression > Regression**.
3. In **Response**, enter the y variable column.
4. In **Predictors**, enter the x variable column.
5. Click **OK**.

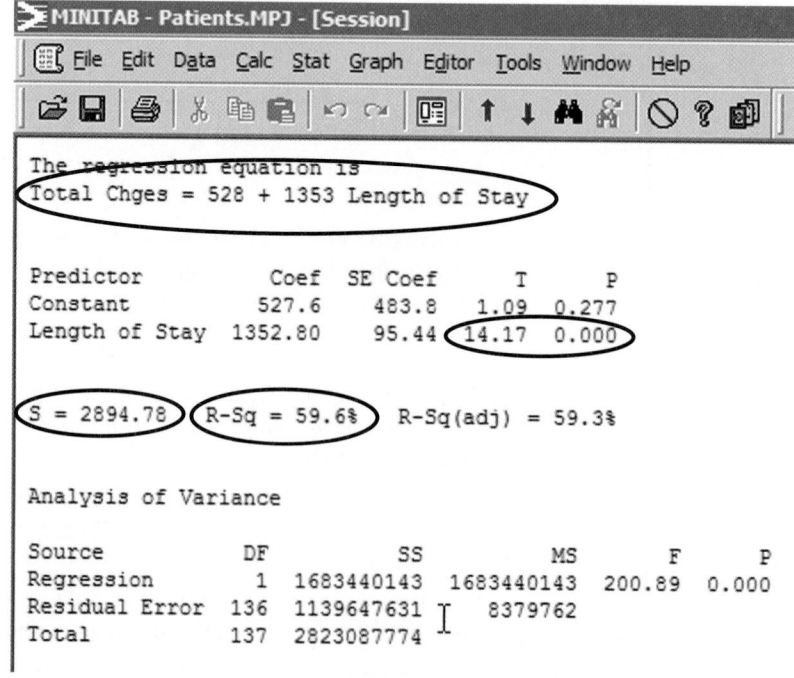

Note that this predicted value is a *point estimate* of the actual charges for this patient. The true charges will be either higher or lower than this amount. The administrator can develop a prediction interval, which is similar to the confidence interval estimates developed in Chapter 8.

Excel and Minitab Tutorial

CHAPTER OUTCOME #6

Confidence Interval for the Average y, Given x The marketing manager might like a 95% confidence interval for *average* charges for all patients who stay in the hospital five days. The confidence interval for the expected value of a dependent variable, given a specific level of the independent variable, is determined by Equation 14.23. Observe that the specific value of *x* used to provide the prediction is denoted as x_p.

Confidence Interval for $E(y)|x_p$

$$\hat{y} \pm ts_\varepsilon \sqrt{\frac{1}{n} + \frac{(x_p - \bar{x})^2}{\Sigma(x - \bar{x})^2}} \tag{14.23}$$

where:

$\hat{y}$ = Point estimate of the dependent variable
t = Critical value with $n - 2\,df$
n = Sample size
x_p = Specific value of the independent variable
$\bar{x}$ = Mean of the independent variable observations in the sample
s_ε = Estimate of the standard error of the estimate

Although the confidence interval estimate can be manually computed using Equation 14.23, using your computer is much easier. Both PHStat and Minitab have built-in options to generate the confidence interval estimate for the dependent variable for a given value of the *x* variable. Figure 14.21 shows the Minitab results when length of stay, *x*, equals five days. Given this length of stay, the point estimate for the mean total charges is rounded by Minitab to $7,292, and at the 95% confidence level, the administrators believe the mean total charges will be in the interval $6,790 to $7,794.

Excel and Minitab Tutorial

Prediction Interval for a Particular y, Given x The confidence interval shown in Figure 14.21 is for the average value of *y* given x_p. The administrator might also be interested in predicting the total charges for a *particular* patient with a five-day stay, rather than the average of the charges for all patients staying five days. Developing this 95% prediction interval requires only a slight modification to Equation 14.23. This prediction interval is given by Equation 14.24.

FIGURE 14.21
_____

**Minitab Output:
Freedom Hospital
Confidence Interval
Estimate**

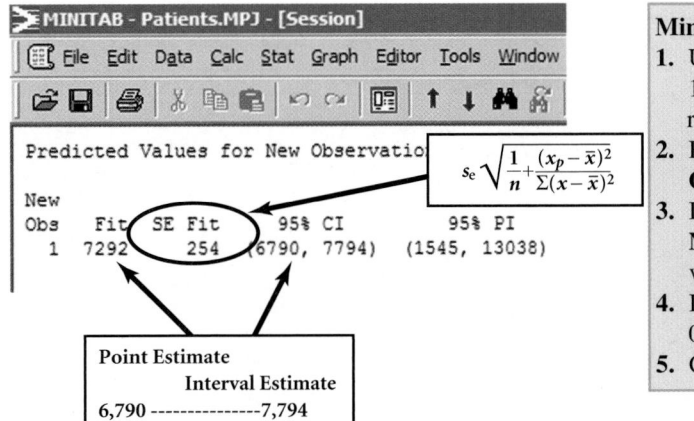

Minitab Instructions:
1. Use Instructions in Figure 14.20 to get regression results.
2. Before clicking **OK**. select **Options**.
3. In **Prediction Interval for New Observations** enter value(s) of *x* variable.
4. In **Confidence level**, enter 0.95.
5. Click **OK. OK.**

Prediction Interval for $y|x_p$

$$\hat{y} \pm ts_{\varepsilon}\sqrt{1 + \frac{1}{n} + \frac{(x_p - \bar{x})^2}{\Sigma(x - \bar{x})^2}} \qquad (14.24)$$

As was the case with the confidence interval application discussed previously, the manual computations required to use Equation 14.24 can be onerous. We recommend using your computer and software such as Minitab or PHStat to find the prediction interval. Figure 14.22 shows the PHStat results. Note that the same PHStat process generates both the prediction and confidence interval estimates.

Based on this regression model, at the 95% confidence level, the hospital administrators can predict total charges for any patient with length of stay of five days to be between $1,545 and $13,038. As you can see, this prediction has extremely poor precision. We doubt any hospital administrator will use a prediction interval that is so wide. Although the regression model explains a significant proportion of variation in the dependent variable, it is relatively imprecise for predictive purposes. To improve the precision, we might decrease the confidence requirements or increase the sample size and redevelop the model.

The prediction interval for a specific value of the dependent variable is wider (less precise) than the confidence interval for predicting the average value of the dependent variable. This will always be the case, as seen in Equations 14.23 and 14.24. From an intuitive viewpoint, we should expect to come closer to predicting an average value than a single value.

Note, the term $(x_p - \bar{x})^2$ has a particular effect on the confidence interval determined by both Equations 14.23 and 14.24. The farther x_p (the value of the independent variable used to predict y), is from $\bar{x}$, the greater $(x_p - \bar{x})^2$ becomes. Figure 14.23 shows two regression lines developed from two samples with the same set of x-values. We have made both lines pass through the same $(\bar{x}, \bar{y})$ point; however, they have different slopes and intercepts.

FIGURE 14.22

Excel 2007 (PHStat) Prediction Interval for Freedom Hospital

Excel 2007 (PHStat) Instructions:
1. Open file: Patients.xls.
2. Click on **Add-Ins > PHStat**.
3. Select **Regression > Simple Linear Regression**.
4. Define y variable range (Total Charges) and x variable range (Length of Stay).
5. Select **Confidence and Prediction Interval** – set $x = 5$ and 95% confidence.

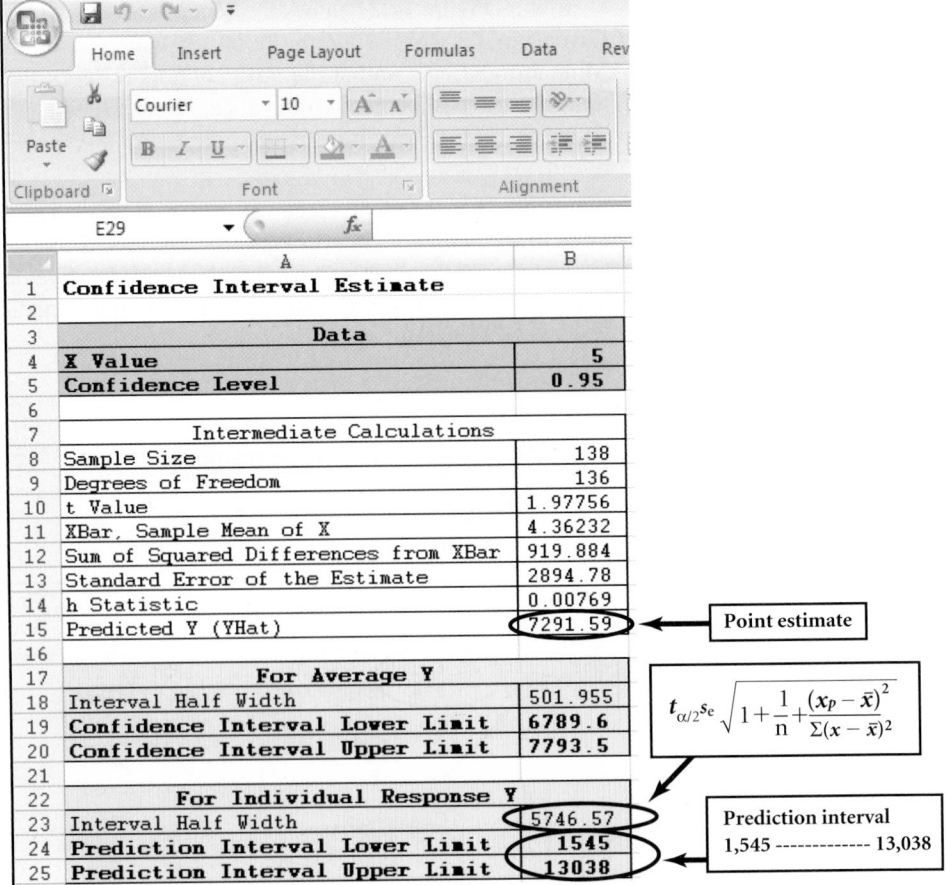

	A	B
1	**Confidence Interval Estimate**	
2		
3	**Data**	
4	**X Value**	**5**
5	**Confidence Level**	**0.95**
6		
7	Intermediate Calculations	
8	Sample Size	138
9	Degrees of Freedom	136
10	t Value	1.97756
11	XBar, Sample Mean of X	4.36232
12	Sum of Squared Differences from XBar	919.884
13	Standard Error of the Estimate	2894.78
14	h Statistic	0.00769
15	Predicted Y (YHat)	7291.59
16		
17	**For Average Y**	
18	Interval Half Width	501.955
19	**Confidence Interval Lower Limit**	**6789.6**
20	**Confidence Interval Upper Limit**	**7793.5**
21		
22	**For Individual Response Y**	
23	Interval Half Width	5746.57
24	**Prediction Interval Lower Limit**	**1545**
25	**Prediction Interval Upper Limit**	**13038**

Point estimate

$$t_{\alpha/2}s_e\sqrt{1 + \frac{1}{n} + \frac{(x_p - \bar{x})^2}{\Sigma(x - \bar{x})^2}}$$

Prediction interval
1,545 ------------ 13,038

FIGURE 14.23

Regression Lines Illustrating the Increase in Potential Variation in y as x_p Moves Farther from $\bar{x}$

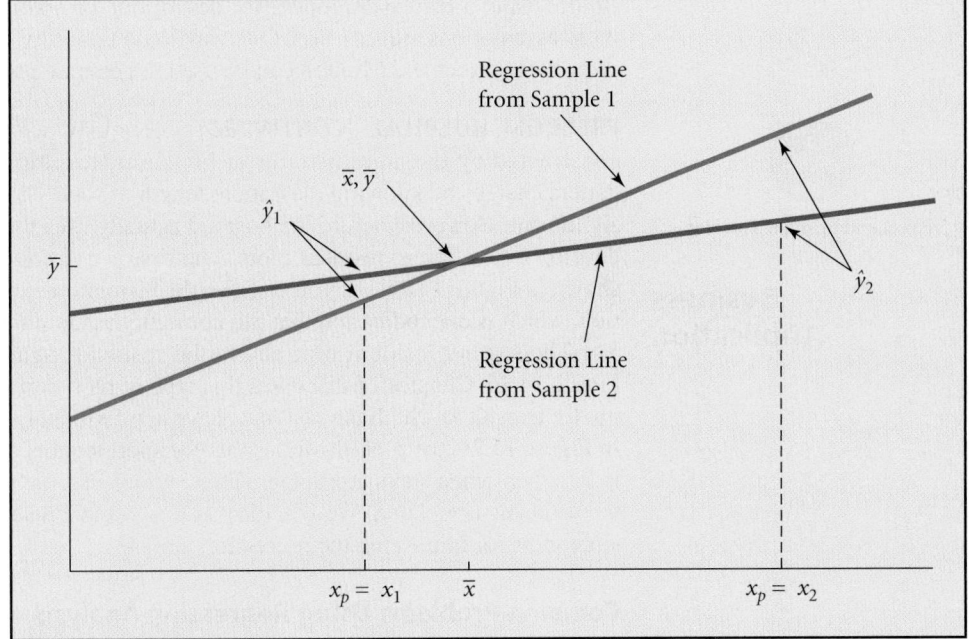

At $x_p = x_1$, the two regression lines give predictions of y that are close to each other. However, for $x_p = x_2$, the predictions of y are quite different. Thus, when x_p is close to $\bar{x}$, the problems caused by variations in regression slopes are not as great as when x_p is far from $\bar{x}$. Figure 14.24 shows the prediction intervals over the range of possible x_p values. The band around the estimated regression line bends away from the regression line as x_p moves in either direction from $\bar{x}$.

Residual Analysis

Recall two important assumptions associated with linear regression analysis.

Assumptions

1. The model errors are normally distributed.
2. The model errors have a constant variance at all levels of the independent variable.

FIGURE 14.24

Confidence Intervals for $y|x_p$ and $E(y)|x_p$

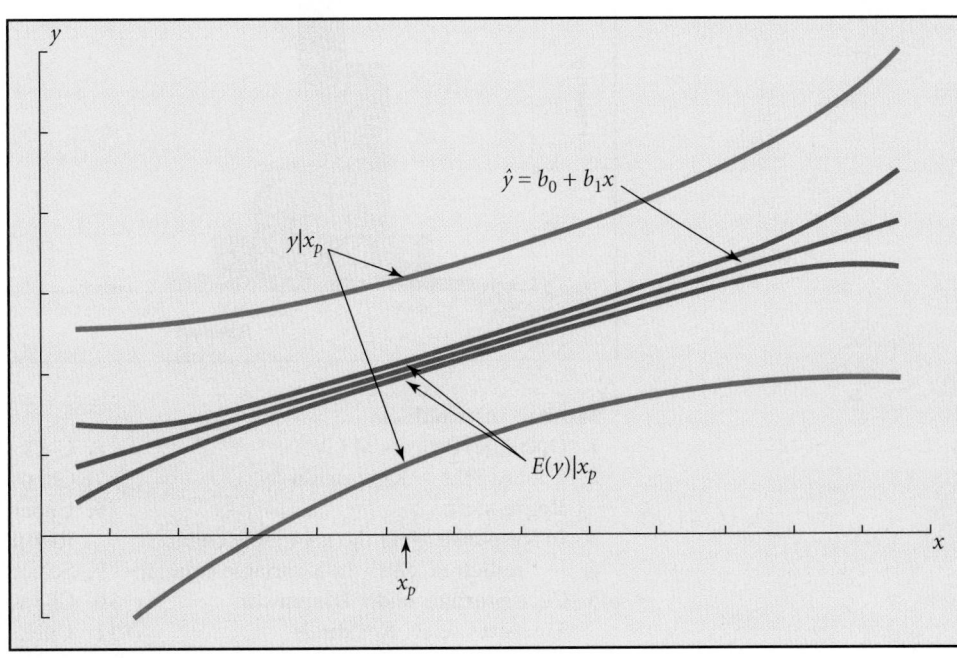

Before using a regression model for description or prediction, you should check to see if these assumptions are satisfied. One way to do this is by examining graphs called *residual plots*. Both Excel and Minitab can be used to generate residual plots.

Excel and Minitab Tutorial

Business Application

FREEDOM HOSPITAL (*CONTINUED*) Previously we showed the regression model constructed by the administrator at Freedom Hospital. He wanted to predict the total patient charges by knowing the patient length of stay. The resulting model was statistically significant. However, before the hospital actually uses this model, the administrator might develop two different residual plots. The first is a *residual frequency histogram*, which is shown in Figure 14.25. As you can see, the histogram closely resembles a normal distribution, which is one indication that the normality assumption is satisfied.

The second residual plot charts the residuals against the *x* variable, as shown in Figure 14.26. Chapter 15 discusses this type of plot more fully. For now, you will be looking for a result in which the residuals have approximately the same spread at all levels of *x*. In Figure 14.26, the plot illustrates that for short lengths of stay, the spread in the residuals is less than when stays are longer. This implies that the assumption of equal variances in the residuals is violated. We will discuss this in more detail in Chapter 15 and suggest possible steps for improving the regression model.

Common Problems Using Regression Analysis

CHAPTER OUTCOME #7

Regression is perhaps the most widely used statistical tool other than descriptive statistical techniques. Because it is so widely used, you need to be aware of the common problems found when the technique is employed.

One potential problem occurs when decision makers apply regression analysis for predictive purposes. The conclusions and inferences made from a regression line are statistically valid only over the range of the data contained in the sample used to develop the regression line. For instance, in the Midwest Distribution example, we analyzed the

FIGURE 14.25

Minitab Residual Frequency Histogram for Freedom Hospital

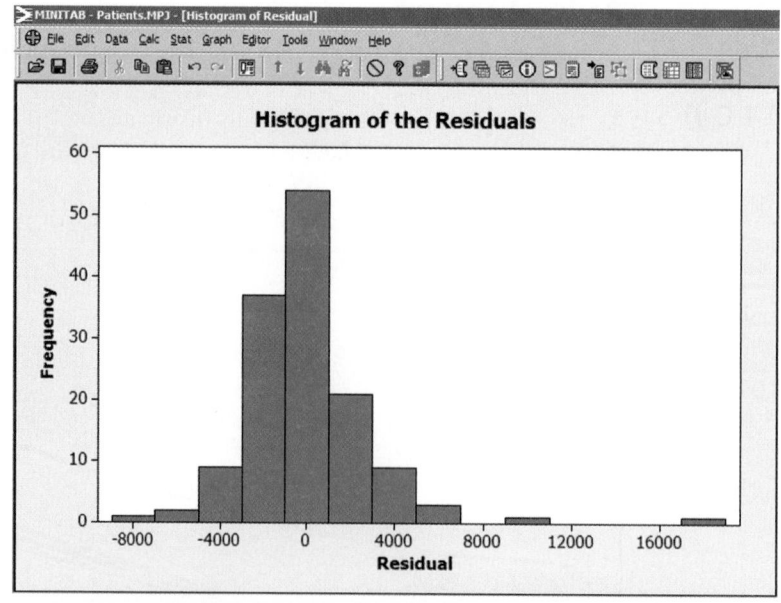

Minitab Instructions:
1. Open file: Patients.MTW.
2. Choose **Stat > Regression > Regression**.
3. In **Response**, enter the *y* variable column.
4. In **Predictors**, enter the *x* variable column.
5. Click **Storage**, under **Diagnostic Measures** select **Residuals**.
6. Click **OK**.
7. Choose **Graphs**.
8. Under **Residuals for Plots**, select **Regular**.
9. Select **Individual Plots**.
10. Choose **Histogram of Residuals**.
11. Click **OK. OK.**

FIGURE 14.26

Minitab Residual Plot for Freedom Hospital Example

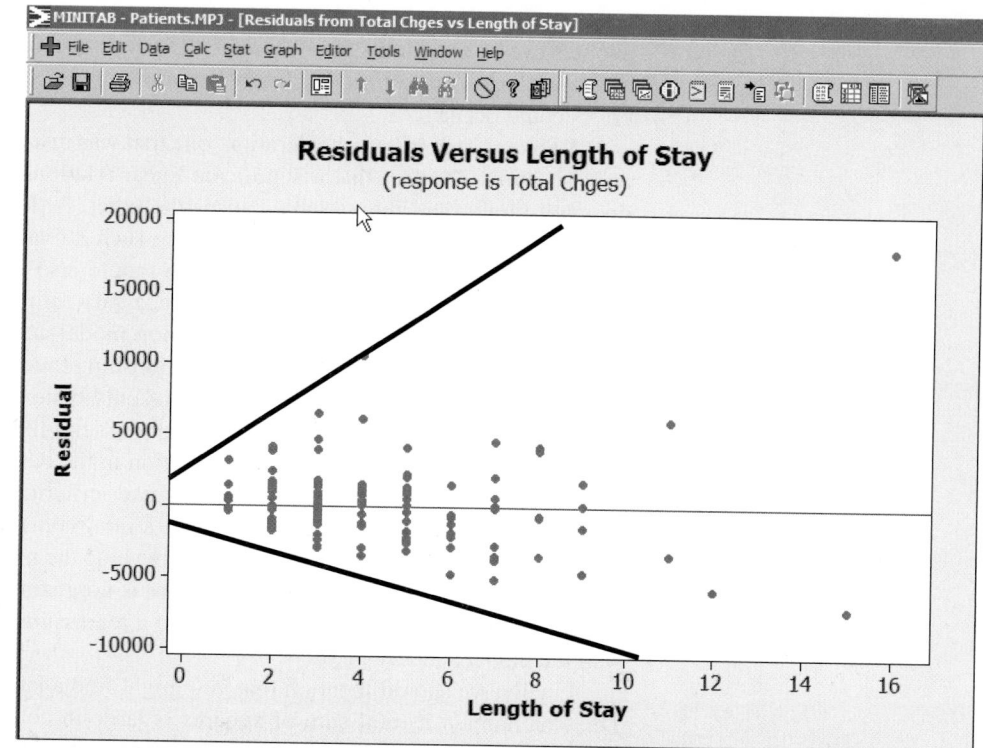

Excel 2007 Instructions (for Similar results):
1. Open file: Patients.xls.
2. Choose **Data > Data Analysis > Regression**.
3. Select data range for *y* variable.
4. Select data range for *x* variable.
5. Check boxes for residuals and residual plots.

Minitab Instructions:
1. Open file: Patients.MTW.
2. Choose **Stat > Regression > Regression**.
3. In **Response** enter the *y* **variable** column.
4. **In Predictors,** enter the *x* variable **column.**
5. Select **Graphs**.
6. In **Residuals versus the variables**, enter the *x* variable column.
7. Click **OK. OK.**

performance of sales representatives with 1 to 9 years of experience. Therefore, predicting sales levels for employees with one to nine years of experience would be justified. However, if we were to try to predict the sales performance of someone with more than nine years of experience, the relationship between sales and experience might be different. Because no observations were taken for experience levels beyond the 1- to 9-year range, we have no information about what might happen outside that range. Figure 14.27 shows a

FIGURE 14.27

Graph for a Sales Peak at 20 Years

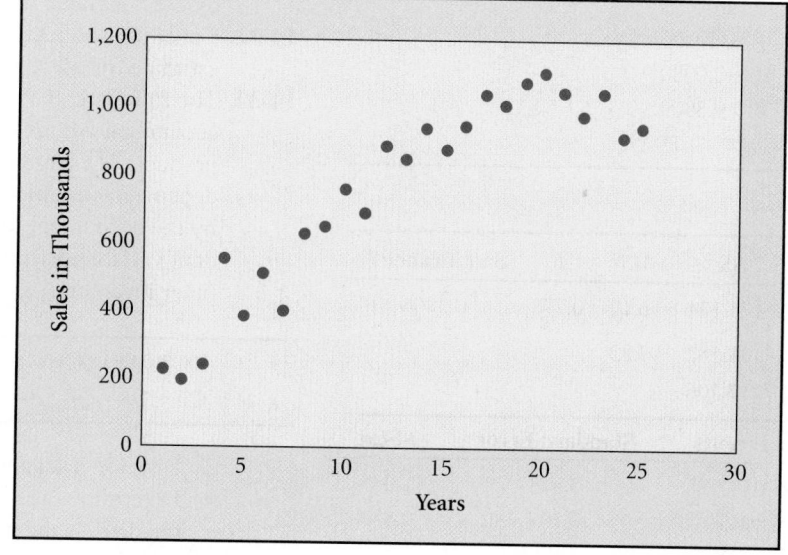

case in which the true relationship between sales and experience reaches a peak value at about 20 years and then starts to decline. If a linear regression equation were used to predict sales based on experience levels beyond the relevant range of data, large prediction errors could occur.

A second important consideration, one that was discussed earlier, involves correlation and causation. The fact that a significant linear relationship exists between two variables does not imply that one variable causes the other. Although there may be a cause-and-effect relationship, you should not infer that such a relationship is present based only on regression and/or correlation analysis. You should also recognize that a cause-and-effect relationship between two variables is not necessary for regression analysis to be an effective tool. What matters is that the regression model accurately reflects the relationship between the two variables and that the relationship remains stable.

Many users of regression analysis mistakenly believe that a high coefficient of determination (R^2) guarantees that the regression model will be a good predictor. You should remember that R^2 is a measure of the variation in the dependent variable explained by the independent variable. Although the least squares criterion assures us that R^2 will be maximized (because the sum of squares error is a minimum) for the given set of sample data, the value applies only to those data used to develop the model. Thus, R^2 measures the fit of the regression line to the sample data. There is no guarantee that there will be an equally good fit with new data. The only true test of a regression model's predictive ability is how well the model actually predicts.

Finally, we should mention that you might find a large R^2 with a large standard error. This can happen if total sum of squares is large in comparison to the SSE. Then, even though R^2 is relatively large, so too is the estimate of the model's standard error. Thus, confidence and prediction errors may be simply too wide for the model to be used in many situations. This is discussed more fully in Chapter 15.

14-3: Exercises

Skill Development

Problems 14-30 and 14-31 refer to the following output for a simple linear regression model:

Summary Output

Regression Statistics

Multiple R	0.1027
R-Square	0.0105
Adjusted R-Square	−0.0030
Standard Error	9.8909
Observations	75

Anova

	df	SS	MS	F	Significance F
Regression	1	76.124	76.12	0.778	0.3806
Residual	73	7141.582	97.83		
Total	74	7217.706			

	Coefficents	Standard Error	t-Stat
Intercept	4.0133	3.878	1.035
x	0.0943	0.107	0.882

	p-value	Lower 95%	Upper 95%
Intercept	0.3041	−3.715	11.742
x	0.3806	−0.119	0.307

14-30. Referring to the displayed regression model, what percent of variation in the y variable is explained by the x variable in the model?

14-31. Construct and interpret a 90% confident interval estimate for the regression slope coefficient.

14-32. The following data have been collected by an accountant who is performing an audit of paper products at a large office supply company. The dependent variable, y, is the time taken (in minutes) by the accountant to count the units. The independent variable, x, is the number of units on the computer inventory record.

y	23.1	100.5	242.9	56.4	178.7	10.5	94.2	200.4	44.2	128.7	180.5
x	24	120	228	56	190	13	85	190	32	120	230

a. Develop a scatter plot for these data.
b. Determine the regression equation representing the data. Is the model significant? Test using a

significance level of 0.10 and the *p*-value approach.

c. Develop a 90% confidence interval estimate for the true regression slope and interpret this interval estimate. Based on this interval, could you conclude the accountant takes an additional minute to count each additional unit?

14-33. You are given the following sample data:

x	y
10	3
6	7
9	3
3	8
2	9
8	5
3	7

a. Develop a scatter plot for these data.
b. Determine the regression equation for the data.
c. Develop a 95% confidence interval estimate for the true regression slope and interpret this interval estimate.
d. Provide a 95% prediction interval estimate for a particular *y*, given $x_p = 7$.

14-34. You are given the following summary statistics from a regression analysis:

$$\hat{y} = 200 + 150x$$
$$SSE = 25.25$$
$$SSX = \text{Sum of squares } X = \Sigma(x - \bar{x})^2 = 99,645$$
$$n = 18$$
$$\bar{x} = 52.0$$

a. Determine the point estimate for *y* if $x_p = 48$ is used.
b. Provide a 95% confidence interval estimate for the average *y*, given $x_p = 48$. Interpret this interval.
c. Provide a 95% prediction interval estimate for a particular *y*, given $x_p = 48$. Interpret.
d. Discuss the difference between the estimates provided in parts b and c.

14-35. The sales manager at Sun City Real Estate Company in Tempe, Arizona, is interested in describing the relationship between condo sales prices and the number of weeks the condo is on the market before it sells. He has collected a random sample of 17 low-end condos that have sold within the past three months in the Tempe area. These data are shown as follows:

Weeks on the Market	Selling Price
23	$76,500
48	$102,000
9	$53,000
26	$84,200
20	$73,000
40	$125,000
51	$109,000
18	$60,000
25	$87,000
62	$94,000
33	$76,000
11	$90,000
15	$61,000
26	$86,000
27	$70,000
56	$133,000
12	$93,000

a. Develop a simple linear regression model to explain the variation in selling price based on the number of weeks the condo is on the market.
b. Test to determine whether the regression slope coefficient is significantly different from 0 using a significance level equal to 0.05.
c. Construct and interpret a 95% confidence interval estimate for the regression slope coefficient.

14-36. A sample of 10 yields the following data:

x	10	8	11	7	10	11	6	7	15	9
y	103	85	115	73	97	102	65	75	155	95

a. Provide a 95% confidence interval for the average *y* when $x_p = 9.4$.
b. Provide a 95% confidence interval for the average *y* when $x_p = 10$.
c. Obtain the margin of errors for both part a and part b. Explain why the margin of error obtained in part b is larger than that in part a.

14-37. A regression analysis from a sample of 15 produced the following:

$$\Sigma(x_i - \bar{x})(y_i - \bar{y}) = 156.4$$
$$\Sigma(x_i - \bar{x})^2 = 173.5$$
$$\Sigma(y_i - \bar{y})^2 = 181.6$$
$$\Sigma(y_i - \hat{y})^2 = 40.621$$
$$\bar{x} = 13.4 \text{ and } \bar{y} = 56.4$$

a. Produce the regression line.
b. Determine if there is a linear relationship between the dependent and independent variables. Use a significance level of 0.05 and a p-value approach.
c. Calculate a 90% confidence interval for the amount the dependent variable changes when the independent variable increases by 1 unit.

Business Applications

14-38. Gym Outfitters sells and services exercise equipment such as treadmills, ellipticals, and stair climbers to gymnasiums and recreational centers. The company's management would like to determine if there is a relationship between the number of minutes required to complete a routine service call and the number of machines serviced. A random sample of 15 records revealed the following information concerning the number of machines serviced and the time (in minutes) to complete the routine service call:

Number of Machines	Service Time (minutes)
11	115
8	60
9	80
10	90
7	55
6	65
8	70
4	33
10	95
5	50
5	40
12	110

a. Estimate the least squares regression equation.
b. If a gymnasium had 6 machines, how many minutes should Gym Outfitters expect a routine service call to require?
c. Provide a 90% confidence interval for the average amount of time required to complete a routine service call when the number of machines being serviced is 9.
d. Provide a 90% prediction interval for the time required to complete a particular routine service call for a gymnasium that has 7 machines.

14-39. The National Association of Realtors Existing-Home Sales Series provides a measurement of the residential real estate market. On or about the 25th of each month, NAR releases statistics on sales and prices of condos and co-ops, in addition to existing single-family homes, for the nation and the four regions. The data presented here indicate the number of (thousands of) existing-home sales as well as condo/co-op sales:

Year		Single-Family Sales	Condo/ Co-op Sales
2005	Apr	6,270	895
	May	6,230	912
	Jun	6,330	943
	Jul	6,220	914
	Aug	6,280	928
	Sept	6,290	908
	Oct	6,180	867
	Nov	6,150	876
	Dec	5,860	885
2006	Jan	5,790	781
	Feb	6,050	852
	Mar	6,040	862
	Apr	5,920	839

a. Construct the regression equation that would predict the number of condo/co-op sales using the number of single-family sales.
b. One might conjecture that these two markets (single-family sales and condo/co-op sales) would be competing for the same audience. Therefore, we would expect that as the number of single-family sales increases, the number of condo/co-op sales would decrease. Conduct a hypothesis test to determine this using a significance level of 0.05.
c. Provide a prediction interval for the number of condo/co-op sales when the number of single-family sales is 6,000 (thousands). Use a confidence level of 95%.

14-40. The following data have been collected by an accountant who is performing an audit of account balances for a major retail company. The population from which the data were collected represented those accounts for which the customer had indicated the balance was incorrect. The dependent variable, y, is the actual account balance as verified by the accountant. The independent variable, x, is the computer account balance.

y	233	10	24	56	78	102	90	200	344	120	18
x	245	12	22	56	90	103	85	190	320	120	23

a. Compute the least squares regression equation.
b. If the computer account balance were 100, what would you expect to be the actual account balance as verified by the accountant?

c. The computer balance for Timothy Jones is listed as 100 in the computer account record. Provide a 90% interval estimate for Mr. Jones's actual account balance.

d. Provide a 90% interval estimate for the average of all customers' actual account balances in which a computer account balance is the same as that of Mr. Jones. (Part c.) Interpret.

14-41. J.D. Power and Associates conducts an initial quality study (IQS) each year to determine the quality of newly manufactured automobiles. IQS measures 135 attributes across nine categories, including ride/handling/braking, engine and transmission, and a broad range of quality problem symptoms reported by vehicle owners. The 2005 Initial Quality Study was based on responses from more than 62,000 purchasers and lessees of new 2005 model-year cars and trucks, who were surveyed after 90 days of ownership. The data given here portray the initial quality industry average of the number of reported problems per 100 vehicles for 1998–2005.

Year	1998	1999	2000	2001	2002	2003	2004	2005
Problems	176	167	154	147	133	133	119	118

a. Construct a scatter plot of the number of reported problems per 100 vehicles as a function of the year.

b. Determine if the average number of reported problems per 100 vehicles declines from year to year. Use a significance level of 0.01 and a *p*-value approach.

c. Assume the relationship between the number of reported problems per 100 vehicles and the year continues into the future. Provide a 95% prediction interval for the initial quality industry average of the number of reported problems per 100 vehicles for 2010.

Computer Database Exercises

14-42. A manufacturer produces a wash-down motor for the food service industry. The company manufactures the motors to order by modifying a base model to meet the specifications requested by the customer. The motors are produced in a batch environment with the batch size equal to the number ordered. The manufacturer has recently sampled 27 customer orders. The motor manufacturer would like to determine if there is a relationship between the cost of producing the order and the order size so that it could estimate the cost of producing a particular size order. The sampled data are contained in the file **Washdown Motors**.

a. Use the sample data to estimate the least squares regression model.

b. Provide an interpretation of the regression coefficients.

c. Test the significance of the overall regression model using a significance level of 0.01.

d. The company has just received an order for 30 motors. Use the regression model developed in part a to estimate the cost of producing this particular order.

e. Referring to part d, what is the 90% confidence interval for an average cost of an order of 30 motors?

14-43. Each month, the Bureau of Labor Statistics (BLS) of the U.S. Department of Labor announces the total number of employed and unemployed persons in the United States for the previous month. At the same time, it also publishes the inflation rate, which is the rate of change in the price of goods and services from one month to the next. It seems quite plausible that there should be some relationship between these two indicators. The file entitled **CPI** provides the monthly unemployment and inflation rates for the period 2000–2005.

a. Construct a scatter plot of the unemployment rate versus inflation rate for the period 2000–2005. Describe the relationship that appears to exist between these two variables.

b. Produce a 95% prediction interval for the unemployment rate for the maximum inflation rate in the period 2000–2005. Interpret the interval.

c. Produce a 95% prediction interval for the unemployment rate when the inflation rate is 0.00.

d. Which of the prediction intervals in parts b and c has the larger margin of error? Explain why this is the case.

14-44. The National Highway Transportation Safety Administration's National Center for Statistics and Analysis released its Vehicle Survivability Travel Mileage Schedules in January 2006. One item investigated was the relationship between the annual vehicle miles traveled (VMT) as a function of vehicle age for passenger cars up to 25 years old. The VMT data were collected by asking consumers to estimate the number of miles driven in a given year. The data were collected over a 14-month period, starting in March 2001 and ending in May 2002. The file entitled **Miles** contains this data.

a. Produce a regression equation modeling the relationship between VMT and the age of the vehicle. Estimate how many more annual vehicle miles would be traveled for a vehicle that is 10 years older than another vehicle.

b. Provide a 90% interval estimate for the average annual vehicle miles traveled when the age of the vehicle is 15 years.

c. Determine if it is plausible for a vehicle that is 10 years old to travel 12,000 miles in a year. Support your answer with statistical reasoning.

Summary and Conclusions

Correlation and regression analysis are two of the most frequently used statistical techniques by business decision makers. This chapter has introduced the basics of these two topics. The discussion of regression analysis has been limited to situations in which you have one dependent variable and one independent variable. In these cases, the technique for modeling the linear relationship between the two variables is referred to as simple linear regression analysis.

If two variables are significantly correlated, then they are said to be linearly related. When that's the case, the resulting simple linear regression model will be statistically significant, which means that the fraction of variation in the dependent variable that is explained by the independent variable (*R*-squared) is significant and the predictions for the *y* variable based on values of *x* will be superior to using the mean of *y* as the predictor.

This chapter introduced the methods used to test whether a correlation is 0 and whether a regression slope coefficient is 0. We also introduced you to the uses of regression for descriptive and predictive purposes and showed how to construct confidence interval estimates for the true regression slope coefficient and prediction intervals.

Chapter 15 will extend the discussion of regression analysis by showing how two or more independent variables are included in the analysis. The focus of that chapter will be on building a model for explaining the variation in the dependent variable. However, the basic concepts presented in this chapter will be carried forward.

Equations

Sample Correlation Coefficient

$$r = \frac{\Sigma(x - \bar{x})(y - \bar{y})}{\sqrt{[\Sigma(x - \bar{x})^2][\Sigma(y - \bar{y})^2]}} \qquad \textbf{(14.1)}$$

or the algebraic equivalent:

$$r = \frac{n\Sigma xy - \Sigma x \Sigma y}{\sqrt{[n(\Sigma x^2) - (\Sigma x)^2][n(\Sigma y^2) - (\Sigma y)^2]}} \qquad \textbf{(14.2)}$$

Test Statistic for Correlation

$$t = \frac{r}{\sqrt{\dfrac{1 - r^2}{n - 2}}} \qquad df = n - 2 \qquad \textbf{(14.3)}$$

Simple Linear Regression Model (Population Model)

$$y = \beta_0 + \beta_1 x + \varepsilon \qquad \textbf{(14.4)}$$

Estimated Regression Model (Sample Model)

$$\hat{y} = b_0 + b_1 x \qquad \textbf{(14.5)}$$

Least Squares Equations (Sample Values)

$$b_1 = \frac{\Sigma(x - \bar{x})(y - \bar{y})}{\Sigma(x - \bar{x})^2} \qquad \textbf{(14.6)}$$

or the algebraic equivalent:

$$b_1 = \frac{\Sigma xy - \dfrac{\Sigma x \Sigma y}{n}}{\Sigma x^2 - \dfrac{(\Sigma x)^2}{n}} \qquad \textbf{(14.7)}$$

and

$$b_0 = \bar{y} - b_1 \bar{x} \qquad \textbf{(14.8)}$$

Sum of Squared Errors

$$SSE = \Sigma y^2 - b_0 \Sigma y - b_1 \Sigma xy \qquad \textbf{(14.9)}$$

Sum of Residuals

$$\sum_{i=1}^{n}(y_i - \hat{y}_i) = 0 \qquad \textbf{(14.10)}$$

Sum of Squared Residuals

$$SSE = \sum_{i=1}^{n}(y_i - \hat{y}_i)^2 \qquad \textbf{(14.11)}$$

Total Sum of Squares

$$SST = \sum_{i=1}^{n}(y_i - \bar{y})^2 \qquad \textbf{(14.12)}$$

Sum of Squares Error

$$SSE = \sum_{i=1}^{n}(y_i - \hat{y}_i)^2 \qquad \textbf{(14.13)}$$

Sum of Squares Regression

$$SSR = \sum_{i=1}^{n} (\hat{y}_i - \bar{y})^2 \qquad \textbf{(14.14)}$$

Coefficient of Determination, R^2

$$R^2 = \frac{SSR}{SST} \qquad \textbf{(14.15)}$$

Coefficient of Determination, Single Independent Variable Case

$$R^2 = r^2 \qquad \textbf{(14.16)}$$

Test Statistic for Significance of the Coefficient of Determination

$$F = \frac{SSR/1}{SSE/(n-2)} \qquad d.f. = D_1 = 1, D_2 = n - 2 \quad \textbf{(14.17)}$$

Simple Regression Standard Deviation of the Slope Coefficient (Population)

$$\sigma_{b_1} = \frac{\sigma_\varepsilon}{\sqrt{\Sigma(x - \bar{x})^2}} \qquad \textbf{(14.18)}$$

Simple Regression Estimator for the Standard Error of the Estimate

$$s_\varepsilon = \sqrt{\frac{SSE}{n-2}} \qquad \textbf{(14.19)}$$

Simple Regression Estimator for the Standard Deviation of the Slope

$$s_{b_1} = \frac{s_\varepsilon}{\sqrt{\Sigma(x - \bar{x})^2}} \qquad \textbf{(14.20)}$$

Simple Linear Regression Test Statistic for Test of the Significance of the Slope

$$t = \frac{b_1 - \beta_1}{s_{b_1}} \qquad df = n - 2 \qquad \textbf{(14.21)}$$

Confidence Interval Estimate for the Regression Slope, Simple Linear Regression

$$b_1 \pm t s_{b_1} \qquad \textbf{(14.22)}$$

or equivalently,

$$b_1 \pm t \frac{s_\varepsilon}{\sqrt{\Sigma(x - \bar{x})^2}} \qquad \text{with } df = n - 2$$

Confidence Interval for $E(y)|x_p$

$$\hat{y} \pm t s_\varepsilon \sqrt{\frac{1}{n} + \frac{(x_p - \bar{x})^2}{\Sigma(x - \bar{x})^2}} \qquad \textbf{(14.23)}$$

Prediction Interval for $y|x_p$

$$\hat{y} \pm t s_\varepsilon \sqrt{1 + \frac{1}{n} + \frac{(x_p - \bar{x})^2}{\Sigma(x - \bar{x})^2}} \qquad \textbf{(14.24)}$$

Key Terms

Coefficient of determination	646	Least squares criterion	635	Scatter plot	622
Correlation coefficient	623	Regression coefficients	634	Simple linear regression	633
Dependent variable	622	Regression slope coefficient	634	Spurious correlation	630
Independent variable	622	Residual	635	Standard error of the estimate	648

Chapter Exercises

Conceptual Questions

14-45. If we select a random sample of data for two variables and, after computing the correlation coefficient, conclude that the two variables may have zero correlation, can we say that there is no relationship between the two variables? Discuss.

14-46. Discuss why prediction intervals that attempt to predict a particular *y*-value are less precise than confidence intervals for predicting an average *y*.

14-47. A statistics student was recently working on a class project that required him to compute a correlation coefficient for two variables. After careful work he arrived at a correlation coefficient of 0.45. Interpret this correlation coefficient for the student who did the calculations.

14-48. Referring to the previous problem, another student in the same class computed a regression equation relating the same two variables. The slope of the equation was found to be −0.735. After trying several times and always coming up with the same result, she felt that she must have been doing something wrong since the value was negative and she knew that this could not be right. Comment on this student's conclusion.

14-49. Consider the two following scenarios:

a. The number of new workers hired per week in your county has a high positive correlation with the average weekly temperature. Can you conclude that an increase in temperature causes an increase in the number of new hires? Discuss.

b. Suppose the stock price and the common dividends declared for a certain company have a high positive correlation. Are you safe in concluding on the basis of the correlation coefficient that an increase in the common dividends declared causes an increase in the stock price? Present other reasons than the correlation coefficient that might lead you to conclude that an increase in common dividends declared causes an increase in the stock price.

14-50. Consider the following set of data:

x	48	27	34	24	49	29	39	38	46	32
y	47	23	31	20	50	48	47	47	42	47

a. Calculate the correlation coefficient of these two variables.

b. Multiply each value of the variable x by 5 and add 10 to the resulting products. Now multiply each value of the variable y by 3 and subtract 7 from the resulting products. Finally, calculate the correlation coefficient of the new x and y variables.

c. Describe the principle that the example developed in parts a and b demonstrates.

14-51. Go to the library and locate an article in a journal related to your major (*Journal of Marketing, Journal of Finance*, etc.) that uses linear regression. Discuss:

a. How the author chose the dependent and independent variables.

b. How the data were gathered.

c. What statistical tests the author used.

d. What conclusions the analysis allowed the author to draw.

Business Applications

14-52. The Farmington City Council recently commissioned a study of park users in their community. Data were collected on the age of the person surveyed and the amount of hours he or she has spent in the park in the past month. The data collected were as follows:

Time in Park	Age
7.2	16
3.5	15
6.6	28
5.4	16
1.5	29
2.3	38
4.4	48
8.8	18
4.9	24
5.1	33
1.0	56

a. Draw a scatter plot for these data and discuss what, if any, relationship appears to be present between the two variables.

b. Compute the correlation coefficient between age and the amount of time spent in the park. Provide an explanation to the Farmington City Council of what the correlation measures.

c. Test to determine whether the amount of time spent in the park increases with the age of the park user. Use a significance level of 0.10. Use a *p*-value approach to conduct this hypothesis test.

14-53. At State University, a study was done to establish whether a relationship existed between student graduating GPA and the SAT verbal score when the student originally entered the university. The sample data are reported as follows:

GPA	2.5	3.2	3.5	2.8	3.0	2.4	3.4	2.9	2.7	3.8
SAT	640	700	550	540	620	490	710	600	505	710

a. Develop a scatter plot for these data and describe what, if any, relationship exists between the two variables, GPA and SAT score.

b. (1) Compute the correlation coefficient. (2) Does it appear that the success of students at State University is related to the SAT verbal scores of those students? Conduct a statistical procedure to answer this question. Use a significance level of 0.01.

c. (1) Compute the regression equation based on these sample data if you wish to predict the university GPA using the student SAT score. (2) Interpret the regression coefficients.

14-54. The Smithfield Organic Milk Company recently studied a random sample of 30 of its distributors and found the correlation between sales and advertising dollars to be 0.67.

   a. Is there a significant linear relationship between sales and advertising? If so, is it fair to conclude that advertising causes sales to increase?

   b. If a regression model were developed using sales as the dependent variable and advertising as the independent variable, determine the proportion of the variation in sales that would be explained by its relationship to advertising. Discuss what this says about the usefulness of using advertising to predict sales.

14-55. A previous exercise citing an article in *USA Today* (Andriene Lewis, "Tuition outstrips inflation," January 5, 2004) discussed the relationship between the average college tuition (in 2003 dollars) for private and public colleges. The data indicated in the article follows:

Period	1983–84	1988–89	1993–94	1998–99	2003–04
Private	9,202	12,146	13,844	16,454	19,710
Public	2,074	2,395	3,188	3,632	4,694

   a. Construct the regression equation that would predict the average college tuition for private colleges using that of the public colleges.

   b. Determine if there is a linear tendency for the average college tuition for private colleges to increase when the average college tuition for public colleges increases. Use a significance level of 0.05 and a *p*-value approach.

   c. Provide a 95% confidence interval for the average college tuition for private colleges when the average college tuition for public colleges reaches $5,000.

   d. Is it plausible that the average college tuition for private colleges would be larger than $25,000 when the average college tuition for public colleges reaches $5,000? Support you assertion with statistical reasoning.

14-56. An American airline company recently performed a customer survey in which it asked a random sample of 100 passengers to indicate their income and the total cost of the airfares they have purchased for pleasure trips during the past year. A regression model was developed for the purposes of determining whether income could be used as a variable to explain the variation in number of times individuals fly on airlines in a year. The following regression results were obtained:

$$\hat{y} = 0.25 + 0.0150x$$
$$s_{\varepsilon} = 721.44$$
$$R^2 = 0.65$$
$$s_{b_1} = 0.0000122$$

   a. Produce an estimate of the maximum and minimum amount of difference in the amounts allocated to purchase airline tickets by two families that have a difference of $20,000 in family income. Assume that you wish to use a 90% confidence level.

   b. Can the intercept of the regression equation be interpreted in this case, assuming that no one who was surveyed had an income of 0 dollars? Explain.

   c. Use the information provided to perform an *F*-test for the significance of the regression model. Discuss your results, assuming the test is performed at the significance level of 0.05.

14-57. One of the advances that have helped to diminish carpal tunnel syndrome is ergonomic keyboards. The ergonomic keyboards may also increase typing speed. Ten administrative assistants were chosen to type on both standard and ergonomic keyboards. The resulting typing speeds follow:

Ergonomic:	69	80	60	71	73	64	63	70	63	74
Standard:	70	68	54	56	58	64	62	51	64	53

   a. Produce a scatter plot of the typing speed of administrative assistants using ergonomic and standard keyboards. Does there appear to be a linear relationship between these two variables? Explain your response.

   b. Calculate the correlation coefficient of the typing speed of administrative assistants using ergonomic and standard keyboards.

   c. Conduct a hypothesis test to determine if a positive correlation exists between administrative assistants using ergonomic and standard keyboards. Use a significance level of 0.05.

14-58. A company is considering recruiting new employees from a particular college and plans to place a great deal of emphasis on the student's college grade point average (GPA). However, the company is aware that not all schools have the same grading standards, so it is possible that a student at this school might have a lower (or higher) GPA than a student from another school, yet really be on par with the other student. To make this comparison between schools, the company has devised a test that it has administered utilizing a sample size of 400 students. With the results of the test, it has developed a regression model that it uses to predict student GPA. The following equation represents the model:

$$\hat{y} = 1.0 + 0.028x$$

The R^2 for this model is 0.88 and the standard error of the estimate is 0.20, based on the sample data used to develop the model. Note that the dependent variable is the GPA and the independent variable is test score, where this score can range from 0 to 100. For the sample data used to develop the model, the following values are known:

$$\bar{y} = 2.76$$
$$\bar{x} = 68$$
$$\Sigma(x - \bar{x})^2 = 148,885.73$$

a. Based on the information contained in this problem, can you conclude that as the test score increases, the GPA will also increase, using a significance level of 0.05?

b. Suppose a student interviews with this company, takes the company test, and scores 80 correct. What is the 90% prediction interval estimate for this student's GPA? Interpret the interval.

c. Suppose the student in part b actually has a 2.90 GPA at this school. Based on this evidence, what might be concluded about this person's actual GPA compared with other students with the same GPA at other schools? Discuss the limitations you might place on this conclusion.

d. Suppose a second student with a 2.45 GPA took the test and scored 65 correct. What is the 90% prediction interval for this student's "real" GPA? Interpret.

Computer Database Exercises

14-59. The Briggs Bank and Trust recently performed a study of its checking account customers. One objective of the study was to determine whether it is possible to explain the variation in average checking account balance by knowing the number of checks written per month. The sample data selected are contained in the data file named **Briggs**.

a. Draw a scatter plot for these data.

b. Develop the least squares regression equation for these data.

c. Develop the 90% confidence interval estimate for the change in the average checking account balance when a person who formerly wrote 25 checks a month doubled the number of checks used.

d. Test to determine if an increase in the number of checks written by an individual can be used to predict the checking account balance of that individual. Use $\alpha = 0.05$. Comment on this result and the result of part c.

14-60. An economist for the state government of Mississippi recently collected the data contained in the file called **Mississippi** on the percentage of people unemployed in the state at randomly selected points in time over the past 25 years and

the interest rate of Treasury bills offered by the federal government at that point in time.

a. (1) Develop a plot showing the relationship between the two variables. (2) Describe the relationship as being either linear or curvilinear.

b. (1) Develop a simple linear regression model with unemployment rate as the dependent variable. (2) Write a short report describing the model and indicating the important measures.

14-61. The Cooley Service Center polishes and cleans automobiles. It has major accounts, such as the Bayview Taxi Service and Bayview Police Department, and also does work for the general public by appointment. Recently, the manager decided to survey customers to determine how satisfied they were with the work performed by the Cooley Service Center. He devised a rating scale between 0 and 100, with 0 being poor and 100 being excellent service. He selected a random sample of 14 customers and asked the customers when they picked up their cars to rate the service. He also recorded the amount of time spent on each customer's car. These data are in the data file named **Cooley**.

a. (1) Draw a scatter plot showing these two variables, with the y variable on the vertical axis and the x variable on the horizontal axis. (2) Describe the relationship between these two variables.

b. (1) Develop a linear regression model to explain the variation in the service rating. (2) Write a short report describing the model and showing the results of pertinent hypothesis tests, using a significance level of 0.10.

14-62. In a press release entitled "College Board Offers Glimpse of New SAT with Writing for Upcoming Class of '06," August 30, 2005, the College Board announced SAT scores for students in the class of 2005, the last to take the former version of the SAT featuring math and verbal sections. The file entitled **MathSAT** contains the math SAT scores for the interval 1967 to 2005. One point of interest concerning the data is the relationship between the average scores of male and female students.

a. Produce a scatter plot depicting the relationship between the average math SAT score of males (the dependent variable) and females (independent variable) over the period 1967 to 2005. Describe the relationship between these two variables.

b. Is there a linear relationship between the average score for males and females over the period 1967 to 2005? Use a significance level of 0.05 and the p-value approach to determine this.

14-63. The National Association of Home Builders published an article ("Housing Facts, Figures, and

Trends," August 2005) summarizing characteristics of the housing market in the United States. Data are listed for the average and median selling prices for houses during the period 1995 to 2004 and also January to July of 2005. The file entitled **House** contains the data. Assume the data can be viewed as samples of the relevant populations.

a. Determine the linear relationship that could be used to predict the average selling prices for January to July of 2005 using the median selling prices for that period.

b. Conduct a hypothesis test to determine if the median selling prices in the period January to July of 2005 could be used to determine the average selling prices in that period. Use a significance level of 0.05 and the p-value approach to conduct the test.

c. Provide an interval estimate of the average selling price of homes in the period 1995 to 2004 for a year in which the median selling price was $195,000. Use a 90% confidence interval.

14-64. The Grinfield Service Company marketing director is interested in analyzing the relationship between her company's sales and the advertising dollars spent. In the course of her analysis, she selected a random sample of 20 weeks and recorded the sales for each week and the amount spent on advertising. These data are contained in the data file called **Grinfield**:

a. Identify the independent and dependent variables.

b. Draw a scatter plot with the dependent variable on the vertical axis and the independent variable on the horizontal axis.

c. The marketing director wishes to know if increasing the amount spent on advertising increases sales. As a first attempt, use a statistical test that will provide the required information. Use a significance level of 0.025. Upon careful consideration, the marketing manager realizes that it takes a certain amount of time for the effect of advertising to register in terms of increased sales. She, therefore, asks you to calculate a correlation coefficient for sales of the current week against amount of advertising spent in the previous week and conduct a hypothesis test to determine if, under this model, increasing the amount spent on advertising increases sales. Again, use a significance level of 0.025.

14-65. Refer to the Grinfield Service Company discussed in Problem 14-64.

a. Develop the least squares regression equation for these variables. Plot the regression line on the scatter plot.

b. Develop a 95% confidence interval estimate for the increase in sales resulting from increasing the advertising budget by $50. Interpret the interval.

c. Discuss whether it is appropriate to interpret the intercept value in this model. Under what conditions is it appropriate? Discuss.

d. Develop a 90% confidence interval for the mean sales amount achieved during all weeks in which advertising is $200 for the week.

e. Suppose you are asked to use this regression model to predict the weekly sales when advertising is to be set at $100. What would you reply to the request? Discuss.

CASE 14.1

A & A Industrial Products

Alex Court, the cost accountant for A & A Industrial Products, was puzzled by the repair cost analysis report he had just reviewed. This was the third consecutive report where unscheduled plant repair costs were out of line with the repair cost budget allocated to each plant. A & A budgets for both scheduled maintenance and unscheduled repair costs for its plants' equipment, mostly large industrial machines. Budgets for scheduled maintenance activities are easy to estimate and are based on the equipment manufacturer's recommendations. The unscheduled repair costs, however, are harder to determine. Historically, A & A Industrial Products has estimated unscheduled maintenance using a formula based on the average number of hours of operation between major equipment failures at a plant.

Specifically, plants were given a budget of $65.00 per hour of operation between major failures. Alex had arrived at this amount by dividing aggregate historical repair costs by the total number of hours between failures. Then plant averages would be used to estimate unscheduled repair cost. For example, if a plant averaged 450 hours of run time before a major repair occurred, the plant would be allocated a repair budget of $450 \times \$65 = \$29,250$ per repair. If the plant was expected to be in operation 3,150 hours per year, the company would anticipate 7 unscheduled repairs (3,150/450) annually and budget $204,750 for annual unscheduled repair costs.

Alex was becoming more and more convinced that this approach was not working. Not only was upper management upset about the variance between predicted and actual costs of repair, plant managers believed that the model did not account for potential differences among the company's three plants when allocating dollars for unscheduled repairs. At the weekly management meeting, Alex was informed that he needed to analyze his cost projections further and produce a report that provided a more reliable

method for predicting repair costs. Upon leaving the meeting, Alex had his assistant randomly pull 64 unscheduled repair reports. The data are in the file **A & A Costs**. The management team is anxiously waiting for Alex's analysis.

CASE 14.2

Sapphire Coffee—Part 1

Jennie Garcia could not believe that her career had moved so far so fast. When she left graduate school with a master's degree in anthropology, she intended to work at a local coffee shop until something else came along that was more related to her academic background. But after a few months she came to enjoy the business, and in a little over a year she was promoted to store manager. When the company for whom she worked continued to grow, Jennie was given oversight of a few stores.

Now, eight years after she started as a barista, Jennie was in charge of operations and planning for the company's southern region. As a part of her responsibilities, Jennie tracks store revenues and forecasts coffee demand. Historically, Sapphire Coffee would base its demand forecast on the number of stores, believing that each store sold approximately the same amount of coffee. This approach seemed to work well when the company had shops of similar size and layout, but as the company grew, stores became more varied. Now, some stores had

drive-thru windows, a feature that top management added to some stores believing that it would increase coffee sales for customers who wanted a cup of coffee on their way to work but who were too rushed to park and enter the store to place an order.

Jennie noticed that weekly sales seemed to be more variable across stores in her region and was wondering what, if anything, might explain the differences. The company's financial vice president had also noticed the increased differences in sales across stores and was wondering what might be happening. In an e-mail to Jennie he stated that weekly store sales are expected to average $5.00 per square foot. Thus, a 1,000-square-foot store would have average weekly sales of $5,000. He asked that Jennie analyze the stores in her region to see if this rule of thumb was a reliable measure of a store's performance.

The VP of finance was expecting the analysis to be completed by the weekend. Jennie decided to randomly select weekly sales records for 53 stores. The data are in the file **Sapphire Coffee-1**. A full analysis would need to be sent to the corporate office by Friday.

CASE 14.3

Alamar Industries

While driving home in northern Kentucky at 8:00 P.M., Juan Alamar wondered whether his father had done him any favor by retiring early and letting him take control of the family machine-tool-restoration business. When his father started the business of overhauling machine tools (both for resale and on a contract basis), American companies dominated the tool manufacturing market. During the past 30 years, however, the original equipment industry had been devastated, first by competition from Germany and then from Japan. Although foreign competition had not yet invaded the overhaul segment of the business, Juan had heard about foreign companies establishing operations on the West Coast.

The foreign competitors were apparently stressing the high-quality service and operations that had been responsible for their great inroads into the original equipment market. Last week Juan had attended a daylong conference on total quality management that had discussed the advantages of competing for the Baldrige Award, the national quality award established in 1987. Presenters from past Baldrige winners, including Xerox, Federal Express, Cadillac, and Motorola, stressed the positive effects on their companies of winning and said similar effects would be possible for any company. This assertion of only positive effects was what Juan questioned. He was certain that the effect on his remaining free time would not be positive.

The Baldrige Award considers seven corporate dimensions of quality. Although the award is not based on a numerical score, an overall score is calculated. The maximum score is 1,000, with most recent winners scoring about 800. Juan did not doubt the award was good for the winners, but he wondered about the nonwinners. In particular, he wondered about any relationship between attempting to improve quality according to the Baldrige dimensions and company profitability. Individual company scores are not released, but Juan was able to talk to one of the conference presenters, who shared some anonymous data, such as companies' scores in the year they applied, their returns on investment in the year applied, and returns on investment in the year after application. Juan decided to commit the company to a total quality management process if the data provided evidence that the process would lead to increased profitability.

Baldrige Score	ROI Application Year	ROI Next Year
470	11%	13%
520	10	11
660	14	15
540	12	12
600	15	16
710	16	16
580	11	12
600	12	13
740	16	16
610	11	14
570	12	13
660	17	19

CASE 14.4

Continental Trucking

Norm Painter is the newly hired cost analyst for Continental Trucking. Continental is a nationwide trucking firm, and, until recently, most of its routes were driven under regulated rates. These rates were set to allow small trucking firms to earn an adequate profit, leaving little incentive to work to reduce costs by efficient management techniques. In fact, the greatest effort was made to try to influence regulatory agencies to grant rate increases.

A recent rash of deregulation moves has made the long-distance trucking industry more competitive. Norm has been hired to analyze Continental's whole expense structure. As part of this study, Norm is looking at truck repair costs. Because the trucks are involved in long hauls, they inevitably break down. In the past, little preventive maintenance was done, and if a truck broke down in the middle of a haul, either a replacement tractor was sent or an independent contractor finished the haul. The truck was then repaired at the nearest local shop. Norm is sure this procedure has led to more expense than if major repairs had been made before the trucks failed.

Norm thinks that some method should be found for determining when preventive maintenance is needed. He believes that fuel consumption is a good indicator of possible breakdowns, as trucks begin to run badly, they will consume more fuel. Unfortunately, the major determinants of fuel consumption are the weight of a truck and headwinds. Norm picks a sample of a single truck model and gathers data relating fuel consumption to truck weight. All trucks in the sample are in good condition. He separates the data by direction of the haul, realizing that winds tend to blow predominantly out of the west.

East-West Haul		West-East Haul	
Miles/Gallon	Haul Weight	Miles/Gallon	Haul Weight
4.1	41,000 lb	4.3	40,000 lb
4.7	36,000	4.5	37,000
3.9	37,000	4.8	36,000
4.3	38,000	5.2	38,000
4.8	32,000	5.0	35,000
5.1	37,000	4.7	42,000
4.3	46,000	4.9	37,000
4.6	35,000	4.5	36,000
5.0	37,000	5.2	42,000
		4.8	41,000

Although he can rapidly gather future data on fuel consumption and haul weight, now that Norm has these data, he is not quite sure what to do with them.

References

Berenson, Mark L., and David M. Levine, *Basic Business Statistics: Concepts and Applications,* 10th ed. (Upper Saddle River, NJ: Prentice Hall, 2006).

Cryer, Jonathan D., and Robert B. Miller, *Statistics for Business: Data Analysis and Modeling,* 2nd ed. (Belmont, CA: Duxbury Press, 1994).

Dielman, Terry E., *Applied Regression Analysis—A Second Course in Business and Economic Statistics*, 4th ed. (Belmont, CA: Duxbury Press, 2005).

Draper, Norman R., and Harry Smith, *Applied Regression Analysis*, 3rd ed. (New York: John Wiley and Sons, 1998).

Frees, Edward W., *Data Analysis Using Regression Models: The Business Perspective* (Upper Saddle River, NJ: Prentice Hall, 1996).

Kleinbaum, David G., Lawrence L. Kupper, Keith E. Muller, and Azhar Nizam, *Applied Regression Analysis and Other Multivariable Methods*, 3rd ed. (Belmont, CA: Duxbury Press, 1998).

Kutner, Michael H., Christopher J. Nachtsheim, John Neter, and William Li, *Applied Linear Statistical Models*, 5th ed. (New York: McGraw-Hill Irwin, 2005).

Microsoft Excel 2007 (Redmond, WA: Microsoft Corp., 2007).

Minitab for Windows Version 14 (State College, PA: Minitab, 2005).

Multiple Regression Analysis and Model Building

CHAPTER OUTCOMES

After studying the material in Chapter 15, you should be able to:

1. Understand the general concepts behind model building using multiple regression analysis.
2. Apply multiple regression analysis to business decision-making situations.
3. Analyze the computer output for a multiple regression model and interpret the regression results.
4. Test hypotheses about the significance of a multiple regression model and test the significance of the independent variables in the model.
5. Recognize potential problems when using multiple regression analysis and take steps to correct the problems.
6. Incorporate qualitative variables into a regression model by using dummy variables.
7. Apply regression analysis to situations where the relationship between the independent variable(s) and the dependent variable is nonlinear.
8. Understand the uses of stepwise regression.

PREPARING FOR CHAPTER FIFTEEN

- Review the methods for testing a null hypothesis using the t-distribution in Chapter 9.

- Review confidence intervals discussed in Chapter 8.

- Make sure you review the discussion about scatter plots in Chapters 2 and 14.

- Review the concepts associated with simple linear regression and correlation analysis presented in Chapter 14.

- In Chapter 14, review the steps involved in using the t-distribution for testing the significance of a correlation coefficient and a regression coefficient.

WHY YOU NEED TO KNOW

Chapter 14 pointed out that decision-makers often need to consider the relationship between two variables when analyzing a problem. Simple linear regression and correlation analyses provide a basis for analyzing the relationship between two variables. If the two variables are correlated, there is a linear relationship between them, and linear regression analysis can be used to model that relationship.

As you might expect, business problems are not limited to linear relationships involving only two variables. Many practical situations involve analyzing the relationships among three or more variables, and these relationships may be nonlinear. For example, a vice president of planning for an automobile manufacturer would be interested in the relationship between her company's automobile sales and the variables that influence those sales. Included in her analysis might be such independent or explanatory variables as automobile price, competitors' sales, and advertising, as well as such economic variables as disposable personal income, the inflation rate, and the unemployment rate.

When multiple independent variables are to be included in an analysis simultaneously, the technique introduced in this chapter—multiple linear regression—is very useful. When a relationship between variables is nonlinear, we may be able to apply variable transformations that allow us to use multiple linear regression analysis to construct a model. This chapter examines the general topic of model building by extending the concepts of simple linear regression analysis. The background information provided in Chapter 14 will be very helpful in understanding and applying multiple regression analysis to business decision-making situations.

15.1 Introduction to Multiple Regression Analysis

Chapter 14 introduced the concept of simple linear regression analysis. The simple regression model is characterized by two variables: y, the *dependent variable*, and x, the *independent*, or *explanatory*, *variable*. The single independent variable explains some variation in the dependent variable, but unless x and y are perfectly correlated, the proportion explained will be less than 100%.

In multiple regression analysis, additional independent variables are added to the regression model to explain some of the yet-unexplained variation in the dependent variable. You will note as we proceed that multiple regression is merely an extension of simple regression analysis. However, as we expand the model for the population from one independent variable to two or more, there are some new considerations.

The general format of a *multiple regression model for the population* is given by Equation 15.1.

Multiple Regression Model (Population Model)

$$y = \beta_0 + \beta_1 x_1 + \beta_2 x_2 + \cdots + \beta_k x_k + \varepsilon \qquad (15.1)$$

where:

β_0 = Population's regression constant
β_j = Population's regression coefficient for each variable x_j; $= 1, 2, \ldots, k$
k = Number of independent variables
ε = Model error

Four assumptions similar to those that apply to the simple linear multiple regression model apply to the multiple regression model.

Assumptions

1. Individual residuals, ε, are statistically independent of one another, and these values represent a random sample from the population of possible residuals at each level of x.
2. For a given value of x, there can exist many values of y, and therefore many possible values for ε. Further, the distribution of possible ε-values for any level of x is normally distributed.
3. The distributions of possible ε-values have equal variances at each level of x.
4. The means of the dependent variable, y, for all specified values of x can be connected with a line called the population regression model.

TABLE 15.1 Sample Data to Illustrate the Difference Between Simple and Multiple Regression Models

| (A) One Independent Variable | | (B) Two Independent Variable | | |
y	x_1	y	x_1	x_2
564.99	50	564.99	50	10
601.06	60	601.06	60	13
560.11	40	560.11	40	14
616.41	50	616.41	50	12
674.96	60	674.96	60	15
630.58	45	630.58	45	16
554.66	53	554.66	53	14

Equation 15.1 represents the multiple regression model for the population. However, in most instances, you will be working with a random sample from the population. Given the preceding assumptions, the estimated multiple regression model, based on the sample data, is of the form shown in Equation 15.2.

Estimated Multiple Regression Model

$$\hat{y} = b_0 + b_1 x_1 + b_2 x_2 + \cdots + b_k x_k \qquad (15.2)$$

This estimated model is an extension of an estimated simple regression model. The principal difference is that, whereas the estimated simple regression model is the equation for a straight line in a two-dimensional space, the estimated multiple regression model forms a hyperplane (or response surface) through multidimensional space. Each regression coefficient represents a different slope. Therefore, for a decision maker, using Equation 15.2, a value of the dependent variable can be estimated using values of two or more independent variables. The **regression hyperplane** represents the relationship between the dependent variable and the k independent variables.

For example, Table 15.1a shows sample data for a dependent variable, y, and one independent variable, x_1. Figure 15.1 shows a scatter plot and the regression line for the simple

Regression Hyperplane
The multiple regression equivalent of the simple regression line. The plane typically has a different slope for each independent variable.

FIGURE 15.1

Simple Regression Line

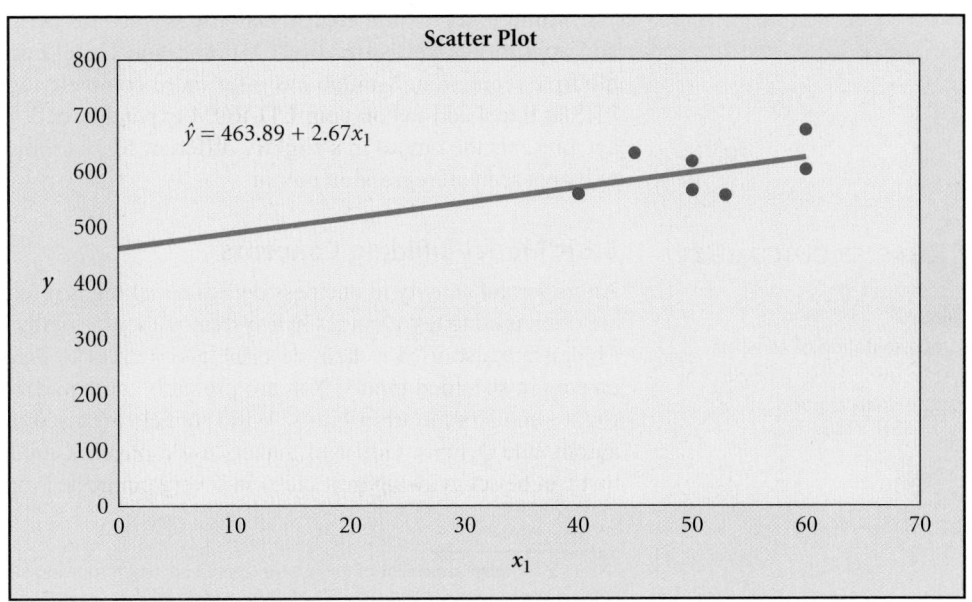

FIGURE 15.2

Multiple Regression Hyperplane for Population

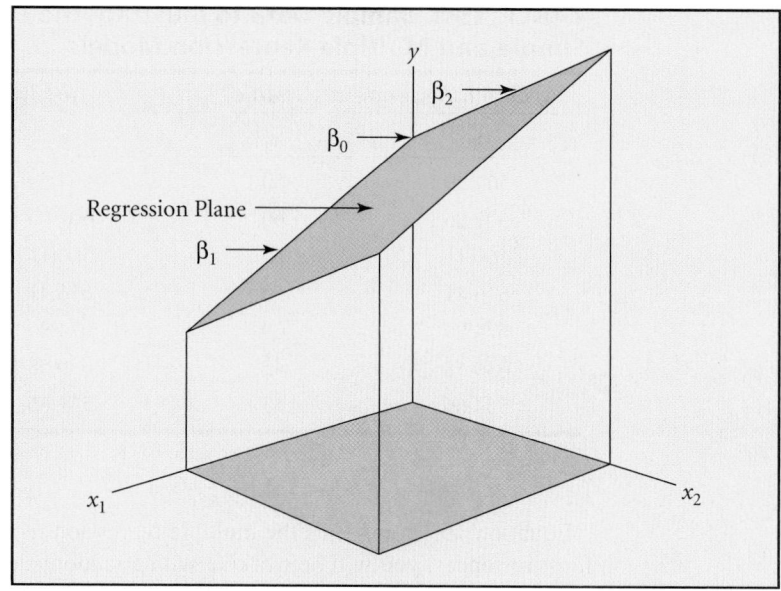

regression analysis for y and x_1. The points are plotted in two-dimensional space, and the regression model is represented by a line through the points such that the sum of squares of error $[SSE = \Sigma(y - \hat{y})^2]$ is minimized.

If we add variable x_2 to the model, as shown in Table 15.1B, the resulting multiple regression equation becomes

$$\hat{y} = 307.71 + 2.85x_1 + 10.94x_2$$

For the time being don't worry about how this equation was computed. That will be discussed shortly. Note, however, that the (y, x_1, x_2) points form a three-dimensional space, as shown in Figure 15.2. The regression equation forms a slice (hyperplane) through the data such that $\Sigma(y - \hat{y})^2$ is minimized. This is the same *least squares criterion* that is used with simple linear regression.

The mathematics for developing the least squares regression equation for simple linear regression involves differential calculus. The same is true for the multiple regression equation. Because the least squares regression coefficients are determined using matrix algebra, the mathematical derivation is beyond the scope of this text.[1]

Multiple regression analysis is virtually always performed with the aid of a computer and appropriate software. Both Minitab and Excel contain procedures for performing multiple regression. Minitab has a far more complete regression procedure. However, the PHStat Excel add-ins on your CD-ROM expand Excel's capabilities. Each software package presents the output in a slightly different format; however, the same basic information will appear in all regression output.

CHAPTER OUTCOME #1

Basic Model-Building Concepts

Model
A representation of an actual system using either a physical or a mathematical portrayal.

An important activity in business decision making is referred to as **model** building. Models are often used to test changes in a system without actually having to change the real system. Models are also used to help describe a system or to predict the output of a system based on certain specified inputs. You are probably quite aware of physical models. Airlines use flight simulators to train pilots. Wind tunnels are used to determine the aerodynamics of automobile designs. Golf ball makers use a physical model of a golfer called "Iron Mike" that can be set to swing golf clubs in a very controlled manner to determine how far a golf

---

[1] For a complete treatment of the matrix algebra approach for estimating multiple regression coefficients, consult *Applied Linear Statistical Models* by Kutner et al.

ball will fly. Although physical models are very useful in business decision making, our emphasis in this chapter is on mathematical models. In particular, we are interested in statistical models that are developed using multiple regression analysis.

People involved in model building frequently conclude that it is both an art and a science. Determining an appropriate model is a challenging task, but it can be made manageable by employing a model-building process consisting of the following three components: model specification, model fitting, and model diagnosis.

Model Specification

Model specification, or model identification, is the process of determining the dependent variable, deciding which independent variables should be included in the model, and obtaining the sample data for all variables. As with any statistical tool, the larger the sample size the better, because the potential for extreme sampling error is reduced when the sample size is large. However, at a minimum, the sample size required to compute a regression model must be at least one greater than the number of independent variables.[2] If we are thinking of developing a regression model with five independent variables, the absolute minimum number of cases required is six. Otherwise, the computer software will indicate an error has been made or will print out meaningless values. However, as a practical matter, the sample size should be at least four times the number of independent variables. Thus, if we had five independent variables ($k = 5$), we would want at least 20 cases to develop the regression model.

SUMMARY Model Specification

In the context of the statistical models discussed in this chapter, this component involves the following three steps:

1. Decide what question you want to ask. The question being asked usually indicates the dependent variable. In the previous chapter, we discussed how simple linear regression analysis could be used to describe

the relationship between a dependent and an independent variable.

2. List the potential independent variables for your model. Here, your knowledge of the situation you are modeling guides you in identifying potential independent variables.

3. Gather the sample data (observations) for all variables.

Model Building *Model building* is the process of actually constructing a mathematical equation in which some or all of the independent variables are used in an attempt to explain the variation in the dependent variable.

Model Diagnosis *Model diagnosis* is the process of analyzing the quality of the model you have constructed by determining how well a specified model fits the data you just gathered. You will examine such output values as R-squared and the standard error of the model. At this stage, you will also assess the extent to which the model's assumptions appear to be satisfied. (Section 15.5 is devoted to examining whether a model meets the regression analysis assumptions.) If the model is unacceptable in any of these areas, you will be forced to revert to the model-specification step and begin again. However, you will be the final judge of whether the model provides acceptable results, and you will always be constrained by time and cost considerations.

An important consideration in practical situations is to use the simplest available model that will meet your needs. The objective of model building is to help you make better decisions. You do not need to feel that a sophisticated model is better if a simpler one will provide acceptable results.

---

[2] There are mathematical reasons for this sample-size requirement that are beyond the scope of this text. In essence, the regression coefficient in Equation 15.2 can't be computed if the sample size is not at least one larger than the number of independent variables.

SUMMARY Developing a Multiple Regression Model

The following steps are employed in developing a multiple regression model:

1. Specify the model by determining the dependent variable, potential independent variables and select the sample data.
2. Formulate the model. This is done by computing the correlation coefficients for the dependent variable and each independent variable and for each independent variable

with all other independent variables. The multiple regression equation is also computed. The computations are performed using computer software such as Excel or Minitab.

3. Perform diagnostic checks on the model to determine how well the specified model fits the data and how well the model appears to meet the multiple regression assumptions.

TRY PROBLEM 15.3

CHAPTER OUTCOME #2

Excel and Minitab Tutorial

EXAMPLE 15-1 Developing a Multiple Regression Model

First City Real Estate First City Real Estate executives wish to build a model to predict sales prices for residential property. Such a model will be valuable when working with potential sellers who might list their homes with First City. This can be done using the following steps:

Step 1 Specify the model.
The question being asked is how can the real estate firm determine the selling price for a house? Thus, the dependent variable is the sales price. This is what the managers want to be able to predict. The managers met in a brainstorming session to determine a list of possible independent (explanatory) variables. Some variables, such as "condition of the house," were eliminated because of lack of data. Others such as "curb appeal" (the appeal of the house to people as they drive by) were eliminated because the values for these variables would be too subjective and difficult to quantify. From a wide list of possibilities, the managers selected the following variables as good candidates:

$$x_1 = \text{Home size (in square free)}$$
$$x_2 = \text{Age of house}$$
$$x_3 = \text{Number of bedrooms}$$
$$x_4 = \text{Number of bathrooms}$$
$$x_5 = \text{Garage size (number of cars)}$$

Data were obtained for a sample of 319 residential properties that had sold within the previous two months in an area served by two of First City's offices. For each house in the sample, the sales price and values for each potential independent variable were collected. The data are in the CD-ROM file **First City**.

Step 2 Formulate the model.
The regression model is developed by including independent variables from among those for which you have complete data. There is no way to determine whether an independent variable will be a good predictor variable by analyzing the individual variable's descriptive statistics, such as the mean and standard deviation. Instead, we need to look at the correlation between the independent variables and the dependent variable, which is measured by the **correlation coefficient**.

Correlation Coefficient
A quantitative measure of the strength of the linear relationship between two variables. The correlation coefficient, r, ranges from -1.0 to $+1.0$.

Correlation Matrix

A table showing the pairwise correlations between all variables (dependent and independent).

When we have multiple independent variables and one dependent variable, we can look at the correlation between all pairs of variables by developing a **correlation matrix**. Each correlation is computed using one of the equations in Equation 15.3. The appropriate formula is determined by whether the correlation is being calculated for an independent variable and the dependent variable or for two independent variables, respectively.

Correlation Coefficient

$$r = \frac{\sum(x - \bar{x})(y - \bar{y})}{\sqrt{\sum(x - \bar{x})^2 \sum(y - \bar{y})^2}} \quad \text{or} \quad r = \frac{\sum(x_i - \bar{x}_i)(x_j - \bar{x}_j)}{\sqrt{\sum(x_i - \bar{x}_i)^2 \sum(x_j - \bar{x}_j)^2}} \quad (15.3)$$

One x variable with v One x variable with another x

The actual calculations are done using Excel's correlation tool or Minitab's correlation command, and the results are shown in Figure 15.3a and Figure 15.3b. The output provides the correlation between y and each x variable and between each pair of independent variables.[3] Recall that in Chapter 14, a t-test (see Equation 14-3) was used to test whether the correlation coefficient is statistically significant.

$$H_0: \rho = 0 \qquad H_A: \rho \neq 0$$

We will conduct the test with a significance level of

$$\alpha = 0.05$$

FIGURE 15.3A

Excel 2007 Results Showing First City Real Estate Correlation Matrix

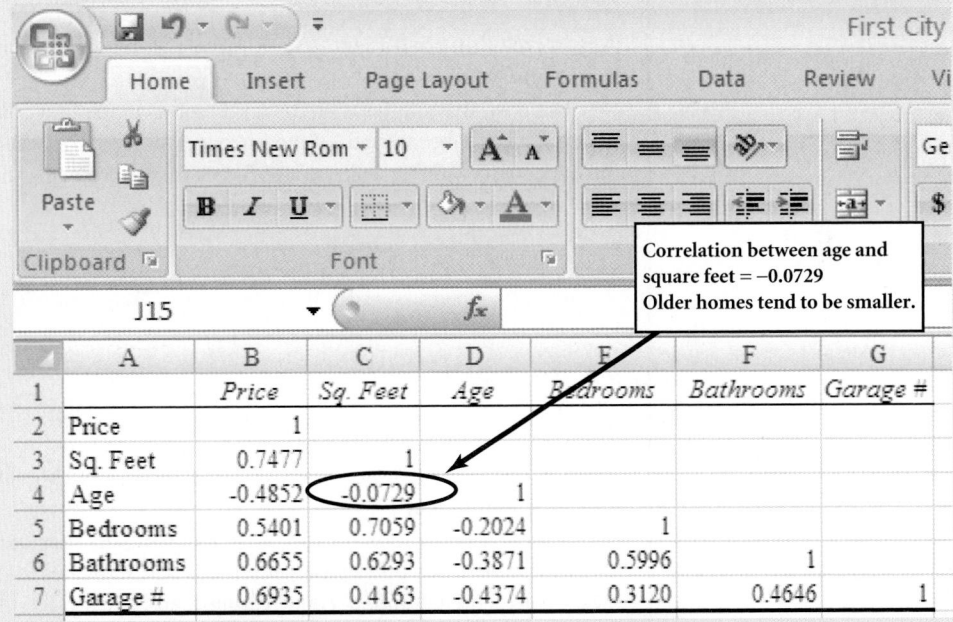

	Price	Sq. Feet	Age	Bedrooms	Bathrooms	Garage #
Price	1					
Sq. Feet	0.7477	1				
Age	-0.4852	-0.0729	1			
Bedrooms	0.5401	0.7059	-0.2024	1		
Bathrooms	0.6655	0.6293	-0.3871	0.5996	1	
Garage #	0.6935	0.4163	-0.4374	0.3120	0.4646	1

Correlation between age and square feet = −0.0729
Older homes tend to be smaller.

Excel 2007 Instructions:
1. Open file: First City.xls.
2. Select Home Sample 1 worksheet.
3. Click on **Data > Data Analysis**.
4. Select **Correlation**.
5. Define y variable range (all rows and columns).
6. Click on **Labels**.
7. Click **OK**.

---

[3] Minitab, in addition to providing the correlation matrix, can provide the p-values for each correlation. If the p-value is less than the specified alpha, the correlation is statistically significant.

FIGURE 15.3B

Minitab Results Showing First CityReal Estate Correlation Matrix

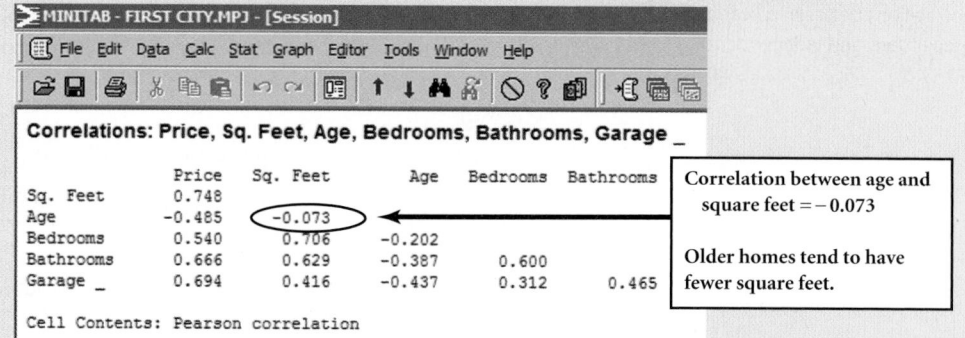

Given degrees of freedom equal to

$$n - 2 = 319 - 2 = 317$$

the critical t (see Appendix E) for a two-tailed test is approximately[4]

$$t_{0.025} = 1.96$$

Any correlation coefficient generating a t-value > 1.96 or less than -1.96 is determined to be significant.

For now, we will focus on the correlations in the first column in Figures 15.3a and 15.3b, which measure the strength of the linear relationship between each independent variable and the dependent variable, sales price. For example, the t statistic for price and square feet is

$$t = \frac{r}{\sqrt{\dfrac{1 - r^2}{n - 2}}} = \frac{0.7477}{\sqrt{\dfrac{1 - 0.7477^2}{319 - 2}}} = 20.048$$

Because

$$t = 20.048 > 1.96$$

we reject H_0 and conclude that the correlation between sales price and square feet is statistically significant.

Similar calculations for the other independent variables with price show that all variables are statistically correlated with price. This indicates that a significant linear relationship exists between each independent variable and sales price. Variable x_1, square feet, has the highest correlation at 0.748. Variable x_2, age of the house, has the lowest correlation at -0.485. The negative correlation implies that older homes tend to have lower sales prices.

As we discussed in Chapter 14, it is always a good idea to develop scatter plots to visually see the relationship between two variables. Figure 15.4 shows the scatter plots for each independent variable and the dependent variable, sales price. In each case, the plots indicate a linear relationship between the independent variable and the dependent

---

[4] You can use the Excel TINV function to get the precise t-value, which is 1.967.

FIGURE 15.4

First City Real Estate Scatter Plots

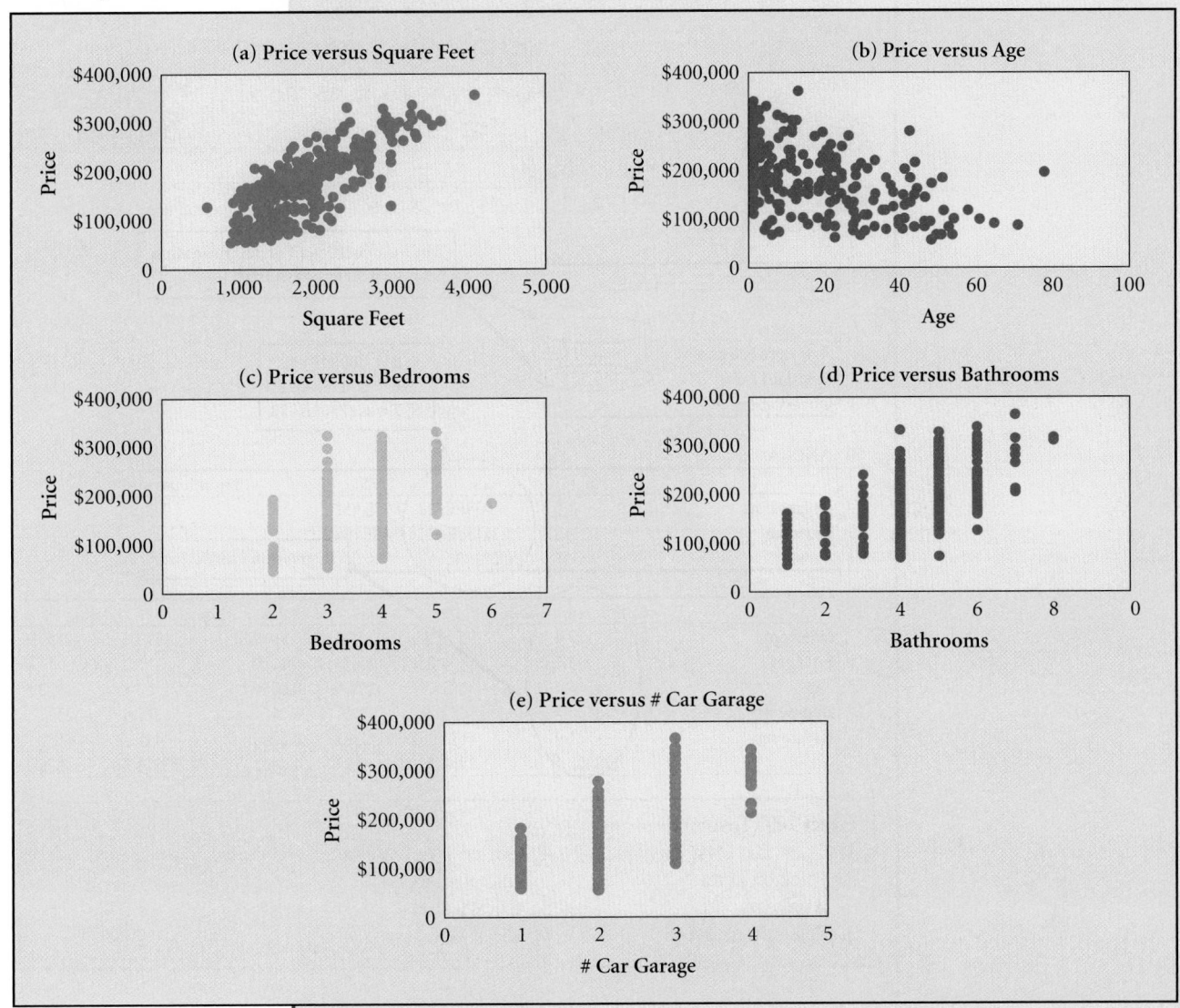

variable. Note that several of the independent variables (bedrooms, bathrooms, garage size) are quantitative but discrete. The scatter plots for these variables show points at each level of the independent variable rather than over a continuum of values.

CHAPTER OUTCOME #3

Computing the Regression Equation First City's goal is to develop a regression model to predict the appropriate selling price for a home, using certain measurable characteristics. The first attempt at developing the model will be to run a multiple regression computer program using all available independent variables. The regression outputs from Excel and Minitab are shown in Figure 15.5a and Figure 15.5b.

The estimate of the multiple regression model given in Figure 15.5a is

$$\hat{y} = 31,127.6 + 63.1(\text{sq. ft.}) - 1,144.4(\text{age}) - 8,410.4(\text{bedrooms})$$
$$+ 3,522.0(\text{bathrooms}) + 28,203.5(\text{garage})$$

The coefficients for each independent variable represent an estimate of the average change in the dependent variable for a 1-unit change in the independent variable, holding all other

FIGURE 15.5A

Excel 2007 Multiple Regression Model Results for First City Real Estate

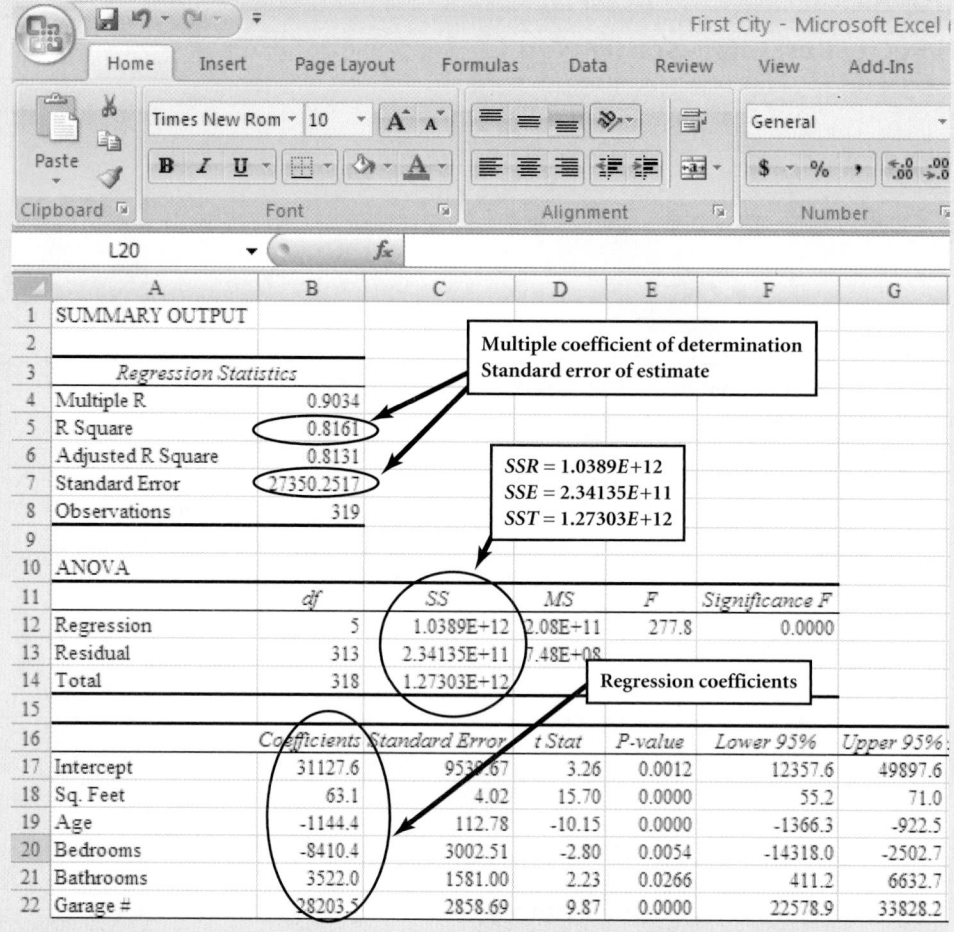

The screenshot shows an Excel 2007 worksheet titled "First City - Microsoft Excel" with the following output:

SUMMARY OUTPUT

Callout: *Multiple coefficient of determination* / *Standard error of estimate*

Regression Statistics	
Multiple R	0.9034
R Square	0.8161
Adjusted R Square	0.8131
Standard Error	27350.2517
Observations	319

Callout:
$SSR = 1.0389E+12$
$SSE = 2.34135E+11$
$SST = 1.27303E+12$

ANOVA

	df	SS	MS	F	Significance F
Regression	5	1.0389E+12	2.08E+11	277.8	0.0000
Residual	313	2.34135E+11	7.48E+08		
Total	318	1.27303E+12			

Callout: *Regression coefficients*

	Coefficients	Standard Error	t Stat	P-value	Lower 95%	Upper 95%
Intercept	31127.6	9538.67	3.26	0.0012	12357.6	49897.6
Sq. Feet	63.1	4.02	15.70	0.0000	55.2	71.0
Age	-1144.4	112.78	-10.15	0.0000	-1366.3	-922.5
Bedrooms	-8410.4	3002.51	-2.80	0.0054	-14318.0	-2502.7
Bathrooms	3522.0	1581.00	2.23	0.0266	411.2	6632.7
Garage #	28203.5	2858.69	9.87	0.0000	22578.9	33828.2

Excel 2007 Instructions:
1. Open file: First City.xls.
2. Click on **Data** > **Analysis**.
3. Select **Regression**.
4. Define *y* variable range and the *x* variable range (include labels).
5. Click **Labels**.
6. Click **OK**.

independent constant. For example, for houses of the same age, with the same number of bedrooms, baths, and garages, a 1-square-foot increase in the size of the house is estimated to increase its price by an average of $63.10. Likewise, for houses with the same square feet, bedrooms, bathrooms, and garages, a 1-year increase in the age of the house is estimated to result in an average drop in sales price of $1,144.40. The other coefficients are interpreted in the same way. Note, in each case, we are interpreting the regression coefficient for one independent variable while holding the other variables constant.

To estimate the value of a residential property, First Real Estate brokers would substitute values for the independent variables into the regression equation. For example, suppose a house with the following characteristics is considered:

$$x_1 = \text{Square feet} = 2,100$$
$$x_2 = \text{Age} = 15$$
$$x_3 = \text{Number of bedrooms} = 4$$
$$x_4 = \text{Number of baths} = 3$$
$$x_5 = \text{Size of garage} = 2$$

FIGURE 15.5B

Minitab Multiple Regression Model Results for First City Real Estate

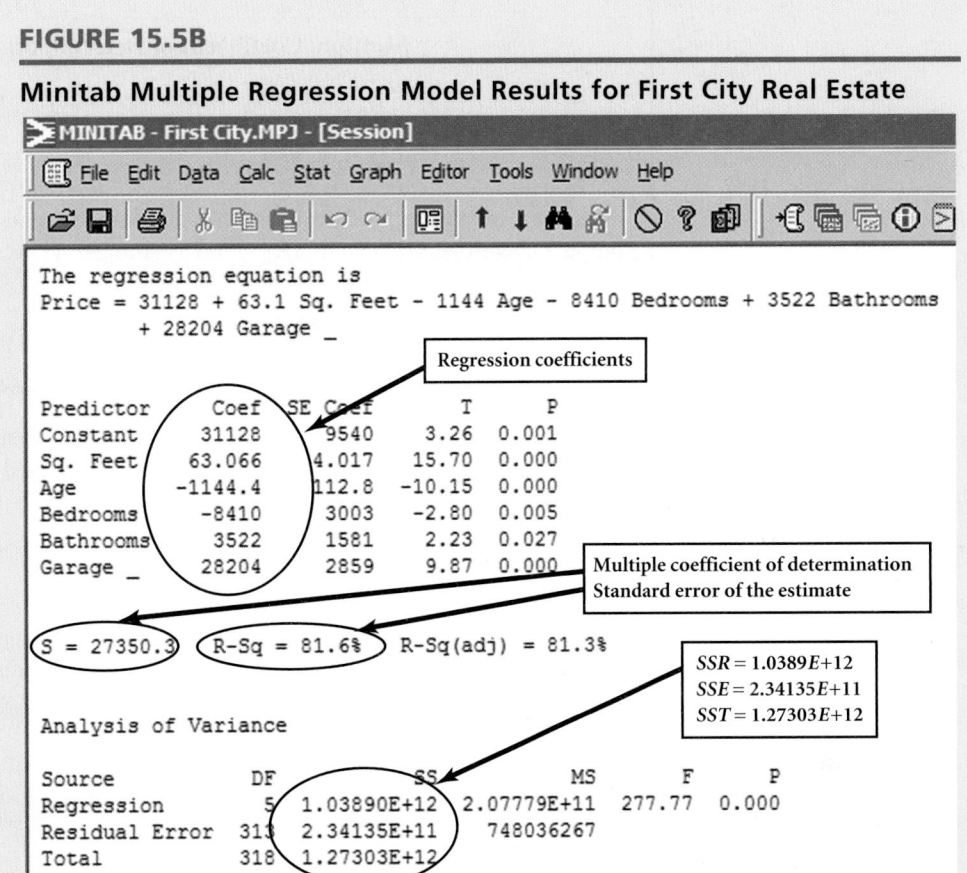

Minitab Instructions:
1. Open file: First City. MTW.
2. Choose **Stat > Regression > Regression**.
3. In **Response**, enter dependent (y) variable.
4. In **Predictors**, enter independent (x) variables.
5. Click **OK**.

The point estimate for the sales price is

$$\hat{y} = 31{,}127.6 + 63.1(\text{sq. ft.}) - 1{,}144.4(\text{age}) - 8{,}410.4(\text{bathrooms}) + 3{,}522.0(\text{bathrooms}) + 28{,}203.5(\text{garage})$$
$$\hat{y} = 31{,}127.6 + 63.1(2{,}100) - 1{,}144.4(15) - 8{,}410.4(4) + 3{,}522.0(3) + 28{,}203.5(2)$$
$$\hat{y} = \$179{,}802.70$$

The Coefficient of Determination You learned in Chapter 14 that the *coefficient of determination*, R^2, measures the proportion of variation in the dependent variable that can be explained by the dependent variable's relationship to a single independent variable. When there are multiple independent variables in a model, R^2 is also used to determine the proportion of variation in the dependent variable that is explained by the dependent variable's relationship to all the independent variables in the model. However, R^2 is now called the **multiple coefficient of determination**. Equation 15.4 is used to compute R^2 for a multiple regression model.

Multiple Coefficient of Determination (R^2)

$$R^2 = \frac{\text{Sum of squares regression}}{\text{Total sum of squares}} = \frac{SSR}{SST} \qquad \textbf{(15.4)}$$

As shown in Figure 15.5a, $R^2 = 0.8161$. Both SSR and SST are also included in the output. Therefore, you can use Equation 15.4 to get R^2, as follows:

$$\frac{SSR}{SST} = \frac{1.0389E+12}{1.27303E+12} = 0.8161$$

More than 81% of the variation in sales price can be explained by the linear relationship of the five independent variables in the regression model to the dependent variable. However, as we shall shortly see, not all independent variables are equally important to the model's ability to explain this variation.

> **Step 3 Diagnose the model.**
> Before First City actually uses this regression model to estimate the sales price of a house, there are several questions that should be answered.
> 1. Is the overall model significant?
> 2. Are the individual variables significant?
> 3. Is the standard deviation of the model error too large to provide meaningful results?
> 4. Is multicollinearity a problem?
> 5. Have the regression analysis assumptions been satisfied?

We shall answer the first four questions in order. We will have to wait until Section 15.5 before we have the tools to answer the fifth important question.

CHAPTER OUTCOME #4

Is the Model Significant? You should keep in mind that the regression model we constructed is based on a sample of data from the population and is subject to sampling error. Therefore, we need to test the statistical significance of the overall regression model. We have previously discussed the multiple coefficient of determination, R^2, which is a measure of how much of the variation in the dependent variable can be explained by the regression model. Because R^2 is a sample statistic, it can be used to make inferences about whether the overall model is statistically significant in explaining the variation in the dependent variable. The specific null and alternative hypotheses tested for First City Real Estate are

$$H_0: \beta_1 = \beta_2 = \beta_3 = \beta_4 = \beta_5 = 0$$
$$H_A: \text{At least one } \beta_i \neq 0.$$

If the null hypothesis is true and all the slope coefficients are simultaneously equal to zero, the overall regression model is not useful for predictive or descriptive purposes.

The F-test is a method for testing whether the regression model explains a significant proportion of the variation in the dependent variable (and whether the overall model is significant). The F-test statistic for a multiple regression model is shown in Equation 15.5.

F-Test Statistic

$$F = \frac{\dfrac{SSR}{k}}{\dfrac{SSE}{n-k-1}} \tag{15.5}$$

where:

$$SSR = \text{Sum of squares regression} = \sum(\hat{y} - \overline{y})^2$$
$$SSE = \text{Sum of squares error} = \sum(y - \hat{y})^2$$
$$n = \text{Number of data points}$$
$$k = \text{Number of independent variables}$$
$$\text{Degrees of freedom} = D_1 = k \quad \text{and} \quad D_2 = (n - k - 1)$$

The ANOVA portion of the output shown in Figure 15.5a contains values for *SSR*, *SSE*, and the *F*-value. The general format of the ANOVA table in a regression analysis is as follows:

ANOVA

Source	df	SS	MS	F	Significance F
Regression	k	SSR	MSR = SSR/k	MSR/MSE	computed p-value
Residual	$n - k - 1$	SSE	MSE = SSE/(n − k − 1)		
Total	$n - 1$	SST			

The ANOVA portion of the output from Figure 15.5a is as follows:

ANOVA

Source	df	SS	MS	F	Significance F
Regression	5	$1.04E + 12$	$2.08E + 11$	277.8	0.0000
Residual	313	$2.34E + 11$	$7.48E + 08$		
Total	318	$1.27303E + 12$			

We can test the model's significance.

$$H_0: \beta_1 = \beta_2 = \beta_3 = \beta_4 = \beta_5 = 0$$
$$H_A: \text{At least one } \beta_i \neq 0.$$

by either comparing the calculated *F*-value, 277.8, with a critical value for a given alpha level

$$\alpha = 0.01$$

and $k = 5$ and $n - k - 1 = 313$ degrees of freedom using Excel's **FINV** function, ($F_{0.01} = 3.079$), or compare the *p*-value in the output with a specified alpha level. Because

$$F = 277.8 > 3.079, \text{ reject } H_0$$

or because

$$p\text{-value} \approx 0.0 < 0.01, \text{ reject } H_0$$

Therefore, we should conclude that the regression model *does* explain a significant proportion of the variation in sales price. Thus, the overall model is statistically significant. This means we can conclude that at least one of the regression slope coefficients is not equal to zero.

Excel and Minitab also provide a measure called the R-sq(adj), which is the **adjusted R-squared** value (see Figure 15.5a and 15.5b). It is calculated by Equation 15.6.

Adjusted R-Squared

A measure of the percentage of explained variation in the dependent variable that takes into account the relationship between the sample size and the number of independent variables in the regression model.

$$R\text{-sq(adj)} = R_A^2 = 1 - (1 - R^2)\left(\frac{n-1}{n-k-1}\right)$$

(15.6)

where:

n = Sample size
k = Number of independent variables
R^2 = Coefficient of determination

Adding independent variables to the regression model will always increase R^2, even if these variables have no relationship to the dependent variable. Therefore, as the number of independent variables is increased (regardless of the quality of the variables), R^2 will increase. However, each additional variable results in the loss of 1 degree of freedom. This is viewed as part of the cost of adding the specified variable. The addition to R^2 may not justify the reduction in degrees of freedom. The R_A^2 value takes into account this cost and adjusts the R_A^2 value accordingly. R_A^2 will always be less than R^2. When a variable is added that does not contribute its fair share to the explanation of the variation in the dependent variable, the R_A^2 may actually decline, even though R^2 will always increase. The adjusted R-squared is a particularly important measure when the number of independent variables is large relative to the sample size. It takes into account the relationship between sample size and number of variables. R^2 may appear artificially high if the number of variables is large compared with the sample size.

In this example, in which the sample size is quite large relative to the number of independent variables, the adjusted R-squared is 81.3%, only slightly less than R^2 = 81.6%.

CHAPTER OUTCOME #4

Are the Individual Variables Significant? We have concluded that the overall model is significant. This means *at least* one independent variable explains a significant proportion of the variation in sales price. This does not mean that *all* the variables are significant, however. To determine which variables are significant, we test the following hypotheses:

$$H_0\text{: } \beta_j = 0$$
$$H_A\text{: } \beta_j \neq 0 \qquad \text{for all } j$$

We can test the significance of each independent variable using significance level

$$\alpha = 0.05$$

and a t-test, as discussed in Chapter 14. The calculated t-values should be compared to the critical t-value with

$$n - k - 1 = 319 - 5 - 1 = 313$$

degrees of freedom, which is approximately

$$t_{0.025} \approx 1.96$$

for $\alpha = 0.05$. The calculated t-value for each variable is provided on the computer printout in Figures 15.5a and 15.5b. Recall that the t statistic is determined by dividing the regression coefficient by the estimator of the standard deviation of the regression coefficient, as shown in Equation 15.9.

t-Test for Significance of Each Regression Coefficient

$$t = \frac{b_j - 0}{s_{b_j}} \qquad df = n - k - 1 \qquad (15.7)$$

where:

b_j = Sample slope coefficient for the *j*th independent variable

s_{b_j} = Estimate of the standard error for the *j*th sample slope coefficient

For example, the *t*-value for square feet shown in Figure 15.5a is 15.70. This was computed using Equation 15.7, as follows:

$$t = \frac{b_j - 0}{s_{b_j}} = \frac{63.1 - 0}{4.02} = 15.70$$

Because

$$t = 15.70 > 1.96, \text{ we reject } H_0,$$

and conclude that the regression slope for square feet is not zero.

We can also look at the Excel or Minitab output and compare the *p*-value for each regression slope coefficient with alpha. If the *p*-value is less than alpha, we reject the null hypothesis and conclude that the independent variable is statistically significant in the model. Both the *t*-test and the *p*-value techniques will give the same results.

You should consider that these *t*-tests are *conditional* tests. This means the null hypothesis is that *the value of each slope coefficient is 0, given that the other independent variables are already in the model.*[5] Figure 15.6 shows the hypothesis tests for each independent variable using a 0.05 significance level. We conclude that all five independent variables in the model are significant. When a regression model is to be used for prediction, the model should contain no insignificant variables. If insignificant variables are present, they should be dropped and a new regression equation obtained before the model is used for prediction purposes. We will have more to say about this later.

Is the Standard Deviation of the Regression Model Too Large? The purpose of developing the First City regression model is to be able to determine values of the dependent variable when corresponding values of the independent variables are known. An indication of how good the regression model is can be found by looking at the relationship between the measured values of the dependent variable and those values that would be predicted by the regression model. The standard deviation of the regression model (also called the *standard error of the estimate),* measures the dispersion of observed home sale values, *y*, around values predicted by the regression model. The standard error of the estimate is shown in Figure 15.5a, and can be computed using Equation 15.8.

Standard Error of the Estimate

$$s_\varepsilon = \sqrt{\frac{SSE}{n - k - 1}} = \sqrt{MSE} \qquad (15.8)$$

where:

SSE = Sum of squares error (residual)

n = Sample size

k = Number of independent variables

---

[5] Note that the *t*-tests may be affected if the independent variables in the model are themselves correlated. A procedure known as the *sum of squares drop F-test*, discussed by Kutner et al. in *Applied Linear Statistical Models*, should be used in this situation. Each *t*-test considers only the marginal contribution of the independent variables and may indicate that none of the variables in the model are significant, even though the ANOVA procedure indicates otherwise.

FIGURE 15.6

Significance Tests for Each Independent Variable in the First City Real Estate Example

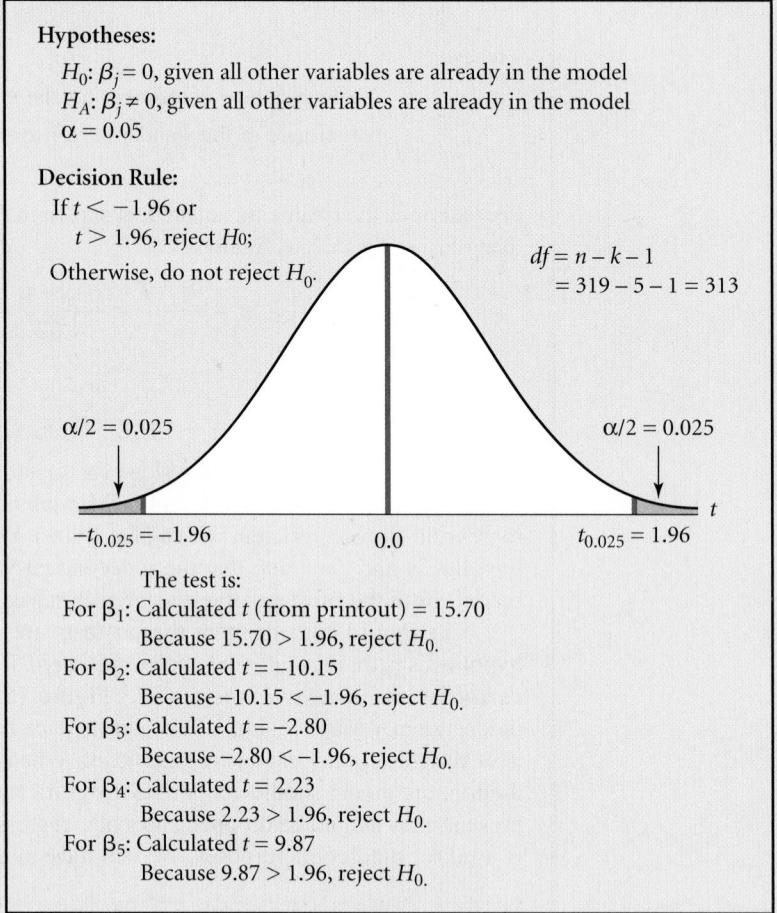

Hypotheses:

$H_0: \beta_j = 0$, given all other variables are already in the model
$H_A: \beta_j \neq 0$, given all other variables are already in the model
$\alpha = 0.05$

Decision Rule:
If $t < -1.96$ or
$t > 1.96$, reject H_0;
Otherwise, do not reject H_0.

$df = n - k - 1$
$= 319 - 5 - 1 = 313$

$\alpha/2 = 0.025$ $\alpha/2 = 0.025$

$-t_{0.025} = -1.96$ 0.0 $t_{0.025} = 1.96$

The test is:
For β_1: Calculated t (from printout) $= 15.70$
        Because $15.70 > 1.96$, reject H_0.
For β_2: Calculated $t = -10.15$
        Because $-10.15 < -1.96$, reject H_0.
For β_3: Calculated $t = -2.80$
        Because $-2.80 < -1.96$, reject H_0.
For β_4: Calculated $t = 2.23$
        Because $2.23 > 1.96$, reject H_0.
For β_5: Calculated $t = 9.87$
        Because $9.87 > 1.96$, reject H_0.

Note: The degrees of freedom for the *t*-distribution is $(n - k - 1)$, where k is the total number of independent variables in the model.

Examining Equation 15.8 closely, we see that this standard error of the estimate is the square root of the mean square error of the residuals found in the analysis of variance table.

Sometimes, even though a model has a high R^2, the standard error of the estimate will be too large to provide adequate precision for confidence and prediction intervals. A rule of thumb that we have found useful is to examine the range $\pm 2s_\varepsilon$. If this range is acceptable from a practical viewpoint, the standard error of the estimate might be considered acceptable.[6]

In this First City Real Estate Company example, the model standard error, shown in Figure 15.5a, is $27,350. Thus, the rough prediction range for the price of an individual home is

$\pm 2(\$27,350)$

$\pm \$54,700$

---

[6] The actual confidence interval for prediction of a new observation requires the use of matrix algebra. However, when the sample size is large and dependent variable values near the means of the dependent variables are used, the rule of thumb given here is a close approximation. Refer to *Applied Linear Statistical Models* by Kutner et al. for further discussion.

From a practical viewpoint, a potential error of $54,700 above or below the true value is probably not acceptable. Not many homeowners would be willing to have their appraisal value set by a model with a possible error this large. The company needs to take steps to reduce the standard deviation of the model error. Subsequent sections of this chapter discuss some ways we can attempt to reduce it.

CHAPTER OUTCOME #5

Is Multicollinearity a Problem? Even if the overall regression model is significant and each independent variable is significant, decision makers should still examine the regression model to determine whether it appears reasonable. This is referred to as checking for *face validity*. Specifically, you should check to see that signs on the regression coefficients are consistent with the signs on the correlation coefficients between the independent variables and the dependent variable. Does any regression coefficient have an unexpected sign?

Before answering this question for the First City Real Estate example, we should review what the regression coefficients mean. First, the constant term, b_0, is the estimate of the model's y intercept. If the data used to develop the regression model contain values of x_1, x_2, x_3, x_4, and x_5 that are simultaneously 0 (such as would be the case for vacant land), b_0 is the mean value of y, given that x_1, x_2, x_3, x_4, and x_5 all equal 0. Under these conditions b_0 would estimate the average value of a vacant lot. However, in the First City example, no vacant land was in the sample, so b_0 has no particular meaning.

The coefficient for square feet, b_1, estimates the average change in sales price corresponding to a change in house size of 1 square foot, holding the other independent variables constant. The value shown in Figure 15.5a for b_1 is 63.1. The coefficient is positive, indicating that an increase in square footage is associated with an increase in sales price. This relationship is expected. All other things being equal, bigger houses should sell for more money.

Likewise, the coefficient for x_5, the size of the garage, is positive, indicating that an increase in size is also associated with an increase in price. This is expected. The coefficient for x_2, the age of the house is negative, indicating that an older house is worth less than a similar younger house. This also seems reasonable. However, the coefficient for variable x_3, the number of bedrooms, is $-\$8,410.4$ meaning that, if we hold the other variables constant but increase the number of bedrooms by one, the average price will *drop* by $8,410.40. This would appear to run counter to conventional thinking about the housing market. Finally, variable x_4 for bathrooms has the expected positive sign.

Referring to the correlation matrix that was shown earlier in Figure 15.3, the correlation between variable x_3, bedrooms, and y, the sales price, is $+0.540$. This indicates that, without considering the other independent variables, the linear relationship between number of bedrooms and sales price is positive. But why does the regression coefficient turn out negative in the model? The answer lies in what is called **multicollinearity**.

Multicollinearity occurs when independent variables overlap with respect to the information they provide in explaining the variation in the dependent variable. For example, x_3 and the other independent variables have the following correlations (see Figure 15.3b):

$$r_{x_3, x_1} = 0.706$$
$$r_{x_3, x_2} = -0.202$$
$$r_{x_3, x_4} = 0.600$$
$$r_{x_3, x_5} = 0.312$$

All four correlations have t-values indicating a significant linear relationship. Refer to the correlation matrix in Figure 15.3 to see that other independent variables are also correlated with each other.

Multicollinearity

A high correlation between two independent variables such that the two variables contribute redundant information to the model. When highly correlated independent variables are included in the regression model, they can adversely affect the regression results.

The problems caused by multicollinearity, and how to deal with them, continue to be of prime concern to statisticians. From a decision maker's viewpoint, you should be aware that multicollinearity can (and usually does) exist and recognize the basic problems it can cause. Some of the most obvious problems and indications of severe multicollinearity are the following:

1. Incorrect signs on the coefficients.
2. A sizable change in the values of the previously estimated coefficients when a new variable is added to the model.
3. A variable that was previously significant in the regression model becomes insignificant when a new independent variable is added.
4. The estimate of the standard deviation of the model error increases when a variable is added to the model.

Mathematical approaches exist for dealing with multicollinearity and reducing its impact. Although these procedures are beyond the scope of this text, one suggestion is to eliminate the variables that are the chief cause of the multicollinearity problems.

If the independent variables in a regression model are correlated and multicollinearity is present, another potential problem is that the *t*-tests for the significance of the individual independent variables may be misleading. That is, a *t*-test may indicate that the variable is not statistically significant when in fact it is.

One method of measuring multicollinearity is known as the **variance inflation factor (VIF)**. Equation 15.9 is used to compute the *VIF* for each independent variable.

Variance Inflation Factor

A measure of how much the variance of an estimated regression coefficient increases if the independent variables are correlated. A *VIF* equal to 1.0 for a given independent variable indicates that this independent variable is not correlated with the remaining independent variables in the model. The greater the multicollinearity, the larger the *VIF*.

Variance Inflation Factor

$$VIF = \frac{1}{(1 - R_j^2)} \tag{15.9}$$

where:

R_j^2 = Coefficient of determination when the *j*th independent variable is regressed against the remaining $k - 1$ independent variables.

Both the PHStat add-ins to Excel and Minitab contain options that provide *VIF* values.[7]

Figure 15.7 shows the Excel (PHStat) output of the variance inflation factors for the First City Real Estate example. The effect of multicollinearity is to decrease the test statistic, thus reducing the probability that the variable will be declared significant. A related impact is to increase the width of the confidence interval estimate of the slope coefficient in the regression model. Generally, if the *VIF* < 5 for a particular independent variable, multicollinearity is not considered a problem for that variable. *VIF* values ≥5 imply that the correlation between the independent variables is too extreme and should be dealt with by dropping variables from the model. As Figure 15.7 illustrates, the *VIF* values for each independent variable are less than 5, so based on variance inflation

---

[7] Excel's Regression procedure in the Data Analysis Tools area does not provide *VIF* values directly. Without PHStat, you would need to compute each regression analysis individually and record the *R*-squared value to compute the *VIF*.

FIGURE 15.7

Excel 2007 (PHStat) Multiple Regression Model Results for First City Real Estate with Variance Inflation Factors

Excel 2007 Instructions:
1. Open file: First City.xls.
2. Click on **Add-Ins PHStat**.
3. Select **Regression >Multiple Regression**.
4. Define *y* variable range and the *x* variable range.

5. Select **Regression Statistics Table** and **ANOVA** and **Coefficients Table**.
6. Select **Various Inflation Factor (VIF)**.
7. Click **OK**. Note VIFs consolidated to one page for display in Figure 15.7.

Minitab Instructions (for similar results):
1. Open file: First City.MTW.
2. Choose **Stat > Regression > Regression**.
3. In **Response** enter dependent (*y*) variable.
4. In **Predictors**, enter independent (*x*) variables.

5. Click **Options**.
6. In **Display**, select Variance Inflation factors.
7. Click **OK. OK**.

factors, even though the sign on the variable, bedrooms, is unexpected, the other multicollinearity issues do not exist among these independent variables.

Confidence Interval Estimation for Regression Coefficients Previously we showed how to determine whether the regression coefficients are statistically significant. This was necessary because the estimates of the regression coefficients are developed from sample data and are subject to sampling error. The issue of sampling error also comes into play when interpreting the slope coefficients.

FIGURE 15.8A

Excel 2007 Multiple Regression Model Results for First City Real Estate

	A	B	C	D	E	F	G
1	SUMMARY OUTPUT						
2							
3	*Regression Statistics*						
4	Multiple R	0.9034					
5	R Square	0.8161					
6	Adjusted R Square	0.8131					
7	Standard Error	27350.2517					
8	Observations	319					
9							
10	ANOVA						
11		*df*	*SS*	*MS*	*F*	*Significance F*	
12	Regression	5	1.0389E+12	2.08E+11	277.8	0.0000	
13	Residual	313	2.34135E+11	7.48E+08			
14	Total	318	1.27303E+12				
15							
16		*Coefficients*	*Standard Error*	*t Stat*	*P-value*	*Lower 95%*	*Upper 95%*
17	Intercept	31127.6	9539.67	3.26	0.0012	12357.6	49897.6
18	Sq. Feet	63.1	4.02	15.70	0.0000	55.2	71.0
19	Age	-1144.4	112.78	-10.15	0.0000	-1366.3	-922.5
20	Bedrooms	-8410.4	3002.51	-2.80	0.0054	-14318.0	-2502.7
21	Bathrooms	3522.0	1581.00	2.23	0.0266	411.2	6632.7
22	Garage #	28203.5	2858.69	9.87	0.0000	22578.9	33828.2

95% Confidence interval estimates for the regression.

Excel 2007 Instructions:
1. Open file: First City.xls.
2. Click on **Data > Data Analysis**.
3. Select **Regression**.
4. Define *y* variable range and the *x* variable range (include labels).
5. Click **Labels**.
6. Click **OK**.

Consider again the regression models for First City Real Estate shown in Figures 15.8a and 15.8b. The regression coefficients shown are *point estimates* for the true regression coefficients. For example, the coefficient for the variable square feet is $b_1 = 63.1$. We interpret this to mean that, holding the other variables constant, for each increase in the size of a home by 1 square foot, the price of a house is estimated to increase by $63.1. But like all point estimates, this is subject to sampling error. In Chapter 14 you were introduced to the concept of confidence interval estimates for the regression coefficients. That same concept applies in multiple regression models. Equation 15.10 is used to develop the confidence interval estimate for the regression coefficients.

Confidence Interval Estimate for the Regression Slope

$$b_j \pm ts_{b_j} \tag{15.10}$$

where:

b_j = Point estimate for the regression coefficient for x_j

t = Critical t-value for the specified confidence level

s_{b_j} = The standard error of the jth regression coefficient

The Excel output in Figure 15.8a provides the confidence interval estimates for each regression coefficient. For example, the 95% interval estimate for square feet is

$$\$55.2 \text{ -------- } \$71.0$$

Minitab does not have a command to generate confidence intervals for the individual regression parameters. However, statistical quantities are provided on the Minitab output in Figure 15.8b to allow the manual calculation of these confidence intervals. As an example, the confidence interval for the coefficient associated with the square feet variable can be computed using Equation 15.10 as[8]

FIGURE 15.8B

Minitab Multiple Regression Model Results for the First City Real Estate

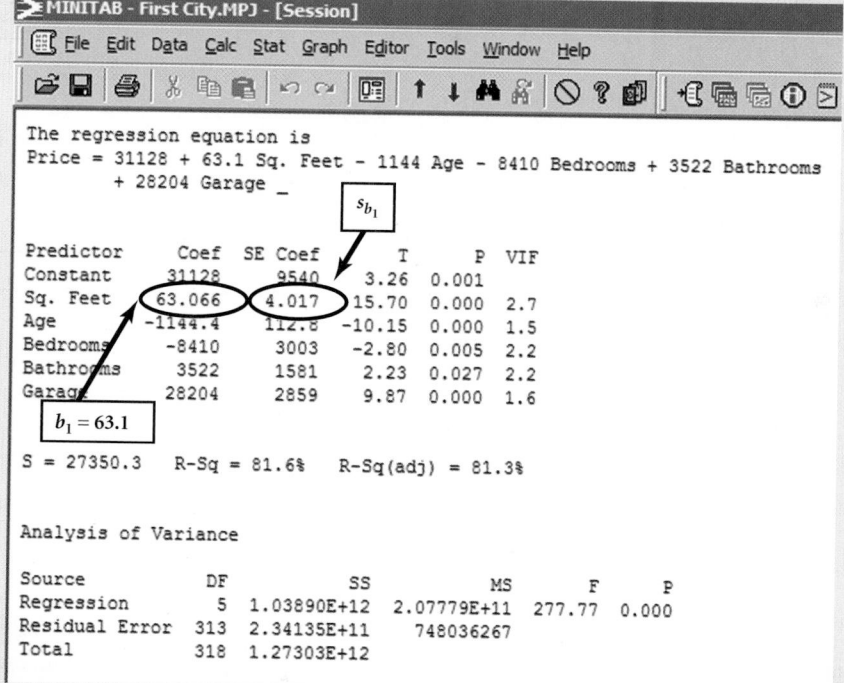

Minitab Instructions:

1. Open file: First City. MTW.
2. Choose **Stat > Regression > Regression**.
3. In **Response**, enter dependent (*y*) variable.
4. In **Predictors**, enter independent (*x*) variable.
5. Click **OK**.

---

[8] Note, we used Excel's TINV function to get the precise *t*-value of 1.967.

$$b_1 \pm ts_{b_1}$$
$$63.1 \pm 1.967(4.017)$$
$$63.1 \pm 7.90$$
$$\$55.2 \text{ -------- } \$71.0$$

We interpret this interval as follows: Holding the other variables constant, using a 95% confidence level, a change in square feet by 1 foot is estimated to generate an average change in home price of between $55.20 and $71.00. Each of the other regression coefficients can be interpreted in the same manner.

15-1: Exercises

Skill Development

15-1. You are given the following estimated regression equation involving a dependent and two independent variables:

$$\hat{y} = 12.67 + 4.14x_1 + 8.72x_2$$

a. Interpret the values of the slope coefficients in the equation.
b. Estimate the value of the dependent variable when $x_1 = 4$ and $x_2 = 9$.

15-2. In working for a local retail store you have developed the following estimated regression equation:

$$\hat{y} = 22{,}167 - 412x_1 + 818x_2 - 93x_3 - 71x_4$$

where:
y = Weekly sales
x_1 = Local unemployment rate
x_2 = Weekly average high temperature
x_3 = Number of activities in the local community
x_4 = Average gasoline price

a. Interpret the values of b_1, b_2, b_3, and b_4 in this estimated regression equation.
b. What is the estimated sales if the unemployment rate is 5.7%, the average high temperature is 61°, there were 14 activities, and gasoline average price was $1.39?

15-3. The following output is associated with a multiple regression model with three independent variables:

	df	SS	MS	F	Significance F
Regression	3	16,646.091	5,548.697	5.328	0.007
Residual	21	21,871.669	1,041.508		
Total	24	38,517.760			

	Coefficients	Standard Error	t Stat	p-value
Intercept	87.790	25.468	3.447	0.002
x_1	−0.970	0.586	−1.656	0.113
x_2	0.002	0.001	3.133	0.005
x_3	−8.723	7.495	−1.164	0.258

	Lower 95%	Upper 95%	Lower 90%	Upper 90%
Intercept	34.827	140.753	43.966	131.613
x_1	−2.189	0.248	−1.979	0.038
x_2	0.001	0.004	0.001	0.004
x_3	−24.311	6.864	−21.621	4.174

a. What is the regression model associated with this data?
b. Is the model statistically significant?
c. How much of the variation in the dependent variable can be explained by the model?
d. Are all of the independent variables in the model significant? If not, which are not and how can you tell?
e. How much of a change in the dependent variable will be associated with a one unit change in x_2? In x_3?
f. Do any of the 95% confidence interval estimates of the slope coefficients contain zero. If so, what does this indicate?

15-4. The following correlation matrix is associated with the same data used to build the regression model in Problem 15-3:

	y	x_1	x_2	x_3
y	1			
x_1	−0.406	1		
x_2	0.459	0.051	1	
x_3	−0.244	0.504	0.272	1

Does this output indicate any potential multi-collinearity problems with the analysis?

15-5. Consider the following set of data:

x_1	29	48	28	22	28	42	33	26	48	44
x_2	15	37	24	32	47	13	43	12	58	19
y	16	46	34	26	49	11	41	13	47	16

a. Obtain the estimated regression equation.
b. Develop the correlation matrix for this set of data. Select the independent variable whose correlation magnitude is the smallest with the dependent variable. Determine if its correlation with the dependent variable is significant.
c. Determine if the overall model is significant. Use a significance level of 0.05.
d. Calculate the variance inflation factor for each of the independent variables. Indicate if multi-collinearity exists between the two independent variables.

15-6. Consider the following set of data:

x_2	10	8	11	7	10	11	6
x_1	50	45	37	32	44	51	42
y	103	85	115	73	97	102	65

a. Obtain the estimated regression equation.
b. Examine the coefficient of determination and the adjusted coefficient of determination. Does it seem that either of the independent variables' addition to R^2 does not justify the reduction in degrees of freedom that results from their addition to the regression model? Support your assertions.
c. Conduct a hypothesis test to determine if the dependent variable increases when x_2 increases. Use a significance level of 0.025 and the p-value approach.
d. Construct a 95% confidence interval for the coefficient of x_1.

Computer Database Exercises

15-7. An article in *BusinessWeek* ("Hot Growth Companies," June 5, 2006) presents a list of the 100 companies perceived as having "hot growth" characteristics. A company's rank on the list is the sum of 0.5 times its rank in return on total capital plus 0.25 times its sales and profit-growth ranks. The file entitled **Growth** contains sales ($million), sales increase (%), return on capital, market value ($million), and recent stock price of the top 20 ranked companies.
a. Produce a correlation matrix for the variables contained in the file entitled **Growth**.
b. Select the two variables that are most highly correlated with the recent stock price and produce the regression equation to predict the recent stock price as a function of the two variables you chose.
c. Determine if the overall model is significant. Use a significance level of 0.10.
d. Examine the coefficient of determination and the adjusted coefficient of determination. Does it seem that either of the independent variables' addition to R^2 does not justify the reduction in degrees of freedom that results from their addition to the regression model? Support your assertions.
e. Select the variable that is most correlated with the stock price and test to see if it is a significant predictor of the stock price. Use a significance level of 0.10 and the p-value approach.

15-8. Refer to Exercise 15-7, which referenced an article in *BusinessWeek* ("Hot Growth Companies," June 5, 2006) that presented a list of the 100 companies perceived as having "hot growth" characteristics. The file entitled **Logrowth** contains sales ($million), sales increase (%), return on capital, market value ($million), and recent stock price of the companies ranked from 81 to 100. In Exercise 15.7, stock prices were the focus. Here examine the sales of the companies.
a. Produce a regression equation that will predict the sales as a function of the other variables.
b. Determine if the overall model is significant. Use a significance level of 0.05.
c. Conduct a test of hypothesis to discover if market value should be removed from this model.
d. To see that a variable can be insignificant in one model but very significant in another, construct a regression equation in which sales is the dependent variable and market value is the independent variable. Test the hypothesis that market

value is a significant predictor of sales for those companies ranked from 81 to 100. Use a significance level of 0.05 and the p-value approach.

15-9. An investment analyst collected data about 20 randomly chosen companies. The data consisted of the 52-week-high stock prices, PE ratio, and the market value of the company. This data is in the file entitled **Investment**.

a. Produce a regression equation to predict the market value using 52-week-high stock price and the PE ratio of the company.

b. Determine if the overall model is significant. Use a significance level of 0.05.

c. OmniVision Technologies (Sunnyvale, CA) in April 2006 had a 52-week-high stock price of 31 and a PE ratio of 19. Estimate its market value for that time period. (*Note*: Its actual market value for that time period was $1,536.)

15-10. The National Association of Theatre Owners is the largest exhibition trade organization in the world, representing more than 26,000 movie screens in all 50 states and in more than 20 countries worldwide. Its membership includes the largest cinema chains and hundreds of independent theatre owners. It publishes statistics concerning the movie sector of the economy. The file entitled **Flicks** contains data on total U.S. box office grosses ($billion), total number of admissions (billion), average U.S. ticket price ($), and number of movie screens.

a. Construct a regression equation in which total U.S. box office grosses are predicted using the other variables.

b. Determine if the overall model is significant. Use a significance level of 0.05.

c. Determine the range of plausible values for the change in box office grosses if the average ticket price were to be increased by $1. Use a confidence level of 95%.

d. Calculate the variance inflation factor for each of the independent variables. Indicate if multicollinearity exists between any two independent variables.

e. Produce the regression equation suggested by your answer to part d.

15-11. The athletic director of State University is interested in developing a multiple regression model that might be used to explain the variation in attendance at football games at his school. A sample of 16 games was selected from home

games played during the past 10 seasons. Data for the following factors were determined:

y = Game attendance
x_1 = Team win/loss percentage to date
x_2 = Opponent win/loss percentage to date
x_3 = Games played this season
x_4 = Temperature at game time

The data collected are in the file called **Football**.

a. Produce scatter plots for each independent variable versus the dependent variable. Based on the scatter plots, produce a model that you believe represents the relationship between the dependent variable and the group of predictor variables represented in the scatter plots.

b. Based on the correlation matrix developed from these data, comment on whether you think a multiple regression model will be effectively developed from these data.

c. Use the sample data to estimate the multiple regression model that contains all four independent variables.

d. What percentage of the total variation in the dependent variable is explained by the four independent variables in the model?

e. Test to determine whether the overall model is statistically significant. Use $\alpha = 0.05$.

f. Which, if any, of the independent variables is statistically significant? Use a significance level of $\alpha = 0.08$ and the p-value approach to conduct these tests.

g. Estimate the standard deviation of the model error and discuss whether this regression model is acceptable as a means of predicting the football attendance at State University at any given game.

h. Define the term *multicollinearity* and indicate the potential problems that multicollinearity can cause for this model. Indicate what, if any, evidence there is of multicollinearity problems with this regression model. Use the variance inflation factor to assist you in this analysis.

i. Develop a 95% confidence interval estimate for each of the regression coefficients and interpret each estimate. Comment on whether the interpretation of the intercept is relevant in this situation.

15.2 Using Qualitative Independent Variables

In Example 15-1 involving the First City Real Estate Company, the independent variables were quantitative and ratio level. However, you will encounter many situations in which you may wish to use a qualitative, lower-level variable as an explanatory variable.

If a variable is nominal, and numerical codes are assigned to the categories, you already know not to perform mathematical calculations using those data. The results would be meaningless. Yet, we may wish to use a variable such as marital status, gender, or geographical location as an independent variable in a regression model. If the variable of interest is coded as an ordinal variable, such as education level or job performance ranking, computing means and variances is also inappropriate. Then how are these variables incorporated into a multiple regression analysis? The answer lies in using what are called **dummy** (or indicator) **variables**.

Dummy Variables
A variable that is assigned a value equal to either 0 or 1, depending on whether the observation possesses a given characteristic.

For instance, consider the variable gender, which can take on two possible values: male or female. Gender can be converted to a dummy variable as follows:

$$x_1 = 1 \text{ if female}$$
$$x_1 = 0 \text{ if male}$$

Thus, a data set consisting of males and females will have corresponding values for x_1 equal to 0s and 1s, respectively. Note that it makes no difference which gender is coded 1 and which is coded 0.

If a categorical variable has more than two mutually exclusive outcome possibilities, multiple dummy variables must be created. Consider the variable marital status, with the following possible outcomes:

never married   married   divorced   widowed

In this case, marital status has four values. To account for all the possibilities, you would create three dummy variables, one less than the number of possible outcomes for the original variable. They could be coded as follows:

$$x_1 = 1 \text{ if never married, 0 if not}$$
$$x_2 = 1 \text{ if married, 0 if not}$$
$$x_3 = 1 \text{ if divorced, 0 if not}$$

Note that we don't need the fourth variable because we would know that a person is widowed if $x_1 = 0$, $x_2 = 0$, and $x_3 = 0$. If the person isn't single, married, or divorced, he or she must be widowed. *Always use one fewer dummy variables than categories.* The mathematical reason that the number of dummy variables must be one less than the number of possible responses is called the *dummy variable trap*. Perfect multicollinearity is introduced, and the least squares regression estimates cannot be obtained, if the number of dummy variables equals the number of possible categories.

EXAMPLE 15-2 Incorporating Dummy Variables

TRY PROBLEM 15.17

Business Executive Salaries   To illustrate the effect of incorporating dummy variables into a regression model, consider the sample data displayed in the scatter plot in Figure 15.9. The population from which the sample was selected consists of executives between the ages of 24 and 60 who are working in U.S. manufacturing businesses. Data for annual salary (y) and age (x_1) are available. The objective is to determine whether a model can be generated to explain the variation in annual salary for business executives. Even though age and annual salary are significantly correlated ($r = 0.686$) at the $\alpha = 0.05$ level, the coefficient of determination is only 47%. Therefore, we would likely search for other independent variables that could help us to further explain the variation in annual salary.

TABLE 15.2
Executive Salary Data Including MBA Variable

Salary	Age	MBA
$ 65,000	26	0
85,000	28	1
74,000	36	0
83,000	35	0
110,000	35	1
160,000	40	1
100,000	41	0
122,000	42	1
85,000	45	0
120,000	46	1
105,000	50	0
135,000	51	1
125,000	55	0
175,000	50	1
156,000	61	1
140,000	63	0

FIGURE 15.9

Executive Salary Data—Scatter Plot

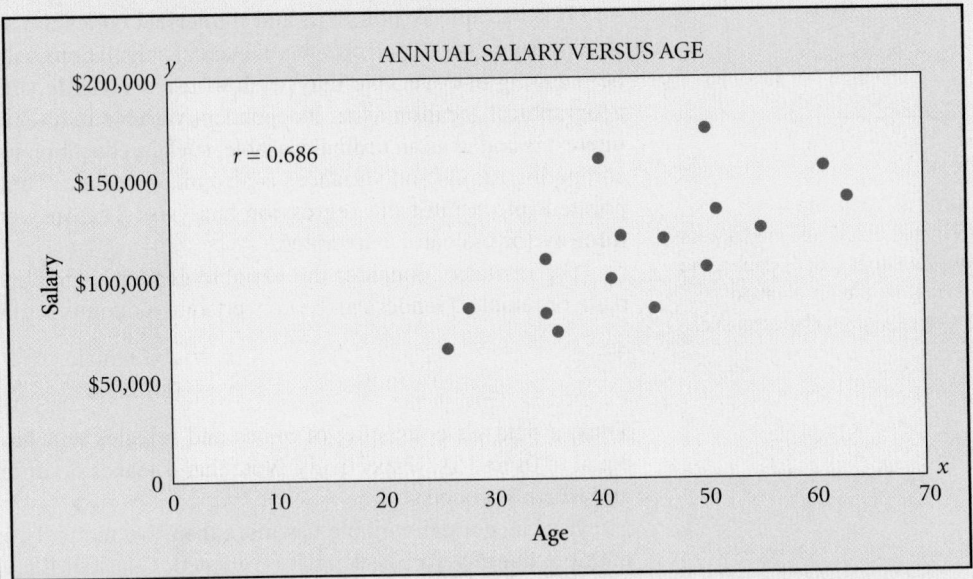

Suppose we can determine which of the 16 people in the sample had an MBA degree. Figure 15.10 shows the scatter plot for these same data, with the MBA data represented by triangles. To incorporate a qualitative variable into the analysis, use the following steps:

Step 1 **Code the qualitative variable as a dummy variable.**
Create a new variable, x_2, which is a dummy variable coded as

$$x_2 = 1 \text{ if MBA, 0 if not}$$

The data with the new variable are shown in Table 15.2.

Step 2 **Develop a multiple regression model with the dummy variables incorporated as independent variables.**
The two-variable population multiple regression model has the following form:

$$y = \beta_0 + \beta_1 x_1 + \beta_2 x_2 + \varepsilon$$

Using either Excel or Minitab, we get the following regression equation as an estimate of the population model:

$$\hat{y} = 6,974 + 2,055 x_1 + 35,236 x_2$$

Because the dummy variable, x_2, has been coded 0 or 1 depending on MBA status, incorporating it into the regression model is like having two simple linear regression lines with the same slopes, but different intercepts. For instance, when $x_2 = 0$, the regression equation is

$$\hat{y} = 6,974 + 2,055 x_1 + 35,236(0)$$
$$= 6,974 + 2,055 x_1$$

FIGURE 15.10

Impact of a Dummy Variable

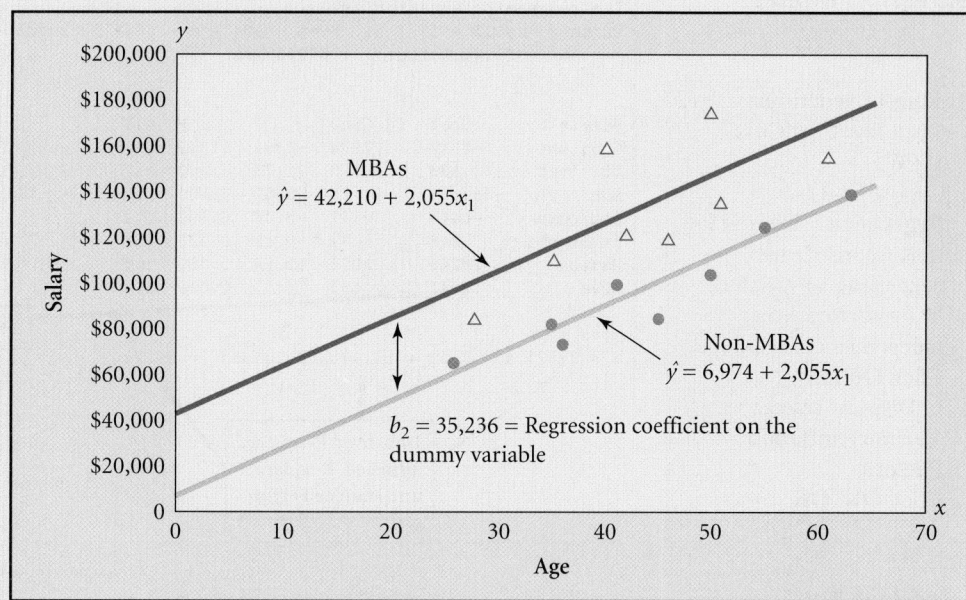

This line is shown in Figure 15.10.

However, when $x_2 = 1$ (the executive has an MBA), the regression equation is

$$\hat{y} = 6,974 + 2,055x_1 + 35,236(1)$$
$$= 42,210 + 2,055x_1$$

This regression line is also shown in Figure 15.10. As you can see, incorporating the dummy variable affects the regression intercept. In this case, the intercept for executives with an MBA degree is $35,236 higher than for those without an MBA. We interpret the regression coefficient on this dummy variable as follows: Based on these data, and holding age (x_1) constant, we estimate that executives with an MBA degree make an average of $35,236 per year more in salary than their non-MBA counterparts.

Business Application

Excel and Minitab Tutorial

FIRST CITY REAL ESTATE (*CONTINUED*) The regression model developed in Example 15-1 for First City Real Estate showed potential because the overall model was statistically significant. Looking back at Figure 15.8, we see that the model explained nearly 82% of the variation in sales prices for the homes in the sample. All of the independent variables were significant, given that the other independent variables were in the model. However, the standard error of the estimate was quite large.

The managers have decided to try to improve the model. First, they have decided to add a new variable: area. However, at this point, the only area variable they can get is whether the house is in the foothills. Because this is a categorical variable with two possible outcomes (foothills or flatland), a dummy variable can be created as follows:

$$x_6 \text{ (area)} = 1 \text{ if foothills, 0 if not}$$

Of the 319 homes in the sample, 249 were homes in the foothills and 70 were in the flatland. Figure 15.11 shows the revised Minitab multiple regression with the variable, area, added.

FIGURE 15.11

Minitab Output—First City Real Estate Revised Regression Model

Minitab Instructions:
1. Open file: First City. MTW.
2. Choose **Stat > Regression > Regression**.
3. In **Response**, enter dependent (*y*) variable.
4. In **Predictors**, enter Independent (*x*) variables.
5. Click **Options**.
6. In **Display**, select **Variance inflation Factors**.
7. Click **OK. OK.**

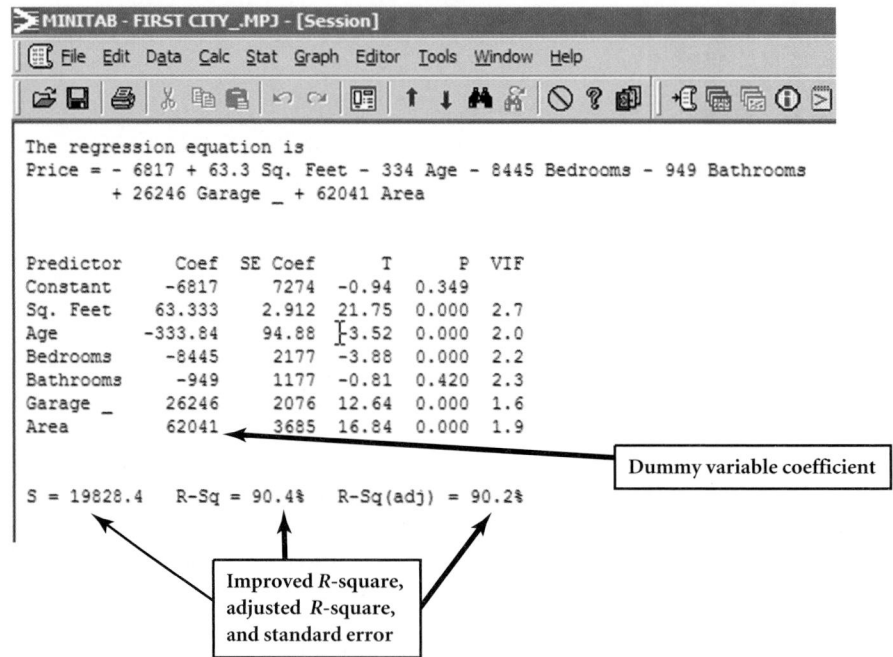

This model is an improvement over the original model because the adjusted *R*-squared has increased from 81.3% to 90.2% and the standard error of the estimate has decreased from $27,350 to $19,828. The conditional *t*-tests show that all of the regression model's slope coefficients, except that for the variable bathrooms, differ significantly from 0. The Minitab output shows that the variance inflation factors are all less than 5.0, so we don't need to be too concerned about the *t*-tests understating the significance of the regression coefficients. (See the Excel Tutorial on the CD-ROM for this example to get the full *VIF* output from PHStat.)

The resulting regression model is

$$\hat{y} = -6,817 + 63.3(\text{sq. ft.}) - 334(\text{age}) - 8,445(\text{bedrooms}) - 949(\text{bathrooms}) + 26,246 \text{ (garage)} + 62,041(\text{area})$$

Because the variable, bathrooms, is not significant in the presence of the other variables, we can remove the variable and rerun the multiple regression. The resulting model is

$$\text{Price} = -7,050 + 62.5(\text{sq. ft.}) - 322(\text{age}) - 8,830(\text{bedrooms}) + 26,054(\text{garage}) + 61,370(\text{area})$$

Based on the sample data and this regression model, we estimate that a house with the same characteristics (square feet, age, bedrooms, and garages) is worth an average of $61,370 more if it is located in the foothills (based on how the dummy variable was coded).

There are still signals of multicollinearity problems. The coefficient on the independent variable, bedrooms, is negative, when we would expect homes with more bedrooms to sell for more. Also, the standard error of the estimate is still too large ($19,817) to provide the precision the managers need to set prices for homes. More work needs to be done before the model is complete.

Possible Improvements to the First City Appraisal Model Because the standard error of the estimate is still too high, we look to improve the model. We could start by identifying possible problems:

1. We may be missing useful independent variables.
2. Independent variables may have been included that should not have been included.

There is no sure way of determining the correct model specification. However, a recommended approach is for the decision maker to try adding variables or removing variables from the model.

We begin by removing the bedrooms variable, which has an unexpected sign on the regression slope coefficient. (*Note*: If the regression model's sole purpose is for prediction, independent variables with unexpected signs do not automatically pose a problem and do not necessarily need to be deleted. However, insignificant variables should be deleted.) The resulting model is shown in Figures 15.12a and 15.12b. Now all the variables in the model have the expected signs. However, the estimate of the model's standard error has increased slightly.

Adding other explanatory variables might help. For instance, consider whether the house has central air conditioning, which might affect sales. If we can identify whether a house has air conditioning, we could add a dummy variable coded as follows:

$$\text{If air conditioning, } x_7 = 1$$
$$\text{If no air conditioning, } x_7 = 0$$

Other potential independent variables might include a more-detailed location variable, a measure of the physical condition, or whether the house has one or two stories. Can you think of others?

The First City example illustrates that even though a regression model may pass the statistical tests of significance, it may not be functional. Good appraisal models can be developed using multiple regression analysis, provided more detail is available about such characteristics as finish quality, landscaping, location, neighborhood characteristics, and so forth. The cost and effort required to obtain these data can be relatively high.

Developing a multiple regression model is more of an art than a science. The real decisions revolve around how to select the best set of independent variables for the model.

FIGURE 15.12A

Excel 2007 Output for the First City Real Estate Revised Model

Excel 2007 Instructions:
1. Open file: First City.xls (worksheet: Homes-Sample-2).
2. Click on **Data** tab—the click on **Data Analysis**.
3. Select **Regression**.
4. Define *y* variable range and the *x* variables range.
5. Click **OK**.

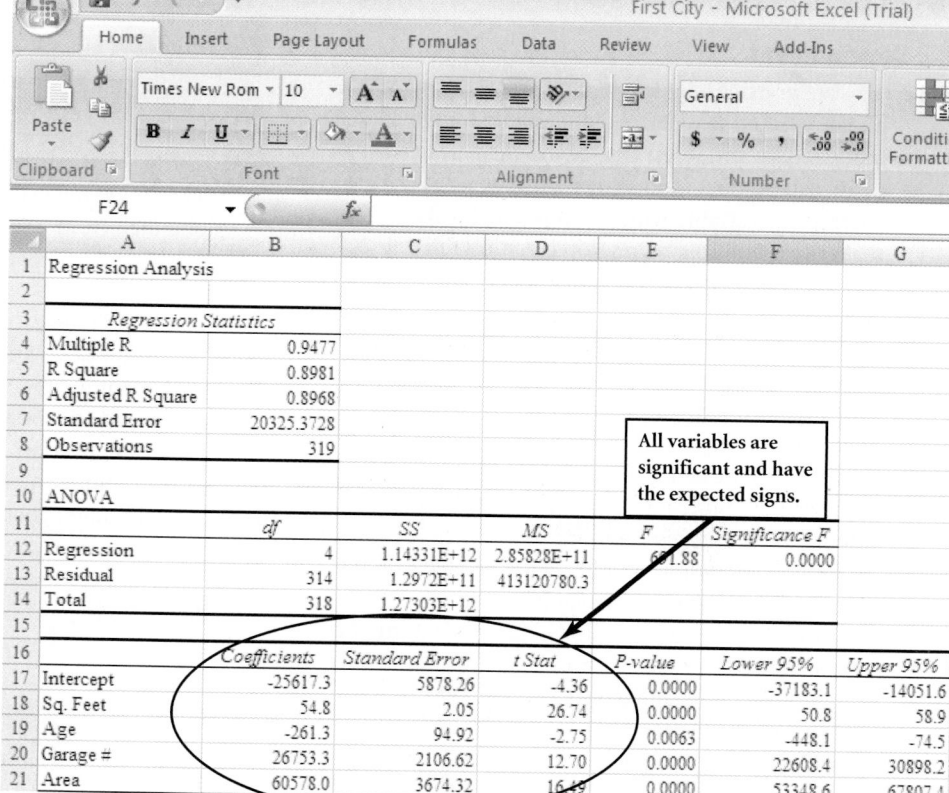

	A	B	C	D	E	F	G
1	Regression Analysis						
2							
3	*Regression Statistics*						
4	Multiple R	0.9477					
5	R Square	0.8981					
6	Adjusted R Square	0.8968					
7	Standard Error	20325.3728					
8	Observations	319			All variables are		
9					significant and have		
10	ANOVA				the expected signs.		
11		*df*	*SS*	*MS*	*F*	*Significance F*	
12	Regression	4	1.14331E+12	2.85828E+11	691.88	0.0000	
13	Residual	314	1.2972E+11	413120780.3			
14	Total	318	1.27303E+12				
15							
16		*Coefficients*	*Standard Error*	*t Stat*	*P-value*	*Lower 95%*	*Upper 95%*
17	Intercept	-25617.3	5878.26	-4.36	0.0000	-37183.1	-14051.6
18	Sq. Feet	54.8	2.05	26.74	0.0000	50.8	58.9
19	Age	-261.3	94.92	-2.75	0.0063	-448.1	-74.5
20	Garage #	26753.3	2106.62	12.70	0.0000	22608.4	30898.2
21	Area	60578.0	3674.32	16.49	0.0000	53348.6	67807.4

FIGURE 15.12B

Minitab Output for the First City Real Estate Revised Model

MINITAB - FIRST CITY_.MPJ - [Session]

File Edit Data Calc Stat Graph Editor Tools Window Help

The regression equation is
Price = - 25617 + 54.8 Sq. Feet - 261 Age + 26753 Garage _ + 60578 Area

Predictor	Coef	SE Coef	T	P
Constant	-25617	5878	-4.36	0.000
Sq. Feet	54.832	2.051	26.74	0.000
Age	-261.30	94.92	-2.75	0.006
Garage _	26753	2107	12.70	0.000
Area	60578	3674	16.49	0.000

S = 20325.4   R-Sq = 89.8%   R-Sq(adj) = 89.7%

All variables are significant and have the expected signs.

Analysis of Variance

Source	DF	SS	MS	F	P
Regression	4	1.14331E+12	2.85828E+11	691.88	0.000
Residual Error	314	1.29720E+11	413120780		
Total	318	1.27303E+12			

Minitab Instructions:
1. Open file: First City. MTW.
2. Choose **Stat > Regression > Regression**.
3. In **Response**, enter dependent (*y*) variable.
4. In **Predictors**, enter Independent (*x*) variables.
5. Click **Options**.
6. In **Display**, select **Variance inflation Factors**.
7. Click **OK. OK**.

15-2: Exercises

Skill Development

15-12. You are considering developing a regression equation relating a dependent variable to two independent variables. One of the variables can be measured on a ratio scale but the other is a categorical variable with two possible levels.
   a. Write a multiple regression equation relating the dependent variable to the independent variables.
   b. Interpret the meaning of the coefficients in the regression equation.

15-13. You are considering developing a regression equation relating a dependent variable to two independent variables. One of the variables can be measured on a ratio scale but the other is a categorical variable with four possible levels.
   a. How many dummy variables are needed to represent the categorical variable?
   b. Write a multiple regression equation relating the dependent variable to the independent variables.
   c. Interpret the meaning of the coefficients in the regression equation.

15-14. Consider the following regression model:

$$y = \beta_0 + \beta_1 x_1 + \beta_2 x_2 + \varepsilon$$

where:

x_1 = a quantitative variable

$$x_2 = \begin{cases} 1 \text{ if } x_1 < 20 \\ 0 \text{ if } x_1 \geq 20 \end{cases}$$

The following estimated regression equation was obtained from a sample of 30 observations:

$$\hat{y} = 24.1 + 5.8x_1 + 7.9x_2$$

   a. Provide the estimated regression equation for instances in which $x_1 < 20$.
   b. Determine the value of $\hat{y}$ when $x_1 = 10$.
   c. Provide the estimated regression equation for instances in which $x_1 \geq 20$.
   d. Determine the value of $\hat{y}$ when $x_1 = 30$.

15-15. A real estate agent wishes to estimate the monthly rental for apartments based upon the size (square feet) and the location of the apartments. She chose the model

$$y = \beta_0 + \beta_1 x_1 + \beta_2 x_2 + \varepsilon$$

where:

x_1 = square footage of the apartment

$$x_2 = \begin{cases} 1 \text{ if located in town center} \\ 0 \text{ if not located in town center} \end{cases}$$

This linear regression model was fitted to a sample of size 50 to produce the following regression equation:

$$\hat{y} = 145 + 1.2x_1 + 300x_2$$

a. Predict the average monthly rental for an apartment located in the town center that has 1,500 square feet.
b. Predict the average monthly rent for an apartment located in the suburbs that has 1,500 square feet.
c. Interpret b_2 in the context of this exercise.

Business Applications

15-16. The Polk Utility Corporation is developing a multiple regression model that it plans to use to predict customers' utility usage. The analyst currently has three quantitative variables (x_1, x_2, and x_3) in the model, but she is dissatisfied with the R-squared and the estimate of the standard deviation of the model's error. Two variables that she thinks might be useful are whether the house has a gas water heater or an electric water heater and whether the house was constructed after the 1974 energy crisis or before.

Provide the model she should use to predict customers' utility usage. Specify the dummy variables to be used, the values these variables could assume, and what each value will represent.

15-17. A study was recently performed by the American Automobile Association in which it attempted to develop a regression model to explain variation in EPA mileage ratings of new cars. At one stage of the analysis, the estimate of the model took the following form:

$$\hat{y} = 34.20 - 0.003x_1 + 4.56x_2$$

where:

$$x_1 = \text{Vehicle weight}$$
$$x_2 = \begin{cases} 1, & \text{if standard transmission} \\ 0, & \text{if automatic transmission} \end{cases}$$

a. Interpret the regression coefficient for variable x_1.
b. Interpret the regression coefficient for variable x_2.
c. Present an estimate of a model that would predict the average EPA mileage rating for an automobile with standard transmission as a function of the vehicle's weight.
d. Cadillac's STS-V with automatic transmission weighs approximately 4,394 pounds. Provide an estimate of the average highway mileage you would expect to obtain from this model.

e. Discuss the effect of a dummy variable being incorporated in a regression equation like this one. Use a graph if it is helpful.

15-18. A real estate agent wishes to determine the selling price of residences using the size (square feet) and whether the residence is a condominium or a single-family home. A sample of 20 residences was obtained with the following results:

Price	Type	Square Feet	Price	Type	Square Feet
199,700	Family	1,500	200,600	Condo	1,375
211,800	Condo	2,085	208,000	Condo	1,825
197,100	Family	1,450	210,500	Family	1,650
228,400	Family	1,836	233,300	Family	1,960
215,800	Family	1,730	187,200	Condo	1,360
190,900	Condo	1,726	185,200	Condo	1,200
312,200	Family	2,300	284,100	Family	2,000
313,600	Condo	1,650	207,200	Family	1,755
239,000	Family	1,950	258,200	Family	1,850
184,400	Condo	1,545	203,100	Family	1,630

a. Produce a regression equation to predict the selling price for residences using a model of the form:

$$y_i = \beta_0 + \beta_1 x_1 + \beta_2 x_2 + \varepsilon$$

where:

$$x_1 = \text{square footage} \quad \text{and} \quad x_2 = \begin{cases} 1 \text{ if a condo} \\ 0 \text{ if a single-family home} \end{cases}$$

b. Interpret the parameters β_1 and β_2 in the model given in part a.
c. Produce an equation that describes the relationship between the selling price and the square footage of (1) condominiums, and (2) single-family homes.
d. Conduct a test of hypothesis to determine if the relationship between the selling price and the square footage is different between condominiums and single-family homes.

15-19. J.D. Power and Associates reported ["2004 Initial Quality Study (IQS)," April 28, 2004] on the initial quality of Korean-branded, European-, and domestic-branded vehicles. The 2004 Initial Quality Study was based on responses from more than 62,000 purchasers and lessors of new-model-year cars and trucks, who were surveyed after 90 days of ownership. Initial quality is measured by the number of problems per 100 vehicles (PP100). The PP100 data from the interval 1998–2004 follow:

	1998	1999	2000	2001	2002	2003	2004
Korean	272	227	222	214	172	152	117
Domestic	182	177	164	153	137	135	123
European	158	171	154	141	137	136	122

a. Produce a regression equation to predict the PP100 for vehicles in the model

$$y_i = \beta_0 + \beta_1 x_1 + \beta_2 x_2 + \varepsilon$$

where:

$$x_1 = \begin{cases} 1 \text{ if Domestic} \\ 0 \text{ if not Domestic} \end{cases} \text{ and } x_2 = \begin{cases} 1 \text{ if European} \\ 0 \text{ if not European} \end{cases}$$

b. Interpret the parameters β_0, β_1, and β_2 in the model given in part a.

c. Conduct a test of hypothesis using the model in part a to determine if the average PP100 is the same for the three international automobile production regions.

Computer Database Exercises

15-20. The Gilmore Accounting firm collected the following data in an effort to explain variation in client profitability. The data are in the data file called **Gilmore**.

y	x_1	x_2
2,345	45	1
4,200	56	2
278	26	3
1,211	56	2
1,406	24	2
500	23	3
−700	34	3
3,457	45	1
2,478	47	1
1,975	24	2
206	32	3

where:

y = Net profit earned from the client
x_1 = Number of hours spent working with the client
x_2 = Type of client:
    1, if manufacturing
    2, if service
    3, if governmental

a. Develop a scatter plot of each independent variable against the client income variable. Comment on what, if any, relationship appears to exist in each case.

b. Run a simple linear regression analysis using only variable x_1 as the independent variable. Describe the resulting estimate fully.

c. Test to determine if the number of hours spent working with the client is useful in predicting the net profit earned by a client.

15-21. Using the data from the Gilmore Accounting firm found in the data file **Gilmore** (see Exercise 15-20),

a. Incorporate the client type into the regression analysis using dummy variables. Describe the resulting multiple regression estimate.

b. Test to determine if this model is useful in predicting the net profit earned from the client.

c. Test to determine if the number of hours spent working with the client is useful in this model in predicting the net profit earned from a client.

d. Considering the tests you have performed, construct a model and its estimate for predicting the net profit earned from the client.

e. Predict the average difference in profit if the client is governmental versus one who is in manufacturing. Also state this in terms of a 95% confidence interval estimate.

15-22. The Energy Information Administration (EIA), created by Congress in 1977, is a statistical agency of the U.S. Department of Energy. It provides data, forecasts, and analyses to promote sound policy-making and public understanding regarding energy and its interaction with the economy and the environment. One of the most important areas of analysis is petroleum. The file entitled **Crude** contains data for the period 1991–2006 concerning the price, supply, and demand for fuel. It has been conjectured that the pricing structure of gasoline changed at the turn of the century.

a. Produce a regression equation to predict the selling price of gasoline

$$y_i = \beta_0 + \beta_1 x_1 + \varepsilon$$

where:

$$x_1 = \begin{cases} 1 \text{ if is in 21st century} \\ 0 \text{ if is in 20th century} \end{cases}$$

b. Conduct a hypothesis test to address the conjecture. Use a significance level of 0.05 and the test statistic approach.

c. Produce a 95% confidence interval to estimate the change of the average selling price of gasoline between the 20th and the 21st centuries.

15-23. In a press release entitled "College Board Offers Glimpse of New SAT with Writing for Upcoming Class of '06," August 30, 2005, the College Board announced SAT scores for students in the class of 2005. The file entitled **MathSAT** contains the average SAT scores for the interval 1967 to 2005. The class of 2005 was the last to take the former version of the SAT featuring math and verbal sections. There has been conjecture indicating a relationship between the average math SAT score and the average verbal SAT score and the gender of the student taking the SAT examination. Consider the following relationship:

$$y_i = \beta_0 + \beta_1 x_1 + \beta_2 x_2 + \varepsilon$$

where:

x_1 = average verbal SAT score   and $x_2 = \begin{cases} 1 \text{ if a female} \\ 0 \text{ if a male} \end{cases}$

   a. Compute the linear regression equation to predict the average math SAT score using the

gender and the average verbal SAT score of the students taking the SAT examination.

   b. Interpret the parameters in the model.

   c. Conduct a hypothesis test to determine if the gender of the student taking the SAT examination is a significant predictor of the student's average math SAT score for a given average verbal SAT score.

   d. Predict the average math SAT score of female students with an average verbal SAT score of 500.

CHAPTER OUTCOME #7

15.3 Working with Nonlinear Relationships

Section 14.1 in Chapter 14 showed there are a variety of ways in which two variables can be related. Correlation and regression analysis techniques are tools for measuring and modeling linear relationships between variables. Many situations in business have a linear relationship between two variables, and regression equations that model that relationship will be appropriate to use in these situations. However, there are also many instances in which the relationship between two variables will be curvilinear, rather than linear. For instance, demand for electricity has grown at an almost exponential rate relative to the population growth in some areas. Advertisers believe that a diminishing returns relationship will occur between sales and advertising if advertising is allowed to grow too large. These two situations are shown in Figures 15.13 and 15.14, respectively. They represent just two of the great many possible curvilinear relationships that could exist between two variables.

   As you will soon see, models with nonlinear relationships become more complicated than models showing only linear relationships. Although complicated models are sometimes

FIGURE 15.13

Exponential Relationship of Increased Demand for Electricity versus Population Growth

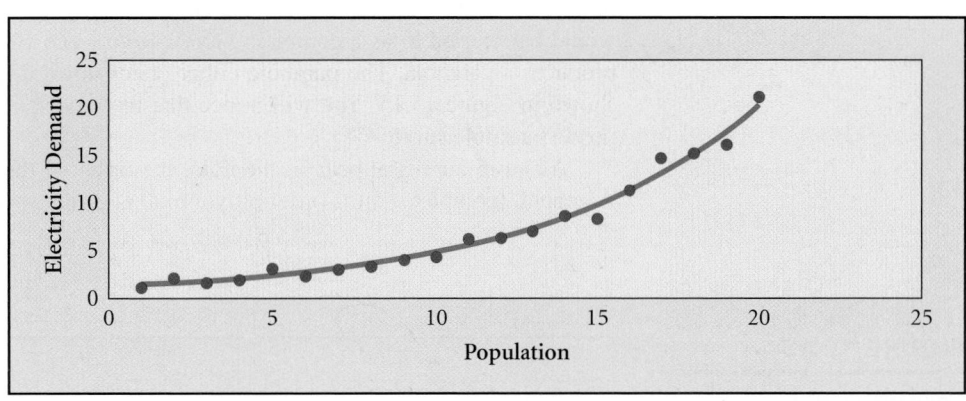

FIGURE 15.14

Diminishing Returns Relationship of Advertising versus Sales

necessary, decision makers should use them with caution for several reasons. First, management researchers and authors have written that people use decision aids they understand and don't use those they don't understand. So, the more complicated a model is, the less likely it is to be used. Second, the scientific principle of parsimony suggests using the simplest model possible that provides a reasonable fit of the data, because complex models typically do not reflect the underlying phenomena that produce the data in the first place.

This section provides a brief introduction into how linear regression analysis can be used in dealing with curvilinear relationships. In order to model such curvilinear relationships, we must incorporate terms into the multiple regression model that will create "curves" in the model we are building. Including terms whose independent variable has an exponent larger than 1 generates these curves. When a model possesses such terms we refer to it as a *polynomial model*. The general equation for a polynomial with one independent variable is given in Equation 15.11.

Polynomial Population Regression Model

$$y = \beta_0 + \beta_1 x + \beta_2 x^2 + \cdots + \beta_p x^p + \varepsilon \qquad (15.11)$$

where:

β_0 = Population regression's constant
β_j = Popultion's regression coefficient for variable x x^j; $j = 1, 2, \ldots, p$
p = Order (or degree) of the polynomial
ε = Model error

The order, or degree, of the model is determined by the largest exponent of the independent variable in the model. For instance, the model

$$y = \beta_0 + \beta_1 x + \beta_2 x^2 + \varepsilon$$

is a second-order polynomial because the largest exponent in any term of the polynomial is 2. You will note that this model contains terms of all orders less than or equal to 2. A polynomial with this property is said to be a *complete* polynomial. Therefore, the previous model would be referred to as a complete *second-order regression model*. A second-order model produces a parabola. The parabola either opens upward ($\beta_2 > 0$) or downward ($\beta_2 < 0$), shown in Figure 15.15. You will notice that the models in Figures 15.13, 15.14 and 15.15 possess a single curve.

As more curves appear in the data, the order of the polynomial must be increased. A general (complete) third-order polynomial is given by the equation

$$y = \beta_0 + \beta_1 x + \beta_2 x^2 + \beta_3 x^3 + \varepsilon$$

FIGURE 15.15

Second-Order Regression Models

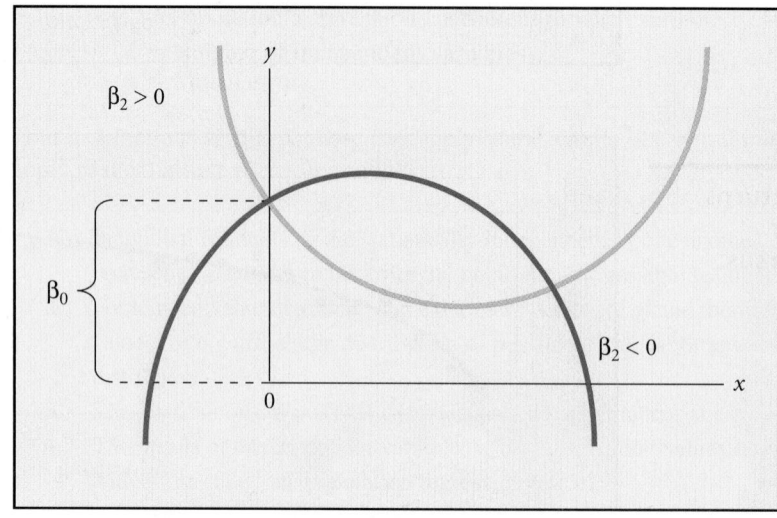

FIGURE 15.16

Third-Order Regression Models

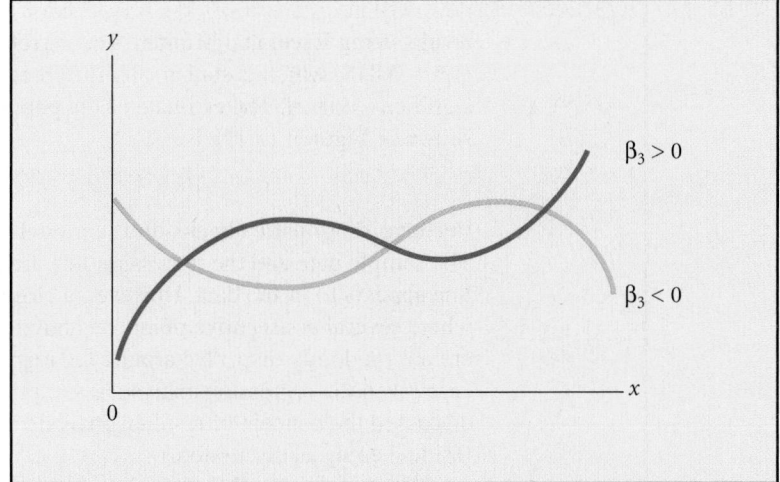

This model produces a curvilinear model that reverses the direction of the initial curve to produce a second curve, as shown in Figure 15.16. Note that there are two curves in the third-order model. In general, a pth-order polynomial will exhibit $p - 1$ curves.

Although polynomials of all orders exist in the business sector, perhaps second-order polynomials are the most common. Sharp reversals in the curvature of a relationship between variables in the business environment usually point to some unexpected or, perhaps, severe changes that were not foreseen. The vast majority of organizations try to avoid such reverses. For this reason, and the fact that this is an introductory business statistics course, we will direct most of our attention to second-order polynomials.

The following examples illustrate two of the most common instances in which curvilinear relationships can be used in decision making. They should give you an idea of how to approach similar situations.

TRY PROBLEM 15.24

CHAPTER OUTCOME #7

Excel and Minitab Tutorial

EXAMPLE 15-3 Modeling Curvilinear Relationships

Ashley Investment Services Ashley Investment Services was severely shaken by the downturn in the stock market after the September 11th attack. To maintain profitability and save as many jobs as possible, since then everyone has been extra busy analyzing new investment opportunities. The director of personnel has noticed an increased number of people suffering from "burnout," in which physical and emotional fatigue hurt job performance. Although he cannot change the job's pressures, he has read that the more time a person spends socializing with coworkers away from the job, the more likely a higher degree of burnout. With the help of the human resources lab at the local university, the personnel director has administered a questionnaire to company employees. A burnout index has been computed from the responses to the survey. Likewise, the survey responses are used to determine quantitative measures of socialization. Sample data from questionnaires are contained in the file **Ashley** on the CD-ROM. The following steps can be used to model the relationship between the socialization index and the burnout index for Ashley employees:

Step 1 **Specify the model by determining the dependent and potential independent variables.**

The dependent variable is the burnout index. The company wishes to explain the variation in burnout level. One potential independent variable is the socialization index.

Step 2 **Formulate the model.**

We begin by proposing that a linear relationship exists between the two variables. Figures 15.17a and 15.17b show the linear regression analysis results using Excel and Minitab. The correlation between the two variables is $r = 0.818$, which is statistically different from zero at any reasonable significance level. The estimate of the population linear regression model shown in Figures 15.17a is

$$\hat{y} = -66.164 + 9.589x$$

Step 3 **Perform diagnostic checks on the model.**

The sample data and the regression line are plotted in Figure 15.18. The line appears to fit the data. However, a closer inspection reveals instances where several consecutive points lie above or below the line. The points are not randomly dispersed around the regression line, as should be the case given the regression analysis assumptions. (In Chapter 14 we briefly discussed the concept of residual analysis. Section 15.5 expands the residual analysis discussion.)

As you will recall from earlier discussions, we can use an F-test to test whether a regression model explains a significant amount of variation in the dependent variable.

FIGURE 15.17A

Excel 2007 Output of a Simple Linear Regression for Ashley Investment Services

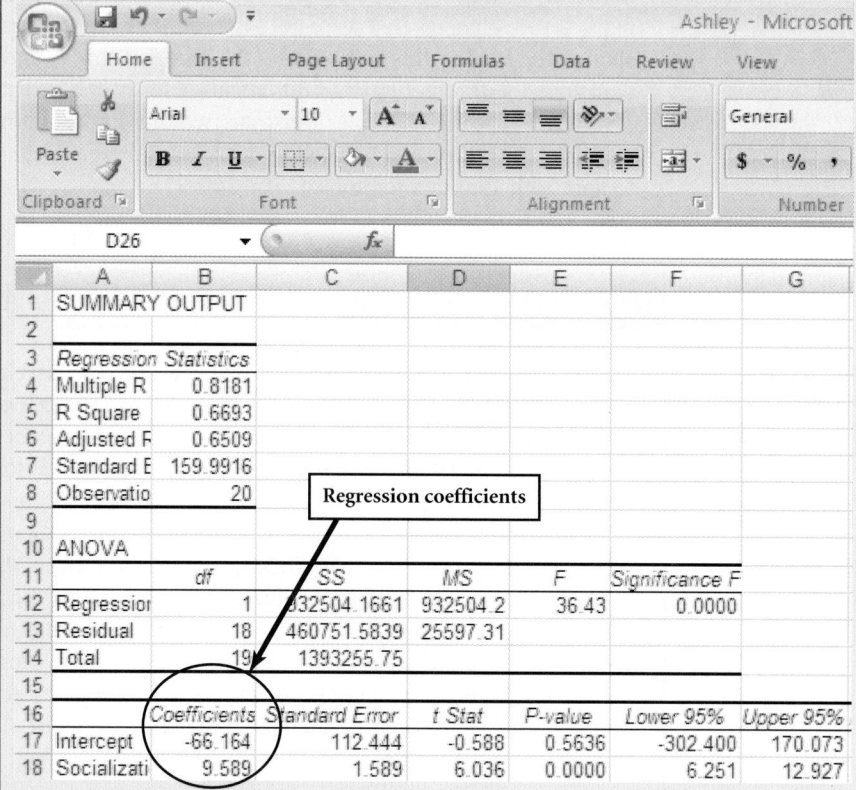

Excel 2007 Instructions:
1. Open file: Ashley.xls.
2. Select **Data > Data Analysis**.
3. Select **Regression**.
4. Specify y variable range and x variable range (include labels).
5. Check **Labels** option.
6. Specify output location.
7. Click **OK**.

FIGURE 15.17B

Minitab Output of a Simple Linear Regression for Ashley Investment Services

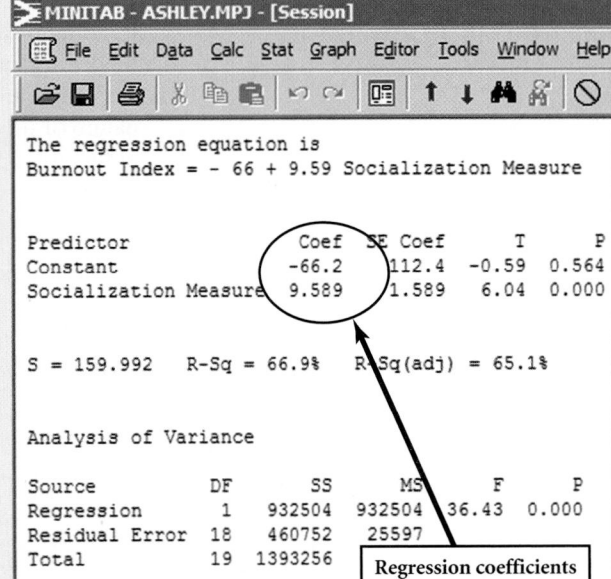

Minitab Instructions:
1. Open file: Ashley.MTW.
2. Choose **Stat > Regression > Regression**.
3. In **Response**, enter the y variable column.
4. In **Predictors**, enter the x variable column.
5. Click **OK**.

FIGURE 15.18

Plot of Regression Line for the Ashley Investment Services Example

$$H_0: \rho^2 = 0$$
$$H_A: \rho^2 > 0$$

From the output in Figure 15.17a,

$$F = 36.43$$

which has a p-value ≈ 0.0000.

Thus, we conclude that the simple linear model is statistically significant. However, we should also examine the data to determine if any curvilinear relationships may be present.

Step 4 Model the curvilinear relationship.

Finding instances of nonrandom patterns in the residuals for a regression model indicates the possibility of using a curvilinear relationship rather than a linear one. One possible approach to modeling the curvilinear nature of the data in the Ashley Investments example is with the use of polynomials. From Figure 15.18, we can see that there appears to be one curve in the data. This suggests fitting the second-order polynomial

$$y = \beta_0 + \beta_1 x + \beta_2 x^2 + \varepsilon$$

Before fitting the estimate for this population model, you will need to create the new independent variable by squaring the socialization measure variable. In Excel, use the formula option, or in Minitab, use the **Calc > Calculator** command to create the new variable. Figures 15.19a and 15.19b show the output after fitting this second-order polynomial model.

FIGURE 15.19A

Excel 2007 Output of a Second-Order Polynomial Fit for Ashley Investment

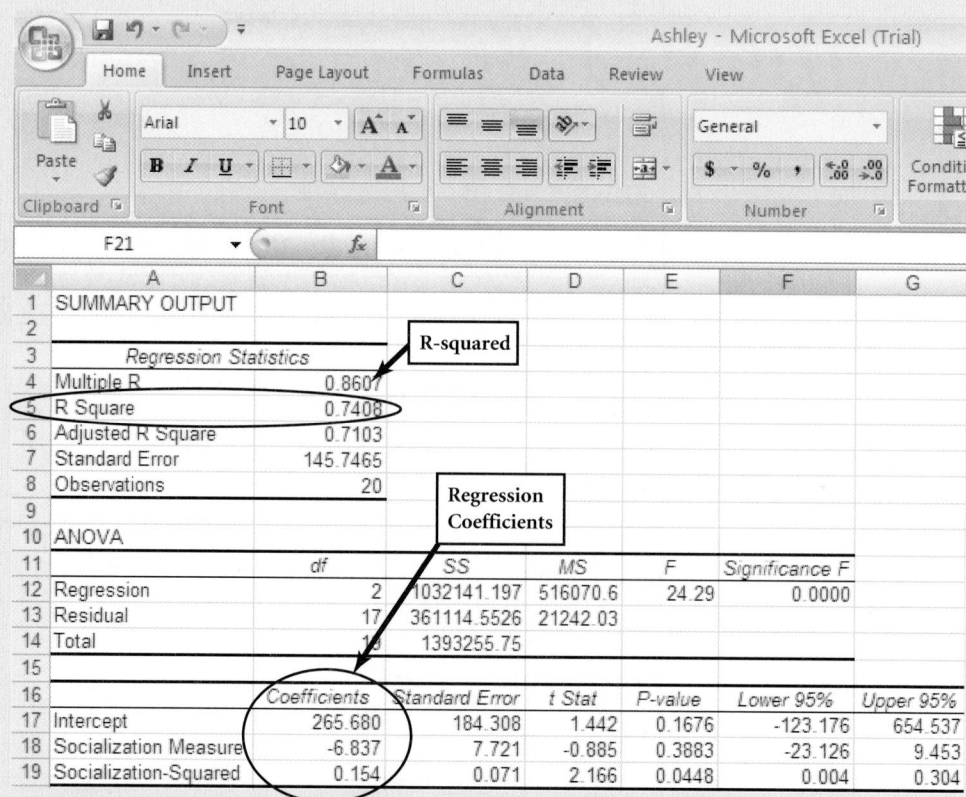

Excel 2007 Instructions:

1. Open file: Ashley.xls.
2. Use Excel equations to create the new variable in column C (i.e. for the first data value use = A2^2. Then copy down).
3. Select **Data > Data Analysis**.
4. Select **Regression**.
5. Specify *y* variable range and *x* variable range (include the new variable and the labels).
6. Check **Labels** option.
7. Specify ouput location.
8. Click **OK**.

FIGURE 15.19B

Minitab Output of a Second-Order Polynomial Fit for Ashley Investment

Minitab Instructions:
1. Open file: Ashley.MTW.
2. Choose **Stat > Regression > Fitted Line Plot**.
3. In **Response**, enter y variable.
4. In **Predictor**, enter x variable.
5. Under **Type of Regression Model**, Choose **Quadratic**.
6. Click **OK**.

Step 5 Perform diagnostics on the revised curvilinear model.

Notice the second-order polynomial provides a model whose estimated regression equation has an R^2 of 74.1%. This is higher than the R^2 of 66.9% for the linear model. Figure 15.20 shows the plot of the second-order polynomial model. Comparing Figure 15.20 with Figure 15.18, we can see that the polynomial model does appear to fit the sample data better than the linear model.

FIGURE 15.20

Plot of Second-Order Polynomial Model for Ashley Investment

Analyzing Interaction Effects

ASHLEY INVESTMENT SERVICES (*CONTINUED*) Referring to Example 15-3 involving Ashley Investment Services, the director of personnel wondered if the effects of burnout differ among male and female workers. He therefore identified the gender of the previously surveyed employees (see the CD-ROM file **Ashley-2**). A multiple scatter plot of the data appears as Figure 15.21.

The personnel director tried to determine the relationship between the burnout index and socialization measure for men and women. The graphical result is presented in Figure 15.21. Note that both relationships appear to be curvilinear with a similarly shaped curve. As we showed earlier, curvilinear shapes often can be modeled by the second-order polynomial

$$\hat{y} = b_0 + b_1 x_1 + b_2 x_1^2$$

However, the regression equations that estimate this second-order polynomial for men and women are not the same. The two equations seem to have different locations and different rates of curvature. Whether an employee is a man or woman seems to change the basic relationship between burnout index (y) and socialization measure (x_1). In order to

FIGURE 15.21

Excel 2007 Multiple Scatter Plot for Ashley Investment Services

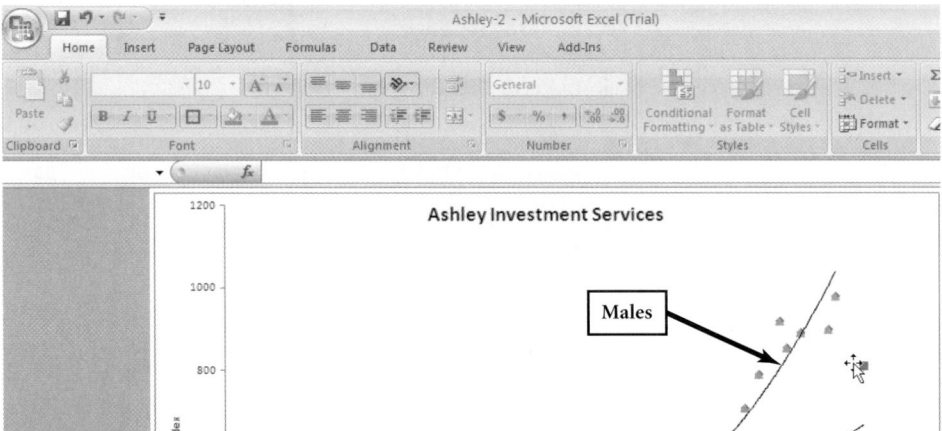

Excel 2007 Instructions:
1. Open file: Ashley-2.xls.
2. Select the Socialization Measure and Burnout Index Columns.
3. Select the **Insert** tab.
4. Select the **XY (Scatter)**.
5. Select **Chart** and click the right mouse button—choose **Select Data**.
6. Click on **Add** on the **Legend Entry (Series)** section.
7. Enter **Series Name**—(Females)— For **Series X Values** select data from Socialization column for row

corresponding to females (rows 2–11). For **Series Y Values** select data from the Burnout column corresponding to females (rows 2–11).
8. Repeat step 7 for males.
9. Click on **layout** tab to remove legend and to add chart and axis titles.
10. Select data points for males—right click and select **Add Trendline > Exponential**.
11. Repeat Step 10 for females.

represent this difference, the equation's coefficients b_0, b_1, and b_2 must be different for men and women employees. Thus, we could use two models, one for each gender. Alternatively, we could use one model for both males and females by incorporating a dummy independent variable with two levels, which is shown as

$$x_2 = 1 \text{ if a male, 0 if a female}$$

As x_2 changes values from 0 to 1, it affects the values of the coefficients b_0, b_1, and b_2. Suppose the director fitted the second-order model for the female employees only. He obtained the following regression equation:

$$\hat{y} = 291.70 - 4.62x_1 + 0.102x_1^2$$

The equation for the male employees only was

$$\hat{y} = 149.59 - 4.40x_1 + 0.160x_1^2$$

Interaction

The case in which one independent variable (such as x_2) affects the relationship between another independent variable (x_1) and a dependent variable (y).

To explain how a change in gender can cause this kind of change, we must introduce the concept of **interaction**. Therefore, in our example, gender (x_2) interacts with the relationship between socialization measure (x_1) and burnout index (y). The question is how do we obtain the interaction terms to model such a relationship? To answer this question, we first obtain the model for the basic relationship between the x_1 and the y variables. The population model is

$$y = \beta_0 + \beta_1 x_1 + \beta_2 x_1^2 + \varepsilon$$

To obtain the interaction terms, multiply the terms on the right-hand side of this equation by the variable that is interacting with this relationship between y and x_1. In this case, that interacting variable is x_2. Then the interaction terms would be

$$\beta_3 x_2 + \beta_4 x_1 x_2 + \beta_5 x_1^2 x_2$$

Composite Model

The model that contains both the basic terms and the interaction terms.

Notice that we have changed the coefficient subscripts so we do not duplicate those in the original model. Then the interaction terms are added to the original model to produce the **composite model**.

$$y = \beta_0 + \beta_1 x_1 + \beta_2 x_1^2 + \beta_3 x_2 + \beta_4 x_1 x_2 + \beta_5 x_1^2 x_2 + \varepsilon$$

Note, the model for women is obtained by substituting $x_2 = 0$ into the composite model. This gives

$$\begin{aligned} y &= \beta_0 + \beta_1 x_1 + \beta_2 x_1^2 + \beta_3(0) + \beta_4 x_1(0) + \beta_5 x_1^2(0) + \varepsilon \\ &= \beta_0 + \beta_1 x_1 + \beta_2 x_1^2 + \varepsilon \end{aligned}$$

Similarly, for men we substitute the value of $x_2 = 1$. The model then becomes

$$\begin{aligned} y &= \beta_0 + \beta_1 x_1 + \beta_2 x_1^2 + \beta_3(1) + \beta_4 x_1(1) + \beta_5 x_1^2(1) + \varepsilon \\ &= (\beta_0 + \beta_3) + (\beta_1 + \beta_4)x_1 + (\beta_2 + \beta_5)x_1^2 + \varepsilon \end{aligned}$$

This illustrates how the coefficients are changed for different values of x_2, and therefore, how x_2 is interacting with the relationship between x_1 and y. Once we know β_3, β_4, and β_5, we know the effect of the interaction of gender on the original relationship between the burnout index (y) and the socialization measure (x_1). In order to estimate the composite model, we need to create the required variables, as shown in Figure 15.22. Figures 15.23a and 15.23b show the regression for the composite model. The estimate for the composite model is

$$\hat{y} = 291.706 - 4.615x_1 + 0.102x_1^2 - 142.113x_2 + 0.215x_1 x_2 + 0.058x_1^2 x_2$$

FIGURE 15.22

Excel 2007 Data Preparation for Estimating Interactive Effects for Second-Order Model for Ashley Investment

Excel 2007 Instructions:
1. Open file: Ashley-2.xls.
2. Use Excel formulas to create new variables in columns C, E and F.

	A	B	C	D	E	F
	Socialization Measure	Burnout Index	Socialization Squared	Gender		
1	x_1	y	x_1^2	x_2	$x_1 x_2$	$x_1^2 x_2$
2	12	296	144	0	0	0
3	35	120	1225	0	0	0
4	60	525	3600	0	0	0
5	68	410	4624	0	0	0
6	70	501	4900	0	0	0
7	75	600	5625	0	0	0
8	77	506	5929	0	0	0
9	79	527	6241	0	0	0
10	86	493	7396	0	0	0
11	92	810	8464	0	0	0
12	20	100	400	1	20	400
13	38	300	1444	1	38	1444
14	59	310	3481	1	59	3481
15	75	709	5625	1	75	5625
16	77	791	5929	1	77	5929
17	80	920	6400	1	80	6400
18	81	855	6561	1	81	6561
19	83	892	6889	1	83	6889
20	87	900	7569	1	87	7569
21	88	980	7744	1	88	7744

We obtain the model for females by substituting $x_2 = 0$, giving

$$\hat{y} = 291.706 - 4.615x_1 + 0.102x_1^2 - 142.113(0) + 0.215x_1(0) + 0.058x_1^2(0)$$
$$\hat{y} = 291.706 - 4.615x_1 + 0.102x_1^2$$

For males, we substitute $x_2 = 1$, giving

$$\hat{y} = 291.706 - 4.615x_1 + 0.102x_1^2 - 142.113(1) + 0.215x_1(1) + 0.058x_1^2(1)$$
$$\hat{y} = 149.593 - 4.40x_1 + 0.160x_1^2$$

Note that these equations for males and females are the same as those we found earlier when we generated two separate regression models, one for each gender.

In this example we have looked at a case in which a dummy variable interacts with the relationship between another independent variable and the dependent variable. However, the interacting variable need not be a dummy variable. It can be any independent variable. Also, strictly speaking, interaction is not said to exist if the only effect of the interaction variable is to change the y intercept of the equation relating another independent variable to the dependent variable. Therefore, when you search a scatter plot to detect interaction, you are trying to determine if the relationships produced, when the interaction variable changes values, are parallel or not. If the relationships are parallel, that indicates that only the y intercept is being affected by the change of the interacting variable and that interaction does not exist. Figure 15.24 demonstrates this concept graphically.

FIGURE 15.23A

Excel 2007 Composite Model for Ashley Investment Services

Excel 2007 Instructions:
1. Open file: Ashley-2.xls.
2. Create new variables (see Figure 15.22 Excel 2007 Instructions).
3. Rearrange columns so all *x* variables are contiguous.
4. Select **Data > Data Analysis**.
5. Select **Regression**.
6. Specify *y* variable range and *x* variable range (include the new variables and the labels).
7. Check **Labels** option.
8. Specify output location.
9. Click **OK**.

FIGURE 15.23B

Minitab Composite Model for Ashley Investment Services

Minitab Instructions:
1. Continue from Figure 15.19b.
2. Choose **Stat > Regression > Regression**.
3. In **Response**, enter dependent (*y*) variable.
4. In **Predictors**, enter independent (*x*) variables.
5. Click **OK**.

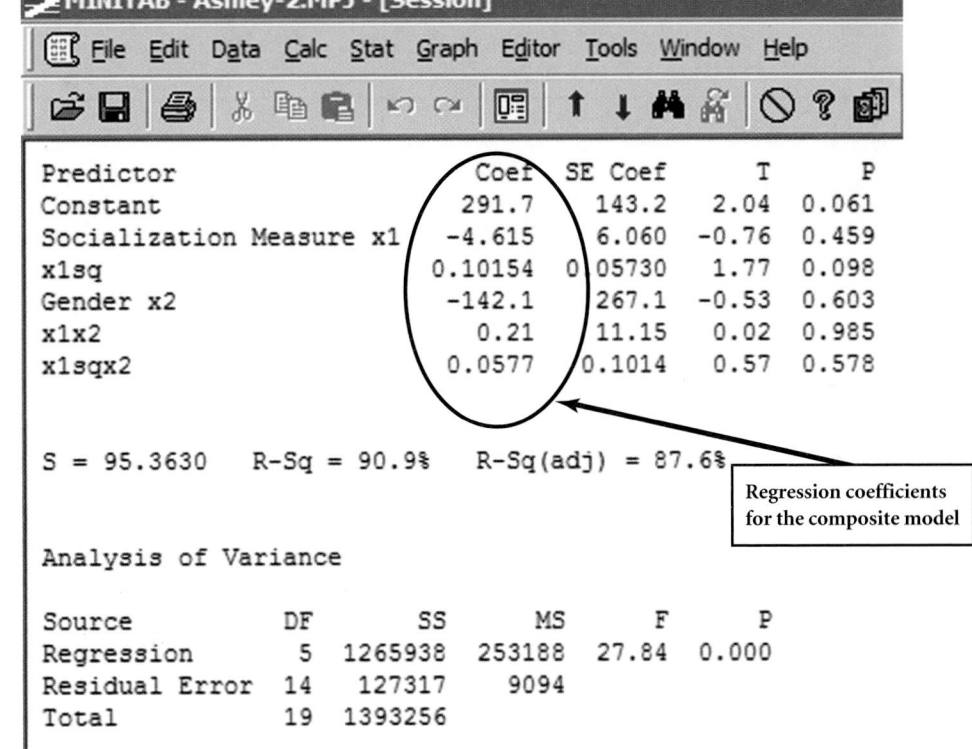

FIGURE 15.24

Graphical Evidence of Interaction

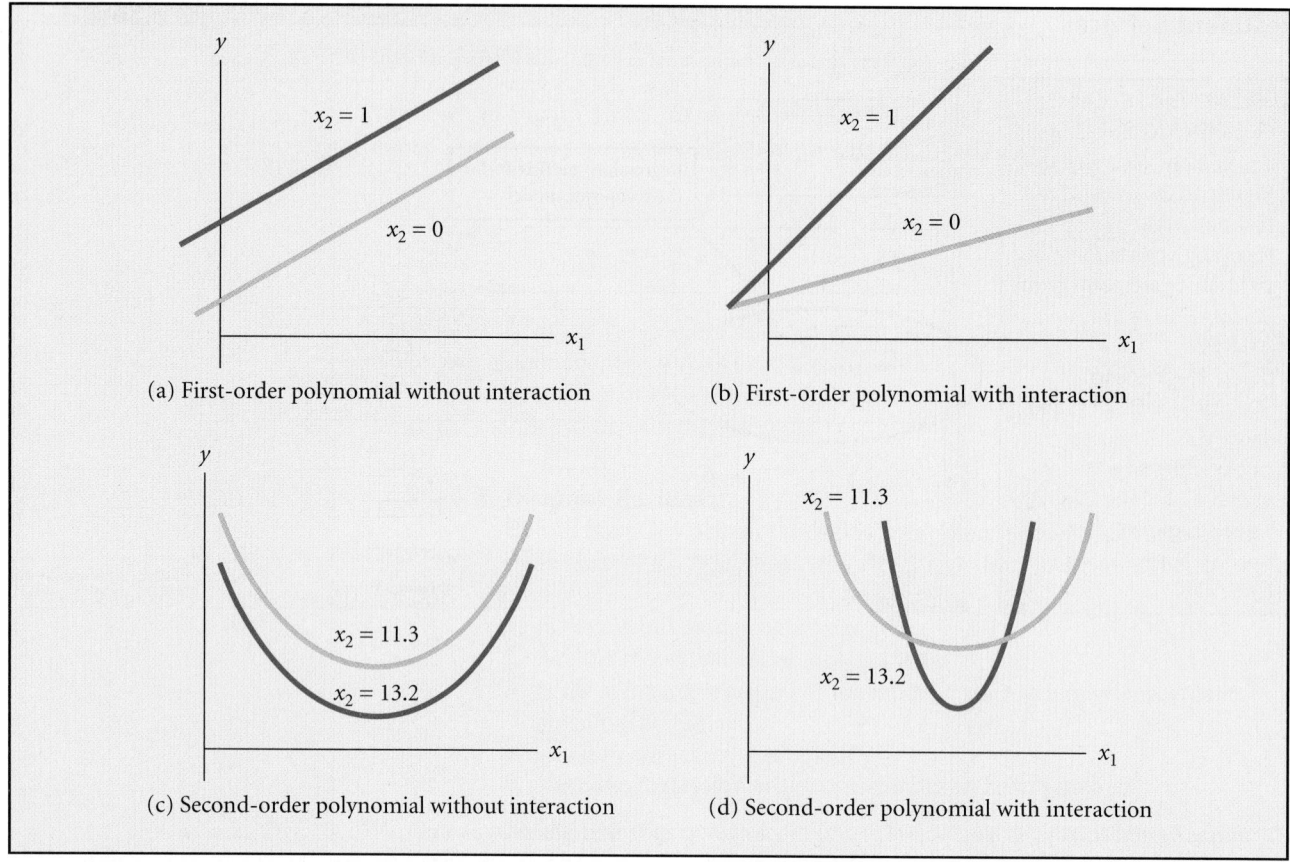

(a) First-order polynomial without interaction

(b) First-order polynomial with interaction

(c) Second-order polynomial without interaction

(d) Second-order polynomial with interaction

15-3: Exercises

Skill Development

15-24. Consider the following values for the dependent and independent variables:

x	y
5	10
15	15
40	25
50	44
60	79
80	112

a. Develop a scatter plot of the data. Does the plot suggest a linear or nonlinear relationship between the dependent and independent variables?

b. Develop an estimated linear regression equation for the data. Is the relationship significant? Test at an $\alpha = 0.05$ level.

c. Develop a regression equation of the form $\hat{y} = b_0 + b_1 x + b_2 x^2$. Does this equation provide a better fit to the data than that found in part b?

15-25. Consider the following values for the dependent and independent variables:

x	y
6	5
9	20
14	28
18	30
22	33
27	35

a. Develop a scatter plot of the data. Does the plot suggest a linear or nonlinear relationship between the dependent and independent variables?

b. Develop an estimated linear regression equation for the data. Is the relationship significant? Test at an $\alpha = 0.05$ level.

c. Develop a regression equation of the form $\hat{y} = b_0 + b_1 \ln(x)$. Does this equation provide a better fit to the data than that found in part b?

15-26. Examine the following data:

x	1	4	5	7	8	12	11	14	19	20
y	1	54	125	324	512	5530	5331	5740	7058	7945

a. Construct a scatter plot of the data. Determine the order of the polynomial that is represented by the data.

b. Obtain an estimate of the model identified in part a.

c. Conduct a test of hypothesis to determine if a third-order, as opposed to a second-order, polynomial is a better representation of the relationship between y and x. Use a significance level of 0.05 and the p-value approach.

15-27. Examine the following two sets of data:

When $x_2 = 1$		When $x_2 = 2$	
x_1	y	x_1	y
1	2	2	3
4	15	3	9
5	23	6	5
7	52	7	10
8	60	9	48
12	154	10	50
11	122	14	87
14	200	13	51
19	381	16	63
20	392	21	202

a. Produce a distinguishable scatter plot for each of the data sets on the same graph. Does it appear that there is interaction between x_2 and the relationship between y and x_1? Support your assertions.

b. Consider the following model to represent the relationship among y, x_1, and x_2:

$$y_i = \beta_0 + \beta_1 x_1 + \beta_2 x_1^2 + \beta_3 x_1 x_2 + \beta_4 x_1^2 x_2 + \varepsilon$$

Produce the estimated regression equation for this model.

c. Conduct a test of hypothesis for each interaction term. Use a significance level of 0.05 and the p-value approach.

d. Based upon the two hypothesis tests in part c, does it appear that there is interaction between x_2 and the relationship between y and x_1? Support your assertions.

Computer Database Exercises

15-28. The Gilmore Accounting firm collected the following in an effort to explain variation in client profitability. The data are also in the data file called **Gilmore**.

y	x_1	x_2
2,345	45	1
4,200	56	2
278	26	3
1,211	56	2
1,406	24	2
500	23	3
-700	34	3
3,457	45	1
2,478	47	1
1,975	24	2
206	32	3

where:

y = Net profit earned from the client
x_1 = Number of hours spent working with the client
x_2 = Type of client:
    1, if manufacturing
    2, if service
    3, if governmental

Gilmore has asked if it needs the client type in addition to the number of hours spent working with the client to predict the net profit earned from the client. You are asked to provide this information.

a. Fit a model to the data that incorporates the number of hours spent working with the client and the type of client as independent variables. (*Hint*: Client type has three levels.)

b. Fit a second-order model to the data, again using dummy variables for client type. Does this model provide a better fit than that found in part a? Which model would you recommend be used?

15-29. McCullom's International Grains is constantly searching out areas in which to expand its market. Such markets present different challenges since tastes in the international market are often different from domestic tastes. India is one country on which McCullom's has recently focused. Paddy is a grain used widely in India but its characteristics are unknown to McCullom's. Charles Walters has been assigned to take charge of the handling of this grain. He has researched its various characteristics. During his research he came across an article, "Determination of Biological Maturity and Effect of Harvesting and Drying conditions on Milling Quality of Paddy" [*Journal of Agricultural Engineering Research* (1975), pp. 353–361], which examines the relationship between y, the yield (kg/ha) of paddy, as a function of x, the number of days after flowering at which harvesting took place. The accompanying data appeared in the article and are in a file called **Paddy** on the CD-ROM.

y	x	y	x
2,508	16	3,823	32
2,518	18	3,646	34
3,304	20	3,708	36
3,423	22	3,333	38
3,057	24	3,517	40
3,190	26	3,241	42
3,500	28	3,103	44
3,883	30	2,776	46

a. Construct a scatter plot of the yield (kg/ha) of paddy as a function of the number of days after flowering at which harvesting took place. Display at least two models that would explain the relationship you see in the scatter plot.

b. Conduct tests of hypotheses to determine if the models you selected are useful in predicting the yield of paddy.

c. Consider the model that includes the second-order term x^2. Would a simple linear regression model be preferable to the model containing the second-order term? Conduct a hypothesis test using the p-value approach to arrive at your answer.

d. Which model should Charles use to predict the yield of paddy? Explain your answer.

15-30. The National Association of Realtors Existing-Home Sales Series provides a measurement of the residential real estate market. One of the measurements it produces is the Housing Affordability Index (HAI). It is a measure of the financial ability of U.S. families to buy a house: 100 means that families earning the national median income have just the amount of money needed to qualify for a mortgage on a median-priced home; higher than 100 means they have more than enough, and lower than 100 means they have less than enough. The file entitled **Index** contains the HAI and associated variables.

a. Construct a scatter plot relating the HAI to the median family income.

b. Determine the order of the polynomial that is suggested by the scatter plot produced in part a. Obtain the estimated regression equation of the polynomial selected.

c. Determine if monthly principle and interest interacts with the relationship between the HAI and the median family income indicated in part b. (*Hint*: You may need to conduct more than one hypothesis test.) Use a significance level of 0.05 and the p-value approach.

15-31. American men have closed the gap with women on life span according to a *USA Today* article (Kim Painter, "Male life span increasing," June 12, 2006). Male life expectancy attained a record 75.2 years and women's reached 80.4 in 2004. The National Center for Health Statistics provided the data given in the file entitled **Life**.

a. Produce a scatter plot depicting the relationship between the life expectancy of women and men.

b. Determine the order of the polynomial that is represented on the scatter plot obtained in part a. Produce the estimated regression equation that represents this relationship.

c. Determine if women's average life expectancy can be used in a second-order polynomial to predict the average life expectancy of men. Use a significance level of 0.05.

d. Use the estimated regression equation computed in part b to predict the average length of life of men when women's length of life equals 100. What does this tell you about the wisdom (or lack thereof) of extrapolation in regression models?

15-32. Badeaux Brothers Louisiana Treats ships packages of Louisiana coffee, cakes, and Cajun spices to individual customers around the United States. The cost to ship these products depends primarily on the weight of the package being shipped. Badeaux charges the customers for shipping and then ships the product itself. As a part of a study of whether it is economically feasible to continue to ship products itself, Badeaux sampled 20 recent shipments to determine what, if any, relationship exists between shipping costs and package weight. These data are in the file called **Badeaux**.

a. Develop a scatter plot of the data with the dependent variable, cost, on the vertical axis and the independent variable, weight, on the horizontal axis. Does there appear to be a relationship between the two variables? Is the relationship linear?

b. Compute the sample correlation coefficient between the two variables. Conduct a test, using a significance level of 0.05, to determine whether the population correlation coefficient is significantly different from zero.

c. Badeaux Brothers has been using a simple linear regression equation to predict the cost of shipping various items. Would you recommend it use a second-order polynomial model instead? Is the second-order polynomial model a significant improvement on the simple linear regression equation?

d. Badeaux Brothers has made a decision to stop shipping products if the shipping charges exceed $100. The company has asked you to determine the maximum weight for future shipments. Do this for both the first- and second-order models you have developed.

15-33. The National Association of Theatre Owners is the largest exhibition trade organization in the world, representing more than 26,000 movie screens in all 50 states and in more than 20 countries worldwide. Its membership includes the largest cinema chains and hundreds of independent theatre owners. It publishes statistics concerning the movie sector of the economy. The file entitled **Flicks** contains data on total U.S. box office grosses ($billion), total number of admissions (billion), average U.S. ticket price ($), and number of movie screens. One concern is the effect the increasing ticket prices have upon the number of individuals who go to the theatres to view movies.

a. Construct a scatter plot depicting the relationship between the total number of admissions and the U.S. ticket price.

b. Determine the order of the polynomial that is suggested by the scatter plot produced in part a.

Obtain the estimated regression equation of the polynomial selected.

c. Examine the p-value associated with the F-test for the polynomial you have selected in part a. Relate these results to those of the t-tests for the individual parameters and the adjusted coefficient of determination. To what is this attributed?

d. Conduct t-tests to remove higher-order components until no components can be removed.

15-34. The Energy Information Administration (EIA), created by Congress in 1977, is a statistical agency of the U.S. Department of Energy. It provides data, forecasts, and analyses to promote sound policy-making and public understanding regarding energy and its interaction with the economy and the environment. One of the most important areas of analysis is petroleum. The file entitled **Crude** contains data for the period 1991–2006 concerning the price, supply, and demand for fuel. One concern has been the increase in imported oil into the United States.

a. Examine the relationship between price of gasoline and the annual amount of imported crude oil. Construct a scatter plot depicting this relationship.

b. Determine the order of the polynomial that would fit the data displayed in part a. Express "Imports" in millions of gallons, i.e., $3,146,454/1,000,000 = 3.146454$. Produce an estimate of this polynomial.

c. Is a linear or quadratic model more appropriate for predicting the price of gasoline using the annual quantity of imported oil? Conduct the appropriate hypothesis test to substantiate your answer.

CHAPTER OUTCOME #8

15.4 Stepwise Regression

One option in regression analysis is to bring all possible independent variables into the model in one step. This is what we have done in the previous sections. We use the term *full regression* to describe this approach. Another method for developing a regression model is called *stepwise regression*. Stepwise regression, as the name implies, develops the least squares regression equation in steps, either through *forward selection, backward elimination*, or *standard stepwise* regression.

Forward Selection

The forward selection procedure begins by selecting a single independent variable from all those available. The independent variable selected at Step 1 is the variable that is most highly correlated with the dependent variable. A t-test is used to determine if this variable explains a significant amount of the variation in the dependent variable. At Step 1, if the variable does explain a significant amount of the dependent variable's variation, it is selected to be part of the final model used to predict the dependent variable. If it does not, the process is terminated. If no variables are found to be significant, the researcher will have to search for different independent variables than the ones already tested.

At Step 2, a second independent variable is selected based on its ability to explain the remaining unexplained variation in the dependent variable. The independent variable

Coefficient of Partial Determination

The measure of the marginal contribution of each independent variable, given that other independent variables are in the model.

selected in the second, and each subsequent, step is the variable with the highest **coefficient of partial determination**.

Recall that the coefficient of determination (R^2) measures the proportion of variation explained by all of the independent variables in the model. Thus, after the first variable (say, x_1) is selected, R^2 will indicate the percentage of variation explained by this variable. The forward selection routine will then compute all possible two-variable regression models, with x_1 included, and determine the R^2 for each model. The coefficient of partial determination at Step 2 is the proportion of the yet unexplained variation (after x_1 is in the model) that is explained by the additional variable. The independent variable that adds the most to R^2, given the variable(s) already in the model, is the one selected. Then a t-test is conducted to determine if the newly added variable is significant. This process continues until either all independent variables have been entered or the remaining independent variables do not add appreciably to R^2. For the forward selection procedure, the model begins with no variables. Variables are entered one at a time, and after a variable is entered, it cannot be removed.

Backward Elimination

Backward elimination is just the reverse of the forward selection procedure. In the backward elimination procedure, all variables are forced into the model to begin the process. Variables are removed one at a time until no more insignificant variables are found. Once a variable has been removed from the model, it cannot be reentered.

EXAMPLE 15-4 Applying Forward Selection Stepwise Regression Analysis

TRY PROBLEM 15.35

B. T. Longmont Company The B. T. Longmont Company operates a large retail department store in Macon, Georgia. Like other department stores, Longmont has incurred heavy losses due to shoplifting and employee pilferage. The store's security manager wants to develop a regression model to explain the monthly dollar loss. The following steps can be used when developing a multiple regression model using stepwise regression:

Step 1 **Specify the model by determining the dependent variable and potential independent variables.**

The dependent variable (y) is the monthly dollar losses due to shoplifting and pilferage. The security manager has identified the following potential independent variables:

x_1 = Average monthly temperature (degrees Fahrenheit)
x_2 = Number of sales transactions
x_3 = Dummy variable for holiday month
(1 if holiday during month, 0 if not)
x_4 = Number of persons on the store's monthly payroll

The data are contained in a CD-ROM file called **Longmont**.

Step 2 **Formulate the regression model.**

The correlation matrix for the data is presented in Figure 15.25. The forward selection procedure will select the independent variable most highly correlated with the dependent variable. By examining the bottom row in the correlation matrix in Figure 15.25, you can see the variable x_2, number of sales transactions, is most highly correlated ($r = 0.6307$) with dollars lost. Once this variable is entered into the model, the remaining independent variables will be entered based on their ability to explain the remaining variation in the dependent variable.

Figure 15.26a shows the PHStat stepwise regression output, and Figure 15.26b has the Minitab output. At Step 1, variable x_2, number of monthly sales transactions, enters the model.

FIGURE 15.25

Excel 2007 Correlation Matrix Output for Longmont

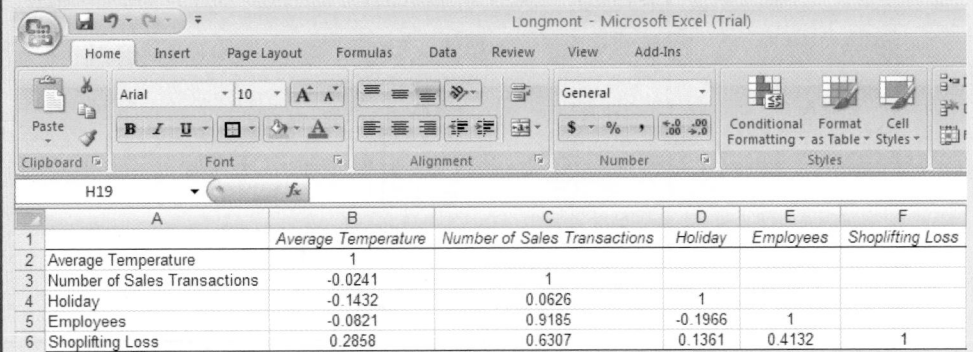

Excel Instructions:
1. Open file: Longmont.xls.
2. Select **Data tab**.
3. Select **Data Analysis > Correlation**.
4. Specify data range (include labels but do not include the Month column).
5. Click **Labels**.
6. Specify output location.
7. Click **OK**.

Step 3 Perform diagnostic checks on the model.

Although PHStat does not provide R^2 or the estimate of the standard error of the estimate directly, they can be computed from the output in the ANOVA section of the printout. Recall from Chapter 14 that R^2 is computed as

$$R^2 = \frac{SSR}{SST} = \frac{1,270,172.193}{3,192,631.529} = 0.398$$

This one independent variable explains 39.8% ($R^2 = 0.398$) of the variation in the dependent variable. The estimate of the standard error of the estimate is the square root of the mean square residual.

$$s_\varepsilon = \sqrt{MSE} = \sqrt{MS \text{ Residual}} = \sqrt{128,163.96} = 358$$

Now at Step 1, we test the following:

$$H_0: \beta_2 = 0 \text{ (slope for variable } x_2 = 0)$$
$$H_A: \beta_2 \neq 0$$
$$\alpha = 0.05$$

As shown in Figure 15.26a, the calculated t-value is 3.1481. We compare this to the critical value from the t-distribution for $\alpha / 2 = (0.05 / 2) = 0.025$ and degrees of freedom equal to

$$n - k - 1 = 17 - 1 - 1 = 15$$

This critical value is

$$t_{0.025} = 2.1315$$

Because

$$t = 3.1481 > 2.1315$$

FIGURE 15.26A

Excel 2007 (PHStat) Forward Selection Results for Longmont Co.—Step 1

R-Square $= SSR/SST =$ 1,270,172/3,192,631

Number of sales transactions entered
$t = 3.1481$
p-value $= 0.0066$

Excel 2007 (PHStat) Instructions:

1. Open file: Longmont.xls.
2. Select **Add-Ins**.
3. Select **PHStat**.
4. Select **Regression > Stepwise Regression**.
5. Define data range for y variable and data range for x variables.
6. Check **p-value** criteria.
7. Select **Forward Selection**.
8. Click **OK**.

we reject the null hypothesis and conclude that the regression slope coefficient for the variable, number of sales transactions, is not zero. Note also, because the

$$p\text{-value} = 0.0066 < \alpha = 0.05$$

we would reject the null hypothesis.

Step 4 Continue to formulate and diagnose the model by adding other independent variables.

The next variable to be selected will be the one that can do the most to increase R^2. If you were doing this manually, you would try each variable to see which one yields the highest R^2, given that the transactions variable is already in the model. Both the PHStat add-in software and Minitab do this automatically. As shown in Figure 15.26a and Figure 15.27, the variable selected in Step 2 is x_4, number of employees. Using the ANOVA section, we can determine R^2 and s_ε as before.

$$R^2 = \frac{SSR}{SST} = \frac{1,833,270.524}{3,192,631.529} = 0.5742 \quad \text{and}$$

$$s_\varepsilon = \sqrt{MS \ \text{Residual}} = \sqrt{97,097.22} = 311.6$$

FIGURE 15.26B

Minitab Forward Selection Results for Longmont Co.—Step 1

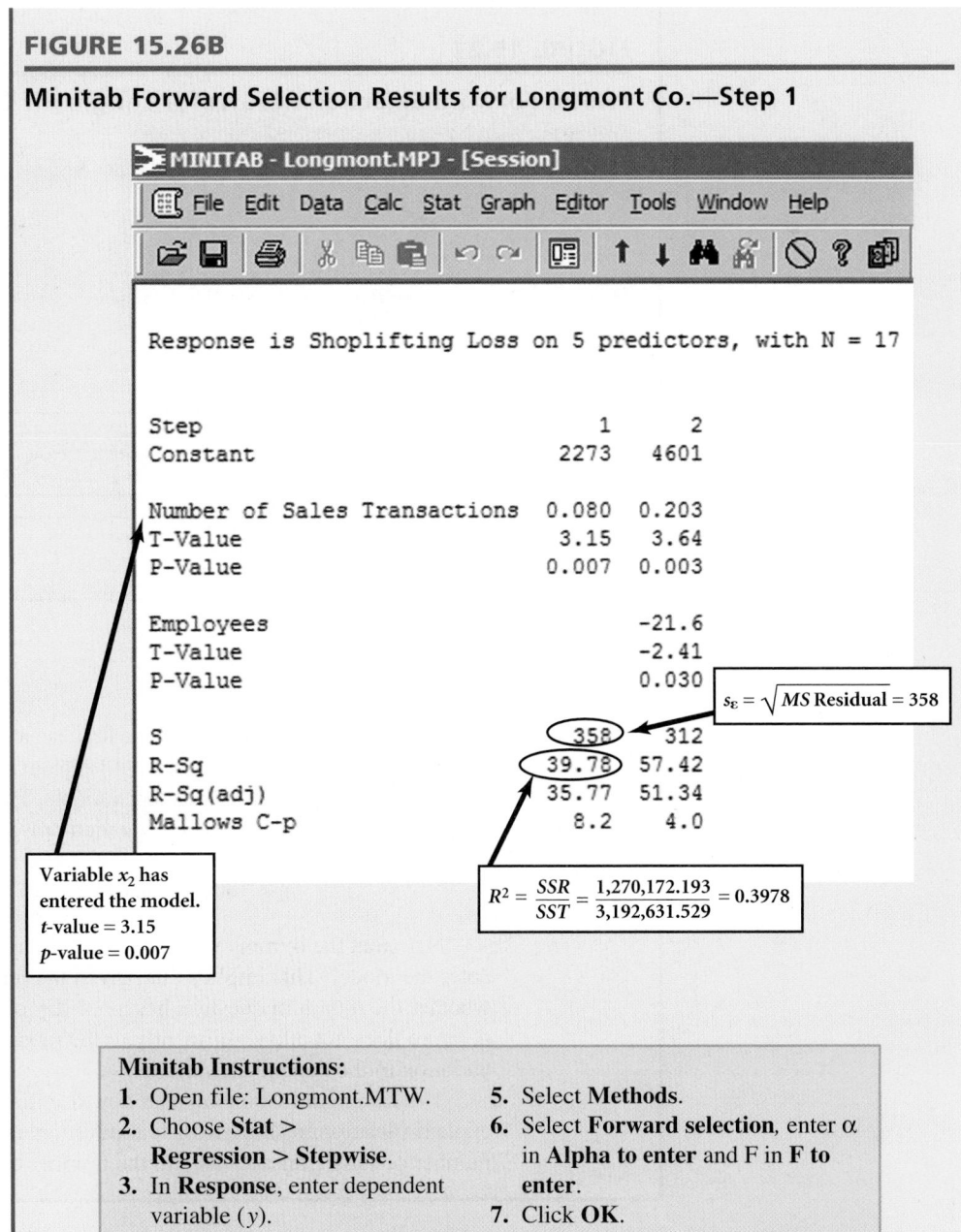

Variable x_2 has entered the model.
t-value = 3.15
p-value = 0.007

$$s_\varepsilon = \sqrt{MS\ Residual} = 358$$

$$R^2 = \frac{SSR}{SST} = \frac{1,270,172.193}{3,192,631.529} = 0.3978$$

Minitab Instructions:	
1. Open file: Longmont.MTW.	5. Select **Methods**.
2. Choose **Stat >**	6. Select **Forward selection**, enter α
Regression > Stepwise.	in **Alpha to enter** and F in **F to**
3. In **Response**, enter dependent	**enter**.
variable (y).	7. Click **OK**.
4. In **Predictors**, enter independent	
variable (x).	

The model now explains 57.42% of the variation in the dependent variable. The t-values for both slope coefficients exceed $t = 2.145$ (the critical value from the t-distribution table with a one-tailed area equal to 0.025 and $17 - 2 - 1 = 14$ degrees of freedom), so we conclude that both variables are significant in explaining the variation in the dependent variable, shoplifting loss.

The forward selection routine continues to enter variables as long as each additional variable explains a significant amount of the remaining variation in the dependent variable. Note that PHStat allows you to set the significance level in terms of a p-value or in terms of the t statistic. Then as long as the calculated p-value for an incoming variable is less than your limit, the variable is allowed to enter the model. Likewise, if the calculated statistic exceeds your t limit, the variable is allowed to enter.

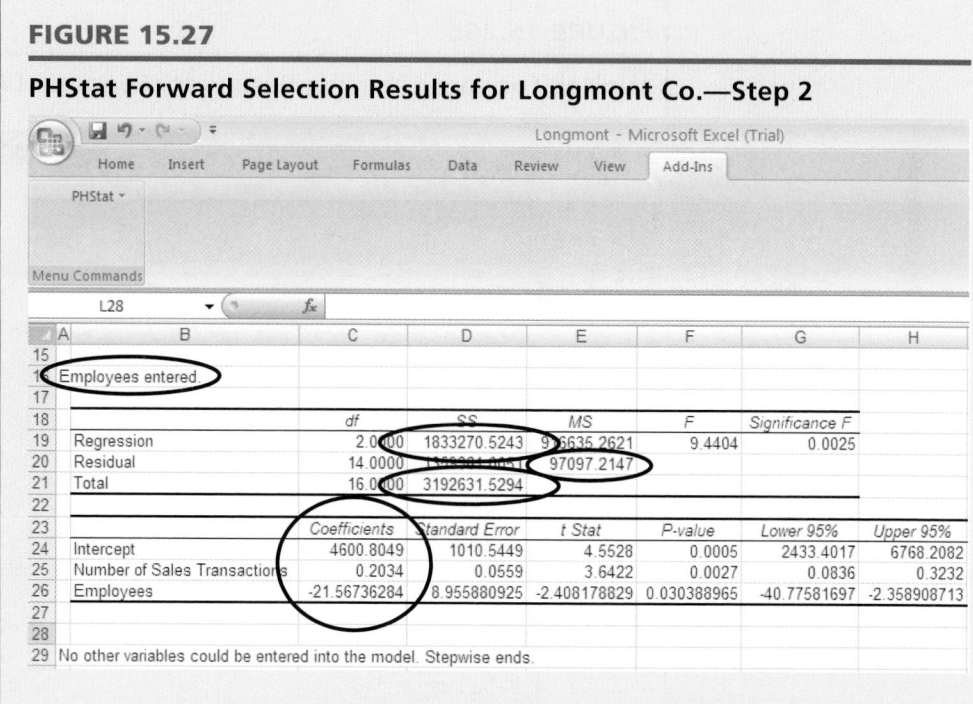

FIGURE 15.27

PHStat Forward Selection Results for Longmont Co.—Step 2

In this example, with the *p*-value limit set at 0.05, neither of the two remaining independent variables would explain a significant amount of the remaining variation in the dependent variable. The procedure is, therefore, terminated. The resulting regression equation provided by forward selection is

$$\hat{y} = 4600.8 + 0.203x_2 - 21.57x_4$$

Note that the dummy variables for holiday and temperature did not enter the model. This implies that, given the other variables, knowing whether the month in question has a holiday or knowing its average temperature does not add significantly to the model's ability to explain the variation in the dependent variable.

The Longmont Company can now use this regression model to explain variation in shoplifting and pilferage losses based on knowing the number of sales transactions and the number of employees.

Standard Stepwise Regression

The standard stepwise procedure (sometimes referred to as forward stepwise regression—not to be confused with forward selection) combines attributes of both backward elimination and forward selection. The standard stepwise method serves one more important function. If two or more variables overlap, a variable selected in an early step may become insignificant when other variables are added at later steps. The standard stepwise procedure will drop this insignificant variable from the model. Standard stepwise regression also offers a means of observing multicollinearity problems, because we can see how the regression model changes as each new variable is added to it.

The standard stepwise procedure is widely used in decision-making applications and is generally recognized as a useful regression method. However, care should be exercised when using this procedure because it is easy to rely too heavily on the automatic selection process. Remember, the order of variable selection is conditional, based on the variables already in the model. There is no guarantee that stepwise regression will lead you to the best set of independent variables from those available. Decision makers still must use common sense in applying regression analysis to make sure they have usable regression models.

Best Subsets Regression

Another method for developing multiple regression models is called the *best subsets* method. As the name implies, the best subsets method works by trying possible subsets from the list of possible independent variables. The user can then select the "best" model based on such measures as R-squared or the estimate of the standard deviation of the model error. Both Minitab and PHStat contain procedures for performing best subsets regression.

TRY PROBLEM 15.44

EXAMPLE 15-5 Applying Best Subsets Regression

Winston Investment Advisors   Charles L. Winston, founder and CEO at Winston Investment Advisors in Burbank, California, is interested in developing a regression model to explain the variation in dividends paid per share by U.S. companies. Such a model would be useful in advising his clients. The following steps can be used to develop such a model using the best subsets regression approach:

Step 1 Specify the model.
Some publicly traded companies pay higher dividends than others. The CEO is interested in developing a multiple regression model to explain the variation in dividends per share paid to shareholders. The dependent variable will be dividends per share. The CEO met with other analysts in his firm to identify potential independent variables for which data would be readily available. The following list of potential independent variables was selected:

x_1 = Return on equity (net income/equity)
x_2 = Earnings per share
x_3 = Current assets in millions of dollars
x_4 = Year-ending stock price
x_5 = Current ratio (current assets/current liabilities)

A random sample of 35 publicly traded U.S. companies was selected. For each company in the sample, data were obtained for the dividends per share paid last year and for year-ending data on the five independent variables. These data are contained in the data file **Company Financials**.

Step 2 Formulate the regression model.
The CEO is interested in developing the "best" regression model for explaining the variation in the dependent variable, dividends per share. The approach taken is to use best subsets, which requires that multiple regression models be developed, each containing a different mix of variables. The models tried will contain from one to five independent variables. The resulting models will be evaluated by comparing values for R-square and the standard error of the estimate. High R-squares and low standard errors are desirable. Another statistic, identified as C_p, is sometimes used to evaluate regression models. This statistic measures the difference between the estimated model and the true population model. Values of C_p close to $p = k + 1$ (k is the number of independent variables in the model) are preferred.

Both the PHStat Excel add-ins and Minitab can be used to perform best subsets regression analysis. Figure 15.28 shows the partial output

FIGURE 15.28

Best Subsets Regression Output for Winston Investment Advisors

	A	B	C	D	E	F
10	Model	Cp	k+1	R Square	Adj. R Square	Std. Error
11	X1	42.306	2	0.0616	0.0331	0.7519
12	X2	20.662	2	0.3387	0.3186	0.6312
13	X3	7.423	2	0.5081	0.4932	0.5444
14	X4	20.684	2	0.3384	0.3183	0.6314
15	X5	46.792	2	0.0042	-0.0260	0.7746
16	X1X2	20.853	3	0.3618	0.3219	0.6297
17	X1X3	7.745	3	0.5296	0.5002	0.5406
18	X1X4	22.657	3	0.3387	0.2974	0.6410
19	X1X5	43.934	3	0.0663	0.0080	0.7616
20	X2X3	1.449	3	0.6102	0.5858	0.4921
21	X2X4	17.751	3	0.4015	0.3641	0.6098
22	X2X5	22.434	3	0.3416	0.3004	0.6396
23	X3X4	3.244	3	0.5872	0.5614	0.5064
24	X3X5	9.419	3	0.5082	0.4774	0.5528
25	X4X5	22.464	3	0.3412	0.3000	0.6398
26	X1X2X3	3.054	4	0.6153	0.5780	0.4967
27	X1X2X4	17.690	4	0.4279	0.3725	0.6057
28	X1X2X5	22.670	4	0.3641	0.3026	0.6386
29	X1X3X4	5.197	4	0.5878	0.5480	0.5141
30	X1X3X5	9.735	4	0.5297	0.4842	0.5492
31	X1X4X5	24.414	4	0.3418	0.2781	0.6497
32	X2X3X4	2.543	4	0.6218	0.5852	0.4925
33	X2X3X5	3.438	4	0.6104	0.5726	0.4999
34	X2X4X5	19.741	4	0.4016	0.3437	0.6195
35	X3X4X5	5.080	4	0.5893	0.5496	0.5132
36	X1X2X3X4	4.028	5	0.6284	0.5789	0.4963
37	X1X2X3X5	5.045	5	0.6154	0.5641	0.5049
38	X1X2X4X5	19.661	5	0.4283	0.3521	0.6156
39	X1X3X4X5	7.052	5	0.5897	0.5350	0.5215
40	X2X3X4X5	4.525	5	0.6220	0.5716	0.5005
41	X1X2X3X4X5	6.000	6	0.6288	0.5648	0.5045

Excel 2007 (PHStat)
Instructions:
1. Open file: Company Financials.xls.
2. Select **Add-Ins**.
3. Select **PHStat**.
4. Select **Regression > Best Subsets Regression**.
5. Define data range for y variable and data range for x variables.
6. Click **OK**.

from PHStat. Notice that all possible combinations of models with $k = 1$ to $k = 5$ independent variables are included. Several models appear to be good candidates based on R-square, adjusted R-square, standard error of the estimate, and C_p values. These are:

Model	C_p	$k+1$	R-square	Adj. R-square	Std. Error
X1X2X3X4	4.0	5	0.628	0.579	0.496
X1X2X3X4X5	6.0	6	0.629	0.565	0.505
X1X2X3X5	5.0	5	0.615	0.564	0.505
X2X3	1.4	3	0.610	0.586	0.492
X2X3X4	2.5	4	0.622	0.585	0.493
X2X3X4X5	4.5	5	0.622	0.572	0.500
X2X3X5	3.4	4	0.610	0.573	0.500

There is little difference in these seven models in terms of the statistics shown. We can examine any of them in more detail by looking at further PHStat output. For instance, the model containing variables x_1, x_2, x_3, and x_5 is shown in Figure 15.29. Note that although this model is among the best with respect to R-square, adjusted R-square, standard error of the estimate, and C_p value, two of the four variables (x_1 = ROE and x_5 = current ratio) have statistically insignificant regression coefficients. Figure 15.30 shows the regression model with the two statistically significant variables remaining. The R-square value is 0.61, the adjusted R^2 has increased, and the overall model is statistically significant.

FIGURE 15.29

One Potential Model for Winston Investment Advisors

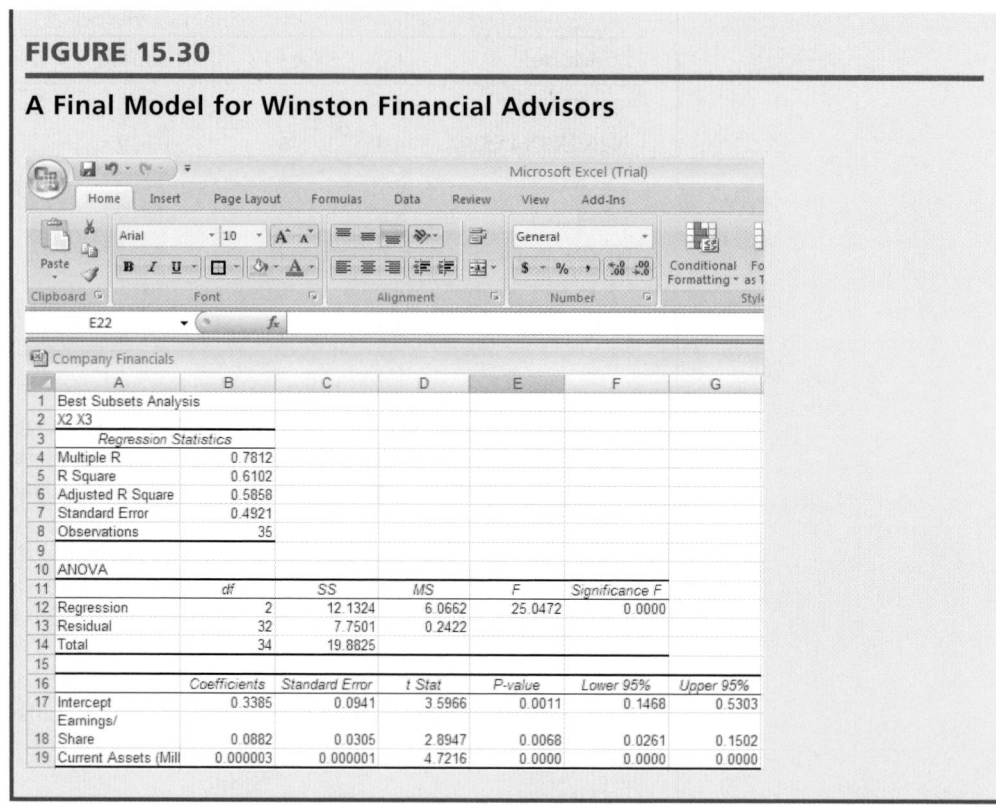

FIGURE 15.30

A Final Model for Winston Financial Advisors

15-4: Exercises

Skill Development

15-35. You are given the following set of data:

y	x_1	x_2	x_3
33	9	192	40
44	11	397	47
34	10	235	37
60	13	345	61
20	11	245	23
30	7	235	35
45	12	296	52
25	9	235	27
53	10	295	57
45	13	335	50
37	11	243	41
44	13	413	51

a. Determine the appropriate correlation matrix and use it to predict which variable will enter in the first step of a stepwise regression model.

b. Use standard stepwise regression to construct a model, entering all significant variables.

c. Construct a full regression model. What are the differences in the model? Which model explains the most variation in the dependent variable?

15-36. You are given the following set of data:

y	x_1	x_2	x_3
45	40	41	39
41	31	41	35
43	45	49	39
38	43	41	41
50	42	42	51
39	48	40	42
50	44	44	41
45	42	39	37
43	37	52	41
34	40	47	40
49	35	44	44
45	39	40	45
40	43	30	42
43	53	34	34

a. Determine the appropriate correlation matrix and use it to predict which variable will enter in the first step of a stepwise regression model.

b. Use standard stepwise regression to construct a model, entering all significant variables.

c. Construct a full regression model. What are the differences in the model? Which model explains the most variation in the dependent variable?

15-37. Suppose you have four potential independent variables, x_1, x_2, x_3 and x_4, from which you want to develop a multiple regression model. Using stepwise regression, x_2 and x_4 entered the model.

a. Why did only two variables enter the model? Discuss.

b. Suppose a full regression with only variables x_2 and x_4 had been run. Would the resulting model be different from the stepwise model that included only these two variables? Discuss.

c. Now suppose a full regression model had been developed, with all four independent variables in the model. Which would have the higher R^2 value, the full regression model or the stepwise model? Discuss.

15-38. The following data represent a dependent variable and four independent variables:

y	x_1	x_2	x_3	x_4
61	37	13	10	21
37	25	7	11	32
22	23	6	7	18
48	12	8	8	30
66	34	15	2	33
69	35	19	9	23
24	23	14	7	31
68	35	17	3	33
65	37	11	17	19
45	30	9	24	31

a. Use the standard stepwise regression to produce an estimate of a multiple regression model to predict y. Use 0.15 as the alpha to enter and to remove.

b. Change the alpha to enter to 0.01. Repeat the standard stepwise procedure.

c. Change the alpha to remove to 0.35, leaving alpha to enter to be 0.15. Repeat the standard stepwise procedure.

d. Change the alpha to remove to 0.15, leaving alpha to enter to be 0.05. Repeat the standard stepwise procedure.

e. Change the alpha to remove and to enter to 0.05. Repeat the standard stepwise procedure.

f. Compare the three estimated regression equations developed in parts a, c, and d.

15-39. Consider the following set of data:

y	x_1	x_2	x_3	x_4
61	37	18	2	13
37	25	5	4	10
22	23	12	7	4
48	12	6	2	15
66	34	14	3	25
69	35	21	2	20
24	23	7	6	9
68	35	15	3	14
65	37	19	2	19
45	30	12	3	12

a. Use standard stepwise regression to produce an estimate of a multiple regression model to predict y.

b. Use forward selection stepwise regression to produce an estimate of a multiple regression model to predict y.

c. Use backwards elimination stepwise regression to produce an estimate of a multiple regression model to predict y.

d. Use best subsets regression to produce an estimate of a multiple regression model to predict y.

Computer Database Exercises

15-40. The Western State Tourist Association gives out pamphlets, maps, and other tourist-related information to people who call a toll-free number and request the information. The association orders the packets of information from a document printing company and likes to have enough available to meet the immediate need without having too many sitting around taking up space. The marketing manager decided to develop a multiple regression model to be used in predicting the number of calls that will be received in the coming week. A random sample of 12 weeks is selected, with the following variables:

  y = Number of calls
  x_1 = Number of advertisements placed the previous week
  x_2 = Number of calls received the previous week
  x_3 = Number of airline tour bookings into Western cities for the current week

These data are in the data file called **Western States**.

a. Develop the multiple regression model for predicting the number of calls received, using backward elimination stepwise regression.

b. At the final step of the analysis, how many variables are in the model?

c. Discuss why the variables were removed from the model in the order shown by the stepwise regression.

15-41. Refer to Problem 15-40.

a. Develop the correlation matrix that includes all independent variables and the dependent variable. Predict the order that the variables will be selected into the model if forward selection stepwise regression is used.

b. Use forward selection stepwise regression to develop a model for predicting the number of calls that the company will receive. Write a report that describes what has taken place at each step of the regression process.

c. Compare the results of the forward selection stepwise regression results in part b and the backward elimination results determined in Problem 15-40. Which model would you choose? Explain your answer.

15-42. The U.S. Energy Information Administration publishes summary statistics concerning the energy sector of the U.S. economy. The electric power industry continues to grow. Electricity generation and sales rose to record levels. The file entitled **Energy** presents the revenue from retail sales ($million) and the net generation by energy source for the period 1993–2004.

a. Produce the correlation matrix of all the variables. Predict the variables that will remain in the estimated regression equation if standard stepwise regression is used to predict the revenues from retail sales of energy.

b. Use standard stepwise regression to develop an estimate of a model that is to predict the revenue from retail sales of energy ($million).

c. Compare the results of parts a and b. Explain any difference between the two models.

15-43. An investment analyst collected data of 20 randomly chosen companies. The data consisted of the 52-week high stock prices, PE ratio, and the market value of the company. These data are in the file entitled **Investment**. The analyst wishes to produce a regression equation to predict the market value using 52-week-high stock price and the PE ratio of the company. He creates a complete second-degree polynomial.

a. Produce two scatter plots: (1) market value versus stock price, and (2) market value versus PE ratio. Do the scatter plots support the analyst's decision to produce a second-order polynomial? Support your assertion with statistical reasoning.

b. Use forward selection stepwise regression to eliminate any unneeded components from the analyst's model.

c. Does forward selection stepwise regression support the analyst's decision to produce a second-order polynomial? Support your assertion with statistical reasoning.

15-44. A variety of sources suggest that individuals assess their health, at least in part, by estimating their percentage of body fat. A widely accepted measure of body fat uses an underwater weighing technique. There are, however, more convenient methods using only a scale and a measuring tape. An article in the *Journal of Statistics Education* 4, no. 1 (1996) (Roger W. Johnson, "Fitting Percentage of Body Fat to Simple Body Measurements") explored regression models to predict body fat. The file entitled **Bodyfat** lists a portion of the data presented in the cited article.

a. Use best subsets stepwise regression to establish the relationship between body fat and the variables in the specified file.

b. Predict the body fat of an individual whose age is 21, weight is 170 pounds, height is 70 inches, chest circumference is 100 centimeters, abdomen is 90 centimeters, hip is 105, and whose thigh is 60 centimeters around.

15-45. The consumer price index (CPI) is a measure of the average change in prices over time in a fixed market basket of goods and services typically purchased by consumers. One of the items in this market basket that affects the CPI is the price of oil and its derivatives. The file entitled **Consumer** contains the price of the derivatives of oil and the CPI adjusted to 2005 levels.

a. Use forward selection stepwise regression to determine which combination of the oil derivative prices drive the CPI. If you encounter difficulties in completing this task, explain what caused the difficulties.

b. Eliminate the source of the difficulties in part a by producing a correlation matrix to determine where the difficulty lies.

c. Delete one of the variables indicated in part b and complete the instructions in part a.

15.5 Determining the Aptness of the Model

In Section 15.1 we discussed the basic steps involved in building a multiple regression model. These are

1. specify the model
2. build the model
3. perform diagnostic checks on the model

The final step is the diagnostic step in which you examine the model to determine how well it performs. In Section 15.2, we discussed several statistics that you need to consider when performing the diagnostic step, including analyzing R^2, adjusted R^2, and the standard error of the estimate. In addition, we discussed the concept of multicollinearity and the impacts that can occur when multicollinearity is present. Section 15.3 introduced another diagnostic step that involves looking for potential curvilinear relationships between the independent variables and the dependent variable. We presented some basic data transformation techniques for dealing with curvilinear situations. However, a major part of the diagnostic process involves an analysis of how well the model fits the regression analysis assumptions.

The assumptions of multiple regression include the following:

Assumptions

1. Individual residuals, ε, are statistically independent of one another, and these values represent a random sample from the population of possible residuals at each level of x.
2. For a given value of x, there can exist many values of y, and therefore many possible values for ε. Further, the distribution of possible ε-values for any level of x is normally distributed.
3. The distributions of possible ε-values have equal variances at each level of x.
4. The means of the dependent variable, y, for all specified values of x can be connected with a line called the population regression model.

The degree to which a regression model satisfies these assumptions is called *aptness*.

Analysis of Residuals

Residual
The difference between the actual value of the dependent variable and the value predicted by the regression model.

The **residual** is computed using Equation 15.12.

Residual
$$e_i = y_i - \hat{y}_i \qquad (15.12)$$

A residual value can be computed for each observation in the data set. A great deal can be learned about the aptness of the regression model by analyzing the residuals. The principal means of residual analysis is a study of residual plots. The following problems can be inferred through graphical analysis of residuals:

1. The regression function is not linear.
2. The residuals do not have a constant variance.
3. The residuals are not independent.
4. The residual terms are not normally distributed.

We will address each of these in order. The regression options in both Minitab and Excel provide extensive residual analysis.

FIGURE 15.31

Residual Plots Showing Linear and Nonlinear Patterns

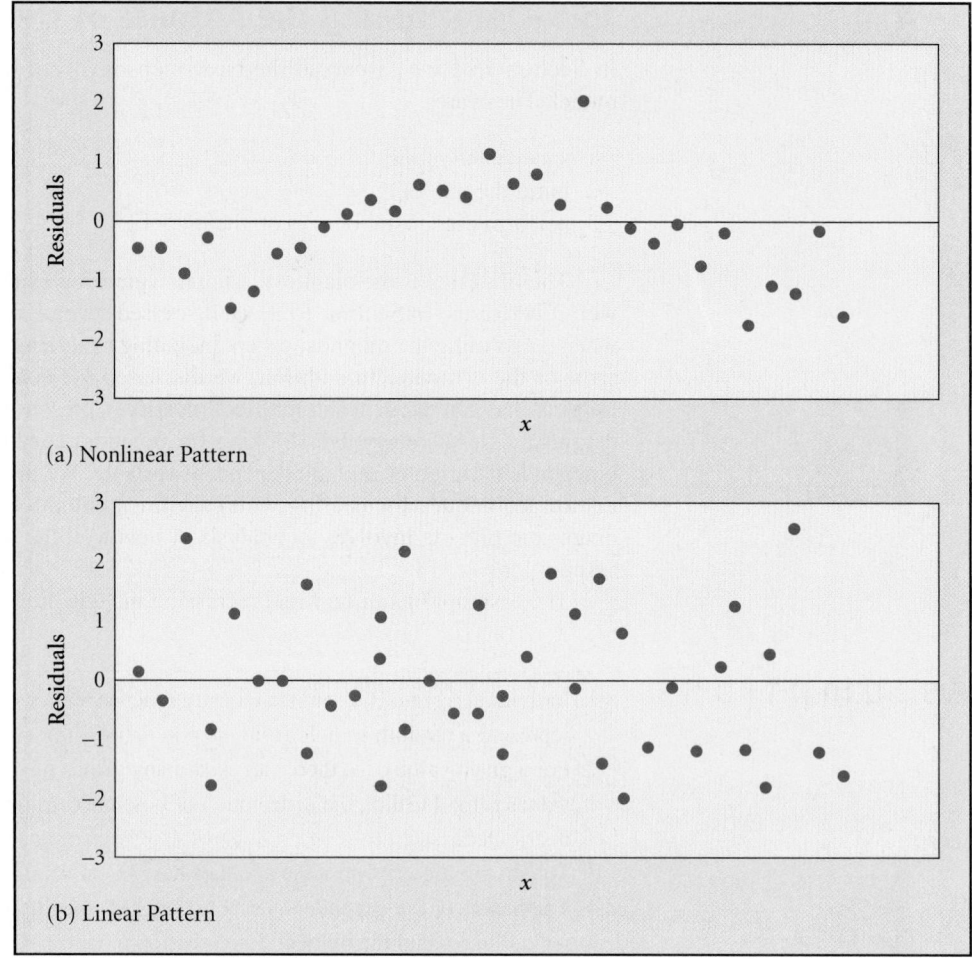

Checking for Linearity A plot of the residuals (on the vertical axis) against the independent variable (on the horizontal axis) is useful for detecting whether a linear function is the appropriate regression function. Figure 15.31 illustrates two different residual plots. Figure 15.31a shows residuals that systematically depart from 0. When x is small, the residuals are negative. When x is in the midrange, the residuals are positive; and for large x-values, the residuals are negative again. This type of plot suggests that the relationship between y and x is nonlinear. Figure 15.31b shows a plot in which residuals do not show a systematic variation from 0, implying that the relationship between x and y is linear.

   If a linear model is appropriate, we expect the residuals to band around 0 with no systematic pattern displayed. If the residual plot shows a systematic pattern, it may be possible to transform the independent variable (refer to Section 15.3) so that the revised model will produce residual plots that will not systematically vary from 0.

Business Application

Excel and Minitab Tutorial

FIRST CITY REAL ESTATE (*CONTINUED*) We have been using First City Real Estate to introduce multiple regression tools throughout this chapter. Remember, the managers wish to develop a multiple regression model for predicting the sales prices of homes in their market. Suppose that the most current model incorporates a transformation of the lot size variable as log of lot size. The output for this model is shown in Figure 15.32. Notice the model now has a R^2 value of 96.9%.

   There are currently four independent variables in the model: square feet, bedrooms, garage, and the log of lot size. Both Minitab and Excel provide procedures for automatically producing residual plots. Figure 15.33 shows the plots of the residuals against each of the independent variables. The transformed variable, log lot size, has a residual pattern that shows a systematic pattern. The residuals are positive for small values of log lot size,

FIGURE 15.32

Minitab Output of First City Real Estate Appraisal Model

Minitab Instructions:
1. Open file: First City-3 MTW.
2. Choose **Stat** > **Regression** > **Regression**.
3. In **Response**, enter dependent (y) variable.
4. In **Predictors**, enter independent (x) variables.
5. Click **OK**.

FIGURE 15.33

First City Real Estate Residual Plots versus the Independent Variables

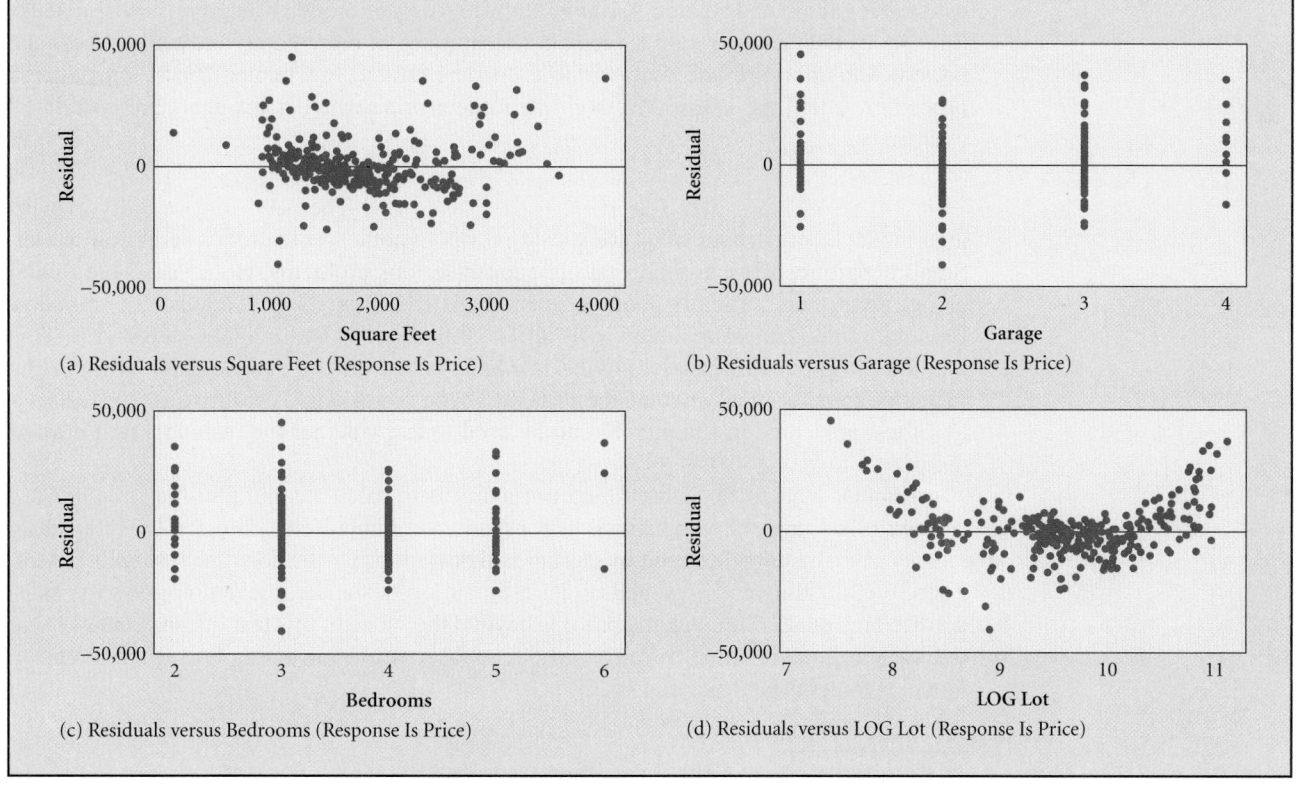

negative for intermediate values of log lot size, and positive again for large values of log lot size. This pattern suggests that the curvature of the relationship between sales prices of homes and lot size is even more pronounced than the logarithm implies. Potentially, a second- or third-degree polynomial in the lot size should be pursued.

Do the Residuals Have Equal Variances at all Levels of Each x Variable? Residual plots also can be used to determine whether the residuals have a constant variance. Consider Figure 15.34, in which the residuals are plotted against an independent variable. The plot in Figure 15.34a shows an example in which, as x increases, the residuals become less variable. Figure 15.34b shows the opposite situation. When x is small, the residuals are tightly packed around 0, but as x increases, the residuals become more variable. Figure 15.34c shows an example in which the residuals exhibit a constant variance around the zero mean.

When a multiple regression model has been employed, we can analyze the equal variance assumption by plotting the residuals against the fitted ($\hat{y}$) values. When the residual plot is cone-shaped, as in Figure 15.35, it suggests that the assumption of equal variance has been violated.

Figure 15.36 shows the residuals plotted against the $\hat{y}$-values for First City Real Estate's appraisal model. We have drawn a band around the residuals that shows that the variance of the residuals stays quite constant over the range of the fitted values.

Are the Residuals Independent? If the data used to develop the regression model are measured over time, a plot of the residuals against time is used to determine whether the residuals are correlated. Figure 15.37a shows an example in which the residual plot against time suggests independence. The residuals in Figure 15.37a appear to be randomly distributed around the mean of zero over time. However, in Figure 15.37b, the plot suggests that the residuals are not independent, because in the early time periods the residuals are negative and in later time periods the residuals are positive. This, or any other nonrandom pattern in the residuals over time, indicates that the assumption of independent residuals has been violated. Generally, this means some variable associated with the passage of time has been omitted from the model. Often, time is used as a surrogate for other time-related variables in a regression model. Chapter 16 will discuss time-series data analysis and forecasting techniques in more detail and will address the issue of incorporating the time variable into the model. In Chapter 16, we introduce a procedure called the Durbin-Watson test to determine whether residuals are correlated over time.

Checking for Normally Distributed Error Terms The need for normally distributed model errors occurs when we want to test a hypothesis about the regression model. Small departures from normality do not cause serious problems. However, if the model errors depart dramatically from a normal distribution, there is cause for concern. Examining the sample residuals will allow us to detect such dramatic departures. One method for graphically analyzing the residuals is to form a frequency histogram of the residuals to determine whether the general shape is normal. The chi-square goodness-of-fit test presented in Chapter 13 can be used to test whether the residuals fit a normal distribution.

Another method for determining normality is to calculate and plot the *standardized residuals*. In Chapter 3 you learned that a random variable is standardized by subtracting its mean and dividing the result by its standard deviation. The mean of the residuals is zero. Therefore, dividing each residual by an estimate of its standard deviation gives the standardized residual.[9] Although the proof is beyond the scope of this text, it can be shown that the standardized residual for any particular observation for a simple linear regression model is found using Equation 15.13.

---

[9] The standardized residual is also referred to as the studentized residual.

FIGURE 15.34

Residual Plots Showing Constant and Nonconstant Variances

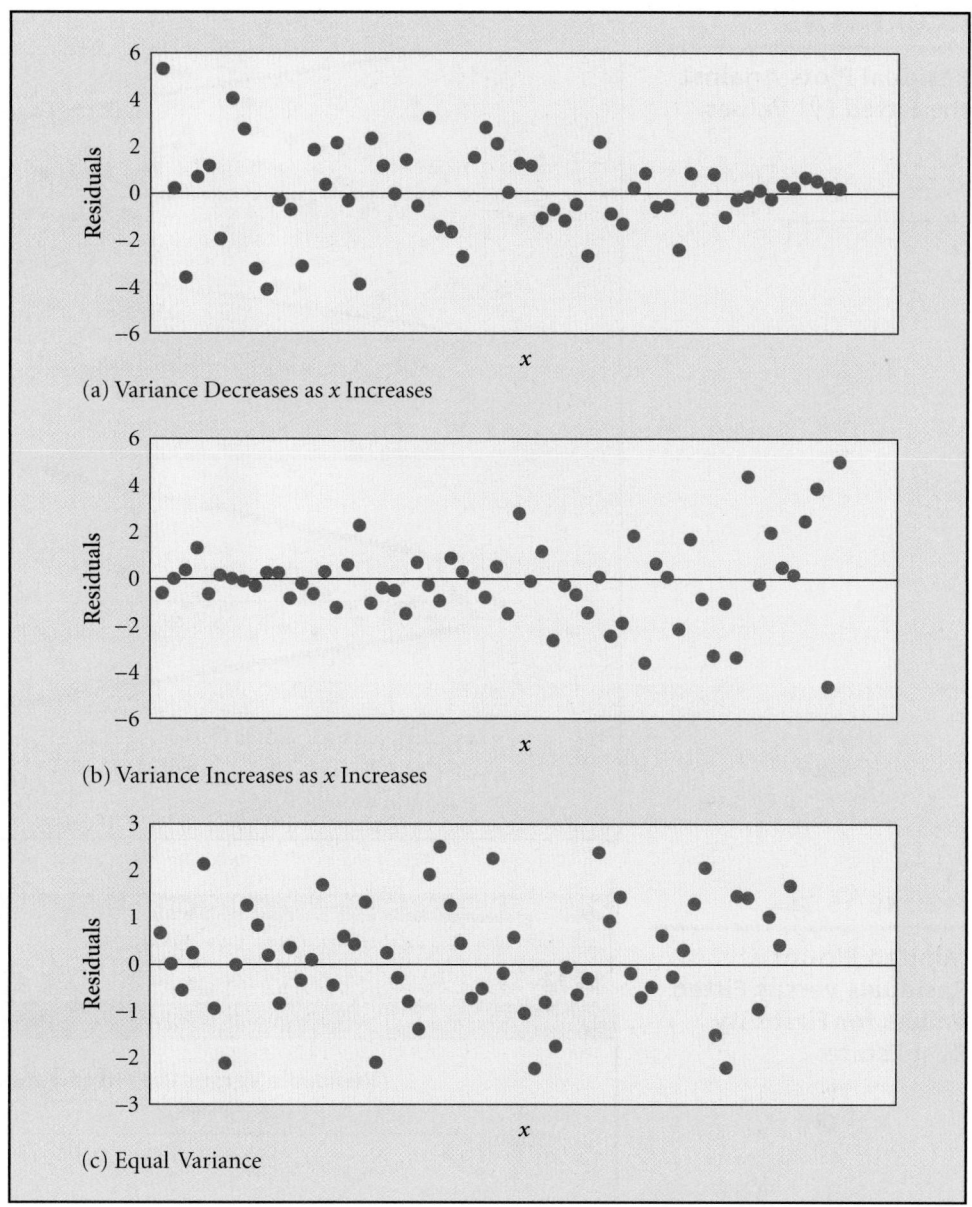

(a) Variance Decreases as x Increases

(b) Variance Increases as x Increases

(c) Equal Variance

Standardized Residual—Simple Linear Regression

$$s_{e_i} = \frac{e_i}{s_\varepsilon \sqrt{1 + \dfrac{1}{n} + \dfrac{(x_i - \bar{x})^2}{\sum x^2 - \dfrac{(\sum x)^2}{n}}}} \qquad (15.13)$$

where:

e_i = ith residual value

s_ε = Standard error of the estimate

x_i = Value of x used to generate the predicted y-value for the ith observation

---

Computing the standardized residual for an observation in a multiple regression model is too complicated to be done by hand. However, the standardized residuals are generated from most statistical software, including Minitab and Excel. The Excel and Minitab tutorials on

FIGURE 15.35

Residual Plots Against the Fitted ($\hat{y}$) Values

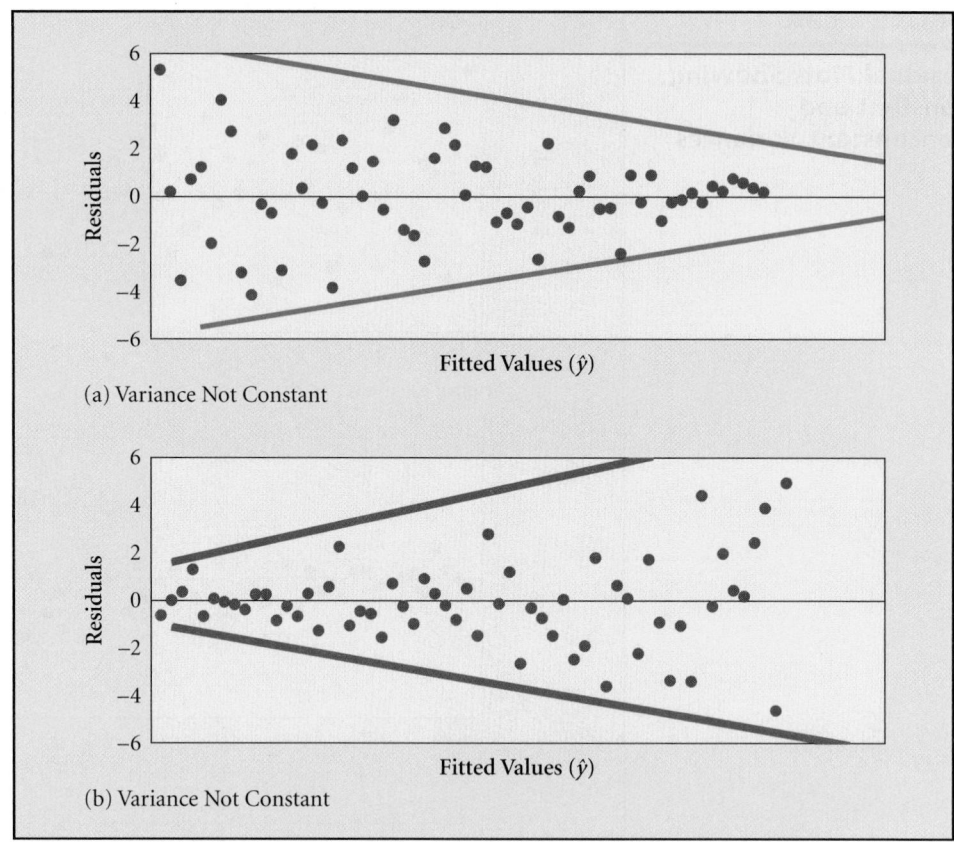

(a) Variance Not Constant

(b) Variance Not Constant

FIGURE 15.36

Minitab Plot of Residuals versus Fitted Values for First City Real Estate

Minitab Instructions:
1. Open file: First City-3. MTW.
2. Choose **Stat > Regression > Regression**.
3. In **Response**, enter dependent (y) variable.
4. In **Predictors**, enter independent (x) variables.
5. Choose **Graphs**.
6. Under **Residual Plots**, select **Residuals versus fits**.
7. Click **OK. OK.**

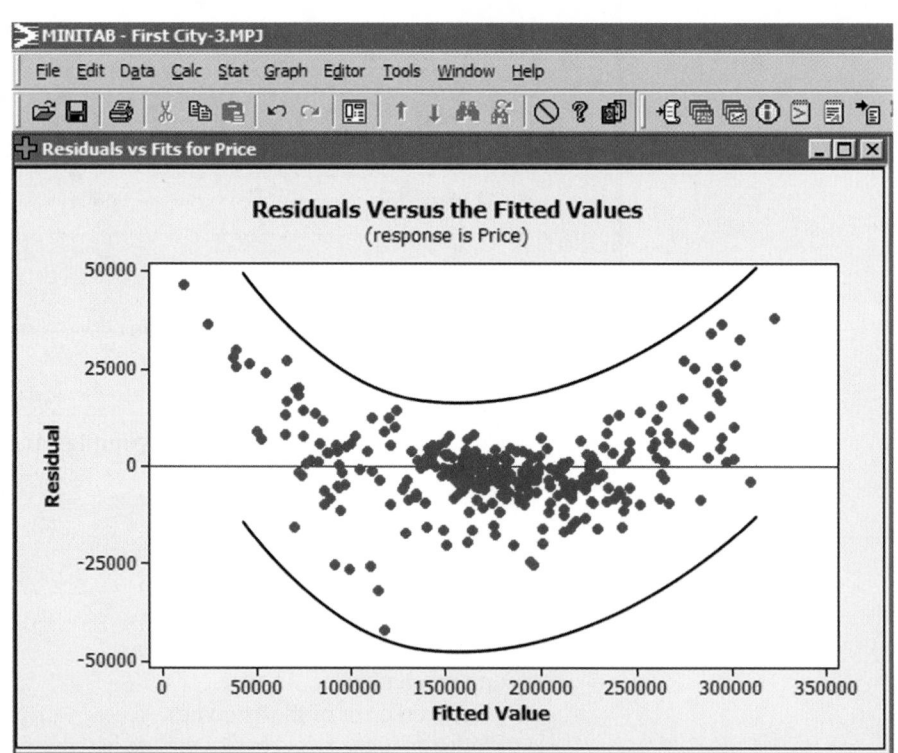

your CD-ROM illustrate the methods required to generate the standardized residuals and residual plots. Because other problems such as nonconstant variance and nonindependent residuals can result in residuals that seem to be abnormal, you should check these other factors before addressing the normality assumption.

FIGURE 15.37

Plot of Residuals Against Time

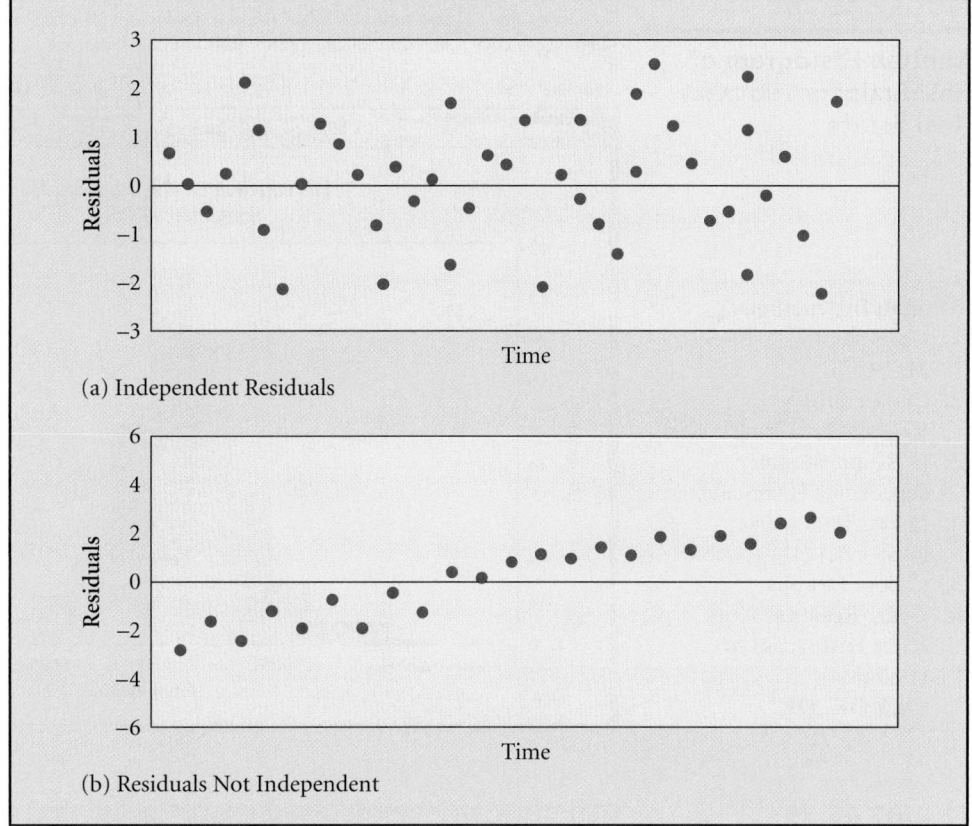

(a) Independent Residuals

(b) Residuals Not Independent

Recall that for a normal distribution, approximately 68% of the values will fall within 1 standard deviation of the mean, 95% within 2 standard deviations of the mean, and virtually all values will fall within 3 standard deviations of the mean.

Figure 15.38 illustrates the histogram of the residuals for the First City Real Estate example. The distribution of residuals looks to be close to a normal distribution. Figure 15.39 shows the histogram for the standardized residuals, which will have the same basic shape as the residual distribution in Figure 15.38.

Another approach for checking for normality of the residuals is to form a *probability plot*. We start by arranging the residuals in numerical order from smallest to largest. The standardized residuals are plotted on the horizontal axis, and the corresponding expected value for the standardized residual is plotted on the vertical axis. Although we won't delve into how the expected value is computed, you can examine the normal probability plot to see whether the plot forms a straight line. The closer the line is to linear, the closer the residuals are to being normally distributed. Figure 15.40 shows the normal probability plot for the First City Real Estate Company example.

You should be aware that Minitab and Excel format their residual plots slightly differently. However, the same general information is conveyed, and you can look for the same signs of problems with the regression model.

Corrective Actions

If, based on analyzing the residuals, you decide the model constructed is not appropriate, but you still want a regression-based model, some corrective action may be warranted. There are three approaches that may work: transform some of the existing independent variables; remove some variables from the model; or start over in the development of the regression model.

Earlier in this chapter, we discussed a basic approach involved in variable transformation. In general, the transformations of the independent variables (such as raising x to a power, taking the square root of x, or taking the log of x) are used to make the data better

FIGURE 15.38

Minitab Histogram of Residuals for First City Real Estate

Minitab Instructions:
1. Open file: First City-3. MTW.
2. Choose **Stat > Regression > Regression**.
3. In **Response**, enter dependent (*y*) variable.
4. In **Predictors**, enter independent (*x*) variables.
5. Choose **Graphs**.
6. Under **Residual Plots**, select **Histogram of residuals**.
7. Click **OK. OK**.

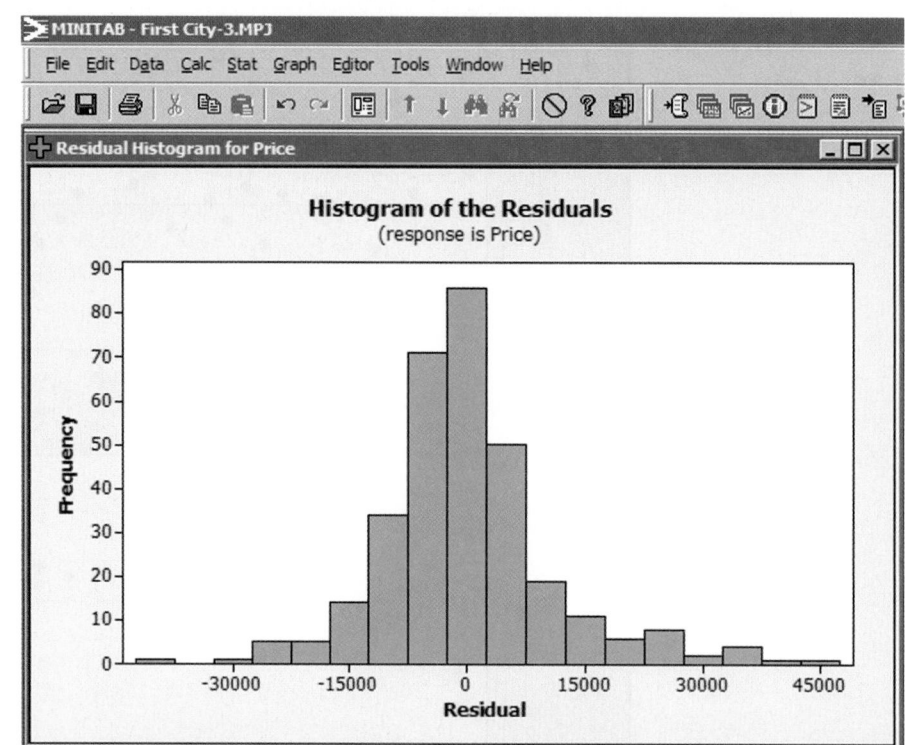

FIGURE 15.39

Minitab Histogram of Standardized Residuals for First City Real Estate

Minitab Instructions:
1. Open file: First City-3. MTW.
2. Choose **Stat > Regression > Regression**.
3. In **Response**, enter dependent (*y*) variable.
4. In **Predictors**, enter independent (*x*) variables.
5. Choose **Graphs**.
6. Under **Residual for Plots**, select **Standadized**.
7. Under **Residual Plots**, select **Histogram of residuals**.
8. Click **OK. OK**.

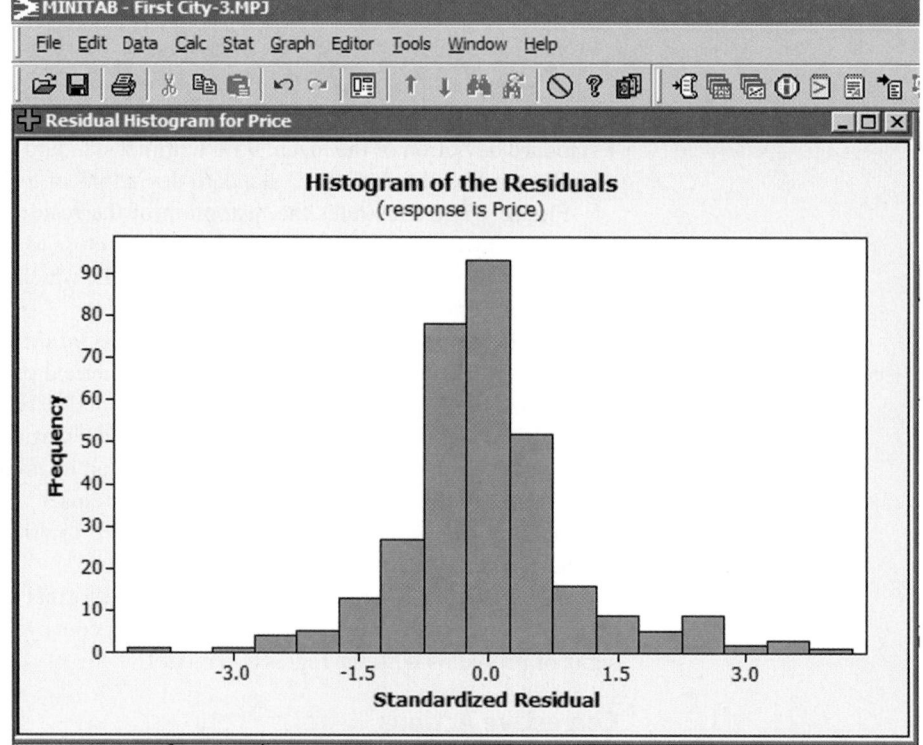

conform to a linear relationship. If the model suffers from nonlinearity and if the residuals have a nonconstant variance, you may want to transform both the independent and dependent variables. In cases in which the normality assumption is not satisfied, transforming the dependent variable is often useful. In many instances, a log transformation works. In some instances, a transformation involving the product of two independent variables will help.

FIGURE 15.40

Minitab Normal Probability Plot of Residuals for First City Real Estate

Minitab Instructions:
1. Open file: First City-3. MTW.
2. Choose **Stat > Regression > Regression**.
3. In **Response**, enter dependent (*y*) variable.
4. In **Predictors**, enter independent (*x*) variables.
5. Choose **Graphs**.
6. Under **Residual** Plots, select **Normal plot of residuals**.
7. Click **OK. OK.**

A more detailed discussion is beyond the scope of this text. However, you can read more about this subject in the Kutner et al. reference listed at the end of the chapter.

The alternative of using a different regression model means that we respecify the model to include new independent variables or remove existing variables from the model. In most modeling situations, we are in a continual state of model respecification. We are always seeking to improve the regression model by finding new independent variables.

15-5: Exercises

Skill Development

15-46. Consider the following values for an independent and dependent variable:

x	*y*
6	5
9	20
14	28
18	30
22	33
27	35
33	45

a. Determine the estimated linear regression equation relating the dependent and independent variables.
b. Is the regression equation you found significant? Test at the $\alpha = 0.05$ level.

c. Determine both the residuals and standardized residuals. Is there anything about the residuals that would lead you to question whether the assumptions necessary to use regression analysis are satisfied? Discuss.

15-47. Consider the following values for an independent and dependent variable:

x	*y*
6	5
9	20
14	28
18	15
22	27
27	31
33	32
50	60
61	132
75	160

a. Determine the estimated linear regression equation relating the dependent and independent variables.

b. Is the regression equation you found significant? Test at the $\alpha = 0.05$ level.

c. Determine both the residuals and standardized residuals. Is there anything about the residuals that would lead you to question whether the assumptions necessary to use regression analysis are satisfied?

15-48. Examine the following data set

y	x
25	10
35	10
14	10
45	20
52	20
41	20
65	30
63	30
68	30

a. Determine the estimated regression equation for this data set.

b. Calculate the residuals for this regression equation.

c. Produce the appropriate residual plot to determine if the linear function is the appropriate regression function for this data set.

d. Use a residual plot to determine if the residuals have a constant variance.

e. Produce a residual plot to determine if the residuals are independent. Assume the order of appearance is the time order of the data.

f. Use a probability plot to determine if the error terms are normally distributed.

15-49. Examine the following data set:

y	x_1	x_2
25	5	25
35	5	5
14	5	5
45	25	40
52	25	5
41	25	25
65	30	30
63	30	30
68	30	25
75	40	30

a. Determine the estimated regression equation for this data set.

b. Calculate the residuals and the standardized residuals for this regression equation.

c. Produce the appropriate residual plot to determine if the linear function is the appropriate regression function for this data set.

d. Use a residual plot to determine if the residuals have a constant variance.

e. Produce the appropriate residual plot to determine if the residuals are independent.

f. Construct a probability plot to determine if the error terms are normally distributed.

Computer Database Exercises

15-50. The Western State Tourist Association gives out pamphlets, maps, and other tourist-related information to people who call a toll-free number and request the information. The association orders the packets of information from a document printing company and likes to have enough available to meet the immediate need without having too many sitting around taking up space. The marketing manager decided to develop a multiple regression model to be used in predicting the number of calls that will be received in the coming week. A random sample of 12 weeks is selected, with the following variables:

   y = Number of calls
   x_1 = Number of advertisements placed the previous week
   x_2 = Number of calls received the previous week
   x_3 = Number of airline tour bookings into Western cities for the current week

The data are in the file called **Western States**.

a. Construct a multiple regression model using all three independent variables. Write a short report discussing the model.

b. Based on the appropriate residual plots, what can you conclude about the constant variance assumption? Discuss.

c. Based on the appropriate residual analysis, does it appear that the residuals are independent? Discuss.

d. Use an appropriate analysis of the residuals to determine whether the regression model meets the assumption of normally distributed error terms. Discuss.

15-51. The athletic director of State University is interested in developing a multiple regression model that might be used to explain the variation in attendance at football games at his school. A sample of 16 games was selected from home games played during the past 10 seasons. Data for the following factors were determined:

   y = Game attendance
   x_1 = Team win/loss percentage to date

x_2 = Opponent win/loss percentage to date

x_3 = Games played this season

x_4 = Temperature at game time

The sample data are in the file called **Football**.

a. Build a multiple regression model using all four independent variables. Write a short report that outlines the characteristics of this model.

b. Develop a table of residuals for this model. What is the average residual value? Why do you suppose it came out to this value? Discuss.

c. Based on the appropriate residual plot, what can you conclude about the constant variance assumption? Discuss.

d. Based on the appropriate residual analysis, does it appear that the model errors are independent? Discuss.

e. Can you conclude, based on the appropriate method of analysis, that the model error terms are approximately normally distributed?

15-52. Refer to Exercise 15-7 which referenced an article in *BusinessWeek* ("Hot Growth Companies," June 5, 2006) that presented a list of the 100 companies perceived as having "hot growth" characteristics. The file entitled **Logrowth** contains sales ($million), sales increase (%), return on capital, market value ($million), and recent stock price of the companies ranked from 81 to 100. In Exercise 15-8, a regression equation was constructed in which the sales of the companies was predicted using their market value.

a. Determine the estimated regression equation for this data set.

b. Calculate the residuals and the standardized residuals for this regression equation.

c. Produce the appropriate residual plot to determine if the linear function is the appropriate regression function for this data set.

d. Use a residual plot to determine if the residuals have a constant variance.

e. Produce the appropriate residual plot to determine if the residuals are independent. Assume the data were extracted in the order listed.

f. Construct a probability plot to determine if the error terms are normally distributed.

15-53. The consumer price index (CPI) is a measure of the average change in prices over time in a fixed market basket of goods and services typically purchased by consumers. One of the items in this market basket that affects the CPI is the price of oil and its derivatives. The file entitled **Consumer** contains the price of the derivatives of oil and the CPI adjusted to 2005 levels. In Exercise 15-45, backward elimination stepwise regression was used to determine the relationship between CPI and two independent variables: the price of heating oil and of diesel fuel.

a. Construct an estimate of the regression equation using the same variables.

b. Produce the appropriate residual plots to determine if the linear function is the appropriate regression function for this data set.

c. Use a residual plot to determine if the residuals have a constant variance.

d. Produce the appropriate residual plot to determine if the residuals are independent. Assume the data were extracted in the order listed.

e. Construct a probability plot to determine if the error terms are normally distributed.

15-54. A variety of sources suggest that individuals assess their health, at least in part, by estimating their percentage of body fat. A widely accepted measure of body fat uses an underwater weighing technique. There are, however, more convenient methods using only a scale and a measuring tape. An article in the *Journal of Statistics Education* 4, no. 1 (1996), (Roger W. Johnson), "Fitting Percentage of Body Fat to Simple Body Measurements") explored regression models to predict body fat. The file entitled **Bodyfat** lists a portion of the data presented in the cited article. Exercise 15-43 utilized best subsets stepwise regression to establish the relationship between body fat and the independent variables weight, abdomen circumference, and thigh circumference.

a. Construct an estimate of the regression equation using the same variables.

b. Produce the appropriate residual plots to determine if the linear function is the appropriate regression function for this data set.

c. Use a residual plot to determine if the residuals have a constant variance.

d. Produce the appropriate residual plot to determine if the residuals are independent. Assume the data were extracted in the order listed.

e. Construct a probability plot to determine if the error terms are normally distributed.

15-55. The National Association of Theatre Owners is the largest exhibition trade organization in the world, representing more than 26,000 movie screens in all 50 states and in more than 20 countries worldwide. Its membership includes the largest cinema chains and hundreds of independent theatre owners. It publishes statistics concerning the movie sector of the economy. The file entitled **Flicks** contains data on total U.S. box office grosses ($billion), total number of admissions (billion), average U.S. ticket price ($), and number of movie screens.

a. Construct a regression equation in which total U.S. box office grosses are predicted using the other variables.

b. Produce the appropriate residual plots to determine if the linear function is the appropriate regression function for this data set.

c. Square each of the independent variables and add them to the model upon which the regression equation in part a was built. Produce the new regression equation.

d. Use a residual plot to determine if the quadratic model in part c alleviates the problem identified in part b.

e. Construct a probability plot to determine if the error terms are normally distributed for the updated model.

Summary and Conclusions

Multiple regression is an extension of simple regression analysis. In multiple regression, two or more independent variables are used to explain the variation in the dependent variable. Just as a manager searches for the best combination of employees to perform a job, the decision maker using multiple regression analysis searches for the best combination of independent variables to explain variation in the dependent variable.

The presentation of multiple regression analysis has largely been an analysis of computer printouts. As a decision maker, you will almost assuredly not be required to manually develop the regression model, but you will have to judge its applicability based on a computer printout. The Excel and Minitab software we have used in Chapters 14 and 15 are representative of the many software packages that are available. You no doubt will encounter printouts that look somewhat different from those shown in this text and some of the terms used may differ slightly. However, the basic information will be the same, as will be the inferences you can make from the model.

This chapter has discussed the difference between R^2 and adjusted R^2, as well as the difference between statistical significance and practical significance. As a decision maker, you must recognize that a regression model can be statistically significant yet have no practical use because the standard error of the estimate is too large or multicollinearity impacts too heavily.

As you continue your study of business, you will find that multiple regression is one of the most widely used statistical tools. You will find it applied particularly to the areas of production, finance, accounting, and economics.

Equations

Population Multiple Regression Model

$$y = \beta_0 + \beta_1 x_1 + \beta_2 x_2 + \cdots + \beta_k x_k + \varepsilon \quad \textbf{(15.1)}$$

Estimated Multiple Regression Model

$$\hat{y} = b_0 + b_1 x_1 + b_2 x_2 + \cdots + b_k x_k \quad \textbf{(15.2)}$$

Correlation Coefficient

$$r = \frac{\Sigma(x - \bar{x})(y - \bar{y})}{\sqrt{\Sigma(x - \bar{x})^2 \, \Sigma(y - \bar{y})^2}}$$

or $\quad r = \dfrac{\Sigma(x_i - \bar{x}_i)(x_j - \bar{x}_j)}{\sqrt{\Sigma(x_i - \bar{x}_i)^2 \, \Sigma(x_j - \bar{x}_j)^2}} \quad \textbf{(15.3)}$

Multiple Coefficient of Determination (R^2)

$$R^2 = \frac{\text{Sum of squares regression}}{\text{Total sum of squares}} = \frac{SSR}{SST} \quad \textbf{(15.4)}$$

F-Test Statistic

$$F = \frac{\dfrac{SSR}{k}}{\dfrac{SSE}{n - k - 1}} \quad \textbf{(15.5)}$$

Adjusted R-Squared

$$R\text{-sq(adj)} = R_A^2 = 1 - (1 - R^2)\left(\frac{n - 1}{n - k - 1}\right) \quad \textbf{(15.6)}$$

t-Test for Significance of Each Regression Coefficient

$$t = \frac{b_j - 0}{s_{b_j}} \qquad df = n - k - 1 \quad \textbf{(15.7)}$$

Standard Error of the Estimate

$$s_\varepsilon = \sqrt{\frac{SSE}{n - k - 1}} = \sqrt{MSE} \quad \textbf{(15.8)}$$

Variance Inflation Factor

$$VIF = \frac{1}{(1 - R_j^2)} \quad \textbf{(15.9)}$$

Confidence Interval Estimate for the Regression Slope

$$b_j \pm s_{b_j} \qquad (15.10)$$

Polynomial Population Regression Model

$$y = \beta_0 + \beta_1 x + \beta_2 x^2 + \cdots + \beta_p x^p + \varepsilon \quad (15.11)$$

Residual

$$e_i = y_i - \hat{y}_i \qquad (15.12)$$

Standardized Residual

$$s_{e_i} = \frac{e_i}{s_\varepsilon \sqrt{1 + \frac{1}{n} + \frac{(x_i - \bar{x})^2}{\sum x^2 - \frac{(\sum x)^2}{n}}}} \qquad (15.13)$$

Key Terms

Aptness   736
Adjusted R-squared (R_A^2)   692
Coefficient of partial
   determination   726
Composite model   719
Correlation coefficient   684
Correlation matrix   685
Dummy variables   703

Interaction   719
Model   682
Multicollinearity   695
Multiple coefficient of determination
  (R^2)   689
Multiple regression model for the
  population   680
Polynomial model   712

Regression hyperplane   681
Residual   737
Second-order regression
  model   712
Standard error of the estimate   693
Standardized residual   740
Variance inflation factor
  (VIF)   696

Chapter Exercises

Conceptual Questions

15-56. Discuss in your own terms the similarities and differences between simple linear regression analysis and multiple regression analysis.

15-57. Discuss what is meant by the least squares criterion as it pertains to multiple regression analysis. Is the least squares criterion any different for simple regression analysis? Discuss.

15-58. List the basic assumptions of regression analysis and discuss in your own terms what each means.

15-59. What does it mean if we have developed a multiple regression model and have concluded that the model is apt?

15-60. Go to the library, or use the Internet, to locate three articles using a regression model with more than one independent variable. For each article write a short summary covering the following points:
  purpose for using the model
  how the variables in the model were selected
  how the data in the model were selected
  any possible violations of the needed assumptions
  the conclusions drawn from using the model

15-61. Consider the following model:

$$\hat{y} = 5 + 3x_1 + 5x_2$$

a. Provide an interpretation of the coefficient of x_1.
b. Is the interpretation provided in part a true regardless of the value of x_2? Explain.
c. Now consider the model $\hat{y} = 5 + 3x_1 + 5x_2 + 4x_1 x_2$. Let $x_2 = 1$. Give an interpretation of the coefficient of x_1 when $x_2 = 1$.
d. Repeat part c when $x_2 = 2$. Is the interpretation provided in part a true regardless of the value of x_2? Explain.
e. Considering your answers to parts b and c, what type of regression components has conditional interpretations?

Computer Database Exercises

The following information applies to Exercises 15-62, 15-63, and 15-64.

A publishing company in New York is attempting to develop a model that it can use to help predict textbook sales for books it is considering for future publication. The marketing department has collected data on several variables from a random sample of 15 books. These data are given in the file **Textbooks**.

15-62. Develop the correlation matrix showing the correlation between all possible pairs of variables. Test statistically to determine which independent variables are significantly correlated with the dependent variable, book sales. Use a significance level of 0.05.

15-63. Develop a multiple regression model containing all four independent variables. Show clearly the regression coefficients. Write a short report discussing the model. In your report make sure you cover the following issues:

a. How much of the total variation in book sales can be explained by these four independent variables? Would you conclude that the model is significant at the 0.05 level?

b. Develop a 95% confidence interval for each regression coefficient and interpret these confidence intervals.

c. Which of the independent variables can you conclude to be significant in explaining the variation in book sales? Test using $\alpha = 0.05$.

d. How much of the variation in the dependent variable is explained by the dependent variable? Is the model statistically significant at the $\alpha = 0.01$ level? Discuss.

e. How much, if at all, does adding one more page to the book impact the sales volume of the book? Develop and interpret a 95% confidence interval estimate to answer this question.

f. Perform the appropriate analysis to determine the aptness of this regression model. Discuss your results and conclusions.

15-64. The publishing company recently came up with some additional data for the 15 books in the original sample. Two new variables, production expenditures (x_5) and number of prepublication reviewers (x_6), have been added. These additional data are as follows:

Book	x_5	x_6	Book	x_5	x_6
1	$38,000	5	9	$51,000	4
2	86,000	8	10	34,000	6
3	59,000	3	11	20,000	2
4	80,000	9	12	80,000	5
5	29,500	3	13	60,000	5
6	31,000	3	14	87,000	8
7	40,000	5	15	29,000	3
8	69,000	4			

Incorporating this additional data, calculate the correlation between each of these additional variables and the dependent variable, book sales.

a. Test the significance of the correlation coefficients, using $\alpha = 0.05$. Comment on your results.

b. Develop a multiple regression model that includes all six independent variables. Which, if any, variables would you recommend be retained if this model is going to be used to predict book sales for the publishing company? For any statistical tests you might perform, use a significance level of 0.05. Discuss your results.

c. Use the F-test approach to test the null hypothesis that all slope coefficients are 0. Test with a significance level of 0.05. What do these results mean? Discuss.

d. Do multicollinearity problems appear to be present in the model? Discuss the potential consequences of multicollinearity with respect to the regression model.

e. Discuss whether the standard error of the estimate is small enough to make this model useful for predicting the sales of textbooks.

f. Plot the residuals against the predicted value of y and comment on what this plot means relative to the aptness of the model.

g. Compute the standardized residuals and form these into a frequency histogram. What does this indicate about the normality assumption?

h. Comment on the overall aptness of this model and indicate what might be done to improve the model.

The following information applies to Exercises 15-65 through 15-74.

The J. J. McCracken Company has authorized its marketing research department to make a study of customers who have been issued a McCracken charge card. The marketing research department hopes to be able to identify the significant variables that explain the variation in purchases. Once these variables are determined, the department intends to try to attract new customers who would be predicted to make a high volume of purchases.

Twenty-five customers were selected at random and values for the following variables were recorded in the file called **McCracken**:

y = Average monthly purchases (in dollars) at McCracken

x_1 = Customer age

x_2 = Customer family income

x_3 = Family size

15-65. A first step in regression analysis often involves developing a scatter plot of the data. Develop the scatter plots of all the possible pairs of variables, and with a brief statement indicate what each plot says about the relationship between the two variables.

15-66. Compute the correlation matrix for these data. Develop the decision rule for testing the significance of each coefficient. Which, if any, correlations are not significant? Use $\alpha = 0.05$.

15-67. Use forward selection stepwise regression to develop the multiple regression model. The variable x_2, family income, was brought into the model. Discuss why this happened.

15-68. Test the significance of the regression model at Step 1 of the computer printout. Justify the significance level you have selected.

15-69. Develop a 95% confidence level for the slope coefficient for the family income variable at Step 1 of the model. Be sure to interpret this confidence interval.

15-70. Describe the regression model at Step 2 of the analysis. In your discussion, be sure to discuss the effect of adding a new variable on the standard error of the estimate and on R^2.

15-71. Referring to Problem 15-70, suppose the manager of McCracken's marketing department questions the appropriateness of adding a second variable. How would you respond to her question?

15-72. Looking carefully at the stepwise regression model, you can see that the value of the slope coefficient for variable x_2, family income, changes each time a new variable is added to the regression model. Discuss why this change takes place.

15-73. Analyze the stepwise regression model at Step 3 and the intermediate results at Steps 1 and 2. Write a report to the marketing manager pointing out the strengths and weaknesses of the model. Be sure to comment on the department's goal of being able to use the model to predict which customers will purchase high volumes from McCracken.

15-74. Plot the residuals against the predicted value of y and comment on what this plot means relative to the aptness of the model.

a. Compute the standardized residuals and form these in a frequency histogram. What does this indicate about the normality assumption?

b. Comment on the overall aptness of this model and indicate what might be done to improve the model.

15-75. Amazon.com has become one of the most successful online merchants. Two measures of its success are sales and net income/loss figures. In an article entitled "Amazon CEO takes long view," *USA Today* (Byron Acohido, July 6, 2005) presented these figures (in $million) for the period 1995 to 2004. They are given here.

Net income/ loss	−0.3	−5.7	−27.5	−124.5	−719.9
Sales	0.5	15.7	147.7	609.8	1,639.8
Net income/ loss	−1,411.2	−567.3	−149.1	35.3	588.5
Sales	2,761.9	3,122.9	3,932.9	5,263.7	6,921.1

a. Produce a scatter plot for Amazon's net income/loss and sales figures for the period 1995 to 2004. Determine the order (or degree) of the polynomial that could be used to predict Amazon's net income/loss using sales figures for the period 1995 to 2004.

b. Produce the polynomial indicated in part a.

c. Test to determine whether the overall model is statistically significant. Use a significance level of 0.10 and the test statistic approach.

d. Conduct a hypothesis test to determine if curvature exists in the model that predicts Amazon's net income/loss using sales figures. Use a significance level of 0.02 and the test statistic approach.

15-76. The National Association of Realtors Existing-Home Sales Series provides a measurement of the residential real estate market. One of the measurements it produces is the Housing Affordability Index (HAI). It is a measure of the financial ability of U.S. families to buy a house. A value of 100 means that families earning the national median income have just the amount of money needed to qualify for a mortgage on a median-priced home; higher than 100 means they have more than enough and lower than 100 means they have less than enough. The file entitled **Index** contains the HAI and associated variables.

a. Produce the correlation matrix of all the variables. Predict the variables that will remain in the estimated regression equation if standard stepwise regression is used.

b. Use standard stepwise regression to develop an estimate of a model that is to predict the HAI from the associated variables found in the file entitled **Index**.

c. Compare the results of parts a and b. Explain any difference between the two models.

15-77. An investment analyst collected data from 20 randomly chosen companies. The data consisted of the 52-week-high stock prices, PE ratio, and the market value of the company. This data are in the file entitled **Investment**. The analyst wishes to produce a regression equation to predict the market value using the 52-week-high stock price and the PE ratio of the company. He creates a complete second-degree polynomial.

a. Construct an estimate of the regression equation using the indicated variables.

b. Produce the appropriate residual plots to determine if the polynomial function is the appropriate regression function for this data set.

c. Use a residual plot to determine if the residuals have a constant variance.

d. Produce the appropriate residual plot to determine if the residuals are independent. Assume the data were extracted in the order listed.

e. Construct a probability plot to determine if the error terms are normally distributed.

15-78. The consumer price index (CPI) is a measure of the average change in prices over time in a fixed market basket of goods and services typically purchased by consumers. One of the items in this market basket that affects the CPI is the price of oil and its derivatives. The file entitled **Consumer** contains the price of the derivatives of oil and the CPI adjusted to 2005 levels.

a. Produce a multiple regression equation depicting the relationship between the CPI and the price of the derivatives of oil.

b. Conduct a *t*-test on the coefficient which has the highest *p*-value. Use a significance level of 0.02 and the *p*-value approach.

c. Produce a multiple regression equation depicting the relationship between the CPI and the price of the derivatives of oil leaving out the variable tested in part b.

d. Referring to the regression results in part c, repeat the tests indicated in part b.

e. Perform a test of hypothesis to determine if the resulting overall model is statistically significant. Use a significance level of 0.02 and the *p*-value approach.

15-79. Refer to the State Department of Transportation data set called **Liabins**. The department was interested in determining the rate of compliance with the state's mandatory liability insurance law, as well as other things. *Assume the data were collected using a simple random sampling process.* Develop the best possible linear regression model using vehicle year as the dependent variable and any or all of the other variables as potential independent variables. Assume that your objective is to develop a predictive model. Write a report that discusses the steps you took to develop the final model. Include a correlation matrix and all appropriate statistical tests. Use an $\alpha = 0.05$. If you are using a nominal or ordinal variable, remember that you must make sure it is in the form of one or more dummy variables.

CASE 15.1

Dynamic Scales, Inc.

In 1985, Stanley Ahlon and three financial partners formed Dynamic Scales, Inc. The company was based on an idea Stanley had for developing a scale to weigh trucks in motion and thus eliminate the need for every truck to stop at weigh stations along highways. This dynamic scale would be placed in the highway approximately one-quarter mile from the regular weigh station. The scale would have a minicomputer that would automatically record truck speed, axle weights, and climate variables, including temperature, wind, and moisture. Stanley Ahlon and his partners believed that state transportation departments in the United States would be the primary market for such a scale.

As with many technological advances, developing the dynamic scale has been difficult. When the scale finally proved accurate for trucks traveling 40 miles per hour, it would not perform for trucks traveling at higher speeds. However, eight months ago, Stanley announced that the dynamic scale was ready to be field-tested by the Nebraska State Department of Transportation under a grant from the federal government. Stanley explained to his financial partners, and to Nebraska transportation officials, that the dynamic weight would not exactly equal the static weight (truck weight on a static scale). However he was sure a statistical relationship between dynamic weight and static weight could be determined, which would make the dynamic scale useful.

Nebraska officials, along with people from Dynamic Scales, installed a dynamic scale on a major highway in Nebraska. Each month for six months data were collected for a random sample of trucks weighed on both the dynamic scale and a static scale. Table 15.3 presents these data.

Once the data were collected, the next step was to determine whether, based on this test, the dynamic scale measurements could be used to predict static weights. A complete report will be submitted to the U.S. government and to Dynamic Scales.

TABLE 15.3 Test Data for the Dynamic Scales Example

Month	Front-Axle Static Weight	Front-Axle Dynamic Weight	Truck Speed	Temperature	Moisture
January	1,800 lb.	1,625 lb.	52 mph	21°F	0.00%
	1,311	1,904	71	17	0.15
	1,504	1,390	48	13	0.40
	1,388	1,402	50	19	0.10
	1,250	1,100	61	24	0.00
February	2,102	1,950	55	26	0.10
	1,410	1,475	58	32	0.20
	1,000	1,103	59	38	0.15
	1,430	1,387	43	24	0.00
	1,073	948	59	18	0.40
March	1,502	1,493	62	34	0.00
	1,721	1,902	67	36	0.00
	1,113	1,415	48	42	0.21
	978	983	59	29	0.32
	1,254	1,149	60	48	0.00
April	994	1,052	58	37	0.00
	1,127	999	52	34	0.21
	1,406	1,404	59	40	0.40
	875	900	47	48	0.00
	1,350	1,275	68	51	0.00
May	1,102	1,120	55	52	0.00
	1,240	1,253	57	57	0.00
	1,087	1,040	62	63	0.00
	993	1,102	59	62	0.10
	1,408	1,400	67	68	0.00
June	1,420	1,404	58	70	0.00
	1,808	1,790	54	71	0.00
	1,401	1,396	49	83	0.00
	933	1,004	62	88	0.40
	1,150	1,127	64	81	0.00

CASE 15.2

Glaser Machine Works

Glaser Machine Works had experienced a significant change in its business operations over the past 50 years. Glaser started business as a machine shop that produced specialty tools and products for the timber and lumber industry. This was a logical fit, given its location in the southern part of the United States. However, over the years Glaser looked to expand its offerings beyond the lumber and timber industry. Initially, its small size coupled with its rural location made it difficult to attract the attention of large companies that could use its products. All of that began to change as Glaser developed the ability to not only fabricate parts and tools but also to assemble products for customers who needed special components in large quantities. Glaser's business really took off when first foreign, and then domestic, automakers began to build automobile plants in the southern United States. Glaser was able to provide quality parts quickly for firms that expected high quality and responsive delivery. Many of Glaser's customers operated with little inventory and required that suppliers be able to provide shipments with short lead times.

As part of its relationship with the automobile industry, Glaser was expected to buy into the lean manufacturing and quality improvement initiatives of its customers. Glaser had always prided itself on its quality, but as the number and variety of its products increased, along with ever higher expectations by its customers, Glaser knew that it would have to respond by ensuring its quality and operations were continually improving. Of recent concern was the performance of its manufacturing line 107B. This line produced a component part for a Japanese automobile company. The Japanese firm had initially been pleased with Glaser's performance, but lately the number of defects was approaching an unacceptable level. Managers of the 107B line knew the line and its workers had been asked to ramp up production to meet increased demand and that some workers were concerned with the amount of overtime being required. There was also concern about the second shift now being run at 107B. Glaser had initially run only one shift, but when demand for its product became so high that there was not sufficient capacity with one shift, additional workers were hired to operate a night shift.

Management was wondering if the new shift had been stretched beyond its capabilities. Glaser plant management asked Kristi Johnson, the assistant production supervisor for line 107B, to conduct an analysis of product defects for the line. Kristi randomly selected several days of output and counted the number of defective parts produced on the 107B line. This information, along with other data, is contained in the file **Glaser Machine Works**. Kristi promised to have a full report for the management team by the end of the month.

CASE 15.3

Hawlins Manufacturing

Ross Hawlins had done it all at Hawlins Manufacturing, a company founded by his grandfather 63 years ago. Among his many duties, Ross oversaw all the plant's operations, a task that had grown in responsibility given the company's rapid growth over the past three decades. When Ross's grandfather founded the company, there were only two manufacturing sites. Expansion and acquisition of competitors over the years had caused that number to grow to over 50 manufacturing plants in 18 states.

Hawlins had a simple process that produced only two products, but the demand for these products was strong and Ross had spent millions of dollars upgrading his facilities over the past decade. Consequently, most of the company's equipment was less than 10 years old on average. Hawlins's two products were produced for local markets, as prohibitive shipping costs prevented shipping the product long distances. Product demand was sufficiently strong to support two manufacturing shifts (day and night) at every plant, and every plant had the capability to produce both products sold by Hawlins. Recently, the management team at Hawlins noticed that there were differences in output levels across the various plants. They were uncertain what, if anything, might explain these differences. Clearly, if some plants were more productive than others, there might be some meaningful insights that could be standardized across plants to boost overall productivity.

Because his duties required him to be involved in a variety of activities, Ross Hawlins has asked Lisa Chandler, an industrial engineer at the company's headquarters, to conduct a study of the plant's productivity. Lisa has randomly sampled 159 weeks of output from various plants together with the number of plant employees working that week, the plants average age in years, the product mix produced that week (either product A or B), and whether the output was from the day or night shift. The sampled data are contained in the file **Hawlins Manufacturing**. The Hawlins management team is expecting a written report and a presentation by Lisa when they meet again next Tuesday.

CASE 15.4

Sapphire Coffee—Part 2

Jennie Garcia could not believe that her career had moved so far so fast. When she left graduate school with a master's degree in anthropology, she intended to work at a local coffee shop until something else came along that was more related to her academic background. But after a few months she came to enjoy the business, and in a little over a year she was promoted to store manager. When the company for whom she worked continued to grow, Jennie was given oversight over a few stores.

Now, eight years after she started as a barista, Jennie was in charge of operations and planning for the company's southern region. As a part of her responsibilities, Jennie tracks store revenues and forecasts coffee demand. Historically, Sapphire Coffee would base its demand forecast on the number of stores, believing that each store sold approximately the same amount of coffee. This approach seemed to work well when the company had shops of similar size and layout, but as the company grew, stores became more varied. Now, some stores had drive-thru windows, a feature that top management added to some stores believing that it would increase coffee sales for customers who wanted a cup of coffee on their way to work but who were too rushed to park and enter the store.

Jennie noticed that weekly sales seemed to be more variable across stores in her region and was wondering what, if anything, might explain the differences. The company's financial vice president had also noticed the increased differences in sales across stores and was wondering what might be happening. In an e-mail to Jennie he stated that weekly store sales are expected to average $5.00 per square foot. Thus, a 1,000-square-foot store would have average weekly sales of $5,000. He asked that Jennie analyze the stores in her region to see if this rule of thumb was a reliable measure of a store's performance.

Jennie had been in the business long enough to know that a store's size, while an important factor, was not the only thing that might influence sales. She had never been convinced of the efficacy of the drive-thru window, believing that it detracted from the coffee house experience that so many of Sapphire Coffee customers had come to expect. The VP of finance was expecting the analysis to be completed by the weekend. Jennie decided to randomly select weekly sales records for 53 stores, along with each store's size, whether it was located close to a college, and whether it had a drive-thru window. The data are in the file **Sapphire Coffee-2**. A full analysis would need to be sent to the corporate office by Friday.

CASE 15.5

Wendell Motors

Wendell Motors manufactures and ships small electric motors and drives to a variety of industrial and commercial customers in and around St. Louis. Wendell is a small operation with a single manufacturing plant. Wendell's products are different from other motor and drive manufacturers because it only produces small motors (25 horsepower or less) and because its products are used in a variety of industries and businesses that appreciate Wendell's quality and speed of delivery. Because it has only one plant, Wendell ships motors directly from the plant to its customers. Wendell's reputation for quality and speed of delivery allows it to maintain low inventories of motors and ship make-to-order products directly.

As part of its ongoing commitment to lean manufacturing and continuous process improvement, Wendell carefully monitors the cost associated with both production and shipping. The manager of shipping for Wendell, Tyler Jenkins, regularly reports the shipping costs to Wendell's management team. Because few finished goods inventories are maintained, competitive delivery times often require that Wendell expedite shipments. This is almost always the case for those customers who operate their business around the clock every day of the week. Such customers might maintain their own backup safety stock of a particular motor or drive, but circumstances often result in cases where replacement products have to be rushed through production and then expedited to the customer.

Wendell's management team wondered if these special orders were too expensive to handle in this way and if it might be less expensive to produce and hold certain motors as finished goods inventory, enabling off-the-shelf delivery using less expensive modes of shipping. This might especially be true for orders that must be filled on a holiday, incurring an additional shipping charge. At the last meeting of the management team, Tyler Jenkins was asked to analyze expedited shipping costs and to develop a model that could be used to estimate the cost of expediting a customer's order.

Donna Layton, an industrial engineer in the plant, was asked to prepare an inventory cost analysis to determine the expenses of holding additional finished goods inventory. To begin his analysis, Tyler randomly selected 45 expedited shipping records. The sampled data can be found in the file **Wendell Motors**. The management team expects a full report in five days. Tyler knew he would need a model for explaining shipping costs for expedited orders and that he would also need to answer the questions as to what effect, if any, shipping on a holiday had on costs.

References

Berenson, Mark L., and David M. Levine, *Basic Business Statistics: Concepts and Applications*, 10th ed. (Upper Saddle River, NJ: Prentice Hall, 2006).

Bowerman, Bruce L., and Richard T. O'Connell, *Linear Statistical Models: An Applied Approach*, 2nd ed. (Belmont, CA: Duxbury Press, 1990).

Cryer, Jonathan D., and Robert B. Miller, *Statistics for Business: Data Analysis and Modeling*, 2nd ed. (Belmont, CA: Duxbury Press, 1994).

Demmert, Henry, and Marshall Medoff, "Game-Specific Factors and Major League Baseball Attendance: An Econometric Study," *Santa Clara Business Review* (1977), pp. 49–56.

Dielman, Terry E., *Applied Regression Analysis: A Second Course in Business and Economic Statistics*, 4th ed. (Belmont, CA: Duxbury Press, 2005).

Draper, Norman R., and Harry Smith, *Applied Regression Analysis*, 3rd ed. (New York: John Wiley and Sons, 1998).

Frees, Edward W., *Data Analysis Using Regression Models: The Business Perspective* (Upper Saddle River, NJ: Prentice Hall, 1996).

Gloudemans, Robert J., and Dennis Miller, "Multiple Regression Analysis Applied to Residential Properties." *Decision Sciences 7* (April 1976) pp. 294–304.

Kleinbaum, David G., Lawrence L. Kupper, Keith E. Muller, and Azhar Nizam, *Applied Regression Analysis and Other Multivariable Methods*, 3rd ed. (Belmont, CA: Duxbury Press, 1998).

Kutner, Michael H., Christopher J. Nachtsheim, John Neter, and William Li, *Applied Linear Statistical Models*, 5th ed. (New York: McGraw-Hill Irwin, 2005).

Microsoft Excel 2007 (Redmond, WA: Microsoft Corp. 2007).

Minitab for Windows Version 14 (State College, PA: Minitab, 2005).

Analyzing and Forecasting Time-Series Data

CHAPTER OUTCOMES

After studying the material in Chapter 16, you should be able to:

1. Identify the components present in a time series.
2. Understand and compute basic index numbers.
3. Apply the fundamental steps in developing and implementing forecasting models.
4. Apply trend-based forecasting models, including linear trend, nonlinear trend, and seasonally adjusted trend.
5. Use smoothing-based forecasting models, including single and double exponential smoothing.

PREPARING FOR CHAPTER SIXTEEN

- Review the steps used to develop a line chart that were discussed in Chapter 2.
- Make sure you understand the steps necessary to construct and interpret linear and nonlinear regression models in Chapters 14 and 15.
- Review the concepts and properties associated with means discussed in Chapter 3.

WHY YOU NEED TO KNOW

No organization, large or small, can function effectively without a forecast for the goods or services it provides. A retail clothing store must forecast the demand for the shirts it sells by shirt size. The concessionaire at Dodger Stadium in Los Angeles must forecast each game's attendance to determine how many soft drinks and hot dogs to have on hand. Your state's elected officials must forecast tax revenues in order to establish a budget each year. These are only a few of the instances in which forecasting is required. For many organizations, the success of the forecasting effort will play a major role in determining the general success of the organization.

When you graduate and join an organization in the public or private sectors, you will almost certainly be required to prepare forecasts or to use forecasts provided by someone else in the organization. You won't have access to a crystal ball on which to rely for an accurate prediction of the future. Fortunately, if you have learned the material presented in this chapter, you will have a basic understanding of forecasting and of how and when to apply various forecasting techniques. We urge you to focus on the material and take with you the tools that will give you a competitive advantage over those who are not familiar with forecasting techniques.

16.1 Introduction to Forecasting, Time-Series Data, and Index Numbers

Decision makers often confuse forecasting and planning. Planning is the process of determining how to deal with the future. On the other hand, *forecasting* is the process of predicting what the future will be like. Forecasts are used as inputs for the planning process.

Experts agree that good planning is essential for an organization to be effective. Because forecasts are an important part of the planning process, you need to be familiar with forecasting methods. There are two broad categories of forecasting techniques: qualitative and quantitative. *Qualitative forecasting* techniques are based on expert opinion and judgment. *Quantitative forecasting* techniques are based on statistical methods for analyzing quantitative historical data. This chapter focuses on quantitative forecasting techniques.

In general, quantitative forecasting techniques are used whenever the following conditions are true: Historical data relating to the variable to be forecast exist; the historical data can be quantified; and you are willing to assume that the historical pattern will continue into the future.

General Forecasting Issues

Decision makers who are actively involved in forecasting frequently say that forecasting is both an art and a science. Operationally, the forecaster is engaged in the process of modeling a real-world system. Determining the appropriate forecasting model is a challenging task, but it can be made manageable by employing the same model-building process discussed in Chapter 15 consisting of **model specification**, **model fitting**, and **model diagnosis**. As we will point out in later sections, guidelines exist for determining which techniques may be more appropriate than others in certain situations. However, you may have to specify (and try) several model forms for a given situation before deciding on one that is acceptable. The idea is that if the future tends to look like the past, a model must adequately fit the past data to have a reasonable chance of forecasting the future. As a forecaster, you will spend much time selecting a model's specification and estimating its parameters to reach an acceptable fit of the past data. You will need to determine how well a model fits past data, how well it performs in mock forecasting trials, and how well its assumptions appear to be satisfied. If the model is unacceptable in any of these areas, you will be forced to revert to the model specification step and begin again.

An important consideration when you are developing a forecasting model is to use the simplest available model that will meet your forecasting needs. The objective of forecasting is to provide good forecasts. You do not need to feel that a sophisticated approach is better if a simpler one will provide acceptable forecasts. As in football, in

Model Specification

The process of selecting the forecasting technique to be used in a particular situation.

Model Fitting

The process of estimating the specified model's parameters to achieve an adequate fit of the historical data.

Model Diagnosis

The process of determining how well a model fits past data and how well the model's assumptions appear to be satisfied.

which some players specialize in defense and others in offense, forecasting techniques have been developed for special situations, which are generally dependent on the **forecasting horizon**. For the purpose of categorizing forecasting techniques in most business situations, the forecast horizon, or lead time, is typically divided into four categories:

Forecasting Horizon
The number of future periods covered by a forecast. It is sometimes referred to as *forecast lead time*.

1. Immediate term—less than one month
2. Short term—one to three months
3. Medium term—three months to two years
4. Long term—two years or more

As we introduce various forecasting techniques, we will indicate the forecasting horizon(s) for which each is typically best suited.

In addition to determining the desired forecasting horizon, the forecaster must determine the **forecasting period**. For instance, the forecasting period might be a day, a week, a month, a quarter, or a year. Thus, the forecasting horizon consists of one or more forecasting periods. If quantitative forecasting techniques are to be employed, historical quantitative data must be available for a similar period. If we want weekly forecasts, weekly historical data must be available. The **forecasting interval** is generally the same length as the forecast period. That is, if the forecast period is one week, then we will provide a new forecast each week.

Forecasting Period
The unit of time for which forecasts are to be made.

Forecasting Interval
The frequency with which new forecasts are prepared.

Components of a Time Series

Most quantitative forecasting models have one factor in common: They use past measurements of the variable of interest to generate a forecast of the future. The past data, measured over time, are called *time-series data*. The decision maker who plans to develop a quantitative forecasting model must analyze the relevant time-series data.

Business Application

SOFTWARE CONSULTING REVENUES For the past four years, a software consulting company has been helping firms to implement enterprise-wide support systems such as SAP and PeopleSoft. In forecasting this company's revenue for next year, managers should consider the historical pattern over the prior four years. They want to know whether demand for consulting services has tended to increase or decrease and whether there have been particular times during the year when demand was typically higher than at other times. The forecasters can perform a time-series analysis of the historical billings.

CHAPTER OUTCOME #1

Table 16.1 presents the time-series data for the revenue generated by the firm's billings for the four-year period. An effective means for analyzing these data is to develop a *time-series plot*, or line chart, as shown in Figure 16.1. By graphing the data, much can be observed about the firm's revenue over the past four years. In fact, the time-series plot

TABLE 16.1 Time-Series Data For Consultant's Billings (Thousands of Dollars)

Month	Billing Total			
	2003	2004	2005	2006
January	170	390	500	750
February	200	350	470	700
March	190	300	510	680
April	220	320	480	710
May	180	310	530	710
June	230	350	500	660
July	220	380	540	630
August	260	420	580	670
September	300	460	630	700
October	330	500	690	720
November	370	540	770	850
December	390	560	760	880

FIGURE 16.1

Time-Series Plot for Consultant Billing Data

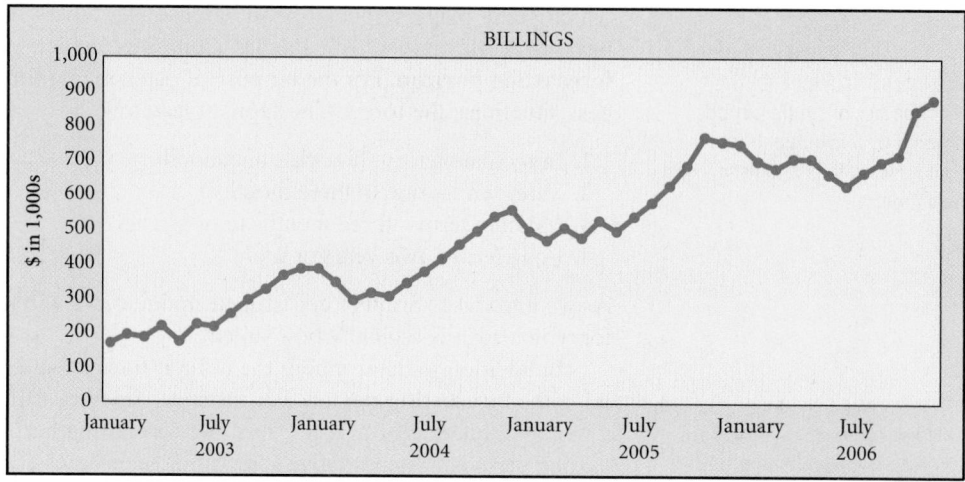

is an important tool in identifying the time-series components. All time-series data exhibit one or more of the following:

1. trend component
2. seasonal component
3. cyclical component
4. random component

Trend Component A *trend* is the long-term increase or decrease in a variable being measured over time. Figure 16.1 shows that the software-consulting company's demand exhibited an upward trend over the four-year period. In other situations, the time series may exhibit a downward trend.

Linear Trend

A long-term increase or decrease in a time series in which the rate of change is relatively constant.

Trends can be classified as **linear** or nonlinear. A trend can be observed when a time series is measured in any time increment, such as years, quarters, months, or days. Figure 16.1 is a good example showing a positive linear trend. Time-series data that exhibit a linear trend will tend to increase or decrease at a fairly constant rate. However, not all trends are linear. Many time series will show a *nonlinear trend*. For instance in the 15 years between 1985 and 1999, Microsoft sales increased at a phenomenal pace, as seen in Figure 16.2. Note that although sales increased over time, the rate of increase was much higher in the latter years of this sequence. You are encouraged to gather data for Microsoft sales since 1999 to see whether the company has been able to sustain this trend in sales.

Seasonal Component

A wavelike pattern that is repeated throughout a time series and has a recurrence period of at most one year.

Seasonal Component Another component that may be present in time-series data is the **seasonal component**. Many time series show a repeating pattern over time. For instance, Figure 16.1 showed a time series that exhibits a wavelike pattern. This pattern repeats itself throughout the time series. The consultant billings reach an annual maximum around January and then decline to an annual minimum around April. This pattern repeats itself every 12 months. The shortest period of repetition for a pattern is known as its *recurrence period*. A seasonal component's recurrence period is at most one year. If the time series exhibits a repetitious pattern with a recurrence period longer than a year, the time series is said to exhibit a cyclical effect—a term to be explored shortly.

In analyzing past sales data for a retail toy store, we would expect to see that sales increase in the months leading into Christmas and then substantially decrease after Christmas. Automobile gasoline sales might show a seasonal increase during the summer months, when people drive more, and a decrease during the cold winter months. These predictable highs and lows at specific times during the year indicate seasonality in data.

In order to view seasonality in a time series, the data must be measured quarterly, monthly, weekly, or daily. Annual data will not show seasonal patterns of highs and lows.

FIGURE 16.2

Microsoft Corporation—a Nonlinear Trend

Excel 2007 Instructions:
1. Open a blank worksheet.
2. Enter Year and Sales for each year.
3. Select the Year and Sales data columns.
4. Click on **Insert > Line Chart**.
5. Click on **Layout > Chart Title** and enter desired title—repeat for axis labels.

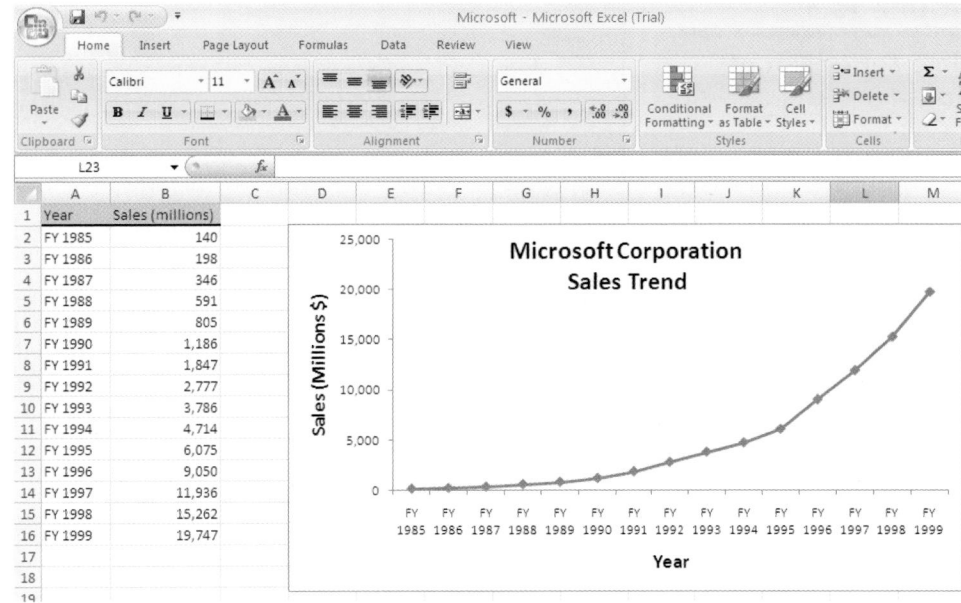

Figure 16.3 shows quarterly sales data for a major hotel chain between June 2001, through December 2006. Notice that the data exhibit a definite seasonal pattern. The local maximums occur in the spring. The recurrence period of the component in the time series is, therefore, one year. The winter quarter tends to be low, whereas the following quarter (spring) is the high quarter each year.

Seasonality can be observed in time-series data measured over time periods shorter than a year. For example, the number of checks processed daily by a bank may show predictable highs and lows at certain times during a month. The pattern of customers arriving at the bank during any hour may be "seasonal" within a day, with more customers arriving near opening time, around the lunch hour, and near closing time.

Cyclical Component

A wavelike pattern within the time series that repeats itself throughout the time series and has a recurrence period of more than one year.

Cyclical Component If you observe time-series data over a long enough time span, you may see sustained periods of high values followed by periods of lower values. If the recurrence period of these fluctuations is larger than a year, the data are said to contain a **cyclical component**.

National economic measures such as the unemployment rate, gross national product, stock market indexes, and personal saving rates tend to cycle. The cycles vary in length

FIGURE 16.3

Hotel Sales by Quarter

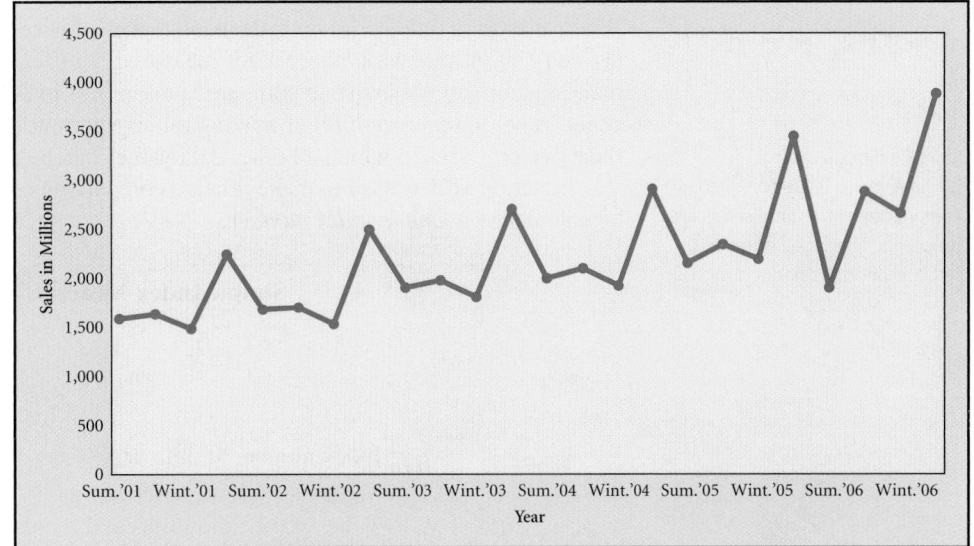

FIGURE 16.4

Time-Series Plot of Housing Starts

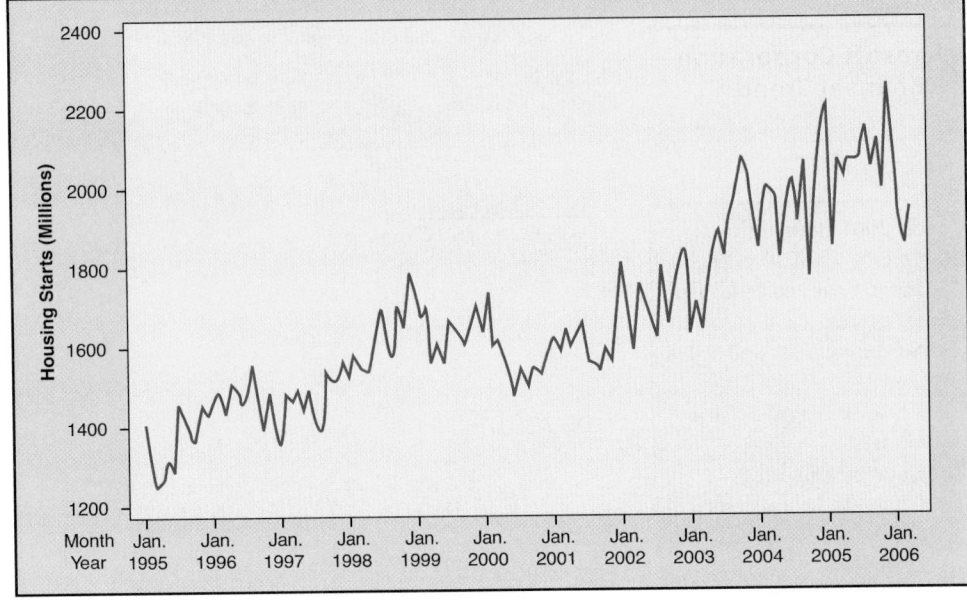

and magnitude. That is, some cyclical time series may have longer runs of high and low values than others. Also, some time series may exhibit deeper troughs and higher crests than others. Figure 16.4 shows quarterly housing starts in the United States between 1995 and 2006. Note the definite cyclical pattern, with low periods in 1995, 1997, and 2000. Although the pattern resembles the shape of a seasonal component, the length of the recurrence period identifies this pattern as being the result of a cyclical component.

Random Component

Changes in time-series data that are unpredictable and cannot be associated with a trend, seasonal, or cyclical component.

Random Component Although not all time series possess a trend, seasonal, or cyclical component, virtually all time series will have a **random component**. The random component is often referred to as "noise" in the data. A time series with no identifiable pattern is completely random and contains only noise. In addition to other components, each of the time series in Figures 16.1 through 16.4 contains random fluctuations.

In the following sections of this chapter, you will see how various forecasting techniques deal with the time-series components. An important first step in forecasting is to identify which components are present in the time series to be analyzed. As we have shown, constructing a time-series plot is the first step in this process.

Introduction to Index Numbers

CHAPTER OUTCOME #2

When analyzing time-series data, decision makers must often compare one value measured at one point in time with other values measured at different points in time. For example, a real estate broker may wish to compare house prices in 2007 with house prices in previous years. A common procedure for making relative comparisons is to begin by determining a **base period index** to which all other data values can be fairly compared.

Base Period Index

The time-series value to which all other values in the time series are compared. The index number for the base period is defined as 100.

Equation 16.1 is used to make relative comparisons for data found in different periods by calculating a *simple index number*.

Simple Index Number

$$I_t = \frac{y_t}{y_0} 100 \tag{16.1}$$

where:

I_t = Index number at time period t

y_t = Value of the time series at time t

y_0 = Value of the time series at the index base period

TRY PROBLEM 16.8

EXAMPLE 16-1 Computing Simple Index Numbers

Armstrong Corporation The Armstrong Corporation is considering purchasing a small textile mill in Georgia. The present mill owners are stressing as a positive attribute to the mill's rapid sales growth over the past 10 years. Armstrong executives wish to convert the sales data to index numbers. The following steps can be used to do this:

Step 1 Obtain the time-series data.
The company has sales data for each of the 10 years since 1997.

Step 2 Select a base period.
Armstrong managers have selected 1997 as the index base period. Sales in 1997 were $14.0 million.

Step 3 Compute the simple index numbers for each year using Equation 16.1.
For instance, sales in 1998 were $15.2 million. Using Equation 16.1, the index for 1998 is

$$I_t = \frac{y_t}{y_0} 100$$

$$I_{1998} = \frac{15.2}{14.0} 100 = 108.6$$

For the 10 years, we get:

Year	Sales (millions)	Index
1997	14.0	100.0
1998	15.2	108.6
1999	17.8	127.1
2000	21.4	152.9
2001	24.6	175.7
2002	30.5	217.9
2003	29.8	212.9
2004	32.4	231.4
2005	37.2	265.7
2006	39.1	279.3

Referring to Example 16-1, we can use the index numbers to determine the percentage change any year is from the base year. For instance, sales in 2004 have an index of 231.4. This means that sales in 2004 are 131.4% above sales in the base year of 1997. Sales in 2006 are 179.3% higher than they were in 1997.

Note that although you can use the index number to compare values between any one time period and the base period, and express the difference in percentage-change terms, you cannot compare period-to-period changes by subtracting the index numbers. For instance, in Example 16-1, when comparing sales for 2005 and 2006, we cannot say that the growth has been

$$279.3 - 265.7 = 13.6\%$$

To determine the actual percentage growth, we do the following:

$$\frac{279.3 - 265.7}{265.7} 100 = 5.1\%$$

Thus, the sales growth rate between 2005 and 2006 has been 5.1%, not 13.6%.

Aggregate Price Indexes

"The dollar's not worth what it once was" is a saying that everyone has heard. The problem is that nothing is worth what it used to be; sometimes it is worth more, and other times it is worth less. The simple index shown in Equation 16.1 works well for comparing prices when we wish to analyze the price of a single item over time. For instance, we could use the simple index to analyze how apartment rents have changed over time or how college tuition has increased over time. However, if we wish to compare prices of a group of items, we might construct an **aggregate price index**.

Equation 16.2 is used to compute an unweighted aggregate price index.

Aggregate Price Index
An index that is used to measure the rate of change from a base period for a group of two or more items.

Unweighted Aggregate Price Index

$$I_t = \frac{\sum p_t}{\sum p_0}(100) \tag{16.2}$$

where:

I_t = Unweighted aggregate index at time period t

$\sum p_t$ = Sum of the prices for the group of items at time period t

$\sum p_0$ = Sum of the prices for the group of items at base time period

---

EXAMPLE 16-2 Computing an Unweighted Aggregate Price Index

TRY PROBLEM 16.8

College Costs There have been many news stories recently discussing the rate of growth of college and university costs. One university is interested in analyzing the growth in the total costs for students over the past five years. The university wishes to consider three main costs: tuition and fees, board and room, and books and supplies. Rather than analyzing these factors individually using three simple indexes, an unweighted aggregate price index can be developed using the following steps:

Step 1 **Define the variables to be included in the index and gather the time-series data.**

The university has identified three main categories of costs: tuition fees, board and room, and books and supplies. Data for the past five years have been collected. Full-time tuition and fees for two semesters are used. The full dorm-and-meal package offered by the university is priced for the board-and-room variable, and the books-and-supplies cost for a "typical" student are used for that component of the total costs. (See page 765.)

Step 2 **Select a base period.**

The base period for this study will be the 2001–2002 academic year.

Step 3 **Use Equation 16.2 to compute the unweighted aggregate price index.**

The equation is

$$I_t = \frac{\sum p_t}{\sum p_0}(100)$$

The sum of the prices for the three components during the base academic year of 2001–2002 is $13,814. The sum of the prices in the 2005–2006 academic year is $19,492. Applying Equation 16.2, the unweighted aggregate price index is

$$I_{2005-2006} = \frac{\$19,492}{\$13,814}(100) = 141.1$$

This means, as a group, the components making up the cost of attending this university have increased by 41.1% since the 2001–2002 academic year. The indexes for the other years are shown as follows:

Academic Year	Tuition & Fees	Board & Room	Books & Supplies	Σp_t	Index
2001–02	$7,300	$5,650	$864	$13,814	100.0
2002–03	7,720	5,980	945	14,645	106.0
2003–04	8,560	6,350	1,067	15,977	115.7
2004–05	9,430	6,590	1,234	17,254	124.9
2005–06	10,780	7,245	1,467	19,492	141.1

Weighted Aggregate Price Indexes

Example 16-2 utilized an unweighted aggregate price index to determine the change in university costs. This was appropriate because each student would incur the same set of three costs. However, in some situations, the items composing a total cost are not equally weighted. For instance, in a consumer price study of a "market basket" of 10 food items, a typical household will not use the same number (or volume) of each item. During a week, a typical household might use the three gallons of milk, but only two loaves of bread. In these types of situations, we need to compute a weighted aggregate price index to account for the different levels of use. Two common weighted indexes are the Paasche Index and the Laspeyres Index.

The Paasche Index Equation 16.3 is used to compute a Paasche Index. Note that the weighting percentage in Equation 16.3 for the Paasche Index is always the percentage for the time period for which the index is being computed. The idea is that the prices in the base period should be weighted relative to their current use, not to what that use level was in other periods.

Paasche Index

$$I_t = \frac{\Sigma q_t p_t}{\Sigma q_t p_0}(100) \tag{16.3}$$

where:

q_t = Weighting percentage at time t
p_t = Price in time period t
p_0 = Price in the base period

TRY PROBLEM 16.12

EXAMPLE 16-3 Computing the Paasche Index

Wage Rates   Before a company makes a decision to locate a new manufacturing plant in a community, the managers will be interested in knowing how the wage rates have changed. Two categories of wages are to be analyzed as a package: production hourly wages and administrative/clerical hourly wages. Annual data showing the average hourly wage rates since 1997 are available. Each year, the makeup of the labor market differs in terms of the percentage of employees in the two categories. To compute a Paasche Index, use the following steps:

Step 1 **Define the variables to be included in the index and gather the time-series data.**
The variables are the mean hourly price for production workers and the mean average price for administrative/clerical workers. Data are collected for the 10-year period through 2006.

Step 2 **Select the base period.**
Because similar data for another community are available only back to 2000, the company will use 2000 as the base period to make comparisons between the two communities easier.

Step 3 **Use Equation 16.3 to compute the Paasche Index.**
The equation is

$$I_t = \frac{\sum q_t p_t}{\sum q_t p_0}(100)$$

The hourly wage rate for production workers in the base year 2000 was $10.80, whereas the average hourly administrative/clerical rate was $10.25.

In 2006, the production hourly rate had increased to $15.45, and the administrative/clerical rate was $13.45. Last year (2006), 60% of the employees in the community were designated as in production and 40% were administrative/clerical. Equation 16.3 is used to compute the Paasche Index for 2006, as follows:

$$I_{2006} = \frac{(0.60)(\$15.45) + (0.40)(\$13.45)}{(0.60)(\$10.80) + (0.40)(\$10.25)}(100) = 138.5$$

This means that, overall, the wage rates in this community have increased by 38.5% since the base year of 2000. The following table shows the Paasche Indexes for all years.

Year	Production Wage Rate	Percent Production	Administrative/Clerical Wage Rate	Percent Admin./Clerical	Paasche Index
1997	8.50	0.78	9.10	0.22	80.8
1998	9.10	0.73	9.45	0.27	86.3
1999	10.00	0.69	9.80	0.31	93.5
2000	10.80	0.71	10.25	0.29	100.0
2001	11.55	0.68	10.60	0.32	105.9
2002	12.15	0.67	10.95	0.33	110.7
2003	12.85	0.65	11.45	0.35	116.5
2004	13.70	0.65	11.90	0.35	123.2
2005	14.75	0.62	12.55	0.38	131.4
2006	15.45	0.60	13.45	0.40	138.5

The Laspeyres Index The Paasche Index is computed using the logic that the index for the current period should be compared to a base period with the current period weightings. An alternate index, called the Laspeyres Index, uses the base-period weighting in its computation, as shown in Equation 16.4.

Laspeyres Index

$$I_t = \frac{\sum q_0 p_t}{\sum q_0 p_0}(100) \tag{16.4}$$

where:

q_0 = Weighting percentage at base period
p_t = Price in time period t
p_0 = Price in base period

TRY PROBLEM 16.13

EXAMPLE 16-4   Computing the Laspeyres Index

Wage Rates   Refer to Example 16-3, in which the managers of a company are interested in knowing how the wage rates have changed in the community in which they are considering building a plant. Two categories of wages are to be analyzed as a package: production hourly wages and administrative/clerical hourly wages. Annual data showing the average hourly wage rate since 1997 are available. Each year, the makeup of the labor market differs in terms of the percentage of employees in the two categories. To compute a Laspeyres Index, use the following steps:

Step 1 Define the variables to be included in the index and gather the time-series data.
The variables are the mean hourly price for production workers and the mean average price for administrative/clerical workers. Data are collected for the 10-year period through 2006.

Step 2 Select the base period.
Because similar data for another community are available only back to 2000, the company will use 2000 as the base period to make comparisons between the two communities easier.

Step 3 Use Equation 16.4 to compute the Laspeyres Index.
The equation is

$$I_t = \frac{\sum q_0 p_t}{\sum q_0 p_0}(100)$$

The hourly wage rate for production workers in the base year of 2000 was $10.80, whereas the average hourly administrative/clerical rate was $10.25. In that year, 71% of the workers were classified as production. In 2006, the production hourly rate had increased to $15.45, and the administrative/clerical rate was at $13.45. Equation 16.4 is used to compute the Laspeyres Index for 2006, as follows:

$$I_{2006} = \frac{(0.71)(\$15.45) + (0.29)(\$13.45)}{(0.71)(\$10.80) + (0.29)(\$10.25)}(100) = 139.7$$

This means that, overall, the wage rates in this community have increased by 39.7% since the base year of 2000. The following table shows the Laspeyres Indexes for all years.

Year	Production Wage Rate	Percent Production	Administrative/Clerical Wage Rate	Percent Admin./Clerical	Laspeyres Index
1997	8.50	0.78	9.10	0.22	81.5
1998	9.10	0.73	9.45	0.27	86.5
1999	10.00	0.69	9.80	0.31	93.4
2000	10.80	0.71	10.25	0.29	100.0
2001	11.55	0.68	10.60	0.32	106.0
2002	12.15	0.67	10.95	0.33	110.9
2003	12.85	0.65	11.45	0.35	116.9
2004	13.70	0.65	11.90	0.35	123.8
2005	14.75	0.62	12.55	0.38	132.6
2006	15.45	0.60	13.45	0.40	139.7

Commonly Used Index Numbers

In addition to converting time-series data to index numbers, you will encounter a variety of indexes in your professional and personal life.

Consumer Price Index To most of us, inflation has come to mean increased prices and less purchasing power for our dollar. The Consumer Price Index (CPI) attempts to measure the overall changes in retail prices for goods and services. The CPI, originally published in 1913 by the U.S. Department of Labor, uses a "market basket" of goods and services purchased by a typical wage earner living in a city. The CPI, a weighted aggregate index similar to a Laspeyres Index, is based on items grouped into seven categories, including food, housing, clothing, transportation, medical care, entertainment, and miscellaneous items. The items in the "market basket" have changed over time to keep pace with the buying habits of our society and as new products and services have become available.

Since 1945, the base period used to construct the CPI has been updated. Currently, the base period, 1982 to 1984, has an index of 100. Table 16.2 shows the CPI index values for 1996 to 2005. For instance, the index for 2005 is 195.3, which means that the price of the "market basket" of goods increased 95.3% between 1984 and 2005. Remember also that you cannot determine the inflation rate by subtracting index values for successive years. Instead, you must divide the difference by the earlier year's index. For instance, the rate of inflation between 2004 and 2005 was

$$\text{Inflation Rate} = \frac{195.3 - 188.9}{188.9}(100) = 3.39\%$$

Thus, in general terms, if your income did not increase by at least 3.39% between 2004 and 2005, you failed to keep pace with inflation and your purchasing power was reduced.

Producer Price Index The U.S. Bureau of Labor Statistics publishes the *Producer Price Index* (PPI) on a monthly basis to measure the rate of change in nonretail prices. Like the CPI, the Producer Price Index is a Laspeyres weighted aggregate index. This index is used as a leading indicator of upcoming changes in the CPI. Table 16.3 shows the PPI between 1996 and 2005.

TABLE 16.2 CPI Index (1996 to 2005)

Year	1996	1997	1998	1999	2000	2001	2002	2003	2004	2005
CPI	156.9	157.0	160.5	166.6	172.2	177.1	179.9	184.0	188.9	195.3

Base = 1982 to 1984 (Index = 100)
Source: Bureau of Labor Statistics: http://www.bls.gov/cpi/home.htm#data

TABLE 16.3 PPI Index (1996 to 2005)

Year	1996	1997	1998	1999	2000	2001	2002	2003	2004	2005
PPI	127.7	127.6	124.4	125.5	132.7	134.2	131.1	138.1	142.7	157.4

Base = 1984 (Index = 100)
Source: Bureau of Labor Statistics: http://www.bls.gov/ppi/home.htm#data

Stock Market Indexes

Every night on the national and local TV news, reporters tell us what happened on the stock market that day by reporting on the *Dow Jones Industrial Average* (DJIA). The Dow, as this index is commonly referred to, is not the same type of index as the CPI or PPI, in that it is not a percentage of a base year. Rather, the DJIA is the sum of the stock prices for 30 large industrial companies whose stocks trade on the New York Stock Exchange divided by a factor that is adjusted for stock splits. Many analysts use the DJIA, which is computed daily, as a measure of the health of the stock market. Other analysts prefer other indexes, such as the *Standard and Poor's 500*. The S&P 500 includes stock prices for 500 companies and is thought by some to be more representative of the broader market.

The *NASDAQ* is an index made up of stocks on the NASDAQ exchange and is heavily influenced by technology-based companies that are traded on this exchange. Publications such as *The Wall Street Journal* and *Barrons* publish all these indexes and others every day for investors to use in their investing decisions.

Using Index Numbers to Deflate a Time Series

A common use of index numbers is to convert values measured at different times into more directly comparable values. For instance, if your wages increase, but at a rate less than inflation, you will in fact be earning less in "real terms." A company experiencing increasing sales at a rate of increase less than inflation is actually not increasing in "real terms."

Business Applications   **WYMAN-GORMAN COMPANY** The Wyman-Gorman Company, located in Massachusetts, designs and produces forgings, primarily for internal combustion engines. The company has recently been experiencing some financial difficulty and has discontinued its agricultural and earthmoving divisions. Table 16.4 shows sales in millions of dollars for the company since 1996. Also shown is the PPI (Producer Price Index) for the same years. Finally, sales, adjusted to 1984 dollars, is also shown.

Equation 16.5 is used to determine the adjusted time-series values.

TABLE 16.4 Deflated Sales Data—Using Producer Price Index

Year	Sales (millions)	PPI (Base = 1984)	Sales (adjusted to 1984 dollars)
1996	610.3	127.7	477.9
1997	473.1	127.6	370.8
1998	383.5	124.4	308.3
1999	425.5	125.5	339.0
2000	384.1	132.7	289.4
2001	341.1	134.2	254.2
2002	310.3	131.1	236.7
2003	271.6	138.1	196.7
2004	371.6	142.7	260.4
2005	390.2	157.4	247.9

Deflation Formula

$$y_{adj_t} = \frac{y_t}{I_t}(100) \qquad\qquad (16.5)$$

where:

y_{adj_t} = Deflated time-series value at time t
y_t = Actual value of the time series at time t
I_t = Index (such as CPI or PPI) at time t

For instance, in 1996 sales were $610.3 million. The producer price index for that year was 127.7. The sales, adjusted to 1984 dollars is

$$y_{adj_{1996}} = \frac{610.3}{127.7}(100) = \$477.9$$

16-1: Exercises

Skill Development

16-1. What are the differences between quantitative and qualitative forecasting techniques? Under what conditions is it appropriate to use a quantitative technique?

16-2. Provide an example of a business decision that requires (1) a short-term forecast (2) a medium-term forecast, (3) a long-term forecast.

16-3. What is meant by time-series data? Give an example.

16-4. Explain the difference between time-series data and cross-sectional data. Are these two types of data sets mutually exclusive? What do they have in common? How do they differ?

16-5. What is meant by the trend component of a time series? How is a linear trend different from a nonlinear trend?

16-6. Must a seasonal component be associated with the seasons (fall, spring, summer, winter) of the year? Provide an example of a seasonal effect that is not associated with the seasons of the year.

16-7. A Greek entrepreneur followed the olive harvests. He noted that olives ripen in September. Each March he would try to determine if the upcoming olive harvest would be especially bountiful. If his analysis indicated it would, he would enter into agreements with the owners of all the olive oil presses in the region. In exchange for a small deposit months ahead of the harvest, he would obtain the right to lease the presses at market prices during the harvest. If he was correct about the harvest and demand for olive oil presses boomed, he could make a great deal of money. Identify the following quantities in the context of this scenario:

a. forecasting horizon
b. category that applies to the forecasting horizon identified in part a
c. forecasting period
d. forecasting interval

16-8. Consider the following median selling prices ($thousands) for homes in a community:

Year	Price
1	320
2	334
3	329
4	344
5	358
6	347
7	383
8	404
9	397
10	411

a. Use year 1 as a base year and construct a simple index number to show how the median selling price has increased.
b. Determine the actual percentage growth in the median selling price between the base year and year 10.
c. Determine the actual percentage growth in the median selling price between the base year and year 5.
d. Determine the actual percentage growth in the median selling price between year 5 and year 10.

16-9. The following values represent advertising rates paid by a regional catalog retailer that advertises either on radio or in newspapers.

Year	Radio Rates	Newspaper Rates
1	300	400
2	310	420
3	330	460
4	346	520
5	362	580
6	380	640
7	496	660

a. Determine a relative index for each type of advertisement using year 1 as the base year.

b. Determine an unweighted aggregate index for the two types of advertisement.

c. In year 1 the retailer spent 30% of the advertisement budget on radio advertising. Construct a Laspeyres index for the data.

d. Using year 1 as the base, construct a Paasche index for the same data.

16-10. Using 1996 as the base year, construct a separate index for each component in the construction of a house.

16-11. Plot both series of data and comment on the trend you see in both plots.

16-12. Construct a Paasche index for 2001 using the data. Use 1996 as the base year and assume that in 2001 sixty percent of the cost of a house was in materials.

16-13. Construct a Laspeyres index using the data, assuming that in 1996, 40% of the cost of a house was labor.

16-14. Retail Forward, Inc. is a global management consulting and market research firm specializing in retail intelligence and strategies. One of their press releases ("June Consumer Outlook: Spending Plans Show Resilience," June 1, 2006) divulged the result of The Retail Forward ShopperScape™ survey conducted each month from a sample of 4,000 U.S. primary household shoppers. A measure of consumer spending is represented by the following figure:

a. Describe the type of index used by Retail Forward to explore consumer spending.

b. Determine the actual percentage change in the Future Spending Index between December 2005 and June 2006.

c. Determine the actual percentage change in the Future Spending Index between June 2005 and June 2006.

Computer Database Exercises

16-15. The federal funds rate is the interest rate charged by banks when banks borrow "overnight" from each other. The funds rate fluctuates according to supply and demand and is not under the direct control of the Federal Reserve Board, but is strongly influenced by the Fed's actions. The file entitled **The Fed** contains the federal funds rate for the period 1955–2005.

a. Construct a time-series plot for the federal funds rate for the period 1955–2005.

Business Applications

Problems 16-10 through 16-13 refer to U.S. Homes, a major developer of housing communities in the New England area. The company has kept a record of the relative cost of labor and materials in its market areas for the last 11 years. These data are as follows:

Year	Hourly Wages	Average Material Cost
1996	30.10	66,500
1997	30.50	68,900
1998	31.70	70,600
1999	32.50	70,900
2000	34.00	71,200
2001	34.50	71,700
2002	35.10	72,500
2003	35.05	73,700
2004	34.90	73,400
2005	33.80	74,100
2006	34.20	74,000

b. Describe the time-series components that are present in the data set.

c. Indicate the recurrence periods for any seasonal or cyclical components.

16-16. The Energy Information Administration (EIA), created by Congress in 1977, is a statistical agency of the U.S. Department of Energy. It provides data, forecasts, and analyses to promote sound policymaking and public understanding regarding energy and its interaction with the economy and the environment. The price of the sources of energy is becoming more and more important as our natural resources are consumed. The file entitled **Prices** contains data for the period 1993–2005 concerning the price of gasoline ($/gal.), natural gas ($/ft^3), and electricity (cents/kilowatt hr.).

a. Using 1993 as the base, calculate an aggregate energy price index for these three energy costs.

b. Determine the actual percentage change in the aggregate energy prices between 1993 and 2005.

c. Determine the actual percentage change in the aggregate energy prices between 1998 and 2005.

16-17. The Census Bureau of the Department of Commerce released the U.S. retail e-commerce sales ("Quarterly Retail e-commerce Sales 1st Quarter 2006," May 18, 2006) for the period 4th Qtr 1999–1st Qtr 2006. The file entitled **E-Commerce** contains that data.

a. Using the fourth quarter of 1999 as the base, calculate a Laspeyres Index for the retail sales for the period of 4th Qtr 1999–1st Qtr 2006.

b. Determine the actual percentage change in the retail sales for the period 4th Qtr 1999–1st Qtr 2004.

c. Determine the actual percentage change in the retail sales for the period 1st Qtr 2004–1st Qtr 2006.

16.2 Trend-Based Forecasting Techniques

As we discussed in Section 16.1, some time series exhibit an increasing or decreasing trend. Further, the trend may be linear or nonlinear. A plot of the data will be very helpful in identifying which, if any, of these trends exist.

Developing a Trend-Based Forecasting Model

In this section, we introduce *trend-based forecasting techniques*. As the name implies, these techniques are used to identify the presence of a trend and to model that trend. Once the trend model has been defined, it is used to provide forecasts for future time periods.

Business Application

Excel and Minitab Tutorial

CHAPTER OUTCOMES #3 AND #4

THE TAFT ICE CREAM COMPANY The Taft Ice Cream Company is a family-operated company selling gourmet ice cream to resort areas, primarily on the North Carolina coast. Figure 16.5 displays the annual sales data for the 10-year period, 1997–2006, and shows the time-series plot that illustrates that sales have trended up in the 10-year period. These data are in a file called **Taft** on the CD-ROM.

Taft's owners are considering expanding their ice cream manufacturing facilities. As part of the bank's financing requirements, the managers are asked to supply a forecast of future sales. Recall from our earlier discussions that the forecasting process has three steps: (1) model specification, (2) model fitting, and (3) model diagnosis.

Step 1 Model Specification
The time-series plot in Figure 16.5 indicates that the sales have exhibited a linear growth pattern. A possible forecasting tool is a linear trend (straight-line) model.

Step 2 Model-Fitting
Because we have specified a linear trend model, the process of fitting can be accomplished using least squares regression analysis of a form described by Equation 16.6.

FIGURE 16.5

Excel 2007 Output Showing Taft Ice Cream Sales Trend Line

Minitab Instructions:
1. Open file: Taft.MTW.
2. Choose **Graph > Time Series Plot**.
3. Select **Simple**.
4. Under **Series**, enter time series' column.
5. Click **Time/Scale**.
6. Under **Time Scale** select **Calendar** and **Year**.
7. Under **Start Values**, insert the starting year.
8. Click **OK. OK.**

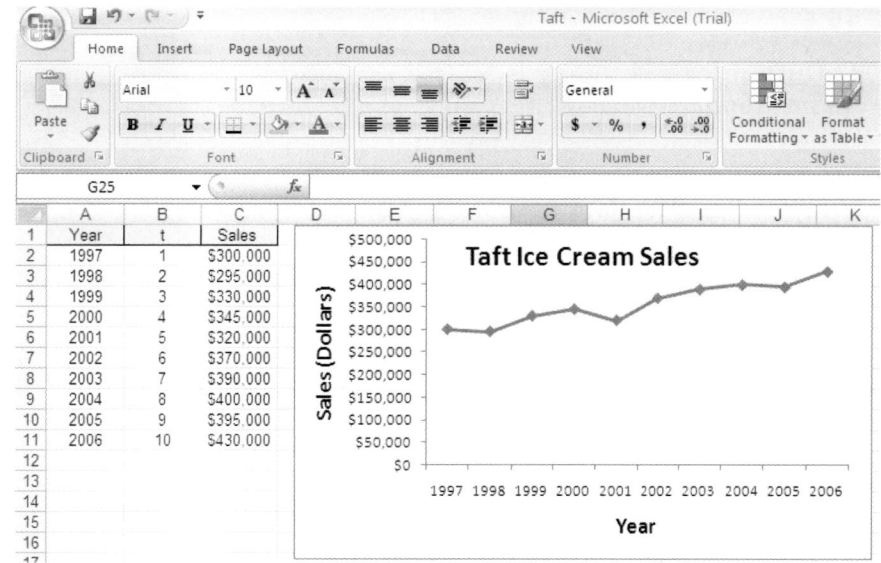

Excel 2007 Instructions:
1. Open file: Taft.xls.
2. Select data in the Sales data column.
3. Click on **Insert > Line Chart**.
4. Click on **Select Data**.
5. Under **Horizontal (categories) Axis Labels**, select data in Year column.
6. Click on **Layout > Chart Title** and enter desired title.
7. Click on **Layout > Axis Titles** and enter horizontal and vertical axis titles.

Linear Trend Model

$$y_t = \beta_0 + \beta_1 t + \varepsilon_t \qquad (16.6)$$

where:

y_t = Value of the trend at time t
β_0 = y intercept of the trend line
β_1 = Slope of the trend line
t = Time ($t = 1, 2, \ldots$)
ε_t = Error at time t

We let the first period in the time series be $t = 1$, the second period be $t = 2$, and so forth. The values for time form the independent variable, with sales being the dependent variable. Referring to Chapter 14, the least squares regression equations for the slope and intercept are estimated by Equations 16.7 and 16.8. Here the sums are taken over the values of t ($t = 1, 2, \ldots$).

Least Squares Equations Estimates

$$b_1 = \frac{\sum t y_t - \dfrac{\sum t \sum y_t}{n}}{\sum t^2 - \dfrac{(\sum t)^2}{n}} \qquad (16.7)$$

$$b_0 = \frac{\sum y_t}{n} - b_1 \frac{\sum t}{n} \qquad (16.8)$$

where:

n = Number of periods in the time series
t = Time period (independent variable)
y_t = Dependent variable at time t

FIGURE 16.6

Excel 2007 Output for Taft Ice Cream Trend Model

Excel 2007 Instructions:
1. Open file: Taft.xls.
2. Select **Data > Data Analysis**.
3. Click on **Regression**.
4. Enter range for the *Y* **variable** (Sales).
5. Enter range for the *X* **variable** ($t = 1, 2 \ldots$).
6. Specify output location.
7. Click on **Labels**.

	A	B	C	D	E	F	G
1	SUMMARY OUTPUT						
2							
3	*Regression Statistics*						
4	Multiple R	0.9551					
5	R Square	0.9123					
6	Adjusted R Square	0.9013					
7	Standard Error	14513.5778					
8	Observations	10					
9							
10	ANOVA						
11		*df*	*SS*	*MS*	*F*	*Significance F*	
12	Regression	1	17527348485	17527348485	83.208	1.67847E-05	
13	Residual	8	1685151515	210643939.4			
14	Total	9	19212500000				
15							
16		*Coefficients*	*Standard Error*	*t Stat*	*P-value*	*Lower 95%*	*Upper 95%*
17	Intercept	277333.33	9914.66	27.97	0.0000	254470.08	300196.58
18	t	14575.76	1597.89	9.12	0.0000	10891.01	18260.50

Linear Trend Equation:
Sales = 277,333.33 + 14,575.76(*t*)

Minitab Instructions (for similar results):
1. Open file: Taft.MTW.
2. Choose **Stat > Regression > Regression**.
3. In **Response**, enter the time series column, *Sales*.
4. In **Predictors**, enter the time variable column, *t*.
5. Click **OK**.

The linear regression procedures in either Excel or Minitab can be used to compute the least squares trend model. Figure 16.6 shows the Excel output for the Taft Ice Cream Company example. The least squares trend model for the Taft Company is

$$\hat{y}_t = b_0 + b_1 t$$
$$\hat{y}_t = 277,333.33 + 14,575.76(t)$$

For a forecast, we use F_t as the forecast value or predicted value at time period t. Thus,

$$F_t = 277,333.33 + 14,575.76(t)$$

Step 3 Model Diagnosis
The linear trend regression output in Figure 16.6 offers some conclusions about the potential capabilities of our model. The *R*-squared = 0.9123 shows that for these 10 years of data, the linear trend model explains more than 91% of the variation in sales. The *p*-value for the regression slope coefficient is 0.0000. This means that time (*t*) explains a significant portion of the variation in sales. Figure 16.7 shows the plot of the trend line through the data. You can see the trend model fits the historical data quite closely. Although these results are a good sign, the model diagnosis step requires further analysis.

Comparing the Forecast Values to the Actual Data

The slope of the trend line indicates the Taft Ice Cream Company has experienced an average increase in sales of $14,575.76 per year over the 10-year period. The linear trend model's fitted sales values for periods $t = 1$ through $t = 10$ can be found by substituting for *t* in the following forecast equation:

$$F_t = 277,333.33 + 14,575.76(t)$$

FIGURE 16.7

Excel 2007 Output for Taft Ice Cream Trend Line

Excel 2007 Instructions:
1. Open file: Taft.xls.
2. Select the Sales data.
3. Click on **Insert > Line Chart**.
4. Click on Select **Data**.
5. Under **Horizontal (categories) Axis Labels**, select data in Year column.
6. Click on **Layout > Chart Title** and enter desired title.
7. Click on **Layout > Axis Titles** and enter horizontal and vertical axes titles.
8. Select the data.
9. Right-click and select **Add Trendline > Linear**.
10. To set color, go to **Trend Line Options** (see step 9).

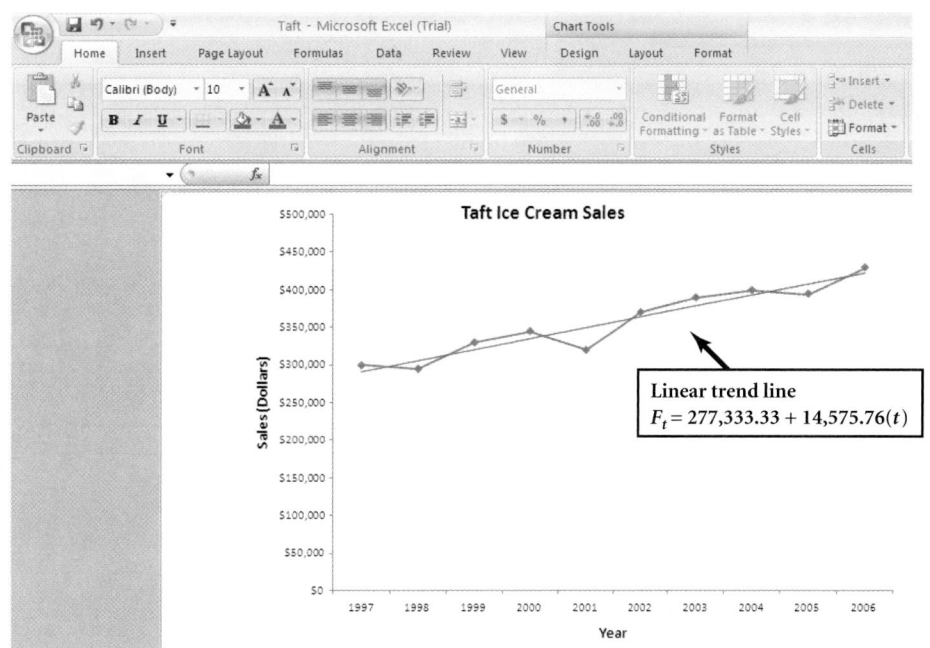

Minitab Instructions:
1. Open file: Taft.MTW.
2. Choose **Stat > Times > Series > Trend Analysis**.
3. In **Variable**, enter the time series column.
4. Under **Model Type** choose **Linear**.
5. Click **OK**.

For example, for $t = 1$, we get

$$F_t = 277{,}333.33 + 14{,}575.76(1)$$
$$= \$\,291{,}909.09$$

Note that the actual sales figure, y_1, for period 1 was \$300,000. The difference between the actual sales in time t and the forecast values in time t, found using the trend model, is called the *forecast error* or the *residual*. Figure 16.8 shows the forecasts for periods 1 through 10 and the forecast errors at each period.

Computing the forecast error by comparing the trend-line values with actual past data is an important part of the model diagnosis step. The errors measure how closely the model fits the actual data at each point. A perfect fit would lead to residuals of 0 each time. We would like to see small residuals and an overall good fit. Two commonly used measures of fit are mean squared residual, or *mean squared error* (*MSE*), and *mean absolute deviation* (*MAD*). These measures are computed using Equations 16.9 and 16.10, respectively. *MAD* measures the average magnitude of the forecast errors. *MSE* is a measure of the variability in the forecast errors. The forecast error is the observed value, y_t, minus the predicted value, F_t.

Mean Squared Error		Mean Absolute Deviation	
$MSE = \dfrac{\sum (y_t - F_t)^2}{n}$	**(16.9)**	$MAD = \dfrac{\sum |y_t - F_t|}{n}$	**(16.10)**

where:

$$y_t = \text{Actual value at time } t$$
$$F_t = \text{Predicted value at time } t$$
$$n = \text{Number of time periods}$$

Figure 16.9 shows the *MSE* and *MAD* calculations using Excel for the Taft Ice Cream example. The *MAD* value of \$11,042 indicates the linear trend model has an average absolute error of \$11,042 per period. The *MSE* (in squared units) equals 168,515,151.52.

FIGURE 16.8

Excel 2007 Residual Output for Taft Ice Cream

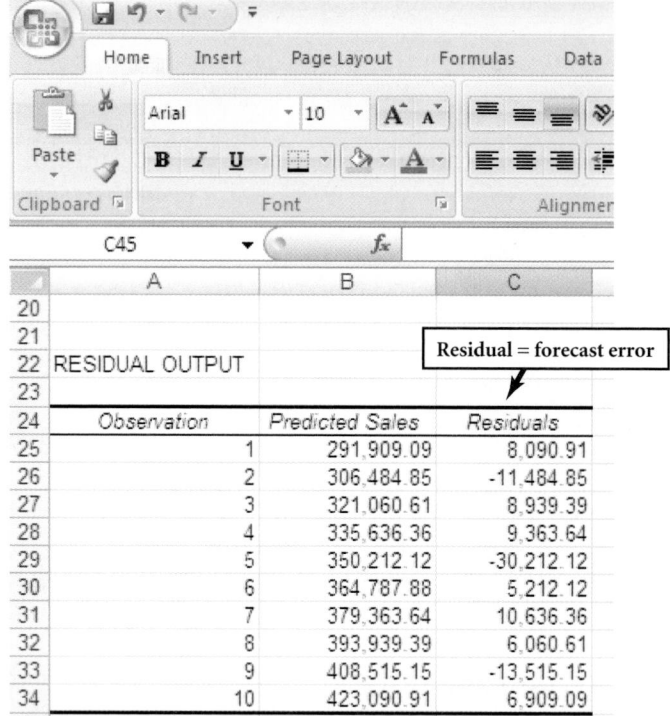

Excel 2007 Instructions:
1. Follow Figure 16.6 Excel Instructions.
2. In **Regression** procedure, click on **Residuals**.

The square root of the *MSE* is $12,981.34, and although it is not equal to the *MAD* value, it does provide similar information about the relationship between the forecast values and the actual values of the time series.[1]

These error measures are particularly helpful when comparing two or more forecasting techniques. We can compute the *MSE* and/or the *MAD* for each forecasting technique. The forecasting technique that gives the smallest *MSE* or *MAD* is generally considered to provide the best fit.

FIGURE 16.9

Excel 2007 *MSE* and *MAD* Computations for Taft Ice Cream

Excel 2007 Instructions:
1. Follow Figure 16.6 Excel Instructions.
2. In **Regression** procedure, click on **Residuals**.
3. Create a new column of squared residuals.
4. Create a column of absolute values of the residuals using the **ABS** function in Excel.
5. Use Equations 16.9 and 16.10 to calculate *MSE* and *MAD*.

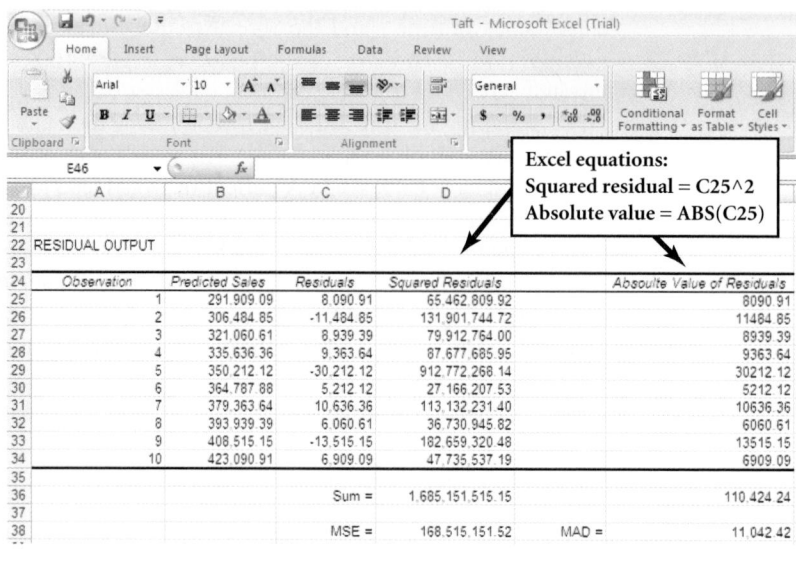

$$MSE = \frac{\sum (y_t - F_t)^2}{n} = 168,515,151.52$$

$$MAD = \frac{\sum |y_t - F_t|}{n} = 11,042.42$$

---

[1] Technically this is the square root of the average squared distance between the forecasts and the observed data values. Algebraically, of course, this is not the same as the average forecast error, but it is comparable.

Autocorrelation In addition to examining the fit of the forecasts to the actual time series, the model-diagnosis step also should examine how a model meets the assumptions of the regression model. One regression assumption is that the error terms are uncorrelated, or independent. When using regression with time-series data, the assumption of independence could be violated. That is, the error terms may be correlated over time. We call this *serial correlation*, or **autocorrelation**.

Autocorrelation

Correlation of the error terms (residuals) occurs when the residuals at points in time are related.

When dealing with a time-series variable, the value of y at time period t is commonly related to the value of y at the previous time periods. If a relationship between y_t and y_{t-1} exists, we conclude that first-order autocorrelation exists. If y_t is related to y_{t-2}, second-order autocorrelation exists, and so forth. If the times-series values are autocorrelated, the assumption that the error terms are independent is violated.

The autocorrelation can be positive or negative. For instance, when the values are first-order positively autocorrelated, we expect a positive residual to be followed by a positive residual in the next period, and we expect a negative residual to be followed by another negative residual. With negative first-order autocorrelation, we expect a positive residual to be followed by a negative residual, followed by a positive residual, and so on. The presence of autocorrelation can have adverse consequences on tests of statistical significance in a regression model. Thus, you need to be able to detect the presence of autocorrelation and take action to remove the problem. The *Durbin-Watson statistic*, which is shown in Equation 16.11, is used to test whether residuals are autocorrelated.

Durbin-Watson Statistic

$$d = \frac{\sum_{t=2}^{n} (e_t - e_{t-1})^2}{\sum_{t=1}^{n} e_t^2} \qquad (16.11)$$

where:

$$d = \text{Durbin-Watson test statistic}$$
$$e_t = (y_t - \hat{y}_t) = \text{Residual at time } t$$
$$n = \text{Number of time periods in the time series}$$

Figure 16.10 shows the Minitab output providing the Durbin-Watson statistic for the Taft Ice Cream data

$$d = \frac{\sum_{t=2}^{n} (e_t - e_{t-1})^2}{\sum_{t=1}^{n} e_t^2} = 2.65$$

Examining Equation 16.11, we see that if successive values of the residual are close in value, the Durbin-Watson d statistic will be small. This situation would describe one in which residuals are positively correlated.

The Durbin-Watson statistic can have a value ranging from 0 to 4. A value of 2 indicates no autocorrelation. However, like any other statistics computed from a sample, the Durbin-Watson d is subject to sampling error. We may wish to test formally to determine whether positive autocorrelation exists.

$$H_0: \rho = 0$$
$$H_A: \rho > 0$$

If the d statistic is too small, we will reject the null hypothesis and conclude that positive autocorrelation exists. If the d statistic is too large, we will not reject and will not be able to conclude that positive autocorrelation exists. Appendix O contains a table of one-tailed Durbin-Watson critical values for $\alpha = 0.05$ and $\alpha = 0.01$ levels. (*Note*: The critical values

FIGURE 16.10

**Minitab Output—
Durbin-Watson Statistic:
Taft Ice Cream Company
Example**

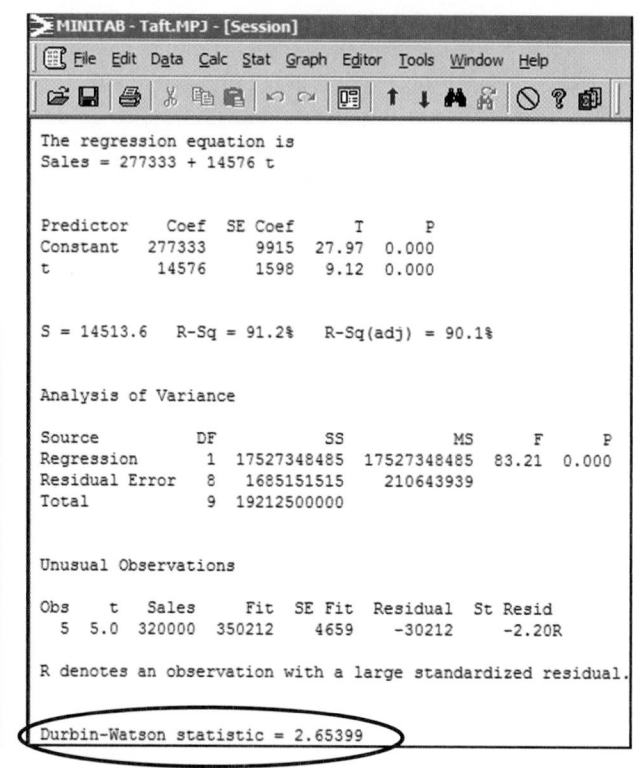

Excel 2007 Instructions (for similar results):
1. Open file: Taft.xls.
2. Click on **Add-Ins**.
3. Select **PHStat**.
4. Select **Regression > Simple Linear Regression**.
5. Define *y* variable.
6. Define *x* variable.
7. Check box for **Durbin-Watson statistic**.
8. Click **OK**.

Minitab Instructions:
1. Open file: Taft.MTW.
2. Choose **Stat > Regression > Regression**.
3. In **Response**, enter the time series column, *Sales*.
4. In **Predictors**, enter the time variable column, *t*.
5. Select **Options**.
6. Under **Display**, select **Durbin-Watson statistic**.
7. Click **OK**. **OK**.

in Appendix O are for one-tailed tests with $\alpha = 0.05$ or 0.01. For a two-tailed test, the alpha is doubled.) The Durbin-Watson table provides two critical values: d_L and d_U. In this test for positive autocorrelation, the decision rule is

If $d < d_L$, reject H_0 and conclude that positive autocorrelation exists.
If $d > d_U$, do not reject H_0 and conclude that no positive autocorrelation exists.
If $d_L < d < d_U$, the test is inconclusive.

The Durbin-Watson test is not reliable for sample sizes smaller than 15. Therefore, for the Taft Ice Cream Company application, we are unable to conduct the hypothesis test for autocorrelation. However, Example 16-5 shows a Durbin-Watson test carried out.

EXAMPLE 16-5 Testing for Autocorrelation

TRY PROLEM 16.18

Grey Harbor Shipping Grey Harbor Shipping is a family-owned freight company located near Providence, Rhode Island. The company has been in business since 1989. During this time, revenues have grown steadily. Figure 16.11 displays the data in a time-series plot. The data are in a CD-ROM file called **Grey Harbor**.

Recently the managers of the company developed a linear trend regression model that they hope to use to forecast revenue for the next two years to determine whether they can support adding another ship to their fleet. They are now interested in determining whether the linear model is subject to positive autocorrelation. To test for this, the following steps can be used:

Step 1 Specify the model.
Based on a study of the line chart, the forecasting model is to be a simple linear trend regression model, with revenue as the dependent variable and time (*t*) as the independent variable.

FIGURE 16.11

Time-Series Plot of Grey Harbor Revenue Data

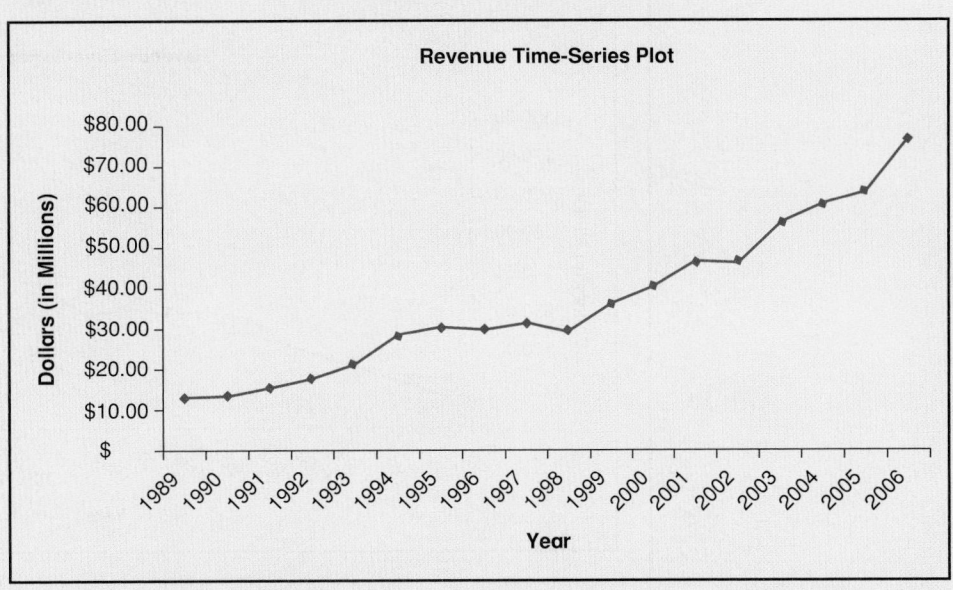

Step 2 Fit the model.

Because we have specified a linear trend model, the process of fitting can be accomplished using least squares regression analysis and Excel or Minitab to estimate the slope and intercept for the model. Fitting the 18 data points with a least squares line, we find the following:

$$F_t = 5.0175 + 3.3014(t)$$

Step 3 Diagnose the model.

The following values were also found:

$$R^2 = 0.935$$
$$F\text{-Statistic} = 230.756$$
$$\text{Standard Error} = 4.78$$

The large F-statistic indicates that the model explains a significant amount of variation in revenue per share over time. However, looking at a plot of the trend line shown in Figure 16.12, we see a pattern of actual revenue values first above, and then below, the trend line. This pattern indicates possible autocorrelation among the error terms. We will test for autocorrelation by calculating the Durbin-Watson d statistic. Both Minitab and the PHStat add-ins for Excel have the option to generate the Durbin-Watson test statistic. The output is shown in Figure 16.13.

Figure 16.13 shows the Durbin-Watson d statistic as

$$d = 0.661$$

The null and alternative hypotheses for testing for positive autocorrelation are

$$H_0: \rho = 0$$
$$H_A: \rho > 0$$

We next go to the Durbin-Watson table (Appendix O) for $\alpha = 0.05$, sample size 18, and number of independent variables, $P = 1$. The values from the table for d_L and d_U are

$$d_L = 1.16 \quad \text{and} \quad d_U = 1.39$$

FIGURE 16.12

Grey Harbor Trend Line

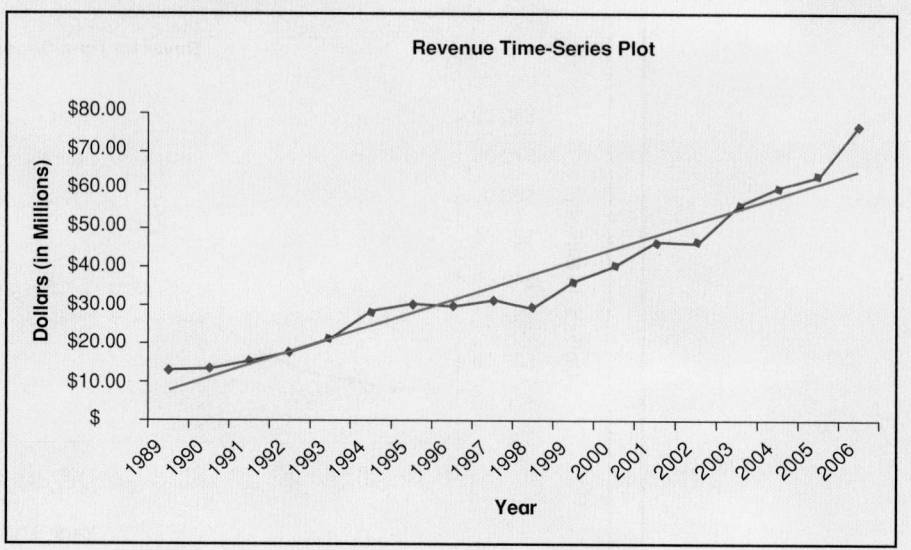

FIGURE 16.13

Excel 2007 (PHStat) Output—Durbin-Watson Statistic for Grey Harbor

Excel 2007 Instructions:
1. Open file: Grey Harbor.xls.
2. Select **Add-Ins**.
3. Select **PHStat**.
4. Select **Regression > Simple Linear Regression**.
5. Define *y* variable data range.
6. Specify *x* variable data range (time = *t* values).
7. Click on **Durbin-Watson Statistic**.
8. Click **OK**.

Minitab Instructions (for similar results):
1. Open file: Grey Harbor.MTW.
2. Choose **Stat > Regression > Regression**.
3. In **Response**, enter the time series column, *Revenue*.
4. In **Predictors**, enter the time variable column, *t*.
5. Select **Options**.
6. Under **Display**, select **Durbin-Watson statistic**.
7. Click **OK. OK**.

> The decision rule for testing whether we have positive autocorrelation is
>
> If $d < 1.16$, reject H_0 and conclude that positive autocorrelation exists.
> If $d > 1.39$, conclude that no positive autocorrelation exists.
> If $1.16 < d < 1.39$, the test is inconclusive.
>
> Because $d = 0.661 < d_L = 1.16$, we must reject the null hypothesis and conclude that significant positive autocorrelation exists in the regression model. This means that the assumption of uncorrelated error terms has been violated in this case. Thus, the linear trend model is not the appropriate model to provide the annual revenue forecasts for the next two years.

There are several techniques for dealing with the problem of autocorrelation. Some of these are beyond the scope of this text. (Refer to books by Nelson and Wonnacott) However, one option is to attempt to fit a nonlinear trend to the data, which is discussed starting on page 782.

True Forecasts Although a decision maker is interested in how well a forecasting technique can fit historical data, the real test comes with how well it forecasts future values. In the Taft example, we had 10 years of historical data. If we wish to forecast ice cream sales for year 11 using the linear trend model, we substitute $t = 11$ into the forecast equation to produce a forecast as follows:

$$F_{11} = 277,333.33 + 14,575.76(11) = \$437,666.69$$

This method of forecasting is called *trend projection*. To determine how well our trend model actually forecasts, we would have to wait until the actual sales amount for period 11 is known.

As we just indicated, a model's true forecasting ability is determined by how well it forecasts future values, not by how well it fits historical values. However, having to wait until after the forecast period to know how effective a forecast is doesn't help us assess a model's effectiveness ahead of time. This problem can be partially overcome by using *split samples*, which involves dividing a time series into two groups. You put the first (n_1) periods of historical data in the first group. These (n_1) periods will be used to develop the forecasting model. The second group contains the remaining (n_2) periods of historical data, which will be used to test the model's forecasting ability. These data are called the *holdout data*. Usually, three to five periods are held out, depending on the total number of periods in the time series.

In the Taft Ice Cream example, we have only 10 years of historical data, so we will hold out the last three periods and use the first seven periods to develop the linear trend model. The computations are performed as before, using Excel or Minitab or Equations 16.7 and 16.8. Because we are using a different data set to develop the linear equation, we get a slightly different trend line than when all 10 periods were used. The new trend line is

$$F_t = 277,142.85 + 14,642.85(t)$$

This model is now used to provide forecasts for periods 8 through 10 by using trend projection. These forecasts are

Year	Actual	Forecast	Error
t	y_t	F_t	$(y_t - F_t)$
8	400,000	394,285.65	5,714.35
9	395,000	408,928.50	−13,928.50
10	430,000	423,571.35	6,428.65

Then we can compute the *MSE* and the *MAD* values for periods 8 through 10.

$$MSE = \frac{[(5,714.35)^2 + (-13,928.50)^2 + (6,428.65)^2]}{3} = 89,328,149.67$$

and

$$MAD = \frac{(|5,714.35| + |-13,928.50| + |6,428.65|)}{3} = 8,690.50$$

These values could be compared with those produced using other forecasting techniques or evaluated against the forecaster's own standards. Smaller values are preferred. Other factors should also be considered. For instance, in some cases, the forecast values might tend to be higher (or lower) than the actual values. This may imply the linear trend model isn't the best model to use. Forecasting models that tend to over- or under-forecast are said to contain *forecast bias*. Equation 16.12 is used as an estimator of the bias.

Forecast Bias

$$\text{Forecast Bias} = \frac{\Sigma(y_t - F_t)}{n} \qquad (16.12)$$

The forecast bias can be either positive or negative. A positive value indicates a tendency to underforecast. A negative value indicates a tendency to overforecast. The estimated bias taken from the forecasts for periods 8 through 10 in our example is

$$\text{Forecast Bias} = \frac{[(5,714.35) + (-13,928.50) + (6,428.65)]}{3} = -595.17$$

This means that, on average, the model overforecasts sales by $595.17.

Suppose that on the basis of our bias estimate we judge that the linear trend model does an acceptable job in forecasting. Then all available data (periods 1 through 10) would be used to develop a linear trend model (see Figure 16.6), and a trend projection would be used to forecast for future time periods by substituting appropriate values for *t* into the trend model.

$$F_t = 277,333.33 + 14,575.76(t)$$

However, if the linear model is judged to be unacceptable, the forecaster will need to try a different technique. For the purpose of the bank loan application, the Taft Ice Cream Company needs to forecast sales for the next three years (periods 11 through 13.) Assuming the linear trend model is acceptable, these forecasts are

$$F_{11} = 277,333.33 + 14,575.76(11) = \$437,666.69$$
$$F_{12} = 277,333.33 + 14,575.76(12) = \$452,242.45$$
$$F_{13} = 277,333.33 + 14,575.76(13) = \$466,818.21$$

Nonlinear Trend Forecasting

As we indicated earlier, you may encounter a time series that exhibits a nonlinear trend. Figure 16.2 showed an example of a nonlinear trend. When the historical data show a nonlinear trend, you should consider using a nonlinear trend forecasting model. A common method for dealing with nonlinear trends is to use an extension of the linear trend method. This extension calls for making a data transformation before applying the least squares regression analysis.

Business Application

HARRISON EQUIPMENT COMPANY Consider Harrison Equipment Company, which leases large construction equipment to contractors in the Southwest. The lease arrangements call for Harrison to perform all repairs and maintenance on this equipment.

FIGURE 16.14

Excel 2007 Time-Series Plot for Harrison Equipment Repair Costs

	A	B	C	D
1	Year	Season	Quarter	Repair Costs
2	2002	Fall	1	$1,459
3		Winter	2	$1,620
4		Spring	3	$1,783
5		Summer	4	$1,794
6	2003	Fall	5	$2,191
7		Winter	6	$2,423
8		Spring	7	$2,677
9		Summer	8	$2,815
10	2004	Fall	9	$2,820
11		Winter	10	$2,600
12		Spring	11	$2,875
13		Summer	12	$3,910
14	2005	Fall	13	$5,820
15		Winter	14	$4,367
16		Spring	15	$6,622
17		Summer	16	$8,092
18	2006	Fall	17	$11,240
19		Winter	18	$10,554
20		Spring	19	$12,348
21		Summer	20	$11,433

Excel 2007 Instructions:
1. Open file: Harrison.xls.
2. Select data in the Repair Cost data column.
3. Click on **Insert > Line Chart**.
4. Click on **Select Data**.
5. Under **Horizontal (categories) Axis Labels**, select data in year and quarter columns.
6. Click on **Layout > Chart Title** and enter desired title.
7. Click on **Layout > Axis Titles** and enter horizontal and vertical axes titles.

Minitab Instructions:
1. Open file: Harrison.MTW.
2. Select **Graph > Time Series Plot**.
3. Select Simple.
4. Under **Series**, enter time series column.
5. Click **Time/Scale**.
6. Under **Time Scale** select **Calendar** and **Quarter Year**.
7. Under **Start Values**, insert the starting quarter and year.
8. Click **OK. OK.**

Excel and Minitab Tutorial

CHAPTER OUTCOME #3

Figure 16.14 shows a line chart for the repair costs for a crawler tractor leased to a contractor in Phoenix for the past 20 quarters. The data are contained in the CD-ROM file **Harrison**.

Step 1 Model Specification
Harrison Equipment is interested in forecasting future repair costs for the crawler tractor. Recall that the first step in forecasting is model specification. Even though the plot in Figure 16.14 indicates a sharp upward nonlinear trend, the forecaster may start by specifying a linear trend model.

Step 2 Model Fitting
As a part of the model-fitting step, she could use Excel's or Minitab's regression procedure to obtain the linear forecasting model shown in Figure 16.15. As shown in Figure 16.15, the linear trend model is

$$F_t = -1,022.7 + 570.9(t)$$

Step 3 Model Diagnosis
The fit is pretty good with an R-squared $= 0.8214$ and a standard error of 1,618.5. But we need to look closer. Figure 16.15 shows a plot of the trend line compared with the actual data. A close inspection indicates the linear trend model may not be best for this case. Notice that the linear model underforecasts, then overforecasts, then underforecasts again. From this we might suspect positive autocorrelation.

We can establish the following null and alternative hypotheses:

$$H_0: \rho = 0$$
$$H_A: \rho > 0$$

FIGURE 16.15

Excel 2007 (PHStat) Output for the Harrison Equipment Company Linear Trend Model

Excel 2007 Instructions:
1. Open file: Harrison.xls.
2. Select **Add-Ins**.
3. Select **PHStat**.
4. Select **Regression > Simple Linear Regression**.
5. Specify *y* variable data range.
6. Specify *x* variable data range (time = *t* values).
7. Check box for **Durbin-Watson Statistic**.
8. Copy Figure 16.4 line chart onto output—add linear trend line.
9. Click **OK**.

Minitab Instructions (for similar results):
1. Open file: Harrison.MTW.
2. Follow Minitab instructions in Figure 16.13.
3. Choose **Stat > Time Series > Trend Analysis**.
4. In **Variable**, enter time-series column.
5. Under **Model Type**, Choose **Linear**.
6. Click **OK**.

Equation 16.11 could be used to manually compute the Durbin-Watson *d* statistic, or more likely, we would use either PHStat or Minitab. The calculated Durbin-Watson is

$$d = 0.505$$

The d_L critical value from the Durbin-Watson table in Appendix O for $\alpha = 0.05$ and a sample size of $n = 20$ and $P = 1$ independent variable is 1.20.

Because $d = 0.505 < d_L = 1.20$, we reject the null hypothesis.

Thus, we conclude that the error terms are significantly positively autocorrelated. The model-building process needs to be repeated.

Step 1 Model Specification

After examining Figure 16.15 and determining the results of the test for positive autocorrelation, a nonlinear trend will likely provide a better fit for these data. To account for the nonlinear growth trend, which starts out slowly and then builds rapidly, the forecaster might consider transforming the time variable by squaring *t* to form a model of the form

$$y = \beta_0 + \beta_1 t + \beta_2 t^2 + \varepsilon$$

This transformation is suggested because the growth in costs appears to be increasing at an increasing rate. Other nonlinear trends may require different types of transformations, such as taking a square root or natural log. Each situation must be analyzed separately. (See the text by Kutner et al. for further discussion of transformations.)

FIGURE 16.16

Excel 2007 (PHStat) Transformed Regression Model for Harrison Equipment

Excel 2007 (PHStat) Instructions:
1. Open data file: Harrison.xls.
2. Select **Add-Ins**.
3. Select **PHStat**.
4. Select **Regression > Multiple Regression**.
6. Specify *y* variable data range.
7. Specify *x* variable data range (time = *t* values and *t* = squared values).
8. Check on **Residuals table** (output not shown here).
9. Check box for **Durbin-Watson Statistic**.
10. Click **OK**.

	A	B	C	D	E	F	G
2							
3	*Regression Statistics*						
4	Multiple R	0.9729					
5	R Square	0.9466					
6	Adjusted R Square	0.9403					
7	Standard Error	910.3486					
8	Observations	20					
9							
10	ANOVA						
11		*df*	*SS*	*MS*	*F*	*Significance F*	
12	Regression	2	249830241.6	124915120.8	150.730	0.0000	
13	Residual	17	14088486.9	828734.5			
14	Total	19	263918728.6				
15							
16		*Coefficients*	*Standard Error*	*t Stat*	*P-value*	*Lower 95%*	*Upper 95%*
17	Intercept	2318.7	677.28	3.42	0.00	889.79	3747.67
18	t	-340.4	148.54	-2.29	0.03	-653.75	-26.97
19	t2	43.4	6.87	6.32	0.00	28.90	57.89
20							
21							
22	Durbin-Watson Calculations						
23							
24	Sum of Squared Difference of Residuals	22965556.38					
25	Sum of Squared Residuals	14088486.90					
26							
27	Durbin-Watson Statistic	1.63					

Minitab Instructions (for similar results):
1. Open File. Harrison.MTW.
2. Choose **Calc > Calculator**.
3. In **Store result in variable**, enter destination column *Qtr²*.
4. With cursed in **Expressions**, enter *Quarter* column then **2.
5. Click **OK**.

6. Choose **Stat > Regression > Regression**.
7. In **Response**, enter *Repair Costs*. In **Predictors**, enter *Qtr²*.
8. Click **Storage**.
9. Under **Diagnostic Measures**, select **Residuals**. Under **Characteristics of Estimated Equation**, select **Fits**.
10. Click **OK. OK**.

Step 2 Model Fitting

Figure 16.16 shows the Excel regression results, and Figure 16.17 shows the revised time-series plot using the polynomial transformation. The resulting nonlinear trend regression model is

$$F_t = 2318.7 - 340.4(t) + 43.4(t^2)$$

Step 3 Model Diagnosis

Visually, the transformed model now looks more appropriate. The fit is much better as the *R*-squared value is increased to 0.9466 and the standard error is reduced to 910.35. The null and alternative hypotheses for testing whether positive autocorrelation exists are

$$H_0: \rho = 0$$
$$H_A: \rho > 0$$

As seen in Figure 16.16, the calculated Durbin-Watson test statistic is equal to

$$d = 1.63$$

The d_L and d_U critical values from the Durbin-Watson table in Appendix O for $\alpha = 0.05$ and a sample size of $n = 20$ and $P = 2$ independent variable are 1.10 and 1.54, respectively.

Because $d = 1.63 > 1.54$, the Durbin-Watson test indicates that there is no positive autocorrelation. Given this result and the improvements to *R*-squared and the standard error of the estimate, the nonlinear model is judged superior to the original linear model.

FIGURE 16.17

Excel 2007 Transformed Model for Harrison Equipment Company

Excel 2007 (PHStat) Instructions:
1. Open data file: Harrison.xls.
2. Follow Figure 16.14 instruction to generate line chart.
3. Select **Add-Ins**.
4. Select **PHStat**.
5. Select **Regression > Multiple Regression**.
6. Specify *y* variable data range
7. Specify *x* variable data range (time = *t* values and *t*-squared values).
8. Click on **Residuals table** (output not shown here).
9. Paste **Predicted Values** on the line chart.

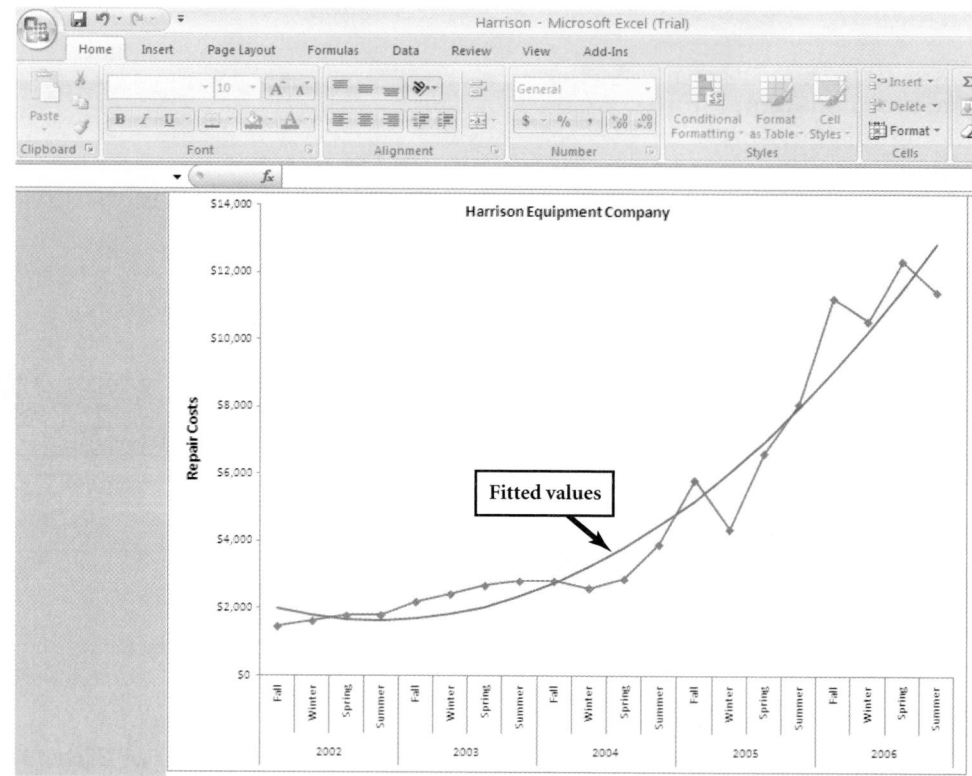

Forecasts for periods 21 and 22, using this latest model, are obtained using the trend projection method.

For period $t = 21$:

$$F_{21} = 2318.7 - 340.4(21) + 43.4(21^2) = \$14,310$$

For period $t = 22$:

$$F_{22} = 2318.7 - 340.4(22) + 43.4(22^2) = \$15,836$$

Using transformations often provides a very effective way of improving the fit of a time series. However, a forecaster should be careful not to get caught up in an exercise of "curve-fitting." One suggestion is that only explainable terms—terms that can be justified—be used for transforming data. For instance, in our example, we might well expect repair costs to increase at a faster rate as a tractor gets older and begins wearing out. Thus, the t^2 transformation seems to make sense.

Some Words of Caution The trend projection method relies on the future behaving in a manner similar to the past. In the previous example, if equipment repair costs continue to follow the pattern displayed over the past 20 quarters, these forecasts may prove acceptable. However, if the future pattern changes, there is no reason to believe these forecasts will be close to actual costs.

Adjusting for Seasonality

In Section 16.1, we discussed seasonality in a time series. The seasonal component represents those changes (highs and lows) in the time series that occur at approximately the same time every period. If the forecasting model that you are using does not already explicitly account for seasonality, you should adjust your forecast to take into account the seasonal component. The linear and nonlinear trend models discussed thus far do not automatically incorporate the seasonal component. Forecasts using these models should be adjusted as illustrated in the following application.

FIGURE 16.18

Excel 2007 Big
Mountain Resort
Quarterly Sales Data

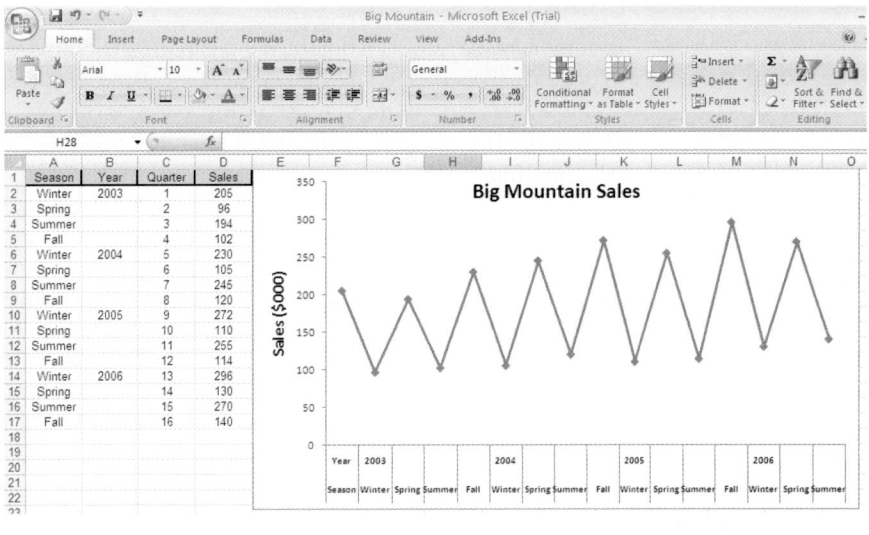

Excel 2007 Instructions:
1. Open file: Big Mountain.xls.
2. Select data in the Repair Cost data column.
3. Click on **Insert > Line Chart**.
4. Click on **Select Data**.
5. Under **Horizontal (categories) Axis**

Labels, select data in Year and Season columns.
6. Click on **Layout > Chart Title** and enter desired title.
7. Click on **Layout > Axis Titles** and enter horizontal and vertical axes titles.

Business Application

Excel and Minitab Tutorial

Seasonal Index
A number used to quantify the effect of seasonality in time-series data.

BIG MOUNTAIN SKI RESORT Most businesses in the tourist industry know that sales are seasonal. For example, at the Big Mountain Ski Resort, business peaks at two times during the year: winter for skiing and summer for golf and tennis. These peaks can be identified in a time series if the sales data are measured on at least a quarterly basis. Figure 16.18 shows the quarterly sales data for the past four years in spreadsheet form. The line chart for these data is also shown. The data are in the CD-ROM file **Big Mountain**. The time-series plot clearly shows that the summer and winter quarters are the busy times. There has also been a slightly increasing linear trend in sales over the four years.

Big Mountain Resort wants to forecast sales for each quarter of the coming year, and it hopes to use a linear trend model. When the historical data show a trend and seasonality, the trend-based forecasting model needs to be adjusted to incorporate the seasonality. One method for doing this involves computing **seasonal indexes**.

For instance, when we have quarterly data, we can develop four seasonal indexes, one each for winter, spring, summer and fall. A seasonal index below 1.00 indicates that the quarter has values that are typically below the average value for the year. On the other hand, an index greater than 1.00 indicates that the quarter's value is higher than the yearly average.

Computing Seasonal Indexes Although there are several methods for computing the seasonal indexes, the procedure introduced here is the *ratio-to-moving-average method*. This method assumes that the actual time-series data can be represented as a product of the four time-series components—trend, seasonal, cyclical, and random—which produces the multiplicative model shown in Equation 16.13.

Multiplicative Time-Series Model

$$y_t = T_t \times S_t \times C_t \times I_t$$

(16.13)

where:

y_t = Value of the time series at time t
T_t = Trend value at time t
S_t = Seasonal value at time t
C_t = Cyclical value at time t
I_t = Irregular or random value at time t

The ratio-to-moving-average method begins by removing the seasonal and irregular components, S_t and I_t, from the data, leaving the combined trend and cyclical components, T_t and C_t. This is done by first computing successive four-period moving averages for the time series. A moving average is the average of n consecutive values of a time series. Using the Big Mountain sales data in Figure 16.19, we find that the **moving average** using the first four quarters is

Moving Averages
The successive averages of n consecutive values in a time series.

$$\frac{205 + 96 + 194 + 102}{4} = 149.25$$

This moving average is associated with the middle time period of the data values in the moving average. The middle period of the first four quarters is 2.5 (between quarter 2 and quarter 3).

The second moving average is found by dropping the value from period 1 and adding the value from period 5, as follows:

$$\frac{96 + 194 + 102 + 230}{4} = 155.50$$

This moving average is associated with time period 3.5, the middle period between quarters 3 and 4.

Figure 16.19 shows the moving averages for the Big Mountain sales data in Excel spreadsheet form.[2] We selected four data values for the moving average because we have quarterly data; with monthly data, 12 data values would have been used.

The next step is to compute the *centered moving averages* by averaging each successive pair of moving averages. Centering the moving averages is necessary so that the resulting moving average will be associated with one of the data set's original time periods. In this example, Big Mountain is interested in quarterly sales data—that is, time periods 1, 2, 3, etc. Therefore, the moving averages we have representing time periods 2.5, 3.5, and so forth are not of interest to Big Mountain. Centering these averaged time series values,

FIGURE 16.19

Excel 2007 Seasonal Index—Step 1: Moving Average Values for Big Mountain Resort

Excel 2007 Instructions:
1. Open file: Big Mountain. xls.
2. Create a new column of 4-period moving averages using Excel's **AVERAGE** function. The first moving average is placed in cell E3 and the equation is =**AVERAGE(D2:D5)**.
3. Copy the equation down to cell E15.

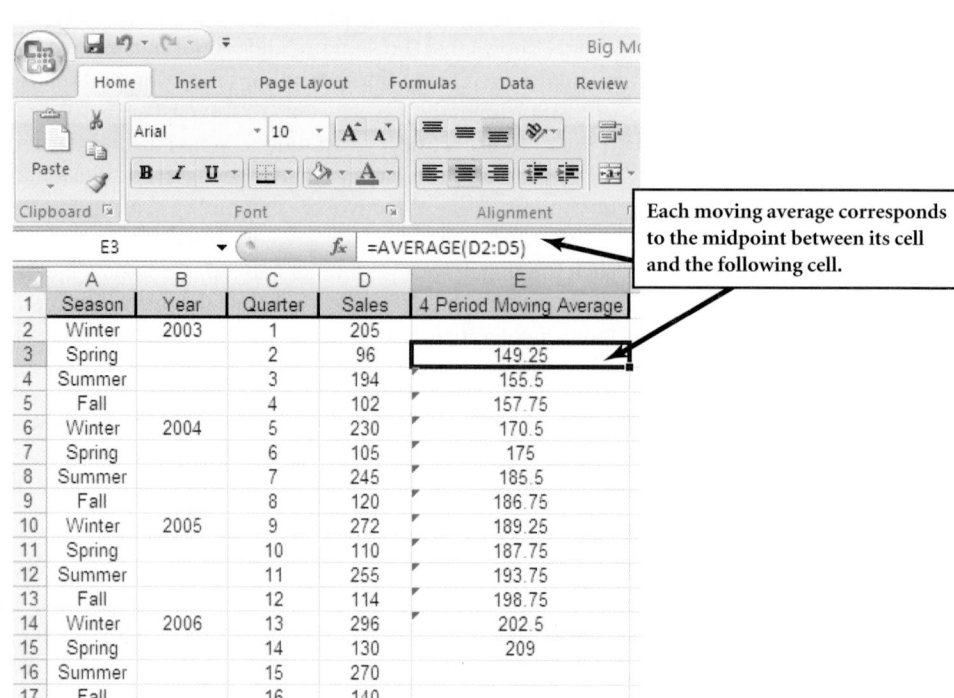

	A	B	C	D	E
1	Season	Year	Quarter	Sales	4 Period Moving Average
2	Winter	2003	1	205	
3	Spring		2	96	149.25
4	Summer		3	194	155.5
5	Fall		4	102	157.75
6	Winter	2004	5	230	170.5
7	Spring		6	105	175
8	Summer		7	245	185.5
9	Fall		8	120	186.75
10	Winter	2005	9	272	189.25
11	Spring		10	110	187.75
12	Summer		11	255	193.75
13	Fall		12	114	198.75
14	Winter	2006	13	296	202.5
15	Spring		14	130	209
16	Summer		15	270	
17	Fall		16	140	

E3 f_x =AVERAGE(D2:D5)

Each moving average corresponds to the midpoint between its cell and the following cell.

---

[2] The Excel process illustrated by Figures 16.19 through 16.23 is also accomplished using Minitab's **Time Series > Decomposition** command, which is illustrated Figure 16.25 on page 793.

however, produces moving averages for the (quarterly) time periods of interest. For example, the first two moving averages are averaged to produce the first centered moving average. We get

$$\frac{149.25 + 155.5}{2} = 152.38$$

This centered moving average is associated with quarter 3. The centered moving averages are shown in Figure 16.20.[3] These values estimate the $T_t \times C_t$ value.

If the number of data values used for a moving average is odd, the moving average will be associated with the time period of the middle observation. In such cases, we would not have to center the moving average, as we did in Figure 16.20, because the moving averages would already be associated with one of the time periods from the original time series.

Next, we estimate the $S_t \times I_t$ value. Dividing the actual sales value for each quarter by the corresponding centered moving average, as in Equation 16.14, does this. As an example, we examine the third time period: summer of 2003. The sales value of 194 is divided by the centered moving average of 152.38, to produce 1.273. This value is called the *ratio-to-moving-average*. Figure 16.21 shows these values for the Big Mountain data.

Ratio-to-Moving-Average

$$S_t \times I_t = \frac{y_t}{T_t \times C_t} \tag{16.14}$$

The final step in determining the seasonal indexes is to compute the mean ratio-to-moving-average value for each season. Each quarter's ratio-to-moving-average is averaged over the years to produce the *seasonal index* for that quarter. Figure 16.22 shows the seasonal indexes. The seasonal index for the winter quarter is 1.441. This indicates that sales for Big Mountain during the winter are 44.1% above the average for the year. Also, sales in the spring quarter are only 60.8% of the average for the year.

FIGURE 16.20

Excel 2007 Seasonal Index—Step 2: Big Mountain Resort Centered Moving Averages

Excel 2007 Instructions:
1. Open File: Big Mountain.xls.
2. Follow instructions in Figure 16.19.
3. Create a new column of centered moving averages using Excel's **AVERAGE** function. The first moving average is placed in cell F4 and the equation is **=AVERAGE (E3:E4)**.
4. Copy the equation down to cell F15.

	A	B	C	D	E	F
						Centered Moving
1	Season	Year	Quarter	Sales	4 Period Moving Average	Average
2	Winter	2003	1	205		
3	Spring		2	96	149.25	
4	Summer		3	194	155.5	152.38
5	Fall		4	102	157.75	156.63
6	Winter	2004	5	230	170.5	164.13
7	Spring		6	105	175	172.75
8	Summer		7	245	185.5	180.25
9	Fall		8	120	186.75	186.13
10	Winter	2005	9	272	189.25	188.00
11	Spring		10	110	187.75	188.50
12	Summer		11	255	193.75	190.75
13	Fall		12	114	198.75	196.25
14	Winter	2006	13	296	202.5	200.63
15	Spring		14	130	209	205.75
16	Summer		15	270		
17	Fall		16	140		
18						

Cell reference: F4   =AVERAGE(E3:E4)

---

[3] Excel's tabular format does not allow the uncentered moving averages to be displayed with their "inter-quarter" time periods. That is, 149.25 is associated with time period 2.5, 155.50 with time period 3.5, and so forth.

FIGURE 16.21

Excel 2007 Seasonal Index—Step 3: Big Mountain Resort Ratio-to-Moving Averages

Excel 2007 Instructions:
1. Open File: Big Mountain.xls.
2. Follow instructions in Figures 16.19 and 16.20.
3. Create a new column of ratio to moving averages using an Excel equation (e.g. **=D4/F4**).
4. Copy the equation down to cell G15.

	A	B	C	D	E	F	G
	Season	Year	Quarter	Sales	4 Period Moving Average	Centered Moving Average	Ratio to Moving Average
2	Winter	2003	1	205			
3	Spring		2	96	149.25		
4	Summer		3	194	155.5	152.38	1.273
5	Fall		4	102	157.75	156.63	0.651
6	Winter	2004	5	230	170.5	164.13	1.401
7	Spring		6	105	175	172.75	0.608
8	Summer		7	245	185.5	180.25	1.359
9	Fall		8	120	186.75	186.13	0.645
10	Winter	2005	9	272	189.25	188.00	1.447
11	Spring		10	110	187.75	188.50	0.584
12	Summer		11	255	193.75	190.75	1.337
13	Fall		12	114	198.75	196.25	0.581
14	Winter	2006	13	296	202.5	200.63	1.475
15	Spring		14	130	209	205.75	0.632
16	Summer		15	270			
17	Fall		16	140			

G4 · fx =D4/F4

One important point about the seasonal indexes is that the sum of the indexes is equal to the number of seasonal indexes. That is, the average seasonal index equals 1.0. In the Big Mountain Resort example, we find:

Summer		Fall		Winter		Spring		
1.323	+	0.626	+	1.441	+	0.608	=	3.998 (difference from 4 due to rounding)

Likewise, in an example with monthly data instead of quarterly data, we would generate 12 seasonal indexes, one for each month. The sum of these indexes should be 12.

The Need to Normalize the Indexes If the sum of the seasonal indexes does not equal the number of time periods in the recurrence period of the time series, an adjustment is necessary. In the Big Mountain Resort example, the sum of the four seasonal indexes may have been something other than 4 (the recurrence period). In such cases, we must adjust the seasonal indexes by multiplying each by the number of time periods in the recurrence period over the sum of the unadjusted seasonal indexes. For quarterly data such as the Big Mountain Resort example, we would multiply each seasonal index by 4/(sum of the unadjusted seasonal indexes). Performing this multiplication will *normalize* the seasonal

FIGURE 16.22

Excel 2007 Seasonal Index—Step 4: Big Mountain Resort Mean Ratios

Excel 2007 Instructions:
1. Open File: Big Mountain.xls.
2. Follow instructions in Figures 16.19 thru 16.21.
3. Rearrange the ratio to moving average value organizing them by season of the year (summer, fall, etc).
4. Total and average the ratio-to-moving averages for each season.

Seasonal indexes:
Summer = 1.323
Fall = 0.626
Winter = 1.441
Spring = 0.608

	A	B	C	D	E
19					
20	Summer	Fall	Winter	Spring	
21	1.273	0.651	1.401	0.608	
22	1.359	0.645	1.447	0.584	
23	1.337	0.581	1.475	0.632	
24					
25	3.969	1.877	4.324	1.823	= Total
26	1.323	0.626	1.441	0.608	= Average

indexes. This adjustment is necessary if the seasonal adjustments are going to even out over the recurrence period.

Deseasonalizing A strong seasonal component may partially mask a trend in the time-series data. Consequently, to identify the trend you should first remove the effect of the seasonal component. This is called *deseasonalizing* the time series.

Again, assume that the multiplicative model shown previously in Equation 16.13 is appropriate:

$$y_t = T_t \times S_t \times C_t \times I_t$$

Deseasonalizing is accomplished by dividing y_t by the appropriate seasonal index, S_t, as shown in Equation 16.15.

Deseasonalization

$$T_t \times C_t \times I_t = \frac{y_t}{S_t} \qquad\qquad (16.15)$$

For time period 1, which is the winter quarter, the seasonal index is 1.441. The deseasonalized value for y_1 is

$$205/1.441 = 142.26$$

Figure 16.23 presents the deseasonalized values and the graph of these deseasonalized sales data for the Big Mountain example. This shows that there has been a gentle upward trend over the four years.

Once the data have been deseasonalized, the next step is to determine the trend based on the deseasonalized data. As in the previous examples of trend estimation, you can use either Excel or Minitab to develop the linear model for the deseasonalized data. The results are shown in Figure 16.24. The linear regression trend line equation is

$$F_t = 142.113 + 4.686(t)$$

You can use this trend line and the trend projection method to forecast sales for period $t = 17$:

$$F_{17} = 142.113 + 4.686(17) = 221.775 = \$221,775$$

This is a **seasonally unadjusted forecast**, because the time-series data used in developing the trend line were deseasonalized.

Seasonally Unadjusted Forecast
A forecast made for seasonal data that does not include an adjustment for the seasonal component in the time series.

FIGURE 16.23

Excel 2007 Deseasonalized Time Series for Big Mountain Sales Data

Excel 2007 Instructions:
1. Open File: Big Mountain.xls.
2. Follow instructions for Figures 16.18 thru 16.22.
3. Create a new column containing the deseasonalized values. Use Excel equations and Equation 16.15.
4. Select the new deseasonalized data and paste onto the line graph.

FIGURE 16.24

Excel 2007 Regression Trend Line of Big Mountain Deseasonalized Data

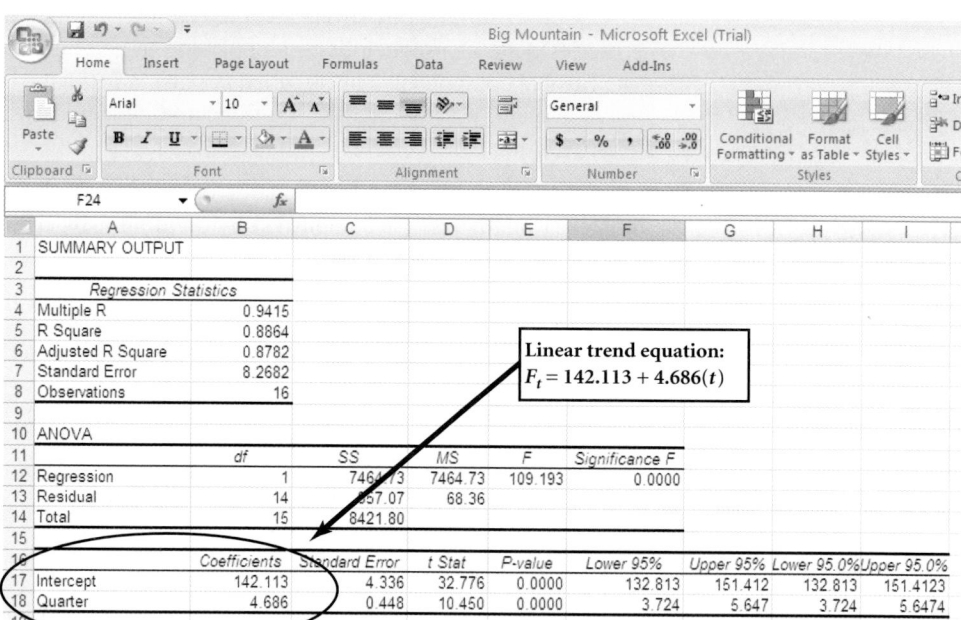

Now we need to adjust the forecast for period 17 to reflect the quarterly fluctuations. We do this by multiplying the unadjusted forecast values by the appropriate seasonal index. In this case, period 17 corresponds to the winter quarter. The winter quarter has a seasonal index of 1.441, indicating a high sales period. The adjusted forecast is

$$F_{17} = (221.775)(1.441) = 319.578, \text{ or } \$319,578$$

The seasonally adjusted forecasts for each quarter in 2007 are

Quarter (2007)	*t*	Unadjusted Forecast	Index	Adjusted Forecast
Winter	17	221.775	1.441	319.578 = $319,578
Spring	18	226.461	0.608	137,688 = $137,688
Summer	19	231.147	1.323	305,807 = $305,807
Fall	20	235.833	0.626	147,631 = $147,631

SUMMARY The Seasonal Adjustment Process: The Multiplicative Model

We can summarize the steps for performing a seasonal adjustment to a trend-based forecast as follows:

1. Compute each moving average from the *k* appropriate consecutive data values, where *k* is the number of values in one period of the time series.
2. Compute the centered moving averages.
3. Isolate the seasonal component by computing the ratio-to-moving-average values.
4. Compute the seasonal indexes by averaging the ratio-to-moving-average values for comparable periods.

5. Normalize the seasonal indexes (if necessary).
6. Deseasonalize the time series by dividing the actual data by the appropriate seasonal index.
7. Use least squares regression to develop the trend line using the deseasonalized data.
8. Develop the unadjusted forecasts using trend projection.
9. Seasonally adjust the forecasts by multiplying the unadjusted forecasts by the appropriate seasonal index.

FIGURE 16.25

Minitab Output Showing Big Mountain Seasonal Indexes

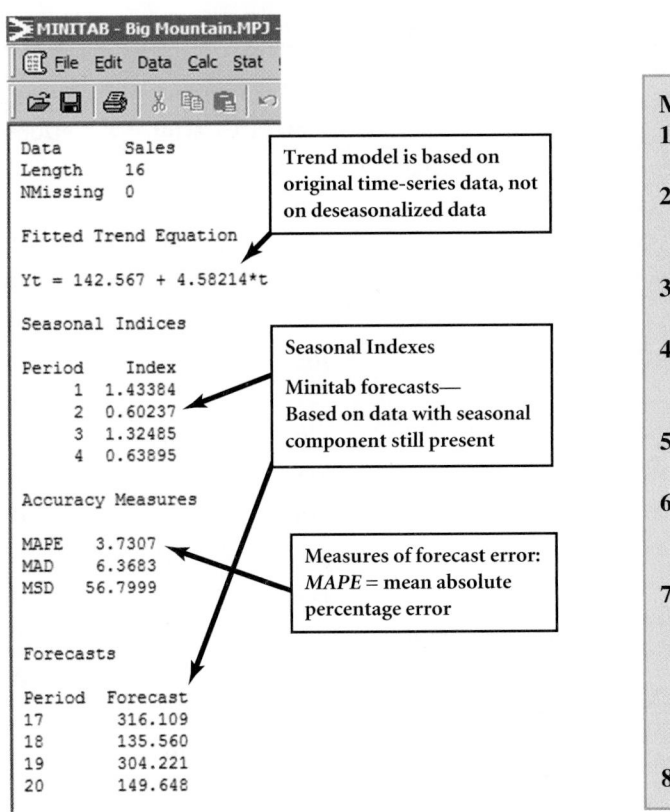

You can use the seasonally adjusted trend model when a time series exhibits both a trend and seasonality. This process allows for a better identification of the trend and produces forecasts that are more sensitive to seasonality in the data.

Minitab contains a procedure for generating seasonal indexes and seasonally adjusted forecasts. Figure 16.25 shows the Minitab results for the Big Mountain Ski Resort example. Notice that the forecast option in Minitab gives different forecasts than we showed earlier. This is because Minitab generates the linear trend model using original sales data rather than deseasonalized data. Our suggestion is to use Minitab to generate the seasonal indexes, but then follow our outline to generate seasonally adjusted forecasts.[4]

Using Dummy Variables to Represent Seasonality The multiplicative model approach for dealing with seasonal data in a time-series forecasting application is one method that is commonly used by forecasters. Another method used to incorporate the seasonal component into a linear trend forecast involves the use of dummy variables. To illustrate, we again use the Big Mountain example, which had four years of quarterly data. Because of quarterly data, start by constructing three dummy variables (one less than the number of data values in the year; if you have monthly data, construct eleven dummy variables). Form dummy variables as:

$x_1 = 1$ if season is winter $x_1 = 0$ if not winter
$x_2 = 1$ if season is spring $x_2 = 0$ if not spring
$x_3 = 1$ if season is summer $x_3 = 0$ if not summer

Table 16.5 shows the revised data set for the Big Mountain Company.

---

[4] Neither Excel nor PHStat offers a procedure for automatically generating seasonal indexes. However, as shown in the Big Mountain example, you can use the spreadsheet formulas to do this. See the Excel Tutorial on your CD-ROM.

TABLE 16.5 Big Mountain Sales Output Using Dummy Variables

Season	Year	y Sales	Quarter = t	x_1 Winter Dummy	x_2 Spring Dummy	x_3 Summer Dummy
Winter	2003	205	1	1	0	0
Spring		96	2	0	1	0
Summer		194	3	0	0	1
Fall		102	4	0	0	0
Winter	2004	230	5	1	0	0
Spring		105	6	0	1	0
Summer		245	7	0	0	1
Fall		120	8	0	0	0
Winter	2005	272	9	1	0	0
Spring		110	10	0	1	0
Summer		255	11	0	0	1
Fall		114	12	0	0	0
Winter	2006	296	13	1	0	0
Spring		130	14	0	1	0
Summer		270	15	0	0	1
Fall		140	16	0	0	0

Next form a multiple regression model:

$$F_t = \beta_0 + \beta_1 t + \beta_2 x_1 + \beta_3 x_2 + \beta_4 x_3 + \varepsilon$$

Note, this model formulation is an extension of the linear trend model where the seasonality is accounted for by adding the regression coefficient for the season to the linear trend fitted value.

Figure 16.26 shows the Excel multiple regression output. The regression equation is

$$F_t = 71.0 + 4.8t + 146.2(x_1) + 0.9(x_2) + 126.8(x_3)$$

The R-square value is very high at 0.9710, indicating the regression model fits the historical data quite well. The F-ratio of 92.07 is significant at any reasonable level of significance, indicating the overall regression model is statistically significant. However, the t-value for x_2, the spring dummy variable, is only 0.082, indicating that variable is insignificant. Consequently, we will drop this variable and rerun the regression analysis with only three independent variables. The resulting model is

$$F_t = 71.5 + 4.8t + 145.7x_1 + 126.4x_3$$

This overall model is significant and all three variables are statistically significant at any reasonable level of alpha. The coefficients on the two dummy variables can be interpreted as the seasonal indexes for winter and summer. The indexes for spring and fall are incorporated into the intercept value. We can now use this model to develop forecasts for year 5 (periods 17–20) as follows:

Winter ($t = 17$): $F_t = 71.5 + 4.8(17) + 145.7(1) + 126.4(0) = 298.80 = \$298,800$
Spring ($t = 18$): $F_t = 71.5 + 4.8(18) + 145.7(0) + 126.4(0) = 157.90 = \$157,900$
Summer ($t = 19$): $F_t = 71.5 + 4.8(19) + 145.7(0) + 126.4(1) = 289.10 = \$289,100$
Fall ($t = 20$): $F_t = 71.5 + 4.8(20) + 145.7(0) + 126.4(0) = 167.50 = \$167,510$

If you compare these forecasts to the ones we previously obtained using the multiplicative model approach, the forecasts for winter and summer are lower with the dummy variable model but higher for spring and fall. You could use the split-sample approach to

FIGURE 16.26

Excel 2007 Regression Output with Dummy Variables Included—Big Mountain Example

Excel 2007 Instructions:
1. Open File: Big Mountain. xls.
2. Create three dummy variables for winter, spring, and summer.
3. Click on **Data**.
4. Select **Data Analysis > Regression**.
5. Specify *y* variable range and *x* variable range (time variable plus three dummies).
6. Click **OK**.

test the two alternative approaches to see which, in this case, seems to provide more accurate forecasts based on *MAD* and *MSE* calculations.

Both the multiplicative and the dummy variable approach have their advantages and both methods are commonly used by business forecasters.

16-2: Exercises

Skill Development

Problems 16-18 to 16-22 refer to Tran's Furniture Store, which has maintained monthly sales records for the past 48 months, with the following results:

Month	Sales
1 (Jan.)	$23,500
2	21,700
3	18,750
4	22,000
5	23,000
6	26,200
7	27,300
8	29,300

Month	Sales
9	31,200
10	34,200
11	39,500
12	43,400
13 (Jan.)	$23,500
14	23,400
15	21,400
16	24,200
17	26,900
18	29,700
19	31,100
20	32,400

(Continued)

Month	Sales
21	34,500
22	35,700
23	42,000
24	42,600
25 (Jan.)	$31,000
26	30,400
27	29,800
28	32,500
29	34,500
30	33,800
31	34,200
32	36,700
33	39,700
34	42,400
35	43,600
36	47,400
37 (Jan)	$32,400
38	35,600
39	31,200
40	34,600
41	36,800
42	35,700
43	37,500
44	40,000
45	43,200
46	46,700
47	50,100
48	52,100

16-18. Based on the Durbin-Watson test, is there evidence of autocorrelation in these data? Use a linear trend model.

16-19. Using the multiplicative model, estimate the $T \times C$ portion by computing a 12-month-moving average and then the centered 12-month moving average.

16-20. Estimate the $S \times I$ portion of the multiplicative model by finding the ratio-to-moving-averages for the time-series data. Determine whether these ratio-to-moving-averages are stable from year to year.

16-21. Extract the irregular component by taking the normalized average of the ratio-to-moving-averages. Make a table that shows the normalized seasonal indexes. Interpret what the index for January means relative to the index for July.

16-22. Based on your work in the previous three problems:
a. Determine a seasonally adjusted linear trend forecasting model. Compare this model with an unadjusted linear trend model. Use both models to forecast Tran's sales for period 49.
b. Which of the two models developed has the lower *MAD* and lower *MSE*?

16-23. Consider the following set of sales data, given in millions of dollars.

2003	2005
1st quarter 152	1st quarter 217
2nd quarter 162	2nd quarter 209
3rd quarter 157	3rd quarter 202
4th quarter 167	4th quarter 221

2004	2006
1st quarter 182	1st quarter 236
2nd quarter 192	2nd quarter 242
3rd quarter 191	3rd quarter 231
4th quarter 197	4th quarter 224

a. Plot these data. Based on your visual observations, what time-series components are present in the data?
b. Determine the seasonal index for each quarter.
c. Fit a linear trend model to the data and determine the *MAD* and *MSE* values. Comment on the adequacy of the linear trend model based on these measures of forecast error.
d. Provide a seasonally unadjusted forecast using the linear trend model for each quarter of the year 2007.
e. Use the seasonal index values computed in part b to provide seasonal adjusted forecasts for each quarter of 2007.

16-24. Examine the following time series:

t	1	2	3	4	5	6	7	8	9	10
y_t	52	72	58	66	68	60	46	43	17	3

a. Produce a scatter plot of this time series. Indicate the appropriate forecasting model for this time series.
b. Construct the equation for the forecasting model identified in part a.
c. Produce forecasts for time periods 11, 12, 13, and 14.
d. Obtain the forecast bias for the forecasts produced in part c if the actual time series values are 35, 14, −9, and −34, for periods 11–14 respectively.

16-25. Examine the following quarterly data:

t	1	2	3	4	5	6	7	8	9	10	11	12
y_t	2	12	23	20	18	32	48	41	35	52	79	63

a. Compute the four-period moving averages for this set of data.
b. Compute the centered moving averages from the moving averages of part a.

c. Compute the ratio-to-moving-averages values.

d. Calculate the seasonal indices. Normalize them if necessary.

e. Deseasonalize the time series.

f. Produce the trend line using the deseasonalized data.

g. Produce seasonally adjusted forecasts for the time periods 13, 14, 15, and 16, respectively.

Business Applications

16-26. The average monthly price of regular gasoline in Southern California is monitored by the Automobile Club of Southern California's monthly Fuel Gauge Report. The prices of the time period July 2004 to June 2006 are given here.

Month	Price	Month	Price	Month	Price
7/04	2.247	5/05	2.532	3/06	2.626
8/04	2.108	6/05	2.375	4/06	2.903
9/04	2.111	7/05	2.592	5/06	3.417
10/04	2.352	8/05	2.774	6/06	3.301
11/04	2.374	9/05	3.031		
12/04	2.192	10/05	2.943		
1/05	1.989	11/05	2.637		
2/05	2.130	12/05	2.289		
3/05	2.344	1/06	2.357		
4/05	2.642	2/06	2.628		

a. Produce a time-series plot of the average price of regular gas in Southern California. Identify any time-series components that exist in the data.

b. Identify the recurrence period of the time series. Determine the seasonal index for each month within the recurrence period.

c. Fit a linear trend model to the deseasonalized data.

d. Provide a seasonally adjusted forecast using the linear trend model for July 2006 and July 2010.

16-27. "The average college senior graduated this year with more than $19,000 in debt" was the beginning sentence of an article in *USA Today* (Sandra Block, "In Debt Before You Start," June 13, 2006). The majority of students have loans that are not due until the student leaves school. This can result in the student ignoring the size of debt that piles up. Federal loans obtained to finance college education are steadily mounting. The data given here shows the amount of loans ($million) from the academic year 1985–86 to 2004–2005.

Year	Amount	Year	Amount	Year	Amount
1985–86	9,914	1992–93	16,221	1999–2000	37,228
1986–87	10,182	1993–94	22,557	2000–2001	39,101
1987–88	12,493	1994–95	26,011	2001–2002	42,761
1988–89	13,195	1995–96	28,737	2002–2003	49,360
1989–90	13,414	1996–97	31,906	2003–2004	57,463
1990–91	13,890	1997–98	33,930	2004–2005	62,614
1991–92	15,232	1998–99	34,376		

a. Produce a time-series plot of this data. Indicate the time-series components that exist in the data.

b. Conduct a test of hypothesis to determine if there exists a linear trend in this data. Use a significance level of 0.10 and the *p*-value approach.

c. Provide a 90% prediction interval for the amount of federal loans for the 2010–11 academic year.

16-28. Manuel Gutierrez correctly predicted the increasing need for home health care services due to the country's aging population. Five years ago, he started a company offering meal delivery, physical therapy, and minor housekeeping services in the Galveston area. Since that time he has opened offices in seven additional Gulf State cities. Manuel is presently analyzing the revenue data from his first location for the first five years of operation.

	Revenue ($10,000s)				
	2002	2003	2004	2005	2006
January	23	67	72	76	81
February	34	63	64	75	72
March	45	65	64	77	71
April	48	71	77	81	83
May	46	75	79	86	85
June	49	70	72	75	77
July	60	72	71	80	79
August	65	75	77	82	84
September	67	80	79	86	91
October	60	78	78	87	86
November	71	89	87	91	94
December	76	94	92	96	99

a. Plot these data. Based on your visual observations, what time-series components are present in the data?

b. Determine the seasonal index for each month

c. (1) Fit a linear trend model to the deseasonalized data for the years 2002–2006 and determine the *MAD* and *MSE* for forecasts for each of the months in 2007. (2) Conduct a test of hypothesis to determine if the linear trend model fits the existing data. (3) Comment on the adequacy of the linear trend model based on the measures of forecast error and the hypothesis test you conducted.

d. Manuel had hoped to reach $2,000,000 in revenue by the time he had been in business for 10 years. From the results in part c, is this a feasible goal based upon the historical data provided? Consider and comment on the size of the standard error for this prediction. What makes this value so large? How does it affect your conclusion?

e. Use the seasonal index values computed in part b to provide seasonal adjusted forecasts for each month of the year 2007.

16-29. A major brokerage company has an office in Miami, Florida. The manager of the office is evaluated based on the number of new clients generated each quarter. The following data reflect the number of new customers added during each quarter between 2003 and 2006.

2003	2004
1st quarter 218	1st quarter 250
2nd quarter 190	2nd quarter 220
3rd quarter 236	3rd quarter 265
4th quarter 218	4th quarter 241

2005	2006
1st quarter 244	1st quarter 229
2nd quarter 228	2nd quarter 221
3rd quarter 263	3rd quarter 248
4th quarter 240	4th quarter 231

a. Plot the time series and discuss the components that are present in the data.

b. Referring to part a, fit the linear trend model to the data for the years 2003–2005. Then use the resulting model to forecast the number of new brokerage customers for each quarter in the year 2006. Compute the *MAD* and *MSE* for these forecasts and discuss the results.

c. Using the data for the years 2003–2005, determine the seasonal indexes for each quarter.

d. Develop a seasonally unadjusted forecast for the four quarters of year 2006.

e. Using the seasonal indexes computed in part d, determine the seasonally adjusted forecast for each quarter for the year 2006. Compute the *MAD* and *MSE* for these forecasts.

f. Examine the values for the *MAD* and *MSE* in parts b and e. Which of the two forecasting techniques would you recommend the manager use to forecast the number of new clients generated each quarter? Support your choice by giving your rationale.

Computer Database Exercises

16-30. Harsin-Williams & Company is a construction company headquartered in Baton Rouge, Louisiana. A very important issue for construction companies is cash management, since they tend to be paid in lump sums when projects are completed or hit milestones. However, their expenses, such as payroll, must be paid regularly. The data file called **Harsin-Williams** contains month-end cash balances for the past 16 months.

a. Plot the data as a time-series graph. Discuss what the graph implies concerning the relationship between cash balance and the time variable, month.

b. Fit a linear trend model to the data. Compute the coefficient of determination for this model and show the trend line on the time-series graph. Discuss the appropriateness of the linear trend model. What are the strengths and weaknesses of the model?

c. Referring to part b, compute the *MAD* and *MSE* for the 16 data points.

d. Use the t^2 transformation approach and recompute the linear model using the transformed time variable. Plot the new trend line against the transformed data. Discuss whether this model appears to provide a better fit than did the model without the transformation. Compare the coefficients of determination for the two models. Which model seems to be superior using the coefficient of determination as the criterion?

e. Refer to part d. Compute the *MAD* and *MSE* for the 16 data values. Discuss how these compare to those that were computed in part c, prior to transformation. Do the measures of fit (R^2, *MSE*, or *MAD*) agree upon the best model to use for forecasting purposes?

16-31. Refer to Problem 16-30.

a. Use the linear trend model (without transformation) for the first 15 months and provide a cash balance forecast for month 16. Then make the t^2 transformation and develop a new linear trend forecasting model based on months 1–15. Forecast the cash balance for month 16. Now compare the accuracy of the forecasts with and without the transformation. Which of the two forecast models would you prefer? Explain your answer.

b. Provide a 95% prediction interval for the cash balance forecast for month 16 using the linear trend model both with and without the transformation. Which interval has the widest width? On this basis, which procedure would you choose?

16-32. The federal funds rate is the interest rate charged by banks when banks borrow "overnight" from each other. The funds rate fluctuates according to supply and demand and is not under the direct control of the Federal Reserve Board, but is strongly influenced by the Fed's actions. The file entitled **The Fed** contains the federal funds rate for the period 1955–2005.

a. Produce a scatter plot of the federal funds rate for the period 1955–2005. Identify any time series components that exist in the data.

b. Identify the recurrence period of the time series. Determine the seasonal index for each month within the recurrence period.

c. Fit a nonlinear trend model that uses coded years and coded years squared as predictors for the deseasonalized data.

d. Provide a seasonally adjusted forecast using the nonlinear trend model for 2006 and 2010.

e. Diagnose the model

16-33. The Census Bureau of the Department of Commerce released the U.S. retail e-commerce sales ("Quarterly Retail E-Commerce Sales 1st Quarter 2006," May 18, 2006) for the period of 4th Qtr 1999–1st Qtr 2006. The file entitled **E-Commerce** contains that data.

a. Produce a time-series plot of this data. Indicate the time-series components that exist in the data.

b. Conduct a test of hypothesis to determine if there exists a linear trend in this data. Use a significance level of 0.10 and the p-value approach.

c. Provide forecasts for the e-commerce retail sales for the next four quarters.

d. Presume the next four quarters exhibit e-commerce retail sales of 25,916, 26,432, 25,096, and 26,807, respectively. Produce the forecast bias. Interpret this number in the context of this exercise.

16.3 Forecasting Using Smoothing Methods

The trend-based forecasting technique introduced in the previous section is widely used and can be very effective in some situations. However, it has a disadvantage in that it gives as much weight to the earliest data in the time series as it does to the data that are close to the period for which the forecast is required. Also, this trend approach does not provide an opportunity for the model to "learn" or "adjust" to changes in the time series.

A class of forecasting techniques called *smoothing models* is widely used to overcome these problems and to provide forecasts in situations in which there is no pronounced trend in the data. These models attempt to "smooth out" the random or irregular component in the time series by an averaging process. In this section we introduce two frequently used smoothing-based forecasting techniques: single exponential smoothing and double exponential smoothing. Double exponential smoothing offers a modification to the single exponential smoothing model that specifically deals with trends.

CHAPTER OUTCOME #5

Exponential Smoothing

The trend-based forecasting methods discussed in Section 16.2 are used in many forecasting situations. As we showed, the least squares trend line is computed using all available historical data. Each observation is given equal input in establishing the trend line, thus allowing the trend line to reflect all the past data. If the future pattern looks like the past, the forecast should be reasonably accurate.

However, in many situations involving time-series data, the more recent the observation, the more indicative it is of possible future values. For example, this month's sales are probably a better indicator of next month's sales than would be sales from 20 months ago. However, the regression analysis approach to trend-based forecasting does not take this fact into account. The data from 20 periods ago will be given the same weight as data from the most current period in developing a forecasting model. This equal valuation can be a drawback to the trend-based forecasting approach.

Exponential Smoothing

A time-series and forecasting technique that produces an exponentially weighted moving average in which each smoothing calculation or forecast is dependent on all previous observed values.

With **exponential smoothing**, current observations can be weighted more heavily than older observations in determining the forecast. Therefore, if in recent periods the time-series values are much higher (or lower) than those in earlier periods, the forecast can be made to reflect this difference. The extent to which the forecast reflects the current data depends on the weights assigned by the decision maker.

We will introduce two classes of exponential smoothing models: single exponential smoothing and double exponential smoothing. Double smoothing is used when a time series exhibits a linear trend. Single smoothing is used when no linear trend is present in the time series. Both single and double exponential smoothing are appropriate for short-term forecasting and for time series that are not seasonal.

Single Exponential Smoothing Just as its name implies, single exponential smoothing uses a single smoothing constant. Equations 16.16 and 16.17 represent two equivalent methods for forecasting using single exponential smoothing.

Exponential Smoothing Model

$$F_{t+1} = F_t + \alpha(y_t - F_t) \tag{16.16}$$

or

$$F_{t+1} = \alpha y_t + (1 - \alpha)F_t \tag{16.17}$$

where:

$$F_{t+1} = \text{Forecast value for period } t + 1$$
$$y_t = \text{Actual value of the time-series at time } t$$
$$F_t = \text{Forecast value for period } t$$
$$\alpha = \text{Alpha (smoothing constant } 0 \leq \alpha \leq 1)$$

The logic of the exponential smoothing model is that the forecast made for the next period will equal the forecast made for the current period, plus or minus some adjustment factor. The adjustment factor is determined by how far this period's forecast is from the actual value $(y_t - F_t)$, times the smoothing constant, α. The idea is that if we forecast low, we will adjust next period's forecast upward, but not by the entire amount of the error.

Excel and Minitab Tutorial

TRY PROBLEM 16.34

EXAMPLE 16-6 Developing a Single Exponential Smoothing Model

Humbolt Electronics Company Consider the past 10 weeks of sales Figures for printed circuits at the Humbolt Electronics Company in Austin, Texas. These data and their line graph are shown in Figure 16.27. The data in thousands of units sold are in the CD-ROM file **Humbolt**. Suppose the current time period is the end of week 10 and we wish to forecast sales for week 11 using a single exponential smoothing model. The following steps can be used:

Step 1 Specify the model.
Because the data do not exhibit a pronounced trend and because we are interested in a short-term forecast (one period ahead), the single exponential smoothing model with a single smoothing constant can be used.

Step 2 Fit the model.
We start by selecting a value for α, the smoothing constant, between 0.0 and 1.0. The closer α is to 0.0, the less influence the current observations have in determining the forecast. Small α values will result in greater smoothing of the time series. Likewise, when α is near 1.0, the current observations have greater impact in determining the forecast and less smoothing will occur. There is no firm rule for selecting the value for the smoothing constant. However, in general, if the time series is quite stable, a small α should be used to lessen the impact of random or irregular fluctuations. Because the time series shown in Figure 16.27 appears to be relatively stable, we will use $\alpha = 0.20$ in this example.

The forecast value for period $t = 11$ is found using Equation 16.17, as follows:

$$F_{11} = 0.20y_{10} + (1 - 0.20)F_{10}$$

FIGURE 16.27

Printed-Circuit Sales Data and Line Graph for Humbolt Electronics

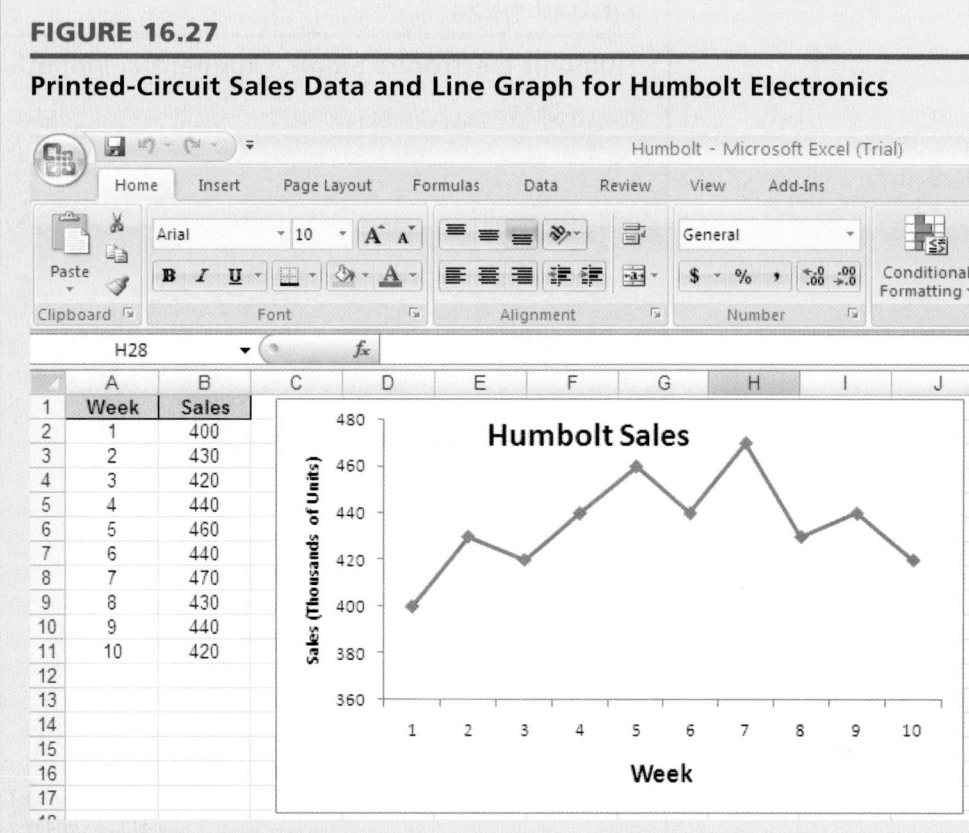

Excel 2007 Instructions:
1. Open data file: Humbolt.xls.
2. Select the Sales data.
3. Click on **Insert > Line**.
4. Click on **Layout**.
5. Use **Chart Titles** and **Axis Titles** to provide appropriate labels.

This demonstrates that the forecast for period 11 is a weighted average of the actual sales in period 10 and the forecast for period 10. Although we know the sales for period 10, we don't know the forecast for period 10. However, we can determine it by

$$F_{10} = 0.20y_9 + (1 - 0.20)F_9$$

Again, this forecast is a weighted average of the actual sales in period 9 and the forecast sales for period 9. We would continue in this manner until we get to

$$F_2 = 0.20y_1 + (1 - 0.20)F_1$$

This requires a forecast for period 1. Because we have no sales data before period 1 from which to develop a forecast, a rule often used is to assume that $F_1 = y_1$.[5]

Forecast for Period 1 = Actual Value in Period 1

Because setting the starting value is somewhat arbitrary, you should obtain as much historical data as possible to "warm" the model and dampen out

---

[5] Another approach for establishing the starting value, F_1, is to use the mean value for some portion of the available data. Regardless of the method used, the quantity of available data should be large enough to dampen out the impact of the starting value.

FIGURE 16.28

Humbolt Electronics Single Exponential Smoothing—Excel Spreadsheet

Minitab Instructions (for similar results):
1. Open file: Humboldt. MTW.
2. Choose **Stat > Time Series > Single Exp Smoothing**.
3. In **Variable**, enter time series column.
4. Under **Weight to use in smoothing**, select **Use** and insert α.
5. Click on **Storage** and select **Fits (one-period-ahead forecasts)**.
6. Click **OK. OK**.

Forecast for period 11 = 432.565 or 433 units

Excel 2007 Instructions:
1. Open data file: Humbolt.xls.
2. Create and label two new columns.
3. Enter the smoothing constant in an empty cell (e.g. B14).
4. Enter initial forecast for period 1 in C3 (400).
5. Use Equation 16.16 to create forecast for period $t + 1$ in D2.
6. Forecast for period t is set equal to forecast for period $t + 1$ from previous period.
7. Copy equations down.

the effect of the starting value. In our example, we have 10 periods of data to warm the model before the forecast for period 11 is made. Note that when using an exponential smoothing model, the effect of the initial forecast is reduced by $(1 - \alpha)$ in the forecast for period 2, then reduced again for period 3, and so on. After sufficient periods, any error due to the arbitrary initial forecast should be very small.

Figure 16.28 shows the results of using the single exponential smoothing equation and Excel for weeks 1 through 10. For week 1, $F_1 = y_1 = 400$. Then, for week 2, we get

$$F_2 = 0.20y_1 + (1 - 0.20)F_1$$
$$F_2 = (0.20)400 + (1 - 0.20)400.00 = 400.00$$

For week 3,

$$F_3 = 0.20y_2 + (1 - 0.20)F_2$$
$$F_3 = (0.20)430 + (1 - 0.20)400.00 = 406.00$$

At the end of week 2, after seeing what actually happened to sales in week 2, our forecasts for week 3 is 406 units. This is a 6-unit increase over the forecast for week 2 of 400 units. The actual amount of sales in week 2 was 430, rather than 400. The amount of sales for week 2 was 30 units higher than the forecast for that time period. Because the actual amount of sales was larger than the forecast, an adjustment must be made. The 6-unit adjustment is determined by multiplying the smoothing constant by the forecast error [0.20(30) = 6], as specified in Equation 16.16. The adjustment compensates for the forecast error in week 2.

Continuing for week 4 again using Equation 16.17,

$$F_4 = 0.20y_3 + (1 - 0.20)F_3$$
$$F_4 = (0.20)420 + (1 - 0.20)406.00 = 408.80$$

Recall that our forecast for week 3 was 406. However, actual sales were higher than forecast at 420 units, and we underforecast by 14 units. The adjustment for week 4 is then 0.20(14) = 2.80, and the forecast for week 4 is 406 + 2.80 = 408.80.

This process continues through the data until we are ready to forecast week 11, as shown in Figure 16.28.

$$F_{11} = 0.20y_{10} + (1 - 0.20)F_{10}$$
$$F_{11} = (0.20)420 + (1 - 0.20)435.70 = 432.56$$

Humbolt managers would forecast sales for week 11 of 432,560 units. If we wished to forecast week 12 sales, we would either use the week 11 forecast or wait until the actual week 11 sales are known and then update the smoothing equations to get a new forecast for week 12.

Step 3 **Diagnose the model.**

However, before we actually use the exponential smoothing forecast for decision-making purposes, we need to determine how successfully the model fits the historical data. Unlike the trend-based forecast, which uses least squares regression, there is no need to use split samples to test the forecasting ability of an exponential smoothing model, because the forecasts are "true forecasts." The forecast for a given period is made before considering the actual value for that period.

Figure 16.29 shows the *MAD* for the forecast model with $\alpha = 0.20$ and a plot of the forecast values versus the actual sales values. This plot shows the smoothing that has occurred. Note, we don't include period 1 in the *MAD* calculation since the forecast is set equal to the actual value.

Our next step would be to try different smoothing constants and find the *MAD* for each new α. The forecast for period 11 would be made using the smoothing constant that generates the smallest *MAD*.

Both Excel and Minitab have single exponential smoothing procedures, although Minitab's procedure is much more extensive. Refer to the Excel and Minitab tutorials on the CD-ROM for instructions on each. Minitab provides optional methods for determining the initial forecast value for period 1 and a variety of useful graphs. Minitab also has an option for determining the optimal smoothing constant value.[6] Figure 16.30 shows the output generated using Minitab. This shows that the best forecast is found using an $\alpha = 0.524$. Note, *MAD* is decreased from 20.86 (when $\alpha = 0.20$) to 17.321 when the optimal smoothing constant is used.

---

[6] The solver in Excel can be used to determine the optimal alpha level to minimize the *MAD*.

FIGURE 16.29

Excel 2007 Output for Humbolt Electronics *MAD* Computation for Single Exponential Smoothing, $\alpha = 0.20$

Excel 2007 Instructions:
1. Open data file: Humbolt.xls.
2. Select the sales data.
3. Click on **Insert > Line**.
4. Click on **Layout**.
5. Use **Chart Titles** and **Axis Titles** to provide appropriate labels.
6. Follow directions for Figure 16.28.

7. Select the Forecast values (F_t) and copy and paste onto the line chart.
8. Create a column of forecast errors using an Excel equation.
9. Create a column of absolute forecast errors using Excel's **ABS** function.
10. Compute the MAD by using the **AVERGE** function for the absolute errors.

FIGURE 16.30

Minitab Output for Humbolt Electronics Single Exponential Smoothing Model

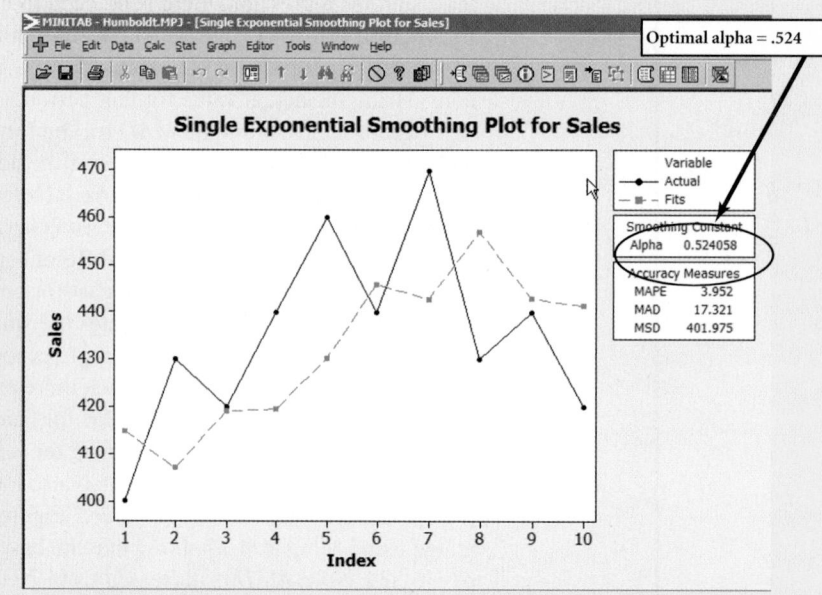

Minitab Instructions:
1. Open file: Humboldt.MTW.
2. Choose **Stat > Time Series > Single Exp Smoothing**.
3. In **Variable**, enter time series column.

4. Under **Weight to Use in Smoothing,** select **Optimal ARIMA**.
5. Click **OK**.

A major advantage of the single exponential smoothing model is that it is easy to update. In Example 16-6, the forecast for week 12 using this model is found by simply plugging the actual sales value in week 11, once it is known, into the smoothing formula.

$$F_{12} = \alpha y_{11} + (1 - \alpha)F_{11}$$

We do not need to go back and recompute the entire model, as would have been necessary with a trend-based regression model.

CHAPTER OUTCOME #5

Double Exponential Smoothing When the time series has an increasing or decreasing trend, a modification to the single exponential smoothing model is used to explicitly account for the trend. The resulting technique is called *double exponential smoothing*. The double exponential smoothing model is often referred to as *exponential smoothing with trend*. In double exponential smoothing, a second smoothing constant, beta (β), is included to account for the trend. Equations 16.18, 16.19, and 16.20 are needed to provide the forecasts.

Double Exponential Smoothing Model

$$C_t = \alpha y_t + (1 - \alpha)(C_{t-1} + T_{t-1}) \qquad (16.18)$$

$$T_t = \beta (C_t - C_{t-1}) + (1 - \beta)T_{t-1} \qquad (16.19)$$

$$F_{t+1} = C_t + T_t \qquad (16.20)$$

where:

y_t = Value of the time-series at time t
α = Constant-process smoothing constant
β = Trend-smoothing constant
C_t = Smoothed constant-process value for period t
T_t = Smoothed trend value for period t
F_{t+1} = Forecast value for period $t + 1$
t = Current time period

Equation 16.18 is used to smooth the time-series data; Equation 16.19 is used to smooth the trend; and Equation 16.20 combines the two smoothed values to form the forecast for period $t + 1$.

EXAMPLE 16-7 Double Exponential Smoothing

Excel and Minitab Tutorial

TRY PROBLEM 16.39

Billingsley Insurance Company The Billingsley Insurance Company has maintained data on the number of automobile claims filed at its Denver office over the past 12 months. These data, which are in the CD-ROM file **Billingsley**, are listed and graphed in Figure 16.31. The claims manager wants to forecast claims for month 13. A double exponential smoothing model can be developed using the following steps:

Step 1 Specify the model.
The time series contains a strong upward trend, so a double exponential smoothing model might be selected.

As was the case with single exponential smoothing, we must select starting values. In the case of the double exponential smoothing model, we must select initial values for C_0, T_0, and the smoothing constants α and β. The choice of smoothing constant values (α and β) depends on the same issues as those discussed earlier for single exponential smoothing. That is, use larger smoothing constants when less smoothing is desired and values closer to 0 when more smoothing is desired. The larger the smoothing

FIGURE 16.31

Excel 2007 Billingsley Insurance Company Data and Time-Series Plot

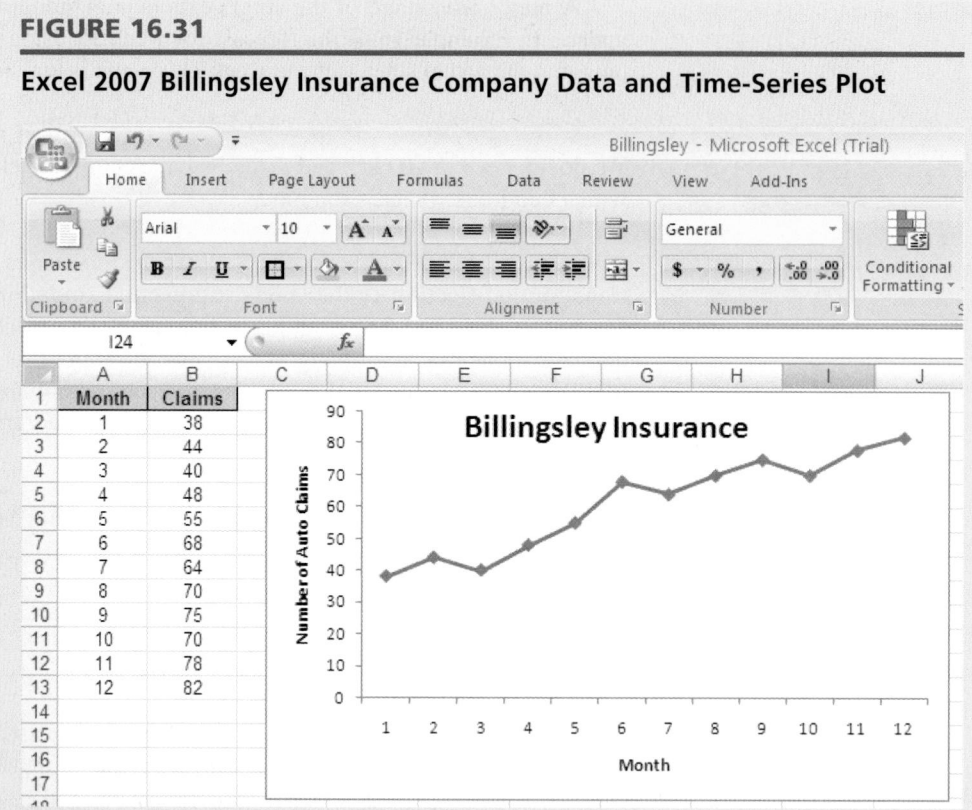

Excel 2007 Instructions:
1. Open file: Billingsly.xls.
2. Select Claims data.
3. Click on **Insert > Line Chart**.

4. Click on **Layout > Chart Title** and enter desired title.
5. Click on **Layout > Axis Titles** and enter horizontal and vertical axes titles.

constant value, the more impact that current data will have on the forecast. Suppose we use $\alpha = 0.20$ and $\beta = 0.30$ in this example. There are several approaches for selecting starting values for C_0 and T_0. The method we use here is to fit the least squares trend to the historical data,

$$\hat{y}_t = b_0 + b_1 t$$

where the y intercept, b_0, is used as the starting value, C_0, and the slope, b_1, is used as the starting value for the trend, T_0. We can use the regression procedure in Excel or Minitab to perform these calculations, giving

$$\hat{y}_t = 34.273 + 4.1119(t)$$

So,

$$C_0 = 34.273 \quad \text{and} \quad T_0 = 4.1119$$

Keep in mind that these are arbitrary starting values and, as with single exponential smoothing, their effect will be dampened out as you proceed through the sample data to the current period. The more historical data you have, the less impact the starting values will have in the forecast.

Step 2 **Fit the model.**

The forecast for period 1 made at the beginning of period 1 is

$$F_1 = C_0 + T_0$$
$$F_1 = 34.273 + 4.1119 = 38.385$$

At the close of period 1, in which actual claims were 38, the smoothing equations are updated as follows.

$$C_1 = 0.20(38) + (1 - 0.20)(34.273 + 4.1119) = 38.308$$
$$T_1 = 0.30(38.308 - 34.273) + (1 - 0.30)(4.1119) = 4.089$$

FIGURE 16.32

Excel 2007 Double Exponential Smoothing Spreadsheet for Billingsley Insurance

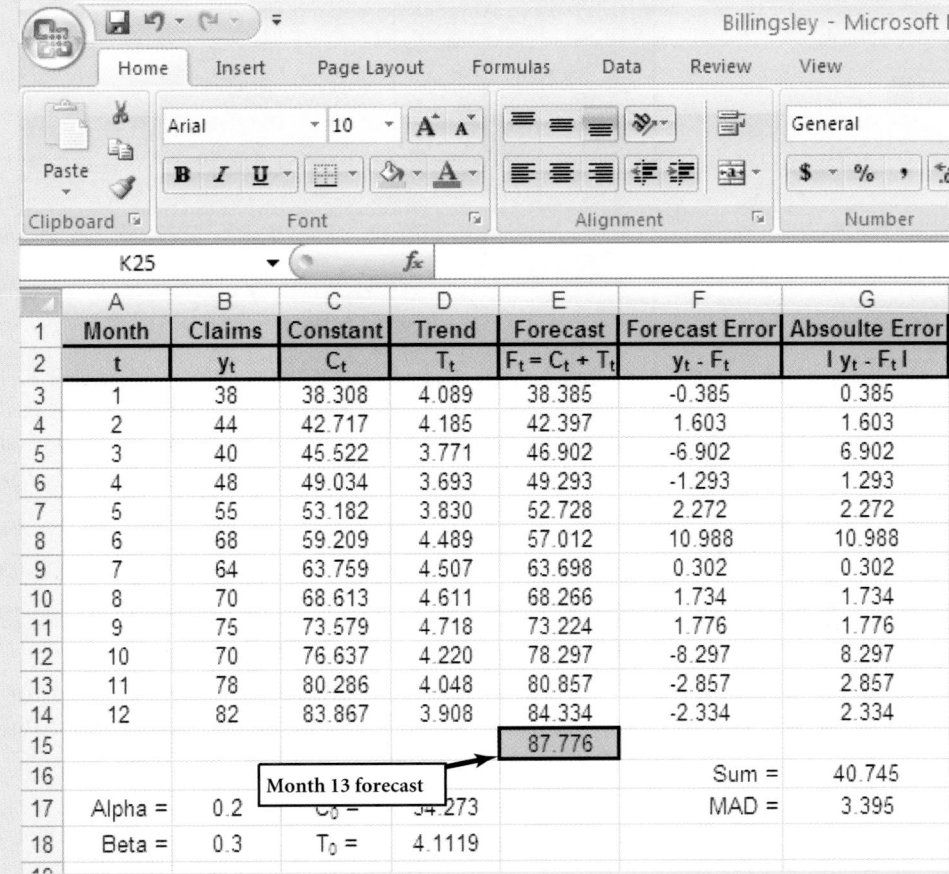

	A	B	C	D	E	F	G
1	Month	Claims	Constant	Trend	Forecast	Forecast Error	Absoulte Error
2	t	y_t	C_t	T_t	$F_t = C_t + T_t$	$y_t - F_t$	$\mid y_t - F_t \mid$
3	1	38	38.308	4.089	38.385	-0.385	0.385
4	2	44	42.717	4.185	42.397	1.603	1.603
5	3	40	45.522	3.771	46.902	-6.902	6.902
6	4	48	49.034	3.693	49.293	-1.293	1.293
7	5	55	53.182	3.830	52.728	2.272	2.272
8	6	68	59.209	4.489	57.012	10.988	10.988
9	7	64	63.759	4.507	63.698	0.302	0.302
10	8	70	68.613	4.611	68.266	1.734	1.734
11	9	75	73.579	4.718	73.224	1.776	1.776
12	10	70	76.637	4.220	78.297	-8.297	8.297
13	11	78	80.286	4.048	80.857	-2.857	2.857
14	12	82	83.867	3.908	84.334	-2.334	2.334
15					87.776		
16				Month 13 forecast		Sum =	40.745
17	Alpha =	0.2	$C_0 =$	34.273		MAD =	3.395
18	Beta =	0.3	$T_0 =$	4.1119			

Excel 2007 Instructions:

1. Open File: Billingsley.xls.
2. Create five new column headings as shown in Figure 16.32.
3. Place the smoothing constants (alpha and beta) in empty cells (B17 and B18).
4. Place the starting values for the constant process and the trend in empty cells (D17 and D18).
5. Use Equations 16.18 and 16.19 to create process columns.
6. Use Equation 16.19 to create the forecast values in the forecast column.
7. Calculate the forecast error by subtracting the forecast column values from the *y* column values.
8. Calculate the absolute forecast errors using the Excel **ABS** function.
9. Calculate the *MAD* by using the Excel **AVERAGE** function.

FIGURE 16.33

Minitab Double Exponential Smoothing Spreadsheet for Billingsley Insurance

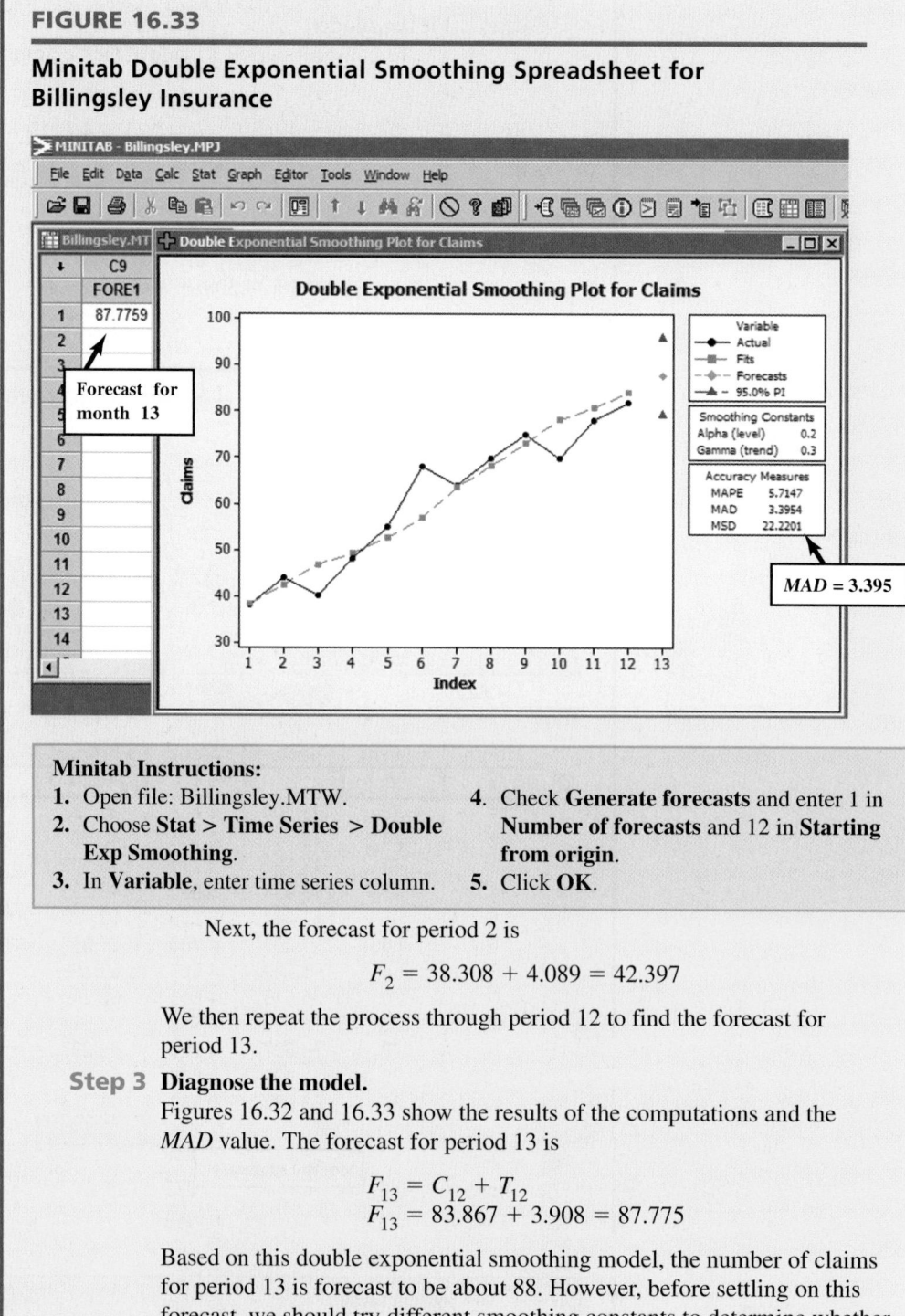

Minitab Instructions:
1. Open file: Billingsley.MTW.
2. Choose **Stat > Time Series > Double Exp Smoothing**.
3. In **Variable**, enter time series column.
4. Check **Generate forecasts** and enter 1 in **Number of forecasts** and 12 in **Starting from origin**.
5. Click **OK**.

Next, the forecast for period 2 is

$$F_2 = 38.308 + 4.089 = 42.397$$

We then repeat the process through period 12 to find the forecast for period 13.

Step 3 **Diagnose the model.**

Figures 16.32 and 16.33 show the results of the computations and the *MAD* value. The forecast for period 13 is

$$F_{13} = C_{12} + T_{12}$$
$$F_{13} = 83.867 + 3.908 = 87.775$$

Based on this double exponential smoothing model, the number of claims for period 13 is forecast to be about 88. However, before settling on this forecast, we should try different smoothing constants to determine whether a smaller *MAD* can be found.

As you can see, the computations required for double exponential smoothing are somewhat tedious and are ideally suited for your computer. Although Excel does not have a double exponential smoothing procedure, in Figure 16.32 we have used Excel formulas to develop our model in conjunction with the regression tool for determining the starting values. Minitab does have a double exponential smoothing routine, as illustrated in Figure 16.33.

The *MAPE* on the Minitab output is the *Mean Absolute Percent Error*, which is computed using Equation 16.21. The *MAPE* = 5.7147, indicating that on average, the double exponential smoothing model produced a forecast that differed from the actual claims by 5.7%.

Mean Absolute Percent Error

$$MAPE = \dfrac{\sum \dfrac{|y_t - F_t|}{y_t}(100)}{n} \qquad (16.21)$$

where:

y_t = Value of time series in time t
F_t = Forecast value for time period t
n = Number of periods of available data

16-3: Exercises

Skill Development

16-34. The following data represents two years of data:

Year 1		Year 2	
1st quarter	242	1st quarter	272
2nd quarter	252	2nd quarter	267
3rd quarter	257	3rd quarter	276
4th quarter	267	4th quarter	281

a. Prepare a single exponential smoothing forecast for the first quarter of year 3 using an alpha value of 0.10. Let the initial forecast value for quarter 1 of year 1 be 250.
b. Prepare a single exponential smoothing forecast for the first quarter of year 3 using an alpha value of 0.25. Let the initial forecast value for quarter 1 of year 1 be 250.
c. Calculate the *MAD* value for the forecasts you generated in parts a and b. Which alpha value provides the smaller *MAD* value at the end of the 4th quarter in year 2?

16-35. The following data represents enrollment in a major at your university for the past six semesters (*note*: semester 1 is the oldest data; semester 6 is the most recent data):

Semester	Enrollment
1	87
2	110
3	123
4	127
5	145
6	160

a. Prepare a graph of enrollment for the six semesters.
b. Based on the graph you prepared in part a, does it appear that a trend is present in the enrollment figures?
c. Prepare a single exponential smoothing forecast for semester 7 using an alpha value of 0.35. Assume that the initial forecast for semester 1 is 90.
d. Prepare a double exponential smoothing forecast for semester 7 using an alpha value of 0.20 and a beta value of 0.25. Assume that the initial smoothed constant value for semester 1 is 80 and the initial smoothed trend value for semester 1 is 10.
e. Calculate the *MAD* value for the simple exponential smoothing model at the end of semester 6 and the *MAD* value for the double exponential smoothing model at the end of semester 6. Which model appears to be doing the better job of forecasting course enrollment? Don't include period 1 in the calculation.

16-36. The following data represents the average number of employees in outlets of a large consumer electronics retailer:

Year	1998	1999	2000	2001	2002	2003	2004	2005	2006	2007
Number	20.6	17.3	18.6	21.5	23.2	19.9	18.7	15.6	19.7	20.4

a. Construct a time-series plot of this time series. Does it appear that a linear trend exists in the time series?
b. Calculate forecasts for each of the years in the time series. Use a smoothing constant of 0.25 and single exponential smoothing.

c. Calculate the *MAD* value for the forecasts you generated in part b.

d. Construct a single exponential smoothing forecast for 2008. Use a smoothing constant of 0.25.

16-37. A brokerage company is interested in forecasting the number of new accounts the office will obtain next month. It has collected the following data for the past 12 months:

Month	Accounts
1	19
2	20
3	21
4	25
5	26
6	24
7	24
8	21
9	27
10	30
11	24
12	30

a. Produce a time-series plot for this data. Specify the exponential forecasting model that should be used to obtain next month's forecast.

b. Assuming a double exponential smoothing model, fit the least squares trend to the historical data, to determine the smoothed constant-process value and the smoothed trend value for period 0.

c. Produce the forecasts for periods 1 through 12 using $\alpha = 0.15$, $\beta = 0.25$. Indicate the number of new accounts the company may expect to receive next month based upon the forecast model.

d. Calculate the *MAD* for this model.

Business Applications

16-38. The fleet manager for a regional sales office is trying to estimate the dollar expenditure for gasoline for next period. The past six months of gasoline expenditures are shown here.

Month	Gasoline Expenditures ($)
April	23,586.41
May	23,539.22
June	23,442.06
July	23,988.71
August	23,727.13
September	23,799.69

Using this past history, prepare a single exponential smoothing forecast for October using an α value of 0.25.

16-39. The human resource manager for a medium-sized business is interested in predicting the dollar value of medical expenditures filed by employees of her company for the year 2007. From her company's database she has collected the following information showing the dollar value of medical expenditures made by employees for the previous seven years:

Year	Medical Claims
2000	$405,642.43
2001	$407,180.60
2002	$408,203.30
2003	$410,088.03
2004	$411,085.64
2005	$412,200.39
2006	$414,043.90

a. Prepare a graph of medical expenditures for the years 2000–2006. Which forecasting technique do you think is most appropriate for this time series, single exponential smoothing or double exponential smoothing? Why?

b. Use an α value of 0.25 and a β value of 0.15 to produce a double exponential forecast for the medical claims data. Use linear trend analysis to obtain the starting values for C_0 and T_0.

c. Compute the *MAD* value for your model for the years 2000 to 2006. Also produce a graph of your forecast values.

16-40. "The average college senior graduated this year with more than $19,000 in debt" was the beginning sentence of an article in *USA Today* (Sandra Block, "In Debt Before You Start," June 13, 2006). The majority of students have loans that are not due until the student leaves school. This can result in the student ignoring the size of debt that piles up. Federal loans obtained to finance college education are steadily mounting. The data given here shows the amount of loans ($million) from the academic years 1985–86 to 2004–05.

Year	Amount	Year	Amount	Year	Amount
1985–86	9,914	1992–93	16,221	1999–2000	37,228
1986–87	10,182	1993–94	22,557	2000–2001	39,101
1987–88	12,493	1994–95	26,011	2001–2002	42,761
1988–89	13,195	1995–96	28,737	2002–2003	49,360
1989–90	13,414	1996–97	31,906	2003–2004	57,463
1990–91	13,890	1997–98	33,930	2004–2005	62,614
1991–92	15,232	1998–99	34,376		

a. Produce a time-series plot for these data. Specify the exponential forecasting model that should be used to obtain next year's forecast.

b. Assuming a double exponential smoothing model, fit the least squares trend to the historical data to determine the smoothed constant-process value and the smoothed trend value for period 0.

c. Using data for periods 1 through 20 and using $\alpha = 0.20$, $\beta = 0.30$ forecast the total student loan volume for the year 2005–06.

d. Calculate the *MAD* for this model.

16-41. Retail Forward, Inc. is a global management consulting and market research firm specializing in retail intelligence and strategies. One of its press releases ("June Consumer Outlook: Spending Plans Show Resilience," June 1, 2006) divulged the result of The Retail Forward ShopperScape™ survey conducted each month from a sample of 4,000 U.S. primary household shoppers. A measure of consumer spending is represented by the following figure:

a. Construct a time-series plot of these data. Does it appear that a linear trend exists in the time series?

b. Calculate forecasts for each of the months in the time series. Use a smoothing constant of 0.25

c. Calculate the *MAD* value for the forecasts you generated in part b.

d. Construct a single exponential smoothing forecast for July 2006. Use a smoothing constant of 0.25.

Computer Database Exercises

16-42. The National Association of Theatre Owners is the largest exhibition trade organization in the world, representing more than 26,000 movie screens in all 50 states and in more than 20 countries worldwide. Its membership includes the largest cinema chains and hundreds of independent theatre owners. It publishes statistics concerning the movie sector of the economy. The file entitled **Flicks** contains data on average U.S. ticket prices ($). One concern is the rapidly increasing price of tickets.

a. Produce a time-series plot for these data. Specify the exponential forecasting model that should be used to obtain next year's forecast.

b. Assuming a double exponential smoothing model, fit the least squares trend to the historical data to determine the smoothed constant-process value and the smoothed trend value for period 0.

c. Using $\alpha = 0.20$, $\beta = 0.30$. Now forecast the average yearly ticket price for the year 2010.

d. Calculate the *MAD* for this model.

16-43. Inflation is a fall in the market value or purchasing power of money. Measurements of inflation are prepared and published by the Bureau of Labor Statistics of the Department of Labor, which measures average changes in prices of goods and services. The file entitled **CPI** contains the monthly CPI and inflation rate for the period January 2000–December 2005.

a. Construct a plot of this time series. Does it appear that a linear trend exists in the time series? Specify the exponential forecasting model that should be used to obtain next month's forecast.

b. Assuming a single exponential smoothing model, calculate forecasts for each of the months in the time series. Use a smoothing constant of 0.15.

c. Calculate the *MAD* value for the forecasts you generated in part b.

d. Construct a single exponential smoothing forecast for January 2006. Use a smoothing constant of 0.15.

16-44. The sales manager at Grossmieller Importers in New York City needs to determine a monthly forecast for the number of men's golf sweaters that will be sold so that he can order an appropriate amount of packing boxes. Grossmieller ships sweaters to retail stores throughout the United States and

Canada. Shirts are packed six to a box. Data for the past 12 months is contained in the data file called **Grossmieller**.

a. Plot the sales data using a time-series plot. Based on the graph, what time series components are present? Discuss.

b. (1) Use a single exponential smoothing model with $\alpha = 0.30$ to forecast sales for month 17. Assume that the initial forecast for period 1 is 36,000. (2) Compute the *MAD* for this model. (3) Graph the smoothing-model-fitted values on the time-series plot.

c. (1) Referring to part b, try different alpha levels to determine which smoothing constant value you would recommend. (2) Indicate why you have selected this value and then develop the forecast for month 17. (3) Compare this to the forecast you got using $\alpha = 0.30$ in part b.

16-45. Referring to Problem 16-44, in which the sales manager for Grossmieller Imports of New York City needs to forecast monthly sales,

a. Discuss why a double exponential smoothing model might be preferred over a single exponential smoothing model.

b. (1) Develop a double exponential smoothing model using $\alpha = 0.20$ and $\beta = 0.30$ as smoothing constants. To obtain the starting values, use the regression trend line approach discussed in this section. (2) Determine the forecast for month 17. (3) Also compute the *MAD* for this model. (4) Graph the fitted values on the time-series graph.

c. Compare the results for this double exponential smoothing model with the "best" single exponential smoothing model developed in part c of Exercise 16-44. Discuss which model is preferred.

d. Referring to part b, try different alpha and beta values in an attempt to determine an improved forecast model for monthly sales. For each model, show the forecast for period 17 and the *MAD*. Write a short report that compares the different models.

e. Referring to part d and to part c for Exercise 16-44, write a report to the Grossmieller sales manager that indicates your choice for the forecasting model, complete with your justification for the selection.

Summary and Conclusions

In this chapter, we have introduced the basics of time-series analysis and forecasting. Although we have included a variety of forecasting techniques, the discussion here does not cover the entire topic of forecasting. The subject of forecasting and time-series analysis could easily require one or more semester-long courses. Our objective has been to provide insight into some of the more frequently used techniques and to acquaint you with the basic terminology of forecasting and time-series analysis.

Quantitative forecasting techniques require historical data for the variable to be forecasted. The success of a quantitative model is determined by two factors:

1. how well the model fits the historical time-series data
2. how closely the future resembles the past

Ultimately, the best forecasting method is the one that provides the most accurate forecasts.

You will find that the techniques introduced in this chapter are used frequently as an initial basis for a forecast. However, in most cases, the decision maker will modify the forecast based on personal judgment and other qualitative inputs that are not considered by the quantitative model. Thus, forecasting is as much an art as it is a science. The more experience you have in a given situation, the more effective you likely will be at identifying and applying the appropriate foreacasting tool.

Equations

Simple Index Number

$$I_t = \frac{y_t}{y_0} 100 \qquad (16.1)$$

Unweighted Aggregate Price Index

$$I_t = \frac{\Sigma p_t}{\Sigma p_0}(100) \qquad (16.2)$$

The Paasche Index

$$I_t = \frac{\Sigma q_t p_t}{\Sigma q_t p_0}(100) \qquad (16.3)$$

Laspeyres Index

$$I_t = \frac{\Sigma q_0 p_t}{\Sigma q_0 p_0}(100) \qquad (16.4)$$

Deflation Formula

$$y_{adj_t} = \frac{y_t}{I_t}(100) \qquad (16.5)$$

Linear Trend Model

$$y_t = \beta_0 + \beta_1 t + \varepsilon_t \qquad (16.6)$$

Least Squares Equations Estimates

$$b_1 = \frac{\sum ty_t - \dfrac{\sum t \sum y_t}{n}}{\sum t^2 - \dfrac{(\sum t)^2}{n}} \qquad (16.7)$$

$$b_0 = \frac{\sum y_t}{n} - b_1 \frac{\sum t}{n} \qquad (16.8)$$

Mean Squared Error

$$MSE = \frac{\sum (y_t - F_t)^2}{n} \qquad (16.9)$$

Mean Absolute Deviation

$$MAD = \frac{\sum |y_t - F_t|}{n} \qquad (16.10)$$

Durbin-Watson Statistic

$$d = \frac{\sum_{t=2}^{n} (e_t - e_{t-1})^2}{\sum_{t=1}^{n} e_t^2} \qquad (16.11)$$

Forecast Bias

$$\text{Forecast Bias} = \frac{\sum (y_t - F_t)}{n} \qquad (16.12)$$

Mulitplicative Time-Series Model

$$y_t = T_t \times S_t \times C_t \times I_t \qquad (16.13)$$

Ratio-to-Moving-Average

$$S_t \times I_t = \frac{y_t}{T_t \times C_t} \qquad (16.14)$$

Deseasonalization

$$T_t \times C_t \times I_t = \frac{y_t}{S_t} \qquad (16.15)$$

Exponential Smoothing Model

$$F_{t+1} = F_t + \alpha(y_t - F_t) \qquad (16.16)$$

or

$$F_{t+1} = \alpha y_t + (1 - \alpha)F_t \qquad (16.17)$$

Double Exponential Smoothing Model

$$C_t = \alpha y_t + (1 - \alpha)(C_{t-1} + T_{t-1}) \qquad (16.18)$$

$$T_t = \beta(C_t - C_{t-1}) + (1 - \beta)T_{t-1} \qquad (16.20)$$

$$F_{t+1} = C_t + T_t \qquad (16.20)$$

Mean Absolute Percent Error

$$MAPE = \frac{\sum \dfrac{|y_t - F_t|}{y_t}(100)}{n} \qquad (16.21)$$

Key Terms

Aggregate price index   764
Autocorrelation   777
Base period index   762
Cyclical component   761
Exponential smoothing   799
Forecasting horizon   759

Forecasting interval   759
Forecasting period   759
Linear trend   760
Model diagnosis   758
Model fitting   758
Model specification   758

Moving averages   788
Random component   762
Seasonal component   760
Seasonal index   787
Seasonally unadjusted forecast   791

Chapter Exercises

Conceptual Questions

16-46. Identify these businesses in your community that might be expected to have sales that exhibit a seasonal component. Discuss.

16-47. Discuss the difference between a cyclical component and a seasonal component. Which component is more predictable, seasonal or cyclical? Discuss and illustrate with examples.

16-48. Go to the library or use the Internet to find data showing your state's population for the past 20 years. Plot these data and indicate which of the time-series components are present.

16-49. A time series exhibits the pattern stated below. Indicate the type of time-series component described.

a. The pattern is "wavelike" with a recurrence period of nine months.

b. The time series is steadily increasing.

c. The pattern is "wavelike" with a recurrence period of two years.

d. The pattern is unpredictable.

e. The pattern steadily decreases, with a "wave-like" shape which reoccurs every 10 years.

16-50. In the simple linear regression model, confidence and prediction intervals are utilized to provide interval estimates for an average and a particular value, respectively, of the dependent variable. The linear trend model in time series is an application of simple linear regression. This being said, discuss whether a confidence or a prediction interval is the relevant interval estimate for a linear trend model's forecast.

Business Applications

Problems 16-51 through 16-54 refer to Malcar Autoparts Company, which has started producing replacement control microcomputers for automobiles. This has been a growth industry since the first control units were introduced in 1985. Sales data since the control unit was introduced are as follows:

Year	Sales
1991	$240,000
1992	218,000
1993	405,000
1994	587,000
1995	795,000
1996	762,000
1997	998,000
1998	1,217,000
1999	1,570,000
2000	1,947,000
2001	2,711,000
2002	3,104,000
2003	2,918,000
2004	4,606,000
2005	5,216,000
2006	5,010,000

16-51. As a start in analyzing these data,

a. Graph these data and indicate whether they appear to have a linear trend.

b. Develop a simple linear regression model with time as the independent variable. Using this regression model, describe the trend and the strength of the linear trend over the 16 years. Is the trend line statistically significant? Plot the trend line against the actual data.

c. Compute the *MAD* value for this model.

d. Provide the Malcar Autoparts Company an estimate of its expected sales for the next 5 years.

e. Provide the maximum and minimum sales Malcar can expect with 90% confidence for the year 2011.

16-52. Develop a single exponential smoothing model using $\alpha = 0.20$. Use as a starting value the average of the first 6 years' data. Determine the forecasted value for year 2007.

a. Compute the *MAD* for this model.

b. Plot the forecast values against the actual data.

c. Use the same starting value but try different smoothing constants (say, 0.05, 0.10, 0.25, and 0.30) in an effort to reduce the *MAD* value.

d. Is it possible to answer part d of Problem 16.51 for this forecasting technique? Explain your answer.

16-53. Develop a double exponential smoothing model using smoothing constants $\alpha = 0.20$ and $\beta = 0.40$. As starting values, use the least squares trend line slope and intercept values.

a. Compute the *MAD* for this model.

b. Plot the forecast values against the actual data.

c. Use the same starting values but try different smoothing constants [say, $(\alpha, \beta) = (0.10, 0.50)$, $(0.30, 0.30)$, and $(0.40, 0.20)$] in an effort to reduce the *MAD* value.

16-54. Using whatever diagnostic tools you are familiar with, determine which of the three forecasting methods utilized to forecast sales for Malcar Autoparts Company in the previous three problems provides superior forecasts. Explain the reasons for your choice.

16-55. Amazon.com has become one of the most successful online merchants. One measure of its success is sales. In an article entitled "Amazon CEO takes long view," *USA Today* (Byron Acohido, July 6, 2005) presented sales Figures (in $million) for the period 1995 to 2004. They are given here.

Year	1995	1996	1997	1998	1999
Sales	0.5	15.7	147.7	609.8	1,639.8
Year	2000	2001	2002	2003	2004
Sales	2,761.9	3,122.9	3,932.9	5,263.7	6,921.1

a. Produce a time-series plot for these data. Specify the exponential forecasting model that should be used to obtain the following years' forecasts.

b. Assuming a double exponential smoothing model, fit the least squares trend to the historical data to determine the smoothed constant-process value and the smoothed trend value for period 0.

c. Produce the forecasts for periods 1 through 10 using $\alpha = 0.10$, $\beta = 0.20$. Indicate the sales Amazon should expect for 2005 based on the forecast model.

d. Calculate the *MAD* for this model.

16-56. College tuition has risen at a pace faster than inflation for more than two decades according to an article in *USA Today* (Andriene Lewis, "Tuition outstrips inflation," January 5, 2004). The following data indicate the average college tuition (in 2003 dollars) for public colleges:

Period	1983–1984	1988–1989	1993–1994	1998–1999	2003–2004
Public	$2,074	$2,395	$3,188	$3,632	$4,694

a. Produce a time-series plot of these data. Indicate the time-series components that exist in the data.

b. Provide a forecast for the average tuition for public colleges in the academic year 2013–14. (*Hint*: One time-series time period represents five academic years.)

c. Provide an interval of plausible values for the average tuition change after five academic periods have gone by. Use a confidence level of 0.90.

Computer Database Exercises

16-57. DataNet is an Internet service where clients can find information and purchase various items such as airline tickets, stereo equipment, and listed stocks. DataNet has been in operation for four years. Data on monthly calls for service for the time that the company has been in business are in the data file called **DataNet**.

a. Plot these data in a times-series graph. Based on the graph, what time-series components are present in the data?

b. Develop the seasonal indexes for each month. Describe what the seasonal index for August means.

c. Fit a linear trend model to the deseasonalized data for months 1–48 and determine the *MAD* value. Comment on the adequacy of the linear trend model based on these measures of forecast error.

d. Provide a seasonally unadjusted forecast using the linear trend model for each month of the year.

e. Use the seasonal index values computed in part b to provide seasonal adjusted forecasts for months 49–52.

16-58. Referring to Problem 16-57, the mangers of DataNet, the Internet company where users can purchase products like airline tickets, need to forecast monthly call volumes in order to have sufficient capacity. Develop a single exponential smoothing model using $\alpha = 0.30$. Use as a starting value the average of the first six months' data.

a. Compute the *MAD* for this model.

b. Plot the forecast values against the actual data.

c. Use the same starting value but try different smoothing constants (say, 0.10, 0.20, 0.40, and 0.50) in an effort to reduce the *MAD* value.

d. Reflect on the type of time series for which the single exponential smoothing model is designed to provide forecasts. Does it surprise you that

the *MAD* for this method is relatively large for these data? Explain your reasoning.

16-59. Continuing with the DataNet forecasting problems, develop a double exponential smoothing model using smoothing constants $\alpha = 0.20$ and $\beta = 0.20$. As starting values, use the least squares trend line slope and intercept values.

a. Compute the *MAD* for this model.

b. Plot the forecast values against the actual data.

c. Compare this with a linear trend model. Which forecast method would you use? Explain your rationale.

d. Use the same starting values but try different smoothing constants [say, $(\alpha, \beta) = (0.10, 0.30)$, $(0.15, 0.25)$, and $(0.30, 0.10)$] in an effort to reduce the *MAD* value. Prepare a short report that summarizes your efforts.

16-60. HSH® Associates, financial publishers, is the nation's largest publisher of mortgage and consumer loan information. Every week it collects current data from 2,000 mortgage lenders from across the nation. It tracks a variety of adjustable rate mortgage (ARM) indexes and makes them available on its Web site. The file entitled **ARM** contains the national monthly average one-year ARM for the time period January 2004 to June 2006.

a. Produce a scatter plot of the federal ARM for the time period January 2004 to June 2006. Identify any time-series components that exist in the data.

b. Identify the recurrence period of the time series. Determine the seasonal index for each month within the recurrence period.

c. Fit a nonlinear trend model containing coded years and coded years squared as predictors for the deseasonalized data.

d. Provide a seasonally adjusted forecast using the nonlinear trend model for July 2006.

e. Diagnose the model.

16-61. In a press release entitled "College Board Offers Glimpse of New SAT with Writing for Upcoming Class of '06" (August 30, 2005), the College Board announced SAT scores for students in the class of 2005, the last to take the former version of the SAT featuring math and verbal sections. The board indicated that for the class of 2005, the average SAT math scores continued their strong upward trend, increasing from 518 in 2004 to 520 in 2005, 14 points above 10 years ago and an all-time high. The file entitled **MathSAT** contains the math SAT scores for the interval 1967 to 2005.

a. Produce a time-series plot for the combined gender math SAT scores for the period 1980 to 2005. Indicate the time-series components that exist in the data.

b. Conduct a test of hypothesis to determine if the average SAT math scores of students continued to increase in the period indicated in part a. Use a significance level of 0.10 and the test statistic approach.

c. Produce a forecast for the average SAT math scores for 2010.

d. Beginning with the March 12, 2005 administration of the exam, the SAT Reasoning Test was modified and lengthened. How does this affect the forecast produced in part c? What statistical concept is exhibited by producing the forecast in part c?

VIDEO CASE 2

Restaurant Location & Re-imaging Decisions @ McDonald's

In the early days of his restaurant company's growth, McDonald's founder Ray Kroc knew that finding the right location was key. He had a keen eye for prime real estate locations. Today, the company is more than 30,000 restaurants strong. When it comes to picking prime real estate locations for its restaurants and making the most of them, McDonald's is way ahead of the competition. In fact, when it comes to global real estate holdings, no corporate entity holds more.

From urban office and airport locations, to Wal-Mart stores and the busiest street corner in your town, McDonald's has grown to become one of the world's most recognized brands. Getting there hasn't been just a matter of buying all available real estate on the market. Instead, the company has used the basic principles and process Ray Kroc believed in to investigate and secure the best possible sites for its restaurants. Factors such as neighborhood demographics, traffic patterns, competitor proximity, workforce, and retail shopping center locations all play a role.

Many of the company's restaurant locations have been in operation for decades. And while the restaurants have adapted to changing times, including diet fads and reporting nutrition information, staff uniform updates and menu innovations such as Happy Meals, Chicken McNuggets and premium salads – there's more to bringing customers back time and again than an updated menu and a good location. Those same factors that played a role in the original location decision need to be periodically examined to learn what's changed, and as a result, what changes the local McDonald's needs to consider.

Beginning in 2003, McDonald's started work on "reimaging" its existing restaurants while continuing to expand the brand globally. More than 6,000 restaurants have been re-imaged to date. Sophia Galassi, Vice President US Restaurant Development is responsible for the new look nationwide. According to Sophia, reimaging is more than new landscaping and paint. In some cases, the entire store is torn down and rebuilt with redesigned drive-thru lanes to speed customers through faster, interiors with contemporary colors and coffee-house seating, entertainment zones with TVs, and free Wi-Fi.

"We work very closely with our owner/operators to collect solid data about their locations, and then help analyze it so we can present the business case to them," says Sophia. Charts and graphs, along with the detailed statistical results are vital to the decision process.

One recent project provides a good example of how statistics supported the reimaging decision. Dave Traub, owner/operator, had been successfully operating a restaurant in Midlothian, Virginia for more than thirty years. The location was still prime, but the architecture and décor hadn't kept up with changing times. After receiving the statistical analysis on the location from McDonald's, Dave had the information he needed to make the decision to invest in reimaging the restaurant. With revenues and customer traffic up, he has no regrets. "We've become the community's gathering place. The local senior citizens group now meets here regularly in the mornings," he says.

The reimaging effort doesn't mean the end to new restaurant development for the company. "As long as new communities are developed and growth continues in neighborhoods across the country, we'll be analyzing data about them to be sure our restaurants are positioned in the best possible locations," states Sophia. Ray Kroc would be proud.

Discussion Questions:

1. Sophia Galassi, Vice President US Restaurant Development for McDonald's, indicated that she and her staff work very closely with owner/operators to collect data about McDonald's restaurant locations. Describe some of the kinds of data that Sophia's staff would collect and the respective types of charts that could be used to present their findings to the owner/operators.

2. At the end of 2001, Sophia Galassi and her team lead a remodel and re-imaging effort for the McDonald's franchises in a major U.S. city. This entailed a total change in store layout and design and a renewed emphasis on customer service. Once this work had been completed, the company put in place a comprehensive customer satisfaction data collection and tracking system. The data in the file called **McDonald's Customer Satisfaction** consist of the overall percentage of customers at the franchise McDonald's in this city who have rated the customer

service as Excellent or Very Good during each quarter since the re-imaging and remodeling was completed. Develop a line chart and discuss what time-series components appear to be contained in these data.

3. Refer to question 2, based upon the available historical data, develop a seasonally adjusted forecast for the percentage of customers who will rate the stores at Excellent or Very Good for Quarter 3 and Quarter 4 of 2006. Discuss the process you used to arrive at these forecasts.

4. Referring to questions 2 and 3, use any other forecasting method discussed in this chapter to arrive at a forecast for Quarters 3 and 4 of 2006. Compare your chosen model with the seasonally adjusted forecast model specified in question 3. Use appropriate measures of forecast error. Prepare a short report outlining your forecasting attempts along with your recommendation of which method you would suggest that McDonald's use in this case.

5. Prior to remodeling or re-imaging a McDonald's store, extensive research is conducted. This includes the use of

"mystery shoppers" who are people hired by McDonald's to go to stores as customers to observe various attributes of the store and the service being provided. The data in the file called **McDonald's Mystery Shopper** contains data pertaining to the "cleanliness" rating provided by the mystery shoppers who visited a particular McDonald's location each month between January 2004 and June 2006. The values represent the average rating on a 0–100 percent scale provided by five shoppers. A score of 100% is considered perfect. Using these time-series data, develop a line chart and discuss what time-series components are present in these data.

6. Referring to question 5, develop a double exponential smoothing model to forecast the rating for July, 2006 (use alpha = .20 and beta = .30 smoothing constants.) Compare the results of this forecasting approach with a simple linear trend forecasting approach. Write a short report describing the methods you have used and the results. Use linear trend analysis to obtain the starting values for C_0 and T_0.

CASE 16.1

Park Falls Chamber of Commerce

Masao Sugiyama is the recently elected president of the Chamber of Commerce in Park Falls, Wisconsin. He is the long-time owner of the only full-service hardware store in this small farming town. Being president of the Chamber of Commerce has been considered largely a ceremonial post because business conditions have not changed in Park Falls for as long as anyone can remember. However, Masao has just read an article in *The Wall Street Journal* that has made him think he needs to take a more active interest in the business conditions of his town.

The article concerned Wal-Mart, the largest retailer in the United States. Wal-Mart has expanded primarily by locating in small towns and avoiding large suburban areas. Although the Park Falls merchants have not had to deal with either Lowes or Home-Depot because these companies have located primarily in large urban centers. In addition, a supplier has recently told Masao that both Lowes and Home-Depot are considering locating stores in smaller towns. Sugiyama knows that Wal-Mart has moved into the outskirts of metropolitan areas and now is considering stores for smaller, untapped markets. He also has heard that Lowes and Home-Depot have recently had difficulty.

Masao decided he needs to know more about all three retailers. He asked the son of a friend to locate the following sales data which are also in a file called Park Falls on the CD-ROM.

Quarterly Sales Values in Millions of Dollars			
	Lowes	Home-Depot	Wal-Mart
Fiscal 1999 Q1	$ 3,772	$ 8,952	$29,819
Q2	$ 4,435	$10,431	$33,521
Q3	$ 3,909	$ 9,877	$33,509
Q4	$ 3,789	$ 9,174	$40,785
Fiscal 2000 Q1	$ 4,467	$11,112	$34,717
Q2	$ 5,264	$12,618	$38,470
Q3	$ 4,504	$11,545	$40,432
Q4	$ 4,543	$10,463	$51,394
Fiscal 2001 Q1	$ 5,276	$12,200	$42,985
Q2	$ 6,127	$14,576	$46,112
Q3	$ 5,455	$13,289	$45,676
Q4	$ 5,253	$13,488	$56,556
Fiscal 2002 Q1	$ 6,470	$14,282	$48,052
Q2	$ 7,488	$16,277	$52,799
Q3	$ 6,415	$14,475	$52,738
Q4	$ 6,118	$13,213	$64,210
Fiscal 2003 Q1	$ 7,118	$15,104	$51,705
Q2	$ 8,666	$17,989	$56,271
Q3	$ 7,802	$16,598	$55,241
Q4	$ 7,252	$15,125	$66,400
Fiscal 2004 Q1	$ 8,681	$17,550	$56,718
Q2	$10,169	$19,960	$62,637
Q3	$ 9,064	$18,772	$62,480
Q4	$ 8,550	$16,812	$74,494

(Continued)

Quarterly Sales Values in Millions of Dollars			
	Lowes	Home-Depot	Wal-Mart
Fiscal 2005 Q1	$ 9,913	$18,973	$64,763
Q2	$11,929	$22,305	$69,722
Q3	$10,592	$30,744	$68,520
Q4	$10,808	$19,489	$82,216

Masao is interested in what all these data tell him. How much faster has Wal-Mart grown than the other two firms? Is there any evidence Wal-Mart's growth has leveled off? Does Lowes seem to be rebounding, based on sales? Are seasonal fluctuations an issue in these sales figures? Is there any evidence that one firm is more affected by the cyclical component than the others? He needs some help in analyzing these data.

CASE 16.2

The St. Louis Companies

An irritated Roger Hatton finds himself sitting in the St. Louis airport after hearing that his flight to Chicago had been delayed—and, if the storm in Chicago continues, possibly cancelled. Because he must get to Chicago if at all possible, Roger is stuck at the airport. He decides he might as well try to get some work done, so he opens his laptop computer and calls up the **Claimnum** file.

Roger was recently assigned as an analyst in the worker's compensation section of the St. Louis Companies, one of the biggest issuers of worker's compensation insurance in the country. Until this year, the revenues and claim costs for all parts of the company were grouped together to determine any yearly profit or loss. Therefore, no one really knew if an individual department was profitable. Now, however, the new president is looking at each part of the company as a profit center. The clear implication is that money-losing departments may not have a future unless they develop a clear plan to become profitable.

When Roger asked the accounting department for a listing, by client, of all policy payments and claims filed and paid, he was told that the information is available but he may have to wait two or three months to get it. He was able to determine, however, that the department has been keeping

track of the clients who file frequent (at least one a month) claims and the total number of firms that purchase worker's compensation insurance. Using the data from this report, Roger divides the number of clients filing frequent claims by the corresponding number of clients. These ratios, kept on the CD-ROM file **Claimnum**, are as follows:

Year	Ratio (%)	Year	Ratio (%)
1	3.8	12	6.1
2	3.6	13	7.8
3	3.5	14	7.1
4	4.9	15	7.6
5	5.9	16	9.7
6	5.6	17	9.6
7	4.9	18	7.5
8	5.6	19	7.9
9	8.5	20	8.3
10	7.7	21	8.4
11	7.1		

Staring at these figures, Roger feels there should be some way to use them to project what the next several years may hold if the company doesn't change its underwriting policies.

CASE 16.3

Wagner Machine Works

Mary Lindsey has recently agreed to leave her upper-level management job at a major paper manufacturing firm and return to her hometown to take over the family machine-products business. The U.S. machine-products industry had a strong position of world dominance until recently, when it was devastated by foreign competition, particularly from Germany and Japan. Among the many problems facing the American industry is that it is made up of many small firms that must compete with foreign industrial giants.

Wagner Machine Works, the company Mary is taking over, is one of the few survivors in its part of the state, but it, too, faces increasing competitive pressure. Mary's father let the business slide as he approached retirement, and Mary sees the need for an immediate modernization of their plant. She has arranged for a loan from the local bank, but now she must forecast sales for the next three years to ensure that the company has enough cash flow to repay the debt. Surprisingly, Mary finds that her father has no forecasting system in place, and she cannot afford the time, or money, to install a system like that used at her previous company.

Wagner Machine Works' quarterly sales (in millions of dollars) for the past 15 years are as follows:

	Quarter			
Year	1	2	3	4
1992	$10,490	$11,130	$10,005	$11,058
1993	11,424	12,550	10,900	12,335
1994	12,835	13,100	11,660	13,767
1995	13,877	14,100	12,780	14,738
1996	14,798	15,210	13,785	16,218
1997	16,720	17,167	14,785	17,725
1998	18,348	18,951	16,554	19,889
1999	20,317	21,395	19,445	22,816
2000	23,335	24,179	22,548	25,029
2001	25,729	27,778	23,391	27,360
2002	28,886	30,125	26,049	30,300
2003	30,212	33,702	27,907	31,096
2004	31,715	35,720	28,554	34,326
2005	35,533	39,447	30,046	37,587
2006	39,093	44,650	30,046	37,587

While looking at these data, Mary wonders whether they can be used to forecast sales for the next three years. She wonders how much, if any, confidence she can have in a forecast made with these data. She also wonders if the recent increase in sales is due to growing business or just to inflationary price increases in the national economy.

References

Armstrong, J. Scott, "Forecasting by Extrapolation: Conclusions from 25 years of Research." *Interfaces*, 14, no. 6 (1984).

The Ombudsman: Research on Forecasting—A Quarter-Century Review, 1960–1984." *Interfaces*, 16, no. 1 (1986).

Bails, Dale G., and Larry C. Peppers, *Business Fluctuations: Forecasting Techniques and Applications* 2nd ed. (Englewood Cliffs, NJ: Prentice Hall, 1992).

Berenson, Mark L., and David M. Levine, *Basic Business Statistics: Concepts and Applications*, 8th ed. (Upper Saddle River, NJ: Prentice Hall 2006).

Bowerman, Bruce L., and Richard T. O'Connell, *Forecasting and Time Series: An Applied Approach*, 3rd ed. (North Scituate, MA: Duxbury Press, 1993).

Brandon, Charles, R. Fritz, and J. Xander, "Econometric Forecasts: Evaluation and Revision." *Applied Economics*, 15, no. 2 (1983).

Cryer, Jonathan D., *Time Series Analysis* (Boston: Duxbury Press, 1986).

Frees, Edward W., *Data Analysis Using Regression Models: The Business Perspective* (Englewood Cliffs, NJ: Prentice Hall, 1996).

Granger, C. W. G., *Forecasting in Business and Economics*, 2nd ed. (New York: Academic Press, 1989).

Makridakis, Spyros, Steven C. Wheelwright, and Rob J. Hyndman, *Forecasting: Methods and Applications*, 3rd ed. (New York: John Wiley & Sons, 1998).

McLaughlin, Robert L., "Forecasting Models: Sophisticated or Naive?" *Journal of Forecasting*, 2, no. 3 (1983).

Microsoft Excel 2007 (Redmond, WA: Microsoft Corp., 2007).

Minitab for Windows Version 14 (State College, PA: Minitab, 2005).

Montgomery, Douglas C., and Lynwood A. Johnson, *Forecasting and Time Series Analysis*, 2nd ed. (New York: McGraw-Hill, 1990).

Nelson, C. R., *Applied Time Series Analysis for Managerial Forecasting* (San Francisco, CA: Holdon-Day, 1983).

Kutner, Michael H., Christopher J. Nachtshein, John Neter, and William Li, *Applied Linear Statistical Models*, 5th ed. (New York: McGraw-Hill Irwin, 2005).

Willis, R. E., *A Guide to Forecasting for Planners* (Englewood Cliffs, NJ: Prentice Hall, 1987).

Wonnacott, T. H., and R. J. Wonnacott, *Econometrics*, 2nd ed. (New York: John Wiley & Sons, 1979).

Introduction to Nonparametric Statistics

CHAPTER OUTCOMES

After studying the material in Chapter 17, you should be able to:

1. Recognize when and how to use the Wilcoxon signed rank test for a population median.
2. Recognize the situations for which the Mann–Whitney U-test for the difference between two population medians applies and be able to use it in a decision-making context.
3. Know when to apply the Wilcoxon matched-pairs signed rank test for related samples.
4. Perform nonparametric analysis of variance using the Kruskal–Wallis one-way ANOVA.

PREPARING FOR CHAPTER SEVENTEEN

- Review the concepts associated with hypothesis testing for a single population mean using the t-distribution in Chapter 9.

- Make sure you are familiar with the steps involved in testing hypotheses for the difference between two population means discussed in Chapter 10.

- Review the concepts and assumptions associated with analysis of variance in Chapter 12.

WHY YOU NEED TO KNOW

A major electronics firm is considering building a new assembly plant in the southeastern United States. Housing prices are particularly important in picking the plant's location because the company would like affordable housing to be available for employees who transfer to the new location. The company has taken a sample of real estate listings from the four cities in contention for the new plant and would like to make a statistically valid comparison of home prices based on this sample information. This comparison then would be used to help determine where the new assembly plant should be located. The same company is also considering what type of employee evaluation system to use in the new plant. It has been experimenting with a group-based, rather than an individual-based, employee evaluation system in one of its plants. As a part of this experiment, the firm has gathered questionnaire data from employees who were asked to rate their experience with the evaluation system as being one with which they were *very satisfied, satisfied, no opinion, dissatisfied,* or *very dissatisfied.*

In previous chapters, you were introduced to a wide variety of statistical techniques that would seem to be useful statistical analysis tools for this company. However, many of the techniques discussed earlier are not appropriate for this situation. For instance, hypothesis tests involving samples and an unknown population standard deviation utilized the *t*-distribution. However, using the *t*-distribution in that situation assumes the population from which the sample is selected is normally distributed. If a situation involves testing the difference between two population means, the *t*-distribution is used under the assumption that both populations are normally distributed. The analysis of variance (ANOVA) *F*-test introduced in Chapter 12 is based on the assumptions that all populations are normally distributed and the population variances are equal. In addition, each of these techniques requires the variables of interest to be either interval or ratio level.

Although in many instances these underlying conditions are satisfied, you will encounter other situations in which either the level of data measurement is too low or the distribution assumptions are clearly violated. This is the case for both of the issues facing the electronics company here. Housing prices are generally not normally distributed because most locations have a few very expensive houses, and the employee questionnaire answers were measured on an ordinal, not on an interval or ratio scale. To handle such cases as these, a class of statistical tools called nonparametric statistics has been developed.

17.1 The Wilcoxon Signed Rank Test for One Population Median

Up to this point, the text has presented a wide array of statistical tools for describing data and for drawing inferences about a population based on sample information from that population. These tools are widely used in decision-making situations. However, you will also encounter decision situations in which major departures from the required assumptions exist. For example, many populations, such as family income levels and house prices, are highly skewed. In other instances, the level of data measurement will be too low (ordinal or nominal) to warrant use of the techniques presented earlier. In such cases, the alternative is to employ a *nonparametric statistical procedure* that has been developed to meet specific inferential needs. Such procedures have fewer restrictive assumptions concerning data level and underlying probability distributions. There are a great many nonparametric procedures that cover a wide range of applications. The purpose of this chapter is to introduce you to the concept of nonparametric statistics and illustrate some of the more frequently used methods.

The Wilcoxon Signed Rank Test—Single Population

CHAPTER OUTCOME #1

In Chapter 9, you were introduced to examples that involved testing hypotheses about a single population mean. Recall that if the data were interval or ratio level and the population was normally distributed, a *t*-test was used to test whether a population mean had a specified value. However, in cases in which the data level is ordinal or when populations are not believed to be approximately normally distributed, the *t*-test is not appropriate. In these instances, a nonparametric statistical technique known as the *Wilcoxon signed rank test* can be used. This test makes no highly restrictive assumption about the shape of the population distribution. (Section 17.2 introduces another Wilcoxon signed rank test for the difference between two population medians.)

The Wilcoxon test is used to test hypotheses about a population median rather than a population mean. The basic logic of the Wilcoxon test is quite straightforward. Because the median is the midpoint in a population, allowing for sampling error, we would expect approximately half the data values in a random sample to lie below the hypothesized median and about half to lie above it. The hypothesized median will be rejected if the actual data distribution shows too large a departure from this expectation.

Business Application

UNIVERSITY UNDERGRADUATE STARTING SALARIES The university placement office is interested in testing to determine whether the median starting salary distribution for undergraduates exceeds $35,000. People in the office believe the salary distribution is highly skewed to the right, so the *t*-test from Chapter 9, which requires that the population be normally distributed, cannot be properly used. In this case, the center of the distribution should be measured by the median. A simple random sample of $n = 10$ graduates is selected. The Wilcoxon signed rank test can be used to test whether the population median exceeds $35,000.

As with all tests, we start by stating the appropriate null and alternative hypotheses. The null and alternative hypotheses for the one-tailed test are

$$H_0: \tilde{\mu} \leq \$35,000$$
$$H_A: \tilde{\mu} > \$35,000$$

The test will be conducted using

$$\alpha = 0.05$$

For small samples, the hypothesis is tested using a *W*-test statistic determined by the following steps.

Step 1 Collect the sample data.

Step 2 Compute d_i, the deviation between each value and the hypothesized median.

Step 3 Convert the d_i values to absolute differences.

Step 4 Determine the ranks for each d_i value, eliminating any zero d_i values. The lowest d_i value receives a rank of 1. If observations are tied, assign the average rank of the tied observations to each of the tied values.

Step 5 For any data value greater than the hypothesized median, place the rank in an $R+$ column. For data values less than the hypothesized median, place the rank in an $R-$ column.

Step 6 The test statistic *W* is the sum of the ranks in the $R+$ column.

Table 17.1 shows the results for a random sample of 10 starting salaries. The hypothesis is tested comparing the calculated *W*-value with the critical values for the Wilcoxon signed rank test that are shown in Appendix P. Both upper and lower critical values are shown, corresponding to $n = 5$ to $n = 25$ for various levels of alpha. Note that *n* equals the number of nonzero d_i values. In this example, we have $n = 9$ nonzero d_i values. The lower critical value for $n = 9$ and a one-tailed $\alpha = 0.05$ is 8. The corresponding upper-tailed critical value is 37.

Because this is an upper-tail test, we are interested only in the upper critical value $W_{0.05}$. Therefore, the decision rule is

If $W > 37$, reject H_0.

TABLE 17.1 Wilcoxon Ranking Table for Starting Salaries Example

Salary = x_i	$d_i = x_i - \$35,000$	$|d_i|$	Rank	R+	R−
$36,400	1,400	1,400	2	2	
38,500	3,500	3,500	3	3	
27,000	−8,000	8,000	8		8
35,000	0	0			
29,000	−6,000	6,000	6.5		6.5
40,000	5,000	5,000	5	5	
52,000	17,000	17,000	9	9	
34,000	−1,000	1,000	1		1
38,900	3,900	3,900	4	4	
41,000	6,000	6,000	6.5	6.5	
				Total = W = 29.5	15.5

Because $W = 29.5 < 37$, we do not reject the null hypothesis and are unable to conclude that the median starting salary for university graduates exceeds $35,000.

Although neither Excel nor PHStat has a Wilcoxon signed rank test, Minitab does. Figure 17.1 illustrates the Minitab output for this example. Note that the p-value = $0.221 > \alpha = 0.05$, which reinforces the conclusion that the null hypothesis should not be rejected.

The starting salary example illustrated how the Wilcoxon signed rank test is used when the sample sizes are small. The W-test statistic approaches a normal distribution as n increases. Therefore, for sample sizes > 20, the Wilcoxon test can be approximated using the normal distribution where the test statistic is a z-value, as shown in Equation 17.1.

FIGURE 17.1

Minitab Output—Wilcoxon Ranked Sum Test for Starting Salaries

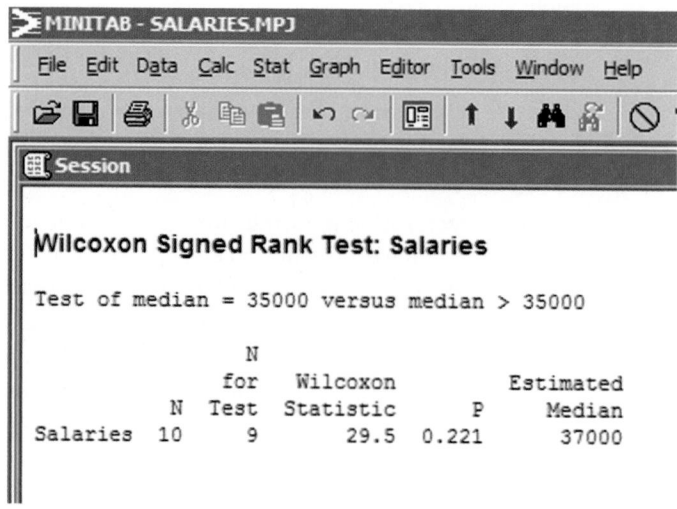

Minitab Instructions:
1. Enter data in column.
2. Choose **Stat > Nonparametric > 1-Samples Wilcoxon**.
3. In **Variable**, enter the data column.
4. Choose **Test median** and enter median value tested.
5. From **Alternative**, select appropriate hypothesis.
6. Click **OK**.

Large-Sample Wilcoxon Signed Rank Test Statistic

$$z = \frac{W - \dfrac{n(n+1)}{4}}{\sqrt{\dfrac{n(n+1)(2n+1)}{24}}} \qquad \textbf{(17.1)}$$

where:

$$W = \text{Sum of the } R+ \text{ ranks}$$
$$n = \text{Number of nonzero } d_i \text{ values}$$

EXAMPLE 17-1 Wilcoxon Signed Rank Test, One Sample, $n > 20$

TRY PROBLEM 17.8

Home Prices A recent article in the business section of a regional newspaper indicated that the median price of houses in the region was less than \$276,200. A legislative intern was assigned to test this statement. A random sample of 25 homes was selected. The large-sample Wilcoxon signed rank test can be conducted using the following steps:

Step 1 Specify the null and alternative hypotheses.
In this case, the null and alternative hypotheses are

$$H_0: \tilde{\mu} \geq \$276,200$$
$$H_A: \tilde{\mu} \geq \$276,200 \text{ (claim)}$$

Step 2 Determine the significance level for the test.
The test will be conducted using

$$\alpha = 0.01$$

Step 3 Collect the sample data and compute the W-test statistic.
Using the steps outlined on page 823, we manually compute the W-test statistic as shown in Table 17.2.

Step 4 Compute the z-test statistic.
The z-test statistic using the sum of the positive ranks is

$$z = \frac{W - \dfrac{n(n+1)}{4}}{\sqrt{\dfrac{n(n+1)(2n+1)}{24}}} = \frac{70 - \dfrac{25(25+1)}{4}}{\sqrt{\dfrac{25(25+1)(2(25)+1)}{24}}} = -2.49$$

Step 5 Reach a decision.
The critical value for a one-tailed test for alpha = 0.01 from the standard normal distribution is -2.33.

Because $z = -2.49 < -2.33$, we reject the null hypothesis.

Step 6 Draw a conclusion.
Thus, based on the sample data, the intern should conclude that the median is less than \$276,200.

TABLE 17.2 Wilcoxon Ranking Table for Home Prices Example

Price = x_i	d_i	$|d_i|$	Rank	R+	R−
$273,000	− 3,200	3,200	1		1
269,900	− 6,300	6,300	2		2
263,500	− 12,700	12,700	3		3
260,600	− 15,600	15,600	4		4
259,200	− 17,000	17,000	5		5
257,200	− 19,000	19,000	6		6
256,500	− 19,700	19,700	7		7
255,400	− 20,800	20,800	8		8
255,200	− 21,000	21,000	9		9
297,750	21,550	21,550	10	10	
254,200	− 22,000	22,000	11		11
300,750	24,550	24,550	12	12	
249,500	− 26,700	26,700	13		13
303,000	26,800	26,800	14	14	
304,900	28,700	28,700	15	15	
245,900	− 30,300	30,300	16		16
243,500	− 32,700	32,700	17		17
237,650	− 38,550	38,550	18		18
316,250	40,050	40,050	19	19	
234,500	− 41,700	41,700	20		20
228,900	− 47,300	47,300	21		21
217,000	− 59,200	59,200	22		22
212,400	− 63,800	63,800	23		23
204,500	− 71,700	71,700	24		24
202,600	− 73,600	73,600	25		25
				70	255

17-1: Exercises

Skill Development

17-1. Consider the following set of observations:

10.21	13.65	12.30	9.51	11.32	12.77	6.16	8.55	11.78	12.32

You should not assume these data come from a normal distribution. Test the hypothesis that these data come from a distribution with a median less than or equal to 10.

17-2. Consider the following set of observations:

3.1	4.8	2.3	5.6	2.8	2.9	4.4

You should not assume these data come from a normal distribution. Test the hypothesis that these data come from a distribution with a median equal to 4.

17-3. Consider the following set of observations:

9.0	15.6	21.1	11.1	13.5	9.2	13.6	15.8	12.5	18.7	18.9

You should not assume these data come from a normal distribution. Test the hypothesis that the median of these data is greater than or equal to 14.

Business Applications

17-4. A telemarketing company located in Los Angeles has established a guideline that states that the median time for each completed call should not exceed 4 minutes. Recently, the operations manager was concerned that calls were taking too long. The operations manager did not wish to make that assertion if the sample data did not strongly indicate it. A sample of 12 calls was selected, and the following times (in seconds) were recorded:

194 278 302 140 245 234 268 208 102 190 220 255

    a. Construct the appropriate null and alternative hypotheses.
    b. Based on the sample data, what should the operations manager conclude? Test at the 0.05 significance level.

17-5. Bowman Electronics sells electronic components for car stereos. The owners claim that the median life of a component exceeds 4,000 hours. To test this claim, they have selected a random sample of $n = 12$ components and have traced their life spans between installation and failure. The following data were obtained:

1,973	4,838	3,805	4,494	4,738	5,249
4,459	4,098	4,722	5,894	3,322	4,800

    a. State the appropriate null and alternative hypotheses.
    b. Assuming that the test is to be conducted using a 0.05 level of significance, what conclusion should be reached based on these sample data? Be sure to examine the required normality assumption.

17-6. A recent trade newsletter reported that during the initial 6-month period of employment, new sales personnel in an insurance company spent a median of 119 hours per month in the field. A random sample of 20 new salespersons was selected. The numbers of hours spent in the field by members in a randomly chosen month are listed here.

163	103	112	96	134
147	102	95	134	126
189	126	135	114	129
142	111	103	89	115

Do the data support the trade newsletter's claim? Conduct the appropriate hypothesis test with a significance level of 0.05.

17-7. The quality control department of a sunblock manufacturer requires the mean weight of its containers to be 11 ounces. The quality control department has answered complaints that the company underfills its containers by using a statistical study that concluded that the average weight of the sunblock containers is indeed 11 ounces. However, a consumer organization, while acknowledging these findings, believes that more than 50% of the containers have less than 11 ounces. A sample of 20 sunblock containers was selected. The data obtained follow:

10.9	11.7	10.5	11.8	10.2
11.5	10.8	11.2	11.8	10.7
10.6	10.9	11.6	11.2	11.0
10.7	10.8	10.5	11.3	10.1

Test the consumer organization's claim at a significance level of 0.05.

17-8. Sylvania's quality control division is constantly monitoring various parameters related to its products. One investigation addressed the life of incandescent light bulbs (in hours). Initially, they were satisfied with examining the average length of life. However, a recent sample taken from the production floor gave them pause for thought. The data follow:

1,100	1,140	1,550	1,210	1,280	840	1,620	1,500
1,460	1,940	2,080	1,350	1,150	730	2,410	1,060
1,150	1,260	1,760	1,250	1,500	1,560	1,210	1,440
1,770	1,270	1,210	1,230	1,230	2,100	1,630	500

Their initial efforts indicated that the average length of life of the light bulbs was 1,440 hours.
    a. Construct a box and whisker plot of this data. On this basis, draw a conclusion concerning the distribution of the population from which this sample was drawn.
    b. Conduct a hypothesis test to determine if the median length of life of the light bulbs is longer than the average length of life. Use $\alpha = 0.05$.

17-9. Mobile Oil Company wished to verify the viscosity of its premium 30-weight oil. A simple random sample of specimens taken from automobiles running at normal temperatures was obtained. The viscosities observed were as follows:

25	24	21	35	25
25	35	38	32	36
35	29	30	27	28
27	31	32	30	30

Determine if the median viscosity at normal running temperatures is equal to 30 as advertised for Mobile's premium 30-weight oil. (Use $\alpha = 0.05$.)

Computer Database Exercises

17-10. The Cell Tone Company sells cellular phones and airtime in several northwestern states. At a recent meeting, the marketing manager stated that the median age of its customers is less than 40. This came up in conjunction with a proposed advertising plan that is to be directed toward a young audience. Before actually completing the advertising plan, Cell Tone decided to randomly sample customers. Among the questions asked in a survey of 50 customers in the Jacksonville, Florida, area was the customers' ages. The data are in the CD-ROM file **Cell Phone Survey**.

a. Examine the sample data. Is the variable being measured a discrete or a continuous variable? Does it seem feasible that this data could have come from a normal distribution?

b. The marketing manager must support his statement concerning customer age in an upcoming board meeting. Using a significance level of 0.10, provide this support for the marketing manager.

17-11. The Wilson Company uses a great deal of water in the process of making industrial milling equipment.

To comply with federal clean-water laws, it has a water purification system that all wastewater goes through before being discharged into a settling pond on the company's property. To determine whether the company is complying with federal requirements, sample measures are taken every so often. One requirement is that the median pH level must be less than 7.4. A sample of 95 pH measures has been taken. The data for these measures are shown in the CD-ROM file **Wilson Water**.

a. Carefully examine the data. Use an appropriate procedure to determine if the data could have been sampled from a normal distribution. (*Hint:* Review the goodness-of-fit test in Chapter 13.)

b. Based on the sample data of pH level, what should the company conclude about its current status on meeting federal requirements? Test the hypothesis at the 0.05 level.

17.2 Nonparametric Tests for Two Population Medians

Chapters 9 through 12 introduced a variety of hypothesis-testing tools and techniques. Included were tests involving two or more population means. These tests carried with them several assumptions and requirements. For some situations in which you are testing about the difference between two population means, the student t-distribution is employed. One of the assumptions for the t-distribution is that the two populations are normally distributed. Another is that the data are restricted to being interval or ratio level. Although in many situations these assumptions and the data requirements will be satisfied, you will often encounter situations in which that is not the case.

In this section we introduce two nonparametric techniques that do not require such stringent assumptions and data requirements: the *Mann–Whitney U-test*[1] and the *Wilcoxon matched-pairs signed rank test*. Both tests can be used with ordinal (ranked) data, and neither requires that the populations be normally distributed. The Mann–Whitney U-test is used when the samples are independent, whereas the Wilcoxon matched-pairs signed rank test is used when the design has paired samples.

The Mann–Whitney U-Test

Business Application

CHAPTER OUTCOME #2

BLAINE COUNTY HIGHWAY DISTRICT The workforce of the Blaine County Highway District (BCHD) is made up of the rural and urban divisions. A few months ago, several rural division supervisors began claiming that the urban division employees waste gravel from the county gravel pit. The supervisors claimed the urban division uses more gravel per mile of road maintenance than the rural division. In response to these claims, the BCHD materials manager performed a test. He selected a random sample from the district's job-cost records of jobs performed by the urban (U) division and jobs performed by the rural (R) division. The yards of gravel per mile for each job are recorded.

Even though the data are of a ratio-level measurement, the manager is not willing to make the normality assumptions necessary to employ the two-sample t-test (discussed in

---

[1] An equivalent test to the Mann–Whitney U-test is the Wilcoxon rank-sum test.

Chapter 10). However, the Mann–Whitney U-test will allow him to compare the gravel use of the two divisions.

The Mann–Whitney U-test is one of the most commonly used nonparametric tests to compare samples from two populations in those cases when the following assumptions are satisfied:

Assumptions

1. The two samples are independent and random.
2. The value measured is a continuous variable.
3. The measurement scale used is at least ordinal.
4. If they differ, the distributions of the two populations will differ only with respect to central location.

The fourth point is instrumental in setting your null and alternative hypotheses. We are interested in determining whether two populations have the same or different medians. The test can be performed using the following steps:

Step 1 State the appropriate null and alternative hypotheses.

In this situation, the variable of interest is cubic yards of gravel used. This is a ratio-level variable; however, the populations are suspected to be skewed, so the material manager has decided to test the following hypotheses, stated in terms of the population medians:

$$H_0: \tilde{\mu}_U \leq \tilde{\mu}_R \text{ (Median urban gravel use is less than or}$$
$$\text{equal to median rural use.)}$$
$$H_A: \tilde{\mu}_U > \tilde{\mu}_R \text{ (Urban median exceeds rural median.)}$$

Step 2 Specify the desired level of significance.

The decision makers have determined that the test will be conducted using

$$\alpha = 0.05$$

Step 3 Select the sample data and compute the appropriate test statistic.

Computing the test statistic manually requires several steps.

1. Combine the raw data from the two samples into one set of numbers, keeping track of the sample from which each value came.
2. Rank the numbers in this combined set from low to high. Note that we expect no ties to occur because the values are considered to have come from continuous distributions. However, in actual situations ties will sometimes occur. When they do, we give tied observations the average of the rank positions for which they are tied. For instance, if the lowest four data points were each 460, each of the four 460s would receive a rank of $(1 + 2 + 3 + 4)/4 = 10/4 = 2.5$.[2]
3. Separate the two samples, listing each observation with the rank it has been assigned. This leads to the rankings shown in Table 17.3.

    The logic of the Mann–Whitney U-test centers on the idea that if the sum of the rankings of one sample differs greatly from the sum of the rankings of the second sample, we should conclude that there is a difference in the population medians.

---

[2] Noether provides an adjustment when ties occur. He, however, points out that using the adjustment has little effect unless a large proportion of the observations are tied or there are ties of considerable extent. See the References at the end of this chapter.

TABLE 17.3 Ranking of Yards of Gravel per Mile for the Blaine County Highway District Example

URBAN ($n_1 = 12$)		RURAL ($n_2 = 12$)	
Yards of Gravel	Rank	Yards of Gravel	Rank
460	2	600	6
830	16	652	9
720	12	603	7
930	20	594	5
500	4	1,402	23
620	8	1,111	21
703	11	902	18
407	1	700	10
1,521	24	827	15
900	17	490	3
750	13	904	19
800	14	1,400	22
	$\sum R_1 = 142$		$\sum R_2 = 158$

4. Calculate a U-value for each sample, as shown in Equations 17.2 and 17.3.

U Statistics

$$U_1 = n_1 n_2 + \frac{n_1(n_1 + 1)}{2} - \sum R_1 \qquad (17.2)$$

$$U_2 = n_1 n_2 + \frac{n_2(n_2 + 1)}{2} - \sum R_2 \qquad (17.3)$$

where:

n_1 and n_2 are the two sample sizes
$\sum R_1$ and $\sum R_2$ = sum of ranks for samples 1 and 2

For our example using the ranks in Table 17.3,

$$U_1 = 12(12) + \frac{12(13)}{2} - 142$$
$$= 80$$
$$U_2 = 12(12) + \frac{12(13)}{2} - 158$$
$$= 64$$

Note that $U_1 + U_2 = n_1 n_2$. This is always the case, and it provides a good check on the correctness of the rankings in Table 17.3.

5. Select the U-value to be the test statistic.

The Mann–Whitney U tables in Appendices L and M give the lower tail of the U-distribution. For one-tailed tests such as our Blaine County example, you need to look at the alternative hypothesis to determine whether U_1 or U_2 should be selected as the test statistic. Recall that

$$H_A: \tilde{\mu}_U > \tilde{\mu}_R$$

If the alternative hypothesis indicates that population 1 has a higher median, as in this case, then U_1 is selected as the test statistic. If population 2 is expected to have a higher median, then U_2 should be selected as the test statistic. The reason is that the population with the larger median should have the larger sum of ranked values, thus producing the smaller U-value. It is very important to note that this logic must be made in terms of the alternative hypothesis and not on the basis of the U-values obtained from the samples.

Now, we select the U-value that the alternative hypothesis indicates should be the smaller and call this U. Because population 1 (urban) should have the smaller U-value (larger median) if the alternative hypothesis is true, the sample data give a

$$U = 80$$

This is actually larger than the U-value for the rural population, but we still use it as the test statistic because the alternative hypothesis indicates that $\tilde{\mu}_U > \tilde{\mu}_R$.[3]

Step 4 Determine the critical value for the Mann–Whitney U-test.

For sample sizes less than 9, use the Mann–Whitney U table in Appendix L for the appropriate sample size. For sample sizes from 9 to 20, as in this example, the null hypothesis can be tested by comparing U with the appropriate critical value given in the Mann–Whitney U table in Appendix M. We begin by locating the part of the table associated with the desired significance level. In this case, we have a one-tailed test with

$$\alpha = 0.05$$

Go across the top of the Mann–Whitney U table to locate the value corresponding to the sample size from population 2 (Rural) and down the left side of the table to the sample size from population 1 (Urban).

In the Blaine County example, both sample sizes are 12, so we will use the Mann–Whitney table in Appendix M for $\alpha = 0.05$. Go across the top of the table to

$$n_2 = 12$$

and down the left-hand side to

$$n_1 = 12$$

The intersection of these column and row values gives a critical value of

$$U_{0.05} = 42$$

We can now form the decision rule as follows:

If $U < 42$, reject H_0;
Otherwise, do not reject H_0.

Step 5 Reach a decision.

Now because

$$U = 80 > 42$$

we do not reject the null hypothesis.

---

[3] For a two-tailed test, you should select the smaller U-value as your test statistic. This will force you toward the lower tail. If the U-value is smaller than the critical value in the Mann–Whitney U table, you will reject the null hypothesis.

Step 6   **Draw a conclusion.**

Therefore, based upon the sample data, there is not sufficient evidence to conclude that the median yards of gravel per mile used by the urban division is greater than that for the rural division.

Neither Excel nor the PHStat add-ins contain a Mann–Whitney U-test. However, PHStat has the equivalent *Wilcoxon Rank Sum Test*. Minitab also has this test procedure. Figure 17.2 shows the output for the Blaine County application. The Wilcoxon test uses, as its test statistic, the sum of the ranks from the population that is supposed to have the larger median. Referring to Table 17.3, Urban is supposed to have the larger median, and the sum of the ranks is 142. As shown in Figure 17.2, the two methods yield the same conclusions.

Mann–Whitney U-Test—Large Samples

When you encounter a situation with sample sizes in excess of 20, the previous approaches to the Mann–Whitney U-test cannot be used because of table limitations. However, the U statistic approaches a normal distribution as the sample sizes increase, and the Mann–Whitney U-test can be conducted using a normal approximation approach, where the mean and standard deviation for the U statistic are as given in Equations 17.4 and 17.5, respectively.

Mean and Standard Deviation for U Statistic

$$\mu = \frac{n_1 n_2}{2} \tag{17.4}$$

$$\sigma = \sqrt{\frac{(n_1)(n_2)(n_1 + n_2 + 1)}{12}} \tag{17.5}$$

where:

n_1 and n_2 = Sample sizes from populations 1 and 2

FIGURE 17.2

Minitab Output— Mann–Whitney U-Test for the Blaine County Example

```
 MINITAB - Blaine County.MPJ - [Session]
 File  Edit  Data  Calc  Stat  Graph  Editor  Tools  Window  Help


Mann-Whitney Test and CI: Urban, Rural

        N  Median
Urban  12   735.0
Rural  12   763.5


Point estimate for ETA1-ETA2 is -78.5
95.4 Percent CI for ETA1-ETA2 is (-327.1,147.1)
W = 142.0
Test of ETA1 = ETA2 vs ETA1 > ETA2


Cannot reject since W is < 150.0
```

Minitab Instructions:
1. Enter data in columns.
2. Choose **Stat** > **Nonparametric** > **Mann–Whitney**.
3. In **First Sample**, enter one data column.
4. In **Second Sample**, enter the other data column.
5. In **Alternative**, select *greater than*.
6. Click **OK**.

Equations 17.4 and 17.5 are used to form the U-test statistic in Equation 17.6.

Mann–Whitney U-Test Statistic

$$z = \frac{U - \dfrac{n_1 n_2}{2}}{\sqrt{\dfrac{(n_1)(n_2)(n_1 + n_2 + 1)}{12}}}$$ (17.6)

**Business
Application**

Excel and Minitab Tutorial

FUTURE-VISION Consider an application involving the managers for a local network television affiliate who were preparing for a national television advertising conference. The theme of the presentation was to center around the advantage for businesses to advertise on network TV rather than on cable. The managers believe that median household income for cable subscribers is less than the median for those who do not subscribe. Therefore, by advertising on network stations, businesses could reach a higher-income audience.

The managers are concerned with the median (as opposed to the mean) income because, as you discovered in Chapter 3, data such as household income are notorious for having large outliers. In such cases, the median is a preferable measure of the center of the data. The large outliers are also an indication that the data do not have a symmetric (such as the normal) distribution—a reason to use a nonparametric procedure such as the Mann–Whitney test.

The managers can use the Mann–Whitney U-test and the following steps to conduct a test about the median incomes for cable subscribers versus nonsubscribers.

Step 1 Specify the null and alternative hypotheses.
Given that the managers believe that median household income for cable subscribers (C) is less than the median for those who do not subscribe (NC) the null and alternative hypotheses to be tested are

$$H_0 : \tilde{\mu}_C \geq \tilde{\mu}_{NC}$$
$$H_A : \tilde{\mu}_C < \tilde{\mu}_{NC} \text{ (claim)}$$

Step 2 Specify the desired level of significance.
The test is to be conducted using

$$\alpha = 0.05$$

Step 3 Select the random sample and compute the test statistic.
In the spirit of friendly cooperation, the network managers joined forces with the local cable provider, Future-Vision, to survey a total of 548 households (144 nonsubscribers and 404 cable subscribers) in the market area. The results of the survey are contained in the CD-ROM file **Future-Vision**. Given the sample size, we can use the large-sample approach to the Mann–Whitney U-test. To compute the test statistic shown in Equation 17.6, use the following steps:

1. The income data must be converted to ranks. The sample data and ranks are in a CD-ROM file called **Future-Vision-Ranks**. Note that when data are tied in value, they share the same rank. For example, if four values are tied for the fifth position, each one is assigned the average of rankings 5, 6, 7, and 8, or $(5 + 6 + 7 + 8)/4 = 6.5$.

2. Next, we use the file data to compute the U-value. The sum of the ranks for noncable subscribers is

$$\Sigma R_1 = 41{,}204$$

and the sum of the ranks for cable subscribers is

$$\Sigma R_2 = 109{,}222$$

3. Based on sample sizes of

$$n_1 = 144$$

noncable subscribers and

$$n_2 = 404$$

cable subscribers, we compute the U-values using Equations 17.2 and 17.3.

$$U_1 = 144(404) + \frac{144(145)}{2} - 41,204 = 27,412$$

$$U_2 = 144(404) + \frac{404(405)}{2} - 109,222 = 30,764$$

Because the alternative hypothesis predicts that noncable subscribers will have a higher median, U_1 is selected to be U. Thus,

$$U = 27,412$$

4. We now substitute appropriate values into Equations 17.4 and 17.5.

$$\mu = \frac{n_1 n_2}{2} = \frac{(144)(404)}{2} = 29,088$$

and

$$\sigma = \sqrt{\frac{(n_1)(n_2)(n_1 + n_2 + 1)}{12}} = \sqrt{\frac{(144)(404)(144 + 404 + 1)}{12}} = 1,631.43$$

5. The test statistic is computed using Equation 17.6.

$$z = \frac{U - \frac{n_1 n_2}{2}}{\sqrt{\frac{(n_1)(n_2)(n_1 + n_2 + 1)}{12}}} = \frac{27,412 - 29,088}{\sqrt{\frac{(144)(404)(144 + 404 + 1)}{12}}}$$

$$= \frac{-1,676}{1,631.43} = -1.027$$

Step 4   Determine the critical value for the test.
Based on a one-tailed test with $\alpha = 0.05$, the critical value from the standard normal distribution table is

$$-z_{0.05} = -1.645$$

Step 5   Reach a decision.
Since $z = -1.027 > -1.645$, the null hypothesis cannot be rejected.

Step 6   Draw a conclusion.
This means that the claim that noncable families have higher median incomes than cable families is not supported by the sample data.

CHAPTER OUTCOME #3   **The Wilcoxon Matched-Pairs Signed Rank Test** The Mann–Whitney U-test is a very useful nonparametric technique. However, as discussed in the Blaine County Highway District example, its use is limited to those situations in which the samples from the two populations are independent. As we discussed in Chapter 10, you will encounter decision situations in which the samples will be paired and, therefore, are not independent.

A nonparametric test called the *Wilcoxon matched-pairs signed rank test* has been developed for situations in which you have related samples and are unwilling or unable (due to data-level limitations) to use the paired-sample t-test. It is useful when the two related samples have a measurement scale that allows us to determine not only whether the pairs of observations differ but also the magnitude of any difference. The Wilcoxon matched-pairs test can be used in those cases in which the following assumptions are satisfied:

Assumptions

1. The differences are measured on a continuous variable.
2. The measurement scale used is at least interval.
3. The distribution of the population differences is symmetric about their median.

EXAMPLE 17-2 | Small-Sample Wilcoxon Test

TRY PROBLEM 17.20

The Quick-Calc Company Consider the Quick-Calc Financial Corporation, which develops and markets software add-ons for common personal-computer spreadsheet packages. To differentiate its products from the other packages on the market, Quick-Calc has built many macros into its software. According to Quick-Calc, once a user learns the macro keystrokes, complicated financial computations become much easier to perform.

As part of its product-development testing program, software engineers at Quick-Calc have selected a focus group of seven people who frequently use spreadsheet packages. Each person is given complicated financial and accounting data and is asked to prepare a detailed analysis. A systems program determines the amount of time each person takes to complete the task. Once the analysis is complete, these same seven individuals are given a training course in Quick-Calc add-ons. After the training course, they are given a similar set of data and are asked to do the same analysis. Again the systems software determines the time needed to complete the analysis.

You should recognize that the samples in this application are not independent because the same subjects are used in both cases. If the software engineers performing the analysis are unwilling to make the normal distribution assumption required of the paired-sample t-test, they can use the Wilcoxon matched-pairs signed rank test. This test can be conducted using the following steps:

Step 1 Specify the appropriate null and alternative hypotheses.
The null and alternative hypotheses being tested are

$$H_0: \tilde{\mu}_b \leq \tilde{\mu}_a$$
$$H_A: \tilde{\mu}_b > \tilde{\mu}_a \quad \text{(Median time will be smaller \textit{after} the Quick-Calc training.)}$$

Step 2 Specify the desired level of significance.
The test will be conducted using

$$\alpha = 0.025$$

Step 3 Collect the sample data and compute the test statistic.
The data are shown in Table 17.4.

TABLE 17.4 Quick-Calc Financial Corporation Ranked Data

Subject	Before Training	After Training	d	Rank of d	Ranks with Smallest Expected Sum
1	24	11	13	7	
2	20	18	2	1	
3	19	23	−4	−3	3
4	20	15	5	4	
5	13	16	−3	−2	2
6	28	22	6	5	
7	15	8	7	6	
					$T = 5$

First, we convert the data in Table 17.4 to differences. The column of differences, d, gives the "before minus after" differences. The next column is the rank of the d-values from low to high. Note that the ranks are determined without considering the sign on the d-value. However, once the rank is determined, the original sign on the d-value is attached to the rank. For example, $d = 13$ is given a rank of 7, whereas $d = -4$ has a rank of -3.

The final column is titled "Ranks with Smallest Expected Sum." To determine the values in this column, we take the absolute values of either the positive or the negative ranks, depending on which group has the smallest expected sum of absolute-valued ranks. We look to the alternative hypothesis, which is

$$H_A: \tilde{\mu}_b > \tilde{\mu}_a$$

Because the before median is predicted to exceed the after median, we would expect the positive differences to exceed the negative differences. Therefore, the negative ranks should have the smaller sum, and therefore should be used in the final column, as shown in Table 17.4. The test statistic, T, is equal to the sum of absolute values of these negative ranks. Thus, $T = 5$.

Step 4   Determine the critical value.
To determine whether T is sufficiently small to reject the null hypothesis, we consult the Wilcoxon table of critical T-values in Appendix N. If the calculated T is less than or equal to the critical T from the table, the null hypothesis is rejected. For instance, with $\alpha = 0.025$ for our one-tailed test and $n = 7$, we get a critical value of

$$T_{0.025} = 2$$

Step 5   Reach a decision.
Because

$$T = 5 > 2, \text{ do not reject } H_0.$$

Step 6   Draw a conclusion.
Based on these sample data, the Quick-Calc Company has no basis for stating that its product will reduce the median time required to perform complicated financial analyses.

Ties in the Data If the two measurements of an observed data pair have the same values and, therefore, a d-value of 0, that case is dropped from the analysis and the sample size is reduced accordingly. You should note that this procedure favors rejecting the null hypothesis because we are eliminating cases in which the two sample points have exactly the same values.

If two or more d-values have the same absolute values, we assign the same rank to each one using the same approach as with the Mann–Whitney U-test. For example, if we have two d-values that tie for ranks 4 and 5, we average them as $(4 + 5)/2 = 4.5$ and assign both a rank of 4.5. Studies have shown that this method of assigning ranks to ties has little effect on the Wilcoxon test results. For a more complete discussion of the effect of ties on the Wilcoxon matched-pairs signed rank test, please see the text by Marascuilo and McSweeney referenced at the end of this chapter.

Large-Sample Wilcoxon Test If the sample size (number of matched pairs) exceeds 25, the Wilcoxon table of critical T-values in Appendix N cannot be used. However, it can be shown that for large samples, the distribution of T-values is approximately normal, with a mean and standard deviation given by Equations 17.7 and 17.8, respectively.

Wilcoxon Mean and Standard Deviation

$$\mu = \frac{n(n+1)}{4} \tag{17.7}$$

$$\sigma = \sqrt{\frac{n(n+1)(2n+1)}{24}} \tag{17.8}$$

where:

$$n = \text{Number of paired values}$$

The *Wilcoxon test statistic* is given by Equation 17.9.

Wilcoxon Test Statistic

$$z = \frac{T - \dfrac{n(n+1)}{4}}{\sqrt{\dfrac{n(n+1)(2n+1)}{24}}} \tag{17.9}$$

Then, the z-value is compared to the critical value from the standard normal table in the usual manner.

17-2: Exercises

Skill Development

17-12. The following sample data have been collected from two independent samples from two populations. Test the claim that the second population median will exceed the median of the first population.

Sample 1		Sample 2	
12	11	9	20
21	14	18	7
15	12	16	12
10	8	17	19

a. State the appropriate null and alternative hypotheses.
b. If you are unwilling to assume that the two populations are normally distributed, based on the sample data, what should you conclude about the null hypothesis? Test using $\alpha = 0.05$.

17-13. For each of the following tests, determine which of the two U statistics (U_1 or U_2) you would choose, the appropriate test statistic, and the rejection region for the Mann–Whitney test:
a. $H_A: \tilde{\mu}_1 < \tilde{\mu}_2, \alpha = 0.05, n_1 = 5, \text{and } n_2 = 10$
b. $H_A: \tilde{\mu}_1 > \tilde{\mu}_2, \alpha = 0.05, n_1 = 15, \text{and } n_2 = 12$
c. $H_A: \tilde{\mu}_1 \neq \tilde{\mu}_2, \alpha = 0.10, n_1 = 12, \text{and } n_2 = 17$

d. $H_A: \tilde{\mu}_1 < \tilde{\mu}_2, \alpha = 0.05, n_1 = 22, \text{and } n_2 = 25$
e. $H_A: \tilde{\mu}_1 \neq \tilde{\mu}_2, \alpha = 0.10, n_1 = 44, \text{and } n_2 = 15$

17-14. The following sample data have been collected from two independent random samples from two populations. Test the claim that the first population median will exceed the median of the second population.

Sample 1		Sample 2	
50	43	38	31
47	46	44	38
44	72	38	39
48	40	37	54
40	55	43	41
36	38	44	40

a. State the appropriate null and alternative hypotheses.
b. Using the Mann–Whitney U-test, based on the sample data, what should you conclude about the null hypothesis? Test using a significance level of 0.01.

17-15. The following sample data have been collected from independent samples from two populations.

The claim is that the first population median will be larger than the median of the second population.

Sample 1		Sample 2	
4.4	2.6	3.7	4.2
2.7	2.4	3.5	5.2
1.0	2.0	4.0	4.4
3.5	2.8	4.9	4.3
2.8		3.1	

a. State the appropriate null and alternative hypotheses.
b. Using the Mann–Whitney U-test, based on the sample data, what should you conclude about the null hypothesis? Test using $\alpha = 0.05$.

17-16. Determine the rejection region for the Mann–Whitney U-test in each of the following cases:
   a. $H_A: \tilde{\mu}_1 < \tilde{\mu}_2, \alpha = 0.05, n_1 = 3,$ and $n_2 = 15$
   b. $H_A: \tilde{\mu}_1 \neq \tilde{\mu}_2, \alpha = 0.10, n_1 = 5,$ and $n_2 = 20$
   c. $H_A: \tilde{\mu}_1 < \tilde{\mu}_2, \alpha = 0.025, n_1 = 9,$ and $n_2 = 12$
   d. $H_A: \tilde{\mu}_1 \neq \tilde{\mu}_2, \alpha = 0.10, n_1 = 124,$ and $n_2 = 25$

17-17. The following sample data have been collected from independent samples from two populations. Do the populations have different medians? Test at a significance level of 0.05. Use the Mann–Whitney U-test.

Sample 1		Sample 2	
550	489	594	538
483	480	542	505
379	433	447	486
438	436	466	425
398	540	560	497
582	415	447	511
528	532	526	576
502	412	446	558
352	572	573	500
488	579	542	467
400	556	473	556
451	383	418	383
571	515	511	515
382	501	510	501
588	353	577	353
465	369	585	
492	475	436	
384	470	461	
563	595	545	
506	361	441	

17-18. For each of the following tests, determine which of the two sums of absolute ranks (negative or positive) you would choose, the appropriate test statistic, and the rejection region for the Wilcoxon matched-pairs signed rank test:
   a. $H_A: \tilde{\mu}_1 < \tilde{\mu}_2, \alpha = 0.025, n = 15$
   b. $H_A: \tilde{\mu}_1 > \tilde{\mu}_2, \alpha = 0.01, n = 12$
   c. $H_A: \tilde{\mu}_1 \neq \tilde{\mu}_2, \alpha = 0.05, n = 9$
   d. $H_A: \tilde{\mu}_1 < \tilde{\mu}_2, \alpha = 0.05, n = 26$
   e. $H_A: \tilde{\mu}_1 \neq \tilde{\mu}_2, \alpha = 0.10, n = 44$

17-19. Given two paired samples with the following information:

Item	Sample 1	Sample 2
1	19.6	21.3
2	22.1	17.4
3	19.5	19.0
4	20.0	21.2
5	21.5	20.1
6	20.2	23.5
7	17.9	18.9
8	23.0	22.4
9	12.5	14.3
10	19.0	17.8

Based on these paired samples, test at the $\alpha = 0.05$ level whether the true median paired difference is 0.

17-20. Given two paired samples with the following information:

Item	Sample 1	Sample 2
1	3.4	2.8
2	2.5	3.0
3	7.0	5.5
4	5.9	6.7
5	4.0	3.5
6	5.0	5.0
7	6.2	7.5
8	5.3	4.2

a. Based on these paired samples, test at the $\alpha = 0.05$ level whether the true median paired difference is 0.
b. Suppose the data given here were sampled from normal distributions with equal variances. Answer part a.

17-21. Given two paired samples with the following information:

Item	Sample 1	Sample 2
1	1,004	1,045
2	1,245	1,145
3	1,360	1,400
4	1,150	1,000
5	1,300	1,350
6	1,450	1,350
7	900	1,140

Based on these paired samples, test at the $\alpha = 0.05$ level whether the true median paired difference is 0.

17-22. From a recent study we have collected the following data from two independent random samples:

Sample 1	Sample 2
405	300
450	340
290	400
370	250
345	270
460	410
425	435
275	390
380	225
330	210
500	395
215	315

Suppose we do not wish to assume normal distributions. Use the appropriate nonparametric test to determine whether the populations have equal medians. Test at $\alpha = 0.05$.

17-23. Given two paired samples with the following information:

Item	Sample 1	Sample 2
1	234	245
2	221	224
3	196	194
4	245	267
5	234	230
6	204	198

Based on these paired samples, test at the $\alpha = 0.05$ level whether the true median paired difference is 0.

17-24. Consider the following data for two paired samples:

Case #	Sample 1	Sample 2
1	258	304
2	197	190
3	400	500
4	350	340
5	237	250
6	400	358
7	370	390
8	130	100

a. Test the following null and alternative hypotheses at an $\alpha = 0.05$ level:

H_0: There is no difference between the two population distributions.

H_A: There is a difference between the two populations.

b. Answer part a as if the samples were independent samples from normal distributions with equal variances.

Business Applications

17-25. The makers of the Plus 20 Hardcard, a plug-in hard disk unit on a PC board, have recently done a marketing research study in which they asked two independently selected groups to rate the Hardcard on a scale of 1 to 100, with 100 being perfect satisfaction. The first group consisted of professional computer programmers. The second group consisted of home computer users. The company hoped to be able to say that the product would receive the same median ranking from each group. The following summary data were recorded:

Professionals	Home Users
$n = 10$	$n = 8$
Sum of ranks = 92	Sum of ranks = 79

Based on these data, what should the company conclude? Test at the $\alpha = 0.02$ level.

17-26. The Acme Speed Reading Company claims that graduates of its program have a higher median reading speed per minute than people who do not take the course. An independent agency conducted a study to determine whether this claim was justified. Researchers from the agency selected a random sample of people who had taken the speed reading course and another random sample of people who had not taken the course. The agency was unwilling to make the assumption that the populations were normally distributed. Therefore, a nonparametric test was needed. The following summary data were observed:

With Course	Without Course
$n = 7$	$n = 5$
Sum of ranks = 42	Sum of ranks = 36

Assuming that higher ranks imply more words per minute being read, what should the testing agency conclude based on the sample data? Test at an $\alpha = 0.05$ level.

17-27. The Tax Commission for a Midwestern state recently conducted a study to determine whether there is a difference in median deductions taken for charitable contributions depending on whether a tax return is filed as a single or a joint return. A random sample from each category was selected, with the following results:

Single	Joint
$n = 6$	$n = 8$
Sum of ranks = 43	Sum of ranks = 62

Based on these data, what should the tax commission conclude? Use an $\alpha = 0.05$ level.

17-28. Property taxes are based on assessed values of property. In most states, the law requires that assessed values be "at or near" market value of the property. In one Washington county, a tax protest group has claimed that assessed values are higher than market values. To address this claim, the county tax assessor, together with representatives from the protest group, has selected 15 properties at random that have sold within the past 6 months. Both parties agree that the sales price was the market value at the time of the sale.

The assessor then listed the assessed values and the sales values side-by-side, as shown.

House	Assessed Value	Market Value
1	$102,000	$98,000
2	76,000	82,400
3	49,000	54,300
4	98,500	98,500
5	114,000	118,000
6	135,000	130,000
7	205,000	198,900
8	87,500	90,000
9	50,000	49,800
10	123,000	122,000
11	78,500	80,000
12	145,000	150,900
13	67,000	65,200
14	119,000	120,700
15	234,000	220,000

a. Assuming that the population of assessed values and the population of market values have the same distribution shape and that they may differ only with respect to medians, state the appropriate null and alternative hypotheses.
b. Test the hypotheses using an $\alpha = 0.01$ level.
c. Discuss why one would not assume that the samples were obtained from normal distributions for this problem. What characteristic about the market values of houses would lead you to conclude that these data were not normally distributed?

17-29. A cattle feedlot operator has collected data for 40 matched pairs of cattle showing weight gain on two different feed supplements. His purpose in collecting the data is to determine whether there is a difference in the median weight gain for the two supplements. He has no preconceived idea about which supplement might produce higher weight gain. He wishes to test using an $\alpha = 0.05$ level.

Assuming that the T-value for these data is 480, what should be concluded concerning which supplement might produce higher weight gain? Use the large-sample Wilcoxon matched-pairs signed rank test normal approximation. Conduct the test using a p-value approach.

17-30. Radio advertisements have been stressing the virtues of an audiotape program to help children learn to read. To test whether this tape program can cause a quick improvement in reading ability, 10 children were given a nationally recognized reading test that measures reading ability. The same 10 children were then given the tapes to listen to for 4 hours spaced over a 2-day period. The children then were tested again. The test scores were as follows:

Child	Before	After
1	60	63
2	40	38
3	78	77
4	53	50
5	67	74
6	88	96
7	77	80
8	60	70
9	64	65
10	75	75

Use the Wilcoxon matched-pairs signed rank test to test whether this tape program produces quick improvement in reading ability. Use an $\alpha = 0.025$.

17-31. The Montgomery Athletic Shoe Company has developed a new shoe sole material it thinks provides superior wear compared with the old material the company has been using for its running shoes. The company selected 10 cross-country runners and supplied each runner with a pair of shoes. Each pair had one sole made of the old material and the other made of the new material. The shoes were monitored until the soles were worn out. The following lifetimes (in hours) were recorded for each material:

Runner	Old Material	New Material
1	45.5	47.0
2	50.0	51.0
3	43.0	42.0
4	45.5	46.0
5	58.5	58.0
6	49.0	50.5
7	29.5	39.0
8	52.0	53.0
9	48.0	48.0
10	57.5	61.0

a. If the populations from which these samples were taken could be considered to have normal distributions, determine if the soles made of the new material have a longer mean lifetime than those made from the old material. Use a significance level of 0.025.

b. Suppose you were not willing to consider that the populations have normal distributions. Make the determination requested in part a.

c. Given only the information in this problem, which of the two procedures indicated in parts a and b would you choose to use? Give reasons for your answer.

Computer Database Exercises

17-32. For at least the past 20 years, there has been a debate over whether children who are placed in child care facilities while their parents work suffer as a result. A recent study of 6,000 children discussed in the March 1999 issue of *Developmental Psychology* found "no permanent negative effects caused by their mothers' absence." In fact, the study indicated that there might be some positive benefits from the day care experience. To investigate this premise, a nonprofit organization called Child Care Connections conducted a small study in which children were observed playing in neutral settings (not at home or at a day care center). Over a period of 20 hours of observation, 15 children who did not go to day care and 21 children who had spent much time in day care were observed. The variable of interest was the total minutes of play in which each child was actively interacting with other students. Child Care Connections leaders hoped to show that the children who had been in day care would have a higher median time in interactive situations than the stay-at-home children. The CD-ROM file **Children** contains the results of the study.

a. Conduct a hypothesis test to determine if the hopes of the Child Care Connections leaders can be substantiated. Use a significance level of 0.05, and write a short statement that describes the results of the test.

b. Based on the outcome of the hypothesis test, which statistical error might have been committed?

17-33. The California State Highway Patrol recently conducted a study on a stretch of interstate highway south of San Francisco to determine whether the mean speed for California vehicles exceeded the mean speed for Nevada vehicles. A total of 140 California cars were included in the study, and 75 Nevada cars were included. Radar was used to measure the speed. The CD-ROM file **Speed-Test** contains the data collected by the California Highway Patrol.

a. Past studies have indicated that the speeds at which both Nevada and California drivers drive have normal distributions. Using a significance level equal to 0.10, obtain the results desired by the California Highway Patrol. Use a *p*-value approach to conduct the relevant hypothesis test. Discuss the results of this test in a short written statement.

b. Describe, in the context of this problem, what a Type I error would be.

17-34. The Sunbeam Corporation makes a wide variety of appliances for the home. One product is a digital blood pressure gauge. For obvious reasons, the blood pressure readings made by the monitor need to be accurate. When a new model is being designed, one of the steps is to test it. To do this, a sample of people is selected. Each person has his or her systolic blood pressure taken by a highly respected physician. They then immediately have their systolic blood pressure taken using the Sunbeam monitor. If the mean blood pressure is the same for the monitor as it is as determined by the physician, the monitor is determined to pass the test.

In a recent test, 15 people were randomly selected to be in the sample. The blood pressure readings for these people using both methods are contained in the CD-ROM file **Sunbeam**.

a. Based on the sample data and a significance level equal to 0.05, what conclusion should the

Sunbeam engineers reach regarding the latest blood pressure monitor? Discuss your answer in a short written statement.

b. Conduct the test as a paired *t*-test.

c. Discuss which of the two procedures in parts a and b is more appropriate to analyze the data presented in this problem.

17-35. The Hersh Corporation is considering two word-processing systems for its computers. One factor that will influence its decision is the ease of use in preparing a business report. Consequently, nine typists were selected from the clerical pool and asked to type a typical report using both word-processing systems. The typists then rated the systems on a scale of 0 to 100. The resulting ratings are in the CD-ROM file **Hersh**.

a. Which measurement level describes the data collected for this analysis?

b. (1) Could a normal distribution describe the population distribution from which these data were sampled? (2) Which measure of central tendency would be appropriate to describe the center of the populations from which these data were sampled?

c. Choose the appropriate hypothesis procedure to determine if there is a difference in the measures of central tendency you selected in part b between these two word-processing systems. Use a significance level of 0.01.

d. Which word-processing system would you recommend the Hersh Corporation adopt? Support your answer with statistical reasoning.

17.3 Kruskal–Wallis One-Way Analysis of Variance

CHAPTER OUTCOME #4

Section 17.2 showed that the Mann–Whitney *U*-test is a useful nonparametric procedure for determining whether two independent samples are from populations with the same median. However, as discussed in Chapter 12, many decisions involve comparing more than two populations. Chapter 12 introduced one-way analysis of variance and showed how, if the assumptions of normally distributed populations with equal variances are satisfied, the *F*-distribution can be used to test the hypothesis of equal population means. However, what if decision makers are not willing to assume normally distributed populations? In that case, they can turn to a nonparametric procedure to compare the populations. *Kruskal–Wallis One-Way Analysis of Variance* is the nonparametric counterpart to the one-way ANOVA procedure presented in Chapter 12. It is applicable any time the variables in question satisfy the following conditions:

Assumptions

1. They have a continuous distribution.
2. The data are at least ordinal.
3. The samples are independent.
4. The samples come from populations whose only possible difference is that at least one may have a different central location than the others.

Business Application

THE EAST HOPE MEDICAL CENTER The East Hope Medical Center is considering acquiring a distributed client-server computer system to handle its online data-processing activities, including patient scheduling, facility assignment, and general accounting and billing. On the basis of cost and performance standards, the medical center's information systems manager has reduced the possible suppliers to three. One critical factor in the decision is downtime (the time when the system is not operational). When the system goes down, the online applications stop and normal hospital activities are interrupted. The information systems manager received from each supplier a list of firms using its system. From these lists, the manager selected random samples of nine users of each computer system. In a telephone interview, she found the number of hours of downtime in the previous month for each system. At issue is whether the centers of the three

TABLE 17.5 Sample Data and Rankings of System Downtimes for the East Hope Medical Center Example

SYSTEM A		SYSTEM B		SYSTEM C	
Data	Ranking	Data	Ranking	Data	Ranking
4.0	11	6.9	19	0.5	1
3.7	10	11.3	23	1.4	4
5.1	15	21.7	27	1.0	2
2.0	6	9.2	20	1.7	5
4.6	12	6.5	17	3.6	9
9.3	21	4.9	14	5.2	16
2.7	8	12.2	25	1.3	3
2.5	7	11.7	24	6.8	18
4.8	13	10.5	22	14.1	26
Sum of ranks = 103		Sum of ranks = 191		Sum of ranks = 84	

populations are different. If the manager is unwilling to make the assumptions of normality and equal variances required for the one-way ANOVA technique introduced in Chapter 12 she can implement the Kruskal–Wallis nonparametric test using the following steps.

Step 1 Specify the appropriate null and alternative hypotheses to be tested.
In this application the information systems manager is interested in determining whether a difference exists between median downtime for the three systems. Thus, the null and alternative hypotheses are

$$H_0: \tilde{\mu}_1 = \tilde{\mu}_2 = \tilde{\mu}_3$$
$$H_A: \text{Not all population medians are equal.}$$

Step 2 Specify the desired level of significance for the test.
The test will be conducted using a significance level equal to

$$\alpha = 0.10$$

Step 3 Collect the sample data and compute the test statistic.
The data represent a random sample of downtimes from each system. The samples are independent. To use the Kruskal–Wallis ANOVA, first replace each downtime measurement by its *relative ranking* within all groups combined. The smallest downtime is given a rank of 1, the next smallest a rank of 2, and so forth, until all downtimes for the three systems have been replaced by their relative rankings. Table 17.5 shows the sample data and the rankings for the 27 observations. Notice that the rankings are summed for each computer system. The Kruskal–Wallis test will determine whether these sums are so different that it is not likely that they came from populations with equal medians.

If the samples actually do come from populations with equal medians (that is, the three systems have the same per-month median downtime), then the H statistic, calculated by Equation 17.10, will be approximately distributed as a chi-square variable with $k - 1$ degrees of freedom, where k equals the number of populations (systems in this application) under study.

H Statistic

$$H = \frac{12}{N(N+1)} \sum_{i=1}^{k} \frac{R_i^2}{n_i} - 3(N+1)$$ (17.10)

where:

N = Sum of the sample sizes from all populations
k = Number of populations
R_i = Sum of ranks in the sample from the ith population
n_i = Size of the sample from the ith population

Using Equation 17.10, the H statistic is

$$H = \frac{12}{N(N+1)} \sum_{i=1}^{k} \frac{R_i^2}{n_i} - 3(N+1)$$

$$= \frac{12}{27(27+1)} \left[\frac{103^2}{9} + \frac{191^2}{9} + \frac{84^2}{9} \right] - 3(27+1) = 11.50$$

Step 4 **Determine the critical value from the chi-square distribution.**
If H is larger than χ^2 from the chi-square distribution with $k - 1$ degrees of freedom in Appendix G, the hypothesis of equal medians should be rejected. The critical value for $\alpha = 0.10$ and

$$k - 1 = 3 - 1 = 2$$

degrees of freedom is

$$\chi^2_{0.10} = 4.6052$$

Step 5 **Reach a decision.**
Since $H = 11.50 > 4.605$, reject the null hypothesis based on these sample data.

Step 6 **Draw a conclusion.**
Thus, the Kruskal–Wallis one-way ANOVA shows the information systems manager should conclude, based on the sample data, that the three computer systems *do not* have equal median downtimes. From this analysis, the supplier of system B would most likely be eliminated from consideration unless other factors such as price or service offset the apparent longer downtimes.

EXAMPLE 17-3 Using Kruskal–Wallis One-Way ANOVA

TRY PROBLEM 17.37

Excel and Minitab Tutorial

Amalgamated Sugar Amalgamated Sugar has recently begun a new effort called total productive maintenance (TPM). The TPM concept is to increase the overall operating effectiveness of the company's equipment. One component of the TPM process attempts to reduce unplanned machine downtime. The first step is to gain an understanding of the current downtime situation. To do this, a sample of 20 days has been collected for each of the three shifts (day, swing, and graveyard). The variable of interest is the minutes of unplanned downtime per shift per day. The minutes are tabulated by summing the downtime minutes for all equipment in the plant. The Kruskal–Wallis test can be performed using the following steps:

Step 1 **State the appropriate null and alternative hypotheses.**
The Kruskal–Wallis one-way ANOVA procedure can test whether the medians are equal, as follows:

$$H_0: \tilde{\mu}_1 = \tilde{\mu}_2 = \tilde{\mu}_3$$
$$H_A: \text{ Not all population medians are equal.}$$

Step 2 Specify the desired significance level for the test.
The test will be conducted using an
$$\alpha = 0.05$$

Step 3 Collect the sample data and compute the test statistic.
The sample data are in the **Amalgamated** file on your CD-ROM.
Both Minitab and Excel (using the PHStat add-ins) can be used to perform
Kruskal–Wallis nonparametric ANOVA tests.* Figures 17.3a and 17.3b
illustrate the Excel and Minitab outputs for these sample data. The calcu-
lated H statistic is

$$H = 0.1859$$

Step 4 Determine the critical value from the chi-square distribution.
The critical value for $\alpha = 0.05$ and $k - 1 = 2$ degrees of freedom is
$$\chi^2_{0.05} = 5.991$$

Step 5 Reach a decision.
Because

$$H = 0.1859 < 5.9915$$
we do not reject the null hypothesis.

Also, the PHStat output provides the p-value associated with the H
statistic. The p-value of 0.9112 far exceeds an alpha of 0.05.

Step 6 Draw a conclusion.
Based on the sample data, the three shifts do not appear to differ with
respect to median equipment downtime. The company can now begin to
work on steps that will reduce the downtime across the three shifts.

FIGURE 17.3A

Excel 2007 (PHStat) Kruskal–Wallis ANOVA Output for Amalgamated Sugar

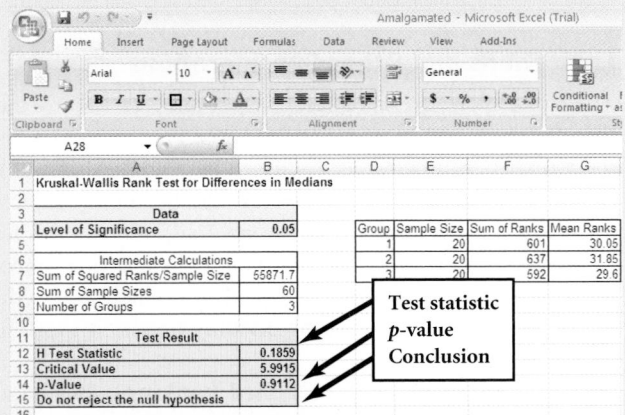

Excel 2007 Instructions:
1. Open File: Amalgamated.xls.
2. Select **Add-Ins**.
3. Select **PHStat**.
4. Select **Multiple Sample Test >**
   Kruskal–Wallis Rank Test.
5. Specify significance level (0.05).
6. Define data range including labels.
7. Click **OK**.

---

* In Minitab, the variable of interest must be in one column. A second column contains the population identifier.
In Excel, the data are placed in separate columns by population. The column headings identify the population.

FIGURE 17.3B

Minitab Kruskal–Wallis ANOVA Output for Amalgamated Sugar

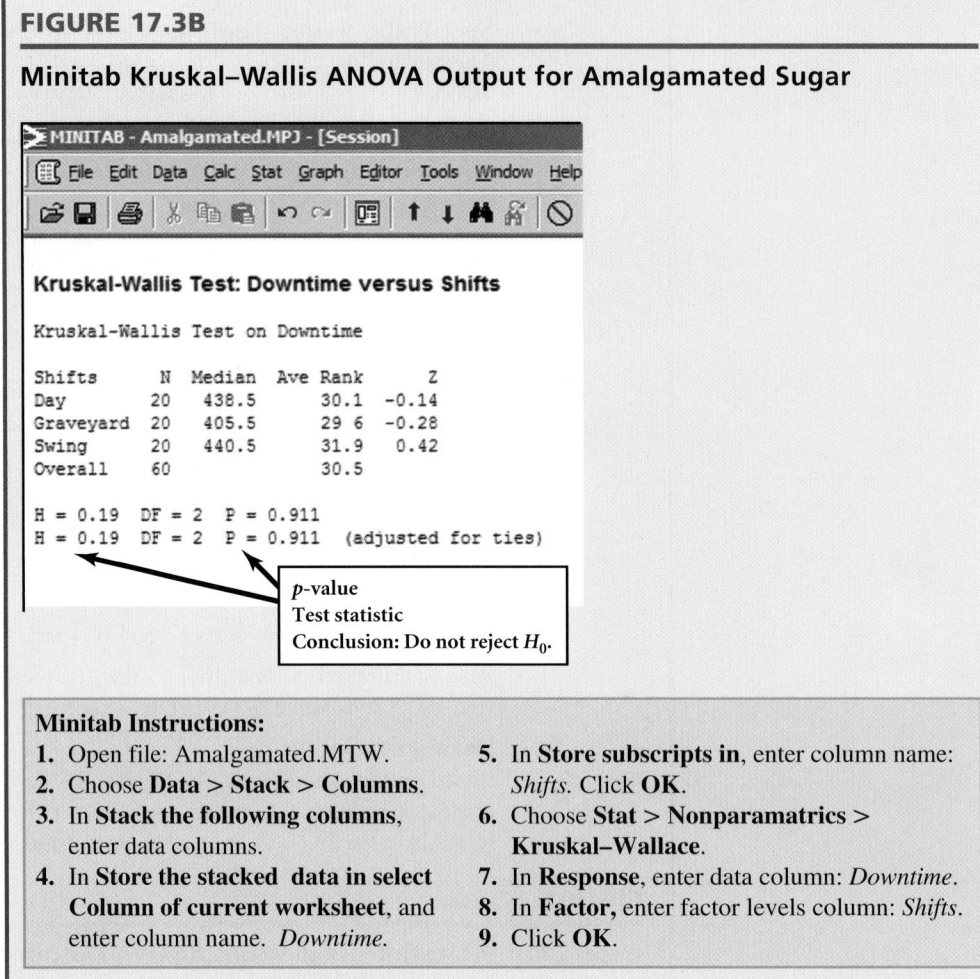

p-value
Test statistic
Conclusion: Do not reject H_0.

Minitab Instructions:
1. Open file: Amalgamated.MTW.
2. Choose **Data > Stack > Columns**.
3. In **Stack the following columns**, enter data columns.
4. In **Store the stacked data in select Column of current worksheet**, and enter column name. *Downtime*.
5. In **Store subscripts in**, enter column name: *Shifts*. Click **OK**.
6. Choose **Stat > Nonparamatrics > Kruskal–Wallace**.
7. In **Response**, enter data column: *Downtime*.
8. In **Factor,** enter factor levels column: *Shifts*.
9. Click **OK**.

Limitations and Other Considerations

The Kruskal–Wallis one-way ANOVA does *not* require the assumption of normality and is, therefore, often used instead of the ANOVA technique discussed in Chapter 12. However, the Kruskal–Wallis test as discussed here applies only if the sample size from each population is at least 5, the samples are independently selected, and each population has the same distribution except for a possible difference in central location.

When ranking observations, you will sometimes encounter ties. When ties occur, each observation is given the average rank for which it is tied. The *H* statistic is influenced by ties and should be corrected by dividing Equation 17.10 by Equation 17.11.

Correction for Tied Rankings—Kruskal–Wallis Test

$$1 - \frac{\sum_{i=1}^{g}(t_i^3 - t_i)}{N^3 - N} \tag{17.11}$$

where:

g = Number of different groups of ties
t_i = Number of tied observations in the *i*th tied group of scores
N = Total number of observations

The correct formula for calculating the Kruskal–Wallis *H* statistic when ties are present is Equation 17.12.

Correcting for ties increases H and thus makes rejecting the null hypothesis more likely than if the correction is not used. A rule of thumb is that if no more than 25% of the observations are involved in ties, the correction factor is not required. Note that if you use Minitab to perform the Kruskal–Wallis test, the adjusted H statistic is provided. The PHStat add-in to Excel for performing the Kruskal–Wallis test does not provide the adjusted H statistic. However, the adjustment is only necessary when the null hypothesis is not rejected and the H statistic is "close" to the rejection region. In that case, making the proper adjustment could lead to rejecting the null hypothesis.

H Statistic Corrected for Tied Rankings

$$H = \frac{\frac{12}{N(N+1)} \sum_{t=1}^{k} \frac{R_i^2}{n_i} - 3(N+1)}{1 - \frac{\sum_{i=1}^{g}(t_i^3 - t_i)}{N^3 - N}} \qquad (17.12)$$

17-3: Exercises

Skill Development

17-36. Given the following sample data:

Group 1	Group 2	Group 3
10	8	13
9	6	12
11	8	12
12	9	11
13	10	13
12	10	15

a. State the appropriate null and alternative hypotheses for determining whether a difference exists in the median value for the three populations.
b. Based on the sample data, use the Kruskal–Wallis ANOVA procedure to test the null hypothesis using $\alpha = 0.05$. What conclusion should be reached?

17-37. Given the following sample data:

Group 1	Group 2	Group3
21	17	29
25	15	38
36	34	28
35	22	27
33	16	14
23	19	26
31	30	39
32	20	36

a. State the appropriate null and alternative hypotheses to test whether there is a difference in the medians of the three populations.
b. Based on the sample data and a significance level of 0.05, what conclusion should be reached about the medians of the three populations if you are not willing to make the assumption that the populations are normally distributed?
c. Test the hypothesis stated in part a, assuming that the populations are normally distributed with equal variances.
d. Which of the procedures described in parts b and c would you select to analyze the data? Explain your reasoning.

17-38. Given the following data:

Group 1	Group 2	Group 3	Group 4
20	28	17	21
27	26	15	23
26	21	18	19
22	29	20	17
25	30	14	20
30	25		
23			

a. State the appropriate null and alternative hypotheses for determining whether a difference exists in the median value for the four populations.

b. Based on the sample data, use the Kruskal–Wallis one-way ANOVA procedure to test the null hypothesis. What conclusion should be reached using a significance level of 0.10? Discuss.

c. Determine the H-value adjusted for ties.

d. Given the results in part b, is it necessary to use the H-value adjusted for ties? If it is, conduct the hypothesis test using this adjusted value of H. If not, explain why not.

17-39. A study was conducted in which samples were selected independently from four populations. The sample size from each population was 20. The data were converted to ranks. The sum of the ranks for the data from each sample is

	Sample 1	Sample 2	Sample 3	Sample 4
Sum of Ranks	640	780	460	1,360

a. State the appropriate null and alternative hypotheses if we wish to determine whether the populations have equal medians.

b. Use the information in this exercise to perform a Kruskal–Wallis one-way ANOVA.

Business Applications

17-40. A study was conducted by the sports department of a national-network television station in which the objective was to determine whether a difference exists between median annual salaries of NBA basketball players, NFL football players, and MLB baseball players. The analyst in charge of the study believes that the normal distribution assumption is violated in this study. Thus, she thinks that a nonparametric test is in order.

The following summary data have been collected:

NBA	NFL	MLB
$n = 20$	$n = 30$	$n = 40$
$\sum R_i = 1,655$	$\sum R_i = 1,100$	$\sum R_i = 1,340$

a. Why would the sports department address the median as the parameter of interest in this analysis, as opposed to the mean? Explain your answer.

b. What characteristics of the salaries of professional athletes suggest that such data are not normally distributed? Explain.

c. Based on these data, what can be concluded about the median salaries for the three sports? Test at an $\alpha = 0.05$. Assume no ties.

17-41. Referring to Exercise 17-40, suppose that there were 40 ties at eight different salary levels. The following shows how many scores were ties at each salary level:

Level	t
1	2
2	3
3	2
4	4
5	8
6	10
7	6
	5

a. Given the results in the previous exercise, is it necessary to use the H-value adjusted for ties?

b. If your answer to part a is yes, conduct the test of hypothesis using this adjusted value of H. If it is not, explain why not.

17-42. The American Beef Growers Association is trying to promote the consumption of beef products. The organization performs numerous studies, the results of which are often used in advertising campaigns. One such study involved a quality perception test. Three grades of beef were involved: choice, standard, and economy. A random sample of people was provided pieces of choice-grade beefsteak and was asked to rate its quality on a scale of 1 to 100. A second sample of people was given pieces of standard-grade beefsteak, and a third sample was given pieces of economy-grade beefsteak, with instructions to rate the beef on the 100-point scale. The following data were obtained:

Choice	Standard	Economy
78	67	65
87	80	62
90	78	70
87	80	66
89	67	70
90	70	73

a. What measurement level do these data possess? Would it be appropriate to assume that such data could be obtained from a normal distribution? Explain your answers.

b. Based on the sample data, what conclusions should be reached concerning the median quality perception scores for the three grades of beef? Test using an $\alpha = 0.01$.

17-43. Suppose as part of your job you are responsible for installing emergency lighting in a series of state office buildings. Bids have been received from four manufacturers of battery-operated emergency lights. The costs are about equal, so the decision will be based on the length of time the lights last before failing. A sample of four lights from each manufacturer has been tested, with the following values (time in hours) recorded for each manufacturer:

Type A	Type B	Type C	Type D
1,024	1,270	1,121	923
1,121	1,325	1,201	983
1,250	1,426	1,190	1,087
1,022	1,322	1,122	1,121

Using $\alpha = 0.01$, what conclusion for the four manufacturers should you reach about the median length of time the lights last before failing? Explain.

Computer Database Exercises

17-44. As purchasing agent for the Horner-Williams Company, you have primary responsibility for securing high-quality raw materials at the best possible prices. One particular material the Horner-Williams Company uses a great deal is aluminum. After careful study, you have been able to reduce the prospective vendors to three. It is unclear whether these three vendors produce aluminum that is equally durable.

To compare durability, the recommended procedure is to put pressure on aluminum until it cracks. The vendor whose aluminum requires the highest median pressure will be judged to be the one that provides the most durable product. To carry out this test, 14 pieces from each vendor have been selected. These data are in the CD-ROM file **Horner-Williams**. (The data are pounds per square inch pressure.) Using $\alpha = 0.05$, what should the company conclude about whether there is a difference in the median strength of the three vendors' aluminum?

17-45. A large metropolitan police force is considering changing from full-size to mid-size cars. The police force sampled cars from each of three manufacturers. The number sampled represents the number that the manufacturer was able to provide for the test. Each car was driven for 5,000 miles, and the operating cost per mile was computed. The operating costs, in cents per mile, for the 21 cars are provided in the CD-ROM file **Police**. Perform the appropriate ANOVA test on these data. Assume a significance level of 0.05. State the appropriate null and alternative hypotheses. Do the experimental data provide evidence that the median operating costs per mile for the three types of police cars are different?

17-46. A nationwide moving company is considering five different types of nylon tie-down straps. The purchasing department randomly selected straps from each company and determined their breaking strengths in pounds. The sample data are contained in the CD-ROM file **Nylon**. Based on your analysis, with a Type I error rate of 0.05, can you conclude that a difference exists among the median breaking strengths of the types of nylon ropes?

Summary and Conclusion

Many people make the mistake of learning one or two statistical techniques and then using these techniques in all situations. Surprisingly, some people even get emotional about being able to analyze a particular problem using their favorite technique. As a future manager and decision maker, you cannot afford the luxury of defining a problem situation so you can apply your favorite technique. Statistics should be an aid to decision making, not an end in itself.

Many powerful statistical tools discussed in this book rest on the assumptions that the data being analyzed can be measured by at least an interval scale and that the underlying populations being analyzed are normal. If these assumptions come close to being satisfied, many of the tools discussed before this chapter apply and are useful. However, in many practical situations these assumptions just do not apply. In such cases the tools discussed in this chapter may be appropriate. In any case, nonparametric statistical tests should be part of every decision maker's tools. There are many other nonparametric statistical techniques that have been developed for specific applications. Many are aimed at situations involving small samples. Figure 17.4 may help you determine which nonparametric test to use in different situations. You should consult the references at the end of the chapter for further reading and discussion.

Equations

Large-Sample Wilcoxon Signed Rank Test Statistic

$$z = \frac{W - \dfrac{n(n+1)}{4}}{\sqrt{\dfrac{n(n+1)(2n+1)}{24}}} \qquad (17.1)$$

FIGURE 17.4

Nonparametric Tests Introduced in Chapter 17

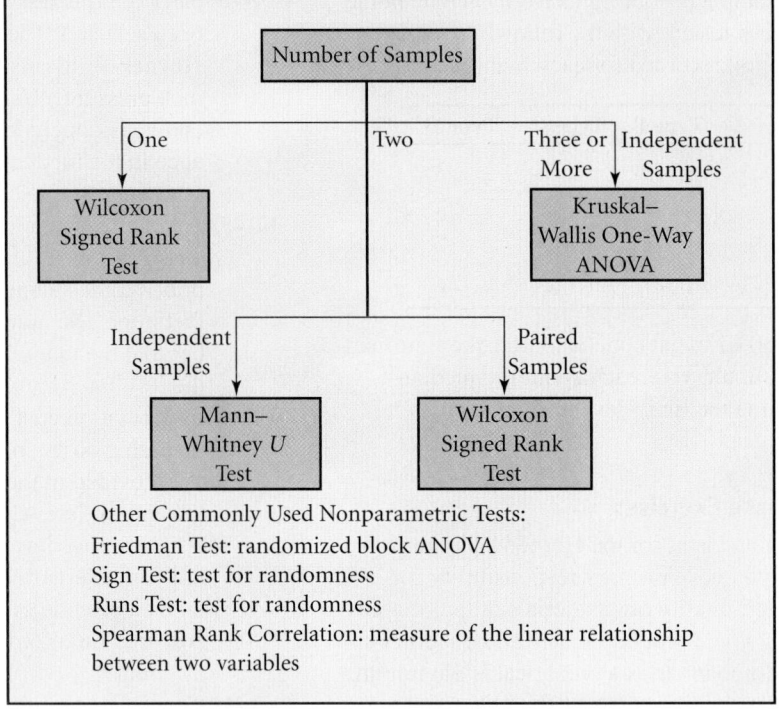

U Statistics

$$U_1 = n_1 n_2 + \frac{n_1(n_1 + 1)}{2} - \sum R_1 \qquad \textbf{(17.2)}$$

$$U_2 = n_1 n_2 + \frac{n_2(n_2 + 1)}{2} - \sum R_2 \qquad \textbf{(17.3)}$$

Mean and Standard Deviation for U Statistic

$$\mu = \frac{n_1 n_2}{2} \qquad \textbf{(17.4)}$$

$$\sigma = \sqrt{\frac{(n_1)(n_2)(n_1 + n_2 + 1)}{12}} \qquad \textbf{(17.5)}$$

Mann–Whitney U-Test Statistic

$$z = \frac{U - \dfrac{n_1 n_2}{2}}{\sqrt{\dfrac{(n_1)(n_2)(n_1 + n_2 + 1)}{12}}} \qquad \textbf{(17.6)}$$

Wilcoxon Mean and Standard Deviation

$$\mu = \frac{n(n + 1)}{4} \qquad \textbf{(17.7)}$$

$$\sigma = \sqrt{\frac{n(n + 1)(2n + 1)}{24}} \qquad \textbf{(17.8)}$$

Wilcoxon Test Statistic

$$z = \frac{T - \dfrac{n(n + 1)}{4}}{\sqrt{\dfrac{n(n + 1)(2n + 1)}{24}}} \qquad \textbf{(17.9)}$$

H Statistic

$$H = \frac{12}{N(N + 1)} \sum_{i=1}^{k} \frac{R_i^2}{n_i} - 3(N + 1) \qquad \textbf{(17.10)}$$

Correction for Tied Rankings—Kruskal–Wallis Test

$$1 - \frac{\displaystyle\sum_{i=1}^{g}(t_i^3 - t_i)}{N^3 - N} \qquad \textbf{(17.11)}$$

H Statistic Corrected for Tied Rankings

$$H = \frac{\dfrac{12}{N(N + 1)} \displaystyle\sum_{i=1}^{k} \dfrac{R_i^2}{n_i} - 3(N + 1)}{1 - \dfrac{\displaystyle\sum_{i=1}^{g}(t_i^3 - t_i)}{N^3 - N}} \qquad \textbf{(17.12)}$$

Chapter Exercises

Conceptual Questions

17-47. Discuss the data conditions that would lead you to use the Kruskal–Wallis test as opposed to the ANOVA procedure introduced in Chapter 12. Present an example illustrating these conditions.

17-48. In the library, locate two journal articles that use one of the nonparametric tests discussed in this chapter. Prepare a brief outline of the articles, paying particular attention to the reasons given for using the particular test.

17-49. Find an organization that you think would be interested in data that would violate the measurement scale or known distribution assumptions necessary to use the statistical tools found in Chapters 10–12 (retail stores are a good candidate). Determine to what extent this organization considers these problems and whether it uses any of the techniques discussed in this chapter.

17-50. As an example of how the sampling distribution for the Mann–Whitney Test is derived, consider two samples with sample sizes $n_1 = 2$ and $n_2 = 3$. The distribution is obtained under the assumption that the two variables, say x and y, are identically distributed. Under this assumption, each measurement is equally likely to obtain one of the ranks between 1 and $n_1 + n_2$.

  a. List all the possible sets of two ranks that could be obtained from five ranks. Calculate the Mann–Whitney U-value for each of these sets of two ranks.

  b. The number of ways in which we may choose n_1 ranks from $n_1 + n_2$ is given by $(n_1 + n_2)!/n_1!n_2!$. Calculate this value for the $n_1 = 2$ and $n_2 = 3$. Now calculate the probability of any one of the possible Mann–Whitney U-values.

  c. List all the possible Mann–Whitney U-values you obtained in part a. Then using part b, calculate the probability that each of these U-values occurs, thereby producing the sampling distribution for the Mann–Whitney U statistic when $n_1 = 2$ and $n_2 = 3$.

17-51. Let us examine how the sampling distribution of the Wilcoxon test statistic is obtained. Consider the sampling distributions of the positive ranks from a sample size of 4. The ranks to be considered are, therefore, 1, 2, 3, and 4. Under the null hypothesis, the differences to be ranked are distributed symmetrically about zero. Thus, each difference is just as likely to be positively as negatively ranked.

  a. For a sample size of four, there are $2^4 = 16$ possible sets of signs associated with the four ranks. List the 16 possible sets of ranks that could be positive—that is, (none), (1), (2) . . . (1, 2, 3, 4). Each of these sets of positive ranks (under the null hypothesis) has the same probability of occurring.

  b. Calculate the sum of the ranks of each set specified in part a.

  c. Using parts a and b, produce the sampling distribution for the Wilcoxon test statistic when $n = 4$.

Business Applications

17-52. The H. F. Houston Company is the parent franchiser for a nationwide fast-food chain, with corporate headquarters in Austin, Minnesota. For the past few months, the company has undertaken a new advertising study. Initially, company executives selected 22 of its retail outlets that were similar with respect to sales volume, profitability, location, climate, economic status of customers, and experience of store management. Each of the outlets was randomly assigned one of two advertising plans promoting a new sandwich product. The accompanying data represent the number of new sandwiches sold during the specific test period at each retail outlet.

Houston executives want you to determine which of the two advertising plans leads to the largest average sales levels for the new product. They are not willing to make the assumptions necessary for you to use the t-test. They do not wish to have an error rate of more than 0.05.

Advertising Plan 1	Advertising Plan 2
1,711	2,100
1,915	2,210
1,905	1,950
2,153	3,004
1,504	2,725
1,195	2,619
2,103	2,483
1,601	2,520
1,580	1,904
1,475	1,875
1,588	1,943

17-53. Two small regional life insurance companies are being studied by the Triangle Life Insurance Company as candidates for a possible merger. Triangle can merge with only one of these regional companies at this time and, as part of its study, wishes to determine whether there is a difference in the average annual premiums received by the two companies. The following data represent sample policy premiums for each company:

Company 1	Company 2
$246	$300
211	305
235	308
270	325
411	340
310	295
450	320
502	330
311	240
200	360

a. Do these data indicate a difference in mean annual premiums for the two companies? Apply the Mann–Whitney U test with a significance level of 0.10.
b. Apply the t-test to determine whether the data indicate a difference between annual premiums for the two regional companies. Use a significance level of 0.10. Indicate what assumptions must be made to apply the t-test.

17-54. The Style-Rite Company of Atlanta makes windbreaker jackets for people who play golf and who are active outdoors during the spring and fall months. The company recently developed a new material and is in the process of test-marketing jackets made from the material. As part of this test-marketing effort, 10 people were each supplied with a jacket made from the original material and were asked to wear it for 2 months, washing it at least twice during that time. A second group of 10 people were each given a jacket made from the new material and asked to wear it for 2 months with the same washing requirements.

Following the 2-month trial period, the individuals were asked to rate the jackets on a scale of 0 to 100, with 0 being the worst performance rating and 100 being the best. The ratings for each material are shown as follows:

Original Material	New Material
76	55
34	90
70	72
23	17
45	56
80	69
10	91
46	95
67	86
75	74

The company expects that, on the average, the performance ratings will be superior for the new material.
a. Examine the data given. What characteristics of these data sets would lead you to reject the assumption that the data came from populations that had normal distributions and equal variances?
b. Do the sample data support this belief at a significance level of 0.05? Discuss.

17-55. A study was recently conducted by the Bonneville Power Association to determine attitudes regarding the association's policies in western U.S. states. One part of the study asked respondents to rate the performance of the BPA on its responsiveness to environmental issues. The following responses were obtained for a sample of 12 urban residents and 10 rural residents. The ratings are on a 1 to 100 scale, with 100 being perfect.

Urban	Rural
76	55
90	80
86	94
60	40
43	85
96	92
50	77
20	68
30	35
82	59
75	
84	

a. Based on the sample data, should the BPA conclude that there is no difference between the urban and rural residents with respect to median environmental rating? Test using a significance level of 0.02.

b. Perform the appropriate parametric statistical test and indicate the assumptions necessary to use this test that were not required by the Mann–Whitney tests. Use a significance level of 0.02. (Refer to Chapter 10, if needed.)

17-56. The Miltmore Corporation performs consulting services for companies that think they have image problems. Recently, the Bluedot Beer Company approached Miltmore. Bluedot executives were concerned that the company's image, relative to its two closest competitors, had diminished. Miltmore conducted an image study in which a random sample of 8 people was asked to rate Bluedot's image. Five people were asked to rate competitor A's image, and 10 people were asked to rate competitor B's image. The image ratings were made on a 100-point scale, with 100 being the best possible rating. Here are the results of the sampling.

Bluedot	Competitor A	Competitor B
40	95	50
60	53	80
70	55	82
40	92	87
55	90	93
90		51
20		63
20		72
		96
		88

a. Based on these sample results, should Bluedot conclude there is an image difference among the three companies? Use a significance level equal to 0.05.

b. Should Bluedot infer that its image has been damaged by last year's federal government recall of its product? Discuss why or why not.

c. Why might the decision maker wish to use parametric ANOVA rather than the corresponding nonparametric test? Discuss.

17-57. During the production of a textbook, there are many steps between when the author begins preparing the manuscript and when the book is finally printed and bound. Tremendous effort is made to minimize the number of errors of any type in the text. One type of error that is especially difficult to eliminate is the typographical error that can creep in when the book is typeset. The Prolythic Type Company does contract work for many publishers. As part of its quality control efforts, it charts the number of corrected errors per page in its manuscripts. In one particularly difficult book to typeset, the following data were observed for a sample of 15 pages (in sequence):

Page	1	2	3	4	5	6	7	8	9	10	11	12	13	14	15
Errors	2	4	1	0	6	7	4	2	9	4	3	6	2	4	2

Is there sufficient evidence to conclude the median number of errors per page is greater than 6?

17-58. A Vermont company is monitoring a process that fills maple syrup bottles. When the process is filling correctly, the median average fill in an 8-ounce bottle of syrup is 8.03 ounces. The last 15 bottles sampled revealed the following levels of fill:

7.95	8.02	8.07	8.06	8.05	8.04	7.97	8.01
8.04	8.05	8.08	8.11	7.99	8.00	8.02	

a. Formulate the null and alternative hypotheses needed in this situation.

b. Do the sample values support the null or alternative hypothesis?

17-59. The manager of credit card operations for a small regional bank has determined that last year's median credit card balance was $1,989.32. A sample of 18 customer balances this year revealed the following figures, in dollars:

Sample 1	Sample 2	Sample 3	Sample 4	Sample 5	Sample 6
1,827.85	1,992.75	2,012.35	1,955.64	2,023.19	1,998.52

Sample 7	Sample 8	Sample 9	Sample 10	Sample 11	Sample 12
2,003.75	1,752.55	1,865.32	2,013.13	2,225.35	2,100.35

Sample 13	Sample 14	Sample 15	Sample 16	Sample 17	Sample 18
2,002.02	1,850.37	1,995.35	2,001.18	2,252.54	2,035.75

Based on the 18 customer balances sampled, is there enough evidence to allow you to conclude the median balance has changed? Test at the 0.05 level of significance.

Computer Database Exercises

17-60. A major car manufacturer is experimenting with three new methods of pollution control. The testing lab must determine whether the three methods produce equal pollution reductions. Readings from a calibrated carbon monoxide meter are taken from groups of engines randomly equipped with one of the three control units. The data are in the CD-ROM file **Pollution**. Determine whether the three pollution-control methods will produce equal results.

17-61. A business statistics instructor at State University has been experimenting with her testing procedure. This term, she has taken the approach of giving two tests over each section of material. The first test is a problem-oriented exam, in which students have to set up and solve applications problems. The exam is worth 50 points. The second test, given a day later, is a multiple-choice test, covering the concepts introduced in the section of the text covered by the exam. This exam is also worth 50 points.

In one class of 15 students, the observed test scores over the first section of material in the course are contained in the CD-ROM file **State University**.

a. If the instructor is unwilling to make the assumptions for the paired-sample *t*-test, what should she conclude based on these data about the distribution of scores for the two tests if she tests at a significance level of 0.05?

b. In the context of this problem, define a Type II error.

17-62. Two brands of tires are being tested for tread wear. To control for vehicle and driver variation, one tire of each brand is put on the front wheels of 10 cars. The cars are driven under normal driving conditions a total of 15,000 miles. The tread wear is then measured using a very sophisticated instrument. The data that were observed are in the CD-ROM file **Tread Wear**. (Note that the larger the number, the less wear in the tread.)

a. What would be the possible objection in this case for employing the paired-sample *t*-test? Discuss.

b. Assuming that the decision makers in this situation are not willing to make the assumptions required to perform the paired-sample *t*-test, what decision should be reached using the appropriate nonparametric test if a significance level of 0.05 is used? Discuss.

17-63. High Fuel Company markets a gasoline additive for automobiles that it claims will increase a car's miles per gallon (MPG) performance. In an effort to determine whether High Fuel's claim is valid, a consumer testing agency randomly selected eight makes of automobiles. Each car's tank was filled with gasoline and driven around a track until empty. Then the car's tank was refilled with

gasoline and the additive, and the car was driven until the gas tank was empty again. The miles per gallon were measured for each car with and without the additive. The results are reported in the CD-ROM file **High Fuel**.

The testing agency is unwilling to accept the assumption that the underlying probability distribution is normally distributed, but it would still like to perform a statistical test to determine the validity of High Fuel's claim.

a. What statistical test would you recommend the testing agency use in this case? Why?

b. Conduct the test that you believe to be appropriate. Use a significance level of 0.025.

c. State your conclusions based on the test you have just conducted. Is High Fuel's claim supported by the test's findings?

17-64. A company assembles remote controls for television sets. The company's design engineers have developed a revised design that they think will make it faster to assemble the controls. To test whether the new design leads to faster assembly, 14 assembly workers were randomly selected and each worker was asked to assemble a control using the current design and then asked to assemble a control using the revised design. The times in seconds to assemble the controls are shown in the CD-ROM file **Remote Control**. The company's engineers are unable to assume that the assembly times are normally distributed, but they would like to test whether assembly times are less using the revised design.

a. What statistical test do you recommend the company use? Why?

b. State the null an alternative hypotheses of interest to the company.

c. At the 0.025 level of significance, is there any evidence to support the engineers' belief that the revised design reduces assembly time?

d. How might the results of the statistical test be used by the company's management?

CASE 17.A

Bentford Electronics—Part 2

On Saturday morning, Jennifer Bentford received a call at her home from the production supervisor at Bentford Electronics Plant 1. The supervisor indicated that she and the supervisors from Plants 2, 3, and 4 had agreed that something must be done to improve company morale and, thereby, increase the production output of their plants. Jennifer Bentford, president of Bentford Electronics,

agreed to set up a Monday morning meeting with the supervisors to see if they could arrive at a plan for accomplishing these objectives.

By Monday each supervisor had compiled a list of several ideas, including a 4-day work week and interplant competition of various kinds.

After listening to the discussion for some time, Jennifer Bentford asked if anyone knew if there was a difference in average daily output for the four plants. When she heard no positive response, she told the supervisors to select a random sample of daily production reports from each plant and test whether there was a difference. They were to meet again on Wednesday afternoon with test results.

By Wednesday morning, the supervisors had collected the following data on units produced:

Plant 1	Plant 2	Plant 3	Plant 4
4,306	1,853	2,700	1,704
2,852	1,948	2,705	2,320
1,900	2,702	2,721	4,150
4,711	4,110	2,900	3,300
2,933	3,950	2,650	3,200
3,627	2,300	2,480	2,975

The supervisors had little trouble collecting the data, but they were at a loss about how to determine whether there was a difference in the output of the four plants. Jerry Gibson, the company's research analyst, told the supervisors that there were statistical procedures that could be used to test hypotheses regarding multiple samples if the daily output was distributed in a bell shape (normal distribution) at each plant. The supervisors expressed dismay because no one thought his or her output was normal. Jerry Gibson indicated that there were techniques that did not require the normality assumption, but he did not know what they were.

The meeting with Jennifer Bentford was scheduled to begin in 3 hours, so he needed some statistical-analysis help immediately.

References

Berenson, Mark L., and David M. Levine, *Basic Business Statistics: Concepts and Applications*, 10th ed. (Upper Saddle River, NJ: Prentice Hall, 2006).

Conover, W. J., *Practical Nonparametric Statistics*, 3rd ed. (New York: John Wiley and Sons, 1999).

Dunn, O. J., "Multiple Comparisons Using Rank Sums," *Technometrics*, 6 (1964), pp. 241–252.

Marascuilo, Leonard A., and Maryellen McSweeney, *Nonparametric and Distribution-Free Methods for Social Sciences*, (Pacific Grove, CA: Brooks/Cole, 1977).

Microsoft Excel 2007 (Redmond, WA: Microsoft Corp., 2007).

Minitab for Windows Version 14 (State College, PA: Minitab, 2005).

Noether, G. E., *Elements of Nonparametric Statistics* (New York: John Wiley & Sons, 1967).

Chapter EIGHTEEN

Introduction to Quality and Statistical Process Control

18.1   Quality Management and Tools for Process Improvement

18.2   Introduction to Statistical Process Control Charts

CHAPTER OUTCOMES

After studying the material in Chapter 18, you should be able to:

1. Use the seven basic tools of quality.
2. Construct and interpret $\bar{x}$-charts and R-charts.
3. Construct and interpret p-charts.
4. Construct and interpret c-charts.

PREPARING FOR CHAPTER EIGHTEEN

Modern quality control is based on many of the statistical concepts you have covered up to now, so to adequately understand the material, you need to review many previous topics.

- Review how to construct and interpret line charts, covered in Chapter 2.

- Make sure you are familiar with the steps involved in determining the mean and standard deviation of the binomial and Poisson distributions, covered in Chapter 5.

- Review how to determine the mean and standard deviation of samples and the meaning of the Central Limit Theorem from Chapter 7.

- Finally, again become familiar with how to determine a confidence interval estimate and test a hypothesis of a single population parameter as covered in Chapters 8 and 9.

WHY YOU NEED TO KNOW

Organizations across the United States and around the world have turned to quality management in an effort to meet the competitive challenges of the international marketplace. Although there is no set approach for implementing quality management, a commonality among most organizations is for employees at all levels to be brought into the effort as members of process improvement teams.

Successful organizations, such as General Electric and Hewlett-Packard, realize that thrusting people together in teams and then expecting process improvement to occur will generally lead to disappointment. They know that their employees need to understand how to work together as a team. In many instances, teams are formed to improve a process so that product or service quality is enhanced. However, teamwork and team building must be combined with training and education in the proper tools if employees are to be successful at making lasting process improvements. Over the past several decades, a number of techniques and methods for process improvement have been developed and used by organizations. As a group, these are referred to as the *Tools of Quality*. Many of these tools are based on statistical procedures and data analysis.

One set of quality tools known as *statistical process control charts* is so prevalent in business today, and is so closely linked to the material in Chapters 5 through 9, that its coverage merits a separate chapter. Today, successful managers must have an appreciation of, and familiarity with, the role of quality in process improvement activities. This chapter is designed to introduce you to the fundamental tools and techniques of quality management and to show you how to construct and interpret statistical process control charts.

18.1 Quality Management and Tools for Process Improvement

From the end of World War II through about the mid-1970s, industry in the United States was kept busy meeting a pent-up demand for its products both at home and abroad. The emphasis in most companies was on getting the "product out the door." The U.S. effort to produce large quantities of goods and services led to less emphasis on quality. During this same time, Dr. W. Edwards Deming and Dr. Joseph Juran were consulting with Japanese business leaders to help them rebuild their economic base after World War II. Deming, a statistician, and Juran, an engineer, emphasized that quality was the key to being competitive and that quality could be best achieved by improving the processes that produced the products and delivered the services.

Employing the process improvement approach was a slow, but effective, method for improving quality, and by the early 1970s Japanese products began to exceed those of the United States in terms of quality. The impact was felt by entire industries, such as automobiles and electronics. Whereas Juran focused on quality planning and helping businesses drive costs down by eliminating waste in processes, Deming preached a new management philosophy, which has become known as **Total Quality Management**, or TQM. There are about as many definitions of TQM as there are companies who have attempted to implement it. The margin definition for TQM is one that has been used by Hewlett-Packard since the early 1980s.

Total Quality Management
A journey to excellence in which everyone in the organization is focused on continuous process improvement directed toward increased customer satisfaction.

In the early 1980s, U.S. business leaders began to realize the competitive importance of providing high-quality products and services and a *quality revolution* was under way in the United States. Deming's 14 points (see Table 18.1) reflected a new philosophy of management that emphasized the importance of leadership. The numbers attached to each point do not indicate an order of importance, rather the 14 points collectively are seen as necessary steps to becoming a world-class company.

Juran's role in the quality movement is virtually on a par with Deming's. Juran is noted for many contributions to TQM, including his 10 steps to quality improvement, which are outlined in Table 18.2. Note that Juran and Deming differed with respect to the use of goals and targets. Juran is also credited with applying the **Pareto Principle** to quality. Juran urges managers to use the Pareto principle to focus on the *vital few* sources of problems and to separate the vital few from the *trivial many*. Pareto charts are used to display data in a way that helps managers find the most important problem issues.

Pareto Principle
80% of the problems come from 20% of the causes.

TABLE 18.1 Deming's 14 Points

1. Create a constancy of purpose toward the improvement of products and services in order to become competitive, stay in business, and provide jobs.

2. Adopt the new philosophy. Management must learn that it is in a new economic age and awaken to the challenge, learn their responsibilities, and take on leadership for change.

3. Stop depending on inspection to achieve quality. Build in quality from the start.

4. Stop awarding contracts on the basis of low bids.

5. Improve continuously and forever the system of production and service to improve quality and productivity, and thus constantly reduce costs.

6. Institute training on the job.

7. Institute leadership. The purpose of leadership should be to help people and technology work better.

8. Drive out fear so that everyone may work effectively.

9. Break down barriers between departments so that people can work as a team.

10. Eliminate slogans, exhortations, and targets for the workforce. They create adversarial relationships.

11. Eliminate quotas and management by objectives. Substitute leadership.

12. Remove barriers that rob employees of their pride of workmanship.

13. Institute a vigorous program of education and self-improvement.

14. Make the transformation everyone's job and put everyone to work on it.

There have been numerous other individuals who have played significant roles in the quality movement. Among these are Philip B. Crosby, who is probably best known for his book *Quality Is Free*, in which he emphasized that in the long run, the costs of improving quality are more than offset by the reductions in waste, rework, returns, and unsatisfied customers. Kauro Ishikawa is credited with developing and popularizing the application of the *Fishbone Diagram* that we will discuss shortly in the section on the Basic 7 Tools of Quality. There is also the work of Masaaki Imai, who popularized the philosophy of *kaizen*, or people-based continuous improvement.

Finally, we must not overlook the contributions of many different managers at companies such as Hewlett-Packard, General Electric, Motorola, Toyota and Federal Express. These leaders synthesized and applied many different quality ideas and concepts to their organizations in order to create world-class corporations. By sharing their successes with other firms, they have inspired and motivated others to continually seek opportunities in which the tools of quality can be applied to improve business processes.

TABLE 18.2 Juran's 10 Steps to Quality Improvement

1. Build awareness of both the need for improvement and the opportunity for improvement.

2. Set goals for improvement.

3. Organize to meet the goals that have been set.

4. Provide training.

5. Implement projects aimed at solving problems.

6. Report progress.

7. Give recognition.

8. Communicate the results.

9. Keep score.

10. Maintain momentum by building improvement into the company's regular systems.

CHAPTER OUTCOME #1

The Tools of Quality for Process Improvement

Once U.S. managers realized that their businesses were engaged in a competitive battle with companies around the world, they reacted in many ways. Some managers ignored the challenge and continued to see their market presence erode. Other managers realized that they needed a system or approach for improving their firms' operations and processes. The *Deming Cycle*, which is illustrated in Figure 18.1, has been effectively used by many organizations as a guide to their quality improvement efforts. The approach taken by the Deming Cycle is that problems should be identified and solved based on data.

Over time, a collection of tools and techniques known as the *Basic 7 Tools* have been developed for quality and process improvement. Some of these tools have already been introduced at various points throughout this text. However, we will briefly introduce all Basic 7 Tools in this section. Section 18.2 will explore one of these tools—Statistical Process Control Charts (SPC)—in greater depth.

Process Flowcharts A flowchart is a diagram that illustrates the steps in a process. Flowcharts provide a visualization of the process and are good beginning points in planning a process improvement effort.

Brainstorming Brainstorming is a tool that is used to generate ideas from the members of the team. Employees are encouraged to share any idea that comes to mind, and all ideas are listed with no ideas being evaluated until all ideas are posted. Brainstorming can be either structured or unstructured. In structured brainstorming, team members are asked for their ideas, in order, around the table. Members may pass if they have no further ideas. With unstructured brainstorming, members are free to interject ideas at any point.

Fishbone Diagram Kauro Ishikawa from Japan is credited with developing the fishbone diagram, which is also called the cause-and-effect diagram or the Ishikawa diagram. The fishbone diagram can be applied as a simple graphical brainstorming tool in which team members are given a problem and several categories of possible causes. They then brainstorm possible causes in any or all of the cause categories.

Histograms You were introduced to histograms in Chapter 2 as a method for graphically displaying quantitative data. Recall that histograms are useful for seeing the center, spread, and shape of a distribution of measurements. As a tool of quality, histograms are used to display measurements to determine whether the output of a process is centered on the target value and whether the process is capable of meeting specifications.

FIGURE 18.1

The Deming Cycle

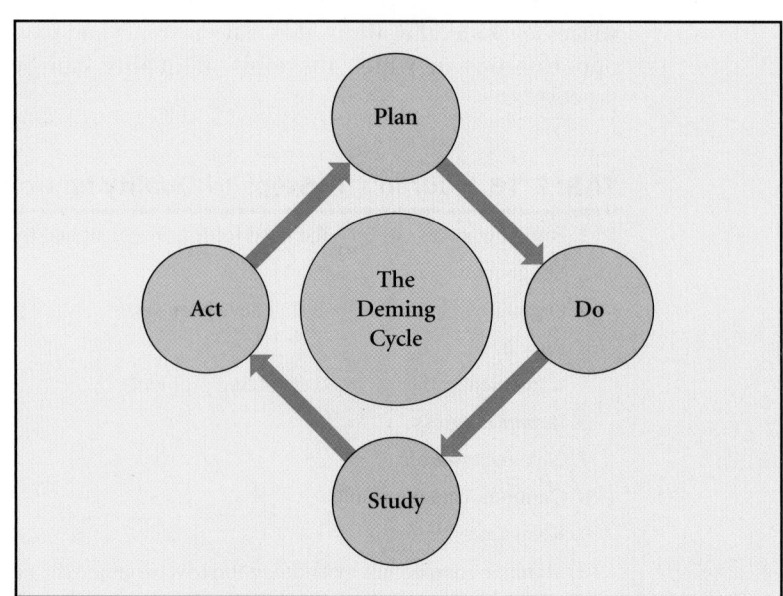

Trend Charts In Chapter 2 we illustrated the use of a line chart to display time-series data. A trend chart is a line chart that is used to track output from a process over time.

Scatter Plots There are many instances in quality improvement efforts in which you will want to examine the relationship between two quantitative variables. A scatter plot is an excellent tool for doing this. You were first introduced to scatter plots in Section 2.3 in Chapter 2. Scatter plots were also used in developing regression models in Chapters 14 and 15.

Statistical Process Control Charts One of the most frequently used Basic 7 Tools is the statistical process control (SPC) chart. SPC charts are a special type of trend chart. In addition to the data, the charts display the process average and the upper and lower control limits. These control limits define the range of random variation expected in the output of a process. SPC charts are used to provide early warnings when a process has gone out of control. There are several types of control charts depending on the type of data generated by the process of interest. Section 18.2 presents an introductory discussion of why control charts work and how to develop and interpret some of the most commonly used SPC charts.

Most organizations (public and private) in the United States and the developed countries of the world are involved in some form of quality improvement effort. Those that are not will likely not survive in the competitive global marketplace that exists today. Statistics plays a key role in the efforts of organizations to improve their quality. You will have the opportunity to use the techniques presented in this chapter and throughout this text as you help your organization meet its quality challenges.

18-1: EXERCISES

Skill Development

18-1. Discuss the similarities and differences between Dr. Deming's 14 points and Dr. Juran's 10 steps to quality improvement.

18-2. Deming is opposed to setting quotas or specific targets for workers.
  a. Use the library or the Internet to locate information that explains his reasoning.
  b. Discuss whether you agree or disagree with him.
  c. If possible, cite one or more examples based on your own experience to support your position.

18-3. Philip Crosby wrote the book *Quality Is Free*. In it he argues that it is possible to have high quality and low price. Do you agree? Provide examples that support your position.

Business Applications

18-4. Develop a process flowchart that describes the registration process at your college or university.

18-5. Generate a process flowchart showing the steps you have to go through to buy a concert ticket at your school.

18-6. Assume that you are a member of a team at your university charged with the task of improving student, faculty, and staff parking. Use brainstorming to generate a list of problems with the current parking plan. After you have generated the list, prioritize the list of problems based on their importance to you.

18-7. Refer to Exercise 18-6.
  a. Use brainstorming to generate a list of solutions for the top-rated parking problem.
  b. Order these possible solutions separately according to each of the following factors: cost to implement, time to implement, and easiest to gain approval.
  c. Did your lists come out in a different order? Why?

18-8. Suppose the computer lab manager at your school has been receiving complaints from students about long waits to use a computer. The "effect" is long wait times. The categories of possible causes are people, equipment, methods/rules, and the environment. Brainstorm specific ideas for each of these causes.

18-9. The city bus line is consistently running behind schedule. Brainstorm possible causes organized by such cause categories as people, methods, equipment, and the environment. Once you have finished, develop a priority order based on which cause is most likely to be the root cause of the problem.

18.2 Introduction to Statistical Process Control Charts

As we stated in Section 18.1, one of the most important tools for quality improvement is the *statistical process control* (SPC) chart. In this section we provide an overview of SPC charts. As you will see, SPC is actually an application of hypothesis testing. The concepts that have been introduced beginning in Chapter 2 provide you with the background needed to understand and use SPC.

The Existence of Variation

After studying the material in Chapters 1 through 17, you should be well aware of the importance of variation in business decision making. Variation exists naturally in the world around us. In any process or activity, the day-to-day outcomes are generally different; rarely are they exactly the same. As a practical example, think about the time it takes you to travel to the university each morning. You know it's about a 15-minute trip, and even though you travel the same route, your actual time will vary somewhat from day to day. You will notice this variation in many daily occurrences. The next time you renew your car license plates, notice that some people seem to get through faster than others. The same is true at a bank, where the time to cash your payroll check varies each payday.

Even in instances when variation is hard to detect, it is present. For example, when you measure a stack of 4-foot-by-8-foot sheets of plywood using a tape measure, they are all 4 feet wide. However, when the stack is measured using an engineer's scale, you may be able to detect slight variations among sheets, and using a caliper you can detect even more (see Figure 18.2).

Therefore, three concepts to remember about variation are

1. Variation is natural; it is inherent in the world around us.
2. No two products or service experiences are exactly the same.
3. With a fine-enough gauge, all things can be seen to differ.

FIGURE 18.2

Plywood Variation

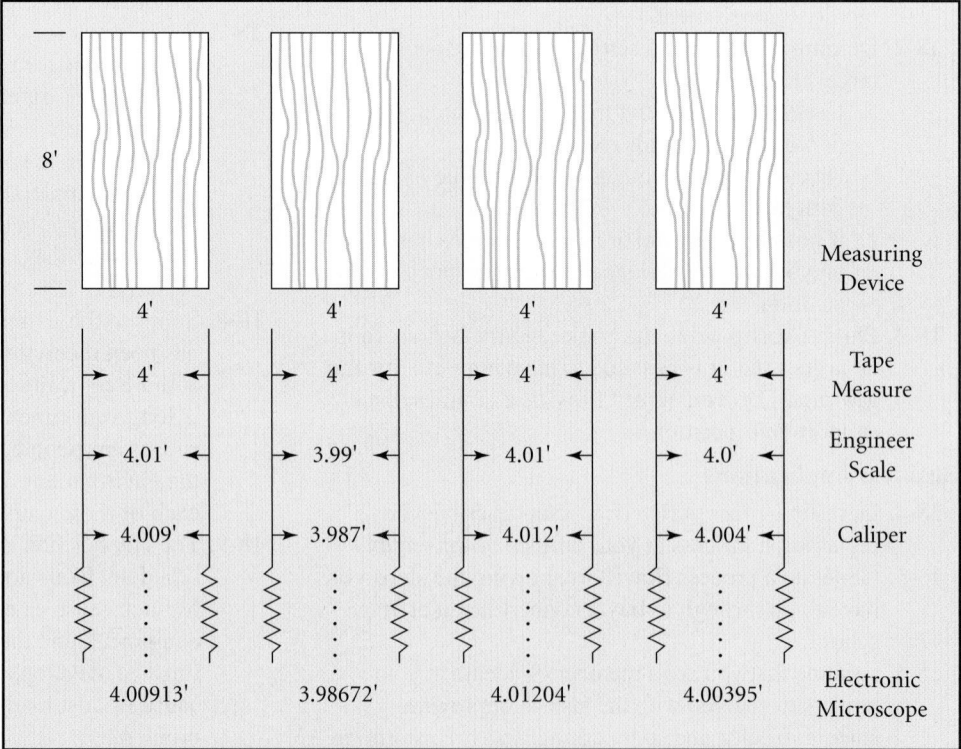

Sources of Variation What causes variation? Variation in the output of a process comes from variation in the inputs to the process. Let's go back to your travel time to school. Why isn't it always exactly the same? Your travel time depends on many factors, such as what route you take, how much traffic you encounter, whether you are in a hurry, how your car is running, and so on.

The six most common sources of variation are

1. people
2. machines
3. materials
4. methods
5. measurement
6. environment

Types of Variation Although variation is always present, we can define two major types that occur. The first is called *common cause variation*, which means it is naturally occurring or expected in the system. Other terms people use for common cause variation include *normal*, *random*, *chance occurrence*, *inherent*, and *stable variation*.

The other type of variation is called *special cause variation*. This type of variation is abnormal, indicating that something out of the ordinary has happened. This type of variation is also called *nonrandom*, *unstable*, and *assignable cause variation*.

In our example of travel time to school, there are common causes of variation such as traffic lights, traffic patterns, weather, and departure time. On the days when it takes you significantly more or less time to arrive at work, there are also special causes of variation occurring. These may be factors such as accidents, road construction detours, or needing to stop for gas. Examples of the two types of variation and some sources are

Sources of Common Cause Variation	Sources of Special Cause Variation
Weather conditions	Equipment not maintained and cleaned
Inconsistent work methods	Poor training
Machine wear	Worker fatigue
Temperature	Procedures not followed
Employee skill levels	Misuse of tools
Computer response times	Incorrect data entry

In any process or system, the total process variation is a combination of common cause and special cause factors. This can be expressed by Equation 18.1.

Variation Components

Total Process Variation = Common Cause Variation + Special Cause Variation (**18.1**)

In process improvement efforts, the goal is to first remove the special cause variation and then to reduce the common cause variation in a system. This requires that the source of a variation be identified and its cause eliminated.

The Predictability of Variation: Understanding the Normal Distribution
Dr. W. Edwards Deming said there is no such thing as consistency. However there is such a thing as a *constant-cause system*. A system that contains only common cause variations is very predictable. Though the outputs vary, they exhibit an important feature called stability. This means that some percentage of the output will continue to lie within given limits hour after hour, day after day, so long as the constant-cause system is operating. When a process exhibits stability, it is in control.

The reason that the outputs vary in a predictable manner is because measurable data, when subgrouped and pictured in a histogram, tend to cluster around the average and spread out symmetrically on both sides. This tendency is a function of the Central Limit Theorem that you first encountered in Chapter 7. This means that the frequency distribution of most processes will begin to resemble the shape of the normal distribution as the values are collected and grouped into classes.

The Concept of Stability We showed in Chapter 6 that the normal distribution can be divided evenly into six sections, the sum of which includes 99.7% of the data values. The width of each of these sections is called the standard deviation. The standard deviation is the primary way the spread (or dispersion) of the distribution is measured. Thus, we expect virtually all (99.7%) of the data in a stable process to fall within plus or minus 3 standard deviations of the mean. Generally speaking, as long as the measurements fall within the 3-standard-deviation boundary, we consider the process to be stable. This concept provides the basis for *statistical process control charts*.

Introducing Statistical Process Control Charts

Most cars are equipped with a temperature gauge that measures engine temperature. We come to rely on the gauge to let us know if "everything is all right." As long as the gauge points to the *normal* range, we conclude that there is no problem. However, if the gauge moves outside the *normal* range toward the *hot* mark, it's a signal that the engine is over-heating and something is wrong. If the gauge moves out of the *normal* range toward the *cold* mark, it's also a signal of potential problems.

Under typical driving conditions, engine temperature will fluctuate. The normal range on the car's gauge defines the expected temperature variation when the car is operating properly. Over time, we come to know what to expect. If something changes, the gauge is designed to give us a signal. The engine temperature gauge is analogous to a process control chart. Like the engine gauge, process control charts are used in business to define the boundaries that represent the amount of variation that can be considered normal.

Figure 18.3 illustrates the general format of a process control chart. The upper and lower *control limits* define the normal operating region for the process. The horizontal axis

FIGURE 18.3

Process Control Chart Format

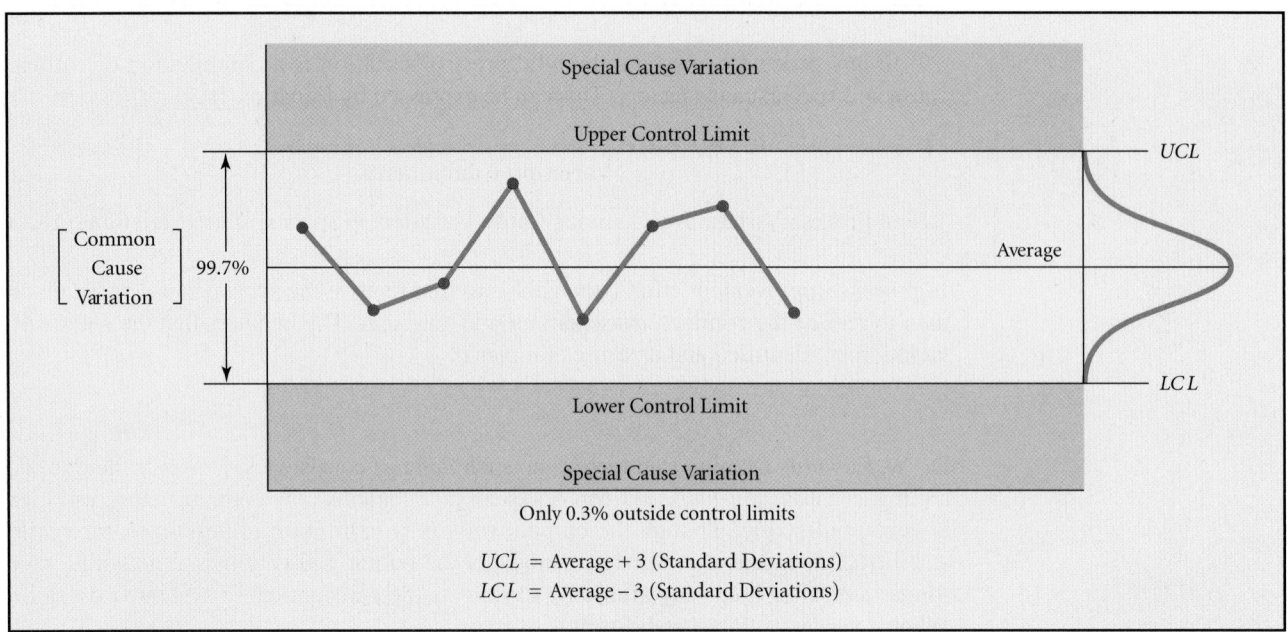

$$UCL = \text{Average} + 3 \text{ (Standard Deviations)}$$
$$LCL = \text{Average} - 3 \text{ (Standard Deviations)}$$

reflects the passage of time, or order of production. The vertical axis corresponds to the variable of interest.

There are a number of different types of process control charts. In this section, we introduce four of the most commonly used process control charts:

- $\bar{x}$-chart
- *R*-chart (range chart)
- *p*-chart
- *c*-chart

Each of these charts is designed for a special purpose. However, as you will see, the underlying logic is the same for each. The $\bar{x}$-chart and *R*-chart are almost always used in tandem. The $\bar{x}$-charts are used to monitor a process average. *R*-charts are used to monitor the variation of individual process values. They require that the variable of interest be quantitative. The next example shows how these two charts are developed and used.

CHAPTER OUTCOME #2

$\bar{x}$-Chart and *R*-Chart

Business Application

Excel and Minitab Tutorial

CATTLEMEN'S BAR AND GRILL The Cattlemen's Bar and Grill in Kansas City has developed a name for its excellent food and service. To maintain this reputation, the owners have established key measures of product and service quality, and they monitor these regularly. One measure is the amount of time customers wait from the time they are seated until they are served.

Every day, each hour that the business is open, four tables are randomly selected. The elapsed time from when customers are seated at these tables until their orders arrive is recorded. The owners wish to use these data to construct an $\bar{x}$-chart and an *R*-chart. These control charts can be developed using the following steps:

Step 1 Collect the initial sample data from which the control charts will be developed.

Four measurements during each hour for 30 hours are contained in a CD-ROM file called **Cattlemen**. The four values recorded each hour make up a *subgroup*. The $\bar{x}$-charts and *R*-charts are typically generated from small subgroups (three to six observations), and the general recommendation is that data from a minimum of 20 subgroups be gathered before a chart is constructed. Once the subgroup size is determined, all subgroups must be the same size. In this case, each subgroup is a sample of four tables.

Step 2 Calculate subgroup means and ranges.

Figure 18.4 shows the Excel worksheet with a partial listing of the data after the means and ranges have been computed for each subgroup.

Step 3 Compute the average of the subgroup means and the average range value.

The average of the subgroup means and the average range value are computed using Equations 18.2 and 18.3.

Average of Subgroup Means

$$\bar{\bar{x}} = \frac{\sum_{i=1}^{k} \bar{x}_i}{k} \tag{18.2}$$

where:

$\bar{x}_i = i$th subgroup average

$k = $ Number of subgroups

FIGURE 18.4

Excel 2007 Worksheet of Cattlemen's Service Time Data, Including Subgroup Means and Ranges

Excel 2007 Instructions:
1. Open file: Cattlemen.xls.
2. Note: Mean and Range values have been computed using Excel functions.

	A	B	C	D	E	F	G	H
1	Hour	Table 1	Table 2	Table 3	Table 4		Mean	Range
2	1	16	18	21	23		19.5	7
3	2	26	20	19	19		21	7
4	3	20	22	18	18		19.5	4
5	4	24	16	22	20		20.5	8
6	5	17	19	24	17		19.25	7
7	6	17	17	15	18		16.75	3
8	7	22	12	20	22		19	10
9	8	24	19	19	17		19.75	7
10	9	18	18	20	14		17.5	6

Minitab Instructions (for similar results):
1. Open file: Cattlemen.MTW.
2. Choose **Calc > Row Statistics**.
3. Under **Statistics**, choose **Mean**.
4. In **Input variables**, enter data column.
5. In **Store result in**, enter storage column.
6. Click **OK**.
7. Repeat 3 through 6 choosing **Range** under **Statistics**.

Average Subgroup Range

$$\bar{R} = \frac{\sum_{i=1}^{k} R_i}{k}$$

(18.3)

where:

$R_i = i$th subgroup range

$k = $ Number of subgroups

Using Equations 18.2 and 18.3, we get:

$$\bar{\bar{x}} = \frac{\sum \bar{x}}{k} = \frac{19.5 + 21 + \cdots + 20.75}{30} = 19.24$$

$$\bar{R} = \frac{\sum R}{k} = \frac{7 + 7 + \cdots + 3}{30} = 5.73$$

Step 4 **Prepare graphs of the subgroup means and ranges as a line chart.**

On one graph, plot the $\bar{x}$-values in time order across the graph and draw a line across the graph at the value corresponding to $\bar{\bar{x}}$. This is shown in Figure 18.5. Likewise, graph the R-values and $\bar{R}$ as a line chart, as shown in Figure 18.6.

The $\bar{\bar{x}}$ and $\bar{R}$ values in Figures 18.5 and 18.6 are called the "process control centerlines." The *centerline* is a graph of the mean value of the sample data. We use $\bar{\bar{x}}$ as the notation for centerline, which represents the current process

FIGURE 18.5

Line Chart for $\bar{x}$-Values for Cattlemen's Data

average. For these sample data, the average time people in the subgroups wait between being seated and being served is 19.24 minutes. However, as seen in Figure 18.5, there is variation around the centerline. The next step is to establish the boundaries that define the limits for what is considered *normal* variation in the process.

Step 5 **Compute the upper and lower control limits for the $\bar{x}$ chart.**

You learned in Chapter 6 that for a normal distribution with mean μ and standard deviation σ, approximately 99.7% of the values will fall within $\mu \pm 3\sigma$. Most process control charts are developed as 3-sigma control charts, meaning that the range of inherent variation is ± 3 standard deviations from the mean.

Because the $\bar{x}$ chart is a graph of subgroup (sample) means, the control limits are established at points ± 3 standard errors from the centerline, $\bar{\bar{x}}$.

FIGURE 18.6

Line Chart for *R*-Values for Cattlemen's Data

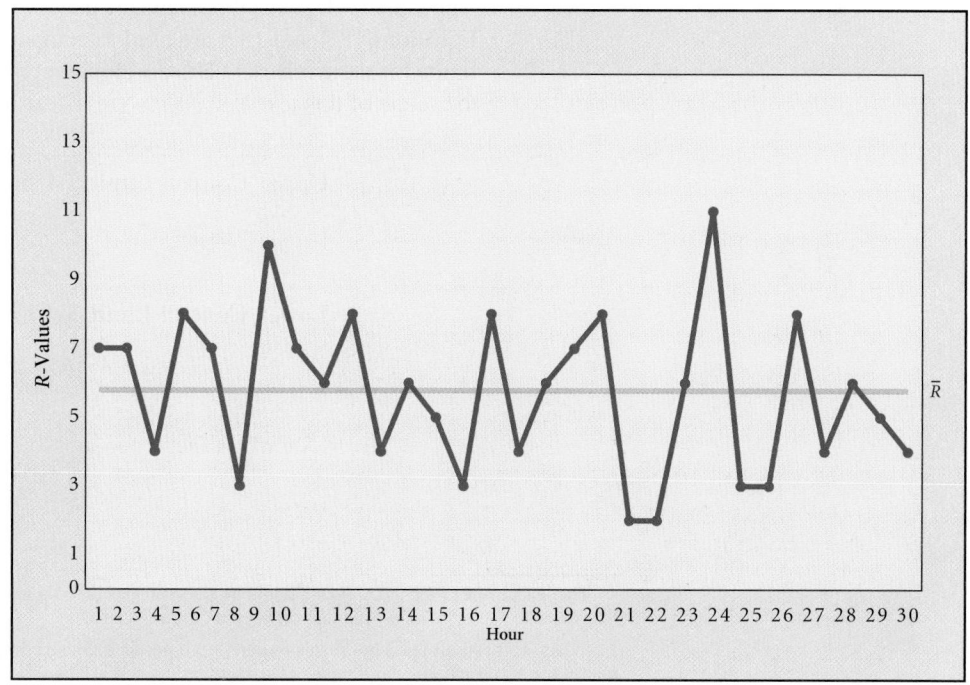

The control limits are analogous to the critical values we establish in hypothesis-testing problems. Using this analogy, the null hypothesis is that the process is in control. We will reject this null hypothesis whenever we obtain a subgroup mean beyond 3 standard errors from the centerline in either direction. Because the control chart is based on sample data, our conclusions are subject to error. Approximately 3 times in 1,000 (0.003), a subgroup mean should be outside the control limits when, in fact, the process is still in control. If this happens, we will have committed a Type I error. The 0.003 value is the significance level for the test. This small alpha level implies that 3-sigma control charts are very conservative when it comes to saying that a process is out of control. We might also conclude that the process is in control when in fact it isn't. If this happens, we have committed a Type II error.

To construct the control limits, we must determine the standard error of the sample means, $\sigma/\sqrt{n}$. Based on what you have learned in previous chapters, you might suspect that we would use $s/\sqrt{n}$. However, in most applications this is not done. In the 1930s, when process control charts were first introduced, there was no such thing as pocket calculators. In order to make control charts usable by people without calculators and without statistical training, a simpler approach was needed. An unbiased estimator of the standard error of the sample means, $\sigma/\sqrt{n}$, that was relatively easy to calculate was developed by Walter Shewhart.[1] The unbiased estimator is

$$\frac{A_2}{3}\bar{R}$$

where:

$\bar{R}$ = the mean of the subgroups' ranges

A_2 = a Shewhart factor that makes $(A_2/3)\bar{R}$ an unbiased estimator of the standard error of the sample means, $\sigma/\sqrt{n}$

Thus, 3 standard errors of the sample means can be estimated by

$$3\left(\frac{A_2}{3}\bar{R}\right) = A_2\bar{R}$$

Appendix Q displays the Shewhart factors for various subgroup sizes. Equations 18.4 and 18.5 are used to compute the upper and lower control limits for the $\bar{x}$-chart.[2] (The development of the *Shewhart table* is outside the scope of this text.)

Upper Control Limit, $\bar{x}$-Chart

$$UCL = \bar{\bar{x}} + A_2(\bar{R})$$

(18.4)

Lower Control Limit, $\bar{x}$-Chart

$$LCL = \bar{\bar{x}} - A_2(\bar{R})$$

(18.5)

where:

A_2 = Shewhart factor for subgroup size = n

---

[1] The leader of a group at the Bell Telephone Laboratories that did much of the original work in SPC, Shewhart is credited with developing the idea of control charts.

[2] When $A_2/3$ is multiplied by $\bar{R}$, this product becomes an unbiased estimator of the standard error, which is the reason for A_2's use here.

For the Cattlemen's Bar and Grill example, the subgroup size is 4. Thus, the A_2 factor from the Shewhart table (Appendix Q) is 0.73. We can compute the upper and lower control limits as follows:

$$UCL = \bar{\bar{x}} + A_2(\bar{R})$$
$$UCL = 19.24 + 0.729(5.73)$$
$$UCL = 23.42$$

$$LCL = \bar{\bar{x}} - A_2(\bar{R})$$
$$LCL = 19.24 - 0.729(5.73)$$
$$LCL = 15.06$$

Step 6 **Compute the upper and lower control limits for the _R_-chart.**

The D_3 and D_4 factors in the Shewhart table presented in Appendix Q are used to compute the 3-sigma control limits for the R-chart. The control limits are established at points ± 3 standard errors from the centerline, $\bar{R}$. However, unlike the case for the $\bar{x}$-chart, the unbiased estimator of the standard error of the sample ranges is a constant multiplied by $\bar{R}$. The constant for the lower control limit is the D_3 value from the Shewhart table. The D_4 value from the Shewhart table is the constant for the upper control limit.

Equations 18.6 and 18.7 are used to find the UCL and LCL values. Because the subgroup size is 4 in our example, $D_3 = 0.0$ and $D_4 = 2.28$.[3]

Upper Control Limit, _R_-chart

$$UCL = D_4(\bar{R})$$

(18.6)

Lower Control Limit, _R_-chart

$$LCL = D_3(\bar{R})$$

(18.7)

where:

D_3 and D_4 are taken from Appendix Q, the Shewhart table, for subgroup size $= n$

Using Equations 18.6 and 18.7, we get:

$$UCL = D_4(\bar{R})$$
$$UCL = 2.282(5.73)$$
$$UCL = 13.08$$

$$LCL = D_3(\bar{R})$$
$$LCL = 0.0(5.73)$$
$$LCL = 0.0$$

Step 7 **Finish constructing the control chart by locating the control limits on the $\bar{x}$ and _R_-charts.**

Graph the UCL and LCL values on the $\bar{x}$-chart and R-chart, as shown in Figures 18.7a and 18.7b and Figures 18.8a and 18.8b, which were constructed using the PHStat add-in to Excel and Minitab.[4]

---

[3] Because a range cannot be negative, the constant is adjusted to indicate that the lower boundary for the range must equal 0.

[4] See the Excel and Minitab Tutorial on the CD-ROM for the specific steps required to obtain the x-bar and R-charts. Minitab provides a much more extensive set of SPC options than PHStat.

FIGURE 18.7A

Excel 2007 (PHStat) Cattlemen's $\bar{x}$-Chart Output

Excel 2007 Instructions:
1. Open File: Cattlemen. xls.
2. Select **Add-Ins**.
3. Select **PHStat**.
4. Select **Control Charts > R and X-Bar Charts**.
5. Specify **Subgroup Size**.
6. Define cell range for the subgroup ranges.
7. Check **R and X-Bar Chart** option.
8. Define cell range for subgroup means.
9. Click **OK**.

FIGURE 18.7B

Minitab Cattlemen's $\bar{x}$-Chart Output

Minitab Instructions:
1. Open file: Cattlemen. MTW.
2. Choose **Stat > Control Charts > Variables Charts for Subgroups > X-bar**.
3. Select *Obervations for a subgroup are in one row of columns*.
4. Enter data columns in box.
5. Because file contains additional data Select **Data Options, Specify which rows to exclude**. Select **Row Numbers** and enter **31, 32, 33, 34, 35, 36. OK**.
6. Click on **Xbar Options** and select **Test tab**.
7. Select *Perform the following tests for special courses* and select the first four tests.
8. Click **OK. OK.**

Both students and people in industry sometimes confuse control limits and specification limits. Specification limits are arbitrary and are defined by a customer, by an industry standard, or by engineers who designed the item. The specification limits are defined as values above and below the "target" value for the item. The specification limits pertain to individual items—an item either meets specifications, or it does not. Process control limits are computed from actual data from the process. These limits define the range of inherent variation that is actually occurring in the process. The control limits are values above and below the current process average (which may be higher or lower than the "target").

Therefore, a process may be operating in a state of control, but it may be producing individual items that do not meet the specifications. Companies interested in improving quality must first bring the process under control before attempting to make changes in the process to reduce the defect level.

Using the Control Charts Once control charts for Cattlemen's service time have been developed, they can be used to determine whether the time it takes to serve customers remains *in control*. The concept involved is essentially a hypothesis test in which the null and alternative hypotheses can be stated as

H_0: The process is in control; the variation around the centerline is a result of common causes inherent in the process.

H_A: The process is out of control; the variation around the centerline is due to some special cause and is beyond what is normal for the process.

In the Cattlemen's Bar and Grill example, the hypothesis is tested every hour, when four tables are selected and the service time is recorded for each table. The $\bar{x}$- and R-values for the new subgroup are computed and plotted on their respective control charts.

FIGURE 18.8A

Excel 2007 (PHStat) Cattlemen's *R*-Chart Output

Excel 2007 Instructions:
1. Open File: Cattlemen.xls.
2. Select **Add-Ins**.
3. Select **PHStat**.
4. Select **Control Charts > R and X-Bar Charts**.
5. Specify **Subgroup Size**.
6. Define cell range for the subgroup ranges.
7. Check **R and X-Bar Chart** option.
8. Define cell range for subgroup means.
9. Click **OK**.

FIGURE 18.8B

Minitab Cattlemen's _R_-Chart Output

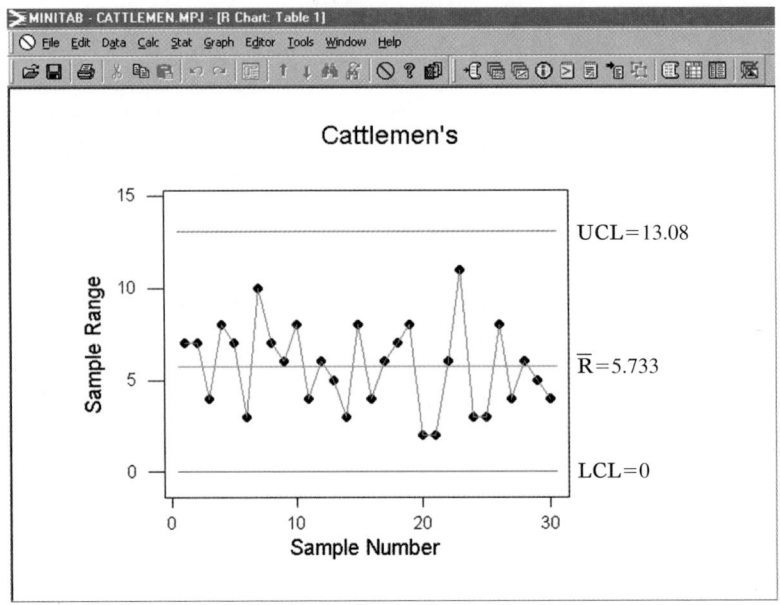

There are three main process changes that can be detected with a process control chart:

1. The process average has shifted up or down from normal.
2. The process average is trending up or down from normal.
3. The process is behaving in such a manner that the existing variation is not random in nature.

If any of these has happened, the null hypothesis is considered false and the process is considered to be _out of control_.

The control charts are used to provide signals that something has changed. There are four primary signals that indicate a change and that, if observed, will cause us to reject the null hypothesis.[5] These are

S i g n a l s

> 1.   one or more points outside the upper or lower control limits
> 2.   nine or more points in a row above (or below) the centerline
> 3.   six or more consecutive points moving in the same direction (increasing or decreasing)
> 4.   fourteen points in a row, alternating up and down

These signals were derived such that the probability of a Type I error is less than 0.01. Thus, there is a very small chance that we will conclude the process has changed when, in fact, it has not. If we examine the control charts in Figures 18.7a and 18.7b and 18.8a and 18.8b, we find that none of these signals occur. Thus, the process is deemed in control during the period in which the initial sample data were collected.

Suppose that the Cattlemen's owners monitor the process for the next 5 hours. Table 18.3 shows these new values, along with the mean and range for each hour. The means are plotted on the $\bar{x}$-chart, and the R-values are plotted on the R-chart, as shown in Figures 18.9 and 18.10.

When $\bar{x}$ and R-charts are used, we first look at the R-chart. Figure 18.10 shows the range (R) has been below the centerline ($\bar{R} = 5.733$) for 7 consecutive hours. Although this doesn't quite come up to the nine points of signal 2, the owners should begin to suspect something unusual might be happening to cause a downward shift in the variation in service time between tables. Although the R-chart does not indicate the reason for the shift, the owners should be pleased, because this might indicate greater consistency in service times. This change

---

[5] There is some minor disagreement on the signals, depending on which process control source you refer to. Minitab actually lets the user define the signals under the option **Define Tests**.

TABLE 18.3 Data for Hours 31 to 35 for Cattlemen's Bar and Grill

Hour	Table 1	Table 2	Table 3	Table 4	Mean	Range
31	20	21	24	22	21.75	4
32	17	22	18	20	19.25	5
33	23	20	22	22	21.75	3
34	24	23	19	20	21.50	5
35	24	25	26	27	25.50	3

FIGURE 18.9

Cattlemen's $\bar{x}$-Chart

FIGURE 18.10

Cattlemen's R-Chart

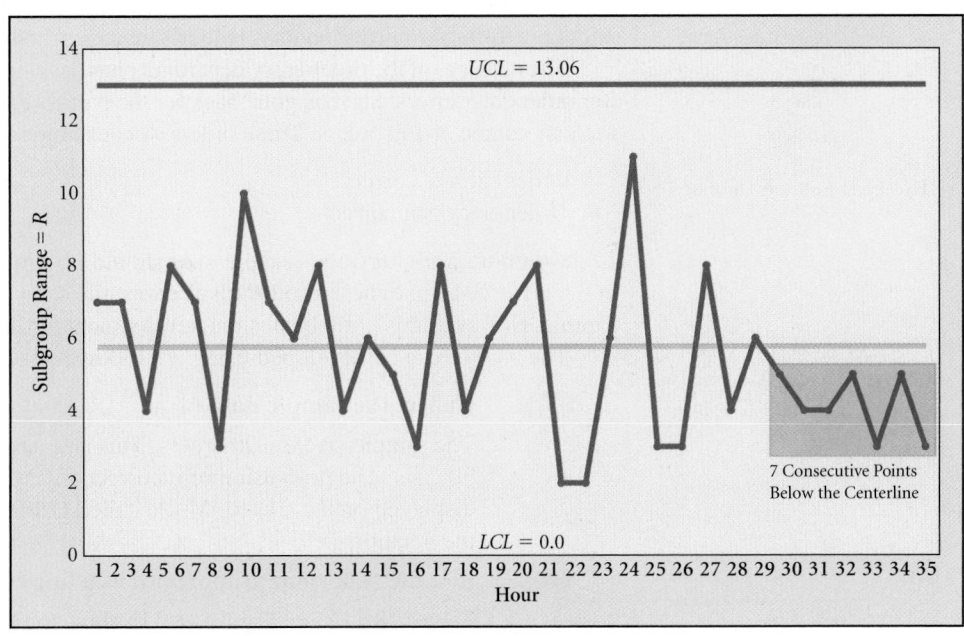

may represent a quality improvement. If this trend continues, the owners will want to study the situation so they will be able to retain these improvements in service time variability.

The $\bar{x}$-chart in Figure 18.9 indicates that the average service time is out of control because in hour 35 the mean service time exceeded the upper control limit of 23.42 minutes. The mean wait time for the four tables during this hour was 25.5 minutes. The chance of this happening is extremely low unless something has changed in the process. This should be a signal to the owners that a special cause exists. They should immediately investigate possible problems to determine if there has been a system change (e.g., training issue) or if this is truly a one-time event (e.g., fire in the kitchen). They could use a brainstorming technique or a fishbone diagram to identify possible causes of the problem.

An important point is that analysis of each of the control charts should not be done in isolation. A moment's consideration will lead you to see that if the variation of the process has gotten out of control (above the upper control limit), then trying to interpret the $\bar{x}$-chart can be very misleading. Widely fluctuating variation could make it much more probable that an $\bar{x}$-value would exceed the control limits even though the process mean had not changed.

Adding (or subtracting) a given number from all of the numbers in a data set does not change the variance of that data set, so a shift in the mean of a process can occur without that shift affecting the variation of the process. However, a change in the variation almost always affects the $\bar{x}$ control chart. For this reason, the general advice is to control the variation of a process before the mean of the process is subjected to control chart analysis.

The process control charts signal the user when something in the process has changed. In order for process control charts to be effective, they must be updated immediately after data have been collected, and action must be taken when the charts signal that a change has occurred.

CHAPTER OUTCOME #3 | **p-Charts** The previous example illustrated how $\bar{x}$-charts and R-charts can be developed and used. They are used in tandem and are applicable when the characteristic being monitored is a variable measured on a continuous scale (e.g., time, weight, length, etc.). However, there are instances when the process issue involves an *attribute* rather than a quantitative variable. An attribute is a quality characteristic that is either present or not present. In many quality control situations, an attribute is whether an item is good (meets specifications) or defective, and in those cases a *p-chart* can be used to monitor the proportion of defects.

Business Application

Excel and Minitab Tutorial

HILDER'S PUBLISHING COMPANY Hilder's Publishing Company sells books and records through a catalog, processing hundreds of mail and phone orders each day. Each customer order requires numerous data-entry steps. Mistakes made in data-entry can be costly, resulting in shipping delays, incorrect prices, or the wrong items being shipped. As part of its ongoing efforts to improve quality, Hilder's managers and employees want to reduce errors.

The manager of the order-entry department has developed a process control chart to monitor order-entry errors. She has gone back for the past 30 days and for each day has selected a random sample of 100 orders. These orders were examined, with the attribute being

- Order entry is correct.
- Order entry is incorrect.

In developing a *p*-chart, the sample size should be large enough such that $np \geq 5$ and $n(1 - p) \geq 5$. Unlike the $\bar{x}$- and R-chart cases, the sample size may differ from sample to sample. However, this complicates the development of the *p*-chart.

The *p*-chart can be developed using the following steps:

Step 1 Collect the sample data.

The sample size is 100 orders. This size sample was selected for each of 30 days. The proportion of incorrect orders, called *nonconformances*, are displayed on the CD-ROM file called **Hilders**. The proportions are given the notation, $\bar{p}$.

Step 2 Plot the subgroup proportions as a line chart.

Figure 18.11a and Figure 18.11b show the line chart for the 30 days.

Step 3 Compute the mean subgroup proportion for all samples using Equation 18.8 or 18.9, depending on whether the sample sizes are equal.

Mean Subgroup Proportion

For equal-size samples

$$\bar{p} = \frac{\sum_{i=1}^{k} p_i}{k} \tag{18.8}$$

where:

$$p_i = \text{Sample proportion for subgroup } i$$
$$k = \text{Number of samples of size } n$$

For unequal sample sizes:

$$\bar{p} = \frac{\sum_{i=1}^{k} n_i p_i}{\sum_{i=1}^{k} n_i} \tag{18.9}$$

where:

$$n_i = \text{The number of items in sample } i$$
$$\sum_{i=1}^{k} = \text{Total number of items sampled in } k \text{ samples}$$
$$k = \text{Number of samples of size } n$$

FIGURE 18.11A

Excel 2007 (PHStat) *p*-Chart for Hilder's Publishing

Excel 2007 (PHStat) Instructions:
1. Open File: Hilders.xls.
2. Select **Add-Ins**.
3. Select **PHStat**.
4. Select **Control Charts > *p*-Charts**.
5. Define cell range for number of nonconformances (note, do not enter cell range for proportions of nonconformances).
6. Check **Sample/Subgroup Size** does not vary.
7. Enter sample/subgroup size.
8. Click **OK**.

FIGURE 18.11B

Minitab *p*-Chart for Hilder's Publishing

Minitab Instructions:
1. Open file: Hilders.MTW.
2. Choose **Stat > Control Charts > Attribute Charts > P**.
3. In **Variable**, enter *number of orders with errors* column.
4. In **Subgroup Sizes** enter size of subgroup.100.

5. Click on **P Chart Options** and select **Tests** tab.
6. Select *Perform all tests for special causes.*
7. Click **OK**. **OK**.

Because we have equal sample sizes, we use Equation 18.8, as follows:

$$\bar{p} = \frac{\sum p_i}{k} = \frac{0.10 + 0.06 + 0.06 + 0.07 + \cdots}{30} = \frac{2.38}{30} = 0.0793$$

Thus, the average proportion of orders with errors is 0.0793.

Step 4 **Compute the standard error of *p* using Equation 18.10.**

Standard Error for the Subgroup Proportions

For equal sample sizes:

$$s_p = \sqrt{\frac{(\bar{p})(1 - \bar{p})}{n}} \qquad \textbf{(18.10)}$$

where:

$$\bar{p} = \text{Mean subgroup proportion}$$
$$n = \text{Common sample size}$$

For unequal sample sizes:

> *Option 1. Compute s_p using largest sample size and s_p using the smallest sample size. Construct control limits using each value.*
>
> *Option 2. Compute a unique value of s_p for each different sample size. Construct control limits for each s_p value.*

We compute $s_{\bar{p}}$ using Equation 18.10, as follows:

$$s_p = \sqrt{\frac{(\bar{p})(1-\bar{p})}{n}} = \sqrt{\frac{(0.0793)(1-0.0793)}{100}} = 0.027$$

Step 5 **Compute the 3-sigma control limits using Equations 18.11 and 18.12.**

Control Limits for p-Chart

$$UCL = \bar{p} + 3s_p \qquad\qquad (18.11)$$

$$LCL = \bar{p} - 3s_p \qquad\qquad (18.12)$$

where:

$\bar{p}$ = Mean subgroup proportion

s_p = Estimated standard error of $p = \sqrt{\dfrac{(\bar{p})(1-\bar{p})}{n}}$

Using Equations 18.11 and 18.12, we get the following control limits:

$$UCL = \bar{p} + 3s_p = 0.079 + 3(0.027) = 0.160$$
$$LCL = \bar{p} - 3s_p = 0.079 - 3(0.027) = -0.002 \rightarrow 0.0$$

Because a proportion of nonconforming items cannot be negative, the lower control limit is set to 0.0.

Step 6 **Plot the centerline and control limits on the control chart.**
Both upper and lower control limits are plotted on the control charts in Figure 18.11a and Figure 18.11b.

Using the p-Chart Once the control chart is developed, the same rules are used as for the $\bar{x}$- and R-charts:[6]

Signals

---

1. one or more points outside the upper or lower control limits
2. nine or more points in a row above (or below) the centerline
3. six or more consecutive points moving in the same direction (increasing or decreasing)
4. fourteen points in a row, alternating up and down

The p-chart shown in Figure 18.11a indicates the process is in control. None of the signals are present in these data. The variation in the nonconformance rates is assumed to be due to the common cause issues.

For future days, the managers would select random samples of 100 orders, count the number with errors, and compute the proportion. This value would be plotted on the p-chart. For each day, the managers would use the control chart to test the hypotheses:

H_0: The process is in control. The variation around the centerline is a result of common causes and is inherent in the process.

H_A: The process is out of control. The variation around the centerline is due to some special cause and is beyond what is normal for the process.

The signals mentioned previously would be used to test the null hypothesis. Remember, control charts are most useful when the charts are updated as soon as the new sample data become available. When a signal of special cause variation is present, you should take action to determine the source of the problem and remove it as quickly as possible.

---

[6] Minitab allows the user to specify the signals. This is done in the Define Tests feature under **Stat—Control Charts**. See the Excel and Minitab Tutorial on the CD-ROM for specifics in developing a p-chart.

CHAPTER OUTCOME #4

c-Charts The *p*-chart just discussed is used when you select a sample of items and you determine the number of the sampled items that possess a specific attribute of interest. Each item either has or does not have that attribute. You will encounter other situations that involve attribute data but differ from the *p*-chart applications. In these situations, you have what is defined as a sampling unit (or experimental unit), which could be a sheet of plywood, a door panel on a car, a textbook page, an hour of service, or any other defined unit of space, volume, time, and so on. Each sampling unit could have one or more of the attributes of interest, and you would be able to count the number of attributes present in each sampling unit. In cases in which the sampling units are the same size, the appropriate control chart is a *c*-chart.

Business Application

Excel and Minitab Tutorial

CHANDLER TILE COMPANY The Chandler Tile Company makes ceramic tile. In recent years, there has been a big demand for tile products in private residences for kitchens and bathrooms and in commercial establishments for decorative counter and wall covering. Although the demand has increased, so has the competition. The senior management at Chandler knows that three factors are key to winning business from contractors: price, quality, and service.

One quality issue is scratches on a tile. The production managers wish to set up a control chart to monitor the level of scratches per tile to determine whether the production process remains in control.

Special Note

> Control charts monitor a process as it currently operates, not necessarily how you would like it to operate. Thus, a process that is in control might still yield a higher number of scratches per tile than the managers would like.

The managers believe that the numbers of scratches per tile are independent of each other and that the prevailing operating conditions are consistent from tile to tile. In this case, the proper control chart is a *c*-chart. Here the tiles being sampled are the same size, and the managers will tally the number of scratches per tile. However, if we asked, "How many opportunities were there to scratch each tile?" we probably would not be able to answer the question. There are more opportunities than we could count. For this reason, the *c*-chart is based on the Poisson probability distribution, rather than the binomial distribution, which was introduced in Chapter 5. You might recall that the Poisson distribution is defined by the mean number of *successes* per interval, or sampling unit, as shown in Equation 18.13. A success can be regarded as a defective, a nonconformance, or any other characteristic of interest. In the Chandler example, a success is a scratch on a tile.

Mean for *c*-Chart

$$\bar{c} = \frac{\sum_{i=1}^{k} x_i}{k} \qquad (18.13)$$

where:

x_i = Number of successes per sampling unit

k = Number of sampling units

Because the Poisson distribution is skewed when the mean of the sampling unit is small, we must define the sampling unit so that it is large enough to provide an average of at least 5 successes per sampling unit ($\bar{c} \geq 5$). This may require that you combine smaller sampling units into a larger unit size. In this case we combine 6 tiles to form a sampling unit.

The mean and the variance of the Poisson distribution are identical. Therefore, the standard deviation of the Poisson distribution is the square root of its mean. For this reason, the estimator of the standard deviation for the Poisson distribution is computed as the square root of the sample mean, as shown in Equation 18.14.

Standard Deviation for *c*-Chart

$$s_c = \sqrt{\overline{c}}$$

(18.14)

Then Equations 18.15 and 18.16 are used to compute the 3-sigma (3 standard deviation) control limits for the *c*-chart.

***c*-Chart Control Limits**

$$UCL = \overline{c} + 3\sqrt{\overline{c}}$$

(18.15)

and

$$LCL = \overline{c} - 3\sqrt{\overline{c}}$$

(18.16)

You can use the following steps to construct a *c*-chart:

Step 1 Collect the sample data.

The original plan called for the Chandler Tile Company to select six tiles each hour from the production line and to perform a thorough inspection to count the number of scratches per tile. Like all control charts, at least 20 samples are desired in developing the initial control chart. After collecting 40 sampling units of six tiles each, the total number of scratches found was 228. The data set is contained in the CD-ROM file **Chandler**.

Step 2 Compute the average number of occurrences per sampling unit using Equation 18.13.

The mean would be

$$\overline{c} = \frac{\sum x}{k} = \frac{228}{40} = 5.70 \text{ scratches per sampling unit}$$

Step 3 Construct the 3-sigma control limits, using Equations 18.15 and 18.16.

The following steps are used.

1. The mean is

$$\overline{c} = \frac{\sum x}{k} = \frac{228}{40} = 5.70$$

2. The standard deviation is computed using Equation 18.14.

$$s_c = \sqrt{\overline{c}} = \sqrt{5.70} = 2.387$$

3. The upper and lower 3-sigma control limits are

$$UCL = \overline{c} + 3\sqrt{\overline{c}} = 5.7 + 3(2.387) = 12.86$$
$$LCL = \overline{c} - 3\sqrt{\overline{c}} = 5.7 - 3(2.387) = -1.46 \rightarrow 0.0$$

As with the *p*-chart, the lower control limit can't be negative. We change it to zero, which is the fewest possible scratches on a tile. The completed *c*-chart is shown in Figure 18.12a and Figure 18.12b.

Note in both figures that four samples of six tiles each had a total number of scratches that fell outside the upper control limit of 12.86. The managers need to consult production records and other information to determine

FIGURE 18.12A

Excel 2007 *c*-Chart for Chandler Tile Company

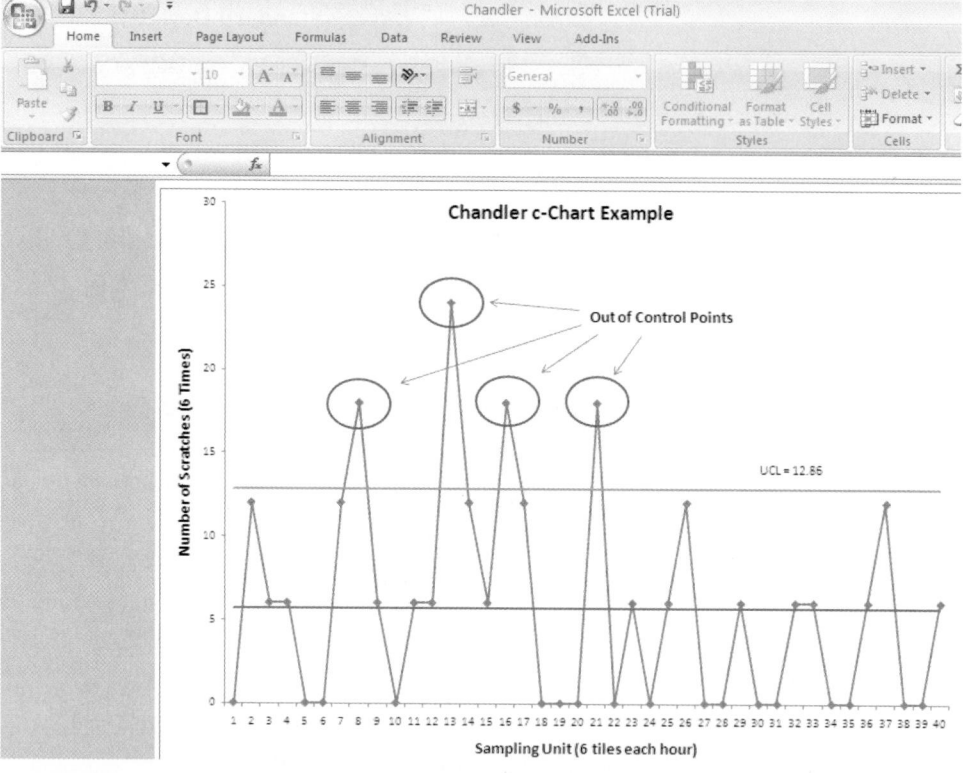

Excel 2007 Instructions:
1. Open File: Chandler.xls.
2. Calculate the *c*-bar value using Excel's **AVERAGE** function and copy this value down in a new column.
3. Calculate the standard deviation as the square root of the mean using Excel's **SQRT** function. Then copy that value down in a new column.
4. Select the three columns.
5. Click **Insert > Line Chart**.
6. Click **Layout** to add axis labels and chart titles.

FIGURE 18.12B

Minitab *c*-Chart for Chandler Tile Company

Minitab Instructions:
1. Open file: Chandler.xls.
2. Choose **Stat > Control Chart > Attributes Charts > C**.
3. In **Variable**, enter number of defectives column.
4. Click on **C Chart Options** and select **Tests** tab.
5. Select *Perform all tests for special causes*.
6. Click **OK. OK.**

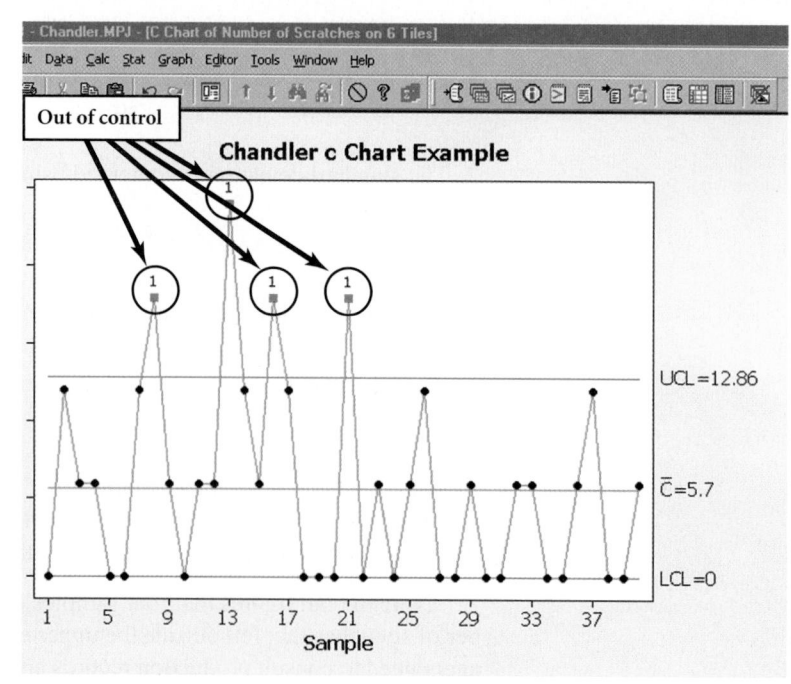

what special cause might have generated this level of scratches. If they can determine the cause, these data points should be removed and the control limits should be recomputed from the remaining 36 values. You might also note that the graph changes beginning with about sample 22. The process seems more stable from sample 22 onward. Managers might consider inspecting for another 13 to 15 hours and recomputing the control limits using data from hours 22 and higher.

Other Control Charts Our purpose in this chapter has been to introduce SPC charts. We have illustrated a few of the most frequently used charts. However, there are many other types of control charts that can be used in special situations. You are encouraged to consult several of the references listed at the end of the chapter for information about these other charts. Regardless of the type of statistical quality control chart you are using, the same general steps are used.

SUMMARY   Constructing SPC charts

The following steps are employed when constructing statistical quality control charts:

1. Collect the sample data.

2. Compute the centerline value. The centerline on the control chart is the average value for the sample data. This is the current process average.

3. Compute the upper and lower control limits.

4. Plot the appropriate data on the control chart, along with the centerline and control limits.

18-2: Exercises

Skill Development

18-10. Data were collected on a quantitative measure with a subgroup size of 5 observations. Thirty subgroups were collected, with the following results:

$$\bar{\bar{x}} = 44.52 \qquad \bar{R} = 5.6$$

   a. Determine the Shewhart factors that will be needed if $\bar{x}$- and R-charts are to be developed.

   b. Compute the upper and lower control limits for the R-chart.

   c. Compute the upper and lower control limits for the $\bar{x}$-chart.

18-11. Data were collected from a process in which the factor of interest was whether the finished item contained a particular attribute. The fraction of items that did not contain the attribute was recorded. A total of 30 samples were selected. The common sample size was 100 items. The total number of nonconforming items was 270. Based on these data, compute the upper and lower control limits for the p-chart.

18-12. Fifty sampling units of equal size were inspected, and the number of nonconforming situations were recorded. The total number of instances was 449.

   a. Determine the appropriate control chart to use for this process.

   b. Compute the mean value for the control chart.

   c. Compute the upper and lower control limits.

18-13. Explain why it is important to update the control charts as soon as new data become available.

Computer Database Exercises

18-14. The Haines Lumber Company makes plywood for residential and commercial construction. One of the key quality measures is plywood thickness. Every hour, five pieces of plywood are selected and the thicknesses are measured. The data (in inches) for the first 20 subgroups are in the CD-ROM file **Haines**.

   a. Construct an $\bar{x}$-chart based on these data. Make sure you plot the centerline and both 3-sigma upper and lower control limits.

   b. Construct an R-chart based on these data.

c. Examine both control charts and determine if there are any special causes of variation that require attention in this process.

18-15. Referring to Exercise 18-14, suppose the process remained in control for the next 40 hours. The thickness measurements for hours 41 through 43 are

Hour 41	0.764	0.737	0.724	0.716	0.752
Hour 42	0.766	0.785	0.777	0.790	0.799
Hour 43	0.812	0.774	0.767	0.799	0.821

a. Based on these data and the two control charts, what should you conclude about the process? Has the process gone out of control? Discuss.

b. Was it necessary to obtain your answer to Exercise 18-14 before part a could be answered? Explain your reasoning.

18-16. Grandfoods, Inc., makes energy supplement bars for use by athletes and others who need an energy boost. One of the critical quality characteristics is the weight of the bars. Too much weight implies that too many liquids have been added to the mix and the bar will be too chewy. If the bars are light, the implication is that the bars are too dry. To monitor the weights, the production manager wishes to use process control charts. Data for 30 subgroups of size 4 bars are contained in the CD-ROM file **Grandfoods**. Note that a subgroup is selected every 15 minutes as bars come off the manufacturing line.

a. Use these data to construct the appropriate process control chart(s).

b. Discuss what each chart is used for. Why do we need both charts?

c. Examine the control charts and indicate which, if any, of the signals are present. Is the process currently in control?

d. Develop a histogram for the energy bar weights. Discuss the shape of the distribution and the implications of this toward the validity of the control chart procedures you have used.

18-17. Referring to the process control charts developed in Exercise 18-16, data for periods 31 to 40 are contained in the CD-ROM file **Grandfoods-Extra**.

a. Based on these data, what would you conclude about the energy bar process?

b. Write a report discussing the results, and show the control charts along with the new data.

18-18. Trinkle & Sons performs subcontract body paint work for one of the "Big Three" automakers. One of its recent contracts called for the company to paint 12,500 door panels. Several quality characteristics are very important to the manufacturer, one of which

is blemishes in the paint. The manufacturer has required Trinkle & Sons to have control charts to monitor the number of paint blemishes per door panels. The panels are all for the same model car and are the same size. To initially develop the control chart, data for 88 door panels were collected and are provided in the CD-ROM file **CarPaint**.

a. Determine the appropriate type of process control chart to develop.

b. Develop a 3-sigma control chart.

c. Based on the control chart and the standard signals discussed in this chapter, what conclusions can you reach about whether the paint process is in control? Discuss.

18-19. Wilson, Ryan, and Reed is a large CPA firm in Charleston, South Carolina. It has been monitoring the accuracy of its employees and wishes to get the number of errors per account under statistical control. It has sampled 100 accounts for each of the last 30 days and has examined them for errors. The data are presented in the CD-ROM file **Accounts**.

a. Construct the relevant control chart for the account process.

b. What does the chart indicate about the statistical stability of the process? Give reasons for your answers.

c. Suppose that for the next 3 days, sample sizes of 100 accounts are examined with the following results:

| Number of Errors | 6 | 7 | 9 |

Plot the appropriate data on the control chart and indicate whether any of the control chart signals are present. Discuss your results.

18-20. Tony Perez is the manager of one of the largest chains of service stores that specialize in oil and lubrication of automobiles, Fastlube, Inc. One of the company's stated goals is to provide a lube and oil change for anyone's automobile in 15 minutes. Tony has thought for some time now that there is a growing disparity among his workers in the time it takes to lube and change the oil of an automobile. To monitor this aspect of Fastlube, Inc., Tony has selected a sample of 20 days and has recorded the time it took five randomly selected employees to service an automobile. The data are located in the CD-ROM file **Fastlube**.

a. Tony glanced through the data and noticed that the longest time it took to service a car was 25.33 minutes. Suppose the distribution of times to service a car was normal, with a mean of 15. Use your knowledge of a normal distribution to let Tony know what the standard deviation is for the time it takes to service a car.

b. Use the **Fastlube** data to construct an $\bar{x}$- and an R-chart.

c. Based on these data, what would you conclude about the service time process?

d. Based on your findings on the R-chart, would it be advisable to draw conclusions based on the $\bar{x}$-chart?

18-21. The Kaiser Corporation makes aluminum at various locations around the country. One of the key factors in being profitable is keeping the machinery running. One particularly troublesome machine is a roller that flattens the sheets to the appropriate thickness. This machine tends to break down for various reasons. Consequently, the maintenance manager has decided to develop a process control chart. Over a period of 10 weeks, 20 subgroups consisting of 5 downtime measures (in minutes) were collected (one measurement at the end of each of the two shifts.) The subgroup means and ranges are shown as follows and are contained in a CD-ROM file called **Kaiser**.

Subgroup Mean	104.8	85.9	78.6	72.8	102.6	84.8	67.0
Subgroup Range	9.6	14.3	8.6	10.6	11.2	13.5	10.8
Subgroup Mean	91.1	79.5	71.9	47.6	106.7	80.7	81.0
Subgroup Range	5.2	14.2	14.1	14.9	12.7	13.3	15.4
Subgroup Mean	57.0	98.9	87.9	64.9	101.6	83.9	
Subgroup Range	15.5	13.8	16.6	11.2	9.6	11.5	

a. Explain why the $\bar{x}$- and R-charts would be appropriate in this case.

b. Find the centerline value for the $\bar{x}$-chart.

c. Calculate the centerline value for the R-chart.

d. Compute the upper and lower control limits for the R-chart, and construct the chart with appropriate labels.

e. Compute the upper and lower control limits for the $\bar{x}$-chart, and construct the chart with appropriate labels.

f. Examine the charts constructed in parts d and e and determine whether the process was in control during the period for which the control charts were developed. Explain.

18-22. Referring to Exercise 18-21, if necessary delete any out-of-control points and construct the appropriate $\bar{x}$- and R-charts. Now, suppose the process stays in control for the next 6 weeks (subgroups 21 through 32). The subgroup means and ranges for subgroups 33 to 38 are as follows:

Subgroup	33	34	35	36	37	38
Subgroup Mean	89.0	88.4	85.2	89.3	97.2	105.3
Subgroup Range	11.4	5.4	14.2	11.7	9.5	10.2

a. Plot the ranges on the R-chart. Is there evidence based on the range chart that the process has gone out of control? Discuss.

b. Plot the subgroup means on the $\bar{x}$-chart. Is there evidence to suggest that the process has gone out of control with respect to the process mean? Discuss.

18-23. The Ajax Taxi company in Manhattan, New York, wishes to set up an $\bar{x}$-chart and an R-chart to monitor the number of miles driven per day by its taxi drivers. Each week, the scheduler selects four taxis and (without the drivers' knowledge) monitors the number of miles driven. He has done this for the past 40 weeks. The data are in the CD-ROM file **Ajax**.

a. Construct the R-chart for these 40 subgroups.

b. Construct the $\bar{x}$-chart for these 40 subgroups. Be sure to label the chart correctly.

c. Look at both control charts and determine if any of the control chart signals are present to indicate that the process is not in control. Explain the implications of what you have found for the Ajax Taxi Company.

18-24. Referring to Exercise 18-23, the data for weeks 41 through 45 are in the **Ajax-Extra** CD-ROM file.

a. Using the control limits developed from the first 40 weeks, do these data indicate that the order-entry process is now out of control? Explain.

b. If a change has occurred, brainstorm some of the possible reasons.

c. What will be the impact on the control charts when the new data are included?

d. Use the data in the files **Ajax** and **Ajax-Extra** to develop the new control charts.

e. Are any of the typical control chart signals present? Discuss.

18-25. Regis Printing Company performs printing services for individuals and business customers. Many of the jobs require that brochures be folded for mailing. The company has a machine that does the folding. It generally does a good job, but it can have problems that cause it to do improper folds. To monitor this process, the company selects a sample of 50 brochures from every order and counts the number of incorrectly folded items in each sample. Until now, nothing has been done with the 300 samples that have been collected. The data are located in the CD-ROM file **Regis**.

a. What is the appropriate control chart to use to monitor this process?

b. Using the data in this file, construct the appropriate control chart and label it properly.

c. Suppose that for the next three orders, sample sizes of 50 brochures are examined with the following results:

Sample Number	301	302	303
Number of Bad Folds	6	9	7

Plot the appropriate data to the control chart and indicate whether any of the control chart signals are present. Discuss your results.

d. Suppose that the next sample of 50 has 14 improperly folded brochures, what conclusion should be reached based on the control chart? Discuss.

18-26. Recall from Exercise 18-20 that Tony Perez is the manager of one of the largest chains of service stores that specialize in oil and lubrication of automobiles, Fastlube, Inc. One of the company's stated goals is to provide a lube and oil change for anyone's automobile in 15 minutes. Tony has thought for some time now that there is a growing disparity among his workers in the time it takes to lube and change the oil of an automobile. To monitor this aspect of Fastlube, Inc., Tony has selected a sample of 24 days and has recorded the time it took to service 100 automobiles each day. The number of times the service was performed in 15 minutes or less (≤ 15) is given in the CD-ROM file **Lubeoil**.

a. (1) Convert the sample data to proportions and plot the data as a line graph. (2) Compute $\bar{p}$ and plot this value on the line graph. (3) Compute s_p and interpret what it measures.

b. Construct a p-chart and determine if the process of the time required for oil and lube jobs is in control.

c. Specify the signals that are used to indicate an out-of-control situation on a p-chart.

18-27. Susan Booth is the director of operations for National Skyways, a small commuter airline with headquarters in Cedar Rapids, Iowa. She has become increasingly concerned about the amount of carry-on luggage passengers have been carrying on board National Skyways' planes. She collected data concerning the number of pieces of baggage that were taken on board over a 1-month period. The data collected are provided in the CD-ROM file **Carryon**.

a. Set up a control chart for the number of carry-on bags per day.

b. Is the process in a state of statistical control? Explain your answer.

c. Suppose that National Skyways' aircraft were full for each of the 30 days. Each Skyways aircraft holds 40 passengers. Describe the control chart you would use. Is it necessary that you use this latter alternative or is it just a preference? Explain your answer.

18-28. Sid Luka is the service manager for Brakes Unlimited, a franchise corporation that specializes in servicing automobile brakes. He wants to study the length of time required to replace the rear drum brakes of automobiles. A subgroup of 10 automobiles needing their brakes replaced was selected on each day for a period of 20 days. The subgroup times required (in hours) for this service were recorded and are presented in the CD-ROM file **Brakes**. (This problem cannot be done using Minitab.)

a. Sid has been trying to get the average time required to replace the rear drum brakes of an automobile to be under 1.65 hours. Use the data Sid has collected to determine if he has reached his goal.

b. Set up the appropriate control charts to determine if this process is under control.

c. Determine whether the process is under control. If the process is not under control, brainstorm suggestions that might help Sid bring it under control. What tools of quality might Sid find useful?

Summary and Conclusions

The quality movement throughout the United States and much of the rest of the world has created great expectations among consumers. We now believe that our televisions, computers, stereo systems, automobiles, and even textbooks should be quality products. This movement was slow getting started in the United States because many managers did not believe that there was a need to increase quality when so many units of their products were already being demanded. However, competitive pressures changed that misconception, and corporate America began to buy into the messages that had been communicated by people such as W. Edwards Deming and Joseph Juran for many years. Ideas such as continuous process improvement and customer focus have become a central part of the operations of many of our successful companies.

Statistics has played a key role in this transition. The enemy of quality is variation. Variation exists in everything. Through the use of appropriate statistical tools and the concept of statistical reasoning, managers and employees have developed better understandings of their processes. Although they haven't yet figured out how to eliminate variation, statistics has helped reduce it and understand how to operate more effectively when it exists.

Statistical process control (SPC) has played a big part in the understanding of variation. SPC is quite likely the most frequently used of the Basic 7 Tools. This chapter has introduced you to the basics of SPC. Hopefully, you realize that these tools are merely extensions of the hypothesis-testing and estimation concepts presented in Chapters 8–10. You will very likely have the opportunity to use SPC in one form or another after you leave this course and enter the workforce. Figure 18.13 summarizes some of the key SPC charts and the conditions under which each is developed.

Equations

Variation Components

$$\text{Total Process Variation} = \text{Common Cause Variation}$$
$$+ \text{ Special Cause Variation} \qquad \textbf{(18.1)}$$

Average Subgroup Means

$$\bar{\bar{x}} = \frac{\sum\limits_{i=1}^{k} \bar{x}_i}{k} \qquad \textbf{(18.2)}$$

Average Subgroup Range

$$\bar{R} = \frac{\sum\limits_{i=1}^{k} R_i}{k} \qquad \textbf{(18.3)}$$

Upper Control Limit, $\bar{x}$-Chart

$$UCL = \bar{\bar{x}} + A_2(\bar{R}) \qquad \textbf{(18.4)}$$

Lower Control Limit, $\bar{x}$-Chart

$$LCL = \bar{\bar{x}} - A_2(\bar{R}) \qquad \textbf{(18.5)}$$

Upper Control Limit, R-Chart

$$UCL = D_4(\bar{R}) \qquad \textbf{(18.6)}$$

FIGURE 18.13

Statistical Process Control Chart Option

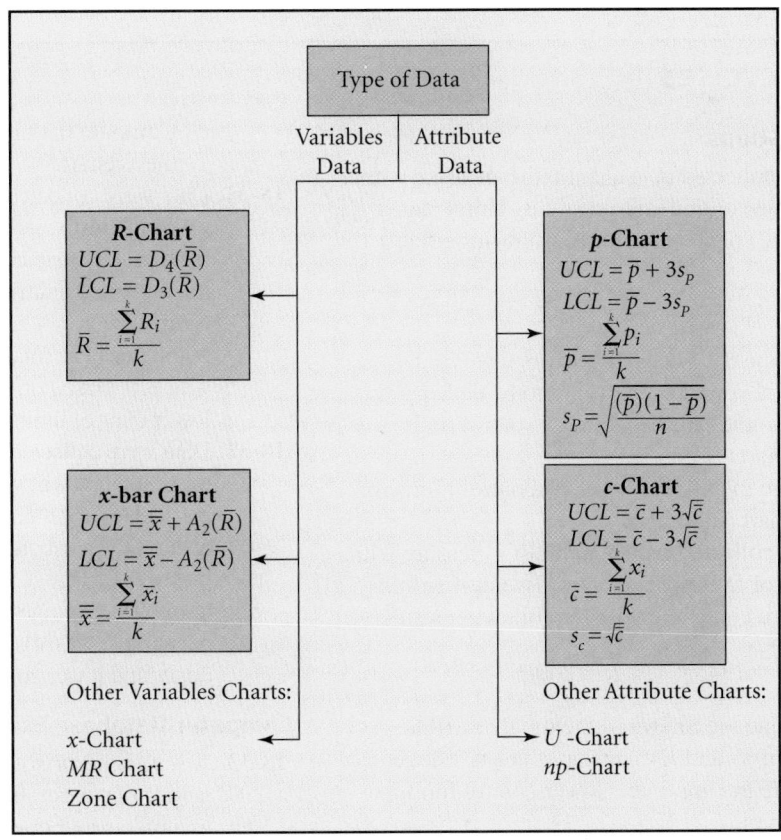

Lower Control Limit, R-Chart

$$LCL = D_3(\bar{R}) \qquad (18.7)$$

Mean Subgroup Proportion.
For equal-size samples:

$$\bar{p} = \frac{\sum_{i=1}^{k} p_i}{k} \qquad (18.8)$$

For unequal sample sizes:

$$\bar{p} = \frac{\sum_{i=1}^{k} n_i p_i}{\sum_{i=1}^{k} n_i} \qquad (18.9)$$

Estimate of the Standard Error for the Subgroup Proportions
For equal sample sizes:

$$s_p = \sqrt{\frac{(\bar{p})(1-\bar{p})}{n}} \qquad (18.10)$$

Control Limits for p-Chart

$$UCL = \bar{p} + 3s_p \qquad (18.11)$$

$$LCL = \bar{p} - 3s_p \qquad (18.12)$$

Mean for c-Chart

$$\bar{c} = \frac{\sum_{i=1}^{k} x_i}{k} \qquad (18.13)$$

Standard Deviation for c-Chart

$$s_c = \sqrt{\bar{c}} \qquad (18.14)$$

c-Chart Control Limits

$$UCL = \bar{c} + 3\sqrt{\bar{c}} \qquad (18.15)$$

$$LCL = \bar{c} - 3\sqrt{\bar{c}} \qquad (18.16)$$

Key Terms

Pareto principle   858

Total quality management (TQM)   858

Chapter Exercises

Conceptual Questions

18-29. Data were collected on a quantitative measure with a subgroup size of three observations. Thirty subgroups were collected, with the following results:

$$\bar{\bar{x}} = 2.33 \qquad \bar{R} = 0.80$$

  a. Determine the Shewhart factors that will be needed if $\bar{x}$- and R-charts are to be developed.
  b. Compute the upper and lower control limits for the R-chart.
  c. Compute the upper and lower control limits for the $\bar{x}$-chart.

18-30. Data were collected on a quantitative measure with subgroups of four observations. Twenty-five subgroups were collected, with the following results:

$$\bar{\bar{x}} = 1345.4 \qquad \bar{R} = 209.3$$

  a. Determine the Shewhart factors that will be needed if $\bar{x}$- and R-charts are to be developed.
  b. Compute the upper and lower control limits for the R-chart.

  c. Compute the upper and lower control limits for the $\bar{x}$-chart.

18-31. Data were collected from a process in which the factor of interest was whether a finished item contained a particular attribute. The fraction of items that did not contain the attribute was recorded. A total of 20 samples were selected. The common sample size was 150 items. The total number of nonconforming items was 720. Based on these data, compute the upper and lower control limits for the p-chart.

18-32. Data were collected from a process in which the factor of interest was whether a finished item contained a particular attribute. The fraction of items that did not contain the attribute was recorded. A total of 30 samples were selected. The common sample size was 100 items. The average number of nonconforming items per sample was 14. Based on these data, construct the upper and lower control limits for the p-chart.

Computer Database Exercises

18-33. A & A Enterprises ships integrated circuits to companies that assemble computers. Because computer manufacturing operations run on little inventory, parts must be available when promised. Thus, a critical element of A & A's customer satisfaction is on-time delivery performance. To ensure that the delivery process is performing as intended, a quality improvement team decided to monitor the firm's distribution and delivery process. From the A & A corporate database, 100 monthly shipping records were randomly selected for the previous 21 months, and the number of on-time shipments was counted. This information is contained in the CD-ROM file **A & A On Time Shipments**. Develop the appropriate 3-sigma control chart(s) for monitoring this process. Does it appear that the delivery process is in control? If not, can you suggest some possible assignable causes?

18-34. Fifi Carpets, Inc., produces carpet for homes and offices. Fifi has recently opened a new production process dedicated to the manufacture of a special type of carpet used by firms who want a floor covering for high-traffic spaces. As a part of their ongoing quality improvement activities, the managers of Fifi regularly monitor their production processes using statistical process control. For their new production process, Fifi managers would like to develop control charts to help them in their monitoring activities. Thirty samples of carpet sections, with each section having an area of 50 square meters, were randomly selected and the numbers of stains, cuts, snags, and tears were counted on each section. The sample data are contained in the CD-ROM file **Fifi Carpets**.

Use the sample data to construct the appropriate 3-sigma control chart(s) for monitoring the production process. Does the process appear to be in statistical control?

18-35. CC, Inc., provides billing services for the health care industry. To ensure that its processes are operating as intended, CC selects 100 billing records at random every day and inspects each record to determine if it is free of errors. A billing record is classified as defective whenever there is an error that requires that the bill be reprocessed and mailed again. Such errors can occur for a variety of reasons. For example, a defective bill could have an incorrect mailing address, a wrong insurance identification number, or an improper doctor or hospital reference. The sample data taken from the most recent 5 weeks of billing records are contained in the CD-ROM file **CC Inc**.

Use the sample information to construct the appropriate 3-sigma control chart. Does CC, Inc.'s billing process appear to be in control? What, if any, comments can you make regarding the performance of their billing process?

18-36. The order-entry, order-processing call center for PS Industries is concerned about the amounts of time that customers must wait before their calls are handled. A quality improvement consultant suggests that it monitor call wait times using control charts. Using call center statistics maintained by the company's database system, the consultant randomly selects four calls every hour for 30 different hours and examines the wait time, in seconds, for each call. This information is contained in the CD-ROM file **PS Industries**.

Use the sample data to construct the appropriate control chart(s). Does the process appear to be in statistical control? What other information concerning the call center's process should the consultant be aware of?

18-37. Varians Controls manufactures a variety of different electric motors and drives. One step in the manufacturing process involves cutting copper wire from large reels into smaller lengths. For a particular motor, there is a dedicated machine for cutting wire to the required length. As a part of their regular quality improvement activities, the continuous process improvement team at Varians took a sample size of 5 cuttings every hour for 30 consecutive hours of operation. At the time the samples were taken, Varians had every reason to believe that its process was working as intended. The automatic cutting machine records the length of each cut, and the results are reported in the CD-ROM file **Varians Controls**.

a. Develop the appropriate 3-sigma control chart(s) for this process. Does the process appear to be working as intended (in control)?

b. A few weeks after the previous data were sampled, a new operator was hired to calibrate the company's cutting machines. The first 5 samples taken from the machine after the calibration adjustments (samples 225 to 229) are shown as follows:

	Cutting 1	Cutting 2	Cutting 3	Cutting 4	Cutting 5
Sample 225	0.7818	0.7760	0.7814	0.7824	0.7702
Sample 226	0.7694	0.7838	0.7675	0.7834	0.7730
Sample 227	0.7875	0.7738	0.7737	0.7594	0.7837
Sample 228	0.7762	0.7711	0.7700	0.7823	0.7673
Sample 229	0.7805	0.7724	0.7748	0.7823	0.7924

Based on these sample values, what can you say about the cutting process? Does it appear to be in control?

CASE 18.1

Izbar Precision Casters, Inc.

Izbar Precision Casters, Inc., manufactures a variety of structural steel products for the construction trade. Currently, there is a strong demand for their I-beam product produced at a mill outside Memphis. Beams at this facility are shipped throughout the Midwest and mid-South, and demand for the product is high due to the strong economy in the regions served by the plant. Angie Schneider, the mill's manager, wants to ensure that the plant's operations are in control, and she has selected several characteristics to monitor. Specifically, she collects data on the number of weekly accidents at the plant, the number of orders shipped on time, and the thickness of the steel I-beams produced.

For the number of reported accidents, Angie selected 30 days at random from the company's safety records. Angie and all the plant employees are very concerned about workplace safety; and management, labor, and government officials have worked together to help create a safe work environment. As a part of the safety program, the company requires employees to report every accident regardless of how minor it may be. In fact, most accidents are very minor, but Izbar still records them and works to prevent them from reoccurring. Because of their strong reporting requirement, Angie was able to get a count of the number of reported accidents for each of the 30 sampled days. These data are shown in Table 18.4.

To monitor the percentage of on-time shipments, Angie randomly selected 50 records from the firm's shipping and billing system every day for 20 different days over the past 6 months. These records contain the actual and promised shipping dates for each order. Angie used a spreadsheet to determine the number of shipments that were made after the promised shipment dates. The number of late shipments from the 50 sampled records was then reported. These data are shown in Table 18.5.

Finally, to monitor the thickness of the I-beam produced at the plant, Angie randomly selected six I-beams every day for 30 days and had each sampled beam measured. The thickness of each beam, in inches, was recorded. All of the data collected by Angie are contained in the CD-ROM file **Izbar**. She wants to use the information she has collected to construct and analyze the appropriate control charts for the plant's production processes. She intends to present this information at the next manager's meeting on Monday morning.

Required Tasks:

a. Use the data that Angie has collected to develop and analyze the appropriate control charts for this process. Be sure to label each control chart carefully and also to identify the type of control chart used.

b. Do the processes analyzed appear to be in control? Why or why not? What would you suggest that Angie do?

c. Does Angie need to continue to monitor her processes on a regular basis? How should she do this? Also, are there other variables that might be of interest to her in monitoring the plant's performance? If so, what do you think they might be?

TABLE 18.4 Accident Data

Day	Number of Reported Accidents	Day	Number of Reported Accidents
1	9	16	4
2	11	17	11
3	9	18	7
4	9	19	7
5	11	20	10
6	10	21	11
7	10	22	6
8	10	23	6
9	4	24	7
10	7	25	4
11	7	26	9
12	8	27	11
13	11	28	9
14	10	29	6
15	7	30	5

TABLE 18.5 Late Shipments

Day	Number of Late Shipments	Day	Number of Late Shipments
1	5	11	8
2	3	12	2
3	1	13	5
4	6	14	6
5	5	15	2
6	8	16	7
7	5	17	7
8	6	18	3
9	4	19	2
10	4	20	7

References

Crosby, Philip B., *Quality Is Free: The Art of Making Quality Certain* (New York: McGraw-Hill, 1979).

Deming, W. Edwards, *Out of the Crisis* (Cambridge, MA: MIT Center for Advanced Engineering Study, 1986).

Evans, James R., and William M. Lindsay, *The Management and Control of Quality*, 6th ed. (Cincinnati, OH: South-Western College Publishing, 2005).

Foster, S. Thomas, *Managing Quality: Integrating the Supply Chain and Student CD PKG*; 3rd ed. (Upper Saddle River, NJ: Prentice Hall, 2007).

Juran, Joseph M. *Quality Control Handbook*, 5th ed. (New York: McGraw-Hill, 1999).

Microsoft Excel 2007 (Redmond, WA: Microsoft Corp., 2007).

Minitab for Windows Version 14 (State College, PA: Minitab, 2005).

Mitra, Amitava, *Fundamentals of Quality Control and Improvement*, 2d ed. (Upper Saddle River, NJ: Prentice Hall, 1998).

Chapter NINETEEN

Introduction to Decision Analysis

CHAPTER OUTCOMES

After studying the material in Chapter 19, you should be able to:

1. Describe the decision-making environments of certainty and uncertainty.
2. Construct both a payoff table and an opportunity-loss table.
3. Define the expected value criterion.
4. Apply the expected value criterion in decision situations.
5. Compute the cost of uncertainty and value of perfect information.
6. Develop a decision tree and explain how it can aid decision making in an uncertain environment.

PREPARING FOR CHAPTER NINETEEN

- Review how to construct tree diagrams, covered in Section 4.1.

- Make sure you are familiar with how to determine expected values introduced in Section 4.2.

WHY YOU NEED TO KNOW

Although this text is devoted to discussing statistical techniques managers can use to help analyze decisions, the term *decision analysis* has a specialized meaning. It applies to the set of tools, some of which are covered in this chapter, that have been developed to help managers analyze multistage decisions that must be made in an uncertain environment.

Putting together this set of tools has been a relatively recent development, starting in the late 1950s, initially by faculty at the Harvard Business School. The individual tools themselves are considerably older than decision analysis, however, and come from three theoretical areas of thought: (1) Bayesian statistics, (2) game theory, and (3) risk-preference analysis.

The bedrock of decision analysis was formed by the eighteenth-century work of the Reverend Thomas Bayes, one of the most enigmatic figures in scientific history. He is credited with being the first person to give a rational account of how statistical inference can be used as a process for understanding situations in the real world. But his pioneering work was not published until after his death in 1761, and during his lifetime he was a scientific unknown. Now,

however, he has become so popular that a whole group of decision analysts refer to themselves as "Bayesians."

A second contribution to modern decision analysis is the game-theory approach of John Von Neumann and Oskar Morgenstern. They demonstrated that the "correct" decision in any situation depends on the objectives of the decision maker and the actions that are likely to be taken by competitors.

The third area is the work of such economists as Milton Friedman and L. J. Savage. They showed that a person's attitude toward risk depends on the person's circumstances; and therefore, different decision makers, when facing the same decision, may make different choices because of their differing risk attitudes.

Since its introduction in the late 1950s, decision analysis has become a common feature in MBA programs and has influenced thousands of decision makers in government and industry.

This chapter introduces the fundamentals of decision analysis and shows, through examples, how several basic decision analysis tools are used in the decision-making process.

19.1 Decision-Making Environments and Decision Criteria

In business, you will encounter a wide variety of decision situations. The analytic methods you use to deal with each situation will depend largely on the decision environment. The two primary decision environments are certainty and uncertainty.

CHAPTER OUTCOME #1

Certainty

Sometimes you will encounter a decision situation in which you can be certain of the outcome for each alternative. This type of decision environment, in which the results of each alternative are known before the decision is made, is termed a **certainty** environment.

Certainty
A decision environment in which the results of selecting each alternative are known before the decision is made.

Business Application

ECONOPRINT COMPANY Consider a decision faced by the Econoprint Company, which makes replacement cartridges for laser printers. The national sales manager has just received a message from a regional sales representative indicating that she has negotiated a deal with a new distributor for 1 million cartridges at $5.00 each. However, the customer wants the cartridges to be packaged in groups of 6, rather than the usual 24 per package. The sales representative points out that the company can modify its packaging equipment "quite easily" to accommodate this change. She urges a quick decision, because a delay is likely to force the customer to go elsewhere, and the efforts to attract this new business will be lost.

Needing information on which to base his decision, the national sales manager contacts the industrial engineering and accounting staffs. He is told that the total production costs for the product grouped 6 to a package will be $4.50 per cartridge. Selling costs and overhead costs are 5% and 1% of sales, respectively.

Table 19.1 shows the projected profits and losses for the two decision alternatives: accept the offer or reject the offer. Because all costs and revenues are known for each

TABLE 19.1 Econoprint Company: Profits and Losses for Two Alternatives

Revenues and Expenses	Alternatives	
	Accept Offer	Reject Offer
Revenues		
Sales (1 million × $5.00)	$5,000,000	0
Costs		
Production (1 million × $4.50)	$4,500,000	0
Selling (5% of sales)	250,000	0
Overhead (1% of sales)	50,000	0
Profit	$ 200,000	0

alternative, the decision is straightforward: The $200,000 profit associated with accepting the offer exceeds the $0 profit associated with not accepting the offer; therefore, the offer should be accepted.

As this example shows, once a certainty model has been specified, the best decision is evident. By "best decision," we mean the alternative course of action, using all available information, that best satisfies the decision criterion. In the Econoprint Company example, the decision criterion was highest profit. Given that the decision model displayed in Table 19.1 utilized all available information, the best decision was to accept the offer. Because this is a certainty environment, the decision will result in an outcome of $200,000 profit. Thus, in a certainty environment, the best decision will always be associated with the best outcome.

CHAPTER OUTCOME #1

Uncertainty

Uncertainty
A decision environment in which the decision maker does not know what outcome will occur when an alternative is selected.

If business decisions were always made in a certainty environment, you would probably not need the academic training you are now receiving to be successful. How many of us would have chosen to reject the offer in the Econoprint Company example if Table 19.1 reflected the total decision picture? In reality, the typical business decision-making environment is not one of certainty but, rather, **uncertainty**.

The certainty environment is predicated on the fact that the outcome from each alternative course of action is known. If we choose alternative A, outcome Y will occur. If alternative B is selected, outcome Z will occur. This makes choosing between the alternatives straightforward. However, in most business situations, although we may be able to specify the possible outcomes for each alternative, we will be uncertain about which outcome will occur. Consider the real estate speculator who is trying to decide whether to purchase land outside of Las Vegas, one of the fastest-growing cities in the country, hoping to resell the land to a developer. If the speculator elects not to purchase the property, the net change in his financial position will be zero. He knows this for sure. However, if he chooses to buy the land, what will the outcome be? Will he make $10,000,000, or $20,000,000, or will he lose $5,000,000? Identifying the possible outcomes is difficult enough, but knowing for certain what outcome definitely will occur is impossible in a competitive real estate market. Thus, the speculator must decide whether to buy in an environment of uncertainty.

Business Application

EAGLE LUMBER COMPANY Consider the Eagle Lumber Company in Glenns Ferry, Wisconsin. About 3 weeks ago, the manager received 4,000 board feet of 2-inch-by-6-inch tongue-and-groove knotty pine, which is used primarily for walls and ceilings. The product is hard to get because the supplier makes only a limited quantity each month. The wholesale price for the recent shipment was $360 per 1,000 board feet. Two days after receiving the material, a customer came in and bought the entire shipment for $450 per 1,000 board feet. However, the customer wanted Eagle Lumber to store the material for 8 weeks.

Two weeks later, another customer arrived and wanted to purchase as much 2-inch-by-6-inch tongue-and-groove knotty pine as possible for immediate use. The only stock on hand at the lumber company at the time was the 4,000 board feet, which had already been sold. After seeing the paid-for knotty pine, the new customer asked whether the manager would consider selling him the 4,000 board feet now and replacing the material before the previous customer returned to pick it up in about 7 weeks.

In a certain environment, the decision would be relatively easy. If the lumber could be replaced at a known price before the first customer returned, the manager could resell the material and both customers would be happy. If the lumber could not be replaced before the first customer returned, the second customer would be turned away. Unfortunately, the decision environment facing Eagle's manager is not one of certainty. For one thing, he does not know whether he will be able to replace the stock within 7 weeks. Furthermore, if he is able to replace the material, he does not know exactly what the cost will be. Therefore, he is uncertain about what price to charge the second customer. He is also uncertain about whether the first customer will arrive early to take his material. As you can see, a seemingly simple situation is actually quite complex due to the uncertainties involved.

The decision analysis techniques presented in this chapter do not eliminate the uncertainty associated with a decision, but they do provide a framework for dealing with the uncertainty. These techniques help you make good decisions under certain conditions, but good decisions don't necessarily result in good outcomes. For instance, suppose after considering all available information that the best decision is not to sell to the new customer. Then, a week later, the original customer calls to say he will be 6 weeks late picking up the material. If the manager had known this, he could have sold the materials to the new customer and received the additional profit. Thus, the best decision at the time did not result in a good outcome.

This concept of decision analysis is contrary to how many people view situations. The tendency is to look at the outcome and, if it is not good, we second-guess our decision. However, if we have properly used all available information in making the decision, it was a good decision. Decision makers must realize that in an uncertain environment, in which they don't have total control over the outcomes of their decisions, bad outcomes will sometimes occur. Decision makers must also continually remind themselves that there is a difference between a good decision and a good outcome. *The goal of decision analysis is to focus on making good decisions, which in the long run should result in an increased number of good outcomes.*

Not all decisions require the use of decision analysis; the complexity of the decision situation usually determines the usefulness of decision analysis. The more complex the decision, the greater the potential benefit from decision analysis. Several factors affect the complexity of a decision, including the number of alternatives available to the decision maker, the number of possible outcomes associated with each alternative, and the general level of uncertainty associated with the decision. For example, marketing decisions regarding product design, product pricing, and distribution are very complex, and decision analysis tools can be helpful to the decision maker. Of course, any decision involving product design or pricing also involves other areas in an organization, including production and finance.

Another characteristic of situations in which decisions can be aided by decision analysis is that they often extend to multiple functional areas of an organization. Production decisions, including process design, aggregate planning, and facilities planning, all lend themselves to decision analysis because of their complexity and long-term importance to the organization. Such financial decision areas as capital budgeting, project financing, and pension investing clearly can benefit from the application of decision analysis.

The types of decisions mentioned here are only a few of those in which decision analysis can be effectively applied. Throughout the remainder of this chapter, we will present further examples in which decision analysis can be used to aid business decision making.

Decision Criteria

When you are faced with choices between two or more options in a business situation, you are required to make a decision. Unless you are willing to flip a coin, "draw straws," or use some other random method, you will need to establish some basis for making the decision. The criteria on which the decision is to be made need to be established. Then, ideally, you will perform an analysis of the decision situation and make the "best" choice by weighing each decision option against the criteria you have established.

Business Application

FISHER FABRICATION Fisher Fabrication has been in business for 10 years in eastern Tennessee. The company was started by two brothers who had worked in the electronics industry in Texas and California. They wanted to get back to where they grew up, and they saw that many electronics companies were beginning to subcontract their assembly work, particularly on small-volume items. They saw an opportunity to get into the subcontracting business and decided to move back home. They found a dedicated workforce and soon employed 150 people.

The brothers concentrated on manual assembly of limited-volume items such as special equipment for oil exploration, vehicles, and military contracts. Business had been extremely good until 2 years ago, when revenues began to decline slightly. By contacting past customers, the brothers determined the drop in sales was due to the increasing use companies were making of surface-mounted components, something the Fishers were not able to do by hand.

This finding made the brothers realize their company must invest in a surface-mount machine, but they were uncertain about the extent of the investment needed. Initial research led them to identify three potential courses of action (alternatives):

A_1: A large investment, which would involve purchasing a full-scale surface-mount system, including robotics, thus allowing them to bid on the majority of current manufacturing contracts. This equipment would give them greater capability.

A_2: A medium investment, which would give them the same general capability as alternative A, but the equipment would operate at a much lower speed. This would prevent them from bidding on large contracts.

A_3: A small investment, which would limit them to bidding on less than half of the potential contracts.

Obviously, the alternative the Fishers should select depended on the future revenues generated by the new equipment. Consequently, the Fishers identified three potential directions that they believed the demand for surface-mounted components could take. In decision analysis terminology, these three demand levels are referred to as **states of nature**. For the Fishers, the states of nature were

States of Nature
The possible outcomes in a decision situation over which the decision maker has no control.

S_1: Rapidly increasing demand due to the capability of the surface-mount equipment

S_2: Moderately increasing demand

S_3: Slight increase in demand as more businesses added their own surface-mount capability

CHAPTER OUTCOME #2

Payoff
The outcome (profit or loss) for any combination of alternative and state of nature. The payoffs associated with all possible combinations of alternatives and states of nature constitute a *payoff table*.

The Fishers wanted to base their investment decision on yearly profit values, but as we can see, there were three potential profit levels, due to the three states of nature, for each alternative. The outcome that is associated with any combination of a particular state of nature and an alternative is called a **payoff**. Because the brothers' decision involved three alternatives and three states of nature, they had nine possible payoffs to consider, as shown in the payoff table (Table 19.2).

In order to decide among the three alternatives, the Fishers had to have some basis for comparison, so they established decision criteria. There are two main categories of decision criteria: *nonprobabilistic* and *probabilistic*. Nonprobabilistic criteria are used when either the probabilities associated with the possible payoffs are unknown or the decision

TABLE 19.2 Fisher Fabrication Payoff Table

	Demand (States of Nature)		
Alternative	S_1 Large Increase	S_2 Moderate Increase	S_3 Small Increase
A_1 Large Investment	$6,000,000	$4,000,000	−$2,600,000
A_2 Medium Investment	2,500,000	5,000,000	−1,000,000
A_3 Small Investment	2,000,000	1,500,000	1,200,000

Note: These values are the Fishers' estimates of the profit associated with each combination of alternative and state of nature.

maker lacks confidence and/or information with which to assess probabilities for the various payoffs. Probabilistic criteria incorporate the decision maker's assessment of the probability of each state of nature occurring.

Nonprobabilistic Decision Criteria

Maximax Criterion

An optimistic decision criterion for dealing with uncertainty without using probability. For each option, the decision maker finds the maximum possible payoff and then selects the option with the greatest maximum payoff.

Maximin Criterion

A pessimistic (conservative) decision criterion for dealing with uncertainty without using probability. For each option, the decision maker finds the minimum possible payoff and selects the option with the greatest minimum payoff.

CHAPTER OUTCOME #2

Opportunity Loss

The difference between the actual payoff that occurs for a decision and the optimal payoff for the same state of nature.

Minimax Regret Criterion

A decision criterion that considers the results of selecting the "wrong" alternative. For each state of nature, the decision maker finds the difference between the best payoff and each other alternative and uses these values to construct an opportunity-loss table. The decision maker then identifies the maximum opportunity loss for each alternative and selects the alternative with the minimum of these maximum values.

Several specific decision criteria fall into the nonprobabilistic category. One of these is the **maximax criterion**. For the Fisher brothers, using this criterion would mean making a major investment in surface-mount equipment, because that was the alternative with the highest possible payoff, $6,000,000 per year (Table 19.2). The maximax criterion might be chosen by optimistic decision makers.

If we are not optimistic, we might select the alternative whose worst possible outcome is better than the worst possible outcome from any other alternative. This pessimistic (or conservative) criterion is called the **maximin criterion**. For the Fishers, using the maximin criterion would mean selecting the small-investment alternative, because its worst outcome, $1,200,000 was better than any other alternative's worst outcome.

A disadvantage of the maximax and maximin criteria is that they use only one value from the payoff table to make a decision. In analyzing the decision situation, the brothers may have been interested in determining how much damage making the wrong choice would cause. For instance, suppose they decided on the medium-investment alternative and later found that the market for surface-mount capability had expanded greatly. The medium-investment decision led to a $2,500,000 yearly profit, but given perfect hindsight, the best decision of making a large investment would have earned $6,000,000. The difference between the actual payoff and the optimal payoff for a given state of nature is an **opportunity loss**; in this case, it is $3,500,000. If the Fishers decided to use the **minimax regret criterion**, they would need to know the value of the opportunity loss.

The minimax regret criterion considers the results of selecting the "wrong" alternative. The first step is to construct an opportunity-loss, or regret, table by finding, for each state of nature, the differences between the payoff for the best decision and the payoffs for all the other alternatives. Table 19.3 shows how this is done. The next step is to find the

TABLE 19.3 Fisher Fabrication: Opportunity-Loss Table

	Demand (States of Nature)		
Alternative	S_1 Large Increase	S_2 Moderate Increase	S_3 Small Increase
A_1 Large Investment	$ 0	$1,000,000	$3,800,000
A_2 Medium Investment	3,500,000	0	2,200,000
A_3 Small Investment	4,000,000	3,500,000	0

Note: The values in this table were found by subtracting each column value in Table 19.2 from the largest value in that column.

TABLE 19.4 Fisher Fabrication Maximum Regret Table

Alternative	Maximum Opportunity Loss, or Regret
A_1 Large Investment	$3,800,000
A_2 Medium Investment	$3,500,000 (smallest regret)
A_3 Small Investment	$4,000,000

maximum regret for each alternative. These values are shown in Table 19.4. The minimax regret criterion now requires selecting the minimum of these maximum regret values. Using this criterion, we would choose the medium-investment decision, because the maximum opportunity loss of $3,500,000 is lower than the maximum opportunity loss for either of the other two alternatives.

Observe that all three criteria lead to different decisions; therefore, the brothers would determine which criterion best described their decision-making philosophy and use it to help them decide on their level of investment.

The maximax, maximin, and minimax regret decision criteria are examples of nonprobabilistic decision criteria. Nonprobabilistic criteria do not take into account the probability associated with the outcomes for each alternative; they merely focus on the dollar value of the outcomes. The criticism of nonprobabilistic decision criteria is aimed at their failure to include important information about the chances of each outcome occurring. Decision analysts argue that if the payoff probabilities are known or can be assessed, a probabilistic decision criterion should be employed.

CHAPTER OUTCOME #3

Probabilistic Decision Criteria

Some decision criteria take into account the probabilities associated with each outcome. One of these is the **expected-value criterion**.

Expected-Value Criterion
A decision criterion that employs probability to select the alternative that will produce the greatest average payoff or minimum average loss.

Expected-Value Criterion The term *expected value* is often used in statistics to refer to the long-run average outcome for a given alternative. In order to determine an expected value, we must have probabilities for each possible outcome. The expected value for a discrete variable is computed as follows:

Expected Value

$$E(x) = \sum_{i=1}^{k} x_i P(x_i) \tag{19.1}$$

where:

x_i = The ith outcome of the specified alternative measured in some units, such as dollars

$P(x_i)$ = The probability of outcome x_i occurring

k = Number of potential outcomes

and:

$$\sum_{i=1}^{k} P(x_i) = 1 \tag{19.2}$$

$$0 \le P(x_i) \le 1 \tag{19.3}$$

Equation 19.1 shows that the expected value is the sum of the weighted outcomes for a specified alternative. This means that if the alternative is repeatedly selected, over the long run the average outcome will equal $E(x)$, the expected value.

TRY PROBLEM 19.10

CHAPTER OUTCOME #4

EXAMPLE 19-1 Employing the Expected-Value Criterion

Xircom, Inc. Consider the following simple decision situation, which involves Xircom, Inc., a mobile connectivity leader. Its products provide notebook PC users the ability to access their corporate networks. Recently, its stock has been trading at $36.50 a share. There has been a rumor of a merger between Xircom and one of its major competitors. The expected-value criterion can be used to determine whether to invest in Xircom using the following steps:

Step 1 Define the decision alternatives.
The alternatives are to invest or don't invest.

Step 2 Define the possible outcomes (states of nature) associated with each alternative.
If the decision is not to invest in Xircom, then the resulting payoff is zero. That is, you are in the same position as you were before making the decision. However, for the do invest alternative, two possible outcomes are thought possible:

1. The merger will occur and the stock price will increase $10 per share.
2. The merger will not occur and the stock price will drop $5 per share.

Step 3 Assign probabilities to the possible outcomes associated with each alternative.
For the don't-invest option, there is 1.0 probability of a zero payoff. For the invest option, analysts believe there is a 0.50 chance of the merger (and likewise a 0.50 chance of no merger).

Step 4 Compute the expected value for each decision alternative.
For the don't-invest option, the expected value (payoff) is $0 because there is 1.0 chance of that outcome occurring. For the buy alternative, we can let $x_1 = \$10$ (merger occurs) and $x_2 = -\$5$ (merger fails). Then, using the analysts' probability assessments, the following probability distribution exists:

x	P(x)
$10	0.50
−$5	0.50
	1.00

The expected value is computed using Equation 19.1.

$$E(x) = \sum_{i=1}^{k} x_i P(x_i)$$

$$E(x) = (\$10)(0.50) + (-\$5)(0.50) = \$2.50$$

This means that over the long run you would have an expected $2.50 gain per share if you elected to purchase the stock. If you don't purchase the stock, the expected gain is $0. Thus, the *best* decision, based on expected value, is to buy the Xircom stock.

When applying the expected-value criterion, the best decision is to select the alternative with the highest average payoff or the lowest average loss. In Example 19-1, the stock purchase example, the best decision, using the expected-value criterion, is to purchase the stock, because $2.50 > $0. The advantage of the expected-value criterion is that it takes into account the information contained in the probabilities.

Expected value is the decision criterion around which the techniques of decision analysis are built and is the one emphasized throughout this chapter. The disadvantage of the expected-value criterion is that it does not take into account the decision maker's attitude toward risk. For instance, in the first case for the stock purchase example, the expected value was $2.50. Clearly, on the basis of expected value we buy the stock, because $2.50 > $0. However, if we purchase stock under these same conditions, we could lose $5. Depending on how averse we are to this outcome, we might decide not to participate after all.

19-1: Exercises

Skill Development

19-1. In decision analysis, what is the difference between a good decision and a good outcome? Do good decisions always produce the "best" outcome? Why or why not?

19-2. What is the goal of decision analysis?

19-3. Varsity Contracting has recently started negotiating to provide custodial service for a local manufacturer at several facilities in the area. The manufacturer has offered to contract for Varsity's services at the rate of $0.10 per square foot per month. To provide nightly custodial service for the 100,000-square-foot plant, Varsity would have to hire two more workers at $8.00 per hour. The new service would require 8 hours per night, 5 nights a week. Supplies would cost $200 per week, and overhead would be charged at 20% of the labor cost.

Given the information presented here, what decision environment exists? Why do you think so? Would you recommend that Varsity sign this contract? Explain your reasoning?

19-4. Given the following decision table:

		States of Nature		
		S_1	S_2	S_3
Alternatives	A_1	150	80	−20
	A_2	60	40	45
	A_3	240	70	−10

  a. Use the maximax criterion to determine which decision alternative to select.
  b. Use the maximin criterion to determine which decision alternative to select.
  c. Use the minimax regret criterion to determine which decision alternative to select.

19-5. The probabilities assessed with the states of nature in the previous exercise are

$$P(S_1) = 0.3, \quad P(S_2) = 0.2, \quad P(S_3) = 0.5$$

Using these probabilities, determine which alternative to select using the expected-value criterion.

19-6. Given the following decision table:

		States of Nature			
		S_1	S_2	S_3	S_4
Alternatives	A_1	170	45	−60	100
	A_2	30	190	175	−65
	A_3	145	−50	120	110
	A_4	−40	80	10	70

  a. Use the maximax criterion to determine which decision alternative to select.
  b. Use the maximin criterion to determine which decision alternative to select.
  c. Use the minimax regret criterion to determine which decision alternative to select.

19-7. The probabilities assessed with the states of nature in the previous problem are

$$P(S_1) = 0.1, \quad P(S_2) = 0.2, \quad P(S_3) = 0.4, \quad P(S_4) = 0.3$$

Using these probabilities, determine which alternative to select using the expected-value criterion.

Business Applications

19-8. Larry Jacava is considering producing a novelty item for golfers that will be sold through pro shops. Larry has decided on a selling price of $3.50 for the item. The item's variable cost of production is $2.00 per unit, with fixed costs of $3,750. Larry has marketed his product to local pro shops and believes the demand for the item will be either 2,000 units, 3,000 units, 4,000 units, or 5,000 units.
  a. Set up the payoff table for Larry's decision.
  b. Determine the number of units that Larry should produce using each of the following criteria:
    1. maximax criterion
    2. maximin criterion
    3. minimax regret criterion

19-9. Sal De Carlo is the manager for food sales for Coyote Stadium. For each home game, Sal must decide how many hot dogs to have available for sale. The number of hot dogs sold depends on the game's attendance. Sal pays $0.75 for each hot dog and $0.15 for each hot dog bun. Hot dogs are sold to fans during the game for $1.75. Any leftover hot dogs are sold to the mens' dorms for $0.25 a piece. Sal estimates that demand for hot dogs for next week's game will be either 10,000, 15,000, 20,000, or 25,000.

a. Set up the payoff table for Sal's decision.
b. How many hot dogs would Sal order if he used each of the following criteria?
   1. maximax criterion
   2. maximin criterion
   3. minimax regret criterion

19-10. A real estate investor in a medium-sized western city is considering three investments: an apartment building, a strip mall, and an office building. Returns from each investment alternative depend on future population growth. The investor has developed three growth scenarios showing the revenue from each investment alternative along with their probabilities of occurrence. This information is shown in the following table:

Population Growth	Probability	Apartment	Mall	Office
Slow	0.20	−$75,000	$15,000	−$200,000
Average	0.30	10,000	30,000	50,000
High	0.50	150,000	75,000	100,000

For the given payoff matrix, what is the best decision and its associated payoff using each of the following?
a. the maximax criterion
b. the maximin criterion
c. the minimax regret criterion
d. the expected-value criterion

19-11. Cooke Collectibles produces fine porcelain miniatures representing famous people and historical events. To avoid production and scheduling problems, Cooke's policy is to make all copies of a figure in one production run. In the event that the demand for any figure exceeds the number produced, each customer's money is returned along with a coupon good for $10.00 toward the purchase of another Cooke miniature. If the company makes too many figures, the extras are sold to a discount outlet, which agrees to hold them for 6 months, for $50 each. This price is half the variable production cost of a figure.

Cooke Collectibles has recently agreed to pay $200,000 for the rights to produce a miniature representing a famous singer. The company plans to sell the figures for $250 each. The marketing department predicts that actual demand will equal one of these possible demand levels: 20,000; 40,000; 60,000; or 80,000.

a. Set up a table showing the payoffs for all combinations of production and demand.

b. Use the maximin criterion to arrive at the appropriate decision and the associated payoff. Contrast this decision with one made using the maximax criterion instead.

19-12. Referring to the previous exercise, suppose the marketing manager at Cooke Collectibles has analyzed the possible demand levels and subjectively assessed the following probabilities for them:

Demand Level	Probability
20,000	0.10
40,000	0.30
60,000	0.40
80,000	0.20
	1.00

Use the expected-value criterion to arrive at the best decision for Cooke and the associated expected value.

19-13. The Special Occasions Company, a nationwide distributor of flowers and greeting cards, has just contracted with Global Floral to purchase up to 500,000 dozen red and yellow roses for sale in the week before Valentine's Day. Special Occasions supplies flower shops and other retail outlets from regional distribution centers throughout the country. The problem now facing the company is how many dozen roses to buy. If the company doesn't buy enough, it loses potential business; if it buys more than are demanded, it loses the costs of purchasing and shipping these unsold roses. Any unsold roses are given to local hospitals and retirement homes or are disposed of at the area landfill.

The contract calls for a basic payment of $150,000 plus $5 per each dozen roses bought by Special Occasions. The company's accounting department has determined that the cost of shipping the roses from Global Floral's greenhouses averages $1.50 per dozen. The marketing department has estimated the demand (in dozens) for roses, and its probability distribution, as follows:

Demand Level	Probability
100,000	0.10
150,000	0.40
200,000	0.20
225,000	0.20
250,000	0.10
	1.00

Assuming the roses sell for an average of $18 per dozen, set up the payoff table and use the expected-value criterion to find how many dozen roses should be purchased for the next Valentine's Day sales and the associated expected profit.

Exercises 19-14, 19-15, and 19-16 refer to Baker Enterprises, a produce wholesaler that supplies fruits and vegetables to local grocery stores and restaurants, which has just received notice that a frost in Florida will have a serious impact on this winter's orange harvest. If Baker's buyer waits until the time he normally buys Florida oranges, the price could be very high. Consequently, Sara Baker, the owner, has decided to enter into a contract now. The Florida supplier will guarantee any quantity of oranges this winter, but only on the following terms:

Fixed finder's fee	$10,000
Fewer than 1,001 boxes	$3.00 per box
1,001 to 5,000 boxes	$2.80 per box
More than 5,000 boxes	$2.50 per box

The sales manager has identified the following possible demand levels for boxes of oranges this winter: 500, 1,000, 2,000, 4,000, and 7,000. The expected selling price will be $9.00 per box, and unsold boxes will be given away.

19-14. Set up a payoff table for this decision problem and use the minimax regret decision criterion to determine how many boxes of oranges Baker Enterprises should buy and the accompanying profit.

19-15. The managers at Baker Enterprises have discussed the situation and, on the basis of their past experience with orange sales, have assessed the following probabilities for each possible demand level:

Demand	Probability
500	0.15
1,000	0.20
2,000	0.20
4,000	0.30
7,000	0.15
	1.00

Incorporate these probabilities into your analysis and determine the "best decision" for Baker Enterprises, as well as the expected profit for this decision, using the expected-value criterion.

19-16. Sara Baker has found an alternative supplier of Florida oranges. The new supplier will not charge a finder's fee but will charge $4.50 per box regardless of the quantity purchased. If Sara Baker decides to buy from the new supplier, how many boxes of oranges should she buy in order to maximize expected profit? Which supplier should she choose? Explain.

19-17. Duckland Enterprises is considering bidding on one or all of the first five franchises offered by a popular Japanese fast-food operation. Each franchise requires a yearly $100,000 payment and the construction of a building at an average cost of $250,000. Duckland plans to keep the franchises for a year and, if the businesses are successful, it should be able to sell them for $600,000 each, including the buildings. If the operations are not successful, Duckland will close them down and sell the buildings for $150,000.

a. Use the maximax decision criterion to determine how many franchises Duckland should purchase and the associated profit.

b. How many franchises should Duckland purchase if the maximin decision criterion is used? Determine the accompanying profit for this decision criterion as well.

c. Suppose Duckland Enterprises has three options for constructing the buildings for its franchises. One option is to construct the buildings as originally planned, at a cost of $250,000 each. A second option is to build smaller facilities in established malls, with building expenses totaling $150,000 each. If the mall operations are not successful, Duckland can recover $100,000 of the $150,000 building cost; and if they are successful, they can be sold for $500,000 each. A third option is to construct larger buildings, at a cost of $400,000 each. If successful, these operations can be sold for $1,000,000 each; and if they are not successful, the buildings can be sold for $200,000 each. Construct a payoff table describing these new alternatives for Duckland Enterprises.

d. Determine how many franchises Duckland should acquire under each building-cost option described in part c, and determine the associated profit. Provide separate answers using the maximin and maximax decision criteria.

e. Referring to part c, suppose Duckland Enterprises assesses the following probability distributions for the number of successful franchises at each building-cost level:

$150,000		$250,000		$400,000	
Number	P(Success)	Number	P(Success)	Number	P(Success)
0	0.05	0	0.06	0	0.09
1	0.10	1	0.10	1	0.15
2	0.15	2	0.20	2	0.25
3	0.25	3	0.40	3	0.40
4	0.30	4	0.12	4	0.07
5	0.15	5	0.12	5	0.04

For each building alternative, use the expected-payoff criterion to determine the optimal number of franchises to purchase and the expected payoff. Then determine which building-cost level Duckland should use for its franchises.

19.2 Cost of Uncertainty

The advantage of making decisions in a certain environment is that the best decision always yields the best outcome. In an uncertain environment, the best decision might not result in the best outcome. Thus, there is a cost of uncertainty associated with not knowing in advance which outcome will occur. An example will show what we mean.

EXAMPLE 19-2   Computing the Cost of Uncertainty

TRY PROBLEMS 19.23

CHAPTER OUTCOME #5

Haroldson's   In the United States, more money is now being spent on take-out and restaurant food than is spent buying groceries. Many grocery chains, in an effort to keep up with this trend, have added extensive deli and take-out sections. Haroldson's is a regional chain that has joined the movement. A popular packaged meal is made up of broiled chicken, potato salad, and a green salad. However, because of several television news specials about potentially spoiled food, Haroldson's has a company policy of giving all unsold food to a local homeless shelter at the end of each day. Although the company doesn't mind giving the food away, it would rather sell all the meals it prepares. Therefore, the question that deli managers face each day is how many meals to make. To answer this question and to compute the cost of uncertainty in this situation, you can use the following steps:

Step 1 Determine the possible outcomes (states of nature).

A deli manager feels that on any weekday, the minimum demand for the broiled-chicken meal will be 50 and the maximum demand will be 90. To simplify the analysis, the following five demand levels are considered possible:

Demand = x = 50	60	70	80	90

Step 2 Assess the probability for each possible outcome.

Based on historical data, the probabilities for each demand level are

Demand = x =	50	60	70	80	90
$P(x)$ =	0.05	0.10	0.20	0.40	0.25

Step 3 Assign appropriate revenue and cost values and establish the payoff function.

The fixed cost of setting up to cook the meals is $120, variable costs amount to $1.50 per meal, and the selling price is $3.70 each. With this information, we find the payoffs associated with different production levels by using the following equation:

$$\text{Payoff} = \$3.70(s) - \$120 - \$1.50(p)$$

where:

$$s = \text{number of units sold}$$
$$p = \text{number of units produced}$$

Step 4 Construct the payoff table.

The payoff when production is 50 and demand is 50 is

$$\text{Payoff} = \$3.70(50) - \$120 - \$1.50(50) = -\$10.00$$

Likewise, if 70 meals are prepared and 90 are demanded, the payoff is

$$\text{Payoff} = \$3.70(70) - \$120 - \$1.50(70) = \$34.00$$

(Notice that even though demand is 90, sales are limited to 70 because only 70 were produced.) The payoffs associated with all combinations of production and demand are displayed in the following payoff table. The demand levels are labeled "states of nature," because demand is outside the control of the decision maker.

Payoff Table					
	Demand (States of Nature)				
Production	50	60	70	80	90
50	−$10	−$10	−$10	−$10	−$10
60	−25	12	12	12	12
70	−40	−3	34	34	34
80	−55	−18	19	56	56
90	−70	−33	4	41	78

Step 5 **Add the probabilities to the payoff table and compute the expected value for each production decision using Equation 19.1.**
The expected values are computed by summing the payoffs times the probabilities. For example, the expected payoff for a production level of 80 meals is

$$E(\text{payoff}) = -\$55(0.05) + -\$18(0.10) + \$19(0.20)$$
$$+ \$56(0.40) + \$56(0.25)$$
$$= \$35.65$$

Therefore, in the long run, the deli manager can expect to make $35.65 if she prepares 80 meals of broiled chicken and potato salad. The other expected values are computed in a similar manner.

Haroldson's Expected Values						
	Demand (States of Nature)					
Production	50 $p = 0.05$	60 $p = 0.1$	70 $p = 0.2$	80 $p = 0.4$	90 $p = 0.25$	E(Payoff)
50	−$10	−$10	−$10	−$10	−$10	−$10.00
60	−25	12	12	12	12	10.15
70	−40	−3	34	34	34	26.60
80	−55	−18	19	56	56	35.65
90	−70	−33	4	41	78	29.90

Step 6 **Determine the best decision using the expected-value decision criterion.**
From Step 5 we see that if the decision criterion of highest expected payoff is used, the best decision is to prepare 80 meals. This production level has a higher expected payoff than any other alternative at $35.65. However, on any single day, the actual payoff from this level could be either −$55, −$18, $19, or $56. This means that for any single situation, the best decision might not give the best outcome. Thus, there is a cost of being uncertain about which demand level will occur.

Step 7 **Compute the expected value under certainty.**
If the deli manager could obtain perfect information about the demand level, her decision environment would change to one of certainty. If she

knew in advance how many meals would be demanded, she could select the production level that would maximize the payoff in each case. For example, if she knew the demand was going to be 70, she would decide to prepare 70 meals, for a profit of $34.00. If she knew demand would be 90, she would decide to prepare 90, for a profit of $78.00.

To compute the *expected value under certainty (EVUC)*, we first assume we know what the demand will be for each day. Therefore, we are able to achieve the optimal decision each time. To determine our overall expected profit, we multiply the probability of each demand level times the payoff associated with the *best* decision *given* that demand level occurs. Therefore, if the deli manager had perfect information (certainty) about what the demand was going to be for each day, her expected payoff would be computed as follows:

$$EVUC = -\$10(0.05) + \$12(0.10) + \$34(0.20)$$
$$+ \$56(0.40) + \$78(0.25)$$
$$= \$49.40$$

With perfect information, the deli would make, on average, a profit of $49.40 per day.

Step 8 Compute the cost of uncertainty.

We determined in Step 6 that the expected payoff for the best decision under uncertainty was $35.65. The expected cost of uncertainty is the difference between the expected payoff given perfect information and the expected payoff under uncertainty. This is

Expected Cost of Uncertainty = $49.40 − $35.65 = $13.75

The expected cost of not having perfect information for this decision situation is $13.75.

Another term for the cost of uncertainty is the *expected value of perfect information (EVPI)*. For Example 19-2, the EVPI is $13.75. This is the most the manager would be willing to pay for perfect information about the meal demand on any weekday. Any information that is not perfect would be worth less than $13.75 per day.

19-2: Exercises

Skill Development

19-18. Consider the following payoff table, in which the probabilities associated with each state of nature are in parentheses:

		States of Nature			
		$S_1(0.2)$	$S_2(0.1)$	$S_3(0.4)$	$S_4(0.3)$
Alternatives	A_1	170	45	−60	100
	A_2	30	190	175	−65
	A_3	145	−50	120	110
	A_4	−40	80	10	70

a. Convert the payoff table to an opportunity-loss table.

b. Find the expected value of perfect information for these alternatives.

19-19. Consider the following payoff table, in which the probabilities associated with each state of nature are shown:

		States of Nature		
		S_1	S_2	S_3
	Probabilities	0.5	0.2	0.3
Alternatives	A_1	145	55	80
	A_2	130	65	100
	A_3	110	80	120

a. Convert the payoff table to an opportunity-loss table.

b. Find the expected value of perfect information for these alternatives.

Business Applications

19-20. Refer to Exercise 19-9 in Section 19.1 concerning the number of hot dogs that Sal De Carlo should order for next week's football game. Suppose that Sal has assigned the probabilities shown here for the different demand levels:

Demand	Probability
10,000	0.20
15,000	0.25
20,000	0.30
25,000	0.25

a. Set up the payoff table for Sal's decision concerning the number of hot dogs to order.
b. What are the expected values for each decision that Sal can make?

c. How much would Sal be willing to pay for perfect information about the number of hot dogs that will be demanded during next week's game?

19-21. Refer to the Cooke Collectibles exercise (Exercise 19-11) in Section 19.1. How much would Cooke be willing to pay for perfect information about the number of miniatures representing a famous singer that it should produce?

19-22. Refer to the Special Occasions Company exercise (Exercise 19-13) in Section 19.1. How much should the company be willing to pay for perfect information in order to determine how many dozen roses it should order for the next Valentine's Day sales?

19-23. Refer to the Baker Enterprises exercise (Exercises 19-14 to 19-16) in Section 19.1. What is the maximum amount that Baker should pay for perfect information to help it determine how many boxes of oranges to order?

CHAPTER OUTCOME #6

19.3 Decision-Tree Analysis

Decision Tree
A diagram that illustrates the correct ordering of actions and events in a decision analysis problem. Each act or event is represented by a branch on the decision tree.

When decision analysis is applied to a real business problem, the process can become quite complex. The decision maker must identify the outcomes for each decision alternative, assess probabilities associated with each outcome, assign cash flows in the form of payoffs or opportunity costs, and somehow keep the sequence of decisions and outcomes in the proper order. Decision-tree analysis is very helpful in dealing with these complex decisions in an orderly manner. A **decision tree** provides a "road map" of the decision problem. In this section, we illustrate the steps involved in using decision trees to help with the decision process.

EXAMPLE 19-3 Decision-Tree Analysis

TRY PROBLEM 19.24

Bighorn Oil Company Bighorn Oil Company has leased the drilling rights on a large parcel of land in Wyoming that may or may not contain an oil reserve. A competitor has offered to lease the land for $200,000 cash in return for drilling rights and all rights to any oil that might be found. The offer will expire in 3 days. If Bighorn does not take the deal, it will be faced with the decision of whether to drill for oil on its own. Drilling costs are projected to be $400,000. The company feels that there are four possible outcomes from drilling:

1. dry hole (no oil or natural gas)
2. natural gas
3. natural gas and some oil
4. oil only

If drilling yields a dry hole, the land will be basically worthless, because it is located in the badlands of Wyoming. If natural gas is discovered, Bighorn will recover only its drilling costs. If natural gas and some oil is discovered, revenue is projected to be $800,000. Finally, if only oil is discovered, revenues will be $1,600,000.

Decision-tree analysis can be used to help make the decision using the following steps:

Step 1 **Grow the decision tree.**

The decision tree is developed by organizing the decisions and events in chronological order. In this example, the initial decision to be made is whether to accept the lease. The tree is started as

If the land is leased, no further decisions are required. However, if the land is not leased, Bighorn faces the decision of whether to drill on the property. The tree then grows to

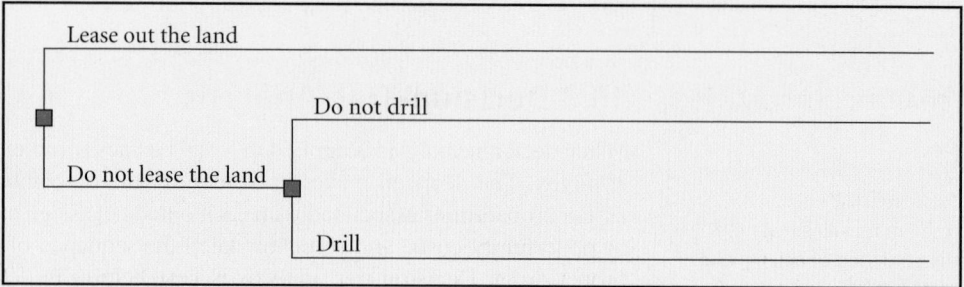

Now, if Bighorn decides to drill, there are four possible events that could occur. These are shown on the decision tree.

When finished, the decision tree should show all the decisions and events.

Step 2 **Assign probabilities to the event outcomes on the tree.**

In this example, the only event deals with the production result if Bighorn decides to drill. The company has subjectively assessed the probability of each of the four possible outcomes as follows:

Outcome	Probability
Dry hole	0.20
Natural gas	0.40
Gas and oil	0.30
Oil only	0.10

The revised decision tree reflects these probabilities and becomes

Step 3 **Assign the cash flows to the tree.**

At each branch of the tree at which a revenue or a cost occurs, show the dollar value. These revenues and costs are then totaled across the tree, and the end values for each branch are determined. These cash flows are placed on the tree as follows:

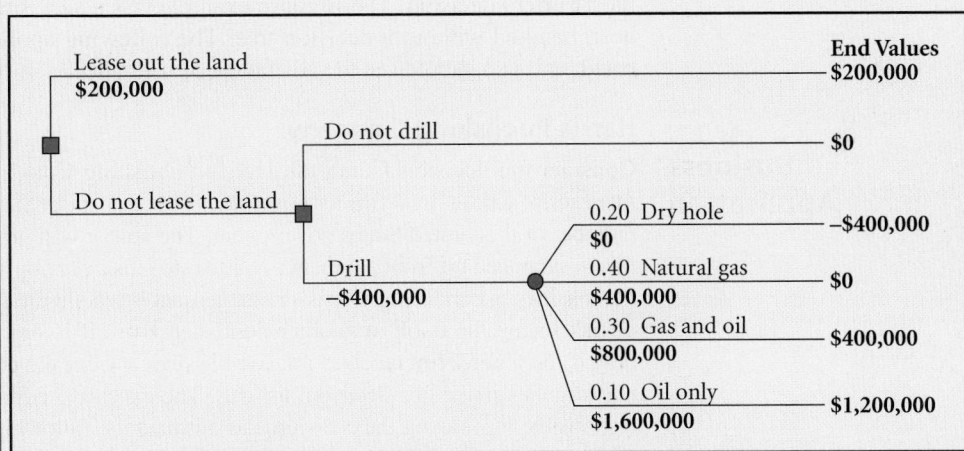

Step 4 **Fold back the decision tree and compute the expected values for each decision.**

We need to compute the expected value for each decision alternative. This is done starting from the right side of the tree and working back to the left. We first determine the expected value for the *Drill* branch as follows:

$$E[\text{Drill}] = -\$400,000(0.20) + \$0(0.40) + \$400,000(0.30)$$
$$+ \$1,200,000(0.10)$$
$$= \$160,000$$

As we fold back the tree, we block all decision alternatives that do not have the highest expected value. This is shown in the decision tree as follows:

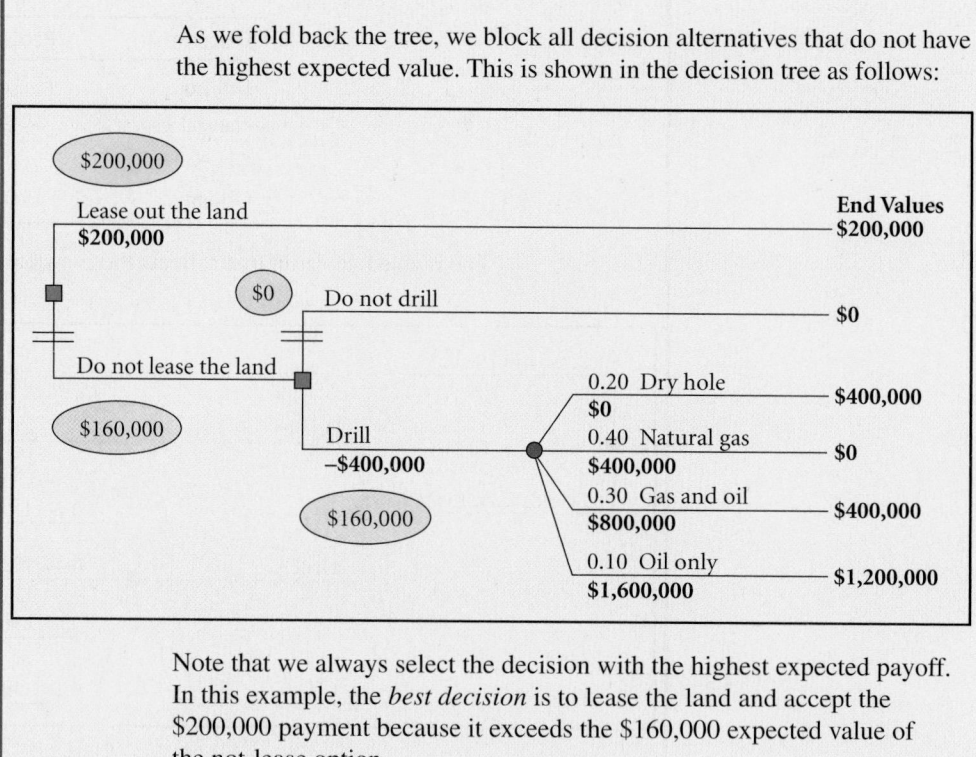

Note that we always select the decision with the highest expected payoff. In this example, the *best decision* is to lease the land and accept the $200,000 payment because it exceeds the $160,000 expected value of the not-lease option.

The value of decision-tree analysis is that a tree helps you to visually structure the decision problem and to systematically analyze the decision alternatives. Decision-tree analysis also provides a way for you to take into account future decisions when making the most current decision. The Bighorn example was a very simple one that could have easily been handled without a decision tree. The following application is a little more complicated, and you should see the advantage of using decision-tree analysis.

Harris Publishing Company

Business Application

Consider the decision facing the Harris Publishing Company, which recently received a manuscript written by a former government official about the private life of a very influential member of the United States government. The author will grant Harris full rights to the book for a guaranteed up-front payment of $400,000 plus a per copy royalty if the book is published. The basic question facing Harris's management is whether to sign the contract with this author or risk losing the book to another publisher. Even if it signs, Harris will publish the book only if the manuscript receives a favorable review from the editorial board. However, several uncertainties make this decision difficult. The executive editor, who is the person ultimately responsible for making the decision, has outlined the following items for consideration:

1. There is an 80% (0.80) chance that the content of the book is accurate. If the content is accurate, the author will be paid $2.00 per copy for each hardcover book sold and $0.80 per copy for each paperback. No royalties will be paid if the manuscript is not accurate.
2. If the content is not accurate, there is a 0.90 chance that a libel suit will be filed; and if so, experience indicates the publisher will settle out of court for $1,800,000.
3. For hardcover publication, the following demand distribution has been assessed:

Demand	Probability
100,000 copies	0.40
1,000,000 copies	0.60

4. The fixed production costs for the hardcover book will be $700,000 before any copies are printed, and the cost of printing and binding is $16.00 per copy. The number of copies to be printed can match any projected demand. The wholesale selling price of the hardcover book will be $24.00.

5. For paperback publication, the following demand distribution has been assessed:

Demand	Probability
50,000 copies	0.30
1,500,000 copies	0.70

6. The fixed costs for paperback publication are $400,000, the printing and binding costs are $2.00 per copy, and the wholesale selling price is $8.00 each.

7. The accuracy of the book's content will be known only after the book has been published and sold.

8. The editor has assessed the probability that the manuscript will get a favorable review from the editorial board as 0.80.

The decision in this case is complicated by the many uncertainties involved. In situations such as these, a decision tree can be used to provide a framework to help make the decision. The following steps are used to develop and apply a decision tree to a decision problem such as the one the Harris Publishing Company is facing.

> **Step 1** **Growing the Tree**
> The decision tree is developed by starting with the initial decision facing the publisher: Sign the contract or don't sign the contract. Figure 19.1 shows the beginnings of the decision tree. The box represents a *decision fork*, the point at which a decision must be made.
>
> If the publisher does not sign the contract, the issue is settled. There are no further branches on that side of the tree. However, if the contract is signed, other branches are needed. Keep in mind that the decision tree is a model of the decision in which alternatives (decisions) are followed by the outcomes (events) that they influence. Usually, but not always, the ordering of alternatives and outcomes follows a chronological sequence. Thus, if the contract is signed, the next step is the review by the editorial board. The outcome of this review is considered an event and is not within control of the company, because it is determined by how well the book is written. A small circle is used to designate an event fork on the decision tree, as is shown in Figure 19.2.

FIGURE 19.1

Harris Publishing Decision Tree: Phase 1

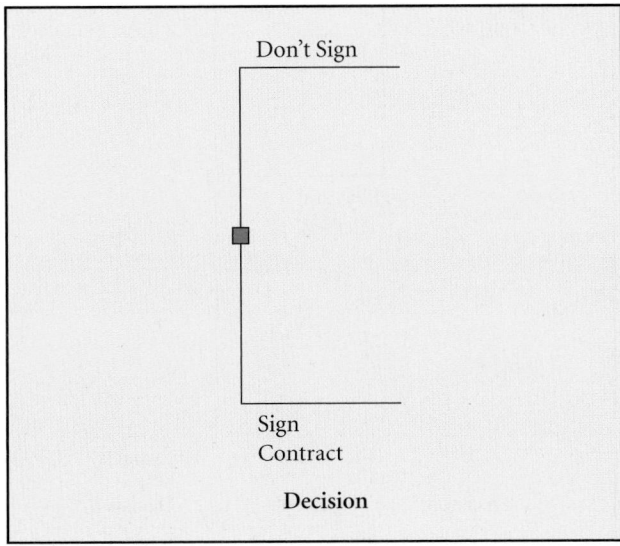

Don't Sign

Sign Contract

Decision

FIGURE 19.2

Harris Publishing Decision Tree: Phase 2

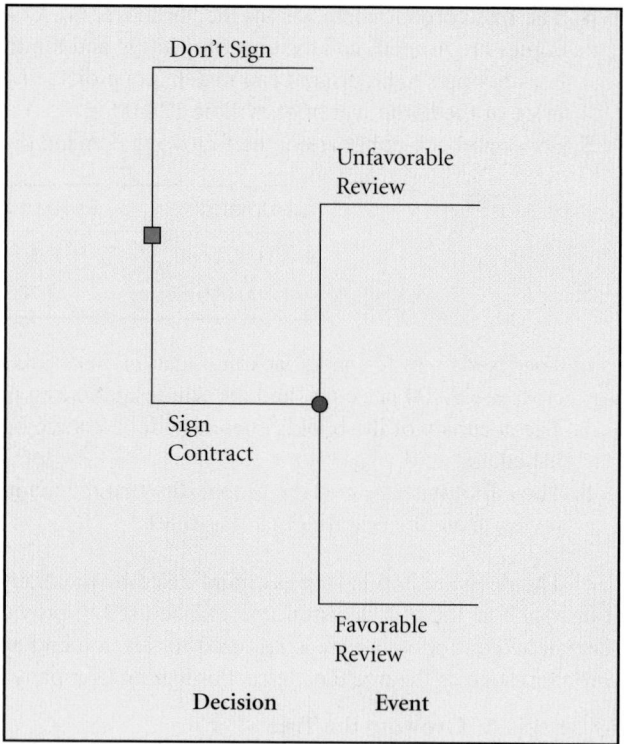

FIGURE 19.3

Harris Publishing Decision Tree: Phase 3

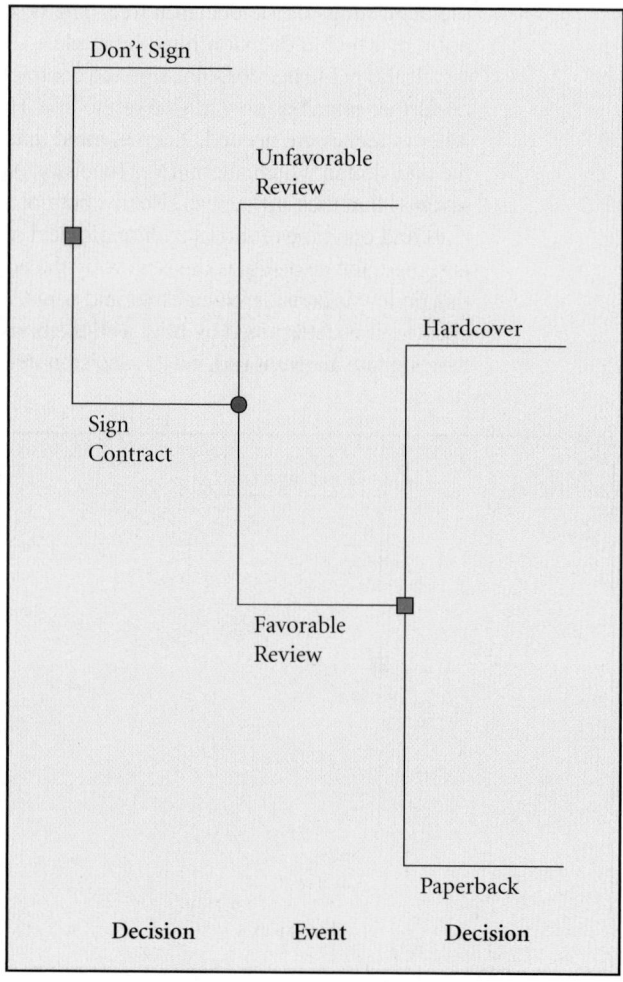

FIGURE 19.4

**Harris Publishing
Decision Tree: Phase 4**

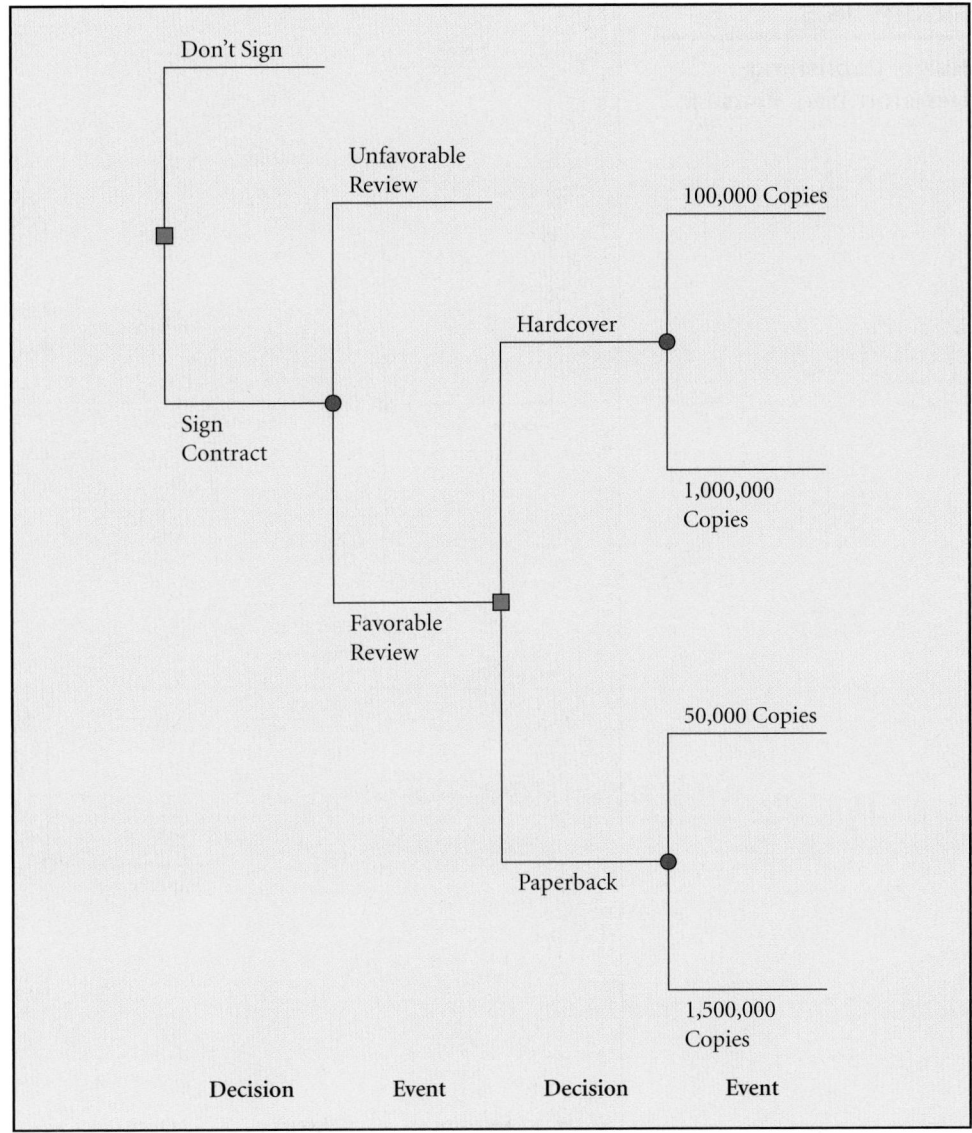

If the editorial review is unfavorable, the book will not be published. If the manuscript review is favorable, the book will be published. Then the company must decide between hardcover or paperback books. This decision fork is shown in Figure 19.3.

Following the hardcover/paperback decision, the book will go on sale and the true demand will be known. (Recall that we assumed production can be set to match demand.) The level of demand is an event and is not controlled by the company. Figure 19.4 shows the event forks and branches associated with demand.

After the book goes on sale, the company will find out whether the content is accurate. This is an event beyond the decision maker's control. Figure 19.5 shows these event branches. As you can see, the tree is growing.

Figure 19.6 shows the final set of branches, which relate to the possibility of a libel suit. If we have correctly described the decision problem, this tree is a model of the decision facing the Harris Publishing Company. After reaching the point at which you think the tree is complete, conferring with someone who has not been involved in developing the tree can be helpful. A fresh perspective is often useful in finding oversights and inconsistencies in a

FIGURE 19.5

Harris Publishing Decision Tree: Phase 5

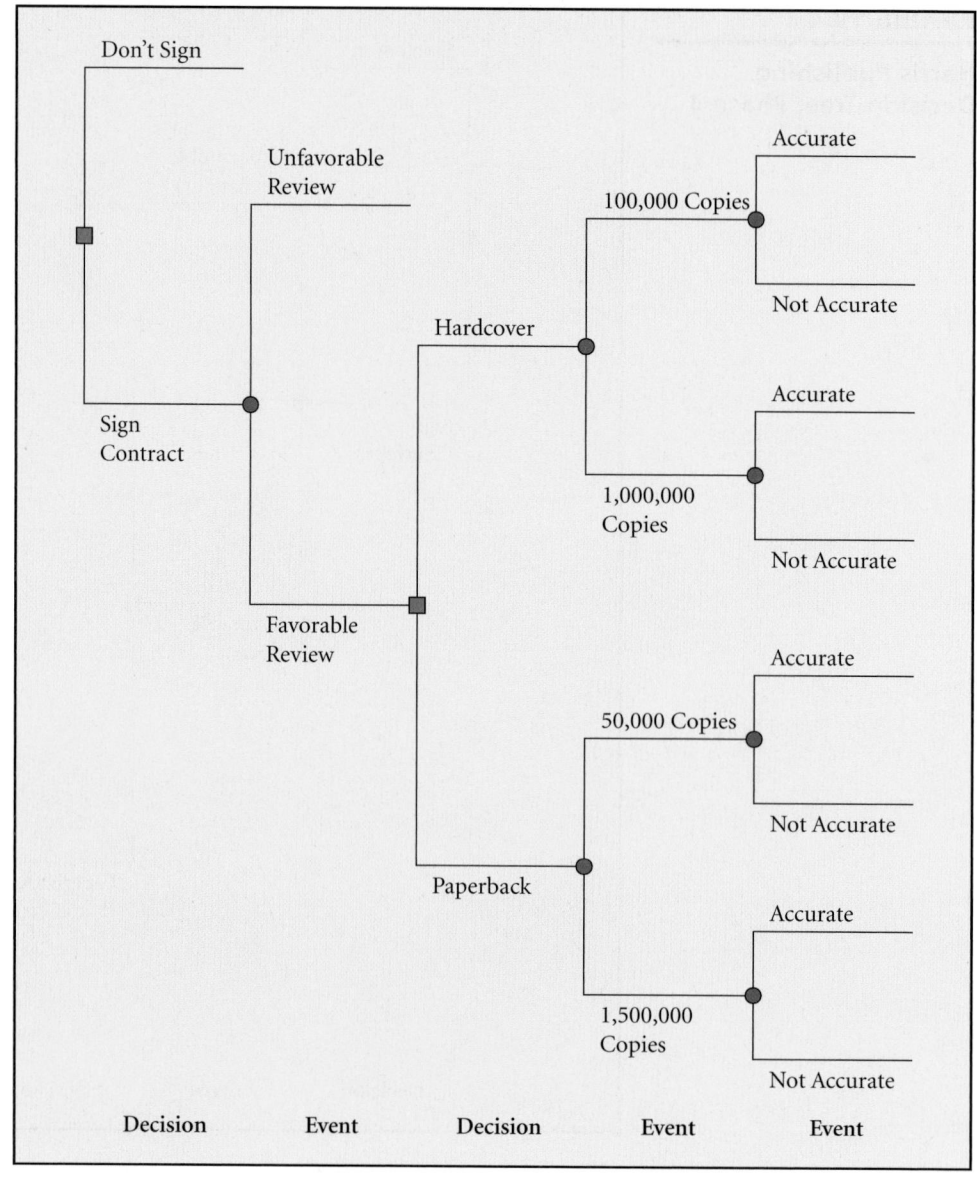

decision tree. *The decision tree should reflect the decision problem as accurately as possible before any further analysis is performed using the tree.*

Step 2 **Assigning the Probabilities**
The decision tree contains a number of *event forks*, represented by small circles. The branches leaving these event forks represent possible outcomes from an uncertain event. To make full use of decision-tree analysis, probabilities must be assigned to each of these event branches. These probabilities can come from classical assessment, relative frequency of occurrence or, most likely, subjective assessment.

In the Harris Publishing Company example, the probabilities were subjective assessments by the executive editor, based on her experience and the available information. We can summarize these as follows:

1. The probability that a manuscript review will be favorable is 0.80; unfavorable, 0.20.
2. If a hardcover edition is printed, there is a 0.40 chance that demand will be 100,000 copies and a 0.60 chance that demand will be 1 million copies.

FIGURE 19.6

Harris Publishing Decision Tree: Phase 6, Final Tree

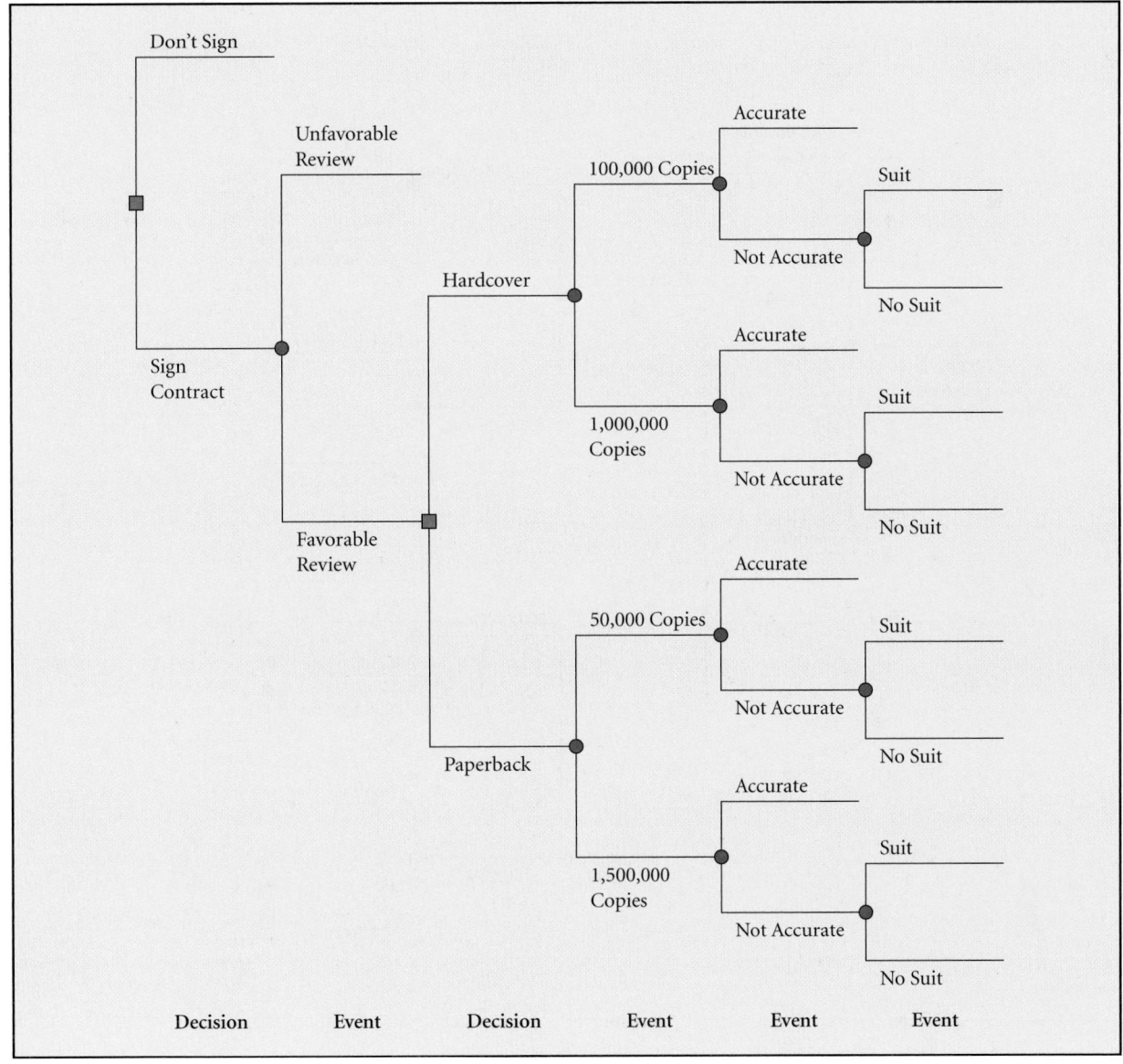

3. If a paperback edition is printed, there is a 0.30 chance that 50,000 copies will be sold and a 0.70 chance that 1.5 million copies will be sold.
4. There is an 0.80 chance that the content of the book will prove accurate.
5. There is a 0.90 chance the publisher will be sued for libel if the book turns out to be inaccurate.

Figure 19.7 shows the decision tree with the probabilities assigned. Remember, probabilities must be assigned to every event branch. The sum of the probabilities for each event fork must be 1.

Step 3 Assigning the Cash Flows

Once probabilities have been assigned to each event, the next step is to assign the cash flows. A *cash flow* is defined here as any dollar change in the decision maker's asset position. For instance, any income or expense that is expressed in dollar terms is considered a cash flow. (In some applications, the "cash flows" might be expressed in something other than dollars,

FIGURE 19.7

Harris Publishing Co.—Assigning Probabilities

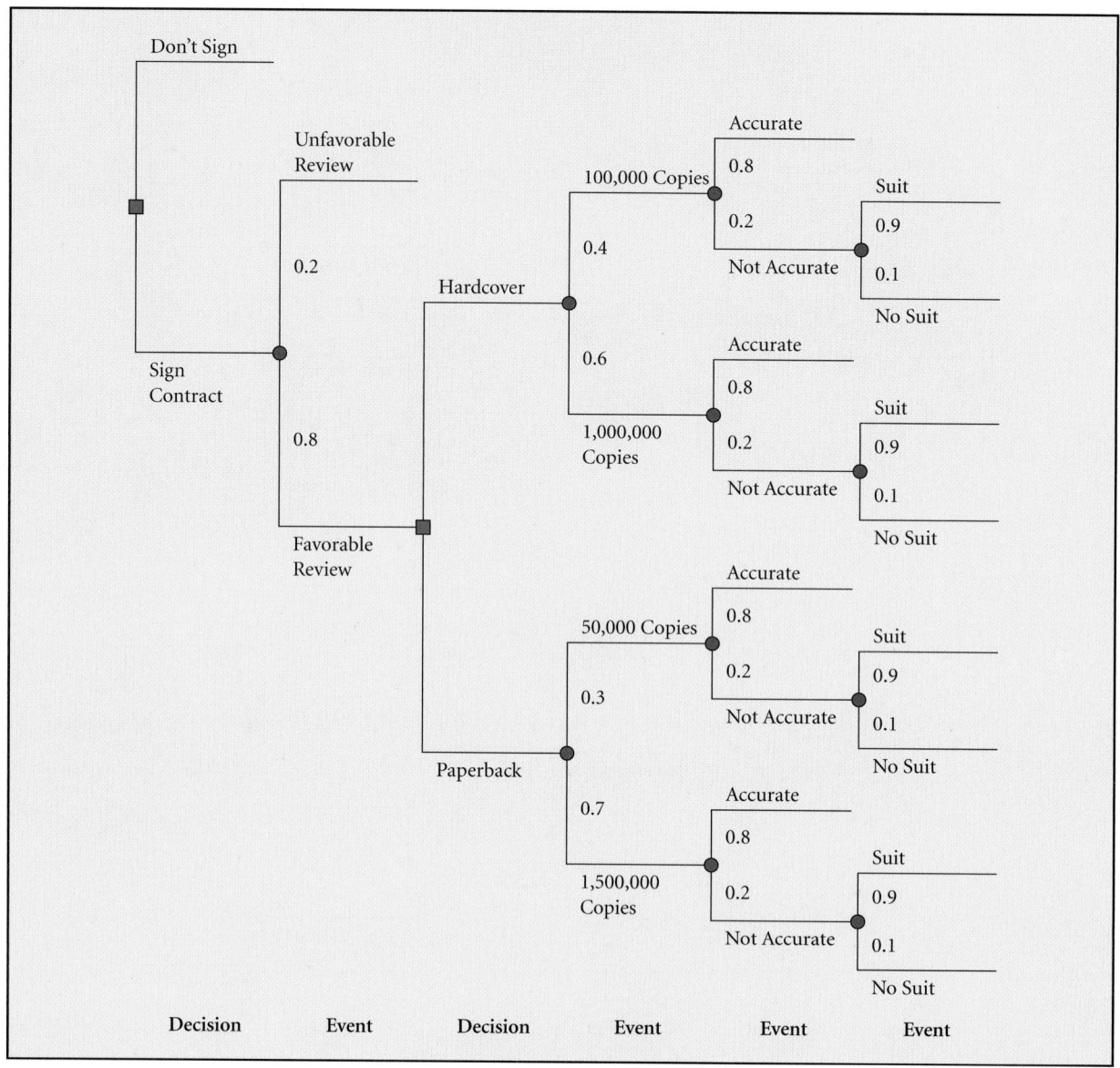

but in this text we will limit our definition of cash flows to dollars.) The cash flows are displayed on the tree branches indicating the time at which they will occur. Unlike probabilities, which are assigned only to events, cash flows can occur for both decisions and events. For Harris Publishing Company, the first cash flow will occur when the author signs the contract. This will be an expense of $400,000. Figure 19.8 shows this as −$400 (amounts are in thousands) directly above the *Sign Contract* branch. The *Don't Sign Contract* branch has a cash flow of $0, indicating that if this decision is made, there will be no change in the company's asset position.

The editorial review is done by salaried staff members. Thus, we can treat this cost as part of administrative overhead and not assign any cash flows to the review branches in Figure 19.8. When the decision to publish hardcover or paperback books is made, a fixed expense occurs. The expense is $700,000 for hardcover and $400,000 for paperback. These cash flows are displayed in Figure 19.8.

FIGURE 19.8

Harris Publishing Co.—Assigning Cash Flows ($ × 1,000)

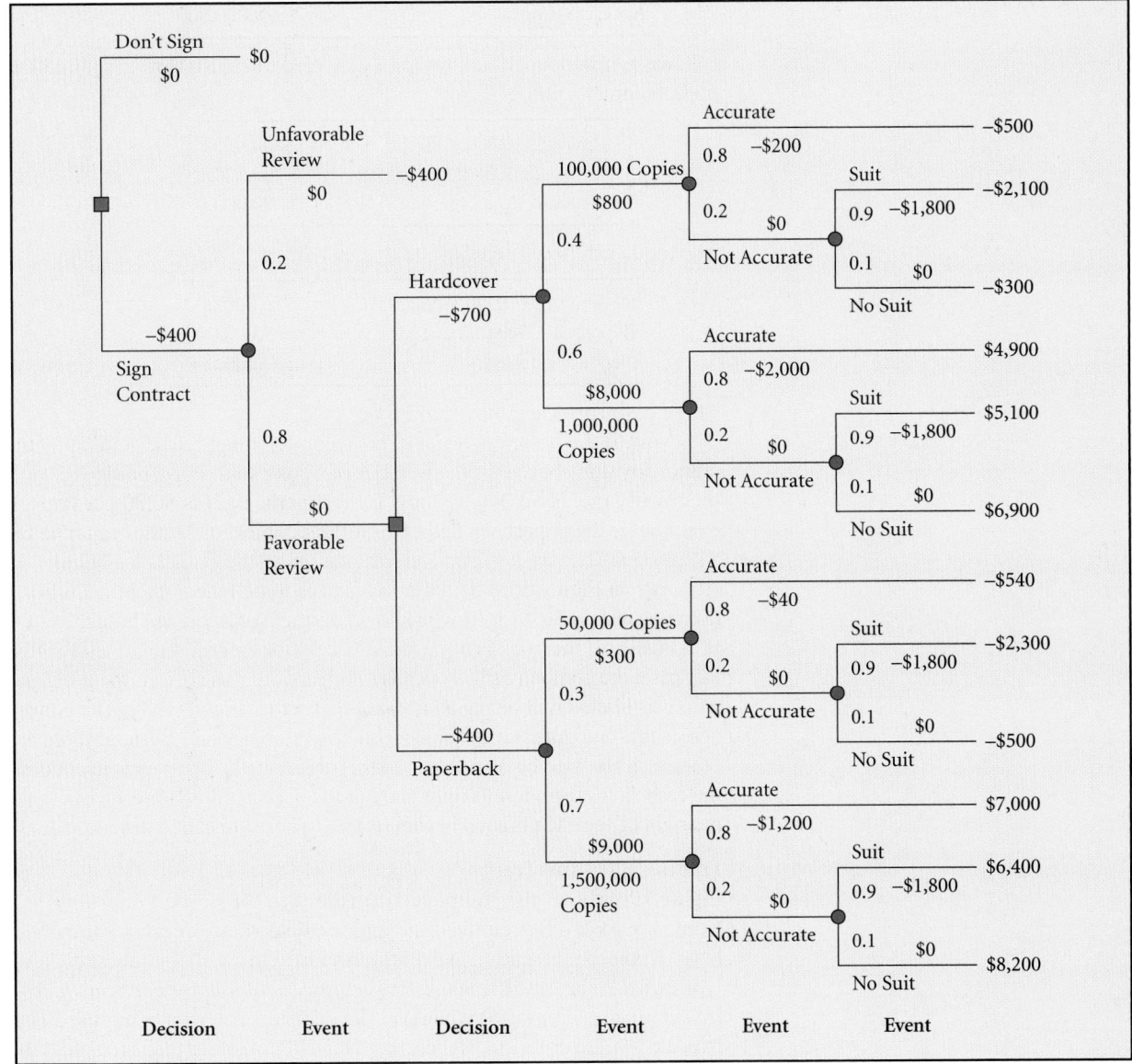

Next, we assign the cash flows associated with the demand levels for hardcover and paperback. For example, if the hardcover decision is selected and demand is 100,000 copies, the following cash flow will occur:

Revenue 100,000 at $24.00 each	=	$2,400,000
Expenses 100,000 at $16.00 each	=	−1,600,000
Net cash flow	=	$ 800,000

This $800,000 cash flow is shown in Figure 19.8. You may be wondering what happened to the author's royalties. These are to be paid only when the book's accuracy has been verified. For purposes of this decision, this is the same as paying the author when the books are sold and having him return the money if the book proves to be inaccurate.

If the hardcover book sells 1,000,000 copies, the cash flow will be

Revenue 1,000,000 at $24.00 each	= $24,000,000
Expenses 1,000,000 at $16.00 each	= −16,000,000
Net cash flow	= $ 8,000,000

Likewise, if the paperback option is selected, the cash flow associated with 50,000 copies will be

Revenue 50,000 at $8.00 each	= $400,000
Expenses 50,000 at $2.00 each	= −100,000
Net cash flow	= $300,000

The total cash flow for 1,500,00 copies will be

Revenue 1,500,000 at $8.00 each	= $12,000,000
Expenses 1,500,000 at $2.00 each	= −3,000,000
Net cash flow	= $ 9,000,000

These cash flows are shown in Figure 19.8.

Now, if the book turns out to be accurate, the publisher must pay the author royalties based on the number of books sold. For a hardcover book, the royalty rate is $2.00 per copy; for a paperback, it is $0.80 per copy. For example, if the paperback sells 1.5 million copies, the author must be paid $1,200,000. The royalty costs are shown under the branches labeled *Accurate* in Figure 19.8. If the book proves to be inaccurate, the author gets no royalties; so $0 cash flow is shown on the *Not Accurate* branch.

Finally, if the book is not accurate, the publisher might be sued for libel. In that case, the company's lawyer has told Harris that the government official who was libeled will be paid $1,800,000 to settle (Figure 19.8). The editor agrees this amount is more than adequate to stop the suit. Because there are no other cash flows to be considered in this decision, the last step is to accumulate the cash flows from left to right and put the net cash flow for each branch to the right of the each branch in Figure 19.8. These are called the end values.

Step 4 **Folding Back the Tree**

Figure 19.9 shows the completed decision tree for Harris Publishing Company. (We have removed the intermediate values from the branches and have expressed the end values in thousands to make the numbers easier to work with.) This sets the stage for the process *of folding back the decision tree*, a process employed whenever the decision criterion being used is the expected-value criterion. Recall that Harris Publishing plans to select the alternative with the highest expected payoff.

Remember that the decision tree is a diagram of the sequence of decisions and events. To fold back the decision tree, we begin with the end values at the right of the tree and work our way back to the initial decision at the far left. To do this, we must determine the expected value of each decision branch. (Please refer to Figure 19.10 as we discuss the fold-back steps.)

Because the Don't *Sign Contract* branch has no following uncertain events, the end value of $0 is the expected value of that decision alternative. This expected value is displayed in a box near the decision fork.

The process of finding the expected value for the *Sign Contract* branch requires a little more effort. To begin, we go to each event branch at which *Suit* and *No Suit* are the possible outcomes. We compute the expected values of these events by multiplying the end value times the probability of each outcome. For instance, for the event branch emanating from the Hardcover, 100,000 *Copies, Not Accurate* branch, the expected value is

$$EV = -\$2,100(0.90) + -\$300(0.10) = -\$1,920$$

FIGURE 19.9

Harris Publishing Co.—Final Decision Tree

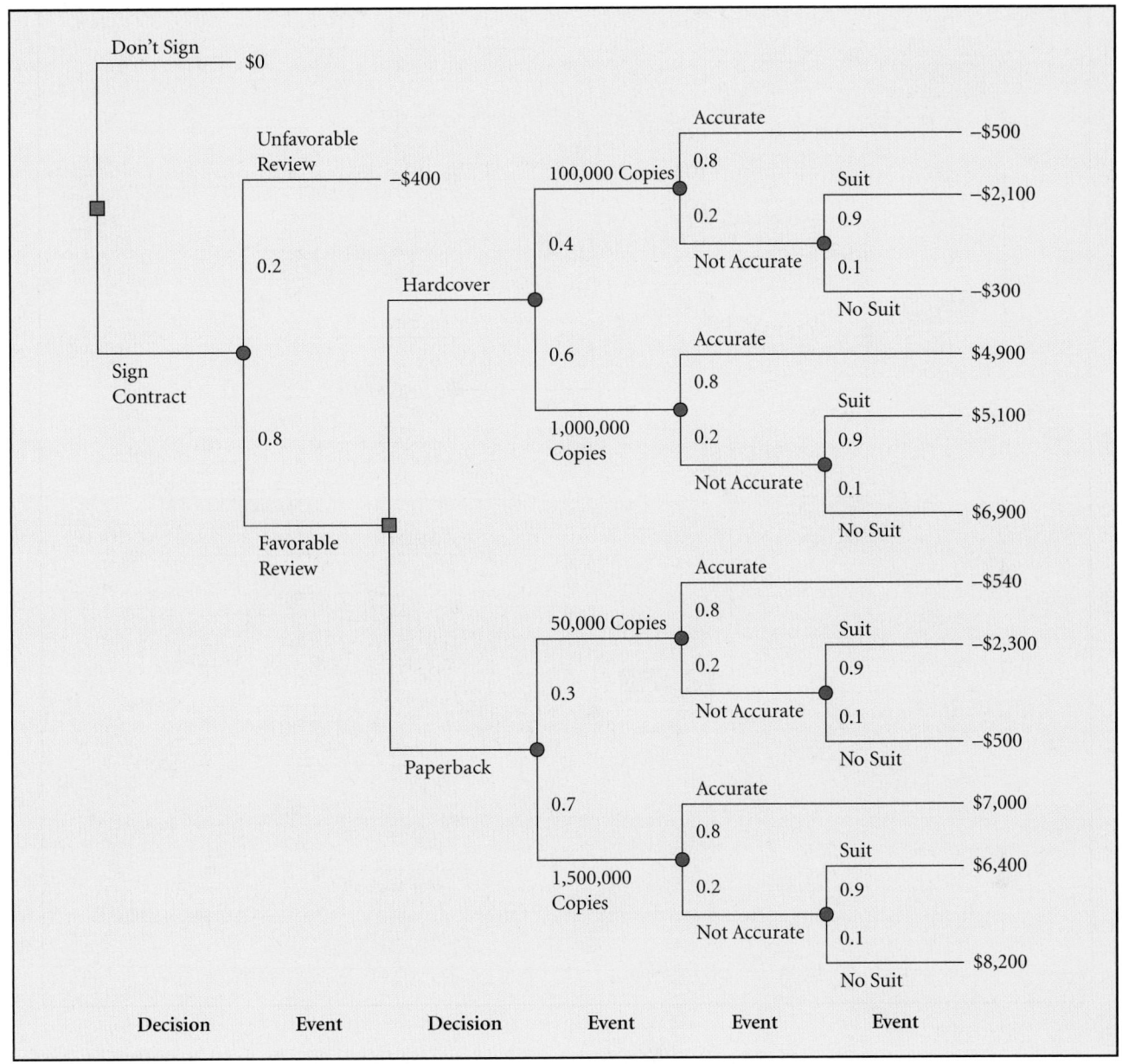

This expected value is displayed inside the oval between the two event branches. We use the same procedure to find expected values for all *Suit/No Suit* event branches, as shown in Figure 19.10. (*Note:* All dollar amounts are in thousands.)

Next, we determine the expected value of the event *Accurate/Not Accurate* in each instance in the tree where the event appears. To illustrate, we will use the event emanating from the *Hardcover, 100,000 Copies* branch. The expected value is

$$EV = -\$500(0.80) + -\$1,920(0.20) = -\$784$$

This value is shown in the oval between the two event branches. Note that in computing the expected value, we used $-\$1,920$, the expected value of the

FIGURE 19.10

Harris Publishing Co.—Folding Back the Decision Tree

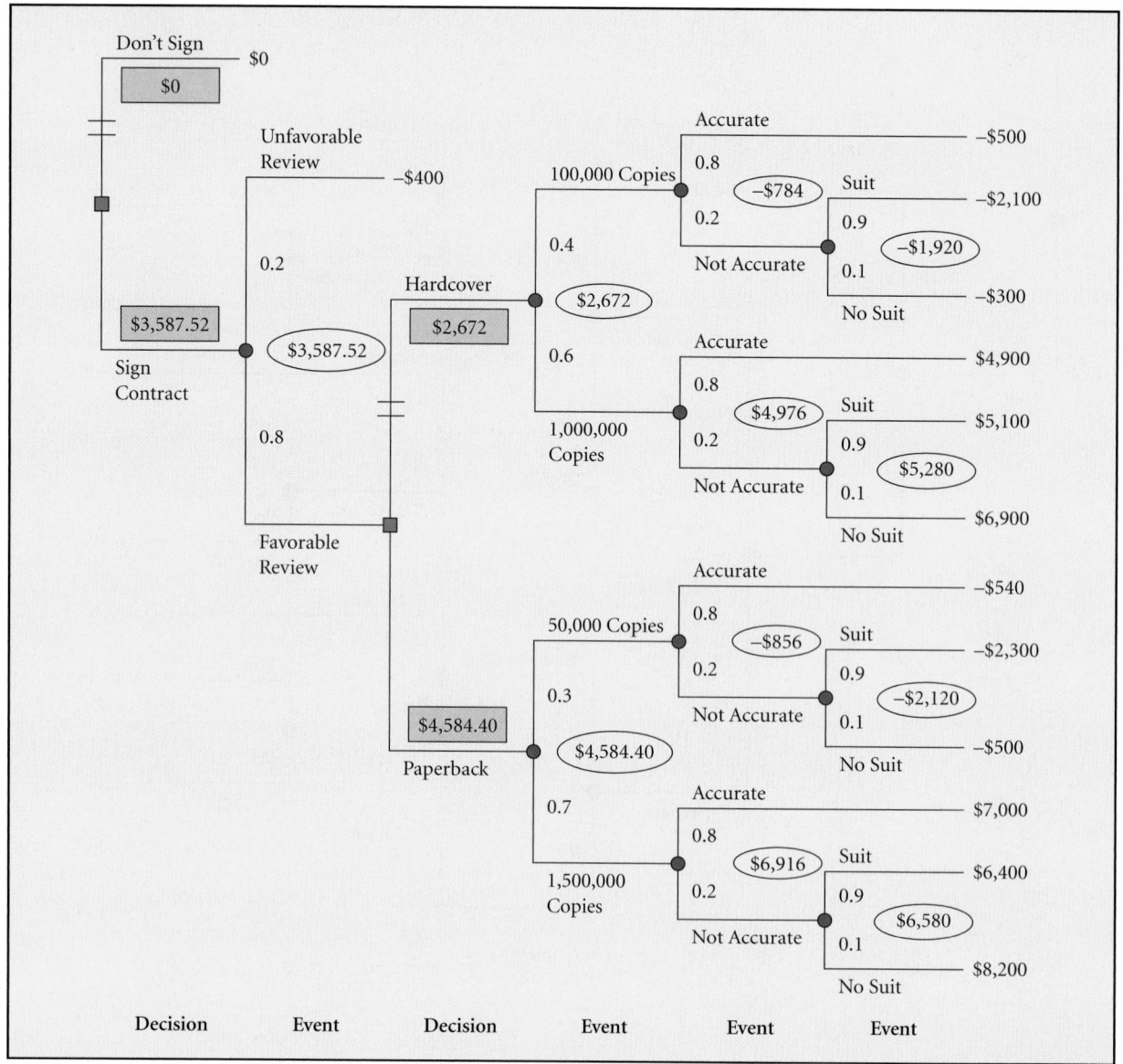

Suit/No Suit event. This value was multiplied by the 0.20 probability that the content of the manuscript will not be accurate. The 0.80 chance that the manuscript will be accurate is multiplied by −$500, because that is the expected value of the *Accurate* branch.

The expected value of the *Accurate/Not Accurate* event emanating from the *Hardcover, 1,000,000 Copies* branch is

$$EV = \$4,900(0.80) + \$5,280(0.20) = \$4,976$$

This value is also shown in Figure 19.10, in the oval between the two outcome branches. The same methodology is used in the lower portion of the tree. This process of moving from right to left is what we mean by "folding back the tree."

We continue by determining the expected values of the demand events. For instance, the expected value for the demand event emanating from the *Hardcover* branch is

$$EV = -\$784(0.40) + \$4,976(0.60) = \$2,672$$

This value is also the expected value of the *Hardcover* decision branch. This means that the expected value of the hardcover alternative is $2,672 (actually $2,672,000).

The expected value for the demand event emanating from the *Paperback* decision branch is

$$EV = -\$856(0.30) + \$6,916(0.70) = \$4,584.40$$

This value is the expected value of the *Paperback* decision alternative. Because $4,584.40 > $2,672, the best decision is to select the paperback option if the editor reaches that decision point. She would expect a net payoff of $4,584.40 (actually $4,584,400) from the paperback decision. Note that the hardcover decision branch is blocked, indicating that it is not the best decision.

The final step in the fold-back process is to determine the expected value of the review event. We again multiply the appropriate cash flows by their probabilities.

$$EV = -\$400(0.20) + \$4,584.40(0.80) = \$3,587.52$$

Thus, as shown in Figure 19.10, the expected value is $3,587.52, which is the expected value of the *Sign Contract* branch. This means that if the company signs the publishing contract, its expected payoff is $3,587.52 (actually $3,587,520). Because this value exceeds the $0 expected payoff for the *Don't Sign Contract* branch, the best decision is to sign the contract. If the editorial review is favorable, then publish in paperback. (Notice that the *Don't Sign* branch is blocked, indicating that this alternative won't be selected.)

This example demonstrates the use of a decision tree to help in making a decision under uncertainty. The decision tree provides a framework for analyzing alternatives and dealing with uncertainties. The decision reached is the best decision given the expected-value criterion. However, as we indicated earlier, the best decision does not always lead to the best outcome. For instance, if the contract is signed and the book is published in paperback, demand may be only 50,000 copies and, worse yet, the contents might not be accurate. If this chain of events occurs, a lawsuit will be filed. Harris Publishing would lose $2,300,000 on the deal. Remember, a "bad outcome" can occur from this one-time decision. But then again, an extremely good outcome could occur if the demand for the book is 1.5 million copies, the book proves inaccurate (no royalties are paid), and no suit is filed. The payoff under this scenario is $8,200,000. The expected-value criterion takes into consideration all the possible payoffs and the probabilities of those payoffs occurring.

SUMMARY Decision-Tree Analysis

To solve a decision-tree problem, the following steps are used:

1. Grow the decision tree. Arrange the decisions and events in the order in which they will occur. This is often difficult with complex decision problems, but unless the decision tree accurately represents the situation, the decision made may not be the best decision.
2. Assign the probabilities. Make the necessary probability assessments and show them on the event branches. These probabilities can be determined using classical assessment,

relative frequency of occurrence, or subjective techniques. (Remember that probabilities are associated with the uncertain events and not with the decision alternatives.)

3. Assign cash flows by showing costs and payoffs on the branches where they occur. Accumulate these cash flows and determine the end value for each branch of the decision tree.
4. Fold back the decision tree. At each decision fork, select the decision that maximizes expected payoff or minimizes expected cost.

This example illustrates an important virtue of decision-tree analysis. That is, the tree allows future decisions that have an influence on the current decision to be systematically considered. Chronologically, the decision about whether to publish in hardcover or paperback comes after the initial decision of whether to sign a contract. However, the decision of whether to sign is made only after the expected profits associated with publishing in hardcover and paperback are determined. In this case, the editor decided to publish in paperback because her analysis indicated the contract should be signed. The ability to use projected future events to help make a current decision is a natural part of the fold-back process.

Sensitivity Analysis In a decision problem such as the one facing Harris Publishing Company, uncertainty in the events is measured by the probabilities assessed for each event outcome. The expected-value criterion utilizes these probability assessments. But a question that arises when decision analysis is applied is how *sensitive* is the decision to the probabilities being assessed. For instance, the company might want to know how much the probability of a favorable review would have to change to make not signing the contract the best decision.

To answer this question, refer to Figure 19.10. Instead of using 0.80 for the probability of a favorable review, let the probability be p. Then the probability of an unfavorable review is $1 - p$. We next solve for p such that the expected value of the *Sign Contract* alternative (now \$3,587.52) is the same as the expected value of the *Don't Sign Contract* alternative, which in this case is \$0.

$$0 = 4{,}584.40p + -400(1 - p)$$
$$0 = 4{,}584.40p - 400 + 400p$$
$$400 = 4{,}984.40p$$
$$400/4{,}984.40 = p$$
$$0.08025 = p$$

Thus, the probability of a favorable report would have to decrease from 0.80 to less than 0.1 in order for the best decision to be not to sign the contract. This means the decision is quite insensitive to the probability assessed for a favorable editorial review, and there is probably no need to investigate this assessment any further.

Another question might be: How sensitive is the decision to publish the softcover book to the probability assessment associated with the number of hardcover books that might be sold? That is, how much higher than 0.60 would the probability of selling 1 million copies have to be before the best decision would be to go with the hardcover books? The approach to answering this question is essentially the same as before. We let $p =$ the probability of selling 1 million copies and $1 - p$ be the probability of selling 100,000 copies. We then solve for p such that the expected payoff for hardcover is equal to that for paperback: \$4,584.40 (see Figure 19.10). We solve for p as follows:

$$4{,}584.40 = 4{,}976p + -784(1 - p)$$
$$4{,}584.40 = 4{,}976p - 784 + 784p$$
$$5{,}368.40 = 5{,}760p$$
$$5{,}368.40/5{,}760 = p$$
$$0.9320 = p$$

The probability of selling 1 million books would have to be higher than 0.9320 for the best decision to be to publish a hardcover book. When this is compared with the current assessment of 0.60, we see the decision is not very sensitive to this probability assessment. Depending on how much information and thought went into the original probability assessment, there does not appear to be a need to allocate substantial resources to study the hardcover-demand issue further.

Sensitivity analysis can also investigate how much a cash-flow value would have to change before the decision would change. The method for determining the sensitivity of a cash-flow item is the same as for a probability. Let the cash-flow value in question equal x, and then solve for x such that the decision branches have the same expected payoff. When sensitivity analysis indicates that the resulting decision is sensitive to a probability or cash-flow value, you will want to spend extra time studying this factor before arriving at the final decision.

19-3: Exercises

Business Applications

19-24. Tom and Joe operate a rock quarry that provides local stone for landscaping. They currently have an offer for $50,000 to sell the quarry. They are hesitant to sell because they believe there will be an increase in demand in the next 2 years that would improve their financial situation. If they decide to keep the quarry, the current buyer would be willing to pay $30,000 in 2 years, regardless of the situation. Tom and Joe think there is a 60% chance of an increase, at which point they would operate at a profit of $75,000 or sell the quarry to a new buyer for $60,000. If demand does not increase, they would operate at a profit of only $10,000. Use a decision tree to determine what they should do.

19-25. Vegetable Farms is a small, family-operated ranch that sells produce to local markets. The owners are currently trying to decide whether they should expand their operation next year. Because this is a fairly new business, the owners have assessed the following demand levels and probabilities: high (probability 0.50), medium (0.30), or low (0.20). The payoffs they expect for each demand/acreage scenario are listed. Use a decision tree to help decide whether to expand the farm.

	DEMAND		
ACREAGE	High	Medium	Low
Expanded	$100,000	$40,000	−$40,000
Same size	50,000	40,000	30,000

19-26. Aquatech currently holds the lease to a site with good potential for geothermal development to generate electricity. Aquatech is now looking at three options for the site: (1) sell the rights to the property for $1.5 million; (2) extend the lease for 25 years at a cost of $0.5 million, with the possibility of selling later; or (3) extend the lease and drill exploratory wells at a total cost of $2 million.

If the company decides to extend the lease in order to drill, future revenue from the site would be determined by the temperature of the water. The following chart lists the probabilities associated

with the three states of nature possible, along with the projected drill revenues:

Water Temperature	Probability	Drill Revenue (in Millions)
High	0.4	$5
Medium	0.4	3
Low	0.2	1

If the company extends the lease in order to sell the property later without drilling, the sale price will be determined by the demand for electricity. The following chart lists the probabilities associated with the three levels of demand and the projected sale prices:

Demand	Probability	Sale Price (in Millions)
High	0.3	$2.5
Medium	0.6	2.0
Low	0.1	1.5

Use a decision tree to diagram Aquatech's possible solutions and determine which option management should choose.

19-27. Paradise Springs is in the position of having to decide what size cross-country ski resort to build. The majority owners are adamant that a resort be built and that future plans for the resort should be determined by revenues generated during the first 2 years of the project.

The developer has the option of building a small complex now and later expanding, if demand warrants, to a large complex or build a large complex now. The expansion project would increase the size of a small complex to that of a large complex and could be completed in the off-season to allow the resort to function as a large resort the second season. The costs of construction are as follows:

Size	Cost (in Millions)
Small	$2.0
Expansion (2nd year)	1.5
Large	3.0

The developer believes that demand for the resort will be either high or low and thinks there will be a 50–50 chance the resort will be popular in its first season. If demand is high the first year, she feels there is a 60% chance the resort will be popular its second season. If demand is low, she would not want to expand. She feels if demand is low the first year, there is a 70% chance it will remain low for the second season. The expected annual revenues for the resort are as follows:

Expected Annual Revenues (in Millions)

Size	High	Low
Small	$2	$1
Large	3	2

Revenue figures do not include the costs of construction. Use a decision tree to determine which size the resort should develop.

Summary and Conclusions

Making decisions under uncertainty is a regular part of business. Although decision makers usually cannot eliminate uncertainty, they can use the tools of decision analysis to help deal with it.

In this chapter, we explained the steps for constructing a payoff table and an opportunity-loss table. We also introduced nonprobabilistic decision criteria, such as maximin, maximax, and minimax regret. More importantly, we discussed the expected-value criterion, which utilizes probabilities assigned to uncertain outcomes. We demonstrated how to determine the cost of uncertainty and how to determine an upper limit on the value of new information using either a payoff or an opportunity-cost approach.

One of the most important decision analysis tools is the decision tree, which provides a chronological ordering of the decisions and events involved in making a decision. In this chapter, we illustrated how to use a decision tree in making a decision under uncertainty. In addition, we showed how decision-tree analysis, through the fold-back process, takes into account future decisions that affect the current decision.

Equations

Expected Value

$$E(x) = \sum_{i=1}^{k} x_i P(x_i) \qquad (19.1)$$

$$\sum_{i=1}^{k} P(x_i) = 1 \qquad (19.2)$$

$$0 \leq P(x_i) \leq 1 \qquad (19.3)$$

Key Terms

Certainty   892
Decision tree   905
Expected-value criterion   897
Maximax criterion   896

Maximin criterion   896
Minimax regret criterion   896
Opportunity loss   896
Payoff   895

States of nature   895
Uncertainty   893

Chapter Exercises

Business Applications

Exercises 19-28 through 19-31 refer to the following situation.

Hatchman Electronics makes specialized fuel-injection units for automobile engines. The company is currently completing its 5-year strategic plan. A major component of this plan involves analyzing the following situation.

Hatchman currently makes an injection unit that it sells to automobile manufacturers for $200. The operating profit (revenue – direct manufacturing costs) for this unit is $90. The company estimates that the probability is 80% that demand for this product will continue, at the same price, for the next 5 years. But if a competitor introduces a better unit, the selling price will be dropped to $140 to maintain the company's market share. Hatchman Electronics is considering trying to develop an improved fuel injector. Whether or not the product is successful, the development costs will be amortized by adding $20 to the cost of every injector sold for the next 5 years. If the development effort is successful, the improved unit will still be sold for $200, but direct manufacturing costs will be reduced to $70. The research and development department estimates that the probability of a successful development effort is 60%.

19-28. Develop a decision tree representing the Hatchman Electronics decision situation.

19-29. Assuming the Hatchman Electronics board of directors is willing to base the decision on expected values, should it decide to develop the new product?

19-30. Hatchman Electronics has the option of contracting with Stewart Consultants to analyze the feasibility of developing the new fuel-injection unit. The feasibility study will cost $5 million and will be added to the production cost of each of the 1 million units the company is planning to make over the next 5 years. If the study indicates the new development is feasible, the probability of the product being successfully developed will be increased to 90%. If the study indicates that the new development is not feasible, the product may still be developed, but the probability of success will drop to 20%. Hatchman's managers don't have enough information to speculate about the probability that the feasibility study will indicate a success, so they assess each outcome—success and not a success—as being equally likely. Develop the decision tree for this new situation.

19-31. Assuming the Hatchman Electronics board of directors is still willing to consider this problem using expected values, should it hire Stewart Consultants? What is the new sequence of decisions that should be taken?

Exercises 19-32 through 19-35 refer to the Far Horizons Development Corporation, which is considering building a vacation condominium project on the Maine coast. The question facing the company is how many units to build.

Because of their central-utility design, the units must be built in blocks of 10. Assume that, for each block of 10, the land will cost $200,000 and construction will cost $250,000 plus an additional $70,000 for each unit. Given that the company has decided to build, the possible production levels are as follows: 10, 20, 30, 40, and 50.

Each unit will be priced at $200,000 for the regular market. However, if demand does not meet supply, Far Horizons will be forced to auction the units at an average price of $75,000.

19-32. Set up a payoff table assuming the following possible demand levels: 0, 10, 20, 30, 40, and 50.

19-33. What is the best decision if the maximin criterion is used? Show how you arrived at your answer.

19-34. What is the best decision for Far Horizons if the maximax criterion is used? Show how you arrived at your answer.

19-35. Assume that Far Horizons has assessed the following probability distribution for condominium demand:

Demand	Probability
0	0.05
10	0.10
20	0.25
30	0.25
40	0.20
50	0.15
	1.00

Use the expected-value criterion to determine how many units should be built. What is the expected value of this alternative?

Exercises 19-36 through 19-39 refer to the following situation.

The production manager for a video-game company has been asked to help upper management decide whether to market a new game based on a popular cartoon character. If the new game is successful, the company will make $50 million; but if it is a failure, the company will lose an estimated $20 million in production and advertising expenses.

19-36. The video-game production manager believes that there is a 60% chance the new game will be successful. Construct the payoff table for the decision faced by the video-game company.

19-37. What decision should the managers of the video-game company make if they wish to maximize the expected payoff?

19-38. Suppose that marketing personnel have determined there are several levels of success and failure possible with the proposed video game. These possibilities (states of nature) and the assessed probabilities are as follows:

Success Level	Probability
Excellent ($70,000,000)	0.30
Good ($50,000,000)	0.30
Fair ($10,000,000)	0.10
Poor (−$20,000,000)	0.30
	1.00

Develop the payoff table that reflects these states of nature.

19-39. Given the payoff table developed in Exercise 19-38, what decision should the company's managers make if they wish to maximize the expected payoff?

19-40. The manager of the Pink Flounder restaurant must decide how many orders of its special butter-broiled catfish to make for Thursday's lunch special. The orders must be made in advance, because the restaurant guarantees lunchtime service in less than 15 minutes and the catfish special takes 45 minutes to prepare. Each order costs $3.50 to prepare and is sold for $7.00. Any leftover orders can be used in the restaurant's fish gumbo, for a savings of $1.50. People who order catfish after it has run out are given a free catfish dinner on their next visit. Sales records from past Thursdays indicate that demand should have the following probability distribution:

Demand Level	Probability
3	0.10
4	0.30
5	0.25
6	0.20
7	0.10
8	0.05
9 or more	0.00
	1.00

Develop a payoff table for the Pink Flounder's decision problem.

19-41. Referring to Exercise 19-40, how many orders of catfish should be prepared on Thursday?

19-42. In Exercises 19-40 and 19-41, you used the expected-value criterion to determine the optimal number of catfish orders to prepare. Convert the table you used in making your decision to an opportunity-loss table. Make the appropriate decision using the opportunity-loss table. What is the EVPI? What is the expected cost of uncertainty?

19-43. In Exercises 19-32 to 19-35, you constructed a payoff table and used expected values to determine the appropriate number of condominiums for Far Horizons to build in Maine. Convert this table to an opportunity-loss table. Using expected opportunity loss as the decision criterion, determine how many units should be built. In this case, what is the EVPI? Suppose for $10,000 someone offered to sell the company perfect information about demand. Would the information be worth that price? Explain.

19-44. East Coast Imports is considering two alternative advertising and marketing plans for a new line of consumer products it buys from a manufacturer in Singapore. The first plan involves contracting with a television shopping channel and is projected to have a monthly cost of $200,000. East Coast's marketing director has analyzed this alternative and, after a joint meeting with the shopping channel's manager, believes that the following probability distribution for additional profit generated is accurate:

Increased Revenue	Probability	Increased Revenue	Probability
$120,000	0.10	260,000	0.20
150,000	0.10	290,000	0.10
200,000	0.20	320,000	0.10
230,000	0.20		1.00

The second marketing alternative—to rely on advertising in airline magazines and newspaper inserts—is projected to have a monthly cost of $120,000. However, the marketing director thinks that this approach would not be as effective for generating added monthly revenue as the shopping channel approach. This is reflected in the following probability distribution:

Increased Revenue	Probability
$70,000	0.10
90,000	0.10
110,000	0.25
140,000	0.25
170,000	0.20
200,000	0.10
	1.00

Because of the fear of "overkill," the company has decided not to try both approaches simultaneously. However, the managers did agree that if the print-advertising approach is chosen and results in $90,000 or less in added revenues, they can switch to the shopping channel for an additional cost of $20,000. They assume that the probabilities would not be affected, but all profit projections will be reduced by this cost.

a. Set up the appropriate decision tree for this problem.

b. Using the criterion of maximizing the expected increase in net revenues, what marketing strategy should be chosen?

Exercises 19-45 through 19-47 refer to the following situation.

The Grimm Group presents in-house training seminars to organizations throughout the United

States. The company currently presents seminars on three topics: quality control, material management, and just-in-time (JIT) manufacturing. The quality control seminar costs each participant $500, and the Grimm Group's gross margin (revenue – direct expenses) is 40% of this amount. The material-management seminar costs $450 for each attendee and also has a 40% gross margin; the JIT seminar costs $600 and has a 35% gross margin. After 5 years of expansion, attendance at the seminars has declined more than 10% in the past year. The revenues from the three operations last year were quality control, $1,200,000; material management, $900,000; and JIT, $1,400,000.

At the yearly forecasting meeting, Graciela Grimm, the company's founder, projects that if no changes are made in marketing philosophy, revenues will be stagnant this year. She is, however, considering two options that should increase demand for the three seminars. The first option is to incorporate a computer simulation game as part of each seminar. Projections indicate that adding this type of game will increase the demand for the quality control seminar by 10% and the demand for the other two seminars by 15% each. Adding a game will increase the cost associated with each seminar participant by $50; but because the market is very competitive, the company will have to hold the line on the price change. The second option is to offer 3-day training seminars on the same topics but at 60% of the price of the 5-day seminars. Unfortunately, the cost of presenting the 3-day seminars will be reduced by only 20% from the cost of the original seminars. The president estimates the demand for the shorter seminars this year will generate revenues equal to 50% of the revenues realized from each 5-day seminar in the past year. Also, adding the shorter seminars will reduce the projected demand for the original seminars to 75% of last year's level.

19-45. Develop a decision tree describing the Grimm Group's decision situation.

19-46. Assuming President Grimm is risk-neutral for this decision, what alternative would you recommend?

19-47. An initial market survey of the acceptance of simulation games indicates they are so popular that there is a 70% chance the Grimm Group will be able to raise the price of the seminars by enough to maintain its previous margins without affecting the demand. Incorporate this new information into your previous problem analysis.

Exercises 19-48 through 19-51 refer to the Major League Corporation, which makes sports-related items at a plant in South Carolina. Before the baseball season, the company was approached by representatives from the Sports Connection,

a company that supplies baseball items to be sold at major league parks and at sports souvenir stores. The Sports Connection has offered to contract to buy 300,000 baseball hats for $3.00 each. The company's production capacity is 500,000 hats. The problem facing Major League is whether to accept this offer or to attempt to independently sell all its baseball hats. If the demand for hats is high, the company will be able to sell hats for much more than $3.00 each, but if demand is low, the hats will have to be sold for much less than $3.00.

At least two uncertainties exist that will affect the demand for hats. First, if the league races are tight, the demand will be high; clear leaders early in the season will lead to low demand. Second, if the players strike this year, demand will be reduced. Using available information on injury levels and team-strength analysis, Major League's executives estimate a 60% probability that the league races will be tight. In addition, the executives estimate the probability of a strike this year to be 30%. Assuming the two events, tight races and a player strike, are independent, the following table shows the possible selling prices for the company's hats and the associated probabilities:

	League Race	
Player Strike	**Tight**	**Not Tight**
No	$5.00	$2.50
	$p = 0.42$	$p = 0.28$
Yes	$4.00	$2.00
	$p = 0.18$	$p = 0.12$

19-48. Assuming Major League will sell its entire output, should it accept the Sports Connection's offer if it wishes to maximize its expected revenue?

19-49. Suppose Major League's executives believe the company will be able to negotiate the following deal with the Sports Connection: The contract price for hats will be reduced to $2.70 per hat; Major League will commit to delivering 150,000 hats at this price, with the option of supplying the remaining 150,000 hats at $2.70 each after it determines whether the players will strike. This decision must be made before the status of the league races is known.

This proposal, if made, will require the services of legal counsel, with a fee estimated to be $25,000. Determine the decision tree describing this situation.

19-50. Should Major League make the proposal? Base your recommendation on expected values.

19-51. Assume you are the purchasing manager for the Sports Connection. If you receive the proposed offer, would you recommend that it be accepted if your only other alternative is to buy 300,000 baseball hats on the open market? Assume that you have assessed the same probabilities as Major League regarding league races and player strikes. Base your conclusions on expected costs.

19-52. New Age Marketing is considering two alternative advertising plans for a client. The first plan uses radio and television commercials that will cost $100,000. The account executive estimates a 40% chance that the client's revenues will increase by $80,000, a 25% chance that revenues will increase by $110,000, and a 35% chance that revenues will increase by $120,000 as a result of this advertising approach.

The second plan is to use newspaper and magazine advertisements, at a cost of $20,000. However, print media are thought to be less effective than radio and television. The account executive estimates the chances are 20% that this plan will increase revenues by $14,000, 50% that revenues will increase by $30,000, and 30% that revenues will increase by $40,000.

If the newspaper and magazine option is chosen, New Age can later take the radio and TV option, but expected revenue will decline by $10,000 from what it would have been had that been the first choice. The account executive has indicated that it would not be feasible to try the newspaper and magazine approach after first choosing radio and TV.

Use a decision-tree approach to determine what decision(s) the New Age agency should make.

19-53. The Gregston Corporation has purchased a petroleum lease tract in the Pacific Ocean that may contain extensive oil deposits. Drilling a dry hole would be very expensive, so Gregston's managers are considering conducting a test to determine

whether the geologic structure is favorable for the presence of oil. Unfortunately, the test is not perfect. Suppose Gregston's managers have determined the correct structure will be found 70% of the time when the reading is positive. Recent industry evidence with the test has shown a correct structure will be found 40% of the time when the reading is negative. Further, records show that when this test was conducted in this region in the past, 40% of the time the reading was positive. However, records also show that oil is struck for only 10% of all holes drilled worldwide.

The test will cost the company $400,000 to perform, and the cost of drilling the hole is $2 million. If Gregston does drill and hit oil, there are three possible outcomes:

Oil Outcome	Revenue	Probability
Small find	$ 2 million	0.40
Medium find	$ 5 million	0.40
Large find	$10 million	0.20

Considering this information, what decision should Gregston make? Base your decision on expected profits.

19-54. In Exercise 19-53, Gregston's managers did not take into account the fact that they had already paid $500,000 for the drilling lease. What, if any, effect does this new information have on the decision facing the company? Discuss.

19-55. Referring to Exercise 19-54, how sensitive is the decision to the probability assessment that the tester will give a positive reading in this region of the ocean? That is, how much would this probability have to change in order to change the decision that Gregston will make?

CASE 19.1

Rockstone International

Rockstone International is one of the world's largest diamond brokers. The firm purchases rough stones and has them cut and polished for sale in the United States and Europe. The diamond business has been very profitable, and from all indications it will continue to be so. However, R. B. Randall, president and chief executive officer for Rockstone, has stressed the need for effective management decisions throughout the organization if the firm is to remain profitable and competitive.

Normally, R. B. does not involve herself in personnel decisions, but today's situation is not typical. Beth Harkness,

Rockstone's personnel manager, is considering whether to hire Hans Marquis, a world-famous diamond cutter, to replace Omar Barboa, who broke both his hands in a freak skateboard accident almost a month ago. If he is hired, Hans Marquis will be paid on a commission basis at the rate of $5,000 for each stone he cuts successfully. (Because of his professional pride, Hans will accept no fee if he is unsuccessful in cutting a stone.)

In the past, the decision of whether to hire Hans would have been simple. If he was available, he would be hired. However, 6 months ago, the Liechtenstein Corporation introduced the world's first diamond-cutting machine. This machine, which can be leased for $1,000,000 per year, is guaranteed to cut stones successfully 90% of the time.

Although Hans Marquis has an excellent reputation, Rockstone International cannot be sure about his success rate because of the extreme secrecy among people in the diamond business. Hans claims that his success rate is 95%, but he has been known to exaggerate. Rockstone executives have made the following assessments, based on all the information they could obtain:

Actual Success Rate	Probability
0.97	0.10
0.95	0.40
0.90	0.30
0.85	0.10
0.80	0.10
	1.00

Rockstone purchases gemstones at a cost of $15,000 each. A successful cut yields four diamonds that can be sold at an average price of $35,000 each. Harry Winkler, sales and purchasing manager, reports that his projections for the next year indicate a need for 100 stones to be cut.

R. B. Randall knows there must be a way to decide whether to hire Hans Marquis or lease the new cutting machine.

CASE 19.2

Hadden Materials and Supplies, Inc.

Mark Hadden and his son, Greg, began Hadden Materials and Supplies, Inc., in the mid-1980s. Both Mark and Greg had had successful careers with major U.S. corporations, but after several years of talking about it they came to the conclusion that they wanted to work together in their own business. They also decided that they wanted to be in manufacturing, where they could take advantage of their previous experience and business contacts.

From the beginning, Mark has run the production shop and Greg has concentrated on sales. About 2 years ago, they got a contract to make an electronic component for natural gas heaters. At first they made this part exclusively for one company, but about 6 months ago they started making the same component for other heater manufacturers. The component is produced in large volume and sells for $30. The variable production cost per unit is $13, making this a very profitable product for the company.

However, until recently there was no way to determine whether a component would work properly until it had actually been installed in the heater unit. Whenever the heater manufacturer found a defect, Hadden Materials and Supplies would refund the full $30 plus pay a penalty of $10. Although the company has made major improvements in its quality control program, this particular component is very difficult to build and to have work properly. As a result, the defect rate has been approximately 25%.

A week ago, the company was approached by a representative of Tech-Notics, Inc., who said her company had a device for testing components such as the one Hadden

makes for gas heaters. By using this tester, Hadden could determine before shipping whether the component would work. This was one sales call that really got Mark and Greg's attention, and the sales representative agreed to bring a unit by for a trial the next morning. Greg called their largest customer and made arrangements to "test the tester" at the customer's plant the next afternoon.

Over the next 2 days, Mark, Greg, and the Tech-Notics sales representative tested 400 components. Of these, 320 tested positive, indicating that they would turn out to be good, however, of the 320 that tested positive, 72 ended up actually being defective. In addition, of the components that got a negative reading, 8 were found to be good: Although the testing device was not perfect, the Haddens were still encouraged.

The sales representative explained that her company preferred to lease the testers, with a financial arrangement that called for the lessor to pay $3 per test. (The tester had an automatic counter.) If the unit were sold outright, it would cost $6 million. Mark and Greg realized that there was no way that they could afford to purchase the unit, so that option was immediately eliminated. However, they were interested in the lease plan and told the sales representative they would call her soon with their decision.

As Mark and Greg conferred over lunch, they estimated the heater component would remain in production for about 2 more years. During that time, they could expect orders for about 100,000 units. They also agreed that if they leased the tester, they would use it to test every component that they built. As Greg said, "Why should we lease it if we don't use it!" They also concluded that if an item tested negative, it would be scrapped and not shipped.

References

Arrow, K. J., "Utilities, Attitudes, Choices: A Review Note." *Econometrica*, 26 (1958).

Baird, Bruce, F., *Managerial Decision Making Under Uncertainty* (New York: Wiley, 1989).

Bell, D., "Regret in Decision Making Under Uncertainty." *Operations Research*, 30 (1982).

Berger, P. D., and A. Gerstenfeld, "Decision Analysis for Increased Highway Safety." *Sloan Management Review* (Spring 1971).

Brown, R. V., "Do Managers Find Decision Theory Useful?" *Harvard Business Review* (January–February 1970).

Brown, R. V., A. S. Kahr, and C. Peterson, *Decision Analysis for the Manager* (New York: Holt, 1974).

Bunn, D. W., *Applied Decision Analysis* (New York: McGraw-Hill, 1984).

Davidson, F., "Dimensions of Utility in a Regional Planning Context." *Decision Sciences* (January 1974).

Farquhar, P., "Utility Assessment Methods." *Management Science*, 30 (1984).

Felson, J., *Decision Making Under Uncertainty* (New York: CBS Educational and Professional Publishing, 1979).

Fishburn, P. C., *Utility Theory for Decision Making* (New York: Wiley, 1970).

Friedman, M., and L. J. Savage, "The Utility Analysis of Choices Involving Risk." *Journal of Political Economy* (August 1948).

Gregory, G., *Decision Analysis* (New York: Plenum, 1988).

Hammond, J. S., "Better Decisions with Preference Theory." *Harvard Business Review*, 45 (November–December 1967).

Hespos, R. F., and P. A. Strassmann, "Stochastic Decision Trees for the Analysis of Investment Decisions." *Management Science*, 11 (1965).

Holloway, C., *Decision Making Under Uncertainty: Models and Choices* (Englewood Cliffs, NJ: Prentice Hall, 1979).

Howard, R. A., "An Assessment of Decision Analysis." *Operations Research*, 28 (1980).

Keeney, R. L., Decision Analysis: An Overview." *Operations Research*, 30 (1982).

Keeney, R. L., and H. Raiffa, *Decisions with Multiple Objectives: Preferences and Value Trade-offs* (New York: Wiley, 1976).

Raiffa, H., *Decision Analysis* (Reading, MA: Addison-Wesley, 1968).

Sampson, D., *Managerial Decision Analysis* (Homewood, IL: Irwin, 1988).

Schlaifer, R., *Analysis of Decisions Under Uncertainty* (New York: McGraw-Hill, 1969).

Stimson, D. H., "Utility, Measurement in Public Health Decision Making." *Management Science*, 16 (1969).

Swalm, R. O., "Utility, Theory Insights into Risk Taking." *Harvard Business Review* (November–December 1966).

Ulvila, J. W., and R. V. Brown, "Decision Analysis Comes of Age." *Harvard Business Review* (September 1982).

Winkler, R., *Introduction to Bayesian Inference and Decision* (New York: Holt, 1972).

List of Appendix Tables

1511	4745	8716	2793	9142	4958	5245	8312	8925
6249	7073	0460	0819	0729	6806	2713	6595	5149
2587	4800	3455	7565	1196	7768	6137	4941	0488
0168	1379	7838	7487	7420	5285	8045	6679	1361
9664	9021	4990	5570	4697	7939	5842	5353	7503
1384	4981	2708	6437	2298	6230	7443	9425	5384
6390	8953	4292	7372	7197	2121	6538	2093	7629
6944	8134	0704	8500	6996	3492	4397	8802	3253
3610	3119	7442	6218	7623	0546	8394	3286	4463
9865	0028	1783	9029	2858	8737	7023	0444	8575
7044	6712	7530	0018	0945	8803	4467	0979	1342
9304	4857	5476	8386	1540	5760	9815	7191	3291
1717	8278	0072	2636	3217	1693	6081	1330	3458
2461	3598	5173	9666	6165	7438	6805	2357	6994
8240	9856	0075	7599	8468	7653	6272	0573	4344
1697	6805	1386	2340	6694	9786	0536	6423	1083
4695	2251	8962	5638	9459	5578	0676	2276	4724
3056	8558	3020	7509	5105	4283	5390	5715	8405
6887	9035	8520	6571	3233	7175	2859	1615	3349
1267	8824	5588	2821	1247	0967	4355	1385	0727
4369	9267	9377	8205	6479	7002	0649	4731	7086
2888	0333	5347	4849	5526	2975	5295	5071	6011
9893	7251	6243	4617	9256	4039	4800	9393	3263
8927	3977	6054	5979	8566	8120	2566	4449	2414
2676	7064	2198	3234	3796	5506	4462	5121	9052
0775	7316	2249	5606	9411	3818	5268	7652	6098
3828	9178	3726	0743	4075	3560	9542	3922	7688
3281	3419	6660	7968	1238	2246	2164	4567	1801
0328	7471	5352	2019	5842	1665	5939	6337	9102
8406	1826	8437	3078	9068	1425	1232	0573	7751
7076	8418	6778	1292	2019	3506	7474	0141	6544
0446	8641	3249	5431	4068	6045	1939	5626	1867
3719	9712	7472	1517	8850	6862	6990	5475	6227
5648	0563	6346	1981	9512	0659	5694	6668	2563
3694	8582	3434	4052	8392	3883	5126	0477	4034
3554	9876	4249	9473	9085	6594	2434	9453	8883
4934	8446	4646	2054	1136	1023	6295	6483	9915
7835	1506	0019	5011	0563	4450	1466	6334	2606
1098	2113	8287	3487	8250	2269	1876	3684	8856
1186	2685	7225	8311	3835	8059	9163	2539	6487
4618	1522	0627	0448	0669	4086	4083	0881	4270
5529	4173	5711	7419	2535	5876	8435	2564	3031
0754	5808	8458	2218	9180	6213	5280	4753	0696
5865	0806	2070	7986	4800	3076	2866	0515	7417
6168	8963	0235	1514	7875	2176	3095	1171	7892
7479	4144	6697	2255	5465	7233	4981	3553	8144
4608	6576	9422	4198	2578	1701	4764	7460	3509
0654	2483	6001	4486	4941	1500	3502	9693	1956
3000	9694	6616	5599	7759	1581	9896	2312	8140
2686	3675	5760	2918	0185	7364	9985	5930	9869
4713	4121	5144	5164	8104	0403	4984	3877	8772
9281	6522	7916	8941	6710	1670	1399	5961	4714
5736	9419	5022	6955	3356	5732	1042	0527	7441
2383	0408	2821	7313	5781	6951	7181	0608	2864
8740	8038	7284	6054	2246	1674	9984	0355	0775

APPENDIX B

Binomial Distribution Table

$$P(x) = \frac{n!}{x!(n-x)!} p^x (1-p)^{n-x}$$

n = 1

x	p = 0.01	p = 0.02	p = 0.03	p = 0.04	p = 0.05	p = 0.06	p = 0.07	p = 0.08	p = 0.09	
0	0.9900	0.9800	0.9700	0.9600	0.9500	0.9400	0.9300	0.9200	0.9100	1
1	0.0100	0.0200	0.0300	0.0400	0.0500	0.0600	0.0700	0.0800	0.0900	0
	p = 0.99	p = 0.98	p = 0.97	p = 0.96	p = 0.95	p = 0.94	p = 0.93	p = 0.92	p = 0.91	x

x	p = 0.10	p = 0.15	p = 0.20	p = 0.25	p = 0.30	p = 0.35	p = 0.40	p = 0.45	p = 0.50	
0	0.9000	0.8500	0.8000	0.7500	0.7000	0.6500	0.6000	0.5500	0.5000	1
1	0.1000	0.1500	0.2000	0.2500	0.3000	0.3500	0.4000	0.4500	0.5000	0
	p = 0.90	p = 0.85	p = 0.80	p = 0.75	p = 0.70	p = 0.65	p = 0.60	p = 0.55	p = 0.50	x

n = 2

x	p = 0.01	p = 0.02	p = 0.03	p = 0.04	p = 0.05	p = 0.06	p = 0.07	p = 0.08	p = 0.09	
0	0.9801	0.9604	0.9409	0.9216	0.9025	0.8836	0.8649	0.8464	0.8281	2
1	0.0198	0.0392	0.0582	0.0768	0.0950	0.1128	0.1302	0.1472	0.1638	1
2	0.0001	0.0004	0.0009	0.0016	0.0025	0.0036	0.0049	0.0064	0.0081	0
	p = 0.99	p = 0.98	p = 0.97	p = 0.96	p = 0.95	p = 0.94	p = 0.93	p = 0.92	p = 0.91	x

x	p = 0.10	p = 0.15	p = 0.20	p = 0.25	p = 0.30	p = 0.35	p = 0.40	p = 0.45	p = 0.50	
0	0.8100	0.7225	0.6400	0.5625	0.4900	0.4225	0.3600	0.3025	0.2500	2
1	0.1800	0.2550	0.3200	0.3750	0.4200	0.4550	0.4800	0.4950	0.5000	1
2	0.0100	0.0225	0.0400	0.0625	0.0900	0.1225	0.1600	0.2025	0.2500	0
	p = 0.90	p = 0.85	p = 0.80	p = 0.75	p = 0.70	p = 0.65	p = 0.60	p = 0.55	p = 0.50	x

n = 3

x	p = 0.01	p = 0.02	p = 0.03	p = 0.04	p = 0.05	p = 0.06	p = 0.07	p = 0.08	p = 0.09	
0	0.9703	0.9412	0.9127	0.8847	0.8574	0.8306	0.8044	0.7787	0.7536	3
1	0.0294	0.0576	0.0847	0.1106	0.1354	0.1590	0.1816	0.2031	0.2236	2
2	0.0003	0.0012	0.0026	0.0046	0.0071	0.0102	0.0137	0.0177	0.0221	1
3	0.0000	0.0000	0.0000	0.0001	0.0001	0.0002	0.0003	0.0005	0.0007	0
	p = 0.99	p = 0.98	p = 0.97	p = 0.96	p = 0.95	p = 0.94	p = 0.93	p = 0.92	p = 0.91	x

x	p = 0.10	p = 0.15	p = 0.20	p = 0.25	p = 0.30	p = 0.35	p = 0.40	p = 0.45	p = 0.50	
0	0.7290	0.6141	0.5120	0.4219	0.3430	0.2746	0.2160	0.1664	0.1250	3
1	0.2430	0.3251	0.3840	0.4219	0.4410	0.4436	0.4320	0.4084	0.3750	2
2	0.0270	0.0574	0.0960	0.1406	0.1890	0.2389	0.2880	0.3341	0.3750	1
3	0.0010	0.0034	0.0080	0.0156	0.0270	0.0429	0.0640	0.0911	0.1250	0
	p = 0.90	p = 0.85	p = 0.80	p = 0.75	p = 0.70	p = 0.65	p = 0.60	p = 0.55	p = 0.50	x

n = 4

x	p = 0.01	p = 0.02	p = 0.03	p = 0.04	p = 0.05	p = 0.06	p = 0.07	p = 0.08	p = 0.09	
0	0.9606	0.9224	0.8853	0.8493	0.8145	0.7807	0.7481	0.7164	0.6857	4
1	0.0388	0.0753	0.1095	0.1416	0.1715	0.1993	0.2252	0.2492	0.2713	3
2	0.0006	0.0023	0.0051	0.0088	0.0135	0.0191	0.0254	0.0325	0.0402	2
3	0.0000	0.0000	0.0001	0.0002	0.0005	0.0008	0.0013	0.0019	0.0027	1
4	0.0000	0.0000	0.0000	0.0000	0.0000	0.0000	0.0000	0.0000	0.0001	0
	p = 0.99	p = 0.98	p = 0.97	p = 0.96	p = 0.95	p = 0.94	p = 0.93	p = 0.92	p = 0.91	x

x	p = 0.10	p = 0.15	p = 0.20	p = 0.25	p = 0.30	p = 0.35	p = 0.40	p = 0.45	p = 0.50	
0	0.6561	0.5220	0.4096	0.3164	0.2401	0.1785	0.1296	0.0915	0.0625	4
1	0.2916	0.3685	0.4096	0.4219	0.4116	0.3845	0.3456	0.2995	0.2500	3
2	0.0486	0.0975	0.1536	0.2109	0.2646	0.3105	0.3456	0.3675	0.3750	2
3	0.0036	0.0115	0.0256	0.0469	0.0756	0.1115	0.1536	0.2005	0.2500	1
4	0.0001	0.0005	0.0016	0.0039	0.0081	0.0150	0.0256	0.0410	0.0625	0
	p = 0.90	p = 0.85	p = 0.80	p = 0.75	p = 0.70	p = 0.65	p = 0.60	p = 0.55	p = 0.50	x

$n = 5$

x	$p = 0.01$	$p = 0.02$	$p = 0.03$	$p = 0.04$	$p = 0.05$	$p = 0.06$	$p = 0.07$	$p = 0.08$	$p = 0.09$	
0	0.9510	0.9039	0.8587	0.8154	0.7738	0.7339	0.6957	0.6591	0.6240	5
1	0.0480	0.0922	0.1328	0.1699	0.2036	0.2342	0.2618	0.2866	0.3086	4
2	0.0010	0.0038	0.0082	0.0142	0.0214	0.0299	0.0394	0.0498	0.0610	3
3	0.0000	0.0001	0.0003	0.0006	0.0011	0.0019	0.0030	0.0043	0.0060	2
4	0.0000	0.0000	0.0000	0.0000	0.0000	0.0001	0.0001	0.0002	0.0003	1
5	0.0000	0.0000	0.0000	0.0000	0.0000	0.0000	0.0000	0.0000	0.0000	0
	$p = 0.99$	$p = 0.98$	$p = 0.97$	$p = 0.96$	$p = 0.95$	$p = 0.94$	$p = 0.93$	$p = 0.92$	$p = 0.91$	x

x	$p = 0.10$	$p = 0.15$	$p = 0.20$	$p = 0.25$	$p = 0.30$	$p = 0.35$	$p = 0.40$	$p = 0.45$	$p = 0.50$	
0	0.5905	0.4437	0.3277	0.2373	0.1681	0.1160	0.0778	0.0503	0.0313	5
1	0.3281	0.3915	0.4096	0.3955	0.3602	0.3124	0.2592	0.2059	0.1563	4
2	0.0729	0.1382	0.2048	0.2637	0.3087	0.3364	0.3456	0.3369	0.3125	3
3	0.0081	0.0244	0.0512	0.0879	0.1323	0.1811	0.2304	0.2757	0.3125	2
4	0.0005	0.0022	0.0064	0.0146	0.0284	0.0488	0.0768	0.1128	0.1563	1
5	0.0000	0.0001	0.0003	0.0010	0.0024	0.0053	0.0102	0.0185	0.0313	0
	$p = 0.90$	$p = 0.85$	$p = 0.80$	$p = 0.75$	$p = 0.70$	$p = 0.65$	$p = 0.60$	$p = 0.55$	$p = 0.50$	x

$n = 6$

x	$p = 0.01$	$p = 0.02$	$p = 0.03$	$p = 0.04$	$p = 0.05$	$p = 0.06$	$p = 0.07$	$p = 0.08$	$p = 0.09$	
0	0.9415	0.8858	0.8330	0.7828	0.7351	0.6899	0.6470	0.6064	0.5679	6
1	0.0571	0.1085	0.1546	0.1957	0.2321	0.2642	0.2922	0.3164	0.3370	5
2	0.0014	0.0055	0.0120	0.0204	0.0305	0.0422	0.0550	0.0688	0.0833	4
3	0.0000	0.0002	0.0005	0.0011	0.0021	0.0036	0.0055	0.0080	0.0110	3
4	0.0000	0.0000	0.0000	0.0000	0.0001	0.0002	0.0003	0.0005	0.0008	2
5	0.0000	0.0000	0.0000	0.0000	0.0000	0.0000	0.0000	0.0000	0.0000	1
6	0.0000	0.0000	0.0000	0.0000	0.0000	0.0000	0.0000	0.0000	0.0000	0
	$p = 0.99$	$p = 0.98$	$p = 0.97$	$p = 0.96$	$p = 0.95$	$p = 0.94$	$p = 0.93$	$p = 0.92$	$p = 0.91$	x

x	$p = 0.10$	$p = 0.15$	$p = 0.20$	$p = 0.25$	$p = 0.30$	$p = 0.35$	$p = 0.40$	$p = 0.45$	$p = 0.50$	
0	0.5314	0.3771	0.2621	0.1780	0.1176	0.0754	0.0467	0.0277	0.0156	6
1	0.3543	0.3993	0.3932	0.3560	0.3025	0.2437	0.1866	0.1359	0.0938	5
2	0.0984	0.1762	0.2458	0.2966	0.3241	0.3280	0.3110	0.2780	0.2344	4
3	0.0146	0.0415	0.0819	0.1318	0.1852	0.2355	0.2765	0.3032	0.3125	3
4	0.0012	0.0055	0.0154	0.0330	0.0595	0.0951	0.1382	0.1861	0.2344	2
5	0.0001	0.0004	0.0015	0.0044	0.0102	0.0205	0.0369	0.0609	0.0938	1
6	0.0000	0.0000	0.0001	0.0002	0.0007	0.0018	0.0041	0.0083	0.0156	0
	$p = 0.90$	$p = 0.85$	$p = 0.80$	$p = 0.75$	$p = 0.70$	$p = 0.65$	$p = 0.60$	$p = 0.55$	$p = 0.50$	x

$n = 7$

x	$p = 0.01$	$p = 0.02$	$p = 0.03$	$p = 0.04$	$p = 0.05$	$p = 0.06$	$p = 0.07$	$p = 0.08$	$p = 0.09$	
0	0.9321	0.8681	0.8080	0.7514	0.6983	0.6485	0.6017	0.5578	0.5168	7
1	0.0659	0.1240	0.1749	0.2192	0.2573	0.2897	0.3170	0.3396	0.3578	6
2	0.0020	0.0076	0.0162	0.0274	0.0406	0.0555	0.0716	0.0886	0.1061	5
3	0.0000	0.0003	0.0008	0.0019	0.0036	0.0059	0.0090	0.0128	0.0175	4
4	0.0000	0.0000	0.0000	0.0001	0.0002	0.0004	0.0007	0.0011	0.0017	3
5	0.0000	0.0000	0.0000	0.0000	0.0000	0.0000	0.0000	0.0001	0.0001	2
6	0.0000	0.0000	0.0000	0.0000	0.0000	0.0000	0.0000	0.0000	0.0000	1
	$p = 0.99$	$p = 0.98$	$p = 0.97$	$p = 0.96$	$p = 0.95$	$p = 0.94$	$p = 0.93$	$p = 0.92$	$p = 0.91$	x

x	$p = 0.10$	$p = 0.15$	$p = 0.20$	$p = 0.25$	$p = 0.30$	$p = 0.35$	$p = 0.40$	$p = 0.45$	$p = 0.50$	
0	0.4783	0.3206	0.2097	0.1335	0.0824	0.0490	0.0280	0.0152	0.0078	7
1	0.3720	0.3960	0.3670	0.3115	0.2471	0.1848	0.1306	0.0872	0.0547	6
2	0.1240	0.2097	0.2753	0.3115	0.3177	0.2985	0.2613	0.2140	0.1641	5
3	0.0230	0.0617	0.1147	0.1730	0.2269	0.2679	0.2903	0.2918	0.2734	4
4	0.0026	0.0109	0.0287	0.0577	0.0972	0.1442	0.1935	0.2388	0.2734	3
5	0.0002	0.0012	0.0043	0.0115	0.0250	0.0466	0.0774	0.1172	0.1641	2
6	0.0000	0.0001	0.0004	0.0013	0.0036	0.0084	0.0172	0.0320	0.0547	1
7	0.0000	0.0000	0.0000	0.0001	0.0002	0.0006	0.0016	0.0037	0.0078	0
	$p = 0.90$	$p = 0.85$	$p = 0.80$	$p = 0.75$	$p = 0.70$	$p = 0.65$	$p = 0.60$	$p = 0.55$	$p = 0.50$	x

$$n = 8$$

x	p = 0.01	p = 0.02	p = 0.03	p = 0.04	p = 0.05	p = 0.06	p = 0.07	p = 0.08	p = 0.09	
0	0.9227	0.8508	0.7837	0.7214	0.6634	0.6096	0.5596	0.5132	0.4703	8
1	0.0746	0.1389	0.1939	0.2405	0.2793	0.3113	0.3370	0.3570	0.3721	7
2	0.0026	0.0099	0.0210	0.0351	0.0515	0.0695	0.0888	0.1087	0.1288	6
3	0.0001	0.0004	0.0013	0.0029	0.0054	0.0089	0.0134	0.0189	0.0255	5
4	0.0000	0.0000	0.0001	0.0002	0.0004	0.0007	0.0013	0.0021	0.0031	4
5	0.0000	0.0000	0.0000	0.0000	0.0000	0.0000	0.0001	0.0001	0.0002	3
6	0.0000	0.0000	0.0000	0.0000	0.0000	0.0000	0.0000	0.0000	0.0000	2
	p = 0.99	p = 0.98	p = 0.97	p = 0.96	p = 0.95	p = 0.94	p = 0.93	p = 0.92	p = 0.91	x

x	p = 0.10	p = 0.15	p = 0.20	p = 0.25	p = 0.30	p = 0.35	p = 0.40	p = 0.45	p = 0.50	
0	0.4305	0.2725	0.1678	0.1001	0.0576	0.0319	0.0168	0.0084	0.0039	8
1	0.3826	0.3847	0.3355	0.2670	0.1977	0.1373	0.0896	0.0548	0.0313	7
2	0.1488	0.2376	0.2936	0.3115	0.2965	0.2587	0.2090	0.1569	0.1094	6
3	0.0331	0.0839	0.1468	0.2076	0.2541	0.2786	0.2787	0.2568	0.2188	5
4	0.0046	0.0185	0.0459	0.0865	0.1361	0.1875	0.2322	0.2627	0.2734	4
5	0.0004	0.0026	0.0092	0.0231	0.0467	0.0808	0.1239	0.1719	0.2188	3
6	0.0000	0.0002	0.0011	0.0038	0.0100	0.0217	0.0413	0.0703	0.1094	2
7	0.0000	0.0000	0.0001	0.0004	0.0012	0.0033	0.0079	0.0164	0.0313	1
8	0.0000	0.0000	0.0000	0.0000	0.0001	0.0002	0.0007	0.0017	0.0039	0
	p = 0.90	p = 0.85	p = 0.80	p = 0.75	p = 0.70	p = 0.65	p = 0.60	p = 0.55	p = 0.50	x

$$n = 9$$

x	p = 0.01	p = 0.02	p = 0.03	p = 0.04	p = 0.05	p = 0.06	p = 0.07	p = 0.08	p = 0.09	
0	0.9135	0.8337	0.7602	0.6925	0.6302	0.5730	0.5204	0.4722	0.4279	9
1	0.0830	0.1531	0.2116	0.2597	0.2985	0.3292	0.3525	0.3695	0.3809	8
2	0.0034	0.0125	0.0262	0.0433	0.0629	0.0840	0.1061	0.1285	0.1507	7
3	0.0001	0.0006	0.0019	0.0042	0.0077	0.0125	0.0186	0.0261	0.0348	6
4	0.0000	0.0000	0.0001	0.0003	0.0006	0.0012	0.0021	0.0034	0.0052	5
5	0.0000	0.0000	0.0000	0.0000	0.0000	0.0001	0.0002	0.0003	0.0005	4
6	0.0000	0.0000	0.0000	0.0000	0.0000	0.0000	0.0000	0.0000	0.0000	3
7	0.0000	0.0000	0.0000	0.0000	0.0000	0.0000	0.0000	0.0000	0.0000	2
	p = 0.99	p = 0.98	p = 0.97	p = 0.96	p = 0.95	p = 0.94	p = 0.93	p = 0.92	p = 0.91	x

x	p = 0.10	p = 0.15	p = 0.20	p = 0.25	p = 0.30	p = 0.35	p = 0.40	p = 0.45	p = 0.50	
0	0.3874	0.2316	0.1342	0.0751	0.0404	0.0207	0.0101	0.0046	0.0020	9
1	0.3874	0.3679	0.3020	0.2253	0.1556	0.1004	0.0605	0.0339	0.0176	8
2	0.1722	0.2597	0.3020	0.3003	0.2668	0.2162	0.1612	0.1110	0.0703	7
3	0.0446	0.1069	0.1762	0.2336	0.2668	0.2716	0.2508	0.2119	0.1641	6
4	0.0074	0.0283	0.0661	0.1168	0.1715	0.2194	0.2508	0.2600	0.2461	5
5	0.0008	0.0050	0.0165	0.0389	0.0735	0.1181	0.1672	0.2128	0.2461	4
6	0.0001	0.0006	0.0028	0.0087	0.0210	0.0424	0.0743	0.1160	0.1641	3
7	0.0000	0.0000	0.0003	0.0012	0.0039	0.0098	0.0212	0.0407	0.0703	2
8	0.0000	0.0000	0.0000	0.0001	0.0004	0.0013	0.0035	0.0083	0.0176	1
9	0.0000	0.0000	0.0000	0.0000	0.0000	0.0001	0.0003	0.0008	0.0020	0
	p = 0.90	p = 0.85	p = 0.80	p = 0.75	p = 0.70	p = 0.65	p = 0.60	p = 0.55	p = 0.50	x

$$n = 10$$

x	p = 0.01	p = 0.02	p = 0.03	p = 0.04	p = 0.05	p = 0.06	p = 0.07	p = 0.08	p = 0.09	
0	0.9044	0.8171	0.7374	0.6648	0.5987	0.5386	0.4840	0.4344	0.3894	10
1	0.0914	0.1667	0.2281	0.2770	0.3151	0.3438	0.3643	0.3777	0.3851	9
2	0.0042	0.0153	0.0317	0.0519	0.0746	0.0988	0.1234	0.1478	0.1714	8
3	0.0001	0.0008	0.0026	0.0058	0.0105	0.0168	0.0248	0.0343	0.0452	7
4	0.0000	0.0000	0.0001	0.0004	0.0010	0.0019	0.0033	0.0052	0.0078	6
5	0.0000	0.0000	0.0000	0.0000	0.0001	0.0001	0.0003	0.0005	0.0009	5
6	0.0000	0.0000	0.0000	0.0000	0.0000	0.0000	0.0000	0.0000	0.0001	4
7	0.0000	0.0000	0.0000	0.0000	0.0000	0.0000	0.0000	0.0000	0.0000	3
	p = 0.99	p = 0.98	p = 0.97	p = 0.96	p = 0.95	p = 0.94	p = 0.93	p = 0.92	p = 0.91	x

x	p = 0.10	p = 0.15	p = 0.20	p = 0.25	p = 0.30	p = 0.35	p = 0.40	p = 0.45	p = 0.50	
0	0.3487	0.1969	0.1074	0.0563	0.0282	0.0135	0.0060	0.0025	0.0010	10
1	0.3874	0.3474	0.2684	0.1877	0.1211	0.0725	0.0403	0.0207	0.0098	9
2	0.1937	0.2759	0.3020	0.2816	0.2335	0.1757	0.1209	0.0763	0.0439	8
3	0.0574	0.1298	0.2013	0.2503	0.2668	0.2522	0.2150	0.1665	0.1172	7
4	0.0112	0.0401	0.0881	0.1460	0.2001	0.2377	0.2508	0.2384	0.2051	6
5	0.0015	0.0085	0.0264	0.0584	0.1029	0.1536	0.2007	0.2340	0.2461	5
6	0.0001	0.0012	0.0055	0.0162	0.0368	0.0689	0.1115	0.1596	0.2051	4
7	0.0000	0.0001	0.0008	0.0031	0.0090	0.0212	0.0425	0.0746	0.1172	3
8	0.0000	0.0000	0.0001	0.0004	0.0014	0.0043	0.0106	0.0229	0.0439	2
9	0.0000	0.0000	0.0000	0.0000	0.0001	0.0005	0.0016	0.0042	0.0098	1
10	0.0000	0.0000	0.0000	0.0000	0.0000	0.0000	0.0001	0.0003	0.0010	0
	p = 0.90	p = 0.85	p = 0.80	p = 0.75	p = 0.70	p = 0.65	p = 0.60	p = 0.55	p = 0.50	x

n = 11

x	p = 0.01	p = 0.02	p = 0.03	p = 0.04	p = 0.05	p = 0.06	p = 0.07	p = 0.08	p = 0.09	
0	0.8953	0.8007	0.7153	0.6382	0.5688	0.5063	0.4501	0.3996	0.3544	11
1	0.0995	0.1798	0.2433	0.2925	0.3293	0.3555	0.3727	0.3823	0.3855	10
2	0.0050	0.0183	0.0376	0.0609	0.0867	0.1135	0.1403	0.1662	0.1906	9
3	0.0002	0.0011	0.0035	0.0076	0.0137	0.0217	0.0317	0.0434	0.0566	8
4	0.0000	0.0000	0.0002	0.0006	0.0014	0.0028	0.0048	0.0075	0.0112	7
5	0.0000	0.0000	0.0000	0.0000	0.0001	0.0002	0.0005	0.0009	0.0015	6
6	0.0000	0.0000	0.0000	0.0000	0.0000	0.0000	0.0000	0.0001	0.0002	5
7	0.0000	0.0000	0.0000	0.0000	0.0000	0.0000	0.0000	0.0000	0.0000	4
	p = 0.99	p = 0.98	p = 0.97	p = 0.96	p = 0.95	p = 0.94	p = 0.93	p = 0.92	p = 0.91	x

x	p = 0.10	p = 0.15	p = 0.20	p = 0.25	p = 0.30	p = 0.35	p = 0.40	p = 0.45	p = 0.50	
0	0.3138	0.1673	0.0859	0.0422	0.0198	0.0088	0.0036	0.0014	0.0005	11
1	0.3835	0.3248	0.2362	0.1549	0.0932	0.0518	0.0266	0.0125	0.0054	10
2	0.2131	0.2866	0.2953	0.2581	0.1998	0.1395	0.0887	0.0513	0.0269	9
3	0.0710	0.1517	0.2215	0.2581	0.2568	0.2254	0.1774	0.1259	0.0806	8
4	0.0158	0.0536	0.1107	0.1721	0.2201	0.2428	0.2365	0.2060	0.1611	7
5	0.0025	0.0132	0.0388	0.0803	0.1321	0.1830	0.2207	0.2360	0.2256	6
6	0.0003	0.0023	0.0097	0.0268	0.0566	0.0985	0.1471	0.1931	0.2256	5
7	0.0000	0.0003	0.0017	0.0064	0.0173	0.0379	0.0701	0.1128	0.1611	4
8	0.0000	0.0000	0.0002	0.0011	0.0037	0.0102	0.0234	0.0462	0.0806	3
9	0.0000	0.0000	0.0000	0.0001	0.0005	0.0018	0.0052	0.0126	0.0269	2
10	0.0000	0.0000	0.0000	0.0000	0.0000	0.0002	0.0007	0.0021	0.0054	1
11	0.0000	0.0000	0.0000	0.0000	0.0000	0.0000	0.0000	0.0002	0.0005	0
	p = 0.90	p = 0.85	p = 0.80	p = 0.75	p = 0.70	p = 0.65	p = 0.60	p = 0.55	p = 0.50	x

n = 12

x	p = 0.01	p = 0.02	p = 0.03	p = 0.04	p = 0.05	p = 0.06	p = 0.07	p = 0.08	p = 0.09	
0	0.8864	0.7847	0.6938	0.6127	0.5404	0.4759	0.4186	0.3677	0.3225	12
1	0.1074	0.1922	0.2575	0.3064	0.3413	0.3645	0.3781	0.3837	0.3827	11
2	0.0060	0.0216	0.0438	0.0702	0.0988	0.1280	0.1565	0.1835	0.2082	10
3	0.0002	0.0015	0.0045	0.0098	0.0173	0.0272	0.0393	0.0532	0.0686	9
4	0.0000	0.0001	0.0003	0.0009	0.0021	0.0039	0.0067	0.0104	0.0153	8
5	0.0000	0.0000	0.0000	0.0001	0.0002	0.0004	0.0008	0.0014	0.0024	7
6	0.0000	0.0000	0.0000	0.0000	0.0000	0.0000	0.0001	0.0001	0.0003	6
7	0.0000	0.0000	0.0000	0.0000	0.0000	0.0000	0.0000	0.0000	0.0000	5
	p = 0.99	p = 0.98	p = 0.97	p = 0.96	p = 0.95	p = 0.94	p = 0.93	p = 0.92	p = 0.91	x

x	p = 0.10	p = 0.15	p = 0.20	p = 0.25	p = 0.30	p = 0.35	p = 0.40	p = 0.45	p = 0.50	
0	0.2824	0.1422	0.0687	0.0317	0.0138	0.0057	0.0022	0.0008	0.0002	12
1	0.3766	0.3012	0.2062	0.1267	0.0712	0.0368	0.0174	0.0075	0.0029	11
2	0.2301	0.2924	0.2835	0.2323	0.1678	0.1088	0.0639	0.0339	0.0161	10
3	0.0852	0.1720	0.2362	0.2581	0.2397	0.1954	0.1419	0.0923	0.0537	9
4	0.0213	0.0683	0.1329	0.1936	0.2311	0.2367	0.2128	0.1700	0.1208	8
5	0.0038	0.0193	0.0532	0.1032	0.1585	0.2039	0.2270	0.2225	0.1934	7
6	0.0005	0.0040	0.0155	0.0401	0.0792	0.1281	0.1766	0.2124	0.2256	6
7	0.0000	0.0006	0.0033	0.0115	0.0291	0.0591	0.1009	0.1489	0.1934	5
8	0.0000	0.0001	0.0005	0.0024	0.0078	0.0199	0.0420	0.0762	0.1208	4
9	0.0000	0.0000	0.0001	0.0004	0.0015	0.0048	0.0125	0.0277	0.0537	3
10	0.0000	0.0000	0.0000	0.0000	0.0002	0.0008	0.0025	0.0068	0.0161	2
11	0.0000	0.0000	0.0000	0.0000	0.0000	0.0001	0.0003	0.0010	0.0029	1
12	0.0000	0.0000	0.0000	0.0000	0.0000	0.0000	0.0000	0.0001	0.0002	0
	p = 0.90	p = 0.85	p = 0.80	p = 0.75	p = 0.70	p = 0.65	p = 0.60	p = 0.55	p = 0.50	x

n = 13

x	p = 0.01	p = 0.02	p = 0.03	p = 0.04	p = 0.05	p = 0.06	p = 0.07	p = 0.08	p = 0.09	
0	0.8775	0.7690	0.6730	0.5882	0.5133	0.4474	0.3893	0.3383	0.2935	13
1	0.1152	0.2040	0.2706	0.3186	0.3512	0.3712	0.3809	0.3824	0.3773	12
2	0.0070	0.0250	0.0502	0.0797	0.1109	0.1422	0.1720	0.1995	0.2239	11
3	0.0003	0.0019	0.0057	0.0122	0.0214	0.0333	0.0475	0.0636	0.0812	10
4	0.0000	0.0001	0.0004	0.0013	0.0028	0.0053	0.0089	0.0138	0.0201	9
5	0.0000	0.0000	0.0000	0.0001	0.0003	0.0006	0.0012	0.0022	0.0036	8
6	0.0000	0.0000	0.0000	0.0000	0.0000	0.0001	0.0001	0.0003	0.0005	7
7	0.0000	0.0000	0.0000	0.0000	0.0000	0.0000	0.0000	0.0000	0.0000	6
8	0.0000	0.0000	0.0000	0.0000	0.0000	0.0000	0.0000	0.0000	0.0000	5
	p = 0.99	p = 0.98	p = 0.97	p = 0.96	p = 0.95	p = 0.94	p = 0.93	p = 0.92	p = 0.91	x

x	p = 0.10	p = 0.15	p = 0.20	p = 0.25	p = 0.30	p = 0.35	p = 0.40	p = 0.45	p = 0.50	
0	0.2542	0.1209	0.0550	0.0238	0.0097	0.0037	0.0013	0.0004	0.0001	13
1	0.3672	0.2774	0.1787	0.1029	0.0540	0.0259	0.0113	0.0045	0.0016	12
2	0.2448	0.2937	0.2680	0.2059	0.1388	0.0836	0.0453	0.0220	0.0095	11
3	0.0997	0.1900	0.2457	0.2517	0.2181	0.1651	0.1107	0.0660	0.0349	10
4	0.0277	0.0838	0.1535	0.2097	0.2337	0.2222	0.1845	0.1350	0.0873	9
5	0.0055	0.0266	0.0691	0.1258	0.1803	0.2154	0.2214	0.1989	0.1571	8
6	0.0008	0.0063	0.0230	0.0559	0.1030	0.1546	0.1968	0.2169	0.2095	7
7	0.0001	0.0011	0.0058	0.0186	0.0442	0.0833	0.1312	0.1775	0.2095	6
8	0.0000	0.0001	0.0011	0.0047	0.0142	0.0336	0.0656	0.1089	0.1571	5
9	0.0000	0.0000	0.0001	0.0009	0.0034	0.0101	0.0243	0.0495	0.0873	4
10	0.0000	0.0000	0.0000	0.0001	0.0006	0.0022	0.0065	0.0162	0.0349	3
11	0.0000	0.0000	0.0000	0.0000	0.0001	0.0003	0.0012	0.0036	0.0095	2
12	0.0000	0.0000	0.0000	0.0000	0.0000	0.0000	0.0001	0.0005	0.0016	1
13	0.0000	0.0000	0.0000	0.0000	0.0000	0.0000	0.0000	0.0000	0.0001	0
	p = 0.90	p = 0.85	p = 0.80	p = 0.75	p = 0.70	p = 0.65	p = 0.60	p = 0.55	p = 0.50	x

n = 14

x	p = 0.01	p = 0.02	p = 0.03	p = 0.04	p = 0.05	p = 0.06	p = 0.07	p = 0.08	p = 0.09	
0	0.8687	0.7536	0.6528	0.5647	0.4877	0.4205	0.3620	0.3112	0.2670	14
1	0.1229	0.2153	0.2827	0.3294	0.3593	0.3758	0.3815	0.3788	0.3698	13
2	0.0081	0.0286	0.0568	0.0892	0.1229	0.1559	0.1867	0.2141	0.2377	12
3	0.0003	0.0023	0.0070	0.0149	0.0259	0.0398	0.0562	0.0745	0.0940	11
4	0.0000	0.0001	0.0006	0.0017	0.0037	0.0070	0.0116	0.0178	0.0256	10
5	0.0000	0.0000	0.0000	0.0001	0.0004	0.0009	0.0018	0.0031	0.0051	9
6	0.0000	0.0000	0.0000	0.0000	0.0000	0.0001	0.0002	0.0004	0.0008	8
7	0.0000	0.0000	0.0000	0.0000	0.0000	0.0000	0.0000	0.0000	0.0001	7
8	0.0000	0.0000	0.0000	0.0000	0.0000	0.0000	0.0000	0.0000	0.0000	6
	p = 0.99	p = 0.98	p = 0.97	p = 0.96	p = 0.95	p = 0.94	p = 0.93	p = 0.92	p = 0.91	x

x	$p = 0.10$	$p = 0.15$	$p = 0.20$	$p = 0.25$	$p = 0.30$	$p = 0.35$	$p = 0.40$	$p = 0.45$	$p = 0.50$	
0	0.2288	0.1028	0.0440	0.0178	0.0068	0.0024	0.0008	0.0002	0.0001	14
1	0.3559	0.2539	0.1539	0.0832	0.0407	0.0181	0.0073	0.0027	0.0009	13
2	0.2570	0.2912	0.2501	0.1802	0.1134	0.0634	0.0317	0.0141	0.0056	12
3	0.1142	0.2056	0.2501	0.2402	0.1943	0.1366	0.0845	0.0462	0.0222	11
4	0.0349	0.0998	0.1720	0.2202	0.2290	0.2022	0.1549	0.1040	0.0611	10
5	0.0078	0.0352	0.0860	0.1468	0.1963	0.2178	0.2066	0.1701	0.1222	9
6	0.0013	0.0093	0.0322	0.0734	0.1262	0.1759	0.2066	0.2088	0.1833	8
7	0.0002	0.0019	0.0092	0.0280	0.0618	0.1082	0.1574	0.1952	0.2095	7
8	0.0000	0.0003	0.0020	0.0082	0.0232	0.0510	0.0918	0.1398	0.1833	6
9	0.0000	0.0000	0.0003	0.0018	0.0066	0.0183	0.0408	0.0762	0.1222	5
10	0.0000	0.0000	0.0000	0.0003	0.0014	0.0049	0.0136	0.0312	0.0611	4
11	0.0000	0.0000	0.0000	0.0000	0.0002	0.0010	0.0033	0.0093	0.0222	3
12	0.0000	0.0000	0.0000	0.0000	0.0000	0.0001	0.0005	0.0019	0.0056	2
13	0.0000	0.0000	0.0000	0.0000	0.0000	0.0000	0.0001	0.0002	0.0009	1
14	0.0000	0.0000	0.0000	0.0000	0.0000	0.0000	0.0000	0.0000	0.0001	0
	$p = 0.90$	$p = 0.85$	$p = 0.80$	$p = 0.75$	$p = 0.70$	$p = 0.65$	$p = 0.60$	$p = 0.55$	$p = 0.50$	x

$n = 15$

x	$p = 0.01$	$p = 0.02$	$p = 0.03$	$p = 0.04$	$p = 0.05$	$p = 0.06$	$p = 0.07$	$p = 0.08$	$p = 0.09$	
0	0.8601	0.7386	0.6333	0.5421	0.4633	0.3953	0.3367	0.2863	0.2430	15
1	0.1303	0.2261	0.2938	0.3388	0.3658	0.3785	0.3801	0.3734	0.3605	14
2	0.0092	0.0323	0.0636	0.0988	0.1348	0.1691	0.2003	0.2273	0.2496	13
3	0.0004	0.0029	0.0085	0.0178	0.0307	0.0468	0.0653	0.0857	0.1070	12
4	0.0000	0.0002	0.0008	0.0022	0.0049	0.0090	0.0148	0.0223	0.0317	11
5	0.0000	0.0000	0.0001	0.0002	0.0006	0.0013	0.0024	0.0043	0.0069	10
6	0.0000	0.0000	0.0000	0.0000	0.0000	0.0001	0.0003	0.0006	0.0011	9
7	0.0000	0.0000	0.0000	0.0000	0.0000	0.0000	0.0000	0.0001	0.0001	8
	$p = 0.99$	$p = 0.98$	$p = 0.97$	$p = 0.96$	$p = 0.95$	$p = 0.94$	$p = 0.93$	$p = 0.92$	$p = 0.91$	x

x	$p = 0.10$	$p = 0.15$	$p = 0.20$	$p = 0.25$	$p = 0.30$	$p = 0.35$	$p = 0.40$	$p = 0.45$	$p = 0.50$	
0	0.2059	0.0874	0.0352	0.0134	0.0047	0.0016	0.0005	0.0001	0.0000	15
1	0.3432	0.2312	0.1319	0.0668	0.0305	0.0126	0.0047	0.0016	0.0005	14
2	0.2669	0.2856	0.2309	0.1559	0.0916	0.0476	0.0219	0.0090	0.0032	13
3	0.1285	0.2184	0.2501	0.2252	0.1700	0.1110	0.0634	0.0318	0.0139	12
4	0.0428	0.1156	0.1876	0.2252	0.2186	0.1792	0.1268	0.0780	0.0417	11
5	0.0105	0.0449	0.1032	0.1651	0.2061	0.2123	0.1859	0.1404	0.0916	10
6	0.0019	0.0132	0.0430	0.0917	0.1472	0.1906	0.2066	0.1914	0.1527	9
7	0.0003	0.0030	0.0138	0.0393	0.0811	0.1319	0.1771	0.2013	0.1964	8
8	0.0000	0.0005	0.0035	0.0131	0.0348	0.0710	0.1181	0.1647	0.1964	7
9	0.0000	0.0001	0.0007	0.0034	0.0116	0.0298	0.0612	0.1048	0.1527	6
10	0.0000	0.0000	0.0001	0.0007	0.0030	0.0096	0.0245	0.0515	0.0916	5
11	0.0000	0.0000	0.0000	0.0001	0.0006	0.0024	0.0074	0.0191	0.0417	4
12	0.0000	0.0000	0.0000	0.0000	0.0001	0.0004	0.0016	0.0052	0.0139	3
13	0.0000	0.0000	0.0000	0.0000	0.0000	0.0001	0.0003	0.0010	0.0032	2
14	0.0000	0.0000	0.0000	0.0000	0.0000	0.0000	0.0000	0.0001	0.0005	1
15	0.0000	0.0000	0.0000	0.0000	0.0000	0.0000	0.0000	0.0000	0.0000	0
	$p = 0.90$	$p = 0.85$	$p = 0.80$	$p = 0.75$	$p = 0.70$	$p = 0.65$	$p = 0.60$	$p = 0.55$	$p = 0.50$	x

$n = 20$

x	$p = 0.01$	$p = 0.02$	$p = 0.03$	$p = 0.04$	$p = 0.05$	$p = 0.06$	$p = 0.07$	$p = 0.08$	$p = 0.09$	
0	0.8179	0.6676	0.5438	0.4420	0.3585	0.2901	0.2342	0.1887	0.1516	20
1	0.1652	0.2725	0.3364	0.3683	0.3774	0.3703	0.3526	0.3282	0.3000	19
2	0.0159	0.0528	0.0988	0.1458	0.1887	0.2246	0.2521	0.2711	0.2818	18
3	0.0010	0.0065	0.0183	0.0364	0.0596	0.0860	0.1139	0.1414	0.1672	17
4	0.0000	0.0006	0.0024	0.0065	0.0133	0.0233	0.0364	0.0523	0.0703	16
5	0.0000	0.0000	0.0002	0.0009	0.0022	0.0048	0.0088	0.0145	0.0222	15
6	0.0000	0.0000	0.0000	0.0001	0.0003	0.0008	0.0017	0.0032	0.0055	14
7	0.0000	0.0000	0.0000	0.0000	0.0000	0.0001	0.0002	0.0005	0.0011	13
8	0.0000	0.0000	0.0000	0.0000	0.0000	0.0000	0.0000	0.0001	0.0002	12
9	0.0000	0.0000	0.0000	0.0000	0.0000	0.0000	0.0000	0.0000	0.0000	11
	$p = 0.99$	$p = 0.98$	$p = 0.97$	$p = 0.96$	$p = 0.95$	$p = 0.94$	$p = 0.93$	$p = 0.92$	$p = 0.91$	x

x	p = 0.10	p = 0.15	p = 0.20	p = 0.25	p = 0.30	p = 0.35	p = 0.40	p = 0.45	p = 0.50	
0	0.1216	0.0388	0.0115	0.0032	0.0008	0.0002	0.0000	0.0000	0.0000	20
1	0.2702	0.1368	0.0576	0.0211	0.0068	0.0020	0.0005	0.0001	0.0000	19
2	0.2852	0.2293	0.1369	0.0669	0.0278	0.0100	0.0031	0.0008	0.0002	18
3	0.1901	0.2428	0.2054	0.1339	0.0716	0.0323	0.0123	0.0040	0.0011	17
4	0.0898	0.1821	0.2182	0.1897	0.1304	0.0738	0.0350	0.0139	0.0046	16
5	0.0319	0.1028	0.1746	0.2023	0.1789	0.1272	0.0746	0.0365	0.0148	15
6	0.0089	0.0454	0.1091	0.1686	0.1916	0.1712	0.1244	0.0746	0.0370	14
7	0.0020	0.0160	0.0545	0.1124	0.1643	0.1844	0.1659	0.1221	0.0739	13
8	0.0004	0.0046	0.0222	0.0609	0.1144	0.1614	0.1797	0.1623	0.1201	12
9	0.0001	0.0011	0.0074	0.0271	0.0654	0.1158	0.1597	0.1771	0.1602	11
10	0.0000	0.0002	0.0020	0.0099	0.0308	0.0686	0.1171	0.1593	0.1762	10
11	0.0000	0.0000	0.0005	0.0030	0.0120	0.0336	0.0710	0.1185	0.1602	9
12	0.0000	0.0000	0.0001	0.0008	0.0039	0.0136	0.0355	0.0727	0.1201	8
13	0.0000	0.0000	0.0000	0.0002	0.0010	0.0045	0.0146	0.0366	0.0739	7
14	0.0000	0.0000	0.0000	0.0000	0.0002	0.0012	0.0049	0.0150	0.0370	6
15	0.0000	0.0000	0.0000	0.0000	0.0000	0.0003	0.0013	0.0049	0.0148	5
16	0.0000	0.0000	0.0000	0.0000	0.0000	0.0000	0.0003	0.0013	0.0046	4
17	0.0000	0.0000	0.0000	0.0000	0.0000	0.0000	0.0000	0.0002	0.0011	3
18	0.0000	0.0000	0.0000	0.0000	0.0000	0.0000	0.0000	0.0000	0.0002	2
	p = 0.90	p = 0.85	p = 0.80	p = 0.75	p = 0.70	p = 0.65	p = 0.60	p = 0.55	p = 0.50	x

n = 25

x	p = 0.01	p = 0.02	p = 0.03	p = 0.04	p = 0.05	p = 0.06	p = 0.07	p = 0.08	p = 0.09	
0	0.7778	0.6035	0.4670	0.3604	0.2774	0.2129	0.1630	0.1244	0.0946	25
1	0.1964	0.3079	0.3611	0.3754	0.3650	0.3398	0.3066	0.2704	0.2340	24
2	0.0238	0.0754	0.1340	0.1877	0.2305	0.2602	0.2770	0.2821	0.2777	23
3	0.0018	0.0118	0.0318	0.0600	0.0930	0.1273	0.1598	0.1881	0.2106	22
4	0.0001	0.0013	0.0054	0.0137	0.0269	0.0447	0.0662	0.0899	0.1145	21
5	0.0000	0.0001	0.0007	0.0024	0.0060	0.0120	0.0209	0.0329	0.0476	20
6	0.0000	0.0000	0.0001	0.0003	0.0010	0.0026	0.0052	0.0095	0.0157	19
7	0.0000	0.0000	0.0000	0.0000	0.0001	0.0004	0.0011	0.0022	0.0042	18
8	0.0000	0.0000	0.0000	0.0000	0.0000	0.0001	0.0002	0.0004	0.0009	17
9	0.0000	0.0000	0.0000	0.0000	0.0000	0.0000	0.0000	0.0001	0.0002	16
10	0.0000	0.0000	0.0000	0.0000	0.0000	0.0000	0.0000	0.0000	0.0000	15
	p = 0.99	p = 0.98	p = 0.97	p = 0.96	p = 0.95	p = 0.94	p = 0.93	p = 0.92	p = 0.91	x

x	p = 0.10	p = 0.15	p = 0.20	p = 0.25	p = 0.30	p = 0.35	p = 0.40	p = 0.45	p = 0.50	
0	0.0718	0.0172	0.0038	0.0008	0.0001	0.0000	0.0000	0.0000	0.0000	25
1	0.1994	0.0759	0.0236	0.0063	0.0014	0.0003	0.0000	0.0000	0.0000	24
2	0.2659	0.1607	0.0708	0.0251	0.0074	0.0018	0.0004	0.0001	0.0000	23
3	0.2265	0.2174	0.1358	0.0641	0.0243	0.0076	0.0019	0.0004	0.0001	22
4	0.1384	0.2110	0.1867	0.1175	0.0572	0.0224	0.0071	0.0018	0.0004	21
5	0.0646	0.1564	0.1960	0.1645	0.1030	0.0506	0.0199	0.0063	0.0016	20
6	0.0239	0.0920	0.1633	0.1828	0.1472	0.0908	0.0442	0.0172	0.0053	19
7	0.0072	0.0441	0.1108	0.1654	0.1712	0.1327	0.0800	0.0381	0.0143	18
8	0.0018	0.0175	0.0623	0.1241	0.1651	0.1607	0.1200	0.0701	0.0322	17
9	0.0004	0.0058	0.0294	0.0781	0.1336	0.1635	0.1511	0.1084	0.0609	16
10	0.0001	0.0016	0.0118	0.0417	0.0916	0.1409	0.1612	0.1419	0.0974	15
11	0.0000	0.0004	0.0040	0.0189	0.0536	0.1034	0.1465	0.1583	0.1328	14
12	0.0000	0.0001	0.0012	0.0074	0.0268	0.0650	0.1140	0.1511	0.1550	13
13	0.0000	0.0000	0.0003	0.0025	0.0115	0.0350	0.0760	0.1236	0.1550	12
14	0.0000	0.0000	0.0001	0.0007	0.0042	0.0161	0.0434	0.0867	0.1328	11
15	0.0000	0.0000	0.0000	0.0002	0.0013	0.0064	0.0212	0.0520	0.0974	10
16	0.0000	0.0000	0.0000	0.0000	0.0004	0.0021	0.0088	0.0266	0.0609	9
17	0.0000	0.0000	0.0000	0.0000	0.0001	0.0006	0.0031	0.0115	0.0322	8
18	0.0000	0.0000	0.0000	0.0000	0.0000	0.0001	0.0009	0.0042	0.0143	7
19	0.0000	0.0000	0.0000	0.0000	0.0000	0.0000	0.0002	0.0013	0.0053	6
20	0.0000	0.0000	0.0000	0.0000	0.0000	0.0000	0.0000	0.0003	0.0016	5
21	0.0000	0.0000	0.0000	0.0000	0.0000	0.0000	0.0000	0.0001	0.0004	4
22	0.0000	0.0000	0.0000	0.0000	0.0000	0.0000	0.0000	0.0000	0.0001	3
	p = 0.90	p = 0.85	p = 0.80	p = 0.75	p = 0.70	p = 0.65	p = 0.60	p = 0.55	p = 0.50	x

Poisson Probability Distribution Table

Values of $P(x) = \dfrac{(\lambda t)^x e^{-\lambda t}}{x!}$

					λt					
x	**0.005**	**0.01**	**0.02**	**0.03**	**0.04**	**0.05**	**0.06**	**0.07**	**0.08**	**0.09**
0	0.9950	0.9900	0.9802	0.9704	0.9608	0.9512	0.9418	0.9324	0.9231	0.9139
1	0.0050	0.0099	0.0196	0.0291	0.0384	0.0476	0.0565	0.0653	0.0738	0.0823
2	0.0000	0.0000	0.0002	0.0004	0.0008	0.0012	0.0017	0.0023	0.0030	0.0037
3	0.0000	0.0000	0.0000	0.0000	0.0000	0.0000	0.0000	0.0001	0.0001	0.0001

					λt					
x	**0.10**	**0.20**	**0.30**	**0.40**	**0.50**	**0.60**	**0.70**	**0.80**	**0.90**	**1.00**
0	0.9048	0.8187	0.7408	0.6703	0.6065	0.5488	0.4966	0.4493	0.4066	0.3679
1	0.0905	0.1637	0.2222	0.2681	0.3033	0.3293	0.3476	0.3595	0.3659	0.3679
2	0.0045	0.0164	0.0333	0.0536	0.0758	0.0988	0.1217	0.1438	0.1647	0.1839
3	0.0002	0.0011	0.0033	0.0072	0.0126	0.0198	0.0284	0.0383	0.0494	0.0613
4	0.0000	0.0001	0.0003	0.0007	0.0016	0.0030	0.0050	0.0077	0.0111	0.0153
5	0.0000	0.0000	0.0000	0.0001	0.0002	0.0004	0.0007	0.0012	0.0020	0.0031
6	0.0000	0.0000	0.0000	0.0000	0.0000	0.0000	0.0001	0.0002	0.0003	0.0005
7	0.0000	0.0000	0.0000	0.0000	0.0000	0.0000	0.0000	0.0000	0.0000	0.0001

					λt					
x	**1.10**	**1.20**	**1.30**	**1.40**	**1.50**	**1.60**	**1.70**	**1.80**	**1.90**	**2.00**
0	0.3329	0.3012	0.2725	0.2466	0.2231	0.2019	0.1827	0.1653	0.1496	0.1353
1	0.3662	0.3614	0.3543	0.3452	0.3347	0.3230	0.3106	0.2975	0.2842	0.2707
2	0.2014	0.2169	0.2303	0.2417	0.2510	0.2584	0.2640	0.2678	0.2700	0.2707
3	0.0738	0.0867	0.0998	0.1128	0.1255	0.1378	0.1496	0.1607	0.1710	0.1804
4	0.0203	0.0260	0.0324	0.0395	0.0471	0.0551	0.0636	0.0723	0.0812	0.0902
5	0.0045	0.0062	0.0084	0.0111	0.0141	0.0176	0.0216	0.0260	0.0309	0.0361
6	0.0008	0.0012	0.0018	0.0026	0.0035	0.0047	0.0061	0.0078	0.0098	0.0120
7	0.0001	0.0002	0.0003	0.0005	0.0008	0.0011	0.0015	0.0020	0.0027	0.0034
8	0.0000	0.0000	0.0001	0.0001	0.0001	0.0002	0.0003	0.0005	0.0006	0.0009
9	0.0000	0.0000	0.0000	0.0000	0.0000	0.0000	0.0001	0.0001	0.0001	0.0002

					λt					
x	**2.10**	**2.20**	**2.30**	**2.40**	**2.50**	**2.60**	**2.70**	**2.80**	**2.90**	**3.00**
0	0.1225	0.1108	0.1003	0.0907	0.0821	0.0743	0.0672	0.0608	0.0550	0.0498
1	0.2572	0.2438	0.2306	0.2177	0.2052	0.1931	0.1815	0.1703	0.1596	0.1494
2	0.2700	0.2681	0.2652	0.2613	0.2565	0.2510	0.2450	0.2384	0.2314	0.2240
3	0.1890	0.1966	0.2033	0.2090	0.2138	0.2176	0.2205	0.2225	0.2237	0.2240
4	0.0992	0.1082	0.1169	0.1254	0.1336	0.1414	0.1488	0.1557	0.1622	0.1680
5	0.0417	0.0476	0.0538	0.0602	0.0668	0.0735	0.0804	0.0872	0.0940	0.1008
6	0.0146	0.0174	0.0206	0.0241	0.0278	0.0319	0.0362	0.0407	0.0455	0.0504
7	0.0044	0.0055	0.0068	0.0083	0.0099	0.0118	0.0139	0.0163	0.0188	0.0216
8	0.0011	0.0015	0.0019	0.0025	0.0031	0.0038	0.0047	0.0057	0.0068	0.0081
9	0.0003	0.0004	0.0005	0.0007	0.0009	0.0011	0.0014	0.0018	0.0022	0.0027
10	0.0001	0.0001	0.0001	0.0002	0.0002	0.0003	0.0004	0.0005	0.0006	0.0008
11	0.0000	0.0000	0.0000	0.0000	0.0000	0.0001	0.0001	0.0001	0.0002	0.0002
12	0.0000	0.0000	0.0000	0.0000	0.0000	0.0000	0.0000	0.0000	0.0000	0.0001

λt

x	3.10	3.20	3.30	3.40	3.50	3.60	3.70	3.80	3.90	4.00
0	0.0450	0.0408	0.0369	0.0334	0.0302	0.0273	0.0247	0.0224	0.0202	0.0183
1	0.1397	0.1304	0.1217	0.1135	0.1057	0.0984	0.0915	0.0850	0.0789	0.0733
2	0.2165	0.2087	0.2008	0.1929	0.1850	0.1771	0.1692	0.1615	0.1539	0.1465
3	0.2237	0.2226	0.2209	0.2186	0.2158	0.2125	0.2087	0.2046	0.2001	0.1954
4	0.1733	0.1781	0.1823	0.1858	0.1888	0.1912	0.1931	0.1944	0.1951	0.1954
5	0.1075	0.1140	0.1203	0.1264	0.1322	0.1377	0.1429	0.1477	0.1522	0.1563
6	0.0555	0.0608	0.0662	0.0716	0.0771	0.0826	0.0881	0.0936	0.0989	0.1042
7	0.0246	0.0278	0.0312	0.0348	0.0385	0.0425	0.0466	0.0508	0.0551	0.0595
8	0.0095	0.0111	0.0129	0.0148	0.0169	0.0191	0.0215	0.0241	0.0269	0.0298
9	0.0033	0.0040	0.0047	0.0056	0.0066	0.0076	0.0089	0.0102	0.0116	0.0132
10	0.0010	0.0013	0.0016	0.0019	0.0023	0.0028	0.0033	0.0039	0.0045	0.0053
11	0.0003	0.0004	0.0005	0.0006	0.0007	0.0009	0.0011	0.0013	0.0016	0.0019
12	0.0001	0.0001	0.0001	0.0002	0.0002	0.0003	0.0003	0.0004	0.0005	0.0006
13	0.0000	0.0000	0.0000	0.0000	0.0001	0.0001	0.0001	0.0001	0.0002	0.0002
14	0.0000	0.0000	0.0000	0.0000	0.0000	0.0000	0.0000	0.0000	0.0000	0.0001

λt

x	4.10	4.20	4.30	4.40	4.50	4.60	4.70	4.80	4.90	5.00
0	0.0166	0.0150	0.0136	0.0123	0.0111	0.0101	0.0091	0.0082	0.0074	0.0067
1	0.0679	0.0630	0.0583	0.0540	0.0500	0.0462	0.0427	0.0395	0.0365	0.0337
2	0.1393	0.1323	0.1254	0.1188	0.1125	0.1063	0.1005	0.0948	0.0894	0.0842
3	0.1904	0.1852	0.1798	0.1743	0.1687	0.1631	0.1574	0.1517	0.1460	0.1404
4	0.1951	0.1944	0.1933	0.1917	0.1898	0.1875	0.1849	0.1820	0.1789	0.1755
5	0.1600	0.1633	0.1662	0.1687	0.1708	0.1725	0.1738	0.1747	0.1753	0.1755
6	0.1093	0.1143	0.1191	0.1237	0.1281	0.1323	0.1362	0.1398	0.1432	0.1462
7	0.0640	0.0686	0.0732	0.0778	0.0824	0.0869	0.0914	0.0959	0.1002	0.1044
8	0.0328	0.0360	0.0393	0.0428	0.0463	0.0500	0.0537	0.0575	0.0614	0.0653
9	0.0150	0.0168	0.0188	0.0209	0.0232	0.0255	0.0281	0.0307	0.0334	0.0363
10	0.0061	0.0071	0.0081	0.0092	0.0104	0.0118	0.0132	0.0147	0.0164	0.0181
11	0.0023	0.0027	0.0032	0.0037	0.0043	0.0049	0.0056	0.0064	0.0073	0.0082
12	0.0008	0.0009	0.0011	0.0013	0.0016	0.0019	0.0022	0.0026	0.0030	0.0034
13	0.0002	0.0003	0.0004	0.0005	0.0006	0.0007	0.0008	0.0009	0.0011	0.0013
14	0.0001	0.0001	0.0001	0.0001	0.0002	0.0002	0.0003	0.0003	0.0004	0.0005
15	0.0000	0.0000	0.0000	0.0000	0.0001	0.0001	0.0001	0.0001	0.0001	0.0002

λt

x	5.10	5.20	5.30	5.40	5.50	5.60	5.70	5.80	5.90	6.00
0	0.0061	0.0055	0.0050	0.0045	0.0041	0.0037	0.0033	0.0030	0.0027	0.0025
1	0.0311	0.0287	0.0265	0.0244	0.0225	0.0207	0.0191	0.0176	0.0162	0.0149
2	0.0793	0.0746	0.0701	0.0659	0.0618	0.0580	0.0544	0.0509	0.0477	0.0446
3	0.1348	0.1293	0.1239	0.1185	0.1133	0.1082	0.1033	0.0985	0.0938	0.0892
4	0.1719	0.1681	0.1641	0.1600	0.1558	0.1515	0.1472	0.1428	0.1383	0.1339
5	0.1753	0.1748	0.1740	0.1728	0.1714	0.1697	0.1678	0.1656	0.1632	0.1606
6	0.1490	0.1515	0.1537	0.1555	0.1571	0.1584	0.1594	0.1601	0.1605	0.1606
7	0.1086	0.1125	0.1163	0.1200	0.1234	0.1267	0.1298	0.1326	0.1353	0.1377
8	0.0692	0.0731	0.0771	0.0810	0.0849	0.0887	0.0925	0.0962	0.0998	0.1033
9	0.0392	0.0423	0.0454	0.0486	0.0519	0.0552	0.0586	0.0620	0.0654	0.0688
10	0.0200	0.0220	0.0241	0.0262	0.0285	0.0309	0.0334	0.0359	0.0386	0.0413
11	0.0093	0.0104	0.0116	0.0129	0.0143	0.0157	0.0173	0.0190	0.0207	0.0225
12	0.0039	0.0045	0.0051	0.0058	0.0065	0.0073	0.0082	0.0092	0.0102	0.0113
13	0.0015	0.0018	0.0021	0.0024	0.0028	0.0032	0.0036	0.0041	0.0046	0.0052
14	0.0006	0.0007	0.0008	0.0009	0.0011	0.0013	0.0015	0.0017	0.0019	0.0022
15	0.0002	0.0002	0.0003	0.0003	0.0004	0.0005	0.0006	0.0007	0.0008	0.0009
16	0.0001	0.0001	0.0001	0.0001	0.0001	0.0002	0.0002	0.0002	0.0003	0.0003
17	0.0000	0.0000	0.0000	0.0000	0.0000	0.0001	0.0001	0.0001	0.0001	0.0001

					λt					
x	**6.10**	**6.20**	**6.30**	**6.40**	**6.50**	**6.60**	**6.70**	**6.80**	**6.90**	**7.00**
0	0.0022	0.0020	0.0018	0.0017	0.0015	0.0014	0.0012	0.0011	0.0010	0.0009
1	0.0137	0.0126	0.0116	0.0106	0.0098	0.0090	0.0082	0.0076	0.0070	0.0064
2	0.0417	0.0390	0.0364	0.0340	0.0318	0.0296	0.0276	0.0258	0.0240	0.0223
3	0.0848	0.0806	0.0765	0.0726	0.0688	0.0652	0.0617	0.0584	0.0552	0.0521
4	0.1294	0.1249	0.1205	0.1162	0.1118	0.1076	0.1034	0.0992	0.0952	0.0912
5	0.1579	0.1549	0.1519	0.1487	0.1454	0.1420	0.1385	0.1349	0.1314	0.1277
6	0.1605	0.1601	0.1595	0.1586	0.1575	0.1562	0.1546	0.1529	0.1511	0.1490
7	0.1399	0.1418	0.1435	0.1450	0.1462	0.1472	0.1480	0.1486	0.1489	0.1490
8	0.1066	0.1099	0.1130	0.1160	0.1188	0.1215	0.1240	0.1263	0.1284	0.1304
9	0.0723	0.0757	0.0791	0.0825	0.0858	0.0891	0.0923	0.0954	0.0985	0.1014
10	0.0441	0.0469	0.0498	0.0528	0.0558	0.0588	0.0618	0.0649	0.0679	0.0710
11	0.0244	0.0265	0.0285	0.0307	0.0330	0.0353	0.0377	0.0401	0.0426	0.0452
12	0.0124	0.0137	0.0150	0.0164	0.0179	0.0194	0.0210	0.0227	0.0245	0.0263
13	0.0058	0.0065	0.0073	0.0081	0.0089	0.0099	0.0108	0.0119	0.0130	0.0142
14	0.0025	0.0029	0.0033	0.0037	0.0041	0.0046	0.0052	0.0058	0.0064	0.0071
15	0.0010	0.0012	0.0014	0.0016	0.0018	0.0020	0.0023	0.0026	0.0029	0.0033
16	0.0004	0.0005	0.0005	0.0006	0.0007	0.0008	0.0010	0.0011	0.0013	0.0014
17	0.0001	0.0002	0.0002	0.0002	0.0003	0.0003	0.0004	0.0004	0.0005	0.0006
18	0.0000	0.0001	0.0001	0.0001	0.0001	0.0001	0.0001	0.0002	0.0002	0.0002
19	0.0000	0.0000	0.0000	0.0000	0.0000	0.0000	0.0001	0.0001	0.0001	0.0001

					λt					
x	**7.10**	**7.20**	**7.30**	**7.40**	**7.50**	**7.60**	**7.70**	**7.80**	**7.90**	**8.00**
0	0.0008	0.0007	0.0007	0.0006	0.0006	0.0005	0.0005	0.0004	0.0004	0.0003
1	0.0059	0.0054	0.0049	0.0045	0.0041	0.0038	0.0035	0.0032	0.0029	0.0027
2	0.0208	0.0194	0.0180	0.0167	0.0156	0.0145	0.0134	0.0125	0.0116	0.0107
3	0.0492	0.0464	0.0438	0.0413	0.0389	0.0366	0.0345	0.0324	0.0305	0.0286
4	0.0874	0.0836	0.0799	0.0764	0.0729	0.0696	0.0663	0.0632	0.0602	0.0573
5	0.1241	0.1204	0.1167	0.1130	0.1094	0.1057	0.1021	0.0986	0.0951	0.0916
6	0.1468	0.1445	0.1420	0.1394	0.1367	0.1339	0.1311	0.1282	0.1252	0.1221
7	0.1489	0.1486	0.1481	0.1474	0.1465	0.1454	0.1442	0.1428	0.1413	0.1396
8	0.1321	0.1337	0.1351	0.1363	0.1373	0.1381	0.1388	0.1392	0.1395	0.1396
9	0.1042	0.1070	0.1096	0.1121	0.1144	0.1167	0.1187	0.1207	0.1224	0.1241
10	0.0740	0.0770	0.0800	0.0829	0.0858	0.0887	0.0914	0.0941	0.0967	0.0993
11	0.0478	0.0504	0.0531	0.0558	0.0585	0.0613	0.0640	0.0667	0.0695	0.0722
12	0.0283	0.0303	0.0323	0.0344	0.0366	0.0388	0.0411	0.0434	0.0457	0.0481
13	0.0154	0.0168	0.0181	0.0196	0.0211	0.0227	0.0243	0.0260	0.0278	0.0296
14	0.0078	0.0086	0.0095	0.0104	0.0113	0.0123	0.0134	0.0145	0.0157	0.0169
15	0.0037	0.0041	0.0046	0.0051	0.0057	0.0062	0.0069	0.0075	0.0083	0.0090
16	0.0016	0.0019	0.0021	0.0024	0.0026	0.0030	0.0033	0.0037	0.0041	0.0045
17	0.0007	0.0008	0.0009	0.0010	0.0012	0.0013	0.0015	0.0017	0.0019	0.0021
18	0.0003	0.0003	0.0004	0.0004	0.0005	0.0006	0.0006	0.0007	0.0008	0.0009
19	0.0001	0.0001	0.0001	0.0002	0.0002	0.0002	0.0003	0.0003	0.0003	0.0004
20	0.0000	0.0000	0.0001	0.0001	0.0001	0.0001	0.0001	0.0001	0.0001	0.0002
21	0.0000	0.0000	0.0000	0.0000	0.0000	0.0000	0.0000	0.0000	0.0001	0.0001

λt

x	8.10	8.20	8.30	8.40	8.50	8.60	8.70	8.80	8.90	9.00
0	0.0003	0.0003	0.0002	0.0002	0.0002	0.0002	0.0002	0.0002	0.0001	0.0001
1	0.0025	0.0023	0.0021	0.0019	0.0017	0.0016	0.0014	0.0013	0.0012	0.0011
2	0.0100	0.0092	0.0086	0.0079	0.0074	0.0068	0.0063	0.0058	0.0054	0.0050
3	0.0269	0.0252	0.0237	0.0222	0.0208	0.0195	0.0183	0.0171	0.0160	0.0150
4	0.0544	0.0517	0.0491	0.0466	0.0443	0.0420	0.0398	0.0377	0.0357	0.0337
5	0.0882	0.0849	0.0816	0.0784	0.0752	0.0722	0.0692	0.0663	0.0635	0.0607
6	0.1191	0.1160	0.1128	0.1097	0.1066	0.1034	0.1003	0.0972	0.0941	0.0911
7	0.1378	0.1358	0.1338	0.1317	0.1294	0.1271	0.1247	0.1222	0.1197	0.1171
8	0.1395	0.1392	0.1388	0.1382	0.1375	0.1366	0.1356	0.1344	0.1332	0.1318
9	0.1256	0.1269	0.1280	0.1290	0.1299	0.1306	0.1311	0.1315	0.1317	0.1318
10	0.1017	0.1040	0.1063	0.1084	0.1104	0.1123	0.1140	0.1157	0.1172	0.1186
11	0.0749	0.0776	0.0802	0.0828	0.0853	0.0878	0.0902	0.0925	0.0948	0.0970
12	0.0505	0.0530	0.0555	0.0579	0.0604	0.0629	0.0654	0.0679	0.0703	0.0728
13	0.0315	0.0334	0.0354	0.0374	0.0395	0.0416	0.0438	0.0459	0.0481	0.0504
14	0.0182	0.0196	0.0210	0.0225	0.0240	0.0256	0.0272	0.0289	0.0306	0.0324
15	0.0098	0.0107	0.0116	0.0126	0.0136	0.0147	0.0158	0.0169	0.0182	0.0194
16	0.0050	0.0055	0.0060	0.0066	0.0072	0.0079	0.0086	0.0093	0.0101	0.0109
17	0.0024	0.0026	0.0029	0.0033	0.0036	0.0040	0.0044	0.0048	0.0053	0.0058
18	0.0011	0.0012	0.0014	0.0015	0.0017	0.0019	0.0021	0.0024	0.0026	0.0029
19	0.0005	0.0005	0.0006	0.0007	0.0008	0.0009	0.0010	0.0011	0.0012	0.0014
20	0.0002	0.0002	0.0002	0.0003	0.0003	0.0004	0.0004	0.0005	0.0005	0.0006
21	0.0001	0.0001	0.0001	0.0001	0.0001	0.0002	0.0002	0.0002	0.0002	0.0003
22	0.0000	0.0000	0.0000	0.0000	0.0001	0.0001	0.0001	0.0001	0.0001	0.0001

λt

x	9.10	9.20	9.30	9.40	9.50	9.60	9.70	9.80	9.90	10.00
0	0.0001	0.0001	0.0001	0.0001	0.0001	0.0001	0.0001	0.0001	0.0001	0.0000
1	0.0010	0.0009	0.0009	0.0008	0.0007	0.0007	0.0006	0.0005	0.0005	0.0005
2	0.0046	0.0043	0.0040	0.0037	0.0034	0.0031	0.0029	0.0027	0.0025	0.0023
3	0.0140	0.0131	0.0123	0.0115	0.0107	0.0100	0.0093	0.0087	0.0081	0.0076
4	0.0319	0.0302	0.0285	0.0269	0.0254	0.0240	0.0226	0.0213	0.0201	0.0189
5	0.0581	0.0555	0.0530	0.0506	0.0483	0.0460	0.0439	0.0418	0.0398	0.0378
6	0.0881	0.0851	0.0822	0.0793	0.0764	0.0736	0.0709	0.0682	0.0656	0.0631
7	0.1145	0.1118	0.1091	0.1064	0.1037	0.1010	0.0982	0.0955	0.0928	0.0901
8	0.1302	0.1286	0.1269	0.1251	0.1232	0.1212	0.1191	0.1170	0.1148	0.1126
9	0.1317	0.1315	0.1311	0.1306	0.1300	0.1293	0.1284	0.1274	0.1263	0.1251
10	0.1198	0.1210	0.1219	0.1228	0.1235	0.1241	0.1245	0.1249	0.1250	0.1251
11	0.0991	0.1012	0.1031	0.1049	0.1067	0.1083	0.1098	0.1112	0.1125	0.1137
12	0.0752	0.0776	0.0799	0.0822	0.0844	0.0866	0.0888	0.0908	0.0928	0.0948
13	0.0526	0.0549	0.0572	0.0594	0.0617	0.0640	0.0662	0.0685	0.0707	0.0729
14	0.0342	0.0361	0.0380	0.0399	0.0419	0.0439	0.0459	0.0479	0.0500	0.0521
15	0.0208	0.0221	0.0235	0.0250	0.0265	0.0281	0.0297	0.0313	0.0330	0.0347
16	0.0118	0.0127	0.0137	0.0147	0.0157	0.0168	0.0180	0.0192	0.0204	0.0217
17	0.0063	0.0069	0.0075	0.0081	0.0088	0.0095	0.0103	0.0111	0.0119	0.0128
18	0.0032	0.0035	0.0039	0.0042	0.0046	0.0051	0.0055	0.0060	0.0065	0.0071
19	0.0015	0.0017	0.0019	0.0021	0.0023	0.0026	0.0028	0.0031	0.0034	0.0037
20	0.0007	0.0008	0.0009	0.0010	0.0011	0.0012	0.0014	0.0015	0.0017	0.0019
21	0.0003	0.0003	0.0004	0.0004	0.0005	0.0006	0.0006	0.0007	0.0008	0.0009
22	0.0001	0.0001	0.0002	0.0002	0.0002	0.0002	0.0003	0.0003	0.0004	0.0004
23	0.0000	0.0001	0.0001	0.0001	0.0001	0.0001	0.0001	0.0001	0.0002	0.0002
24	0.0000	0.0000	0.0000	0.0000	0.0000	0.0000	0.0000	0.0001	0.0001	0.0001

λt

x	11.00	12.00	13.00	14.00	15.00	16.00	17.00	18.00	19.00	20.00
0	0.0000	0.0000	0.0000	0.0000	0.0000	0.0000	0.0000	0.0000	0.0000	0.0000
1	0.0002	0.0001	0.0000	0.0000	0.0000	0.0000	0.0000	0.0000	0.0000	0.0000
2	0.0010	0.0004	0.0002	0.0001	0.0000	0.0000	0.0000	0.0000	0.0000	0.0000
3	0.0037	0.0018	0.0008	0.0004	0.0002	0.0001	0.0000	0.0000	0.0000	0.0000
4	0.0102	0.0053	0.0027	0.0013	0.0006	0.0003	0.0001	0.0001	0.0000	0.0000
5	0.0224	0.0127	0.0070	0.0037	0.0019	0.0010	0.0005	0.0002	0.0001	0.0001
6	0.0411	0.0255	0.0152	0.0087	0.0048	0.0026	0.0014	0.0007	0.0004	0.0002
7	0.0646	0.0437	0.0281	0.0174	0.0104	0.0060	0.0034	0.0019	0.0010	0.0005
8	0.0888	0.0655	0.0457	0.0304	0.0194	0.0120	0.0072	0.0042	0.0024	0.0013
9	0.1085	0.0874	0.0661	0.0473	0.0324	0.0213	0.0135	0.0083	0.0050	0.0029
10	0.1194	0.1048	0.0859	0.0663	0.0486	0.0341	0.0230	0.0150	0.0095	0.0058
11	0.1194	0.1144	0.1015	0.0844	0.0663	0.0496	0.0355	0.0245	0.0164	0.0106
12	0.1094	0.1144	0.1099	0.0984	0.0829	0.0661	0.0504	0.0368	0.0259	0.0176
13	0.0926	0.1056	0.1099	0.1060	0.0956	0.0814	0.0658	0.0509	0.0378	0.0271
14	0.0728	0.0905	0.1021	0.1060	0.1024	0.0930	0.0800	0.0655	0.0514	0.0387
15	0.0534	0.0724	0.0885	0.0989	0.1024	0.0992	0.0906	0.0786	0.0650	0.0516
16	0.0367	0.0543	0.0719	0.0866	0.0960	0.0992	0.0963	0.0884	0.0772	0.0646
17	0.0237	0.0383	0.0550	0.0713	0.0847	0.0934	0.0963	0.0936	0.0863	0.0760
18	0.0145	0.0255	0.0397	0.0554	0.0706	0.0830	0.0909	0.0936	0.0911	0.0844
19	0.0084	0.0161	0.0272	0.0409	0.0557	0.0699	0.0814	0.0887	0.0911	0.0888
20	0.0046	0.0097	0.0177	0.0286	0.0418	0.0559	0.0692	0.0798	0.0866	0.0888
21	0.0024	0.0055	0.0109	0.0191	0.0299	0.0426	0.0560	0.0684	0.0783	0.0846
22	0.0012	0.0030	0.0065	0.0121	0.0204	0.0310	0.0433	0.0560	0.0676	0.0769
23	0.0006	0.0016	0.0037	0.0074	0.0133	0.0216	0.0320	0.0438	0.0559	0.0669
24	0.0003	0.0008	0.0020	0.0043	0.0083	0.0144	0.0226	0.0328	0.0442	0.0557
25	0.0001	0.0004	0.0010	0.0024	0.0050	0.0092	0.0154	0.0237	0.0336	0.0446
26	0.0000	0.0002	0.0005	0.0013	0.0029	0.0057	0.0101	0.0164	0.0246	0.0343
27	0.0000	0.0001	0.0002	0.0007	0.0016	0.0034	0.0063	0.0109	0.0173	0.0254
28	0.0000	0.0000	0.0001	0.0003	0.0009	0.0019	0.0038	0.0070	0.0117	0.0181
29	0.0000	0.0000	0.0001	0.0002	0.0004	0.0011	0.0023	0.0044	0.0077	0.0125
30	0.0000	0.0000	0.0000	0.0001	0.0002	0.0006	0.0013	0.0026	0.0049	0.0083
31	0.0000	0.0000	0.0000	0.0000	0.0001	0.0003	0.0007	0.0015	0.0030	0.0054
32	0.0000	0.0000	0.0000	0.0000	0.0001	0.0001	0.0004	0.0009	0.0018	0.0034
33	0.0000	0.0000	0.0000	0.0000	0.0000	0.0001	0.0002	0.0005	0.0010	0.0020
34	0.0000	0.0000	0.0000	0.0000	0.0000	0.0000	0.0001	0.0002	0.0006	0.0012
35	0.0000	0.0000	0.0000	0.0000	0.0000	0.0000	0.0000	0.0001	0.0003	0.0007
36	0.0000	0.0000	0.0000	0.0000	0.0000	0.0000	0.0000	0.0001	0.0002	0.0004
37	0.0000	0.0000	0.0000	0.0000	0.0000	0.0000	0.0000	0.0000	0.0001	0.0002
38	0.0000	0.0000	0.0000	0.0000	0.0000	0.0000	0.0000	0.0000	0.0000	0.0001
39	0.0000	0.0000	0.0000	0.0000	0.0000	0.0000	0.0000	0.0000	0.0000	0.0001

APPENDIX D

Standard Normal Distribution Table

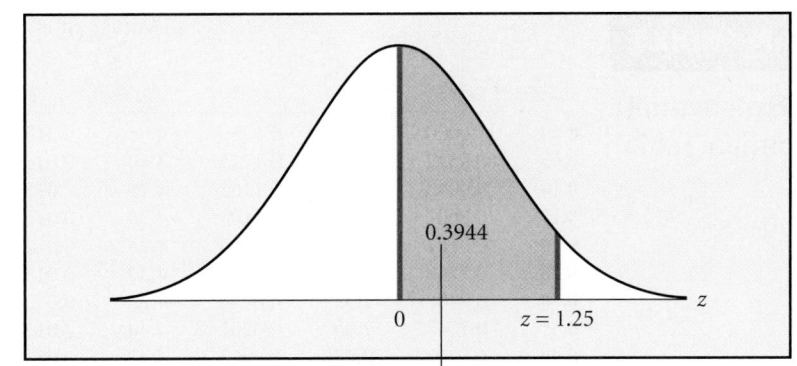

z	0	0.01	0.02	0.03	0.04	0.05	0.06	0.07	0.08	0.09
0.0	0.0000	0.0040	0.0080	0.0120	0.0160	0.0199	0.0239	0.0279	0.0319	0.0359
0.1	0.0398	0.0438	0.0478	0.0517	0.0557	0.0596	0.0636	0.0675	0.0714	0.0753
0.2	0.0793	0.0832	0.0871	0.0910	0.0948	0.0987	0.1026	0.1064	0.1103	0.1141
0.3	0.1179	0.1217	0.1255	0.1293	0.1331	0.1368	0.1406	0.1443	0.1480	0.1517
0.4	0.1554	0.1591	0.1628	0.1664	0.1700	0.1736	0.1772	0.1808	0.1844	0.1879
0.5	0.1915	0.1950	0.1985	0.2019	0.2054	0.2088	0.2123	0.2157	0.2190	0.2224
0.6	0.2257	0.2291	0.2324	0.2357	0.2389	0.2422	0.2454	0.2486	0.2517	0.2549
0.7	0.2580	0.2611	0.2642	0.2673	0.2704	0.2734	0.2764	0.2794	0.2823	0.2852
0.8	0.2881	0.2910	0.2939	0.2967	0.2995	0.3023	0.3051	0.3078	0.3106	0.3133
0.9	0.3159	0.3186	0.3212	0.3238	0.3264	0.3289	0.3315	0.3340	0.3365	0.3389
1.0	0.3413	0.3438	0.3461	0.3485	0.3508	0.3531	0.3554	0.3577	0.3599	0.3621
1.1	0.3643	0.3665	0.3686	0.3708	0.3729	0.3749	0.3770	0.3790	0.3810	0.3830
1.2	0.3849	0.3869	0.3888	0.3907	0.3925	0.3944	0.3962	0.3980	0.3997	0.4015
1.3	0.4032	0.4049	0.4066	0.4082	0.4099	0.4115	0.4131	0.4147	0.4162	0.4177
1.4	0.4192	0.4207	0.4222	0.4236	0.4251	0.4265	0.4279	0.4292	0.4306	0.4319
1.5	0.4332	0.4345	0.4357	0.4370	0.4382	0.4394	0.4406	0.4418	0.4429	0.4441
1.6	0.4452	0.4463	0.4474	0.4484	0.4495	0.4505	0.4515	0.4525	0.4535	0.4545
1.7	0.4554	0.4564	0.4573	0.4582	0.4591	0.4599	0.4608	0.4616	0.4625	0.4633
1.8	0.4641	0.4649	0.4656	0.4664	0.4671	0.4678	0.4686	0.4693	0.4699	0.4706
1.9	0.4713	0.4719	0.4726	0.4732	0.4738	0.4744	0.4750	0.4756	0.4761	0.4767
2.0	0.4772	0.4778	0.4783	0.4788	0.4793	0.4798	0.4803	0.4808	0.4812	0.4817
2.1	0.4821	0.4826	0.4830	0.4834	0.4838	0.4842	0.4846	0.4850	0.4854	0.4857
2.2	0.4861	0.4864	0.4868	0.4871	0.4875	0.4878	0.4881	0.4884	0.4887	0.4890
2.3	0.4893	0.4896	0.4898	0.4901	0.4904	0.4906	0.4909	0.4911	0.4913	0.4916
2.4	0.4918	0.4920	0.4922	0.4925	0.4927	0.4929	0.4931	0.4932	0.4934	0.4936
2.5	0.4938	0.4940	0.4941	0.4943	0.4945	0.4946	0.4948	0.4949	0.4951	0.4952
2.6	0.4953	0.4955	0.4956	0.4957	0.4959	0.4960	0.4961	0.4962	0.4963	0.4964
2.7	0.4965	0.4966	0.4967	0.4968	0.4969	0.4970	0.4971	0.4972	0.4973	0.4974
2.8	0.4974	0.4975	0.4976	0.4977	0.4977	0.4978	0.4979	0.4979	0.4980	0.4981
2.9	0.4981	0.4982	0.4982	0.4983	0.4984	0.4984	0.4985	0.4985	0.4986	0.4986
3.0	0.4987	0.4987	0.4987	0.4988	0.4988	0.4989	0.4989	0.4989	0.4990	0.4990

Exponential Distribution Table

Values of $e^{-\lambda a}$

λa	$e^{-\lambda a}$	λa	$e^{-\lambda a}$	λa	$e^{-\lambda a}$	λa	$e^{-\lambda a}$	λa	$e^{-\lambda a}$
0.00	1.0000	2.05	0.1287	4.05	0.0174	6.05	0.0024	8.05	0.0003
0.05	0.9512	2.10	0.1225	4.10	0.0166	6.10	0.0022	8.10	0.0003
0.10	0.9048	2.15	0.1165	4.15	0.0158	6.15	0.0021	8.15	0.0003
0.15	0.8607	2.20	0.1108	4.20	0.0150	6.20	0.0020	8.20	0.0003
0.20	0.8187	2.25	0.1054	4.25	0.0143	6.25	0.0019	8.25	0.0003
0.25	0.7788	2.30	0.1003	4.30	0.0136	6.30	0.0018	8.30	0.0002
0.30	0.7408	2.35	0.0954	4.35	0.0129	6.35	0.0017	8.35	0.0002
0.35	0.7047	2.40	0.0907	4.40	0.0123	6.40	0.0017	8.40	0.0002
0.40	0.6703	2.45	0.0863	4.45	0.0117	6.45	0.0016	8.45	0.0002
0.45	0.6376	2.50	0.0821	4.50	0.0111	6.50	0.0015	8.50	0.0002
0.50	0.6065	2.55	0.0781	4.55	0.0106	6.55	0.0014	8.55	0.0002
0.55	0.5769	2.60	0.0743	4.60	0.0101	6.60	0.0014	8.60	0.0002
0.60	0.5488	2.65	0.0707	4.65	0.0096	6.65	0.0013	8.65	0.0002
0.65	0.5220	2.70	0.0672	4.70	0.0091	6.70	0.0012	8.70	0.0002
0.70	0.4966	2.75	0.0639	4.75	0.0087	6.75	0.0012	8.75	0.0002
0.75	0.4724	2.80	0.0608	4.80	0.0082	6.80	0.0011	8.80	0.0002
0.80	0.4493	2.85	0.0578	4.85	0.0078	6.85	0.0011	8.85	0.0001
0.85	0.4274	2.90	0.0550	4.90	0.0074	6.90	0.0010	8.90	0.0001
0.90	0.4066	2.95	0.0523	4.95	0.0071	6.95	0.0010	8.95	0.0001
0.95	0.3867	3.00	0.0498	5.00	0.0067	7.00	0.0009	9.00	0.0001
1.00	0.3679	3.05	0.0474	5.05	0.0064	7.05	0.0009	9.05	0.0001
1.05	0.3499	3.10	0.0450	5.10	0.0061	7.10	0.0008	9.10	0.0001
1.10	0.3329	3.15	0.0429	5.15	0.0058	7.15	0.0008	9.15	0.0001
1.15	0.3166	3.20	0.0408	5.20	0.0055	7.20	0.0007	9.20	0.0001
1.20	0.3012	3.25	0.0388	5.25	0.0052	7.25	0.0007	9.25	0.0001
1.25	0.2865	3.30	0.0369	5.30	0.0050	7.30	0.0007	9.30	0.0001
1.30	0.2725	3.35	0.0351	5.35	0.0047	7.35	0.0006	9.35	0.0001
1.35	0.2592	3.40	0.0334	5.40	0.0045	7.40	0.0006	9.40	0.0001
1.40	0.2466	3.45	0.0317	5.45	0.0043	7.45	0.0006	9.45	0.0001
1.45	0.2346	3.50	0.0302	5.50	0.0041	7.50	0.0006	9.50	0.0001
1.50	0.2231	3.55	0.0287	5.55	0.0039	7.55	0.0005	9.55	0.0001
1.55	0.2122	3.60	0.0273	5.60	0.0037	7.60	0.0005	9.60	0.0001
1.60	0.2019	3.65	0.0260	5.65	0.0035	7.65	0.0005	9.65	0.0001
1.65	0.1920	3.70	0.0247	5.70	0.0033	7.70	0.0005	9.70	0.0001
1.70	0.1827	3.75	0.0235	5.75	0.0032	7.75	0.0004	9.75	0.0001
1.75	0.1738	3.80	0.0224	5.80	0.0030	7.80	0.0004	9.80	0.0001
1.80	0.1653	3.85	0.0213	5.85	0.0029	7.85	0.0004	9.85	0.0001
1.85	0.1572	3.90	0.0202	5.90	0.0027	7.90	0.0004	9.90	0.0001
1.90	0.1496	3.95	0.0193	5.95	0.0026	7.95	0.0004	9.95	0.0000
1.95	0.1423	4.00	0.0183	6.00	0.0025	8.00	0.0003	10.00	0.0000
2.00	0.1353								

APPENDIX F

Values of *t* for Selected Probabilities

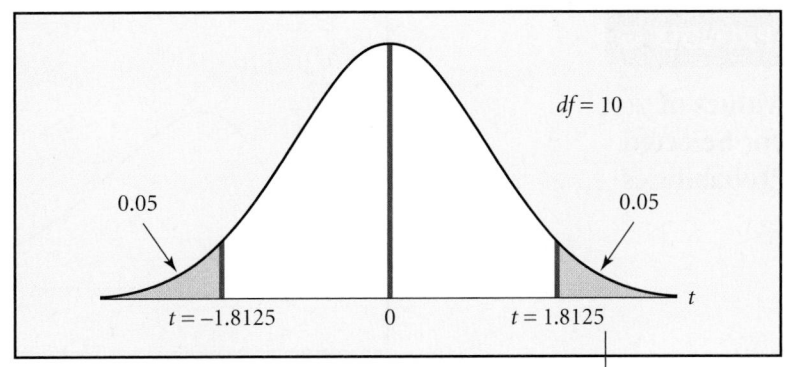

$df = 10$

0.05

0.05

$t = -1.8125$ 0 $t = 1.8125$

PROBABILITES (OR AREAS UNDER *t*-DISTRIBUTION CURVE)

Conf. Level	0.1	0.3	0.5	0.7	0.8	0.9	0.95	0.98	0.99
One Tail	0.45	0.35	0.25	0.15	0.1	0.05	0.025	0.01	0.005
Two Tails	0.9	0.7	0.5	0.3	0.2	0.1	0.05	0.02	0.01
df						Values of *t*			
1	0.1584	0.5095	1.0000	1.9626	3.0777	6.3137	12.7062	31.8210	63.6559
2	0.1421	0.4447	0.8165	1.3862	1.8856	2.9200	4.3027	6.9645	9.9250
3	0.1366	0.4242	0.7649	1.2498	1.6377	2.3534	3.1824	4.5407	5.8408
4	0.1338	0.4142	0.7407	1.1896	1.5332	2.1318	2.7765	3.7469	4.6041
5	0.1322	0.4082	0.7267	1.1558	1.4759	2.0150	2.5706	3.3649	4.0321
6	0.1311	0.4043	0.7176	1.1342	1.4398	1.9432	2.4469	3.1427	3.7074
7	0.1303	0.4015	0.7111	1.1192	1.4149	1.8946	2.3646	2.9979	3.4995
8	0.1297	0.3995	0.7064	1.1081	1.3968	1.8595	2.3060	2.8965	3.3554
9	0.1293	0.3979	0.7027	1.0997	1.3830	1.8331	2.2622	2.8214	3.2498
10	0.1289	0.3966	0.6998	1.0931	1.3722	1.8125	2.2281	2.7638	3.1693
11	0.1286	0.3956	0.6974	1.0877	1.3634	1.7959	2.2010	2.7181	3.1058
12	0.1283	0.3947	0.6955	1.0832	1.3562	1.7823	2.1788	2.6810	3.0545
13	0.1281	0.3940	0.6938	1.0795	1.3502	1.7709	2.1604	2.6503	3.0123
14	0.1280	0.3933	0.6924	1.0763	1.3450	1.7613	2.1448	2.6245	2.9768
15	0.1278	0.3928	0.6912	1.0735	1.3406	1.7531	2.1315	2.6025	2.9467
16	0.1277	0.3923	0.6901	1.0711	1.3368	1.7459	2.1199	2.5835	2.9208
17	0.1276	0.3919	0.6892	1.0690	1.3334	1.7396	2.1098	2.5669	2.8982
18	0.1274	0.3915	0.6884	1.0672	1.3304	1.7341	2.1009	2.5524	2.8784
19	0.1274	0.3912	0.6876	1.0655	1.3277	1.7291	2.0930	2.5395	2.8609
20	0.1273	0.3909	0.6870	1.0640	1.3253	1.7247	2.0860	2.5280	2.8453
21	0.1272	0.3906	0.6864	1.0627	1.3232	1.7207	2.0796	2.5176	2.8314
22	0.1271	0.3904	0.6858	1.0614	1.3212	1.7171	2.0739	2.5083	2.8188
23	0.1271	0.3902	0.6853	1.0603	1.3195	1.7139	2.0687	2.4999	2.8073
24	0.1270	0.3900	0.6848	1.0593	1.3178	1.7109	2.0639	2.4922	2.7970
25	0.1269	0.3898	0.6844	1.0584	1.3163	1.7081	2.0595	2.4851	2.7874
26	0.1269	0.3896	0.6840	1.0575	1.3150	1.7056	2.0555	2.4786	2.7787
27	0.1268	0.3894	0.6837	1.0567	1.3137	1.7033	2.0518	2.4727	2.7707
28	0.1268	0.3893	0.6834	1.0560	1.3125	1.7011	2.0484	2.4671	2.7633
29	0.1268	0.3892	0.6830	1.0553	1.3114	1.6991	2.0452	2.4620	2.7564
30	0.1267	0.3890	0.6828	1.0547	1.3104	1.6973	2.0423	2.4573	2.7500
40	0.1265	0.3881	0.6807	1.0500	1.3031	1.6839	2.0211	2.4233	2.7045
50	0.1263	0.3875	0.6794	1.0473	1.2987	1.6759	2.0086	2.4033	2.6778
60	0.1262	0.3872	0.6786	1.0455	1.2958	1.6706	2.0003	2.3901	2.6603
70	0.1261	0.3869	0.6780	1.0442	1.2938	1.6669	1.9944	2.3808	2.6479
80	0.1261	0.3867	0.6776	1.0432	1.2922	1.6641	1.9901	2.3739	2.6387
90	0.1260	0.3866	0.6772	1.0424	1.2910	1.6620	1.9867	2.3685	2.6316
100	0.1260	0.3864	0.6770	1.0418	1.2901	1.6602	1.9840	2.3642	2.6259
250	0.1258	0.3858	0.6755	1.0386	1.2849	1.6510	1.9695	2.3414	2.5956
500	0.1257	0.3855	0.6750	1.0375	1.2832	1.6479	1.9647	2.3338	2.5857
∞					See Normal Distribution				

APPENDIX G

Values of χ^2 for Selected Probabilities

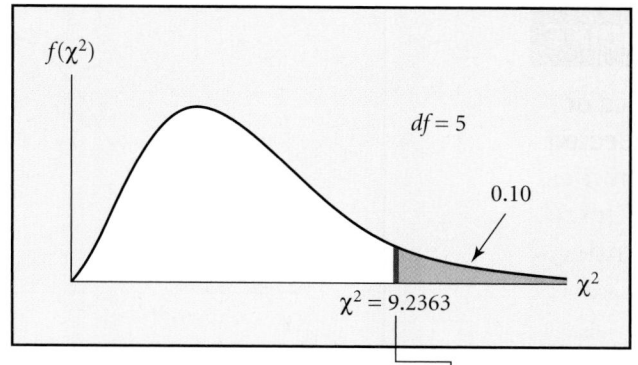

PROBABILITIES (OR AREAS UNDER CHI-SQUARE DISTRIBUTION CURVE ABOVE GIVEN CHI-SQUARE VALUES)

df	0.995	0.99	0.975	0.95	0.90	0.10	0.05	0.025	0.01	0.005
						Values of Chi-Squared				
1	0.0000	0.0002	0.0010	0.0039	0.0158	2.7055	3.8415	5.0239	6.6349	7.8794
2	0.0100	0.0201	0.0506	0.1026	0.2107	4.6052	5.9915	7.3778	9.2104	10.5965
3	0.0717	0.1148	0.2158	0.3518	0.5844	6.2514	7.8147	9.3484	11.3449	12.8381
4	0.2070	0.2971	0.4844	0.7107	1.0636	7.7794	9.4877	11.1433	13.2767	14.8602
5	0.4118	0.5543	0.8312	1.1455	1.6103	9.2363	11.0705	12.8325	15.0863	16.7496
6	0.6757	0.8721	1.2373	1.6354	2.2041	10.6446	12.5916	14.4494	16.8119	18.5475
7	0.9893	1.2390	1.6899	2.1673	2.8331	12.0170	14.0671	16.0128	18.4753	20.2777
8	1.3444	1.6465	2.1797	2.7326	3.4895	13.3616	15.5073	17.5345	20.0902	21.9549
9	1.7349	2.0879	2.7004	3.3251	4.1682	14.6837	16.9190	19.0228	21.6660	23.5893
10	2.1558	2.5582	3.2470	3.9403	4.8652	15.9872	18.3070	20.4832	23.2093	25.1881
11	2.6032	3.0535	3.8157	4.5748	5.5778	17.2750	19.6752	21.9200	24.7250	26.7569
12	3.0738	3.5706	4.4038	5.2260	6.3038	18.5493	21.0261	23.3367	26.2170	28.2997
13	3.5650	4.1069	5.0087	5.8919	7.0415	19.8119	22.3620	24.7356	27.6882	29.8193
14	4.0747	4.6604	5.6287	6.5706	7.7895	21.0641	23.6848	26.1189	29.1412	31.3194
15	4.6009	5.2294	6.2621	7.2609	8.5468	22.3071	24.9958	27.4884	30.5780	32.8015
16	5.1422	5.8122	6.9077	7.9616	9.3122	23.5418	26.2962	28.8453	31.9999	34.2671
17	5.6973	6.4077	7.5642	8.6718	10.0852	24.7690	27.5871	30.1910	33.4087	35.7184
18	6.2648	7.0149	8.2307	9.3904	10.8649	25.9894	28.8693	31.5264	34.8052	37.1564
19	6.8439	7.6327	8.9065	10.1170	11.6509	27.2036	30.1435	32.8523	36.1908	38.5821
20	7.4338	8.2604	9.5908	10.8508	12.4426	28.4120	31.4104	34.1696	37.5663	39.9969
21	8.0336	8.8972	10.2829	11.5913	13.2396	29.6151	32.6706	35.4789	38.9322	41.4009
22	8.6427	9.5425	10.9823	12.3380	14.0415	30.8133	33.9245	36.7807	40.2894	42.7957
23	9.2604	10.1957	11.6885	13.0905	14.8480	32.0069	35.1725	38.0756	41.6383	44.1814
24	9.8862	10.8563	12.4011	13.8484	15.6587	33.1962	36.4150	39.3641	42.9798	45.5584
25	10.5196	11.5240	13.1197	14.6114	16.4734	34.3816	37.6525	40.6465	44.3140	46.9280
26	11.1602	12.1982	13.8439	15.3792	17.2919	35.5632	38.8851	41.9231	45.6416	48.2898
27	11.8077	12.8785	14.5734	16.1514	18.1139	36.7412	40.1133	43.1945	46.9628	49.6450
28	12.4613	13.5647	15.3079	16.9279	18.9392	37.9159	41.3372	44.4608	48.2782	50.9936
29	13.1211	14.2564	16.0471	17.7084	19.7677	39.0875	42.5569	45.7223	49.5878	52.3355
30	13.7867	14.9535	16.7908	18.4927	20.5992	40.2560	43.7730	46.9792	50.8922	53.6719

APPENDIX H

F-Distribution Table: Upper 5% Probability (or 5% Area) Under *F*-Distribution Curve

DENOMINATOR
$df = D_2$

NUMERATOR $df = D_1$

	1	2	3	4	5	6	7	8	9	10
1	161.446	199.499	215.707	224.583	230.160	233.988	236.767	238.884	240.543	241.882
2	18.513	19.000	19.164	19.247	19.296	19.329	19.353	19.371	19.385	19.396
3	10.128	9.552	9.277	9.117	9.013	8.941	8.887	8.845	8.812	8.785
4	7.709	6.944	6.591	6.388	6.256	6.163	6.094	6.041	5.999	5.964
5	6.608	5.786	5.409	5.192	5.050	4.950	4.876	4.818	4.772	4.735
6	5.987	5.143	4.757	4.534	4.387	4.284	4.207	4.147	4.099	4.060
7	5.591	4.737	4.347	4.120	3.972	3.866	3.787	3.726	3.677	3.637
8	5.318	4.459	4.066	3.838	3.688	3.581	3.500	3.438	3.388	3.347
9	5.117	4.256	3.863	3.633	3.482	3.374	3.293	3.230	3.179	3.137
10	4.965	4.103	3.708	3.478	3.326	3.217	3.135	3.072	3.020	2.978
11	4.844	3.982	3.587	3.357	3.204	3.095	3.012	2.948	2.896	2.854
12	4.747	3.885	3.490	3.259	3.106	2.996	2.913	2.849	2.796	2.753
13	4.667	3.806	3.411	3.179	3.025	2.915	2.832	2.767	2.714	2.671
14	4.600	3.739	3.344	3.112	2.958	2.848	2.764	2.699	2.646	2.602
15	4.543	3.682	3.287	3.056	2.901	2.790	2.707	2.641	2.588	2.544
16	4.494	3.634	3.239	3.007	2.852	2.741	2.657	2.591	2.538	2.494
17	4.451	3.592	3.197	2.965	2.810	2.699	2.614	2.548	2.494	2.450
18	4.414	3.555	3.160	2.928	2.773	2.661	2.577	2.510	2.456	2.412
19	4.381	3.522	3.127	2.895	2.740	2.628	2.544	2.477	2.423	2.378
20	4.351	3.493	3.098	2.866	2.711	2.599	2.514	2.447	2.393	2.348
24	4.260	3.403	3.009	2.776	2.621	2.508	2.423	2.355	2.300	2.255
30	4.171	3.316	2.922	2.690	2.534	2.421	2.334	2.266	2.211	2.165
40	4.085	3.232	2.839	2.606	2.449	2.336	2.249	2.180	2.124	2.077
50	4.034	3.183	2.790	2.557	2.400	2.286	2.199	2.130	2.073	2.026
100	3.936	3.087	2.696	2.463	2.305	2.191	2.103	2.032	1.975	1.927
200	3.888	3.041	2.650	2.417	2.259	2.144	2.056	1.985	1.927	1.878
300	3.873	3.026	2.635	2.402	2.244	2.129	2.040	1.969	1.911	1.862

DENOMINATOR
$df = D_2$

NUMERATOR $df = D_1$

	11	12	13	14	15	16	17	18	19	20
1	242.981	243.905	244.690	245.363	245.949	246.466	246.917	247.324	247.688	248.016
2	19.405	19.412	19.419	19.424	19.429	19.433	19.437	19.440	19.443	19.446
3	8.763	8.745	8.729	8.715	8.703	8.692	8.683	8.675	8.667	8.660
4	5.936	5.912	5.891	5.873	5.858	5.844	5.832	5.821	5.811	5.803
5	4.704	4.678	4.655	4.636	4.619	4.604	4.590	4.579	4.568	4.558
6	4.027	4.000	3.976	3.956	3.938	3.922	3.908	3.896	3.884	3.874
7	3.603	3.575	3.550	3.529	3.511	3.494	3.480	3.467	3.455	3.445
8	3.313	3.284	3.259	3.237	3.218	3.202	3.187	3.173	3.161	3.150
9	3.102	3.073	3.048	3.025	3.006	2.989	2.974	2.960	2.948	2.936
10	2.943	2.913	2.887	2.865	2.845	2.828	2.812	2.798	2.785	2.774
11	2.818	2.788	2.761	2.739	2.719	2.701	2.685	2.671	2.658	2.646
12	2.717	2.687	2.660	2.637	2.617	2.599	2.583	2.568	2.555	2.544
13	2.635	2.604	2.577	2.554	2.533	2.515	2.499	2.484	2.471	2.459
14	2.565	2.534	2.507	2.484	2.463	2.445	2.428	2.413	2.400	2.388
15	2.507	2.475	2.448	2.424	2.403	2.385	2.368	2.353	2.340	2.328
16	2.456	2.425	2.397	2.373	2.352	2.333	2.317	2.302	2.288	2.276

(continued)

DENOMINATOR
df = D_2

NUMERATOR *df* = D_1

	11	12	13	14	15	16	17	18	19	20
17	2.413	2.381	2.353	2.329	2.308	2.289	2.272	2.257	2.243	2.230
18	2.374	2.342	2.314	2.290	2.269	2.250	2.233	2.217	2.203	2.191
19	2.340	2.308	2.280	2.256	2.234	2.215	2.198	2.182	2.168	2.155
20	2.310	2.278	2.250	2.225	2.203	2.184	2.167	2.151	2.137	2.124
24	2.216	2.183	2.155	2.130	2.108	2.088	2.070	2.054	2.040	2.027
30	2.126	2.092	2.063	2.037	2.015	1.995	1.976	1.960	1.945	1.932
40	2.038	2.003	1.974	1.948	1.924	1.904	1.885	1.868	1.853	1.839
50	1.986	1.952	1.921	1.895	1.871	1.850	1.831	1.814	1.798	1.784
100	1.886	1.850	1.819	1.792	1.768	1.746	1.726	1.708	1.691	1.676
200	1.837	1.801	1.769	1.742	1.717	1.694	1.674	1.656	1.639	1.623
300	1.821	1.785	1.753	1.725	1.700	1.677	1.657	1.638	1.621	1.606

DENOMINATOR
df = D_2

NUMERATOR *df* = D_1

	24	30	40	50	100	200	300
1	249.052	250.096	251.144	251.774	253.043	253.676	253.887
2	19.454	19.463	19.471	19.476	19.486	19.491	19.492
3	8.638	8.617	8.594	8.581	8.554	8.540	8.536
4	5.774	5.746	5.717	5.699	5.664	5.646	5.640
5	4.527	4.496	4.464	4.444	4.405	4.385	4.378
6	3.841	3.808	3.774	3.754	3.712	3.690	3.683
7	3.410	3.376	3.340	3.319	3.275	3.252	3.245
8	3.115	3.079	3.043	3.020	2.975	2.951	2.943
9	2.900	2.864	2.826	2.803	2.756	2.731	2.723
10	2.737	2.700	2.661	2.637	2.588	2.563	2.555
11	2.609	2.570	2.531	2.507	2.457	2.431	2.422
12	2.505	2.466	2.426	2.401	2.350	2.323	2.314
13	2.420	2.380	2.339	2.314	2.261	2.234	2.225
14	2.349	2.308	2.266	2.241	2.187	2.159	2.150
15	2.288	2.247	2.204	2.178	2.123	2.095	2.085
16	2.235	2.194	2.151	2.124	2.068	2.039	2.030
17	2.190	2.148	2.104	2.077	2.020	1.991	1.981
18	2.150	2.107	2.063	2.035	1.978	1.948	1.938
19	2.114	2.071	2.026	1.999	1.940	1.910	1.899
20	2.082	2.039	1.994	1.966	1.907	1.875	1.865
24	1.984	1.939	1.892	1.863	1.800	1.768	1.756
30	1.887	1.841	1.792	1.761	1.695	1.660	1.647
40	1.793	1.744	1.693	1.660	1.589	1.551	1.537
50	1.737	1.687	1.634	1.599	1.525	1.484	1.469
100	1.627	1.573	1.515	1.477	1.392	1.342	1.323
200	1.572	1.516	1.455	1.415	1.321	1.263	1.240
300	1.554	1.497	1.435	1.393	1.296	1.234	1.210

(continued)

**F-Distribution
Table: Upper 2.5%
Probability (or 2.5%
Area) Under
F-Distribution
Curve**

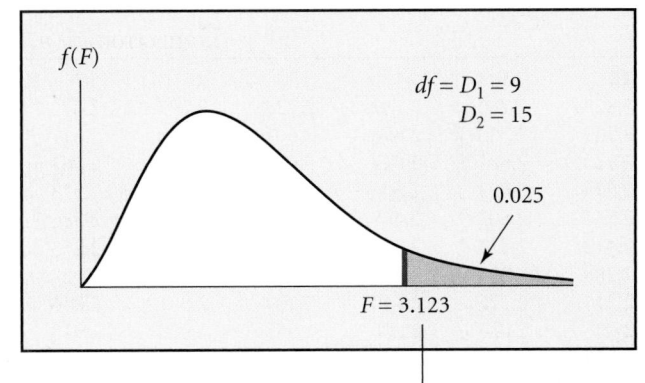

DENOMINATOR
$df = D_2$

NUMERATOR $df = D_1$

	1	2	3	4	5	6	7	8	9	10	11
1	647.793	799.482	864.151	899.599	921.835	937.114	948.203	956.643	963.279	968.634	973.028
2	38.506	39.000	39.166	39.248	39.298	39.331	39.356	39.373	39.387	39.398	39.407
3	17.443	16.044	15.439	15.101	14.885	14.735	14.624	14.540	14.473	14.419	14.374
4	12.218	10.649	9.979	9.604	9.364	9.197	9.074	8.980	8.905	8.844	8.794
5	10.007	8.434	7.764	7.388	7.146	6.978	6.853	6.757	6.681	6.619	6.568
6	8.813	7.260	6.599	6.227	5.988	5.820	5.695	5.600	5.523	5.461	5.410
7	8.073	6.542	5.890	5.523	5.285	5.119	4.995	4.899	4.823	4.761	4.709
8	7.571	6.059	5.416	5.053	4.817	4.652	4.529	4.433	4.357	4.295	4.243
9	7.209	5.715	5.078	4.718	4.484	4.320	4.197	4.102	4.026	3.964	3.912
10	6.937	5.456	4.826	4.468	4.236	4.072	3.950	3.855	3.779	3.717	3.665
11	6.724	5.256	4.630	4.275	4.044	3.881	3.759	3.664	3.588	3.526	3.474
12	6.554	5.096	4.474	4.121	3.891	3.728	3.607	3.512	3.436	3.374	3.321
13	6.414	4.965	4.347	3.996	3.767	3.604	3.483	3.388	3.312	3.250	3.197
14	6.298	4.857	4.242	3.892	3.663	3.501	3.380	3.285	3.209	3.147	3.095
15	6.200	4.765	4.153	3.804	3.576	3.415	3.293	3.199	3.123	3.060	3.008
16	6.115	4.687	4.077	3.729	3.502	3.341	3.219	3.125	3.049	2.986	2.934
17	6.042	4.619	4.011	3.665	3.438	3.277	3.156	3.061	2.985	2.922	2.870
18	5.978	4.560	3.954	3.608	3.382	3.221	3.100	3.005	2.929	2.866	2.814
19	5.922	4.508	3.903	3.559	3.333	3.172	3.051	2.956	2.880	2.817	2.765
20	5.871	4.461	3.859	3.515	3.289	3.128	3.007	2.913	2.837	2.774	2.721
24	5.717	4.319	3.721	3.379	3.155	2.995	2.874	2.779	2.703	2.640	2.586
30	5.568	4.182	3.589	3.250	3.026	2.867	2.746	2.651	2.575	2.511	2.458
40	5.424	4.051	3.463	3.126	2.904	2.744	2.624	2.529	2.452	2.388	2.334
50	5.340	3.975	3.390	3.054	2.833	2.674	2.553	2.458	2.381	2.317	2.263
100	5.179	3.828	3.250	2.917	2.696	2.537	2.417	2.321	2.244	2.179	2.124
200	5.100	3.758	3.182	2.850	2.630	2.472	2.351	2.256	2.178	2.113	2.058
300	5.075	3.735	3.160	2.829	2.609	2.451	2.330	2.234	2.156	2.091	2.036

DENOMINATOR
$df = D_2$

NUMERATOR $df = D_1$

	12	13	14	15	16	17	18	19	20	24	30
1	976.725	979.839	982.545	984.874	986.911	988.715	990.345	991.800	993.081	997.272	1001.405
2	39.415	39.421	39.427	39.431	39.436	39.439	39.442	39.446	39.448	39.457	39.465
3	14.337	14.305	14.277	14.253	14.232	14.213	14.196	14.181	14.167	14.124	14.081
4	8.751	8.715	8.684	8.657	8.633	8.611	8.592	8.575	8.560	8.511	8.461
5	6.525	6.488	6.456	6.428	6.403	6.381	6.362	6.344	6.329	6.278	6.227
6	5.366	5.329	5.297	5.269	5.244	5.222	5.202	5.184	5.168	5.117	5.065
7	4.666	4.628	4.596	4.568	4.543	4.521	4.501	4.483	4.467	4.415	4.362
8	4.200	4.162	4.130	4.101	4.076	4.054	4.034	4.016	3.999	3.947	3.894
9	3.868	3.831	3.798	3.769	3.744	3.722	3.701	3.683	3.667	3.614	3.560
10	3.621	3.583	3.550	3.522	3.496	3.474	3.453	3.435	3.419	3.365	3.311
11	3.430	3.392	3.359	3.330	3.304	3.282	3.261	3.243	3.226	3.173	3.118
12	3.277	3.239	3.206	3.177	3.152	3.129	3.108	3.090	3.073	3.019	2.963
13	3.153	3.115	3.082	3.053	3.027	3.004	2.983	2.965	2.948	2.893	2.837
14	3.050	3.012	2.979	2.949	2.923	2.900	2.879	2.861	2.844	2.789	2.732
15	2.963	2.925	2.891	2.862	2.836	2.813	2.792	2.773	2.756	2.701	2.644
16	2.889	2.851	2.817	2.788	2.761	2.738	2.717	2.698	2.681	2.625	2.568

(continued)

DENOMINATOR

df = D_2 NUMERATOR *df* = D_1

	12	13	14	15	16	17	18	19	20	24	30
17	2.825	2.786	2.753	2.723	2.697	2.673	2.652	2.633	2.616	2.560	2.502
18	2.769	2.730	2.696	2.667	2.640	2.617	2.596	2.576	2.559	2.503	2.445
19	2.720	2.681	2.647	2.617	2.591	2.567	2.546	2.526	2.509	2.452	2.394
20	2.676	2.637	2.603	2.573	2.547	2.523	2.501	2.482	2.464	2.408	2.349
24	2.541	2.502	2.468	2.437	2.411	2.386	2.365	2.345	2.327	2.269	2.209
30	2.412	2.372	2.338	2.307	2.280	2.255	2.233	2.213	2.195	2.136	2.074
40	2.288	2.248	2.213	2.182	2.154	2.129	2.107	2.086	2.068	2.007	1.943
50	2.216	2.176	2.140	2.109	2.081	2.056	2.033	2.012	1.993	1.931	1.866
100	2.077	2.036	2.000	1.968	1.939	1.913	1.890	1.868	1.849	1.784	1.715
200	2.010	1.969	1.932	1.900	1.870	1.844	1.820	1.798	1.778	1.712	1.640
300	1.988	1.947	1.910	1.877	1.848	1.821	1.797	1.775	1.755	1.688	1.616

DENOMINATOR

df = D_2 NUMERATOR *df* = D_1

	40	50	100	200	300
1	1005.596	1008.098	1013.163	1015.724	1016.539
2	39.473	39.478	39.488	39.493	39.495
3	14.036	14.010	13.956	13.929	13.920
4	8.411	8.381	8.319	8.288	8.278
5	6.175	6.144	6.080	6.048	6.037
6	5.012	4.980	4.915	4.882	4.871
7	4.309	4.276	4.210	4.176	4.165
8	3.840	3.807	3.739	3.705	3.693
9	3.505	3.472	3.403	3.368	3.357
10	3.255	3.221	3.152	3.116	3.104
11	3.061	3.027	2.956	2.920	2.908
12	2.906	2.871	2.800	2.763	2.750
13	2.780	2.744	2.671	2.634	2.621
14	2.674	2.638	2.565	2.526	2.513
15	2.585	2.549	2.474	2.435	2.422
16	2.509	2.472	2.396	2.357	2.343
17	2.442	2.405	2.329	2.289	2.275
18	2.384	2.347	2.269	2.229	2.215
19	2.333	2.295	2.217	2.176	2.162
20	2.287	2.249	2.170	2.128	2.114
24	2.146	2.107	2.024	1.981	1.966
30	2.009	1.968	1.882	1.835	1.819
40	1.875	1.832	1.741	1.691	1.673
50	1.796	1.752	1.656	1.603	1.584
100	1.640	1.592	1.483	1.420	1.397
200	1.562	1.511	1.393	1.320	1.293
300	1.536	1.484	1.361	1.285	1.255

(continued)

F-Distribution Table: Upper 1% Probability (or 1% Area) Under F-Distribution Curve

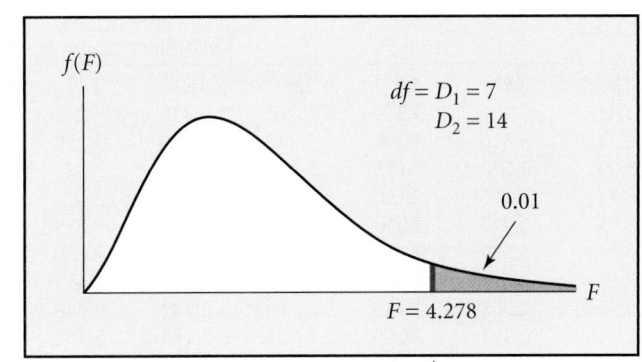

$f(F)$

$df = D_1 = 7$
$D_2 = 14$

0.01

F

$F = 4.278$

DENOMINATOR
$df = D_2$ NUMERATOR $df = D_1$

	1	2	3	4	5	6	7	8	9	10	11
1	4052.185	4999.340	5403.534	5624.257	5763.955	5858.950	5928.334	5980.954	6022.397	6055.925	6083.399
2	98.502	99.000	99.164	99.251	99.302	99.331	99.357	99.375	99.390	99.397	99.408
3	34.116	30.816	29.457	28.710	28.237	27.911	27.671	27.489	27.345	27.228	27.132
4	21.198	18.000	16.694	15.977	15.522	15.207	14.976	14.799	14.659	14.546	14.452
5	16.258	13.274	12.060	11.392	10.967	10.672	10.456	10.289	10.158	10.051	9.963
6	13.745	10.925	9.780	9.148	8.746	8.466	8.260	8.102	7.976	7.874	7.790
7	12.246	9.547	8.451	7.847	7.460	7.191	6.993	6.840	6.719	6.620	6.538
8	11.259	8.649	7.591	7.006	6.632	6.371	6.178	6.029	5.911	5.814	5.734
9	10.562	8.022	6.992	6.422	6.057	5.802	5.613	5.467	5.351	5.257	5.178
10	10.044	7.559	6.552	5.994	5.636	5.386	5.200	5.057	4.942	4.849	4.772
11	9.646	7.206	6.217	5.668	5.316	5.069	4.886	4.744	4.632	4.539	4.462
12	9.330	6.927	5.953	5.412	5.064	4.821	4.640	4.499	4.388	4.296	4.220
13	9.074	6.701	5.739	5.205	4.862	4.620	4.441	4.302	4.191	4.100	4.025
14	8.862	6.515	5.564	5.035	4.695	4.456	4.278	4.140	4.030	3.939	3.864
15	8.683	6.359	5.417	4.893	4.556	4.318	4.142	4.004	3.895	3.805	3.730
16	8.531	6.226	5.292	4.773	4.437	4.202	4.026	3.890	3.780	3.691	3.616
17	8.400	6.112	5.185	4.669	4.336	4.101	3.927	3.791	3.682	3.593	3.518
18	8.285	6.013	5.092	4.579	4.248	4.015	3.841	3.705	3.597	3.508	3.434
19	8.185	5.926	5.010	4.500	4.171	3.939	3.765	3.631	3.523	3.434	3.360
20	8.096	5.849	4.938	4.431	4.103	3.871	3.699	3.564	3.457	3.368	3.294
24	7.823	5.614	4.718	4.218	3.895	3.667	3.496	3.363	3.256	3.168	3.094
30	7.562	5.390	4.510	4.018	3.699	3.473	3.305	3.173	3.067	2.979	2.906
40	7.314	5.178	4.313	3.828	3.514	3.291	3.124	2.993	2.888	2.801	2.727
50	7.171	5.057	4.199	3.720	3.408	3.186	3.020	2.890	2.785	2.698	2.625
100	6.895	4.824	3.984	3.513	3.206	2.988	2.823	2.694	2.590	2.503	2.430
200	6.763	4.713	3.881	3.414	3.110	2.893	2.730	2.601	2.497	2.411	2.338
300	6.720	4.677	3.848	3.382	3.079	2.862	2.699	2.571	2.467	2.380	2.307

DENOMINATOR
$df = D_2$ NUMERATOR $df = D_1$

	12	13	14	15	16	17	18	19	20	24	30
1	6106.682	6125.774	6143.004	6156.974	6170.012	6181.188	6191.432	6200.746	6208.662	6234.273	6260.350
2	99.419	99.422	99.426	99.433	99.437	99.441	99.444	99.448	99.448	99.455	99.466
3	27.052	26.983	26.924	26.872	26.826	26.786	26.751	26.719	26.690	26.597	26.504
4	14.374	14.306	14.249	14.198	14.154	14.114	14.079	14.048	14.019	13.929	13.838
5	9.888	9.825	9.770	9.722	9.680	9.643	9.609	9.580	9.553	9.466	9.379
6	7.718	7.657	7.605	7.559	7.519	7.483	7.451	7.422	7.396	7.313	7.229
7	6.469	6.410	6.359	6.314	6.275	6.240	6.209	6.181	6.155	6.074	5.992
8	5.667	5.609	5.559	5.515	5.477	5.442	5.412	5.384	5.359	5.279	5.198
9	5.111	5.055	5.005	4.962	4.924	4.890	4.860	4.833	4.808	4.729	4.649
10	4.706	4.650	4.601	4.558	4.520	4.487	4.457	4.430	4.405	4.327	4.247
11	4.397	4.342	4.293	4.251	4.213	4.180	4.150	4.123	4.099	4.021	3.941
12	4.155	4.100	4.052	4.010	3.972	3.939	3.910	3.883	3.858	3.780	3.701
13	3.960	3.905	3.857	3.815	3.778	3.745	3.716	3.689	3.665	3.587	3.507
14	3.800	3.745	3.698	3.656	3.619	3.586	3.556	3.529	3.505	3.427	3.348
15	3.666	3.612	3.564	3.522	3.485	3.452	3.423	3.396	3.372	3.294	3.214
16	3.553	3.498	3.451	3.409	3.372	3.339	3.310	3.283	3.259	3.181	3.101

(continued)

DENOMINATOR

$df = D_2$					NUMERATOR $df = D_1$						
	12	**13**	**14**	**15**	**16**	**17**	**18**	**19**	**20**	**24**	**30**
17	3.455	3.401	3.353	3.312	3.275	3.242	3.212	3.186	3.162	3.083	3.003
18	3.371	3.316	3.269	3.227	3.190	3.158	3.128	3.101	3.077	2.999	2.919
19	3.297	3.242	3.195	3.153	3.116	3.084	3.054	3.027	3.003	2.925	2.844
20	3.231	3.177	3.130	3.088	3.051	3.018	2.989	2.962	2.938	2.859	2.778
24	3.032	2.977	2.930	2.889	2.852	2.819	2.789	2.762	2.738	2.659	2.577
30	2.843	2.789	2.742	2.700	2.663	2.630	2.600	2.573	2.549	2.469	2.386
40	2.665	2.611	2.563	2.522	2.484	2.451	2.421	2.394	2.369	2.288	2.203
50	2.563	2.508	2.461	2.419	2.382	2.348	2.318	2.290	2.265	2.183	2.098
100	2.368	2.313	2.265	2.223	2.185	2.151	2.120	2.092	2.067	1.983	1.893
200	2.275	2.220	2.172	2.129	2.091	2.057	2.026	1.997	1.971	1.886	1.794
300	2.244	2.190	2.142	2.099	2.061	2.026	1.995	1.966	1.940	1.854	1.761

DENOMINATOR

$df = D_2$			NUMERATOR $df = D_1$		
	40	**50**	**100**	**200**	**300**
1	6286.427	6302.260	6333.925	6349.757	6355.345
2	99.477	99.477	99.491	99.491	99.499
3	26.411	26.354	26.241	26.183	26.163
4	13.745	13.690	13.577	13.520	13.501
5	9.291	9.238	9.130	9.075	9.057
6	7.143	7.091	6.987	6.934	6.916
7	5.908	5.858	5.755	5.702	5.685
8	5.116	5.065	4.963	4.911	4.894
9	4.567	4.517	4.415	4.363	4.346
10	4.165	4.115	4.014	3.962	3.944
11	3.860	3.810	3.708	3.656	3.638
12	3.619	3.569	3.467	3.414	3.397
13	3.425	3.375	3.272	3.219	3.202
14	3.266	3.215	3.112	3.059	3.040
15	3.132	3.081	2.977	2.923	2.905
16	3.018	2.967	2.863	2.808	2.790
17	2.920	2.869	2.764	2.709	2.691
18	2.835	2.784	2.678	2.623	2.604
19	2.761	2.709	2.602	2.547	2.528
20	2.695	2.643	2.535	2.479	2.460
24	2.492	2.440	2.329	2.271	2.251
30	2.299	2.245	2.131	2.070	2.049
40	2.114	2.058	1.938	1.874	1.851
50	2.007	1.949	1.825	1.757	1.733
100	1.797	1.735	1.598	1.518	1.490
200	1.694	1.629	1.481	1.391	1.357
300	1.660	1.594	1.441	1.346	1.309

Critical Values of Hartley's F_{max} Test

$$F_{max} = \frac{S^2_{largest}}{S^2_{smallest}} \sim F_{max_{1-a\,(c,v)}}$$

UPPER 5% POINTS ($\alpha = 0.05$)

c / v	2	3	4	5	6	7	8	9	10	11	12
2	39.0	87.5	142	202	266	333	403	475	550	626	704
3	15.4	27.8	39.2	50.7	62.0	72.9	83.5	93.9	104	114	124
4	9.60	15.5	20.6	25.2	29.5	33.6	37.5	41.1	44.6	48.0	51.4
5	7.15	10.8	13.7	16.3	18.7	20.8	22.9	24.7	26.5	28.2	29.9
6	5.82	8.38	10.4	12.1	13.7	15.0	16.3	17.5	18.6	19.7	20.7
7	4.99	6.94	8.44	9.70	10.8	11.8	12.7	13.5	14.3	15.1	15.8
8	4.43	6.00	7.18	8.12	9.03	9.78	10.5	11.1	11.7	12.2	12.7
9	4.03	5.34	6.31	7.11	7.80	8.41	8.95	9.45	9.91	10.3	10.7
10	3.72	4.85	5.67	6.34	6.92	7.42	7.87	8.28	8.66	9.01	9.34
12	3.28	4.16	4.79	5.30	5.72	6.09	6.42	6.72	7.00	7.25	7.48
15	2.86	3.54	4.01	4.37	4.68	4.95	5.19	5.40	5.59	5.77	5.93
20	2.46	2.95	3.29	3.54	3.76	3.94	4.10	4.24	4.37	4.49	4.59
30	2.07	2.40	2.61	2.78	2.91	3.02	3.12	3.21	3.29	3.36	3.39
60	1.67	1.85	1.96	2.04	2.11	2.17	2.22	2.26	2.30	2.33	2.36
∞	1.00	1.00	1.00	1.00	1.00	1.00	1.00	1.00	1.00	1.00	1.00

UPPER 1% POINTS ($\alpha = 0.01$)

c / v	2	3	4	5	6	7	8	9	10	11	12
2	199	448	729	1036	1362	1705	2063	2432	2813	3204	3605
3	47.5	85	120	151	184	21(6)	24(9)	28(1)	31(0)	33(7)	36(1)
4	23.2	37	49	59	69	79	89	97	106	113	120
5	14.9	22	28	33	38	42	46	50	54	57	60
6	11.1	15.5	19.1	22	25	27	30	32	34	36	37
7	8.89	12.1	14.5	16.5	18.4	20	22	23	24	26	27
8	7.50	9.9	11.7	13.2	14.5	15.8	16.9	17.9	18.9	19.8	21
9	6.54	8.5	9.9	11.1	12.1	13.1	13.9	14.7	15.3	16.0	16.6
10	5.85	7.4	8.6	9.6	10.4	11.1	11.8	12.4	12.9	13.4	13.9
12	4.91	6.1	6.9	7.6	8.2	8.7	9.1	9.5	9.9	10.2	10.6
15	4.07	4.9	5.5	6.0	6.4	6.7	7.1	7.3	7.5	7.8	8.0
20	3.32	3.8	4.3	4.6	4.9	5.1	5.3	5.5	5.6	5.8	5.9
30	2.63	3.0	3.3	3.4	3.6	3.7	3.8	3.9	4.0	4.1	4.2
60	1.96	2.2	2.3	2.4	2.4	2.5	2.5	2.6	2.6	2.7	2.7
∞	1.00	1.0	1.0	1.0	1.0	1.0	1.0	1.0	1.0	1.00	1.0

Note: $S^2_{largest}$ is the largest and the $s^2_{smallest}$ the smallest in a set of c independent mean squares, each based on v degrees of freedom.

Source: Reprinted from E. S. Pearson and H. O. Hartley, eds., *Biometrika Tables for Statisticians*, 3d ed., 1966, by permission of the Biometrika Trustees.

$p = 0.95$

D_2 \ D_1	2	3	4	5	6	7	8	9	10
1	17.97	26.98	32.82	37.08	40.41	43.12	45.40	47.36	49.07
2	6.08	8.33	9.80	10.88	11.74	12.44	13.03	13.54	13.99
3	4.50	5.91	6.82	7.50	8.04	8.48	8.85	9.18	9.46
4	3.93	5.04	5.76	6.29	6.71	7.05	7.35	7.60	7.83
5	3.64	4.60	5.22	5.67	6.03	6.33	6.58	6.80	6.99
6	3.46	4.34	4.90	5.30	5.63	5.90	6.12	6.32	6.49
7	3.34	4.16	4.68	5.06	5.36	5.61	5.82	6.00	6.16
8	3.26	4.04	4.53	4.89	5.17	5.40	5.60	5.77	5.92
9	3.20	3.95	4.41	4.76	5.02	5.24	5.43	5.59	5.74
10	3.15	3.88	4.33	4.65	4.91	5.12	5.30	5.46	5.60
11	3.11	3.82	4.26	4.57	4.82	5.03	5.20	5.35	5.49
12	3.08	3.77	4.20	4.51	4.75	4.95	5.12	5.27	5.39
13	3.06	3.73	4.15	4.45	4.69	4.88	5.05	5.19	5.32
14	3.03	3.70	4.11	4.41	4.64	4.83	4.99	5.13	5.25
15	3.01	3.67	4.08	4.37	4.59	4.78	4.94	5.08	5.20
16	3.00	3.65	4.05	4.33	4.56	4.74	4.90	5.03	5.15
17	2.98	3.63	4.02	4.30	4.52	4.70	4.86	4.99	5.11
18	2.97	3.61	4.00	4.28	4.49	4.67	4.82	4.96	5.07
19	2.96	3.59	3.98	4.25	4.47	4.65	4.79	4.92	5.04
20	2.95	3.58	3.96	4.23	4.45	4.62	4.77	4.90	5.01
24	2.92	3.53	3.90	4.17	4.37	4.54	4.68	4.81	4.92
30	2.89	3.49	3.85	4.10	4.30	4.46	4.60	4.72	4.82
40	2.86	3.44	3.79	4.04	4.23	4.39	4.52	4.63	4.73
60	2.83	3.40	3.74	3.98	4.16	4.31	4.44	4.55	4.65
120	2.80	3.36	3.68	3.92	4.10	4.24	4.36	4.47	4.56
∞	2.77	3.31	3.63	3.86	4.03	4.17	4.29	4.39	4.47

D_2 \ D_1	11	12	13	14	15	16	17	18	19	20
1	50.59	51.96	53.20	54.33	55.36	56.32	57.22	58.04	58.83	59.56
2	14.39	14.75	15.08	15.38	15.65	15.91	16.14	16.37	16.57	16.77
3	9.72	9.95	10.15	10.35	10.52	10.69	10.84	10.98	11.11	11.24
4	8.03	8.21	8.37	8.52	8.66	8.79	8.91	9.03	9.13	9.23
5	7.17	7.32	7.47	7.60	7.72	7.83	7.93	8.03	8.12	8.21
6	6.65	6.79	6.92	7.03	7.14	7.24	7.34	7.43	7.51	7.59
7	6.30	6.43	6.55	6.66	6.76	6.85	6.94	7.02	7.10	7.17
8	6.05	6.18	6.29	6.39	6.48	6.57	6.65	6.73	6.80	6.87
9	5.87	5.98	6.09	6.19	6.28	6.36	6.44	6.51	6.58	6.64
10	5.72	5.83	5.93	6.03	6.11	6.19	6.27	6.34	6.40	6.47
11	5.61	5.71	5.81	5.90	5.98	6.06	6.13	6.20	6.27	6.33
12	5.51	5.61	5.71	5.80	5.88	5.95	6.02	6.09	6.15	6.21
13	5.43	5.53	5.63	5.71	5.79	5.86	5.93	5.99	6.05	6.11
14	5.36	5.46	5.55	5.64	5.71	5.79	5.85	5.91	5.97	6.03
15	5.31	5.40	5.49	5.57	5.65	5.72	5.78	5.85	5.90	5.96
16	5.26	5.35	5.44	5.52	5.59	5.66	5.73	5.79	5.84	5.90
17	5.21	5.31	5.39	5.47	5.54	5.61	5.67	5.73	5.79	5.84
18	5.17	5.27	5.35	5.43	5.50	5.57	5.63	5.69	5.74	5.79
19	5.14	5.23	5.31	5.39	5.46	5.53	5.59	5.65	5.70	5.75
20	5.11	5.20	5.28	5.36	5.43	5.49	5.55	5.61	5.66	5.71
24	5.01	5.10	5.18	5.25	5.32	5.38	5.44	5.49	5.55	5.59
30	4.92	5.00	5.08	5.15	5.21	5.27	5.33	5.38	5.43	5.47
40	4.82	4.90	4.98	5.04	5.11	5.16	5.22	5.27	5.31	5.36
60	4.73	4.81	4.88	4.94	5.00	5.06	5.11	5.15	5.20	5.24
120	4.64	4.71	4.78	4.84	4.90	4.95	5.00	5.04	5.09	5.13
∞	4.55	4.62	4.68	4.74	4.80	4.85	4.89	4.93	4.97	5.01

Note: $D_1 = K$ populations and $D_2 = N - K$.

$p = 0.99$

D_2 \ D_1	2	3	4	5	6	7	8	9	10
1	90.03	135.0	164.3	185.6	202.2	215.8	227.2	237.0	245.6
2	14.04	19.02	22.29	24.72	26.63	28.20	29.53	30.68	31.69
3	8.26	10.62	12.17	13.33	14.24	15.00	15.64	16.20	16.69
4	6.51	8.12	9.17	9.96	10.58	11.10	11.55	11.93	12.27
5	5.70	6.98	7.80	8.42	8.91	9.32	9.67	9.97	10.24
6	5.24	6.33	7.03	7.56	7.97	8.32	8.61	8.87	9.10
7	4.95	5.92	6.54	7.01	7.37	7.68	7.94	8.17	8.37
8	4.75	5.64	6.20	6.62	6.96	7.24	7.47	7.68	7.86
9	4.60	5.43	5.96	6.35	6.66	6.91	7.13	7.33	7.49
10	4.48	5.27	5.77	6.14	6.43	6.67	6.87	7.05	7.21
11	4.39	5.15	5.62	5.97	6.25	6.48	6.67	6.84	6.99
12	4.32	5.05	5.50	5.84	6.10	6.32	6.51	6.67	6.81
13	4.26	4.96	5.40	5.73	5.98	6.19	6.37	6.53	6.67
14	4.21	4.89	5.32	5.63	5.88	6.08	6.26	6.41	6.54
15	4.17	4.84	5.25	5.56	5.80	5.99	6.16	6.31	6.44
16	4.13	4.79	5.19	5.49	5.72	5.92	6.08	6.22	6.35
17	4.10	4.74	5.14	5.43	5.66	5.85	6.01	6.15	6.27
18	4.07	4.70	5.09	5.38	5.60	5.79	5.94	6.08	6.20
19	4.05	4.67	5.05	5.33	5.55	5.73	5.89	6.02	6.14
20	4.02	4.64	5.02	5.29	5.51	5.69	5.84	5.97	6.09
24	3.96	4.55	4.91	5.17	5.37	5.54	5.69	5.81	5.92
30	3.89	4.45	4.80	5.05	5.24	5.40	5.54	5.65	5.76
40	3.82	4.37	4.70	4.93	5.11	5.26	5.39	5.50	5.60
60	3.76	4.28	4.59	4.82	4.99	5.13	5.25	5.36	5.45
120	3.70	4.20	4.50	4.71	4.87	5.01	5.12	5.21	5.30
∞	3.64	4.12	4.40	4.60	4.76	4.88	4.99	5.08	5.16

D_2 \ D_1	11	12	13	14	15	16	17	18	19	20
1	253.2	260.0	266.2	271.8	277.0	281.8	286.3	290.4	294.3	298.0
2	32.59	33.40	34.13	34.81	35.43	36.00	36.53	37.03	37.50	37.95
3	17.13	17.53	17.89	18.22	18.52	18.81	19.07	19.32	19.55	19.77
4	12.57	12.84	13.09	13.32	13.53	13.73	13.91	14.08	14.24	14.40
5	10.48	10.70	10.89	11.08	11.24	11.40	11.55	11.68	11.81	11.93
6	9.30	9.48	9.65	9.81	9.95	10.08	10.21	10.32	10.43	10.54
7	8.55	8.71	8.86	9.00	9.12	9.24	9.35	9.46	9.55	9.65
8	8.03	8.18	8.31	8.44	8.55	8.66	8.76	8.85	8.94	9.03
9	7.65	7.78	7.91	8.03	8.13	8.23	8.33	8.41	8.49	8.57
10	7.36	7.49	7.60	7.71	7.81	7.91	7.99	8.08	8.15	8.23
11	7.13	7.25	7.36	7.46	7.56	7.65	7.73	7.81	7.88	7.95
12	6.94	7.06	7.17	7.26	7.36	7.44	7.52	7.59	7.66	7.73
13	6.79	6.90	7.01	7.10	7.19	7.27	7.35	7.42	7.48	7.55
14	6.66	6.77	6.87	6.96	7.05	7.13	7.20	7.27	7.33	7.39
15	6.55	6.66	6.76	6.84	6.93	7.00	7.07	7.14	7.20	7.26
16	6.46	6.56	6.66	6.74	6.82	6.90	6.97	7.03	7.09	7.15
17	6.38	6.48	6.57	6.66	6.73	6.81	6.87	6.94	7.00	7.05
18	6.31	6.41	6.50	6.58	6.65	6.73	6.79	6.85	6.91	6.97
19	6.25	6.34	6.43	6.51	6.58	6.65	6.72	6.78	6.84	6.89
20	6.19	6.28	6.37	6.45	6.52	6.59	6.65	6.71	6.77	6.82
24	6.02	6.11	6.19	6.26	6.33	6.39	6.45	6.51	6.56	6.61
30	5.85	5.93	6.01	6.08	6.14	6.20	6.26	6.31	6.36	6.41
40	5.69	5.76	5.83	5.90	5.96	6.02	6.07	6.12	6.16	6.21
60	5.53	5.60	5.67	5.73	5.78	5.84	5.89	5.93	5.97	6.01
120	5.37	5.44	5.50	5.56	5.61	5.66	5.71	5.75	5.79	5.83
∞	5.23	5.28	5.35	5.40	5.45	5.49	5.54	5.57	5.61	5.65

Source: Reprinted with permission from E. S. Pearson and H. O. Hartley, *Biometrika Tables for Statisticians* (New York: Cambridge University Press, 1954).

APPENDIX K

Critical Values of *r* in the Runs Test

a. Lower Tail: Too Few Runs

n_1 \ n_2	2	3	4	5	6	7	8	9	10	11	12	13	14	15	16	17	18	19	20
2											2	2	2	2	2	2	2	2	2
3			2	2	2	2	2	2	2	2	2	2	2	3	3	3	3	3	3
4			2	2	2	3	3	3	3	3	3	3	3	3	4	4	4	4	4
5			2	2	3	3	3	3	3	4	4	4	4	4	4	4	5	5	5
6		2	2	3	3	3	3	4	4	4	4	5	5	5	5	5	5	6	6
7		2	2	3	3	3	4	4	5	5	5	5	5	6	6	6	6	6	6
8		2	3	3	3	4	4	5	5	5	6	6	6	6	6	7	7	7	7
9		2	3	3	4	4	5	5	5	6	6	6	7	7	7	7	8	8	8
10		2	3	3	4	5	5	5	6	6	7	7	7	7	8	8	8	8	9
11		2	3	4	4	5	5	6	6	7	7	7	8	8	8	9	9	9	9
12	2	2	3	4	4	5	6	6	7	7	7	8	8	8	9	9	9	10	10
13	2	2	3	4	5	5	6	6	7	7	8	8	9	9	9	10	10	10	10
14	2	2	3	4	5	5	6	7	7	8	8	9	9	9	10	10	10	11	11
15	2	3	3	4	5	6	6	7	7	8	8	9	9	10	10	11	11	11	12
16	2	3	4	4	5	6	6	7	8	8	9	9	10	10	11	11	11	12	12
17	2	3	4	4	5	6	7	7	8	9	9	10	10	11	11	11	12	12	13
18	2	3	4	5	5	6	7	8	8	9	9	10	10	11	11	12	12	13	13
19	2	3	4	5	6	6	7	8	8	9	10	10	11	11	12	12	13	13	13
20	2	3	4	5	6	6	7	8	9	9	10	10	11	12	12	13	13	13	14

b. Upper Tail: Too Many Runs

n_1 \ n_2	2	3	4	5	6	7	8	9	10	11	12	13	14	15	16	17	18	19	20
2																			
3																			
4				9	9														
5			9	10	10	11	11												
6			9	10	11	12	12	13	13	13	13								
7				11	12	13	13	14	14	14	14	15	15	15					
8				11	12	13	14	14	15	15	16	16	16	16	17	17	17	17	17
9					13	14	14	15	16	16	16	17	17	18	18	18	18	18	18
10					13	14	15	16	16	17	17	18	18	18	19	19	19	20	20
11					13	14	15	16	17	17	18	19	19	19	20	20	20	21	21
12					13	14	16	16	17	18	19	19	20	20	21	21	21	22	22
13						15	16	17	18	19	19	20	20	21	21	22	22	23	23
14						15	16	17	18	19	20	20	21	22	22	23	23	23	24
15						15	16	18	18	19	20	21	22	22	23	23	24	24	25
16							17	18	19	20	21	21	22	23	23	24	25	25	25
17							17	18	19	20	21	22	23	23	24	25	25	26	26
18							17	18	19	20	21	22	23	24	25	25	26	26	27
19							17	18	20	21	22	23	23	24	25	26	26	27	27
20							17	18	20	21	22	23	24	25	25	26	27	27	28

Mann-Whitney
U Test Probabilities
($n < 9$)

$n_2 = 3$

U \ n_1	1	2	3
0	.250	.100	.050
1	.500	.200	.100
2	.750	.400	.200
3		.600	.350
4			.500
5			.650

$n_2 = 4$

U \ n_1	1	2	3	4
0	.200	.067	.028	.014
1	.400	.133	.057	.029
2	.600	.267	.114	.057
3		.400	.200	.100
4		.600	.314	.171
5			.429	.243
6			.571	.343
7				.443
8				.557

$n_2 = 5$

U \ n_1	1	2	3	4	5
0	.167	.047	.018	.008	.004
1	.333	.095	.036	.016	.008
2	.500	.190	.071	.032	.016
3	.667	.286	.125	.056	.028
4		.429	.196	.095	.048
5		.571	.286	.143	.075
6			.393	.206	.111
7			.500	.278	.155
8			.607	.365	.210
9				.452	.274
10				.548	.345
11					.421
12					.500
13					.579

$n_2 = 6$

U \ n_1	1	2	3	4	5	6
0	.143	.036	.012	.005	.002	.001
1	.286	.071	.024	.010	.004	.002
2	.428	.143	.048	.019	.009	.004
3	.571	.214	.083	.033	.015	.008
4		.321	.131	.057	.026	.013
5		.429	.190	.086	.041	.021
6		.571	.274	.129	.063	.032
7			.357	.176	.089	.047
8			.452	.238	.123	.066
9			.548	.305	.165	.090
10				.381	.214	.120
11				.457	.268	.155
12				.545	.331	.197
13					.396	.242
14					.465	.294
15					.535	.350
16						.409
17						.469
18						.531

$n_2 = 7$

U \ n_1	1	2	3	4	5	6	7
0	.125	.028	.008	.003	.001	.001	.000
1	.250	.056	.017	.006	.003	.001	.001
2	.375	.111	.033	.012	.005	.002	.001
3	.500	.167	.058	.021	.009	.004	.002
4	.625	.250	.092	.036	.015	.007	.003
5		.333	.133	.055	.024	.011	.006
6		.444	.192	.082	.037	.017	.009
7		.556	.258	.115	.053	.026	.013
8			.333	.158	.074	.037	.019
9			.417	.206	.101	.051	.027
10			.500	.264	.134	.069	.036
11			.583	.324	.172	.090	.049
12				.394	.216	.117	.064
13				.464	.265	.147	.082
14				.538	.319	.183	.104
15					.378	.223	.130
16					.438	.267	.159
17					.500	.314	.191
18					.562	.365	.228
19						.418	.267
20						.473	.310
21						.527	.355
22							.402
23							.451
24							.500
25							.549

$n_2 = 8$

U \ n_1	1	2	3	4	5	6	7	8	t	Normal
0	.111	.022	.006	.002	.001	.000	.000	.000	3.308	.001
1	.222	.044	.012	.004	.002	.001	.000	.000	3.203	.001
2	.333	.089	.024	.008	.003	.001	.001	.000	3.098	.001
3	.444	.133	.042	.014	.005	.002	.001	.001	2.993	.001
4	.556	.200	.067	.024	.009	.004	.002	.001	2.888	.002
5		.267	.097	.036	.015	.006	.003	.001	2.783	.003
6		.356	.139	.055	.023	.010	.005	.002	2.678	.004
7		.444	.188	.077	.033	.015	.007	.003	2.573	.005
8		.556	.248	.107	.047	.021	.010	.005	2.468	.007
9			.315	.141	.064	.030	.014	.007	2.363	.009
10			.387	.184	.085	.041	.020	.010	2.258	.012
11			.461	.230	.111	.054	.027	.014	2.153	.016
12			.539	.285	.142	.071	.036	.019	2.048	.020
13				.341	.177	.091	.047	.025	1.943	.026
14				.404	.217	.114	.060	.032	1.838	.033
15				.467	.262	.141	.076	.041	1.733	.041
16				.533	.311	.172	.095	.052	1.628	.052
17					.362	.207	.116	.065	1.523	.064
18					.416	.245	.140	.080	1.418	.078
19					.472	.286	.168	.097	1.313	.094
20					.528	.331	.198	.117	1.208	.113
21						.377	.232	.139	1.102	.135
22						.426	.268	.164	.998	.159
23						.475	.306	.191	.893	.185
24						.525	.347	.221	.788	.215
25							.389	.253	.683	.247
26							.433	.287	.578	.282
27							.478	.323	.473	.318
28							.522	.360	.368	.356
29								.399	.263	.396
30								.439	.158	.437
31								.480	.052	.481
32								.520		

Source: Reproduced from H. B. Mann and D. R. Whitney, "On a test of whether one of two random variables is stochastically larger than the other," *Ann. Math Statist*, 18 (1947): 52–54, with the permission of the publisher.

APPENDIX M

Mann-Whitney U Test Critical Values ($9 \le n \le 20$)

Critical Values of U for a One-Tailed Test at $\alpha = 0.001$ or for a Two-Tailed Test at $\alpha = 0.002$

n_1 \ n_2	9	10	11	12	13	14	15	16	17	18	19	20
1												
2												
3									0	0	0	0
4		0	0	0	1	1	1	2	2	3	3	3
5	1	1	2	2	3	3	4	5	5	6	7	7
6	2	3	4	4	5	6	7	8	9	10	11	12
7	3	5	6	7	8	9	10	11	13	14	15	16
8	5	6	8	9	11	12	14	15	17	18	20	21
9	7	8	10	12	14	15	17	19	21	23	25	26
10	8	10	12	14	17	19	21	23	25	27	29	32
11	10	12	15	17	20	22	24	27	29	32	34	37
12	12	14	17	20	23	25	28	31	34	37	40	42
13	14	17	20	23	26	29	32	35	38	42	45	48
14	15	19	22	25	29	32	36	39	43	46	50	54
15	17	21	24	28	32	36	40	43	47	51	55	59
16	19	23	27	31	35	39	43	48	52	56	60	65
17	21	25	29	34	38	43	47	52	57	61	66	70
18	23	27	32	37	42	46	51	56	61	66	71	76
19	25	29	34	40	45	50	55	60	66	71	77	82
20	26	32	37	42	48	54	59	65	70	76	82	88

Critical Values of U for a One-Tailed Test at $\alpha = 0.01$ or for a Two-Tailed Test at $\alpha = 0.02$

n_1 \ n_2	9	10	11	12	13	14	15	16	17	18	19	20
1												
2					0	0	0	0	0	0	1	1
3	1	1	1	2	2	2	3	3	4	4	4	5
4	3	3	4	5	5	6	7	7	8	9	9	10
5	5	6	7	8	9	10	11	12	13	14	15	16
6	7	8	9	11	12	13	15	16	18	19	20	22
7	9	11	12	14	16	17	19	21	23	24	26	28
8	11	13	15	17	20	22	24	26	28	30	32	34
9	14	16	18	21	23	26	28	31	33	36	38	40
10	16	19	22	24	27	30	33	36	38	41	44	47
11	18	22	25	28	31	34	37	41	44	47	50	53
12	21	24	28	31	35	38	42	46	49	53	56	60
13	23	27	31	35	39	43	47	51	55	59	63	67
14	26	30	34	38	43	47	51	56	60	65	69	73
15	28	33	37	42	47	51	56	61	66	70	75	80
16	31	36	41	46	51	56	61	66	71	76	82	87
17	33	38	44	49	55	60	66	71	77	82	88	93
18	36	41	47	53	59	65	70	76	82	88	94	100
19	38	44	50	56	63	69	75	82	88	94	101	107
20	40	47	53	60	67	73	80	87	93	100	107	114

Critical Values of U for a One-Tailed Test at $\alpha = 0.025$ or for a Two-Tailed Test at $\alpha = 0.05$

n_1 \ n_2	9	10	11	12	13	14	15	16	17	18	19	20
1												
2	0	0	0	1	1	1	1	1	2	2	2	2
3	2	3	3	4	4	5	5	6	6	7	7	8
4	4	5	6	7	8	9	10	11	11	12	13	13
5	7	8	9	11	12	13	14	15	17	18	19	20
6	10	11	13	14	16	17	19	21	22	24	25	27
7	12	14	16	18	20	22	24	26	28	30	32	34
8	15	17	19	22	24	26	29	31	34	36	38	41
9	17	20	23	26	28	31	34	37	39	42	45	48
10	20	23	26	29	33	36	39	42	45	48	52	55
11	23	26	30	33	37	40	44	47	51	55	58	62
12	26	29	33	37	41	45	49	53	57	61	65	69
13	28	33	37	41	45	50	54	59	63	67	72	76
14	31	36	40	45	50	55	59	64	67	74	78	83
15	34	39	44	49	54	59	64	70	75	80	85	90
16	37	42	47	53	59	64	70	75	81	86	92	98
17	39	45	51	57	63	67	75	81	87	93	99	105
18	42	48	55	61	67	74	80	86	93	99	106	112
19	45	52	58	65	72	78	85	92	99	106	113	119
20	48	55	62	69	76	83	90	98	105	112	119	127

Critical Values of U for a One-Tailed Test at $\alpha = 0.05$ or for a Two-Tailed Test at $\alpha = 0.10$

n_1 \ n_2	9	10	11	12	13	14	15	16	17	18	19	20
1											0	0
2	1	1	1	2	2	2	3	3	3	4	4	4
3	3	4	5	5	6	7	7	8	9	9	10	11
4	6	7	8	9	10	11	12	14	15	16	17	18
5	9	11	12	13	15	16	18	19	20	22	23	25
6	12	14	16	17	19	21	23	25	26	28	30	32
7	15	17	19	21	24	26	28	30	33	35	37	39
8	18	20	23	26	28	31	33	36	39	41	44	47
9	21	24	27	30	33	36	39	42	45	48	51	54
10	24	27	31	34	37	41	44	48	51	55	58	62
11	27	31	34	38	42	46	50	54	57	61	65	69
12	30	34	38	42	47	51	55	60	64	68	72	77
13	33	37	42	47	51	56	61	65	70	75	80	84
14	36	41	46	51	56	61	66	71	77	82	87	92
15	39	44	50	55	61	66	72	77	83	88	94	100
16	42	48	54	60	65	71	77	83	89	95	101	107
17	45	51	57	64	70	77	83	89	96	102	109	115
18	48	55	61	68	75	82	88	95	102	109	116	123
19	51	58	65	72	80	87	94	101	109	116	123	130
20	54	62	69	77	84	92	100	107	115	123	130	138

Source: Adapted and abridged from Tables 1, 3, 5, and 7 of D. Auble, "Extended tables for the Mann-Whitney statistic," *Bulletin of the Institute of Educational Research at Indiana University* 1, No. 2 (1953) with the permission of the publisher.

APPENDIX N

Critical Values of *T* in the Wilcoxon Matched-Pairs Signed-Ranks Test (*n* ≤ 25)

	LEVEL OF SIGNIFICANCE FOR ONE-TAILED TEST		
	0.025	0.01	0.005
n	LEVEL OF SIGNIFICANCE FOR TWO-TAILED TEST		
	0.05	0.02	0.01
6	0	—	—
7	2	0	—
8	4	2	0
9	6	3	2
10	8	5	3
11	11	7	5
12	14	10	7
13	17	13	10
14	21	16	13
15	25	20	16
16	30	24	20
17	35	28	23
18	40	33	28
19	46	38	32
20	52	43	38
21	59	49	43
22	66	56	49
23	73	62	55
24	81	69	61
25	89	77	68

Source: Adapted from Table 1 of F. Wilcoxon, *Some Rapid Approximate Statistical Procedures* (New York: American Cyanamid Company, 1949), 13, with the permission of the publisher.

Critical Values d_L
and d_U of the
Durbin-Watson
Statistic D (Critical
Values Are
One-Sided)

	$\alpha = .05$									
	$P = 1$		$P = 2$		$P = 3$		$P = 4$		$P = 5$	
n	d_L	d_U	d_L	d_U	d_L	d_U	d_L	d_U	d_L	d_U
15	1.08	1.36	.95	1.54	.82	1.75	.69	1.97	.56	2.21
16	1.10	1.37	.98	1.54	.86	1.73	.74	1.93	.62	2.15
17	1.13	1.38	1.02	1.54	.90	1.71	.78	1.90	.67	2.10
18	1.16	1.39	1.05	1.53	.93	1.69	.82	1.87	.71	2.06
19	1.18	1.40	1.08	1.53	.97	1.68	.86	1.85	.75	2.02
20	1.20	1.41	1.10	1.54	1.00	1.68	.90	1.83	.79	1.99
21	1.22	1.42	1.13	1.54	1.03	1.67	.93	1.81	.83	1.96
22	1.24	1.43	1.15	1.54	1.05	1.66	.96	1.80	.86	1.94
23	1.26	1.44	1.17	1.54	1.08	1.66	.99	1.79	.90	1.92
24	1.27	1.45	1.19	1.55	1.10	1.66	1.01	1.78	.93	1.90
25	1.29	1.45	1.21	1.55	1.12	1.66	1.04	1.77	.95	1.89
26	1.30	1.46	1.22	1.55	1.14	1.65	1.06	1.76	.98	1.88
27	1.32	1.47	1.24	1.56	1.16	1.65	1.08	1.76	1.01	1.86
28	1.33	1.48	1.26	1.56	1.18	1.65	1.10	1.75	1.03	1.85
29	1.34	1.48	1.27	1.56	1.20	1.65	1.12	1.74	1.05	1.84
30	1.35	1.49	1.28	1.57	1.21	1.65	1.14	1.74	1.07	1.83
31	1.36	1.50	1.30	1.57	1.23	1.65	1.16	1.74	1.09	1.83
32	1.37	1.50	1.31	1.57	1.24	1.65	1.18	1.73	1.11	1.82
33	1.38	1.51	1.32	1.58	1.26	1.65	1.19	1.73	1.13	1.81
34	1.39	1.51	1.33	1.58	1.27	1.65	1.21	1.73	1.15	1.81
35	1.40	1.52	1.34	1.58	1.28	1.65	1.22	1.73	1.16	1.80
36	1.41	1.52	1.35	1.59	1.29	1.65	1.24	1.73	1.18	1.80
37	1.42	1.53	1.36	1.59	1.31	1.66	1.25	1.72	1.19	1.80
38	1.43	1.54	1.37	1.59	1.32	1.66	1.26	1.72	1.21	1.79
39	1.43	1.54	1.38	1.60	1.33	1.66	1.27	1.72	1.22	1.79
40	1.44	1.54	1.39	1.60	1.34	1.66	1.29	1.72	1.23	1.79
45	1.48	1.57	1.43	1.62	1.38	1.67	1.34	1.72	1.29	1.78
50	1.50	1.59	1.46	1.63	1.42	1.67	1.38	1.72	1.34	1.77
55	1.53	1.60	1.49	1.64	1.45	1.68	1.41	1.72	1.38	1.77
60	1.55	1.62	1.51	1.65	1.48	1.69	1.44	1.73	1.41	1.77
65	1.57	1.63	1.54	1.66	1.50	1.70	1.47	1.73	1.44	1.77
70	1.58	1.64	1.55	1.67	1.52	1.70	1.49	1.74	1.46	1.77
75	1.60	1.65	1.57	1.68	1.54	1.71	1.51	1.74	1.49	1.77
80	1.61	1.66	1.59	1.69	1.56	1.72	1.53	1.74	1.51	1.77
85	1.62	1.67	1.60	1.70	1.57	1.72	1.55	1.75	1.52	1.77
90	1.63	1.68	1.61	1.70	1.59	1.73	1.57	1.75	1.54	1.78
95	1.64	1.69	1.62	1.71	1.60	1.73	1.58	1.75	1.56	1.78
100	1.65	1.69	1.63	1.72	1.61	1.74	1.59	1.76	1.57	1.78

(continued)

n = number of observations; P = number of independent variables.

Source: This table is reproduced from *Biometrika*, 41 (1951): 173 and 175, with the permission of the *Biometrika* Trustees.

$\alpha = .01$

n	P = 1		P = 2		P = 3		P = 4		P = 5	
	d_L	d_U	d_L	d_U	d_L	d_U	d_L	d_U	d_L	d_U
15	.81	1.07	.70	1.25	.59	1.46	.49	1.70	.39	1.96
16	.84	1.09	.74	1.25	.63	1.44	.53	1.66	.44	1.90
17	.87	1.10	.77	1.25	.67	1.43	.57	1.63	.48	1.85
18	.90	1.12	.80	1.26	.71	1.42	.61	1.60	.52	1.80
19	.93	1.13	.83	1.26	.74	1.41	.65	1.58	.56	1.77
20	.95	1.15	.86	1.27	.77	1.41	.68	1.57	.60	1.74
21	.97	1.16	.89	1.27	.80	1.41	.72	1.55	.63	1.71
22	1.00	1.17	.91	1.28	.83	1.40	.75	1.54	.66	1.69
23	1.02	1.19	.94	1.29	.86	1.40	.77	1.53	.70	1.67
24	1.04	1.20	.96	1.30	.88	1.41	.80	1.53	.72	1.66
25	1.05	1.21	.98	1.30	.90	1.41	.83	1.52	.75	1.65
26	1.07	1.22	1.00	1.31	.93	1.41	.85	1.52	.78	1.64
27	1.09	1.23	1.02	1.32	.95	1.41	.88	1.51	.81	1.63
28	1.10	1.24	1.04	1.32	.97	1.41	.90	1.51	.83	1.62
29	1.12	1.25	1.05	1.33	.99	1.42	.92	1.51	.85	1.61
30	1.13	1.26	1.07	1.34	1.01	1.42	.94	1.51	.88	1.61
31	1.15	1.27	1.08	1.34	1.02	1.42	.96	1.51	.90	1.60
32	1.16	1.28	1.10	1.35	1.04	1.43	.98	1.51	.92	1.60
33	1.17	1.29	1.11	1.36	1.05	1.43	1.00	1.51	.94	1.59
34	1.18	1.30	1.13	1.36	1.07	1.43	1.01	1.51	.95	1.59
35	1.19	1.31	1.14	1.37	1.08	1.44	1.03	1.51	.97	1.59
36	1.21	1.32	1.15	1.38	1.10	1.44	1.04	1.51	.99	1.59
37	1.22	1.32	1.16	1.38	1.11	1.45	1.06	1.51	1.00	1.59
38	1.23	1.33	1.18	1.39	1.12	1.45	1.07	1.52	1.02	1.58
39	1.24	1.34	1.19	1.39	1.14	1.45	1.09	1.52	1.03	1.58
40	1.25	1.34	1.20	1.40	1.15	1.46	1.10	1.52	1.05	1.58
45	1.29	1.38	1.24	1.42	1.20	1.48	1.16	1.53	1.11	1.58
50	1.32	1.40	1.28	1.45	1.24	1.49	1.20	1.54	1.16	1.59
55	1.36	1.43	1.32	1.47	1.28	1.51	1.25	1.55	1.21	1.59
60	1.38	1.45	1.35	1.48	1.32	1.52	1.28	1.56	1.25	1.60
65	1.41	1.47	1.38	1.50	1.35	1.53	1.31	1.57	1.28	1.61
70	1.43	1.49	1.40	1.52	1.37	1.55	1.34	1.58	1.31	1.61
75	1.45	1.50	1.42	1.53	1.39	1.56	1.37	1.59	1.34	1.62
80	1.47	1.52	1.44	1.54	1.42	1.57	1.39	1.60	1.36	1.62
85	1.48	1.53	1.46	1.55	1.43	1.58	1.41	1.60	1.39	1.63
90	1.50	1.54	1.47	1.56	1.45	1.59	1.43	1.61	1.41	1.64
95	1.51	1.55	1.49	1.57	1.47	1.60	1.45	1.62	1.42	1.64
100	1.52	1.56	1.50	1.58	1.48	1.60	1.46	1.63	1.44	1.65

n = number of observations; P = number of independent variables.
Source: This table is reproduced from *Biometrika*, 41 (1951): 173 and 175, with the permission of the *Biometrika* Trustees.

**Lower and Upper
Critical Values W
of Wilcoxon
Signed-Ranks Test**

n	One-Tailed: $\alpha = .05$ Two-Tailed: $\alpha = .10$	$\alpha = .025$ $\alpha = .05$	$\alpha = .01$ $\alpha = .02$	$\alpha = .005$ $\alpha = .01$
	(Lower, Upper)			
5	0,15	—,—	—,—	—,—
6	2,19	0,21	—,—	—,—
7	3,25	2,26	0,28	—,—
8	5,31	3,33	1,35	0,36
9	8,37	5,40	3,42	1,44
10	10,45	8,47	5,50	3,52
11	13,53	10,56	7,59	5,61
12	17,61	13,65	10,68	7,71
13	21,70	17,74	12,79	10,81
14	25,80	21,84	16,89	13,92
15	30,90	25,95	19,101	16,104
16	35,101	29,107	23,113	19,117
17	41,112	34,119	27,126	23,130
18	47,124	40,131	32,139	27,144
19	53,137	46,144	37,153	32,158
20	60,150	52,158	43,167	37,173

Source: Adapted from Table 2 of F. Wilcoxon and R. A. Wilcox, *Some Rapid Approximate Statistical Procedures* (Pearl River, NY: Lederle Laboratories, 1964), with permission of the American Cyanamid Company.

Control Chart Factors

Number of Observations in Sample	d_2	d_3	D_3	D_4	A_2
2	1.128	0.853	0	3.267	1.880
3	1.693	0.888	0	2.575	1.023
4	2.059	0.880	0	2.282	0.729
5	2.326	0.864	0	2.114	0.577
6	2.534	0.848	0	2.004	0.483
7	2.704	0.833	0.076	1.924	0.419
8	2.847	0.820	0.136	1.864	0.373
9	2.970	0.808	0.184	1.816	0.337
10	3.078	0.797	0.223	1.777	0.308
11	3.173	0.787	0.256	1.744	0.285
12	3.258	0.778	0.283	1.717	0.266
13	3.336	0.770	0.307	1.693	0.249
14	3.407	0.763	0.328	1.672	0.235
15	3.472	0.756	0.347	1.653	0.223
16	3.532	0.750	0.363	1.637	0.212
17	3.588	0.744	0.378	1.622	0.203
18	3.640	0.739	0.391	1.609	0.194
19	3.689	0.733	0.404	1.596	0.187
20	3.735	0.729	0.415	1.585	0.180
21	3.778	0.724	0.425	1.575	0.173
22	3.819	0.720	0.435	1.565	0.167
23	3.858	0.716	0.443	1.557	0.162
24	3.895	0.712	0.452	1.548	0.157
25	3.931	0.708	0.459	1.541	0.153

Source: Reprinted from ASTM-STP 15D by kind permission of the American Society for Testing and Materials.

Answers to Selected Odd-Numbered Problems

Chapter 1

1-1. This application is primarily descriptive in nature. The owner wishes to develop a presentation. He will most likely use charts, graphs, tables, and numerical measures to describe his data.

1-3. A bar chart is used whenever you want to display data that has already been categorized, whereas a histogram is used to display data over a range of values for the factor under consideration. Another fundamental difference is that there typically are gaps between the bars on a bar chart but there are no gaps between the bars of a histogram.

1-5. Statistical inference tools are useful in situations where a decision maker needs to reach an estimate about a population based on a subset of data taken from the population. For example, a decision maker might want to know the starting annual salary of all attorneys in the United States. If it is not feasible or possible to look at the salary data for all attorneys, the decision maker could look at a subset of attorneys and use statistical inference to reach a conclusion about the population of all attorneys.

1-7. Hypothesis testing is used whenever one is interested in testing claims that concern a population. Using information taken from samples, hypothesis testing evaluates the claim and makes a conclusion about the population from which the sample was taken. Estimation is used when one is interested in knowing something about all the data, but the population is too large, or the data set is too big to work with all the data. In estimation, no claim is being made or tested.

1-9. The major advantage of a graph is it allows a more complete representation of information in the data. Not only can a decision maker visualize the center of the data but also how spread out the data are. An average, for instance, nicely represents the center of a data set, but contains no information of how spread out the data are.

1-11. The company could use statistical inference to determine whether its light bulbs last longer. Because it is not possible to examine every light bulb that could be produced, the company could examine a subset of its light bulbs and compare the average life of the subset to the average life of a subset of the competitor's bulb. By using statistical inference tools the company could reach a conclusion about whether its bulbs last longer or not.

1-13. Student answers will vary depending on the periodical selected and the periodical's issue date, but all should address the three parts of the question.

1-15. a. A commonly used measure of the center of the data is the mean or average. The executive could calculate the average age of the people in the market area and use the average as the center value.

b. To determine a value for the percentage of people in the market area who are senior citizens, the executives would rely on estimation—a set of statistical techniques that allow one to know something about a data set by using a subset of the data whenever the data set is too large to work with all the data.

c. The executives might want to test the hypothesis that the percentage of senior citizens in the market area is greater than the percentage of senior citizens nationwide. The executives could also test the hypothesis that the percentage of senior citizens is greater than or less than a specific value—say, 27%.

1-17. A leading question is one that is designed to elicit a specific response, or one that might influence the respondent's answer by its wording. The question is posed so that the respondent believes the researcher has a specific answer in mind when the question is asked or is worded in such a way that the respondent feels obliged to provide an answer consistent with the question. For example, a question such as "Do you agree with the experts who recommend that more tax dollars be given to clean up dangerous and unhealthy pollution?" could cause respondents to provide the answer that they think will be consistent with the "experts" with whom they do not want to disagree. Leading questions should be avoided in surveys because they may introduce bias.

1-19. No. The bank would most likely use a written survey or a telephone survey to collect the customer satisfaction data.

1-21. a. Observation would be the most likely method. Observers could be located at various bike routes and observe the number of riders with and without helmets. This would likely be better than asking people if they wear a helmet since the popular response might be to say yes even when they don't always do so.

b. A telephone survey to gas stations in the state. This could be a cost-effective way of getting data from across the state. The respondent would have the information and be able to provide the correct price.

c. A written survey of passengers. This could be given out on the plane before the plane lands and passengers could drop the surveys in a box as they deplane. This method would likely garner higher response rates compared to sending the survey to passengers' mailing address and asking them to return the completed survey by mail.

1-23. The two types of validity mentioned in the section are internal validity and external validity. For this problem, external validity is easier to address. It simply means the sampling method chosen will be sufficient to ensure that the results based on the sample can be generalized to the population of all students. Internal validity would involve making sure the data gathering method, for instance a questionnaire, accurately determines the respondent's attitude toward the registration process.

1-25. This data could have been collected through observation or experiment. Employees of the USDA could provide periodic reports of fire ant activity in their region. Likewise, scientists studying the spread of fire ants may have conducted experiments that indicate the rate of spread under certain conditions.

1-27. There are many potential sources of bias associated with data collection. If data are to be collected using personal interviews, it will be important that the interviewer is trained so that interviewer bias, arising from the way survey questions are asked, is not injected into the survey. If the survey is conducted using either a mail survey or a telephone survey, then it is important to be aware of nonresponse bias from those who do not respond to the mailing or refuse to answer your calls. You must also be careful when selecting your survey subjects that selection bias is not a problem. In order to have useful, reliable data that are representative of the true student opinions regarding campus food service, it is necessary that the data collection process be conducted in a manner that reduces or eliminates the potential for these and other sources of potential bias.

1-29. Student answers will vary. However, the issue questions should be designed to gather the desired data regarding customers' preferences for the use of the space. Demographic questions should provide data that can be broken down appropriately so that Gold's Gym managers can determine which subset of customers has what opinion about this issue. Regarding questionnaire layout, look at neatness and answer location space. Make sure questions are properly worded, use reasonable vocabulary, and are not leading questions.

1-31. The results of the survey are based on telephone interviews with 1,007 national adults, aged 18 and older (http://www.gallup.com/poll/content/?ci=18286). Students may also answer that the survey could have been conducted using personal interviews. Because telephone interviews were used to collect the survey data there are nonresponse biases associated with sampled adults who are not at home when phoned or adults who refuse to participate in the survey. There is also the problem that some adults do not have a phone. If personal interviews are used to collect the data, then it is important to guard against nonresponse bias from those sampled adults who refuse to be interviewed. There is also the problem of selection bias. In phone interviews we may miss the people who work evenings and nights. If personal interviews are used, we must be careful to select a representative sample of the adult population, not just those who appear willing or interested in participating.

1-33. a. Because the population is spread over a large geographical area, a cluster random sample could be selected to reduce travel costs.
b. A stratified random sample would probably be used to keep sample size as small as possible.
c. Most likely a convenience sample would be used since doing a statistical sample would be too difficult. It might be possible to survey every 15th customer using a systematic random sampling method.

1-35. From a numbered list of all customers who own a certificate of deposit the bank would need to randomly determine a starting point between 1 and k, where k would be equal to 25,000/1,000 = 25. This could be done using a random number table or by having a statistical package or a spreadsheet generate a random number between 1 and 25. Once this value is determined the bank would select that numbered customer as the first sampled customer and then select every 25th customer after that until 100 customers are sampled.

1-37. Statistical sampling techniques consist of those sampling methods that select samples based on chance. Nonstatistical sampling techniques consist of those methods of selecting samples using convenience, judgment, or other non-chance processes. In convenience sampling samples are chosen because they are easy or convenient to sample. There is no attempt to randomize the selection of the selected items. In convenience sampling not every item in the population has a random chance of being selected. Rather, items are sampled based on their convenience alone. Thus, convenience sampling is not a statistical sampling method.

1-39. A census is an enumeration of the entire set of measurements taken from the population as a whole. While in some cases the items of interest are obtained from people such as through a survey, in many instances the items of interest come from a product or other inanimate object. For example, a study could be conducted to determine the defect rate for items made on a production line. The census would consist of all items produced on the line in a defined period of time.

1-41. a. Stratified random sampling
b. Simple random sampling or possibly cluster random sampling
c. Systematic random sampling
d. Stratified random sampling

1-43. These percentages would be parameters since all U.S. colleges are included.

1-45. a. Student answers will vary.
b. Cluster sampling could be used to ensure that you get all types of food. Make each cluster the area where certain foods are located (that is, aisle, row, shelf, etc.).
c. Cluster sampling would give you a better idea of the inventory of all types of food. Simple random sampling could possibly end up with looking at only two or three food types.

1-47. a. The population should be all users of cross-country ski lots in Colorado.
b. Several sampling techniques could be selected. Be sure that some method of ensuring randomness is discussed. In addition, some students might give greater weight to frequent users of the lots, in which case the population would really be user days rather than individual users.
c. Students using Excel should use the Data Tab – Data Analysis – Random Number Generation process. Students' answers will differ since Excel generates different streams of random numbers each time it is used. Because the application requires integer numbers, the Decrease Decimal option should be used.

1-49. Qualitative data are categories or numerical values that represent categories. Quantitative data are data that are purely numerical.

1-51. a. Time-series
b. Cross-sectional
c. Time-series
d. Cross-sectional

1-53. Since the circles involve a ranking from best to worst, this would be ordinal data.

1-55. a. Nominal data
  b. Ratio data
  c. Nominal data
  d. Ratio data
  e. Ratio data
  f. Nominal data
  g. Ratio data
1-57. Vehicle Name—Nominal
  Sports Car—Nominal
  Sport Utility—Nominal
  Wagon—Nominal
  Minivan—Nominal
  Pickup—Nominal
  All-Wheel-Drive—Nominal
  Rear-Wheel-Drive—Nominal
  Suggested Retail Price—Ratio
  Dealer Cost—Ratio
  Engine Size—Ratio
  Number of Cylinders—Ratio
  Horsepower—Ratio
  City MPG—Ratio
  Highway MPG—Ratio
  Weight—Ratio
  Wheelbase—Ratio
  Length—Ratio
  Width—Ratio
1-59. Nominal data or ordinal data
1-61. Ratings are typical uses of ordinal scale data. And since ratings are based on personal opinion, even though people are using the same scale a direct comparison between the two ratings is not possible. This is a common problem when people are asked to rate an object using an ordinal scale.
1-63. Answers will vary with the student, but a good discussion should include the following factors:
  sampling techniques and possible problems selecting a representative sample
  determining how to measure confidence
  structuring questions to avoid bias
  the measurement scale associated with the questions
  the fact this poll is specifically intended to develop time-series data
1-65. Answers will vary with the student.
1-67. a. They would probably want to sample the cartons as they come off the assembly line at the Illinois plant for a specified time period. They would want to use a random sample. One method would be to take a systematic random sample. They could then calculate the percentage of the sample that had an unacceptable texture.
  b. The product is going to be ruined after testing it. You would not want to ruin the entire product that comes off the assembly line.

Chapter 2

2-1. Given $n = 2,000$, the minimum number of groups for a grouped data frequency distribution determined using the $2^k \geq n$ guideline is

$$2^k \geq n \quad \text{or} \quad 2^{11} = 2,048 \geq 2,000$$
Thus, use $k = 11$ groups.

2-3.

x	Frequency
0	1
1	0
2	2
3	4
4	1
5	2
6	5
7	6
8	1
9	1
10	1
11	0
12	1
	Total = 25

2-5.

Class	Frequency	Relative Frequency	Cumulative Relative Frequency
7.85 – <7.95	6	0.12	0.12
7.95 – <8.05	18	0.36	0.48
8.05 – <8.15	12	0.24	0.72
8.15 – <8.25	5	0.10	0.82
8.25 – <8.35	9	0.18	1.00

2-7. a. Proportion of days in which no shortages occurred = $1 -$ proportion of days in which shortages occurred = $1 - 0.24 = 0.76$.
  b. Less than $20 off implies that overage was less than $20 and the shortage was less than $20 = (proportion of overages less $20) $-$ (proportion of shortages at most $20) = $0.56 - 0.08 = 0.48$.
  c. Proportion of days with less than $40 over or at most $20 short = proportion of days with less than $40 over $-$ proportion of days with more than $20 short = $0.96 - 0.08 = 0.86$.

2-9. a.

CLASS	FREQUENCY	RELATIVE FREQUENCY
2–3	2	0.0333
4–5	25	0.4167
6–7	26	0.4333
8–9	6	0.1000
10–11	1	0.0167

b. The cumulative frequency distribution is

CLASS	FREQUENCY	CUMULATIVE FREQUENCY
2–3	2	2
4–5	25	27
6–7	26	53
8–9	6	59
10–11	1	60

c.

CLASS	FREQUENCY	RELATIVE FREQUENCY	CUM. REL. FREQ.
2–3	2	0.0333	0.0333
4–5	25	0.4167	0.4500
6–7	26	0.4333	0.8833
8–9	6	0.1000	0.9833
10–11	1	0.0167	1.0000

The relative frequency histogram is

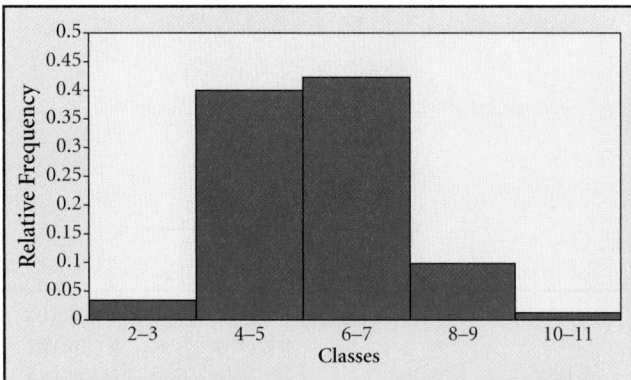

d. The ogive is a graph of the cumulative relative frequency distribution.

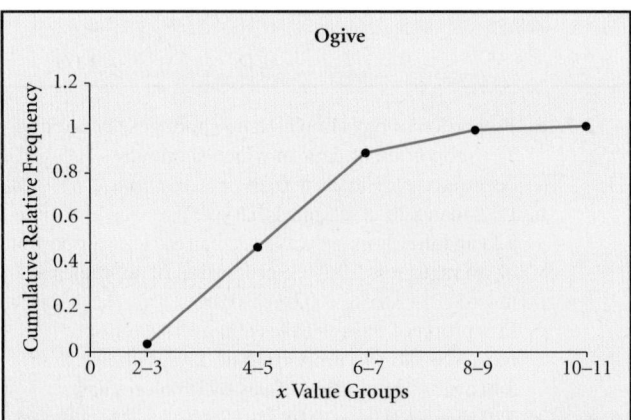

2-11. a.

	Knowledge Level			
	Savvy	**Experienced**	**Novice**	**Total**
Online Investors	32	220	148	400
Traditional Investors	8	58	134	200
Total	40	278	282	600

b.

	Knowledge Level		
	Savvy	**Experienced**	**Novice**
Online Investors	0.0533	0.3667	0.2467
Traditional Investors	0.0133	0.0967	0.2233

c. The proportion that were both online and experienced is 0.3667.

d. The proportion of online investors is 0.6667.

2-13. a. The turnaround times are sorted from smallest to largest to create the data array.

77	79	80	83	84	85	86
86	86	86	86	86	87	87
87	88	88	88	88	89	89
89	89	89	90	90	91	91
92	92	92	92	93	93	93
94	94	94	94	94	95	95
95	96	97	98	98	99	101

b.

Turnaround Time (Classes)	Frequency
77–81	3
82–86	9
87–91	16
92–96	16
97–101	5
	Total = 49

c.

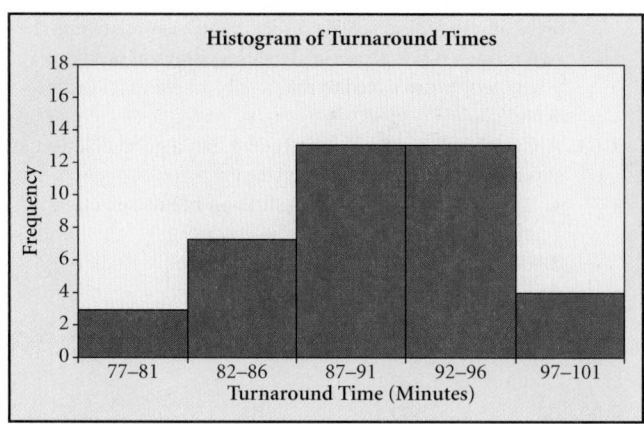

d.

Turnaround Time (Classes)	Frequency	Relative Frequency	Cumulative Relative Frequency
77–81	3	0.0612	0.0612
82–86	9	0.1837	0.2449
87–91	16	0.3265	0.5714
92–96	16	0.3265	0.8980
97–101	5	0.1020	1.0000
Total =	49		

The percentage of sampled planes with turnaround times greater than 96 minutes is 10.20%.

2-15. a.

Classes	Frequency	Relative Frequency	Cumulative Relative Frequency
(105<115)	1	0.04	0.04
(115<125)	1	0.04	0.08
(125<135)	2	0.08	0.16
(135<145)	1	0.04	0.20
(145<155)	1	0.04	0.24
(155<165)	7	0.28	0.52
(165<175)	4	0.16	0.68
(175<185)	3	0.12	0.80
(185<195)	2	0.08	0.88
(195<205)	0	0.00	0.88
(205<215)	3	0.12	1.00

b. The data show 8 of the 25, or 0.32, of the salaries greater than 175.

c. The data show 18 of the 25, or 0.72, having salaries that are at most $205,000 and at least $135,000.

2-17. a.

Classes	Frequency
51–53	7
54–56	15
57–59	28
60–62	16
63–65	21
66–68	9
69–71	2
72–74	2

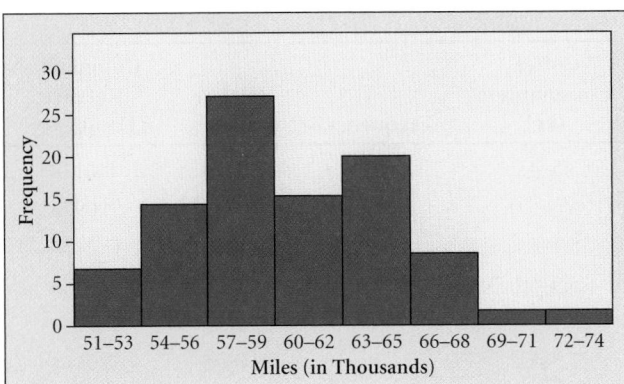

b. The tread life of at least 50% of the tires is 60,000 or more. The top 10% is greater than 66,000 and the longest tread life is 74,000.

c.

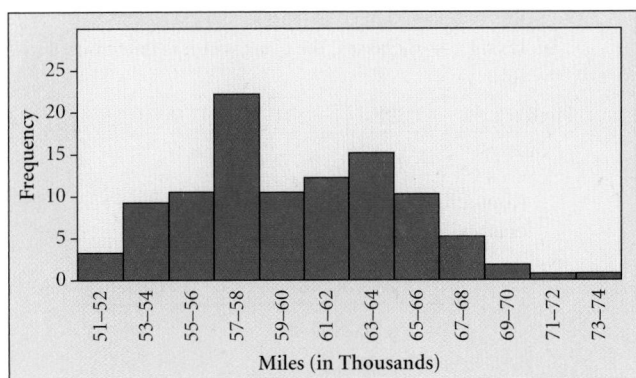

Classes	Frequency
51–52	3
53–54	9
55–56	10
57–58	22
59–60	10
61–62	12
63–64	15
65–66	10
67–68	5
69–70	2
71–72	1
73–74	1

Students will probably say that the 12 classes give better information because they allow you to see more detail about the number of miles the tires can go.

2-19. a.

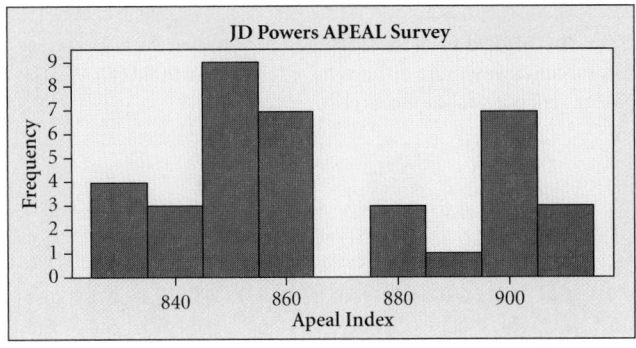

b. The 2005 average is $\bar{x} = (32{,}043/37) = 866.03$, which is larger than the past industry average.

c. The fifth class is vacant. This suggests that there is a distinct gap in consumers' satisfaction between the low- and high-rated automobiles.

2-21. a. There are $n = 59$ different airlines that flew into and out of Orlando in 2004. Then using the $2^k \geq n$ guideline, we would need at least $k = 6$ classes.

b. Using $k = 6$ classes, the class width is determined as follows:

$$w = \frac{\text{High} - \text{Low}}{\text{Classes}} = \frac{5,398,141 - 234}{6} = \frac{5,397,907}{6} = 899,651.17$$

Rounding this up to the nearest 1,000 passengers, the class width is 900,000.

c.

Passengers	Frequency
0–899,999	48
900,000–1,799,999	7
1,800,000–2,699,999	1
2,700,000–3,599,999	1
3,600,000–4,499,999	1
4,500,000–5,399,999	1

This shows that most airlines load and unload a passenger total of under 900,000.

d. Based on the results in part c, the frequency histogram is as follows:

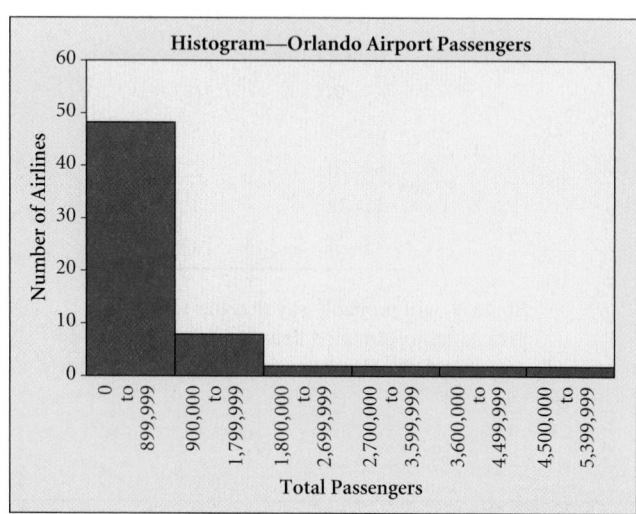

Based on the data from the Orlando International Airport, we see that far and away more airlines have fewer than 900,000 passengers per year at the airport.

2-23. a.

3.5	3.8	4.4	4.5	4.6	4.6	4.7	4.7	4.8	4.8	5.0	5.0
5.0	5.0	5.2	5.3	5.3	5.3	5.3	5.3	5.3	5.4	5.4	5.4
5.4	5.5	5.5	5.6	5.6	5.7	5.7	5.7	5.7	5.8	5.8	5.9
5.9	6.0	6.0	6.0	6.0	6.0	6.0	6.0	6.0	6.1	6.1	6.1
6.1	6.1	6.2	6.2	6.2	6.3	6.3	6.3	6.3	6.3	6.3	6.4
6.4	6.4	6.4	6.4	6.4	6.4	6.5	6.5	6.5	6.5	6.5	6.5
6.5	6.5	6.5	6.6	6.6	6.6	6.6	6.6	6.7	6.7	6.7	6.7
6.7	6.8	6.8	6.8	6.8	6.8	6.8	6.8	6.8	6.9	6.9	7.0
7.0	7.0	7.0	7.1	7.1	7.1	7.2	7.2	7.2	7.2	7.2	7.3
7.4	7.4	7.4	7.5	7.5	7.5	7.5	7.5	7.6	7.6	7.6	7.6
7.6	7.6	7.6	7.7	7.7	7.8	7.8	7.8	7.9	7.9	7.9	7.9
8.0	8.0	8.0	8.0	8.0	8.3	8.4	8.4	8.4	8.6	8.9	10.1

b.

Coffee Consumption (kg)	Frequency
3.5–4.2	2
4.3–5.0	12
5.1–5.8	21
5.9–6.6	45
6.7–7.4	31
7.5–8.2	26
8.3–9.0	6
9.1–9.8	0
9.9–10.6	1

c.

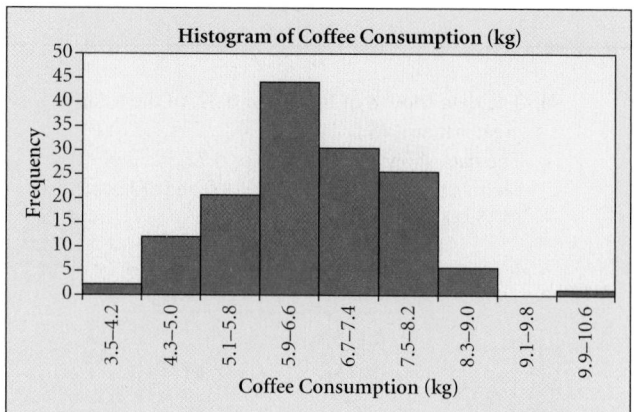

The histogram shows the shape of the distribution. This histogram is showing that fewer people consume small and large quantities and that most individuals consume between 5.1 and 8.2 kg of coffee, with the most individuals consuming between 5.9 and 6.6.

d.

Coffee Consumption (kg)	Frequency	Relative Freqency	Cumulative Relative Frequency
3.5–4.2	2	0.0139	0.0139
4.3–5.0	12	0.0833	0.0972
5.1–5.8	21	0.1458	0.2431
5.9–6.6	45	0.3125	0.5556
6.7–7.4	31	0.2153	0.7708
7.5–8.2	26	0.1806	0.9514
8.3–9.0	6	0.0417	0.9931
9.1–9.8	0	0.0000	0.9931
9.9–10.6	1	0.0069	1.0000
Total	144		

2-25. a.

b.

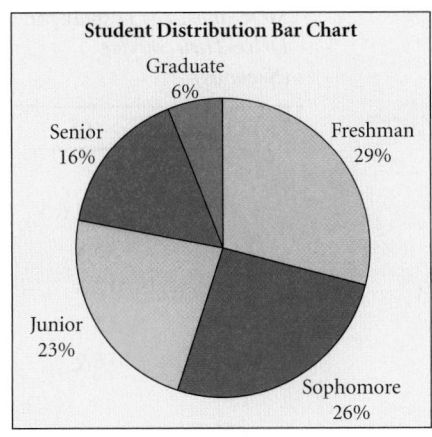

c. A case can be made for either a bar chart or a pie chart. Pie charts are especially good at showing how the total is divided into parts. The bar chart is best to draw attention to specific results. In this case, a discussion might be centered on the apparent attrition that takes place in the number of students between the Freshman and Senior years.

2-27.

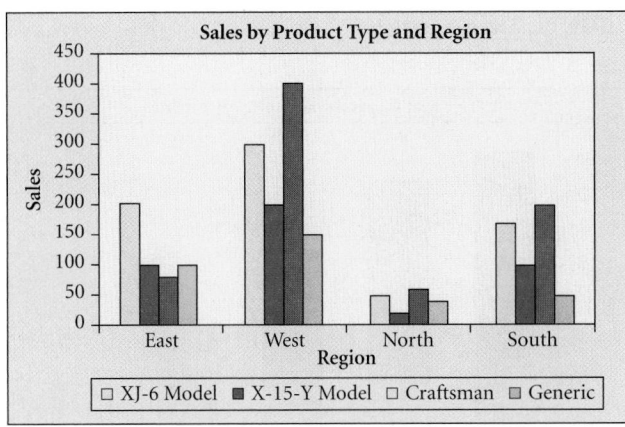

Still another possible way is a "stacked" bar chart.

2-29. a.

b.

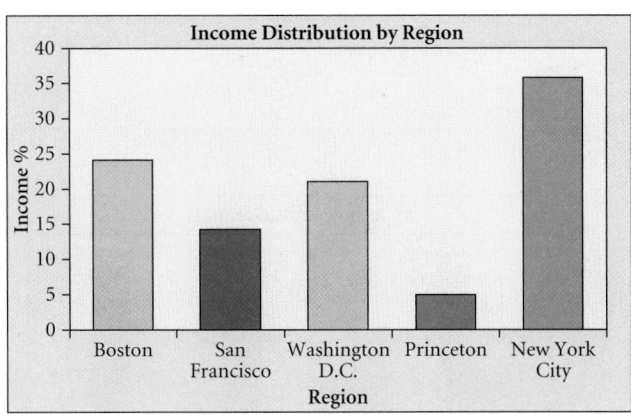

c. Both charts clearly indicate which regions produce the greatest percentage of income. The bar chart, however, makes it easier to compare percentages across regions.

2-31. a.

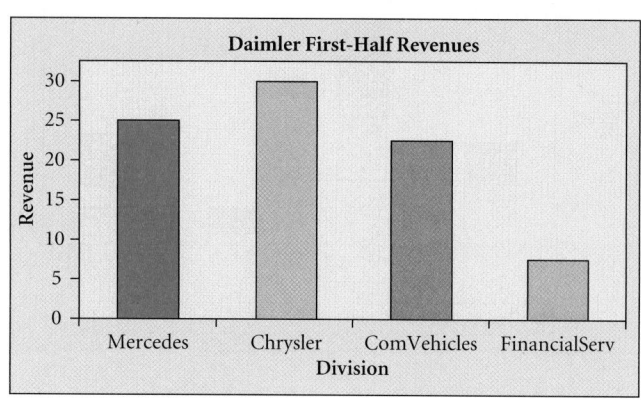

b. Proportion of Vehicle Revenue
= 1 − Proportion of Financial Services
= 1 − 0.0985 = 0.9015

2-33. a. Pie charts are typically used to show how a total is divided into parts. In this case, the total of the five ratios is not a meaningful value. Thus, a pie chart showing each ratio as a fraction of the total would not be meaningful, and so a pie chart is not the most appropriate tool. A bar chart would be appropriate.

b.

2-35.

2-37. a.

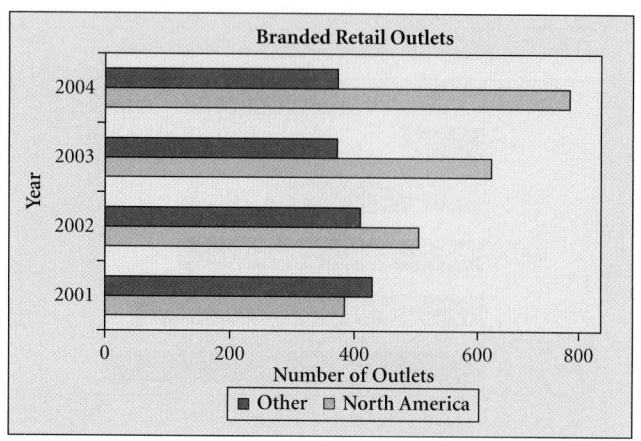

Stem-and-Leaf Display for Drive-Thru Service (Seconds)

Stem Unit	10
6	8
7	1 3 4 6 9
8	3 5 8
9	0 2 3
10	3 5
11	0 6 9
12	
13	0 4 8
14	5 6 7
15	6 6
16	2
17	8
18	1

b. The most frequent speed of service is between 70 and 79 seconds.

2-39. a. The bar graph is

b.

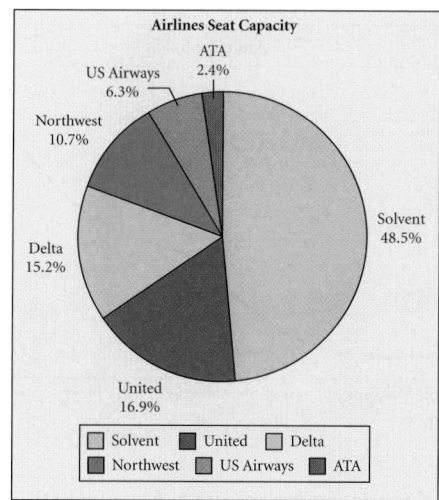

c. The percent of seat capacity of those in bankruptcy =
16.9 + 15.2 + 10.7 + 6.3 + 2.4 = 51.5%.
Since this is larger than 50%, their statement was
correct.

2-41. a. A bar chart is an appropriate graph since there are two
categories, males and females. A pie chart could also
be used to display the data.

b.

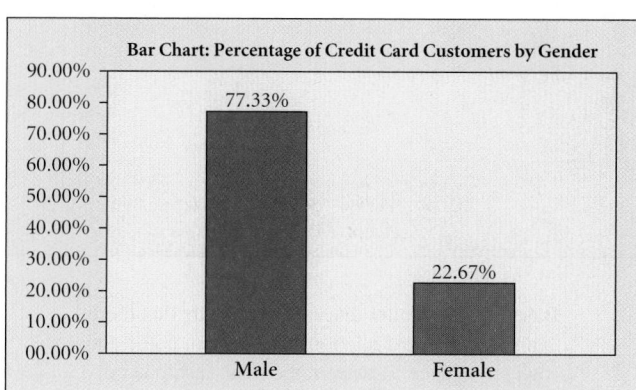

2-43. a.

Stem-and-Leaf Display: Days

Stem-and-leaf of Days N = 50	
Stem Unit = 10.0	**Leaf Unit = 1.0**
0	4
0	7
1	0344
1	566677889
2	00012244
2	5666777888999
3	000122344
3	5669
4	0

b. The shape of the data is slightly skewed to the left.
The center of the data appears to be between 24
and 26.

$$\bar{x} = \frac{2428}{50} = 24.28$$

This and the data indicate that the mean is larger than
indicated by J.D. Power.

2-45. a.

UNIVERSITY RELATED	RELIGIOUS AFFILIATED	MUNICIPALLY OWNED	PRIVATELY HELD
$6,398	$3,591	$4,613	$5,191

b.

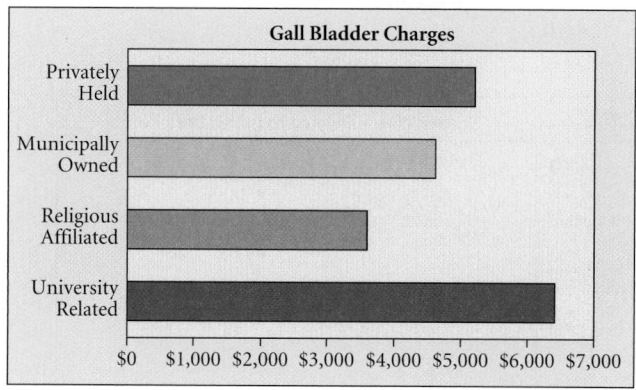

c. A pie chart is used to display the parts of a total.
In this case, the total charges of the four hospital
types is not a meaningful number, so a pie
chart showing how that total is divided among the
four hospital types would not be useful or
appropriate.

2-47.

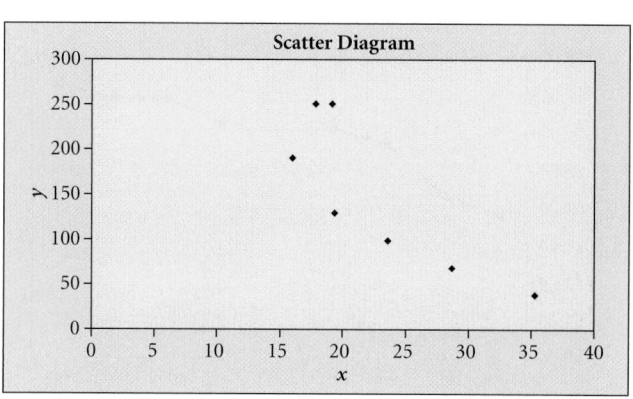

There is negative linear relationship between the two
variables.

2-49. a.

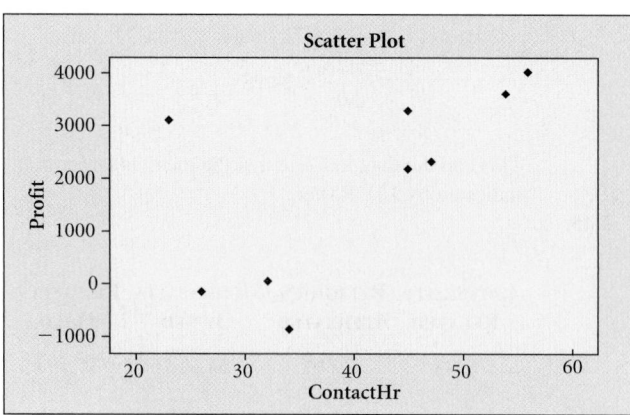

There appears to be a curvilinear relationship between the dependent and independent variables.

b.

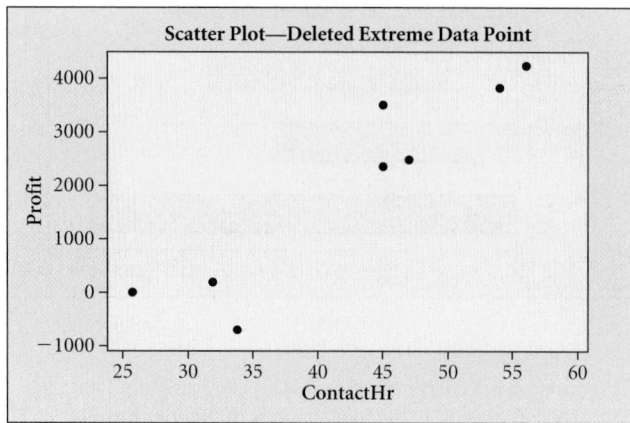

Having removed the extreme data point, the relationship between dependent and independent variables seems to be linear and positive.

2-51.

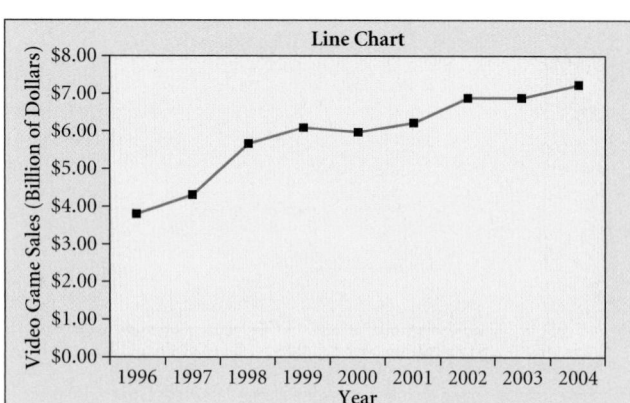

The line chart illustrates that over the 9-year period between 1996 and 2004, video game sales in the United States have grown quite steadily from just below $4 billion to over $7 billion.

2-53. a.

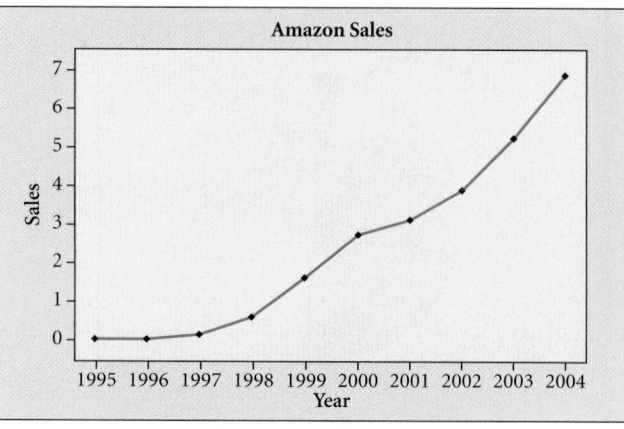

b. The relationship appears to be curvilinear.
c. The largest difference in sales occurred between 2003 and 2004. That difference was $6.9211 - 5.2637 = 1.6574$ $billions.

2-55.

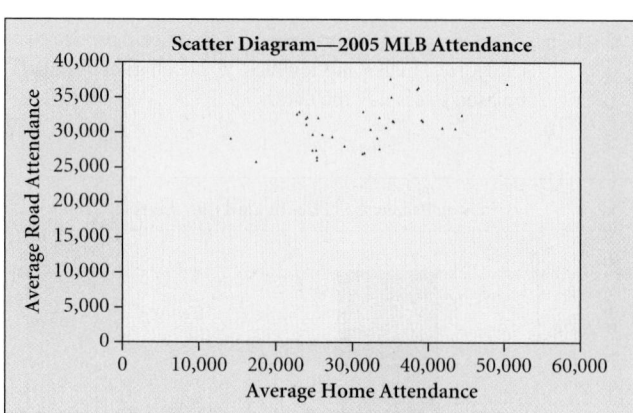

Based on the scatter diagram, it appears that there is a positive linear relationship between home and road attendance. However, the relationship is not perfect.

2-57.

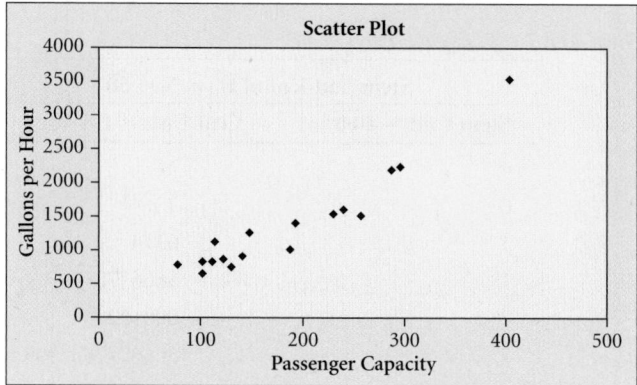

Based on the scatter diagram, we see there is a strong positive linear relationship between passenger capacity and fuel consumption per hour.

2-59. a.

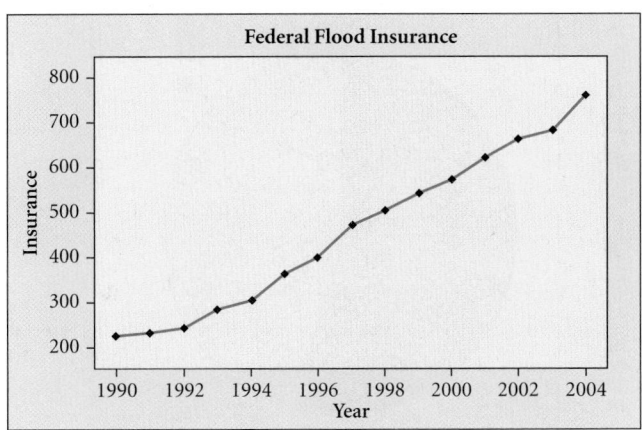

b. The relationship appears to be linear and positive.
c. The average equals the sum divided by the number of data points: 6,830/15 = 455.33.

2-61. a.

Gasoline prices have trended upward over the 36-year period with some short periods of decline. However, price rises have been very steep since 1999.

b.

c. Thus, while gasoline prices were high in California in 2005, they were not the worst that have occurred in that state.

2-63. A relative frequency distribution deals with the percentage of the total observations that fall into each class rather than the number that fall into each class. Sometimes decision makers are more interested in percentages than numbers. Politicians, for instance, are often more interested in the percentage of voters who will vote for them (more than 50%) than the total number of votes they will get. Relative frequencies are also valuable when comparing distributions from two populations that have different total numbers.

2-65. Pie charts are effectively used when the data set is made up of parts of a whole, and therefore each part can be converted to a percentage. For instance, if the data involve a budget, a pie chart can represent the percentage of the budget each category represents. Or, if the data involve total company sales, a pie chart can be used to represent the percentage contribution to sales for each major product line.

2-67. a.

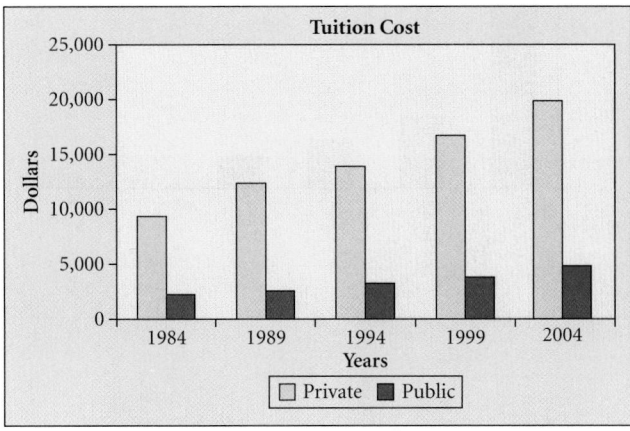

b. Student answers will vary but should include identifying that both private and public college tuition costs have more than doubled in the 20 years of data.

2-69. a.

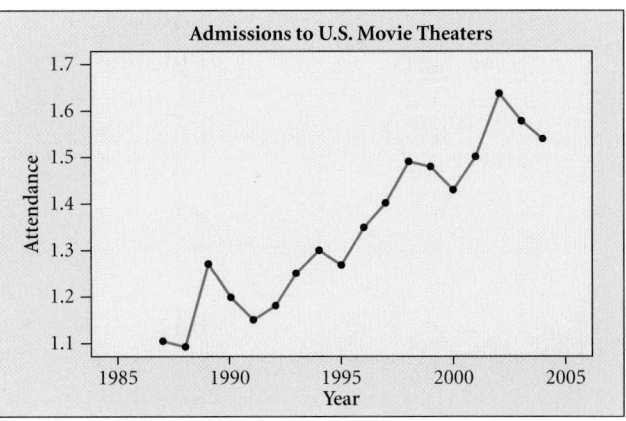

b. It appears that there is a positive linear relationship between the attendance and the year. However, there does appear to be a sharp decline in the last two years. It could be evidence of a normal cycle since a similar decline occurred in 1990/91, which was followed by a steady climb in attendance for six of the next seven years.

2-71. a.

Classes	Frequency
0.1 to 3	27
3.1 to 6.0	9
6.1 to 9.0	6
9.1 to 12.0	4
12.1 to 15.0	0
15.1 to 18.0	2

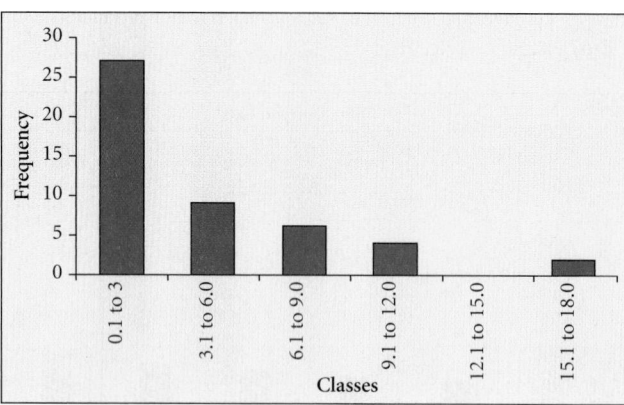

b.

Stem-and-Leaf Display	
Stem unit	**1**
0	3 4 5 7
1	0 0 0 0 4 5 5 9
2	0 0 0 0 4 5 5 5 7
3	0 0 0 0 0 2 5 5 5 5 6
4	0 0 0
5	
6	4 5
7	5
8	3
9	0 0 2
10	
11	0
12	0 0
13	
14	
15	
16	0
17	5

c.

d.

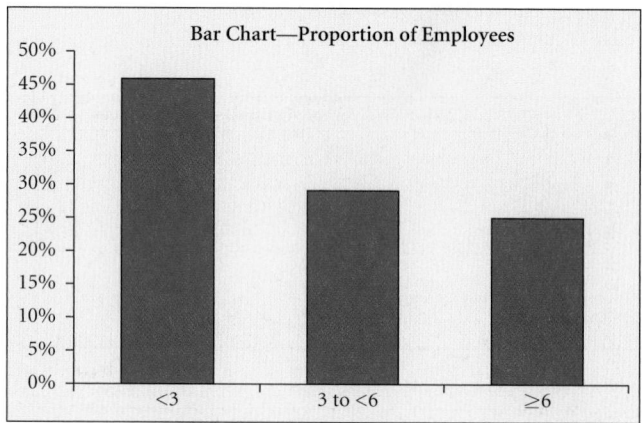

2-73. a. The independent variable is hours and the dependent variable is sales.

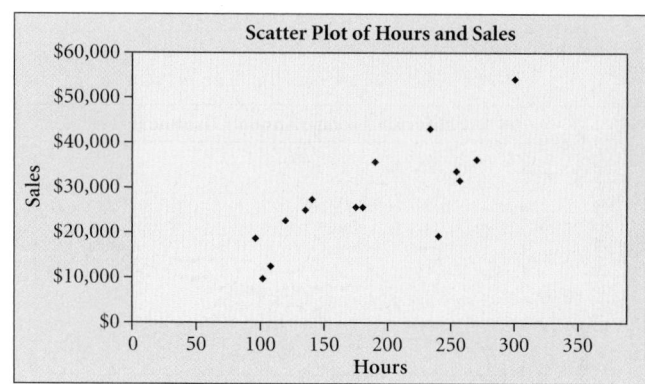

b. It appears that there is a positive linear relationship between hours worked and weekly sales. It appears that the more hours worked, the greater the sales. No stores seem to be substantially different in terms of the general relationship between hours and sales.

2-75. a. Using the $2^k \geq n$, $2^k \geq 100$, so $2^7 = 128$. Determine the width: $(310,495 - 70,464)/7 = 34,290$; round to 35,000.

Classes	Frequency
70,000–105,000	43
105,001–140,000	34
140,001–175,000	13
175,001–210,000	5
210,001–245,000	2
245,001–280,000	1
280,001–315,000	2

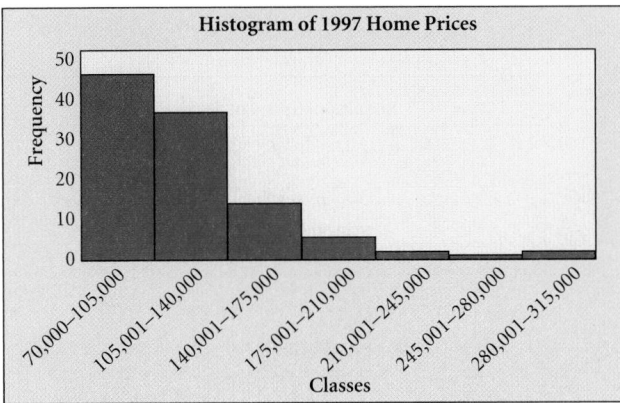

b.

	Frequency	Relative Frequency	Cumulative Relative Frequency
70,000–105,000	43	0.43	0.43
105,001–140,000	34	0.34	0.77
140,001–175,000	13	0.13	0.90
175,001–210,000	5	0.05	0.95
210,001–245,000	2	0.02	0.97
245,001–280,000	1	0.01	0.98
280,001–315,000	2	0.02	1.00

c. Using four classes,

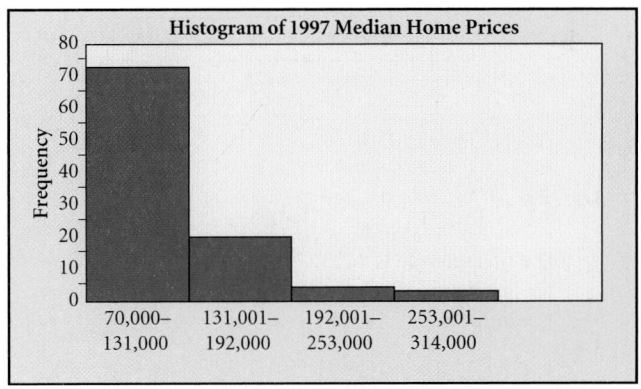

Distribution with four classes appears to be more skewed than when seven classes are used. Less detail is available.

Cumulative Frequency Ogive

2-77. a.

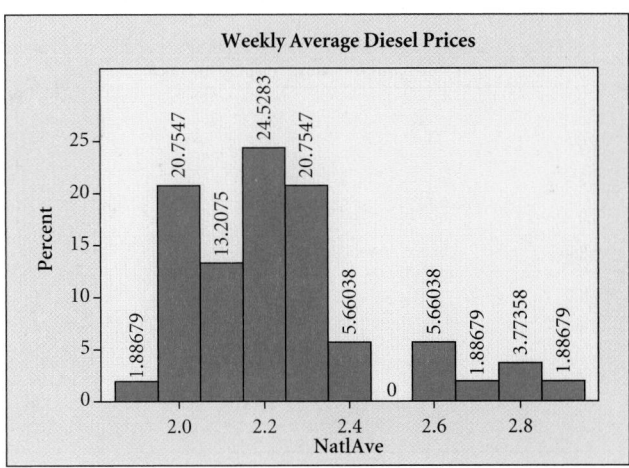

b. Notice that the class interval with no observations is the seventh class, which has boundaries of $2.45 and $2.55.

Chapter 3

3-1. a. $\mu = \dfrac{\Sigma x}{N} = \dfrac{58}{24} = 2.42$

b. $M_d = \dfrac{2+3}{2} = 2.5$

c. The mode is 3.

3-3. $\bar{x} = \dfrac{74,349}{15} = 4,956.60$

The first quartile is 4423.
The median is 5002.
The third quartile is 5381.

3-5.

3-7. a. The 80th percentile is 32.7.
b. The 25th percentile is 28.95.
c. The median is 21.8.

3-9. a. $\bar{x} = \dfrac{\sum\limits_{i=1}^{n} x_i}{n} = 456/24 = 19$

Median $= (19 + 19)/2 = 19$
Mode $= 19$
b. This data is symmetrical since the mean $=$ median $=$ mode.
c.

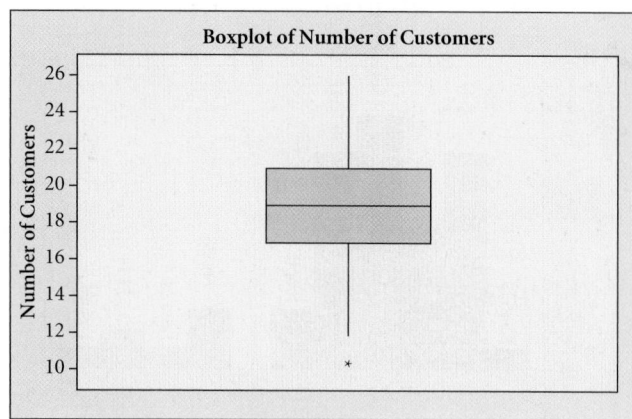

3-11. $\bar{x} = \dfrac{989}{40} = 24.73$

$M_d = \dfrac{26+26}{2} = 26$

Half the data values fall below 26 and half the data values fall above 26.
The mode is 30 minutes.
The mean is 25 and the median is 26. The data are slightly left skewed.

3-13. a. The mean is 114.21. The median is 107.50. The mode is 156.

b. Because the mean is larger than the median, the data are skewed right.

c.

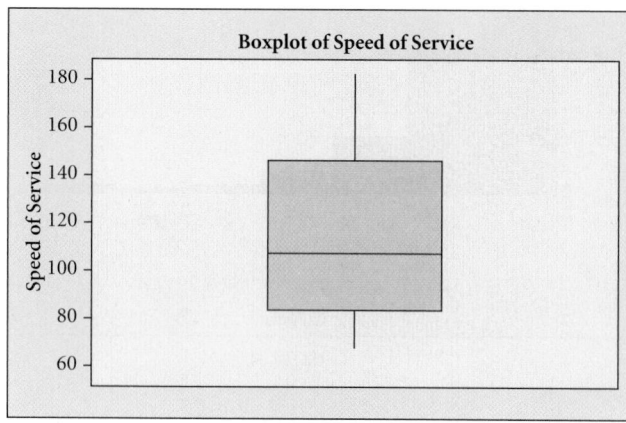

The whisker going up is longer than the whisker going down, which indicates that the data are skewed to the right. This supports the conclusion that the data are not symmetric, but skewed.

3-15. a. Average = 562.99

b. The 17th observation is quite a bit larger than the rest of the data, an *outlier*. Averages, but not medians, are highly affected by outliers. Therefore, the median would be an appropriate measure for this data set.

c. Deleting the outlier, average = 562.9.

3-17. a. FDIC Average = 768,351,603.83

Bank of America Average = 113,595,000

b. The ratio between the FDIC and BA averages is 768,351,603.83/113,595,000 = 6.76. The discrepancy may be due to the use of the word *bank*. The FDIC in referring to "bank" may consider a corporation such as BA to be a "bank," whereas the BA term *banking center* refers to its branches.

c. The answer to this question depends upon the intent of the measurements. If they were attempting to characterize only the specified years, they would be considered to be parameters. If, however, these data were considered "typical" and were to be used to describe past current averages, they would be considered statistics.

3-19. Excel or Minitab can be used to compute the statistics shown as follows:

	Mean	**Median**	**Mode**
White	599.7727	577.5	817
Wheat	530.4091	503	#N/A
Multigrain	470.3636	426	#N/A
Black	383.5909	362.5	#N/A
Cinnamon Raisin	139.7272727	137.5	100
Sour Dough French	127.0909091	120	104
Light Oat	261.6364	260	224

3-21. The 20th percentile is \$15,933. Homeowners aged 65 or older with incomes at or below \$15,933 will be eligible for property tax relief.

3-23. a. $\bar{x} = \frac{2448.30}{20} = 122.465$; $i = (50/100)20 = 10$;

Median = 123.45. Since the mean < median, this suggests that the distribution is left skewed.

b. The average = 0.925.

c. The weights would be: $w_1 = 0.925$, $w_2 = 2(0.925), \ldots, w_8 = 8(0.925)$. Therefore, the weighted average is 1,126.36.

d. The weighted average does seem more appropriate since the PHSI continues to increase each month. We expect that the most recent observations give a better appraisal as to the current, average PHSI.

3-25. a. Range = 8 − 0 = 8
b. $s^2 = 3.99$
c. $s = 1.998$

3-27. a. $\sigma^2 = 16.87$
b. $\sigma = 4.11$

3-29. $Q_1 = 7.65$
$Q_3 = 12.1$
IQR = 4.45
$s^2 = 7.86$
$s = 2.8$

3-31. a. Range = 24
$s^2 = 51.95$, $s = 7.21$
$Q_1 = 12$
$Q_3 = 24$
IQR = 12

b. Range = 24
$\sigma^2 = 48.49$, $\sigma = 6.96$
$Q_1 = 12$
$Q_3 = 24$
IQR = 12

c. σ^2 is smaller than s^2 by a factor of $(N-1)/N$. σ is smaller than s by a factor of $\sqrt{(N-1)/N}$. The range is not affected.

3-33. a. Range = 115
$Q_1 = 67.5$
$Q_3 = 100$
IQR = 32.5
$s^2 = 815.79$
$s = 28.56$

b. The interquartile range overcomes the susceptibility of the range to being highly influenced by extreme values.

3-35. a. Range = 12
$s = 4.0675$
$Q_1 = 23$
$Q_3 = 28$
IQR = 5

b. Student answers will vary but they should look at the number of standard deviations the new mean is from the old mean. Old mean (37.8) − new mean (26.1) = 11.7, which is 11.7/4.0657 = 2.8, or almost 3 standard deviations from the old mean.

3-37. a. Using Minitab,

Variable	StDev	Variance	Range	IQR
Speed of Service	34.89	1217.14	113.00	62.25

b. No, the interquartile is not affected by changes to the extreme values.
c. Adding a constant to all the data values leaves the variance unchanged.

3-39. a. 2004: $\bar{x} = 0.442$
$s = 1.00$
IQR = 1.7

2005: $\bar{x} = 1.075$
$s = 0.629$
IQR = 0.75

b. $\bar{x}_2 = 1.075$ and $\bar{x}_1 = 0.422$; the index has risen substantially.
c. $s_1 = 1.000$ and $s_2 = 0.629$; this indicates the price indices for 2005 do not fluctuate as much as those in 2004.

3-41.

	Pre-MBA Salary (Average)	Post-MBA Salary (Average)	Percentage Increase in Salary	Undergraduate GPA (Average)	GMAT Score (Average)	Annual Tuition	Expected Annual Student Cost
Mean	43337.63	98902	123.29%	3.4025	631.125	15967.5	27980.75
Median	39077	82203	116.32%	3.455	635	13163.5	23169.5
Standard Deviation	12334.73	38787.1	21.75%	0.134881	48.47514	7698.981	11921.58
Sample Variance	1.52E+08	1.5E+09	4.73%	0.018193	2349.839	59274313	1.42E+08
Range	32737	97077	55.85%	0.33	139	20896	31744
Minimum	32763	68423	104.15%	3.2	553	8000	17860
Maximum	65500	165500	160.00%	3.53	692	28896	49604
Sum	346701	791216	986.28%	27.22	5049	127740	223846
Count	8	8	8	8	8	8	8

Student reports will differ but should contain a discussion of the measures of the center and the measures of the spread.

3-43. Using Excel's pivot table feature,

a.
Data	F	M
Average of Price	98	117
StdDev of Price	36.14	68.06

b.
Data	Business	Home
Average of Price	166.67	105.74
StdDev of Price	57.74	56.40

3-45. a. The 20th percentile = 5.5. The 40th, 60th, and 80th percentiles are 10.5, 15.5, and 20.5, respectively.

b.

	μ	σ^2	σ
Top-Ranked	103,056	616,184,957	24,883
2nd-Ranked	82,678	641,965,420	25,337
3rd-Ranked	84,300	360,030,000	18,975
4th-Ranked	87,725	570,233,125	23,880
5th-Ranked	71,047	78,214,458	8,844

c. The ranking of the first- and fifth-ranked subgroups appears to coincide to their average tuition. However, the rankings of the middle three ranked subgroups seemed to be the inverse of their average tuitions.

3-47. a. Population 1 – $CV = 7\%$ Population 2 – $CV = 17\%$
b. Population 2 is more variable relative to the size of the population mean than is population 1.

3-49. Distribution A: $z = 0.695$ Distribution B: $z = 1.63$
The smaller the z-value, the relatively closer the x-value is to the mean. The value from distribution A is relatively closer to its mean.

3-51. a. $z = 2$

A bulb that lasts 500 hours is 2 standard deviations higher than the population mean.
b. If the time distribution is bell-shaped, the Empirical Rule can be used. Only 2.5% of all bulbs are expected to last longer than 500 hours, assuming that the distribution is approximately bell-shaped.

3-53. a. $z = -0.80$ **b.** $z = 0.80$ **c.** $z = 0.00$
3-55. a. $\bar{x} = 51$, $s = 22.60$
b. There are $(19/30)100\% = 63.3\%$ of the data within $(28.4, 73.6)$, $(30/30)100\% = 100\%$, of the data within $(5.8, 96.2)$, $(30/30)100\% = 100\%$, of the data within $(-16.8, 118.8)$.
c. The Empirical Rule indicates that the percentages should be approximately 68%, 95%, and 100% in these intervals.

3-57. a.

	Mean	Standard Deviation
English-Speaking	111.36	22.42

b.

	Mean	Standard Deviation
Spanish-Speaking	150.86	26.84

c. CV for English $= 20.13\%$
CV for Spanish $= 17.79\%$
d.

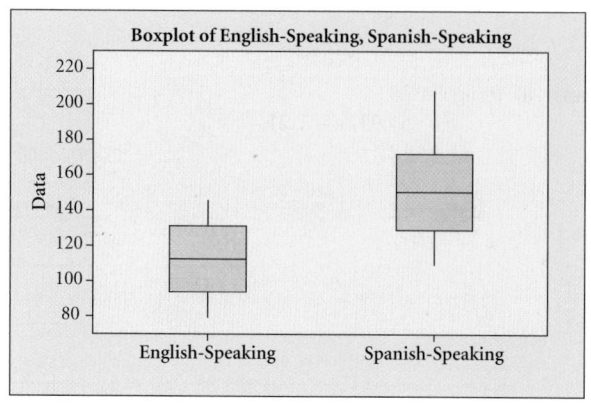

3-59. At issue is relative variability.

Existing supplier: $CV = 2.08\%$ New supplier: $CV = 0.75\%$

Students should show the results of the coefficient of variation computations and conclude that the new supplier has the potential to produce parts with less variation than the existing supplier.

3-61. a. Public: $CV = 54.6\%$ Private: $CV = 47.1\%$

b. Using the Empirical Rule, $\mu \pm 3\sigma = 21{,}235 \pm 3(10{,}000) = -8{,}765$ to 51,235.

c. It does not appear that the data values are bell-shaped since about 15% [= {0 – (–8,765)}/{51,235 – (–8,765)} = 0.146] of the range of the data is negative. Since tuition and fees are not negative, this casts doubt on the assertion that it is bell-shaped.

3-63. a. $\bar{x} = 1.6848$ and $s = 0.00383$

b. Except for random variation, the diameter of the golf balls should not be smaller than 1.682. The larger the diameter, the shorter the distance when driving a golf ball, so the data should be bunched around 1.682 but not smaller. This would create a right-skewed distribution whereas the bell-shaped distribution is symmetric.

c. $\bar{x} \pm 2s = 1.6848 \pm 2(0.00383) = (1.6771, 1.6925)$ contained 43 of the data points = 96%, versus Tchebysheff's stipulation at least $(1 - 1/2^2) \, 100 = 75\%$, $\bar{x} \pm 3s = 1.6848 \pm 3(0.00383) = (1.6733, 1.6963) = (1.6695, 1.7001)$ contained all 45, implying 100% compared to at least $(1 - 1/3^2)100 = 89\%$, $\bar{x} \pm 4s = 1.6848 \pm 4(0.00383)$ contained all 45, implying 100% compared to at least $(1 - 1/4^2)100 = 93.75\%$.

3-65. a. LAX/SFO: $\bar{x} = 336$ and $s = 162.8$
LAX/BCN: $\bar{x} = 1997$ and $s = 203.4$

b. For LAX/SFO, $CV = 48.5\%$.
For LAX/BCN, $CV = 10.2\%$.

c. The CV won't change since both elements of the ratio are multiplied by the same constant.

3-67. Convert the growth rates to standardized z-values. Only Afghanistan had a growth rate more than 2 standard deviations above the mean. This country was 3.84 standard deviations above the mean. No countries were more than 2 standard deviations below the mean. The closest was the Ukraine and $z = -1.96$.

3-69. The first interval, so the area in the left-hand tail is 32/2. Therefore, the lower endpoint is the 16th percentile. The upper endpoint is 84th percentile. The second interval is $\mu \pm 2\sigma$. The lower endpoint is the 2.5th percentile and the upper endpoint is the 97.5th percentile. The third interval is $\mu \pm 3\sigma$; it contains 100% of the data. Therefore, the lower endpoint is the 0th percentile. The upper endpoint is the 100th percentile.

3-71. Some problems are that it does not look at total hours taken. It also does not look at the difficulty of the classes taken. Comparing across two universities has the same problems as mentioned previously, along with the fact that all universities are different and the type of classes and difficulty level of classes will be completely different. None of this is accounted for in calculating a grade point average.

3-73. The mode is a useful measure of location of a set of data if the data set is large and involves nominal or ordinal data.

3-75. a. The standardized sample data for 507 is 1 standard deviation from the mean; $z = (507 - 407)/100 = 1$. The Empirical Rule indicates that 68% of the data is within 1 standard deviation from the mean. Thus, the proportion of airfares less than 507 is 0.68/2 + 0.50 = 0.84.

b. Being in a 25th percentile would mean that 0.25 of the area is to its left. The Empirical Rule says that 68% of the data is within 1 standard deviation of the mean. That means there is $(100 - 68)/2 = 0.16$ in each tail. Therefore, we need only produce a number less than 1 standard deviation below the mean: $407 - 1(100) = 307$, so a number between 307 and 407.

c. $z = -1.57$. Tchebysheff's Theorem indicates that $1 - (1/k^2) = 1 - [1/(1.57^2)] = 0.59$ of the data lies within 1.57 standard deviations from the mean. Thus, the proportion beyond 1.57 standard deviations is $1 - 0.59 = 0.41$. Therefore, the largest percentile that could be attributed to an airfare of $250 is the 41st percentile.

3-77. Student answers will vary but one approach would be to standardize the results for each manager:

Plant 1: $(810 - 700)/200 = .55$ standard deviation
Plant 2: $(2{,}600 - 2{,}300)/350 = .86$ standard deviation
Plant 3: $(1{,}320 - 1{,}200)/30 = 4$ standard deviations

Based upon this, the manager of Plant 3 performed far better than the other plant managers on a relative basis.

3-79. a. $\bar{x} = 364.42$

b. $s^2 = 16{,}662.69$
$s = 129.08$

3-81. a. $\bar{x} = 39.0556$

b. Median = 35

c. $s^2 = 219.232$
$s = 14.8065$

d. Use Excel's histogram feature to create the frequency distribution.

Classes	Frequency
15–24	4
25–34	5
35–44	4
45–54	2
55–64	2
65–74	1

e. Use Excel's histogram feature to create the histogram.

f.

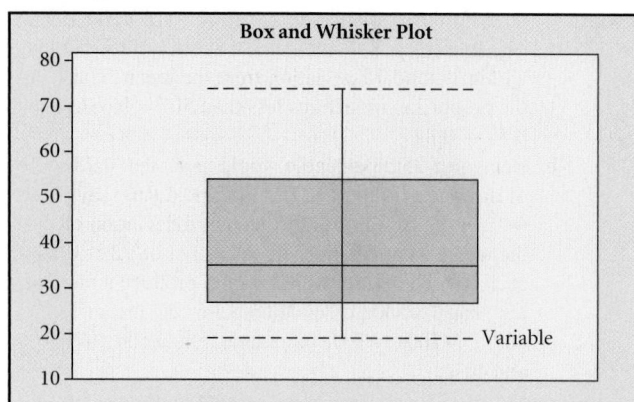

g. $Q_3 = 54$

3-83. Student answers will vary but one thing they might do is calculate the mean and standard deviation and then calculate the coefficient of variation in order to compare the data sets.

Idaho Power: $\bar{x} = 131.1267$
$s = 34.6578$

S&P: $\bar{x} = 152.5628$
$s = 58.943$

EEI100: $\bar{x} = 122.4233$
$s = 25.3535$

Coefficient of Variation:
Idaho Power $= 26.43\%$
S&P $= 38.64\%$
EEI100 $= 20.71\%$

3-85. a.

Variable	Mean	StDev
Price	22.000	3.813

b. $\bar{x} \pm 1s = 22 \pm (3.813) = (18.187, 25.813),$
$\bar{x} \pm 2s = (14.374, 29.626), \quad \bar{x} \pm 3s = (10.561, 33.439)$

c. The Empirical Rule indicates that 95% of the data is contained within $\bar{x} \pm 2s$. This would mean that each tail has $(1 - 0.95)/2 = 0.025$ of the data. Therefore, the costume should be priced at $14.37.

3-87. a.

Variable	Mean	StDev	Median
Close–Open	−0.0354	0.2615	−0.0600

b. The closing price for GE stock is an average of approximately 4 ($0.0354) cents lower than the opening price.

c.

Variable	Mean	StDev	Median
Open	33.947	0.503	33.980
Close–Open	−0.0354	0.2615	−0.0600

Variable	CoefVar
Open	1.48
Close–Open	738.47

3-89. a.

Mileage, Highway	
Mean	24.8333
Standard Error	0.76276
Median	24
Mode	21
Standard Deviation	4.1778
Sample Variance	17.454
Kurtosis	−1.2915
Skewness	0.01937
Range	14
Minimum	18
Maximum	32
Sum	745
Count	30

Mileage City	
Mean	18.4
Standard Error	0.539476119
Median	18.5
Mode	19
Standard Deviation	2.954832395
Sample Variance	8.731034483
Kurtosis	0.496563717
Skewness	−0.25743034
Range	13
Minimum	11
Maximum	24
Sum	552
Count	30

Yes, the data support the premise.

b. Highway $CV = 4.1778/24.8333 = 16.8\%$
City $CV = 2.9548/18.4 = 16.1\%$

c. Calculate how many standard deviations the mean of city driving is from the highway driving mean (24.8):

$$(24.8333 - 18.4)/2.9548 = 2.17$$

Using the Empirical Rule, $\frac{1}{2}$ of the remaining 5% would be at least 24.8333, which means 2.5%.

3-91. a. Sorting the data and determining what position 45,000 is in, you can solve the percentile equation for the percentile.

$$i = \frac{p}{100} n = (75/100) * (200) = 150;$$

The 75th percentile is the average of the 150th and 151st value in the data. You can use PHStat's Stack feature under Data Preparation to reorganize the data. Then sorting the data you get the following:

148	44,879
149	44,879
150	44,904
151	44,980
152	45,052
153	45,148
154	45,153
155	45,227
156	45,228
157	45,276

Thus, the 75th percentile is the average of 44,904 and 44,980, or 44,942.

b. Using Excel's Average and Median functions you can find that

Mean = 42,261

Median = 42,326

c. Using the $2^k \geq n$ guideline, the appropriate number of classes should be 8 since $2^8 = 256$.

The class width is

$$w = \frac{52,774 - 31,476}{8} = 2,662.25$$

We choose to round this to 2,750 and start at 31,000, giving the following histogram:

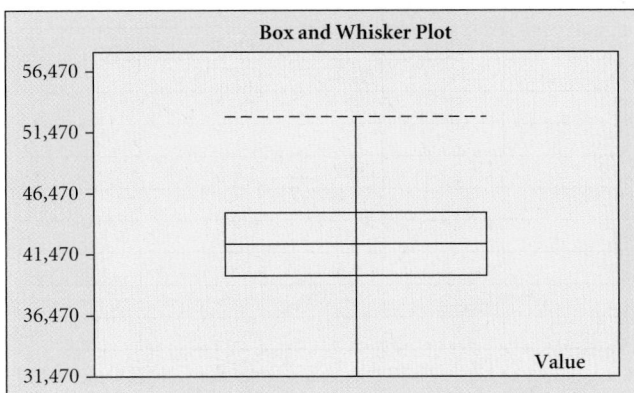

Chapters 1–3 Special Review

SR.1. a–c. Student answers will vary but class limits should be set so that classes are mutually exclusive and all-inclusive. Class intervals should be of equal size and chosen so that observations are approximately equally distributed over the interval.

SR.3. Student reports will vary. We look for effective use of visual tools indicating trends, not just reliance on tables and numbers. Superior students might compare Intel graphs with competitors or benchmark companies.

SR.5. a.

	Revenues	**Profits**	**Employees**
Mean	6,354.71	803.43	21,530.3
Median	3,428	401	11,000
Std. Deviation	7,457.66	881.812	21,269.35

b. The standardized *z*-values need to be computed. Mellon Bank Corporation is slightly below the average for profits ($z = -.03$) and revenues ($z = -.16$) and slightly above the average for number of employees ($z = .28$).

c. You need to calculate the coefficient of variation for each variable.

	Revenues	**Profits**	**Employees**
Coefficient of variation	1.173564	1.097558	0.9878812

Revenues has the largest relative variation.

d.

Classes	**Frequency**
0.000–0.014	1
0.015–0.029	16
0.030–0.044	25
0.045–0.059	5
0.060–0.074	2
0.075–0.089	2

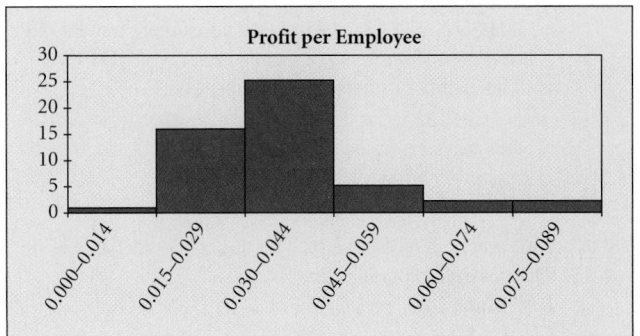

	Profits per Employee
Mean	0.0365
Median	0.0353
Standard Deviation	0.0140

e. 2 standard deviations above the mean is

$$0.0365 + 2(0.0140) = 0.0645$$

Three banks have a profit-per-employee ratio above 0.0645.

Chapter 4

4-1. For two customers, the sample space is

V, V
V, C
V, S
C, V
C, C
C, S
S, V
S, C
S, S

4-3. The concept is independent events.

4-5. a. Subjective probability based on expert opinion
  b. Relative frequency based on previous customer return history
  c. 1/5 = 0.20

4-7. Using Equation 4.1,

$$P(\text{Commons}) = 1/3$$

4-9. Probability, using the classical probability assessment method, is computed using the following steps:
  a. Since each position is chosen randomly, each outcome is equally likely.
  b. There are 16 equally likely events.
  c. The event of interest is that both positions are filled with candidates from the Ivy League.
  d. The event of interest is comprised of $e_7, e_8, e_{11}, e_{12}, e_{15}, e_{16}$.
  e. $P(E_i) = \dfrac{6}{16} = 0.375$

4-11. a. Step 1: Since each decision is assumed to be equally likely, each outcome is equally likely.
$$P(e_i) = (1/2)^3 = 1/8$$
  b. There are 8 equally likely events.
  c. The events of interest are (1) only two consumers buy a HDTV (E_1), (2) at most two consumers buy HDTVs (E_2), and (3) at least two consumers buy HDTVs (E_3).
  d. The events of interest are comprised of
  (1) $E_1 = \{e_2, e_3, e_4\}$, (2) $E_2 = \{e_2, e_3, e_4, e_5, e_6, e_7, e_8\}$,
  and $E_3 = \{e_1, e_2, e_3, e_4\}$.
  e. $P(E_1) = \dfrac{3}{8} = 0.375$

4-13. Nine weeks can be covered with this schedule. (see Figure)

4-15. The possible outcomes are
  B = Buick sold
  C = Cadillac sold
  P = Pontiac sold
  U = Used car sold
  For two cars sold, the sample space is
  B, B
  B, C
  B, P
  B, U
  C, C
  C, B
  C, P
  C, U
  P, P
  P, B
  P, C
  P, U
  U, U
  U, B
  U, C
  U, P

4-17. a. Subjective assessment
  b. Manager 3 since that manager stated the probability is 0.90
  c. Subjective probability assessments reflect the state of mind of the individual doing the assessment.

4-19. a. The relative frequency probability assessment method
  b. N = (Number of Times E_i Occurs)/
  (Relative Frequency of E_i) = (9560)/(1/6)
  = 57,360
  c. The number of large corporations that were not audited = 57,360 − 9,560 = 47,800.

$$\text{Relative Frequency of } E_i = \frac{\text{Number of Times } E_i \text{ Occurs}}{N}$$

$$= \frac{47,800}{57,360} = 0.8333$$

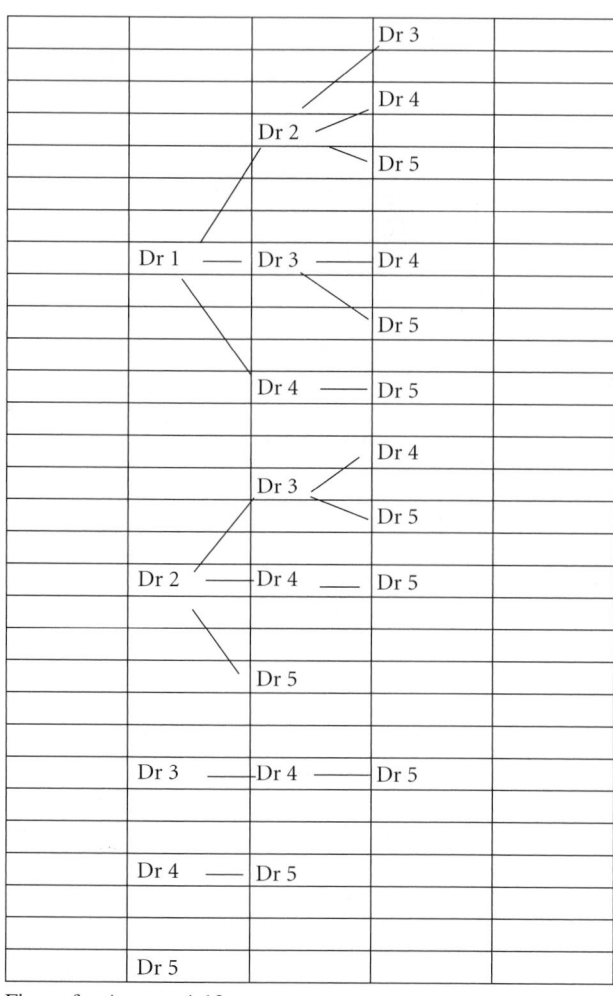

Figure for Answer 4-13.

4-21. a.

Count of Delivery Method

Delivery Method	Total
Caesarean	22
Normal	28
Grand Total	50

$$P(\text{Caesarean}) = \frac{22}{50} = 0.44$$

b. The number of births observed (50) is not very large. Any new birth may not exactly match the 50 in this study.

4-23. Using the following joint frequency table,

	Electrical	Mechanical	Total
Lincoln	28	39	67
Tyler	64	69	133
Total	92	108	200

a. $133/200 = 0.665$
b. $108/200 = 0.54$
c. $28/200 = 0.14$

4-25. a. Relative Frequency of $E_i = \dfrac{43}{100} = 0.43$

b. Relative Frequency of E_i

$$= \frac{\text{Number of Times } E_i \text{ Occurs}}{N}$$

$$= \frac{5+6+6}{100} = 0.17$$

c. For Pepsi, probability = 0.486
For Coke, probability = 0.514

d. For Pepsi, probability = 0.4
For Coke, probability = 0.6

4-27. a. $P(\text{Soft Drink}) * P(\text{No Fries}) = (0.9)(1 - 0.5) = 0.45$
b. $P(\text{Hamburger \& FF}) = P(\text{Hamburger})$
$P(FF|\text{Hamburger}) = (0.6)(0.8) = 0.48$

4-29. a. $P(\text{Matched}) = 2/3$
b. $P(\text{Both Wrong}) = (1/3) * (1/3) = 1/9$

4-31. a. Because the two outcomes are independent, Probability Rule 9 (Multiplication Rule for Independent Events) can be used to find the probability of winning both: $P(\text{H})P(\text{O}) = (0.40)(0.25) = 0.10$.

Using Probability Rule 4 (Addition Rule for Any Two Events). This is equal to $P(\text{H}) + P(\text{O}) - P(\text{H})P(\text{O}) = 0.40 + 0.25 - (0.40 * 0.25) = 0.55$.

b. Using the Complement Rule and Probability Rule 9, the probability of losing both contracts is therefore $(0.60) * (0.75) = 0.45$.

4-33. a. Using the relative frequency assessment method,

$$P(\text{B}) = 0.28$$

b. $P(\text{Defect}) = 0.07$

c. $P(\text{Defect}|\text{B}) = \dfrac{\text{Number of Defective Drives from B}}{\text{Number of Drives from B}}$

$$= \frac{15}{195} = 0.076$$

4-35. a. Let E_1 = the driver is a woman; E_2 = the driver stops to ask for directions.
$P(E_1 \text{ and } E_2) = P(E_2|E_1) \, P(E_1) = (0.61)(0.518)$
$= 0.316$

b. Determine the probability of each event: $P(E_1) = 0.518$, $P(\overline{E}_1) = 1 - 0.518 = 0.482$, $P(E_2|E_1) = 0.61$, $P(E_2|\overline{E}_1) = 0.42$; $P(\overline{E}_1 \text{ and } E_2) = P(E_2|\overline{E}_1) \, P(\overline{E}_1) = (0.42)(0.482) = 0.202$. Compute the probability using Rule 5: $P[(E_1 \text{ and } E_2) \text{ or } (\overline{E}_1 \text{ and } E_2)] = P(E_1 \text{ and } E_2) + P(\overline{E}_1 \text{ and } E_2) = 0.316 + (0.42)(0.482) = 0.316 + 0.202 = 0.518$.

c. $P(\overline{E}_1 | E_2) = P(\overline{E}_1 \text{ and } E_2) / P(E_2)$
$= 0.202 / 0.518 = 0.39$

4-37. If they purchase four black-and-white copiers, their probability of being able to provide a color copy is 0.0. Their probability of being able to provide a black-and-white copy on demand is $1 - [(0.1)(0.1)(0.1)(0.1)] = 0.9999$. If they buy all color copiers, the probability of providing a black-and-white copy is the same as providing a color copy since color copiers can make black-and-white copies. This probability is $1 - [(0.2)(0.2)(0.2)(0.2)] = 0.9984$. They cannot get to 99.9% on color copies regardless of the configuration.

4-39. The probability of three consecutive 9s assuming each number is equally likely is $(1/10)(1/10)(1/10)$, but since only 30% are eligible for free gas, the probability is $(1/10)(1/10)(1/10)(0.3) = 0.0003$

4-41. a. $P(>7 \text{ days}) = 0.41 + 0.17 = 0.58$
b. For two events to be independent, the following must hold:

$P(1-7 \text{ and } \$200-\$500) = P(1-7) \times P(\$200-\$500)$

$P(1-7 \text{ and } \$200-\$500) = \dfrac{200}{2,020} = 0.099$

$P(1-7) = \dfrac{850}{2,020} = 0.42$

$P(\$200-\$500) = \dfrac{450}{2,020} = 0.22$

$P(1-7) \times P(\$200-\$500) = 0.42 \times 0.22 = 0.09 \neq 0.099$

Thus, the two events are not independent.

c. $P(\text{under } \$200 | 1-7 \text{ days}) = \dfrac{125}{850} = 0.15$

$P(\$200-\$500 | 1-7 \text{ days}) = \dfrac{200}{850} = 0.24$

$P(\$501-\$1,000 | 1-7 \text{ days}) = \dfrac{400}{850} = 0.47$

$P(\text{over } \$1,000 | 1-7 \text{ days}) = \dfrac{125}{850} = 0.15$

Given that the house sold in 1–7 days, it most likely was in the $501 – $1,000 price range at a 0.47 probability.

4-43. The probability that no overseas plants are selected is equal to the probability that all four randomly selected plants are domestic. There are seven domestic plants. The probability that only domestic plants are randomly selected is equal to $(7/11) * (6/10) * (5/9) * (4/8) = 0.1061$. Therefore, the probability of one or more overseas plants being selected is $1 - 0.1061 = 0.8939$.

4-45. $P(\text{Line 1}|\text{Defective}) = (0.05)(0.4)/0.0725 = 0.2759$
$P(\text{Line 2}|\text{Defective}) = (0.10)(0.35)/0.0725 = 0.4828$
$P(\text{Line 3}|\text{Defective}) = (0.07)(0.25)/0.0725 = 0.2413$
The unsealed cans probably came from Line 2.

4-47. Let D = defective

F = Franklin

W = Wilson

E = Evergreen

S = Scott

We can use Bayes' Theorem to determine the probability of interest.

$$P(F|D) = \frac{P(F)P(D|F)}{P(F)P(D|F) + P(W)P(D|W) + P(E)P(D|E) + P(S)P(D|S)}$$

$$P(F|D) = \frac{(0.40)(0.03)}{(0.40)(0.03) + (0.30)(0.06) + (0.20)(0.02) + (0.10)(0.08)}$$

$$P(F|D) = 0.29$$

4-49. a. Let B = voted for President Bush, V = voted in the election, R = registered to vote. $P(B \text{ and } V) = P(B|V)P(V) = 0.508(0.607) = 0.308$

Let E_1 = an individual voted for President Bush; E_2 = an individual voted in the election.

$P(E_2) = 0.607$, $P(E_1|E_2) = 0.508$

Since $P(E_1|E_2) = 0.508$ and $P(E_1|\overline{E}_2) = 0$, E_1 and E_2 are not independent.

Compute the probability using Rule 8:

$$P(E_1 \text{ and } E_2) = P(E_1|E_2)P(E_2) = 0.508(0.607) = 0.308$$

b. Since one cannot vote without registering, $P(V) = P(V \text{ and } R) = 0.607$. Since $P(V|R) = P(V \text{ and } R)/P(R)$, $P(R) = P(V \text{ and } R)/P(V|R) = 0.607/0.853 = 0.712$.

Let E_1 and E_2 be defined as in part a. Let E_3 = an individual registered to vote.

$P(E_2) = 0.607$, $P(E_1|E_2) = 0.508$. Since one cannot vote without registering, $P(E_2) = P(E_2 \text{ and } E_3) = 0.607$. $P(E_1|E_3) = 0.853$

Since $P(E_1|E_3) = 0.853$ and $P(E_1|\overline{E}_3) = 0$, E_1 and E_3 are not independent.

Compute the probability using Rule 8:

Since $P(E_1|E_3) = P(E_1 \text{ and } E_3)/P(E_3)$, $P(E_3) = P(E_1 \text{ and } E_3)/P(E_1|E_3) = 0.607/0.853 = 0.712$.

4-51. Use Excel's pivot table feature to answer this question.

a. $P(\text{neither on business}) = 1 - (27/62)(26/61) = 1 - 0.1856 = 0.81454$

b. $P(\text{business or no hotel problem}) = 27/62 + 48/62 - 17/62 = 58/62 = 0.936$

c. $P(\text{pleasure and in-state area code}) = 2/62 = 0.0323$

4-53. Using the values in the file:

a. Let E_1 = the respondents 36 or older; E_2 = would not use a wireless phone exclusively because of some type of difficulty in placing and receiving calls.

$$P(E_2|E_1) = P(E_1 \text{ and } E_2)/P(E_1)$$
$$= 0.074/0.627 = 0.119$$

b. For ease of typing, let not E_1 indicate the complement of E_1. Then, $P(E_2| \text{ not } E_1) = P(\text{not } E_1 \text{ and } E_2)/P(E_2) = 0.55/0.373 = 0.148$.

c. Let A_i = the ith respondent stated that the most important reason for not using a wireless exclusively was that they need a line for Net access.

$P(\text{at least one}) = 1 - P(\text{none}) = 1 - P(\text{ not } A_1 \text{ and not } A_2 \text{ and not } A_3) = 1 - P(\text{not } A_1)P(\text{not } A_2) P(\text{ not } A_3) = 1 - [1 - P(A_1)][1 - P(A_2)] [1 - P(A_3)] = 1 - (1 - 0.148) (1 - 0.148) (1 - 0.148) = 1 - 0.6186 = 0.3814$

4-55. The following joint frequency table (developed using Excel's pivot table feature) summarizes the data:

	Electrical	**Mechanical**	**Total**
Lincoln	28	39	67
Tyler	64	69	133
Total	92	108	200

a. $P(\text{Electrical/Tyler}) = P(\text{Electrical and Tyler})/P(\text{Tyler}) = (64/200)/(133/200) = 0.4812$

b. The probability of a mechanical problem is not independent of the plant where the scooter was assembled.

c. $P(\text{Electrical and Tyler}) * 500 \text{ Scooters} * \$100 = \$16,000$

$P(\text{Mechanical and Tyler}) * 500 \text{ Scooters} * \$75 = \$12,937.50$

$P(\text{Electrical and Lincoln}) * 500 \text{ Scooters} * \$100 = \$7,000$

$P(\text{Mechanical and Lincoln}) * 500 \text{ Scooters} * \$75 = \$7,312.50$

Total budgeted expense would be \$43,250. Of this total, \$28,937.50 would be assigned to Tyler and \$14,312.50 would be assigned to Lincoln.

4-57. The relative frequency assessment approach takes the number of times the item of interest occurred and divides it by the total number of times the event or activity was done. An example of this might be that a health insurance company is interested in the number of errors that occur in claims. It could look at a sample of claims and count the number of times errors occurred divided by the sample size that was reviewed.

4-59. Classical probability assessment is the method of determining probability based on the ratio of the number of ways the event of interest can occur to the total number of ways any event can occur when the individual elementary events are equally likely. Classical probability assessment is rarely applied in business situations.

4-61. a.

$P(A) = 500/2000 = 0.25$, $P(\overline{A}) = 1 - P(A) = 1 - 0.25 = 0.75$

$P(A | B) = P(A \text{ and } B)/P(B) = (200/2000)/[(200 + 800)/2000] = 0.20$

$P(\overline{A} | B) = P(\overline{A} \text{ and } B)/P(B) = (800/2000)/[(200 + 800)/2000] = 0.80$

$P(A | \overline{B}) = P(A \text{ and } \overline{B})/P(\overline{B}) = (300/2000)/[(300 + 700)/2000] = 0.30$

and $P(\overline{A} | \overline{B}) = P(\overline{A} \text{ and } \overline{B})/P(\overline{B}) = (700/2000)/[(300 + 700)/2000] = 0.70$

b. So (1) $P(A|B) = 0.20 \neq 0.25 = P(A)$ and A and B are dependent;

(2) $P(\overline{A}|B) = 0.80 \neq 0.75 = P(\overline{A})$ and $\overline{A}$ and B are dependent;

(3) $P(A|\overline{B}) = 0.30 \neq 0.25 = P(A)$ and A and $\overline{B}$ are dependent;

(4) $P(\overline{A}|\overline{B}) = 0.70 \neq 0.75 = P(\overline{A})$ and A and B are dependent.

$P(A) = 0.25 = P(A|B)$ if A and B are independent. This says that 25% of the sample space and 25% of B's 1000 elementary events must be A's. This means that 25% of B's elementary events must also be A's. A similar argument for $\bar{A}$ yields 750 elementary events in ($\bar{A}$ and B) and in ($\bar{A}$ and $\bar{B}$). And the relevant probabilities become $P(A|B) = P(A \text{ and } B)/P(B) = (250/2000)/[(250 + 750)/2000] = 0.25 = P(A)$. A and B are independent, $P(\bar{A}|B) = P(\bar{A} \text{ and } B)/P(B) = (750/2,000)/[(250 + 750)/2,000] = 0.75 = P(\bar{A})$. $\bar{A}$ and B are independent, $P(A|\bar{B}) = P(A \text{ and } \bar{B}')/P(\bar{B}) = (250/2,000)/[(250 + 750)/2,000] = 0.25 = P(A)$. A and $\bar{B}$ are independent. And $P(\bar{A}|\bar{B}) = P(\bar{A} \text{ and } \bar{B})/P(\bar{B}) = (750/2,000)/[(250 + 750)/2,000] = 0.75 = P(\bar{A})$. $\bar{A}$ and $\bar{B}$ are independent.

4-63. The probability of correctly guessing on any one question is 0.25. The questions are independent.

a. $P(C \text{ and } C \text{ and } C) = 0.25 \times 0.25 \times 0.25 = 0.0156$

b. Sample space is

$P(C \text{ and } C \text{ and } C) = 0.25 \times 0.25 \times 0.25 = 0.0156$

Or

$P(C \text{ and } C \text{ and } W) = 0.25 \times 0.25 \times 0.75 = 0.0469$

Or

$P(C \text{ and } W \text{ and } C) = 0.25 \times 0.75 \times 0.25 = 0.0469$

Or

$P(W \text{ and } C \text{ and } C) = 0.75 \times 0.25 \times 0.25 = 0.0469$

$P(\text{Passing}) = 0.0156 + 0.0469 + 0.0469 + 0.0469$
$= 0.1563$

c. For a, $P(C \text{ and } C \text{ and } C) = 0.5 \times 0.5 \times 0.5 = 0.125$. For b, sample space is

$P(C \text{ and } C \text{ and } C) = 0.5 \times 0.5 \times 0.5 = 0.125$

Or

$P(C \text{ and } C \text{ and } W) = 0.5 \times 0.5 \times 0.5 = 0.125$

Or

$P(C \text{ and } W \text{ and } C) = 0.5 \times 0.5 \times 0.5 = 0.125$

Or

$P(W \text{ and } C \text{ and } C) = 0.5 \times 0.5 \times 0.5 = 0.125$

$P(\text{Passing}) = 0.125 + 0.125 + 0.125 + 0.125 = 0.50$

4-65. a. Let E_1 = a randomly selected wealthy individual is audited. $P(E_1) = 1/63 = 0.016$ and $P(\text{not } E_1) = 1 - P(E_1) = 1 - 0.016 = 0.984$.

$P(\text{at least one}) = 1 - P(\text{none}) = 1 - 0.851 = 0.149$

b. Let E_2 = a randomly selected corporation with assets of at least \$250 million would be audited. $P(E_2) = 0.44$ and $P(\text{not } E_2) = 1 - P(E_2) = 1 - 0.44 = 0.56$.

$P(\text{at least one}) = 1 - P(\text{none}) = 1 - 0.003 = 0.997$

c. $P(E_1 \text{ or } E_2) = P(E_1) + P(E_2) - P(E_1)P(E_2) = 0.016 + 0.44 - (0.016)(0.44) = 0.449$

4-67. $P(\text{Plant A}) = 0.5$
$P(\text{Plant B}) = 0.3$
$P(\text{Plant C}) = 0.2$
$P(\text{Incorrect Mix}|\text{Plant A}) = 0.1$

$P(\text{Incorrect Mix}|\text{Plant B}) = 0.05$
$P(\text{Incorrect Mix}|\text{Plant C}) = 0.20$

$P(\text{Incorrect Mix}) = P(\text{Incorrect Mix}|\text{Plant A})P(\text{Plant A})$
$+ P(\text{Incorrect Mix}|\text{Plant B})P(\text{Plant B})$
$+ P(\text{Incorrect Mix}|\text{Plant C}) P(\text{Plant C})$
$= (0.1)(0.5) + (0.05)(0.3)$
$+ (0.2)(0.2) = 0.105$

$P(\text{Plant A}|\text{Incorrect Mix}) = (0.1)(0.5)/0.105 = 0.4762$
$P(\text{Plant B}|\text{Incorrect Mix}) = (0.05)(0.3)/0.105 = 0.1429$
$P(\text{Plant C}|\text{Incorrect Mix}) = (0.2)(0.2)/0.105 = 0.3809$

Cost to Plant A = $(0.4762)(\$10,000) = \$4,762$
Cost to Plant B = $(0.1429)(\$10,000) = \$1,429$
Cost to Plant C = $(0.3809)(\$10,000) = \$3,809$

4-69. $P(\text{Clerk 1}) = 0.4$
$P(\text{Clerk 2}) = 0.3$
$P(\text{Clerk 3}) = 0.3$
$P(\text{Defective}|\text{Clerk 1}) = 0.02$
$P(\text{Defective}|\text{Clerk 2}) = 0.025$
$P(\text{Defective}|\text{Clerk 3}) = 0.015$

$P(\text{Defective}) = P(\text{Defective}|\text{Clerk 1})P(\text{Clerk 1})$
$+ P(\text{Defective}|\text{Clerk 2})P(\text{Clerk 2})$
$+ P(\text{Defective}|\text{Clerk 3})P(\text{Clerk 3})$
$= (0.02)(0.4) + (0.025)(0.3)$
$+ (0.015)(0.3) = 0.02$

$P(\text{Clerk 1}|\text{Defective}) = (0.02)(0.4)/0.02 = 0.4$
$P(\text{Clerk 2}|\text{Defective}) = (0.025)(0.3)/0.02 = 0.375$
$P(\text{Clerk 3}|\text{Defective}) = (0.015)(0.3)/0.02 = 0.225$

Clerk 1 is most likely responsible for the boxes that raised the complaints.

4-71. Students can use Excel's pivot table feature to answer these questions.

a. $P(\text{Salt Lake}) = 24/110 = 0.2182$

b. $P(\text{Wiring}) = 23/110 = 0.2091$

c. $P(\text{Salt Lake and Wiring}) = 8/110 = 0.0727$

d. $P(\text{Day Shift and Salt Lake and Cracked Lens}) = 8/110 = 0.0727$

e. The most likely profile would be the largest number, which would be the Boise day shift for cracked lens.

4-73. a. Relative frequency of W $= \dfrac{100}{300} = 0.33$

b. Relative frequency of (W and E) $= \dfrac{30}{300} = 0.10$

c. Note: East = NE + SE.

Relative frequency of East $= \dfrac{50 + 25}{300} = 0.25$

Relative frequency of C $= \dfrac{100}{300} = 0.333$

Relative frequency of (East and C) $= \dfrac{18 + 13}{300} = 0.103$

Therefore, $P(\text{East or C}) = P(\text{East}) + P(\text{C}) - P(\text{East and C}) = 0.25 + 0.333 - 0.103 = 0.48$.

d. $P(\text{C}|\text{East}) = P(\text{C and East})/P(\text{East}) = 0.103/0.25 = 0.41$

4-75. a.

	Boomer	**GenX**	**GenY**	**Silent**
email	13	13	10	10
	13.00	13.00	10.00	10.00
	3.250	3.250	2.500	2.500
Face-to-face	39	38	52	39
	39.00	38.00	52.00	39.00
	9.750	9.500	13.000	9.750
Gp Meeting	41	42	36	40
	41.00	42.00	36.00	40.00
	10.250	10.500	9.000	10.000
Other	7	7	2	11
	7.00	7.00	2.00	11.00
	1.750	1.750	0.500	2.750
All	100	100	100	100
	100.00	100.00	100.00	100.00
	25.000	25.000	25.000	25.000
Cell Contents:	Count			
	% of Column			
	% of Total			

b. Let E_1 = a member of the Silent generation, E_2 = Boomer generation, E_3 = X generation, E_4 = Y generation, and B = prefers face-to-face communication.

$P(E_1) P(B|E_1) + P(E_2) P(B|E_2) + \cdots + P(E_4) P(B|E_4)$
$= 0.39(0.075) + 0.39(0.42) + 0.38(0.295) + 0.52(0.21) = 0.4144$

c.

$$P(E_i|B) = \frac{P(E_i)P(B|E_i)}{P(E_1)P(B|E_1)+P(E_2)P(B|E_2)+\cdots+P(E_k)P(B|E_k)} =$$

For Silent Generation:

$$\frac{(0.39)(0.075)}{(0.39)(0.075)+(0.39)(0.42)+(0.38)(0.295)+0.52(0.21)} = \frac{0.0281}{0.4144} = 0.0678$$

For Baby Boomers:

$$\frac{(0.39)(0.42)}{(0.39)(0.075)+(0.39)(0.42)+(0.38)(0.295)+0.52(0.21)} = \frac{0.1638}{0.4144} = 0.3953$$

For X generation:

$$\frac{(0.38)(0.295)}{(0.39)(0.075)+(0.39)(0.42)+(0.38)(0.295)+0.52(0.21)} = \frac{0.1121}{0.4144} = 0.2705$$

For Y generation:

$$\frac{(0.52)(0.21)}{(0.39)(0.075)+(0.39)(0.42)+(0.38)(0.295)+0.52(0.21)} = \frac{0.1092}{0.4144} = 0.2635$$

The most likely generation of which the individual is a member is the Baby Boomers.

Chapter 5

5-1. The variable, x, is a discrete random variable because x can take on only specific integer values.
  a. The possible values for x are
  $x = \{0, 1, 2, 3, 4, 5, 6\}$

5-3. The sample space can be developed using a tree diagram as follows:

Draw 1	Draw 2	Total
2	2	4
	4	6
	6	8
	8	10
2	2	4
	4	6
	6	8
	8	10
4	2	6
	2	6
	6	10
	8	12
6	2	8
	4	10
	2	8
	8	14
8	2	10
	4	12
	6	14
	2	10

The random variable, x, and the frequency and relative frequency distributions are shown as follows:

Total	**Frequency**	**Rel. Freq.**
4	2	0.1
6	4	0.2
8	4	0.2
10	6	0.3
12	2	0.1
14	2	0.1
	20	

The graph of the probability distribution is shown as follows:

5-5. a. $E(x) = (100)(0.25) + (125)(0.30) + (150)(0.45) = 130$

b. The calculations are

x	$P(x)$	$xP(x)$	$[x-E(x)]$	$[x-E(x)]^2 P(x)$
100	0.25	25	-30	225
125	0.3	37.5	-5	7.5
150	0.45	67.5	20	180

The variance of x is equal to $225 + 7.5 + 180 = 412.50$.

c. $\sigma_x = \sqrt{412.50} = 20.31$

5-7. a. The expected value of the sum of two randomly rolled dice is equal to $(2)(1/36) + (3)(2/36) + (4)(3/36) + (5)(4/36) + (6)(5/36) + (7)(6/36) + (8)(5/36) + (9)(4/36) + (10)(3/36) + (11)(2/36) + (12)(1/36) = 7$.

b. The variance is equal to $\Sigma[x - E(x)]^2 P(x) = 5.833$.

c. $\sigma_x = \sqrt{5.833} = 2.415$

5-9. a. $E(y) = \Sigma yP(y) = 10(0.13) + \cdots + 19(0.60) = 16.66$

$\sigma^2 = \Sigma[y - E(y)]^2 P(y) = (-6.66)^2(0.13)$
$\qquad + \cdots + 2.34^2(0.60) = 10.7247$

$\sigma = \sqrt{\sigma^2} = \sqrt{10.7247} = 3.2749$

b. $E(z) = \Sigma zP(z) = 21(0.13) + \cdots + 84(0.60)$
$\qquad = 67.62 = 7(9.66)$

$\sigma^2 = \Sigma[z - E(z)]^2 P(z) = (-46.62)^2(0.13)$
$\qquad + \cdots + 16.38^2(0.60) = 525.51 = 7^2(10.7247)$

$\sigma = \sqrt{\sigma^2} = \sqrt{525.51} = 22.924 = 7(3.2749)$

c. Neither is affected.

d. When each of the values of the random variable is multiplied by a constant, the variance is increased by a multiple equal to the constant squared. The standard deviation is increased by a multiple equal to the constant.

5-11. a. $E(x) = \Sigma xP(x) = 2(0.27) + \cdots + 7(0.03) = 3.51$

b. $\sigma^2 = \Sigma[x - E(x)]^2 P(x)$
$\qquad = (-1.51)^2(0.27) + \cdots + 3.49^2(0.03) = 1.6499$

$\sigma = \sqrt{\sigma^2} = \sqrt{1.6499} = 1.2845$

5-13. The average number of minutes spent in the Bittercreek Grille is 85.5.
The variance is 134.75 minutes squared.
The standard deviation is 11.61 minutes.

5-15. a. The average lead time can be computed using Equation 5-1: $E(x) = \Sigma xP(x) = (2)(0.15) + (3)(0.45) + (4)(0.30) + (5)(0.075) + (6)(0.025) = 3.375$ days.

b. The standard deviation is equal to

$\sqrt{\Sigma[x - E(x)]^2 P(x)} = \sqrt{0.834375} = 0.913441$ days.

The expected value was found in (a) above. Therefore, the coefficient of variation $= (0.913441/3.375) * 100\% = 27.065\%$.

c. There is a relationship among lead times, customer service, safety stock, and inventory costs. By reducing lead times, the company can reduce the amount of inventory in its pipeline. By reducing lead time variability, the manufacturing firm can reduce the amount of safety stock it must carry. By knowing its average lead time and its standard deviation, the firm can better plan its ordering and inventory requirements.

5-17. a. $P(x = 0) = P(\bar{I}_1 \text{ and } \bar{I}_2) = P(\bar{I}_1)P(\bar{I}_2) = (1/4)(2/4)$,

$P(x = 1) = P(I_1 \text{ and } \bar{I}_2) + P(\bar{I}_1 \text{ and } I_2) = P(I_1)P(\bar{I}_2) + P(\bar{I}_1)P(\bar{I}_2) = (3/4)(2/4) + (1/4)(2/4) = 1/2$,

$P(x = 2) = P(I_1 \text{ and } I_2) = P(I_1)P(I_2) = (3/4)(2/4) = 3/8$

x	0	1	2
$P(x)$	$1/8 = 0.125$	$1/2 = 0.5$	$3/8 = 0.375$

b. P (both from Ivy League) $= P(2) = 0.375$

c. $E(x) = \Sigma xP(x) = 0(0.125) + 1(0.5) + 2(0.375) = 1.25$

$\sigma^2 = \Sigma(x - E(x))^2 P(x) = (-1.25)^2(0.125)$
$\qquad + (-0.25)^2(0.5) + 0.75^2(0.375) = 0.7187$

$\sigma = \sqrt{\sigma^2} = \sqrt{0.7187} = 0.8478$

5-19. a.

x	14	15	16	17	18	19	20	21	22	23
$P(x)$	0.008	0.024	0.064	0.048	0.184	0.216	0.240	0.128	0.072	0.016

b. $E(x) = \Sigma xP(x) = 14(0.008) + 15(0.024) + \cdots + 23(0.016) = 19.168$

c. $\sigma^2 = \Sigma[x - E(x)]^2 P(x) = (-4.168)^2(0.008) + (-3.168)^2(0.024) + \cdots + 3.832^2(0.016) = 3.1634$

(2) $\sigma = \sqrt{\sigma^2} = \sqrt{3.1634} = 1.7787$

d. The median would have to be at most 19. Here, $P(X \leq 19) = 0.544 > 0.50$ and $P(X \geq 19) = 0.672 > 1 - 0.50$. Therefore, the median is 19 and the quality control department is incorrect.

5-21. a.

x	25	26	27	28	29	30	31	32	33
P(x)	0.005	0.0	0.015	0.120	0.255	0.265	0.185	0.120	0.035

b. $E(x) = \Sigma xP(x) = 25(0.005) + 26(0.0) + \cdots + 33(0.035)$
$= 29.965$

$\sigma^2 = \Sigma[x - E(x)]^2 P(x) = (-4.965)^2(0.005) + (-3.965$
$(0.0) + \cdots + 3.035^2(0.035) = 1.973,$

$\sigma = \sqrt{\sigma^2} = \sqrt{1.973} = 1.405$

c. 90% of the cast remain protected for 18 days.

5-23. a. $n = 15, p = .20, x = 4$

The event of interest is: $P(x = 4) = 0.1876.$

b. $P(x \leq 4) = 0.1876 + 0.2501 + 0.2309 + 0.1319 + 0.0352$

$P(x \leq 4) = 0.8358$

5-25. $P(x \leq 2) = 0.0031 + 0.0005 + 0.0000$
$P(x \leq 2) = 0.0036$

5-27. $P(x = 5) = 0.1029$

5-29. $P(x \geq 8) = P(8) + P(9) + P(10) + P(11) = 0.0462$
$+ 0.0126 + 0.0021 + 0.0002 = 0.0611$

5-31. a. $P(x = 3) = 0.1442$

b. $P(x \geq 4) = P(4) + P(5) + P(6) + P(7) = 0.2679$
$+ 0.2985 + 0.1848 + 0.0490 = 0.8002$

c. $P(x = 7) = 0.0490$

d. $E(x) = np = (7)(0.65) = 4.55$

5-33. a. $E(x) = np = 8(0.40) = 3.2$

b. $\sigma = \sqrt{npq} = \sqrt{8(0.4)(1 - 0.4)} = \sqrt{1.92} = 1.386$

c. $P(x > 3.2) = P(x \geq 4) = P(x = 4) + P(x = 5) +$
$P(x = 6) + P(x = 7) + P(x = 8) = 0.2322 + 0.1239 +$
$0.0413 + 0.0079 + 0.0007 = 0.4060$

d. $P(\mu - 2\sigma \leq x \leq \mu + 2\sigma) = P[3.2 - 2(1.386) \leq$
$x \leq 3.2 + 2(1.386)] = P(0.428 \leq x \leq 5.972) = P(1 \leq$
$x \leq 5) = P(x = 1) + P(x = 2) + P(x = 3) + P(x = 4) +$
$P(x = 5) = 0.0896 + 0.2090 + 0.2787 + 0.2322 +$
$0.1239 = 0.9334$

5-35. a. $\mu_x = E(x) = np = 10(0.308) = 3.08$

b. $P(x = 10) = \binom{10}{10} 0.607^{10}(0.393)^{10-10} = 0.0068$

c. $P(x \geq 8) = P(x = 8) + P(x = 9) + P(x = 10) =$

$\binom{10}{8} 0.308^8 (0.692)^{10-8} + \binom{10}{9} 0.308^9 (0.692)^{10-9} +$

$\binom{10}{10} 0.308^{10} (0.692)^{10-10} = \frac{10!}{8!(10-8)!} 0.308^8 \ 0.692^2 +$

$\frac{10!}{9!(10-9)!} 0.308^9 0.692^1 + \frac{10!}{10!(10-10)!} 0.308^{10} 0.692^0 =$

$0.0017 + 0.0002 + 0.0000 = 0.0019$

d. It is quite unlikely that the employees followed the national trend. The probability of such an occurrence is very small—for voting, only 0.0068, and for voting for President Bush, only 0.0019, assuming they were following the national trend.

5-37. a. $E(x) = np = (20)(0.80) = 16$

b. $P(x \leq 11) = 0.0074 + 0.0020 + \cdots + 0.0000$
$P(x \leq 11) = 0.0100$

c. Given this very small chance of 11 or fewer happening if 80% in the population would be able to identify, we would conclude that the 80% figure is too high. If so, then by the McNeal executives' definition, the advertising campaign will not be successful.

5-39. a. Expected Number $= 8(0.37) = 2.96$

b. Variance $= 8(0.37)(0.63) = 1.8648,$
Standard Deviation $= 1.3656$

c. $P(x \leq 2) = 0.0248 + 0.1166 + 0.2397 = 0.3811$

5-41. a. From the binomial table in Appendix B, we find the probability that $x = 5$ for $p = 0.15 = 0.1028.$

b. $E(x) = np = (20)(0.15) = 3.0$

c. From the binomial table, we find $P(15) = 0.1028 +$
$P(16) = 0.1821 + P(17) = 0.2428 + P(18) = 0.2293 +$
$P(19) = 0.1368 + P(20) = 0.0388 = 0.9326.$

5-43. a. $P(x = 5) = 0.156378,$ found using Excel.

b. $P(x = 3) = 0.2174$

c. $P(x = 0) + P(x = 1) + P(x = 2) = 0.01720 +$
$0.07587 + 0.16067 = 0.25374$

5-45. a. $\bar{x}_w = \dfrac{\sum w_i x_i}{\sum w_i} = \dfrac{30(0.50) + 10(0.10) + 50(0.35)}{30 + 10 + 50} = 0.372$

b. $\mu_x = E(x) = np = 20(0.60) = 12.$ Given that the average obtained is 12, 4 seems to be extremely small. It would seem that Vericours' estimate may be too high.

c. $P(x \leq 4) = P(x = 0) + P(x = 1) + P(x = 2) +$
$P(x = 3) + P(x = 4)$

$P(x = 4) = \binom{20}{0} 0.372^0 (0.628)^{20-0} + \binom{20}{1} 0.372^1$

$(0.628)^{20-1} + \binom{20}{2} 0.372^2 (0.628)^{20-2} + \binom{20}{3} 0.372^3$

$(0.628)^{20-3} + \binom{20}{4} 0.372^4 (0.628)^{20-4} = \dfrac{20!}{0!(20-0)!}$

$0.372^0 0.628^{20} + \dfrac{20!}{1!(20-1)!} 0.372^1 \ 0.628^{20-1} +$

$\dfrac{20!}{2!(20-2)!} 0.372^2 0.628^{20-2} + \dfrac{20!}{3!(20-3)!} 0.372^3$

$0.628^{20-3} + \dfrac{20!}{4!(20-4)!} 0.372^4 0.628^{20-4} =$

$0.0001 + 0.0011 + 0.0061 + 0.0216 + 0.0543 =$
0.0832

d. 0.0003

e. The redemption rate is lower than either the Vericours or TCA fulfillment estimate.

5-47. a. The number of pairs of wrong-size shoes that were delivered to customers is 13.

b. $P(x \geq 13) = 1 - P(x \leq 12) = 1 - 0.989994 =$
0.010006

c. It is very unusual to obtain 13 or more successes in 125 trials if the proportion of successes is 0.05.

d. $E(x) = np = 5,000,000(13/125).$ This indicates that the $E(\text{Cost}) = 520,000(4.75) = \$2,470,000.$

5-49. a.

	0	**1**	**All**
Number	113	37	150
Percent	75.33	24.67	100.00

b. $E(x) = np = 135(0.325) = 43.875$

c. $P(x \le 36) = 0.086047$
$P(x \ge 37)\ 1 - P(x \le 36) = 1 - 0.086047 = 0.913953$

d. Since there is a very large probability that the outcome we observed or something larger would occur, it seems quite plausible that the California percentage agrees with that obtained by the Bureau of Labor Statistics.

5-51. The desired probability is:
$P(x > 3) = 1 - [0.1687 + 0.1125 + 0.0500 + .0111]$
$P(x > 3) = 1 - 0.3423 = 0.6577$

5-53. $P(x_1 = 3, x_2 = 2, x_3 = 0) = \dfrac{C_{x_1}^{X_1} * C_{x_2}^{X_2} * C_{x_3}^{X_3}}{C_n^N}$

$= \dfrac{C_3^5 * C_2^4 * C_0^5}{C_5^{14}} = \dfrac{(10)(6)(1)}{2,002}$

$= \dfrac{60}{2,002} = 0.03$

5-55. a. $P(x) = \dfrac{C_{n-x}^{N-X} * C_x^X}{C_n^N} = P(x = 1) = \dfrac{C_{4-1}^{11-4} * C_1^4}{C_4^{11}} = 0.4242$

b. $P(x) = \dfrac{C_{n-x}^{N-X} * C_x^X}{C_n^N} = P(x = 3) = \dfrac{C_{4-3}^{11-7} * C_3^7}{C_4^{11}} = 0.4242$

c. $P(x = 2) = \dfrac{C_{4-2}^{11-4} * C_2^4}{C_4^{11}} = 0.3818$

$P(x = 3) = \dfrac{C_{4-3}^{11-4} * C_3^4}{C_4^{11}} = 0.0848$

$P(x = 4) = \dfrac{C_{4-4}^{11-4} * C_4^4}{C_4^{11}} = 0.0030$

Therefore, the $P(x > 2) = 0.4696$.

5-57. a. $P(x \le 3) = P(x = 0) + P(x = 1) + P(x = 2) + P(x = 3) = 0.0498 + 0.1494 + 0.2240 + 0.2240 = 0.6472$

b. $P(x > 3) = P(x \ge 4) = 1 - P(x \le 3) = 1 - 0.6472 = 0.3528$

c. $P(2 \le x \le 5) = P(x = 3) + P(x = 4) + P(x = 5) = 0.2240 + 0.1680 + 0.1008 = 0.4928$

d. From part a, $P(x \le 3) = 0.6472$ and $P(x \le 2) = 0.4232$. Therefore, $x' = 3$ is the smallest x', so $P(x \le x') > 0.50$.

5-59. Using the Poisson Table in Appendix C for $\lambda t = 17$, we find $P(26) = 0.0101$, $P(27) = 0.0063$, $P(28) = 0.0038$, $P(29) = 0.0023$, $P(30) = 0.0013$, $P(31) = 0.0007$, $P(32) = 0.0004$, $P(33) = 0.0002$, $P(34) = 0.0001$, $P(35) = 0.0000$, and all subsequent probabilities are essentially 0 above $P(35)$. The sum of these individual probabilities is the $P(x \ge 26) = 0.0252$.

5-61. The event of interest is

$P(x_1 = 7, x_2 = 0, x_3 = 0) = \dfrac{C_{x_1}^{X_1} * C_{x_2}^{X_2} * C_{x_3}^{X_3}}{C_n^N} = \dfrac{C_7^{10} * C_0^5 * C_0^5}{C_7^{20}}$

$= \dfrac{(120)(1)(1)}{77,520} = \dfrac{120}{77,520} = 0.0015$

It is very likely that the sampling was not done using random selection as directed by the customer.

5-63. a. $P(x = 0) = 0.000123$

b. $P(x > 14) = P(x \ge 15) = 1 - P(x \le 14)$
$= 1 - 0.9585 = 0.0415$

c. $P(x < 9) = P(x \le 8) = 0.4557$

d. The error rate is probably higher than 3 per 400.

5-65. The probability of rejecting the box of fasteners is $0.21672 + 0.03096 + 0.001032 = 0.24871$. The probability of accepting the shipment is equal to the probability of 1 or fewer defective in the sample. Therefore, the probability of accepting the shipment is $P(0) = 0.28173 + P(1) = 0.46956 = 0.7513$.

5-67. a. $P(x = 4)\dfrac{C_{n-x}^{N-X} C_x^X}{C_n^N} = \dfrac{C_{5-4}^{20-16} C_4^{16}}{C_5^{20}} = \dfrac{4(1,820)}{15,504} = 0.4696$

b. $P(x = 3)\dfrac{C_{n-x}^{N-X} C_x^X}{C_n^N} = \dfrac{C_{5-3}^{20-16} C_3^{16}}{C_5^{20}} = \dfrac{6(560)}{15,504} = 0.2167$

c. $P(x = 5) = \dfrac{C_{5-5}^{20-16} C_5^{16}}{C_5^{20}} = \dfrac{1(4,368)}{15,504} = 0.2817$

$P(x \ge 3) = 0.4696 + 0.2167 + 0.2817 = 0.9680$

5-69. a. $P(x_1, x_2, x_3) = \dfrac{C_{x_1}^{X_1} C_{x_2}^{X_2} C_{x_3}^{X_3}}{C_n^N} = \dfrac{C_5^{15} C_3^{26} C_2^9}{C_{10}^{50}}$

$= \dfrac{3,003(2,600)(36)}{10,272,278,170}$

$= 0.0274$

b. $P(10,0,0) = \dfrac{C_{x_1}^{X_1} C_{x_2}^{X_2} C_{x_3}^{X_3}}{C_n^N} = \dfrac{C_{10}^{15} C_0^{26} C_0^9}{C_{10}^{50}} = \dfrac{3,003(1)(1)}{10,272,278,170}$

$= 0.0000$

c. $P(6,0,4) = \dfrac{C_{x_1}^{X_1} C_{x_2}^{X_2} C_{x_3}^{X_3}}{C_n^N} = \dfrac{C_6^{15} C_0^{26} C_4^9}{C_{10}^{50}} = \dfrac{5,005(1)(126)}{10,272,278,170}$

$= 0.0001$

5-71. c. $P(x \ge 8) = 1 - P(x \le 7) = 1 - 0.9881 = 0.0119$

d. It is very unlikely that as many or more than 8 scratches would occur in 48 balls if the company's goal had been met. Therefore, we believe that the goal has not been met.

5-73. Both the binomial and Poisson distributions are discrete distributions. There are several differences in the two distributions. In the binomial distribution, you must be able to count the number of successes and number of failures. In the Poisson distribution, the outcomes of interest are rare relative to the possible outcomes.

5-75. a. The trials are dependent.

b. The probability of a success is the same (2/3) for all three trials. This indicates that the probability of a success being constant does not imply that the trials are independent.

5-77. $P(x = 9) = 0.0020$
We would likely conclude that the process is not in control. The filling process tends to overfill.

5-79. a. $P(x \le 2) = 0.0746 + 0.3151 + 0.5987 = 0.9884$

b. $P(x \le 2) = 0.1937 + 0.3874 + 0.3487 = 0.9298$

c. While the sampling plan is very good ($p = 0.9884$) at keeping shipments that actually contain 0.05 defects, the sampling plan also keeps most ($p = 0.9298$) of the shipments that contain twice ($p = 0.10$) as many defects as allowed. Thus the plan is one-sided. It favors the supplier.

5-81. $P(x \geq 1) = 1 - P(x = 0)$

$$P(0) = \frac{C_{4-0}^{20-4} \cdot C_0^4}{C_4^{20}}$$

$$= \frac{1{,}820 \cdot 1}{4{,}845} = 0.3756$$

$$1 - 0.3756 = 0.6244$$

5-83. a. Expected Number of Packages = 1.1

  b. Var. = 0.89, Standard Deviation = 0.9434

  c. The production cost would be $3(3) = \$9$; \$7.29 per package in order to break even.

5-85. a. The expected number of defectives is equal to 2. This means that on the average of several shipments Bentfield should expect the number of defectives to be 2. It does not mean that each shipment will have exactly 2 defects.

  b. The standard deviation is equal to 1.4142. It is a measure of average deviation from the mean number of defective products based on the probability distribution.

  c. This probability distribution is called a Uniform Distribution since the probability of each outcome is equally likely (0.2).

5-87. a. $P(x = 6) = \dfrac{C_{10-6}^{20-12} C_6^{12}}{C_{10}^{20}}$

$$= \frac{70(924)}{184{,}756} = 0.3501$$

  b. $P(x \leq 5) = 1 - P(x \geq 6) = 1 - P(x = 6) - P(x = 7) -$
  $P_x(x = 8) - P(x = 9) - P(x = 10) = 1 - 0.3501 -$

$$\frac{C_{10-7}^{20-12} C_7^{12}}{C_{10}^{20}} - \frac{C_{10-8}^{20-12} C_8^{12}}{C_{10}^{20}} - \frac{C_{10-9}^{20-12} C_9^{12}}{C_{10}^{20}} - \frac{C_{10-10}^{20-12} C_{10}^{12}}{C_{10}^{20}} =$$

  $1 - 0.3501 - 0.2400 - 0.075 - 0.0095 - 0.0004 =$
  0.3250

5-89. a. Proportion of defectives is $38/[20(90)] = 0.02$.

  b. $E(x) = \mu = np = 20(0.02) = 0.4$;

$$\sigma = \sqrt{npq} = \sqrt{20(0.02)(1-0.02)} = 0.6261$$

  c. $\mu \pm 3\sigma = 0.4 \pm 3(0.6261) = (-1.4783, 2.2783)$. Since it is impossible to have a negative number here, the limits are (0, 2.2783).

  d. $P(0 \leq x \leq 2.2783) = P(0 \leq x \leq 2)$, $1 - P(x \leq 2) = 1 - 0.9929 = 0.0071$

Chapter 6

6-1. a. The probability from the standard normal table associated with $z = 1.50$ is 0.4332. This corresponds to the area between $z = 1.50$ and the mean. The desired probability is found by subtracting 0.4332 from 0.5000, giving 0.0668.

  b. The probability from the standard normal table associated with $z = -0.50$ is 0.1915. This corresponds to the area between $z = -0.50$ and the mean. The desired probability is found by subtracting 0.1915 from 0.5000, giving 0.3085.

  c. $P(90 \leq x \leq 130) = 0.1915 + 0.4332 = 0.6247$

6-3.

  a. $z = \dfrac{x - \mu}{\sigma} = \dfrac{225 - 200}{20} = \dfrac{25}{20} = 1.25$

  b. $z = \dfrac{x - \mu}{\sigma} = \dfrac{190 - 200}{20} = \dfrac{-10}{20} = -0.50$

  c. $z = \dfrac{x - \mu}{\sigma} = \dfrac{240 - 200}{20} = \dfrac{40}{20} = 2.00$

6-5. a. $1.29 = \dfrac{x - 5.5}{0.50}$

  $x = 1.29(0.50) + 5.5 = 6.145$

  Thus, the desired value is $x = 6.145$.

  b. Solve for μ as follows:

$$1.65 = \frac{6.145 - \mu}{.50}$$

  $\mu = 6.145 - (1.65)(.50) = 5.32$

  Thus, the population mean must be reduced from 5.5 to 5.32 in order for the probability of a value exceeding 6.145 to be reduced from 0.10 to 0.05.

6-7. a. $P(z > 2.78) = 0.5 - 0.4973 = 0.0027$
  Therefore, $P(x > 1{,}550) = 0.0027$.

  b. $P(z < -0.83) = 0.5 - 0.2967 = 0.2033$
  Therefore, $P(x < 1{,}485) = 0.2033$.

  c. $P(z < -1.39) = 0.5 - 0.4177 = 0.0823$
  $P(z > 1.94) = 0.5 - 0.4738 = 0.0262$
  $P(x < 1{,}475 \text{ or } x > 1{,}535) = 0.0823 + 0.0262 = 0.1085$

6-9. a. $P(z < -1.5) = 0.5 - 0.4332 = 0.0668$
  Therefore, $P(x < 46.5) = 0.0668$.

  b. $P(z > 1.11) = 0.5 - 0.3665 = 0.1335$
  Therefore, $P(x > 78) = 0.1335$.

  c. $P(-1 < z < 1.5) = 0.3413 + 0.4332 = 0.7745$
  Therefore, $P(51 < x < 73.5) = 0.7745$.

6-11. a. $P(0 < z < 1.96) = 0.4750$

  b. $P(z > 1.645) = \dfrac{0.4495 + 0.4505}{2} = 0.4500$

  c. $P(1.28 < z \leq 2.33) = P(0 < z \leq 2.33) - P(0 < z \leq 1.28) = 0.4901 - 0.3997 = 0.0904$

  d. $P(-2 \leq z \leq 3) = P(-2 < z \leq 0) + P(0 < z \leq 3) = P(0 < z \leq 2) + P(0 < z \leq 3) = 0.4772 + 0.49865 = 0.97585$

  e. $P(z > -1) = P(-1 < z \leq 0) + P(z \geq 0) = P(0 < z \leq 1) + P(z \geq 0) = 0.3413 + 0.5000 = 0.8513$

6-13. a. $P(z > 1.645) = 0.05$; $x_0 = \mu + z_0\sigma$, so $x_0 = 13.6 + 1.645(2.90) = 18.37$

  b. $P(0 \leq z \leq 1.96) = 0.4750$, so $P(z \leq 1.96) = 0.05 + 0.475$; $x_0 = \mu + z_0\sigma$, so $x_0 = 13.6 + 1.96(2.90) = 19.284$

  c. $P(0 \leq z \leq 1.96) = 0.4750$, so $P(-1.96 \leq z \leq 1.96) = 0.4750 + 0.4750 = 0.95$; $x_0 = \mu + z_0\sigma$, so $\mu - x_0 = z_0\sigma = 1.96(2.90) = 5.684$. Therefore, $x_0 = \mu - 5.684 = 13.6 - 5.684 = 7.916$.

6-15. a. Since $P(0 \leq z \leq 1.67) = 0.4525$, $P(z \geq 1.67) = P(z > 1.67) = 0.5 - 0.4525 = 0.0475 = P(x > 3.5)$.

b. Since $P(-0.83 \leq z \leq 0) = 0.2967$, $P(z > -0.83) = P(-0.83 \leq z \leq 0) + 0.5 P(z > -0.83) = 0.2967 + 0.5 = 0.7967$.

c. Since $x_0 = \mu + z_0\sigma$, $x_0 = 3 + 1.28(0.3) = 3.384$ years. Therefore, the length of life values for the 10% of the watches' batteries that last the longest are those greater than 3.384 years.

6-17. a. $P(x < 49.5) = P(z < (49.5 - 50)/1.25 = P(z < -0.40) = 0.5 - 0.1554 = 0.3446$

b. $P(48.5 < z < 51) = P((48.5 - 50)/1.25 < z < (51 - 50)/1.25) = P(-1.2 < z < 0.8) = 0.3849 + 0.2881 = 0.6730$

c. $1.04 = \dfrac{x - 50}{1.25}$

Solving for x,

$x = 50 + 1.04(1.25) = 51.30$

d. $2.055 = \dfrac{52 - 50}{\sigma}$

Solving for σ,

$\sigma = (52 - 50)/2.055 = 0.9732$

6-19. a. $2,500 + 1.96(300) = 2,500 + 588 = 3,088$ toys

b. $P(x > 2,750) = P(z) > \dfrac{2750 - 2500}{300}$

$= P(z > 0.8333) = 0.2023$

c. If $\sigma = 500$, the retailer will need to stock $2,500 + 1.96(500) = 2,500 + 980 = 3,480$ toys. This is an increase of $3,480 - 3,088 = 392$ toys over the case where the standard deviation of demand was 300 per week.

6-21. $P(x > 35) = 0.3413 + 0.5000 = 0.8413$

6-23. Thus, there is a 0.67 probability that a loan selected at random from the Wells Fargo real estate portfolio will have a balance less than $170,000; thus, 67 loans.

6-25. a. $P(x > 1500) = P\left(z > \dfrac{1500 - 1200}{350}\right)$

$= P(z > 0.86) = 0.50 - P(0 \leq z \leq 0.86)$

$= 0.5 - 0.3051 = 0.1949$

b. $\mu \pm 2\sigma = 1,200 \pm 2(350) = (500, 1900)$

$P(500 \leq x \leq 1900) = P\left(\dfrac{500 - 1200}{350} \leq z \leq \dfrac{1900 - 1200}{350}\right)$

$= P(-2 \leq z \leq 2) = P(-2 \leq z \leq 0) + P(0 \leq z \leq 2)$

$= 2P(0 \leq z \leq 2) = 2(0.4772) = 0.9544$

c. The mean and the median are the same for a normal distribution. Here the mean is $1,200 and so is the median.

6-27. a. $P(11.98 \leq x \leq 12.02) = 0.2157 + 0.2157 = 0.4314$

b. $-1.65 = \dfrac{11.97 - \mu}{0.035}$

$\mu = 11.97 + (1.65)(0.035) = 12.03$

6-29. a.

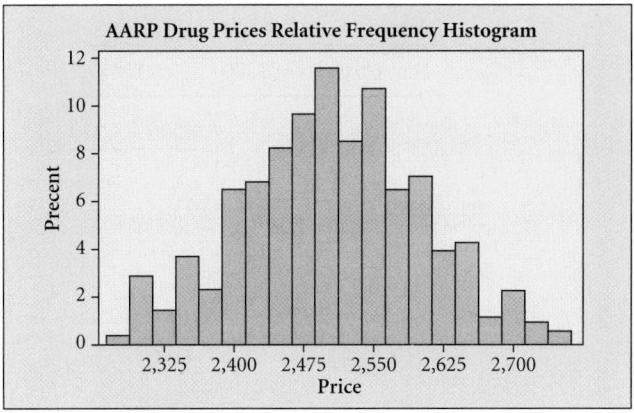

Although the distribution is not perfectly "mound-shaped," the histogram appears to be approximately so.

b. Descriptive Statistics: Price

Variable	Mean	StDev
Price	2.5052	0.0961

c. $P(x \leq 2.12) = P\left(z \leq \dfrac{2.12 - 2.51}{0.0961}\right)$

$= P(z \leq -4.06)$

Since $P(0 \leq z \leq 3.09) = 0.4990$, then $P(z > 3.09) = P(-3.09 < z) = 0.5 - 0.4990 = 0.0010$.
Since $P(z \leq -4.06) < P(-3.09 < z) = 0.0010$, $P(z \leq -4.06) < 0.0010 \approx 0$.

6-31. a.

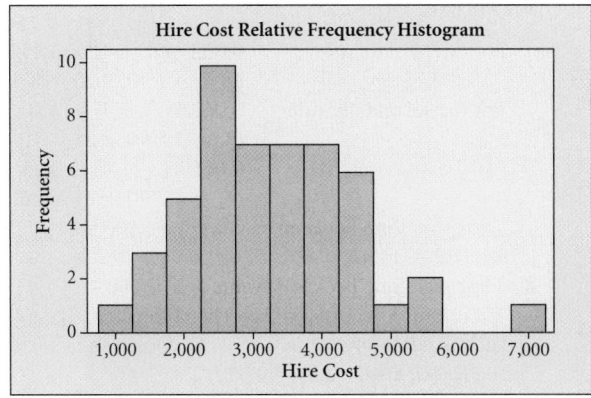

The histogram seems to be "bell-shaped" with the exception of three or four observations. These could be due to sampling error.

b. Descriptive Statistics: Hire Cost

Variable	Mean	StDev
Hire Cost	3270	1181

c. The $P(2{,}000 < x < 3{,}000) = P\left(\dfrac{2{,}000 - 3{,}270}{1{,}181} < z < \right.$

$\left.\dfrac{3{,}000 - 3{,}270}{1{,}181}\right) = P(-1.08 < z < -0.23) = P(-1.08 \le$

$z \le 0) - P(-0.23 \le z < 0) = P(0 \le z < 1.08) -$
$P(0 \le z \le 0.23) = 0.3599 - 0.0910 = 0.2689.$

d. Then $P(x > 2{,}500 | 2{,}000 < x < 3{,}000) =$
$\dfrac{P(2{,}500 < x < 3{,}000)}{P(2{,}000 < x < 3{,}000)} = \dfrac{0.1512}{0.2689} = 0.5623.$

6-33. a. $P(c \le x \le d) = f(x)(d - c) = 0.25(8 - 5.5) =$
0.625

b. $P(x > 7) = P(7 < x \le 9) = f(x)(d - c) =$
$0.25(9 - 7) = 0.50$

c. $\mu = \dfrac{b + a}{2} = \dfrac{9 + 5}{2} = 7, \quad \sigma = \sqrt{\dfrac{(b - a)^2}{12}}$

$= \sqrt{\dfrac{(9 - 5)^2}{12}} = \sqrt{1.333} = 1.155$

d. $(\mu \pm 2\sigma) = [7 \pm 2(1.155)] = 7 \pm 2.31 =$
(4.69, 9.31). Since the distributions limits are 5 and 9,
$P(4.69 \le x \le 9.31) = 1$, or 100%.

6-35. a. $P(x < 0.75) = 1 - e^{-(0.6667)(0.75)} = 1 - 0.6065 =$
0.3935

b. In this case, $a = 112.5$ seconds, which is 112.5/60 =
1.875 minutes. $P(x > 112.5 \text{ seconds}) = e^{-\lambda a} =$
$e^{-(0.6667)(1.875)} = e^{-1.25} = 0.2865$

6-37. a. Using the Addition Rule for two events, $P[(10 \le x \le$
20) or $(15 \le x \le 25)] = P(10 \le x \le 20) + P(15 \le$
$x \le 25) - P[(10 \le x \le 20)$ and $(15 \le x \le 25)] =$
$P(10 \le x \le 20) + P(15 \le x \le 25) - P[(15 \le x \le$
$20)] = 0.5 + 0.5 - 0.05(20 - 15) = 0.75.$

b. $f(x) = \dfrac{1}{b - a} = \dfrac{1}{20 - 4} = 0.0625$

For the first quartile	$0.0625(Q_1 - 4) = 0.25$
	$Q_1 = 4.25/0.0625 = 8$
For the second quartile	$0.0625(Q_2 - 4) = 0.50$
	$Q_2 = 4.50/0.0625 = 12$
For the third quartile	$0.0625(Q_3 - 4) = 0.75$
	$Q_3 = 4.75/0.0625 = 16$

c. The mean time between events equals $1/\lambda =$
$1/0.069 = 14.43.$

d. The mean time between events $= 1/\lambda = 0.4.$
Therefore, $\lambda = 1/0.4 = 2.5$. The 90th percentile is
such that $0.90 = 1 - e^{-2.5x}$. Therefore, $x =$
$[\ln(1 - 0.90)]/(-2.5) = 0.92.$

6-39. Students can use Excel's EXPONDIST function to solve
this problem.

a. $\lambda = 1/4{,}000 = 0.00025; P(x < 2{,}100) =$
EXPONDIST(2100,0.00025, true) = 0.4084. Yes,
because this is a pretty high probability of a failure at
less than 2,100.

b. $100{,}000(0.4084) = 40{,}840$

6-41. a. $f(x) = \dfrac{1}{b - a} = \dfrac{1}{20 - 0} = 0.05$

$P(x > 10) = 1 - P(x \le 10) = 1 - 0.05(10 - 0) = 0.50$

b. $P(x \le 6) = 0.05(6 - 0) = 0.30$

c. $P(8 \le x \le 15) = 0.05(15 - 8) = 0.35$

6-43. a. $P(x \le 3) = 1 - e^{-\lambda a} = 1 - e^{-0.75(3)} = 0.1054$

b. $P(x \ge 12) = e^{-\lambda a} = e^{-0.75(12)} = 0.00012$

c. $P(4 \le x \le 6) = e^{-0.75(4)} - e^{-0.75(6)} = 0.0498 -$
$0.0111 = 0.0387$

6-45. a. $P(347 \le x \le 350) = f(x)(d - c) = 0.033(350 - 347) =$
0.099

b. $P(320 \le x \le 332) = f(x)(d - c) = 0.033(332 - 320) =$
0.396

c. $\mu = \dfrac{b + a}{2} = \dfrac{350 + 320}{2} = 335$

d. $\sigma^2 = \dfrac{(b - a)^2}{12} = \dfrac{(350 - 320)^2}{12} = 75$

6-47. a. $P(x > 5{,}000) = 1 - P(0 \le x \le 5{,}000) = 1 -$
$[1 - e^{-0.0008(5000)}] = 0.0183$

b. $P(x > 1{,}250) = 1 - P(0 \le x \le 1{,}250) = 1 -$
$[1 - e^{-0.0008(1250)}] = 0.3679$

c. For the exponential distribution, the average = standard deviation = $1/\lambda$. Therefore, 1 standard deviation
below the mean = $1{,}250 - 1{,}250 = 0$. So this exercise is requiring $P(x > 0) = 1.$

6-49. a.

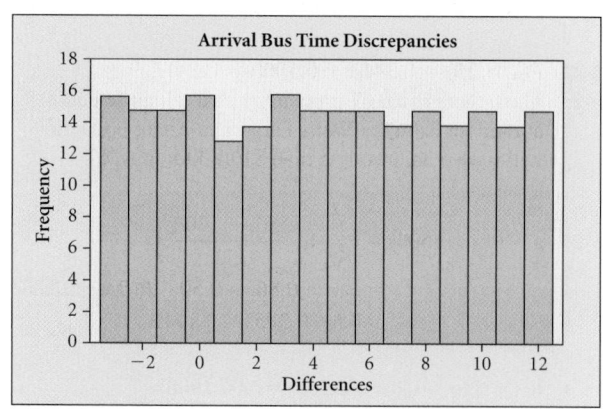

The frequency for each difference seems to be very
close to the same, a characteristic of a uniform
distribution.

b. $f(x) = \dfrac{1}{b - a} = \dfrac{1}{12 - (-3)}$
$= 0.067$

c. $P(11 < x \le 12) = f(x)(d - c) = 0.067(12 - 11) =$
0.067

d. Median $= \mu = \dfrac{b + a}{2} = \dfrac{12 + (-3)}{2} = 4.5$

6-51. The exponential distribution is defined by a sample parameter, its mean. It is not a symmetric distribution.

6-53. A discrete distribution allows you to list the individual outcomes. A continuous distribution can take on any value over some range of values.

6-55. a. The average $= 1/\lambda = 0.5$. Therefore, $\lambda = 1/(0.5) = 2$. Since $P(0 \le x \le a) = 1 - e^{-\lambda a}$, $P(x > 1) = 1 - P(0 \le x \le 1) = 1 - [1 - e^{-2(1)}] = e^{-2} = 0.1353$.

b. $P(x > 1 + 2 \mid X > 2) = \dfrac{P[(x > 3) \text{ and } (x > 2)]}{P(x > 2)}$

$= \dfrac{P(x > 3)}{P(x > 2)} = \dfrac{1 - [1 - e^{-2(3)}]}{1 - [1 - e^{-2(2)}]}$

$= \dfrac{e^{-2(3)}}{e^{-2(2)}} = e^{-2} = 0.1353$

6-57. Machine #1:

$P(11.9 \le x \le 12.0) = P\left(\dfrac{11.9 - 11.9}{0.07} \le z \le \dfrac{12.0 - 11.9}{0.07}\right)$

$= P(0 \le z \le 1.43) = 0.4236$

Machine #2:

$P(11.9 \le x \le 12.0) = P\left(\dfrac{11.9 - 12.0}{0.05} \le z \le \dfrac{12.0 - 12.0}{0.05}\right)$

$= P(-2 \le z \le 0) = P(0 \le z \le 2) = 0.4772$

Machine #2 should be selected.

6-59. a. $f(x) = 1/(b - a) = 1/(0.35 - 0.15) = 5$

b. $P(0.15 \le x \le 0.20) = f(x)(d - c) = 5(0.20 - 0.15) = 0.25$

c. $P(x > 0.325) = P(0.325 \le x \le 0.35) = f(x)(d - c) = 5(0.35 - 0.325) = 0.125$

d. $P(x > 0.325 \mid x > 0.2) = \dfrac{P[(x > 0.325) \text{ and } (x > 0.2)]}{P(x > 0.2)}$

$= \dfrac{P(x > 0.325)}{P(x > 0.2)} = \dfrac{0.125}{0.75} = 0.167$

6-61. $\lambda = 12/\text{hour} = 0.2$ per minute; $P(x < 4) = 1 - e^{-(.2)(4)} = 1 - 0.4493 = 0.5507$

6-63. a. $P(5.85 < x < 6.15) = P[(5.85 - 6)/0.1 < z < (6.15 - 6)/0.1] = P(-1.5 < z < 1.5) = 2(0.4332) = 0.8664$. Since this is less than 99%, Bryce Brothers should not purchase this machine.

b. For 99%, chance z would be $+2.575$.

$2.575 = (6.15 - 6)/\text{standard deviation}$; standard deviation $= 0.058$ inch

6-65. a. $P(x < 10) = P(z < (10 - 14.25)/2.92) = P(z < -1.46) = 0.5 - 0.4279 = 0.0721$

b. $P(x < 9.375) = P(z < (9.375 - 14.25)/2.92) = P(z < -1.67) = 0.5 - 0.4525 = 0.0475$

6-67. a.

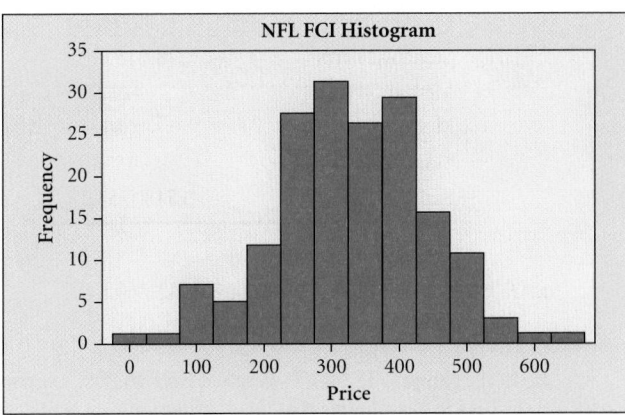

The histogram seems to be "bell-shaped" with the exception of a few observations. These could be due to sampling error.

b. Descriptive Statistics: Price

Variable	Mean	StDev
Price	329.82	112.41

c. Minitab output:

Inverse Cumulative Distribution Function

Normal with mean = 329.82 and standard deviation = 112.41

$P(X <= x)$	x
0.9	473.879

d. 347 is the 56th percentile.

6-69. a.

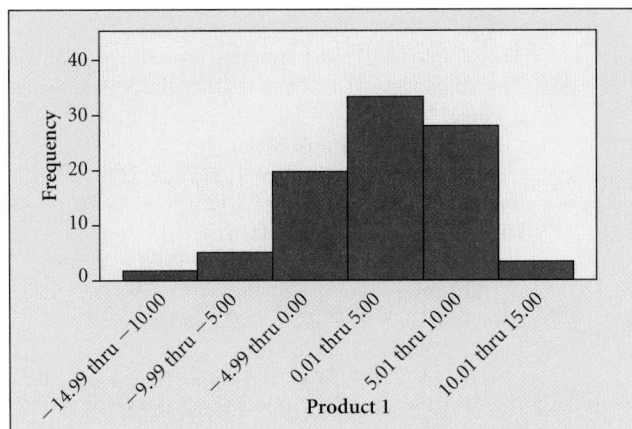

It does appear that the distribution is approximately normally distributed.

b. Mean $= 2.453$; Standard Deviation $= 4.778$

c. $P(x < -12) = P(z < (-12 - 2.4527)/4.7775) = P(z < -3.03) = 0.5 - 0.4988 = 0.0012$

d. No, this would not be an appropriate claim.

6-71.

Garbage Truck Weights	
Mean	42260.64
Standard Error	278.2153265
Median	42325.5
Mode	40010
Standard Deviation	3934.55888
Sample Variance	15480753.58

a. $P(x > 46,000) = P(z > (46,000 - 42,260.64)/3,934.55888) = P(z > 0.95) = 0.5 - 0.3289 = 0.1711$

b. In the sample, 35 of 200 weighed over 46,000, which is 0.175; this implies that the distribution is nearly normally distributed.

c. $P(x < 38,000) = P(z < ((38,000 - 42,260.64)/3,934.56) = P(z < -1.08) = 0.50 - 0.3599 = 0.1401$

Chapter 7

7-1. Sampling Error $= \bar{x} - \mu = 10.17 - 11.38 = -1.21$

7-3. Sampling Error $= \bar{x} - \mu = 106.5 - 125 = -18.50$

7-5. a. Sampling Error $= \bar{x} - \mu = 24.5 - 25 = -0.5$

b. The mean of the 8 largest data points is

$\bar{x} = \dfrac{\sum x_i}{n} = \dfrac{247}{8} = 30.875$. This produces a

sampling error of $\bar{x} - \mu = 30.875 - 25 = 5.875$.

c. The mean of the 8 smallest data points is

$\bar{x} = \dfrac{\sum x_i}{n} = \dfrac{152}{8} = 19$. This produces a sampling

error of $\bar{x} - \mu = 19 - 25 = -6$.

7-7. a. Sampling Error $= \bar{x} - \mu = 18 - 22.125 = -4.125$
The sample of 10 has a sampling error of -4.125.
The sample has a smaller mean than the population as a whole.

b. Lowest Possible Sample Mean
$= (6 + 6 + 9 + 10 + 10 + 11)/6 = 52/6 = 8.667$
Sampling Error $= 8.667 - 22.125 = -13.458$
Highest Possible Sample Mean
$= (32 + 32 + 33 + 33 + 34 + 35)/6 = 199/6$
$= 33.167$
Sampling Error $= 33.167 - 22.125 = 11.042$

c. Lowest Possible Sample Mean
$= (6 + 6 + 9 + 10 + 10 + 11 + 13 + 14 + 14 + 19 + 19 + 24)/12 = 155/12 = 12.917$
Sampling Error $= 12.917 - 22.125 = -9.208$
Highest Possible Sample Mean
$= (27 + 28 + 30 + 30 + 31 + 31 + 32 + 32 + 33 + 33 + 34 + 35)/12 = 376/12 = 31.333$
Sampling Error $= 31.333 - 22.125 = 9.208$

7-9. a. $\mu = 35,802/25 = 1,432.08$

b. $\bar{x} = 7,596/5 = 1,591.2$
Sampling Error $= 1,591.2 - 1,432.08 = 87.12$

c. The range of extreme sampling error for a sample of size $n = 7$ is -175.937 to 178.634.

7-11. a. The range in sampling error for a sample of size 6 is -194.33 to 225.67.

b. The range in sampling error for a sample of size 10 is -164.33 to 178.67. Larger sample sizes will yield a lower range in the potential sampling error.

7-13. Sampling Error $= \bar{x} - \mu = 6.8 - 6.16 = 0.64$

7-15. Sampling Error $= \bar{x} - \mu = 5.24 - 7.4 = -2.16$
The sample mean is 2.16 lower than the population mean of 7.4.

7-17. a. $\mu = \dfrac{\sum x}{N} = \dfrac{13,364.664}{1,345} = 9,936.55$

b. Student answers will vary depending on the sample selected.

c. Again, student responses are going to differ because each one will select a different sample.

d. Student answers will vary depending on the sample selected.

e. Student reports will vary depending on individual results.

7-19. a. $\bar{x} = \dfrac{\sum x}{n} = \dfrac{\$2,629}{166} = \$15.84$

Sampling Error $= \bar{x} - \mu = \$15.84 - \$20.00 = -\$4.16$

b. It is possible that this sample constitutes a random sample. However, there is no way to be assured of that.

7-21. a.

Diameter	Mean Value
6	$ 7.90
7	$ 11.13
8	$ 16.55
9	$ 21.54
10	$ 28.87
11	$ 35.40
12	$ 41.80
13	$ 48.54
14	$ 58.86
15	$ 65.97
16	$ 76.48
17	$ 85.33
18	$ 93.63
19	$105.01
20	$109.89
21	$120.31

b. Assuming that the sample means calculated in part a are based on a random sample from the population of all logs to be used by the company, there is no way to predict with any certainty what the sampling error is.

7-23. $P(\bar{x} > 2,100) = 0.5000 - 0.3907 = 0.1093$

7-25. From the standard normal table, the probability associated with $z = 1.50 = 0.4332$. Therefore, $P(\bar{x} < 1325) = P(z < 1.5) = 0.5 + 0.4332 = 0.9332$.

7-27. From the standard normal table, the probability associated with $z = -0.75 = 0.2734$. Therefore, $P(\bar{x} < 95) = P(z < -0.75) = 0.5 - 0.2734 = 0.2266$.

7-29. a. $P(\bar{x} > \bar{x}_0) = P\left(z > \dfrac{\bar{x}_0 - \mu}{\sigma / \sqrt{n}}\right)$, so $P(\bar{x} > 37)$

$$= P\left(z > \dfrac{37 - 40}{13 / \sqrt{49}}\right) = P(z > -1.62)$$

$$= 0.5 + P(0 \le z \le 1.62) = 0.5 + 0.4474$$
$$= 0.9474$$

b. $P(\bar{x} \le 43) = P\left(z \le \dfrac{43 - 40}{13 / \sqrt{49}}\right) = P(z \le 1.62)$

$$= 0.5 + P(0 \le z \le 1.62) = 0.5 + 0.4474$$
$$= 0.9474$$

c. $P(37 < \bar{x} < 43) = P\left(\dfrac{37 - 40}{13 / \sqrt{49}} < z < \dfrac{43 - 40}{13 / \sqrt{49}}\right)$

$$= P(-1.62 \le z \le 1.62)$$
$$= 2P(0 \le z \le 1.62) = 2(0.4474)$$
$$= 0.8948$$

d. $P(43 < \bar{x} < 45) = P\left(\dfrac{43 - 40}{13 / \sqrt{49}} < z < \dfrac{45 - 40}{13 / \sqrt{49}}\right)$

$$= P(1.62 \le z \le 2.69)$$
$$= P(0 \le z \le 2.69) - P(0 \le z \le 1.62)$$
$$= 0.4964 - 0.4474 = 0.0490$$

e. $P(\bar{x} \le 35) = P\left(z \le \dfrac{35 - 40}{13 / \sqrt{49}}\right) = P(z \le -2.69)$

$$= 0.5 - P(0 \le z \le 2.69) = 0.5 - 0.4964$$
$$= 0.0036$$

7-31. a. From the standard normal table, the probability associated with $z = -0.50 = 0.1915$ and the probability associated with $z = 0.50 = 0.1915$. Therefore, $P(70 \le \bar{x} \le 80) = P(-0.50 \le z \le 0.50) = 0.1915 + 0.1915 = 0.3830$.

b. From the standard normal table, the probability associated with $z = -2.00 = 0.4772$ and the probability associated with $z = 2.00 = 0.4772$. Therefore, $P(70 \le \bar{x} \le 80) = P(-2.00 \le z \le 2.00) = 0.4722 + 0.4722 = 0.9444$.

c. From the standard normal table, the probability associated with $z = -2.22 = 0.4868$ and the probability associated with $z = 2.22 = 0.4868$. Therefore, $P(70 \le \bar{x} \le 80) = P(-2.22 \le z \le 2.22) = 0.4868 + 0.4868 = 0.9736$.

7-33. From the standard normal table, the probability associated with $z = 1.00 = 0.3413$. Therefore, $P(\bar{x} \le 12.5) = P(z \le 1.00) = 0.50 + 0.3413 = 0.8413$.

a. Step 1: Compute the sample mean. The sample mean is

$$\bar{x} = \frac{\Sigma x}{n} = \frac{450}{36} = 12.5.$$

Step 2: From the standard normal table, the probability associated with $z = 1.00 = 0.3413$. Therefore, $P(\bar{x} < 12.5) = P(z > 1.00) = 0.50 - 0.3413 = 0.1587$.

b. Although the population of returns processed daily is not normally distributed, the sample size is sufficiently large so that the sampling distribution of $\bar{x}$ is normally distributed.

7-35. $P(\bar{x} \ge 4.2) = 0.5000 - 0.4989 = 0.0011$
The manager should be concerned that the waiting time has increased.

7-37. a. $P(\bar{x} \ge 15.7) = P(z \ge 2.80) = 0.5 - P(0 \le z \le 2.80)$
$$= 0.5 - 0.4974 = 0.0026$$

b. $P(\bar{x} \ge 15.7) = P(z \ge 5.00) = 0$

c. $P(13.44 \le \bar{x} \le 15.12)$
$$= P(-1.72 \le z \le 1.64)$$
$$= P(0 \le z \le 1.72) + P(0 \le z \le 1.64)$$
$$= 0.4573 + 0.4495 = 0.9068$$

7-39. $\bar{x} = \dfrac{\Sigma x}{n} = \dfrac{718.39}{60} = 11.97$

$z = \dfrac{\bar{x} - \mu}{\dfrac{\sigma}{\sqrt{n}}} = \dfrac{11.97 - 12}{\dfrac{0.05}{\sqrt{60}}} = -4.65$

$P(\bar{x} \le 11.97) = 0.5000 - 0.5000 = 0.0$

7-41. a. The population mean is 55.68 years with a population standard deviation equal to 6.75 years.

b. Student answers will vary depending on what sample is selected.

c. Student answers to parts b and c will vary depending on the sample selected.

7-43. a.

Median of HD Costs	Mean of HD Costs
Median of HD Costs = 144.89	Mean of HD Costs = 141.99

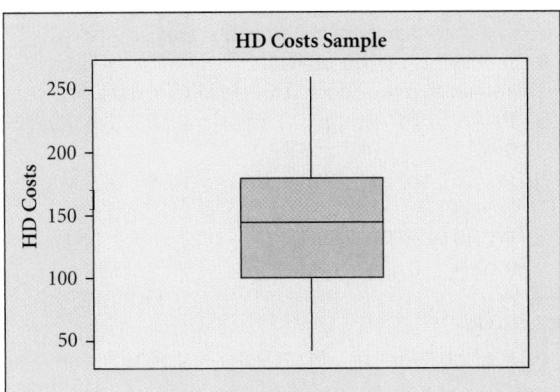

b. $\sigma_{\bar{x}} = \dfrac{\sigma}{\sqrt{n}} = \dfrac{50}{\sqrt{150}} = 4.082$

$$P(\bar{x} < 136.99) = P\left(z < \dfrac{136.99 - 150}{4.082}\right)$$
$$= P(z < -3.19) \cong 0$$

$$P(\bar{x} > 146.99) = P\left(z > \frac{146.99 - 150}{4.082}\right)$$
$$= P(z > -0.74) = 0.5000 + 0.2704$$
$$= 0.7704$$

c. The boxplot presents differing evidence indicating both positive and negative skewness. This could very well signal either sampling error or a nonnormal distribution of the population. However, since the sample size is considerably larger than 30, there is not a requirement that the population be normally distributed in order to make these procedures valid.

7-45. $P(p \le 0.27)$ or $P(z \le -0.93) = 0.5 - 0.3238 = 0.1762$

7-47. a. $P(0.18 \le p \le 0.23)$ or $P(-1.12 \le z \le 1.68) = 0.3686 + 0.4535 = 0.8221$

b. $P(0.18 \le p \le 0.23)$ or $P(-0.71 \le z \le 1.06) = 0.2611 + 0.3554 = 0.6165$

7-49. a. Sampling Error $= p - \pi = 0.65 - 0.70 = -0.05$

b. The probability associated with $z = -1.09$ is 0.3621. This, the desired probability is

$$P(p \le 0.65) = 0.5000 = 0.3621 = 0.1379$$

7-51. a. $p = \dfrac{x}{n} = \dfrac{27}{60} = 0.45$

b. $P(p \ge 0.45) = 0.5000 - 0.2852 = 0.2148$

7-53. a. $P(p \le 0.35)$ or $P(z \le 1.09) = 0.50 + 0.3621 = 0.8621$

b. Using the same steps outlined above:
$$P(p > 0.40)\quad \text{or}\quad P(z > 2.18) = 0.50 - 0.4854$$
$$= 0.0146$$

c. $P(0.25 \le p \le 0.40)$ or $P(-1.09 \le z \le 2.18) = 0.3621 + 0.4854 = 0.8475$

d. $P(p \ge 0.27)$ or $P(z \ge -0.65) = 0.50 + 0.2422 = 0.7422$

7-55. $p = \dfrac{x}{n} = \dfrac{190}{200} = 0.95$

$$\sigma_p = \sqrt{\frac{\pi(1-\pi)}{n}} = \sqrt{\frac{0.97(1-0.97)}{200}} = 0.012$$

From the standard normal distribution table in Appendix D, the probability associated with $z = -1.67$ is 0.4525. Therefore, $P(p \le 0.95) = 0.5 - 0.4525 = 0.0475$.

7-57. a. $P(p \ge 0.60)$ or $P(z \ge 1.54) = 0.50 - 0.4382 = 0.0618$

b. $P(p \ge 0.60)$ or $P(z \ge 0.63) = 0.50 - 0.2357 = 0.2643$

c. $P(0.40 \le p \le 0.60)$ or $P(-0.27 \le z \le 1.54) = 0.1064 + 0.4382 = 0.5446$

7-59. a. $P(p \ge 0.25)$ or $P(z \ge -1.47) = 0.50 + 0.4292 = 0.9292$

b. $P(p \ge 0.400)$ or $P(z \ge 2.21) = 0.5000 - 0.4864 = 0.0136$.

c. $P(0.278 \le p \le 0.389)$ or $P(-1.05 \le z \le 1.19) = 0.3531 + 0.3830 = 0.7361$

7-61. a. There are 131 1s, which means 131 sampled subscribers have annual incomes over \$100,000 and 65 0s which means 65 sampled subscribers have incomes of \$100,000 or less.

b. $p = 131/196 = 0.668$

c. $P(p > 0.668) = P\left(z > \dfrac{0.668 - 0.65}{\sqrt{\dfrac{0.65(1-0.65)}{196}}} = 0.53\right)$
$$= 0.5 - 0.2019 = 0.2981$$

d. It would be a judgment call. The sample proportion of 0.668 is higher than the claimed population proportion of 0.65. But because the chance of getting a sample proportion of 0.668 or higher if the true proportion is 0.65 is about almost 30%, the value seen could be due to sampling error.

7-63. a. The sample proportion $= 0.72$.

b. The sampling error $= p - \pi = 0.72 - 0.66 = 0.06$.

c. $P(p \ge 0.72) = 1 - P(p \le 0.72) = 1 - 0.963374 = 0.0366$

d. It is very unlikely (0.0366) that a sample proportion of 0.72 or more would be obtained from a population whose proportion was 0.66.

7-65. Examples will vary.

7-67. The finite correction factor should be used if the sample size is greater than 5% of the population size and sampling is performed without replacement.

7-69. The standard deviation and the standard error both measure the dispersion or spread of data sets or variables. The difference between them is that the standard error measures the spread of the sampling distribution of a statistic. That statistic is a function of the data sets or variables whose spread is measured by a standard deviation.

7-71. A sample size of 1 would be sufficient since the population itself is normal. Large samples would also produce normally distributed sampling distributions.

7-73. $P(p \ge 0.33) = P\left(z \ge \dfrac{0.33 - 0.30}{\sqrt{\dfrac{0.30(1-0.30)}{200}}}\right)$
$$= P(z \ge 0.93) = 0.5 - 0.3238 = 0.1762$$

7-75. a. $\mu = \dfrac{3+6}{2} = 4.5$

$$\sigma = \sqrt{\frac{(b-a)^2}{12}} = \sqrt{\frac{(6-3)^2}{12}} = 0.8660$$

b. $P(\bar{x} \ge 4.25) = P(z \ge -2.02)$
$$= 0.4783 + 0.50 = 0.9783$$

c. Although the population of service times is not normally distributed, but uniformly distributed, the sample size is sufficiently large so that the sampling distribution of $(\bar{x})$ is normally distributed.

7-77. a. $P(p > 0.14) = P(z > (0.14 - 0.10)/\sqrt{[0.10(1-0.10)]/100})$
$$= P(z > 1.33) = 0.5 - 0.4082 = 0.0918$$

b. $P(p > 0.14) = P(z > (0.14 - 0.10)/\sqrt{[0.10(1-0.10)]/200})$
$$= P(z > 1.89) = 0.5 - 0.4706 = 0.0294$$

7-79. a. $P(\bar{x} > 50) = P(z > (50 - 45)/[(5/\sqrt{16})])$
$$= P(z > 4) = 0$$

b. Yes, since the probability of a sample of size 16 having a mean of 50 or more is essentially 0.

7-81. Finite correction factor is used.

a. $P(\bar{x} \le 5.9)$

$= P(z < (5.9 - 6.2)/[(3/\sqrt{100})\sqrt{(300-100)/(300-1)}])$

$= P(z \le -1.22) = 0.5 - 0.3888 = 0.1112$

b. Based on this low probability, either the mean or the standard deviation or both may have changed.

c. $P(\bar{x} \le 5.9)$

$= P(z \le (5.9 - 6.2)/[(3/\sqrt{40})\sqrt{(300-40)/(300-1)}])$

$= P(z < -0.68) = 0.5 - 0.2517 = 0.2483$

d. The probabilities differ because the spread of the sampling distribution is smaller for the larger sample.

7-83. a. $P(\bar{x} \le 88,626) = P\left(\dfrac{88,626 - 92,500}{40,000/\sqrt{5,829}} \ge z\right)$

$= P(-7.39 \ge z) = 0$

b. A sample mean of at most \$88,626 from a population with a mean of \$92,500 is highly unlikely,

c. $P(x \ge 5/2) = P(x \ge 3) = P(x=3) + P(x=4) + P(x=5)$

$= \binom{5}{3} 0.5^3 (1-0.5)^{5-3} + \binom{5}{4} 0.5^4 (1-0.5)^{5-4}$

$+ \binom{5}{5} 0.5^5 (1-0.5)^{5-5}$

$= 0.3125 + 0.1562 + 0.0312 = 0.4999$

7-85. a.

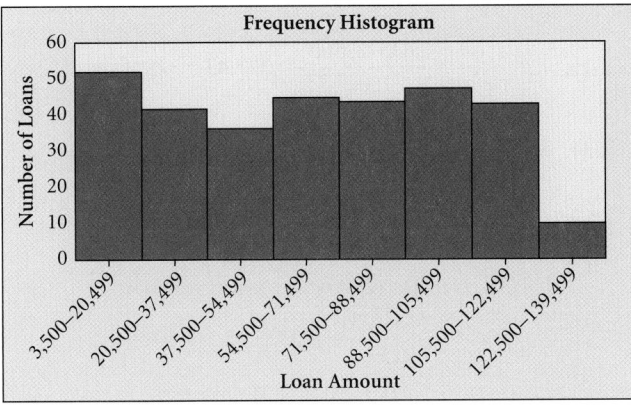

Based upon this distribution, the data do not appear to be normally distributed.

b. Mean $= 63,668.57$

c. Standard Deviation $= 35,938.16$

d. Student answers will vary depending upon the sample selected.

7-87. a. $P(p < 0.4855)$

$= P(z < (0.4855 - 0.70)/\sqrt{[0.70(1-0.70)]/138})$

$= P(z < -5.50) = 0$

b. $P(p > 0.8406)$

$= P(z > (0.8406 - 0.80)/\sqrt{[0.80(1-0.80)]/138})$

$= P(z > 1.19) = 0.5 - 0.383 = 0.117$

7-89. a. Proportion of adults who connect to the Internet using a computer is 0.79.

b. The sampling error $= p - \pi = 0.79 - 0.74 = 0.05$. The standard error of the sample's proportion equals

$$\sqrt{\frac{\pi(1-\pi)}{n}} = \sqrt{\frac{0.74(1-0.74)}{202}} = 0.031$$

c. $P(0.69 < p < 0.79)$

$= P\left(\dfrac{0.69 - 0.76}{0.031} < z < \dfrac{0.79 - 0.74}{0.031}\right)$

$= P(-1.61 < z < 1.61) = 0.4463 + 0.4463 = 0.8926$

d. $P(0.72 \le p \le 0.76) = 0.9794 - 0.0206 = 0.9588$

Chapter 8

8-1. The confidence interval is

$300 \pm 1.96 \dfrac{55}{\sqrt{250}}$

300 ± 6.82

$293.18\text{-------------------------}306.82$

8-3. $70 \pm 1.645(1.86)$

70 ± 3.06

$66.94 \text{--------------}73.06$

8-5. $3 \pm 2.2622 \dfrac{2.26}{\sqrt{10}}$

3 ± 1.62

$1.38 \text{-------------------------}4.62$

8-7. $\bar{x} \pm z\dfrac{\sigma}{\sqrt{n}} = 1200 \pm 1.645 \dfrac{121}{\sqrt{100}} = 1,200 \pm 19.90$

$1,180.10\text{--------------------------}1,219.90$

8-9. $\bar{x} \pm z\dfrac{\sigma}{\sqrt{n}} = 50 \pm 1.645 \dfrac{5}{\sqrt{9}} = 50 \pm 2.74$

$= 47.26 \text{--------------------------}52.74$

8-11. a. $\bar{x} \pm t\dfrac{s}{\sqrt{n}} = 13.4 \pm 1.8331(0.9804)$

$= 13.4 \pm 1.7972 = (11.6028,\ 15.1972)$

b. $\bar{x} \pm t\dfrac{s}{\sqrt{n}} = 31.2 \pm 1.6578(0.7486) = 31.2 \pm 1.241$

$= (29.9590,\ 32.4410)$

c. $\bar{x} \pm z\dfrac{s}{\sqrt{n}} = 4.5 \pm 1.645(0.9667) = 4.5 \pm 1.5902$

$= (2.9098,\ 6.0902)$

d. $\bar{x} \pm t\dfrac{s}{\sqrt{n}} = 21.7 \pm 1.7056(1.9822) = 21.7 \pm 3.3808$

$= (18.3192,\ 25.0808)$

8-13. a. Point Estimate $= \bar{x} = \$1.875$

b. The population will have to be a normal distribution in this situation. The critical value can then come from the t-distribution.

c. The population must be normally distributed.

d. $1.875 \pm 1.7959(0.735/\sqrt{12})$; 1.875 ± 0.3810;

$1.494\text{-------------------------}2.256$

8-15. a. $\bar{x} \pm z\dfrac{\sigma}{\sqrt{n}} = 5,000 \pm 1.96\left(\dfrac{1500}{\sqrt{179}}\right) = 5,000 \pm 219.75$

$= (4,780.25,\ 5,219.75)$

b. The margin of error is $z \dfrac{\sigma}{\sqrt{n}} = 1.96\left(\dfrac{1,500}{\sqrt{179}}\right) = 219.75.$

c. Reducing the margin of error by 50% would produce a margin of error $= 219.75/2 = 109.875$. So

$$z \dfrac{\sigma}{\sqrt{n}} = 1.96\left(\dfrac{1,500}{\sqrt{n}}\right) = 109.875. \text{ Solving,}$$

$$n = \left(\dfrac{1.96(1,500)}{109.875}\right)^2 = 715.97 \approx 716.$$

8-17. a. $\$9.18 \pm 2.0452 \dfrac{\$10.41}{\sqrt{30}}$

$\$9.18 \pm 3.89$

$\$5.29 \text{ -------------------- } \$13.07$

b. The interval includes the $11.35 mean value determined in the American Express study. Therefore, these sample data do not dispute the American Express study.

8-19. a. $\bar{x} = \dfrac{\sum x}{n} = \dfrac{630}{36} = \$17.50$

b. $\bar{x} \pm t \dfrac{s}{\sqrt{n}} = 17.50 \pm 2.03 \dfrac{7.52}{\sqrt{36}}$

$\qquad = 17.50 \pm 2.54 = 14.96 \text{----------------} 20.04$

c. Yes

8-21. a.

Company A—Passenger Car:	$\bar{x} = 60.2$
Company B—Passenger Car:	$\bar{x} = 65.4$
Company C—Passenger Car:	$\bar{x} = 76.8$
Company A—SUV:	$\bar{x} = 97.2$
Company B—SUV:	$\bar{x} = 92.6$
Company C—SUV:	$\bar{x} = 101.0$

b. The critical t-value for $n - 1 = 4$ degrees of freedom and 95% confidence is 2.7765.

Company A—Passenger Car: $60.2 \pm 2.7765 \dfrac{12.7}{\sqrt{5}}$

60.2 ± 15.8

$44.4 \text{ --------------} 76.0$

Company B—Passenger Car: $65.4 \pm 2.7765 \dfrac{11.3}{\sqrt{5}}$

65.4 ± 14.0

$51.4 \text{ ----------------} 79.4$

Company C—Passenger Car: $76.8 \pm 2.7765 \dfrac{9.0}{\sqrt{5}}$

76.8 ± 11.2

$65.6 \text{ --------------} 88.0$

Company A—SUV: $97.2 \pm 2.7765 \dfrac{18.7}{\sqrt{5}}$

97.2 ± 23.2

$74.0 \text{ -------------} 120.4$

Company B—SUV: $92.6 \pm 2.7765 \dfrac{5.4}{\sqrt{5}}$

92.6 ± 6.7

$85.9 \text{ -------------} 99.3$

Company C—SUV: $101 \pm 2.7765 \dfrac{14.1}{\sqrt{5}}$

101 ± 17.5

$83.5 \text{ -------------} 118.5$

c. Companies B and C SUV brake installation time means exceed the mean time for passenger cars for Companies A and B. Company A's SUV mean time overlaps the mean time for passenger cars from all companies.

8-23. a. $\bar{x} \pm t \dfrac{s}{\sqrt{n}} = 167.52 \pm 1.9722 \dfrac{28.5179}{\sqrt{196}} = 167.52 \pm 4.0174$

$\qquad = 163.5026 \text{ ---------------} 171.5374$

b. The margin of error can be reduced by increasing the sample size or by decreasing the level of confidence.

8-25. a.

Descriptive Statistics: ChickWt

Variable	Mean	StDev
ChichWt	86.71	24.90

b.

One-Sample Z: ChickWt
THE ASSUMED STANDARD DEVIATION = 24.9

Variable	N	Mean	StDev	SE Mean	99% CI
ChickWt	200	86.7100	24.8989	1.7607	(82.1747, 91.2453)

c. The 99% confidence interval indicates that the plausible values for the 2006 per capita consumption of chicken are between 82.2 and 91.2 pounds. Since 88 is contained in this interval, it is one of the plausible values and the trend seems to be continuing.

8-27. $n = \dfrac{z^2 \sigma^2}{e^2} = \left(\dfrac{z\sigma}{e}\right)^2 = \left(\dfrac{(1.96)(680)}{44}\right)^2 = 917.54 \approx 918$

8-29. $n = \dfrac{z^2 \sigma^2}{e^2} = \dfrac{1.645^2 27500^2}{2500^2} = 327.43 = 328$

8-31. $n = \dfrac{z^2 \sigma^2}{e^2} = \dfrac{1.96^2 350^2}{50^2} = 188.24 = 189$

8-33. a. $n = \dfrac{z^2 \sigma^2}{e^2} = \dfrac{1.96^2 (16)^2}{4^2} = 61.47, n = 62$

b. (1) $e = 0.5$, (2) $\sigma = 23$, (3) $z = 1.645$,

$\quad$ (4) $n = \dfrac{1.645^2 (23)^2}{0.5^2} = 5725.95, n = 5726$

c. (1) $e = 1$, (2) $\sigma = 0.5$, (3) $z = 2.575$,

$\quad$ (4) $n = \dfrac{2.575^2 (0.5)^2}{1^2} = 1.658, n = 2$

d. (1) $e = 0.2$, (2) $\sigma = 1.5$, (3) $z = 2.33$,

$\quad$ (4) $n = \dfrac{2.33^2 (1.5)^2}{0.2^2} = 305.38, n = 306$

e. (1) $e = 4$, (2) $\sigma = 16$, (3) $z = 1.96$,

$\quad$ (4) $n = \dfrac{1.96^2 (16)^2}{4^2} = 61.47, n = 62$

8-35. $n = \dfrac{z^2 \sigma^2}{e^2} = \dfrac{1.645^2 1,225^2}{100^2} = 406.07 = 407$ samples must be taken.

8-37. a. $n = \dfrac{z^2 \sigma^2}{e^2} = \left(\dfrac{z\sigma}{e}\right)^2 = \left(\dfrac{(1.96)(3.79)}{.25}\right)^2 = 882.898 \cong 883$

The required sample size is 883 bags from the population. However, the 20 items in the pilot sample can be used, so the net required sample is $883 - 20 = 863$.

b. 1. Reduce the confidence level to something less than 95%.
   2. Increase the margin of error beyond 0.25 pounds.
   3. Some combination of decreasing the confidence level and increasing the margin of error.

8-39. a. $n = \dfrac{z^2\sigma^2}{e^2} = \left(\dfrac{z\sigma}{e}\right)^2 = \left(\dfrac{(2.575)(1.4)}{.2}\right)^2 = 324.9 \cong 325$

Net required sample is $325 - 50 = 275$.

8-41. a. $n = \dfrac{z^2\sigma^2}{e^2} = \dfrac{2.575^2 30^2}{10^2} = 59.68 = 60$ samples must be taken.

b. $n = \dfrac{z^2\sigma^2}{e^2} = \dfrac{2.575^2 30^2}{5^2} = 238.70 = 239$

8-43. a. $n = \dfrac{z^2\sigma^2}{e^2} = \dfrac{1.96^2 10^2}{(1.25)^2} = 245.86, n = 246$

b. $n = \dfrac{z^2\sigma^2}{e^2} = \dfrac{1.96^2 10^2}{(0.25)^2} = 6,146.56, n = 6147$

c. For $n = 1,500$, $\sigma = 10$, 1.96, $e = \dfrac{z\sigma}{\sqrt{n}} = \dfrac{1.96(10)}{\sqrt{1500}} = 0.5061$

For $n = 2,000$, $\sigma = 10$, 1.96, $e = \dfrac{z\sigma}{\sqrt{n}} = \dfrac{1.96(10)}{\sqrt{2000}} = 0.4383$

The range of values for the margin of error is from $0.44 to $0.51.

8-45. a. $n = \dfrac{z^2\sigma^2}{e^2} = \left(\dfrac{z\sigma}{e}\right)^2 = \left(\dfrac{(1.96)(3.2)}{0.15}\right)^2 = 1,748.35 \approx 1,749$

The net required sample is $1,749 - 150 = 1,599$.

b. Reduce the confidence level (lowers the z-value) or increase the margin of error or some combination of the two.

8-47. a. The confidence interval is $36.616 \pm 1.195 = 35.421$ to 37.811.

b. $n = \dfrac{z^2\sigma^2}{e^2} = \left(\dfrac{z\sigma}{e}\right)^2 = \left(\dfrac{(2.33)(6.22)}{1.4}\right)^2 = 107.16 \cong 108$

c. The 98% confidence interval (35.421 to 37.811) is considerably below the mean hourly compensation below $44.82.

8-49. $p \pm z\sqrt{\dfrac{p(1-p)}{n}}$

$0.28 \pm 1.96\sqrt{\dfrac{0.28(1-0.28)}{240}}$

0.28 ± 0.056

0.224 ------------------------- 0.336

8-51. $p \pm z\sqrt{\dfrac{p(1-p)}{n}} = 0.4 \pm 1.645\sqrt{\dfrac{0.4(1-0.4)}{100}}$

$= 0.4 \pm 0.0806$

0.3194 -------------------- 0.4806

8-53. a. $p = \dfrac{x}{n} = \dfrac{144}{200} = 0.72$

b. $= 0.72 \pm 1.96\sqrt{\dfrac{0.72(1-0.72)}{200}} = 0.72 \pm 0.0622$

0.6578 ------------------------- 0.7822

8-55. a. $p = \dfrac{x}{n} = \dfrac{7}{40} = 0.175$

b. $p \pm z\sqrt{\dfrac{p(1-p)}{n}} = 0.175 + 1.96\sqrt{\dfrac{0.175(1-0.175)}{40}}$

$= 0.175 \pm 0.118 = (0.057, 0.293)$

c. $n = \dfrac{z^2 p(1-p)}{e^2} = \dfrac{1.96^2(0.175)(1-0.175)}{(0.025)^2}$

$= 887.4, n = 888$

8-57. $0.33 \pm 1.96\sqrt{\dfrac{0.33(1-0.33)}{1,100}}$

0.33 ± 0.028

0.302 ------------------------------ 0.358

8-59. $0.91 \pm 1.645\sqrt{\dfrac{0.91(1-0.91)}{1,000}}$

0.91 ± 0.015

0.895 ------------------------------ 0.925

8-61. a. $n = \dfrac{z^2 \pi(1-\pi)}{e^2} = \dfrac{1.96^2\, 0.5(1-0.5)}{0.03^2} = 1,067.22, \, or\, 1,068$

b. $n = \dfrac{z^2 \pi(1-\pi)}{e^2} = \dfrac{1.96^2\, 0.14(1-0.14)}{0.03^2} = 513.92, \, or\, 514$

8-63. a. $p \pm z\sqrt{\dfrac{p(1-p)}{n}} = 0.1377 \pm 1.645\sqrt{\dfrac{0.1377(1-0.1377)}{363}}$

$= 0.1377 \pm 0.0298 = 0.1079$ ---------------- 0.1675

8-65. a. $p \pm e = 0.66 \pm 0.05 = (0.61, 0.71)$

b. $n = \dfrac{z^2 p(1-p)}{e^2} = \dfrac{1.96^2 0.66(1-0.66)}{(0.05)^2}$

$= 344.82, n = 345$

For Baby Boomers

$n = \dfrac{z^2 p(1-p)}{e^2} = \dfrac{1.96^2 0.61(1-0.61)}{(0.05)^2} = 365.57, n = 366$

For Generation X

$n = \dfrac{z^2 p(1-p)}{e^2} = \dfrac{1.96^2 0.58(1-0.58)}{(0.05)^2} = 374.33, n = 375$

8-67. a. $0.3889 \pm 1.96\sqrt{\dfrac{0.3889(1-0.3889)}{144}} = 0.3889 \pm 0.0796$

$= 0.3093$ --------------- 0.4685

b. No

8-69. a. The margin of error $= (0.6229 - 0.5365)/2 = 0.0432$.

b. 0.5365 ------------ 0.6229

c. $n = \dfrac{z^2 p(1-p)}{e^2} = \dfrac{1.96^2 0.58(1-0.58)}{(0.0324)^2} = 891.45, n = 892$

8-71. The t will be greater than z for a given confidence level and $s/\sqrt{n}$ will be a larger value when n is small.

8-73. This is not correct.

8-75. a. $n = (1.96)^2(200)^2/(50)^2 = 61.4656$, or 62, so you would need to sample $62 - 40 = 22$ more.

b. $(62)(\$10) = \$620$. Without pilot: $n = (1.96)^2(300)^2/(50)^2 = 138.29$, or 139 @ \$10 = \$1,390; so savings of $\$1,390 - \$620 = \$770$.

8-77. a. $0.76 \pm 1.645\left(\sqrt{[(0.76)(1-0.76)/441]}\right)$;

0.7265 ----------------- 0.7935

b. $0.7265(35,000)$ --------------- $0.7935(35,000)$;

$25,427.50$ --------------- $27,772.50$

8-79. a. $\bar{x} = \dfrac{\sum x_i}{n} = \dfrac{250,000}{48,000} = 5.21$

b. $n = \dfrac{z^2\sigma^2}{e^2} = \dfrac{1.645^2 1.5^2}{(1/8)^2} = 389.67, n = 390$

c. $e = \dfrac{z\sigma}{\sqrt{n}} = \dfrac{1.645(1.5)}{\sqrt{100}} = 0.25$ work days

$= 2.00$ work hours

8-81. $11.9991 \pm 1.96(0.2002/\sqrt{5000})$;

11.9936 -------------- 12.0046

8-83. a. $p = 404/548 = 0.7372$

$0.7372 \pm 1.96(\sqrt{[(0.7372)(1-0.7372]/548})$;

0.7372 ± 0.0369;

0.7003 ----------------- 0.7741

b. $32801.095 \pm 1.96(6230.097/\sqrt{548})$;

$32,279.4674$ ------------- $33,322.7227$

8-85. a. The population mean $= 9987.44$.

b.

Classes	Frequency
5,001–6,000	0
6,001–7,000	1
7,001–8,000	4
8,001–9,000	24
9,001–10,000	100
10,001–11,000	79
11,001–12,000	40
12,001–13,000	2

c.

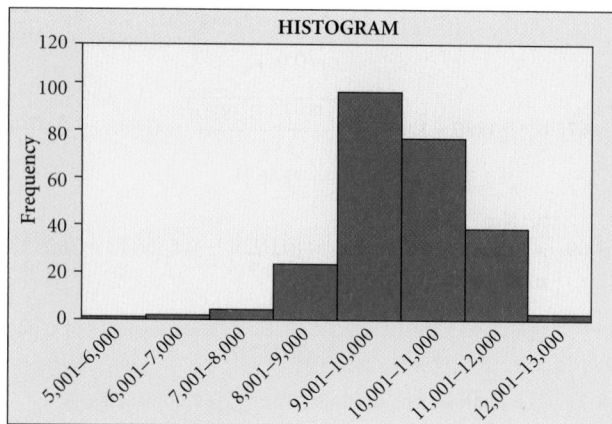

COUNT OF SALES	
Region	**Total**
East	39.60%
Midwest	17.60%
South	31.60%
West	11.20%
Grand Total	100.00%

d, e, and f. Student answers will vary depending upon the sample selected.

Chapter 9

9-1. a. $z = 1.96$

b. $t = -1.6991$

c. $t = \pm 2.4033$

d. $z = \pm 1.645$

9-3. a. Reject the null hypothesis if the calculated value of the test statistic, t, is less than the critical value of -2.0639. Otherwise, do not reject.

b. $t = (20-23)/(8/\sqrt{25}) = -1.875$

c. Because $t = -1.875 > t = -2.0639$, do not reject.

9-5. a. Reject if $t < -2.1448$ or $t > 2.1448$. Otherwise, do not reject.

b. $t = (62.2-60.5)/(7.5/\sqrt{15}) = 0.878$

c. Because $t = 0.878 > -2.1448$ and $t = 0.878 < 2.1448$, do not reject.

9-7. a. p-value $= P(z > 1.34) = 0.5000 - 0.4099 = 0.0901$

b. p-value $= P(z > 2.09) = 0.5000 - 0.4817 = 0.0183$

c. p-value $= P(z < -1.55) = 0.5000 - 0.4394 = 0.0606$

9-9. a. p-value $= 0.5 - 0.4772 = 0.0228$

b. p-value $= 2(0.01) = 0.02$

c. p-value $= 2(0.5 - 0.4922) = 0.0156$

d. The calculated t-value falls between the 0.005 and 0.01 columns in the t-distribution table, so the p-value is in this range (p-value $= 0.0071$ found using Excel).

9-11. a. If the null hypothesis is rejected, a Type I error would be committed.

b. If the null hypothesis is not true, a Type II error would be committed.

c. If the null hypothesis is true, a Type I error would be committed.

d. No error is made.

e. If the null hypothesis is not rejected, a Type II error would be committed.

f. No error is made.

9-13. Because $t = 1.0326$ is less than 1.8595, do not reject H_0.

9-15. a. $H_0: \mu = 24$ ounces

$H_a: \mu \neq 24$ ounces

b. Because $-2.1315 < 1.83 < 2.1315$, do not reject H_0 and conclude that the filling machine remains all right to operate.

c. Because the production control manager does not want the boxes underfilled or overfilled.

d. Using Excel's TDIST function, p-value $= 0.0872 > 0.025$; therefore, do not reject H_0

e. Type II error may have been committed.

9-17. a. H_0: $\mu \geq 55$
H_a: $\mu > 55$

b. Because $t = -0.93 > -2.4620$, the null hypothesis is not rejected.

9-19. Because p-value $= 0.2546 > $ alpha $= 0.10$, we do not reject the null hypothesis.

9-21. a. Because $t = 2.1953 < 2.8073$, do not reject H_0.

b. Type I error

9-23. a. $z = 1.96$

b. $z = -1.645$

c. $z = \pm 2.33$

d. $z = \pm 1.645$

9-25. a. If $z < z = -1.96$, otherwise, do not reject.

b. $z = (0.66 - 0.75)/(\sqrt{0.75 * (1-0.75)/100})$
$= -2.0785$

c. Because $z = -2.0785 < -1.96$, reject.

9-27. Since $-2.17 > -2.33$, the null hypothesis is not rejected.

9-29. a. p-value $= 2[P(z \leq -1.964)] = 2(0.5 - 0.475) = 0.05$

b. p-value $= 2[P(z \geq 0.5454)] = 2(0.5 - 0.2054) = 0.5892$

c. p-value $= 2[P(z \geq 1.3093)] = 2(0.5 - 0.4049) = 0.1902$

d. p-value $= 2[P(z \geq 2.1822)] = 2(0.5 - 0.4854) = 0.0292$

9-31. Because $z = -3.145$ is less than -2.055, reject H_0.

9-33. a. H_0: $\pi = 0.69$
H_a: $\pi \neq 0.69$

b. Since $z = -3.19 < -1.96$, we reject the null hypothesis.

9-35. a. H_0: $\pi \leq 0.40$
H_a: $\pi > 0.40$

b. Since $z = 1.43 < 1.645$, we do not reject the null hypothesis.

9-37. a. Since the p-value $= 0.0192$ is less than $\alpha = 0.025$, reject H_0.

b. A Type II error would be concluding that the poll does not indicate that more than 70% of adults prefer seeing movies in their homes when, in fact, they do.

9-39. a. Since $z = -0.7107 > -1.645$, do not reject.

b. $0.0075 \pm 1.96\left(\sqrt{(0.0075)(1-0.0075)/800}\right)$;
0.0075 ± 0.006; 0.0015 -------- 0.0135

9-41. Because $z = -2.021$ is less than -1.96, reject H_0.

9-43. a. H_0: $\pi = 0.50$
H_a: $\pi \neq 0.50$

b. Since $z = -1.41 > -1.645$, we do not reject.

9-45. a. H_0: $\pi \geq 0.95$
H_a: $\pi \leq 0.95$

b. Since $z = -4.85 < -1.645$, we reject the null hypothesis.

9-47. a. $\bar{x}_\alpha = 4,350 - 1.645(200/\sqrt{100})$; $\bar{x}_\alpha = 4,317.10$

$P(z > (4,317.10 - 4,345)/(200/\sqrt{100})) =$
$P(z > -1.40) = 0.5 + 0.4192 = 0.9192$

b. Power $= 1 - $ Beta $= 1 - 0.9192 = 0.0808$

c. The power increases, and beta decreases, as the sample size increases. We could also increase alpha since alpha and beta are inversely related.

d. Since $\bar{x} = 4,337.5 > 4,317.1$, do not reject the null hypothesis.

9-49. Type II Error $= P(-0.895 \leq z \leq 2.395) \approx 0.3146 + 0.4917 = 0.8063$

9-51. Beta $= 0.5000 - 0.1772 = 0.3228$

9-53. a. $\beta = P(2.39 < z < 6.31) = 0.5 - 0.4916 = 0.0084$

b. $\beta = P(0.76 < z < 4.68) = 0.5 - 0.2764 = 0.2236$

c. $\beta = P(-1.42 \leq z \leq 2.50) = 0.4222 + 0.4938 = 0.9160$

9-55. a. $\beta = 0.5000 + 0.3665 = 0.8665$. We then solve for the power as:
$$\text{Power} = 1 - \beta$$
$$= 1 - 0.8665 = 0.1335$$

b. $\beta = 0.5000 + 0.3749 = 0.8749$. We then solve for the power as:
$$\text{Power} = 1 - \beta$$
$$= 1 - 0.8749 = 0.1251$$

c. $\beta = 0.5000 + 0.3888 = 0.8888$. We then solve for the power as:
$$\text{Power} = 1 - \beta = 1 - 0.8888 = 0.1122$$

9-57. a. H_0: $\mu \geq 15$
H_a: $\mu < 15$

b. Beta $= 0.5000 - 0.4394 = 0.0606$

9-59. a. H_0: $\mu \geq \$41,000$
H_a: $\mu < \$41,000$

b. Beta $= 0.5000 - 0.2704 = 0.2296$

9-61. $\beta = P(z > 1.0047) = 0.5 - 0.3413 = 0.1587$

9-63. $\beta = P(z > -0.2386) = 0.5 + 0.0948 = 0.5948$
Power $= 1 - \beta = 1 - 0.5948 = 0.4052$

9-65. $\beta = P(-4.7042 < z < -0.7842) = 0.5 - 0.2823 = 0.2177$

9-67. A Type I error occurs when the decision maker rejects a true null hypothesis. A Type II error occurs when a false null hypothesis is accepted.

9-69. The critical value is the cut-off point or demarcation between acceptance and rejection regions in a hypothesis test.

9-71. The probability of committing a Type I error is denoted by alpha (α) and is usually specified by the decision maker. The choice of alpha reflects the cost of making a Type I error.

9-73. You use the population proportion to calculate the standard error.

9-75. a. $z = \dfrac{\bar{x} - \mu}{\dfrac{\sigma}{\sqrt{n}}}$

b. $t = \dfrac{\bar{x} - \mu}{\dfrac{s}{\sqrt{n}}}$

c. $z = \dfrac{p - \pi}{\sqrt{\dfrac{\pi(1-\pi)}{n}}}$; should not be used since $n(1-p) < 5$.

d. A hypothesis test using a small (<30) sample from a skewed distribution cannot be conducted using procedures in this text.

9-77. a. If α is decreased, the rejection region is smaller, making it easier to accept H_0, so β is increased.

    b. If n is increased, the test statistic is also increased, making it harder to accept H_0, so β is decreased.

    c. If n is increased, the test statistic is also increased, making it harder to accept H_0, so β is decreased and power is increased.

    d. If α is decreased, the rejection region is smaller, making it easier to accept H_0, so β is increased and power is decreased.

9-79. a. Since $z = 1.98 > 1.2991$, reject H_0.

    b. $1.2991 = (\bar{x} - 100)/50/\sqrt{50}$; $x = 109.186$

9-81. a. Since $z = -1.5275 > -1.645$, do not reject.

    b. A Type II error in this problem would mean that the proportion of students passing the test is actually less than 0.70 but the sample results lead the administrators to believe that it is actually 70% or better.

9-83. a. $n\pi = 883(0.21) = 185.43 > 5$ and $n(1 - \pi) = 883(1 - 0.21) = 697.57 > 5$. The normal approximation to the binomial is warranted.

    b. Since $z = -1.4401 > -1.645$, do not reject H_0.

9-85. a. $P(z > (17.4175 - 16.5)/(2.4/\sqrt{60})) = P(z > 2.96) = 0.5 - 0.4985 = 0.0015$

    b. $P(z > (17.4175 - 17.3)/(2.4/\sqrt{60})) = P(z > 0.38) = 0.50 - 0.1480 = 0.352$. As the mean selected from H_a moves closer to the mean specified in H_0, the harder it is for the hypothesis test to distinguish and, thus, the larger β becomes and the smaller the Power becomes.

    c. The probability of a Type II error would be smaller.

    d. The probabilities of Type II errors would be reduced for larger sample sizes.

9-87. a. H_0: $\mu = 6$ inches

       H_a: $\mu \neq 6$ inches

    b. If $\bar{x} < 5.9818$, reject the null hypothesis.

       If $\bar{x} > 6.0182$, reject the null hypothesis. Otherwise, do not reject.

    c. Since $\bar{x} = 6.03 > 6.0182$, reject the null hypothesis.

9-89. a. $n\pi = 2500(0.75) = 1875 > 5$; $n(1 - \pi) = 625 > 5$ The normal approximation to the binomial is warranted.

    b. Since $z = -1.1547 > -1.96$ do not reject H_0.

9-91. a. Because $z = 3.567 > 2.24$, we reject H_0.

    b. $\bar{x} \pm z \dfrac{\sigma}{\sqrt{n}} = 61834.12 \pm 1.645 \dfrac{1734.23}{\sqrt{55}} =$

       $(61834.12 \pm 384.67(61449.45, 62218.797)$.

       The largest plausible average balance in the GM workers' 401(k) in which you could have 90% confidence = \$62218.79.

9-93. a. H_0: $\mu \leq 7.4$

       H_a: $\mu > 7.4$

    b. Since $t = 10.1335 > 1.6612$, reject H_0 and conclude that the average pH level is higher than 7.4.

9-95. a. Since $z = -1.1711 > -1.645$, do not reject.

    b. In this case, a Type II error may have been committed.

    c. As long as the sample size is sufficiently large such that np and $n(1 - p)$ are both greater than 5, you are justified in using the standard normal distribution.

    d. Since $z = -1.8047 < -1.645$, reject H_0.

9-97. a. H_0: $\mu \geq 40$

       H_a: $\mu < 40$

    b. Since $z = -0.8052 > -1.2991$, do not reject H_0 and conclude that the average age is not less than 40.

    c. Type II error

    d. $\bar{x}_\alpha = 40 - 1.2991(12.9965)/\sqrt{50}$; $\bar{x}_\alpha = 37.6123$

    e. p-value $= 0.2122$, which is greater than 0.10

    f. Given a sample size of $n = 50$, the sampling distribution for $\bar{x}$ will be approximately normal based on the Central Limit Theorem. Thus, the use of the distribution to find the critical t-value and the p-value is appropriate.

9-99. a. The p-value $= P(t \geq 1.575)$. Using Excel's TDIST option, this probability is 0.0644. Since the p-value is greater than α, we do not reject H_0.

    b. $P(x \geq 2) = 1 - P(x \leq 1)$

$$= 1 - \left[\frac{C_4^6 x C_0^4}{C_4^{10}} + \frac{C_3^6 x C_1^4}{C_4^{10}} \right] = 1 - 95/210$$

$$= 1 - 0.4524 = 0.5476$$

Chapter 10

10-1. $5 \pm 2.0086(18.21)\sqrt{\dfrac{1}{24} + \dfrac{1}{28}}$

$$= 5 \pm 10.17 = -5.17 \leq (\mu_1 - \mu_2) \leq 15.17$$

10-3. $(355 - 320) \pm 1.96\sqrt{\dfrac{34^2}{50} + \dfrac{40^2}{80}}$

$$= 35 \pm 12.87$$

$$= 22.13 \leq \mu_1 - \mu_2 \leq 47.87$$

10-5. $df = \dfrac{\left(s_1^2\big/n_1 + s_2^2\big/n_2 \right)^2}{\left[\dfrac{\left(s_1^2\big/n_1 \right)^2}{n_1 - 1} + \dfrac{\left(s_2^2\big/n_2 \right)^2}{n_2 - 1} \right]}$

$$= \dfrac{\left(42.5^2\big/12 + 41.9^2\big/12 \right)^2}{\left[\dfrac{\left(42.5^2\big/12 \right)^2}{11} + \dfrac{\left(41.9^2\big/12 \right)^2}{11} \right]} = \dfrac{88,103}{4,004.68} = 22$$

$$(400.67 - 375.33) \pm 2.0739\sqrt{\dfrac{42.5^2 + 41.9^2}{12 + 12}}$$

$$= 25.34 \pm 25.27$$

$$= 0.07 \leq (\mu_1 - \mu_2) \leq 50.61$$

10-7. a. $\bar{x}_1 - \bar{x}_2 = 24.96 - 25.01 = -0.05$

b. $-0.0974 \le (\mu_1 - \mu_2) \le -0.0026$

c. Since the interval does not contain zero, the managers can conclude the two lines do not fill bags with equal average amounts.

10-9. $-19.47 \le \mu_1 - \mu_2 \le -7.93$

10-11. a. $(41.5 - 39) \pm 1.9695(4.36)\sqrt{(1/200)+(1/200)}$;

1.6413 -------------- 3.3587; yes

Company A:

$$-1.6602 = (\bar{x} - 41.5)/(3.6/\sqrt{200}); \quad \bar{x} = 41.0774$$

Company B:

$$-1.6602 = (\bar{x} - 39)/(5/\sqrt{200}); \quad \bar{x} = 38.4130$$

10-13. a. The ratio between the two variances is 200. It seems highly unlikely sample variances that are so different would come from populations with the same variance.

$$df = \frac{(s_1^2/n_1 + s_2^2/n_2)^2}{\left(\frac{(s_1^2/n_1)^2}{n_1-1} + \frac{(s_2^2/n_2)^2}{n_2-1}\right)}$$

$$= \frac{(64/1442 + 0.36/1442)^2}{\left(\frac{(64/1442)^2}{1442-1} + \frac{(0.36/1442)^2}{1442-1}\right)}$$

$$= 1457.2 \approx 1457$$

Therefore, the critical value = 2.5792.

$$(\bar{x}_1 - \bar{x}_2) \pm t\sqrt{\frac{s_1^2}{n_1} + \frac{s_2^2}{n_1}} = (38.9 - 2) \pm 2.5792\sqrt{\frac{64}{1442} + \frac{0.36}{1442}}$$

$$= 36.9 \pm 0.5449 = (36.3551, 37.4449)$$

b. 36.3551 ------------------------- 37.4449

c. Since both 36.5 and 37 are in this interval, this indicates that both values are plausible values for the difference in the average number of job applications. This is not a contradiction. All values contained in the interval are plausible values for the difference in the means. Sampling error produces the uncertainty.

10-15. $(7.44 - 5.71) \pm 2.0244(5.08)\sqrt{\frac{1}{15} + \frac{1}{25}}$

$$= 1.73 \pm 3.36$$

$$= -1.63 \le \mu_1 - \mu_2 \le 5.09$$

10-17. a. The percentage decline is $= \dfrac{72{,}400 - 70{,}700}{72{,}400}100\% =$

b. 2.35%; -1527.32 ------------------------- 4926.82

It is plausible that there is no difference.

c. Margin of Error $= \dfrac{4{,}926.82 - (-1{,}527.32)}{2} = 3{,}227$

10-19. Since $t = -4.80 < -2.1199$, we reject and conclude that the mean for population 1 is not equal to the mean for population 2.

10-23. a. Because $t = -2.7200 < -2.3685$, the null hypothesis is rejected.

b. The p-value $= P(\bar{x}_1 - \bar{x}_2 \le 25.4 - 33.2)$
$$= P(t \le -2.7200) < 0.005.$$

c. Since the null hypothesis was rejected, the only statistical error that could have been made would be a Type I error = reject H_0 given that H_0 is true.

10-25. Because the calculated value of $t = 1.17$ is neither less than the lower-tail critical value of $t = -1.6686$, nor greater than the upper-tail critical value of $t = 1.6686$, do not reject the null hypothesis.

10-27. Since $t = 2.56 > 2.4233$, we reject the null hypothesis and conclude that the mean for population 1 exceeds the mean for population 2.

10-29. Since $t = -4.30 < -1.6510$, we reject the null hypothesis and conclude that the mean for population 2 exceeds the mean for population 1.

10-31. a. The ratio of these two standard deviations is $2{,}084/2{,}050 = 1.02$.

b. Because the p-value $= P(t \le 3.93) \cong 1.00$, the null hypothesis is not rejected.

10-33. a. $H_0: \mu_1 - \mu_2 = 0$
$H_a: \mu_1 - \mu_2 \ne 0$

b. Because $t = -1.833 > -1.9725$, we do not reject the null hypothesis.
Because p-value $= 0.068 > $ alpha $= 0.05$, we do not reject the null hypothesis.

10-35. a. -13.746 ------------------ -1.0000

b. $H_0: \mu(06 \text{ fares}) - \mu(05 \text{ fares}) \ge \$10.00$
$H_a: \mu(06 \text{ fares}) - \mu(05 \text{ fares}) < \$10.00$
Since the p-value is greater than 0.025, we do not reject the null hypothesis.

c. You should be able to reach the same conclusion using either a confidence interval estimate on a hypothesis test.

10-37. $\bar{d} \pm t\dfrac{s_d}{\sqrt{n}}$

$$= -3.727 \pm 2.2281\frac{3.409}{\sqrt{11}}$$

$$= -3.727 + 2.29$$

$$= -6.017 \le \mu_d < -1.437$$

10-39. Because $t = 5.06 > 2.0930$, reject the null hypothesis.

10-41. a. $10.5333 \pm 2.9101 = (7.6232, 13.4434)$

b. Because $t = 0.37 < 1.459$, the null hypothesis cannot be rejected.

10-43. Because the calculated $t = -2.499$ is less than the critical $t = -1.7959$, reject the null hypothesis.

10-45. a. This study was set up as a paired-sample experiment. The reason is to control the outside influences due to driver and car differences.

b. The following steps can be taken to answer this question involving two paired samples:
$H_0: \mu_d \ge 0$ (Using no additive will provide at least as high mean mpg.)
$H_a: \mu_d < 0$ (Acetone additive is associated with higher mean mpg.)
Because $t = -1.66 > -1.8331$, do not reject the null hypothesis.

10-47. a. Because $t = -9.24 < -2.3646$, the null hypothesis is rejected.

b. $s_1 = \sqrt{\dfrac{\sum(x - \bar{x})^2}{n - 1}} = \sqrt{\dfrac{61.66}{22}} = 1.6741;$

$s_2 = \sqrt{\dfrac{70.87}{22}} = 1.7948$

$s_p = \sqrt{\dfrac{(n_1 - 1)s_1^2 + (n_2 - 1)s_2^2}{n_1 + n_2 - 2}}$

$= \sqrt{\dfrac{(23 - 1)(1.6741)^2 + (23 - 1)(1.7948)^2}{23 + 23 - 2}} = 1.7355$

$s_p\sqrt{\dfrac{1}{n_1} + \dfrac{1}{n_2}} = 1.7355\sqrt{\dfrac{1}{23} + \dfrac{1}{23}} = 0.5118;$

$\dfrac{s_d}{\sqrt{n}} = \dfrac{0.63849}{\sqrt{23}} = 0.13313$

A smaller standard error means that the test can detect smaller differences in the population means.

10-49. a. Knowing that the average selling price in 2004 was $274,500, say, makes it more likely that the median selling price would be in this neighborhood. Therefore, the samples are dependent.

b. 31,044.5 -------------------- 42,4215.5

c. It is plausible to assert that the mean of the average selling prices for houses during the period 1995 to 2004 is more than mean of the median selling prices during this period.

d. Since the p-value $= 0.029 < 0.05 = \alpha$, it is plausible to assert that the mean of the average selling prices for houses during the period 1995 to 2004 is more than $30,000 larger than the mean of the median selling prices during this period.

10-51. $z = \dfrac{(0.35 - 0.38) - (0)}{\sqrt{0.367(1 - 0.367)\left(\dfrac{1}{120} + \dfrac{1}{150}\right)}} = -0.508$

The p-value is $2 * 0.3050 = 0.61$. Because the p-value is greater than α, we do not reject the null hypothesis.

10-53. a. For sample 1, we have $p_1 = \dfrac{40}{200} = 0.20$. Thus, $np = 200(0.2) = 40$ and $n(1 - p) = 200(1 - 0.20) = 160$. For sample 2, we have $p_2 = \dfrac{27}{150} = 0.18$. Thus, $np = 150(0.18) = 27$ and $n(1 - p) = 150(1 - 0.18) = 123$. Therefore, we conclude that the sample sizes are sufficiently large.

b. $(0.20 - 0.18) \pm 1.96\sqrt{\dfrac{(0.20)(1 - 0.20)}{200} + \dfrac{(0.18)(1 - 0.18)}{150}}$

$= 0.02 + 0.083$

$= -0.063 \leq (\pi_1 - \pi_2) \leq 0.103$

10-55. a. Since $z = 2.538 > 1.96$, reject H_0.
There is sufficient evidence to conclude that $\pi_1 - \pi_2 \neq 0$.

b. Since $z = 2.538 > -1.645$, fail to reject H_0.

c. Since $z = 2.538 > 1.96$, reject H_0.

d. Since $z = 2.08 < 2.33$, fail to reject H_0.

10-57. $H_0: \pi_s = \pi_M$
$H_a: \pi_s \neq \pi_M$

$z = \dfrac{(p_1 - p_2) - (\pi_1 - \pi_2)}{\sqrt{\bar{p}(1 - \bar{p})\left(\dfrac{1}{n_1} + \dfrac{1}{n_2}\right)}}$

$= \dfrac{(0.33 - 0.35) - (0)}{\sqrt{0.3395(1 - 0.3395)\left(\dfrac{1}{200} + \dfrac{1}{180}\right)}} = -0.4111$

Since the test statistic, -0.4111, is not less than the critical value of -2.575, do not reject the null hypothesis.

10-59. a. Since the p-value $= 0.0244 < 0.05$, reject H_0.

b. The margin of error is

$\pm 1.96\sqrt{\dfrac{0.149(0.851)}{23,601} + \dfrac{0.103(0.897)}{23,601}} = 0.00597.$

c. The smallest difference equals the margin of error, 0.00597.

10-61. $z = \dfrac{(p_1 - p_2) - (\pi_1 - \pi_2)}{\sqrt{\bar{p}(1 - \bar{p})\left(\dfrac{1}{n_1} + \dfrac{1}{n_2}\right)}}$

$= \dfrac{(0.28 - 0.3467) - (0)}{\sqrt{0.3133(1 - 0.3133)\left(\dfrac{1}{150} + \dfrac{1}{150}\right)}} = -1.2454$

Since the test statistic, -1.2454, is not less than the critical value of -2.575, do not reject the null hypothesis.

10-63. a. $n_1 p_1 = 147(72/147) = 72 > 5$, $n_1 q_1 = 147(75/147) = 75 > 5$; $n_2 p_2 = 120(48/120) = 48 > 5$, $n_2 q_2 = 120(72/120) = 72 > 5$. Therefore, the sampling distribution can be approximated with a normal distribution.

b. Since the p-value $= 0.095 > 0.01$, the null hypothesis is not rejected.

c. Given the sample sizes, the difference, 0.09, is not large enough to support the assertion that the difference in the population proportions is more than 0.01.

10-65. The t-distribution is used instead of the z-distribution, since the t-distribution is always larger than the z.

10-67. a. $5 \pm (2.0687)(3.4262)\sqrt{\left(\dfrac{1}{15} + \dfrac{1}{10}\right)} = 5 \pm 2.8936$

$= (2.1064, 7.8936)$

b. -2.0687

c. 2.0687

d. To conduct a two-tailed hypothesis test using a confidence interval, simply compare the value stated in H_0. If that value is contained in the confidence interval, do not reject H_0. If that value is not contained in the confidence interval, reject H_0.

10-69. $4.54 \pm 1.7109(3.27)\sqrt{\dfrac{1}{13} + \dfrac{1}{13}}$

$= 4.54 \pm 2.19$

$= 2.35 \leq \mu_1 - \mu_2 \leq 6.73$

10-71. Because the calculated $t = -1.529$ is not less than the critical $t = -3.2498$, nor > 3.2498, do not reject the null hypothesis.

10-73. a. Because $t = 1.89 > 1.6479$, the null hypothesis is rejected.
b. The required assumptions are the three listed on page 445.

10-75. a. The critical values for the one-tailed test is 2.3499; the calculated t-value is 5.25. The null hypothesis is rejected.
b. Type I error = rejecting H_0 when in fact H_0 was true.

10-77. a. $H_0: \mu_H \geq \mu_A$
$H_A: \mu_H > \mu_A$
Since the test statistic of -1.7832 is not less than the critical value for a one-tail lower tail test of -2.345, do not reject the null hypothesis.
b. The $P(T \leq t)$ one-tail value of 0.038 is the p-value, which means that all alpha values greater than 0.038 would change your decision.
c. $H_0: \mu_H \geq \mu_A$
$H_A: \mu_H < \mu_A$
For any alpha values less than 0.0354, you would not reject the null hypothesis, and for any alpha values greater than 0.0354, you would reject the null hypothesis.

Chapter 11

11-1. Because $\chi^2 = 12.39 > 10.1170$, do not reject the null hypothesis.

11-3. The 95% confidence interval is:
$$\frac{(20-1)129,600}{32.8523} \leq \sigma^2 \leq \frac{(20-1)129,600}{8.9065}$$
$$74,953.7 \leq \sigma^2 \leq 276,472.2$$

11-5. a. Because $\chi^2 = 17.82 < \chi^2_{0.05} = 19.6752$ and because, $\chi^2 = 17.82 > \chi^2_{0.95} = 4.5748$, do not reject the null hypothesis.
b. Because $\chi^2 = 12.96 < \chi^2_{0.025} = 31.5264$ and because $\chi^2 = 12.96 > \chi^2_{0.975} = 8.2307$, we do not reject the null hypothesis.

11-7. a. Since the p-value $< \alpha$, reject H_0.
b. $\alpha = 0.10 < p$-value $= 0.94$
Fail to reject H_0.

11-9. a. Because the test statistic $t = 0.19 < t = 2.2622$, do not reject the null hypothesis.
b. Because $\chi^2 = 30.8 > 19.0228$, we reject the null hypothesis.
c. The consultants are justified in using a mean of 30 minutes for the downtime per occurrence at this machine center, but they are going to want to modify their standard deviation.

11-11. $\frac{(14-1)672.39}{24.7356} \leq \sigma^2 \leq \frac{(14-1)672.39}{5.0087} = $
$353.38 \leq \sigma^2 \leq 1,745.18$

11-13. a. $H_0: \mu \leq 10$
$H_a: \mu > 10$
b. Since $1.2247 < 1.383$, do not reject H_0.
c. $H_0: \sigma^2 \leq 16$
$H_a: \sigma^2 > 16$
Since $3.75 < 14.6837$, do not reject H_0.

11-15. a. $\sigma^2 = 4.637$
b. Since the test statistic $= 11.03 <$ the χ^2 critical value $= 13.8484$, reject the null hypothesis.
Since $t = -17.57 < -1.7109$, reject H_0.

11-17. a. p-value $= 0.017 < 0.025$; the null hypothesis is rejected.
b. Box and Whisker Plot

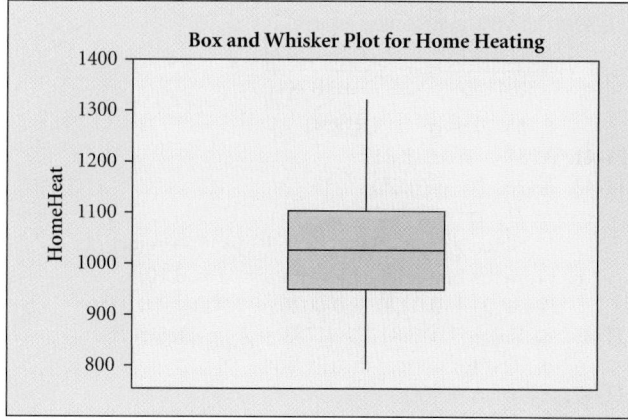

11-19. a. $F = 3.619$
b. $F = 3.106$
c. $F = 3.051$

11-21. a. If the calculated $F > 2.278$, reject H_0, otherwise do not reject H_0.
b. $F = 1,450/1,320 = 1.0985$. Since $1.0985 < 2.278$, do not reject H_0.

11-23. a. Since $F = 1.154 < 6.388 = F_{0.05}$, fail to reject H_0. Based on these sample data, there is not sufficient evidence to conclude that population 1's variance is larger than population 2's variance.
b. p-value $= P(F \geq 1.154)$. Using the F table, $P(F \geq 6.388) = 0.05 \rightarrow p$-value > 0.05. Using Excel, p-value $= 0.4465$.
c. If the two population variances were equal, the probability of the ratio of the two sample variances being larger than 1.154 is 0.4465.

11-25. $H_0: \sigma_m^2 \leq \sigma_F^2$
$H_A: \sigma_m^2 > \sigma_F^2$
$F = 2.5^2/1.34^2 = 3.4807$
Since $3.4807 > 1.984$, reject H_0.

11-27. a. $H_0: \sigma_A^2 \leq \sigma_T^2$
$H_A: \sigma_A^2 > \sigma_T^2$
If the calculated $F > 2.534$, reject H_0; otherwise, do not reject H_0.
$F = 0.202^2/0.14^2 = 2.0818$
Since $2.0818 < 2.534$, do not reject H_0.
b. You would have rejected a true null hypothesis, which is a Type I error. You could decrease the alpha level to decrease the probability of a Type I error or you could increase the sample sizes.

11-29. a. Since $F = 3.035 > 2.526 = F_{0.05}$, reject H_0.
b. $P(x < 39448) = P\left(z = \frac{39,448 - 43,809}{2,636}\right)$
$= P(z < -1.65) = 0.5000 - 0.4505$
$= 0.0495$

11-31. $F = 34.434^2/29.9187^2 = 1.3246$
Since $1.3246 < 1.4341$, do not reject H_0.

11-33. a. p-value $= 0.0000$

b. $P(x > 1.398) = P\left(z = \dfrac{1.398 - 9.603}{8.545}\right)$

$P(z > -0.96) = 0.5000 + 0.3315 = 0.8315$

11-35. Answers will vary.

11-37. Student answers will vary with the article.

11-39. The 90% confidence interval is
$$\dfrac{(25-1)47^2}{36.4150} \le \sigma^2 \le \dfrac{(25-1)47^2}{13.8484}$$

$1{,}455.89 \le \sigma^2 \le 3{,}828.31$

11-41. $0.753 \le \sigma^2 \le 2.819$

11-43. a. $H_0: \sigma^2 = (0.05)^2$
$H_A: \sigma^2 \ne 0.0025$
Since $\chi^2 = 37.24 > \chi_U^2 = 30.1435 \to$ reject H_0.

b. From the binomial table with $p = \alpha = 0.10$:
$P(x \ge 3) = 0.0230 + 0.0026 + 0.0002 = 0.0256$

11-45. a. Since $F = 3.817 > 1.752 = F_{0.025}$, reject H_0.

b. Test for normal distributions.

11-47. $H_0: \sigma^2 \le 3{,}900^2$
$H_a: \sigma^2 > 3{,}900^2$
Since $202.5424 < 224.9568$, do not reject the null hypothesis

11-49. $H_0: \sigma^2{}_M \le \sigma^2_F$
$H_a: \sigma^2{}_M > \sigma^2_F$
Since $2.0609 > 1.4953$, reject the null hypothesis.

11-51. a. Since the p-value $= 0.195 > 0.05 = \alpha = 0.05$, fail to reject the null hypothesis.

b. Use the two-sample t since the two population variances were determined to be equal to each other. The populations must have normal distributions.

Chapter 12

12-1. a. $F = 1{,}474{,}542{,}579/87{,}813{,}791 = 16.79$

b. Because the F-test statistic $= 16.79 > F_\alpha = 2.3778$, we reject the null hypothesis.

12-3. Because $F = 4.18 < 20.6$, do not reject the null hypothesis. Thus, there is no evidence to suggest that population variances are not equal.
Since the test statistic $= F = 5.905 > 3.239$, reject the null hypothesis. p-value $= 0.0065 < 0.05$; we reject the null hypothesis.

12-7. a. Because $F = 2.729 < 15.5$, we conclude that the population variances could be equal.
Since $F = 5.03 > 3.885$, we reject H_0.
There is sufficient evidence to indicate that at least two of the population means differ.

b. The contrasts are
$|\bar{x}_1 - \bar{x}_2| = |14 - 16.75| = 2.75 > 2.311,$

$|\bar{x}_1 - \bar{x}_3| = |14 - 15.33| = 1.33 < 2.086,$ and

$|\bar{x}_2 - \bar{x}_3| = |16.75 - 15.33| = 1.42 < 2.224$

12-9. a. Because $1.462 < 85$, we conclude that the population variances could be equal.
Since $F = 504.88 > 8.022$, we reject H_0.

b. The contrasts are
$|\bar{x}_1 - \bar{x}_2| = |4976.8 - 3309.8| = 1667 > 202.86,$

$|\bar{x}_1 - \bar{x}_3| = |4976.8 - 3970.8| = 1006 > 202.86,$ and

$|\bar{x}_2 - \bar{x}_3| = |3309.8 - 3970.8| = 661 > 202.86$

12-11. a. Because $3.125 < 15.5$, we conclude that the population variances could be equal.
Since $F = 1459.78 > 3.885$, we reject H_0.

b. The contrasts are
$|\bar{x}_1 - \bar{x}_2| = |163 - 308.2| = 145.2 > 9.36,$

$|\bar{x}_1 - \bar{x}_3| = |163 - 341.4| = 178.4 > 9.36,$ and

$|\bar{x}_2 - \bar{x}_3| = |308.2 - 341.4| = 33.2 > 9.36$

12-13. a. Since $10.48326 > 5.9525$, reject H_0 and conclude that at least two populations means are different.

b.

	Absolute Difference	Critical Range	Significant?
Type A − Type B	231.5	222.02	Yes
Type A − Type C	54.25	222.02	No
Type A − Type D	75.75	222.02	No
Type B − Type C	177.25	222.02	No
Type B − Type D	307.25	222.02	Yes
Type C − Type D	130.00	222.02	No

Based on the Tukey–Kramer test, you can eliminate Types D and A since the mean life is less than B.

12-15. a. $H_0: \mu_1 = \mu_2 = \mu_3$
$H_A:$ At least two population means are different
Since $0.01 < 0.05$, reject H_0 and conclude that at least two populations means are different.

b.

	Absolute Differences	Critical Range	Significant?
Car 1 − Car 2	0.633	1.264	No
Car 1 − Car 3	1.175	1.161	Yes
Car 2 − Car 3	1.808	1.322	Yes

c. $\$293.40 ----- \$803.40$

12-17. a. p-value $= 0.000 < \alpha = 0.05$

b. There is sufficient evidence to conclude that the average length of life differs between Delphi and Exide and also between Delphi and Johnson. There is, however, not enough evidence to indicate that the average lifetimes for batteries made by Exide and Johnson differ.

12-19. a. F (textbooks) $= 1{,}511.3/38.7 = 39.05$
F (retailer) $= 1.2/38.7 = 0.031$

b. Since $F = 39.05 > F_{\alpha = 0.10} = 1.88$, reject the null hypothesis.

c. $H_0: \mu_{On} = \mu_{Off} = \mu_I$
$H_A:$ Not all populations have the same mean
$F = 0.031$
Since $F = 0.031 < F_{\alpha = 0.10} = 2.56$, do not reject the null hypothesis.

12-21. Because $F = 14.3 >$ critical $F = 3.326$, we reject the null hypothesis and conclude that blocking is effective.
Because $F = 0.1515 <$ critical $F = 4.103$, we do not reject the null hypothesis and conclude that the three populations may have the same mean value.

12-23. a. Since $F = 23.72 > F_{0.05} = 9.277$, reject H_0. Conclude that blocking was effective.

b. Since $F = 3.37 < F_{0.05} = 10.126$, fail to reject H_0. Conclude that the two types of lettuce may have equal means

c. $|\bar{x}_1 - \bar{x}_2| = |106.50 - 161.50| = 55.00 > 21.457$,

$|\bar{x}_1 - \bar{x}_3| = |106.50 - 144.00| = 37.50 > 21.457$,

$|\bar{x}_1 - \bar{x}_4| = |106.50 - 144.50| = 38.00 > 21.457$,

$|\bar{x}_2 - \bar{x}_3| = |161.50 - 144.00| = 17.50 < 21.457$,

$|\bar{x}_2 - \bar{x}_4| = |161.50 - 144.50| = 17.00 < 21.457$, and

$|\bar{x}_3 - \bar{x}_4| = |144.00 - 144.50| = 0.50 < 21.457$,

12-25. a. Because $F = 32.12 > F_{\alpha = 0.01} = 9.78$, reject the null hypothesis. Thus, based on these sample data we conclude that blocking is effective.

b. Because $F = 1.673 < F_{\alpha = 0.01} = 10.925$, do not reject the null hypothesis.

12-27. a. It was attempting to remove the effect of items selected.

b. Since $952.6155 > 1.8673$, reject H_0 and conclude that there is an indication that blocking was effective.

c. Since the p-value of 2.68E-10 < 0.05, reject H_0 and conclude that at least two means are different

d. Least Significant Difference (LSD): 1.3962405

	Mean Difference	Absolute Mean Difference	Significant?
D1 − D2	−6.29	6.29	Yes
D1 − D3	−3.032	3.032	Yes
D2 − D3	3.258	3.258	Yes

12-29. a. The p-value $= 0.000 < \alpha = 0.05$.

b. The p-value $= 0.004 < \alpha = 0.05$.

c. Since

$|\bar{x}_1 - \bar{x}_2| = |9.06 - 8.24| = 0.82 < 1.550$,

$|\bar{x}_1 - \bar{x}_3| = |9.06 - 11.37| = 2.31 > 1.550$, and

$|\bar{x}_2 - \bar{x}_3| = |8.24 - 11.37| = 3.13 > 1.550$

12-31. a. Since $0.4617 < 3.8853$, do not reject H_0 and conclude that Factors A and B do not interact.

b. Since $2.3766 < 3.8853$, do not reject H_0 and conclude that all means are equal.

c. Since $5.7532 > 4.7472$, reject H_0 and conclude that not all means are equal.

12-33. a. p-value $= 0.854 > \alpha = 0.05$; therefore, fail to reject H_0. $H_0 : \mu_{A1} = \mu_{A2} = \mu_{A3}$.

b. Since $F = 47.10 > F_{0.05} = 5.143$, reject H_0.

c. p-value $= 0.039 < \alpha = 0.05$; therefore, reject H_0.

12-35. a. Since $F = 39.63 > F_{0.05} = 3.633$, reject H_0. Conclude that there is sufficient evidence to indicate that interaction exists between Factors A and B.

b. Since $F = 2.90 < F_{0.05} = 9.552$, fail to reject H_0.

c. Since $F = 3.49 < F_{0.05} = 9.552$, fail to reject H_0. Since $F = 57.73 > F_{0.05} = 9.552$, reject H_0. Conclude that there is sufficient evidence to indicate that at least two levels of Factor A have different mean responses at Level 2 of Factor B.

12-37. a. Because $F = 0.168 < F_{\alpha = 0.10} = 2.108$, do not reject the null hypothesis.

b. Because $F = 0.322 < F_{\alpha = 0.10} = 2.456$, do not reject the null hypothesis.

c. Because $F = 35.401 > F_{\alpha = 0.10} = 2.456$, reject the null hypothesis.

12-39. a.

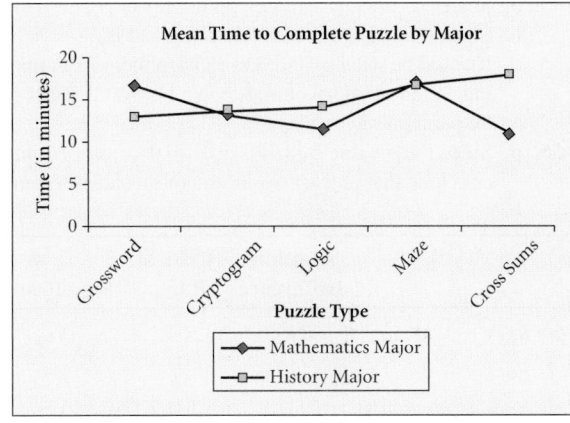

b. Because $F = 26.247 > F_{\alpha = 0.05} = 2.606$, reject the null hypothesis.

c. Because $F = 14.183 > F_{\alpha = 0.05} = 2.866$, reject the null hypothesis.

Because $F = 30.765 > F_{\alpha = 0.05} = 2.866$, reject the null hypothesis.

12-41. a. $\alpha = 0.025 < p$-value $= 0.849$. Therefore, fail to reject H_0.

b. Since $F = 15.61 > F_{0.025} = 3.353$, reject H_0.

c. Conclude that there is not sufficient evidence to indicate that at least two plant sites have different averages of percent of crude fat.

d. Since $-2.0595 < t = -0.69 < 2.0595$, fail to reject H_0.

12-43. Answers will vary with the student.

12-45. We would expect that the Tukey–Kramer procedure for multiple comparisons would show no significant difference in any pairwise comparison.

12-47. Using the MSW enables us to incorporate all the information related to the estimate of the common population variance, not just some of it as would be the case with the two-sample t-test approach.

12-49. a. Since $9.7555 > 5.9525$, reject H_0.

b.

	Absolute Difference	Critical Range	Significant?
Supplier A − Supplier B	226.5	226.23	Yes
Supplier A − Supplier C	54.25	226.23	No
Supplier A − Supplier D	75.75	226.23	No
Supplier B − Supplier C	172.25	226.23	No
Supplier B − Supplier D	302.25	226.23	Yes
Supplier C − Supplier D	130	226.23	No

Based on the Tukey–Kramer test, you can eliminate Types D and A since the mean life is less than B.

12-51. a. Because $F = 25.004 < 403$, we conclude that the population variances could be equal. Since $F = 3.752 > 2.657$, we reject H_0.

b. For $n_1 = n_2 = \cdots = n_8 = 3$, critical range $=$

$$4.90\sqrt{\frac{11.3}{2}\left(\frac{1}{3} + \frac{1}{3}\right)} = 9.5099. \text{ Tukey–Kramer,}$$

therefore, indicates that $\mu_I > \mu_B$, $\mu_I > \mu_{IF}$ and $\mu_I > \mu_G$. Other pairwise comparison were deemed to be equal.

12-53. a. Since $0.59153 < 2.16795$, do not reject H_0.
   b. Since $0.74628 < 3.0648$, do not reject H_0.
   c. It could be used by Gordon to keep them from making a claim that was not true, which would affect public perception.

12-55. a. Since the p-value $= 8.74E$-$30 < 0.05$, reject H_0 and conclude that at least two of the means are different.
   b.

	Absolute Difference	Critical Range	Significant?
Little Rock − Wichita	5773.6	1504.72	Yes
Little Rock − Tulsa	1157.6	1504.72	No
Little Rock − Memphis	2931.8	1504.72	Yes
Wichita − Tulsa	6931.2	1504.72	Yes
Wichita − Memphis	8705.4	1504.72	Yes
Tulsa − Memphis	1774.2	1504.72	Yes

   c. $n = 1.96^2(6,368,664)/500^2 = 97.8634$, or 98

12-57. a. Since $F = 5.37 > F_{0.05} = 3.682$, reject H_0.
   b. Since $F = 142.97 > F_{0.05} = 5.192$, reject H_0.
   c. Since $F = 129.91 > F_{0.05} = 5.192$, reject H_0.
   Since $F = 523.33 > F_{0.05} = 5.192$, reject H_0.

Chapters 8–12 Special Review

SR.1. Decision: $z = 1.4731 < 1.645 = z_\alpha \Rightarrow$ do not reject H_0.
SR.3. Decision: $z = -3.2011 < -1.96 = -z_{\alpha/2} \Rightarrow$ reject H_0.
SR.5. Decision: $F_\alpha = 3.137 > 1.1703 = F \Rightarrow$ do not reject H_0.
   Decision: $t_{\alpha/2} = 2.0930 < 6.0689 = t \Rightarrow$ reject H_0.
SR.7. Decision: $F_H = 10.8 > 1.3123 = F \Rightarrow$ do not reject H_0.
   Decision: $F_\alpha = 3.682 > 0.10 = F \Rightarrow$ do not reject H_0.
SR.9. Test for Factor 1: Glass type
   p-value $= 0.065 > 0.05 = \alpha$. Therefore, do not reject the null hypothesis that the average brightness of the monitors is not different between the glass types.
   Test for Factor 2: Phosphor type
   p-value $= 0.000 < 0.05 = \alpha$. Therefore, reject the null hypothesis that the average brightness of the monitors is not different among the Phosphor types.

SR.11. $p_1 - p_2 \pm z \sqrt{\dfrac{p_1(1-p_1)}{n_1} + \dfrac{p_2(1-p_2)}{n_2}}$

$= \left(\dfrac{16}{250} - \dfrac{9}{250}\right) \pm 1.96 \sqrt{\dfrac{0.064(0.936)}{250} + \dfrac{0.036(0.964)}{250}}$

$= 0.028 \pm 0.0381$

$= (0.0019, 0.0781)$

Chapter 13

13-1. Because $\chi^2 = 35.725 > 11.0705$, reject the null hypothesis.
13-2. Because $\chi^2 = 119.3 > 18.3070$, we reject the null hypothesis.
13-3. Because $\chi^2 = 6.4607 < 13.2767$, do not reject the null hypothesis.

13-5. Because the calculated value of $595.657 > 13.2767$, we do not reject H_0.
13-7. Because $\chi^2 = 2.1229 < 9.2104$, we do not reject the null hypothesis.
13-9. Because the calculated value of 4.48727 is less than the critical value of 12.8345, we do not reject H_0.
13-11. a. H_0: distribution of dollars spent per person is normally distributed
   H_A: distribution of dollars spent is not normally distributed
   b.

Amount Spent	Frequency
under $44	24
$44 < $74	108
$74 < $104	224
$104 < $134	172
$134 < $164	65
$164 < $194	7
	600

   c.

Amount Spent	o Frequency	z-value	Normal Probability	e Expected Frequency
under $44	24	−1.75	0.0401	24.06
$44 < $74	108	−0.76	0.1835	110.1
$74 < $104	224	0.24	0.3712	222.72
$104 < $134	172	1.23	0.2959	177.54
$134 < $164	65	2.22	0.0961	57.66
$164 < $194	7	3.21	0.0132	7.92
	600		1.0000	

   d. Because $\chi^2 = 1.26 < 7.8147$, do not reject the null hypothesis.
13-13. The calculated χ^2 is 3.6549, which is less than 7.3778, so do not reject H_0.
13-15. a. Because the calculated value of 1.97433 is less than the critical value of 14.0671, we do not reject H_0.
   b. Since $\alpha = 0.05$, the critical value is 1.645. Reject H_0 if $z > 1.645$.
   Since $z = -4.16 < 1.645$, do not reject H_0.
13-17. Because $\chi^2 = 50.3115 > 21.666$, reject the null hypothesis.
13-19. Because $\chi^2 = 300.531 > 16.8119$, reject the null hypothesis.
13-21. Because $\chi^2 = \sum\sum \dfrac{(o-e)^2}{e} = 87.3 > 15.507$, we
   would reject the null hypothesis. Because we reject, we need to take care of the small expected frequencies.
   Because revised $\chi^2 = \sum\sum \dfrac{(o-e)^2}{e} = 86.9 > 12.5916$,
   we reject the null hypothesis.
13-23. The p-value for a chi-square value of 30.2753 and 6 df is 0.00003484. Since the p-value is less than $\alpha = 0.02$, we reject the null hypothesis.
13-25. a. Because p-value $> 0.025 = \alpha$, do not reject H_0.

b. Examine the average number of heads per SAR level for Salinas and Sniper:

$$\bar{x}_1 = \frac{\sum x_i}{n} = \frac{539}{4} = 134.75 \quad \text{and}$$

$$\bar{x}_2 = \frac{\sum x_i}{n} = \frac{574}{4} = 143.50$$

Since H_0 was not rejected in part a even though a difference exists, it could be due to sampling error.

13-27. Because $\chi^2 = \sum\sum\frac{(o-e)^2}{e} = 12.9 > 7.8147$, we would reject the null hypothesis. Thus, we need to take care of the small expected frequencies.

Because revised $\chi^2 = \sum\sum\frac{(o-e)^2}{e} = 11.6 > 5.9915$, we reject the null hypothesis.

13-29. a. Minitab output:

Tabulated statistics: Severity, Emotions

ROWS: SEVERITY   COLUMNS: EMOTIONS

	Anger	Hostility	Irritability	All
A little	166	151	367	684
Extreme	110	55	113	278
Moderate	101	70	189	360
Quite a bit	81	55	131	267
All	458	331	800	1589
Cell Contents:	Count			

b. Because $\chi^2 = 24.439 > 12.5916$, reject the null hypothesis.

13-31. Since $0.307967 < 5.9915$, do not reject H_0.

13-33. Student answers will vary.

13-35. The hypothesis-test procedure allows the researcher to conduct a one-tail test to determine if one proportion is larger than the other, whereas the contingency analysis establishes independence/dependence (equal proportions/unequal proportions). The second advantage is that the test of proportions allows the test of difference between the two proportions to be something other than zero; the contingency analysis only tests the equality of the proportions.

13-37. Since $25.2975 > 16.8118$, reject H_0.

13-39. a. Students will need to collapse rows to make the expected cell frequencies reach 5 or more.

Readmissions Last Year	Observed Frequency	Poisson Probability Distribution	Expected Frequency
0	139	0.3012	90.3583
1	87	0.3614	108.4299
2	48	0.2169	65.0579
3	14	0.0867	26.0232
4 or more	12	0.0338	10.1400

b. Since $40.7889 > 9.4877$, reject H_0.

13-41. Because p-value $> 0.995 > \alpha = 0.05$, reject the null hypothesis.

13-43. a. There is no one right way to break these data into classes to perform the goodness-of-fit test. If students use different groupings, they will get a different χ^2. However, they should reach the same conclusion with respect to the null hypothesis.

Classes	Observed Frequency	Normal Distribution Probability	Expected Frequency	$(O-E)^2/E$
less than 4	1	0.0668	6.6807229	4.8304073
4 and under 8	9	0.2417	24.17303	9.523871827
8 and under 12	25	0.3829	38.292493	4.614230005
12 and under 16	32	0.2417	24.17303	2.534289635
16 and over	33	0.0668	6.6806942	103.6877063
				125.190505

The calculated χ^2 value of 125.1905 is greater than the critical value of 9.4877, so reject H_0.

b. Since $116.55 < 117.4069$, do not reject H_0.

c. Yes, it is appropriate to construct a confidence interval for the mean since the confidence interval is based upon $\bar{x}$ and the standard deviation and we have established that the standard deviation could be equal to 4.

d. $13.839 \pm 2.575(4/\sqrt{100})$; 12.81 ----- 14.87; no, since the 99% confidence interval estimate for the true mean is between 12.81 and 14.87. This does not include the value of 10.

13-45. a. Minitab output:

Tabulated statistics: Invest, Race

ROWS: INVESTS   COLUMNS: RACE

	African American	White	All
Don't Invest	175	90	265
	132.5	132.5	265.0
Invest	325	410	735
	367.5	367.5	735.0
All	500	500	1000
	500.0	500.0	1000.0
Cell Contents:		Count	
		Expected count	

b. Because $\chi^2 = 37.094 > 3.8415$, reject the null hypothesis.

13-46. Since the calculated value $= 1.155$ is less than $\chi^2 = 7.8147$, do not reject.

Chapter 14

14-1. a.

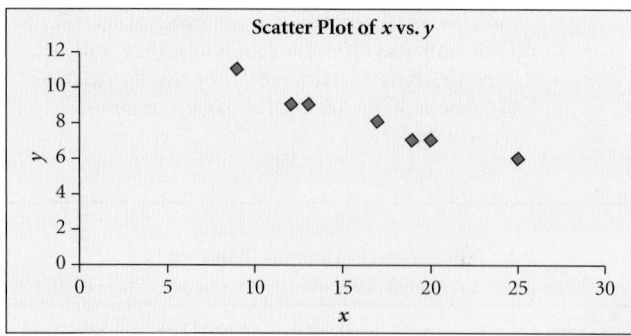

From the scatter plot it appears that a negative linear relationship exists between the two variables x and y.

b. $r = -0.9707$

c. Because $t = -9.895 < -1.9432$, reject the null hypothesis.

14-3. Because $t = 2.50 > 1.7709$, reject the null hypothesis.

14-5. a. $r = 0.206$

b. Because $-1.8595 < t = 0.59 < 1.8595$, we do not reject H_0.

14-7. a. There appears to be a fairly strong positive correlation.

b. Because $t = 7.856 > 2.4066$, reject the null hypothesis.

14-9. a. The dependent variable is average credit card balance. The independent variable is income.

b.

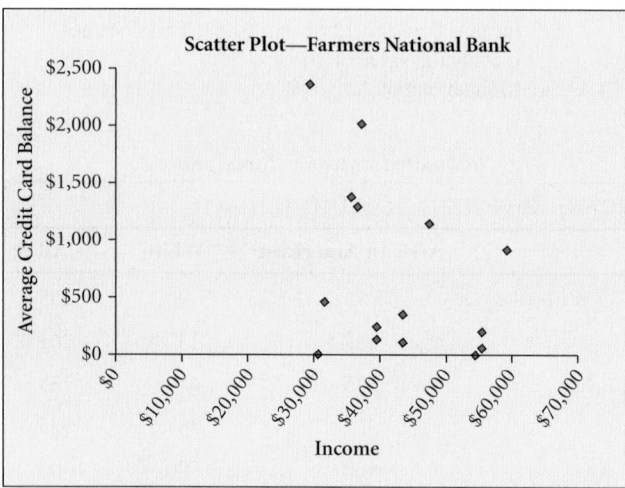

Based on this scatter plot, there does not appear to be a strong relationship.

c. $r = -0.397$

Because $t = -1.56 > -1.7709$, do not reject the null hypothesis.

14-11. a. $r = 0.979$

b. Because $6.791 > t = 2.9200$, we reject H_0.

14-13. a.

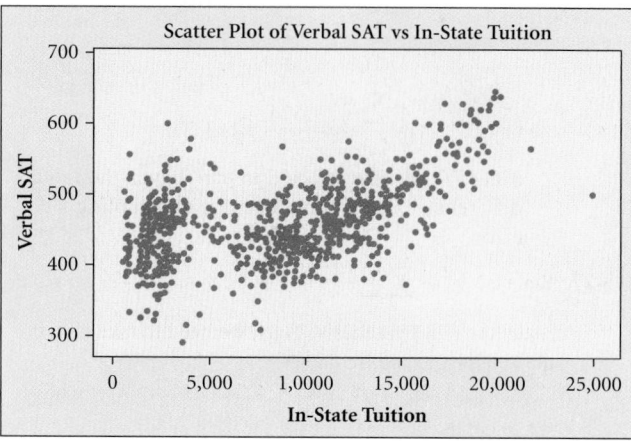

Based on this scatter plot, it appears that there is a positive linear relationship between verbal SAT scores and in-state tuition.

b. $r = 0.51$

c. Because $t = 15.87 > 1.647$, reject the null hypothesis.

14-15. a.

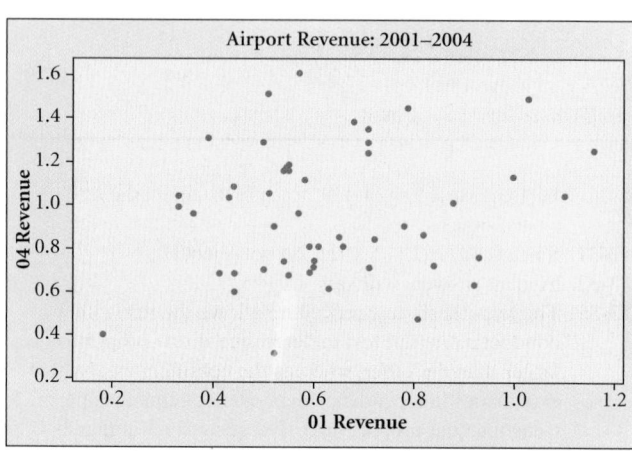

b. $r = 0.186$

c. Because $1.325 < t = 1.67655$, we do not reject H_0.

14-17. a. The following steps can be used to obtain the regression equation based on these sample data:

Step 1: Specify the independent and dependent variables. The x and y variables are specified in the problem data labels.

Step 2: $\hat{y} = 36.7 + 8.33x$

b. $R^2 = \dfrac{SSR}{SST} = 1 - \dfrac{SSE}{SST} = 1 - \dfrac{1{,}467}{7{,}050} = 0.79$

c. $s_e = \sqrt{\dfrac{SSE}{n-2}} = \sqrt{\dfrac{1{,}467}{8}} = 13.54$

d. $s_{b_1} = \dfrac{s_e}{\sqrt{\sum x^2 - \dfrac{\left(\sum x\right)^2}{n}}} = \dfrac{13.54}{\sqrt{2,452 - \dfrac{154^2}{10}}} = 1.51$

e. $t = 5.52 > 2.8965$; we reject the null hypothesis.

14-19. a. $\hat{y} = 26.830 - 0.4923x$

b. When $x = 10$, $\hat{y} = 26.830 - 0.4923(10) = 21.907$.

c. What is being sought here is 10 times the slope: $10(-0.4923) = -4.923$ (a decrease of 4.923 units). The t-test statistic of -3.67 is less than the t-critical value of -2.4469. Reject the null hypothesis.

14-21. a.

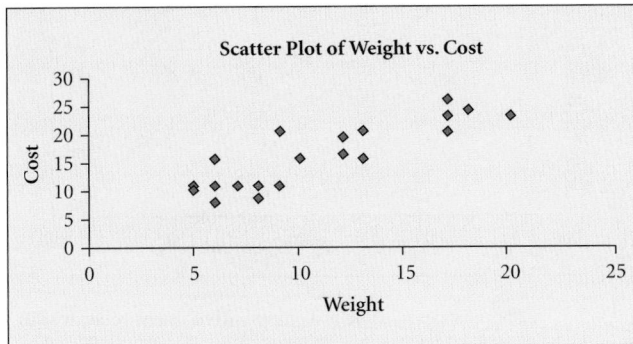

b. $\hat{y} = 4.5 + 1.101(x)$

c. Because $t = 7.7171 > 2.1009$, reject H_0.

d. $R^2 = 0.7680$

14-23. a. The t-test statistic of 9.72 is greater than the upper t-critical value of 2.3534.

b. An increase in the average public college tuition of \$100 would accompany an increase in the average private college tuition of \$3.80(100) = \$380.

c. $\hat{y} = 2109 + 3.80(7500) = \$30,609$

14-25. a. $R^2 = \dfrac{SSR}{SST} = \dfrac{93,223,985.89}{2,360,447,414} = 0.0395$

b. $s_e = \sqrt{\dfrac{SSE}{n-2}} = \sqrt{\dfrac{2,267,222,428}{30}} = 8,693.34$

c. Because $t = 1.11 < 2.0423$, do not reject the null hypothesis.

d. After analyzing the regression model, it is clear that using the number of wins in the season to predict average home attendance is not effective.

14-27. a.

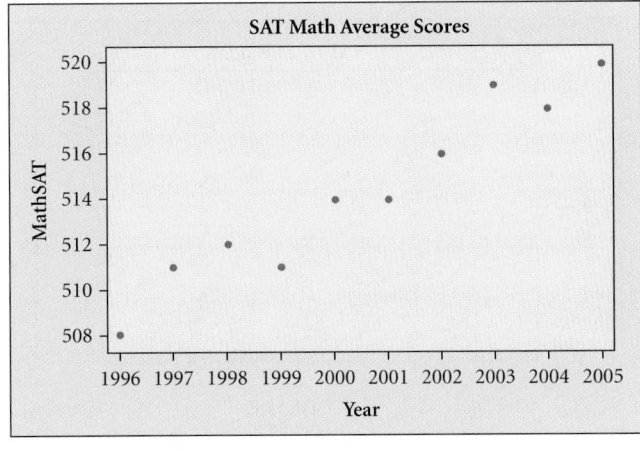

b. $\hat{y} = -1995 + 1.25x$
The t-test statistic of -1.301 is greater than the t-critical value of -1.8595. Therefore, do not reject the null hypothesis.

14-29. a. $\hat{y} = 145,000,000 + 1.3220x$

b. The t-test statistic of 7.02 is greater than the t-critical value of 2.2281. Therefore, reject the null hypothesis.

c. $1,000,000\hat{y} = 1000000(1.322) = \$1,322,000$

14-31. 0.0943 ± 0.179
-0.0847 ----------------- $+0.2733$

14-33. a.

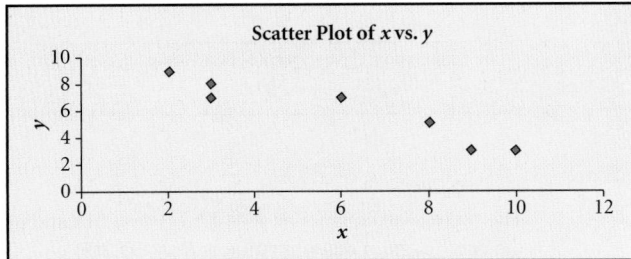

b. $\hat{y} = 10.1 + (-0.7)(x)$

c. -0.7 ± 0.2594
-0.9594 ------------------ -0.4406

d. $\hat{y} = 10.1 + (-0.7)(7) = 5.2$
95% prediction interval: 2.98165 ----- 7.41835

14-35. a. $\hat{y} = \$58,766.11 + \$943.58(x)$

b. $t = \dfrac{b_1 - \beta_1}{s_{b_1}} = \dfrac{943.58 - 0}{244.43} = 3.86$
$t = 3.86 > 2.1315$; reject the null hypothesis.

c. $\$943.58 \pm \$521$
$\$422.58$ -------------------- $\$1,464.58$

14-37. a. $\hat{y} = 44.3207 + 0.9014x$

b. $t = \dfrac{b_1 - \beta_1}{s_{b_1}} = \dfrac{0.9014 - 0}{0.1342} = 6.717$; the null hypothesis is rejected.

c. $0.9014 \pm 1.7709(0.1342) = (0.6637, 1.1391)$

14-39. a. $\hat{y} = -371.9 + 0.20470x$

b. The scatter plot is

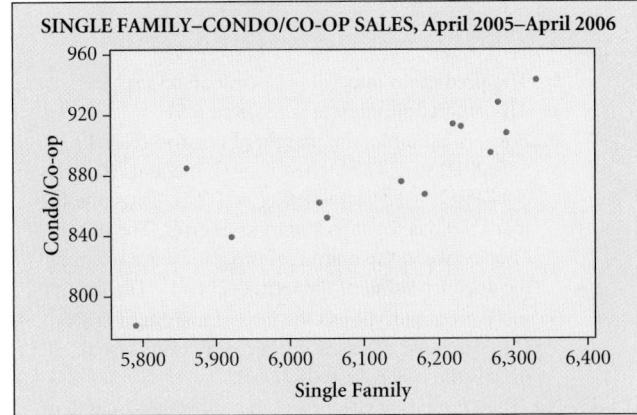

$r = 0.841$
$t = 5.16$; therefore, do not reject the null hypothesis.

c. $\hat{y} = -371.9 + 0.2047(6000) = 856.30$
The 95% prediction interval for an individual response is 799.87 to 912.1.

14-41. a.

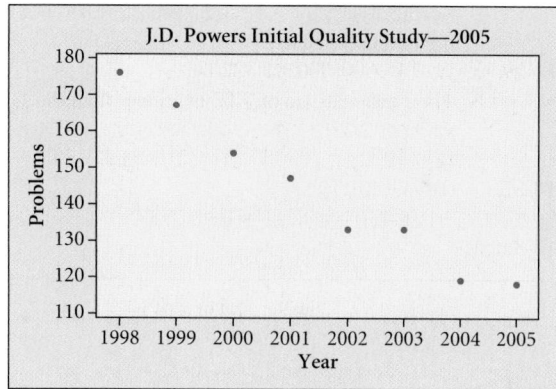

b. $r = -0.986$

The regression equation is $\hat{y} = 17,371 - 8.61x$ and the coefficient of determination is $R^2 = 97.2\%$. The p-value $= 0.000 < \alpha = 0.01$. Therefore, reject the null hypothesis.

c. The 95% prediction interval for the initial quality industry average of the number of reported problems per 100 vehicles for 2010 is (54.19 to 86.23).

14-43. a. Minitab scatter plot:

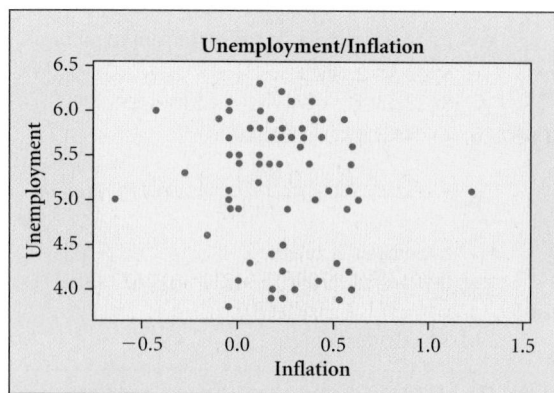

b. The prediction interval is (3.2426, 6.4325).

c. The prediction interval is (3.78 to 6.5).

d. For this example, the margin of error = (6.7249 − 3.7800)/2 = 1.4724 when $x_p = 0$. It equals (6.4325 − 3.2426)/2 = 1.5950 when $x_p = 1.223$. Thus, the former case has the larger margin of error. The difference between the margin of error for parts b and c is the specific value of the term $(x_p - \bar{x})^2$. The former prediction interval has the largest margin of error since its $x_p (= 1.223)$ is further away from $\bar{x}(= 0.2201)$ than is the other $x_p (= 0)$.

14-45. No. The correlation coefficient measures the strength of the linear relationship between two variables.

14-47. The correlation is a quantitative measure of the strength of the linear relationship between two variables. The correlation coefficient may range in value between −1.00 and +1.00.

14-49. a. No, you cannot assume this because correlation does not assume cause and effect. Two unconnected variables could be highly correlated.

b. On the basis of the correlation coefficient case, you can still not assume cause and effect, although an increase in the common dividends may well cause an increase in the stock price.

14-51. The answer will vary depending on the article the students select.

14-53. a.

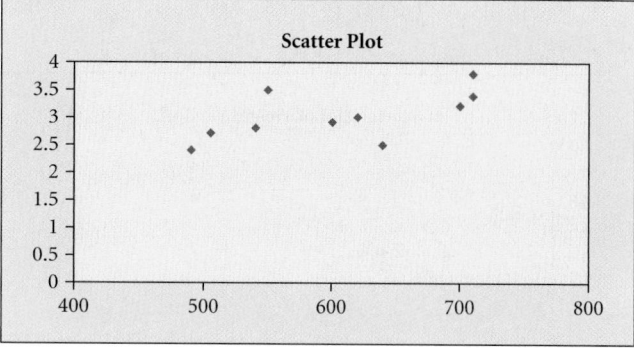

There appears to be a weak positive linear relationship.

b. $r = 0.6239$

Since $2.2580 < 3.3554$, do not reject H_0 and conclude that there is not a correlation between SAT scores and final GPA.

c. $\hat{y} = 0.9772 + 0.0034(x)$

(2). The y intercept would indicate the average university GPA of all students who received an SAT score of 0. Such a situation seems highly unlikely. Therefore, the y intercept has no interpretation in this case. The slope indicates that the average university GPA increases by 0.0034 for each increase of 1 unit in the SAT score.

14-55. a. $\hat{y} = 2109 + 3.80x$

b. $t = \dfrac{b_1 - \beta_1}{s_{b_1}} = \dfrac{3.8048 - 0}{0.3913} = 9.72$; the degrees of

freedom $= n - 2 = 5 - 2 = 3$. Therefore, the p-value $< 0.001 < \alpha = 0.05$ and the null hypothesis is rejected.

c. The 95% confidence interval is ($18,605, $23,660).

d. Since $25,000 is larger than $23,660, it does not seem to be a plausible value.

14-57. a. Minitab scatter plot:

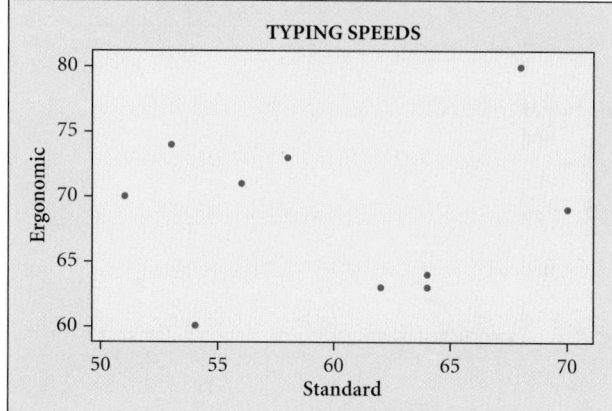

b. $r = 0.071$

c. Because $0.2013 < t = 1.8595$, we fail to reject H_0.

14-59. a.

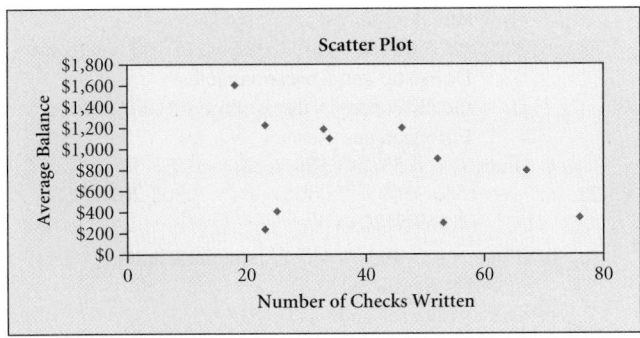

b. The regression model is $\hat{y} = 1219.8035 + (-9.1196)(x)$.

c. Lower 90%: $25 \times -22.7314 = -568.285$; Upper 90%: $25 \times 4.4922 = 112.305$

d. Since $1.5 < 5.117$, do not reject H_0.

14-61. a.

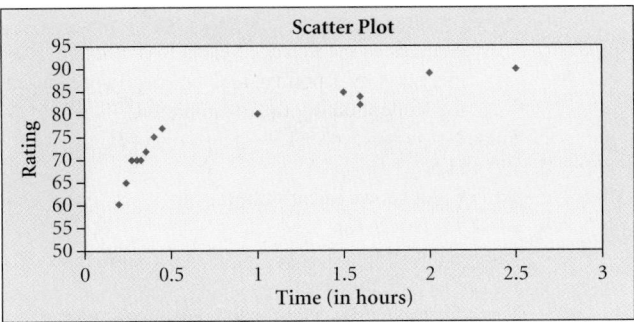

b. $\hat{y} = 66.7111 + 10.6167(x)$

Since $F = 62.14236$, conclude that the overall model is significant at the 0.10 level.

14-63. a. $\hat{y} = 165537 + 0.525x$

b. $r = 0.826$

The coefficient of determination is $R^2 = 68.3\%$. The p-value $= 0.022 < \alpha = 0.05$. Therefore, we reject the null hypothesis.

c. $\hat{y} = -22,194 + 1.35x$ and the estimate of the standard error of the estimate is 2,327.92. ($239,177, $243,125)

14-65. a.

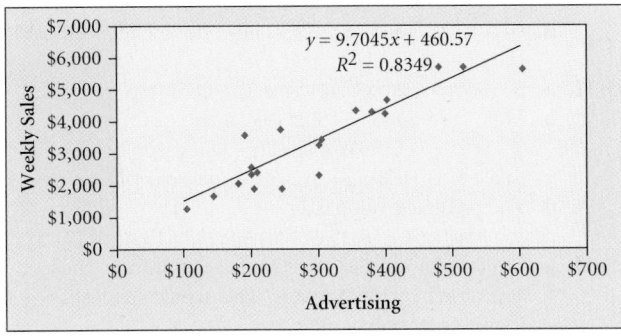

b. Lower 95%: $50 \times 7.5673 = 378.365$; Upper 95%: $50 \times 11.8416 = 592.08$

A $50 increase in advertising will result in an increase in sales of $378.365 to $592.08.

c. No, it is not appropriate in this case. It is appropriate if the value 0 is in the range of x-values in the sample.

d.

For Average Predicted (YH)	
Interval Half Width 286.0036653	
Confidence Interval Lower Limit	2115.458156
Confidence Interval Upper Limit	2687.465486

e. The conclusions and inferences made from a regression line are statistically valid only over the range of the data contained in the sample used to develop the regression line. The $100 is outside of the range of the sample.

Chapter 15

15-1. a. $b_1 = 4.14 \qquad b_2 = 8.72$

b. $\hat{y} = 12.67 + 4.14(4) + 8.72(9) = 107.71$

15-3. a. $\hat{y} = 87.7897 - 0.9705x_1 + 0.0023x_2 - 8.7233x_3$

b. $F = 5.3276 > F_{0.05} = 3.0725$ (using Excel's FINV). Also, p-value $= 0.00689 <$ any reasonable alpha. Therefore, reject H_0.

c. $R^2 = \dfrac{SSR}{SST} = \dfrac{16,646.09124}{38,517.76} = 0.432167$

d. X_1 (p-value $= 0.1126 > \alpha = 0.05 \rightarrow$ fail to reject H_0: $\beta_1 = 0$) and x_3 (p-value $= 0.2576 > \alpha = 0.05 \rightarrow$ fail to reject H_0: $\beta_3 = 0$) are not significant.

e. $b_2 = 0.0023 \quad b_3 = -8.7233$

f. The confidence intervals for β_1 and β_3 contain 0.

15-5. a. $y_i = 5.05 - 0.051 X_1 + 0.888 X_2$

b. 0.206. Since $t = -2.306 < 0.5954 < t = 2.306$; we fail to reject H_0.

c. Since $F = 19.07 > 4.737$, reject H_0.

d. Both x_1 and x_2 have VIFs equal to 1.1. Therefore, multicollinearity does not exist between the two independent variables.

15-7. a.

Correlations: Sales, Sales Increa, Return on Ca, Market Value, Stock Price

	Sales	Sales Increa	Return on Ca	Market Value
Sales Increa	0.157			
Return on Ca	−0.037	−0.122		
Market Value	0.910	0.158	0.028	
Stock Price	0.397	0.018	−0.087	0.430

b. $\hat{y} = 32.1 + 0.0037x_1 + 0.00587x_2$

c. Since $F = 1.93 < 2.64464$, fail to reject H_0.

d. The coefficient of determination equals 18.5% and the adjusted coefficient of determination equals 8.9%. At least one of the variables might be removed.

e. Since the p-value $= 0.058 < 0.10$, reject H_0.

15-9. a. $\hat{y} = -977.1 + 11.252 \text{WK HI} + 177.72 \text{ P-E}$

b. Since $F = 39.80 > 3.592$, we reject H_0.

c. $\hat{y} = 1607$

15-11. a. Positive linear relationship between team win/loss percentage and game attendance.

Positive linear relationship between opponent win/loss percentage and game attendance.

Positive linear relationship between games played and game attendance.

No relationship between temperature and game attendance.

b. There is a significant relationship between game attendance and team win/loss% and games played.

c. Multiple regression equation using x_1, x_2, x_3, x_4 as independent variables to predict y.

$y = 12{,}122.24 + 63.14 \text{ (Win/Loss\%)}$
$+ 10.09 \text{ (opp Win/Loss\%)} + 31.51 \text{(Games)}$
$- 55.46 \text{ (Temperature)}$

d. $R^2 = 0.7753$

e. Since p-value (Significance F) $= 0.00143$, reject H_0.

f. Significant variables:

Win/Loss% the p-value $= 0.0014 < 0.08$

g. 1184.1274; no practical significance.

h.

	VIF
Team Win/Loss percentage and all other x	1.569962033
Temperature and all other x	1.963520336
Games played and all other x	1.31428258
Opponent Win/Loss percentage and all other x	1.50934547

The low VIF values indicate multicollinearity is not a problem since no VIF is greater than 5.

i. The interpretation of the intercept would not be relevant since none of the predictor variables is likely to be zero.

15-13. a. 3

b. $y = \beta_0 + \beta_1 x_1 + \beta_2 x_2 + \beta_3 x_3 + \beta_4 x_4 + \varepsilon$; $x_1 = \{1$ for level 1, 0 otherwise$\}$, $x_2 = \{1$ for level 2, 0 otherwise$\}$, $x_3 = \{1$ for level 3, 0 otherwise$\}$

c. $\beta_0 =$ the average value of y for the fourth level of the categorical variable and when $x_4 = 0$.

$\beta_i =$ the difference in the average value of y when the categorical variable at level i is changed from level i to level four while holding x_4 constant; $i = 1$, 2, and 3.

$\beta_4 =$ the amount of change in the average value of y when x_4 is increased by 1 unit while holding all other x_i constant.

15-15. a. 2,245

b. 1,945

c. b_2 indicates the average premium paid for living in the city's town center.

15-17. a. Average highway mileage rating would decrease by 0.003 for a specified type of transmission.

b. Highway mileage rating will increase by an average of 4.56, holding the weight constant.

c. $\hat{y} = 38.76 - 0.003 x_1$

d. $\hat{y} = 21.02$

e. Incorporating the dummy variable essentially gives two regression equations with the same slope but

different intercepts, depending upon whether the automobile is an automatic or standard transmission.

15-19. a. $\hat{y} = 197 - 43.6 x_1 - 51 x_2$

b. $\beta_0 =$ the average PP100 of the Korean-branded vehicles

$\beta_1 =$ the difference in the average PP100 between Domestic and Korean vehicles

$\beta_2 =$ the difference in the average PP100 between European and Korean vehicles

c. Since $F = 4.53 > 3.555$, we reject H_0.

15-21. a. $\hat{y} = -586.2556 + 22.8611 (x_1) + 2{,}302.2670 (x_2)$
$+ 1{,}869.8130 (x_3)$

b. Since $F = 5.3934 > 4.347$, conclude that the overall model is significant.

c. The p-value for hours is 0.4613.

d. $\hat{y} = 71 + 2{,}689(x_2) + 2{,}127(x_3)$

e. $(2{,}760 - 71) \pm 2.3060(951.07)$; 495.8326 -----
4882.1674

15-23. a. $\hat{y} = 390 - 37.0 x_1 + 0.263 x_2$

b. $\beta_0 =$ the average math SAT score for females who score 0 on the verbal

$\beta_1 =$ the difference in the average math SAT scores between males and females

$\beta_2 =$ the amount the average math SAT score changes as the average verbal SAT score increases by 1 point given the specific gender of the student taking the examination

c. Since $t = -20.45 < -1.9921$, we reject H_0.

d. $\hat{y} = 484.5$

15-25. a. Scatter plot shows linear relationship.

b. $\hat{y} = 4.937 + 1.2643 x$

The p-value $= 0.015 < \alpha = 0.05$. Therefore, reject H_0.

c. $\hat{y} = -25.155 + 18.983 \ln x$

The adjusted R^2 (91.5%) for the curvilinear model exceeds the R^2 of the simple linear model.

15-27. a. Scatter plot shows curvilinear relationship.

b. The equation is $\hat{y}_i = 4.9 - 3.58 x_1 - 0.014 x_1^2$
$+ 1.42 x_1 x_2 + 0.528 x_1^2 x_2$.

c. Since the p-value $= 0.488 > 0.05$, we fail to reject H_0.

d. There was sufficient evidence to conclude that there is interaction between x_2 and the quadratic relationship between x_1 and y.

15-29. a. Scatter plot shows curvilinear relationship.

b. For the simple linear model $F = 1.1829 < 4.6001$, so conclude that the simple linear model is not a significant model.

For the 2nd Order Model $F = 25.0765 > 3.8056$ so conclude that the 2nd order model is a significant model.

c. The second-order model with a squared term would be preferred to the simple linear model.

d. Charles should use the second-order model with days squared.

15-31. a. Scatter plot shows curvilinear relationship

b. Men $= 758.0664 - 19.2549 \text{Women}$
$+ 0.1339 \text{Women Sq}$

c. Since $F = 1030.737 > 3.3852$, we reject H_0.

d. The predicted value is
$\hat{y} = 758.0664 - 19.2549(100) + 0.1339(100)^2 = 171.58$.

15-33. a. Scatter plot shows a curvilinear relationship. There appear to be three "curves." This would suggest a fourth-order polynomial.

b. F-test has a p-value of 0.000. However, the individual t-tests all have very large p-values.

c. p-value $= 0.572 > 0.05$; we fail to reject H_0.

p-value $= 0.488 > 0.05$; there is sufficient evidence to remove the third-order component.

Since its p-value $= 0.000 < 0.05$, there is sufficient evidence to retain the second-order component.

$$\hat{y}_i = -2.68 + 1.47x_1 - 0.129x_1^2$$

15-35. a. x_3

b. $\hat{y} = -3.097 + 0.973x_3$

c. Using the adjusted R^2, it is apparent that the equation developed using Standard Selection explains the most variation in the dependent variable, adjusting for the number of independent variables in the model.

15-37. a. x_2 and x_4 were the only variables to enter the model.

b. The stepwise model and the "full" model with the same variables would be identical.

c. Stepwise regression cannot have a larger R^2 than the full model, since R^2 is increased every time a new variable is added.

15-39. a. $\hat{y} = 32.08 + 0.76x_1 - 5x_3 + 0.95x_4$

b. $\hat{y} = 32.08 + 0.76x_1 - 5x_3 + 0.95x_4$

c. $\hat{y} = 32.08 + 0.76x_1 - 5x_3 + 0.95x_4$

d. $\hat{y} = 32.08 + 0.76x_1 - 5x_3 + 0.95x_4$

15-41. a. The expected order would be Calls Received the Previous Week, Ads Placed the Previous Week, and then Airline Bookings.

b. Calls Received the Previous Week was the first variable to enter the model.

c. The two models developed are identical.

15-43. a. Scatter plots show there are two outliers.

b. $\hat{y} = 1110 + 1.60x_2^2$

c. The forward selection stepwise regression agrees with the analyst's decision.

15-45. a. There is multicollinearity among the predictor variables.

b. Either crude oil or diesel prices should be removed since they have the same correlation coefficient with the dependent variable and a correlation coefficient with each other of 1.

c. $\hat{y} = 0.8741 + 0.00089x_2 - 0.00023x_3$

15-47. a. $\hat{y} = -16.02 + 2.1277x$

b. The p-value equals 0.000; reject the null hypothesis.

c. The error terms are not independent of each other.

No evidence is available to refute the assumption that the residuals have equal variances at each value of the independent variable.

A second-order term might be placed into the model. The normal probability plot indicates that the assumption that the residuals possess a normal distribution cannot be rejected.

15-49. a. $\hat{y} = 17.0 + 1.54x_1 - 0.119x_2$

b. See Student Solutions Manual.

c. This residual plot shows the residuals scattered about 0.

d. The residual plot does not display any nonrandom pattern.

e. This residual plot shows positive residuals early in the experiment. In the middle of the experiment, the residuals are negative, and at the end they are positive again.

f. The probability plot shows all of the standardized residuals within the confidence bounds. This indicates that the error terms are normally distributed.

15-51. a. The overall model is significant and only the team win/loss percentage variable is significant.

b. The residuals are the difference between the actual values and the predicted values from the model.

c. The plot of residuals does not appear to have a pattern.

d. The plot of the residuals against time shows a systematic variation about 0, indicating that the residuals are dependent.

e. Based upon the normal probability plot, which is almost a straight line, we can assume the model error terms are approximately normally distributed.

15-53. a. The equation is $\hat{y} = 0.874 + 0.000887x_1 - 0.00235x_2$.

b. The residual plot supports the choice of the linear model.

c. The residuals do not have constant variances.

d. Residual plot shows the residuals scattered about 0. The residuals, however, follow a pattern of being negative, positive, negative, and positive. The linear model appears to be insufficient.

e. The probability plot shows all of the standardized residuals within the confidence bounds. This indicates that the error terms are normally distributed.

15-55. a. $\hat{y} = -6.81 + 5.29x_1 + 1.51x_2 - 0.000033x_3$

b. The residual plot indicates that a higher-order model may be in order.

c. $\hat{y} = 0.97 - 3.20x_1 + 0.285x_2 + 0.000029x_3 + 3.12x_1^2 + 0.103x_2^2 + 0.000000x_3^2$

d. The addition of the quadratic terms has alleviated the nonrandomness with the residuals.

e. The error terms are normally distributed.

15-57. The least squares objective is the same for both simple linear and multiple linear regression.

15-59. A model is apt if it satisfies the regression assumptions.

15-61. a. The coefficient of x_1 indicates that the average y increases by 3 units *holding x_2 constant*.

b. The interpretation provided in part a is true

c. The coefficient of x_1 indicates that the average y increases by 7 units *when $x_2 = 1$*.

d. The coefficient of x_1 indicates that the average y increases by 11 units when $x_2 = 1$. For this model, the interpretation in part a is no longer true.

e. When interaction terms exist in the model, those coefficients affected by the interaction terms have conditional interpretations.

15-63. a. $R^2 = 0.8448$; $F = 13.6076 > 3.4780$; conclude that the overall model is significant.

b.

	Coefficients	Lower 95%	Upper 95%
Intercept	$-125,307.8062$	$-194,563.0421$	$-56,052.6$
Pages X1	175.8963214	87.28373715	264.5089
Competing Books X2	$-1,573.777885$	$-6,020.812614$	$2,873.257$
Advertising Budget X3	1.591706487	0.601381026	2.582032
Age of Author X4	$1,613.747496$	221.1082826	$3,006.387$

c. Pages: $t = 4.4229 > 2.2281$; conclude pages is significant.

Competing books: $t = -0.7885 > -2.2281$; conclude competing books is insignificant.

Advertising budget: $t = 3.5812 > 2.2281$; conclude advertising budget is significant.

Age of author: $t = 2.5819 > 2.2281$; conclude age of author is significant.

d. 87.2852 ----- 264.5074

15-65. Negative linear relationship between age and purchases. Slight positive linear relationship between purchases and family income.

Based on the scatter plot, it is difficult to detect any pattern of relationship between family size and purchases.

There does not appear to be any relationship between age and family income.

There appears to be a slightly positive linear relationship between age and family size.

There seems to be little correlation between income and family size.

15-67. Family income was brought into the model because it had the highest correlation with average monthly purchases.

15-69. $0.000329 - 0.003653$.

15-71. There are several issues to address when deciding whether to add a new variable to the regression model. Among these are:

1. R^2 increased from 0.2108 to 0.3905.
2. The standard error decreased from 36.3553 to 32.5313.
3. Since the calculated $t = -2.593 < -2.074$, we conclude the variable is significant.
4. Age is negatively correlated with the dependent variable. This is consistent with the resulting sign on the regression coefficient when age is entered. The low correlation between x_1 and x_2 is an indication that the addition of x_1 will not introduce much of a multicollinearity problem.

15-73. For reasonable levels of alpha, only two variables will enter the model.

15-75. **a.** The scatter plot suggests that the polynomial should be a second-order polynomial.

b. $\hat{y} = 35 - 0.443x + 0.000078x^2$

c. Since $F = 5.10 > 3.257$, conclude the overall model is significant.

d. Since $t = 3.10 > 2.9979$, there is sufficient evidence to conclude that curvature exists in the model that predicts Amazon's net income/loss using sales figures.

15-77. **a.** $\hat{y} = 2857 - 26.4x_1 - 80.6x_2 + 0.115x_1^2 + 2.31x_2^2 + 0.542x_1x_2$

b. The residual plot supports the choice of the linear model.

c. The residuals do have constant variances.

d. The linear model appears to be insufficient. The addition of an independent variable representing time is indicated.

e. The probability plot shows two of the standardized residuals beyond the confidence bounds. This indicates that the error terms are not normally distributed.

A transformation of the independent or dependent variables is required.

15-79. So only the driver's gender (male or female), years education, and the dummy variable associated with not being required to wear a seat belt are significant in the model. However, only 14.959% of the variation in the year of the vehicle can be explained by the available data.

Chapter 16

16-1. Generally, quantitative forecasting techniques can be used whenever historical data related to the variable of interest exist; the historical data can be quantified and the past is prologue to the future.

16-3. Past measurement of the variable of interest measured at successive points in time is a good definition of time-series data.

16-5. The trend component is one of four generally recognized components of time-series data. These components are the trend, the seasonal, the cyclical, and the random. The trend is the long-term increase or decrease in a variable being measured over time.

16-7. **a.** The forecasting horizon is the lead time: the number of periods between when the forecast is made and time period to which it applies.

b. The medium-term forecast has a forecasting horizon of 3 months to 2 years.

c. The forecasting period is the unit of time for which forecasts are to be made. Here, that unit of time is a month.

d. The forecasting interval is the frequency with which new forecasts are prepared. Here, a forecast is made each year (every 12 months). Therefore, the forecasting interval is 12 months.

16-9. **a.**

Year	Radio Advertising	Index	Newspaper Ad	Index
1	300	100.00	400	100
2	310	103.33	420	105
3	330	110.00	460	115
4	346	115.33	520	130
5	362	120.67	580	145
6	380	126.67	640	160
7	496	165.33	660	165

b.

Year	Radio Advertising	Newspaper Ad	Sum	Index
1	300	400	700	100.00
2	310	420	730	104.29
3	330	460	790	112.86
4	346	520	866	123.71
5	362	580	942	134.57
6	380	640	1020	145.71
7	496	660	1156	165.14

c.

Year	Radio	% Radio	Newspaper	Laspeyres
1	300	0.3	400	100
2	310	0.42	420	104.59
3	330	0.42	460	113.78
4	346	0.4	520	126.43
5	362	0.38	580	139.08
6	380	0.37	640	151.89
7	496	0.43	660	165.08

d.

Year	Radio	% Radio	Newspaper	Paasche
1	300	0.3	400	100
2	310	0.42	420	104.41
3	330	0.42	460	113.22
4	346	0.4	520	124.77
5	362	0.38	580	136.33
6	380	0.37	640	148.12
7	496	0.43	660	165.12

16-11. The graphs show an upward trend with random components. The average material cost time series exhibits a cyclical component with a recurrence period of 5 years. The hourly wages time series may be indicating a cyclical component with a recurrence period of 9 years. However, there is not enough data to determine if this pattern will repeat.

16-13.

Year	Labor Costs	Materials Costs	% Materials	% Labor	Laspeyres Index
1996	44333	66500	60	40	100.00
1997	49893	68900	58	42	106.36
1998	57764	70600	55	45	113.59
1999	58009	70900	55	45	114.07
2000	55943	71200	56	44	112.95
2001	61078	71700	54	46	117.03
2002	67015	72600	52	48	122.09
2003	73700	73700	50	50	127.88
2004	67754	73400	52	48	123.44
2005	74100	74100	50	50	128.57
2006	83447	74000	47	53	134.95

16-15. a.

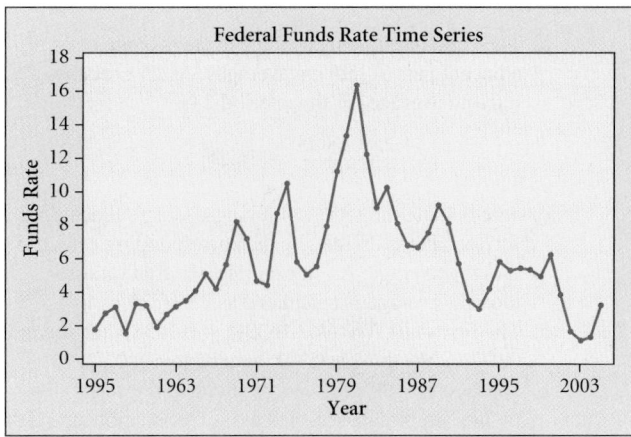

b. Two trend sections, a cycle, and random fluctuations

c. The recurrence period is 5 years.

16-17. a. The Laspeyres Index (for instance) for the 1st Qtr of 2000 is calculated as

$$I_t = \frac{\sum q_o p_t}{\sum q_o p_o} = \frac{736784(0.994) + 5838(0.006)}{720122(0.994) + (4615)(0.006)}(100) = 1.31.$$

b. The Laspeyres Index for 1st Qtr of 2004 is 115.41

c. 14.43%

16-19. This exercise follows the procedure outlined in Figures 16–19 and 16–20.

16-21. The normalized index for January, 0.849, compared to July, 0.966

16-23. a. There appears to be an upward linear trend, but you also see a seasonal component as a slight drop in the 3rd quarter.

b. Because the seasonal index numbers do not add to 4, we normalize them by multiplying each by 4/4.00445 to get the following values:

QUARTER	SEASONAL INDEX
1	1.035013
2	1.020898
3	0.959934
4	0.984154

c. $MSE = 36.995$; $MAD = 4.831$

d. and e.

Quarter	Period	Seasonally Unadjusted Forecast	Seasonal Index	Seasonally Adjusted Forecast
Quarter 1 2007	17	250.15	1.0350	258.91
Quarter 2 2007	18	256.17	1.0209	261.52
Quarter 3 2007	19	262.18	0.9599	251.68
Quarter 4 2007	20	268.20	0.9842	263.95

16-25. a. As an example, the first moving average is calculated as

$$\frac{2+12+23+20}{4} = 14.25$$

b. The centered moving average is the average of each adjacent pair of moving averages. As an example, the moving average for time period 2 is

$$\frac{14.25+18.25}{2} = 16.25$$

c. To calculate the ratio-to-moving-averages, each time-series value is divided by the corresponding centered moving average. As an example, the first ratio-to-moving-average is calculated as $23/16.25 = 1.41538$.

d. The first $= [0.70676/4.01632]4 = 0.70389$, the second 0.97116, the third 1.35302, and the fourth 0.97194.

e. We deseasonalize the data by dividing the actual data by the appropriate seasonal index. As example, the first observation is deseasonalized by $2/0.70389 = 2.84135$.

f. $\hat{y}_t = -0.607 + 5.24t$

g. $\hat{y}_{13} = 0.70389(69.845) = 49.1632$, $\hat{y}_{14} =$

$0.97116(75.265) = 73.0944$, $\hat{y}_{15} = 1.35302(80.684) =$

109.1671, and $\hat{y}_{16} = 0.97194(86.103) = 83.6870$.

16-27. a. There appears to be a linear trend evidenced by the slope from low to high values.

b. $\hat{y} = 990 + 2623t$; $R^2 = 93.6\%$
p-value as 0.000; therefore, reject the null hypothesis.

c. $(60614$ to $77752)$ in $ millions.

16-29. a. A seasonal component is present in the data.

b. $\hat{y} = 211.89 + 3.47(t)$

$$MAD = 29.89;\ MSE = 976.34$$

c.

QUARTER	INDEX
1	1.0290
2	0.9207
3	1.0789
4	0.9714

d.

2006	PERIOD	FORECAST
Qtr. 1	13	256.5620033
Qtr. 2	14	260.0884382
Qtr. 3	15	263.614873
Qtr. 4	16	267.1413079

e. $MAD = 29.60;\ MSE = 926.12$

f. Deseasonalized data model

16-31. a. Forecast for period 16 without transformation $=$
$36.0952 + 10.8714(16) = 210.0376$.
Forecast for period 16 with transformation $=$
$65.2986 + 0.6988(16)^2 = 244.1914$.
Transformed model is preferred.

b. Select the model with the transformation.

16-33. a. Linear trend evidenced and randomness

b. $\hat{y} = 3141 + 769t;\ R^2 = 97.6\%$. Reject the null hypothesis.

c. $F_{27} = 23,894$, $F_{28} = 24,662$, $F_{29} = 25,431$, and $F_{30} = 26,200$.

d. The model overforecasts the e-commerce retail sales by $1,016 million on average.

16-35. a.

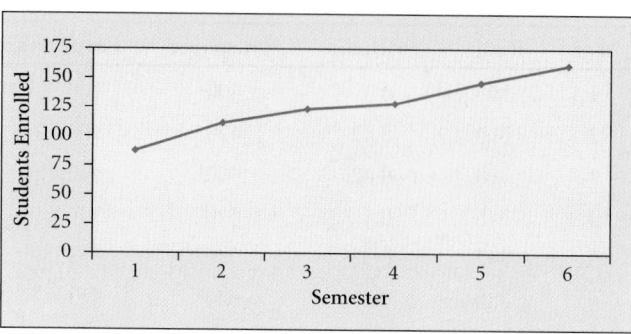

b. Trend is present.

c. $MAD = 23.278$

d. $MAD = 7.655$

e. Double exponential smoothing model

16-37. a. Strong upward trend; use double exponential smoothing

b. $\hat{y}_t = 19.364 + 0.7517t$. Since $C_0 = b_0$, $C_0 = 19.364$.
$T_0 = b_1 = 0.7517$.

c. $F_1 = C_0 + T_0 = 19.3644 + 0.7517 = 20.1154$
$C_1 = \alpha y_1 + (1 - \alpha)(C_0 + T_0)$
$\quad = 0.15(19) + (1 - 0.15)(20.1154) = 19.9481$
$T_1 = \beta(C_1 - C_0) + (1 - \beta)T_0$
$\quad = 0.25(19.948 - 19.3644) + 0.75(0.7517)$
$\quad = 0.7099$
$F_2 = C_1 + T_1 = 19.9483 + 0.7098 = 20.6580$
Period 13 forecast $= 29.105$

d.

ACCURACY MEASURES	
MAPE	8.58150
MAD	2.08901
MSD	6.48044

16-39. a. Strong upward linear trend

b. Use Equations 16-18, 19 and 20 and follow the steps in Example 16-7 using regression coefficients for initial constant and trend.

$$\hat{y} = 404,331 + 1,361.65(t)$$

c. $MAD = 208.7$

16-41. a. There does not appear to be any trend component in this time series.

b. The forecast is calculated as an example; $F_1 = F_2 = 99.1$. Then, $F_3 = 0.25y_2 + (1 - 0.25)F_2 = 0.25(102.8) + 0.75(99.1) = 100.025$.

c. $MAD = 3.2652$

d. $F_{14} = 0.25y_{13} + (1 - 0.25)F_{13} = 0.25(101.3) + 0.75(100.22) = 100.49$

16-43. a. No trend; use single exponential smoothing model.

b. The forecast is calculated as an example; $F_1 = F_2 = 0.296$. Then, $F_3 = 0.15y_2 + (1 - 0.15)F_2 = 0.15(0.413) + 0.85(0.296) = 0.3136$.

c. $MAD = 15.765/71 = 0.222$

d. $F_{73} = 0.15y_{72} + (1 - 0.15)F_{72} = 0.15(-0.051) + 0.85(0.259) = 0.212$

16-45. a. The time-series plot of the data indicates an upward trend over time. The double exponential smoothing model will incorporate the trend effect.

b. *MAD* = 5836.06; double exponential smoothing preferred.
c. alpha = 0.05; beta = 0.05; *MAD* = 5136.51
d. and **e.** Student reports will vary.

16-47. A seasonal component is one that is repeated throughout a time series and has a recurrence period of at most 1 year. A cyclical component is one that is represented by wavelike fluctuations and has a recurrence period of more than 1 year. Seasonal components are more predictable.

16-49. a. Seasonal component exists in the time series.
b. A linear trend component exists.
c. A cyclical component exists.
d. A random component exists.
e. A cyclical component exists.

16-51. a. An upward linear trend
b. Slope = \$342,385.2941; *r* = 0.9479. Since 123.9719 > 4.6001, you would conclude that there is a significant relationship.
c. *MAD* = 461,216.73
d.

YEAR	FORECAST
2007	4,929,275.00
2008	5,271,660.29
2009	5,614,045.59
2010	5,956,430.88
2011	6,298,816.18

e. 5,667,720.9 to 7,530,911.5

16-53. Use Equations 16-18, 19, 20 and follow the steps outlined in Example 15-7.
a. *MAD* = 526,262.5
b. See Student Solutions Manual.

	Beta Values			
	0.5	**0.4**	**0.3**	**0.2**
0.1	\$568,793.54	\$547,728.21	\$523,915.68	\$498,375.36
0.2	\$538,592.87	\$526,262.47	\$515,577.21	\$497,639.06
0.3	\$481,539.18	\$466,164.76	\$459,595.63	\$452,681.23
0.4	\$454,803.56	\$449,962.38	\$436,850.70	\$421,877.56

Alpha Values (leftmost column label)

16-55. a. Strong upward trend, so a double exponential smoothing model is selected.
b. $\hat{y}_t = -1778.7 + 767.33t$

Since $C_0 = b_0$, $C_0 = -1778.7$. $T_0 = b_1 = 767.33$.
c. $F_1 = C_0 + T_0 = -1,778.7 + 767.33 = -1,011.37$
$C_1 = \alpha y_1 + (1 - \alpha)(C_0 + T_0) =$
$0.10(0.5) + (1 - 0.10)(-1011.37) = -910.183$
$T_1 = \beta(C_1 - C_0) + (1 - \beta)T_0 =$
$0.20(-910.183 - (-1,778.7)) + 0.80(767.33) = 787.567$
$F_2 = C_1 + T_1 = -910.183 + 787.567 = -122.6156$
$F_{2005} = 5,854.24 + 768.665 = \$6,622.91$

d.

ACCURACY MEASURES	
MAPE	20382
MAD	521
MSD	395364

16-57. a. Slight linear trend as well as a seasonal trend
b.

MONTH	INDEX
Jan.	0.8488
Feb.	0.8627
March	0.7889
April	0.8662
May	0.9249
June	0.9329
July	0.9660
Aug.	1.0161
Sept.	1.0754
Oct.	1.1349
Nov.	1.2560
Dec.	1.3272

c. MAD = 1424.27.
d.

MONTH	PERIOD	FORECAST
January	49	41,807.4369
February	50	42,247.1405
March	51	42,597.3731
April	52	42,927.3412
May	53	43,267.3072
June	54	43,607.2753
July	55	43,947.2434
August	56	44,287.2115
September	57	44,627.1796
October	58	44,967.1477
November	59	45,307.1157
December	60	45,647.0837

e.

Month	Period	Unadjusted Forecast	Seasonal Index	Adjusted Forecast
January	49	41,907.4368	0.8488	35,572.333
February	50	42,247.405	0.8627	36,445.963
March	51	42,587.3731	0.7889	33,595.260
April	52	42,927.3412	0.8662	37,182.217

16-59. a. *MAD* = 5,181.12
b. See Student Solutions Manual.
c. Recommend the linear trend model.
d. Alpha = 0.30 and beta = 0.10 provide the lowest MAD of those smoothing constants tested.

16-61. a. Upward linear trend
b. $\hat{y}_t = 490.249 + 1.09265t$; $R^2 = 95.7\%$

The *t*-test statistic of 23.19 is larger than the upper *t*-critical value of 1.3178. Therefore, reject the null hypothesis.

c. Forecast is $\hat{y}_t = 490.249 + 1.09265(31) = 524.1212$.

d. Time-series forecasts are based on the assumption that the structure which has occurred in the past will continue to occur in the future.

Chapter 17

17-1. $W = 39$. Since this is an upper-tail test, and $n = 10$, letting $\alpha = 0.05$, we reject if $W > 45$. Therefore, there is not enough evidence to reject the null hypothesis.

17-3. $W = 36$. Since this is an lower-tail test, and $n = 11$, letting $\alpha = 0.05$, we reject if $W < 13$. Therefore, there is not enough evidence to reject the null hypothesis.

17-5. **a.** The hypotheses are: $H_0: \tilde{\mu} \le 4{,}000$

$$H_A: \tilde{\mu} > 4{,}000$$

b. $W = 59$. Since this is an upper-tail test and $n = 12$, letting $\alpha = 0.05$, sum the positive ranks and reject if $W > 61$. Therefore, there is not enough evidence to reject the null hypothesis and the manager can not conclude the median time is greater than 4,000 hours.

17-7. $W = 92$. Since one of the differences equaled 0, we only rank 19 values. This is a lower-tail test with $n = 19$ and $\alpha = 0.05$. We reject if $W < 53$. Therefore, there is not enough evidence to support the consumer group's claim.

17-9. $W = 71.5$ and $W = 81.5$. Because some of the differences are 0, $n = 17$. From Appendix P, the upper and lower values for the Wilcoxon test are 34 and 119 for $\alpha = 0.05$. We do not reject the hypothesis.

17-11. **a.** Since the calculated $\chi^2 = 3.5002$, we do not reject the hypothesis the data come from a normal distribution.

b. $z = \dfrac{7.6306 - 7.4}{\dfrac{0.2218}{\sqrt{95}}} = 10.13$

Therefore, we do not reject the null hypothesis and conclude the average pH level is at least 7.4.

17-13. **a.** Use U_2; reject if $U \le 11$.

b. Use U_1; reject if $U \le 55$.

c. Use smallest of U_1 or U_2; reject if $U \le 64$.

d. Use z-value from Equation 17-8. Reject if $z < -1.645$.

e. Use z-value from Equation 17-8. Reject if $z < -1.645$ or $z > 1.645$.

17-15. **a.** Statistical evidence is associated with rejecting the null hypothesis; therefore, the hypotheses are

$$H_0: \tilde{\mu}_1 - \tilde{\mu}_2 \le 4{,}000$$
$$H_A: \tilde{\mu}_1 - \tilde{\mu}_2 > 4{,}000$$

b. Using Appendix L with $n_1 = 9$ and $n_2 = 9$, the decision rule becomes: reject if $U \le 21$. Since $U = 73$, we cannot reject the null hypothesis.

17-17. $W = 1384.0$

Test of ETA1 = ETA2 vs. ETA1 not = ETA2 is significant at 0.1502.

The test is significant at 0.1501 (adjusted for ties). Cannot reject at alpha = 0.05.

17-19. Reject if $T \le 8$. Since $T = 23.5$, we do not reject the null hypothesis.

17-21. Reject if $T \le 2$. Since $T = 13$, we do not reject the null hypothesis.

17-23. If $T \le 0$, reject H_0; otherwise, do not reject H_0. Since $8 > 0$ do not reject H_0 and conclude that the medians are the same.

17-25. If $U \le 13$, reject H_0; otherwise, do not reject H_0. Since $37 > 13$, do not reject H_0.

17-27. The p-value = 0.426; do not reject H_0.

17-31. **a.** Since $-1.785 > t$ critical $= -2.2622$, do not reject H_0.

b. If $T \le 6$, reject H_0; otherwise, do not reject H_0. Since $5.5 < 6$, reject H_0 and conclude that the medians are not the same.

c. Because you cannot assume the underlying populations are normal, you must use the technique from part b.

17-33. This exercise can be done following the steps shown in the Future Vision example.

a. $z = (4{,}297 - 5250)/434.7413 = -2.19$
p-value $= 0.5 - 0.4857 = 0.0143$
Since $0.0143 < 0.10$, reject H_0.

b. A Type I error

17-35. **a.** The data are ordinal.

b. No, because the data is not at least interval; the median would be the best measure.

c. Since $T = 12.5 > 2$, do not reject H_0 and conclude that the medians are the same for both types of word-processing systems.

d. Since there is no significant difference in the measures of central tendency, the decision could be made based on some other factor, such a cost.

17-37. This exercise can be done following the steps shown in Example 17-3.

a. $H_0: \tilde{\mu}_1 = \tilde{\mu}_2 = \tilde{\mu}_3$
H_A: not all population medians are equal

b. $H = 5.415 < 5.99$; do not reject.

c. Since $F = 3.447 < 3.4668$, do not reject H_0 and conclude that all population means are equal.

d. Use the Kruskal–Wallis test.

17-39. **a.** $H_0: \tilde{\mu}_1 = \tilde{\mu}_2 = \tilde{\mu}_3 = \tilde{\mu}_4$
H_A: not all population medians are equal

b. Selecting $\alpha = 0.05$, $\chi_\alpha^2 = 7.8147$; since $H = 42.11$, we reject the null hypothesis of equal medians.

17-41. **a.** No

b. It is not necessary because the adjustment is only necessary when the null hypothesis is not rejected and the null hypothesis was rejected.

17-43. Adjusting for ties, the test statistic is 11.21, which is smaller than the critical value (11.34488). Therefore, the null hypothesis is not rejected.

17-45. Since $H = 13.9818 > 5.9915$, reject H_0 and conclude that not all population medians are equal.

17-47. The Kruskal–Wallis one-way analysis of variance is the nonparametric counterpart to the analysis of variance procedure and is used if the decision makers are not willing to assume normally distributed populations. Examples will vary.

17-49. Student answers will vary depending upon the organization selected.

17-51. Solution

a. **a** and **b**:

POSSIBLE SETS	SUM OF RANKS	PROBABILITY
none	—	1/16
1	1	1/16
2	2	1/16
3	3	1/16
4	4	1/16
1,2	3	1/16
1,3	4	1/16
1,4	5	1/16
2,3	5	1/16
2,4	6	1/16
3,4	7	1/16
1,2,3	6	1/16
1,2,4	7	1/16
1,3,4	8	1/16
2,3,4	9	1/16
1,2,3,4	10	1/16

b.

T	0	1	2	3	4	5	6	7	8	9	10
$P(T)$	1/16	1/16	1/16	2/16	2/16	2/16	2/16	2/16	1/16	1/16	1/16

17-53. **a.** Since Utest = 42 > 27, do not reject H_0 and conclude that the medians are not different.

b. $F = (105.2386)^2/(32.1906)^2 = 10.6879$

$F_{0.05} = 3.179$

Reject hypothesis of equal variances. If $t > 1.8125$ or $t < -1.8125$, reject H_0; otherwise, do not reject H_0.

$$t = (314.60 - 312.30)/\sqrt{\frac{105.2386^2}{10} + \frac{32.1906^2}{10}} = 0.0661$$

Since $t = 0.0661 < 1.8125$, do not reject H_0.

17-55. **a.** Utest = 58

If $\alpha = 0.02$, $U_\alpha = 24$. Since 58 > 24, do not reject H_0.

b. Testing for equal variances:

$F = 24.9909^2/20.7806^2 = 1.4463$

$F_\alpha = 5.178$ at $\alpha = 0.01$

Accept hypothesis of equal variances. Since $t = -0.2518 > -2.5280$, do not reject H_0.

17-57. Putting the claim in the alternate hypothesis, we find the following:

H_0: $\tilde{\mu} \le 6$

H_A: $\tilde{\mu} > 6$

$W = 7.5$. If $\alpha = 0.05$, using Appendix P, we reject if $W > 74$. Do not reject.

17-59. The hypotheses being tested are

H_0: $\tilde{\mu} = 1,989.32$

H_A: $\tilde{\mu} \neq 1,989.32$

Absolute	
$W = 103$	$W = 68$

$W = 103$ and 68. With $\alpha = 0.05$, using Appendix P, we reject if $W \le 40$ or $W > 131$. Do not reject.

17-61. **a.** Using Appendix P, with $\alpha = 0.05$, reject if $T \le 21$ or if $T \ge 84$. Since 44.5 > 21, do not reject H_0 and conclude that the medians are the same.

b. A Type II error

17-63. **a.** They should use the Wilcoxon Matched-Pairs Signed Rank test.

b. $T = 6$. Using $\alpha = 0.025$, critical $T_\alpha = 4$.

c. Since 6 > 4, do not reject H_0.

Chapter 18

18-1. Both Deming and Juran emphasized that quality was the key component to business competitiveness and that the best way to improve quality came from improving the processes and systems that produce products and deliver services. There are, however, some differences in the philosophies of the two quality pioneers. Student discussions will vary.

18-3. Student answers will vary.

18-5. Student answers will vary depending on the process at their school.

18-7. Student answers will vary depending upon answers to Exercise 18.6.

18-9. Student answers will vary. Some possible causes by category are:

People: Too Few Drivers, High Driver Turnover

Methods: Poor Scheduling, Improper Route Assignments

Equipment: Buses Too Small, Bus Reliability, Too Few Buses

Environment: Weather, Traffic Congestion, Road Construction

18-11. $\bar{p} = 270 / (30 * 100) = 0.090$

$$UCL = 0.090 + 3 * \sqrt{\frac{0.090 * (1 - 0.090)}{100}} = 0.176$$

$$LCL = 0.090 - 3 * \sqrt{\frac{0.090 * (1 - 0.090)}{100}} = 0.004$$

18-13. Because a process can go out of control rather quickly, it is imperative that the control charts be updated as soon as information becomes available

18-15. **a.** At this time, end of Hour 43, there is no evidence that a special cause of variation is present in the process.

b. Yes. Without the control chart limits it would not be possible for us to see the natural, inherent variation of the process.

18-17. a. Looking at the mean values of these observations, it appears that the process has gone out of control since several observations are below the LCL.
  b. The report will vary with the student, but should certainly comment on the R-chart being in control but the x-bar chart going out of control in periods 31–38. An assignable cause should be found.

18-19. a. The 3-sigma upper control limit is $0.0793 + (3 * 0.0270) = 0.1603$. The 3-sigma lower control limit is $0.0793 - (3 * 0.0270) = -0.0017$, which is then set equal to 0.0000.
  b. The process appears to be in control.
  c. The process still appears to be in statistical control.

18-21. a. The x-bar and R-charts are used together to monitor a process where the characteristic of interest is a variable (i.e., a characteristic measured on a continuous scale).
  b. The centerline for the x-bar chart is the average of the subgroup means and equals 82.46.
  c. The centerline for the R-chart is the average of the subgroup ranges and equals 12.33.
  d. $UCL = 2.114 * 12.33 = 26.07$ and $LCL = 0 * 12.33 = 0$
  e. $UCL = 82.46 + (0.577 * 12.33) = 89.57$
  $LCL = 82.46 - (0.577 * 12.33) = 75.35$
  f. While the range chart has no points outside the control chart limits, there is a run of 9 values above the centerline, which indicates a possible loss of statistical control.

18-23. a. $UCL = 2.282 * 100.375 = 229.056$
  $CL = 100.375$
  $LCL = 0 * 100.375 = 0$
  b. $UCL = 415.3 + 0.729(100.375) = 488.473$
  $CL = 415.3$
  $LCL = 415.3 - 0.729(100.375) = 342.127$
  c. The process appears to have lost control with respect to its variability, which is measured by the R-chart.

18-25. a. The appropriate control chart for these data is the p-chart.
  b. $\bar{p} = 441/(300 * 50) = 0.0294$
  $s = \sqrt{(0.0294)(1-0.0294)/50} = 0.0239$
  $UCL = 0.0294 + 3(0.0239) = 0.1011$
  $LCL = 0.0294 - 3(0.0239) = -0.0423$, so set to 0
  c. All of these points are above the UCL, which indicates that the process has gone out of control.
  d. The new sample proportion would be 0.28, which is again above the UCL. This suggests that the process is still out of control and getting further out of control.

18-27. a. $\bar{c} = 29.3333$
  $UCL = 29.3333 + 3(\sqrt{29.3333}) = 45.5814$
  $LCL = 29.3333 - 3(\sqrt{29.3333}) = 13.0852$
  b. The process seems to be out of control since several observations are above the UCL or right at the LCL, there seems to be a run (observation 4–12) below the centerline, and observations 27–30 seem to be alternating one above or near the upper UCL and the next below the LCL, etc.

$CL = 29.333/40 = 0.7333$
$UCL = 0.7333 + 3 * \sqrt{0.7333/40} = 1.1395$
$LCL = 0.7333 - 3 * \sqrt{0.7333/40} = 0.3271$

18-29. a. The Shewart factor for the x-bar chart with a subgroup size of 3 is A2 = 1.023. The Shewart factors for the range chart are D3 = 0.0 and D4 = 2.575 for the lower and upper control limits, respectively.
  b. $UCL = 2.575 * 0.80 = 2.06$ $LCL = 0 * 0.80 = 0$
  c. $UCL = 2.33 + (1.023 * 0.80) = 3.147$
  $LCL = 2.33 - (1.023 * 0.80) = 1.512$

18-31. The centerline of the control chart is the average proportion of defective $= 720/(20 * 150) = 0.240$. For 3-sigma control chart limits, we find

$$UCL = 0.240 + 3 * \sqrt{\frac{0.240 * (1-0.240)}{150}} = 0.345$$

$$LCL = 0.240 - 3 * \sqrt{\frac{0.240 * (1-0.240)}{150}} = 0.135$$

18-33. The appropriate control chart is the p-chart.
  $LCL = 0.9152 - 3 * 0.0279 = 0.8315$
  $CL = 0.9152$
  $UCL = 0.9152 + 3 * 0.0279 = 0.9989$
  The delivery process appears to be in statistical control.

18-35. The appropriate chart is the p-chart: $\bar{p} = 0.0524$.

$$\sqrt{\frac{0.0524 * (1-0.0524)}{100}} = 0.0223$$

The 3-sigma control limits are computed as follows:
  $LCL = 0.0524 - 3 * 0.0223 = -0.0145$, so set to 0
  $CL = 0.0524$
  $UCL = 0.0524 + 3 * 0.0223 = 0.1193$
  The process appears to be in control.

18-37. a. x-bar chart: $CL = 0.7499$
  $UCL = 0.7499 + (0.577)(0.0115) = 0.7565$
  $LCL = 0.7499 - (0.577)(0.0115) = 0.7433$
  R-chart: $CL = 0.0115$
  $UCL = (0.0115)(2.114) = 0.0243$
  $LCL = (0.0115)(0) = 0$
  The process appears to be in control.
  b. It now appears that the process is out of control. All of the averages are above the UCL and in the range chart one value is above the UCL.

Chapter 19

19-1. A good outcome occurs whenever the "best" outcome results, or at the very least, the worst outcome does not occur.

19-3. Given that Varsity will realize an annual profit of $69,664, Varsity should sign the contract.

19-5. Select the alternative with the largest expected value, $A_3 = 81$.

19-7. Select the alternative with the largest expected value, $A_2 = 91.5$.

19-9. a.

	DEMAND			
Purchase	10,000	15,000	20,000	25,000
10,000	8,500	8,500	8,500	8,500
15,000	5,250	12,750	12,750	12,750
20,000	2,000	9,500	17,000	17,000
25,000	(1,250)	6,250	13,750	21,250

b. 1. The maximum values are 8,500, 12,750, 17,000, and 21,250, in order, so purchase 25,000 hot dogs and buns.
2. The minimum values are 8,500, 5,250, 2,000, and −1,250, in order, so purchase 10,000 hot dogs and buns.
3. The maximum regret values are 12,750, 8,500, 6,500, and 9,750, so purchase 20,000 hot dogs and buns.

19-11. a.

	DEMAND			
Production	20,000	40,000	60,000	80,000
20,000	$2,800,000.00	$2,600,000.00	$2,400,000.00	$ 2,200,000.00
40,000	$1,800,000.00	$5,800,000.00	$5,600,000.00	$ 5,400,000.00
60,000	$ 800,000.00	$4,800,000.00	$8,800,000.00	$ 8,600,000.00
80,000	$ (200,000.00)	$3,800,000.00	$7,800,000.00	$11,800,000.00

Acquisition Cost	$200,000.00
Selling Price	$250.00
Discount Price	$50.00
Coupon (Demand Exceeds Supply)	$10.00
Variable Production Cost	$100.00

b. Maximin: Max(2,200,000, 1,800,000, 800,000, −200,000), so produce 20,000.
Maximax: Max(2,800,000, 5,800,000, 8,800,000, 11,800,000), so produce 80,000.

19-13.

	DEMAND				
Purchases	100,000	150,000	200,000	225,000	250,000
100,000	1,000,000	1,000,000	1,000,000	1,000,000	1,000,000
150,000	675,000	1,575,000	1,575,000	1,575,000	1,575,000
200,000	350,000	1,250,000	2,150,000	2,150,000	2,150,000
225,000	187,500	1,087,500	1,987,500	2,437,500	2,437,500
250,000	25,000	925,000	1,825,000	2,275,000	2,725,000

Fixed Cost	150,000					
Variable Cost	5					
Shipping	1.5					
Sales Price	18					
Probabilities		0.1	0.4	0.2	0.2	0.1

PURCHASES	EXPECTED VALUE
100,000	1,000,000
150,000	1,485,000
200,000	1,610,000
225,000	1,582,500
250,000	1,465,000

Using the expected value criterion, 200,000 dozen roses should be purchased. The expected profit of purchasing this amount is $1,610,000.

19-15. Supply 4,000 for $EV = 1,075$.

19-17. a. The maximum values for each alternative are 0; 250,000; 500,000; 750,000; 1,000,000; and 1,250,000, so purchase 5 restaurants for a maximum profit of $1,250,000.
b. The minimum values for each alternative are 0; −200,000; −400,000; −600,000; −800,000; and −1,000,000, so purchase no restaurants for a profit of $0.
c. Mall option:

Revenue per unit	$500,000
Variable Cost per unit	$250,000 (includes franchise cost)
Salvage Cost per unit	$100,000

STATES OF NATURE (POSSIBLE SUCCESSFUL RESTAURANTS)

Purchase	0	1	2	3	4	5
0	—	—	—	—	—	—
1	(150,000)	250,000	250,000	250,000	250,000	250,000
2	(300,000)	100,000	500,000	500,000	500,000	500,000
3	(450,000)	(50,000)	350,000	750,000	750,000	750,000
4	(600,000)	(200,000)	200,000	600,000	1,000,000	1,000,000
5	(750,000)	(350,000)	50,000	450,000	850,000	1,250,000

Larger buildings:

Revenue per unit	$1,000,000
Variable Cost per unit	$500,000 (includes franchise cost)
Salvage Cost per unit	$200,000

STATES OF NATURE (POSSIBLE SUCCESSFUL RESTAURANTS)

Purchase	0	1	2	3	4	5
0	—	—	—	—	—	—
1	(300,000)	500,000	500,000	500,000	500,000	500,000
2	(600,000)	200,000	1,000,000	1,000,000	1,000,000	1,000,000
3	(900,000)	(100,000)	700,000	1,500,000	1,500,000	1,500,000
4	(1,200,000)	(400,000)	400,000	1,200,000	2,000,000	2,000,000
5	(1,500,000)	(700,000)	100,000	900,000	1,700,000	2,500,000

d. Mall option:
Maximax: The maximum values for each alternative are 0; 250,000; 500,000; 750,000; 1,000,000; 1,250,000, so purchase 5 franchises for a maximum profit of 1,250,000.

Maximin: The minimum values for each alternative are 0; −150,000; −300,000; −450,000; −600,000; −750,000, so purchase 0 franchises for a profit of $0.

Larger building option:

Maximax: The maximum values for each alternative are 0; 500,000; 1,000,000; 1,500,000; 2,000,000; 2,500,000, so purchase 5 franchises for a maximum profit of 2,500,000.

Maximin: The minimum values for each alternative are 0; −300,000; −600,000; −900,000; −1,200,000; −1,500,000, so purchase 0 franchises for a profit of $0.

e. Based on the expected value criteria, they should purchase 3 franchises with the larger building option for an expected profit of $844,000.

19-19. a.

OPPORTUNITY LOSS TABLE

	States of Nature		
Probabilities	0.5	0.2	0.3
Alternative	S_1	S_2	S_3
A_1	0	25	40
A_2	15	15	20
A_3	35	0	0

b. EVUC = 0.5(145) + 0.2(80) + 0.3(120) = 124.5
EVPI = 124.5 − 108.0 = 16.5

19-21. EVPI = $7,900,000 − $6,760,000 = $1,140,000

19-23. EVPI = $8,395 − $1,075 = $7,320

19-25. The owners should expand.

19-27. The developer should build the large resort.

19-29. The expected value of the *Do Not Develop* branch on the decision tree is $78 per unit, while the expected value of the *Develop* branch is $82. The best decision is to work on the improved model.

19-31. The expected value of the *Don't Contract* branch is $82. By evaluating the *Contract* branch of the decision tree, we find an expected value of $81. So the best decision is not to sign the contract and develop the improved model.

19-33. Max (−400,000; −800,000; −1,200,000; −1,600,000; −2,000,000), so Max = −400,000, which is associated with build 10.

19-35. The optimal decision based on expected value would be build 40 at an expected profit of $1,837.50.

19-37. Based on the expected value, the company should market the product.

19-39. Based on the expected value, the company should market the product.

19-41. Based on the expected value, they should prepare 6 orders for an expected value of $13.975.

19-43. To minimize the EOL, you would build 40 units for an expected opportunity loss of $607,500. This is the EVPI. The $607,500 is the most you would pay for perfect information, so if someone is willing to sell it to you for $10,000, you would definitely purchase it.

19-45.

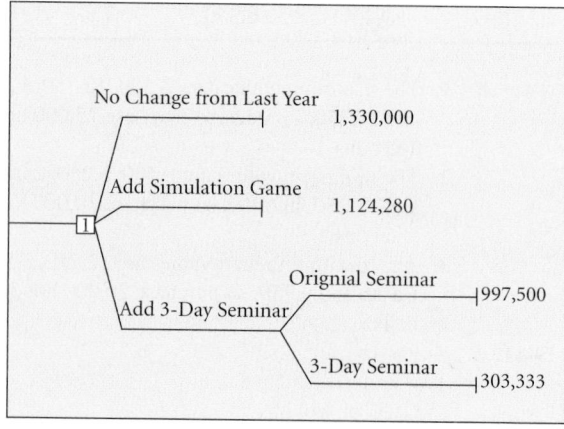

19-47. The total profit is $1,505,430 if margins can be maintained. The best decision now is to add the simulation game.

19-49.

LEAGUE RACE

Player Strike	*Tight*	*Not Tight*
No	$5.00	$2.50
	$p = 0.42$	$p = 0.28$
Yes	$4.00	$2.00
	$p = 0.18$	$p = 0.12$

19-51. The expected cost to you for the proposal above is $944,000. The expected cost of buying them on the open market is $1,128,000. You would accept the proposal if you were the purchasing manager.

19-53. By folding back the decision tree, the expected values for the various alternatives are determined. Based on expected profits, Gregston should Not Test and Drill.

19-55. For the decision to change, the expected value of the Test branch will have to be greater than the expected value of the Do Not Test branch.

$(x)(960,000) + (1 − x)(−400,000) \geq 496,000,\ x \geq 0.66$

Glossary

Aggregate Price Index. An index that is used to measure the rate of change from a base period for a group of two or more items.

All-Inclusive Classes. A set of classes that contains all the possible data values.

Alternative Hypothesis. The hypothesis that includes all population values not included in the null hypothesis. The alternative hypothesis is deemed to be true if the null hypothesis is rejected.

Autocorrelation. Correlation of the error terms (residuals) occurs when the residuals at points in time are related.

Balanced Design. An experiment has a balanced design if the factor levels have equal sample sizes.

Bar Chart. A graphical representation of a categorical data set in which a rectangle or bar is drawn over each category or class. The length or height of each bar represents the frequency or percentage of observations or some other measure associated with the category. The bars may be vertical or horizontal. The bars may all be the same color or they may be different colors depicting different categories. Additionally, multiple variables can be graphed on the same bar chart.

Base Period Index. The time-series value to which all other values in the time series are compared. The index number for the base period is defined as 100.

Between-Sample Variation. Dispersion among the factor sample means is called the *between-sample variation*.

Binomial Probability Distribution Characteristics. A distribution that gives the probability of x successes in n trials in a process that meets the following conditions:

1. A trial has only two possible outcomes: a success or a failure.
2. There is a fixed number, n, identical trials.
3. The trials of the experiment are independent of each other. This means that if one outcome is a success, this does not influence the chance of another outcome being a success.
4. The process must be consistent in generating successes and failures. That is, the probability, p, associated with a success remains constant from trial to trial.
5. If p represents the probability of a success, then $(1 - p) = q$ is the probability of a failure.

Box and Whisker Plot. A graph that is composed of two parts: a box and the whiskers. The box has a width that ranges from the first quartile ($Q1$) to the third quartile ($Q3$). A vertical line through the box is placed at the median. Limits are located at a value that is 1.5 times the difference between $Q1$ and $Q3$ below $Q1$ and above $Q3$. The whiskers extend to the left to the lowest value within the limits and to the right to the highest value within the limits.

Business Statistics. A collection of tools and techniques that are used to convert data into meaningful information in a business environment.

Census. An enumeration of the entire set of measurements taken from the whole population.

Certainty. A decision environment in which the results of selecting each alternative are known before the decision is made.

Class Boundaries. The upper and lower values of each class.

Class Width. The distance between the lowest possible value and the highest possible value for a frequency class.

Classical Probability Assessment. The method of determining probability based on the ratio of the number of ways an outcome or event of interest can occur to the number of ways *any* outcome or event can occur when the individual outcomes are equally likely.

Closed-end Questions. Questions that require the respondent to select from a short list of defined choices.

Cluster Sampling. A method by which the population is divided into groups, or clusters, that are each intended to be minipopulations. A simple random sample of m clusters is selected. The items chosen from a cluster can be selected using any probability sampling technique.

Coefficient of Determination. The portion of the total variation in the dependent variable that is explained by its relationship with the independent variable. The coefficient of determination is also called R-squared and is denoted as R^2.

Coefficient of Partial Determination. The measure of the marginal contribution of each independent variable, given that other independent variables are in the model.

Coefficient of Variation. The ratio of the standard deviation to the mean expressed as a percentage. The coefficient of variation is used to measure variation relative to the mean.

Complement. The complement of an event E is the collection of all possible outcomes not contained in event E.

Completely Randomized Design. An experiment is completely randomized if it consists of the independent random selection of observations representing each level of one factor.

Composite Model. The model that contains both the basic terms and the interaction terms.

Conditional Probability. The probability that an event will occur *given* that some other event has already happened.

Confidence Interval. An interval developed from sample values such that if all possible intervals of a given width were constructed, a percentage of these intervals, known as the confidence level, would include the true population parameter.

Confidence Level. The percentage of all possible confidence intervals that will contain the true population parameter.

Consistent Estimator. An unbiased estimator is said to be a consistent estimator if the difference between the estimator and the parameter tends to become smaller as the sample size becomes larger.

Contingency Table. A table used to classify sample observations according to two or more identifiable characteristics. It is also called a *crosstabulation table*.

Continuous Data. Data whose possible values are uncountable and which may assume any value in an interval.

Continuous Random Variables. Random variables that can assume any value in an interval.

Convenience Sampling. A sampling technique that selects the items from the population based on accessibility and ease of selection.

Correlation Coefficient. A quantitative measure of the strength of the linear relationship between two variables. The correlation ranges from −1.0 to +1.0. A correlation of ±1.0 indicates a perfect linear relationship, whereas a correlation of 0 indicates no linear relationship.

Correlation Matrix. A table showing the pairwise correlations between all variables (dependent and independent).

Critical Value. The value corresponding to a significance level that determines those test statistics that lead to rejecting the null hypothesis and those that lead to a decision not to reject the null hypothesis.

Cross-sectional Data. A set of data values observed at a fixed point in time.

Cumulative Frequency Distribution. A summary of a set of data that displays the number of observations with values less than or equal to the upper limit of each of its classes.

Cumulative Relative Frequency Distribution. A summary of a set of data that displays the proportion of observations with values less than or equal to the upper limit of each of its classes.

Cyclical Component. A wavelike pattern within the time series that repeats itself throughout the time series and has a recurrence period of more than one year.

Data Array. Data that have been arranged in numerical order.

Decision Tree. A diagram that illustrates the correct ordering of actions and events in a decision analysis problem. Each act or event is represented by a branch on the decision tree.

Degrees of Freedom. The number of independent data values available to estimate the population's standard deviation. If k parameters must be estimated before the population's standard deviation can be calculated from a sample of size n, the degrees of freedom are equal to $n - k$.

Demographic Questions. Questions relating to the respondents' characteristics, backgrounds, and attributes.

Dependent Events. Two events are dependent if the occurrence of one event impacts the probability of the other event occurring.

Dependent Variable. A variable whose values are thought to be a function of, or dependent on, the values of another variable called the *independent variable*. On a scatter plot, the dependent variable is placed on the y axis and is often called the response variable.

Discrete Data. Data that can take on a countable number of possible values.

Discrete Random Variable. A random variable that can only assume a finite number of values or an infinite sequence of values such as 0, 1, 2 . . . .

Dummy Variables. A variable that is assigned a value equal to either 0 or 1, depending on whether the observation possesses a given characteristic.

Empirical Rule. If the data distribution is bell-shaped, then the interval

$\mu \pm 1\sigma$ contains approximately 68% of the values

$\mu \pm 2\sigma$ contains approximately 95% of the values

$\mu \pm 3\sigma$ contains virtually all of the data values

Equal-Width Classes. The distance between the lowest possible value and the highest possible value in each class is equal for all classes.

Event. A collection of experimental outcomes.

Expected Value. The mean of a probability distribution. The average value when the experiment that generates values for the random variable is repeated over the long run.

Expected-Value Criterion. A decision criterion that employs probability to select the alternative that will produce the greatest average payoff or minimum average loss.

Experiment. A process that produces a single outcome whose result cannot be predicted with certainty.

Experimental Design. A plan for performing an experiment in which the variable of interest is defined. One or more factors are identified to be manipulated, changed, or observed so that the impact (or influence) on the variable of interest can be measured or observed.

Experiment-Wide Error Rate. The proportion of experiments in which at least one of the set of confidence intervals constructed does not contain the true value of the population parameter being estimated.

Exponential Smoothing. A time-series and forecasting technique that produces an exponentially weighted moving average in which each smoothing calculation or forecast is dependent on all previous observed values.

External Validity. A characteristic of an experiment whose results can be generalized beyond the test environment so that the outcomes can be replicated when the experiment is repeated.

Factor. A quantity under examination in an experiment as a possible cause of variation in the response variable.

Forecasting Horizon. The number of future periods covered by a forecast. It is sometimes referred to as *forecast lead time*.

Forecasting Interval. The frequency with which new forecasts are prepared.

Forecasting Period. The unit of time for which forecasts are to be made.

Frequency Distribution. A summary of a set of data that displays the number of observations in each of the distribution's distinct categories or classes.

Frequency Histogram. A graph of a frequency distribution with the horizontal axis showing the classes, the vertical axis showing the frequency count, and (for equal class widths) the rectangles having a height equal to the frequency in each class.

Hypergeometric Distribution. The hypergeometric distribution is formed by the ratio of the number of ways an event of interest can occur over the total number of ways any event can occur.

Independent Events. Two events are independent if the occurrence of one event in no way influences the probability of the occurrence of the other event.

Independent Samples. Samples selected from two or more populations in such a way that the occurrence of values in one sample has no influence on the probability of the occurrence of values in the other sample(s).

Independent Variable. A variable whose values are thought to impact the values of the *dependent variable*. The independent variable, or explanatory variable, is often within the direct control of the decision maker. On a scatter plot, the independent variable, or explanatory variable, is graphed on the *x* axis.

Interaction. The case in which one independent variable (such as x_2) affects the relationship between another independent variable (x_1) and a dependent variable (y).

Internal Validity. A characteristic of an experiment in which data are collected in such a way as to eliminate the effects of variables within the experimental environment that are not of interest to the researcher.

Interquartile Range. The interquartile range is a measure of variation that is determined by computing the difference between the third and first quartiles.

Least Squares Criterion. The criterion for determining a regression line that minimizes the sum of squared prediction errors.

Left-Skewed Data. A data distribution is left skewed if the mean for the data is smaller than the median.

Levels. The categories, measurements, or strata of a factor of interest in the current experiment.

Line Chart. A two-dimensional chart showing time on the horizontal axis and the variable of interest on the vertical axis.

Linear Trend. A long-term increase or decrease in a time series in which the rate of change is relatively constant.

Margin of Error. The amount that is added and subtracted to the point estimate to determine the endpoints of the confidence interval. Also, a measure of how close we expect the point estimate to be to the population parameter with the specified level of confidence.

Maximax Criterion. An optimistic decision criterion for dealing with uncertainty without using probability. For each option, the decision maker finds the maximum possible payoff and then selects the option with the greatest maximum payoff.

Maximin Criterion. A pessimistic (conservative) decision criterion for dealing with uncertainty without using probability. For each option, the decision maker finds the minimum possible payoff and selects the option with the greatest minimum payoff.

Mean. A numerical measure of the center of a set of quantitative measures computed by dividing the sum of the values by the number of values in the data.

Median. The median is a center value that divides a data array into two halves. We use $\tilde{\mu}$ to denote the population median and M_d to denote the sample median.

Minimax Regret Criterion. A decision criterion that considers the results of selecting the "wrong" alternative. For each state of nature, the decision maker finds the difference between the best payoff and each other alternative and uses these values to construct an opportunity-loss table. The decision maker then selects the alternative with the minimum opportunity loss (or regret).

Mode. The mode is the value in a data set that occurs most frequently.

Model. A representation of an actual system using either a physical or a mathematical portrayal.

Model Diagnosis. The process of determining how well a model fits past data and how well the model's assumptions appear to be satisfied.

Model Fitting. The process of estimating the specified model's parameters to achieve an adequate fit of the historical data.

Model Specification. The process of selecting the forecasting technique to be used in a particular situation.

Moving Averages. The successive averages of *n* consecutive values in a time series.

Multicollinearity. A high correlation between two independent variables such that the two variables contribute redundant information to the model. When highly correlated independent variables are included in the regression model, they can adversely affect the regression results.

Mutually Exclusive Classes. Classes that do not overlap so that a data value can be placed in only one class.

Mutually Exclusive Events. Two events are mutually exclusive if the occurrence of one event precludes the occurrence of the other event.

Nonstatistical Sampling Techniques. Those methods of selecting samples using convenience, judgment, or other nonchance processes.

Normal Distribution. The normal distribution is a bell shaped distribution with the following properties.

1. It is *unimodal*; that is, the normal distribution peaks at a single value.

2. It is *symmetrical*; this means that the two areas under the curve between the mean and any two points equidistant on either side of the mean are identical. One side of the distribution is the mirror image of the other side.

3. The mean, median, and mode are equal.

4. The normal approaches the horizontal axis on either side of the mean toward plus and minus infinity (∞). In more formal terms, the normal distribution is *asymptotic* to the x axis.

5. The amount of variation in the random variable determines the height and spread of the normal distribution.

Null Hypothesis. The statement about the population parameter that will be tested. The null hypothesis will be rejected only if the sample data provide substantial contradictory evidence.

One-tailed Test. A hypothesis test in which the entire rejection region is located in one tail of the sampling distribution. In a one-tailed test, the entire alpha level is located in one tail of the distribution.

One-Way Analysis of Variance. An analysis of variance design in which independent samples are obtained from k levels of a single factor for the purpose of testing whether the k levels have equal means.

Open-end Questions. Questions that allow respondents the freedom to respond with any value, words, or statements of their own choosing.

Opportunity Loss. The difference between the actual payoff that occurs for a decision and the optimal payoff for the same state of nature.

Paired Samples. Samples that are selected in such a way that values in one sample are matched with the values in the second sample for the purpose of controlling for extraneous factors. Another term for paired samples is *dependent samples*.

Parameter. A measure computed from the entire population. As long as the population does not change, the value of the parameter will not change.

Pareto Principle. 80% of the trouble comes from 20% of the causes.

Payoff. The outcome (profit or loss) for any combination of alternative and state of nature. The payoffs associated with all possible combinations of alternatives and states of nature constitute a *payoff table*.

Percentiles. The pth percentile in a data array is a value that divides the data set into two parts. The lower segment contains at least $p\%$, and the upper segment contains at least $(100 - p)\%$, of the data. The 50th percentile is the median.

Pie Chart. A graph in the shape of a circle. The circle is divided into "slices" corresponding to the categories or classes to be displayed. The size of each slice is proportional to the magnitude of the displayed variable associated with each category or class.

Pilot Sample. A sample taken from the population of interest of a size smaller than the anticipated sample size that is used to provide an estimate for the population standard deviation.

Point Estimate. A single statistic, determined from a sample, that is used to estimate the corresponding population parameter.

Population. The set of all objects or individuals of interest or the measurements obtained from all objects or individuals of interest.

Population Proportion. The fraction of values in a population that have a specific attribute.

Power. The probability that the hypothesis test will reject the null hypothesis when the null hypothesis is false.

Power Curve. A graph showing the probability that the hypothesis test will correctly reject a false null hypothesis for a range of possible "true" values for the population parameter.

Probability. The probability value will be in the range 0 to 1. A value of 0 means the event will not occur. A probability of 1 means the event will occur. Anything between 0 and 1 reflects the uncertainty of the event occurring. The definition given is for a countable number of events. The chance that a particular event will occur.

p-value. The probability (assuming the null hypothesis is true) of obtaining a test statistic at least as extreme as the test statistic we calculated from the sample. The p-value is also known as the *observed significance level*.

Qualitative Data. Data whose measurement scale is inherently categorical.

Quantitative Data. Measurements whose values are inherently numerical.

Quartiles. Quartiles in a data array are those values that divide the data set into four equal-sized groups. The median corresponds to the second quartile.

Random Component. Changes in time-series data that are unpredictable and cannot be associated with a trend, seasonal, or cyclical component.

Random Variable. A variable that takes on different numerical values based on chance.

Range. The range is a measure of variation that is computed by finding the difference between the maximum and minimum values in a data set.

Regression Hyperplane. The multiple regression equivalent of the simple regression line. The plane typically has a different slope for each independent variable.

Regression Slope Coefficient. The average change in the dependent variable for a unit change in the independent variable. The slope coefficient may be positive or negative, depending on the relationship between the two variables.

Relative Frequency. The proportion of total observations that are in a given category. Relative frequency is computed by dividing the frequency in a category by the total number of observations. The relative frequencies can be converted to percentages by multiplying by 100.

Relative Frequency Assessment. The method that defines probability as the number of times an event occurs divided by the total number of times an experiment is performed in a large number of trials.

Research Hypothesis. The hypothesis the decision maker attempts to demonstrate to be true. Because this is the hypothesis deemed to be the most important to the decision maker, it will be declared true only if the sample data strongly indicates that it is true.

Residual. The difference between the actual value of $\hat{y}$ and the predicted value $\hat{y}$ for a given level of the independent variable, x.

Right-Skewed Data. A data distribution is right skewed if the mean for the data is larger than the median.

Sample. A subset of the population.

Sample Proportion. The fraction of items in a sample that have the attribute of interest.

Sample Space. The collection of all outcomes that can result from a selection, decision, or experiment.

Sampling Distribution. The distribution of all possible values of a statistic for a given sample size that has been randomly selected from a population.

Sampling Error. The difference between a measure computed from a sample (a statistic) and the corresponding measure computed from the population (a parameter).

Sampling Error. The difference between a measure (a statistic) computed from a sample and the corresponding measure (a parameter) computed from the population.

Scatter Diagram. A two-dimensional graph of plotted points in which the vertical axis represents values of one quantitative variable and the horizontal axis represents values of the other quantitative variable. Each plotted point has coordinates whose values are obtained from the respective variables.

Scatter Plot. A two-dimensional plot showing the values for the joint occurrence of two variables. The scatter plot may be used to graphically represent the relationship between two variables. It is also known as a scatter diagram.

Seasonal Component. A wavelike pattern that is repeated throughout a time series and has a recurrence period of at most one year.

Seasonal Index. A number used to quantify the effect of seasonality in time-series data.

Seasonally Unadjusted Forecast. A forecast made for seasonal data that does not include an adjustment for the seasonal component in the time series.

Significance Level. The maximum allowable probability of committing a Type I statistical error. The probability is denoted by the symbol α.

Simple Linear Regression. The method of regression analysis in which a single independent variable is used to predict the dependent variable.

Simple Random Sample. A sample selected in such a manner that each possible sample of a given size has an equal chance of being selected.

Simple Random Sampling. A method of selecting items from a population such that *every possible sample of a specified size has an equal chance of being selected.*

Skewed Data. Data sets that are not symmetric. For skewed data, the mean will be larger or smaller than the median.

Standard Deviation. The standard deviation is the positive square root of the variance.

Standard Error. A value which measures the spread of the sample means around the population mean. The standard error is reduced when the sample size is increased.

Standard Normal Distribution. A normal distribution that has a mean = 0.0 and a standard deviation = 1.0. The horizontal axis is scaled in z-values that measure the number of standard deviations a point is from the mean. Values above the mean have positive z-values. Values below the mean have negative z-values.

Standardized Data Values. The number of standard deviations a value is from the mean. Standardized data values are sometimes referred to as z-scores.

States Of Nature. The possible outcomes in a decision situation over which the decision maker has no control.

Statistic. A measure computed from a sample that has been selected from a population. The value of the statistic will depend on which sample is selected.

Statistical Inference Tools. Tools that allow a decision maker to reach a conclusion about a set of data based on a subset of that data.

Statistical Sampling Techniques. Those sampling methods that use selection techniques based on chance selection.

Stratified Random Sampling. A statistical sampling method in which the population is divided into subgroups called *strata* so that each population item belongs to only one stratum. The objective is to form strata such that the population values of interest within each stratum are as much alike as possible. Sample items are selected from each stratum using the simple random sampling method.

Structured Interview. Interviews in which the questions are scripted.

Student's *t*-Distributions. A family of distributions that is bell-shaped and symmetric like the standard normal distribution but with greater area in the tails. Each distribution in the *t*-family is defined by its degrees of freedom. As the degrees of freedom increase, the *t*-distribution approaches the normal distribution.

Subjective Probability Assessment. The method that defines probability of an event as reflecting a decision maker's state of mind regarding the chances that the particular event will occur.

Symmetric Data. Data sets whose values are evenly spread around the center. For symmetric data, the mean and median are equal.

Systematic Random Sampling. A statistical sampling technique that involves selecting every *k*th item in the population after a randomly selected starting point between 1 and *k*. The value of *k* is determined as the ratio of the population size over the desired sample size.

Tchebysheff's Theorem. Regardless of how data are distributed, *at least* $(1 - 1/k^2)$ of the values will fall within *k* standard deviations of the mean. For example:

At least $\left(1 - \dfrac{1}{1^2}\right) = 0 = 0\%$ of the values will fall

within $k = 1$ standard deviation of the mean.

At least $\left(1 - \dfrac{1}{2^2}\right) = \dfrac{3}{4} = 75\%$ of the values will lie

within $k = 2$ standard deviation of the mean.

At least $\left(1 - \dfrac{1}{3^2}\right) = \dfrac{8}{9} = 89\%$ of the values will lie

within $k = 3$ standard deviation of the mean.

Test Statistic. A function of the sampled observations that provides a basis for testing a statistical hypothesis.

Time-series Data. A set of consecutive data values observed at successive points in time.

Total Quality Management. A journey to excellence in which everyone in the organization is focused on continuous process improvement directed toward increased customer satisfaction.

Total Variation. The aggregate dispersion of the individual data values across the various factor levels is called the *total variation* in the data.

Two-tailed Test. A hypothesis test in which the entire rejection region is split into the two tails of the sampling distribution. In a two-tailed test, the alpha level is split evenly between the two tails.

Type I Error. *Rejecting* the null hypothesis when it is, in fact, true.

Type II Error. *Failing to reject* the null hypothesis when it is, in fact, false.

Unbiased Estimator. A characteristic of certain statistics in which the average of all possible values of the sample statistic equals a parameter.

Uncertainty. A decision environment in which the decision maker does not know what outcome will occur when an alternative is selected.

Unstructured Interview. Interviews that begin with one or more broadly stated questions, with further questions being based on the responses.

Variance. The population variance is the average of the squared distances of the data values from the mean.

Variance Inflation Factor. A measure of how much the variance of an estimated regression coefficient increases if the independent variables are correlated. A *VIF* equal to 1.0 for a given independent variable indicates that this independent variable is not correlated with the remaining independent variables in the model. The greater the multicollinearity, the larger the *VIF*.

Variation. A set of data exhibits variation if all the data are not the same value.

Weighted Mean. The mean value of data values that have been weighted according to their relative importance.

Within-Sample Variation. The dispersion that exists among the data values within a particular factor level is called the *within-sample variation*.

Index